Statistical Techniques in
BUSINESS AND ECONOMICS

The Irwin/McGraw-Hill Series
Operations and Decision Sciences

Tenth Edition

Statistical Techniques in
BUSINESS AND
ECONOMICS

Robert D. Mason
Late of The University of Toledo

Douglas A. Lind
William G. Marchal
Both of The University of Toledo

Irwin
McGraw-Hill

Boston • Burr Ridge, IL • Dubuque, IA • Madison, WI
New York • San Francisco • St. Louis
Bangkok • Bogotá • Caracas • Lisbon • London
Madrid • Mexico City • Milan • New Delhi • Seoul
Singapore • Sydney • Taipei • Toronto

Irwin/McGraw-Hill

*A Division of The **McGraw·Hill** Companies*

STATISTICAL TECHNIQUES IN BUSINESS AND ECONOMICS

This book is printed on acid-free paper.

International   2 3 4 5 6 7 8 9 0 VNH/VNH 9 3 2 1 0 9
Domestic   2 3 4 5 6 7 8 9 0 VNH/VNH 9 3 2 1 0 9

ISBN 0-07-303935-7 (student's edition)
ISBN 0-07-303936-5 (instructor's edition)

Vice president and editorial director: *Michael W. Junior*
Publisher: *Jeffrey J.Shelstad*
Executive editor: *Richard T. Hercher, Jr.*
Senior developmental editor: *Gail Korosa*
Marketing manager: *Zina Craft*
Project manager: *Carrie Sestak*
Production supervisor: *Scott M. Hamilton*
Senior designer: *Crispin Prebys*
Senior photo research coordinator: *Keri Johnson*
Supplement coordinator: *Rose M. Range*
Compositor: *GAC/Shepard Poorman Communications*
Typeface: *9.5/11 Helvetica Neue 45*
Printer: *Von Hoffman Press*

Library of Congress Cataloging-in-Publication Data

Mason, Robert Deward
    Statistical techniques in business and economics / Robert D.
Mason, Douglas A. Lind, William G. Marchal. — 10th ed.
      p.   cm.
    ISBN 0-07-303935-7 (student's ed.). — ISBN 0-07-303936-5
(instructor's ed.)
    Includes bibliographical references and index.
    1. Social sciences—Statistical methods.   2. Economics-
-Statistical methods.   3. Commercial statistics.   I. Lind, Douglas
A. II. Marchal, William G.   III. Title.
HA29.M268   1999
519.5—dc21   98-26640

To Jane and Andrea

In memory of Robert D. Mason
Author, mentor, colleague, and friend

Preface

As the name implies, the objective of *Statistical Techniques in Business and Economics* is to provide students majoring in economics, finance, marketing, accounting, management, and other fields of business administration, with an introductory survey of the many business applications of descriptive and inferential statistics.

When Bob Mason wrote the first edition of this text back in 1967, locating relevant data was a problem. That has changed! Today, locating data is not a problem. The number of items you purchase at the grocery store is automatically recorded. The phone company keeps track of the length of a call, the time of the day the call was made, and the number of the people called. Medical devices automatically monitor and record our heart rate, blood pressure, and temperature. A large amount of business information is recorded and reported almost instantly. CNN, *USA Today*, and NBC News, for example, have web sites where you can track stock prices with a delay of less than 20 minutes. There are volumes of information on sports.

Today, skills are needed to deal with all this numerical information. First, we need to be critical consumers of information presented by others. Second, we need to be able to reduce large amounts of data into a meaningful form so that we can make effective decisions.

When we began teaching, only a few students had calculators. Today, many students have a computer at home or in their dorm room, and most have access to a computer in a Computer Lab. Statistical software is widely available, as is electronically stored data. In response to these changes, we have made some changes in the text, such as adding Excel screen captures within chapters and commands at the end of chapters, replacing some calculation examples with interpretation ones, and so forth. In this edition we continue the use of MINITAB software but add Excel spreadsheet examples because much of the current world uses Microsoft applications.

Users of previous editions will notice another change, the addition of William G. Marchal as a coauthor. Bill is a longtime friend and colleague at The University of Toledo. We have collaborated for years on book writing projects, including, informally, this one. I am pleased to welcome him and acknowledge his significant contribution to this edition. On a sad note, Bob Mason, the original author of this text, passed away during this revision. We dedicate this edition to his memory. We will miss him as a coauthor, mentor, colleague, and most importantly as a friend.

▌ Acknowledgments

The tenth edition of *Statistical Techniques in Business and Economics* is the product of many people: students, colleagues, reviewers, and the staff at Irwin/McGraw-Hill. We thank them all. We wish to express our sincere gratitude to the reviewers:

Paul Arnold
McNeese State University

John McCreery
North Carolina State University

Mary Jo Boehms
Jackson State Community College

Chester Piascik
Bryant College

Frederick Derrick
Loyola College—Maryland

Anastasia Pikas
Niagara University

Jonas Falik
Queensborough Community College

Elizabeth Polenzani
Pasadena Community College

Charles Fishburn
Pacific Christian College

Christopher Rogers
Miami-Dade Community College

Leonard Gaston
Central State University

Sue Schou
Idaho State University

Creig Kronstedt
Cardinal Stritch University

Dang Tran
California State University—Los Angeles

Denise Kummer
St. Louis Community College

Rama Yelkur
Texas A&M International University

John Leipold
University of Phoenix

Their suggestions and thorough review of the previous edition and the manuscript for this edition made this a better text.

Special thanks go to a number of people. Dr. Louis A. Patille, of the University of Phoenix, and Mr. Ray Pohlman each solved all of the exercises and checked our answers for accuracy. Gwen H. Terwilliger and Walter H. Lange, both of The University of Toledo, prepared the Test Bank and the Study Guide, respectively. Ms. Denise Heban and the text authors prepared the Instructor's Manual, and Mr. Christopher B. X. Marchal the Power Point Presentation. We appreciate their efforts on the project.

We also would like to thank the staff at Irwin/McGraw-Hill. This includes: Richard T. Hercher, Jr, the Executive Editor; Gail Korosa, Senior Development Editor; Carrie Sestak, Project Manager; and others who we don't know personally, but who we know made valuable contributions.

D.A.L.
W.G.M.

A Note to the Student

As the name implies, the purpose of the tenth edition of *Statistical Techniques in Business and Economics* is to provide students in marketing, accounting, finance, international business, sales, management, marketing, and other fields of business and economics with a sound introduction to descriptive and inferential statistics. The book, however, is also appropriate for use in other subject areas, such as the various social sciences. You will find the text provides excellent preparation for decision-making problems in various facets of business and economics and a good background for advanced courses involving statistical analysis.

▌ Learning Aids

We have designed the text to assist you in approaching the course without the anxiety often associated with statistics. These learning aids are all intended to help you in your study.

Objectives   Each chapter begins with a set of learning objectives. They are designed to provide focus for the chapter and to motivate learning. These objectives indicate what you should be able to do after completing the chapter. We include a photo that ties these chapter objectives to one of the exercises within the chapter.

Introduction   At the start of each chapter, we review the important concepts of the previous chapter(s) and provide a link to what the current chapter will cover.

Definitions   Definitions of new terms or terms unique to the study of statistics are set apart from the text and highlighted. This allows easy reference and review.

Formulas   Formulas used for the first time are boxed and numbered for easy reference. In addition, a formula card that summarizes these key formulas is bound into the text.

Margin Notes   There are more than 300 concise notes in the margin. Each emphasizes the key concept being presented immediately adjacent to it.

Examples/Solutions   We include numerous examples with solutions. These are designed to show applications of the concepts being presented.

Statistics in Action   Statistics in Action articles are scattered throughout the text, usually about two per chapter. They provide unique and interesting applications and historical insights into statistics.

Self-Reviews   Self-reviews are interspersed throughout the chapter and each is closely patterned after the preceding **Example/Solution.** They will help you monitor your progress and provide immediate reinforcement for that particular technique. The answers and methods of solution are located at the end of the chapter.

Exercises   We include exercises within the chapter, after the **Self-Reviews,** and at the end of the chapter. The answers and method of solution for all odd-numbered exercises are at the end of the book. For exercises with more than 20 observations, the data can be found on the CD-ROM supplied with the text.

Chapter Outline   As a summary, each chapter includes a chapter outline. This learning aid provides an opportunity to review material, particularly vocabulary, and to see and review the formulas again.

Web Exercises   Almost all chapters have references to Internet Web sites for companies, government organizations, and university data sets. These Web sites contain interesting and relevant information to enhance the exercises at the end of the chapters.

Computer Data Exercises   In most chapters, the last four exercises are written around four data sets. A complete listing of the data is available in the back of the text and on the CD-ROM included with the text.

Section Reviews   After selected groups of chapters, a section review is included. This includes a brief review of the chapters, a glossary of the key terms, and a practice examination of the material covered. This review also includes cases that let you make decisions using tools and techniques from a variety of chapters.

▍ Supplements

Student CD-ROM packaged free with all copies of the text, features practice quizzes, PowerPoint slides, the data files (in MINITAB, Excel, and ASCII formats) for the end of book large data sets and for exercises having 20 or more data values, and an Internet link to the text web site and to the web sites listed in the Web exercises in the text. Also included is MegaStat for Excel, by J. B. Orris, software that enhances the power of Excel in statistical analysis.

A comprehensive **Study Guide,** written by Professor Walter Lange, is organized much like the textbook. Each chapter includes objectives, a brief summary of the chapter, problems and their solution, self-review exercises, and assignments.

Douglas A. Lind
William G. Marchal

Brief Contents

Contents

4 Describing Data: Measures of Dispersion   97

5 A Survey of Probability Concepts   141

6 Discrete Probability Distributions 185

7 The Normal Probability Distribution 220

8 Sampling Methods and Sampling Distributions 257

9   Tests of Hypothesis: Large Samples   304

10   Tests of Hypothesis: Small Samples   352

11   Analysis of Variance   385

Chapter One

What Is Statistics?

GOALS

When you have completed this chapter, you will be able to:

ONE
Define what is meant by statistics.

TWO
Explain what is meant by *descriptive statistics* and *inferential statistics*.

THREE
Distinguish between a *qualitative variable* and a *quantitative variable*.

FOUR
Distinguish between a *discrete variable* and a *continuous variable*.

FIVE
Distinguish among the *nominal, ordinal, interval,* and *ratio* levels of measurement.

SIX
Define the terms *mutually exclusive* and *exhaustive*.

From a random sample of 500 potential customers, 400 persons rated a new tooth-paste excellent, 32 rated it fair, and the remaining had no opinion. Based on this sample, make an inference about the reaction of all customers to the new tooth-paste. (See Goal Two and Exercise 12.)

▌ Introduction

More than 100 years ago H. G. Wells, an English author and historian, noted that "statistical thinking will one day be as necessary for efficient citizenship as the ability to read." He made no mention of business because the Industrial Revolution was just beginning. Were he to comment on statistical thinking today, he would probably say that "statistical thinking is necessary not only for effective citizenship but also for effective decision making in various facets of business."

The late W. Edwards Deming, a noted statistician and quality-control expert, insisted that statistics education should begin before high school. He liked to tell the story of an 11-year old who devised a quality-control chart to track the on-time performance of his school bus. Deming commented, "He's got a good start in life." We hope that this book will give you a solid foundation in statistics for your future life in marketing, management, accounting, sales, or some other facet of business.

Almost daily we apply statistical concepts in our lives. For example, to start the day you turn on the shower and let it run for a few moments. Then you put your hand in the shower to sample the temperature and decide to add more hot water or more cold water, or you conclude that the temperature is just right and enter the shower. As a second example, suppose you are at the grocery store looking to buy a frozen pizza. One of the pizza makers has a stand, and they offer a small wedge of their pizza. After sampling the pizza, you decide whether to purchase the pizza or not. In both the shower and pizza examples, you make a decision and select a course of action based on a sample.

Businesses are faced with similar problems. The Kellogg Company must ensure that the mean amount of Raisin Bran in the 25.5 gram package meets the label specifications. To do so, they select periodic random samples from the production area and weigh the contents.

On a national level, a candidate for the office of President of the United States wants to know what percent of the voters in Illinois will support him in the upcoming election. There are several ways he could go about answering this question. He could have his staff call all those people in Illinois who plan to vote in the upcoming election and ask for whom they plan to vote. He could go out on a street in Chicago, stop 10 people that look to be of voting age and ask them for whom they plan to vote. He could select a random cross-section of about 2,000 voters from the state, contact these voters and, based on this cross-section, make an estimate of the percent who will vote for him in the upcoming election. In this text we will show you why the third choice is the best course of action.

▌ What Is Meant by Statistics?

How do we define the word *statistics*? We encounter it frequently in our everyday language. It really has two meanings. In the more common usage, statistics refers to numerical information. Examples include the average starting salary of college graduates, the average number of Fords sold per month at Kistler Ford over the last year, the percentage of undergraduates attending Harvard who will attend graduate school, the number of deaths due to alcoholism last year, the change in the Dow Jones Industrial Average from yesterday to today, or the number of home runs hit by the Chicago Cubs during the 1997 season. In these examples statistics are a number or a percentage. Other examples include:

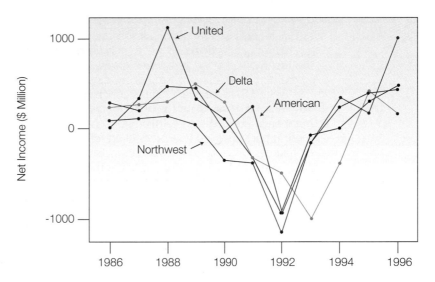

Chart 1–1   Net Income of Selected Airlines, 1986–1996

- The typical automobile in the United States travels 11,099 miles per year, the typical bus 9,353 miles per year, and the typical truck 13,942 miles per year. In Canada the corresponding information is 10,371 miles for automobiles, 19,823 miles for buses, and 7,001 miles for trucks.
- The mean time spent on hold waiting for technical support is 17 minutes.
- The Bureau of the Census projects the population of the United States to be 335,050,000 by the year 2025.
- The mean length of the nine business cycles since 1945 (measured from peak to peak) is 61 months.

The above are examples of a **statistic**. A collection of more than one figure is called **statistics** (plural).

Statistics can appear in graphic form as well as in sentence form. A graph is often used to capture reader attention and portray a large amount of data over an extended period of time. For example, 44 plots were used to construct Chart 1–1. However, it takes only a quick glance to discover that all airlines lost money in 1992 and 1993, that United had the highest income in the period, making more than $1.1 billion in 1988, and that American Airlines had the highest net income in 1996.

The subject of statistics, as we will explore it in this text, has a much broader mean-ing than just collecting and publishing numerical information. We define statistics as:

| **Statistics**   The science of collecting, organizing, presenting, analyzing, and in-terpreting data to assist in making more effective decisions. |

As the definition suggests, the first step in investigating a problem is to collect relevant data. It must be organized in some way and perhaps presented in a chart, such as Chart 1–1. Only after the data have been organized are we then able to analyze and interpret it. Here are some examples of the need for data collection.

- Research analysts for Merrill Lynch evaluate many facets of a particular stock before making a "buy" or "sell" recommendation. They collect the past sales data of the company and estimate future earnings. Other factors, such as the projected world-wide demand for the company's products, the strength of the competition, and the effect of the new union-management contract, are also considered before making a recommendation.
- The marketing department at Lever Brothers, a manufacturer of soap products, has the responsibility of making recommendations regarding the potential profitability of

a newly developed group of face soaps having fruit smells, such as grape, orange, and pineapple. Before making a final decision, they will test it in several markets. That is, they may advertise and sell it in Topeka, Kansas, and Tampa, Florida. Based on the test marketing in these two regions, Lever Brothers will make a decision whether to market the soaps in the entire country.

- The United States government is concerned with the present condition of our economy and with predicting future economic trends. The government conducts a large number of surveys to determine consumer confidence and the outlook of management regarding sales and production for the next 12 months. Indexes, such as the Consumer Price Index (described in Chapter 17), are constructed each month to assess inflation. Information on department store sales, housing starts, money turnover, and industrial production are just a few of the hundreds of items used to form the basis of the projections. These evaluations are used by banks to decide on their prime lending rate and by the Federal Reserve Board to decide on the level of control to place on the money supply.

- Management must make decisions on the quality of production. For example, automatic drill presses do not produce a perfect hole that is always 1.30 inches in diameter each time the hole is drilled (because of drill wear, vibration of the machine, and other factors). Slight tolerances are permitted, but when the hole is too small or too large, production is defective and the products cannot be used. The Quality Assurance Department is charged with continually monitoring production by using sampling techniques (described in Chapter 16).

▌ Why Study Statistics?

If you look through your university catalog, you will find that statistics is required for many college programs. Why is this so? What are the differences in the statistics courses taught in the Engineering College, Psychology or Sociology Departments in the Liberal Arts College, and that of the College of Business? The biggest difference is the examples used. The course content is basically the same. In the College of Business we are interested in such things as profits, hours worked, and wages. In the Psychology Department they are interested in test scores, and in Engineering they may be interested in how many units are manufactured on a particular machine. However, all three are interested in what is a typical value and how much variation there is in the data. There may also be a difference in the level of mathematics required. An engineering statistics course usually requires calculus. Statistics courses in colleges of business and education usually teach the course at a more applied level. You should be able to handle the mathematics in this text if you have completed high school algebra.

So why is statistics required in so many majors? The first reason is that numerical information is everywhere. Look in the newspapers (*USA Today*), news magazines (*Time, Newsweek,* and *U. S. News and World Report*), business magazines (*Business Week* or *Forbes*), or general interest magazines (*People*), women's magazines (*Home and Garden*), or sports magazines (*Sports Illustrated, Sport*), and you will be bombarded with numerical information.

Examples of why we study statistics

Here are some examples:

- Ford reports that in 1996 sales were $146.9 billion, up 7.2 percent, profit was $4.4 billion, up 7.0 percent, and net cash on hand was $7.2 billion.
- Graduates of the University of Notre Dame Masters of Business Administration Program had a mean starting salary of $54,000 and 91 percent were employed within three months of graduation.
- For golfers who play on public golf courses, the greens fees average $176.20 per year.
- The USA drinks more coffee than any other country, an average of 1.75 cups per person per day.

How are we to determine if the conclusions reported are reasonable? Was the sample large enough? How were the sampled units selected? To be an educated consumer of this information, we need to be able to read the charts and graphs and understand the discussion of the numerical information. An understanding of the concepts of basic statistics will be a big help.

The second reason for taking a statistics course is that statistical techniques are used to make decisions that affect our daily lives. That is, they affect our personal welfare. Here are a few examples:

- Insurance companies use statistical analysis to set rates for home, automobile, life, and health insurance. Tables are available that summarize the probability that a 25-year-old woman will survive the next year, the next five years, and so on. On the basis of these probabilities, life insurance premiums can be established.
- The Environmental Protection Agency is interested in the water quality of Lake Erie. They periodically take water samples to establish the level of contamination and maintain the level of quality.
- Medical researchers study the cure rates for diseases, based on the use of different drugs and different forms of treatment. For example, what is the effect of treating a certain type of knee injury surgically or with physical therapy? If you take an aspirin each day, does that reduce your risk of a heart attack?

A third reason for taking a statistics course is that the knowledge of statistical methods will help you understand why decisions are made and give you a better understanding of how they affect you.

No matter what line of work you select, you will find yourself faced with decisions where an understanding of data analysis is helpful. In order to make an informed decision, you will need to be able to:

1. Determine whether the existing information is adequate or additional information is required.
2. Gather additional information, if it is needed, in such a way that it does not provide misleading results.
3. Summarize the information in a useful and informative manner.
4. Analyze the available information.
5. Draw conclusions and make inferences while assessing the risk of an incorrect conclusion.

The statistical methods presented in the text will provide you with a framework for the decision-making process.

In summary, there are at least three reasons for studying statistics: (1) data is everywhere, (2) statistical techniques are used to make many decisions that affect our lives, and (3) no matter what your future line of work, you will make decisions that involve data. An understanding of statistical methods will help you make these decisions more effectively.

▌ Types of Statistics

Descriptive Statistics

The study of statistics is usually divided into two categories: descriptive statistics and inferential statistics. The definition of statistics given earlier referred to "organizing, presenting, analyzing . . . data." This facet of statistics is usually referred to as **descriptive statistics.**

▌ **Descriptive statistics**   Methods of organizing, summarizing, and presenting ▌
data in an informative way.

For instance, when the United States government reports that, on the basis of the decennial census counts, the population of the United States was 179,323,175 in 1960,

203,302,031 in 1970, 226,542,203 in 1980, and 248,709,783 in 1990, this information belongs to the field of descriptive statistics. This would also be the case if we calculated the percentage growth from one decade to the next. It would *not* have been the case, however, if we used the data to predict the population of the United States in the year 2010 or the percentage growth from 1990 to 2010.

The following are some other examples of descriptive statistics.

- Gallup makes ongoing studies of Americans' knowledge of the Bible. Gallup found that 49 percent of those studied knew the name of the first book in the Bible. The statistic "49" describes the number per 100 persons who got the correct answer.
- According to the Bureau of Labor Statistics, the average hourly earnings of retail trade workers was $8.45 in October 1997. This is up from $6.12 in 1987 and $7.12 in 1992. This value of $8.45 describes the average hourly earnings of a typical employee in such firms as Dayton-Hudson, Sears, Wal-Mart, and Osterman Jewelers.
- The Internal Revenue Service reports that the mean time to file Form 1040EZ is 2 hours and 46 minutes. This compares with 7 hours and 34 minutes for Form 1040A, and 10 hours and 53 minutes for Form 1040. The average time to complete a return via the TeleFile system is 37 minutes.

Masses of unorganized data — such as the census of population, the weekly earnings of thousands of computer programmers, and the individual responses of 2,340 registered voters regarding their choice for President of the United States — are of little value as is. However, statistical techniques are available to organize this type of data into a meaningful form. Some data can be organized into a **frequency distribution.** (The procedure for doing this is covered in Chapter 2.) Various **charts** may be used to describe data; several basic chart forms are also presented in Chapter 2.

Specific averages, such as the mean, may be computed to describe the central value of a group of numerical data. These averages are presented in Chapter 3. A number of statistical measures may be used to describe how closely the data are clustered about an average. These measures are examined in Chapter 4.

Inferential Statistics

Another facet of statistics is **inferential statistics** — also called **statistical inference** and **inductive statistics.** Our main concern regarding inferential statistics is finding out something about a population based on a sample taken from that population. For example, based on a sample survey by the federal government reported in *USA Today,* only 46 percent of high school seniors can solve problems involving fractions, decimals, and percentages. And only 77 percent of high school seniors correctly totaled the cost of soup, a burger, fries, and a cola on a restaurant menu. Since these are inferences about the population (all high school seniors) based on sample data, we refer to them as inferential statistics.

> **Inferential statistics**   The methods used to find out something about a population, based on a sample.

Note the words "population" and "sample" in the definition of inferential statistics. We often make reference to the population living in the United States or the 1 billion population of China. However, in statistics the word *population* has a broader meaning. A **population** may consist of *individuals* — such as all the students enrolled at Utah State University, all the students in Accounting 201, or all the inmates at Attica prison. A population may also consist of *objects,* such as all the XB-70 tires produced during the week at the Cooper Tire and Rubber Company in Findlay, Ohio, or all the trout in a stock pond. A population may also consist of a group of *measurements,* such as all the weights of the defensive linemen on the Penn State University football team or all the heights of the basketball players in the Southeastern Conference. Thus, a population in the statistical sense of the word does not necessarily refer to people.

> **Population**   A collection of all possible individuals, objects, or measurements of interest.

To infer something about a population, we usually take a **sample** from the population.

> **Sample**   A portion, or part, of the population of interest.

Reasons for sampling   Why take a sample instead of studying every member of the population? A sample of registered voters is necessary because of the prohibitive cost of contacting millions of voters before an election. Testing wheat for moisture content destroys the wheat, thus making a sample imperative. If the wine tasters tested all the wine, none would be available for sale. It would be physically impossible for a few marine biologists to capture and tag all the seals in the ocean. (These and other reasons for sampling are discussed in Chapter 8.)

As noted, taking a sample to learn something about a population is done extensively in business, agriculture, politics, and government, as cited in the following examples:

- Television networks constantly monitor the popularity of their programs by hiring Nielsen and other organizations to sample the preferences of TV viewers. These program ratings are used to set advertising rates and to cancel programs.
- A public accounting firm selects a random sample of 100 invoices and checks each invoice for accuracy. There were errors on 5 of the invoices; hence the accounting firm estimates that 5 percent of the entire population of invoices contain an error.
- A random sample of 1,260 accounting graduates from four-year schools showed that the mean starting salary was $32,694. We therefore conclude that the mean starting salary for all accounting graduates of four-year institutions is $32,694.

The relationship between a sample and a population is portrayed below.

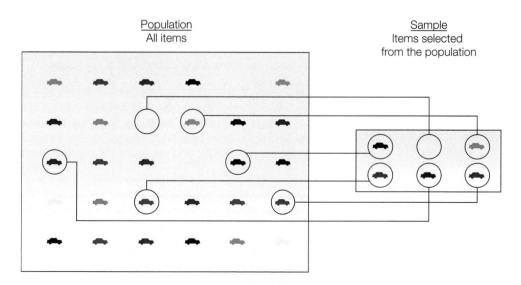

Population
All items

Sample
Items selected
from the population

*We strongly suggest
you do the
Self-Review exercises*

Following is a self-review problem. There are a number of them interspersed throughout each chapter. They test your comprehension of the preceding material. The answer and method of solution are given at the end of the chapter. We recommend that you solve each one and then check your answer.

SELF-REVIEW 1–1

The answers are at the end of the chapter.

Chicago-based Market Facts asked a sample of 1,960 consumers to try a newly developed frozen fish dinner by Morton called Fish Delight. Of the 1,960 sampled, 1,176 said they would purchase the dinner if it is marketed.

(a)   What would Market Facts report to Morton Foods regarding acceptance of Fish Delight in the population?
(b)   Is this an example of descriptive statistics or inferential statistics? Explain.

▌ Types of Variables

There are two basic types of data: (1) those obtained from a qualitative population and (2) those obtained from a quantitative population. When the characteristic or variable being studied is nonnumeric, it is called a **qualitative variable** or an **attribute.** Examples of qualitative variables are gender, religious affiliation, type of automobile owned, state of birth, and eye color. When the data being studied are qualitative, we are usually interested in how many or what proportion fall in each category. For example, what percent of the population has blue eyes? How many Catholics and how many Protestants are there in the United States? What percent of the total number of cars sold last month were Buicks? Qualitative data are often summarized in charts and bar graphs (Chapter 2).

Qualitative variable

When the variable studied can be reported numerically, the variable is called a **quantitative variable,** and the population is called a quantitative population. Examples of quantitative variables are the balance in your checking account, the ages of company presidents, the life of a battery (such as 42 months), the speeds of automobiles traveling along Interstate 5 near Seattle, and the number of children in a family.

Quantitative variable

Quantitative variables are either discrete or continuous. **Discrete variables** can assume only certain values, and there are usually "gaps" between the values. Examples of discrete variables are the number of bedrooms in a house (1, 2, 3, 4, etc.), the number of cars arriving at a tollbooth on I-75 at Berea, Kentucky, over an hour (16, 19, 30, etc.), and the number of students in each section of a statistics course (25 in section A, 42 in section B, and 18 in section C). Notice that a home can have 3 or 4 bedrooms, but it cannot have 3.56 bedrooms. Thus, there is a "gap" between possible values. Typically, discrete variables result from counting. We count, for example, the number of cars arriving at the Berea exit on I-75, and we count the number of statistics students in each section.

Observations of a **continuous variable** can assume any value within a specific range. Examples of continuous variables are the air pressure in a tire and the weight of a shipment of grain (which, depending on the accuracy of the scales, could be 15.0 tons, 15.01 tons, 15.03 tons, etc.). The amount of raisin bran in a box and the time it took to fly from Orlando to San Diego are other variables of a continuous nature. The Orlando–San Diego flight could take 7 hours and 30 minutes; or 7 hours, 30 minutes, and 45 seconds; or 7 hours, 30 minutes, and 45.1 seconds, depending on the accuracy of the timing device. Typically, continuous variables result from measuring something.

The types of variables are summarized in the following diagram.

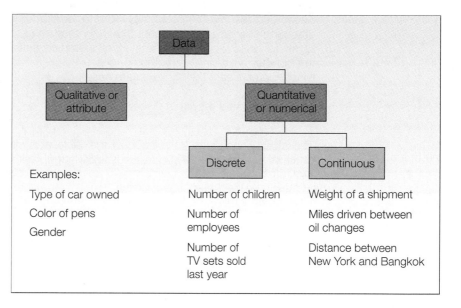

Examples:

Qualitative or attribute	Discrete	Continuous
Type of car owned	Number of children	Weight of a shipment
Color of pens	Number of employees	Miles driven between oil changes
Gender	Number of TV sets sold last year	Distance between New York and Bangkok

▌ Sources of Statistical Data

Reseaching problems involving such topics as crime, health, imports and exports, production, and hourly wages generally requires published data. We may want figures on the total value of timber cut in 1996 ($918,000,000), the earnings per share of Delta Airlines in 1996 ($1.42), the state with the largest number of inmates in prisons in 1994 (California, with 121,084), and countries projected to have more than 2 million persons age 65 and over in the year 2020 (China, India, and the United States). These and thousands of other assorted statistics can be found in publications such as the *Statistical Abstract of the United States* and the *World Almanac and Book of Facts.*

What if we wanted to know the hourly wages of employees in manufacturing, mining, and retail trades since 1975? We would find these in the *Monthly Labor Review,* published monthly by the U.S. Department of Labor. These and other historical data are released regularly by the federal government, each state, and the United Nations.

In addition to regularly published data, prestigious publications such as *Fortune, Business Week,* and *The Wall Street Journal* contain a multitude of statistics with emphasis on business and economic topics. In addition to these publications, which come out on a regular basis, Gallup and other pollsters release studies on the popularity of political candidates.

Published data are not always available on every subject of interest. Persons may be contacted in a shopping mall, at their homes, over the telephone, or by mail. The respondents' answers are usually tabulated either by hand or using a computer. You have probably seen and completed many questionnaires. Perhaps you will be presented with such a questionnaire at the end of this course. Here are the results from surveys in the recent literature.

Midsized manufacturers were surveyed by the Grant Thornton Survey of Manufacturers. One question asked was, "Do you plan to add full-time employees next year?" The choices were "Yes," "No," and "Undecided." Sixty-three percent of the manufacturers responding said yes. Another question from the same survey was, "Are you hiring extra part-time employees?" Forty-two percent indicated yes.

Working Mother commissioned Gallup to study how satisfied working mothers are with their dual role. Gallup polled 1,000 working mothers nationwide. Some of the findings were:

1. Seven out of 10 women said they work to feel good about themselves, regardless of the job they do or the amount of money they make.
2. Eight out of 10 working mothers were "extremely satisfied" or "very satisfied" with the job they are doing as mothers.
3. Ninety percent said their children are happy.
4. Three quarters said they "like" or "love" their jobs.
5. Four percent said they "hate" their work.

The study concerning knowledge of the Bible was cited previously. While testing respondents on their biblical and religious knowledge, Gallup asked these questions:

1. What country ruled Jerusalem during the time of Jesus? (Thirty-five percent knew it was Rome.)
2. What is the Holy Trinity? (Forty percent knew the answer.)
3. Who delivered the Sermon on the Mount? (Thirty-four percent knew it was Jesus.)

The sponsor of the questionnaire (Princeton Religion Research Center) learned that about one out of three respondents could answer questions similar to these.

Following are two examples of questionnaires. The first is a survey by the RCA Label Group regarding the purchase of CDs. The second is a survey by the Hertz Corporation regarding customer satisfaction with car rentals.

The RCA Label Group would like to welcome you to our family of music owners. Only with your help can we continue to produce the best in pre-recorded entertainment. Your opinion counts. All you need to do is listen to this CD a few times and answer the questions below. Then just drop this card in the mail (the postage is on us). Please be sure to print your name and address so we can include you in future promotions.

1. Title of CD purchased: _____

2. Including this purchase, how many COUNTRY music CDs/Cassettes have you purchased in the past 6 months?
   ❑ Less than 4   ❑ 5-9   ❑ 10 or more

3. Do you consider yourself to be a: ❑ Country music fan
   ❑ Country music occasional listener   ❑ Don't like country music

4. How did you learn this album was available? (check one)
   ❑ Heard song on radio   ❑ Saw video on TV
   ❑ Read an article/review   ❑ Saw on sale at store
   ❑ Heard ad on radio   ❑ Saw artist on TV
   ❑ Word-of-mouth   ❑ Found information on Internet

5. What are your favorite 3 songs on this album? (fill in track #)

   [ ][ ] [ ][ ] [ ][ ]

6. Do you actively participate in the following? (check all that apply)
   ❑ Boating   ❑ Family vacations   ❑ Attend football games
   ❑ Fishing   ❑ Go to movies   ❑ Attend baseball games
   ❑ Camping   ❑ Rent videos   ❑ Attend basketball games
                                         ❑ Attend soccer games

7. Are you a homeowner?   ❑ YES   ❑ NO

8. Are you: ❑ Male   ❑ Female

9. What is your age?
   ❑ 16 & under   ❑ 17-24   ❑ 25-34   ❑ 35-44   ❑ 45 & older

10. Marital status: ❑ Single   ❑ Married   ❑ Divorced   ❑ Widow

11. Do you want to participate in future RCA programs where your feedback helps us learn about your music preferences?   ❑ YES   ❑ NO

12. Would you like to receive information about special offers from RCA?
    ❑ YES   ❑ NO

PLEASE PRINT CLEARLY:

First Name _____

Last Name _____

Address _____

City _____   State ___   ZIP _____

Phone ___ - ___ - _____   E-mail Address: _____

RLG0197-2

How Do We Rate?

City where car was:

Rented _____

Date _____ Time _____

☐ Airport   ☐ Downtown   ☐ Other

City where car was:

Returned _____

Date _____ Time _____

☐ Airport   ☐ Downtown   ☐ Other

Rental record number? _____

Did you make a reservation? ☐ Yes   ☐ No

If yes; through a travel agent? ☐

Or direct with Hertz? ☐

Name and address (optional)

Name _____

Company _____

Street address _____

City _____

State _____ Zip code _____

Day telephone: ( ) _____-_____

Evening telephone: ( ) _____-_____

Hertz rents Fords and other fine cars.

1. Type of service used this rental?

At rental:	At return:	Used Hertz courtesy bus:
☐ #1 Club Gold-Canopy	☐ Instant (at car)	
	☐ Express (box)	
☐ #1 Club Gold-Counter	☐ Self-service	☐ Yes
	☐ Standard	☐ No
☐ Standard		

2. Speed of service this rental?

	Excellent	Good	Fair	Poor
At rental	☐	☐	☐	☐
At return	☐	☐	☐	☐
Courtesy bus pickup	☐	☐	☐	☐

3. Vehicle condition this rental?

	Excellent	Good	Fair	Poor
Cleanliness	☐	☐	☐	☐
Mechanical	☐	☐	☐	☐

4. Courtesy and friendliness of Hertz personnel this rental?

	Excellent	Good	Fair	Poor
At reservation	☐	☐	☐	☐
At rental	☐	☐	☐	☐
At return	☐	☐	☐	☐
On courtesy bus	☐	☐	☐	☐

5. Competence of Hertz personnel this rental?

	Excellent	Good	Fair	Poor
At reservation	☐	☐	☐	☐
At rental	☐	☐	☐	☐
At return	☐	☐	☐	☐
On courtesy bus	☐	☐	☐	☐

6. Overall experience?

	Excellent	Good	Fair	Poor
This rental	☐	☐	☐	☐
Prior rentals	☐	☐	☐	☐

7. Additional comments?

_____

_____

_____

_____

_____

_____

_____

_____

Thank you for your time.

The Internet is changing the way we live and the way we do business. It is an excellent source of data. It is estimated that more than 10 million people had access to the Internet at the beginning of 1997 and that more than 75 million will have access by the year 2005. By using the Internet you can find statistics on the sales and profits of companies like IBM and Ford. You can find data on school systems from the state departments of education. You can even find the salaries of Major League Baseball players by accessing the *USA Today* Web site.

▌ Levels of Measurement

Data can be classified according to levels of measurement. The level of measurement of the data often dictates the calculations that can be done to summarize and present the data and the statistical tests that can be performed. For example, there are six colors of candies in a bag of M&M's candies. Suppose we assign the brown a value of 1, yellow 2, blue 3, orange 4, green 5, and red 6. From a bag of candies, we add the assigned color values and divide by the number of candies and report that the mean color is 3.56.

Does this mean that the average color is blue or orange? As a second example, in a high school track meet there are 8 competitors in the 400 meter run. We report the order of finish and that the mean finish is 4.5. What does the mean finish tell us? In both of these instances, we have not properly used the level of measurement.

There are actually four levels of measurement: nominal, ordinal, interval, and ratio. The "lowest," or the most primitive, measurement is the nominal level. The highest, or the level that gives us the most information about the observation, is the ratio level of measurement.

Nominal Level Data

In the **nominal level** of measurement, the observations can only be classified or counted. There is no particular order to the labels. The classification of the six colors of M&M's candies is an example of the nominal level of measurement. We simply classify the candies by color. There is no natural order. That is, we could report the brown candies first, the orange first, or any of the colors first. Gender is another example of the nominal level of measurement. Suppose we count the number of students entering a football game with a student ID and report how many are men and how many are women. We could report either the men or the women first. For the nominal level of measurement there is no measurement involved, only counts. Table 1–1 shows a breakdown of U.S. long distance telephone usage. This is the nominal level of measurement because we counted the number of times each long distance carrier was used.

Table 1–1   Long Distance Telephone Usage by Carrier

Carrier	Number of Calls	Percent
AT&T	108,115,800	75
MCI	20,577,310	14
Sprint	8,238,740	6
Other	7,130,620	5
Total	144,062,470	100

The arrangement of the carriers in Table 1–1 could have been changed. That is, we could have reported MCI first, Sprint second, and so on. This essentially indicates the major feature of the nominal level of measurement: there is no particular order to the categories.

These categories are **mutually exclusive,** meaning, for example, that a particular phone call cannot originate with both AT&T and MCI.

Mutually exclusive   An individual, object, or measurement is included in only one category.

The categories in Table 1–1 are also **exhaustive,** meaning that every member of the population, or sample, must appear in one of the categories. So if a call did not originate with AT&T, MCI, or Sprint, it is classified as Other.

Exhaustive   Each individual, object, or measurement must appear in a category.

In order to process data on telephone usage, gender, employment by industry, and so forth, the categories are often coded 1, 2, 3, and so on, with 1 representing AT&T, 2 representing MCI, and so on. This facilitates counting by the computer. However, because we have assigned numbers to the various companies, this does not give us license to manipulate the numbers. For example, 1 + 2 does not equal 3, that is, AT&T + MCI does not equal Sprint. To summarize, the nominal level data has the following properties:

1. Data categories are mutually exclusive, so an object belongs to only one category.
2. Data categories have no logical order.

Ordinal Level Data

The next higher level of data is the **ordinal level.** Table 1–2 lists the student ratings of Professor James Brunner in an Introduction to Finance course. Each student in the class answered the question "Overall how did you rate the instructor in this class?" This illustrates the use of the ordinal scale of measurement. One category is "higher" or "better" than the next one. That is "Superior" is better than "Good," "Good" is better than "Average," and so on. However, we are not able to distinguish anything about the magnitude of the differences between groups. Is the difference between "Superior" and "Good" the same as the difference between "Poor" and "Inferior"? We cannot tell. If we substitute a 5 for "Superior" and a 4 for "Good," we can conclude that the rating of "Superior" is better than the rating of "Good," but we cannot add a ranking of "Superior" and a ranking of "Good," with the result being meaningful. Further we cannot conclude that a rating of "Good" (rating is 4) is necessarily twice as good as a "Poor" (rating is 2). We can only conclude that a rating of "Good" is better than a rating of "Poor." We cannot conclude how much better the rating is.

Table 1–2 Rating of a Finance Professor

Rating	Frequency
Superior	6
Good	28
Average	25
Poor	12
Inferior	3

In summary, the properties of ordinal level data are:

1. The data categories are mutually exclusive and exhaustive.
2. Data categories are ranked or ordered according to the particular trait they possess.

Interval Level Data

The **interval level** of measurement is the next highest level. It includes all the characteristics of the ordinal level, but in addition, the difference between values is a constant size. An example of the interval level of measurement is temperature. Suppose the high temperatures on three consecutive winter days in Boston are 28, 31, and 20 degrees Fahrenheit. These temperatures can be easily ranked, but we can also determine the difference between temperatures. This is possible because 1 degree Fahrenheit represents a constant unit of measurement. Equal differences between two temperatures are the same, regardless of their position on the scale. That is, the difference between 10 degrees Fahrenheit and 15 degrees is 5, the difference between 50 and 55 degrees is also 5 degrees. It is also important to note that 0 is just a point on the scale. It does not represent the absence of the condition. Zero degrees Fahrenheit does not represent the absence of heat, just that it is cold! In fact 0 degrees Fahrenheit is about −18 degrees on the Celsius scale.

The properties of the interval scale are:

1. Data categories are mutually exclusive and exhaustive.
2. Data categories are scaled according to the amount of the characteristic they possess.

3. Equal differences in the characteristic are represented by equal differences in the numbers assigned to the categories.

Ratio Level Data

The **ratio level** is the "highest" level of measurement. The ratio level of measurement has all the characteristics of the interval level, but in addition, the 0 point is meaningful and the ratio between two numbers is meaningful. Examples of the ratio scale of measurement include wages, units of production, weight, and height. Money is a good illustration. If you have zero dollars, then you have no money. Weight is another example. If the dial on the scale is at zero, then there is a complete absence of weight. The ratio of two numbers is also meaningful. If Jim earns $30,000 per year selling insurance and Rob earns $60,000 per year selling cars, then Rob earns twice as much as Jim.

The properties of the ratio level are:

1. Data categories are mutually exclusive and exhaustive.
2. Data categories are scaled according to the amount of the characteristic they possess.
3. Equal differences in the characteristic are represented by equal differences in the numbers assigned to the categories.
4. The point 0 reflects the absence of the characteristic.

Table 1–3 illustrates the use of the ratio scale of measurement. It reports the incomes of four father–son combinations.

Table 1–3 Father–Son Salary Combinations

| | Incomes | |
Name	Father	Son
Jones	$80,000	$ 40,000
White	90,000	30,000
Rho	60,000	120,000
Scazzro	75,000	130,000

Observe that the senior Jones earns twice as much as his son. In the Rho family the son makes twice as much as the father.

SELF-REVIEW 1–2

What is the level of measurement reflected by the following data?

a. The age of adults who listen to the nearly 700 Oldies radio stations in the United States is:

Age (years)	Percent of Listeners
18 up to 25	12
25 up to 35	22
35 up to 45	32
45 up to 55	23
55 or older	11

b. In a survey of 200 luxury-car owners, 100 were from California, 50 from New York, 30 from Illinois, and 20 from Ohio.

▌ Exercises

The answers to the odd-numbered exercises are at the end of the book.

1. What is the level of measurement for each of the following variables?
   a. Student grade point averages.
   b. Distance students travel to class.
   c. Student scores on the first statistics test.
   d. A classification of students by state of birth.
   e. A ranking of students by freshman, sophomore, junior, and senior.
   f. Number of hours students study per week.
2. What is the level of measurement for these items related to the newspaper business?
   a. The number of papers sold each Sunday during 1998.
   b. The number of employees in each of the departments, such as editorial, advertising, sports, etc.
   c. A summary of the number of papers sold by county.
   d. The number of years with the paper for each employee.
3. Look in the latest edition of *USA Today* or your local newspaper and find examples of each level of measurement. Write a brief memo summarizing your findings.
4. For each of the following, determine whether the group is a sample or a population.
   a. The participants in a study of a new diabetes drug.
   b. All the drivers who received a speeding ticket in Kansas City last month.
   c. All those on welfare in Cook County (Chicago), Illinois.
   d. The 30 stocks reported as a part of the Dow Jones Industrial Average.

▌ Uses and Abuses of Statistics

You have probably heard the old saying that there are three kinds of lies: lies, damn lies, and statistics. This saying is attributable to Benjamin Disraeli and is over a century old. It has also been said that "figures don't lie: liars figure." Both of these statements refer to the abuses of statistics in which data are presented in ways that are misleading. Many abusers of statistics are simply ignorant or careless, while others have an objective to mislead the reader by emphasizing data that support their position while leaving out data that may be detrimental to their position. One of our major goals in this text is to make you a more critical consumer of information. When you see charts or data in a newspaper, in a magazine, or on TV, always ask yourself: What is the person trying to tell me? Does that person have an agenda? Following are several examples of the abuses of statistical analysis.

An average may not be representative of all the data.

The term *average* refers to several different measures of central tendency that we discuss in Chapter 3. To most people, an average is found by adding the values involved and dividing by the number of values. So if a real estate developer tells a client that the average home in a particular subdivision sold for $150,000, we assume that $150,000 is a representative selling price for all the homes. But suppose there are only 5 homes in the subdivision and they sold for $50,000, $50,000, $60,000, $90,000, and $500,000. We can correctly claim that the average selling price is $150,000, but does $150,000 really seem like a "typical" selling price? Would you like to also know that the same number of homes sold for more than $60,000 as less than $60,000? Or that $50,000 is the selling price that occurred most frequently? So what selling price really is the most "typical"? This example illustrates that a reported average can be misleading, because it can be one of several numbers that could be used to represent the data. There is really no objective set of criteria that states what average should be reported on each occasion. We want to educate you as a consumer of data about how a person or group might report one value that favors their position and exclude other values. We will discuss averages, or measures of central tendency, in Chapter 3.

Graphs can also be misleading.

Charts and graphs can also be used to visually mislead. Suppose the school taxes in a particular school district increased from $100 a year to $200 a year; that is, the taxes doubled. To show this change, the dollar sign below on the right is twice as tall as the one on the left. It is also twice as wide, however, so the area of the dollar sign on the right is 4 times (not twice) that of the one on the left.

$ $ $

When we double the dimensions of two-dimensional objects, we increase the area by a factor of four.

The figure is misleading because visually the increase is much larger than it really is. We discuss the construction of tables and charts in Chapter 2.

Study the sampling methods.

Several years ago, a series of TV advertisements reported that "2 out of 3 dentists surveyed indicated they would recommend Brand X toothpaste to their patients." The implication is that 67 percent of all dentists would recommend the product to their patients. The trick is that the manufacturer of the toothpaste could take *many* surveys of 3 dentists and report *only* the survey of 3 dentists that had 2 indicating they would recommend Brand X. Undoubtedly, a survey of more than 3 is needed, and it must be unbiased and representative of the population of all dentists. We discuss sampling methods in Chapter 8.

Another area where there can be a misrepresentation of data is the association between variables. In statistical analysis often we find there is a strong *association* between variables. We find there is a strong association between the number of hours a student studies for an exam and the score he or she receives. Does this mean that studying causes the higher score? No. It means the two variables are related, that is, they tend to act together in a predictable fashion. We study the association between variables in Chapters 12 and 13.

Sometimes numbers themselves can be deceptive. The mean price of homes sold last month in the Tampa, Florida, area is $134,891.58. This sounds like a very precise value and may instill a high degree of confidence in its accuracy. To report that the mean selling price is $135,000 doesn't convey the same precision and accuracy. However, a statistic that is very precise and carries 5 or even 10 decimal places is not necessarily accurate.

There are many other ways that statistical information can be deceiving. Entire books have been written about the subject. The most famous of these is *How to Lie with Statistics* by Darrell Huff. Understanding these practices will make you a better consumer of statistical information and help you defend yourself against those who might wish to mislead.

▌ Computer Applications

Computers are now available for student use at most colleges and universities, as are such statistical software systems as MINITAB, SAS, and CBS (published by Irwin/McGraw-Hill). Spreadsheets, such as Microsoft Excel, which have many statistical functions, are also available in most computer labs and on most home computers. We have selected MINITAB and Excel for most of the statistical applications in the text. Check with your instructor or computing consultant for any instructions that are required at your site.

The following example shows the wide application of computers in statistical analysis. In chapters 2, 3, and 4 we illustrate methods for summarizing and describing data. An example used in those chapters refers to the price of 80 vehicles sold at Whitner Pontiac last month. The following MINITAB output reveals, among other things, that (1) 80 automobiles were sold last month, (2) the mean (average) selling price was $20,227, and (3) the selling prices ranged from a minimum of $12,546 to a maximum of $33,625. The various headings will be explained later, beginning in Chapter 2.

```
Descriptive Statistics

Variable        N       Mean     Median    Tr Mean      StDev     SE Mean
Price          80      20227      19831      20005       4381         490


Variable      Min        Max         Q1         Q3
Price       12546      33625      17074      22795
```

The Excel output that follows contains much of the same information, although it is ordered somewhat differently.

Column 1	
Mean	20226.91
Standard Error	489.8015
Median	19831
Mode	17642
Standard Deviation	4380.917
Sample Variance	19192438
Kurtosis	0.680418
Skewness	0.762864
Range	21079
Minimum	12546
Maximum	33625
Sum	1618153
Count	80
Confidence Level(95.0%)	974.9263

Had we used a calculator to arrive at these measures and others needed to fully analyze the selling prices, many hours of calculations would have been required. The likelihood of an error in arithmetic is high when a large number of values are concerned. On the other hand, statistical software packages and spreadsheets can provide accurate information in seconds.

At the option of your instructor, and depending on the operating system available, we urge you to apply a computer package to the exercises in the **Computer Data Exercises** section in each chapter. It will relieve you of the tedious calculations and allow you to concentrate on data analysis.

I   Chapter Outline

I. Statistics is the science of collecting, organizing, analyzing, and interpreting data for the purpose of making better decisions.

II.　There are two types of statistics.
　　A.　Descriptive statistics are procedures used to organize and summarize data.
　　B.　Inferential statistics involve taking a sample from a population and making estimates about a population based on the sample results.
　　　　1.　A population is the total collection of individuals or objects.
　　　　2.　A sample is a part of the population.
III.　There are two types of variables.
　　A.　A qualitative variable is nonnumeric.
　　　　1.　Usually we are interested in the number or percent of the observations in each category.
　　　　2.　Qualitative data are usually summarized in graphs and bar charts.
　　B.　There are two types of quantitative variables and they are usually reported numerically.
　　　　1.　Discrete variables can assume only certain values, and there are usually gaps between values.
　　　　2.　A continuous variable can assume any value within a specified range.
IV.　There are four levels of measurement.
　　A.　With the nominal level, the data are sorted into categories with no particular order to the categories.
　　　　1.　The categories are mutually exclusive. An individual or object appears in only one category.
　　　　2.　The categories are exhaustive. An individual or object appears in at least one of the categories.
　　B.　The ordinal level of measurement presumes that one category is ranked higher than another.
　　C.　The interval level of measurement has the ranking characteristic of the ordinal level of measurement plus the characteristic that the distance between values is meaningful.
　　D.　The ratio level of measurement has all the characteristics of the interval level, plus there is a zero point and the ratio of two values is meaningful.

▌ Chapter Exercises

5.　Explain the difference between qualitative and quantitative data. Give an example of qualitative and quantitative data.
6.　Explain the difference between a sample and a population.
7.　List the four levels of measurement and give an example (different from those used in the book) of each level of measurement.
8.　Define the term *mutually exclusive.*
9.　Define the term *exhaustive.*
10.　Using data from such publications as the *Statistical Abstract of the United States,* the *World Almanac, Forbes,* or your local newspaper, give examples of the nominal, ordinal, interval and ratio level of measurement.
11.　A random sample of 300 executives out of 2,500 employed by a large firm showed that 270 would move to another location if it meant a substantial promotion. Based on these findings, write a brief note to management regarding all executives in the firm.
12.　A random sample of 500 customers was asked to test a new toothpaste. Of the 500, 400 said it was excellent, 32 thought it was fair, and the remaining customers had no opinion. Based on these sample findings, make an inference about the reaction of all customers to the new toothpaste.
13.　Explain the difference between a discrete and a continuous variable. Give an example of each not included in the text.
14.　A survey of U.S. households regarding satisfaction with the U.S. economy revealed the following data, which is portrayed graphically. Note that 1991 = 100. A value of 100 suggests an "average" satisfaction of Americans during the given year. A value of 75 would indicate

that consumer satisfaction in the economy for that year is 25 percent below normal. Write an analysis of consumer satisfaction from 1986 to 1997.

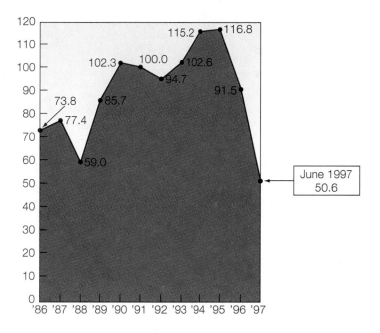

Consumer Satisfaction: From a Survey of U.S. Households, 1991 = 100

▌ Computer Data Exercises

15. Refer to Data Set 1 at the back of the text, which reports information on homes sold in the Venice, Florida, area last year. Consider the following variables: selling price, number of bedrooms, township, and distance from the center of the city.
    a. Which of the variables are qualitative and which are quantitative?
    b. Determine the level of measurement for each of the variables.
16. Refer to Data Set 2, which reports information on the 28 Major League Baseball teams for 1997. Consider the following variables: team salary, attendance, and number of errors.
    a. Which of the variables are qualitative and which are quantitative?
    b. Determine the level of measurement for each of the variables.
17. Refer to Data Set 3, which reports information on the circulation of 48 magazines. Consider the following variables: name of magazine, circulation, median subscriber age, and the per page color advertising cost.
    a. Which of the variables are qualitative and which are quantitative?
    b. Determine the level of measurement for each of the variables.
18. Refer to Data Set 4, which refers to the 94 school districts in Northwest Ohio. Consider the following variables: number of students in the district, the name of the school, amount spent per pupil, and the mean salary of the teachers.
    a. Which of the variables are qualitative and which are quantitative?
    b. Determine the level of measurement for each of the variables.

C H A P T E R 1   *Answers to Self-Review*

1–1 a. Based on the sample of 1,960 consumers, we estimate that, if it is marketed, 60 percent of all consumers will purchase Fish Delight (1,176/1,960) $\times$ 100 = 60 percent.

   b. Inferential statistics, because a sample was used to make an inference about how all consumers in the population would react if Fish Delight were marketed.

1–2 a. Age is a ratio scale variable. A 40-year-old is twice as old as someone 20-years-old.

   b. Nominal scale. We could arange the states in any order.

Chapter Two

Describing Data

Frequency Distributions and Graphic Presentation

GOALS

When you have completed this chapter, you will be able to:

ONE

Organize data into a frequency distribution.

TWO

Portray a frequency distribution in a histogram, frequency polygon, and cumulative frequency polygon.

THREE

Develop a stem-and-leaf display.

FOUR

Present data using such graphic techniques as line charts, bar charts, and pie charts.

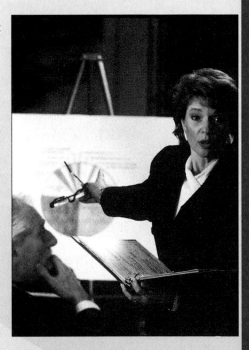

Given a list of selected companies and their shareholders, how would you graphically portray the frequency distribution of the number of shareholders? (See Goal Two and Exercise 38.)

▌ Introduction

Rob Whitner is the owner of Whitner Pontiac in Columbia, South Carolina. Rob's father founded the dealership in 1964, and for more than 30 years they sold exclusively

Pontiacs. In the early 1990s Rob's father's health began to fail, and Rob took over more of the day-to-day operation of the dealership. At this same time, the automobile business began to change — dealers began to sell vehicles from several manufacturers — and Rob was faced with some major decisions. The first came when another local dealer, who handled Volvos, Saabs, and Volkswagens, approached Rob about purchasing his dealership. After considerable thought and analysis, Rob purchased that dealership. More recently, the local Jeep Eagle dealership got into difficulty and Rob bought them out. So now, on the same lot, Rob sells the complete line of Pontiacs, the expensive Volvos, Saabs, Volkswagens, and the Chrysler products, including the popular Jeep line. Whitner Pontiac employs 83, including 23 full-time salespeople. Because of the diverse product line, there is quite a bit of variation in the selling price of the vehicles. A top-of-the-line Volvo sells for more than twice that of a Pontiac Grand Am. Rob would like to develop some charts and graphs that he could review monthly to see where the selling prices tend to cluster, to see the variation in the selling prices, and to note any trends. In this chapter we present techniques that will be useful to Rob in managing his business.

▌ Constructing a Frequency Distribution

Recall from Chapter 1 that we refer to techniques used to describe a set of data as *descriptive statistics.* To put it another way, we use descriptive statistics to organize data in various ways to point out where the data values tend to concentrate and help distinguish the largest and the smallest values. The first method we are going to use to describe a set of data is a **frequency distribution.**

> **Frequency Distribution** A grouping of data into categories showing the number of observations in each mutually exclusive category.

How do we develop a frequency distribution? The first step is to tally the data into a table that shows the classes (categories) and the number of observations in each category. The steps in constructing a frequency distribution are best described using an example. Remember, our goal is to establish a table that will quickly reveal the underlying shape of the data.

Example

In the Introduction we describe a case where Rob Whitner, owner of Whitner Pontiac, is interested in collecting information on the selling prices of vehicles sold at his dealership. What is the typical selling price? What is the largest selling price? What is the smallest selling price? Around what value do the selling prices tend to cluster? In order to answer these questions, we need to collect data. According to sales records, Whitner Pontiac sold 80 vehicles last month. The price paid by the customer for each vehicle is shown in Table 2–1. Summarize the selling prices of the vehicles sold last month. Around what value do the selling prices tend to cluster?

Table 2–1   Selling Prices of Vehicles Sold Last Month at Whitner Pontiac

$20,197	$20,372	$17,454	$20,591	$23,651	$24,453	$14,266	$15,021	$25,683	$27,872
16,587	20,169	32,851	16,251	17,047	21,285	21,324	21,609	25,670	12,546
12,935	16,873	22,251	22,277	25,034	21,533	24,443	16,889	17,004	14,357
17,155	16,688	20,657	23,613	17,895	17,203	20,765	22,783	23,661	29,277
17,642	18,981	21,052	22,799	12,794	15,263	33,625	14,399	14,968	17,356
18,442	18,722	16,331	19,817	16,766	17,633	17,962	19,845	23,285	24,896
26,076	29,492	15,890	18,740	19,374	21,571	22,449	25,337	17,642	20,613
21,220	27,655	19,442	14,891	17,818	23,237	17,445	18,556	18,639	21,296

Lowest

Highest

Solution

We refer to the unorganized information in Table 2–1 as **raw data** or **ungrouped data.** With a little searching, we can find the lowest selling price ($12,546) and the highest selling price ($33,625), but that is about all. It is difficult to determine what is a typical selling price. It is also difficult to visualize where the typical selling prices tend to occur. The raw data are more easily interpreted if organized into a frequency distribution.

*The steps for orga-
nizing data into a
frequency distribution*

Step 1. Set up groupings, called **classes.** In this problem the first class might include all the vehicles with selling prices from $12,000 up to $15,000; the next class might include all vehicles that sold for $15,000 up to $18,000; and so on. We need to be clear about the class limits. In this case a selling price from $12,000 up to but not including $15,000 is tallied in the first class. This means that a vehicle selling for $12,000 is included in this class. A vehicle selling for $14,999.99 is included in this class. But one selling for $15,000 is not. Each class has an upper and a lower limit. In this case the lower limit of the first class is $12,000 and the upper limit is $15,000.

The usual practice is to let the lower limit of the first class be slightly lower than the lowest value in the data set and the upper limit of the largest class somewhat larger than the largest value. That is, we do not necessarily make the lower limit of the first class equal to the smallest value. The classes are **mutually exclusive,** meaning that a particular observation can fit in only one category. For example, a vehicle that sold for $16,876 falls only in the $15,000 up to $18,000 class.

Step 2. Tally the vehicle selling prices into the classes. To begin, the selling price of the first vehicle in Table 2–1 is $20,197. It is tallied in the $18,000 up to $21,000 class. The second selling price in the first column of Table 2–1 is $16,587. It is tallied in the $15,000 up to $18,000 class. The other selling prices are tallied in a similar manner. When all the selling prices are tallied, the table would appear as:

Class	Tallies
$12,000 up to $15,000	ЖЖ III
$15,000 up to $18,000	ЖЖ ЖЖ ЖЖ ЖЖ III
$18,000 up to $21,000	ЖЖ ЖЖ ЖЖ II
$21,000 up to $24,000	ЖЖ ЖЖ ЖЖ III
$24,000 up to $27,000	ЖЖ III
$27,000 up to $30,000	IIII
$30,000 up to $33,000	I
$33,000 up to $36,000	I

What happens to a vehicle that sells for the amount at the upper limit? That is, where would we classify a vehicle that sold for $18,000? Note that the class limits of the second class are stated as "$15,000 up to (but not including) $18,000." The limits of the third class are $18,000 up to $21,000. Hence, the vehicle selling price of exactly $18,000 is included in the third class, $18,000 up to $21,000. A vehicle selling for $17,999.99 is included in the second class. To put it another way, the class includes the lower limit, but not the upper limit. Thus, there is no overlap and a particular selling price can occur in only one class.

Step 3. Count the number of items in each class. The number of observations in each class is called the **class frequency.** In the $12,000 up to $15,000 class there are 8 observations, and in the $15,000 up to $18,000 there are 23 observations. Therefore, the class frequency in the first class is 8 and the class frequency in the second class is 23. There is a total of 80 observations or frequencies in the entire set of data.

Often it is useful to express the data in thousands, or some convenient units, rather than the actual data. Table 2–2 reports the vehicle selling prices in thousands of dollars, rather than dollars.

Table 2–2   **Frequency Distribution of Selling Prices at Whitner Pontiac Last Month**

Selling Prices ($ thousands)	Frequency
12 up to 15	8
15 up to 18	23
18 up to 21	17
21 up to 24	18
24 up to 27	8
27 up to 30	4
30 up to 33	1
33 up to 36	1
Total	80

Now that we have organized the data into a frequency distribution, we can summarize the pattern in the selling prices of the vehicles for Rob Whitner. Observe the following:

1.   The selling prices ranged from about $12,000 up to about $36,000.
2.   The selling prices are concentrated between $15,000 and $24,000.
3.   A total of 58, or 72.5 percent, of the vehicles sold within this range.
4.   The largest concentration is in the $15,000 up to $18,000 class. The middle of this class is $16,500, so we say that a typical selling price is $16,500.
5.   Two of the vehicles sold for $30,000 or more, and 8 sold for less than $15,000.

By presenting this information to Mr. Whitner, we give him a clear picture of the distribution of selling prices for last month.

We admit that arranging the information on selling prices into a frequency distribution does result in the loss of some detailed information. That is, by organizing the data into a frequency distribution, we cannot pinpoint the exact selling price, such as $20,197 or $23,372. Or, we cannot tell that the actual selling price for the least expensive vehicle was $12,546 and for the most expensive $33,625. However, the lower limit of the first class and the upper limit of the largest class convey essentially the same meaning. Rob will make the same judgment if he knows the lowest price is about $12,000 that he will if he knows the exact price is $12,546. The advantages of condensing the data into a more understandable form more than offset this disadvantage.

SELF-REVIEW 2–1

The answers are at the end of the chapter.

The commissions earned for the first quarter of last year by the eight members of the sales staff at Master Chemical Company are:

$1,650, $1,475, $1,760, $1,540, $1,495, $1,590, $1,625, and $1,510.

(a)   What are the values such as $1,650 and $1,475 called?
(b)   Using $1,400 up to $1,500 as the first class, $1,500 up to $1,600 as the second class, and so forth, organize the monthly incomes into a frequency distribution.
(c)   What are the numbers in the right column of your frequency distribution called?
(d)   Describe the distribution of monthly incomes, based on the frequency distribution. What is the largest amount of commission earned? What is the smallest? What is the typical amount earned?

Class Intervals and Class Midpoints

We will use two other terms frequently: **class midpoint** and **class interval.** The midpoint, also called the **class mark,** is halfway between the lower and the upper class limit. It can be computed by adding the lower class limit to the upper class limit and dividing by 2. Referring to Table 2–2, for the first class the lower class limit is $12,000 and the upper limit is $15,000. The class midpoint is $13,500, found by ($12,000 + $15,000)/2. The midpoint of $13,500 best represents, or is typical of, the selling price of the vehicles in that class.

To determine the class interval, subtract the lower limit of the class from the lower limit of the next class. The class interval of the vehicle selling price data is $3,000, which we find by subtracting the lower limit of the first class, $12,000 from the lower limit of the next class; that is, $15,000 − $12,000 = $3,000. You can also determine the class interval by finding the distance between consecutive midpoints. The midpoint of the first class is $13,500, and the midpoint of the second class is $16,500. The difference is $3,000.

▮ A Computer Software Example

As we mentioned in Chapter 1, there are many software packages that perform statistical calculations and output the results. Throughout this text we will show the output from MINITAB, Excel, and Computerized Business Statistics by Hall. The commands required to generate the outputs are given in the **Computer Commands** section at the end of each chapter.

The following is a frequency distribution, produced by MINITAB, showing the selling prices of the 80 vehicles sold last month at Whitner Pontiac. The form of the output is somewhat different than the frequency distribution of Table 2–2, but the overall conclusions are the same.

```
Character Histogram
Histogram of Price   N = 80
Midpoint      Count
   13500          8   ********
   16500         23   ***********************
   19500         17   *****************
   22500         18   ******************
   25500          8   ********
   28500          4   ****
   31500          1   *
   34500          1   *
```

Suggestions on Constructing Frequency Distributions

How do you determine the class interval or the number of classes? Today we can ask the computer software package to develop a frequency distribution for us. But what standards are programmed into the software? Here are some guidelines. You should look at them as guidelines for the construction of frequency distributions, not as absolute rules. For most data sets, there is no single correct answer for the construction of a frequency distribution.

1. *The class intervals used in the frequency distribution should be equal.* Unequal class intervals present problems in graphically portraying the distribution. Unequal class intervals, however, may be necessary in certain situations in order to avoid a large number of empty, or almost empty, classes. Such is the case in Table 2–3. The Internal Revenue Service used unequal-sized class intervals to report the adjusted gross income on individual tax returns. Had the IRS used an equal-sized interval of $1,000, more than 1,000 classes would have been required to describe all the incomes. A frequency distribution with 1,000 classes would be difficult to interpret. In this case the frequency distribution is more interpretable, in spite of the unequal classes. Note also that the number of frequencies is reported in thousands. This also makes the information easier to interpret.

Table 2–3   Adjusted Gross Income for Individuals Filing Income Tax Returns

Adjusted Gross Income	Number of Returns (in thousands)
Under $ 2,000	135
$ 2,000 up to 3,000	3,399
3,000 up to 5,000	8,175
5,000 up to 10,000	19,740
10,000 up to 15,000	15,539
15,000 up to 25,000	14,944
25,000 up to 50,000	4,451
50,000 up to 100,000	699
100,000 up to 500,000	162
500,000 up to 1,000,000	3
$1,000,000 and over	1

2. *The following formula, based on the number of classes, is useful for determining the class interval.* Suppose you have a mass of raw data to organize into a frequency distribution and want to use the same class interval for each class. What class interval should you use? The following formula gives a suggested common class interval. Note the formula number (2–1) is to the right of the formula. We will use these numbers to identify this particular formula in future discussions.

CLASS INTERVAL	$$i = \frac{\text{Highest value} \quad - \quad \text{Lowest value}}{\text{Number of classes}}$$	**[2–1]**

The lower case letter i refers to the class interval. Suppose you want to condense the raw data for the car prices in Table 2–1 into eight classes. The lowest value is $12,546 and the highest value is $33,625. What is the suggested class interval?

$$i = \frac{\$33,625 \quad - \quad \$12,546}{8} = \$2,635$$

A class interval of $2,635 would be awkward to work with. It would be easier to tally the car prices into a frequency distribution if the interval were rounded up to, say, $3,000.

3. *The class interval can also be estimated based on the number of observations.* To estimate the class interval, use the following formula, which uses logs to the base 10.

SUGGESTED INTERVAL BASED ON THE NUMBER OF OBSERVATIONS	$$i = \frac{\text{Highest value} \quad - \quad \text{Lowest value}}{1 + 3.322(\text{log of the total frequencies})}$$	**[2–2]**

For the vehicle selling price:

$$i = \frac{\$33,625 \quad - \quad \$12,546}{1 + 3.322(\log 80)} = \$2,879.$$

To find the logarithm of 80 using a scientific hand calculator, depress 80 then the key marked **log.** (Make sure you press the **log** key for the base 10 logarithms *not* the **ln** key for the base e logarithms.) The display will show 1.90309. From there, complete the arithmetic; the result is a suggested interval of $2,879. This is a rather awkward value, so a nearby value such as $3,000 is easier.

4. *Your professional judgment can determine the number of classes.* Too many classes or too few classes might not reveal the basic shape of the set of data. In the vehicle selling price problem, for example, an interval of $9,000 would not give much insight into the pattern of the data (see Table 2–4). With such a class interval, all we could say is that more than half of the vehicles sell for less than $21,000. As a general rule, it is best to not use less than 5 nor more than 15 classes in the construction of a frequency distribution.

Table 2–4 An Example of Too Few Classes

Vehicle Selling Price ($)	Number of Vehicles
12,000 up to 21,000	48
21,000 up to 30,000	30
30,000 up to 39,000	2
Total	80

5. *The "2 to the k rule" is also used to determine the number of classes.* To estimate the number of classes, we select the smallest integer (whole number) such that $2^k \geq n$ where n is the total number of observations. Using the Whitner Pontiac example, recall that there were 80 vehicles sold, so $n = 80$. If we try $k = 6$, which means we would use 6 classes, $2^6 = 64$, which is less than 80. Hence, 6 is not enough classes. If we let $k = 7$, then $2^7 = 128$, which is greater than 80. So the recommended number of classes is 7. Recall that in Table 2–2 we actually used eight. Based on this guideline, the following table shows the number of classes for a specific number of observations.

Total Number of Observations	Recommended Number of Classes
9–16	4
17–32	5
33–64	6
65–128	7
129-256	8
257–512	9
513–1,024	10

6. *The lower limit of the first class should be an even multiple of the class interval.* In the Whitner Pontiac problem, the class interval was $3,000. Multiplying this by 4 (an even multiple) gives $12,000, the lower limit of the first class. As another example, suppose a sample of company invoices ranged from $23 (low) to $69 (high). We want to organize the invoices into a frequency distribution with class interval of $10. The lower limit of the first class would be $20, found by multiplying 2 (the even multiple) by $10, the class interval.

7. *Avoid overlapping stated class limits.* Class limits such as $1,300–$1,400 and $1,400–$1,500 should not be used. Classes established in this way are not mutually exclusive, thus violating the definition of a frequency distribution. With overlapping classes it would not be clear where to tally a value of $1,400. Does it belong in the $1,300–$1,400 class or in the $1,400–$1,500 class?

8. *Try to avoid open-ended classes.* The classes "Under $2,000" and "$1,000,000 and over" used by the Internal Revenue Service in Table 2–3 are examples of open-ended classes. They cause problems in graphing, described in the next section, and in determining certain measures of central tendency and dispersion, described in chapters 3 and 4.

SELF-REVIEW 2–2

1. The monthly salaries of a sample of the 87 employees of Acklin Stamping were rounded to the nearest dollar. They ranged from a low of $1,041 to a high of $2,348.
   (a) Suppose we want to condense the data into seven classes. Using the same interval for each class, determine a suggested class interval.
   (b) What class interval would be easier to work with?
   (c) What are the class limits for the first class? The next class?
2. Suppose classes are written as:

   20–40
   40–60
   60–90
   90–150
   150 and greater

   These classes illustrate three practices that should be avoided. What are they?

Relative Frequency Distribution

A relative frequency distribution converts the distribution to a percent.

It may be desirable to convert class frequencies to **relative class frequencies** to show the percent of the total number of observations in each class. In our vehicle sales example, we may want to know what percent of the vehicle prices are in the $18,000 up to $21,000 class. In another study, we may want to know what percent of the employees are absent between one and three days per year due to illness.

To convert a frequency distribution to a relative frequency distribution, each of the class frequencies is divided by the total number of observations. Using the distribution of vehicle sales again (Table 2–2, where the selling price is reported in thousands of dollars), the relative frequency for the $12,000 up to $15,000 class is 0.10, found by dividing 8 by 80. That is, the selling price of 10 percent of the vehicles sold at Whitner Pontiac is between $12,000 and $15,000. The relative frequencies for the remaining classes are shown in Table 2–5.

Table 2–5 Relative Frequency Distribution of the Selling Prices of Vehicles Sold Last Month at Whitner Pontiac

Selling Price ($ thousands)	Frequency	Relative Frequency	Found by
12 up to 15	8	0.1000 ←	8/80
15 up to 18	23	0.2875	23/80
18 up to 21	17	0.2125	17/80
21 up to 24	18	0.2250	18/80
24 up to 27	8	0.1000	8/80
27 up to 30	4	0.0500	4/80
30 up to 33	1	0.0125	1/80
33 up to 36	1	0.0125	1/80
Total	80	1.0000	

SELF-REVIEW 2-3

Refer to Table 2–5, which shows the relative frequency distribution for the vehicles sold last month at Whitner Pontiac.

(a) How many vehicles sold for $15,000 up to $18,000?
(b) What percent of the vehicles sold for a price between $15,000 and $18,000?
(c) What percent of the vehicles sold for $27,000 or more?

Exercises

The answers to the odd-numbered exercises are at the end of the book.

1. A set of data consists of 38 observations. How many classes would you recommend for the frequency distribution?
2. A set of data consists of 45 observations, ranging from $0 to $29. What size would you recommend for the class interval?
3. A set of data consists of 230 observations that range from $235 to $567. What class interval would you recommend?

4. A set of data contains 53 observations. The lowest value is 42 and the largest is 129. The data are to be organized into a frequency distribution.
    a. What would you suggest as the lower limit of the first class?
    b. How many classes would you suggest?

5. The director of the honors program at Western University has 16 applications for admission next fall. The composite ACT scores of the applicants are:

27	27	27	28	27	25	25	28
26	28	26	28	31	30	26	26

    The ACT scores are to be organized into a frequency distribution.
    a. How many classes would you recommend?
    b. What class interval would you suggest?
    c. What lower limit would you recommend for the first class?
    d. Organize the scores into a frequency distribution and determine the relative frequency distribution.
    e. Comment on the shape of the distribution.

6. The Quick Change Oil Company has a number of outlets in the metropolitan area. The numbers of oil changes at the Oak Street outlet in the past 20 days are:

65	98	55	62	79	59	51	90	72	56
70	62	66	80	94	79	63	73	71	85

    The data are to be organized into a frequency distribution.
    a. How many classes would you recommend?
    b. What class interval would you suggest?
    c. What lower limit would you recommend for the first class?
    d. Organize the number of oil changes into a frequency distribution.
    e. Comment on the shape of the frequency distribution. Also determine the relative frequency distribution.

7. The local manager of Food Queen is interested in the number of times a customer shops at her store during a two-week period. The responses of 51 customers were:

5	3	3	1	4	4	5	6	4	2	6	6	6	7	1
1	14	1	2	4	4	4	5	6	3	5	3	4	5	6
8	4	7	6	5	9	11	3	12	4	7	6	5	15	1
1	10	8	9	2	12									

    a. Starting with 0 as the lower limit of the first class and using a class interval of 3, organize the data into a frequency distribution.
    b. Describe the distribution. Where do the data tend to cluster?
    c. Convert the distribution to a relative frequency distribution.

8. Moore Travel Agency, a nationwide travel agency, offers special rates on certain Caribbean cruises to senior citizens. The president of Moore Travel wants additional information on the ages of those people taking cruises. A random sample of 40 customers taking a cruise last year revealed these ages.

77	18	63	84	38	54	50	59	54	56	36	26	50	34	44
41	58	58	53	51	62	43	52	53	63	62	62	65	61	52
60	60	45	66	83	71	63	58	61	71					

    a. Organize the data into a frequency distribution, using seven classes and 15 as the lower limit of the first class. What class interval did you select?
    b. Where do the data tend to cluster?
    c. Describe the distribution.
    d. Determine the relative frequency distribution.

▌ Stem-and-Leaf Displays

In the previous section, we showed how to organize data into a frequency distribution so we could summarize the raw data into a meaningful form. The major advantage to organizing the data into a frequency distribution is that we get a quick visual picture of the shape of the distribution without doing any further calculation. That is, we can see where the data are concentrated and also determine whether there are any extremely large or small values. There are two disadvantages, however, to organizing the data into a frequency distribution: (1) we lose the exact identity of each value and (2) we are not sure how the values within each class are distributed. To explain, the following frequency distribution shows the number of advertising spots purchased by the 45 members of the Greater Buffalo Automobile Dealer's Association in 1997. We observe that 7 of the 45 dealers purchased between 90 and 99 spots (but less than 100). However, is the number of spots purchased within this class clustered about 90, spread evenly throughout the class, or clustered near 99? We cannot tell for sure.

Number of Spots Purchased	Frequency
80 up to 90	2
90 up to 100	7
100 up to 110	6
110 up to 120	9
120 up to 130	8
130 up to 140	7
140 up to 150	3
150 up to 160	3
Total	45

One technique that is used to display quantitative information in a condensed form is the **stem-and-leaf display.** An advantage of the stem-and-leaf display over a frequency distribution is that we do not lose the identity of each observation. In the above example, we would not know the identity of the values in the 90 up to 100 class. To illustrate the construction of a stem-and-leaf display using the number of advertising spots purchased, suppose the seven observations in the 90 up to 100 class are: 96, 94, 93, 94, 95, 96, and 97. The **stem** value is the leading digit or digits, in this case 9. The **leaves** are the trailing digits. The stem is placed to the left of a vertical line and the leaf values to the right.

The values in the 90 up to 100 class would appear as follows:

9 | 6 4 3 4 5 6 7

Finally, we sort the values within each stem from smallest to largest. Thus, the first row of the stem-and-leaf display would appear as follows:

9 | 3 4 4 5 6 6 7

With the stem-and-leaf display, we can quickly observe that there were two dealers who purchased 94 spots and that the number of spots purchased ranged from 93 to 97. A stem-and-leaf display is really a histogram with more information, i.e., data values instead of tallies.

> **Stem-and-Leaf Display** A statistical technique for displaying a set of data. Each numerical value is divided into two parts; The leading digit(s) becomes the *stem,* and the trailing digit the *leaf.* The stems are located along the main vertical axis, and the leaf for each observation along the horizontal axis.

The final table would appear as follows, where we have sorted all of the leaf values.

Stem	Leaf
8	8 9
9	3 4 4 5 6 6 7
10	3 3 4 6 7 8
11	1 2 2 3 3 7 7 8 9
12	0 0 4 5 5 5 7 7
13	2 4 5 6 8 9 9
14	2 3 8
15	5 5 6

You can draw several conclusions from the stem-and-leaf display. First the lowest number of spots purchased is 88 and the largest is 156. Two dealers purchased less than 90 spots, and three purchased 150 or more. You can observe, for example, that the three dealers who purchased more than 150 spots actually purchased 155, 155, and 156 spots. The concentration of the number of spots is between 110 and 130. There were 9 dealers who purchased between 110 and 119 spots and 8 who purchased between 120 and 129 spots. We can also tell that within the 120 to 129 group the actual number of spots purchased was spread evenly throughout. That is, two dealers purchased 120 spots, three dealers purchased 125 spots, and two purchased 127 spots.

We can also generate this information on the MINITAB software system. We have named the variable *Spots.* The MINITAB output is below. You can find the MINITAB commands that will produce this output at the end of the chapter.

```
Stem-and-leaf of Spots     N = 45
Leaf Unit = 1.0

      2     8  89
      9     9  3445667
     15    10  334678
    (9)    11  122337789
     21    12  00455577
     13    13  2456899
      6    14  238
      3    15  556
```

The MINITAB solution provides some additional information regarding cumulative totals. In the column to the left of the stem values are numbers such as 2, 9, 15, and so on. The number 9 indicates that there are 9 observations that have occurred before the value of 100. The number 15 indicates that 15 observations have occurred prior to 110. About halfway down the column the number 9 appears in parentheses. The parentheses indicate that the middle value appears in that row. In this case, we describe the middle value as the value below which half of the observations occur. There are a total of 45 observations, so the middle value, if the data were arranged from smallest, would be the 23rd observation. In this example there are 15 observations below 110. The value of 9 in parentheses indicates that there are nine observations in the row with a stem of 11. The middle value would be the 23rd observation or the 8th value in this row. Hence the middle value, or the median as it is called, is 118, found by counting over 8 values in that row. After the median row, the values begin to decline. These values represent the "more than" cumulative totals. There are 21 observations of 120 or more, 13 of 130 or more, and so on.

SELF-REVIEW 2–4

The price-earning ratios for 21 stocks in the retail trade category are:

8.3	9.6	9.5	9.1	8.8	11.2	7.7	10.1	9.9	10.8	
10.2	8.0	8.4	8.1	11.6	9.6	8.8	8.0	10.4	9.8	9.2

Organize this information into a stem-and-leaf display.

(a) How many values are there less than 9.0?
(b) List the values in the 10.0 up to 10.9 category.
(c) What is the middle value?
(d) What are the largest and the smallest price-earnings ratios?

▌ Exercises

9.   The first row of a stem-and-leaf chart appears as follows: 62 | 1 3 3 7 9.
    a.   What is the possible range of the values in this row?
    b.   How many data values are in this row?
    c.   List the actual values in this row of data.
10.   The third row of a stem-and-leaf chart appears as follows: 21 | 0 1 3 5 7 9.
    a.   What is the possible range of the values in this row?
    b.   How many data values are in this row?
    c.   List the actual values in this row of data.
11.   The following stem-and-leaf chart shows the number of units produced per day in a factory.

1	3 8	
1	4	
2	5 6	
9	6	0133559
(7)	7	0236778
9	8	59
7	9	00156
2	10	36

    a.   How many days were studied?
    b.   How many observations are in the first class?
    c.   What are the smallest value and the largest value?
    d.   List the actual values in the fourth row.
    e.   List the actual values in the second row.
    f.   How many values are less than 70?
    g.   How many values are 80 or more?
    h.   What is the middle value?
    i.   How many values are there between 60 and 89?
12.   The following stem-and-leaf chart reports the number of movies rented per day at Video Connection.

```
 3      12 689
 6      13 123
10      14 6889
13      15 589
15      16 35
20      17 24568
23      18 268
(5)     19 13456
22      20 034679
16      21 2239
12      22 789
 9      23 00179
 4      24 8
 3      25 13
 1      26
 1      27 0
```

a.   How many days were studied?
b.   How many observations are in the last class?
c.   What are the largest and the smallest values in the entire set of data?
d.   List the actual values in the fourth row.
e.   List the actual values in the next to the last row.
f.   On how many days were less than 160 movies rented?
g.   On how many days were 220 or more movies rented?
h.   What is the middle or the median value?
i.   On how many days were between 170 and 210 movies rented?

13.   A survey of the number of calls received by a sample of Southern Phone Company subscribers last week revealed the following information. Develop a stem-and-leaf chart. Summarize the data on the number of calls received: How many calls did a typical subscriber receive? What were the largest and the smallest number of calls received? Around what values did the number of calls tend to cluster?

52	43	30	38	30	42	12	46	39
37	34	46	32	18	41	5		

14.   Aloha Banking Co. is studying the number of times their automatic teller, located in Loblaws Supermarket, is used each day. The following is the number of times it was used during each of the last 30 days. Develop a stem-and-leaf chart. Summarize the data on the number of times the automatic teller was used: How many times was the teller used on a typical day? What were the largest and the smallest number of times the teller was used? Around what values did the number of times the teller was used tend to cluster?

83	64	84	76	84	54	75	59	70	61
63	80	84	73	68	52	65	90	52	77
95	36	78	61	59	84	95	47	87	60

▌ Graphic Presentation of a Frequency Distribution

Sales managers, stock analysts, hospital administrators, and other busy executives often need a quick picture of the trends in sales, stock prices, or hospital costs. These trends can often be depicted by the use of charts and graphs. Three charts that will help portray a frequency distribution graphically are the histogram, the frequency polygon, and the cumulative frequency polygon.

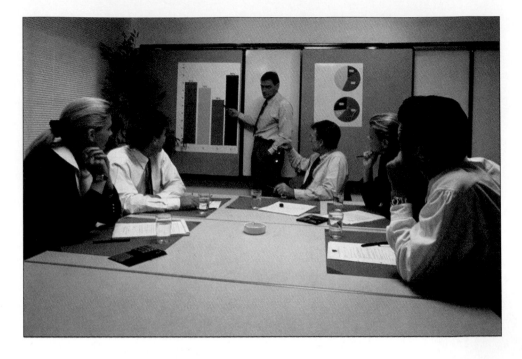

Histogram

One of the most common ways to portray a frequency distribution is with a **histogram.**

> **Histogram**   A graph in which the classes are marked on the horizontal axis and the class frequencies on the vertical axis. The class frequencies are represented by the heights of the bars, and the bars are drawn adjacent to each other.

Thus, a histogram describes a frequency distribution using a series of adjacent rectangles, where the height of each rectangle is proportional to the frequency the class represents. The construction of a histogram is best illustrated by reintroducing the selling prices of the 80 vehicles sold last month at Whitner Pontiac.

Example

Below is the frequency distribution of the selling prices of vehicles sold at Whitner Pontiac last month.

Selling Prices ($ thousands)	Frequency
12 up to 15	8
15 up to 18	23
18 up to 21	17
21 up to 24	18
24 up to 27	8
27 up to 30	4
30 up to 33	1
33 up to 36	1
Total	80

Construct a histogram. What conclusions can you reach based on the information presented in the histogram?

Solution

To construct a histogram, the class frequencies are scaled along the vertical axis (*Y*-axis) and either the class limits or the class midpoints along the horizontal axis. To illustrate the construction of the histogram, the first three classes are shown in Chart 2–1.

Chart 2–1   Construction of a Histogram

From Chart 2–1 we note that there are eight vehicles in the $12,000 up to $15,000 class. Therefore, the height of the column for that class is 8. There are 23 vehicles in the $15,000 up to $18,000 class, so, logically, the height of that column is 23. The height of the bar represents the number of observations in the class.

This procedure is continued for all classes. The complete histogram is shown in Chart 2–2. Note that there is no space between the bars. This is a feature of the histogram. In bar charts, which are described in a later section, the vertical bars are separated slightly.

Chart 2–2   Histogram of the Selling Prices of 80 Vehicles at Whitner Pontiac

Based on the histogram in Chart 2–2, we conclude:

1. The lowest selling price is about $12,000, and the largest is about $36,000.

2. The largest class frequency is the $15,000 up to $18,000 class. A total of 23 of the 80 vehicles sold are within this price range.
3. Fifty-eight of the vehicles, or 72.5 percent, had a selling price of between $15,000 and $24,000.

Thus, the histogram provides an easily interpreted visual representation of a frequency distribution. We should also point out that we would have reached the same conclusions and the shape of the histogram would have been the same had we used a relative frequency distribution instead of the actual frequencies. That is, if we had used the relative frequencies of Table 2–5, found on page 29, we would have had a histogram of the same shape as Chart 2–2. The difference is that the vertical axis would have been reported in percent of vehicles instead of the number of vehicles.

Frequency Polygon

In a frequency polygon the class midpoints are connected with a line segment.

A **frequency polygon** is similar to a histogram. It consists of line segments connecting the points formed by the intersections of the class midpoints and the class frequencies. The construction of a frequency polygon is illustrated in Chart 2–3 on the next page. We use the vehicle selling prices for the cars sold last month at Whitner Pontiac. The midpoint of each class is scaled on the *X*-axis and the class frequencies on the *Y*-axis. Recall that the class midpoint is the value at the center of a class and represents the values in that class. The class frequency is the number of observations in a particular class. The vehicle selling prices at Whitner Pontiac are:

Selling Price ($ thousands)	Midpoint	Frequency
12 up to 15	13.5	8
15 up to 18	16.5	23
18 up to 21	19.5	17
21 up to 24	22.5	18
24 up to 27	25.5	8
27 up to 30	28.5	4
30 up to 33	31.5	1
33 up to 36	34.5	1
Total		80

As noted previously, the $12,000 up to $15,000 class is represented by the midpoint, $13,500. To construct a frequency polygon, move horizontally on the graph to the midpoint, $13.5, and then vertically to 8, the class frequency, and place a dot. The *X* and the *Y* values of this point are called the *coordinates*. The coordinates of the next point are *X* = $16.5 and *Y* = 23. The process is continued for all classes. Then the points are connected in order. That is, the point representing the lowest class is joined to the one representing the second class and so on.

Note in Chart 2–3 that, to complete the frequency polygon, midpoints of $10.5 and $37.5 are added to the *X*-axis to "anchor" the polygon at zero frequencies. These two values, $10.5 and $37.5, were derived by subtracting the class interval of $3.0 from the lowest midpoint ($13.5) and by adding $3.0 to the highest midpoint ($34.5) in the frequency distribution.

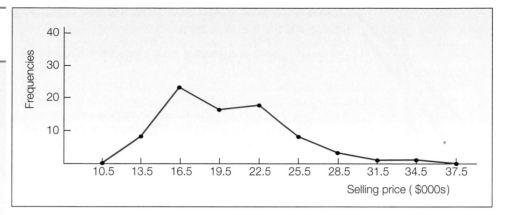

Chart 2–3   Frequency Polygon of the Selling Prices of 80 Vehicles at Whitner Pontiac

Both the histogram and the frequency polygon allow us to get a quick picture of the main characteristics of the data (highs, lows, points of concentration, etc.). Although the two representations are similar in purpose, the histogram has the advantage of depicting each class as a rectangle, with the area of the rectangular bar representing the number in frequencies of each class. The frequency polygon, in turn, has an advantage over the histogram. It allows us to compare directly two or more frequency distributions. Suppose that Rob Whitner, the owner of Whitner Pontiac, wants to compare the sales last month at his dealership with those at Midtown Cadillac. To do this, two frequency polygons are constructed, one on top of the other, as in Chart 2–4. It is clear from Chart 2–4 that the typical vehicle selling price is higher at the Cadillac dealership.

The total number of frequencies at Whitner Pontiac and at Midtown Cadillac is about the same, so a direct comparison is possible. If the difference in the total number of frequencies is quite large, converting the actual frequencies to relative frequencies and then plotting the two distributions would allow a clearer comparison.

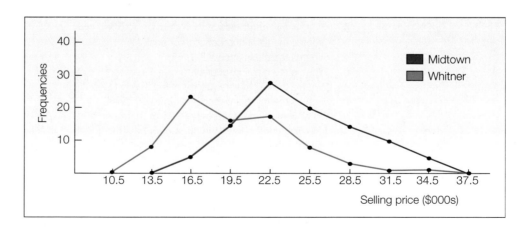

Chart 2–4   Distribution of Vehicle Selling Prices at Whitner Pontiac and Midtown Cadillac

SELF-REVIEW 2-5

The annual imports of a selected group of electronic suppliers are shown in the following frequency distribution.

Imports ($ millions)	Number of Suppliers
2 up to 5	6
5 up to 8	13
8 up to 11	20
11 up to 14	10
14 up to 17	1

(a) Portray the imports in the form of a histogram.
(b) Portray the imports in the form of a relative frequency polygon.
(c) Summarize the important facets of the distribution (such as low and high, concentration, etc.)

▌ Exercises

15. Molly's Candle Shop has several retail stores in the coastal areas of North and South Carolina. Many of Molly's customers ask her to ship their purchases. The chart below shows the number of packages shipped per day for the last 100 days.

    a. What is this chart called?
    b. What is the total number of frequencies?
    c. What is the class interval?
    d. What is the class frequency for the 10 up to 15 class?
    e. What is the relative frequency of the 10 up to 15 class?
    f. What is the midpoint of the 10 up to 15 class?
    g. On how many days were there 25 or more packages shipped?

16. The following chart shows the number of patients admitted to Memorial Hospital through the emergency room.

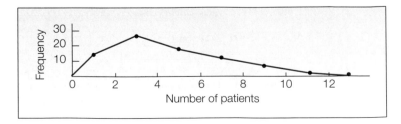

    a. What is the midpoint of the 2 up to 4 class?
    b. How many days were there 2 up to 4 patients admitted?
    c. How many days were studied?
    d. What is the class interval?
    e. What is this chart called?

17. The following frequency distribution represents the number of days during a year that employees at the E. J. Wilcox Manufacturing Company were absent from work due to illness.

Number of Days Absent	Number of Employees
0 up to 3	5
3 up to 6	12
6 up to 9	23
9 up to 12	8
12 up to 15	2
Total	50

    a. Assuming that this is a sample, what is the sample size?
    b. What is the midpoint of the first class?
    c. Construct a histogram.
    d. A frequency polygon is to be drawn. What are the coordinates of the plot for the first class?
    e. Construct a frequency polygon.
    f. Interpret the rate of employee absenteeism using the two charts.

18. A large retailer is studying the lead time (elapsed time between when an order is placed and when it is filled) for a sample of recent orders. The lead times are reported in days.

Lead Time (days)	Frequency
0 up to 5	6
5 up to 10	7
10 up to 15	12
15 up to 20	8
20 up to 25	7
Total	40

    a. How many orders were studied?
    b. What is the midpoint of the first class?
    c. What are the coordinates of the first class?
    d. Draw a histogram.
    e. Draw a frequency polygon.
    f. Interpret the lead times using the two charts.

Less-Than Cumulative Frequency Polygons

Consider once again the distribution of the selling prices of vehicles at Whitner Pontiac. Suppose we were interested in the number of vehicles that sold for less than $18,000, or the value below which 40 percent of the vehicles sold. These numbers can be approximated by developing a **cumulative frequency distribution** and portraying it graphically in a **cumulative frequency polygon.**

Example   The frequency distribution of the vehicle selling prices at Whitner Pontiac is repeated from Table 2–2.

Selling Price ($ thousands)	Frequency
12 up to 15	8
15 up to 18	23
18 up to 21	17
21 up to 24	18
24 up to 27	8
27 up to 30	4
30 up to 33	1
33 up to 36	1
Total	80

Construct a less-than cumulative frequency polygon. Answer these questions: Fifty percent of the vehicles were sold for less than what amount? Twenty-five of the vehicles were sold for less than what amount?

Solution   As the name implies, a cumulative frequency distribution and a cumulative frequency polygon require *cumulative frequencies.* To construct a less-than cumulative frequency distribution, refer to the preceding table and note that there were eight vehicles sold for less than $15,000. Those 8 vehicles, plus the 23 in the next higher class, for a total of 31, were sold for less than $18,000. The cumulative frequency for the next higher class is 48, found by 8 + 23 + 17. This process is continued for all the classes. All the vehicles were sold for less than $36,000. (See Table 2–7.)

Table 2–7   Less-Than Cumulative Frequency Distribution for Vehicle Selling Price

Selling Price ($ thousands)	Frequency	Cumulative Frequency	Found by
12 up to 15	8	8	
15 up to 18	23	31 ←	8 + 23
18 up to 21	17	48	8 + 23 + 17
21 up to 24	18	66	8 + 23 + 17 + 18
24 up to 27	8	74	
27 up to 30	4	78	
30 up to 33	1	79	
33 up to 36	1	80	
Total	80		

To plot a less-than cumulative frequency distribution, scale the upper limit of the class along the *X*-axis and the cumulative frequencies along the *Y*-axis. To provide additional information, you can scale the vertical axis on the left in units and the vertical axis on the right in percent. In the Whitner Pontiac example, the vertical axis on the left is scaled from 0 to 80 and on the right from 0 to 100 percent. The value of 50 percent corresponds to 40 vehicles sold.

To begin the plotting, 8 vehicles sold for less than $15,000, so the first plot is at *X* = 15 and *Y* = 8. The coordinates for the next plot are *X* = 18 and *Y* = 31. The rest of the points are plotted and then the dots connected to form the chart (see Chart 2–5). To find the selling price below which half the cars sold, we draw a line from the 50 percent mark on the right-hand vertical axis over to the polygon, then drop down to the *X*-axis and read the selling price. The value on the *X*-axis is about 19.5, so we estimate that 50 percent of the vehicles sold for less than $19,500.

Chart 2–5   Less-Than Cumulative Frequency Distribution for Vehicle Selling Price

To find the value below which 25 of the vehicles sold, we locate the value of 25 on the left-hand vertical axis. Next, we draw a horizontal line from the value of 25 to the polygon, and then drop down to the *X*-axis and read the value. It is about 17.5, so we estimate that 25 of the vehicles sold for less than $17,500. We can also make estimates of the percent of vehicles that sold for less than a particular amount. To explain, suppose we want to estimate the percent of vehicles that sold for less than $25,500. We begin by locating the value of 25.5 on the *X*-axis, move vertically to the polygon, and then horizontally to the vertical axis on the right. The value is about 87.5 percent, so we conclude that 87.5 percent of the vehicles sold for less than $25,500.

SELF-REVIEW 2-6

A sample of the hourly wages of 80 employees at Food City Supermarkets was organized into the following table.

Hourly Wages	Number of Wages
$ 6 up to $ 8	18
8 up to 10	36
10 up to 12	20
12 up to 14	6

(a) What is the table called?
(b) Develop a less-than cumulative frequency distribution and portray the distribution in a less-than cumulative frequency polygon.
(c) Based on the cumulative frequency polygon, how many employees earn $9 an hour or less? Half of the employees earn an hourly wage of how much or more? Twenty employees earn how much or less?

▌ Exercises

19. The following chart shows the hourly wages of certified welders in the Atlanta, Georgia, area.

   a. How many welders were studied?
   b. What is the class interval?
   c. About how many welders earn less than $10.00 per hour?
   d. About 75 percent of the welders make less than what amount?
   e. Ten of the welders studied made less than what amount?
   f. What percent of the welders make less than $20.00 per hour?

20. The following chart shows the selling price ($000) of houses sold in the Billings, Montana, area.

a. How many homes were studied?
b. What is the class interval?
c. One hundred homes sold for less than what amount?
d. About 75 percent of the homes sold for less than what amount?
e. Estimate the number of homes in the $150 up to $200 class.
f. About how many homes sold for less than $225?

21. The frequency distribution representing the number of days annually the employees at the E. J. Wilcox Manufacturing Company were absent from work due to illness is repeated from Exercise 17.

Number of Days Absent	Frequency
0 up to 3	5
3 up to 6	12
6 up to 9	23
9 up to 12	8
12 up to 15	2
Total	50

a. How many employees were absent less than three days annually? How many were absent less than six days due to illness?
b. Convert the frequency distribution to a less-than cumulative frequency distribution.
c. Portray the cumulative distribution in the form of a less-than cumulative frequency polygon.
d. Based on the cumulative frequency polygon, about three out of four employees were absent for how many days or less due to illness?

22. The frequency distribution of the lead time to fill an order from Exercise 18 is repeated below.

Lead Time (days)	Frequency
0 up to 5	6
5 up to 10	7
10 up to 15	12
15 up to 20	8
20 up to 25	7
Total	40

a. How many orders were filled in less than 10 days? In less than 15 days?
b. Convert the frequency distribution to a less-than cumulative frequency distribution.
c. Develop a less-than cumulative frequency polygon.
d. About 60 percent of the orders were filled in less than how many days?

Other Graphic Presentations of Data

The histogram, the frequency polygon, and the less-than cumulative frequency polygon all have strong visual appeal. That is, they are designed to capture the attention of the reader. In this section we will examine some other graphical forms, namely the line chart, the bar chart, and the pie chart. These charts are seen extensively in *USA Today, U.S. News and World Report, Business Week,* and other newspapers, magazines, and government reports.

Charts 2–6 and 2–7 are examples of **line charts.** Line charts are particularly effective in business because we can show the change in a variable over time. The variable, such as the number of units sold or the total value of sales, is scaled along the vertical axis and time along the horizontal axis. Chart 2–6 shows the Dow Jones Average, one of the most widely reported measures of business activity, on Thursday, January 15, 1998. The Dow was at 7695.21, which was down 89.18 for the day.

Chart 2–6   Market Summary on January 15, 1998

Chart 2–7 is also a line chart. It shows the average total number of points scored (number scored by the winner plus the number scored by the loser) in Division I men's college basketball games beginning with the 1985–86 season through the 1996–97 season. The interesting point of this chart is that, because of the relatively low scoring, the 3-point shot was added after the 1985–86 season. For the next several years, the total points increased to a high of 152.9 per game in the 1990–91 season. For the last 6 seasons, however, the total number of points scored has declined. Does the NCAA need to do something again to increase scoring?

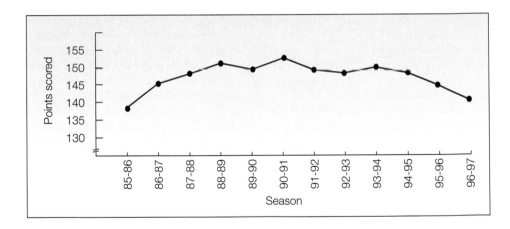

Chart 2–7   Total Points Scored in NCAA Men's Basketball, 1985–86 to 1996–97

Quite often two or more series of figures are plotted on the same line chart. Thus, one chart can show the trend of several series. This allows for a quick comparison of several series over a period of time. Chart 2–8 is an illustration. It shows the earnings per share of common stock for the telecommunications company GTE for the years 1992 through 1996. On the same chart are the dividends declared per share of common stock. We can easily see that the declared dividends have stayed fairly constant, but that the earnings per share increased during the five-year period.

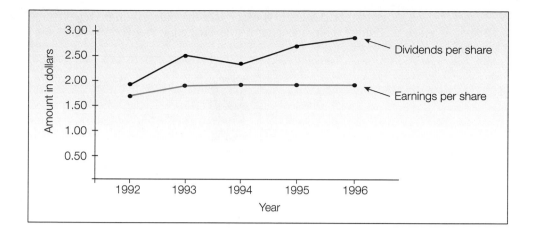

Chart 2–8   Earnings and Dividends per Share of Common Stock, GTE, 1992–96

A **bar chart** can be used to depict any of the levels of measurement — nominal, ordinal, interval, or ratio. (We discussed levels of measurement at some length in Chapter 1.) Suppose we want to portray the percentage increase for selected civilian jobs (nominal level of data) from 1988 to the year 2000. The need for medical assistants is projected to be up 70 percent by 2000, travel agents up 54 percent, computer employees up 53 percent, and so on. We plot these figures in the form of a *horizontal bar chart.* We extend the bar for medical assistants to 70 percent, showing the percent increase from 1988 to 2000. This process is continued for all the civilian jobs shown in Chart 2–9.

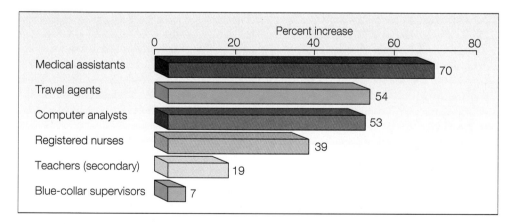

Chart 2–9   Percent Increases in Civilian Jobs for Selected Occupations, 1988 to 2000

Suppose we want to show the religious affiliation of the U.S. population in the form of a **vertical bar chart.** From the *Yearbook of American and Canadian Churches,* we find that 79 million persons of age 14 years and older stated that their religion is Protestant, 31 million stated that their religion is Roman Catholic, 4 million identified themselves as Jewish, and 2 million had other religions. This information is depicted in Chart 2–10. It shows clearly, for example, that there are more than twice as many Protestants as Roman Catholics. Note that there is space between the bars representing the various groups. This is one of the ways in which a histogram and a vertical bar chart differ. There is no space between the bars of a histogram because the data are interval or ratio level data, but this is not the case for the data in a bar chart. The Protestants and Roman Catholics represent nominal level groups; therefore, the bars are separated.

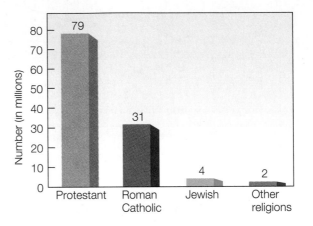

Chart 2–10   Religious Affiliation of the U.S. Population 14-Years-Old and Over (self-reported)

A **pie chart** is especially useful for depicting nominal level data. We will use the information in Table 2–8, which shows a breakdown of state lottery proceeds since 1964, to explain the details of constructing a pie chart.

Table 2–8   State Lottery Proceeds

Use of Profits	Percent Share
Education	56
General fund	23
Cities	10
Senior citizens	9
Other	2
Total	100

The first step is to record the percentages 0, 5, 10, 15, and so on evenly around the circumference of a circle. To plot the 56 percent share for education, draw a line from 0 to the center of the circle and then another line from the center to 56 percent on the circle. The area of this "slice" represents the lottery proceeds that were given to education. Next, add the 56 percent transferred to education to the 23 percent transferred to the general fund; the result is 79 percent. Draw a line from the center of the circle to 79 percent, so the area from 56 percent to 79 percent represents the percent of the lottery proceeds transferred to the general fund of the state. Continuing, add 10, the component given to the cities, which gives us a total of 89 percent. Draw a line from the center out to the value 89, so the area between 79 and 89 represents the share transferred to cities. Continue the same process for the senior citizen programs and "Other." Because the areas of the pie represent the relative share of each category, we can quickly compare them: The largest percent of the proceeds go to education; this amount is more than half the total, and it is more than twice the amount given to the next largest category.

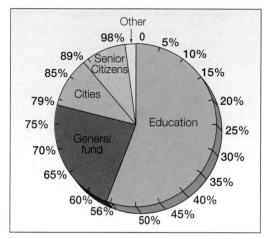

Percent of State Lottery Proceeds

The Excel system will develop a pie chart and output the result. Following is an Excel chart showing the percentage of viewers watching each of the major television networks during prime time.

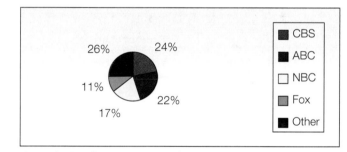

Share of Prime-Time Viewing for Major Networks

SELF-REVIEW 2–7

The Clayton County Commissioners want to design a chart to show taxpayers attending the forthcoming meeting what happens to their tax dollars. The total amount of taxes collected is $2 million. Expenditures are: $440,000 for schools, $1,160,000 for roads, $320,000 for administration, and $80,000 for supplies. A pie chart seems ideal to show the portion of each tax dollar going for schools, roads, administration, and supplies. Convert the dollar amounts to percents of the total and portray the percents in the form of a pie chart.

▌ Misuses of Statistics

When you purchase a computer for your home or office, it usually includes some graphics and spreadsheet software, such as Excel. This software will produce effective charts and graphs. However, you must be careful not to mislead or misrepresent. In this section we present several examples of charts and graphs that are misleading. Whenever you see a chart or graph, study it carefully. Ask yourself: What is the writer trying to show me? Could the writer have any bias?

One of the easiest ways to mislead the reader is to make the range of the *Y*-axis very small in terms of the units used for that axis. A second method is to begin at some value other than 0 on the *Y*-axis. In the chart below, it looks like there has been a dramatic increase in sales from 1985 to 1996. However, during the period, sales increased only 2 percent (from $5.0 million to $5.1 million)! In addition, observe that the *Y*-axis does not begin at 0.

Sales of Matsui Nine-Passenger Vans, 1985–1996

The chart below gives the correct impression of the trend in sales. Sales are almost flat from 1985 to 1996; that is, there has been practically no change in sales during the 10-year period.

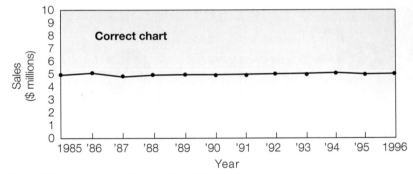

Sales of Matsui Nine-Passenger Vans, 1985–1996

Without much comment, we ask you to look at each of the following charts and carefully decide whether the intended message is accurate.

1. The following chart was adapted from an advertisement for the new Wilson ULTRA DISTANCE golf ball. The chart shows that the new ball gets the longest distance, but what is the scale for the horizontal axis? How was the test conducted?

Maybe everybody can't hit a ball like John Daly. But everybody wants to. That's why Wilson© is introducing the new ULTRA© DISTANCE ball. ULTRA DISTANCE is the longest, most accurate ball you'll ever hit.

Wilson has totally redesigned this ball from the inside out, making ULTRA DISTANCE a major advancement in golf technology.

ULTRA© DISTANCE	**591.2 Yds.**
DUNLOP© DDH IV	**584.6 Yds.**
MAXFLI MD©	**571.2 Yds.**
TITLEIST© HVC	**569.3 Yds.**
TOP-FLITE© Tour 90	**565.9 Yds.**
TOP-FLITE© MAGNA	**564.3 Yds.**

Combined yardage with a driver, #5 iron and #9 iron, ULTRA DISTANCE is clearly measurably longer.

2. Fibre Tech, in Largo, Florida, makes and installs fiberglass coatings for swimming pools. The following chart was included in a brochure. Is the comparison fair? What is the scale for the vertical axis? Is the scale in dollars or in percent?

Fibre Tech Reduces Chemical Use, Saving You Time and Money.

- Saves up to 60% on chemical costs alone.
- Reduces water loss, which means less need to replace chemicals and up to 10% warmer water (reducing heating costs, too).
- Fibre Tech pays for itself in reduced maintenance and chemical costs.

Again, we caution you. When you see a chart or graph, particularly as part of an advertisement, be careful. Look at the scales used on the *X*-axis and the *Y*-axis.

❙ Exercises

23. The Marketing Research Department is investigating the performance of several corporations in the coal, mining, and gas industries. The fourth-quarter sales in 1997 (in millions of dollars) for these corporations are:

Corporation	Fourth-Quarter Sales ($ millions)
American Hess	$ 1,645.2
Atlantic Richfield	4,757.0
Chevron	8,913.0
Diamond Shamrock	627.1
Exxon	24,612.0
Quaker State	191.9

The Department wants to include a chart in their report comparing the fourth-quarter sales of the six corporations. Use a bar chart to compare the fourth quarter sales of these corporations and write a brief report summarizing the bar chart.

24. The Blair Corporation, located in Warren, Pennsylvania, sells fashion apparel for men and women plus a broad range of home products. It services its customers by mail. Listed below are the net sales for Blair from 1992 through 1996. Draw a line chart depicting the net sales

over the time period and write a brief report summarizing the bar chart.

Year	Net Sales ($ millions)
1992	500.0
1993	519.2
1994	535.8
1995	560.9
1996	544.1

25. A headline in the *Toledo Blade* reported that crime was on the decline. Listed below are the number of homicides from 1986 to 1996. Draw a line chart to summarize the data and write a brief summary of the homicide rates for the last 11 years.

Year	Homicides	Year	Homicides
1986	21	1992	44
1987	34	1993	45
1988	26	1994	40
1989	42	1995	35
1990	37	1996	30
1991	37		

26. A report prepared for the governor of a western state indicated that 56 percent of the state's tax revenue went to education, 23 percent to the general fund, 10 percent to the counties, 9 percent to senior programs, and the remainder to other social programs. Develop a pie chart to show the breakdown of the budget.

27. Listed below, in millions, is the population of the United States in 5-year intervals from 1950 to 1995. Develop a line chart depicting the population growth and write a brief report summarizing your findings.

Year	Population (millions)	Year	Population (millions)
1950	152.30	1975	216.00
1955	165.90	1980	227.70
1960	180.70	1985	238.50
1965	194.30	1990	249.90
1970	205.10	1995	263.00

28. Shown below are the military and civilian personnel expenditures for the eight largest military locations in the United States. Develop a bar chart and summarize the results in a brief report.

Location	Amount Spent (billions)	Location	Amount Spent (billions)
St. Louis, MO	$6,087	Norfolk, VA	$3,228
San Diego, CA	4,747	Marietta, GA	2,828
Pico Rivera, CA	3,272	Fort Worth, TX	2,492
Arlington, VA	3,284	Washington, DC	2,347

▮ Chapter Outline

I. A frequency distribution is a grouping of data into categories showing the number of observations in each mutually exclusive category.

    A. The steps in constructing a frequency distribution are:

        1. Decide on the size of the class interval.

2. Tally the raw data into the classes.
3. Count the number of tallies in each class.
   B. The class frequency is the number of observations in each class.
   C. The class interval is the difference between the lower limits of two consecutive classes.
   D. The class midpoint is halfway between the lower limits of two consecutive classes.
   E. The criteria for constructing a frequency distribution are:
      1. Avoid having fewer than 5 or more than 15 classes.
      2. Avoid open-ended classes.
      3. Keep the class intervals the same size.
      4. Do not have overlapping classes.
II. A relative frequency distribution shows the percent of the observations in each class.
III. A stem-and-leaf display is an alternative to a frequency distribution.
   A. The leading digit is the stem and the trailing digit the leaf.
   B. The advantages of the stem-and-leaf chart over a frequency distribution include:
      1. The identity of each observation is not lost.
      2. The digits themselves give a picture of the distribution.
      3. The cumulative frequencies are also reported.
IV. There are two methods for graphically portraying a frequency distribution.
   A. A histogram portrays the number of frequencies in each class in the form of rectangles.
   B. A frequency polygon consists of line segments connecting the points formed by the intersections of the class midpoints and the class frequencies.
V. A less-than cumulative frequency polygon shows the number of observations below a certain value.
VI. There are many charts used in newspapers and magazines.
   A. A line chart is ideal for showing the trend of sales or income over time.
   B. Bar charts are similar to line charts and are useful for showing changes in business or economic data over time.
   C. Pie charts are useful for showing the percent that various components are of the total.

▌ Chapter Exercises

29. A data set consists of 83 observations. How many classes would you recommend for a frequency distribution?
30. A data set consists of 145 observations that range from 56 to 490. What size class interval would you recommend?
31. The following is the number of minutes to commute from home to work for a group of automobile executives.

| 28 | 25 | 48 | 37 | 41 | 19 | 32 | 26 | 16 | 23 | 23 | 29 | 36 |
| 31 | 26 | 21 | 32 | 25 | 31 | 43 | 35 | 42 | 38 | 33 | 28 | |

   a. How many classes would you recommend?
   b. What class interval would you suggest?
   c. What would you recommend as the lower limit of the first class?
   d. Organize the data into a frequency distribution.
   e. Comment on the shape of the frequency distribution.
32. The following data give the weekly amounts spent on groceries for a sample of households.

$271	$363	$159	$ 76	$227	$337	$295	$319	$250
279	205	279	266	199	177	162	232	303
192	181	321	309	246	278	50	41	335
116	100	151	240	474	297	170	188	320
429	294	570	342	279	235	434	123	325

    a.   How many classes would you recommend?
    b.   What class interval would you suggest?
    c.   What would you recommend as the lower limit of the first class?
    d.   Organize the data into a frequency distribution.

33.   The following stem-and-leaf display shows the number of minutes of daytime TV viewing for a sample of college students.

2	0	05
3	1	0
6	2	137
10	3	0029
13	4	499
24	5	00155667799
30	6	023468
	7	1366789
33	8	01558
28	9	1122379
21	10	022367899
12	11	2457
8	12	4668
4	13	249
1	14	5

    a.   How many college students were studied?
    b.   How many observations are in the second class?
    c.   What are the smallest value and the largest value?
    d.   List the actual values in the fourth row.
    e.   How many students watched less than 60 minutes of TV?
    f.   How many students watched 100 minutes or more of TV?
    g.   What is the middle value?
    h.   How many students watched at least 60 minutes but less than 100 minutes?

34.   The following stem-and-leaf display reports the number of orders received per day by a mail-order firm.

1	9	1
2	10	2
5	11	235
7	12	69
8	13	2
11	14	135
15	15	1229
22	16	2266778
27	17	01599
11	18	00013346799
17	19	03346
12	20	4679
8	21	0177
4	22	45
2	23	17

a. How many days were studied?
b. How many observations are in the fourth class?
c. What are the smallest value and the largest value?
d. List the actual values in the sixth class.
e. How many days did the firm receive less than 140 orders?
f. How many days did the firm receive 200 or more orders?
g. On how many days did the firm receive 180 orders?
h. What is the middle value?

35. The following frequency polygon shows the scores on the first statistics exam.

a. How many students took the exam?
b. What is the class interval?
c. What is the class midpoint for the first class?
d. How many students earned a score of less than 70?

36. The following chart summarizes the selling price of homes sold last month in the Sarasota, Florida, area.

a. What is the chart called?
b. How many homes were sold during the last month?
c. What is the class interval?
d. About 75 percent of the houses sold for less than what amount?
e. One hundred seventy-five of the homes sold for less than what amount?

37. A chain of sport shops catering to beginning skiers, headquartered in Aspen, Colorado, plans to conduct a study of how much a beginning skier spends on his or her initial purchase of equipment and supplies. Based on these figures, they want to explore the possibility of offering combinations, such as a pair of boots and a pair of skis, to induce customers to buy more. A sample of their cash register receipts revealed these initial purchases:

$140	$ 82	$265	$168	$ 90	$114	$172	$230	$142
86	125	235	212	171	149	156	162	118
139	149	132	105	162	126	216	195	127
161	135	172	220	229	129	87	128	126
175	127	149	126	121	118	172	126	

a. Arrive at a suggested class interval. Use five classes, and let the lower limit of the first class be $80.
b. What would be a better class interval?
c. Organize the data into a frequency distribution.
d. Interpret your findings.

38. The numbers of shareholders for a selected group of large companies (in thousands) are:

Company	Number of Shareholders (thousands)	Company	Number of Shareholders (thousands)
Pan American World Airways	144	Northeast Utilities	200
General Public Utilities	177	Standard Oil (Indiana)	173
Occidental Petroleum	266	Atlantic Richfield	195
Middle South Utilities	133	Detroit Edison	220
Chrysler Corporation	209	Eastman Kodak	251
Standard Oil of California	264	Dow Chemical	137
Bethlehem Steel	160	Pennsylvania Power	150
Long Island Lighting	143	American Electric Power	262
RCA	246	Ohio Edison	158
Greyhound Corporation	151	Transamerica Corporation	162
Pacific Gas & Electric	239	Columbia Gas System	165
Niagrara Mohawk Power	204	International Telephone &	
E. I. du Pont de Nemours	204	Telegraph	223
Westinghouse Electric	195	Union Electric	158
Union Carbide	176	Virginia Electric and Power	162
BankAmerica	175	Public Service Electric & Gas	225
		Consumers Power	161

The numbers of shareholders are to be organized into a frequency distribution and several graphs drawn to portray the distribution.
a. Using seven classes and a lower limit of 130, construct a frequency distribution.
b. Portray the distribution in the form of a frequency polygon.
c. Portray the distribution in a less-than cumulative frequency polygon.
d. Based on the polygon, three out of four (75 percent) of the companies have how many shareholders or less?
e. Write a brief analysis of the number of shareholders based on the frequency distribution and graphs.

39. A recent survey showed that the typical American car owner spends $2,950 per year on operating expenses. Below is a breakdown of the various expenditure items. Draw an appropriate chart to portray the data and summarize your findings in a brief report.

Expenditure Item	Amount
Fuel	$ 603
Interest on car loan	279
Repairs	930
Insurance and license	646
Depreciation	492
Total	$2,950

40. The Midland National Bank selected a sample of 40 student checking accounts. Below are their end-of-the-month balances.

$404	$ 74	$234	$149	$279	$215	$123	$ 55	$ 43	$321
87	234	68	489	57	185	141	758	72	863
703	125	350	440	37	252	27	521	302	127
968	712	503	489	327	608	358	425	303	203

   a. Tally the data into a frequency distribution using $100 as a class interval and $0 as the starting point.
   b. Draw a less-than cumulative frequency polygon.
   c. The bank considers any student with an ending balance of $400 or more a "preferred customer." Estimate the percentage of preferred customers.
   d. The bank is also considering a service charge to the lowest 10 percent of the ending balances. What would you recommend as the cutoff point between those who have to pay a service charge and those who do not?

41. The United States Department of Transportation keeps track of the percentage of flights that arrive within 15 minutes of the scheduled time, by airline. Below is the information for July 1998. Construct a stem-and-leaf chart from these data. Summarize your conclusion.

Airline	Percent on Time	Airline	Percent on Time
Pan Am	82.7	American	78.1
America West	82.7	United	76.4
Northwest	81.0	Delta	76.1
USAir	80.1	Continental	76.9
Southwest	79.7	British Airways	80.4
Alaska	79.7	Japan Airlines	81.4

42. A breakfast cereal is supposed to include 200 raisins in each box. A sample of 60 boxes produced yesterday showed the following number of raisins in each box. Develop a frequency distribution for the process. What class interval do you suggest? Summarize your findings.

200	200	202	204	206	197	199	200	204	195	206
193	196	200	195	202	199	202	200	206	197	202
198	203	201	198	198	200	205	205	206	200	197
203	201	198	202	206	205	207	196	199	199	200
196	205	203	201	200	191	199	200	193	200	198
202	201	193	204	204						

43. Listed below are the part-time, full-time, and total headcount enrollments at the University of Toledo from 1979 through 1997. Write a memo to Dr. John Fornof, Vice President of Academic Affairs, describing the enrollment trends for the three groups over the period. Be sure to include an appropriate chart.

Year	Full-time	Part-time	Total
1979	10,127	8,112	18,239
1980	11,684	8,586	20,270
1981	12,173	8,944	21,117
1982	12,540	8,846	21,386
1983	12,748	8,841	21,589
1984	12,612	8,427	21,039
1985	12,725	8,513	21,238
1986	12,826	8,350	21,176
1987	13,341	8,399	21,740
1988	14,433	8,373	22,806
1989	15,430	8,498	23,928
1990	16,227	8,554	24,781
1991	16,811	8,158	24,969
1992	16,878	7,663	24,541
1993	16,786	7,402	24,188
1994	15,971	7,136	23,107
1995	15,192	6,799	21,991
1996	15,018	6,674	21,692
1997	13,352	6,955	20,307

44. Listed below are the number of subscribers, in thousands, for GTE for the period from 1990 to 1996. Develop an appropriate chart or graph to depict the results. Write a brief report summarizing any trends.

Year	Subscribers	Year	Subscribers
1990	594	1994	2,339
1991	811	1995	3,011
1992	1,090	1996	3,273
1993	1,585		

45. Annual revenues, by type of tax, for the state of Georgia are as follows. Develop an appropriate chart or graph and write a brief report summarizing the information.

Type of Tax	Amount (000)
Sales	$2,812,473
Income (Individual)	2,732,045
License	185,198
Corporate	525,015
Property	22,647
Death and Gift	37,326
Total	$6,314,704

46. Annual imports from selected Canadian trading partners are listed on the next page. Develop an appropriate chart or graph and write a brief report summarizing the information.

Partner	Annual Imports (million)
Japan	$9,550
United Kingdom	4,556
South Korea	2,441
China	1,182
Australia	618

47. Farming has changed from the early 1900s to the 1990s. In the early 20th century, machinery gradually replaced animal power. For example, in 1910 U.S. farms used 24.2 million horses and mules and only about 1,000 tractors. By 1960, 4.6 million tractors were used and only 3.2 million horses and mules. In 1920 there were over 6 million farms in the United States. Today there are less than 2 million. Listed below is the number of farms, in thousands, for each of the 50 states in 1997. Show these data in an appropriate chart or graph and write a paragraph summarizing your findings.

47	1	8	46	76	26	4	3	39	45
4	21	80	63	100	65	91	29	7	15
7	52	87	39	106	25	55	2	3	8
14	38	59	33	76	71	37	51	1	24
35	86	185	13	7	43	36	20	79	9

48. One of the most popular candies in the United States is M&M's, which is produced by the Mars Company. For many years the M&M's plain candies were produced in six colors: red, green, orange, tan, brown, and yellow. Recently, tan was replaced by blue. Did you ever wonder how many candies were in a bag, or how many of each color? Are there about the same number of each color, or are there more of some colors than others? Here is some information for a one-pound bag of M&M's plain candies. It contained a total of 544 candies. There were 135 brown, 156 yellow, 128 red, 22 green, 50 blue, and 53 orange. Develop a chart depicting this information and a brief report summarizing the information.

49. The following graph compares the average selling prices of the Ford Taurus and the Toyota Camry from 1990 to 1997. Write a brief report summarizing the information in the graph. Be sure to include the selling price of the two cars, the change in the selling price, and the direction of the change in the eight-year period.

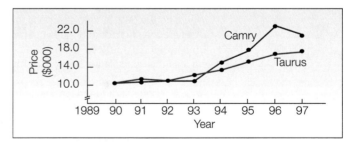

www.Exercises.com

50. A systematic sample where every 10th company was selected from an alphabetical list of the Forbes List of 500 companies is available at the Web site: *http://lib.stat.cmu.edu/DASL/Datafiles/Companies.html.* (This address is sensitive to capitalization so enter exactly as shown, including the capital letters.) Select the variable "sales" and develop a frequency distribution. Comment on the histogram.

51. Data on the percentage of waste, which is called run-up, for suppliers to a Levi-Strauss clothing manufacturing plant are given at the Web site: *http://lib.stat.cmu.edu/DASL/*

Datafiles/wasterunupdat.html. This address is sensitive to capitalization so enter exactly as shown, including the capital letter. The results are from five different suppliers. Combine all the information and develop a stem-and-leaf chart. There are a total of 95 observations. What conclusions can you reach from the chart?

▌ Computer Data Exercises

52. Refer to Data Set 1, which reports information on homes sold in the Venice, Florida, area during the last year.
    a. Select an appropriate class interval and organize the selling prices into a frequency distribution.
       1. Around what values do the data tend to cluster?
       2. What is the largest selling price? What is the smallest selling price?
       3. What percent of the homes sold for less than $125,000?
    b. Draw a less-than cumulative frequency distribution based on the frequency distribution developed in Part a.
       1. How many homes sold for less than $200,000?
       2. Estimate the percent of the homes that sold for more than $220,000.
       3. What percent of the homes sold for less than $125,000?
    c. Write a report summarizing the selling prices of the homes.
53. Refer to Data Set 2, which reports information on the 28 Major League Baseball teams for 1997.
    a. Organize the information on the team salaries into a frequency distribution. Select an appropriate class interval.
       1. What is a typical team salary? What is the range of salaries?
       2. Comment on the shape of the distribution. Does it appear that any of the team salaries are out of line with the others?
    b. Draw a less-than cumulative frequency distribution based on the frequency distribution developed in Part a.
       1. Forty percent of the teams are paying less than what amount in total team salary?
       2. About how many teams have total salaries of less than $50,000,000?
       3. Below what amount do the lowest five teams pay in total salary?
54. Refer to Data Set 3, which reports information on the circulation of 48 magazines.
    a. Select an appropriate class interval and organize the information on the circulation of magazines into a frequency distribution.
       1. Where do the data tend to be concentrated?
       2. What are the smallest and the largest circulations?
       3. Do any of the magazines seem to be out of line with respect to the others?
    b. Draw a less-than cumulative frequency distribution based on the frequency distribution developed in Part a.
       1. About 75 percent of the magazines have a circulation less than what amount?
       2. Keeping in mind that the circulation data is reported in thousands, what percent of them have a circulation of less than 5,000 (which is actually 5,000,000)?
55. Refer to Data Set 4, which refers to the 94 school districts in Northwest Ohio. Organize the average teachers' salaries into a stem-and-leaf display.
    a. What is the lowest salary among the 94 districts? The highest salary?
    b. What is a typical salary?
    c. How many school districts have average salaries of $30,000 or more?
    d. Write a brief report summarizing your findings.

I Computer Commands

1. MINITAB commands for the frequency distribution on page 26.
   a. Import the data from the data disk. The file name is **Tbl2-1.**
   b. Select **Graph, Character Graphs,** then click on **Histogram.**
   c. Select **Price** as the variable, **First Midpoint** 13500, and **Interval Width** 3000. Then click **OK.**

Histogram	✕
C1　Price C2　Sorted	**Variables:** `Price`
	☐ **By variable:**
	☐ **Same scale for all variables**
	First midpoint: `13500`
	Last midpoint:
	Interval width: `3000`
Select	
Help	OK　　Cancel

2. MINITAB commands for stem-and-leaf display on page 33.
   a. Import the data from the data disk. The file name is **Tbl2-6.**
   b. Select **Stat, EDA,** then click on **Stem-and-Leaf.**
   c. Select the variable **Spots,** and then click on **Increment** and put in the number 10.
   d. Click **OK.**

Stem-and-Leaf	✕
C1　Spots	**Variables:** `Spots`
	☐ **By variable:**
	☐ **Trim outliers**
Select	**Increment:** `10`
Help	OK　　Cancel

3. Excel commands for pie chart on page 49.
    a. Set cell A1 as the active cell and type the words *Market Share.* In cells A2 through A6 enter the major networks: CBS, ABC, NBC, Fox, and Other.
    b. Set cell B1 as the active cell and type the word *Percent.* In cells B2 through B6 enter the values 24, 22, 26, 17, and 11.
    c. From the **Tool Bar** select the **Chart Wizard.** Select **Pie** as the chart type, select the chart type in the upper left corner, and then click on **Next.**
    d. For the Data Range type *A1:B6,* indicate that the data are in a column, and finally click on **Next.**
    e. Click on the chart title area and type *Share of Prime-Time Viewing for the Major Networks.* Then click **Finish.**

CHAPTER 2   *Answers to Self-Review*

2–1 (a) The raw data.

(b)

Commission	Number of Salespeople
$1,400 up to $1,500	2
1,500 up to 1,600	3
1,600 up to 1,700	2
1,700 up to 1,800	1
Total	8

(c) Class frequencies.

(d) The largest concentration of commissions is $1,500 up to $1,600. The smallest commission is about $1,400 and the largest is about $1,800.

2–2 1. (a) $186.71, found by ($2,348 − $1,041)/7
   (b) $200
   (c) $1,000 up to $1,200
       $1,200 up to $1,400
2. Unequal size class intervals
   Open-ended class
   Overlapping classes

2–3 (a) 23
   (b) 28.75%, found by (23/80) × 100
   (c) 7.5%, found by (6/80) × 100.

2–4

```
 7 | 7
 8 | 0013488
 9 | 1256689
10 | 1248
11 | 26
```

(a) 8
(b) 10.1, 10.2, 10.4, 10.8
(c) 9.5
(d) 7.7, 11.6

2–5 (a)

(b)

(c) The smallest annual sales volume of imports by a supplier is about $2 million, the highest about $17 million. The concentration is between $8 million and $11 million.

2–6 (a) A frequency distribution.

(b)

Hourly Wages	Cumulative Number
Less than $6	0
Less than $8	18
Less than $10	54
Less than $12	74
Less than $14	80

(c) About 36 employees earn $9.00 or less. About half the employees earn $9.25 or more. About 20 employees earn $8.25 or less.

2–7

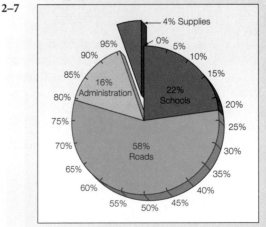

Chapter Three

Describing Data

Measures of Location

GOALS

When you have completed this chapter, you will be able to:

ONE

Calculate the arithmetic mean, median, mode, weighted mean, and the geometric mean.

TWO

Explain the characteristics, uses, advantages, and disadvantages of each measure of location.

THREE

Identify the position of the arithmetic mean, median, and mode for both symmetric and skewed distributions.

In an effort to study phone usage, sample data on the number and frequency of phone calls for the previous month were gathered. Estimate the mean and median number of calls. (See Goal One and Exercise 58.)

STATISTICS
IN ACTION

Did you ever meet the
"average" American
man? Well, his name
is Robert (that is the
nominal level of
measurement), he is
31 years old (that is the
ratio level), he is 69.5
inches tall (again the
ratio level of measure-
ment), weighs 172
pounds, wears a size
9½ shoe, has a 34-inch
waist, and wears a size
40 suit. In addition,
the average man eats
4 pounds of potato
chips, watches 2,567
hours of TV, receives
598 pieces of mail, and
eats 26 pounds of
bananas each year.
Also, he sleeps 7.7
hours per night. Is this
really an "average" man
or would it be better
to refer to him as a
"typical" man? Would
you expect to find a
man with all these
characteristics?

Introduction

Chapter 2 began our study of descriptive statistics. In order to transform raw or un-grouped data into a meaningful form, we organized the data into a frequency distribution and portrayed it graphically in a histogram or a frequency polygon. We also described other tools for describing data, such as stem-and-leaf displays, line charts, bar charts, and pie charts.

In this chapter we continue to develop methods to describe data by finding a single value to describe a set of data. We refer to this single value as a **measure of central tendency** or, more commonly, an **average.**

| **Measure of Central Tendency** A single value that summarizes a set of data. It locates the center of the values.

You are familiar with the concept of an average. The sports world is full of them. During the 1996 National Football League season, Jerry Rice, of the San Francisco 49ers, averaged 13.4 yards per reception. Michael Jordan, of the Chicago Bulls, averaged 29.8 points per game during the 1996–97 NBA season. Some other averages include:

- The average cost to drive a mile in Los Angeles is 55.8 cents, in Boston it is 49.8 cents, and it is 49.0 cents in Philadelphia. This includes the cost of insurance, depre-ciation, license, fees, fuel, oil, tires, and maintenance.
- Each person receives an average of 598 pieces of mail per year.
- Hertz Corporation reports that the average annual maintenance expense is $269 for a new car and $565 for a car more than one year old.
- The average U.S. home changes ownership every 11.8 years. The fastest turn-arounds are in Arizona, where the average for the state is 6.2 years. For other selected states: Nevada 6.5 years, North Carolina 7.4 years, Utah 8.4 years, and Tennessee 8.8 years.

There is not just one measure of central tendency; in fact, there are many. We will consider five: the arithmetic mean, the weighted mean, the median, the mode, and the geometric mean. We will begin by discussing the most widely used and widely reported measure of central tendency, the arithmetic mean.

The Population Mean

Many studies involve all the values in a population. If we report that the mean ACT score of all students entering the University of Toledo in the Fall of 1997 is 19.6, this is an example of a population mean because we have a score for *all* students who entered in the fall of 1997. There are 12 sales associates employed at the Reynolds Road outlet of New York Carpet World. The mean amount of commission they earned last month was $1,345. We consider this a population value because we considered *all* the sales asso-ciates. Other examples of a population mean would be: the mean closing price for John-son and Johnson stock for the last five days is $53.75; the mean annual rate of return for the last 10 years for Berger Funds, Ultra, is 8.67 percent; and the mean number of hours of overtime worked last week by the six welders in the welding department of the Struthers Wells Corp. is 6.45 hours.

For raw data, that is, data that has not been grouped in a frequency distribution or a stem-and-leaf display, the population mean is the sum of all the values in the popula-tion divided by the number of values in the population. To find the population mean, we use the following formula.

$$\text{Population mean} = \frac{\text{Sum of all the values in the population}}{\text{Number of values in the population}}$$

Instead of writing out in words the full directions for computing the population mean (or any other measure), it is more convenient to use the shorthand symbols of mathematics. The mean of a population using mathematical symbols is:

POPULATION MEAN	$\mu = \dfrac{\Sigma X}{N}$	**[3–1]**

where:

μ represents the population mean. It is the Greek lowercase letter "mu."
N is the number of items in the population.
X represents any particular value.
Σ is the Greek capital letter "sigma" and indicates the operation of adding.
ΣX is the sum of the X values.

Any measurable characteristic of a population is called a **parameter.** The mean of a population is a parameter. So is the range (the difference between the largest and smallest value in a set of data).

| **Parameter**   A characteristic of a population.

Example

There are 12 automobile companies in the United States. Listed below is the number of patents granted by the United States government to each company last year.

Company	Number of Patents Granted	Company	Number of Patents Granted
General Motors	511	Mazda	210
Nissan	385	Chrysler	97
Daimler-Benz	275	Porsche	50
Toyota	257	Mitsubishi	36
Honda	249	Volvo	23
Ford	234	BMW	13

Is this information a sample or a population? What is the arithmetic mean number of patents granted?

Solution

This is a population because we are considering all the automobile companies obtaining patents. We add the number of patents for each of the 12 companies. The total number of patents for the 12 companies is 2,340. To find the arithmetic mean, we divide this total by 12. So the arithmetic mean is 195, found by 2340/12. Using formula (3–1):

$$\mu = \frac{511 + 385 + \cdots + 13}{12} = \frac{2340}{12} = 195$$

How do we interpret the value of 195? The typical number of patents received by an automobile company is 195. Because we considered all the companies receiving patents, this value is a population parameter.

▌ The Sample Mean

As explained in Chapter 1, frequently we select a sample from the population in order to find out something about a specific characteristic of the population. The quality assurance department, for example, needs to be assured that the ball bearings being produced have an acceptable outside diameter. It would be very expensive and time consuming to check the outside diameter of all the bearings being produced. Therefore, a sample of five bearings might be selected and the mean outside diameter of the five bearings calculated in order to estimate the mean diameter of all the bearings produced.

For raw data, that is, ungrouped data, *the mean is the sum of all the values divided by the total number of values.* To find the mean for a sample:

Mean of ungrouped sample data

$$\text{Sample mean} = \frac{\text{Sum of all the values in the sample}}{\text{Number of values in the sample}}$$

The mean of a sample and the mean of a population are computed in the same way, but the shorthand notation used is different. The formula for the mean of a *sample* is:

SAMPLE MEAN	$\bar{X} = \dfrac{\Sigma X}{n}$	[3–2]

where $\bar{X}$ stands for the sample mean. It is read "X bar." The lower case *n* is the number in the sample.

The mean of a sample, or any other measure based on sample data, is called a **statistic.** If the mean outside diameter of a sample of ball bearings is 0.625 inches, this is an example of a statistic.

▌ **Statistic** A characteristic of a sample. ▌

Example

The Merrill Lynch Global Fund specializes in long-term obligations of foreign countries. We are interested in the interest rate on these obligations. A random sample of six bonds revealed the following.

Issue	Interest Rate
Australian government bonds	9.50%
Belgian government bonds	7.25
Canadian government bonds	6.50
French government "B-TAN"	4.75
Buoni Poliennali de Tesora (Italian government bonds)	12.00
Bonos del Estado (Spanish government bonds)	8.30

What is the arithmetic mean interest rate on this sample of long-term obligations?

Solution

Using formula (3–2), the sample mean is:

$$\text{Sample mean} = \frac{\text{Sum of all the values in the sample}}{\text{Number of all the values in the sample}}$$

$$\bar{X} = \frac{\Sigma X}{n} = \frac{9.50 + 7.25 + \cdots + 8.30}{6} = \frac{48.3}{6} = 8.05$$

The arithmetic mean interest rate of the sample of long-term obligations is 8.05 percent.

▌ The Properties of the Arithmetic Mean

The arithmetic mean interest rate is a widely used measure of central tendency. It has several important properties:

1. Every set of interval-level and ratio-level data has a mean. (Recall from Chapter 1 that interval- and ratio-level data include such data as ages, incomes, and weights, with the distance between numbers being constant.)
2. All the values are included in computing the mean.
3. A set of data has only one mean. The mean is unique. (Later in the chapter we will discover an average that might appear twice, or more than twice, in a set of data.)
4. The mean is a useful measure for comparing two or more populations. It can, for example, be used to compare the performance of the production employees on the first shift at the Chrysler transmission plant with the performance of those on the second shift.
5. The arithmetic mean is the only measure of location where *the sum of the deviations of each value from the mean will always be zero.* Expressed symbolically:

DEVIATIONS FROM THE MEAN SUM TO ZERO	$\Sigma(X - \bar{X}) = 0$	**[3–3]**

As an example, the mean of 3, 8, and 4 is 5. Then:

$$\Sigma(X - \bar{X}) = (3 - 5) + (8 - 5) + (4 - 5)$$
$$= -2 + 3 - 1$$
$$= 0$$

Mean as a balance point   Thus, we can consider the mean as a balance point for a set of data. To illustrate, suppose we had a long board with the numbers 1, 2, 3, . . . , *n* evenly spaced on it. Suppose three gold bars of equal weight were placed on the board at numbers 3, 4, and 8, and the balance point was set at 5, the mean of the three numbers. We would find that the board balanced perfectly! The deviations below the mean (−3) are equal to the deviations above the mean (+3). Shown schematically:

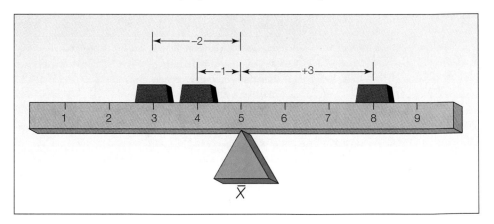

Mean unduly affected by unusually large or small values   The mean does have several disadvantages, however. Recall that the mean uses the value of every item in a sample, or population, in its computation. If one or two of these values are either extremely large or extremely small, the mean might not be an appropriate average to represent the data. For example, suppose the annual incomes of a small group of stockbrokers at Merrill Lynch are $62,900, $61,600, $62,500, $60,800, and $1.2 million. The mean income is $289,560. Obviously, it is not representative of this group, because all but one broker has an income in the $60,000 to $63,000 range. One income ($1.2 million) is unduly affecting the mean.

Cannot determine mean for open-ended data

The mean is also inappropriate if there is an *open-ended class* for data tallied into a frequency distribution. If a frequency distribution has the open-ended class "$100,000 and more," and there are 10 persons in that class, we really do not know whether their incomes are close to $100,000, $500,000, or $16 million. Since we lack information about their incomes, the arithmetic mean income for this distribution cannot be determined.

SELF-REVIEW 3–1

1. The annual incomes of a sample of several middle-management employees at Westinghouse are: $42,900, $49,100, $38,300, and $56,800.
   (a) Give the formula for the sample mean.
   (b) Find the sample mean.
   (c) Is the mean you computed in (b) a statistic or a parameter? Why?
   (d) What is your best estimate of the population mean?
2. All the students in advanced Computer Science 411 are considered the population. Their course grades are 92, 96, 61, 86, 79, and 84.
   (a) Give the formula for the population mean.
   (b) Compute the mean course grade.
   (c) Is the mean you computed in (b) a statistic or a parameter? Why?

▌ Exercises

The answers to the odd-numbered exercises are at the end of the book.

1. Compute the mean of the following population values: 6 3 5 7 6
2. Compute the mean of the following population values: 7 5 7 3 7 4
3. a. Compute the mean of the following sample values: 5, 9, 4, 10.
   b. Show that $\Sigma(X - \bar{X}) = 0$.
4. a. Compute the mean of the following sample values: 1.3, 7.0, 3.6, 4.1, 5.0.
   b. Show that $\Sigma(X - \bar{X}) = 0$.
5. Compute the mean of the following sample values: 16.25, 12.91, 14.58.
6. Compute the mean hourly wage paid to carpenters who earned the following wages: $15.40, $20.10, $18.75, $22.76, $30.67, $18.00.

For questions 7–10, (a) compute the arithmetic mean and (b) indicate whether it is a sample statistic or a population parameter.

7. There are 10 salespeople employed by Midtown Ford. The numbers of new cars sold last month by the respective salespeople were: 15, 23, 4, 19, 18, 10, 10, 8, 28, 19.
8. The accounting department at a mail-order company counted the following numbers of incoming calls per day to the company's toll-free number during the first seven days in May 1998: 14, 24, 19, 31, 36, 26, 17.
9. The Cambridge Power and Light Company selected 20 residential customers at random. Following are the amounts, to the nearest dollar, the customers were charged for electrical service last month:

54	48	58	50	25	47	75	46	60	70
67	68	39	35	56	66	33	62	65	67

10. The personnel director at Mercy Hospital began a study of the overtime hours of the registered nurses. Fifteen RNs were selected at random, and these overtime hours during June were noted:

13	13	12	15	7	15	5	12
6	7	12	10	9	13	12	

▌ Weighted Mean

The weighted mean is a special case of the arithmetic mean. It occurs when there are several observations of the same value which might occur if the data have been grouped into a frequency distribution. To explain, suppose the nearby Burger King Restaurant sold medium, large, and Biggie-sized soft drinks for $.50, $.75, and $.90, respectively. Of the last ten drinks sold, 3 were medium, 4 were large, and 3 were Biggie-sized. To find the mean amount of the last ten drinks sold, we could use formula (3–2).

$$\bar{X} = \frac{\$0.50 + \$0.50 + \$0.50 + \$0.75 + \$0.75 + \$0.75 + \$0.75 + \$0.90 + \$0.90 + \$0.90}{10} = \frac{\$7.20}{10} = \$0.72$$

The mean selling price of the last ten drinks is $0.72.

An easier way to find the mean selling price is to determine the weighted mean. That is we multiply each observation by the number of times it happens. We will refer to the weighted mean as $\bar{X}_w$. This is read "X bar sub w."

$$\bar{X}_w = \frac{3(\$0.50) + 4(\$0.75) + 3(\$0.90)}{10} = \frac{\$7.20}{10} = \$0.72$$

In general the weighted mean of a set of numbers designated $X_1, X_2, X_3, \ldots, X_n$ with the corresponding weights $w_1, w_2, w_3, \ldots, w_n$ is computed by:

WEIGHTED MEAN	$$\bar{X}_w = \frac{w_1X_1 + w_2X_2 + w_3X_3 + \cdots + w_nX_n}{w_1 + w_2 + w_3 + \cdots + w_n}$$	**[3–4]**

This may be shortened to:

$$\bar{X}_w = \frac{\Sigma(wX)}{\Sigma w}$$

Example

The Carter Construction Company pays its hourly employees $6.50, $7.50, or $8.50 per hour. There are 26 hourly employees, 14 are paid at the $6.50 rate, 10 at the $7.50 rate, and 2 at the $8.50 rate. What is the mean hourly rate paid the 26 employees?

Solution

To find the mean hourly rate, we multiply each of the hourly rates by the number of employees earning that rate. Using formula (3–4), the mean hourly rate is

$$\bar{X}_w = \frac{14(\$6.50) + 10(\$7.50) + 2(\$8.50)}{14 + 10 + 2} = \frac{\$183.00}{26} = \$7.038$$

The weighted mean hourly wage is rounded to $7.04.

SELF-REVIEW 3–2

Springers sold 95 Antonelli men's suits for the regular price of $400. For the spring sale the suits were reduced to $200 and 126 were sold. At the final clearance, the price was reduced to $100 and the remaining 79 suits were sold.

(a) What was the weighted mean price of an Antonelli suit?
(b) Springers paid $200 a suit for the 300 suits. Comment on the store's profit per suit if a salesperson receives a $25 commission for each one sold.

I Exercises

11. Calico Pizza sells colas in three sizes: small, medium, and large. The small size costs $0.50, the medium $0.75, and the large $1.00. Yesterday 20 small, 50 medium, and 30 large colas were sold. What was the weighted mean price per cola?
12. A specialty bookstore concentrates mainly on used books. Paperbacks are $1.00 each, and hardcover books are $3.50. Of the 50 books sold last Tuesday morning, 40 were paperback and the rest were hardcover. What was the weighted mean price of a book?
13. Metropolitan Hospital employs 200 persons on the nursing staff. Fifty are nurse's aides, 50 are practical nurses, and 100 are registered nurses. Nurse's aides receive $8 an hour, practical nurses $10 an hour, and registered nurses $14 an hour. What is the weighted mean hourly wage?
14. Andrews and Associates specialize in corporate law. They charge $100 an hour for researching a case, $75 an hour for consultations, and $200 an hour for writing a brief. Last week one of the associates spent 10 hours consulting with her client, 10 hours researching the case, and 20 hours writing the brief. What was the weighted mean hourly charge for her legal services?

I The Median

It has been pointed out that for data containing one or two very large or very small values, the arithmetic mean may not be representative. The center point for such problems can be better described using a measure of central tendency called the **median.**

To illustrate the need for a measure of central tendency other than the arithmetic mean, suppose you are seeking to buy a condominium in Palm Aire. Your real estate agent says that the average price of the units currently available is $110,000. Would you still want to look? If you had budgeted your maximum purchase price between $60,000 and $75,000, you might think they are out of your price range. However, checking the individual prices of the units might change your mind. They are $60,000, $65,000, $70,000, $80,000, and a superdeluxe penthouse costs $275,000. The arithmetic mean price is $110,000, as the real estate agent reported, but one price ($275,000) is pulling the arithmetic mean upward, causing it to be an unrepresentative average. It does seem that a price between $65,000 and $75,000 is a more typical or representative average, and it is. In cases such as this, the median provides a more accurate measure of central tendency.

Median The midpoint of the values after they have been ordered from the smallest to the largest, or the largest to the smallest. Fifty percent of the observations are above the median and 50 percent below the median.

The median price of the units available is $70,000. To determine this, we ordered the prices from low ($60,000) to high ($275,000) and selected the middle value ($70,000).

Prices Ordered from Low to High		Prices Ordered from High to Low
$ 60,000		$275,000
65,000		80,000
70,000	← Median →	70,000
80,000		65,000
275,000		60,000

Median unaffected by extreme values

Note that there are the same number of prices below the median of $70,000 as above it. The median is, therefore, unaffected by extremely low or high observations. Had the highest price been $90,000, or $300,000, or even $1 million, the median price would still be $70,000. Likewise, had the lowest price been $20,000 or $50,000, the median price would still be $70,000.

In the previous illustration there is an *odd* number of observations (five). How is the median determined for an *even* number of observations? As before, the observations are ordered. Then the usual practice is to find the arithmetic mean of the two middle observations. Note that for an even number of observations, the median may not be one of the given values.

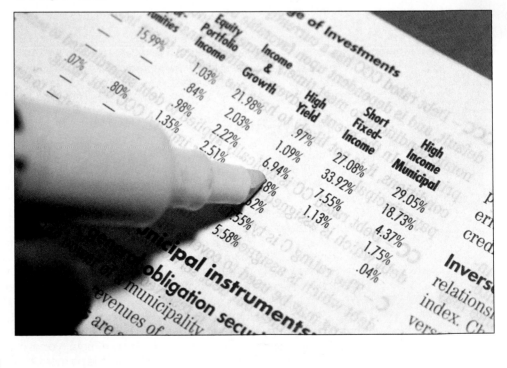

Example

The five-year annualized total returns of the six top-performing stock mutual funds with emphasis on aggressive growth are listed below. What is the median annualized return?

Name of Fund	Annualized Total Return
PBHG Growth	28.5%
Dean Witter Developing Growth	17.2
AIM Aggressive Growth	25.4
Twentieth Century Giftrust	28.6
Robertson Stevens Emerging Growth	22.6
Seligman Frontier A	21.0

Solution   Note that the number of returns is *even* (6). As before, the returns are first ordered from low to high. Then the two middle returns are identified. The arithmetic mean of the two middle observations gives us the median return. Arranging from low to high:

```
17.2%
21.0
22.6  ◄
25.4  ◄          48.0/2 = 24.0 percent, the median return
28.5
28.6
```

Notice that the median is not one of the values. Also, half of the returns are below the median and half are above it.

The major properties of the median are:

1. The median is unique; that is, like the mean, there is only one median for a set of data.
2. It is not affected by extremely large or small values and is therefore a valuable measure of central tendency when such values do occur.
3. It can be computed for a frequency distribution with an open-ended class if the median does not lie in an open-ended class. (We will show the computations for the median of data grouped in a frequency distribution shortly.)

Median can be determined for all levels of data except nominal

4. It can be computed for ratio-level, interval-level, and ordinal-level data. (Recall from Chapter 1 that ordinal-level data can be ranked from low to high — such as the responses "excellent," "very good," "good," "fair," and "poor" to a question on a marketing survey.) To use a simple illustration, suppose five people rated a new fudge bar. One person thought it was excellent, one rated it very good, one called it good, one rated it fair, and one considered it poor. The median response is "good." Half of the responses are above "good"; the other half are below it.

▌ The Mode

The **mode** is another measure of central tendency.

▌ **Mode**   The value of the observation that appears most frequently.   ▌

The mode is especially useful in describing nominal and ordinal levels of measurement. As an example of its use for nominal-level data, a company has developed five bath oils. Chart 3–1 shows the results of a marketing survey designed to find out which bath oils consumers prefer. The largest number of respondents favored Lamoure, as evidenced by the highest bar. Thus, Lamoure is the mode.

Chart 3–1   Number of Respondents Favoring Various Bath Oils

Example   The annual salaries of quality-control managers in selected states are shown below. What is the modal annual salary?

Arizona	$35,000	Illinois	$58,000	Ohio	$50,000
California	49,100	Louisiana	60,000	Tennessee	60,000
Colorado	60,000	Maryland	60,000	Texas	71,400
Florida	60,000	Massachusetts	40,000	West Virginia	60,000
Idaho	40,000	New Jersey	65,000	Wyoming	55,000

Solution   A perusal of the salaries reveals that the annual salary of $60,000 appears more often (six times) than any other salary. The mode is, therefore, $60,000.

In summary, we can determine the mode for all levels of data — nominal, ordinal, interval, and ratio. The mode also has the advantage of not being affected by extremely high or low values. Like the median, it can be used as a measure of central tendency for distributions with open-ended classes.

Disadvantages of the mode   The mode does have a number of disadvantages, however, that cause it to be used less frequently than the mean or median. For many sets of data, there is no mode because no value appears more than once. For example, there is no mode for this set of price data: $19, $21, $23, $20, and $18. Since every value is different, however, it could be argued that every value is the mode. Conversely, for some data sets there is more than one mode. Suppose the ages of a group are 22, 26, 27, 27, 31, 35, and 35. Both the ages 27 and 35 are modes. Thus, this grouping of ages is referred to as *bimodal* (having two modes). One would question the use of two modes to represent the central tendency of this set of age data.

S E L F - R E V I E W   3 – 3

1. A sample of single persons in Towson, Texas, receiving Social Security payments revealed these monthly benefits: $426, $299, $290, $687, $480, $439, and $565.
    (a) What is the median monthly benefit?
    (b) How many observations are below the median? Above it?
2. The numbers of work stoppages in the automobile industry for selected months are 6, 0, 10, 14, 8, and 0.
    (a) What is the median number of stoppages?
    (b) How many observations are below the median? Above it?
    (c) What is the modal number of work stoppages?

▌ Exercises

15. What would you report as the modal value for a set of observations if there were a total of:
     a. 10 observations and no two values were the same?
     b. 6 observations and they were all the same?
     c. 6 observations and the values were 1, 2, 3, 3, 4, and 4?

For exercises 16–19, (a) determine the median and (b) the mode.

16. The following is the number of oil changes for the last seven days at the Jiffy Lube located at the corner of Elm Street and Pennsylvania Ave.

    | 41 | 15 | 39 | 54 | 31 | 15 | 33 |

17. The following is the percent change in net income from 1997 to 1998 for a sample of 12 construction companies in Denver.

    | 5 | 1 | −10 | −6 | 5 | 12 | 7 | 8 | 2 | 5 | −1 | 11 |

18. The following are the ages of the 10 people in the video arcade at the Southwyck Shopping Mall at 10 A.M. this morning.

    | 12 | 8 | 17 | 6 | 11 | 14 | 8 | 17 | 10 | 8 |

19. Listed below are several indicators of long-term economic growth in the United States. The projections are through the year 2005.

Economic Indicator	Percent Change	Economic Indicator	Percent Change
Inflation	4.5	Real GNP	2.9
Exports	4.7	Investment (residential)	3.6
Imports	2.3	Investment (nonresidential)	2.1
Real disposable income	2.9	Productivity (total)	1.4
Consumption	2.7	Productivity (manufacturing)	5.2

     a. What is the median percent change?
     b. What is the modal percent change?

20. Listed below are the total automobile sales (in millions) in the United States for the last 14 years. During this period, what was the median number of automobiles sold? What are the modes?

9.0   8.5   8.0   9.1   10.3   11.0   11.5   10.3   10.5   9.8   9.3   8.2   8.2   8.5

▮ Computer Solution

A computer can be used to organize raw data and determine the various measures of central tendency.

Example

Table 2–1 on page 23 shows the price of the 80 vehicles sold last month at Whitner Pontiac. Determine the mean and the median selling price.

Solution

The mean and the median vehicle selling prices are reported in the following Excel output. (Reminder: The commands needed to create this output are shown at the end of the chapter.) There are 80 vehicles in the study, so calculations by hand or a calculator would be tedious.

	F	G
2	*Selling price*	
4	Mean	20226.91
5	Standard Error	489.8015
6	Median	19831
7	Mode	17642
8	Standard Deviation	4380.917
9	Sample Variance	19192438
10	Kurtosis	0.680418
11	Skewness	0.762864
12	Range	21079
13	Minimum	12546
14	Maximum	33625
15	Sum	1618153
16	Count	80

The mean selling price is $20,227, the median is $19,831, and the mode is $17,642. The mean and the median are less than $400 apart, so to report either value is reasonable. We conclude that the typical vehicle sold for about $20,000. How would Mr. Whitner use this value? He could use it in his revenue projections. If the dealership could increase the number sold in a month from 80 to 90, that would result in an additional $200,000 of revenue, found by 10($20,000).

▮ The Geometric Mean

The geometric mean is useful in finding the average of percentages, ratios, indexes, or growth rates. It has a wide application in business and economics because we are often interested in finding the percentage change in sales, salaries, or economic figures, such as the Gross National Product. The geometric mean of a set of n positive numbers is defined as the nth root of the product of n values. The formula for the geometric mean is written:

GEOMETRIC MEAN	$GM = \sqrt[n]{(X_1)(X_2) \cdots (X_n)}$	**[3–5]**

The geometric mean will always be less than or equal to (never more than) the arithmetic mean. Note also that all the data values must be positive to determine the geometric mean.

As a brief example of the interpretation of the geometric mean, suppose you receive a 5 percent increase in salary this year and a 15 percent increase next year. The average percent increase is 9.886, not 10.0. We begin by calculating the geometric mean. Recall, for example, that a 5 percent increase in salary is 105 or 1.05. We will write it as 1.05.

$$GM = \sqrt{(1.05)(1.15)} = 1.09886$$

This can be verified by assuming that your monthly earning was $3,000 to start and you received two increases of 5 percent and 15 percent.

$$\text{Raise 1} = \$3,000 \,(.05) = \$150.00$$
$$\text{Raise 2} = \$3,150 \,(.15) = \underline{\quad 472.50}$$
$$\text{Total} \qquad\qquad\quad \$622.50$$

Your total salary raise is $622.50. This is equivalent to:

$$\$3,000.00 \,(.09886) = \$296.58$$
$$\$3,296.58 \,(.09886) = \underline{\quad 325.90}$$
$$\$622.48 \text{ is about } \$622.50$$

The following example shows the geometric mean of several percentages.

Example

The profits earned by Atkins Construction Company on four recent projects were 3 percent, 2 percent, 4 percent, and 6 percent. What is the geometric mean profit?

Solution

The geometric mean is 3.46 percent, found by

$$GM = \sqrt[n]{(X_1)(X_2) \cdots (X_n)} = \sqrt[4]{(3)(2)(4)(6)} = \sqrt[4]{144}$$

The geometric mean is the fourth root of 144 or 3.46[1]. The geometric mean profit is 3.46 percent.

---

[1]Finding the nth root using a hand calculator is quite easy, but the details vary among calculator brands. Check the operating instructions of your particular calculator for the details. For a Texas Instruments TI-35X, first multiply 3(2)(4)(6), so that 144 appears. Next hit the 2nd, then $\sqrt[x]{y}$, then 4, and finally the "=" sign. The result is 3.464101615. We would round this value to 3.46.

The arithmetic mean profit is 3.75 percent, found by $(3 + 2 + 4 + 6)/4$. Although the profit of 6 percent is not extremely large, it draws the arithmetic mean upward. The geometric mean of 3.46 gives a more conservative profit figure because it is not being drawn by the large value. It will always, in fact, be less than or equal to the arithmetic mean.

A second application of the geometric mean is to find an average percent increase over a period of time. For example, if you earned \$30,000 a year in 1990 and \$50,000 in the year 2000, what is your annual rate of increase over the period? The rate of increase is determined from the following formula.

AVERAGE PERCENT INCREASE OVER TIME	$$GM = \sqrt[n]{\dfrac{\text{Value at end of period}}{\text{Value at beginning of period}}} - 1$$	**[3–6]**

An example will show the details of finding the average annual percent increase.

Example

The population of Haarlan, Alaska, in 1988 was 2 persons, by 1998 it was 22. What is the average annual rate of percentage increase during the period?

Solution

There are 10 years between 1988 and 1998 so $n = 10$. The formula (3–6) for the geometric mean as applied to this type of problem is:

$$GM = \sqrt[n]{\frac{\text{Value at end of period}}{\text{Value at beginning of period}}} - 1$$

$$= \sqrt[10]{\frac{22}{2}} - 1 = 1.271 - 1 = 0.271$$

The final value is .271. So the annual rate of increase is 27.1 percent. This means that the rate of population growth in Haarlan is 27.1 percent per year[2].

SELF-REVIEW 3–4

1. The annual dividends, in percent, of four oil stocks are: 4.91, 5.75, 8.12, and 21.60.
   (a) Find the geometric mean dividend.
   (b) Find the arithmetic mean dividend.
   (c) Is the arithmetic mean equal to or greater than the geometric mean?
2. Production of Cablos trucks increased from 23,000 units in 1978 to 120,520 units in 1998. Find the geometric mean annual percent increase.

---

[2]Again, the method of solution will depend on the calculator used. For the Texas Instrument TI-35X, the first step is to divide 22 by 2. The result is 11. Next hit 2nd, then $\sqrt[x]{y}$, then 10, and finally "=." The value is 1.270981615. We subtract 1.00 from this value, which leaves 0.270981615. We round this value to .271, or 27.1 percent.

▌ Exercises

21. Compute the geometric mean of the following values: 8, 12, 14, 26, 5.
22. Compute the geometric mean of the following values: 2, 8, 6, 4, 10, 6, 8, 4.
23. In 1950 there were 51 countries that belonged to the United Nations. By 1996 this number had increased to 185. What was the geometric mean annual rate of increase in membership during this period?
24. Listed below is the percent increase in sales for the MG Corporation for the last 5 years. Determine the geometric mean percent increase in sales over the period.

| 9.4 | 13.8 | 11.7 | 11.9 | 14.7 |

25. Darenfest and Associates stated that in 1988 hospitals spent $3.9 billion on computer systems. They estimate that by the year 2000 this will increase to $14.0 billion. If the expenditures do increase to $14.0 billion, what is the geometric mean annual rate of increase for the period?
26. In 1988 there were 9.19 million cable TV subscribers. By 1998 the number had increased to 54.87 million. What is the yearly rate of increase?

▌ The Mean, Median, and Mode of Grouped Data

Quite often data on incomes, ages, and so on are grouped and presented in the form of a frequency distribution. It is usually impossible to secure the original raw data. Thus, if we are interested in a typical value to represent the data, we must *estimate* it based on the frequency distribution.

The Arithmetic Mean

To approximate the arithmetic mean of data organized into a frequency distribution, we begin by assuming the observations in each class are represented by the *midpoint* of the class. The mean of a sample of data organized in a frequency distribution is computed by:

ARITHMETIC MEAN OF GROUPED DATA	$\bar{X} = \dfrac{\Sigma fX}{n}$	**[3–7]**

where:

$\bar{X}$ is the designation for the arithmetic mean.

X is the mid-value, or midpoint, of each class.

f is the frequency in each class.

fX is the frequency in each class times the midpoint of the class.

ΣfX is the sum of these products.

n is the total number of frequencies.

Example

The computations for the arithmetic mean of data grouped into a frequency distribution will be shown based on the Whitner Pontiac data. Recall in Chapter 2, in Table 2–2 on page 24 we constructed a frequency distribution for the vehicle selling prices. The information is repeated below. Determine the arithmetic mean vehicle selling price.

Selling Price ($ thousands)	Frequency
12 up to 15	8
15 up to 18	23
18 up to 21	17
21 up to 24	18
24 up to 27	8
27 up to 30	4
30 up to 33	1
33 up to 36	1
Total	80

Solution

The mean vehicle selling price can be estimated from data grouped into a frequency distribution. To find the estimated mean, assume the midpoint of each class is representative of all the data values in that class. Recall that the midpoint of a class is halfway between the upper and the lower class limit. To find the midpoint of a particular class, we add the upper and the lower class limits and divide by 2. Hence, the midpoint of the first class is $13.5, found by ($12 + $15)/2. We assume that the value of $13.5 is representative of the eight values in that class. To put it another way, we assume the actual sum of the eight values in this class is $108, found by 8($13.5). We continue the process of multiplying the class midpoint by the class frequency for each class and then sum these products. The results are summarized in Table 3–1.

Table 3–1   Selling Price of 80 New Vehicles Sold Last Month at Whitner Pontiac

Selling Price ($ thousands)	Frequency (f)	Midpoint (X)	fX
12 up to 15	8	$13.5	$108.0
15 up to 18	23	16.5	379.5
18 up to 21	17	19.5	331.5
21 up to 24	18	22.5	405.0
24 up to 27	8	25.5	204.0
27 up to 30	4	28.5	114.0
30 up to 33	1	31.5	31.5
33 up to 36	1	34.5	34.5
Total	80		$1,608.0

Solving for the arithmetic mean using formula (3–7), we get:

$$\overline{X} = \frac{\Sigma fX}{n} = \frac{\$1,608}{80} = \$20.1 \text{ (thousands)}$$

So we conclude that the mean vehicle selling price is about $20,100.

The mean of data grouped into a frequency distribution may be different from that of raw data. The grouping results in some loss of information. In the vehicle selling price problem, the mean of the raw data, reported in the Excel output on page 76 is $20,227. This value is quite close to that estimated mean just computed. The difference is $127 or about 0.63 percent.

SELF-REVIEW 3 – 5

The net incomes of a sample of large importers of antiques were organized into the following table:

Net Income ($ millions)	Number of Importers
2 up to 6	1
6 up to 10	4
10 up to 14	10
14 up to 18	3
18 up to 22	2

(a) What is the table called?
(b) Based on the distribution, what is the estimate of the arithmetic mean net income?

▌ Exercises

27. When we compute the mean of a frequency distribution, why do we refer to this as an *estimated* mean?
28. Determine the estimated mean of the following frequency distribution.

Class	Frequency
0 up to 5	2
5 up to 10	7
10 up to 15	12
15 up to 20	6
20 up to 25	3

29. Determine the estimated mean of the following frequency distribution.

Class	Frequency
20 up to 30	7
30 up to 40	12
40 up to 50	21
50 up to 60	18
60 up to 70	12

30. The selling prices of a sample of 60 antiques sold in Erie, Pennsylvania, last month were organized into the following frequency distribution. Estimate the mean selling price.

Selling Price ($ thousands)	Frequency
70 up to 80	3
80 up to 90	7
90 up to 100	18
100 up to 110	20
110 up to 120	12

31. FM radio station WLQR recently changed its format from easy listening to contemporary. A recent sample of 50 listeners revealed the following age distribution. Estimate the mean age of the listeners.

Age	Frequency
20 up to 30	1
30 up to 40	15
40 up to 50	22
50 up to 60	8
60 up to 70	4

32. Advertising expenses are a significant component of the cost of goods sold. Listed below is a frequency distribution showing the advertising expenditures for 60 manufacturing companies located in the Southwest. Estimate the mean advertising expense.

Advertising Expenditure ($ millions)	Number of Companies
25 up to 35	5
35 up to 45	10
45 up to 55	21
55 up to 65	16
65 up to 75	8
Total	60

The Median

Median: Half the values are above it, half below

Recall that the median is defined as the value below which half of the values lie and above which the other half of the values lie. Since the raw data have been organized into a frequency distribution, some of the information is not identifiable. As a result we cannot determine the exact median. It can be estimated, however, by (1) locating the class in which the median lies and then (2) interpolating within that class to arrive at the median. The rationale for this approach is that the members of the median class are assumed to be evenly spaced throughout the class. The formula is:

MEDIAN OF GROUPED DATA
$$\text{Median} = L + \frac{\frac{n}{2} - CF}{f}(i)$$
[3–8]

where:

L is the lower limit of the class containing the median.

n is the total number of frequencies.

f is the frequency in the median class.

CF is the cumulative number of frequencies in all the classes preceding the class containing the median.

i is the width of the class in which the median lies.

First, we shall estimate the median by locating the class in which it falls and interpolating. Then the formula for the median will be applied to check our answer.

Example

The data involving the selling prices of vehicles at Whitner Pontiac is again used to show the procedure for estimating the median. (See Table 3–2.) The cumulative frequencies in the right column will be used shortly. What is the median selling price for a new vehicle sold by Whitner Pontiac?

Table 3–2 Selling Prices of 80 New Vehicles Sold Last Month at Whitner Pontiac

Selling Price ($ thousands)	Number Sold (f)	Cumulative Frequency (CF)
12 up to 15	8	8
15 up to 18	23	31
18 up to 21	17	48
21 up to 24	18	66
24 up to 27	8	74
27 up to 30	4	78
30 up to 33	1	79
33 up to 36	1	80
Total	80	

Solution

To find the median selling price we need to locate the 40th observation (there are a total of 80) when the data are arranged from smallest to largest. Why the 40th? Recall that half the observations in a set of data are less than the median and half are more than the median. So if we thought of arranging all the vehicle selling prices from smallest to largest, the one in the middle, the 40th, would be the median. To be technically correct, and consistent with how we found the median for ungrouped data, we should use $(n + 1)/2$ instead of $n/2$. However, because the number of observations is usually large for data grouped into a frequency distribution, we usually ignore this small difference.

The class containing the selling price of the 40th vehicle is located by referring to the right-hand column of Table 3–2, which is the cumulative frequency. There were 31 vehicles that sold for less than $18,000 and 48 that sold for less than $21,000. Hence, the 40th vehicle must be in the range of $18,000 up to $21,000. We have, therefore, located the median selling price as somewhere between the two limits of $18,000 and $21,000.

To locate the median more precisely, we need to interpolate in this class containing the median. Recall that there are 17 vehicles in the "$18,000 up to $21,000" class. Assume the selling prices are evenly distributed between the lower ($18,000) and the upper ($21,000) class limits. There are nine vehicle selling prices between the 31st and the 40th vehicle. The median is, therefore, 9/17 of the distance between $18,000 and $21,000. See Chart 3–2. The class width is $3,000 and 9/17 of $3,000 is $1,588. We add $1,588 to the lower class limit of $18,000, so the estimated median vehicle selling price is $19,588.

Chart 3–2 Location of the Median

We could use formula 3–8 to determine the median of data grouped into a frequency distribution, where L is the lower limit of the class containing the median, which is $18,000. There are 80 selling prices, so $n = 80$. CF is the cumulative number of selling prices preceding the median class (31), f is the frequency of the number of observations in the median class (17), and *i* is the interval of the class containing the median ($3,000). Substituting these values:

$$Median = L + \frac{\frac{n}{2} - CF}{f} (i)$$

$$= \$18,000 + \frac{\frac{80}{2} - 31}{17} (\$3,000)$$

$$= \$18,000 + \$1,588 = \$19,588$$

The assumption underlying the approximation of the median, that the frequencies in the median class are evenly distributed between $18,000 and $21,000, may not be exactly correct. Therefore, it is safer to say that *about half* of the selling prices are less than $19,588 and about half are more. The median estimated from grouped data and the median determined from raw data are usually not exactly equal. In this case, the median computed from raw data using Excel is $19,831 and the median estimated from the frequency distribution is $19,588. The difference in the two estimates is $243 or about 1 percent.

Median can be determined for distributions having open ends.
A final note: The median is based only on the frequencies and the class limits of the median class. The open-ended classes that occur at the extremes are rarely needed. Therefore, the median of a frequency distribution having open ends can be determined. The arithmetic mean of a frequency distribution with an open-ended class cannot be accurately computed — unless, of course, the midpoints of the open-ended classes are estimated. Further, the median can be determined if *percentage frequencies* are given instead of the actual frequencies. This is because the median is the value with 50 percent of the distribution above it and 50 percent below it and does not depend on actual counts. The percents are considered substitutes for the actual frequencies. In a sense, they are actual frequencies whose total is 100.0.

The Mode

Class midpoint of the modal class is the estimated mode
Recall that the mode is defined as the value that occurs most often. For data grouped into a frequency distribution, the mode can be approximated by the *midpoint of the class containing the largest number of class frequencies.* For Problem 2 in Self-Review 3–6, the modal net sales are found by first locating the class containing the greatest number of percents. It is the $7 up to $10 million class because it has the largest number of percents (40). The midpoint of that class ($8.5 million) is the estimated mode. This indicates that more stamping plants had net sales of $8.5 million than any other amount.

Two values may occur a large number of times. The distribution is then called *bimodal.* Suppose the ages of a sample of workers are 22, 27, 30, 30, 30, 30, 34, 58, 60, 60, 60, 60, and 65. The two modes are 30 years and 60 years. Often two points of concentration develop because the population being sampled is probably not homogeneous. In this illustration, the population might be composed of two distinct groups — one a group of relatively young employees who have been recently hired to meet the increased demand for a product, and the other a group of older employees who have been with the company a long time.

If the set of data has more than two modes, the distribution is referred to as being *multimodal.* In such cases we would probably not consider any of the modes as being representative of the central value of the data.

SELF-REVIEW 3–6

1. A sample of the daily production of transceivers at Scott Electronics was organized into the following distribution. Estimate the median daily production.

Daily Production	Frequency
80 up to 90	5
90 up to 100	9
100 up to 110	20
110 up to 120	8
120 up to 130	6
130 up to 140	2

2. The net sales of a sample of small stamping plants were organized into the following percentage frequency distribution. What is the estimated median net sales?

Net Sales ($ millions)	Percent of Total
1 up to 4	13
4 up to 7	14
7 up to 10	40
10 up to 13	23
13 and greater	10

▌ Exercises

33. Refer to Exercise 28. Compute the median. What is the modal value?
34. Refer to Exercise 29. Compute the median. What is the modal value?
35. The chief accountant at Betts Machine, Inc. wants to prepare a report on the company's accounts receivable. Below is a frequency distribution showing the amount outstanding.

Amount	Frequency
$ 0 up to $ 2,000	4
$ 2,000 up to $ 4,000	15
$ 4,000 up to $ 6,000	18
$ 6,000 up to $ 8,000	10
$ 8,000 up to $10,000	4
$10,000 up to $12,000	3

   a. Determine the median amount.
   b. What is the modal amount owed?
36. At the present time there are about 1.2 million enlisted men and women on active duty in the United States Army, Navy, Marines, and Air Force. Shown below is a percent breakdown by age. Determine the median age of enlisted personnel on active duty. What is the mode?

Age (years)	Percent
Up to 20	15
20 up to 25	33
25 up to 30	19
30 up to 35	17
35 up to 40	11
40 up to 45	4
45 or more	1

▌ Selecting an Average for Data in a Frequency Distribution

For a symmetric distribution, mean, median, and mode are equal.

Refer to the frequency polygon in Chart 3–3. It is symmetrical, meaning that *the distribution has the same shape on either side of the center.* If the polygon were folded in half, the two halves would be identical. For a symmetric distribution, the mode, median, and mean are located at the center and are always equal. They are all 20 years in Chart 3–3.

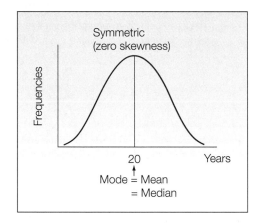

Chart 3–3   A Symmetric Distribution

The number of years corresponding to the highest point of the curve is the *mode* (20 years). Because the frequency curve is symmetrical, the *median* corresponds to the point where the distribution is cut in half (20 years). The total number of frequencies representing many years is offset by the total number representing few years, resulting in an *arithmetic mean* of 20 years. Logically, any of the three averages would be appropriate to represent this distribution.

A skewed distribution is not symmetrical.

As the distribution becomes nonsymmetrical, or **skewed,** the relationship among the three averages changes. In a **positively skewed distribution,** the arithmetic mean is the largest of the three averages. Why? Because the mean is influenced more than the median or mode by a few extremely high values. The median is generally the next largest average in a positively skewed frequency distribution. The mode is the smallest of the three averages.

If the distribution is highly skewed, such as the weekly incomes in Chart 3–4, the mean would not be a good average to use. The median and mode would be more representative.

Conversely, in a distribution that is **negatively skewed,** the mean is the lowest of the three averages. The mean is, of course, influenced by a few extremely low observations. The median is greater than the arithmetic mean, and the modal value is the largest of the three averages. Again, if the distribution is highly skewed, such as the distribution of tensile strengths shown in Chart 3–5, the mean should not be used to represent the data.

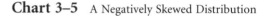

Chart 3–4 A Positively Skewed Distribution

Chart 3–5 A Negatively Skewed Distribution

SELF-REVIEW 3–7

The weekly sales from a sample of Hi-Tec electronic supply stores were organized into a frequency distribution. The mean of weekly sales was computed to be $105,900, the median $105,000, and the mode $104,500.

(a) Sketch the sales in the form of a smoothed frequency polygon. Note the location of the mean, median, and mode on the X-axis.

(b) Is the distribution symmetrical, positively skewed, or negatively skewed? Explain.

▌ Chapter Outline

I. A measure of location is a value used to describe the center of a set of data.

   A. The arithmetic mean is the most widely reported measure of location.

   1. It is calculated by adding the values of the observations and dividing by the total number of observations.

   a. The formula for a population mean of ungrouped or raw data is:

$$\mu = \frac{\Sigma X}{N}$$

[3–1]

   b. The formula for the mean of a sample is

$$\bar{X} = \frac{\Sigma X}{n}$$

[3–2]

   c. For data grouped into a frequency distribution, the formula is:

$$\bar{X} = \frac{\Sigma fX}{n}$$

[3–7]

STATISTICS IN ACTION

Most colleges report the "average class size." This information can be misleading because average class size can be found several ways. If we find the number of students *in each class* at a particular university, the result is the mean number of students per class. If we compiled a list of the class sizes for each student and find the mean class size, we might find the mean to be quite different. One school found the mean number of students in each of their 747 classes to be 40. But when they found the mean from a list of the class sizes of each student it was 147. Why the disparity? Because there are few students in the small classes and a larger number of students in the larger class, which has the effect of increasing the mean class size when it is calculated this way. A school could reduce this mean class size for each student by reducing the number of students in each class. That is, cut out the large freshman lecture classes.

2. The major characteristics of the arithmetic mean are:
   a. At least the interval scale of measurement is required.
   b. All the data values are used in the calculation.
   c. A set of data has only one mean. That is, it is unique.
   d. The sum of the deviations from the mean equals 0.
B. The weighted mean is found by multiplying each observation by its corresponding weight.
   1. The formula for determining the weighted mean is:

$$\bar{X}_w = \frac{w_1 X_1 + w_2 X_2 + w_3 X_3 + \cdots + w_n X_n}{w_1 + w_2 + w_3 + \cdots + w_n} \qquad \text{[3–4]}$$

   2. It is a special case of the arithmetic mean.
C. The geometric mean is the *n*th root of the product of *n* values.
   1. The formula for the geometric mean is:

$$GM = \sqrt[n]{(X_1)(X_2)(X_3) \cdots (X_n)} \qquad \text{[3–5]}$$

   2. The geometric mean is also used to find the annual rate of change from one period to another.

$$GM = \sqrt[n]{\frac{\text{Value at end of period}}{\text{Value at beginning of period}}} - 1 \qquad \text{[3–6]}$$

   3. The geometric mean is always equal to or less than the arithmetic mean.
D. The median is the value in the middle of a set of ordered data.
   1. To find the median, sort the observations from smallest to largest and identify the middle value.
   2. The formula for estimating the median from grouped data is:

$$\text{Median} = L + \frac{\frac{n}{2} - CF}{f} (i) \qquad \text{[3–8]}$$

   3. The major characteristics of the median are:
      a. At least the ordinal scale of measurement is required.
      b. It is not influenced by extreme values.
      c. Fifty percent of the observations are larger than the median.
      d. It is unique to a set of data.
E. The mode is the value that occurs most often in a set of data.
   1. The mode can be found for nominal level data.
   2. A set of data can have more than one mode.

Pronunciation Key

SYMBOL	MEANING	PRONUNCIATION
μ	Population mean	*mu*
Σ	Operation of adding	*sigma*
ΣX	Adding a group of values	*sigma X*
$\bar{X}$	Sample mean	*X bar*
$\bar{X}_w$	Weighted mean	*X bar sub w*
GM	Geometric mean	*G M*
ΣfX	Adding the product of the frequencies and the class midpoints	*sigma f X*

▌ Chapter Exercises

37. The accounting firm of Crawford and Associates has five senior partners. Yesterday the senior partners saw six, four, three, seven, and five clients, respectively.
    a. Compute the mean number and median number of clients seen by a partner.
    b. Is the mean a sample mean or a population mean?
    c. Verify that $\Sigma(X - \mu) = 0$.

38. Owens Orchards sells apples in a large bag by weight. A sample of seven bags contained the following numbers of apples: 23, 19, 26, 17, 21, 24, 22.
    a. Compute the mean number and median number of apples in a bag.
    b. Verify that $\Sigma(X - \overline{X}) = 0$.

39. A sample of households that subscribe to the United Bell Phone Company revealed the following numbers of calls received last week. Determine the mean and the median number of calls received.

52	43	30	38	30	42	12	46	39	37
34	46	32	18	41	5			

40. The Citizens Banking Company is studying the number of times the automatic teller, located in a Loblaws Supermarket, is used per day. Following are the numbers of times the machine was used over each of the last 30 days. Determine the mean number of times the machine was used per day.

83	64	84	76	84	54	75	59	70	61
63	80	84	73	68	52	65	90	52	77
95	36	78	61	59	84	95	47	87	60

41. The numbers of Temban camcorders produced during eight-hour shifts for 50 shifts selected at random are listed below. Determine the mean number of camcorders produced during an eight-hour shift.

348	371	360	369	376	397	368	361	374
410	374	377	335	356	322	344	399	362
384	365	380	349	358	343	432	376	347
385	399	400	359	329	370	398	352	396
366	392	375	379	389	390	386	341	351
354	395	338	390	333				

42. Trudy Green works for the True-Green Lawn Company. Her job is to solicit lawn-care business via the telephone. Listed below are the number of appointments she made in each of the last 25 hours of calling. What is the arithmetic mean number of appointments she made per hour? What is the median number of appointments per hour? Write a brief report summarizing the findings.

9	5	2	6	5	6	4	4	7	2	3	6	3
4	4	7	8	4	4	5	5	4	8	3	3	

43. The Split-A-Rail Fence Company sells three types of fence to homeowners in suburban Seattle, Washington. Grade A costs $5.00 per running foot to install, Grade B costs $6.50 per running foot, and Grade C, the premium quality, costs $8.00 per running foot. Yesterday, Split-A-Rail installed 270 feet of Grade A, 300 feet of Grade B, and 100 feet of Grade C. What was the mean cost per foot of fence installed?

44. Rolland Poust is a sophomore in the College of Business at Scandia Tech. Last semester he took courses in statistics and accounting, 3 hours each, and earned an A in both. He earned a B in a five-hour history course and a B in a two-hour history of jazz course. In addition, he took a one-hour course dealing with the rules of basketball so he could get his license to officiate high school basketball games. He got an A in this course. What was his GPA for the semester? Assume that he receives 4 points for an A, 3 for a B, and so on. What measure of central tendency did you just calculate?

45. The table below shows the percent of the labor force that is unemployed and the size of the labor force for three counties in Northwest Ohio. Jon Elsas is the Regional Director of Economic Development. He must present a report to several companies that are considering locating in Northwest Ohio. What would be an appropriate unemployment rate to show for the entire region?

County	Percent Unemployed	Size of Workforce
Wood	4.5	15,300
Ottawa	3.0	10,400
Lucas	10.2	150,600

46. *Modern Healthcare* reported the average patient revenues (in $millions) for five types of hospitals. What is the median patient revenue?

Hospital Type	Patient Revenue (millions)
Catholic	$46.6
Other church	59.1
Nonprofit	71.7
Public	93.1
For profit	32.4

47. The *Bank Rate Monitor* reported the following savings rates. What is the median savings rate?

Instrument	Savings Rate (percent)	Instrument	Savings Rate (percent)
Money market mutual fund	3.01	1-year CD	3.51
Bank money market account	2.96	2.5-year CD	4.25
6-month CD	3.25	5-year CD	5.46

48. The American Automobile Association checks the prices of gasoline before many holiday weekends. Listed below are the self-service prices for a sample of 15 retail outlets during the May 1997 Memorial Day weekend in the Detroit, Michigan, area.

1.24	1.22	1.15	1.19	1.29	1.29	1.21	1.26	1.21	1.29
1.25	1.28	1.19	1.26	1.24					

a. What is the arithmetic mean selling price?
b. What is the median selling price?
c. What is the modal selling price?

49. The following table shows major earthquakes by country between 1983 and 1995. Also reported is the size of the earthquake, as measured on the Richter Scale, and the number of deaths reported. Compute the mean and the median for both the size of the earthquake as measured on the Richter scale and the number of deaths. Which measure of central tendency would you report for each of the variables? Tell why.

Country	Richter	Deaths	Country	Richter	Deaths
Colombia	5.5	250	Iran	7.7	40,000
Japan	7.7	81	Philippines	7.7	1,621
Turkey	7.1	1,300	Pakistan	6.8	1,200
Chile	7.8	146	Turkey	6.2	4,000
Mexico	8.1	4,200	USA	7.5	1
Ecuador	7.3	4,000	Indonesia	7.5	2,000
India	6.5	1,000	India	6.4	9,748
China	7.3	1,000	Indonesia	7.0	215
Armenia	6.8	55,000	Colombia	6.8	1,000
USA	6.9	62	Algeria	6.0	164
Peru	6.3	114	Japan	7.2	5,477
Romania	6.5	8	Russia	7.6	2,000

50. The metropolitan area of Los Angeles–Long Beach, California, is the area expected to show the largest increase in the number of jobs between 1989 and 2010. The number of jobs is expected to increase from 5,164,900 to 6,286,800. What is the geometric mean expected yearly rate of increase?

51. Wells Fargo Mortgage and Equity Trust gave these occupancy rates in their annual report for various office income properties the company owns. What is the geometric mean occupancy rate?

Pleasant Hills, California	100%
Lakewood, Colorado	90
Riverside, California	80
Scottsdale, Arizona	20
San Antonio, Texas	62

52. A recent article suggested that if you earn $25,000 a year today and the inflation rate continues at 3 percent per year, you'll need to make $33,598 in 10 years to have the same buying power. You would need to make $44,771 if the inflation rate jumped to 6 percent. Confirm that these statements are accurate by finding the geometric mean rate of increase.

53. Wells Fargo Mortgage and Equity Trust also reported these occupancy rates for some of its industrial income properties. What is the geometric mean occupancy rate?

Tucson, Arizona	81%
Irvine, California	100
Carlsbad, California	74
Dallas, Texas	80

54. The 12-month returns on five aggressive-growth mutual funds were 32.2 percent, 35.5 percent, 80.0 percent, 60.9 percent, and 92.1 percent. Determine the arithmetic mean and the geometric mean rates of return.

55. An automatic machine that fills containers appears to be performing erratically. A check of the weights of the contents of a number of cans revealed:

Weight (grams)	Number of Cans
130 up to 140	2
140 up to 150	8
150 up to 160	20
160 up to 170	15
170 up to 180	9
180 up to 190	7
190 up to 200	3
200 up to 210	2

    a.   Estimate the arithmetic mean weight of the contents of a can.

    b.   Estimate the median weight of the contents of a can.

56.   The Department of Commerce, Bureau of the Census, reported on the number of income earners in American families:

Number of Earners	Number (in thousands)
0	7,083
1	18,621
2	22,414
3	5,533
4 or more	2,797

    a.   What is the modal number of income earners?

    b.   What is the median number of income earners?

    c.   Tell why you cannot compute the arithmetic mean number of earners.

57.   The following frequency distribution shows a percentage distribution of household incomes in Alaska. What are the median and modal incomes?

Incomes	Percent of Households
Less than $20,000	18.3
$20,000 up to 30,000	21.2
30,000 up to 40,000	18.4
40,000 up to 50,000	15.1
50,000 up to 60,000	11.3
60,000 and greater	15.7

58.   There is intense competition among AT&T, MCI, and Sprint for the long distance phone business. In an effort to study the actual phone usage of residential customers, an independent agency gathered the following sample information on the *number* of phone calls per household for the last month. Estimate the arithmetic mean number of calls and the median number of calls.

Phone Calls	Frequency
3 up to 6	5
6 up to 9	19
9 up to 12	20
12 up to 15	20
15 up to 18	4
18 up to 20	2

59.   The following table shows the amount of mortgage payment for a sample of 60 homeowners in the Twin Cities area of Minnesota. Estimate the arithmetic mean amount of payment and the median amount of payment.

Monthly Mortgage Payment	Number of Homeowners
$ 100 up to $ 500	1
500 up to 900	9
900 up to 1,300	11
1,300 up to 1,700	23
1,700 up to 2,100	11
2,100 up to 2,500	4
2,500 up to 2,900	1
Total	60

60. A sample of 50 antique dealers in the southeast United States revealed the following sales last year:

Sales ($ thousands)	Number of Firms
100 up to 120	5
120 up to 140	7
140 up to 160	9
160 up to 180	16
180 up to 200	10
200 up to 220	3

    a. Estimate the mean sales.
    b. Estimate the median sales.
    c. What is the modal sales amount?

61. Shown below are the mean hourly wage for full-time and part-time registered nurses by size of the hospital, location of the hospital, and type of hospital.

	Full-time	Part-time
Number of beds:		
Under 100	$17.05	$17.10
100 up to 300	18.35	19.40
300 up to 500	18.50	20.15
500 or more	19.40	20.10
Location of hospital:		
Suburban	19.20	20.15
Urban	18.70	20.25
Rural	16.80	16.70
Type of hospital:		
Private, nonprofit	18.80	*
University	18.70	19.85
Community, nonprofit	18.50	19.10
Private, for profit	17.90	18.85
Public	17.45	*

*Insufficient data

Write a paragraph summarizing the results. Be sure to include information on the difference in the wages of full-time versus part-time nurses as well as among the categories of hospitals.

62. The information below profiles the typical home buyer in the United States for 1995 and 1996. Write a brief report summarizing the results. What changes do you note between 1995 and 1996? What are some of the differences between first-time buyers and repeat buyers?

	First-Time Buyers		Repeat Buyers	
	1995	1996	1995	1996
Mean cost of single-family home	$156,400	$147,400	$195,300	212,700
Homes visited before buying	12.9	12.5	15.6	15.7
Mean monthly mortgage payment	$950	$945	$1,076	$1,114
Mean age	31.6	31.6	41.0	41.7

www.Exercises.com

63. Ms. Wendy Lamberg is a financial consultant for Merrill Lynch Financial Services. She must recommend to one of her clients whether to purchase Johnson and Johnson or Pepsico stock. She checks the Internet for each and finds that 23 brokers evaluated each stock.

Brokers rate the stock a "1" if it is a strong buy and a "5" if it is a strong sell. The results are shown in the table below. Determine the mean broker ratings of the two stocks. Which stock do you think Wendy should recommend and why?

Recommendation	Rating	Johnson & Johnson	Pepsico
Strong buy	1	6	10
Moderate buy	2	10	7
Hold	3	7	6
Moderate sell	4	0	0
Strong sell	5	0	0

You can compare the ratings as of today with those at the time the text was revised. Go to: *http://quote.yahoo.com.* To the left of "Get Quotes," type the two stock symbols JNJ and PEP then click on **Get Quote.** Finally, in the column head "More Info" click on **Research.**

64. One of the most famous averages, the Dow Jones Industrial Average (DJIA), is not really an average. Below is a listing of the 30 stocks that make up the DJIA and their selling price. Compute the average of the selling price of these 30 stocks. Compare this to the closing value of the DJIA today, which was 8049.66. Then go to the following Web site and read about the DJIA and how it is actually computed: *http://foxnews.com/news/features/dow/.* Or go to the Web site of the Dow Jones Company: *http://www.dowjones.com/,* then click on "about Dow Jones." Explain how the DJIA is actually computed.

The Dow Jones Industrial Average, Updated as of: Dec 09, 1997 @ 4:02 pm ET

Symbol	Company Name	Last	Symbol	Company Name	Last
ALD	Allied-Signal Inc.	38.5000	HWP	Hewlett-Packard Co.	64.7500
AA	Aluminum Co. of America	71.1875	IBM	International Business Machines	110.000
AXP	American Express	87.5625	IP	International Paper	44.3750
T	AT&T	58.0000	JNJ	Johnson & Johnson	65.2500
BA	Boeing Co.	50.8125	MCD	McDonald's Corp.	47.5625
CAT	Caterpillar Inc.	50.4375	MRK	Merck & Co.	105.0000
CHV	Chevron Corp.	78.0000	MMM	Minnesota Mining/Mfg.	94.2500
KO	Coca-Cola Co.	63.3750	JPM	Morgan (J.P.)	122.0000
DIS	Disney Co.	93.875	MO	Philip Morris Cos.	44.3125
DD	DuPont	63.875	PG	Procter & Gamble	79.1250
EK	Eastman Kodak	57.8175	S	Sears, Roebuck	46.1875
XON	Exxon Corp.	62.1250	TRV	Travelers Group Inc.	54.5625
GE	General Electric	74.437	UK	Union Carbide	46.6250
GM	General Motors	63.1875	UTX	United Technologies	75.8125
GT	Goodyear Tire & Rubber	65.0625	WMT	Wal-Mart Stores Inc.	39.8125

▌ Computer Data Exercises

65. Refer to Data Set 1, which reports information on homes sold in the Venice, Florida, area during the last year.
    a. Determine the mean and the median selling prices of the homes. Does one measure of central tendency seem better, or more representative, than the other?
    b. How many bedrooms are there in a typical house?
    c. How many bathrooms are there in a typical house?
    d. How many miles is the typical home from the center of the city?
66. Refer to Data Set 2, which reports information on the 28 Major League Baseball teams for the 1997 season.
    a. Determine the mean team salary and the median team salary. Does one measure of central tendency seem better, or more representative, than the other?

b. Determine the mean attendance and the median attendance per team. Does one measure of central tendency seem better, or more representative, than the other?

c. Determine the rate of increase in players' salaries from 1989 to 1997.

67. Refer to Data Set 3, which reports information on the circulation of 48 popular magazines.

a. Determine the mean and the median circulation for the group of magazines. Does one measure of central tendency seem better, or more representative, than the other?

b. Determine the mean and the median cost of black and white advertising for the group of magazines. Does one measure of central tendency seem better, or more representative, than the other?

c. Determine the mean and the median cost of color advertising for the group of magazines. Does one measure of central tendency seem better, or more representative, than the other?

68. Refer to Data Set 4, which refers to the 94 school districts in Northwest Ohio.

a. Determine the mean and the median average teacher salary for the group of schools. Does one average appear more representative than the other?

b. Determine the mean and the median number of students for the group of schools. Does one average appear more representative than the other?

c. Determine the mean and the median income for the school districts. Does one average appear more representative than the other?

▌ Computer Commands

1. The Excel commands for the descriptive statistics on page 76 are:

a. From the data disk retrieve the Whitner data file, which is called **Tbl 2-1.**

b. From the menu bar select **Tools** and then **Data Analysis.** Select **Descriptive statistics** and then click **OK.**

c. For the Input range, type A1:A81, indicate that the data are grouped by column and that there are labels in the first row, click on the output range, indicate that the output is to go to F2 and that you want summary statistics, then click **OK.**

d. After you get your results, double-check the count in the output to be sure it contains the correct number of items.

Descriptive Statistics   ?✕

Input
Input Range: $A$1:$A$81   OK

Grouped By: ⦿ Columns   Cancel
      ○ Rows

☑ Labels in First Row   Help

Output options
⦿ Output Range: $F$2
○ New Worksheet Ply:
○ New Workbook
☑ Summary statistics
☐ Confidence Level for Mean: 95 %
☐ Kth Largest: 1
☐ Kth Smallest: 1

CHAPTER 3   *Answers to Self-Review*

3–1 1. (a) $\overline{X} = \dfrac{\Sigma X}{n}$

(b) $\overline{X} = \dfrac{\$187{,}100}{4} = \$46{,}775.$

(c) Statistic, because it is a sample value.

(d) $46,775. The sample mean is our best estimate of the population mean.

2. (a) $\mu = \dfrac{\Sigma X}{N}$

(b) $\mu = \dfrac{498}{6} = 83$

(c) Parameter, because it was computed using all the population values.

3–2 (a) $237, found by:

$$\frac{(95 \times \$400) + (126 \times \$200) + (79 \times \$100)}{95 + 126 + 79} = \$237$$

(b) The profit per suit is $12, found by $237 − $200 cost − $25 commission. The total profit for the 300 suits is $3,600, found by 300 × $12.

3–3 1. (a) $439.

(b) 3, 3.

2. (a) 7, found by (6 + 8)/2 = 7.

(b) 3, 3.

(c) 0.

3–4 1. (a) About 8.39 percent.

(b) About 10.1 percent.

(c) Yes, 10.1 > 8.39.

2. 8.63 percent found by, $\sqrt[20]{\dfrac{120{,}520}{23{,}000}} - 1 = 1.0863$
   − 1.

3–5 1. (a) Frequency distribution.

(b)

f	X	fX
1	4	4
4	8	32
10	12	120
3	16	48
2	20	40
20		244

$$\overline{X} = \frac{\Sigma fX}{n} = \frac{\$244}{20} = \$12.2$$

3–6 (a)

Production	Frequency	CF
80 up to 90	5	5
90 up to 100	9	14
100 up to 110	20	34
110 up to 120	8	42
120 up to 130	6	48
130 up to 140	2	50
	50	

$$\text{Median} = 100 + \frac{25 - 14}{20}(10)$$

$$= 100 + 5.5 = 105.5$$

(b)

Net Sales	Cumulative Percent
$ 1 up to $ 4	13
4 up to 7	27
7 up to 10	67
10 up to 13	90
13 and over	100

$$\$7 + \frac{50 - 27}{40}(\$3) = \$8.725 \text{ or } \$8{,}725{,}000$$

3–7 (a)

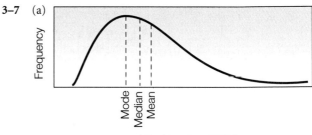

Weekly sales ($000)

(b) Positively skewed, because the mean is the largest average and the mode is the smallest.

Chapter Four

Describing Data

Measures of Dispersion

GOALS

When you have completed this chapter, you will be able to:

ONE

Compute and interpret the range, the mean deviation, the variance, and the standard deviation from raw data.

TWO

Compute and interpret the range, the variance, and the standard deviation from grouped data.

THREE

Explain the characteristics, uses, advantages, and disadvantages of each measure of dispersion.

FOUR

Understand Chebyshev's theorem and the Normal, or Empirical Rule, as they relate to a set of observations.

FIVE

Compute and interpret quartiles and the interquartile range.

SIX

Construct and interpret box plots.

SEVEN

Compute and understand the coefficient of variation and the coefficient of skewness.

The distribution of weight of a sample of 1,400 cargo containers is normally distributed. Based on the Empirical Rule, what percent of the weight will lie between the mean + or − 2 standard deviations? (See Goal 5 and Exercise 25.)

Introduction

Chapter 2 began our study of descriptive statistics. We organized a mass of raw data into a table called a frequency distribution and then portrayed the distribution graphically in a histogram or a frequency polygon. This allowed us to visualize where the data tended to cluster and the general shape of the distribution. In Chapter 3 we computed several measures of central tendency, or averages, as they are commonly called. This allowed us to define a typical value in a set of observations. In this chapter we continue to develop measures to describe a set of data, concentrating on measures that describe the dispersion or variability of the data.

Why Study Dispersion?

An average, such as the mean or the median, only locates the center of the data. It is valuable from that standpoint, but an average does not tell us anything about the spread of the data. For example, if your nature guide told you that the river ahead averaged 3 feet in depth, would you cross it without additional information? Probably not. You would want to know something about the variation in the depth. Is the maximum depth of the river 3.25 feet and the minimum 2.75 feet? If that is the case, you would probably agree to cross. What if you learned the river depth ranged from 0.50 feet to 5.5 feet? Your decision would probably be not to cross. Before making a decision about crossing the river, you want information on both the typical depth and the variation in the depth of the river.

A small value for a measure of dispersion indicates that the data are clustered closely, say, around the arithmetic mean. The mean is therefore considered representative of the data. That is, the mean is a reliable average. Conversely, a large measure of dispersion indicates that the mean is not reliable — it is not representative of the data. Such is the case with Chart 4–1. Note that the ages of the employees range from 18 to 85. The large spread results in a measure of location (50 years) that is not very meaningful.

The average is not representative because of the large spread.

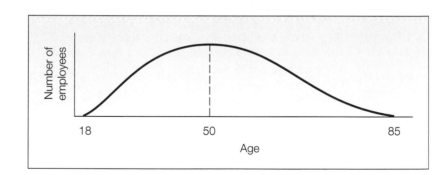

Chart 4–1   Ages of Employees

A second reason for studying the dispersion in a set of data is to compare the spread in two or more distributions. Suppose, for example, that the new PDM/3 computer is assembled in Baton Rouge and also in Tucson. The arithmetic mean daily output in the Baton Rouge plant is 50, and in the Tucson plant the mean output is also 50. Based on the two means, one might conclude that the distributions of the daily outputs are identical. Production records for nine days at the two plants, however, reveal that this conclusion is not correct. (See Chart 4–2.) Baton Rouge production varies from 48 to 52 assemblies a day. Production at the Tucson plant is more erratic, ranging from 40 to 60 a day.

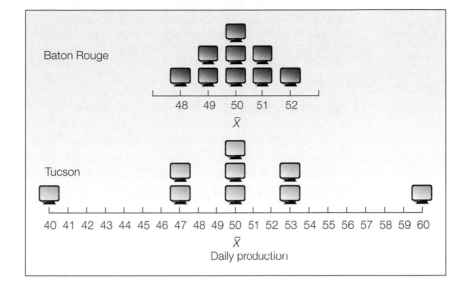

A measure of dispersion can be used to evaluate the reliability of two or more averages.

Chart 4–2   Daily Production of Computers at the Baton Rouge and Tucson Plants

▌ Measures of Dispersion

We will consider several measures of dispersion. The range is based on the location of the largest and the smallest values in the data set. The mean deviation, the variance, and the standard deviation are all based on deviations from the mean.

Range

The simplest measure of dispersion is the **range.** It is the difference between the highest and the lowest values in a data set. In the form of an equation:

THE RANGE	Range = Highest value − Lowest value	[4–1]

The range is widely used in statistical process control (SPC) applications. For these applications, see Chapter 16.

Example

Refer to Chart 4–2. Find the range in the number of computers produced for the Baton Rouge and the Tucson plants. Interpret the two ranges.

Solution

The range of the daily production of computers at the Baton Rouge plant is 4, found

by the difference between the largest daily production of 52 and the smallest of 48. The range in the daily production for the Tucson plant is 20 computers, found by 60 − 40. We therefore conclude that (1) there is less dispersion in the daily production in the Baton Rouge plant than in the Tucson plant because the range of 4 computers is less than a range of 20 computers, and (2) the production is clustered more closely around the mean of 50 at the Baton Rouge plant than at the Tucson plant (because a range of 4 is less than a range of 20). Thus, the mean production in the Baton Rouge plant (50 computers) is a more representative average than the mean of 50 computers for the Tucson plant.

Mean Deviation

A serious defect of the range is that it is based on only two values, the highest and the lowest; it does not take into consideration all of the values. The **mean deviation** does. It measures the mean amount by which the values in a population, or sample, vary from their mean. In terms of a definition:

> **Mean Deviation**   The arithmetic mean of the absolute values of the deviations from the arithmetic mean.

In terms of a formula, the mean deviation, designated *MD,* is computed for a sample by:

MEAN DEVIATION	$$MD = \frac{\Sigma|X - \bar{X}|}{n}$$	**[4–2]**

where:

   X is the value of each observation.
   $\bar{X}$ is the arithmetic mean of the values.
   n is the number of observations in the sample.
   $\|$ indicates the absolute value. In other words, the signs of the deviations from the mean are disregarded.

Why do we ignore the signs of the deviations from the mean? If we didn't, the positive and negative deviations from the mean would exactly offset each other, and the mean deviation would always be zero. Such a measure (zero) would be a useless statistic. Because we use absolute deviations, the mean deviation is also called the **mean absolute deviation,** or **MAD.** It is usually written *MD.*

Example

The number of patients seen in the emergency room at St. Luke's Memorial Hospital for a sample of 5 days last year were: 103, 97, 101, 106, and 103. Determine the mean deviation and interpret.

Solution

The mean deviation is the mean of the amounts that individual observations differ from the arithmetic mean. To find the mean deviation of a set of data, we begin by finding the arithmetic mean. The mean number of patients is 102, found by (103 + 97 + 101 + 106 + 103) / 5. Next we find the amount by which each observation differs from the mean. Then we sum these differences, ignoring the signs, and divide the sum by the number of observations. The result is the mean amount the observations differ from the mean. A small value for the mean deviation indicates the mean is representative of the data, whereas a large value for the mean deviation indicates dispersion in the data. Below are the details of the calculations using formula (4–2).

Number of Cases	$(X - \bar{X})$	Absolute Deviation
103	$(103 - 102) = 1$	1
97	$(97 - 102) = -5$	5
101	$(101 - 102) = -1$	1
106	$(106 - 102) = 4$	4
103	$(103 - 102) = 1$	1
		Total 12

$$MD = \frac{\Sigma|X - \bar{X}|}{n} = \frac{12}{5} = 2.4$$

The mean deviation is 2.4 patients per day. The number of patients deviates, on average, by 2.4 patients per day from the mean of 102 patients per day.

The mean deviation has two advantages. First, it uses all the values in the sample in the computation. Recall that the range uses only the highest and the lowest values. Second, it is easy to understand — it is the average amount by which values deviate from the mean. However, its major drawback is the use of absolute values. Generally, absolute values are difficult to work with, so the mean deviation is not used as frequently as other measures of dispersion, such as the standard deviation.

SELF-REVIEW 4–1

The weights of a group of crates being shipped to Ireland are (in pounds):
95, 103, 105, 110, 104, 105, 112, and 90.

(a) What is the range of the weights?
(b) Compute the arithmetic mean weight.
(c) Compute the mean deviation of the weights.

Exercises

For questions 1 through 6 calculate the (a) range, (b) arithmetic mean, (c) mean deviation and (d) interpret the range and the mean deviation.

1. There were five customer service representatives on duty at the Electronic Super Store during last Friday's sale. The respective numbers of VCRs these representatives sold are: 5, 8, 4, 10, and 3.
2. The Department of Statistics at Western State University offers eight sections of basic statistics. Following are the numbers of students enrolled in these sections: 34, 46, 52, 29, 41, 38, 36, and 28.
3. Dave's Automatic Door installs automatic garage door openers. The following list indicates the number of minutes needed to install a sample of 10 doors: 28, 32, 24, 46, 44, 40, 54, 38, 32, and 42.
4. A sample of eight companies in the aerospace industry was surveyed as to their return on investment last year. The results are (in percent): 10.6, 12.6, 14.8, 18.2, 12.0, 14.8, 12.2, and 15.6.
5. Ten experts rated a newly developed pizza on a scale of 1 to 50. The ratings were: 34, 35, 41, 28, 26, 29, 32, 36, 38, and 40.
6. A sample of the personnel files of eight male employees employed by Acme Carpet revealed that, during a six-month period, they lost the following numbers of days due to illness: 2, 0, 6, 3, 10, 4, 1, and 2.

Variance and Standard Deviation

Variance and standard deviation are based on squared deviations from the mean.

The **variance** and **standard deviation** are also based on the deviations from the mean.

| **Variance**   The arithmetic mean of the squared deviations from the mean. |

| **Standard Deviation**   The positive square root of the variance. |

Note in the definition of variance that the deviations from the mean are squared. The signs of the deviations (+ or −) are not ignored as they were for the mean deviation. Squaring the deviations from the mean eliminates the chance of having negative numbers, because multiplying two negative numbers gives a positive number.

Population Variance   The formulas for the population variance and the sample variance are slightly different. The population variance is considered first. (Recall that a population is the totality of all observations being studied.) The **population variance** for ungrouped data, that is, data not tabulated into a frequency distribution, is found by:

$$\text{POPULATION VARIANCE} \qquad \sigma^2 = \frac{\Sigma(X - \mu)^2}{N} \qquad \text{[4–3]}$$

where:

σ^2 is the symbol for the population variance (σ is the lower-case Greek letter sigma). It is usually referred to as "sigma squared."

X is the value of an observation in the population.

μ is the arithmetic mean of the population.

N is the total number of observations in the population.

Example

The ages of all the patients in the isolation ward of Yellowstone Hospital are 38, 26, 13, 41, and 22 years. What is the population variance?

Solution

Age (X)	X − μ	(X − μ)²
38	+10	100
26	− 2	4
13	−15	225
41	+13	169
22	− 6	36
140	0*	534

*Sum of the deviations from mean must equal zero.

$$\mu = \frac{\Sigma X}{N} = \frac{140}{5} = 28$$

$$\sigma^2 = \frac{\Sigma(X - \mu)^2}{N}$$

$$= \frac{534}{5} = 106.8$$

Like the range and the mean deviation, the variance can be used to compare the dispersion in two or more sets of observations. For example, the variance for the ages of the patients in isolation was just computed to be 106.8. If the variance in the ages of all the cancer patients in the hospital is 342.9, it can be said: (1) There is less dispersion in the distribution of the ages of patients in isolation than in the age distribution of all cancer patients (because 106.8 is less than 342.9). (2) The ages of the patients in isolation are clustered more closely about the mean of 28 years than are the ages of those in the cancer ward. Thus, the mean age for the patients in isolation is a more representative average than the mean for all cancer patients.

Variance is difficult to interpret because of the units.

Population Standard Deviation Both the range and the mean deviation are easy to interpret. The range is the difference between the high and low values of a set of data, and the mean deviation is the mean of the deviations from the mean. However, the variance is difficult to interpret for a single set of observations. The variance of 106.8 for the ages of the patients in isolation is not in terms of years, but rather "years squared."

Standard deviation is in the same units as the data.

There is a way out of this dilemma. By taking the square root of the population variance, we can transform it to the same unit of measurement used for the original data. The square root of 106.8 years-squared is 10.3 years. The square root of the population variance is called the **population standard deviation.** In terms of a formula for ungrouped data:

POPULATION STANDARD DEVIATION	$\sigma = \sqrt{\dfrac{\Sigma(X - \mu)^2}{N}}$	**[4–4]**

SELF-REVIEW 4–2

The Philadelphia office of Arthur Andersen, Inc. hired five accounting trainees this year. Their monthly starting salaries were: $2,536; $2,173; $2,448; $2,121; and $2,622.

(a) Compute the population mean.
(b) Compute the population variance.
(c) Compute the population standard deviation.
(d) The Pittsburgh office hired 6 trainees. Their mean monthly salary was $2,550, and the standard deviation was $250. Compare the two groups.

▌ Exercises

7. Consider these five values a population: 8, 3, 7, 3, and 4.
    a. Determine the mean of the population.
    b. Determine the variance.
8. Consider these six values a population: 13, 3, 8, 10, 8, and 6.
    a. Determine the mean of the population.
    b. Determine the variance.
9. The annual report of Dennis Industries cited these primary earnings per common share for the past five years: $2.68, $1.03, $2.26, $4.30, and $3.58. If we assume these are population values, what is:
    a. The arithmetic mean primary earnings per share of common stock?
    b. The variance?
10. Referring to Exercise 9, the annual report of Dennis Industries also gave these returns on stockholder equity for the same five-year period (in percent): 13.2, 5.0, 10.2, 17.5, and 12.9.
    a. What is the arithmetic mean return?
    b. What is the variance?
11. Plywood, Inc. reported these returns on stockholder equity for the past five years: 4.3, 4.9, 7.2, 6.7, and 11.6. Consider these as population values.
    a. Compute the range, the arithmetic mean, the variance, and the standard deviation.
    b. Compare the return on stockholder equity for Plywood, Inc. with that for Dennis Industries cited in Exercise 10.
12. The annual income of the five vice presidents of TMV Industries are: $75,000; $78,000; $72,000; $83,000; and $90,000. Consider this a population.
    a. What is the range?
    b. What is the arithmetic mean income?
    c. What is the population variance? The standard deviation?
    d. The annual incomes of officers of another firm similar to TMV Industries were also studied. $\mu = \$79,900$, and $\sigma = \$8,612$. Compare the means and dispersions in the two firms.

Sample Variance   The formula for the population mean given in Chapter 3 is $\mu = \Sigma X/N$. We just changed the symbols for the sample mean, that is $\bar{X} = \Sigma X/n$. Unfortunately, the conversion from the population variance to the sample variance is not as direct. It requires a change in the denominator. Instead of substituting n (number in the sample) for N (number in the population), the denominator is $n - 1$. Thus the formula for the **sample variance** is:

SAMPLE VARIANCE, CONCEPTUAL FORMULA	$s^2 = \dfrac{\Sigma(X - \bar{X})^2}{n - 1}$	**[4–5]**

where:

    s^2 is the symbol for the sample variance.

    X is the value of each observation in the sample.

    $\bar{X}$ is the mean of the sample.

    n is the total number of observations in the sample.

Why is this seemingly insignificant change made in the denominator? Although the use of n is logical, it tends to underestimate the population variance, σ^2. The use of $(n - 1)$ in the denominator provides the appropriate correction for this tendency. Because the primary use of sample statistics like s^2 is to estimate population parameters like σ^2, $(n - 1)$ is preferred to n when defining the sample variance. We will also use this convention when computing the sample standard deviation.

    We can show that

$$\Sigma(X - \bar{X})^2 = \Sigma X^2 - \frac{(\Sigma X)^2}{n}$$

The second term is much easier to use, even with a hand calculator, because it avoids all but one subtraction. Hence, we recommend formula (4–6) for calculating a sample variance.

SAMPLE VARIANCE, COMPUTATIONAL FORMULA	$s^2 = \dfrac{\Sigma X^2 - \dfrac{(\Sigma X)^2}{n}}{n - 1}$	**[4–6]**

Example   The hourly wages for a sample of part-time employees at Fruit Packers, Inc. are: $2, $10, $6, $8, and $9. What is the sample variance?

Solution   The sample variance is computed using two methods. On the left is the deviation method, using formula (4–5). On the right is the direct method, using formula (4–6).

$$\bar{X} = \frac{\Sigma X}{n} = \frac{\$35}{5} = \$7$$

Using squared deviations from the mean:

Using the direct formula:

Hourly Wage (X)	X − X̄	(X − X̄)²
$ 2	−$5	25
10	3	9
6	− 1	1
8	1	1
9	2	4
$35	0	40

Hourly Wage (X)	X²
$ 2	4
10	100
6	36
8	64
9	81
$35	285

$$s^2 = \frac{\Sigma(X - \bar{X})^2}{n - 1} = \frac{40}{5 - 1}$$

$$= 10 \text{ in dollars squared}$$

$$s^2 = \frac{\Sigma X^2 - \frac{(\Sigma X)^2}{n}}{n - 1}$$

$$= \frac{285 - \frac{(35)^2}{5}}{5 - 1} = \frac{40}{5 - 1}$$

$$= 10 \text{ in dollars squared}$$

Sample Standard Deviation   The sample standard deviation is used as an estimator of the population standard deviation. As noted previously, the population standard deviation is the square root of the population variance. Likewise, the *sample standard deviation is the square root of the sample variance.* The sample standard deviation for ungrouped data is most easily determined by:

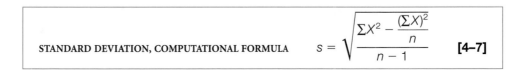

STANDARD DEVIATION, COMPUTATIONAL FORMULA	$s = \sqrt{\dfrac{\Sigma X^2 - \dfrac{(\Sigma X)^2}{n}}{n - 1}}$	**[4–7]**

Example   The sample variance in the previous example involving hourly wages was computed to be 10. What is the sample standard deviation?

Solution   The sample standard deviation is $3.16, found by $\sqrt{10}$. Note again that the sample variance is in terms of dollars squared, but taking the square root of 10 gives us $3.16, which is in the same units (dollars) as the original data.

SELF-REVIEW 4-3

The weights of the contents of several small aspirin bottles are (in grams): 4, 2, 5, 4, 5, 2, and 6. What is the sample variance? Compute the sample standard deviation.

Exercises

For questions 13–17, do the following:

a. Compute the variance by squaring the individual deviations from the mean.
b. Compute the variance by squaring the original values.
c. Determine the sample standard deviation.

13. Consider these values a sample: 7, 2, 6, 2, and 3.
14. The following five values are a sample: 11, 6, 10, 6, and 7.
15. Dave's Automatic Door, referred to in Exercise 3, installs automatic garage door openers. Based on a sample, following are the times, in minutes, required to install 10 doors: 28, 32, 24, 46, 44, 40, 54, 38, 32, and 42.
16. The sample of eight companies in the aerospace industry, referred to in Exercise 4, was surveyed as to their return on investment last year. The results are: 10.6, 12.6, 14.8, 18.2, 12.0, 14.8, 12.2, and 15.6.
17. Trout, Inc. feeds fingerling trout in special ponds and markets them when they attain a certain weight. A sample of 10 trout were isolated in a pond and fed a special food mixture, designated RT-10. At the end of the experimental period, the weights of the trout were (in grams): 124, 125, 125, 123, 120, 124, 127, 125, 126, and 121.
18. Refer to Exercise 17. Another special mixture, AB-4, was used in another pond. The mean of a sample was computed to be 126.9 grams, and the standard deviation 1.2 grams. Which food results in a more uniform weight?

Measures of Dispersion for Data Grouped into a Frequency Distribution

Range

Recall that the range is defined as the difference between the highest and lowest values. To estimate the range from data already grouped into a frequency distribution, subtract the lower limit of the smallest class from the upper limit of the largest class. For example, suppose a sample of 47 hourly wages was grouped into this frequency distribution:

Hourly Earnings	Number
$ 5 up to $10	6
10 up to 15	12
15 up to 20	19
20 up to 25	7
25 up to 30	3

The range is $25, found by $30 − $5.

Standard Deviation

Recall that for *ungrouped* data, one formula for the sample standard deviation is:

$$s = \sqrt{\frac{\Sigma X^2 - \frac{(\Sigma X)^2}{n}}{n-1}}$$

If the data of interest are in *grouped* form (in a frequency distribution), the sample standard deviation can be approximated by substituting ΣfX^2 for ΣX^2 and ΣfX for ΣX. The formula for the *sample standard deviation* then converts to:

STANDARD DEVIATION, GROUPED DATA	$s = \sqrt{\dfrac{\Sigma fX^2 - \dfrac{(\Sigma fX)^2}{n}}{n-1}}$	[4–8]

where:

    s is the symbol for the sample standard deviation.

    X is the midpoint of a class.

    f is the class frequency.

    n is the total number of sample observations.

Example

A sample of the semimonthly amounts invested in the Dupree Paint Company's profit-sharing plan by employees was organized into a frequency distribution for further study. (See Table 4–1.) What is the standard deviation of the data? What is the sample variance?

Table 4–1 A Sample of Semimonthly Amounts Invested by Employees in the Profit-Sharing Plan

Amount Invested	Number of Employees
$30 up to $35	3
35 up to 40	7
40 up to 45	11
45 up to 50	22
50 up to 55	40
55 up to 60	24
60 up to 65	9
65 up to 70	4

Solution

Following the same practice used in Chapter 3 for computing the arithmetic mean of data grouped into a frequency distribution, X represents the midpoint of each class. For example, the midpoint of the "$30 up to $35" class is $32.50. (See Table 4–2.) It is assumed that the amounts invested in the "$30 up to $35" class average about $32.50. Similarly, the seven amounts in the "$35 up to $40" class are assumed to average about $37.50, and so on.

Table 4–2   **Calculations Needed for the Sample Standard Deviation**

Amount Invested	Number, f	Midpoint, X	fX	$fX \times X$ or fX^2
\$30 up to \$35	3	\$32.50	\$ 97.50	3,168.75
35 up to 40	7	37.50	262.50	9,843.75
40 up to 45	11	42.50	467.50	19,868.75
45 up to 50	22	47.50	1,045.00	49,637.50
50 up to 55	40	52.50	2,100.00	110,250.00
55 up to 60	24	57.50	1,380.00	79,350.00
60 up to 65	9	62.50	562.50	35,156.25
65 up to 70	4	67.50	270.00	18,225.00
Total	120		\$6,185.00	325,500.00

To find the standard deviation of these data grouped into a frequency distribution:

Step 1. Each class frequency is multiplied by its class midpoint. That is, multiply f times X. Thus, for the first class $3 \times \$32.50 = \$97.50$, for the second class $fX = 7 \times \$37.50 = \$262.50$, and so on.

Step 2. Calculate fX^2. This could be written $fX \cdot X$. For the first class it would be $\$97.50 \times \$32.50 = 3,168.75$, for the second class $\$262.50 \times \$37.50 = 9,843.75$, and so on.

Step 3. Sum the fX and the fX^2 columns. The totals are $\$6,185$ and $325,500$, respectively.

Inserting these sums in formula (4–8) and solving for the sample standard deviation:

$$s = \sqrt{\frac{\Sigma fX^2 - \dfrac{(\Sigma fX)^2}{n}}{n - 1}}$$

$$= \sqrt{\frac{325,500 - \dfrac{(6,185)^2}{120}}{120 - 1}}$$

$$= \sqrt{\frac{325,500 - 318,785.2}{119}}$$

$$= \$7.51$$

The sample standard deviation is \$7.51. The sample variance is $(\$7.51)^2$, or about 56.40 (in dollars squared).

S E L F - R E V I E W   4 – 4

The ages of a sample of quarter-inch drills available for rental at Tool Rental, Inc. were organized into the following frequency distribution.

Age (months)	Frequency
2 up to 4	2
4 up to 6	5
6 up to 8	10
8 up to 10	4
10 up to 12	2

(a) Estimate the range.
(b) Estimate the sample standard deviation.
(c) Estimate the sample variance.

▌ Exercises

For exercises 19–22 compute the range, the standard deviation, and the variance.

19. Refer to the following frequency distribution.

Class	Frequency
0 up to 5	2
5 up to 10	7
10 up to 15	12
15 up to 20	6
20 up to 25	3

20. Refer to the following frequency distribution.

Class	Frequency
20 up to 30	7
30 up to 40	12
40 up to 50	21
50 up to 60	18
60 up to 70	12

21. Each person who applies for an assembly job at North Carolina Furniture is given a mechanical aptitude test. One part of the test involves assembling a dresser based on numbered instructions. A sample of the lengths of time it took 42 persons to assemble the dresser was organized into the following frequency distribution.

Length of Time (minutes)	Number
2 up to 4	4
4 up to 6	8
6 up to 8	14
8 up to 10	9
10 up to 12	5
12 up to 14	2

22. A sample of the amounts paid for parking on Saturday at the Downtown Parking Garage in Toronto was organized into the following frequency distribution.

Amount Paid	Number
$0.50 up to $0.75	2
0.75 up to 1.00	7
1.00 up to 1.25	15
1.25 up to 1.50	28
1.50 up to 1.75	14
1.75 up to 2.00	9
2.00 up to 2.25	3
2.25 up to 2.50	2

Interpretation and Uses of the Standard Deviation

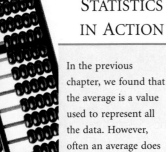

STATISTICS IN ACTION

In the previous chapter, we found that the average is a value used to represent all the data. However, often an average does not give the full picture. Stockbrokers are often faced with this problem when they are considering two investments, where the mean rate of return is the same. They usually calculate the standard deviation of the rates of return to assess the risk associated with the two investments. The investment with the larger standard deviation is considered to have the greater risk. In this context the standard deviation plays a vital part in making critical decisions regarding the composition of an investor's portfolio.

The standard deviation is commonly used as a measure to compare the spread in two or more sets of observations. For example, the standard deviation of the semimonthly amounts invested in the Dupree Paint Company profit-sharing plan was just computed to be $7.51. Suppose these employees are located in the South. If the standard deviation for a group of employees in the West is $10.47, and the means are about the same, it indicates that the amounts invested by the southern employees are not dispersed as much as those in the West (because $7.51 < $10.47). Since the amounts invested by the southern employees are clustered more closely about the mean, the mean for the southern employees is a more reliable measure than the mean for the western group.

Chebyshev's Theorem

We have stressed that a small standard deviation for a set of values indicates that these values are located close to the mean. Conversely, a large standard deviation reveals that the observations are widely scattered about the mean. The Russian mathematician P. L. Chebyshev (1821–1894) developed a theorem that allows us to determine the minimum proportion of the values that lie within a specified number of standard deviations of the mean. For example, based on **Chebyshev's theorem,** at least three of four values, or 75 percent, must lie between the mean plus two standard deviations and the mean minus two standard deviations. This relationship applies regardless of the shape of the distribution. Further, at least eight of nine values, or 88.9 percent, will lie between plus three standard deviations and minus three standard deviations of the mean. At least 24 of 25 values, or 96 percent, will lie between plus and minus five standard deviations of the mean.

In general terms, Chebyshev's theorem states:

> **Chebyshev's Theorem** For any set of observations (sample or population), the proportion of the values that lie within k standard deviations of the mean is at least $1 - 1/k^2$, where k is any constant greater than 1.

Example

In the previous example and solution, the arithmetic mean semimonthly amount contributed by the Dupree Paint employees to the company's profit-sharing plan was $51.54, and the standard deviation was computed to be $7.51. At least what percent of the contributions lie within plus 3.5 standard deviations and minus 3.5 standard deviations of the mean?

Solution

About 92 percent, found by

$$1 - \frac{1}{k^2} = 1 - \frac{1}{(3.5)^2} = 1 - \frac{1}{12.25} = 0.92$$

The Empirical Rule

Empirical Rule applies only to symmetrical, bell-shaped distributions.

Chebyshev's theorem is concerned with any set of values; that is, the distribution of values can have any shape. However, for a symmetrical, bell-shaped distribution such as the one in Chart 4–3, we can be more precise in explaining the dispersion about the mean. These relationships involving the standard deviation and the mean are included in the **Empirical Rule**, sometimes called the **Normal Rule**.

> **Empirical Rule** For a symmetrical, bell-shaped frequency distribution, approximately 68 percent of the observations will lie within plus and minus one standard deviation of the mean; about 95 percent of the observations will lie within plus and minus two standard deviations of the mean; and practically all (99.7 percent) will lie within plus and minus three standard deviations of the mean.

These relationships are portrayed graphically in Chart 4–3.

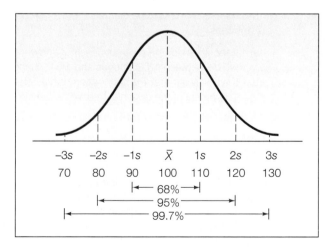

Chart 4–3 A Symmetrical, Bell-Shaped Curve Showing the Relationships between the Standard Deviation and the Mean

It has been noted that if a distribution is symmetrical and bell-shaped, practically all of the observations lie between the mean plus and minus three standard deviations.

Thus, if $\bar{X} = 100$ and $s = 10$, practically all the observations lie between $100 + 3(10)$ and $100 - 3(10)$, or 70 and 130. The range is therefore 60, found by $130 - 70$.

Conversely, if we know that the range is 60, we can approximate the standard deviation by dividing the range by 6. For this illustration: range $\div 6 = 60 \div 6 = 10$, the standard deviation.

Example

A sample of the monthly amounts spent for food by a senior citizen living alone approximates a symmetrical, bell-shaped frequency distribution. The sample mean is $150; the standard deviation is $20. Using the empirical rule:

1. About 68 percent of the monthly food expenditures are between what two amounts?
2. About 95 percent of the monthly food expenditures are between what two amounts?
3. Almost all of the monthly expenditures are between what two amounts?

Solution

1. About 68 percent are between $130 and $170, found by $\bar{X} \pm 1s = \$150 \pm 1(\$20)$.
2. About 95 percent are between $110 and $190, found by $\bar{X} \pm 2s = \$150 \pm 2(\$20)$.
3. Almost all (99.7 percent) are between $90 and $210, found by $\bar{X} \pm 3s = \$150 \pm 3(\$20)$.

SELF-REVIEW 4–5

The Pitney Pipe Company is one of several domestic manufacturers of PVC pipe. The quality control department sampled 600 10-foot lengths. At a point 1 foot from the end of the pipe they measured the outside diameter. The mean was 14.0 inches and the standard deviation 0.1 inches.

(a) If the shape of the distribution is not known, at least what percent of the observations will be between 13.85 inches and 14.15 inches?
(b) If we assume that the distribution of diameters is symmetrical and bell-shaped, about 95 percent of the observations will be between what two values?

❙ Exercises

23. According to Chebyshev's theorem, at least what percent of any set of observations will be within 1.8 standard deviations of the mean?
24. The mean income of a group of sample observations is $500; the standard deviation is $40. According to Chebyshev's theorem, at least what percent of the incomes will lie between $400 and $600?
25. The distribution of the weights of a sample of 1,400 cargo containers is somewhat normally distributed. Based on the Empirical Rule, what percent of the weights will lie:
    a. Between $\bar{X} - 2s$ and $\bar{X} + 2s$?
    b. Between $\bar{X}$ and $\bar{X} + 2s$? Below $\bar{X} - 2s$?
26. The following figure portrays the symmetrical appearance of a sample distribution of efficiency ratings.

a. Estimate the mean efficiency rating.
b. Estimate the standard deviation to the nearest whole number.
c. About 68 percent of the efficiency ratings are between what two values?
d. About 95 percent of the efficiency ratings are between what two values?

▌ Relative Dispersion

A direct comparison of two or more measures of dispersion — say, the standard devia-

tion for a distribution of annual incomes and the standard deviation of a distribution of absenteeism for this same group of employees — is impossible. Can we say that the standard deviation of $1,200 for the income distribution is greater than the standard deviation of 4.5 days for the distribution of absenteeism? Obviously not, because we cannot directly compare dollars and days absent from work. In order to make a meaningful comparison of the dispersion in incomes and absenteeism, we need to convert each of these measures to a *relative* value — that is, a percent. Karl Pearson (1857–1936), pictured at left, who contributed significantly to the science of statistics, developed a relative measure called the **coefficient of variation** (*CV*). It is a very useful measure when:

When to use CV
1. The data are in different units (such as dollars and days absent).
2. The data are in the same units, but the means are far apart (such as the incomes of the top executives and the incomes of the unskilled employees).

▌ **Coefficient of Variation**   The ratio of the standard deviation to the arithmetic mean, expressed as a percent. ▌

In terms of a formula for a sample:

| COEFFICIENT OF VARIATION | $CV = \dfrac{s}{\overline{X}}(100)$ ⟵ | Multiplying by 100 converts the decimal to a percent | **[4–9]** |

Example

A study of the test scores for an in-plant course in management principles and the years of service of the employees enrolled in the course resulted in these statistics: The mean score was 200; the standard deviation was 40. The mean number of years of service was 20 years; the standard deviation was 2 years. Compare the relative dispersion in the two distributions using the coefficient of variation.

Solution

The distributions are in different units (test scores and years of service). Therefore, they are converted to coefficients of variation.

For the test scores:

$$CV = \frac{s}{\overline{X}}(100)$$

$$= \frac{40}{200}(100)$$

$$= 20 \text{ percent}$$

For years of service:

$$CV = \frac{s}{\overline{X}}(100)$$

$$= \frac{2}{20}(100)$$

$$= 10 \text{ percent}$$

Interpreting, there is more dispersion relative to the mean in the distribution of test scores compared with the distribution of years of service (because 20 percent > 10 percent).

The same procedure is used when the data are in the same units but the means are far apart. (See the following example.)

Example

The variation in the annual incomes of executives is to be compared with the variation in incomes of unskilled employees. For a sample of executives, $\overline{X}$ = \$500,000 and s = \$50,000. For a sample of unskilled employees, $\overline{X}$ = \$22,000, and s = \$2,200. We are tempted to say that there is more dispersion in the annual incomes of the executives because \$50,000 > \$2,200. The means are so far apart, however, that we need to convert the statistics to coefficients of variation to make a meaningful comparison of the variation in annual incomes.

Solution

For the executives:

$$CV = \frac{s}{\overline{X}}(100)$$

$$= \frac{\$50,000}{\$500,000}(100)$$

$$= 10 \text{ percent}$$

For the unskilled employees:

$$CV = \frac{s}{\overline{X}}(100)$$

$$= \frac{\$2,200}{\$22,000}(100)$$

$$= 10 \text{ percent}$$

There is no difference in the relative dispersion of the two groups.

SELF-REVIEW 4–6

A large group of Air Force inductees was given two experimental tests — a mechanical aptitude test and a finger dexterity test. The arithmetic mean score on the mechanical aptitude test was 200, with a standard deviation of 10. The mean and standard deviation for the finger dexterity test were: $\overline{X}$ = 30, s = 6. Compare the relative dispersion in the two groups.

▌ Exercises

27. For a sample of students in the College of Business Administration at Mid-Atlantic University, the mean grade point average is 3.10 with a standard deviation of 0.25. Compute the coefficient of variation.

28. United Airlines is studying the weight of luggage for each passenger. For a large group of domestic passengers, the mean is 47 pounds with a standard deviation of 10 pounds. For a large group of overseas passengers, the mean is 78 pounds and the standard deviation is 15 pounds. Compute the relative dispersion of each group. Comment on the difference in relative dispersion.

29. The research analyst for the Sidde Financial stock brokerage firm wants to compare the dispersion in the price-earnings ratios for a group of common stocks with the dispersion of their return on investment. For the price-earnings ratios, the mean is 10.9 and the standard deviation 1.8. The mean return on investment is 25 percent and the standard deviation 5.2 percent.
    a. Why should the coefficient of variation be used to compare the dispersion?
    b. Compare the relative dispersion for the price-earnings ratios and return on investment.

30. The spread in the annual prices of stocks selling for under $10 and the spread in prices of those selling for over $60 are to be compared. The mean price of the stocks selling for under $10 is $5.25 and the standard deviation $1.52. The mean price of those stocks selling for over $60 is $92.50 and the standard deviation $5.28.
    a. Why should the coefficient of variation be used to compare the dispersion in the prices?
    b. Compute the coefficients of variation. What is your conclusion?

▌ Skewness

Chapter 3 described the central tendency of a set of observations using the mean, median, and mode. This chapter has shown several measures that describe the spread in the data. Another characteristic that can be measured is the degree of **skewness** of a distribution. Recall that if a frequency distribution is *symmetrical*, it has no skewness — that is, the skewness is zero. If one or more observations are extremely large, the mean of the distribution becomes greater than the median or mode. In such cases the distribution is said to be **positively skewed.** Conversely, if one or more extremely small observations are present, the mean is the smallest of the three measures of central tendency, and the distribution is said to be **negatively skewed.** (See Chart 4–4.)

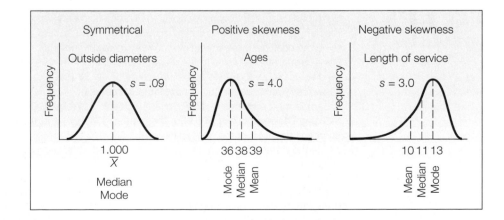

Chart 4–4 Shapes of Frequency Polygons Depicting Skewness

Karl Pearson also developed a measure to describe the degree of skewness, called the **coefficient of skewness:**

COEFFICIENT OF SKEWNESS	$Sk = \dfrac{3(\text{mean} - \text{median})}{\text{Standard deviation}}$	[4–10]

Example

The lengths of stay on the cancer floor of Sunnyside Hospital were organized into a frequency distribution. The mean length of stay was 28 days, the median 25 days, and the modal length 23 days. The standard deviation was computed to be 4.2 days.

1. Is the distribution symmetrical, positively skewed, or negatively skewed?
2. What is the coefficient of skewness? Interpret.

Solution

1. The distribution is positively skewed because the mean is the largest of the three measures of central tendency.
2. The coefficient of skewness is 2.14, found by

$$Sk = \frac{3(\text{mean} - \text{median})}{\text{Standard deviation}} = \frac{3(28 - 25)}{4.2} = \frac{9}{4.2} = 2.14$$

Interpreting, the coefficient of skewness generally lies between -3 and $+3$. In this case the coefficient of $+2.14$ indicates a substantial amount of positive skewness. Apparently, a few cancer patients are staying in the hospital for a long time, causing the mean to be larger than the median or mode.

SELF-REVIEW 4–7

A sample of experienced data entry clerks revealed that their mean typing speed is 87 words per minute and the median is 73. The standard deviation is 16.9 words per minute. What is the coefficient of skewness? Interpret.

▌ Exercises

31. For a particular distribution of wages, the arithmetic mean was computed to be $25,000, the median $25,000, and the mode also $25,000. The standard deviation was $1,000. Determine the coefficient of skewness. Comment on your findings.
32. For a group of executives in the electronics industry, the mean salary is $542,000, and the median is $400,000. The standard deviation is $448,500. Determine the coefficient of skewness. Comment on the shape of the distribution.
33. A sample of the homes currently offered for sale in Walla Walla, Washington, revealed that the mean asking price is $75,900, the median $70,100, and the modal price $67,200. The standard deviation of the distribution is $5,900.
     a. Is the distribution of prices symmetrical, negatively skewed, or positively skewed?
     b. What is the coefficient of skewness? Interpret.
34. A study of the net sales of a sample of small corporations revealed that the mean net sales is $2.1 million, the median $2.4 million, and the modal sales $2.6 million. The standard deviation of the distribution is $500,000.
     a. Is the distribution of net sales symmetrical, negatively skewed, or positively skewed?
     b. What is the coefficient of skewness? Interpret.

▍ Other Measures of Dispersion

The variance and the standard deviation are the most widely used measures of dispersion. However, there are other ways of describing the variation or spread in a set of data. One method is to determine the *location* of values that divide a set of observations into equal parts. These measures include *quartiles, deciles,* and *percentiles.*

Quartiles divide a set of observations into four equal parts. To explain further, think of any set of values arranged from smallest to largest. In Chapter 3 we called the middle value of a set of data arranged from smallest to largest the median. That is, 50 percent of the observations are larger than the median and 50 percent are smaller. The median is a measure of location because it pinpoints the center of the data. In a similar fashion quartiles divide a set of observations into four equal parts. The first quartile, usually labeled Q_1, is the value below which 25 percent of the observations occur and the third quartile, usually labeled Q_3, is the value below which 75 percent of the observations occur. Logically, Q_2 is the median. The values corresponding to Q_1, Q_2, and Q_3 divide a set of data into four equal parts. Q_1 can be thought of as the "median" of the lower half of the data and Q_3 the "median" of the upper half of the data.

In a similar fashion deciles divide a set of observations into 10 equal parts and percentiles into 100 equal parts. So if you found that your GPA was in the 8th decile at your university, you could conclude that 80 percent of the students had a GPA lower than yours and 20 percent had a higher GPA. A GPA in the 33rd percentile means that 33 percent of the students have a lower GPA and 67 percent have a higher GPA. Percentile scores are frequently used to report results on such national standardized tests as the SAT, ACT, GMAT (used to judge entry into many Master of Business Administration programs), and LSAT (used to judge entry into law school).

Quartiles, Deciles, and Percentiles

To formalize the procedure, let L_p refer to the location of a desired percentile. So if we wanted to find the 33rd percentile we would use L_{33} and if we wanted the median, the 50th percentile, then L_{50}. The number of observations is *n,* so if we want to locate the middle observation, its position is at $(n + 1)/2$, or we could write this as $(n + 1)\dfrac{P}{100}$, where P is the desired percentile.

LOCATION OF A PERCENTILE $\qquad\qquad L_p = (n + 1)\dfrac{P}{100}$ **[4–11]**

An example will help to explain further.

Example

Listed below are the commissions earned last month by a sample of 15 brokers at Smith Barney's Oakland, California, office. Smith Barney is an investment company with offices located throughout the United States.

$2,038	$1,758	$1,721	$1,637	$2,097	$2,047	$2,205	$1,787	$2,287
$1,940	$2,311	$2,054	$2,406	$1,471	$1,460			

Locate the median, the first quartile, and the third quartile for the commissions earned.

Solution   The first step is to organize the data from the smallest commission to the largest.

| $1,460 | $1,471 | $1,637 | $1,721 | $1,758 | $1,787 | $1,940 | $2,038 |
| $2,047 | $2,054 | $2,097 | $2,205 | $2,287 | $2,311 | $2,406 | |

The median value is the observation in the center. The center value is located at $(n + 1)/2$, where n is the total number of observations. In this case that is position number 8, found by $(15 + 1)/2$. The eighth largest commission is $2,038. So we conclude this is the median and that half the brokers earned commissions more than $2,038 and half earned less than $2,038.

Recall the definition of a quartile. Quartiles divide a set of observations into four equal parts. Hence 25 percent of the observations will be less than the first quartile. Seventy-five percent of the observations will be less than the third quartile. To locate the first quartile, we use formula (4–11), where $n = 15$ and $P = 25$,

$$L_p = (n + 1)\frac{P}{100} = (15 + 1)\frac{25}{100} = 4$$

and to locate the third quartile: $n = 15$ and $P = 75$:

$$L_p = (n + 1)\frac{P}{100} = (15 + 1)\frac{75}{100} = 12$$

Therefore, the first and third quartile values are located at positions 4 and 12. The fourth value in the ordered array is $1,721 and the twelfth is $2,205. These are the first and third quartiles, respectively.

In the above example the location formula yielded a whole number result. That is, we were looking to find the first quartile and there were 15 observations, so the location formula indicated we should look to the fourth ordered value. What if there were 20 observations in the sample, that is $n = 20$, and we wanted to locate the first quartile? From the location formula (4–11):

$$L_p = (n + 1)\frac{P}{100} = (20 + 1)\frac{25}{100} = 5.25$$

We would locate the fifth value in the ordered array and then move .25 of the distance between the 5th and 6th value and report that as the first quartile. Like the median, the quartile does not need to be one of the actual values in the data set.

To explain further, suppose a data set contained the following six values: 91, 75, 61, 101, 43, and 104. We want to locate the first quartile. We order the values from smallest to largest: 43, 61, 75, 91, 101, and 104. The first quartile is located at

$$L_p = (n + 1)\frac{P}{100} = (6 + 1)\frac{25}{100} = 1.75$$

The position formula tells us that the first quartile is located between the first and the second value and that it is .75 of the distance between the first and the second value. The first value is 43 and the second is 61, so the distance between these two values is 18. To locate the first quartile, we need to move .75 of the distance between the first and second value, so .75(18) = 13.5. To complete the procedure, we add 13.5 to the first value and report that the first quartile is located at 56.5.

We can extend the idea to include both deciles and percentiles. If we wanted to locate the 23rd percentile in a sample of 80 observations, we would look for the 18.63 position.

$$L_p = (n + 1)\frac{P}{100} = (80 + 1)\frac{23}{100} = 18.63$$

To find the value corresponding to the 23rd percentile, we would locate the 18th and 19th observations and determine the distance between these two values. Next we would multiply this difference by .63 and add the result to the smaller value. The result would be the 23rd percentile.

With a computer it is quite easy to sort the data from smallest to largest and to locate percentiles and deciles. Both MINITAB and Excel will find the first and third quartiles. Listed below is the MINITAB output that includes the first and third quartiles as well as the mean, median, and standard deviation for the Whitner Pontiac data. (See Table 2–1.) We conclude that 25 percent of the vehicles sold for less than $17,074 and that 75 percent sold for less than $22,795.

```
MTB > Describe 'Price'

Descriptive Statistics

Variable        N       Mean     Median    Tr Mean      StDev     SE Mean
Price          80      20227      19831      20005       4381         490


Variable      Min        Max         Q1         Q3
Price       12546      33625      17074      22795
```

SELF-REVIEW 4–8

The Quality Control Department at the Plainsville Peanut Company is responsible for checking the total weight of the peanuts in a jar that is labeled as containing 8 ounces. The weights of a sample of 9 jars produced last hour revealed the following:

| 7.69 | 7.72 | 7.80 | 7.86 | 7.90 | 7.94 | 7.97 | 8.06 | 8.09 |

(a) What is the median weight?
(b) Determine the weights corresponding to Q_1 and Q_3.

▌ Exercises

35. Determine the median and the values corresponding to the first and third quartiles in the following data.

| 46 | 47 | 49 | 49 | 51 | 53 | 54 | 54 | 55 | 55 | 59 |

36. Determine the median and the values corresponding to the first and third quartiles in the following data.

| 5.24 | 6.02 | 6.67 | 7.30 | 7.59 | 7.99 | 8.03 | 8.35 | 8.81 | 9.45 |
| 9.61 | 10.37 | 10.39 | 11.86 | 12.22 | 12.71 | 13.07 | 13.59 | 13.89 | 15.42 |

37. Anderson, Inc. is a distributor of small electrical motors. As with any business, the length of time customers take to pay their invoices is important. Listed below, arranged from smallest to largest, is the time, in days, for a sample of Anderson, Inc. invoices.

13	13	13	20	26	27	31	34	34	34	35	35	36	37	38
41	41	41	45	47	47	47	50	51	53	54	56	62	67	82

   a. Determine the first and third quartiles.
   b. Determine the 2nd decile and the 8th decile.
   c. Determine the 67th percentile.

38. Wendy Hagel is the national sales manager for National Textbooks, Inc. She has a sales staff of 40 who visit college professors all over the United States. Each Saturday morning she requires her sales staff to send her a report. This report includes, among other things, the number of professors visited during the previous week. Listed below, ordered from smallest to largest, are the number of visits last week.

38	40	41	45	48	48	50	50	51	51	52	52	53	54	55	55	55	56	56	57
59	59	59	62	62	62	63	64	65	66	66	67	67	69	69	71	77	78	79	79

   a. Determine the median number of calls.
   b. Determine the first and third quartiles.
   c. Determine the 1st decile and the 9th decile.
   d. Determine the 33rd percentile.

Box Plots

A **box plot** is a graphical display, based on quartiles, that helps us to picture a set of data. To construct a box plot, we need only five statistics: the minimum value, Q_1 (the first quartile), the median, Q_3 (the third quartile), and the maximum value. An example will help to explain.

Example

Alexander's Pizza offers free delivery of its pizza within 15 miles. Alex, the owner, wants some information on the time it takes for delivery. How long does a typical delivery take? Within what range of times will most deliveries be completed? For a sample of 20 deliveries, he determined the following information:

$$\text{Minimum value} = 13 \text{ minutes}$$

$$Q_1 = 15 \text{ minutes}$$

$$\text{Median} = 18 \text{ minutes}$$

$$Q_3 = 22 \text{ minutes}$$

$$\text{Maximum value} = 30 \text{ minutes}$$

Develop a box plot for the delivery times. What conclusions can you make about the delivery times?

Solution

The first step in drawing a box plot is to create an appropriate scale along the horizontal axis. Next, we draw a box that starts at Q_1 (15 minutes) and ends at Q_3 (22 minutes). Inside the box we place a vertical line to represent the median (18 minutes). Finally, we extend horizontal lines from the box out to the minimum value (13 minutes) and the maximum value (30 minutes). These horizontal lines outside of the box are sometimes called "whiskers" because they look a bit like a cat's whiskers.

The box plot shows that the middle 50 percent of the deliveries take between 15 minutes and 22 minutes. The distance between the ends of the box, 7 minutes, is called the **interquartile range.** The interquartile range is the distance between the first and the third quartile.

The box plot also reveals that the distribution of delivery times is positively skewed. How do we know this? In this case there are actually two pieces of information that suggest that the distribution is positively skewed. First, the dashed line to the right of the box from 22 minutes (Q_3) to the maximum time of 30 minutes is longer than the dashed line from the left of 15 minutes (Q_1) to the minimum value of 13 minutes. To put it another way, the 25 percent of the data larger than the third quartile is more spread out than the 25 percent less than the first quartile. A second indication of positive skewness is that the median is not in the center of the box. The distance from the first quartile to the median is smaller than the distance from the median to the third quartile. We know that the number of delivery times between 15 minutes and 18 minutes is the same as the number of delivery times between 18 minutes and 22 minutes.

Example

Refer to the Whitner Pontiac data in Table 2–1. Develop a box plot of the data. What can we conclude about the distribution of vehicle selling prices?

Solution

The MINITAB statistical software system was used to develop the following chart.

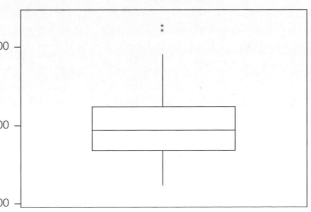

We conclude that the median vehicle selling price is about $20,000, that about 25 percent of the vehicles sell for less than $17,000 and about 25 percent sell for more than $23,000. About 50 percent of the vehicles sell for between $17,000 and $23,000. The distribution is somewhat positively skewed, because the line above $23,000 is somewhat longer than the line below $17,000.

There are two asterisks (**) above the $30,000 selling price. An asterisk indicates an outlier. An **outlier** is a value that is inconsistent with the rest of the data. The standard definition of a outlier, which is used in MINITAB, is a value that is more than 1.5 times the interquartile range larger than Q_3 or smaller than Q_1. In this example an outlier would be a value greater than $32,000, found by

$$\text{Outlier} = Q_3 + 1.5(Q_3 - Q_1) = 23,000 + 1.5\,(23,000 - 17,000) = 32,000$$

A value less than $8,000 would also be an outlier.

$$\text{Outlier} = Q_1 - 1.5(Q_3 - Q_1) = 17,000 - 1.5\,(23,000 - 17,000) = 8,000$$

In the Whitner Pontiac data, there were two outliers, vehicles that sold for more than $32,000. Box plots are available from many computer software packages and offer a quick way to evaluate a set of observations.

SELF-REVIEW 4–9

The following box plot is given.

What are the median, the largest and smallest values, and the first and third quartiles? Would you agree that the distribution is symmetrical?

▌ Exercises

39. Refer to the box plot.

a. Estimate the median.
b. Estimate the first and third quartiles.
c. Determine the interquartile range.
d. Beyond what point is a value considered an outlier?

e.　Identify any outliers and estimate their value.

f.　Is the distribution symmetrical or positively or negatively skewed?

40.　Refer to the box plot.

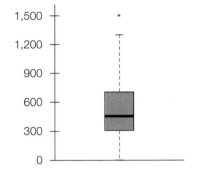

a.　Estimate the median.

b.　Estimate the first and third quartiles.

c.　Determine the interquartile range.

d.　Beyond what point is a value considered an outlier?

e.　Identify any outliers and estimate their value.

f.　Is the distribution symmetrical or positively or negatively skewed?

41.　In a study of the mileage of automobiles manufactured in 1997, the mean number of miles per gallon was 27.5 and the median was 26.8. The smallest value in the study was 12.70 miles per gallon, and the largest was 50.20. The first and third quartiles were 17.95 and 35.45 miles per gallon, respectively. Develop a box plot and comment on the distribution. Is it a symmetric distribution?

42.　A sample of 28 hospitals in Florida revealed the following daily charges for a semiprivate room. For convenience the data are ordered from largest to smallest. Construct a box plot to represent the data. Comment on the distribution. Be sure to identify the first and third quartiles and the median, and comment on the shape of the distribution of daily charges.

$116	$121	$157	$192	$207	$209	$209
229	232	236	236	239	243	246
260	264	276	281	283	289	296
307	309	312	317	324	341	353

❙ Chapter Outline

I.　The dispersion is the variation in a set of data.

A.　The range is the difference between the largest and the smallest value in a set of data.

1.　The formula for the range is:

$$\text{Range} = (\text{Highest value} - \text{Lowest value}) \qquad \textbf{[4–1]}$$

2.　The major characteristics of the range are:

a.　Only two values are used in its calculation.

b.　It is influenced by extreme values.

c.　It is easy to compute and to understand.

B.　The mean absolute deviation is the sum of the absolute deviations divided by the number of observations.

1.　The formula for computing the mean absolute deviation is

$$MD = \frac{\Sigma |X - \bar{X}|}{n} \qquad \textbf{[4–2]}$$

2.　The major characteristics are:

a.　It is not unduly influenced by large or small values.

      b.   All values are used in the calculation.

      c.   The absolute values are somewhat difficult to work with.

  C.   The variance is the mean of the squared deviations from the arithmetic mean.

    1.   The major characteristics of the variance are:

      a.   All observations are used in the calculation.

      b.   It is not unduly influenced by extreme observations.

      c.   The units are somewhat difficult to work with; they are the original units squared.

    2.   The formula for the population variance is:

$$\sigma^2 = \frac{\Sigma(X - \mu)^2}{N} \qquad \text{[4–3]}$$

    3.   The formula for the sample variance is

$$s^2 = \frac{\Sigma(X - \bar{X})^2}{n - 1} \qquad \text{[4–5]}$$

  D.   The standard deviation is the square root of the variance.

    1.   The following two formulas are for the sample standard deviation.

$$s = \sqrt{\frac{\Sigma(X - \bar{X})^2}{n - 1}} = \sqrt{\frac{\Sigma X^2 - \frac{(\Sigma X)^2}{n}}{n - 1}} \qquad \text{[4–5], [4–7]}$$

    2.   The major characteristics of the standard deviation are:

      a.   It is in the same units as the original data.

      b.   It is the square root of the average squared distance from the mean.

      c.   It cannot be negative.

      d.   It is the most widely reported measure of dispersion.

 II. Chebyshev's theorem states that regardless of the shape of the distribution, at least $1 - 1/k^2$ of the observations will be within k standard deviations of the mean.

III. The coefficient of variation is a measure of relative dispersion.

  A.   The formula for the coefficient of variation is:

$$CV = \frac{s}{\bar{X}}(100) \qquad \text{[4–9]}$$

  B.   It reports the variation relative to the mean.

  C.   It is useful for comparing distributions with different units.

 IV. The coefficient of skewness measures the symmetry of a distribution.

  A.   The formula for the coefficient of skewness is:

$$Sk = \frac{3(\bar{X} - \text{Median})}{s} \qquad \text{[4–10]}$$

  B.   The major characteristics are:

    1.   It may range from −3.00 up to 3.00.

    2.   A value near 0 means the distribution is symmetric.

    3.   Positive skewness is indicated when there is a long tail to the right.

    4.   Negative skewness is indicated when there is a long tail to the left.

  V. Measures of location also describe the spread in a set of observations.

  A.   A quartile divides a set of observations into four equal parts.

    1.   Twenty-five percent of the observations are less than the first quartile, 50 percent are less than the second quartile (the median), and 75 percent are less than the third quartile.

    2.   The interquartile range is the difference between the third and the first quartile.

  B.   Deciles divide a set of observations into 10 equal parts.

  C.   Percentiles divide a set of observations into 100 equal parts.

   D. A box plot is a graphic display of a set of data.
       1. A box is drawn connecting the first and third quartiles.
           a. A line through the inside of the box shows the median.
           b. Dotted line segments from the third quartile to the largest value and from the first quartile to the smallest value shows the range of the largest 25 percent of the observations and the smallest 25 percent.
       2. A box plot is based on five statistics: the largest and smallest observation, the first and third quartiles, and the median.

▌ Pronunciation Key

SYMBOL	MEANING	PRONUNCIATION
σ^2	Population variance	*sigma squared*
σ	Population standard deviation	*sigma*
$\Sigma f X^2$	Sum of the product of the class midpoints squared and the class frequency	*sigma f X squared*
L_p	Location of percentile	*L sub p*
Q_1	First quartile	*Q sub 1*
Q_3	Third quartile	*Q sub 3*

▌ Chapter Exercises

Exercises 43 through 51 are based on the following data. The quality control department at Clegg Industries constantly monitors three assembly lines producing ovens for private homes. The oven is designed to preheat to 240 degrees Fahrenheit in four minutes and then shut off. However, the oven may not reach 240 in the allotted time because of improper installation of the insulation and other reasons. Likewise, the temperature might go beyond 240 degrees during the four-minute preheating cycle. A large sample from each of the three production lines revealed the following information.

	Temperature (°F)		
Statistical Measure	Line 1	Line 2	Line 3
Arithmetic mean	238.1	240.0	242.9
Median	240.0	240.0	240.0
Mode	241.5	240.0	239.1
Standard deviation	3.0	0.4	3.9
Mean deviation	1.9	0.2	2.2
Quartile deviation	1.0	0.1	1.7

43. Which of the lines has a bell-shaped distribution?
44. Which line has the most variation in the temperature? How do you know?
45. According to the Empirical Rule, about 95 percent of the temperature readings for line 2 are between what values?
46. The distribution of temperatures for which lines is positively skewed?
47. For line 2, approximate the first and the third quartiles.
48. For line 3, according to Chebyshev's theorem, about 89 percent of the temperatures will be between what two values?
49. Determine the coefficient of variation for line 3.
50. Determine the coefficient of skewness for line 1.
51. Determine the variance for line 1.

52. In a study of data from the personnel files of a large company, the coefficient of variation for the number of years with the company is 20 percent and the coefficient of variation for the amount of commission earned last year is 30 percent. Comment on the relative dispersion of the two variables.

53. In the same study discussed in exercise 52, the coefficient of skewness for the age of the employees is −2.25. Comment on the shape of the distribution. Which measure of central tendency is the largest? Which direction is the longer tail? What would you conclude about the ages of the employees?

54. The hourly outputs of a group of employees assembling plug-in units at Zenith were selected at random. The sample outputs were: 8, 9, 8, 10, 9, 10, 12, and 10.
    a. Compute the range.
    b. Compute the mean deviation.
    c. Compute the standard deviation.

55. The ages of a sample of Canadian tourists flying from Toronto to Hong Kong were: 32, 21, 60, 47, 54, 17, 72, 55, 33, and 41.
    a. Compute the range.
    b. Compute the mean deviation.
    c. Compute the standard deviation.

56. The weights (in pounds) of a sample of five boxes being sent by UPS are: 12, 6, 7, 3, and 10.
    a. Compute the range.
    b. Compute the mean deviation.
    c. Compute the standard deviation.

57. A southern state has seven state universities in its system. The numbers of volumes (in thousands) held in their libraries are 83, 510, 33, 256, 401, 47, and 23.
    a. Is this a sample or a population?
    b. Compute the standard deviation.
    c. Compute the coefficient of variation. Interpret.

58. A recent report in *Woman's World* magazine suggested that the typical family of four with an intermediate budget spends about $96 per week on food. The following frequency distribution was included in the report. Compute (a) the range and (b) the standard deviation.

Amount Spent	Frequency
$ 80 up to $ 85	6
85 up to 90	12
90 up to 95	23
95 up to 100	35
100 up to 105	24
105 up to 110	10

59. Bidwell Electronics, Inc. recently surveyed a sample of employees to determine how far they lived from corporate headquarters. The results are shown below. Compute the range and the standard deviation.

Distance (miles)	Frequency
0 up to 5	4
5 up to 10	15
10 up to 15	27
15 up to 20	18
20 up to 25	6

60. Health issues are a concern of managers, especially as they evaluate the cost of medical insurance. In a recent survey of 150 executives at Elvers Industries, a large insurance and

financial firm located in the Southwest, the number of pounds by which the executives were overweight was reported. Compute the range and the standard deviation.

Pounds Overweight	Frequency
0 up to 6	14
6 up to 12	42
12 up to 18	58
18 up to 24	28
24 up to 30	8

61. A major airline wanted some information on those enrolled in their "frequent flyer" program. A sample of 48 members resulted in the following number of miles flown, to the nearest 1,000 miles, by each participant. Develop a box plot of the data and comment on the information.

22	29	32	38	39	41	42	43	43	43	44	44
45	45	46	46	46	47	50	51	52	54	54	55
56	57	58	59	60	61	61	63	63	64	64	67
69	70	70	70	71	71	72	73	74	76	78	88

62. The National Muffler Company claims they will change your muffler in less than 30 minutes. An undercover consumer reporter for WTOL Channel 11 monitored 30 consecutive muffler changes at the National outlet on Liberty Street. The number of minutes to perform changes is reported below.

44	12	22	31	26	22	30	26	18	28	12
40	17	13	14	17	25	29	15	30	10	28
16	33	24	20	29	34	23	13			

a. Develop a box plot for the time to change a muffler.
b. Does the distribution show any outliers?
c. Summarize your findings in a brief report.

63. The Walter Gogel Company is an industrial supplier of fasteners, tools, and springs. The amounts of their invoices vary widely, from less than $20.00 to over $400.00. During the month of January they sent out 80 invoices. Here is a box plot of these invoices. Write a brief report summarizing the amounts of their invoices. Be sure to include information on the values of the first and third quartile, the median, and whether there is any skewness. If there are any outliers, approximate the value of these invoices.

64. The box plot shows the number of daily newspapers published in each state and the District of Columbia. Write a brief report summarizing the number published. Be sure to include information on the values of the first and third quartile, the median, and whether there is any skewness. If there are any outliers, estimate their value.

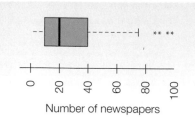

Number of newspapers

65. The previous problem presented a box plot of the number of daily newspapers by state and the District of Columbia. Listed below is a summary from Excel showing statistics for the same data set.

Number of Papers	
Mean	30.05882
Standard Error	3.409837
Median	23
Mode	22
Standard Deviation	24.35111
Sample Variance	592.9765
Kurtosis	0.933851
Skewness	1.271859
Range	96
Minimum	2
Maximum	98
Sum	1533
Count	51

a. Chebyshev's theorem states that at least 75 percent of the observations will be within two standard deviations of the mean. What are these limits?
b. Determine the coefficient of variation. Interpret.
c. Do the values tend to show a positive or a negative skewness? How do you know?

66. Danfoss Electronics, Inc. has 150 suppliers throughout the United States and Canada. Listed below are MINITAB summary statistics on the sales volume to its suppliers.

Variable	N	Mean	Median	Tr Mean	StDev	SE Mean
Sales	150	128.1	81.0	102.2	162.7	13.3

Variable	Min	Max	Q1	Q3
Sales	2.0	1019.0	38.7	138.2

a. What is the range?
b. Determine the interquartile range.
c. Determine the coefficient of variation.
d. Determine the coefficient of skewness.
e. Draw a box plot.

67. The following data are the estimated market values (in $ millions) of 50 companies in the auto parts business.

26.8	8.6	6.5	30.6	15.4	18.0	7.6	21.5	11.0	10.2
28.3	15.5	31.4	23.4	4.3	20.2	33.5	7.9	11.2	1.0
11.7	18.5	6.8	22.3	12.9	29.8	1.3	14.1	29.7	18.7
6.7	31.4	30.4	20.6	5.2	37.8	13.4	18.3	27.1	32.7
6.1	0.9	9.6	35.0	17.1	1.9	1.2	16.6	31.1	16.1

a. Determine the mean and the median of the market values.
b. Determine the standard deviation of the market values.
c. Using Chebyshev's theorem, between what values would you expect about 56 percent of the market values to occur?
d. Using the Empirical Rule, about 95 percent of the values would occur between what values?
e. Determine the coefficient of variation.
f. Determine the coefficient of skewness.
g. Estimate the values of Q_1 and Q_3. Draw a box plot.
h. Write a brief report summarizing the results.

www.Exercises.com

68. The following Web site presents information from a study regarding the amount consumers spend in a grocery store: *http://lib.stat.cmu.edu/DASL/Datafiles/Shoppers.html.* Develop a box plot of the data. What can you conclude about the shape of the distribution? Compute the mean, median, and the standard deviation and then find the coefficient of skewness. What does this statistic indicate about the shape of the data?

69. In problem 64 in Chapter 3, we presented information on the Dow Jones Industrial Average (DJIA). That information is repeated below.

The Dow Jones Industrial Average, Updated as of: Dec 09, 1997 @ 4:02 pm ET

Symbol	Company Name	Last	Symbol	Company Name	Last
ALD	Allied-Signal Inc.	38.5000	HWP	Hewlett-Packard Co.	64.7500
AA	Aluminum Co. of America	71.1875	IBM	International Business Machines	110.000
AXP	American Express	87.5625	IP	International Paper	44.3750
T	AT&T	58.0000	JNJ	Johnson & Johnson	65.2500
BA	Boeing Co.	50.8125	MCD	McDonald's Corp.	47.5625
CAT	Caterpillar Inc.	50.4375	MRK	Merck & Co.	105.0000
CHV	Chevron Corp.	78.0000	MMM	Minnesota Mining/Mfg.	94.2500
KO	Coca-Cola Co.	63.3750	JPM	Morgan (J.P.)	122.0000
DIS	Disney Co.	93.875	MO	Philip Morris Cos.	44.3125
DD	DuPont	63.875	PG	Procter & Gamble	79.1250
EK	Eastman Kodak	57.8175	S	Sears, Roebuck	46.1875
XON	Exxon Corp.	62.1250	TRV	Travelers Group Inc.	54.5625
GE	General Electric	74.437	UK	Union Carbide	46.6250
GM	General Motors	63.1875	UTX	United Technologies	75.8125
GT	Goodyear Tire & Rubber	65.0625	WMT	Wal-Mart Stores Inc.	39.8125

a. Develop a box plot for these 30 observations and write a brief report. Is the distribution symmetrical? What are your estimates of the first and third quartiles, and the median. Are there any outliers?
b. Determine the standard deviation of these stock prices. Do the prices show much variation?

c.   You may want to go to the following Web site to find current information about the Dow: *http://foxnews.com/news/features/dow/.* Has there been much change since the above data were collected? You might even check to see whether any of the companies included in the calculation have changed.

▌ Computer Data Exercises

70.   Refer to Data Set 1, which reports information on homes sold in the Venice, Florida, area last year.
   a.   For the variable "selling price":
      1.   Compute the mean, median, and standard deviation.
      2.   Determine the coefficient of skewness. Is the distribution positively or negatively skewed?
      3.   Determine the largest and smallest selling price and the first and third quartiles. From this information develop a box plot.
      4.   Write a brief summary regarding the distribution of the selling prices.
   b.   For the variable "area of the home in square feet":
      1.   Compute the mean, median, and standard deviation.
      2.   Determine the coefficient of skewness. Is the distribution positively or negatively skewed?
      3.   Determine the largest and smallest areas and the first and third quartiles. From this information develop a box plot.
      4.   Write a brief summary regarding the distribution of the area of the homes.
71.   Refer to Data Set 2, which reports information on the 28 Major League Baseball teams for the 1997 season.
   a.   For the variable "team salary":
      1.   Compute the mean, median, and standard deviation.
      2.   Determine the coefficient of skewness. Is the distribution positively or negatively skewed?
      3.   Determine the largest and smallest team salary and the first and third quartiles. From this information develop a box plot.
      4.   Write a brief summary regarding the distribution of the team salaries.
   b.   For the variable "team attendance":
      1.   Compute the mean, median, and standard deviation.
      2.   Determine the coefficient of skewness. Is the distribution positively or negatively skewed?
      3.   Determine the largest and smallest team attendance and the first and third quartiles. From this information develop a box plot.
      4.   Write a brief summary regarding the distribution of the attendance.
72.   Refer to Data Set 3, which reports information on the circulation of 48 popular magazines.
   a.   For the variable "circulation":
      1.   Compute the mean, median, and standard deviation.
      2.   Determine the coefficient of skewness. Is the distribution positively or negatively skewed?
      3.   Determine the largest and smallest circulation and the first and third quartiles. From this information develop a box plot.
      4.   Write a brief summary regarding the distribution of circulation.
   b.   For the variable "color advertising":
      1.   Compute the mean, median, and standard deviation.
      2.   Determine the coefficient of skewness. Is the distribution positively or negatively skewed?

3. Determine the largest and smallest cost of color advertising and the first and third quartiles. From this information develop a box plot.
4. Write a brief summary regarding the distribution of cost of color advertising.

73. Refer to Data Set 4, which reports information on the 94 school districts in Northwest Ohio.
    a. For the variable "teacher salary":
        1. Compute the mean, median, and standard deviation.
        2. Determine the coefficient of skewness. Is the distribution positively or negatively skewed?
        3. Determine the largest and smallest salary and the first and third quartiles. From this information develop a box plot.
        4. Write a brief summary regarding the distribution of salaries.
    b. For the variable "number of students in the school district":
        1. Compute the mean, median, and standard deviation.
        2. Determine the coefficient of skewness. Is the distribution positively or negatively skewed?
        3. Determine the largest and smallest number of students and the first and third quartiles. From this information develop a box plot.
        4. Write a brief summary regarding the distribution of number of students.

▌ Computer Commands

1. MINITAB commands for the summary of descriptive statistics on page 119.
    a. Import the data from the data disk. The file name is **Tbl2-1.**
    b. Select **Stat, Basic Statistics,** and then click on **Descriptive Statistics.**
    c. Select the variable **Price** and click on **OK.**

2. The MINITAB commands for the box plot on page 121.
    a. Import the data from the data disk. The file name is **Tbl2-1.**
    b. Select **Graph,** and then **Boxplots.**

c. Select **Price** as the variable and then click on **OK.**

Boxplot

C1   Price
C2   Sorted

Variable: Price

☐ By variable:
Use levels:

☐ Notch, confidence level: 90.0

Axis

Minimum position:

Maximum position:

Tick increment:

Select

☐ Condensed display

Help   OK   Cancel

CHAPTER 4 *Answers to Self-Review*

4–1 (a) 22, found by $112 - 90$.

(b) $\overline{X} = \dfrac{824}{8} = 103$

(c)

X	$|X - \overline{X}|$	Absolute Deviation
95	$|-8|$	8
103	$|\ 0|$	0
105	$|+2|$	2
110	$|+7|$	7
104	$|+1|$	1
105	$|+2|$	2
112	$|+9|$	9
90	$|-13|$	13
	Total	42

$$MD = \frac{42}{8} = 5.25 \text{ pounds}$$

4–2 (a) $\mu = \dfrac{11,900}{5} = 2380$

(b) $\sigma^2 = \dfrac{\begin{array}{c}(2536 - 2380)^2 + (2173 - 2380)^2 \\ + (2448 - 2380)^2 + (2121 - 2380)^2 \\ + (2622 - 2380)^2\end{array}}{5}$

$= \dfrac{(156)^2 + (-207)^2 + (68)^2 + (-259)^2 + (242)^2}{5}$

$= \dfrac{197,454}{5} = 39,490.8$

(c) $\sigma = \sqrt{39,490.8} = 198.72$

(d) There is more variation in the Pittsburgh office because the standard deviation is larger. The mean is also larger in the Pittsburgh office.

4–3 2.33, found by:

$$\overline{X} = \frac{\Sigma X}{n} = \frac{28}{7} = 4$$

X	$X - \overline{X}$	$(X - \overline{X})^2$	X^2
4	0	0	16
2	-2	4	4
5	1	1	25
4	0	0	16
5	1	1	25
2	-2	4	4
6	2	4	36
28	0	14	126

$$s^2 = \frac{\Sigma(X - \overline{X})^2}{n - 1} \quad \text{or} \quad s^2 = \frac{\Sigma X^2 - \dfrac{(\Sigma X)^2}{n}}{n - 1}$$

$$= \frac{14}{7 - 1} \qquad\qquad = \frac{126 - \dfrac{(28)^2}{7}}{7 - 1}$$

$$= 2.33 \qquad\qquad\quad = \frac{126 - 112}{6}$$

$$= 2.33$$

$$s = \sqrt{2.33} = 1.53$$

4–4 (a) $12 - 2 = 10$ months

(b) 2.130 months, found by:

Months	f	X	fX	fX^2
2 up to 4	2	3	6	18
4 up to 6	5	5	25	125
6 up to 8	10	7	70	490
8 up to 10	4	9	36	324
10 up to 12	2	11	22	242
	23		159	1,199

$$s = \sqrt{\frac{1,199 - \dfrac{(159)^2}{23}}{23 - 1}}$$

$$= \sqrt{\frac{1,199 - 1,099.1739}{22}}$$

$$= \sqrt{4.53755}$$

$$= 2.130 \text{ months}$$

(c) $s^2 = (2.130)^2 = 4.5369.$

4–5 (a) $k = \dfrac{14.15 - 14.00}{.10} = 1.5$

$$1 - \frac{1}{(1.5)^2} = 1 - .44 = .56$$

(b) 13.8 and 14.2

4–6 *CV* for mechanical is 5 percent, found by $(10/200)$ (100). For finger dexterity, *CV* is 20 percent, found by $(6/30)(100)$. Thus, relative dispersion in finger dexterity scores is greater than relative dispersion in mechanical, because 20 percent $>$ 5 percent.

4–7 2.49, found by:

$$Sk = \frac{3(87 - 73)}{16.9} = 2.49$$

There is considerable positive skewness in the distribution of the typing speeds. A few extremely fast typists are causing the mean to be greater than the median or mode.

4–8 (a) 7.90

(b) $Q_1 = 7.76$, $Q_2 = 8.015$

4–9 The smallest value is 10 and the largest 85; the first quartile is 25 and the third 60. About 50 percent of the values are between 25 and 60. The median value is 40. The distribution is somewhat positively skewed.

A REVIEW OF CHAPTERS 1–4

This section is a review of the major concepts and terms introduced in Chapters 1 through 4. These chapters were concerned with describing a set of data by organizing it into a *frequency distribution* and then portraying the distribution in the form of a *histogram,* a *frequency polygon,* and a *cumulative frequency polygon.* The purpose of these graphs is to visually reveal the important characteristics of the data.

Computing a central value to represent the data is a numerical way of summarizing a mass of observations. Chapter 3 looked at several measures of central tendency, including the *mean, weighted mean, geometric mean, median,* and *mode.* Chapter 4 described the *dispersion,* or *spread,* in the data by computing the *range, standard deviation,* and other measures. Further, *skewness,* or lack of symmetry in the data, was described by determining the *coefficient of skewness.*

We stressed the importance of computer software packages, including Excel and Minitab. Several computer outputs in these chapters demonstrated how quickly and accurately a mass of raw data can be organized into a frequency distribution and a histogram. Also, we noted that the computer outputs present a large number of descriptive measures, including the mean, the variance, and the standard deviation.

▌ Glossary

Chapter 1

Descriptive statistics   The techniques used to describe the important characteristics of a set of data. These may include organizing the values into a frequency distribution and computing measures of central tendency and measures of spread and skewness.

Exhaustive   Each observation must fall into one of the categories.

Inferential statistics, also called **statistical inference** or **inductive statistics**   This facet of statistics deals with estimating a population parameter based on a sample statistic. For example, if 2 out of the 10 hand calculators sampled are defective, we might infer that 20 percent of the production is defective.

Interval measurement   If one observation is greater than another by a certain amount, and the zero point is arbitrary, the measurement is on an interval scale. For example, the difference between temperatures of 70 degrees and 80 degrees is 10 degrees. Likewise, a temperature of 90 degrees is 10 degrees more than a temperature of 80 degrees, and so on.

Mutually exclusive   An observation cannot fall into more than one category.

Nominal measurement   The "lowest" level of measurement. If data are classified into categories and the order of those categories is not important, it is the nominal level of measurement. Examples are gender (male, female) and political affiliation (Republican, Democrat, Independent, all others). If it makes no difference whether male or female is listed first, the data are nominal level.

Ordinal measurement   Data that can be logically ranked are referred to as ordinal measures. For example, consumer response to the sound of a new speaker might be excellent, very good, fair, or poor.

Population   The collection, or set, of all individuals, objects, or measurements whose properties are being studied.

Ratio measurement   If the distances between numbers are of a known constant size and *there is a true zero point,* and the ratio of two values is meaningful, the measurement is ratio scale. For example, the distance between $200 and $300 is $100, and in the case of money there is a true zero point. If you have zero dollars, there is an absence of money (you have none). Also the ratio between $200 and $300 is meaningful.

Sample   A portion, or subset, of the population being studied.

Statistics   The science of collecting, organizing, analyzing, and interpreting numerical data for the purpose of making more effective decisions.

Chapter 2

Charts   Special graphical formats used to portray a frequency distribution, including histograms, frequency polygons, and cumulative frequency polygons. Other graphical devices used to portray data are line charts, bar charts, and pie charts. They are very useful, for example, for depicting the trend in long-term debt or percent changes in profit from last year to this year.

Class   The interval in which the data are tallied. For example, $4 up to $7 is a class; $7 up to $11 is another class.

Class frequency   The number of observations in each class. If there are 16 observations in the "$4 up to $6" class, 16 is the class frequency.

Frequency distribution   A grouping of data into categories showing the number of observations in each of the non-overlapping classes. For example, data are organized into classes, such as $1,000 up to $2,000, $2,000 up to $3,000 and so on to summarize the information.

Midpoint   The value that divides the class into two equal parts. For the classes $10 up to $20 and $20 up to $30, the midpoints are $15 and $25, respectively.

Chapter 3

Arithmetic mean   The sum of the values divided by the number of values. The symbol for the mean of a sample is $\bar{X}$, and the symbol for a population mean is μ.

Geometric mean   The nth root of the product of all the values. It is especially useful for averaging rates of change and index numbers. It minimizes the importance of extreme values. A second use of the geometric mean is determining the mean annual percent change over a period of time. For example, if gross sales were $245 million in 1985 and $692 million in 1998, what is the average annual percent increase?

Measure of central tendency   A number that describes the central tendency of the data. There are several such measures, including the arithmetic mean, weighted mean, median, mode, and geometric mean.

Median   The value of the middle observation after all the observations have been arranged from low to high. For example, if observations 6, 9, 4 are rearranged to read 4, 6, 9, the middle value is 6, the median.

Mode   The value that appears most frequently in a set of data. For grouped data, it is the *midpoint* of the class containing the largest number of values.

Weighted mean   Each value is weighted according to its relative importance. For example, if 5 shirts cost $10 each and 20 shirts cost $8 each, the weighted mean price is $8.40: [(5 × $10) + (20 × $8)]/25 = $210/25 = $8.40.

Chapter 4

Coefficient of skewness   A measure that describes the lack of symmetry in a distribution. For a symmetrical distribution there is no skewness, so the coefficient of skewness is zero. Otherwise, it is either positive or negative, with the limits at ±3.0.

Coefficient of variation   The standard deviation divided by the mean, expressed as a percent. It is especially useful for comparing the relative dispersion in two or more sets of data where (1) they are in different units or (2) one mean is much larger than the other mean.

Dispersion or spread   A measure of central tendency pinpoints a single value that is typical of the data. A measure of dispersion indicates how close or far apart the values are from the mean or other measure of central tendency. Such a measure of dispersion indicates how reliable the average is.

Interquartile range   The distance between the third quartile and the first quartile.

Mean deviation   The mean of the deviations from the mean, disregarding signs. It is abbreviated as *MD*.

Range   Difference between the highest and lowest values.

Standard deviation   Square root of the variance.

Variance   Mean of the squared deviations from the mean.

▌ Exercises

The answers to the odd-numbered exercises are at the end of the book.

1. A small number of employees were selected from all the employees at NED Electronics and their hourly rates recorded. The rates were: $9.50, $9.00, $11.70, $14.80, and $13.00.
   a. Are the hourly rates a sample or a population?
   b. What is the level of measurement?
   c. What is the arithmetic mean hourly rate?
   d. What is the median hourly rate? Interpret.
   e. What is the variance?
   f. What is the coefficient of skewness? Interpret.

2. The weekly overtime hours worked by all the employees at the Public Market are: 1, 4, 6, 12, 5, and 2.
   a. Is this a sample or a population?
   b. What is the mean number of overtime hours worked?
   c. What is the median? Interpret.
   d. What is the mode?
   e. What is the mean deviation?
   f. What is the standard deviation?
   g. What is the coefficient of variation?

3. The tourist bureaus of St. Thomas and other Caribbean islands surveyed a sample of tourists as they left to return to the United States. One of the questions was: How many rolls of film did you expose when visiting our island? The sample responses were:

8	6	3	11	14	8	9	16	9	10
5	11	7	8	8	10	9	12	13	9

a. Using five classes, organize the sample data into a frequency distribution.
b. Portray the distribution in the form of a frequency polygon.
c. What is the mean number of rolls exposed? Use the actual raw data.
d. What is the median? Use the actual raw data.
e. What is the mode? Use the actual raw data.
f. What is the range? Use the actual raw data.
g. What is the sample variance? Use the actual raw data.
h. What is the sample standard deviation? Use the actual raw data.
i. Assuming that the distribution is symmetrical and bell-shaped, about 95 percent of the tourists exposed between _____ and _____ rolls.

4. The annual amounts spent on research and development for a sample of electronic component manufacturers are (in $ millions):

8	34	15	24	15	28	12	20	22	23
14	26	18	23	10	21	16	17	22	31
13	25	20	28	6	20	19	27	16	22

a. What is the level of measurement?
b. Using six classes, organize the expenditures into a frequency distribution.
c. Portray the distribution in the form of a histogram.
d. Portray the distribution in the form of a less-than cumulative frequency polygon.
e. Based on the less-than cumulative frequency polygon, what is the *estimated* median amount spent on research and development? Interpret.
f. What is the mean amount spent on research and development?
g. Based on the less-than cumulative frequency polygon, what is the interquartile range?

5. The rates of growth of Bardeen Chemicals for the past five years are 5.2 percent, 8.7 percent, 3.9 percent, 6.8 percent, and 19.5 percent.
a. What is the arithmetic mean annual growth rate?
b. What is the geometric mean annual growth rate?
c. Should the arithmetic mean or geometric mean be used to represent the average annual growth rate? Why?

6. The Currin Manufacturing Co. noted in its 1997 second-quarter report that as of June 30, 1997, notes payable amounted to $284.0 million. For the same date in 1987, they were $113.0 million. What is the geometric mean yearly percent increase (June to June) from June 1987 to June 1997?

7. BFI in its annual report revealed that working capital was (in billions) $4.4, $3.4, $3.0, $4.8, $7.8, and $8.3 consecutively for the years 1993–1998. Present these figures in either a simple line chart or a simple bar chart.

8. Refer to the following diagram.

a. What is the graph called?
b. What are the median, and first and third quartile values?
c. Is the distribution positively skewed. Tell how you know.
d. Are there any outliers? If yes, estimate these values.
e. Can you determine the number of observations in the study?

For exercises 9–18, fill in the blanks.

9. Employees in a company training course were asked to rate it as either outstanding, very good, good, fair, or poor. The level of measurement is _____.

10. A sample of senior citizens revealed that their mean annual retirement income is $16,900. Since the mean is based on a sample, the $16,900 is called a _____.

11. Refer to the following picture. It is called a _____. The third quartile is about _____, the first quartile _____, the interquartile range _____, and the range _____.

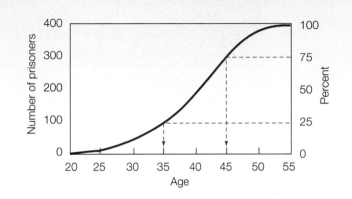

12. Refer to the following picture, which is based on a frequency distribution. It is called a _____. Describe the skewness in the distribution. Explain.

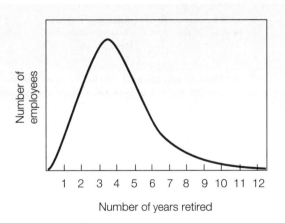

13. For a set of observations we have the following information: mean = $64, median = $61, mode = $60, standard deviation = $6, and range = $40. The coefficient of variation is

_____.

14. Refer to Exercise 13. The coefficient of skewness is _____.

15. A useful measure to compare the relative dispersion in two or more distributions, if they are in different units, is the _____.

16. For a set of observations we have the following information: mean = 100, median = 100, mode = 100, and $s = 4$. The range is about _____.

17. Refer to Exercise 16. About 95 percent of the values lie between _____ and _____.

18. Fine Furniture, Inc. produced 2,460 desks in 1988 and 6,520 in 1998. To find the average annual percent increase in production, the _____ should be used.

19. A sample of the amounts of funds customers first deposited in First Federal's MCA (miniature checking account) revealed the following.

$124	$ 14	$150	$289	$ 52	$156	$203	$ 82	$ 27	$248
39	52	103	58	136	249	110	298	251	157
186	107	142	185	75	202	119	219	156	78
116	152	206	117	52	299	58	153	219	148
145	187	165	147	158	146	185	186	149	140

Using the preceding raw data and a statistical package (such as MINITAB):
a. Organize the data into a frequency distribution.
b. Calculate the mean, median, and other descriptive measures. Include charts, if available. You decide on the class interval.
c. Interpret the computer output; that is, describe the central tendency, spread, skewness, and other measures.

20. If a computer is not available, organize the miniature checking accounts into a frequency distribution. You decide on the class interval. Portray the distribution in chart form, and compute measures of central tendency, spread, and skewness. Then interpret the important characteristics of the miniature checking accounts.

21. Between 1789 and 1996, 85 judges served as associate justices of the Supreme Court of the United States. Their lengths of service are given below. Analyze the data.
a. What is the typical length of service?
b. What is the variation in the lengths of service?
c. Is the distribution skewed?
d. Develop a stem-and-leaf chart.

8	1	20	5	9	0	13	15	30	3
30	16	18	23	33	20	2	31	14	32
4	28	14	18	27	5	23	5	8	23
18	28	14	34	10	21	9	33	6	7
20	11	5	20	15	10	2	16	13	26
29	19	3	4	5	26	4	10	26	22
5	15	16	7	16	15	6	34	19	23
36	9	1	13	6	13	17	7	16	5
23	2	3	15	14					

22. The per capita personal income by state (including the District of Columbia), in thousands of dollars, follows.
a. Organize these data into a frequency distribution.
b. What is a "typical" per capita income for a state?
c. How much variation in the income data is there?
d. Is the distribution symmetrical?
e. Summarize your findings.

11.1	17.7	13.2	10.7	16.8	15.1	19.2	15.1
18.9	14.3	13.2	14.7	11.4	15.4	12.9	13.2
14.4	11.1	11.2	12.7	16.6	17.5	14.1	14.7
9.5	13.6	11.9	13.8	15.1	15.9	18.3	11.1
17.1	12.2	12.3	13.7	12.4	12.2	13.9	14.7
11.1	11.9	11.8	13.5	10.7	12.8	15.4	14.5
10.5	13.8	13.2					

23. Following are the ages at which the 43 U.S. presidents began their terms in office. Organize the data into a stem-and-leaf chart. Determine a typical age at the time of inauguration. Comment on the variation in age.

57	61	57	57	58	57	61	54	68	51	65
49	64	50	48	65	52	56	46	54	49	46
50	47	55	55	54	42	51	56	55	51	47
54	51	60	62	43	55	56	61	52	69	

▎ Cases

A. Century National Bank

The following case will appear in the review sections. Assume that you work in the Planning Department of the Century National Bank and report to Ms. Lamberg. You will need to do some data analysis and prepare a short written report. Remember, Mr. Selig is the president of the bank, so you will want to ensure that your report is complete and accurate. A copy of the data appears in Appendix N.

The Century National Bank has offices in several cities in the Midwest and the southeastern part of the United States. Mr. Dan Selig, president and CEO, would like to know the characteristics of his checking account customers. What is the balance of a typical customer? How many other bank services do the checking account customers use? Do the customers use the ATM service and, if so, how often? What about debit cards? Who uses them, and how often are they used?

To better understand the customers, Mr. Selig asked Ms. Wendy Lamberg, Director of Planning, to select a sample of customers and prepare a report. To begin, she has appointed a team from her staff. You are the head of the team and responsible for preparing the report. You select a random sample of 60 customers. In addition to the balance in each account at the end of last month, you determine: (1) the number of ATM (automatic teller machine) transactions in the last month; (2) the number of other bank services (a savings account, a certificate of deposit, etc.) the customer uses; (3) whether the customer has a debit card (this is a relatively new bank service in which charges are made directly to the customer's account); and (4) whether or not interest is paid on the checking account. The sample includes customers from the branches in Cincinnati, Ohio; Atlanta, Georgia; Louisville, Kentucky; and Erie, Pennsylvania.

1. Develop a graph or table that portrays the checking balances. What is the balance of a typical customer? Do many customers have more than $2,000 in their accounts? Does it appear that there is a difference in the distribution of the accounts among the four branches? Around what value do the account balances tend to cluster?

2. Determine the mean and median of the checking account balances. Compare the mean and the median balances for the four branches. Is there a difference among the branches? Be sure to explain the difference between the mean and the median in your report.

3. Determine the range and the standard deviation of the checking account balances. What do the first and third quartiles show? Determine the coefficient of skewness and indicate what it shows. Because Mr. Selig does not deal with statistics daily, include a brief description and interpretation of the standard deviation and other measures.

B. Wildcat Plumbing Supply, Inc.: Do We Have Gender Differences?

Wildcat Plumbing Supply has served the plumbing needs of Southwest Arizona for more than 40 years. The company was founded by Mr. Terrence St. Julian and is run today by his son Cory. The company has grown from a handful of employees to more than 500 today. Cory is concerned about several positions within the company where he has men and women doing essentially the same job but at different pay. To investigate, he collected the information below. Suppose you are a student intern in the Accounting Department and have been given the task to write a report summarizing the situation.

Yearly Salary ($000)	Women	Men
Less than 30	2	0
30 up to 40	3	1
40 up to 50	17	4
50 up to 60	17	24
60 up to 70	8	21
70 up to 80	3	7
80 or more	0	3

To kick off the project, Mr. Cory St. Julian held a meeting with his staff and you were invited. At this meeting it was suggested that you calculate several measures of location, draw charts, such as a more-than cumulative frequency distribution, and determine the quartiles for both men and women. Develop the charts and write the report summarizing the yearly salaries of employees at Wildcat Plumbing Supply. Does it appear that there are gender differences?

C.   Kimble Products:
Is There a Difference in the Commissions?

At the January national sales meeting, the CEO of Kimble Products was questioned extensively regarding the company policy for paying commissions to its sales representatives. The company sells sporting goods to two major markets. There are 40 sales representatives who call directly on large volume customers, such as the athletic departments at major colleges and universities and professional sports franchises. There are 30 sales representatives who represent the company to retail stores located in shopping malls and large discounters such as Kmart and Target.

Upon his return to corporate headquarters, the CEO asked the sales manager for a report comparing the commissions earned last year by the two parts of the sales team. The information is reported below. Write a brief report. Would you conclude that there is a difference? Be sure to include information in the report on both the central tendency and dispersion of the two groups.

Commissions Earned by Sales Representatives Calling on Athletic Departments ($)

354	87	1,676	1,187	69	3,202	680	39	1,683	1,106
883	3,140	299	2,197	175	159	1,105	434	615	149
1,168	278	579	7	357	252	1,602	2,321	4	392
416	427	1,738	526	13	1,604	249	557	635	527

Commissions Earned by Sales Representatives Calling on Large Retailers ($)

1,116	681	1,294	12	754	1,206	1,448	870	944	1,255
1,213	1,291	719	934	1,313	1,083	899	850	886	1,556
886	1,315	1,858	1,262	1,338	1,066	807	1,244	758	918

Chapter Five

A Survey of Probability Concepts

GOALS

When you have completed this chapter, you will be able to:

ONE

Define *probability*.

TWO

Describe the classical, the empirical, and the subjective approaches to probability.

THREE

Understand the terms: *experiment, event, outcome, permutations,* and *combinations.*

FOUR

Define the terms: *conditional probability* and *joint probability.*

FIVE

Calculate probabilities applying the rules of addition and the rules of multiplication.

SIX

Use a tree diagram to organize and compute probabilities.

SEVEN

Calculate a probability using Bayes' theorem.

Thirty-five percent of executives read Time *magazine, 20 percent read* Newsweek, *40 percent read* U.S. News & World Report *and 10 percent read both* Time *and* U.S. News & World Report. *What is the probability that a particular executive reads either* Time *or* U.S. News? *(See Goal 5 and Exercise 27.)*

▌ Introduction

The emphasis in Chapters 2 through 4 was on descriptive statistics. In Chapter 2 the prices of 80 vehicles sold last month at Whitner Pontiac were organized into a frequency distribution to show the lowest and the highest selling prices and where the largest concentration of data occurred. In Chapters 3 and 4 we used a number of measures of central tendency and dispersion to locate a typical selling price (about $20,000) and to examine the spread in the data. We described the spread in the selling prices with such measures of dispersion as the range and the standard deviation. Descriptive statistics is concerned with summarizing that which has already happened. For example, we described the vehicle selling prices last month at Whitner Pontiac.

We now turn to the second facet of statistics, namely, *computing the chance that something will occur in the future*. This facet of statistics is called **statistical inference** or **inferential statistics**.

Seldom does a decision maker have complete information from which to make a decision. For example:

- Toys and Things, a toy and puzzle manufacturer, has developed a new game based on sports trivia and wants to know whether sports buffs will purchase the game. "Slam Dunk" and "Home Run" are two of the names under consideration. One way to minimize the risk of making a wrong decision is to hire pollsters to take a sample of, say, 2,000 from the population and ask each respondent for a reaction to the new game and its proposed titles.
- The quality assurance department of a Bethlehem Steel mill must assure management that the quarter-inch wire being produced has an acceptable tensile strength. Obviously, not all the wire produced can be tested for tensile strength because test-

ing requires the wire to be stretched until it breaks — thus destroying it. So a random sample of 10 pieces is selected and tested. Based on the test results, all the wire produced is deemed to be either satisfactory or unsatisfactory.
- Other questions involving uncertainty are: Should the daytime drama "Mama Knows Best" be discontinued immediately? Should the New York Giants select Sammy Uwea or Clint Murray in the first round of the college draft? Will a

newly developed mint-flavored cereal be profitable if marketed? Should I marry Jean? Should I buy a new Rolls Royce? Should I vote for Charles Linden for town commissioner?

Statistical inference deals with conclusions about a population based on a sample taken from that population. (The populations for the preceding illustrations are: all consumers who like sports trivia games, all the quarter-inch steel wire produced, all television viewers who watch soaps, all the college football players to be drafted by the professional teams, and so on.)

Since there is considerable uncertainty in decision making, it is important that all the known risks involved be scientifically evaluated. Helpful in this evaluation is *probability theory,* which has often been referred to as the science of uncertainty. The use of probability theory allows the decision maker with only limited information to analyze the risks and minimize the gamble inherent, for example, in marketing a new product or accepting an incoming shipment possibly containing defective parts.

Because probability concepts are so important in the field of statistical inference (to be discussed starting with Chapter 8), this chapter introduces the basic language of probability, including such terms as *experiment, event, subjective probability,* and *addition* and *multiplication rules.*

❚ What Is a Probability?

No doubt you are familiar with terms such as *probability, chance,* and *likelihood.* They are often used interchangeably. The weather forecaster announces that there is a 70 percent chance of rain for Super Bowl Sunday. Based on a survey of consumers who tested a newly developed pickle with a banana taste, the probability is .03 that, if marketed, it will be a financial success. (This means that the chance of the banana-tasting pickle being accepted by the public is rather remote.) What is a probability? In general, it is the chance that something will happen.

> **Probability**   A value between zero and one, inclusive, describing the relative possibility (chance or likelihood) an event will occur.

Three key words are used in the study of probability: **experiment, outcome,** and **event.** These terms are used in our everyday language, but in statistics they have specific meanings.

> **Experiment**   A process that leads to the occurrence of one (and only one) of several possible observations.

This definition is more general than the one used in the physical sciences, where we picture someone manipulating test tubes or microscopes. In reference to probability, an experiment has two or more possible results, and it is uncertain which will occur.

> **Outcome**   A particular result of an experiment.

For example, the tossing of a coin is an experiment. You may observe the toss of the coin, but you are unsure whether it will come up "heads" or "tails." Similarly, asking 500 college students whether they would purchase a new IBM Aptiva computer at a particular price is an experiment. If the coin is tossed, one particular outcome is a "head." The alternative outcome is a "tail." In the computer purchasing experiment, one possible outcome is that 273 students indicate they would purchase the computer. Another outcome is that 317 students would purchase the computer. Still another outcome is that 423 students indicate that they would purchase it. When one or more of the experiment's outcomes are observed, we call this an event.

> **Event**   A collection of one or more outcomes of an experiment.

On the next page are some examples to clarify the definitions of the terms *experiment, outcome,* and *event.*

In the die-rolling experiment there are six possible outcomes, but there are many possible events. When counting the number of members of the board of directors for Fortune 500 companies over 60 years of age, the number of possible outcomes can be anywhere from zero to the total number of members. There are an even larger number of possible events in this experiment.

A probability is expressed as a decimal, such as .70, .27, or .50. However, it may be given as a fraction such as $7/10$, $27/100$, or $\frac{1}{2}$. It can assume any number from 0 to 1, inclusive. If a company has only five sales regions, and each region's name or number

Experiment	Roll a die	Count the number of members of the board of directors for Fortune 500 companies who are over 60 years of age
All possible outcomes	Observe a 1 Observe a 2 Observe a 3 Observe a 4 Observe a 5 Observe a 6	None are over 60 One is over 60 Two are over 60 ... 29 are over 60 ... ... 48 are over 60
Some possible events	Observe an even number Observe a number greater than 4 Observe a number 3 or less	More than 13 are over 60 Fewer than 20 are over 60

is written on a slip of paper and the slips put in a hat, the probability of selecting one of the five regions is 1. The probability of selecting from the hat a slip of paper that reads "Pittsburgh Steelers" is 0. Thus, the probability of 1 represents something that is certain to happen, and the probability of 0 represents something that cannot happen.

The closer a probability is to 0, the more improbable it is that something will happen. The closer the probability is to 1, the more sure we are it will happen. The relationship is shown in the following diagram along with a few of our personal beliefs. You might, however, select a different probability to Slo Poke's chances to win the Kentucky Derby or to an increase in federal taxes.

Cannot happen										Sure to happen
0.00	0.10	0.20	0.30	0.40	0.50	0.60	0.70	0.80	0.90	1.00
↑		↑			↑		↑			↑
Probability our sun will disappear this year		Chance Slo Poke will win the Kentucky Derby			Chance of a head in single toss of a coin		Chance of an increase in federal taxes			Chance of rain in Florida this year

What role does probability have in decision making? This question can be answered by citing two cases that will be discussed in forthcoming chapters.

Case 1

Based on past experience, a publishing company has determined that at least 20 percent of a certain group, such as musicians, must subscribe to a monthly magazine to make it a financial success. The company is considering a monthly magazine for bird-watchers. A special copy was designed and mailed to a sample of 1,000 bird-watchers. In response, 190 out of 1,000, or 19 percent, said they would subscribe to the magazine if it were published. Should we state that this proportion is less than 20 percent and make an immediate decision not to publish the magazine? Or could the difference between the required percent (20) and the sample percent (19) be attributed to sampling, that is, chance? Probability will help us arrive at a decision for this type of problem, which will be discussed in Chapter 9.

Case 2

A very large construction project requires thousands of concrete blocks. Specifications state that the blocks must stand up to pressures of 1,050 pounds per square inch (psi) on the average. Two firms manufacturing these blocks submitted samples for testing. The arithmetic mean strength of the Strong Block Company blocks was 1,070 psi; those from the Taylor Company tested at 1,062 psi. Strong Block thinks it should be awarded the contract because its blocks have a higher mean strength. Taylor disagrees, saying that the difference of only 8 psi could be due to sampling (chance). If Strong Block's claim is correct, it will be awarded the contract. If Taylor's statement is correct, the contract will be divided between the two companies. Probability will help us reach a decision for a problem such as this in Chapter 9.

❙ Approaches to Probability

Two approaches to probability will be discussed, namely, the *objective* and the *subjective* viewpoints. **Objective probability** can be subdivided into (1) *classical* probability and (2) the *empirical* probability.

Classical Probability

Classical probability is based on the assumption that the outcomes of an experiment are *equally likely*. Using the classical viewpoint, the probability of an event happening is computed by dividing the number of favorable outcomes by the total number of possible outcomes:

DEFINITION OF CLASSICAL PROBABILITY	Probability of an event $= \dfrac{\text{Number of favorable outcomes}}{\text{Total number of possible outcomes}}$	**[5–1]**

Example

Consider the experiment of rolling a six-sided die. What is the probability of the event "an even number of spots appear face up?"

Solution

The possible outcomes are:

There are three "favorable" outcomes (a two, a four, and a six) in the collection of six equally likely possible outcomes. Therefore:

$$\text{Probability of an even number} = \frac{3}{6} \leftarrow \boxed{\begin{array}{l} \text{Number of favorable outcomes} \\ \hline \text{Total number of possible outcomes} \end{array}}$$

$$= .5$$

If *only one* of several events can occur at one time, we refer to the events as **mutually exclusive.**

> **Mutually Exclusive**   The occurrence of any one event means that none of the others can occur at the same time.

In the die-tossing experiment, the event "an even number" and the event "an odd number" are mutually exclusive. If an even number occurred, it could not also be an odd number.

If an experiment has a set of events that includes every possible outcome, such as the events "an even number" and "an odd number" in the die-tossing experiment, then the set of events is called **collectively exhaustive.**

> **Collectively Exhaustive**   At least one of the events must occur when an experiment is conducted.

For the die-tossing experiment, every outcome will be either even or odd. So the set is collectively exhaustive.

Sum of probabilities = 1   If the set of events is collectively exhaustive and the events are mutually exclusive, the sum of the probabilities equals 1. For a coin-tossing experiment:

	Probability
Event: Head	.5
Event: Tail	.5
Total	1.0

For the classical approach to be applied, the events must have the same chance of occurring (called *equally likely* events). Also, the set of events must be mutually exclusive and collectively exhaustive.

Historically, the classical approach to probability was developed and applied in the 17th and 18th centuries to games of chance, such as cards and dice. Note that it is unnecessary to do an experiment to determine the probability of an event occurring using the classical approach; we can logically arrive, for example, at the probability of getting a tail on the toss of one coin or three heads on the toss of three coins. Nor do we have to conduct an experiment to determine the probability that your income tax return will be audited if there are 2 million returns mailed to your district office and 2,400 are to be audited. Assuming that each return has an equal chance of being audited, your probability is .0012—found by 2,400 divided by 2 million. Obviously, the chance of your return being audited is rather remote.

Empirical Concept

Another way to define probability is based on **relative frequencies.** The probability of an event happening in the long run is determined by observing what fraction of the time similar events happened in the past. In terms of a formula:

$$\frac{\text{Probability of}}{\text{event happening}} = \frac{\text{Number of times event occurred in past}}{\text{Total number of observations}}$$

Example

A study of 751 business administration graduates at the University of Toledo was conducted. It revealed that 383 of the 751 were *not* employed in their major area of study in college. For illustration, a person who majored in accounting is now the marketing manager of a tomato-processing firm. What is the probability that a particular business graduate will be employed in an area other than his or her college major?

Solution

$$\frac{\text{Probability of}}{\text{event happening}} = \frac{\text{Number of times event occurred in past}}{\text{Total number of observations}}$$

$$P(A) = \frac{383}{751}$$

$$= .51$$

To simplify, letters or numbers may be used. *P* stands for probability, and in this case *P(A)* stands for the probability a graduate is not employed in his or her major area of college study.

Since 383 out of 751, or .51 in terms of a probability, are in a different field of employment from their major in college, we can use this as an estimate of the probability. In other words, based on past experience, the probability is .51 that a business graduate will be employed in a field other than his or her college major.

Subjective Probability

If there is little or no past experience on which to base a probability, it may be arrived at subjectively. Essentially, this means evaluating the available opinions and other information and then estimating or assigning the probability. This probability is aptly called a **subjective probability.**

Subjective Concept of Probability   The likelihood (probability) of a particular event happening that is assigned by an individual based on whatever information is available.

Illustrations of subjective probability are:

1. Estimating the likelihood that the New England Patriots will play in the Super Bowl next year.
2. Estimating the probability that General Motors Corp. will lose its number 1 ranking in total units sold to Ford Motor Co. or Chrysler Corp. within two years.
3. Estimating the likelihood that you will earn an *A* in this course.

In summary, there are two viewpoints regarding probability—the objective and the subjective viewpoints. We noted that a probability statement always constitutes an estimate of an unknown value that will govern an event that has not yet occurred. There is, of course, a considerable latitude in the degree of uncertainty that surrounds this estimate, based primarily on the knowledge possessed by the individual concerning the underlying process. The individual possesses a great deal of knowledge about the toss of a die and can state that the probability that a one-spot will appear face up on the toss of a true die is one sixth. But we know very little concerning the acceptance in the marketplace of a new and untested product. For example, even though a market research director tests a newly developed product in 40 retail stores and states that there is a 70 percent chance that the product will have sales of more than 1 million units, she still has little knowledge of how consumers will react when it is marketed nationally. In both cases (the case of the person rolling a die and the testing of a new product) the individual is assigning a probability value to an event of interest, and a difference exists only in the predictor's confidence in the precision of the estimate. However, regardless of the viewpoint, the same laws of probability (presented in the following sections) will be applied.

SELF-REVIEW 5–2

1. One card will be randomly selected from a standard 52-card deck. What is the probability the card will be a queen? Which approach to probability did you use to answer this question?
2. The National Center for Health Statistics reports that of 883 deaths, 24 resulted from an automobile accident, 182 from cancer, and 333 from heart disease. What is the probability that a particular death is due to an automobile accident? Which approach to probability did you use to answer this question?
3. What is the probability that the Dow Jones Industrial Average will exceed the value 10,000 before the millennium? Which approach to probability did you use to answer this question?

❙ Exercises

1. Some people are in favor of reducing Social Security benefits in order to achieve a balanced budget and others are against it. Two persons are selected and their opinions are recorded. List the possible outcomes.
2. A quality control inspector selects a part to be tested. The part is then declared acceptable, repairable, or scrapped. Then another part is tested. List all of the possible outcomes of this experiment.

3. A survey of a class of 34 students in a business school showed the following selection of majors:

Accounting	10
Finance	5
Info. Systems	3
Management	6
Marketing	10

    Suppose you select a student and observe his or her major.
    a. What is the probability he or she is a management major?
    b. Which concept of probability did you use to make this estimate?

4. A university planning to hire a new president prepares a final list of five candidates, all of whom are equally qualified. Two of these candidates are members of a minority group. The university decides to select the president by lottery.
    a. What is the probability one of the minority is hired?
    b. Which concept of probability did you use to make this estimate?

5. The Streets Department in Whitehouse, Illinois, is considering widening Indiana Avenue to three lanes. Before a final decision is made, 500 citizens are asked if they support the widening.
    a. What is the experiment?
    b. What are some of the possible events?
    c. List two possible outcomes.

6. The chairman of the board of Rudd Industries is delivering a speech to the company stockholders tomorrow explaining his position that the company should merge with Zimmerman Plastics. He has received six pieces of mail on the issue and is interested in the number of writers who agree with him.
    a. What is the experiment?
    b. What are some of the possible events?
    c. List two possible outcomes.

7. In each of the following cases, indicate whether classical, empirical, or subjective probability is used.
    a. A basketball player makes 30 out of 50 foul shots. The probability is .6 that she makes the next foul shot attempted.
    b. A seven-member committee of students is formed to study environmental issues. What is the likelihood that any one of the seven is chosen as the spokesperson?
    c. You purchase one of 5 million tickets sold for Lotto Canada. What is the likelihood you win the $1 million jackpot?
    d. The probability of an earthquake in northern California in the next 10 years is .80.

8. A firm will promote two employees out of a group of six men and three women.
    a. List the outcomes of this experiment if there is particular concern about gender equity.
    b. Which concept of probability would you use to estimate these probabilities?

9. There are 52 cards in a standard deck.
    a. What is the probability that the first card selected is a spade?
    b. What is the probability that the first card selected is the jack of spades?
    c. What concept of probability do a. and b. illustrate?

10. A single die is rolled.
    a. What is the probability that a two-spot will show face up?
    b. What concept of probability does this illustrate?
    c. Are the outcomes for the numbers 1 through 6 equally likely and mutually exclusive? Explain.

11. Before a nationwide survey was conducted, 40 people were selected to test the questionnaire. One question about whether or not abortions should be legal required a yes or no answer.
    a. What is the experiment?
    b. List one possible event.

c. Ten of the 40 favored the legalization of abortions. Based on these sample responses, what is the probability that a particular person will be in favor of the legalization of abortions?

d. What concept of probability does this illustrate?

e. Are each of the possible outcomes equally likely and mutually exclusive?

12. A large number of automobile drivers were selected at random, and the number of traffic violations they had, if any, were recorded.

Number of Violations	Number of Drivers
0	1,910
1	46
2	18
3	12
4	9
5 or more	5

a. What is the experiment?

b. List one possible event.

c. What is the probability that a particular driver had exactly two violations?

d. What concept of probability does this illustrate?

13. Bank customers select their own three-digit personal identification number (PIN) for use on most secure ATMs.

a. Think of this as an experiment and list four possible outcomes.

b. What is the probability Mr. Jones and Mrs. Smith select the same PIN?

c. Which concept of probability did you use to answer the question above?

14. An investor buys 100 shares of AT&T stock and records its price change daily.

a. List several possible events for this experiment.

b. Estimate the probability for each event you described in a.

c. Which concept of probability did you use in b.?

▌ Some Rules of Probability

Now that we have defined probability and described the different approaches to probability, we turn our attention to combining events by applying rules of addition and multiplication.

Rules of Addition

Two mutually exclusive events cannot both happen at one time

Special Rule of Addition   To apply the **special rule of addition,** the events must be mutually exclusive. Recall that *mutually exclusive* means that when one event occurs, none of the other events can occur at the same time. An illustration of mutually exclusive events in the die-tossing experiment is the events "a number 4 or larger," and "a number 2 or smaller." If the outcome is in the first group {4, 5, and 6}, then it cannot also be in the second group {1 and 2}. And a product coming off the assembly line cannot be defective and satisfactory at the same time.

If two events A and B are mutually exclusive, the special rule of addition states that the probability of one *or* the other event's occurring equals the sum of their probabilities. This rule is expressed in the following formula:

SPECIAL RULE OF ADDITION	$P(A \text{ or } B) = P(A) + P(B)$	**[5–2]**

For three mutually exclusive events designated A, B, and C, the rule is written:

$$P(A \text{ or } B \text{ or } C) = P(A) + P(B) + P(C)$$

Example

An automatic Shaw machine fills plastic bags with a mixture of beans, broccoli, and other vegetables. Most of the bags contain the correct weight, but because of the slight variation in the size of the beans and other vegetables, a package might be slightly underweight or overweight. A check of 4,000 packages filled in the past month revealed:

Weight	Event	Number of Packages	Probability of Occurrence	
Underweight	A	100	.025	← $\frac{100}{4{,}000}$
Satisfactory	B	3,600	.900	
Overweight	C	300	.075	
		4,000	1.000	

What is the probability that a particular package will be either underweight or overweight?

Solution

The outcome "underweight" is the event A. The outcome "overweight" is the event C. Applying the special rule of addition:

$$P(A \text{ or } C) = P(A) + P(C)$$
$$= .025 + .075$$
$$= .10$$

Note that the events are mutually exclusive, meaning that a package of mixed vegetables cannot be underweight, satisfactory, and overweight at the same time. (Also, $P(A \text{ or } B \text{ or } C) = 1.000$.)

A Venn diagram is a useful tool to depict addition or multiplication rules.

English logician J. Venn (1834–1888) developed a diagram to portray graphically the outcome of an experiment. The *mutually exclusive* concept and various other rules for combining probabilities can be illustrated using this device. To construct a Venn diagram, a space is first enclosed representing the total of all possible outcomes. This space is usually in the form of a rectangle. An event is represented by an oval area which is drawn proportional to the probability of the event. The following Venn diagram represents the *mutually exclusive* concept. There is no overlapping of events, meaning that the events are mutually exclusive.

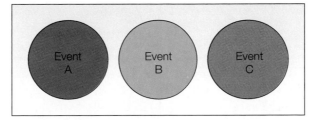

The probability that a bag of mixed vegetables selected is underweight, $P(A)$, plus the probability that it is not an underweight bag, written $P(\sim A)$ and read "not A, must logically equal 1. This is written:

$$P(A) + P(\sim A) = 1$$

This can be revised to read:

| **COMPLEMENT RULE** | $P(A) = 1 - P(\sim A)$ | **[5–3]** |

This is referred to as the **complement rule.**

The complement rule is used to determine the probability of an event occurring by subtracting the probability of the event *not* occurring from 1. A Venn diagram illustrating the complement rule might appear as:

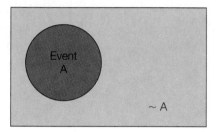

Example

Recall that the probability that a bag of mixed vegetables is underweight is .025 and that the probability of an overweight bag is .075. Use the complement rule to show that the probability of a satisfactory bag is .900. Show the solution using a Venn diagram.

Solution

The probability that the bag is unsatisfactory equals the probability that the bag is overweight plus the probability that it is underweight. That is, $P(A \text{ or } C) = P(A) + P(C) = .025 + .075 = .100$. The bag is satisfactory if it is not underweight or overweight, so $P(B) = 1 - [P(A)] + P(C)] = 1 - [.025 + .075] = 0.900$. The Venn diagram portraying this situation is:

The complement rule is important in the study of probability. Often it is easier to calculate the probability of an event happening by determining the probability of it not happening and subtracting the result from 1.

SELF-REVIEW 5–3

A selected group of employees of Worldwide Enterprises is to be surveyed about a new pension plan. In-depth interviews are to be conducted with each employee selected in the sample. The employees are classified as followed:

Classification	Event	Number of Employees
Supervisors	A	120
Maintenance	B	50
Production	C	1,460
Management	D	302
Secretarial	E	68

(a) What is the probability that the first person selected is:
  (i) either in maintenance or a secretary?
  (ii) not in management?
(b) Draw a Venn diagram illustrating your answers to part (a).
(c) Are the events in part (a)(i) complementary or mutually exclusive or both?

STATISTICS IN ACTION

The General Rule of Addition The outcomes of an experiment may not be mutually exclusive. Suppose, for illustration, that the Florida Tourist Commission selected a sample of 200 tourists who visited the state during the year. The survey revealed that 120 tourists went to Disney World and 100 went to Busch Gardens near Tampa. What is the probability that a person selected visited either Disney World or Busch Gardens? If the special rule of addition is used, the probability of selecting a tourist who went to Disney World is .60, found by 120/200. Similarly, the probability of a tourist going to Busch Gardens is .50. The sum of these probabilities is 1.10. We know, however, that this probability cannot be greater than 1. The explanation is that many tourists visited both attractions and are being counted twice! A check of the survey responses revealed that 60 out of 200 sampled did, in fact, visit both attractions.

To answer our question, "What is the probability that a person selected visited either Disney World or Busch Gardens?" (1) add the probability that a tourist visited Disney World and the probability he/she visited Busch Gardens, and (2) subtract the probability of visiting both. Thus:

$$P(\text{Disney or Busch}) = P(\text{Disney}) + P(\text{Busch}) - P(\text{both Disney and Busch})$$

$$= \frac{120}{200} + \frac{100}{200} - \frac{60}{200}$$

$$= \frac{160}{200} = .80, \text{ or}$$

$$= .60 + .50 - .30 = .80$$

When two events overlap, the probability is called a **joint probability.** The probability that a tourist visits both attractions (.30) is an example of a joint probability.

Joint Probability A probability that measures the likelihood that two or more events will happen concurrently.

In summary, the general rule of addition is used to combine events that are not mutually exclusive. This rule for two events designed *A* and *B* is written:

GENERAL RULE OF ADDITION	$P(A \text{ or } B) = P(A) + P(B) - P(A \text{ and } B)$	**[5–4]**

For the expression $P(A \text{ or } B)$, the word *or* suggests that *A* may occur or *B* may occur. This also includes the possibility that *A* and *B* may occur. This use of *or* is sometimes called an **inclusive.** To put it another way, you are happy when both *A* and *B* occur or when either one occurs.

Example

An example involving joint probability

What is the probability that a card chosen at random from a standard deck of cards will be either a king or a heart?

Solution

We may be inclined to add the probability of a king and the probability of a heart. But this creates a problem. If we do that, the king of hearts is counted with the kings and also with the hearts. So, if we simply add the probability of a king (there are 4 in a deck of 52 cards) to the probability of a heart (there are 13 in a deck of 52 cards) and report that 17 out of 52 cards meet the requirement, we have counted the king of hearts twice. We need to subtract 1 card from the 17 so that the king of hearts is counted only once. Thus, there are 16 cards that are either hearts or kings. So the probability is 16/52 = .3077.

Card	Probability	Explanation
King	$P(A)$ = 4/52	4 kings in a deck of 52 cards
Heart	$P(B)$ = 13/52	13 hearts in a deck of 52 cards
King of hearts	$P(A \text{ and } B)$ = 1/52	1 king of hearts in a deck of 52 cards

Using formula (5–4):

$$P(A \text{ or } B) = P(A) + P(B) - P(A \text{ and } B)$$

$$= 4/52 + 13/52 - 1/52$$

$$= 16/52, \text{ or } .3077$$

A Venn diagram portrays these outcomes, which are not mutually exclusive.

SELF-REVIEW 5–4

Routine physical examinations are conducted annually as part of a health service program for General Cement employees. It was discovered that 8 percent of the employees need corrective shoes, 15 percent need major dental work, and 3 percent need both corrective shoes and major dental work.

(a) What is the probability that an employee selected at random will need either corrective shoes or major dental work?
(b) Show this situation in the form of a Venn diagram.

▌ Exercises

15. The events *A* and *B* are mutually exclusive. Suppose $P(A) = .30$ and $P(B) = .20$. What is the probability of either *A* or *B* occurring? What is the probability that neither *A* nor *B* will happen?

16. The events *X* and *Y* are mutually exclusive. Suppose $P(X) = .05$ and $P(Y) = .02$. What is the probability of either *X* or *Y* occurring? What is the probability that neither *X* nor *Y* will happen?

17. A study of 200 grocery chains revealed these incomes after taxes:

Income after Taxes	Number of Firms
Under $1 million	102
$1 million to $20 million	61
$20 million or more	37

    a. What is the probability that a particular chain has under $1 million in income after taxes?
    b. What is the probability that a grocery chain selected at random has either an income between $1 million and $20 million, or an income of $20 million or more? What rule of probability was applied?

18. A study of the opinions of designers with respect to the primary color most desirable for use in executive offices showed:

Primary Color	Number of Opinions	Primary Color	Number of Opinions
Red	92	Blue	37
Orange	86	Indigo	46
Yellow	46	Violet	2
Green	91		

    a. What is the experiment?
    b. What is one possible event?
    c. What is the probability of selecting a particular response and discovering that the designer prefers red or green?
    d. What is the probability that a designer does not prefer yellow?

19. The Chair of the Board of Directors says, "There is a 50% chance this company will earn a profit, a 30% chance it will break even, and a 20% chance it will lose money next quarter."
    a. Use an addition rule to find the probability they will not lose money next quarter.
    b. Use the complement rule to find the probability they will not lose money next quarter.

20. Suppose the probability you will get a grade of *A* in this class is .25 and the probability you will get a *B* is .50. What is the probability your grade will be above *C*?

21. A single die is rolled. Let *A* be the event "the die shows 4," *B* be the event "the die shows an even number," and *C* be the event "the die shows an odd number." Consider each pair

of these events and describe whether they are mutually exclusive. Then identify whether they are complementary.

22. Two coins are tossed. If *A* is the event "two heads" and *B* is the event "two tails," are *A* and *B* mutually exclusive? Are they complements?

23. The probabilities of the events *A* and *B* are .20 and .30, respectively. The probability that both *A* and *B* occur is .15. What is the probability of either *A* or *B* occurring?

24. Let $P(X) = .55$ and $P(Y) = .35$. Assume the probability that they both occur is .20. What is the probability of either *X* or *Y* occurring?

25. Suppose the two events *A* and *B* are mutually exclusive. What is the probability of their joint occurrence?

26. A student is taking two courses, history and math. The probability that the student will pass the history course is .60, and the probability of passing the math course is .70. The probability of passing both is .50. What is the probability of passing at least one?

27. A survey of top executives revealed that 35 percent of them regularly read *Time* magazine, 20 percent read *Newsweek,* and 40 percent read *U.S. News and World Report.* Ten percent read both *Time* and *U.S. News and World Report.*
    a. What is the probability that a particular top executive reads either *Time* or *U.S. News and World Report* regularly?
    b. What is the probability .10 called?
    c. Are the events mutually exclusive? Explain.

28. A study by the National Park Service revealed that 50 percent of vacationers going to the Rocky Mountain region visit Yellowstone Park, 40 percent visit the Tetons, and 35 percent visit both.
    a. What is the probability that a vacationer will visit at least one of these magnificent attractions?
    b. What is the probability .35 called?
    c. Are the events mutually exclusive? Explain.

Rules of Multiplication

Special Rule of Multiplication   The special rule of multiplication requires that two events *A* and *B* be **independent.** Two events are independent if the occurrence of one does not alter the probability of the other. So if the events *A* and *B* are independent, the occurrence of *A* does not alter the probability of *B*.

| **Independent**   The occurrence of one event has no effect on the probability of the occurrence of any other event. |

For two independent events *A* and *B*, the probability that *A* and *B* will both occur is found by multiplying the two probabilities. This is called the **special rule of multiplication** and is written symbolically as:

| THE SPECIAL RULE OF MULTIPLICATION | $P(A \text{ and } B) = P(A)P(B)$ | **[5–5]** |

This rule for combining probabilities presumes that a second outcome is *not* affected by the first outcome. To illustrate what is meant by independence of outcomes, suppose two coins are tossed. The outcome of one coin (head or tail) is unaffected by the outcome of the other coin (head or tail). To put it another way, two events are independent if the outcome of the second event does not depend on the outcome of the first event.

For three independent events *A, B,* and *C,* the special rule of multiplication used to determine the probability that all three events will occur is:

$$P(A \text{ and } B \text{ and } C) = P(A)P(B)P(C)$$

Example

Two coins are tossed. What is the probability that both will land tail up?

Solution

The probability of a tail showing face up on one of the coins, written $P(A)$, is one half, or .50. The probability that the other coin will land tail up, written $P(B)$, is one half, or .50. Using formula (5–5), the probability that both will happen is one fourth, or .25, found by:

$$P(A \text{ and } B) = P(A)P(B)$$

$$= \left(\frac{1}{2}\right)\left(\frac{1}{2}\right)$$

$$= \frac{1}{4}, \text{ or } .25$$

This can be shown by listing all of the possible outcomes. Two tails is only one of the four possible outcomes:

SELF-REVIEW 5–5

1. From long experience, Teton Tire knows that the probability is .80 that their XB-70 will last 60,000 miles before it becomes bald or fails. An adjustment is made on any tire that does not last 60,000 miles. You purchase four XB-70s. What is the probability that all four tires will last at least 60,000 miles?

2. As cited in an earlier example, an automatic Shaw machine inserts mixed vegetables into a plastic bag. Past experience revealed that some packages were underweight and some overweight, but most of them had satisfactory weight.

Weight	Probability
Underweight	.025
Satisfactory	.900
Overweight	.075

(a) What is the probability of selecting three packages from the food processing line today and finding that all three of them are underweight?

(b) What does this probability mean?

If two events are not independent, they are referred to as *dependent*. To illustrate dependency, suppose there are 10 rolls of film in a box, and it is known that 3 are defective. A roll of film is selected from the box. Obviously, the probability of selecting a defective roll is ³⁄₁₀, and the probability of selecting a good roll is ⁷⁄₁₀. Then a second roll is selected from the box without the first one being returned to the box. The probability that it is defective *depends on* whether the first roll selected was defective or good. The probability that the second roll is defective is:

²⁄₉, if the first roll was defective. (Only two defective rolls remain in the box containing nine rolls.)

³⁄₉, if the first roll selected was good. (All three defective rolls are still in the box containing nine rolls.)

The fraction ²⁄₉ (or ³⁄₉) is aptly called a **conditional probability** because its value is conditional on (dependent on) whether a defective or a good roll of film is chosen in the first selection from the box.

| **Conditional Probability**   The probability of a particular event occurring, given that another event has occurred.

If we want to determine the probability that two defective rolls of film are selected one after the other, the general rule of multiplication is applied.

General Rule of Multiplication   The **general rule of multiplication** is used to find the *joint probability* that two events will occur, such as selecting 2 defective rolls from the box of 10 rolls, one after the other. In general, the rule states that for two events *A* and *B,* the joint probability that both events will happen is found by multiplying the probability that event *A* will happen by the conditional probability of event *B* occurring. Symbolically, the joint probability $P(A \text{ and } B)$ is found by:

| GENERAL RULE OF MULTIPLICATION | $P(A \text{ and } B) = P(A)P(B \mid A)$ | **[5–6]** |

where $P(B \mid A)$ stands for the probability that *B* will occur *given that A has already occurred.* The vertical line means "given that."

Example

To illustrate the formula, let's use the problem with 10 rolls of film in a box, 3 of which are defective. Two rolls are to be selected, one after the other. What is the probability of selecting a defective roll followed by another defective roll?

Solution

The first roll of film selected from the box being found defective is event *A*. $P(A) = ³⁄₁₀$ because 3 out of the 10 are defective. The second roll selected being found defective is event *B*. Therefore, $P(B \mid A) = ²⁄₉$, because after the first selection was found to be defective, only 2 defective rolls of film remained in the box containing 9 rolls. Determining the probability of two defectives [see formula (5–6)]:

$$P(A \text{ and } B) = P(A)P(B \mid A)$$
$$= \left(\frac{3}{10}\right)\left(\frac{2}{9}\right) = \frac{6}{90}, \text{ or about .07}$$

Incidentally, it is assumed that this experiment was conducted *without replacement*—that is, the defective roll of film was not thrown back in the box before the next roll was selected. It should also be noted that the general rule of multiplication can be extended to more than two events. For three events, *A, B,* and *C,* the formula would be:

$$P(A \text{ and } B \text{ and } C) = P(A)P(B \mid A)P(C \mid A \text{ and } B)$$

For illustration, the probability that the first three rolls chosen from the box will all be defective is .00833, found by:

$$P(A \text{ and } B \text{ and } C) = P(A)P(B \mid A)P(C \mid A \text{ and } B)$$

$$= \left(\frac{3}{10}\right)\left(\frac{2}{9}\right)\left(\frac{1}{8}\right) = \frac{6}{720} = .00833$$

SELF-REVIEW 5–6

The board of directors of Tarbell Industries consists of eight men and four women. A four-member search committee is to be chosen at random to recommend a new company president.

(a)   What is the probability that all four members of the search committee will be women?
(b)   What is the probability that all four members will be men?
(c)   Does the sum of the probabilities for 1 and 2 equal 1? Explain.

Another application of the general rule of multiplication follows. A survey of executives dealt with their loyalty to the company. One of the questions asked was, "If you were given an offer by another company equal to or slightly better than your present position, would you remain with the company or take the other position?" The responses of the 200 executives in the survey were cross-classified with their length of service with the company. (See Table 5–1.) The type of table that resulted is usually referred to as a **contingency table.**

Table 5–1   Loyalty of Executives and Length of Service with Company

| | Length of Service | | | | |
Loyalty	Less than 1 Year	1–5 Years	6–10 Years	More than 10 Years	Total
Would remain	10	30	5	75	120
Would not remain	25	15	10	30	80
					200

Example

What is the probability of randomly selecting an executive who is loyal to the company (would remain) and who has more than 10 years of service?

Solution

Note that two events occur at the same time — the executive would remain with the company, and he or she has more than 10 years of service.

1.   Event *A* is an executive who would remain with the company despite an equal or slightly better offer from another company. To find the probability that event *A* will happen, refer to Table 5–1. Note that there are 120 executives out of the 200 in the survey who would remain with the company, so *P(A)* = 120/200, or .60.
2.   Event *B* is an executive who has more than 10 years of service with the company. Thus, *P(B | A)* is the conditional probability that an executive with more than 10 years of service would remain with the company despite an equal or slightly

better offer from another company. Referring to the contingency table, Table 5–1, 75 of the 120 executives who would remain have more than 10 years of service, so $P(B \mid A) = 75/120$.

Solving for the probability that an executive randomly selected will be the one who would remain with the company and who has more than 10 years of service with the company, using the general rule of multiplication in formula (5–6):

$$P(A \text{ and } B) = P(A)P(B \mid A)$$

$$= \left(\frac{120}{200}\right)\left(\frac{75}{120}\right) = \frac{9,000}{24,000} = .375$$

SELF-REVIEW 5–7

Refer to Table 5–1. Using the general rule of multiplication, what is the probability of selecting at random an executive who would not remain with the company and has less than one year of service?

❚ Tree Diagrams

The *tree diagram* is a graphical device that is helpful in organizing calculations that involve several stages. Each segment in the tree is one stage of the problem. The probabilities written near the branches are conditional probabilities for that experiment. We will use the data in Table 5–1 to show the construction of a tree diagram.

Steps in constructing a tree diagram

1. To construct a tree diagram, we begin by drawing a heavy dot on the left to represent the trunk of the tree (see Chart 5–1).
2. For this problem, two main branches go out from the trunk, the upper one representing "would remain" and the lower one "would not remain." Their probabilities are written on the branches, namely, 120/200 and 80/200. These are $P(A)$ and $P(\sim A)$.
3. Four branches "grow" out of each of the two main branches. These branches represent the length of service—less than 1 year, 1–5 years, 6–10 years, and more than 10 years. The conditional probabilities for the upper branch of the tree, 10/120, 30/120, 5/120, and so on are written on the appropriate branches. These are $P(B_1 \mid A)$, $P(B_2 \mid A)$, $P(B_3 \mid A)$, and $P(B_4 \mid A)$, where B_1 refers to less than 1 year of service, B_2 1 to 5 years, B_3 6 to 10 years, and B_4 more than 10 years. Next, write the conditional probabilities for the lower branch.
4. Finally, joint probabilities, that A and B will occur together, are shown on the right side. For example, the joint probability of randomly selecting an executive who would remain with the company and who has less than one year of service, using formula (5–6), is:

$$P(A \text{ and } B_1) = P(A)P(B_1 \mid A)$$

$$= \left(\frac{120}{200}\right)\left(\frac{10}{120}\right) = .05$$

Because the joint probabilities represent all possible selections (would remain, 6–10 years service; would not remain, more than 10 years of service; etc.), they must sum to 1.00. (See chart 5–1.)

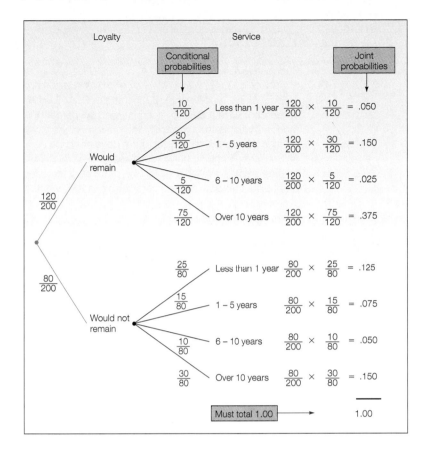

Chart 5–1 Tree Diagram Showing Loyalty and Length of Service

SELF-REVIEW 5–8

1. Refer to the tree diagram in Chart 5–1. Explain the path you would follow to find the joint probability of selecting an executive at random who has 6–10 years' service and who would not remain with the company upon receipt of an equal or slightly better offer from another company.

2. A random sample of the employees of the Hardware Manufacturing Company was chosen to determine their retirement plans after age 65. Those selected in the sample were divided into management and production. The results were:

Employee	Plans after Age 65		
	Retire	Not Retire	Total
Management	5	15	20
Production	30	50	80
			100

(a) What is the table called?
(b) Draw a tree diagram, and determine the joint probabilities.
(c) Do the joint probabilities total 1.00? Why?

▌ Exercises

29. Suppose $P(A) = .40$ and $P(B \mid A) = .30$. What is the joint probability of A and B?
30. Suppose $P(X_1) = .75$ and $P(Y_2 \mid X_1) = .40$. What is the joint probability of X_1 and Y_2?
31. A local bank reports that 80 percent of its customers maintain a checking account, 60 percent have a savings account, and 50 percent have both. If a customer is chosen at random, what is the probability the customer has either a checking or a savings account? What is the probability the customer does not have either a checking or a savings account?
32. All Seasons Plumbing has two service trucks which frequently break down. If the probability the first truck is available is .75, the probability the second truck is available is .50, and the probability that both trucks are available is .30, what is the probability that neither truck is available?
33. Refer to the following table.

	First Event			
Second Event	A_1	A_2	A_3	Total
B_1	2	1	3	6
B_2	1	2	1	4
Total	3	3	4	10

  a. Determine $P(A_1)$.
  b. Determine $P(B_1 \mid A_2)$.
  c. Determine $P(B_2$ and $A_3)$.

34. Three defective electric toothbrushes were accidentally shipped to a drugstore by Clean-brush Products along with 17 nondefective ones.
  a. What is the probability that the first two electric toothbrushes sold will be returned to the drugstore because they are defective?
  b. What is the probability that the first two electric toothbrushes sold will not be defective?
35. Each salesperson at Stiles-Compton is rated either below average, average, or above average with respect to sales ability. Each salesperson is also rated with respect to his or her potential for advancement — either fair, good, or excellent. These traits for the 500 sales-people were cross-classified into the following table.

	Potential for Advancement		
Sales Ability	Fair	Good	Excellent
Below average	16	12	22
Average	45	60	45
Above average	93	72	135

  a. What is this table called?
  b. What is the probability that a salesperson selected at random will have above average sales ability and excellent potential for advancement?
  c. Construct a tree diagram showing all the probabilities, conditional probabilities, and joint probabilities.
36. An investor owns three common stocks. Each stock, independently of the other, has equally likely chances of (1) increasing in value, (2) decreasing in value, or (3) remaining the same value. List the possible outcomes of this experiment. Estimate the probability that at least two of the stocks increase in value.
37. The board of directors of a small company consists of five people. Three of those are "strong leaders." If they buy an idea, the entire board will agree. The other "weak" members have no influence. Three salesmen are scheduled, one after the other, to make sales presentations to

a board member of the salesman's choice. The salesmen are convincing but do not know who the "strong leaders" are. However, they will know who the previous salesmen spoke to. The first salesman to find a strong leader will win the account. Do the three salesmen have the same chance of winning the account? If not, find their respective probabilities of winning.

38. If you ask three strangers on campus, what is the probability: (a) All were born on Wednesday? (b) All were born on different days of the week? (c) None were born on Saturday?

Bayes' Theorem

In the 18th century Reverend Thomas Bayes, an English Presbyterian minister, pondered this question: Does God really exist? Being interested in mathematics, he attempted to develop a formula to arrive at the probability that God does exist based on evidence that was available to him on earth. Later Laplace refined Bayes' work and gave it the name "Bayes' theorem." In a workable form, **Bayes' theorem** is:

BAYES' THEOREM	$P(A_1 \mid B) = \dfrac{P(A_1)P(B \mid A_1)}{P(A_1)P(B \mid A_1) + P(A_2)P(B \mid A_2)}$	**[5–7]**

(The meaning of each of these letters will be explained in the following example, but note that they refer to conditional probabilities.)

Consider the following problem. Suppose 5 percent of the population of Umen, a fictional Third World country, have a disease that is peculiar to that country. We will let A_1 refer to the event "has the disease" and A_2 refer to the event "does not have the disease." Thus, we know that if we select a person from Umen at random, the probability that the individual chosen has the disease is .05, or $P(A_1) = .05$. This probability, $P(A_1) = P(\text{has the disease}) = .05$, is called the **prior probability.** It is given this name because the probability is assigned before any empirical data are obtained.

Prior Probability The initial probability based on the present level of information.

The prior probability that a person is not afflicted with the disease is therefore .95, or $P(A_2) = .95$, found by $1 - .05$.

There is a diagnostic technique to detect the disease, but it is not very accurate. Let B denote the event "test shows the disease is present." Assume that historical evidence shows that if a person actually has the disease, the probability that the test will indicate the presence of the disease is .90. Using the conditional probability definitions developed earlier in this chapter, this statement is written as:

$$P(B \mid A_1) = .90$$

Assume the probability is .15 that a person actually does not have the disease but the test indicates the disease is present.

$$P(B \mid A_2) = .15$$

Let's randomly select a person from Umen and perform the test. The test results indicate the disease is present. What is the probability that the person actually has the disease? In symbolic form, we want to know $P(A_1 \mid B)$, which is interpreted as: $P(\text{has the disease}) \mid (\text{the test results are positive})$. The probability $P(A_1 \mid B)$ is called a **posterior probability.**

Posterior Probability A revised probability based on additional information.

With the help of Bayes' theorem, formula (5–7), we can determine the posterior or revised probability.

$$P(A_1 \mid B) = \frac{P(A_1)P(B \mid A_1)}{P(A_1)P(B \mid A_1) + P(A_2)P(B \mid A_2)}$$

$$= \frac{(.05)(.90)}{(.05)(.90) + (.95)(.15)} = \frac{.0450}{.1875} = .24$$

So the probability that a person has the disease, given that he or she tested positive, is .24. How is the result interpreted? If a person is selected at random from the population, the probability that he or she has the disease is .05. If the person is tested and the test result is positive, the probability that the person actually has the disease is increased about fivefold, from .05 to .24.

The preceding problem included only two events, A_1 and A_2, as prior probabilities. If there are more than two prior probabilities, the denominator of Bayes' theorem requires additional terms. If the prior probability distribution consists of n mutually exclusive events, Bayes' theorem, formula (5–7), becomes

$$P(A_i \mid B) = \frac{P(A_i)P(B \mid A_i)}{P(A_1)P(B \mid A_1) + P(A_2)P(B \mid A_2) + \cdots + P(A_n)P(B \mid A_n)}$$

where A_i refers to any of the n possible outcomes.

Using the preceding notation, the calculations for the Umen problem are summarized in the following table.

Event, A_i	Prior Probability, $P(A_i)$	Conditional Probability, $P(B \mid A_i)$	Joint Probability, $P(A_i \text{ and } B)$	Posterior Probability, $P(A_i \mid B)$
Disease, A_1	.05	.90	.0450	.0450/.1875 = .24
No disease, A_2	.95	.15	.1425	.1425/.1875 = .76
			$P(B) = .1875$	1.00

Another illustration of Bayes' theorem follows.

Example

A manufacturer of VCRs purchases a particular microchip, called the LS-24, from three suppliers: Hall Electronics, Schuller Sales, and Crawford Components. Thirty percent of the LS-24 chips are purchased from Hall Electronics, 20 percent from Schuller Sales, and the remaining 50 percent from Crawford Components. The

manufacturer has extensive histories on the three suppliers and knows that 3 percent of the LS-24 chips from Hall Electronics are defective, 5 percent of chips from Schuller Sales are defective, and 4 percent of the chips purchased from Crawford Components are defective.

When the LS-24 chips arrive at the manufacturer, they are placed directly in a bin and not inspected or otherwise identified by supplier. A worker selects a chip for installation in a VCR and finds it defective. What is the probability that it was manufactured by Schuller Sales?

Solution   As a first step, let's summarize some of the information given in the problem statement.

- There are three events, that is, three suppliers.

    A_1 The LS-24 was purchased from Hall Electronics
    A_2 The LS-24 was purchased from Schuller Sales
    A_3 The LS-24 was purchased from Crawford Components

- The prior probabilities are:

    $P(A_1)$ = .30 The probability the LS-24 was manufactured by Hall Electronics
    $P(A_2)$ = .20 The probability the LS-24 was manufactured by Schuller Sales
    $P(A_3)$ = .50 The probability the LS-24 was manufactured by Crawford Components

- The additional information is that the LS-24 chip is defective.

    B_1 The LS-24 is defective
    B_2 The LS-24 is not defective

- The following conditional probabilities are given.

    $P(B_1 \mid A_1)$ = .03 The probability that an LS-24 chip produced by Hall Electronics is defective
    $P(B_1 \mid A_2)$ = .05 The probability that an LS-24 chip produced by Schuller Sales is defective
    $P(B_1 \mid A_3)$ = .04 The probability that an LS-24 chip produced by Crawford Components is defective

- A chip is selected from the bin. Because the chips are not identified by supplier, we are not certain which supplier manufactured the chip. We want to determine the probability that the defective chip was purchased from Schuller Sales. The probability is written $P(A_2 \mid B_1)$.

Look at Schuller's quality record. It is the worst of the three suppliers. Now that we have found a defective LS-24 chip, we suspect that $P(A_2 \mid B_1)$ is greater than $P(A_2)$. That is, we expect the revised probability to be greater than .20. But how much greater? Bayes' theorem can give us the answer. As a first step, consider the tree diagram in Chart 5–2.

The events are dependent, so the prior probability in the first branch is multiplied by the conditional probability in the second branch to obtain the joint probability. The joint probability is reported in the last column of Chart 5–2. To construct the tree diagram of Chart 5–2, we used a time sequence that moved from the supplier to the determination of whether the chip was acceptable or unacceptable.

What we need to do is reverse the time process. That is, instead of moving from left to right in Chart 5–2, we need to move from right to left. We have a defective chip, and we want to determine the likelihood that it was purchased from Schuller Sales. How is that accomplished? We first look at the joint probabilities as relative frequencies out of 1,000 cases. For example, the likelihood of a defective LS-24 chip that was produced by Hall Electronics is .009. So of 1,000 cases we would expect to find 9 defective chips produced by Hall Electronics. We observe that in 39 of 1,000 cases the LS-24 chip selected for assembly will be defective, found by 9 + 10 + 20. Of these 39 defective chips, 10 were produced by Schuller Sales. Thus, the probability that the defective LS-24 chip was purchased from Schuller Sales is 10/39 = .2564. We have now determined the revised probability of $P(A_2 \mid B_1)$. Before we found the defective chip, the likelihood that it was purchased from Schuller Sales was .20. This likelihood has been increased to .2564.

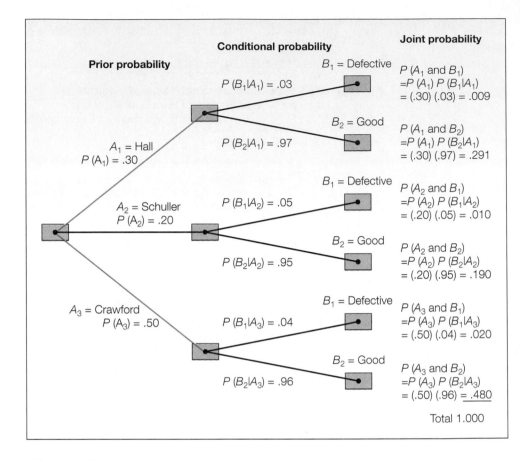

Chart 5–2   Tree Diagram of VCR Manufacturing Problem

This information is summarized in the following table.

Event, A_i	Prior Probability, $P(A_i)$	Conditional Probability, $P(B_1 \mid A_i)$	Joint Probability, $P(A_i \text{ and } B_1)$	Posterior Probability, $P(A_i \mid B_1)$
Hall	.30	.03	.009	.009/.039 = .2308
Schuller	.20	.05	.010	.010/.039 = .2564
Crawford	.50	.04	.020	.020/.039 = .5128
			$P(B_1) = \overline{.039}$	$\overline{1.0000}$

The probability that the defective LS-24 chip came from Schuller Sales can be formally found by using Bayes' theorem. We want to compute $P(A_2 \mid B_1)$, where A_2 refers to Schuller Sales and B_1 to the fact that the selected LS-24 chip was defective.

$$P(A_2 \mid B_1) = \frac{P(A_2)P(B_1 \mid A_2)}{P(A_1)P(B_1 \mid A_1) + P(A_2)P(B_1 \mid A_2) + P(A_3)P(B_1 \mid A_3)}$$

$$= \frac{(.20)(.05)}{(.30)(.03) + (.20)(.05) + (.50)(.04)} = \frac{.010}{.039} = .2564$$

This is the same result obtained from Chart 5–2 and from the conditional probability table.

SELF-REVIEW 5–9

Refer to the preceding example and solution.
(a) Design a formula to find the probability that the part selected came from Crawford Components, given that it was a good chip.
(b) Compute the probability using Bayes' theorem.

▌ Exercises

39. $P(A_1) = .60$, $P(A_2) = .40$, $P(B_1 \mid A_1) = .05$, and $P(B_1 \mid A_2) = .10$. Use Bayes' theorem to determine $P(A_1 \mid B_1)$.

40. $P(A_1) = .20$, $P(A_2) = .40$, and $P(A_3) = .40$. $P(B_1 \mid A_1) = .25$. $P(B_1 \mid A_2) = .05$, and $P(B_1 \mid A_3) = .10$. Use Bayes' theorem to determine $P(A_3 \mid B_1)$.

41. The Ludlow Wildcats baseball team, a minor league team in the Cleveland Indians organization, plays 70 percent of their games at night and 30 percent during the day. The team wins 50 percent of their night games and 90 percent of their day games. According to today's newspaper, they won yesterday. What is the probability the game was played at night?

42. Dr. Stallter has been teaching basic statistics for many years. She knows that 80 percent of the students will complete the assigned problems. She has also determined that among those who do their assignments, 90 percent will pass the course. Among those students who do not do their homework, 60 percent will pass. Mike Fishbaugh took statistics last semester from Dr. Stallter and received a passing grade. What is the probability that he completed the assignments?

43. The credit department of Lion's Department Store in Anaheim, California, reported that 30 percent of their sales are cash, 30 percent are paid by for check at the time of the purchase, and 40 percent are charged. Twenty percent of the cash purchases, 90 percent of the checks, and 60 percent of the charges are for more than $50. Ms. Tina Stevens just purchased a new dress that cost $120. What is the probability that she paid cash?

44. A municipal bond rating service has three categories (A, B, and C). In the last year, of the municipal bonds issued throughout the United States, 60 percent were rated A, 30 percent B, and 10 percent C. Of the bonds rated A, 40 percent were issued by cities, 40 percent by suburbs, and 20 percent by rural areas. Of the bonds rated B, 50 percent were from cities, 30 percent from suburbs, and 20 percent from rural areas. Of the bonds rated C, 80 percent were from cities, 10 percent from suburbs, and 10 percent from rural areas. A bond is selected at random.
   a. What is the conditional probability of selecting a bond from a rural area, given that it is rated C?
   b. What is the joint probability of selecting a bond rated C that is from a rural area?
   c. What is the probability that the bond is rated C, given that it is from a rural area?

▌ Principles of Counting

If the number of possible outcomes in an experiment is small, it is relatively easy to list and count all of the possible events. There are six possible events, for example, resulting from the roll of a die, namely:

If, however, there are a large number of possible outcomes, such as the number of boys and girls for families with 10 children, it would be tedious to list and count all the possibilities. They could have all boys, one boy and nine girls, two boys and eight girls, and so on. To facilitate counting, three counting formulas will be examined: the **multiplication formula** (not to be confused with the multiplication *rule* described earlier in the chapter), the **permutation formula,** and the **combination formula.**

The Multiplication Formula

| **Multiplication Formula**   If there are *m* ways of doing one thing and *n* ways of doing another thing, there are *m* × *n* ways of doing both. |

In terms of a formula:

| MULTIPLICATION FORMULA | Total number of arrangements = $(m)(n)$ | **[5–8]** |

This can be extended to more than two events. For three events *m, n,* and *o*:

$$\text{Total number of arrangements} = (m)(n)(o)$$

Example

An automobile dealer wants to advertise that for $19,999 you can buy a convertible, a two-door, or a four-door model with your choice of either wire wheel covers or solid wheel covers. How many different arrangements of models and wheel covers can the dealer offer?

Solution

Of course the dealer could determine the total number of arrangements by picturing and counting them. There are six.

Convertible with wire wheels — Convertible with solid wheels
Two-door with wire wheels — Two-door with solid wheels
Four-door with wire wheels — Four-door with solid wheels

We can employ the multiplication formula as a check (where *m* is the number of models and *n* the wheel cover type). Using formula (5–8):

$$\text{Total possible arrangements} = (m)(n) = (3)(2) = 6$$

It was not difficult to list and count all the possible model and wheel cover combinations in this example. Suppose, however, that the dealer decided to offer eight models and six types of wheel covers. It would be tedious to picture and count all the possible alternatives. Instead, the multiplication formula can be used. In this case, $(m)(n) = (8)(6) = 48$ possible arrangements.

Note in the preceding applications of the multiplication formula that there were *two or more groupings* from which you made selections. The automobile dealer, for example, offered a choice of models and a choice of wheel covers. If a home builder offered you four different exterior styles of a home to choose from and three interior floor plans, the multiplication formula would be used to find how many different arrangements were possible.

SELF-REVIEW 5–10

1. Stiffin Lamps has developed five lamp bases and four lamp shades that can be used together. How many different arrangements of base and shade can be offered?
2. Pioneer manufactures three models of stereo receivers, two cassette decks, four speakers, and three CD carousels. When the four types of compatible components are sold together, they form a "system." How many different systems can the electronics firm offer?

The Permutation Formula

As noted, the multiplication formula is applied to find the number of possible arrangements for two or more groups. The **permutation formula** is applied to find the possible number of arrangements when there is only *one* group of objects. As illustrations of this type of problem:

- Three electronic parts are to be assembled into a plug-in unit for a television set. The parts can be assembled in any order. The question involving counting is: In how many different ways can the three parts be assembled?
- A machine operator must make four safety checks before starting his machine. It does not matter in which order the checks are made. In how many different ways can the operator make the checks?

One order for the first illustration might be: the transistor first, the LEDs second, and the synthesizer third. This arrangement is called a **permutation.**

| **Permutation** Any arrangement of r objects selected from a single group of n possible objects.

Note that the arrangements $a, b, c,$ and b, a, c are *different* permutations. The formula to count the total number of different permutations is:

$$\text{PERMUTATION FORMULA} \qquad {}_nP_r = \frac{n!}{(n-r)!} \qquad \text{[5–9]}$$

where:

P is the number of permutations, or ways the objects can be arranged.

n is the total number of objects. In the first illustration, there are three electronic parts, so $n = 3$.

r   is the number of objects to be used at one time. In the electronics problem, all the objects (electronic parts) are to be assembled, so $r = 3$. If only two out of the three electronic parts were to be inserted in the plug-in unit, r would be 2.

Before we solve the two problems illustrated, note that permutations and combinations (to be discussed shortly) use a notation called *n factorial*. It is written $n!$ and means the product of $n(n - 1)(n - 2)(n - 3) \ldots (1)$. For instance, $5! = 5 \cdot 4 \cdot 3 \cdot 2 \cdot 1 = 120$.

As shown below, numbers can be canceled when the same numbers are included in the numerator and denominator.

$$\frac{6!3!}{4!} = \frac{6 \cdot 5 \cdot 4 \cdot 3 \cdot 2 \cdot 1(3 \cdot 2 \cdot 1)}{4 \cdot 3 \cdot 2 \cdot 1} = 180$$

$0! = 1$ By definition, zero factorial, written $0!$, is set equal to 1. That is, $0! = 1$.

Example

Referring to the group of three electronic parts that are to be assembled in any order, in how many different ways can they be assembled?

Solution

$n = 3$ because there are three electronic parts to be assembled. $r = 3$ because all three are to be inserted in the plug-in unit. Solving using formula (5–9):

$$_nP_r = \frac{n!}{(n - r)!} = \frac{3!}{(3 - 3)!} = \frac{3!}{0!} = \frac{3!}{1} = 6$$

A check can be made to the number of permutations arrived at using the permutation formula. To check, we merely determine how many spaces have to be filled and the possibilities for each space and apply the multiplication formula. In the problem involving three electronic parts, there are three locations in the plug-in unit for the three parts. There are three possibilities for the first place, two for the second (one has been used up), and one for the third, as follows:

$$(3)(2)(1) = 6 \text{ permutations}$$

The six ways in which the three electronic parts, lettered *A, B, C,* can be arranged are:

$$ABC \quad BAC \quad CAB \quad ACB \quad BCA \quad CBA$$

Another example utilizing this principle follows.

Example

Suppose there are eight machines available but only three spaces on the floor of a machine shop for the machines. In how many different ways can eight machines be arranged in the three available spaces?

Solution

There are eight possibilities for the first space, seven for the second space (one has been used up), and six for the third space. Then:

$$(8)(7)(6) = 336 \text{ permutations}$$

As before, this may also be expressed mathematically by saying that the number of permutations, P, of n items is dependent on the number of spaces, r, available:

$$_nP_r = \frac{n!}{(n-r)!} = \frac{8!}{(8-3)!} = \frac{8!}{5!} = \frac{(8)(7)(6)5!}{5!} = 336$$

SELF-REVIEW 5–11

1. A musician wants to write a score based on only five chords: B-flat, C, D, E, and G. However, only three chords out of the five will be used in succession, such as C, B-flat, and E. Repetitions, such as B-flat, B-flat, and E, will not be permitted.
   (a) How many permutations of the five chords, taken three at a time, are possible?
   (b) Using formula (5–9), how many permutations are possible?
2. Recall that a machine operator must make four safety checks before starting to machine a part. It does not matter in which order the checks are made. In how many different ways can the operator make the checks?
3. The 10 numbers 0 through 9 are to be used in code groups of four to identify an item of clothing. Code 1083 might identify a blue blouse, size medium; the code group 2031 might identify a pair of pants, size 18; and so on. Repetitions of numbers are not permitted. That is, the same number cannot be used twice (or more) in a total sequence. For example, 2256, 2562, or 5559 would not be permitted. How many different code groups can be designed?

The Combination Formula

For a permutation, each different order of objects is counted.

To qualify as a *permutation,* the *order of the objects for each possible outcome is different.* For three objects, *a, b,* and *c,* the order *a, b, c,* is one order (permutation); *b, a, c* is another permutation; *c, a, b,* is another permutation; and so on. There are six possible arrangements of these three objects taken three at a time. Using the permutation formula:

$$_nP_r = \frac{n!}{(n-r)!} = \frac{3!}{(3-3)!} = \frac{3\cdot2\cdot1}{1} = 6$$

For a combination, order ab is considered the same as order ba.

If the order of the objects is not important, the total number of orders is called a *combination.*

| **Combination** The number of ways to choose r objects from a group of n objects without regard to order.

The **combination formula** is:

COMBINATION FORMULA	$_nC_r = \dfrac{n!}{r!(n-r)!}$	**[5–10]**

For example, if executives Able, Baker, and Chauncy are to be chosen as a committee to negotiate a merger, there is only one possible combination of these three; the committee of Able, Baker, and Chauncy is the same as the committee of Baker, Chauncy, and Able. Using the combination formula:

$$_nC_r = \frac{n!}{r!(n-r)!} = \frac{3\cdot2\cdot1}{3\cdot2\cdot1(1)} = 1$$

Example

The marketing department has been given the assignment of designing color codes for the 42 different lines of compact discs sold by Goody Records. Three colors are to be used on each CD, but a combination of three colors used for one CD cannot be rearranged and used to identify a different CD. This means that if green, yellow, and violet were used to identify one line, then yellow, green, and violet (or any other combination of these three colors) cannot be used to identify another line. Would seven colors taken three at a time be adequate to color code the 42 lines?

Solution

Using formula (5–10), there are 35 combinations, found by

$$_7C_3 = \frac{n!}{r!(n-r)!} = \frac{7!}{3!(7-3)!} = \frac{7!}{3!4!} = 35$$

The seven colors taken three at a time (i.e., three colors to a line) would not be adequate to color code the 42 different lines because they would provide only 35 combinations. Eight colors taken three at a time would give 56 different combinations. This would be more than adequate to color code the 42 different lines.

SELF-REVIEW   5–12

(a)   In the preceding solution, we said that eight colors taken three at a time would give 56 different combinations. Using formula (5–10), is that true?

(b)   As an alternative plan for color coding the 42 different lines, it has been suggested that only two colors be placed on a disc. Would 10 colors be adequate to color code the 42 different lines? (Again, a combination of two colors could be used only once—that is, if pink and blue were coded for one line, blue and pink could not be used to identify a different line.)

▎Exercises

45.   Solve the following:
    a. $40!/35!$
    b. $_7P_4$
    c. $_5C_2$

46.   Solve the following:
    a. $20!/17!$
    b. $_9P_3$
    c. $_7C_2$

47.   A pollster randomly selected 4 of 10 available people. How many different groups of 4 are possible?

48.   A telephone number consists of seven digits, the first three representing the exchange. How many different telephone numbers are possible within the 537 exchange?

49.   An overnight express company must include five cities on its route. How many different routes are possible, assuming that it does not matter in which order the cities are included in the routing?

50.   A representative of the Environmental Protection Agency (EPA) wants to select samples from 10 landfills. The director has 15 landfills from which she can collect samples. How many different samples are possible?

51.   A national pollster has developed 15 questions designed to rate the performance of the president of the United States. The pollster will select 10 of these questions. How many different arrangements are there for the order of the 10 selected questions?

52. A company is creating three new divisions and seven managers are eligible to be appointed head of a division. How many different ways could the three new heads be appointed?

▌ Chapter Outline

I. A probability is a value between 0 and 1 inclusive that represents the likelihood that a particular event will happen.
  A. An experiment is the observation of some activity or the act of taking some measurement.
  B. An outcome is a particular result of an experiment.
  C. An event is the collection of one or more outcomes of an experiment.

II. There are three definitions of probability.
  A. The classical definition applies when there are n equally likely outcomes to an experiment.
  B. The empirical definition occurs when the number of times an event happens is divided by the total number of observations.
  C. A subjective probability is based on whatever information is available.

III. Two events are mutually exclusive if by virtue of one event happening the other cannot happen.

IV. Events are independent if the occurrence of one event does not affect the occurrence of another event.

V. The rules of addition are used to combine events.
  A. The special rule of addition is used to combine events that are mutually exclusive.

$$P(A \text{ or } B) = P(A) + P(B) \qquad \textbf{[5–2]}$$

  B. The general rule of addition is

$$P(A \text{ or } B) = P(A) + P(B) - P(A \text{ and } B) \qquad \textbf{[5–4]}$$

  C. The complement rule is used to determine the probability of an event happening by subtracting the probability of the event not happening from 1.

$$P(A) = 1 - P(\sim A) \qquad \textbf{[5–3]}$$

VI. The rules of multiplication are also used to combine events.
  A. The special rule of multiplication is used to combine events that are independent.

$$P(A \text{ and } B) = P(A)P(B) \qquad \textbf{[5–5]}$$

  B. The general rule of multiplication is

$$P(A \text{ and } B) = P(A)P(B \mid A) \qquad \textbf{[5–6]}$$

  C. A joint probability is the likelihood that two or more events will happen at the same time.
  D. A conditional probability is the likelihood that an event will happen, given that another event has already happened.
  E. Bayes' theorem is a method of revising a probability, given that additional information is obtained. For two events:

$$P(A_1 \mid B) = \frac{P(A_1)P(B \mid A_1)}{P(A_1)P(B \mid A_1) + P(A_2)P(B \mid A_2)} \qquad \textbf{[5–7]}$$

VII. There are three counting rules that are useful in determining the total number of ways in which events can occur.
  A. The multiplication rule states that if there are m ways one event can happen and n ways another event can happen, then there are mn ways the two events can happen.

$$\text{Number of arrangements} = (m)(n) \qquad \textbf{[5–8]}$$

B. A permutation is an arrangement in which the order of the objects selected from a specific pool of objects is important.

$$_nP_r = \frac{n!}{(n - r)!}$$ **[5–9]**

C. A combination is an arrangement where the order of the objects selected from a specific pool of objects is not important.

$$_nC_r = \frac{n!}{r!(n - r)!}$$ **[5–10]**

▎ Pronunciation Key

SYMBOL	MEANING	PRONUNCIATION
$P(A)$	Probability of A	P of A
$P(\sim A)$	Probability of not A	P of not A
$P(A$ and $B)$	Probability of A and B	P of A and B
$P(A$ or $B)$	Probability of A or B	P of A or B
$P(A/B)$	Probability of A given B has happened	P of A given B
$_nP_r$	Permutation of n items selected r at a time	Pnr
$_nC_r$	Combination of n items selected r at a time	Cnr

▎ Chapter Exercises

53. The marketing research department at Vernors plans to survey teenagers about a newly developed soft drink. They will be asked to compare it with their favorite soft drink.
  a. What is the experiment?
  b. What is one possible event?

54. The number of times a particular event occurred in the past is divided by the total number of occurrences. What is this approach to probability called?

55. The probability that the cause and the cure of cancer will be discovered before the year 2000 is .02. What viewpoint of probability does this statement illustrate?

56. Is it true that, if there is absolutely no chance a person will recover from 50 bullet wounds, the probability assigned to this event is −1.00? Why?

57. On the throw of one die, what is the probability that a one-spot or a two-spot or a six-spot will appear face up? What definition of probability is being used?

58. A study of the weekly offering in the envelopes at the First Baptist Church in Warren, Pennsylvania, revealed the following:

Offering in Envelope	Number
$ 0 up to $ 5	200
5 up to 10	100
10 up to 20	75
20 up to 50	75
50 or more	50
Total	500

   a. What is the probability of selecting an envelope at random and finding $50 or more in it?
   b. Are the classes "$0 up to $5," "$5 up to $10," and so on considered mutually exclusive?
   c. If the probabilities associated with each class were totaled, what would the total be?
   d. What is the probability of selecting an envelope at random and finding it to contain up to $10?
   e. What is the probability of finding less than $50 in an envelope selected at random?

59. Define each of these items:
   a. Conditional probability.
   b. Event.
   c. Joint probability.

60. The first card selected from a standard 52-card deck was a king.
   a. If it is returned to the deck, what is the probability that a king will be drawn on the second selection?
   b. If the king is not replaced, what is the probability that a king will be drawn on the second selection?
   c. What is the probability that a king will be selected on the first draw from the deck and another king on the second draw (assuming that the first king was not replaced)?

61. Armco, a manufacturer of traffic light systems, found that under accelerated-life tests, 95 percent of the newly developed systems lasted three years before failing to change signals properly.
   a. If a city purchased four of these systems, what is the probability that all four systems would operate properly for at least three years?
   b. Which rule of probability does this illustrate?
   c. Using letters to represent the four systems, design an equation to show how you arrived at the answer to part a.

62. Refer to the following picture.

   a. What is the picture called?
   b. What rule of probability is illustrated?
   c. *B* represents the event of choosing a family that receives welfare payments. What does $P(B) + P(\sim B)$ equal?

63. In a management trainee program at Claremont Enterprises, 80 percent of the trainees are female and 20 percent male. Ninety percent of the females attended college, and 78 percent of the males attended college.
   a. A management trainee is selected at random. What is the probability that the person selected is a female who did not attend college?
   b. Construct a tree diagram showing all the probabilities, conditional probabilities, and joint probabilities.
   c. Do the joint probabilities total 1.00? Why?

64. A coin is tossed four times.
    a. What is the probability that each of the four tosses will result in a head face up?
    b. Using the letters *A, B, C,* and *D,* write the formula for the probability of this outcome.
    c. Suppose four heads did appear face up on the tosses of the coin. What is the probability that a head will appear face up on the next toss of the coin?

65. Of every 100 employees at Kiddie Carts, 57 are production workers (designated as *A*), 40 are supervisors (designated as *B*), 2 are secretaries (designated as *C*), and 1 is with either middle or top management (designated as *D*). If an employee is selected at random, what does *P(A* or *B* or *C)* equal?

66. Alex Rodriguez led major league baseball in hitting during 1996. During that time his batting average was .358. Assume that the probability of getting a hit is .358 for each time at bat. (To put it another way, for every 1,000 times at bat, he had 358 hits.) In a particular game he batted three times.
    a. What is the probability that he had three hits?
    b. What is the probability that he did not get any hits in the game?

67. The probability that a bomber hits its target on any particular run is .80. If four bombers are sent after the same target, what is the probability that they all hit the target? What is the probability that none of the bombers hits the target?

68. Ninety students will graduate from Lima Shawnee High School this year. Out of the 90 graduates, 50 are planning to attend college. Two students are selected at random to carry the flag at graduation. What is the probability that both of them are planning to attend college?

69. The board of directors of Saner Automatic Door Company consists of 12 members, 3 of whom are women. A new policy and procedures manual is to be written for the company. A committee of 3 is randomly selected from the board to do the writing.
    a. What is the probability that all members of the committee are men?
    b. What is the probability that at least 1 member of the committee is a woman?

70. A survey of undergraduate students in the School of Business at Northern University revealed the following regarding the gender and majors of the students:

Gender	Major			Total
	Accounting	Management	Finance	
Male	100	150	50	300
Female	100	50	50	200
Total	200	200	100	500

    a. What is the probability of selecting a female student?
    b. What is the probability of selecting a finance or accounting major?
    c. What is the probability of selecting a female or an accounting major? Which rule of addition did you apply?
    d. What is the probability of selecting an accounting major, given that the person selected is a male?
    e. Suppose two students are selected randomly to attend a lunch with the president of the university. What is the probability that both of those selected are accounting majors?

71. The Wood County sheriff classifies crimes by age (in years) of the criminal and whether the crime is violent or nonviolent. As shown below, a total of 150 crimes were reported by the sheriff last year.

Type of Crime	Age (in years)			Total
	Under 20	20 to 40	Over 40	
Violent	27	41	14	82
Nonviolent	12	34	22	68
Total	39	75	36	150

    a. What is the probability of selecting a case to analyze and finding it involved a violent crime?

    b. What is the probability of selecting a case to analyze and finding the crime was committed by someone less than 40 years old?

    c. What is the probability of selecting a case that involved a violent crime or an offender less than 20 years old? Which rule of addition did you apply?

    d. Given that a violent crime is selected for analysis, what is the probability the crime was committed by a person under 20 years old?

    e. Two crimes are selected for review by Judge Tybo. What is the probability that both are violent crimes?

72. Mr. and Mrs. Wilhelms are both retired and living in a retirement community in Arizona. Suppose the probability that a retired man will live another 10 years is .60. The probability that a retired woman will live another 10 years is .70.

    a. What is the probability that both Mr. and Mrs. Wilhelms will be alive 10 years from now?

    b. What is the probability that in 10 years Mr. Wilhelms is not living and Mrs. Wilhelms is living?

    c. What is the probability that in 10 years at least one is living?

73. Flashner Marketing Research, Inc. specializes in providing assessments of the prospects for women's apparel shops in shopping malls. Al Flashner, president, reports that he assesses the prospects as good, fair, or poor. Records from previous assessments show that 60 percent of the time the prospects were rated as good, 30 percent of the time fair, and 10 percent of the time poor. Of those rated good, 80 percent made a profit the first year; of those rated fair, 60 percent made a profit the first year; and of those rated poor, 20 percent made a profit the first year. Connie's Apparel was one of Flashner's clients. Connie's Apparel made a profit last year. What is the probability that it was given an original rating of poor?

74. There are 400 employees at G. G. Greene Manufacturing Co., and 100 of them smoke. There are 250 males working for the company, and 75 of them smoke. What is the probability that an employee selected at random:

    a. Is a male?

    b. Smokes?

    c. Is male and smokes?

    d. Is male or smokes?

75. With each purchase of a large pizza at Tony's Pizza, the customer receives a coupon that can be scratched to see if a prize will be awarded. The odds of winning a free soft drink are 1 in 10, and the odds of winning a free large pizza are 1 in 50. You plan to eat lunch tomorrow at Tony's. What is the probability:

    a. That you will win either a large pizza or a soft drink?

    b. That you will not win a prize?

    c. That you will not win a prize on three consecutive visits to Tony's?

    d. That you will win at least one prize on one of your next three visits to Tony's?

76. For the daily lottery game in Illinois, participants select three numbers between 0 and 9. A number cannot be selected more than once, so a winning ticket could be, say, 307. Purchasing one ticket allows you to select one set of numbers. The winning numbers are announced on TV each night.

    a. How many different outcomes (three-digit numbers) are possible?

    b. If you purchase a ticket for the game tonight, what is the likelihood you will win?

    c. Suppose you purchase three tickets for tonight's drawing and select a different number for each ticket. What is the probability that you will not win with any of the tickets?

77. A new job consists of assembling four different parts. All four have different color codes, and they can be assembled in any order. The production department wants to determine the most efficient way to assemble the four parts. The supervisors are going to conduct some experiments to solve the problem. First, they plan to assemble the parts in this order—green, black, yellow, and blue—and record the time. Then the assembly will be accomplished in a different order. In how many different ways can the four parts be assembled?

78. It was found that 60 percent of the tourists to China visited the Forbidden City, the Temple of Heaven, the Great Wall, and other historical sites in or near Beijing. Forty percent visited Xi'an with its magnificent terracotta soldiers, horses, and chariots, which lay buried for over 2,000 years. Thirty percent of the tourists went to both Beijing and Xi'an. What is the probability that a tourist visited at least one of these places?

79. Two boxes of men's Arrow shirts were received from the factory. Box 1 contained 25 sport shirts and 15 dress shirts. Box 2 contained 30 sport shirts and 10 dress shirts. One of the boxes was selected at random, and a shirt was chosen at random from that box to be inspected. The shirt was a sport shirt. Given this information, what is the probability that the sport shirt came from box 1?

80. The operators of Riccardo's Restaurant want to advertise that they have a large number of different meals. They offer 4 soups, 3 salads, 12 entrees, 6 vegetables, and 5 desserts. How many different meals do they offer? In addition, Riccardo's has an "early bird" special: You may omit any part of the meal except the entrees for a reduced price. How many different meals do they have for the "early birds"?

81. Several years ago Wendy's Hamburgers advertised that there are 256 different ways to order your hamburger. You may choose to have, or omit, any combination of the following on your hamburger: mustard, ketchup, onion, pickle, tomato, relish, mayonnaise, and lettuce. Is the advertisement correct? Show how you arrive at your answer.

82. Reynolds Construction Company has agreed not to erect all "look-alike" homes in a new subdivision. Five exterior designs are offered to potential home buyers. The builder has standardized three interior plans that can be incorporated in any of the five exteriors. How many different ways can the exterior and interior plans be offered to potential home buyers?

83. A small rug weaver has decided to use seven compatible colors in her new line of rugs. However, in weaving a rug, only five spindles can be used. In her advertising she wants to indicate the number of different color groupings for sale. How many color groupings using the seven colors taken five at a time are there? (This assumes that five different colors will go into each rug—i.e., there are no repetitions of color.)

84. Consideration is being given to forming a Super Ten football conference. The top 10 football teams in the country, based on past records, would be members of the Super Ten conference. Each team would play every other team in the conference during the season. The team winning the most games would be declared the national champion. How many games would the conference commissioner have to schedule each year? (Remember, Oklahoma versus Michigan is the same as Michigan versus Oklahoma.)

85. A new chewing gum has been developed that is helpful to those who want to stop smoking. If 60 percent of those people chewing the gum are successful in stopping smoking, what is the probability that in a group of four smokers using the gum at least one quits smoking?

86. The state of Maryland has license plates with three numbers followed by three letters. How many different license plates are possible?

87. A new sports car model has defective brakes 15 percent of the time and a defective steering mechanism 5 percent of the time. Let's assume (and hope) that these problems occur independently. If one or the other of these problems is present, the car is called a "lemon." If both of these problems are present, the car is a "hazard." Your instructor purchased one of these cars yesterday. What is the probability it is:
    a. A lemon?
    b. A hazard?

88. Tim Bleckie is the owner of Bleckie Investment and Real Estate Company. The company recently purchased four tracts of land in Holly Farms Estates and six tracts in Newburg Woods. The tracts are all equally desirable and sell for about the same amount.
    a. What is the probability that the next two tracts sold will be in Newburg Woods?
    b. What is the probability that of the next four sold at least one will be in Holly Farms?
    c. Are these events independent or dependent?

89. There are four people being considered for the position of chief executive officer of Dalton Enterprises. Three of the applicants are over 60 years of age. Two are female, of which only one is over 60. All four applicants are either over 60 years of age or female.

    a. What is the probability that a candidate is over 60 and female?
    b. Given that the candidate is male, what is the probability he is less than 60?
    c. Given that the person is over 60, what is the probability the person is female?

90. A case of 24 cans contains 1 can that is contaminated. Three cans are to be chosen randomly for testing.
    a. How many different combinations of 3 cans could be selected?
    b. What is the probability that the contaminated can is selected for testing?

91. The ages of drunk drivers in Ohio and whether the drunk drivers were first-time or repeat offenders are reported below. The data are reported in thousands.

Age	First-time	Repeat	Total
16–20	5.3	.5	5.8
21–25	10.7	4.1	14.8
26–30	10.3	5.7	16.0
31–35	8.2	4.3	12.5
36–40	5.4	2.6	8.0
41–45	3.5	1.7	5.2
Total	43.4	18.9	62.3

    A drunk driver is selected at random.
    a. What is the probability that the driver is a repeat offender?
    b. What is the probability that the driver is under 21 or a first-time offender?
    c. What is the probability that the driver is a repeat offender, given that the driver is over 30?
    d. Is a first-time offender or a repeat offender more likely to be over 30?
    e. What is the probability of selecting two drunk drivers and finding they are both first-time offenders?

92. Betts Electronics, Inc. purchases TV picture tubes from four different suppliers. Tyson Wholesale supplies 20 percent of the tubes, Fuji Importers 30 percent, Kirkpatricks 25 percent, and Parts, Inc. 25 percent. Tyson Wholesale tends to have the best quality, as only 3 percent of their tubes arrive defective. Fuji Importers tubes are 4 percent defective, Kirkpatricks 7 percent, and Parts, Inc. 6.5 percent defective.
    a. What is the overall (average) percent defective?
    b. A defective picture tube was discovered in the latest shipment. What is the probability that it came from Tyson Wholesale?
    c. What is the probability that the defective tube came from Fuji Importers? From Kirkpatricks? From Parts, Inc.?

93. The following diagram represents a system of two components, A and B, which are in series. (Being in series means that for the system to operate, both components A and B must work.) Suppose that the probability that A functions is .90, and the probability that B functions is also .90. Assume that these two components are independent. What is the probability that the system operates?

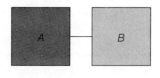

94. Refer to the system diagram above, but suppose the system works if *either* A or B works. What is the probability the system works under these conditions?

95. A puzzle in the newspaper presents a matching problem. The names of 10 U.S. presidents are listed in one column, and their vice presidents are listed in random order in the second column. The puzzle asks the reader to match each president with his vice president. If you make the matches randomly, how many matches are possible? What is the probability all 10 of your matches are correct?

96. To reduce theft, the Meredeth Company screens all its employees with a lie detector test that is known to be correct 90 percent of the time (for both guilty and innocent subjects). George Meredeth decides to fire all employees who fail the test. Suppose 5 percent of the employees are guilty of theft.
    a. What proportion of the workers are fired?
    b. Of the workers fired, what proportion are actually guilty?
    c. Of the workers not fired, what proportion are guilty?
    d. What do you think of George's policy?

97. Peterson's Vitamins, an advertiser in the magazine *Healthy Living,* estimates that 1 percent of the subscribers will buy vitamins from Peterson's. They also estimate that 0.5 percent of nonsubscribers will buy the product and that there is one chance in 20 that a person is a subscriber.
    a. Find the probability that a randomly selected person will buy the vitamins.
    b. If a person buys the vitamins, what is the probability he subscribes to *Healthy Living*?
    c. If a person does not buy the vitamins, what is the probability she subscribes to *Healthy Living*?

98. ABC Auto Insurance classifies drivers as good, medium, or poor risks. Drivers who apply to them for insurance fall into these three groups in the proportions: 30%, 50%, and 20%, respectively. The probability a "good" driver will have an accident is 0.01, the probability a "medium" risk driver will have an accident is 0.03, and the probability a "poor" driver will have an accident is 0.10. The company sells Mr. Brophy an insurance policy and he has an accident. What is the probability Mr. Brophy is:
    a. A "good" driver?   b. A "medium" risk driver?   c. A "poor" driver?

99. A hospital administrator is looking over the Knox County Medical Society survey of its members, which records their gender and age. The following table summarizes the results.

	Under 35	Between 35 and 54	Over 54	Total
Male	27	87	26	140
Female	14	25	3	42
Total	41	112	29	182

If you randomly select a member of the society, what is the probability they are:
    a. Male?
    b. Between the ages of 35 and 54?
    c. Both male and between the ages of 35 and 54?
    d. Both female and over 54?
    e. Either male or between the ages of 35 and 54?
    f. Either female or over 54?
    g. Male, given that they are under 35?
    h. Male, given that they are over 54?
    i. Over 54, given that they are male?
    j. Over 54, given that they are female?
    k. Are the events "male" and "between the ages of 35 and 54" independent?
    l. Are the events "female" and "over 54" independent?
    m. Are the events "male" and "over 54" mutually exclusive?
    n. Are the events "female" and "male" mutually exclusive?

▌ Computer Data Exercises

100. Refer to Data Set 1, which reports information on homes sold in the Venice, Florida, area during the last year.
    a. Sort the data into a table that shows the number of homes that have a pool versus the number that don't have a pool in each of the five townships. If a home is selected at random, compute the following probabilities.
        (1) The home is in Township 1 or has a pool.
        (2) Given that it is in Township 3, that it has a pool.
        (3) Has a pool and is in Township 3.
    b. Sort the data into a table that shows the number of homes that have a garage versus those that don't have a garage in each of the five townships. If a home is selected at random, compute the following probabilities:
        (1) The home has a garage.
        (2) Given that it is in Township 5, that it does not have a garage.
        (3) The home has a garage and is in Township 3.
        (4) Does not have a garage or is in Township 2.
101. Refer to Data Set 2, which reports information on the 28 Major League Baseball teams for the 1997 season. Set up a variable that divides the teams into two groups, those that had a winning season and those that did not. That is, create a variable to count the teams that won 81 games or more, and those that won 80 or less. Next create a new variable for attendance, using three categories: attendance less than 1,500,000 (shown in the data as 1.5), attendance of 1.5 million up to 2.5 million, and attendance of 2.5 million or more.
    a. Create a table that shows the number of teams with a winning season versus those with a losing season by the three categories of attendance. If a team is selected at random, compute the following probabilities:
        (1) Having a winning season.
        (2) Having a winning season or attendance of more than 2.5 million.
        (3) Given attendance of more than 2.5 million, having a winning season.
        (4) Having a losing season and drawing less than 1.5 million.
    b. Create a table that shows the number of teams that play on artificial turf fields by winning and losing records. If a team is selected at random, compute the following probabilities:
        (1) Selecting a team with a home field that is turf.
        (2) Is the likelihood of selecting a team with a winning record larger for teams with grass or turf fields?
        (3) Having a winning record or playing on a turf field.
102. Refer to Data Set 3, which reports information on the circulation of 48 magazines. First, set up a variable that divides the magazines into two groups: those that have male readership of 50 percent or more and those that have less than 50 percent male readership. Create a second variable that divides the circulation into magazines with less than 3,000 (remember, this is in thousands) and those with 3,000 or more. If a magazine is randomly selected, what is the probability that:
    a. More than half the readers are male?
    b. More than half the readers are male and the circulation is 3,000 or more?
    c. More than half the readers are male or the circulation is 3,000 or more?
    d. Given that the circulation is 3,000 or more, more than half the readers are male?
103. Refer to Data Set 4, which refers to 94 school districts in Northwest Ohio.
    a. Group the districts based on the percent of students on welfare: "low" (less than 5 percent), "moderate" (between 5 and 10 percent, inclusive), and "high" (more than 10 percent).

    (1)   A school district is randomly selected. Then a student within that district is chosen. What is the probability the student passed the proficiency exam?

    (2)   If it is a "low" welfare district, what is the probability the student passed the exam?

    (3)   What is the probability the student is from a "high" welfare district and passes the exam?

    (4)   Find the probability the student is either from a "moderate" welfare district or failed the exam.

b.   Now arrange the districts by size: "small" (less than 1,000 students), "medium" (between 1,000 and 3,000 students), or "large" (more than 3,000 students).

    (1)   What percent of the districts are "small"?

    (2)   If a district is "small," estimate the probability it is a "low" welfare district.

    (3)   What percent of the districts are both "small" and "low" welfare?

    (4)   What percent are either "small" or "low" welfare?

    (5)   If three districts are randomly chosen, what is the probability they are all "medium" sized?

CHAPTER 5 *Answers to Self-Review*

5–1 (a) Testing of the new computer game.
(b) Seventy-three players liked the game.
(c) No. Probability cannot be greater than 1. The probability that the game, if put on the market, will be successful is $^{65}/_{80}$, or .8125.
(d) Cannot be less than 0. Perhaps a mistake in arithmetic.
(e) More than half of the persons testing the game liked it. (Of course, other answers are possible.)

5–2 1. $\dfrac{4 \text{ queens in deck}}{52 \text{ cards total}} = \dfrac{4}{52} = .0769$
Classical.

2. $\dfrac{24}{883} = .027$ Empirical.

3. The author's view of the chance that the DJIA will climb to 10,000 is .25. You may be more optimistic or less optimistic.
Subjective.

5–3 (a) (i) $\dfrac{(50 + 68)}{2,000} = 0.059$

(ii) $1 - \dfrac{302}{2,000} = 0.849$

(b)

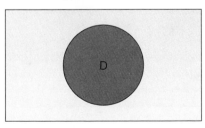

(c) They are not complementary, but are mutually exclusive.

5–4 (a) Need for corrective shoes is event *A*. Need for major dental work is event *B*.

$$P(A \text{ or } B) = P(A) + P(B) - P(A \text{ and } B)$$
$$= .08 + .15 - .03$$
$$= .20$$

(b) One possibility is:

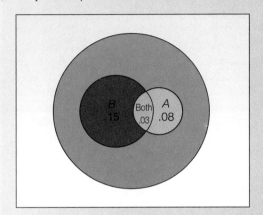

5–5 1. $(.80)(.80)(.80)(.80) = .4096$.
2. (a) .0000156, found by: $(.025)(.025)(.025)$.
(b) The chance of selecting three bags and finding them all underweight is rather remote.

5–6 (a) .002, found by:

$$\left(\frac{4}{12}\right)\left(\frac{3}{11}\right)\left(\frac{2}{10}\right)\left(\frac{1}{9}\right) = \frac{24}{11,880} = .002$$

(b) .14, found by:

$$\left(\frac{8}{12}\right)\left(\frac{7}{11}\right)\left(\frac{6}{10}\right)\left(\frac{5}{9}\right) = \frac{1,680}{11,880} = .1414$$

(c) No, because there are other possibilities, such as three women and one man.

5–7 $P(A \text{ and } B) = P(A)P(B \mid A)$

$$= \left(\frac{80}{200}\right)\left(\frac{25}{80}\right) = .125$$

5–8 1. Go out from the tree trunk on the lower branch, "would not remain." The probability of that event is 80/200. Continuing on the same path, find the branch labeled "6–10 years." The conditional probability is 10/80. To get the joint probability:

$$P(A \text{ and } B) = \left(\frac{80}{200}\right)\left(\frac{10}{80}\right)$$

$$= \frac{800}{16,000} = .05$$

2. (a) Contingency table.

(b)

Employee	Plans		Joint
	$\frac{5}{20}$ Retire	$\left(\frac{20}{100}\right)\left(\frac{5}{20}\right) = \frac{100}{2,000}$	$= .05$
$\frac{20}{100}$ Management	$\frac{15}{20}$ Not retire	$\left(\frac{20}{100}\right)\left(\frac{15}{20}\right) = \frac{300}{2,000}$	$= .15$
$\frac{80}{100}$ Production	$\frac{30}{80}$ Retire	$\left(\frac{80}{100}\right)\left(\frac{30}{80}\right) = \frac{2,400}{8,000}$	$= .30$
	$\frac{50}{80}$ Not retire	$\left(\frac{80}{100}\right)\left(\frac{50}{80}\right) = \frac{4,000}{8,000}$	$= .50$

(c) Yes, all possibilities are included.

5–9 (a) $P(A_3 \mid B_2) = \dfrac{P(A_3)P(B_2 \mid A_3)}{P(A_1)P(B_2 \mid A_1) + P(A_2)P(B_2 \mid A_2) + P(A_3)P(B_2 \mid A_3)}$

$$= \frac{.50(.96)}{(.30)(.97) + (.20)(.95) + (.50)(.96)}$$

$$= \frac{.480}{.961} = .499$$

5–10 1. There 20, found by $(5)(4)$
2. There are 72, found by $(3)(2)(4)(3)$

5–11 1. (a) 60, found by $(5)(4)(3)$.
(b) 60, found by:

$$\frac{5!}{(5-3)!} = \frac{5 \cdot 4 \cdot 3 \cdot \cancel{2 \cdot 1}}{\cancel{2 \cdot 1}}$$

2. 24, found by:

$$\frac{4!}{(4-4)!} = \frac{4!}{0!} = \frac{4!}{1} = \frac{4 \cdot 3 \cdot 2 \cdot 1}{1}$$

3. 5,040, found by:

$$\frac{10!}{(10-4)!} = \frac{10 \cdot 9 \cdot 8 \cdot 7 \cdot \cancel{6 \cdot 5 \cdot 4 \cdot 3 \cdot 2 \cdot 1}}{\cancel{6 \cdot 5 \cdot 4 \cdot 3 \cdot 2 \cdot 1}}$$

5–12 (a) 56 is correct, found by:

$$_8C_3 = \frac{n!}{r!(n-r)!} = \frac{8!}{3!(8-3)!} = 56$$

(b) Yes. There are 45 combinations, found by:

$$_{10}C_2 = \frac{n!}{r!(n-r)!} = \frac{10!}{2!(10-2)!} = 45$$

Chapter Six

Discrete Probability Distributions

GOALS

When you have completed this chapter, you will be able to:

ONE
Define the terms *probability distribution* and *random variable.*

TWO
Distinguish between discrete and continuous probability distributions.

THREE
Calculate the mean, variance, and standard deviation of a discrete probability distribution.

FOUR
Describe the characteristics and compute probablities using the binomial probability distribution.

FIVE
Describe the characteristics and compute probabilities using the hypergeometric distribution.

SIX
Describe the characteristics and compute probabilities using the Poisson distribution.

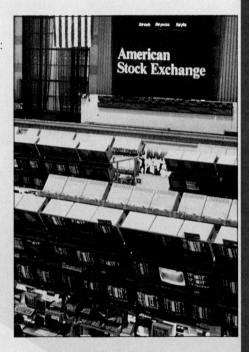

According to the "January theory," if the stock market is up for the month of January, it will be up for the year. If it is down, it will be down for the year. This theory has held for 29 of the last 34 years. If the theory is false, what is the probability this could happen by chance? (See Goal 4 and Exercise 58.)

▌ Introduction

Chapters 2 through 4 were devoted to descriptive statistics. We described raw data by organizing them into a frequency distribution and portraying the distribution in charts. Also, we computed a measure of central tendency—such as the arithmetic mean, median, or mode—to locate a typical value near the center of the distribution. The range and the standard deviation were used to describe the spread in the data. These chapters focused on describing *something that has already happened.*

Starting with Chapter 5, the emphasis changed—we began examining *something that would probably happen.* We noted that this facet of statistics is called *statistical inference.* The objective is to make inferences (statements) about a population based on a small number of observations, called a sample, selected from the population. In Chapter 5, we stated that a probability is a value between 0 and 1 inclusive, and we examined how probabilities can be combined using rules of addition and multiplication.

This chapter will begin the study of **probability distributions.** A probability distribution gives the entire range of values that can occur based on an experiment. A probability distribution is similar to a frequency distribution. However, instead of describing the past, it describes how likely some future event is. For example, a drug manufacturer may claim a treatment will cause weight loss for 80 percent of the population. A consumer protection agency may test the treatment on a sample of six people. If the manufacturer's claim is true, it is *almost impossible* to have an outcome where no one in the sample loses weight and it is *most likely* that 5 out of the 6 do lose weight.

The mean, variance, and standard deviation for probability distributions as well as three frequently occurring families of probability distributions (the binomial, hypergeometric, and Poisson) are also presented in this chapter.

▌ What Is a Probability Distribution?

A probability distribution shows the possible outcomes of an experiment and the probability of each of these outcomes.

▏ **Probability Distribution**   A listing of all the outcomes of an experiment and ▕
▏ the probability associated with each outcome.

How can we generate a probability distribution?

Example

Suppose we are interested in the number of heads showing face up on three tosses of a coin. This is the experiment. The possible results are: zero heads, one head, two heads, and three heads. What is the probability distribution for the number of heads?

Solution

There are eight possible outcomes. A tail might appear face up on the first toss, another tail on the second toss, and another tail on the third toss of the coin. Or we might get a tail, tail, and head, in that order.

| Possible | Coin Toss | | | Number of |
Result	First	Second	Third	Heads
1	T	T	T	0
2	T	T	H	1
3	T	H	T	1
4	T	H	H	2

Possible Result	Coin Toss			Number of Heads
	First	Second	Third	
5	H	T	T	1
6	H	T	H	2
7	H	H	T	2
8	H	H	H	3

Note that the outcome "zero heads" occurred only once, "one head" occurred three times, "two heads" occurred three times, and the outcome "three heads" occurred only once. That is, "zero heads" happened one out of eight times. Thus, the probability of zero heads is one eighth, the probability of one head is three eighths, and so on. The distribution of probabilities is shown in Table 6–1. Note that the total of the probabilities of all possible events is 1.000. This is always true. The same information can be shown using a chart. (See Chart 6–1.)

Table 6–1 Probability Distribution for the Events of Zero, One, Two, and Three Heads Showing Face Up on Three Tosses of a Coin

Number of Heads, x	Probability of Outcome, $P(x)$
0	$\frac{1}{8}$ = .125
1	$\frac{3}{8}$ = .375
2	$\frac{3}{8}$ = .375
3	$\frac{1}{8}$ = .125
Total	$\frac{8}{8}$ = 1.000

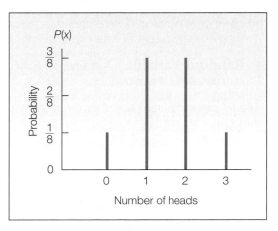

Chart 6–1 Graphical Presentation of the Number of Heads Resulting from Three Tosses of a Coin and the Corresponding Probability

Characteristics of a probability distribution

Before continuing, we should note two important characteristics of a probability distribution.

1. The probability of a particular outcome must always be between 0 and 1, inclusive. (The probabilities of *x,* written *P(x)* in the coin tossing example, were .125, .375, etc.)
2. The sum of the probabilities of all mutually exclusive outcomes is 1.000. (Referring to Table 6–1, .125 + .375 + .375 + .125 = 1.000.)

SELF-REVIEW 6–1

The possible outcomes of an experiment involving the roll of a six-sided die are: a one-spot, a two-spot, a three-spot, a four-spot, a five-spot, and a six-spot.

(a) Develop a probability distribution for these outcomes.
(b) Portray the probability distribution graphically.
(c) What is the total of the probabilities?

▌ Random Variables

In any experiment of chance, the outcomes occur randomly. For example, rolling a single die is an experiment: any one of six possible outcomes can occur. Some experiments result in outcomes that are quantitative (such as dollars, weight, or number of children), and others result in qualitative outcomes (such as color or religious preference). A few examples will further illustrate what is meant by a **random variable.**

- If we count the number of employees absent from the day shift on Monday, the number might be 0, 1, 2, 3, ... The number absent is the random variable.
- If we weigh a steel ingot, it might be 2,500 pounds, 2,500.1 pounds, 2,500.13 pounds, and so on, depending on the accuracy of the scale. The weight is the random variable.
- If we toss two coins and count the number of heads, there could be zero, one, or two heads. Because the exact number of heads resulting from this experiment is due to chance, the number of heads appearing is the random variable.
- Other random variables might be: the number of defective light bulbs produced during the week, the heights of the members of the girls' basketball team, the number of runners in the Boston Marathon, and the daily number of drivers charged with driving under the influence of alcohol in Texas.

▐ **Random Variable**   A quantity resulting from an experiment that, by chance, can assume different values. ▐

The following diagram illustrates these three related terms: outcome, event, and random variable.

Possible *outcomes* for three coin tosses

The *event* {one head} occurs and the *random variable x* = 1.

A random variable may be either *discrete* or *continuous.*

Discrete Random Variable

A discrete random variable can assume only a certain number of separated values. If there are 100 employees, then the count of the number absent on Monday can only be 0, 1, 2, 3, . . . , 100. A discrete random variable is usually the result of counting something. By way of a definition:

> **Discrete Random Variable** A variable that can assume only certain clearly separated values resulting from a count of some item of interest.

It should be noted that a discrete variable can, in some cases, assume fractional or decimal values. These values must be separated, that is, have distance between them. As an example, the scores awarded by judges for technical competence and artistic form in figure skating are decimal values, such as 7.2, 8.9, and 9.7. Such values are discrete because there is a distance between scores of, say, 8.3 and 8.4. A score cannot be 8.34 or 8.347, for example.

Continuous Random Variable

If we measure something such as the width of a room, the height of a person, or the outside diameter of a bushing, the variable is called a *continuous random variable.* It can assume one of an infinitely large number of values, within certain limitations. As examples:

- The distance between Atlanta and Los Angeles could be 2,254 miles, 2,254.1 miles, 2,254.162 miles, and so on, depending on the accuracy of our measuring device.
- Tire pressure could be 28 pounds per square inch (psi), 28.6 psi, 28.62 psi, 28.624 psi, and so on, depending on the accuracy of the gauge.

Logically, if we organize a set of discrete random variables in a probability distribution, the distribution is called a **discrete probability distribution.**

The tools used, as well as the probability interpretations, are different for discrete and continuous random variables. This chapter is limited to the discrete probability distributions. The next chapter will address one important example of continuous probability distributions.

▌ The Mean, Variance, and Standard Deviation of a Probability Distribution

In Chapters 3 and 4, measures of location and variation were discussed for a frequency distribution. The mean reports the central location of the data, and the variance describes the spread in the data. In a similar fashion, a probability distribution is summarized by its mean and variance. The mean of a probability distribution is denoted by the lower-case Greek letter mu (μ) and the standard deviation by the square of the lower-case Greek letter sigma (σ).

Mean

The mean is a typical value used to represent a probability distribution. It also is the long-run average value of the random variable. The mean of a probability distribution is also referred to as its expected value, $E(x)$. It is a weighted average where the possible values are weighted by their corresponding probabilities of occurrence.

The mean of a discrete probability distribution is computed by the formula:

MEAN OF A PROBABILITY DISTRIBUTION	$\mu = E(x) = \Sigma[xP(x)]$	**[6–1]**

where $P(x)$ is the probability of the possible values of the random variable x. In other words, multiply each x value by its probability of occurrence, and then add these products.

Variance and Standard Deviation

As noted, the mean is a typical value used to represent a discrete probability distribution. However, it does not describe the amount of spread (variation) in a distribution. The variance does this. As explained in Chapter 4, a comparison of two variances allows you to compare the variation in two distributions having the same mean but different spreads. The formula for the variance of a probability distribution is:

VARIANCE OF A PROBABILITY DISTRIBUTION	$\sigma^2 = \Sigma[(x - \mu)^2 P(x)]$	**[6–2]**

The computational steps are:

1. Subtract the mean from each value, and square this difference.
2. Multiply each squared difference by its probability.
3. Sum the resulting products to arrive at the variance.

The standard deviation, σ, is found by taking the square root of σ^2; that is, $\sigma = \sqrt{\sigma^2}$.

Example

John Ragsdale sells new cars for Pelican Ford. John usually sells the largest number of cars on Saturday. He has established the following probability distribution for the number of cars he expects to sell on a particular Saturday.

Number of Cars Sold, x	Probability, $P(x)$
0	.10
1	.20
2	.30
3	.30
4	.10
Total	1.00

1. What type of distribution is this?
2. On a typical Saturday, how many cars should John expect to sell?
3. What is the variance of the distribution?

Solution

1. This is an example of a discrete probability distribution. Note that John expects to sell only within a certain range of cars; he does not expect to sell 5 cars or 50 cars. Further, he cannot sell half a car. He can sell only 0, 1, 2, 3, or 4 cars. Also, the outcomes are mutually exclusive—he cannot sell a total of both 3 and 4 cars on the same Saturday.
2. The mean number of cars sold is computed by weighting the number of cars sold by the probability of selling that number and totaling the products using formula (6–1):

$$\mu = E(x) = \Sigma[xP(x)]$$

$$= 0(.10) + 1(.20) + 2(.30) + 3(.30) + 4(.10)$$

$$= 2.1$$

These calculations are summarized in the following table.

Number of Cars Sold, x	Probability, P(x)	x · P(x)
0	.10	0.00
1	.20	0.20
2	.30	0.60
3	.30	0.90
4	.10	0.40
Total	1.00	E(x) = 2.10

How do we interpret a mean of 2.1? This value indicates that, over a large number of Saturdays, John Ragsdale expects to sell a mean of 2.1 cars a day. (Of course, it is not possible for him to sell *exactly* 2.1 cars on any particular Saturday.) Thus, the mean is sometimes called the expected value.

3. Again, a table is useful for systemizing the computations for the variance, which is 1.290.

Number of Cars Sold, x	Probability, P(x)	$(x - \mu)$	$(x - \mu)^2$	$(x - \mu)^2 P(x)$
0	.10	0 − 2.1	4.41	0.441
1	.20	1 − 2.1	1.21	0.242
2	.30	2 − 2.1	0.01	0.003
3	.30	3 − 2.1	0.81	0.243
4	.10	4 − 2.1	3.61	0.361
				$\sigma^2 = 1.290$

Recall that the standard deviation, σ, is the square root of the variance. In this problem, $\sqrt{\sigma^2} = \sqrt{1.290} = 1.136$ cars. How do we interpret a standard deviation of 1.136 cars? If salesperson Rita Kirsch also sold a mean of 2.1 cars on Saturdays, and the standard deviation in her sales was 1.91 cars, we would conclude that there is more variability in the Saturday sales of Ms. Kirsch than in those of Mr. Ragsdale (because 1.91 > 1.136).

Here is an alternative formula for the variance of a discrete probability distribution. It has the advantage that it avoids most of the subtractions:

$$\sigma^2 = \Sigma x^2 P(x) - \mu^2$$

For the Ragsdale data, we have:

x	x^2	P(x)	$x^2 P(x)$
0	0	.1	0.00
1	1	.2	0.20
2	4	.3	1.20
3	9	.3	2.70
4	16	.1	1.60
			5.70

The variance using the above formula is: $\sigma^2 = \Sigma x^2 P(x) - \mu^2 = 5.70 - (2.1)^2 = 1.29$, which is the same value we found before.

SELF-REVIEW 6–2

The Pizza Palace offers three sizes of cola—small, medium, and large—to go with its pizza. The colas are sold for 50 cents, 75 cents, and 90 cents, respectively. Thirty percent of the orders are for small, 50 percent are for medium, and 20 percent are for the large sizes. Organize the size of the colas and the probability of a sale into a probability distribution.

(a) Is this a discrete probability distribution? Indicate why or why not.
(b) Compute the mean amount charged for a cola.
(c) What is the variance in the amount charged for a cola? The standard deviation?

Exercises

1. Compute the mean and variance of the following discrete probability distribution.

x	P(x)
0	.20
1	.40
2	.30
3	.10

2. Compute the mean and variance of the following discrete probability distribution.

x	P(x)
2	.50
8	.30
10	.20

3. Three tables listed below show "random variables" and their "probabilities." However, only one of these is actually a probability distribution.
   a. Which is it?

x	P(x)		x	P(x)		x	P(x)
5	.3		5	.1		5	.5
10	.3		10	.3		10	.3
15	.2		15	.2		15	−.2
20	.4		20	.4		20	.4

   b. Using the correct probability distribution, find that the probability x is:
      (1) Exactly 15.   (2) No more than 10.   (3) More than 5.
   c. Compute the mean, variance, and standard deviation of this distribution.
4. Which of these variables are discrete?
   a. The number of new accounts established by a salesperson in a year.
   b. The time between customer arrivals to a bank ATM.
   c. The number of customers in Big Nick's barber shop.
   d. The amount of fuel in your car's gas tank.
   e. The number of minorities on a jury.
   f. The outside temperature today.

5. Dan Woodward is the owner and manager of Dan's Truck Stop. Dan offers free refills on all coffee orders. He gathered the following information on the number of coffee refills. Compute the mean, variance, and standard deviation for the distribution of number of refills.

Refills	Percent
0	30
1	40
2	20
3	10

6. The director of admissions at Kinzua University in Nova Scotia estimated the student admissions for the fall semester based on past experience. What is the expected number of admissions for the fall semester? Compute the variance and the standard deviation.

Admissions	Probability
1,000	.60
1,200	.30
1,500	.10

7. The following table lists the probability distribution for cash prizes in a lottery conducted at Lawson's Department Store.

Prize ($)	Probability
0	.45
10	.30
100	.20
500	.05

If you buy a single ticket, what is the probability that you win:
a. Exactly $100?   b. At least $10?   c. No more than $100?
d. Compute the mean, variance, and standard deviation of this distribution.

8. You are asked to match three songs with the performers who made those songs famous. If you guess, the probability distribution for the number of correct matches is:

Probability	.333	.500	0	.167
Number correct	0	1	2	3

What is the probability you get:
a. Exactly one correct?   b. At least one correct?   c. Exactly two correct?
d. Compute the mean, variance, and standard deviation of this distribution.

9. A group of 3 people is drawn at random from a pool of 10 that includes 4 minorities. You are interested in the number of minorities in the group.
a. What are the possible values of this random variable?
b. Find the probability distribution for this random variable.
c. What is the probability you have: exactly one? at least one? two or more?
d. Compute the mean, variance, and standard deviation of this number.

10. A fair coin is tossed until the first time a tail comes up or until three heads occur.
a. What is the probability distribution for the number of tosses until this process ends?
b. Find its mean and standard deviation.
c. What is the probability the number of tosses required is more than one?

▌ Binomial Probability Distribution

The **binomial probability distribution** is an example of a discrete probability distribution. One characteristic of a binomial distribution is that there are only two possible outcomes on a particular trial of an experiment. For example, the statement in a true/false question is either true or false. The outcomes are *mutually exclusive,* meaning that the answer to a true/false question cannot be both true and false at the same time. As other examples, a product is classified as either acceptable or not acceptable by the quality control department, a worker is classified as employed or unemployed, and a sales call results in the customer either purchasing the product or not purchasing the product. Frequently, we classify the two possible outcomes as "success" and "failure." However, this classification does *not* imply that one outcome is good and the other is bad.

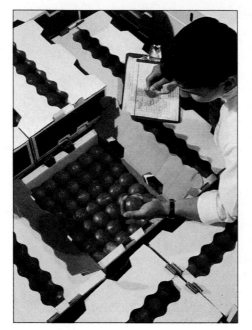

Another characteristic of the binomial distribution is that the random variable is the result of counts. That is, we count the number of successes in the total number of trials. We flip a fair coin five times and count the number of times a head appears; we select 10 workers and count the number who are over 60 years old, or we select 20 boxes of Kellogg's Raisin Bran and count the number that weigh more than the amount indicated on the package.

Another characteristic of a binomial distribution is that the probability of a success remains the same from one trial to another. Examples:

- The probability that you will guess the first question of a true/false test correctly (a success) is one half. This is the first "trial." The probability that you will guess right on the second question (the second trial) is also one half, the probability of success on the third trial is one half, and so on.
- If past experience revealed that the drawbridge over the Gulf Intracoastal Waterway was raised one out of every five times you approach it, then the probability is one fifth that it will be raised (a success) the next time you approach it, one fifth the following time, and so on.

The final characteristic of a binomial probability distribution is that one trial is *independent* of any other trial. This means that there is no rhythmic pattern with respect to the outcomes. As an example, the answers to a true/false test are not arranged T, T, T, F, F, F, T, T, T, and so forth.

A binomial distribution has these characteristics.

In summary, a binomial distribution has these characteristics:

1. An outcome on each trial of an experiment is classified into one of two mutually exclusive categories—a success or a failure.
2. The random variable is the result of counting the number of successes in a fixed number of trials.

3. The probability of a success stays the same for each trial. So does the probability of a failure.
4. The trials are independent, meaning that the outcome of one trial does not affect the outcome of any other trial.

How Is a Binomial Probability Distribution Constructed?

To construct a particular binomial probability distribution, we must know (1) the number of trials and (2) the probability of success on each trial. For example, if an examination at the conclusion of a management seminar consists of 20 multiple-choice questions, the number of trials is 20. If each question has five choices and only one choice is correct, the probability of success for a person with no knowledge of the subject on each trial is .20. Thus, the probability is .20 that a person with no knowledge of the subject matter will guess the answer to a question correctly. So the conditions of the binomial distribution just noted are met.

The binomial probability distribution can be described using the formula:

BINOMIAL PROBABILITY DISTRIBUTION	$P(x) = \dfrac{n!}{x!\,(n-x)!}\,\pi^x\,(1-\pi)^{n-x}$	**[6–3]**

where:

n is the number of trials.

x is the number of successes.

π is the probability of a success on each trial.

Note that we use the Greek letter π to denote a population parameter. Do not confuse it with the mathematical constant 3.1416.

Example

As we all know, the answer to a true/false question is either correct or incorrect. Assume that (1) an examination consists of four true/false questions and (2) a student has no knowledge of the subject matter. The chance (probability) that the student will guess the correct answer to the first question is .50. Likewise, the probability of guessing each of the remaining questions correctly is .50. What is the probability of:

1. Getting exactly none of four correct?
2. Getting exactly one of four correct?

Solution

1. The probability of guessing none of the four correctly is .0625, found by applying formula (6–3). (Recall from Chapter 5 that 0! is equal to 1.)

$$P(0) = \frac{4!}{0!(4-0)!}\,(.50)^0(1-.50)^{4-0} = .0625$$

2. The probability of getting exactly one of four correct is .2500, found by:

$$P(1) = \frac{4!}{1!(4-1)!}\,(.50)^1(1-.50)^{4-1} = .2500$$

The probabilities of getting exactly zero, one, two, three, and four true/false questions correct out of a total of four questions are shown in Table 6–2.

Table 6–2 Binomial Probability Distribution for $n = 4$, $\pi = .50$

Number of Correct Guesses	Probability Fraction	Probability Decimal
0	$\frac{1}{16}$	.0625
1	$\frac{4}{16}$	.2500
2	$\frac{6}{16}$	.3750
3	$\frac{4}{16}$	.2500
4	$\frac{1}{16}$	.0625
Total	$\frac{16}{16}$	1.000

The random variable in Table 6–2 is plotted in Chart 6–2. Note that this distribution is symmetrical. This is always the case when π, the probability of a success, is .50.

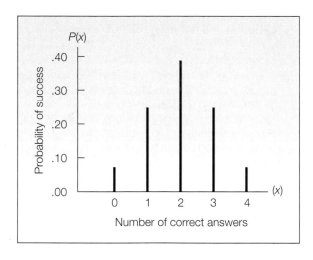

Chart 6–2 Binomial Probability Distribution for $n = 4$, $\pi = .50$

Using Binomial Probability Tables

Binomial table: Quick way of determining a probability

A binomial probability distribution is a theoretical distribution that, as has been shown, can be generated mathematically. However, except for problems involving small n (say, $n = 3$ or 4), the calculations for the probabilities of 0, 1, 2, . . . successes can be rather tedious. As an aid in finding the needed probabilities, an extensive table has been developed that gives the probabilities of 0, 1, 2, 3, . . . successes for various values of n and π. This table is in Appendix A, and a small portion of the table needed for the following example is shown in Table 6–3.

Table 6–3 Binomial Probabilities for $n = 6$

x	.05	.1	.2	.3	.4	.5	.6	.7	.8	.9	.95
0	.735	.531	.262	.118	.047	.016	.004	.001	.000	.000	.000
1	.232	.354	.393	.303	.187	.094	.037	.010	.002	.000	.000
2	.031	.098	.246	.324	.311	.234	.138	.060	.015	.001	.000
3	.002	.015	.082	.185	.276	.313	.276	.185	.082	.015	.002
4	.000	.001	.015	.060	.138	.234	.311	.324	.246	.098	.031
5	.000	.000	.002	.010	.037	.094	.187	.303	.393	.354	.232
6	.000	.000	.000	.001	.004	.016	.047	.118	.262	.531	.735

Example

Based on recent experience, 5 percent of the worm gears produced by an automatic, high-speed Carter-Bell milling machine are defective. What is the probability that out of six gears selected at random, exactly zero gears will be defective? Exactly one? Exactly two? Exactly three? Exactly four? Exactly five? Exactly six out of six? (Note: $n = 6$, $\pi = .05$).

Solution

Note that the binomial conditions are met: (1) There is a constant probability of success (.05), (2) there is a fixed number of trials (6), (3) the trials are independent, and (4) there are only two possible outcomes (a particular gear is either defective or acceptable).

Refer to Table 6–3 for the probability of exactly zero defective gears. Go down the left margin to an x of 0. Now move horizontally to the column headed by a π of .05 to find the probability. It is .735.

The probability of exactly one defective in a sample of six worm gears is .232. The complete binomial probability distribution for $n = 6$ and $\pi = .05$ is:

Number of Defective Gears, x	Probability of Occurrence, P(x)	Number of Defective Gears, x	Probability of Occurrence, P(x)
0	.735	4	.000
1	.232	5	.000
2	.031	6	.000
3	.002		

Of course, there is a slight chance of getting exactly five defective gears out of six random selections. It is .00000178, found by inserting the appropriate values in the binomial formula:

$$P(5) = \frac{6!}{5!(6-5)!}(.05)^5(.95)^1$$

$$= (6)(.05)^5(.95) = .00000178$$

For six out of the six, the probability is .000000016. Thus, the probability is very small that five or six defective gears will be selected in a sample of six.

This problem can also be solved on the MINITAB system. The output is as follows:

```
MTB > PDF c1;
SUBC>   Binomial 6 .05.
         K              P( X = K)
        0.00              0.7351
        1.00              0.2321
        2.00              0.0305
        3.00              0.0021
        4.00              0.0001
        5.00              0.0000
```

The output is the same as in Table 6–3 except for the difference in the number of digits after the decimal.

SELF-REVIEW 6–3

The Florida Tourism Agency reports a particular drawbridge over the Gulf Intracoastal Waterway is in the raised position, blocking vehicular traffic, 20 percent of the time. You are going to drive this route once each day for the next seven days and are interested in predicting the number of days on which the drawbridge will be raised when you approach.

(a) Does this situation fit the assumptions of the binomial probability distribution?
(b) Without the aid of formula (6–3) or the table in Appendix A, compute the probability the bridge will be raised every time you approach it.
(c) Use formula (6–3) to find the probability it will be raised on exactly three of your seven trips.
(d) Use formula (6–3) to find the probability it will be raised exactly once.
(e) Use the binomial probability table in Appendix A to verify your answers to parts (b), (c), and (d).

Appendix A is somewhat limited in that it gives probabilities only for n values of 1 to 20 and 25 and π values of .05, .10, .20, . . . , .95. There are two methods for arriving at a binomial distribution for an n over 25 or a π not found in the table (say, .07): (1) The normal approximation to the binomial may be used. This will be presented in Chapter 7. (2) A computer can generate the probabilities for a specified number of successes, given an n and a π. To illustrate, the following are two MINITAB outputs—one for an n of 40 and a π of .09, and the other for an n of 27 and a π of .376.

```
MTB > set c1
DATA>    1( 0 : 13 / 1 )1
DATA>    End.
MTB > PDF c1;
SUBC>    Binomial 40 .09.
         K              P( X = K)
        0.00             0.0230
        1.00             0.0910
        2.00             0.1754
        3.00             0.2198
        4.00             0.2011
        5.00             0.1432
        6.00             0.0826
        7.00             0.0397
        8.00             0.0162
        9.00             0.0057
       10.00             0.0017
       11.00             0.0005
       12.00             0.0001
       13.00             0.0000
```

```
MTB > PDF c1;
SUBC>    Binomial 27 .376.
         K              P( X = K)
        1.00             0.0000
        2.00             0.0004
        3.00             0.0019
        4.00             0.0068
        5.00             0.0189
        6.00             0.0418
        7.00             0.0756
        8.00             0.1139
        9.00             0.1448
       10.00             0.1571
       11.00             0.1463
       12.00             0.1175
       13.00             0.0817
       14.00             0.0492
       15.00             0.0257
       16.00             0.0116
       17.00             0.0045
       18.00             0.0015
       19.00             0.0004
       20.00             0.0001
       21.00             0.0000
```

As π approaches .50, the binomial distribution becomes more symmetrical.

Several additional points should be made about binomial distributions:

1. If n remains the same but π increases from .05 to .95, the shape of the distribution changes. Note in Table 6–4 that the probabilities for a π of .05 are positively skewed. As π approaches .50, the distribution approaches a symmetrical distribution. As π goes beyond .50 and moves toward .95, the probability distribution becomes negatively skewed. Table 6–4 gives probabilities for $n = 10$ and probabilities of success of .05, .10, .20, .50, and .70. The plots of these values are shown in Chart 6–3.

Table 6–4 Probability of 0, 1, 2, . . . Successes for a π of .05, .10, .20, .50, and .70 and an n of 10

x	.05	.1	.2	.3	.4	.5	.6	.7	.8	.9	.95
0	.599	.349	.107	.028	.006	.001	.000	.000	.000	.000	.000
1	.315	.387	.268	.121	.040	.010	.002	.000	.000	.000	.000
2	.075	.194	.302	.233	.121	.044	.011	.001	.000	.000	.000
3	.010	.057	.201	.267	.215	.117	.042	.009	.001	.000	.000
4	.001	.011	.088	.200	.251	.205	.111	.037	.006	.000	.000
5	.000	.001	.026	.103	.201	.246	.201	.103	.026	.001	.000
6	.000	.000	.006	.037	.111	.205	.251	.200	.088	.011	.001
7	.000	.000	.001	.009	.042	.117	.215	.267	.201	.057	.010
8	.000	.000	.000	.001	.011	.044	.121	.233	.302	.194	.075
9	.000	.000	.000	.000	.002	.010	.040	.121	.268	.387	.315
10	.000	.000	.000	.000	.000	.001	.006	.028	.107	.349	.599

Chart 6–3   Chart Representing the Binomial Probability Distribution for a π of .05, .10, .20, .50, and .70 and an n of 10

2.   If π, the probability of success, remains the same but n becomes larger, the shape of the binomial distribution becomes more symmetrical. Chart 6–4 shows a situation where π remains constant at .10 but n increases from 7 to 40.

Chart 6–4   Chart Representing the Binomial Probability Distribution for a π of .10 and an n of 7, 12, 20, and 40

3.   The mean (μ) and the variance (σ^2) of a binomial distribution can be computed in a "shortcut" fashion by:

| MEAN OF A BINOMIAL DISTRIBUTION | $\mu = n\pi$ | **[6–4]** |

VARIANCE OF A BINOMIAL DISTRIBUTION	$\sigma^2 = n\pi(1 - \pi)$	**[6–5]**

For the previous example regarding defective worm gears, recall that $\pi = .05$ and $n = 6$. Hence:

$$\mu = n\pi = 6(.05) = .30$$

$$\sigma^2 = n\pi(1 - \pi) = 6(.05)(1 - .05) = .285$$

The mean of .30 and the variance of .285 can be verified from the general definitions using formulas (6–1) and (6–2). The probability distribution from Table 6–3 is repeated below.

Number of Defects, x	$P(x)$	$xP(x)$	$x - \mu$	$(x - \mu)^2$	$(x - \mu)^2 P(x)$
0	.735	0	−0.30	0.09	0.06615
1	.232	0.232	0.70	0.49	0.11368
2	.031	0.062	1.70	2.89	0.08959
3	.002	0.006	2.70	7.29	0.01458
4	.000	0	3.70	13.69	0
5	.000	0	4.70	22.09	0
6	.000	0	5.70	32.49	0
		0.30			0.284*

*The slight discrepancy between .285 and .284 is due to rounding.

▌ Exercises

11. In a binomial situation $n = 4$ and $\pi = .25$. Determine the following probabilities using the binomial formula (6–3).
    a. $x = 2$
    b. $x = 3$
12. In a binomial situation $n = 5$ and $\pi = .40$. Determine the following probabilities using the binomial formula.
    a. $x = 1$
    b. $x = 2$
13. Assume a binomial distribution where $n = 3$ and $\pi = .60$.
    a. Refer to Appendix A, and list the probabilities of a success for values of x from 0 to 3.
    b. Determine the mean and standard deviation of the distribution from the general definitions given in formulas (6–1) and (6–2).
14. Assume a binomial distribution where $n = 5$ and $\pi = .30$.
    a. Refer to Appendix A, and list the probabilities of a success for values of x from 0 to 5.
    b. Determine the mean and standard deviation of the distribution from the general definitions given in formulas (6–1) and (6–2).
15. A brokerage survey reports that 30 percent of individual investors have used a discount broker; that is, one which does not charge the full commissions. In a random sample of nine individuals, what is the probability:
    a. Exactly two of the sampled individuals have used a discount broker?
    b. Exactly four of them have used a discount broker?
    c. None of them have used a discount broker?
16. It is claimed that 95 percent of first class mail within the same city is delivered within two days of the time of mailing. Six letters are randomly sent to different locations.

a. What is the probability that all six arrive within two days?
b. What is the probability that exactly five arrive within two days?
c. Find the mean number of letters that will arrive within two days.
d. Compute the variance and standard deviation of the number that will arrive within two days.

17. Ten percent of new automobiles will require warranty service within the first year. Jones Honda sells 12 automobiles in April.
a. What is the probability that none of these automobiles requires warranty service?
b. Find the probability exactly one of them requires warranty service.
c. Determine the probability that exactly two automobiles require warranty service.
d. Compute the mean and standard deviation of this probability distribution.

18. A telemarketer makes six phone calls per hour and is able to make a sale on 30 percent of these contacts. During the next two hours, find:
a. The probability of making exactly 4 sales.
b. The probability of making no sales.
c. The probability of making exactly 2 sales.
d. The mean number of sales in the two-hour period.
e. The variance and standard deviation in the number of sales during the two-hour period.

19. Ten percent of the production employees at Nome Steel are absent from work on a typical summer day. Suppose 10 production employees are selected at random for a special in-depth study on absenteeism.
a. What is the random variable?
b. Is the random variable discrete or continuous?
c. What is the probability that none of the 10 selected employees are absent?
d. Develop a binomial probability distribution for the experiment.
e. Compute the mean, variance, and standard deviation of the distribution.

20. The marketing department of the Kellogg Company plans to conduct a national survey to find whether consumers of flake cereals can distinguish one of their favorite flake cereals from other flake cereals. To test the questionnaire and procedure to be used, eight persons were asked to cooperate in an experiment. Five very small bowls of flake cereals were placed in front of a person. The bowls were labeled A, B, C, D, and E. The person was informed that only one bowl contained his or her favorite flake cereal.
a. Suppose a person could not identify his or her favorite cereal and just guessed that it was in bowl C. What is the probability that the person guessed correctly?
b. What is the random variable in this problem?
c. Is the random variable discrete or continuous? Why?
d. Suppose that all eight persons in the experiment were unable to identify their favorite cereal and just guessed which bowl it was in. What is the probability that none of the eight guessed correctly?
e. Develop a binomial probability distribution for this experiment.
f. Compute the mean, variance, and standard deviation of the distribution.
g. Portray the binomial probability distribution in the form of a chart.
h. Suppose seven of the eight persons identified the cereal they liked best. Is it reasonable to assume that they were just guessing? Explain. What would you conclude?
i. Why is the binomial probability distribution appropriate for this problem?

Cumulative Probability Distributions

We may want to know the probability of correctly guessing the answers to 6 *or more* true/false questions out of 10. Or we may be interested in the probability of selecting *less than two* defectives at random from production during the previous hour. This sounds like we need cumulative frequency distributions similar to the ones developed in Chapter 2. The following example will illustrate.

Example

A recent study by the American Highway Patrolman's Association revealed that 60 percent of American drivers use their seat belts. A sample of 10 drivers on the Florida Turnpike is selected.

1. What is the probability that exactly 7 are wearing seat belts?
2. What is the probability that 7 or fewer of the drivers are wearing seat belts?

Solution

This situation meets the binomial requirements, namely:

- A particular driver either is wearing a seat belt or is not. There are only two possible outcomes.
- The probability of "success" (wearing a seat belt) is the same from driver to driver: 60 percent.
- The trials are independent. If the fourth driver selected in the sample is wearing a seat belt, for example, it has no effect on whether the fifth driver selected is or is not wearing a seat belt.
- There is a fixed number of trials — 10 in this case, because 10 drivers were checked.

1. To find the likelihood of *exactly* 7 drivers, we use Appendix A. Locate the page for $n = 10$. Next find the column for $\pi = .60$ and the row for $x = 7$. The value is .215. Thus, the probability of finding 7 out of 10 drivers in the sample wearing their seat belts is .215. This is often written as follows:

$$P(x = 7 \mid n = 10 \text{ and } \pi = .60) = .215$$

where x refers to the number of successes, n the number of trials, and π the probability of a success. The bar "|" means "given that."

2. To find the probability that 7 or fewer of the drivers will be wearing seat belts, we apply the special rule of addition, formula (5–2), from Chapter 5. Because the events are mutually exclusive, we determine the probability that of the 10 drivers stopped, none was wearing a seat belt, 1 was wearing a seat belt, 2 were wearing a seat belt, and so on up to 7 drivers. The probabilities of the eight possible outcomes are then totaled. From Appendix A, $n = 10$, and $\pi = .60$.

$$
\begin{aligned}
P(x \le 7 \mid n = 10 \text{ and } \pi = .60) &= P(x = 0) + P(x = 1) + P(x = 2) + P(x = 3) \\
&\quad + P(x = 4) + P(x = 5) + P(x = 6) + P(x = 7) \\
&= .000 + .002 + .011 + .042 + .111 + .201 \\
&\quad + .251 + .215 \\
&= .833
\end{aligned}
$$

So the probability of stopping 10 cars at random and finding 7 or fewer of the drivers wearing their seat belts is .833.

This value may also be determined, with less computation, using the complement rule. First, find $P(x > 7)$ given that $n = 10$ and $\pi = .60$. This probability is .167, found by $P(x = 8) + P(x = 9) + P(x = 10) = .121 + .040 + .006$. The probability that $x \le 7$ is equal to $1 - P(x > 7)$, so $P(x \le 7) = 1 - .167 = .833$, the same as computed above.

SELF-REVIEW 6–4

For a case where $n = 4$ and $\pi = .60$, determine the probability that:

(a) $x = 2$.
(b) $x \leq 2$.
(c) $x > 2$.

▌ Exercises

21.   In a binomial distribution $n = 8$ and $\pi = .30$. Find the following probabilities.
  a. $x = 2$.
  b. $x \leq 2$ (the probability that x is equal to or less than 2).
  c. $x \geq 3$ (the probability that x is equal to or greater than 3).

22.   In a binomial distribution $n = 12$ and $\pi = .60$. Find the following probabilities.
  a. $x = 5$.
  b. $x \leq 5$.
  c. $x \geq 6$.

23.   In a recent study 90 percent of the homes in the United States were found to have color TVs. In a sample of nine homes, what is the probability that:
  a.   All nine have color TVs?
  b.   Less than five have color TVs?
  c.   More than five have color TVs?
  d.   At least seven homes have color TVs?

24.   A manufacturer of window frames knows from long experience that 5 percent of the production will have some type of minor defect that will require a slight adjustment. What is the probability that in a sample of 20 window frames:
  a.   None will need adjustment?
  b.   At least 1 will need adjustment?
  c.   More than 2 will need adjustment?

▌ Hypergeometric Probability Distribution

We pointed out that for the binomial distribution to be applied, the probability of a success must stay the same for each trial. For example, the probability of guessing the correct answer to a true/false question is .50. This probability remains the same for each question on an examination. Likewise, suppose that 40 percent of the registered voters in a precinct are Republicans. If 27 registered voters are to be selected at random, the probability of choosing a Republican on the first selection is .40. The chance of choosing a Republican on the next selection is also .40, assuming that the sampling is done *with replacement,* meaning that the person selected is put back in the population before the next person is selected.

   Most sampling is done *without replacement.* Thus, if the population is small, the probability for each observation will change. For example, if the population consists of 20 items, the probability of selecting a particular item from that population is $\frac{1}{20}$. If the sampling is done without replacement, after the first selection there are only 19 items remaining; the probability of selecting a particular item on the second selection is only $\frac{1}{19}$. For the third selection, the probability is $\frac{1}{18}$, and so on. This assumes that the population is **finite**—that is, the number in the population is known and relatively small in number.

▌ **Finite Population**   A population consisting of a small number of individuals, objects, or measurements. ▌

Examples of a finite population are 2,842 Republicans in the precinct, 9,241 applications for medical school, and the 18 Pontiac Sunbirds currently in stock at North Pontiac.

Recall that one of the criteria for using the binomial distribution is that the probability of success remain the same from trial to trial. Since the probability of success does not remain the same from trial to trial when sampling from a relatively small population without replacement, the binomial distribution should not be used. Instead, the **hypergeometric distribution** should be applied. Therefore, (1) if a sample is selected from a finite population without replacement and (2) if the size of the sample n is greater than 5 percent of the size of the population N, then the hypergeometric distribution is used to determine the probability of a specified number of successes or failures. It is especially appropriate when the size of the population is small.

The formula for the hypergeometric distribution is:

$$\textbf{HYPERGEOMETRIC DISTRIBUTION} \qquad\qquad P(x) = \frac{({}_S C_x)({}_{N-S} C_{n-x})}{{}_N C_n} \qquad\qquad \textbf{[6–6]}$$

where:

- N is the size of the population.
- S is the number of successes in the population.
- x is the number of successes of interest. It may be 0, 1, 2, 3, ...
- n is the size of the sample or the number of trials.
- C is the symbol for a combination.

Example

Suppose 50 PlayStations were manufactured during the week ($N = 50$). Forty operated perfectly ($S = 40$), and 10 had at least one defect. A sample of 5 is selected at random ($n = 5$). Using the hypergeometric formula, what is the probability that 4($x = 4$) of the 5 will operate perfectly? (Note that sampling is done without replacement, and the sample size of 5 is $\frac{5}{50}$, or 10 percent of the population. This is greater than the 5 percent requirement.)

Solution

In this problem,

$N = 50$, the number of PlayStations manufactured,

$n = 5$, the size of the sample.

$S = 40$, the number of PlayStations in the population operating perfectly.

$x = 4$, the number in the sample operating perfectly.

We want to find the probability that 4 PlayStations of the 5 selected will operate perfectly.

Inserting these values in formula (6–6) and solving for the probability that 4 out of 5 PlayStations in the sample operate perfectly:

$$P(x) = \frac{({}_S C_x)({}_{N-S} C_{n-x})}{({}_N C_n)}$$

$$P(4) = \frac{({}_{40} C_4)({}_{50-40} C_{5-4})}{{}_{50} C_5}$$

$$= \frac{\left(\dfrac{40!}{4!36!}\right)\left(\dfrac{10!}{1!9!}\right)}{\dfrac{50!}{5!45!}} = \frac{(91{,}390)(10)}{2{,}118{,}760} = .431$$

Thus, the probability of selecting 5 PlayStations at random out of 50 and finding that 4 of the 5 operate perfectly is .431.

The hypergeometric probabilities of finding 0, 1, 2, 3, 4, and 5 working PlayStations of the 5 PlayStations selected at random are given in Table 6–5.

Table 6–5   **Hypergeometric Probabilities ($n = 5$, $N = 50$, $S = 40$)**
That PlayStations Operate Correctly

Number Operating Correctly	Probability
0	.000*
1	.004
2	.044
3	.210
4	.431
5	.311

*Actually .0001.

Table 6–6 gives the hypergeometric and binomial probabilities for the PlayStation problem. (Since 40 of the 50 PlayStations operated correctly, the binomial probability of selecting a perfect PlayStation on one trial is $40/50 = .80$. The binomial probabilities for Table 6–6 come from the binomial table in Appendix A, $n = 5$, $\pi = .80$.)

Table 6–6   **Hypergeometric and Binomial Probabilities for the PlayStation Problem**

Number of PlayStations in Sample Operating Correctly, x	Hypergeometric Probability, $P(x)$	Binomial Probability ($n = 5$, $\pi = 40/50 = .80$)
0	.000	.000
1	.004	.006
2	.044	.051
3	.210	.205
4	.431	.410
5	.311	.328

We pointed out that when the binomial requirement of a constant probability of success cannot be met, the hypergeometric distribution should be used in its place. However, as Table 6–6 shows, under many conditions the results of the binomial closely approximate those of the hypergeometric. As a rule of thumb, if the selected items are not returned to the population and the sample size is less than 5 percent of the population, the binomial distribution can be used to approximate the hypergeometric distribution. That is, when $n < .05N$, the binomial approximation should suffice.

SELF-REVIEW 6–5

Refer to the PlayStation example and Table 6–5. Verify the hypergeometric probability of .210 that three of the five randomly selected PlayStations will operate correctly.

▮ Exercises

25. Suppose a population consists of 10 items, 6 of which are defective. A sample of 3 items is selected. What is the probability that exactly 2 are defective?
26. Suppose a population consists of 15 items, 10 of which are acceptable. A sample of 4 items is selected. What is the probability that exactly 3 are acceptable?
27. Kolzak Appliance Outlet just received a shipment of 10 TV sets. Shortly after they were received, the manufacturer called to report that he had inadvertently shipped 3 defective sets. Ms. Kolzak, the owner of the outlet, decided to test 2 of the 10 sets she received. What is the probability that neither of the 2 sets tested was defective?
28. The Computer Systems Department consists of eight faculty, six of whom are tenured. Dr. Vonder, the chairman, wants to establish a committee of three department faculty members to review the curriculum. If she selects the committee at random:
    a. What is the probability all members of the committee are tenured?
    b. What is the probability that at least one member is not tenured? (Hint: For this question use the complement rule.)
29. Keith's Florists has 15 delivery trucks, used mainly to deliver flowers and flower arrangements in the Tulsa area. Suppose 6 of the 15 trucks have brake problems. Five trucks were selected at random to be tested. What is the probability that 2 of those tested have defective brakes?
30. Professor Jon Hammer has a pool of 15 multiple-choice questions regarding probability distributions. Four of these questions involve the hypergeometric distribution. What is the probability at least 1 of these hypergeometric questions will appear on the 5-question quiz on Monday?

▮ Poisson Probability Distribution

The binomial probability distributions for probabilities of success (π) less than .05 could be computed, but the calculations would be quite time consuming (especially for a large n of, say, 100 or more). The distribution of probabilities would become more and more skewed as the probability of success became smaller. The limiting form of the binomial distribution where the probability of success is very small and n is large is called the **Poisson probability distribution.** It is often referred to as the "law of improbable events," meaning that the probability, π, of a particular event's happening is quite small. The Poisson distribution is a discrete probability distribution because it is formed by counting something.

This distribution has many applications. It is used as a model to describe the distribution of errors in data entry, the number of scratches and other imperfections in newly painted car panels, the number of defective parts in outgoing shipments, the number of customers waiting to be served at a restaurant or waiting to get into an attraction at Disney World, and the number of accidents on I-75 during a three-month period.

The Poisson distribution can be described mathematically using the formula:

POISSON DISTRIBUTION	$$P(x) = \frac{\mu^x e^{-\mu}}{x!}$$	**[6–7]**

where:

μ (mu)   is the arithmetic mean number of occurrences (successes) in a particular interval of time.

e is the constant 2.71828 (base of the Naperian logarithmic system).

x is the number of occurrences (successes).

$P(x)$ is the probability to be computed for a specified value of x.

The mean number of successes, μ, can be determined in Poisson situations by $n\pi$, where n is the total number of trials and π the probability of success.

MEAN OF A POISSON DISTRIBUTION	$\mu = n\pi$	**[6–8]**

The variance of the Poisson is also equal to $n\pi$. If, for example, the probability that a check cashed by a bank will bounce is .0003, and 10,000 checks are cashed, the mean number of bad checks is 3.0, found by $\mu = n\pi = 10,000(.0003) = 3.0$.

Recall that for a binomial distribution there is a fixed number of trials. For example, for a four-question multiple-choice test there can only be zero, one, two, three, or four successes (correct answers). The random variable, x, for a Poisson distribution, however, can assume an *infinite number of values* — that is, 0, 1, 2, 3, 4, 5, ... However, *the probabilities become very small after the first few occurrences* (successes).

To illustrate the Poisson probability computation, assume baggage is rarely lost by Northwest Airlines. Most flights do not experience any mishandled bags; some have one bag lost; a few have two bags lost; rarely a flight will have three lost bags; and so on. Suppose a random sample of 1,000 flights shows a total of 300 bags were lost. Thus, the arithmetic mean number of lost bags per flight is 0.3, found by 300/1,000. If the number of lost bags per flight follows a Poisson distribution with $\mu = 0.30$, we can compute the various probabilities by the formula:

$$P(x) = \frac{\mu^x e^{-\mu}}{x!}$$

For example, the probability of not losing any bags is:

$$P(0) = \frac{(0.3)^0 (e^{-0.30})}{0!} = 0.7408$$

In other words, 74 percent of the flights will have no lost baggage. The probability of exactly one lost bag is:

$$P(0) = \frac{(0.3)^1 (e^{-0.30})}{1!} = 0.2222$$

Thus, we would expect to find exactly one lost bag on 22 percent of the flights. Poisson probabilities can also be found in the table in Appendix C.

Example

Recall from the previous illustration that the number of lost bags follows a Poisson distribution with a mean of 0.3. Use Appendix C to find the probability that no bags will be lost on a particular flight. What is the probability exactly one bag will be lost on a particular flight? When should the supervisor become suspicious that a flight is having too many lost bags?

Solution   Part of Appendix C is repeated as Table 6–7. To find the probability of no lost bags, locate the column headed "0.3" and read down that column to the row labeled "0." The probability is .7408. That is the probability of no lost bags. The probability of one lost bag is .2222, which is in the next row of the table, in the same column. The probability of two lost bags is .0333, in the row below; for three lost bags it is .0033; and for four lost bags it is .0003. Thus, a supervisor should not be surprised to find one lost bag but should expect to see more than one lost bag infrequently.

Table 6–7   **Poisson Table for Various Values of μ (from Appendix C)**

| | | | | | μ | | | | |
x	0.1	0.2	0.3	0.4	0.5	0.6	0.7	0.8	0.9
0	0.9048	0.8187	0.7408	0.6703	0.6065	0.5488	0.4966	0.4493	0.4066
1	0.0905	0.1637	0.2222	0.2681	0.3033	0.3293	0.3476	0.3595	0.3659
2	0.0045	0.0164	0.0333	0.0536	0.0758	0.0988	0.1217	0.1438	0.1647
3	0.0002	0.0011	0.0033	0.0072	0.0126	0.0198	0.0284	0.0383	0.0494
4	0.0000	0.0001	0.0003	0.0007	0.0016	0.0030	0.0050	0.0077	0.0111
5	0.0000	0.0000	0.0000	0.0001	0.0002	0.0004	0.0007	0.0012	0.0020
6	0.0000	0.0000	0.0000	0.0000	0.0000	0.0000	0.0001	0.0002	0.0003
7	0.0000	0.0000	0.0000	0.0000	0.0000	0.0000	0.0000	0.0000	0.0000

These probabilities can also be found using the MINITAB system. The commands necessary are reported at the end of the chapter. The output appears below. A graph of the distribution of the number of errors is shown in Chart 6–5. Note that the distribution is severely skewed in the positive direction.

```
MTB > Set c1
DATA>    0:5
DATA>    End.
MTB > PDF c1:
SUBC>    Poisson .3.
          K            P( X = K)
         0.00            0.7408
         1.00            0.2222
         2.00            0.0333
         3.00            0.0033
         4.00            0.0003
         5.00            0.0000
```

Chart 6–5   Poisson Probability Distribution for $\mu = 0.3$

SELF-REVIEW   6–6

A hybrid seed grower is experiencing trouble with corn borers. A random check of 5,000 ears revealed the following: Many of the ears contained no borers; some ears had one borer; a few had two borers; and so on. The distribution of the number of borers per ear approximates the Poisson distribution. The grower counted 3,500 borers in the 5,000 ears.

(a)   What is the probability that an ear of corn selected at random will contain no borers?
(b)   Develop a Poisson probability distribution for this experiment.

The Poisson probability distribution is always positively skewed. Also, the Poisson random variable has no specific upper limit. The Poisson distributions for the lost bags illustration, where $\mu = 0.3$, and for the corn borer experiment in Self-Review 6–6, where $\mu = 0.7$, are highly skewed. As μ becomes larger, the Poisson distribution becomes more symmetrical. For example, Chart 6–6 shows the distributions of the number of transmission services, muffler replacements, and oil changes per day at Avellino's Auto Shop. They follow Poisson distributions with means of 0.7, 2.0, and 6.0, respectively.

Chart 6–6   Poisson Probability Distributions for Means of 0.7, 2.0, and 6.0

Only μ needed to construct Poisson

In brief summary, the Poisson distribution is actually a group of discrete distributions. To apply it, n must be large, such as 1,000 pieces. Conversely, the probability, π, of a defect, error, and the like must be small. All that is needed to construct a Poisson probability distribution is the mean number of defects, errors, and so on — designated as μ. It is computed by $n\pi$.

▌ Exercises

31. In a Poisson distribution $\mu = 0.4$.
    a. What is the probability that $x = 0$?
    b. What is the probability that $x > 0$?
32. In a Poisson distribution $\mu = 4$.
    a. What is the probability that $x = 2$?
    b. What is the probability that $x \leq 2$?
    c. What is the probability that $x > 2$?
33. Ms. Bergen is a loan officer at Coast Bank and Trust. Based on her years of experience, she estimates that the probability is .025 that an applicant will not be able to repay his or her installment loan. Last month she made 40 loans.
    a. What is the probability that 3 loans will be defaulted?
    b. What is the probability that at least 3 loans will be defaulted?
34. Automobiles arrive at the Elkhart exit of the Indiana Toll Road at the rate of two per minute. The distribution of arrivals approximates a Poisson distribution.
    a. What is the probability that no automobiles arrive in a particular minute?
    b. What is the probability that at least one automobile arrives during a particular minute?
35. It is estimated that 0.5 percent of the callers to the billing department of the U.S. West Telephone Company will receive a busy signal. What is the probability that of today's 1,200 callers at least 5 received a busy signal?
36. Textbook authors and publishers work very hard to minimize the number of errors in a text. However, some errors are unavoidable. Mr. J. A. Carmen, statistics editor, reports that the mean number of errors per chapter is 0.8. What is the probability that there are less than 2 errors in a particular chapter?

▌ Chapter Outline

I. A random variable is a numerical value determined by the outcome of an experiment.
II. A probability distribution is a listing of all the possible outcomes of an experiment and the probability associated with each outcome.
   A. A discrete probability distribution can assume only certain values. The main features are:
       1. The sum of the probabilities is 1.00.
       2. The probability of a particular outcome is between 0.00 and 1.00.
       3. The outcomes are mutually exclusive.
   B. A continuous distribution can assume an infinite number of values within a specific range.
III. The mean and variance of a probability distribution are computed as follows.
   A. The mean is equal to:

$$\mu = \Sigma[xP(x)] \tag{6-1}$$

   B. The variance is equal to:

$$\sigma^2 = \Sigma[(x - \mu)^2 P(x)] \tag{6-2}$$

IV. The binomial distribution has the following characteristics.
   A. Each outcome is classified into one of two mutually exclusive categories.
   B. The probability of a success remains the same from trial to trial.
   C. Each trial is independent.
   D. The distribution results from a count of the number of successes in a fixed number of trials.

E. A binomial probability is determined as follows:

$$P(x) = \frac{n!}{x!(n-x)!}\, \pi^x (1-\pi)^{n-x}$$ **[6–3]**

F. The mean is computed as:

$$\mu = n\pi$$ **[6–4]**

G. The variance is

$$\sigma^2 = n\pi(1-\pi)$$ **[6–5]**

V. The hypergeometric distribution has the following characteristics.
   A. There are only two possible outcomes.
   B. The probability of a success is not the same on each trial.
   C. The distribution results from a count of the number of successes in a fixed number of trials.
   D. A hypergeometric probability is computed from the following equation.

$$P(x) = \frac{(_sC_x)(_{N-s}C_{n-x})}{(_NC_n)}$$ **[6–6]**

VI. The Poisson distribution has the following characteristics.
   A. Each outcome is classified into one of two mutually exclusive categories.
   B. The probability of a success remains the same from trial to trial.
   C. Each trial is independent.
   D. The distribution results from a count of the number of successes in a fixed number of trials.
   E. A Poisson probability is determined from the following equation.

$$P(x) = \frac{\mu^x e^{-\mu}}{x!}$$ **[6–7]**

F. The probability of a success is usually small, and the number of trials is usually large.
G. The mean and variance of a Poisson distribution are the same and are equal to $n\pi$.

❙ Chapter Exercises

37. The local Democratic party has received 12 requests for endorsement for four positions to be selected during the next general election. Of these 12 people, 4 are female and 8 are male. In order to avoid controversy, the committee agrees to pick their endorsed candidates by lot, that is, at random. Use the hypergeometric distribution to find the probability that:
   a. Exactly two of the endorsed candidates will be female.
   b. All four of the endorsed candidates will be female.
   c. At most one of the endorsed candidates will be female.
   Suppose you were to use the binomial distribution in this situation, what would be your estimates of these probabilities?
38. What is a binomial distribution?
39. Under what conditions will the Poisson and the binomial distributions give roughly the same results?
40. One percent of all video cameras sold by Phil's Photo Shop have a defect in their carrying case. Four cases are randomly selected from recent sales, find the probability that:
   a. Exactly one case is defective.
   b. Exactly two cases are defective.
   c. No cases are defective.
   Use the Poisson distribution to estimate the same probabilities.

41. Samson Apartments has a large number of units available to rent each month. A concern of management is the number of vacant apartments each month. A recent study revealed the percent of the time that a given number of apartments are vacant. Compute the mean and standard deviation of the number of vacant apartments.

Number of Vacant Units	Probability
0	.10
1	.20
2	.30
3	.40

42. An investment will be worth $1,000, $2,000, or $5,000 at the end of the year. The probabilities of these values are .25, .60, and .15, respectively. Determine the mean and variance of the worth of the investment.

43. The personnel manager of the Cumberland Pig Iron Company is studying the number of on-the-job accidents over a period of one month. He developed the following probability distribution. Compute the mean, variance, and standard deviation of the number of accidents in a month.

Number of Accidents	Probability
0	.40
1	.20
2	.20
3	.10
4	.10

44. Corso Bakery offers special decorated cakes for birthdays, weddings, and other occasions. They also have regular cakes available in their bakery. The following table gives the total number of cakes sold per day and the corresponding probability. Compute the mean, variance, and standard deviation of the number of cakes sold per day.

Number of Cakes Sold in a Day	Probability
12	.25
13	.40
14	.25
15	.10

45. A Tamiami shearing machine is producing 10 percent defective pieces, which is abnormally high. The quality control engineer has been checking the output by almost continuous sampling since the abnormal condition began. What is the probability that in a sample of 10 pieces:
    a. Exactly 5 will be defective?
    b. 5 or more will be defective?

46. Thirty percent of the population in a southwestern community are Spanish-speaking Americans. A Spanish-speaking person is accused of killing a non-Spanish-speaking American. Of the first 12 potential jurors, only 2 are Spanish-speaking Americans, and 10 are not. The defendant's lawyer challenges the jury selection, claiming bias against her client. The government lawyer disagrees, saying that the probability of this particular jury composition is common. What do you think?

47. A new flavor of toothpaste has been developed. It was tested by a group of 10 people. Six of the group said they liked the new flavor, and the remaining 4 indicated they did not. Four of the 10 are selected to participate in an in-depth interview. What is the probability that of those selected for the in-depth interview two liked the new flavor and two did not?

48. Suppose it is known that 5 of 25 Chrysler subcompact automobiles require adjustment of some kind. Four subcompacts are selected at random. We are interested in the probability that exactly one will require adjustment.
    a. Solve the problem assuming that of the 25 subcompacts, the samples are drawn without replacement.
    b. Solve the problem assuming the sampling is done with replacement.
    c. Assuming replacement, work the problem using the Poisson distribution.
    d. Compare the results in parts a., b., and c. Comment on your findings.

49. The law firm of Hagel and Hagel is located in downtown Cincinnati. There are 10 partners in the firm; 7 live in Ohio and 3 in northern Kentucky. Ms. Wendy Hagel, the managing partner, wants to appoint a committee of three partners to look into moving the firm to northern Kentucky. If the committee is selected at random from the 10 partners, what is the probability that:
    a. One member of the committee lives in northern Kentucky and the others live in Ohio?
    b. At least one member of the committee lives in northern Kentucky?

50. According to recent information published by the U.S. Environmental Protection Agency, four of the top nine cars in terms of fuel economy are manufactured by Honda. Determine the probability distribution for the number of Hondas in a sample of three cars chosen from the top nine. What is the likelihood that in the sample of three at least one Honda is included?

51. The position of chief of police in the city of Corry is open. The search committee, charged with the responsibility of recommending a new chief to the city council, received 12 applications for the position. Four of the 12 applicants are either female or members of a minority. The search committee decides to interview all 12 of the applicants. To begin, they randomly select four applicants to be interviewed on the first day, and none of the four is female or a member of a minority. The local newspaper, the *Corry Press,* suggests discrimination in an editorial. What is the likelihood of this occurrence?

52. A box of electric hedge trimmers contains six Cummings Trimmers. Two are defective; four operate correctly. Three trimmers are selected from the box.
    a. What is the probability that exactly one of the Cummings trimmers is defective?
    b. What is the probability that two trimmers of the three selected are defective?

53. The sales of Lexus automobiles in the Detroit area follow a Poisson distribution with a mean of 3.00 per day.
    a. What is the probability that no Lexus is sold on a particular day?
    b. What is the probability that for five consecutive days at least one Lexus is sold?

54. Suppose 1.5 percent of the plastic spacers produced by a Corson high-speed mold injection machine are defective. The distribution of defectives follows a Poisson distribution. For a random sample of 200 spacers, find the probability that:
    a. None of the spacers is defective.
    b. Three or more of the spacers are defective.

55. A study of the lines at the checkout registers of Safeway Supermarket revealed that, during a certain period at the rush hour, the number of customers waiting averaged four. What is the probability that during that period:
    a. No customers were waiting?   c. Four or fewer were waiting?
    b. Four customers were waiting?   d. Four or more were waiting?

56. L. L. Bean advertised same-day service. Unfortunately, the movement of orders did not go as planned, and there were a large number of complaints. A complete change in the handling of incoming and outgoing orders was then made. An internal goal was set to have fewer than five unfilled orders on hand (per picker) at the end of 95 out of every 100 working days. Frequent checks of the unfilled orders at the end of the day revealed that the distribution of

the unfilled orders approximated a Poisson distribution; that is, most of the days there were no unfilled orders, some of the days there was one order, and so on. The mean number of unfilled orders per picker was 2.0.

  a.   Has L. L. Bean lived up to its internal goal? Cite evidence.

  b.   Draw a histogram representing the Poisson probability distribution of unfilled orders at the end of the day.

57. On January 29, 1986, the space shuttle *Challenger* exploded at an altitude of 46,000 feet, resulting in the death of all seven astronauts. A 1985 study published by the National Aeronautics and Space Administration (NASA) suggested that the probability of a catastrophic occurrence such as this was about 1 in 60,000. A similar report by the Air Force set the likelihood of a catastrophe at 1 in 35. The *Challenger* flight was the 25th mission in the shuttle program. Use the Poisson distribution to compare the probabilities of at least one disaster in 25 missions using both estimates of the probability of occurrence.

58. According to the "January theory," if the stock market is up for the month of January, it will be up for the year. If it is down in January, it will be down for the year. According to an article in *The Wall Street Journal,* this theory held for 29 out of the last 34 years. Suppose there is no truth to this theory. What is the probability this could happen by chance? (You will probably need a computer. Use the binomial distribution.)

59. During the second round of the 1989 U.S. Open golf tournament, four golfers each made a hole in one on the sixth hole. The odds of a professional golfer making a hole in one are 3,708 to 1, so the probability is 1/3709. There were 155 golfers participating in the second round that day. Estimate the probability that four golfers would score a hole in one on the sixth hole.

▍ Computer Data Exercises

60. Refer to Data Set 1, which reports information on homes sold in the Venice, Florida, area last year.

  a.   Create a probability distribution for the number of bedrooms. Compute the mean and the standard deviation of this distribution.

  b.   Create a probability distribution for the number of bathrooms. Compute the mean and the standard deviation of this distribution.

61. Refer to Data Set 2, which contains information on the 1997 Major League Baseball season. There are 28 teams in the major leagues, and 8 of them have home fields with artificial playing surfaces. As part of the negotiations with the players' union, a study regarding injuries on grass versus artificial surfaces will be conducted. Five teams will be selected to participate in the study, and the teams will be selected at random. What is the likelihood that 2 of the 5 teams selected for study play their home games on artificial surfaces?

▍ Computer Commands

1. The MINITAB commands to generate the first binomial distribution on page 198.

  a.   First, type the values of interest in a column. In this instance put the numbers 0 through 5 in the first column.

  b.   Then select **Calc** > **Probability Distributions** > **Binomial.**

  c.   In the dialog box select **Probability,** set the number of trials to 6, the probability of success to .05, and the **Input column** to C1. Refer to the following graphic to see how the resulting box appears. Then click **OK.**

Binomial Distribution   ☒

C1   ⦿ **P**robability
            ○ **C**umulative probability
            ○ **I**nverse cumulative probability

            N**u**mber of trials: │6   │
            Pro**b**ability of success: │.05   │

            ⦿ Input col**u**mn: │c1   │
              Optional s**t**orage: │   │

            ○ Input con**s**tant: │   │
              Optional sto**r**age: │   │

  │ Select │

  │ **?** │PDF   │   **O**K   │   │ Cancel │

2. The MINITAB commands to generate the second binomial distribution on page 199.
   a. Type the values of interest in a column. In this example put the numbers 0 through 13 in the first column.
   b. Then select **Calc > Probability Distributions > Binomial.**
   c. In the dialog box select **Probability,** set the number of trials to 40, the probability of success to .09, and the **Input column** to C1. Refer to the graphic below to see how the resulting box appears.

Binomial Distribution   ☒

C1   ⦿ **P**robability
            ○ **C**umulative probability
            ○ **I**nverse cumulative probability

            N**u**mber of trials: │40   │
            Pro**b**ability of success: │.09   │

            ⦿ Input col**u**mn: │c1   │
              Optional s**t**orage: ││   │

            ○ Input con**s**tant: │   │
              Optional sto**r**age: │   │

  │ Select │

  │ **?** │PDF   │   **O**K   │   │ Cancel │

3. The MINITAB commands to generate the third binomial distribution on page 199.
   a. Type the numbers 1 through 21 in the first column.
   b. Then select **Calc > Probability Distributions > Binomial.**
   c. In the dialog box select **Probability,** set the number of trials to 27, the probability of success to .376, and the **Input column** to C1. Refer to the following graphic to see how the resulting box appears.

Binomial Distribution

C1

- ○ **P**robability
- ○ **C**umulative probability
- ○ **I**nverse cumulative probability

Number of trials: `27`

Pro**b**ability of success: `.376`

- ● **I**nput column: `c1`
  - Optional st**o**rage: ` `
- ○ Input con**s**tant: ` `
  - Optional sto**r**age: ` `

Select

? PDF   **OK**   Cancel

4. The MINITAB commands to generate the Poisson distribution on page 209.
   a. Put the numbers 0 through 5 in the first column.
   b. Then select **Calc** > **Probability Distributions** > **Poisson.**
   c. In the dialog box select **Probability,** set the mean to .3, and the **Input column** to C1. Refer to the graphic below to see the completed box.

Poisson Distribution

- ● **P**robability
- ○ **C**umulative probability
- ○ **I**nverse cumulative probability

Mean: `.3`

- ● **I**nput column: `c1`
  - Optional st**o**rage: ` `
- ○ Input con**s**tant: ` `
  - Optional sto**r**age: ` `

Select

? PDF   **OK**   Cancel

5. The Excel commands to find binomial probabilities.
   a. Choose **Insert** > **Function** or else click on the **Function Wizard** button.
   b. In the first dialog box, select **Statistical** in the **Function Category** and **Binomdist** in the **Function Name** list box. Then click **Next.**
   c. In the second dialog box, enter four items:
      i. The number of "successes," such as 7.
      ii. The number of trials, such as 10.

iii. The probability of success on each trial, such as .6.
iv. Enter 0 or "false" for the individual probability; or 1 or "true" for the cumulative probability.

Refer to the graphic below to see the completed dialog box.

Function Wizard - Step 2 of 2   ? X

BINOMDIST   Value: 0.214990848

Returns the individual term binomial distribution probability.

Cumulative (required)
is a logical value that determines the form of the function.

number_s *fx*	7	7
trials *fx*	10	10
probability_s *fx*	.6	0.6
cumulative *fx*	0	FALSE

| Help | Cancel | < Back | Next > | Finish |

CHAPTER 6   *Answers to Self-Review*

6–1 (a)

Number of Spots	Probability
1	$\frac{1}{6}$
2	$\frac{1}{6}$
3	$\frac{1}{6}$
4	$\frac{1}{6}$
5	$\frac{1}{6}$
6	$\frac{1}{6}$
Total	$\frac{6}{6} = 1.00$

(b)

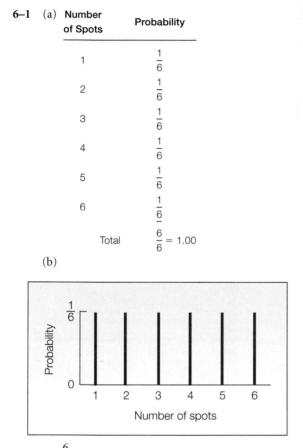

(c) $\frac{6}{6}$, or 1.

6–2 (a) It is discrete, because the values 50, 75, and 90 are clearly separated from each other, the sum of the probabilities is 1.00, and the outcomes are mutually exclusive.

(b)

x	$P(x)$	$xP(x)$
50	.30	15.0
75	.50	37.5
90	.20	18.0
		70.5

The mean is 70.5 cents.

(c)

x	$P(x)$	$(x - \mu)$	$(x - \mu)^2 P(x)$
50	.30	−20.5	126.075
75	.50	4.5	10.125
90	.20	19.5	76.050
			212.250

The variance is 212.25, and the standard deviation is 14.57 cents.

6–3 (a) It would appear reasonable because: each day the bridge is either raised or not, we are only counting how many days the bridge is raised, the probability is .2 each day, and the days are independent of each other.

(b) $(.2)^7 = .0000128$

(c) $\dfrac{7!}{3!(7-3)!}(.2)^3(.8)^4 = .1147$

(d) $\dfrac{7!}{1!(7-1)!}(.2)^1(.8)^6 = .3670$

(e) They are all in agreement.

6–4 $n = 4$, $\pi = .60$

(a) $P(x = 2) = .346$

(b) $P(x \le 2) = .526$

(c) $P(x > 2) = 1 - .526$
$= .474$

6–5 .210, found by:

$$P(3) = \frac{(_{40}C_3)(_{10}C_2)}{_{50}C_5}$$

$$= \frac{\left(\dfrac{40 \cdot 39 \cdot 38}{3 \cdot 2 \cdot 1}\right)\left(\dfrac{10 \cdot 9}{2}\right)}{\left(\dfrac{50 \cdot 49 \cdot 48 \cdot 47 \cdot 46}{5 \cdot 4 \cdot 3 \cdot 2 \cdot 1}\right)}$$

$$= \frac{(9,880)(45)}{(2,118,760)} = .210$$

6–6 (a) .4966. $\mu = 0.7$, found by 3,500/5,000. Refer to Appendix C, for a μ of 0.7 and an x of 0.

(b)

Number of Occurrences, x	Probability of Occurrence, $P(x)$
0	.4966
1	.3476
2	.1217
3	.0284
4	.0050
5	.0007
6	.0001

Chapter Seven

The Normal Probability Distribution

GOALS

When you have completed this chapter, you will be able to:

ONE

List the characteristics of the normal probability distribution.

TWO

Define and calculate *z* values.

THREE

Determine the probability that an observation will lie between two points using the standard normal distribution.

FOUR

Determine the probability that an observation will be above (or below) a given value using the standard normal distribution.

FIVE

Compare two or more observations that are on different probability distributions.

SIX

Use the normal distribution to approximate the binomial probability distribution.

The probability of a disaster such as the January 28, 1986 explosion of the space shuttle Challenger was 1 in 35. What is the probability of at least one disaster in 25 missions? (See Goal 6 and Exercise 42.)

▌ Introduction

Chapter 6 dealt with three families of *discrete* probability distributions: the binomial distribution, the hypergeometric distribution, and the Poisson distribution. Recall that these distributions are based on discrete random variables, which can assume only specified values. For example, the number of correct answers on a 10-question examination can only be 0, 1, 2, 3, . . . , 10. There cannot be a negative number of correct answers, such as −7, nor can there be 7¼ or 15 correct answers.

We will continue our study of probability distributions in this chapter by examining a very important *continuous* probability distribution, namely, the **normal probability distribution.** As noted in the preceding chapter, a continuous random variable is one that

can assume an *infinite* number of possible values within a specified range. It usually results from measuring something, such as the weight of an individual. The weight might be 112.0 kilograms, 112.1 kilograms, 112.12 kilograms, and so on, depending on the accuracy of the scale. Other continuous random variables are the life expectancy of alkaline batteries, the volume of a shipping container, and the weight of impurities in a steel ingot.

The probability distributions of the life expectancies of some products, such as batteries, tires, and light bulbs, tend to follow a "normal" pattern. So do the weights of boxes of Kellogg's Special K cereal, the lengths of rolls of aluminum, and other variables measured on a continuous scale.

In this chapter the main characteristics of a normal probability distribution and the normal curve are examined first. Then the **standard normal distribution** and its uses are presented. Finally, we will look at how the normal distribution is used to estimate binomial probabilities.

▌ The Family of Normal Probability Distributions

The normal probability distribution and its accompanying normal curve have the following characteristics:

1. The normal curve is **bell-shaped** and has a single peak at the center of the distribution. The arithmetic mean, median, and mode of the distribution are equal and located at the peak. Thus, half the area under the curve is above this center point, and the other half is below it.
2. The normal probability distribution is **symmetrical** about its mean. If we cut the normal curve vertically at this central value, the two halves will be mirror images.
3. The normal curve falls off smoothly in either direction from the central value. It is **asymptotic,** meaning that the curve gets closer and closer to the *X*-axis but never actually touches it. That is, the "tails" of the curve extend indefinitely in both directions.

These characteristics are shown graphically in Chart 7–1, on the following page.

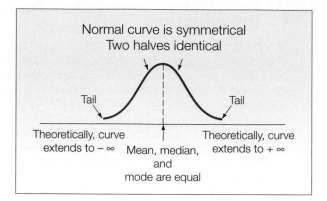

Chart 7–1   Characteristics of a Normal Distribution

There is not just one normal probability distribution, but rather a "family" of them. There is one normal probability distribution for the lengths of service of the employees in our Camden plant, where the mean is 20 years and the standard deviation is 3.1 years. There is another normal probability distribution for the lengths of service in our Dunkirk plant, where $\mu = 20$ years and $\sigma = 3.9$ years. Chart 7–2 portrays three normal distributions, where the means are the same but the standard deviations are different.

Equal means, unequal standard deviations

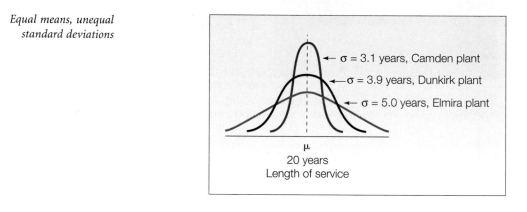

Chart 7–2   Normal Probability Distributions with Equal Means but Different Standard Deviations

Chart 7–3 shows the distribution of weights of three different cereals. The weights are normally distributed with different means but identical standard deviations.

Unequal means, equal standard deviations

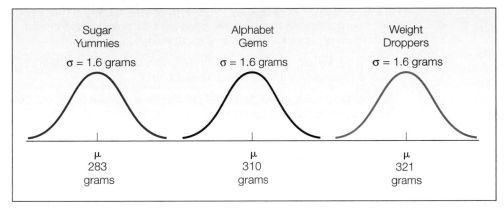

Chart 7–3   Normal Probability Distributions Having Different Means but Equal Standard Deviations

Finally, Chart 7–4 shows three normal distributions having different means and standard deviations. They show the distribution of tensile strengths, measured in pounds per square inch (psi) for three types of cables.

Unequal means, unequal standard deviations

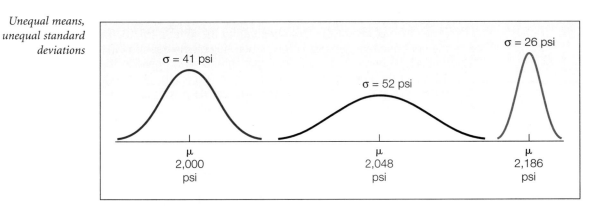

Chart 7–4   Normal Probability Distributions with Different Means and Standard Deviations

▌ The Standard Normal Probability Distribution

We noted that there is a family of normal distributions. Each distribution may have a different mean (μ) or standard deviation (σ). The number of normal distributions is therefore unlimited. It would be physically impossible to provide a table of probabilities (such as for the binomial and Poisson) for each combination of μ and σ. Fortunately, one member of the family of normal distributions can be used for all problems where the normal distribution is applicable. It has a mean of 0 and a standard deviation of 1 and is called the **standard normal distribution.** Any normal distribution can be converted into the "standard normal distribution" by subtracting the mean from each observation and dividing by the standard deviation.

First, it is necessary to convert, or *standardize,* the actual distribution to a standard normal distribution using a *z value,* also called a *z score,* a *z statistic,* the *standard normal deviate,* or just the *normal deviate.*

| **z Value**   The distance between a selected value, designed X, and the mean μ, divided by the standard deviation, σ.

So, a *z* value is the distance from the mean, measured in units of the standard deviation. In terms of a formula:

THE STANDARD NORMAL VALUE	$$z = \frac{X - \mu}{\sigma}$$	**[7–1]**

where:

    X is the value of any particular observation or measurement.

    μ is the mean of the distribution.

    σ is the standard deviation of the distribution.

As noted in the above definition, a *z* value measures the distance between a particular value of *X* and the arithmetic mean in units of the standard deviation. By determining the *z* value using formula (7–1), we can find the area or the probability under any normal curve by referring to Appendix D (also on the inside back cover).

To explain, suppose we computed *z* to be 1.91. What is the area under the normal curve between the mean and *X*? A portion of Appendix D is repeated as Table 7–1. Go down the column of the table headed by the letter *z* to 1.9. Then move horizontally to the right and read the probability under the column headed 0.01. It is .4719. This means that 47.19 percent of the area under the curve is between the mean and the *X* value 1.91 standard deviations above the mean. This is the *probability* that an observation is between 0 and 1.91 standard deviations of the mean.

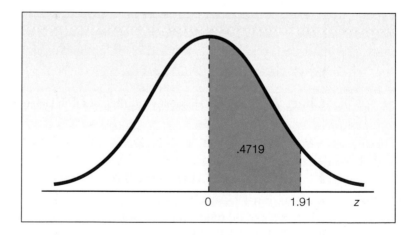

Table 7–1 Areas under the Normal Curve

z	0.00	0.01	0.02	0.03	0.04	0.05	...
⋮							
1.0	0.3413	0.3438	0.3461	0.3485	0.3508	0.3531	
1.1	0.3643	0.3665	0.3686	0.3708	0.3729	0.3749	
1.2	0.3849	0.3869	0.3888	0.3907	0.3925	0.3944	
1.3	0.4032	0.4049	0.4066	0.4082	0.4099	0.4115	
1.4	0.4192	0.4207	0.4222	0.4236	0.4251	0.4265	
1.5	0.4332	0.4345	0.4357	0.4370	0.4382	0.4394	
1.6	0.4452	0.4463	0.4474	0.4484	0.4495	0.4505	
1.7	0.4554	0.4564	0.4573	0.4582	0.4591	0.4599	
1.8	0.4641	0.4649	0.4656	0.4664	0.4671	0.4678	
1.9	0.4713	0.4719	0.4726	0.4732	0.4738	0.4744	
⋮							

Applications of the Standard Normal Distribution

What is the area under the curve between the mean and X for the following z values? Check your answers against those given. Not all the values are available in Table 7–1. You will need to use Appendix D or the table located in the back endpapers of the text.

Computed z Value	Area under Curve
2.84	.4977
1.00	.3413
0.49	.1879

Now we will compute the z value given the population mean, μ, the population standard deviation, σ, and a selected X.

Example

The weekly incomes of a large group of middle managers are normally distributed with a mean of \$1,000 and a standard deviation of \$100. What is the z value for an income X of \$1,100? For \$900?

Solution

Using formula (7–1), the z values for the two X values (\$1,100 and \$900) are computed as follows:

For $X = \$1,100$:

$$z = \frac{X - \mu}{\sigma}$$

$$= \frac{\$1,100 - \$1,000}{\$100}$$

$$= 1.00$$

For $X = \$900$:

$$z = \frac{X - \mu}{\sigma}$$

$$= \frac{\$900 - \$1,000}{\$100}$$

$$= -1.00$$

The *z* of 1.00 indicates that a weekly income of $1,100 for a middle manager is one standard deviation above the mean, and a *z* of −1.00 shows that a $900 income is one standard deviation below the mean. Note that both incomes ($1,100 and $900) are the same distance ($100) from the mean.

SELF-REVIEW 7–1

Using the same information as in the preceding example (μ = $1,000, σ = $100), convert:

(a)   The weekly income of $1,225 to a standard unit (*z* value).
(b)   The weekly income of $775 to a *z* value.

Areas under the Normal Curve

Before examining various applications of the standard normal probability distribution, we will consider three areas under the normal curve that will be used extensively in the following chapters. They were also called the Empirical Rule in Chapter 4.

1.   About 68 percent of the area under the normal curve is within plus one and minus one standard deviation of the mean. This can be written as $\mu \pm 1\sigma$.
2.   About 95 percent of the area under the normal curve is within plus and minus two standard deviations of the mean, written $\mu \pm 2\sigma$.
3.   Practically all of the area under the normal curve is within three standard deviations of the mean, written $\mu \pm 3\sigma$.

Shown diagrammatically, using more precise percentages:

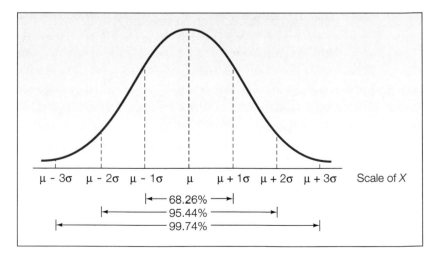

Transforming measurements to standard normal deviates changes the scale. The conversions are shown in the following graph. For example, $\mu + 1\sigma$ is converted to a z value of $+1.00$. Likewise, $\mu - 2\sigma$ is transformed to a z value of -2.00. Note that the center of the z distribution is zero, indicating no deviation from the mean, μ

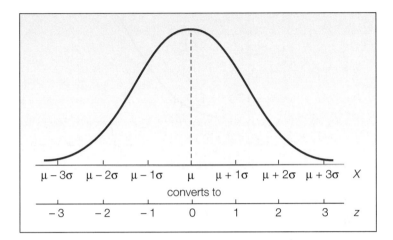

Total area under the normal curve is 1. These concepts can be stated somewhat differently: The area under the normal curve within plus and minus one standard deviation of the mean is .6826. The area within plus and minus two standard deviations of the mean is .9544. The area within three standard deviations of the mean is .9974. The total area under the normal curve is 1.0000.

Example

A life test on a large number of type D alkaline batteries revealed that the mean life for a particular use before failure is 19.0 hours. The distribution of the lives approximated a normal distribution. The standard deviation of the distribution was 1.2 hours.

1. About 68 percent of the batteries failed between what two values?
2. About 95 percent of the batteries failed between what two values?
3. Virtually all of the batteries failed between what two values?

Solution

1. About 68 percent failed between 17.8 hours and 20.2 hours, found by 19.0 ± 1(1.2).
2. About 95 percent failed between 16.6 hours and 21.4 hours, found by 19.0 ± 2(1.2).
3. Virtually all failed between 15.4 hours and 22.6 hours, found by 19.0 ± 3(1.2).

Shown in a diagram:

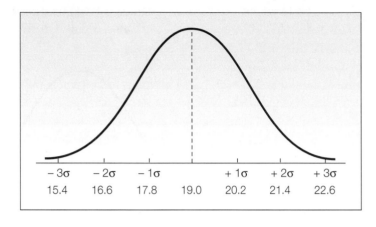

	−3σ	−2σ	−1σ		+1σ	+2σ	+3σ
	15.4	16.6	17.8	19.0	20.2	21.4	22.6

SELF-REVIEW 7–2

The distribution of the annual incomes of a group of middle-management employees at Compton Plastics approximates a normal distribution with a mean of $37,200 and a standard deviation of $800.

(a) About 68 percent of the incomes lie between what two amounts?
(b) About 95 percent of the incomes lie between what two amounts?
(c) Virtually all of the incomes lie between what two amounts?
(d) What are the median and the modal incomes?
(e) Is the distribution of incomes symmetrical?

❚ Exercises

1. Explain what is meant by this statement: "There is not just one normal probability distribution but a 'family' of them."
2. List the major characteristics of a normal probability distribution.
3. The mean of a normal probability distribution is 500; the standard deviation is 10.
    a. About 68 percent of the observations lie between what two values?
    b. About 95 percent of the observations lie between what two values?
    c. Practically all of the observations lie between what two values?
4. The mean of a normal probability distribution is 60; the standard deviation is 5.
    a. About what percent of the observations lie between 55 and 65?
    b. About what percent of the observations lie between 50 and 70?
    c. About what percent of the observations lie between 45 and 75?

   The first application of the standard normal distribution involves the determination of the area under the normal curve between the mean and a selected value, designated X. Using the same problem as in the previous weekly income example ($\mu = \$1,000$, $\sigma = \$100$), what is the area under the normal curve between $1,000 and $1,100?

   We have already converted $1,100 to a z value of 1.00 using formula (7–1). To repeat:

$$z = \frac{X - \mu}{\sigma} = \frac{\$1,100 - \$1,000}{\$100} = 1.00$$

The probability associated with a z of 1.00 has been computed and is found in Appendix D. A small portion of that appendix table follows. To locate the area, go down the left column to 1.0. Then move horizontally to the right, and read the area under the curve in the column marked .00. It is .3413.

z	.00	.01	.02
0.7	.2580	.2611	.2642
0.8	.2881	.2910	.2939
0.9	.3159	.3186	.3212
1.0	.3413	.3438	.3461
1.1	.3643	.3665	.3686

Shown in a diagram:

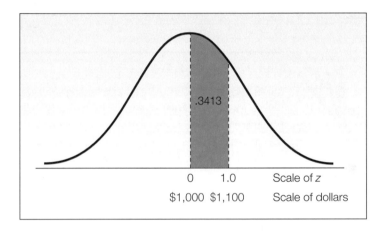

The area under the normal curve between $1,000 and $1,100 is .3413. One can also say that 34.13 percent of the weekly incomes are between $1,000 and $1,100 and that the probability of a particular income being between $1,000 and $1,100 is .3413.

Example

Refer to the previous problem ($\mu = \$1,000$, $\sigma = \$100$).

1. What is the probability that a particular weekly income selected at random is between $790 and $1,000?
2. What is the probability that the income is less than $790?

Solution

Computing the z value for $790 using formula (7–1):

$$z = \frac{X - \mu}{\sigma} = \frac{\$790 - \$1,000}{\$100} = \frac{-\$210}{\$100} = -2.10$$

1. The area under the normal curve between μ and X corresponding to a z value of −2.10 is .4821 (from Appendix D). The minus sign in front of 2.10 indicates that the area is to the left of the mean but does not change its size.

2. The mean divides the normal curve into two identical halves. The area under the half to the left of the mean is .5000, and the area to the right of the mean is also .5000. Since the area under the curve between $790 and $1,000 is .4821, the area below $790 can be found by subtracting .4821 from .5000. Thus, .5000 − .4821 = .0179. Shown in a diagram:

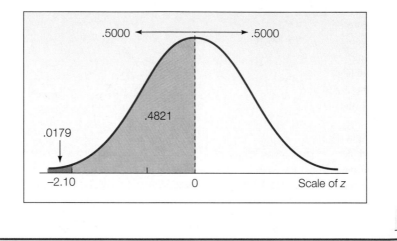

SELF-REVIEW 7–3

The employees of Cartwright Manufacturing are awarded efficiency ratings. The distribution of the ratings approximates a normal distribution. The mean is 400, the standard deviation 50.

(a) What is the area under the normal curve between 400 and 482?
(b) What is the area under the normal curve for ratings greater than 482?
(c) Show the facets of this problem in a chart.

▌ Exercises

5. A normal population has a mean of 20.0 and a standard deviation of 4.0.
    a. Compute the z value associated with 25.0.
    b. What proportion of the population is between 20.0 and 25.0?
    c. What proportion of the population is less than 18.0?
6. A normal population has a mean of 12.2 and a standard deviation of 2.5.
    a. Compute the z value associated with 14.3.
    b. What proportion of the population is between 12.2 and 14.3?
    c. What proportion of the population is less than 10.0?
7. A recent study of the hourly wages of maintenance crews for major airlines showed that the mean hourly salary was $16.50, with a standard deviation of $3.50. If we select a crew member at random, what is the probability the crew member earns:
    a. Between $16.50 and $20.00 per hour?
    b. More than $20.00 per hour?
    c. Less than $15.00 per hour?
8. The mean of a normal distribution is 400 pounds. The standard deviation is 10 pounds.
    a. What is the area between 415 pounds and the mean of 400 pounds?
    b. What is the area between the mean and 395 pounds?
    c. What is the probability of selecting a value at random and discovering that it has a value of less than 395 pounds?

A second application of the standard normal distribution involves combining two areas, one to the right and the other to the left of the mean.

Example

Returning to the distribution of weekly incomes (μ = $1,000, σ = $100), what is the area under the normal curve between $840 and $1,200?

Solution

The problem can be divided into two parts. For the area between $840 and the mean of $1,000:

$$z = \frac{\$840 - \$1,000}{\$100} = \frac{-\$160}{\$100} = -1.60$$

For the area between the mean of $1,000 and $1,200:

$$z = \frac{\$1,200 - \$1,000}{\$100} = \frac{\$200}{\$100} = 2.00$$

The area under the curve for a z of -1.60 is .4452 (from Appendix D). The area under the curve for a z of 2.00 is .4772. Adding the two areas: .4452 + .4772 = .9224. Thus, the probability of selecting an income between $840 and $1,200 is .9224. In other words, 92.24 percent of the managers have weekly incomes between $840 and $1,200. Shown in a diagram:

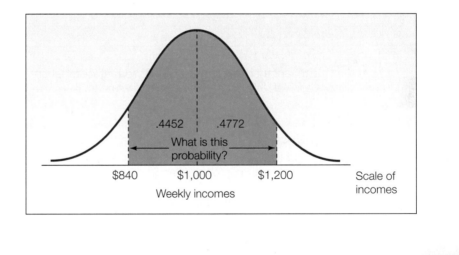

Another application of the normal distribution is finding the area above, or below, a specified value.

Example

Returning again to the weekly incomes illustration (μ = $1,000, σ = $100), what percent of the executives earn weekly incomes of $1,245 or more?

Solution

We first need to find the area between the mean of $1,000 and $1,245. We will first use formula (7–1) to find z.

$$z = \frac{X - \mu}{\sigma} = \frac{\$1,245 - \$1,000}{\$100} = \frac{\$245}{\$100} = 2.45$$

Then, referring to Appendix D, the area associated with a z of 2.45 is .4929. This is the area between $1,000 and $1,245. Logically, the area for $1,245 and beyond is found by subtracting .4929 from .5000. This area is .0071, indicating that only 0.71 percent of the executives earn weekly incomes of $1,245 or more.

The following diagram shows the various facets of this problem.

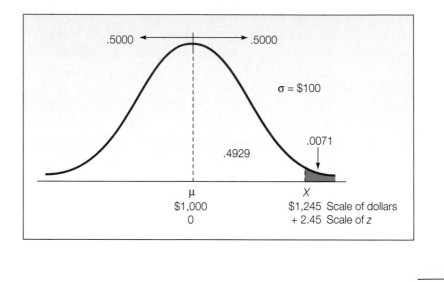

Still another application of the normal distribution involves determining the area between values on the *same* side of the mean.

Example

Returning to the weekly incomes example ($\mu = \$1,000$, $\sigma = \$100$), what is the area under the normal curve between $1,150 and $1,250?

Solution

The problem is again separated into two parts, and formula (7–1) is used. First, we find the z value associated with a weekly salary of $1,250:

$$z = \frac{\$1,250 - \$1,000}{\$100} = 2.50$$

Next we find the z value for a weekly salary of $1,150:

$$z = \frac{\$1,150 - \$1,000}{\$100} = 1.50$$

From Appendix D the area associated with a z value of 2.50 is .4938. So the probability of a weekly salary between $1,000 and $1,250 is .4938. Similarly, the area associated with a z value of 1.50 is .4332, so the probability of a weekly salary between $1,000 and $1,150 is .4332. The probability of a weekly salary between $1,150 and $1,250 is found by subtracting the area associated with a z value of 1.50 (.4332) from that associated with a z of 2.50 (.4938). Thus, the probability of a weekly salary between $1,150 and $1,250 is .0606. Shown in a diagram:

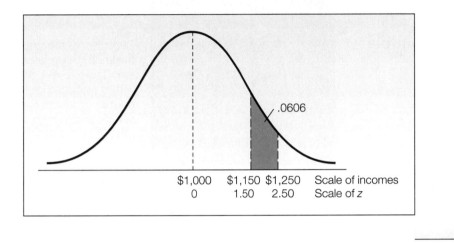

In brief, there are only four situations in which you may wish to find the area under the standard normal distribution.

1. If you wish to find the area between 0 and z (or $-z$), then you can look up the value directly in the table.
2. If you wish to find the area beyond z or $(-z)$, then locate the probability of z in the table and subtract that value from .5000.
3. If you wish to find the area between two points on different sides of the mean, determine the z values and add the corresponding areas.
4. If you wish to find the area between two points on the same side of the mean, determine the z values and subtract the smaller area from the larger.

SELF-REVIEW 7–4

Refer to the previous example, where the mean weekly salary is $1,000 and σ is $100.

(a) What percent of the executives earn a weekly income between $750 and $1,225? Draw a normal curve and shade the desired area on your diagram.
(b) What percent of the executives earn a weekly income between $1,100 and $1,225? Draw a normal curve and shade the desired area on your diagram.

Previous examples required finding the percent of the observations located between two observations or the percent of the observations above, or below, a particular obser-

vation *X*. A further application of the normal distribution involves finding the value of the observation *X* when the percent above or below the observation is given.

Example

Suppose a tire manufacturer wants to set a minimum mileage guarantee on its new MX100 tire. Tests reveal the mean mileage is 47,900 with a standard deviation of 2,050 miles and a normal distribution. The manufacturer wants to set the minimum guaranteed mileage so that no more than 4 percent of the tires will have to be replaced. What minimum guaranteed mileage should the manufacturer announce?

Solution

The facets of this problem are shown in the following diagram, where *X* represents the minimum guaranteed mileage.

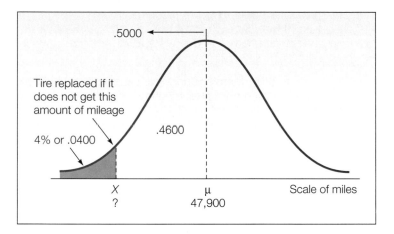

Inserting these values in formula (7–1) for *z*:

$$z = \frac{X - \mu}{\sigma} = \frac{X - 47,900}{2,050}$$

There are two unknowns, *z* and *X*. To find *z*, notice the area under the normal curve to the left of *μ* is .5000. The area between *μ* and *X* is .4600, found by .5000 − .0400. Now refer to Appendix D. Search the body of the table for the area closest to .4600, namely .4599. Move to the margins from this value and read the *z* value of 1.75. Because the value is to the left of the mean, it is actually −1.75. These steps are summarized in Table 7–2.

Table 7–2   Selected Areas under the Normal Curve

z	.03	.04	.05	.06
⋮				
1.5	.4370	.4382	.4394	.4406
1.6	.4484	.4495	.4505	.4515
1.7	.4582	.4591	.4599	.4608
1.8	.4664	.4671	.4678	.4686

Knowing that the distance between μ and X is -1.75σ, we can now solve for X (the minimum guaranteed mileage):

$$z = \frac{X - 47{,}900}{2{,}050}$$

$$-1.75 = \frac{X - 47{,}900}{2{,}050}$$

$$-1.75(2{,}050) = X - 47{,}900$$

$$X = 47{,}900 - 1.75(2{,}050) = 44{,}312$$

So the manufacturer can advertise that it will replace for free any tire that wears out before it reaches 44,312 miles, and the company will know that only 4 percent of the tires will be replaced under this plan.

SELF-REVIEW   7–5

An analysis of the final test scores for a computer programming seminar revealed that they approximate a normal curve with a mean of 75 and a standard deviation of 8. The instructor wants to award the grade of A to the upper 10 percent of the test grades. What is the dividing point between an A and a B grade?

A fourth application of the normal distribution is to compare two or more observations that are on different scales or in different units. That is, the observations are in different distributions.

Example
Comparing observations on different scales

Suppose a study of the inmates at a correctional institution is concerned with the social responsibility of the inmates in prison and their prospects for rehabilitation upon being released. Each inmate is given a test regarding social responsibility. The scores are normally distributed, with a mean of 100 and a standard deviation of 20. Prison psychologists rated each of the inmates with respect to the prospect for rehabilitation. These ratings are also normally distributed, with a mean of 500 and a standard deviation of 100.

Tora Carney scored 146 on the social responsibility test, and her rating with respect to rehabilitation is 335. How does Tora compare to the group with respect to social responsibility and the prospect for rehabilitation?

Solution   Converting her social responsibility test score of 146 to a *z* value using formula (7–1):

$$z = \frac{X - \mu}{\sigma} = \frac{146 - 100}{20}$$

$$= \frac{46}{20} = 2.30$$

Converting her rehabilitation rating of 335 to a *z* value:

$$z = \frac{X - \mu}{\sigma} = \frac{335 - 500}{100}$$

$$= \frac{-165}{100} = -1.65$$

The standardized test score and the standardized rating are shown below.

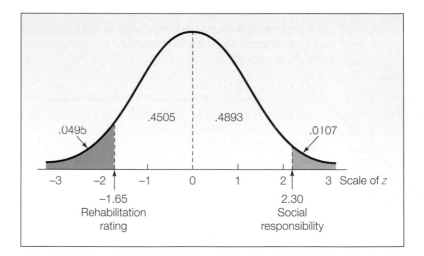

With respect to social responsibility, therefore, Tora Carney is in the highest 1 percent of the group. However, compared with the other inmates, she is among the lowest 5 percent with regard to the prospects for rehabilitation.

Self-Review 7–6 illustrates the use of the standard normal distribution for comparing data in different units — ratios and percent changes, in this case. The ratios are in one distribution and the percent changes in another.

SELF-REVIEW 7–6

The price-earnings (PE) ratios and the changes in price over a three-year period for selected stocks were studied. For the PE ratios, $\mu = 10.0$ and $\sigma = 2.0$. For the price changes, $\mu = 50$ percent and $\sigma = 10$ percent. Both distributions are normally distributed. Radnor Industries had a PE of 11.2 and a 75 percent increase in price in the three-year period.

(a) Convert Radnor's PE and percent change to z values.
(b) Show the two z values on a standardized normal curve.
(c) Compare Radnor's PE ratio and percent change with those of the other selected stocks.

▌ Exercises

9. A normal population has a mean of 50.0 and a standard deviation of 4.0.
   a. Compute the probability of a value between 44.0 and 55.0.
   b. Compute the probability of a value greater than 55.0.
   c. Compute the probability of a value between 52.0 and 55.0.
   d. Determine the value of X below which 95 percent of the values will occur.
10. A normal population has a mean of 80.0 and a standard deviation of 14.0.
    a. Compute the probability of a value between 75.0 and 90.0.
    b. Compute the probability of a value 75.0 or less.
    c. Compute the probability of a value between 55.0 and 70.0.
    d. Determine the value of X above which 80 percent of the values will occur.
11. A cola-dispensing machine is set to dispense on average 7.00 ounces of cola per cup. The standard deviation is 0.10 ounces. What is the probability that a machine will dispense:
    a. Between 7.10 and 7.25 ounces of cola?
    b. 7.25 ounces of cola or more?
    c. Between 6.8 and 7.25 ounces of cola?
    d. How much cola is dispensed in the largest 1 percent of the drinks?
12. The amounts of money requested in home loan applications at Dawn River Federal Savings are approximately normally distributed with a mean of $70,000 and a standard deviation of $20,000. A loan application is received this morning. What is the probability that:
    a. The amount requested is $80,000 or more?
    b. The amount requested is between $65,000 and $80,000?
    c. The amount requested is $65,000 or more?
    d. Twenty percent of the loans are larger than what amount?
13. WNAE, an FM stereo station with a rock and roll format, finds that the mean length of time a person is tuned to the station is 15.0 minutes with a standard deviation of 3.5 minutes. What is the probability that a particular listener will tune in:
    a. For 20 minutes or more?
    b. For 20 minutes or less?
    c. Between 10 and 12 minutes?
    d. Seventy percent of the listeners are tuned in for how many minutes or less?

▌ The Normal Approximation to the Binomial

Chapter 6 described the binomial probability distribution, which is a discrete distribution. The table of binomial probabilities in Appendix A goes successively from an n of 1 to an n of 20, and then to $n = 25$. Suppose a problem involved taking a sample of 60. Generating a binomial distribution for that large a number would be very time consuming—even using a computer. A more efficient approach is to apply the *normal approximation to the binomial*.

Using the normal distribution (a continuous distribution) as a substitute for a binomial distribution (a discrete distribution) for large values of *n* seems reasonable because, as *n* increases, a binomial distribution gets closer and closer to a normal distribution. The change in the shape of a binomial distribution with $\pi = .50$ from an *n* of 1 to an *n* of 20 is depicted in Chart 7–5.

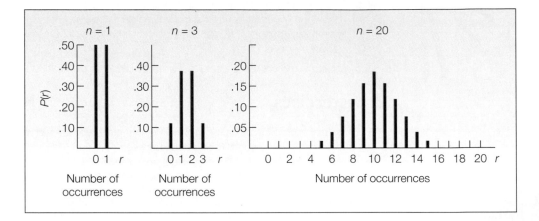

Chart 7–5   Binomial Distributions for an *n* of 1, 3, and 20, Where $\pi = .50$

When to use the normal approximation

When can we use the normal approximation to the binomial? The normal probability distribution is generally deemed a good approximation to the binomial probability distribution when $n\pi$ and $n(1 - \pi)$ are both at least 5. However, before we apply the normal approximation, we must make sure that our distribution of interest is in fact a binomial distribution. Recall from Chapter 6 that four criteria must be met:

1. There are only two mutually exclusive outcomes to an experiment: a "success" and a "failure."
2. The distribution results from counting the number of successes in a fixed number of trials.
3. Each trial is independent.
4. The probability, π, remains the same from trial to trial.

Continuity Correction Factor

To show the application of the normal approximation to the binomial and the need for a correction factor, suppose that the management of the Santoni Pizza Restaurant found that 70 percent of their new customers return for another meal. For a week in which 80 new (first-time) customers dined at Santoni's, what is the probability that 60 or more will return for another meal?

Notice that the binomial conditions are met: (1) There are only two possible outcomes—a customer either returns for another meal or does not return. (2) We can count the number of successes, meaning, for example, that 57 of the 80 customers return. (3) The trials are independent, meaning that if the 34th person returns for a second meal, that does not affect whether the 58th person returns. (4) The probability of a customer returning remains at .70 for all 80 customers.

Therefore, we could use the binomial formula (6–3)

$$P(x) = \frac{n!}{x!(n - x)!} (\pi)^x (1 - \pi)^{(n - x)}$$

The binomial probabilities for the distribution of between 43 and 68 returning customers are shown in the table below.

Number Returning	Probability	Number Returning	Probability
43	0.001	56	0.097
44	0.002	57	0.095
45	0.003	58	0.088
46	0.006	59	0.077
47	0.009	60	0.063
48	0.015	61	0.048
49	0.023	62	0.034
50	0.033	63	0.023
51	0.045	64	0.014
52	0.059	65	0.008
53	0.072	66	0.004
54	0.084	67	0.002
55	0.093	68	0.001

We can find the probability of 60 or more returning by summing 0.063 + 0.048 + · · · + 0.001, which is 0.197. However, a look at the plot below shows the similarity of this distribution to a normal distribution. All we need do is smooth out the discrete probabilities into a continuous distribution. Furthermore, working with a normal distribution will involve far fewer calculations than working with the binomial.

The trick is to let the discrete probability for 56 customers be represented by an area under the curve between 55.5 and 56.5. Then let the probability for 57 customers be represented by an area between 56.5 and 57.5 and so on. This is just the opposite of rounding off the numbers to a whole number.

Because we are going to use the normal curve to determine the binomial probability of 60 or more successes, we must subtract, in this case, .5 from 60. The value .5 is called the **continuity correction factor.** This small adjustment must be made because a continuous distribution (the normal distribution) is being used to approximate a discrete distribution (the binomial distribution). Subtracting, 60 − .5 = 59.5.

Continuity Correction Factor   The value .5 subtracted or added, depending on the problem, to a selected value when a discrete probability distribution is being approximated by a continuous probability distribution.

How to Apply the Correction Factor

Only four cases may arise. These cases are:

1. For the probability *at least X* occur, use the area *above* $(X - .5)$.
2. For the probability that *more than X* occur, use the area *above* $(X + .5)$.
3. For the probability that *X or fewer* occur, use the area *below* $(X + .5)$.
4. For the probability that *fewer than X* occur, use the area *below* $(X - .5)$.

To use the normal distribution to approximate the probability that 60 or more first-time Santoni customers out of 80 will return, follow the procedure shown below.

Step 1.   Find the z corresponding to an X of 59.5 using formula (7–1), and formulas (6–4) and (6–5) for the mean and the variance of a binomial distribution:

$$\mu = n\pi = 80(.70) = 56$$

$$\sigma^2 = n\pi(1 - \pi) = 80(.70)(1 - .70) = 16.8$$

$$\sigma = \sqrt{16.8} = 4.10$$

$$z = \frac{X - \mu}{\sigma} = \frac{59.5 - 56}{4.10} = 0.85$$

Step 2.   Determine the area under the normal curve between a μ of 56 and an X of 59.5. From step 1, we know that the z value corresponding to 59.5 is 0.85. So we go to Appendix D and read down the left margin to 0.8, and then we go horizontally to the area under the column headed by .05. That area is .3023.

Step 3.   Calculate the area beyond 59.5 by subtracting .3023 from .5000 $(.5000 - .3023 = .1977)$. Thus, .1977 is the approximate probability that 60 or more first-time Santoni customers out of 80 will return for another meal.

The facets of this problem are shown graphically:

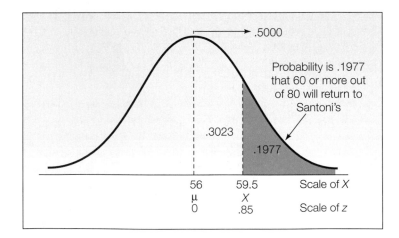

No doubt you will agree that using the normal approximation to the binomial is a much more efficient method of estimating the probability of 60 or more first-time customers returning.

SELF-REVIEW 7-7

A study by Great Southern Home Insurance revealed that none of the stolen goods were recovered by the homeowners in 80 percent of reported thefts.

(a) During a period in which 200 thefts occurred, what is the probability that no stolen goods were recovered in 170 or more of the robberies?
(b) During a period in which 200 thefts occurred, what is the probability that no stolen goods were recovered in 150 or more robberies?

▌Exercises

14. Landrum Airline flies the route between Chicago and Pittsburgh. The mean number of passengers per flight is 160 with a standard deviation of 20. The aircraft used for the route has 200 seats.
    a. What percent of the flights are sold out?
    b. The airline must sell 150 seats to break even on this particular flight. On what percent of the flights does the airline make money?
    c. The airline would like to reduce the number of flight attendants on 20 percent of the flights. This will be done on the flights with the fewest passengers. Below what number of passengers on a flight will the airline reduce the number of flight attendants?
15. Suppose X has a binomial probability distribution with $n = 50$ and $\pi = .25$. Compute the following:
    a. The mean and standard deviation of the random variable.
    b. The probability that X is 15 or more.
    c. The probability that X is 10 or less.
16. Suppose X has a binomial probability distribution with $n = 40$ and $\pi = .55$. Compute the following:
    a. The mean and standard deviation of the random variable.
    b. The probability that X is 25 or greater.
    c. The probability that X is 15 or less.
    d. The probability that X is between 15 and 25 inclusive.
17. Theresa's Tax Service specializes in federal tax returns. A recent audit by the IRS of the returns she prepared indicated that an error was made on 10 percent of the returns she prepared last year. Assuming this rate continues into this year and she prepares 60 returns, what is the probability that she makes:
    a. More than nine errors?
    b. At least nine errors?
    c. Exactly nine errors?
18. Shorty's Muffler advertises that they can change a muffler in 30 minutes or less. However, the work standards department at corporate headquarters recently conducted a study and found that 20 percent of the mufflers were not installed in 30 minutes or less. The Maumee branch installed 50 mufflers last month. If the corporate report is correct:
    a. How many of the installations at the Maumee branch would you expect to take more than 30 minutes?
    b. What is the likelihood that fewer than eight installations took more than 30 minutes?
    c. What is the likelihood that eight or fewer installations took more than 30 minutes?
    d. What is the likelihood that exactly eight of the 50 installations took more than 30 minutes?
19. A study conducted by the nationally known Taurus Health Club revealed that 30 percent of its new members are significantly overweight. A membership drive in a metropolitan area resulted in 500 new members.
    a. It has been suggested that the normal approximation to the binomial be used to

determine the probability that 175 or more of the new members are significantly overweight. Does this problem qualify as a binomial problem? Explain.

b. What is the probability that 175 or more of the new members are overweight?

c. What is the probability that 140 or more new members are significantly overweight?

20. Research on new juvenile delinquents who were put on probation by Judge Conners revealed that 38 percent of them committed another crime.

a. What is the probability that of the last 100 new juvenile delinquents put on probation, 30 or more will commit another crime?

b. What is the probability that 40 or fewer of the delinquents will commit another crime?

c. What is the probability that between 30 and 40 of the delinquents will commit another crime?

❙ Chapter Outline

I. The normal distribution is a continuous probability distribution with the following major characteristics.

    A. It is bell-shaped, and the mean, median, and mode are equal.

    B. It is symmetrical.

    C. It is asymptotic, meaning the curve approaches but never touches the X-axis.

    D. It is completely described by the mean and the standard deviation.

    E. There is a family of normal distributions. Each time the mean or the standard deviation changes, a new distribution is created.

II. The standard normal distribution is a particular normal distribution.

    A. It has a mean of 0.00 and a standard deviation of 1.00.

    B. Any normal distribution can be converted to the standard normal distribution by the following formula.

$$z = \frac{X - \mu}{\sigma} \qquad \text{[7–1]}$$

    C. By standardizing a normal distribution, we can report the distance from the mean in units of the standard deviation.

III. The normal distribution can be used to approximate a binomial distribution under certain conditions.

    A. $n\pi$ and $n(1 - \pi)$ must both be at least 5.

        1. n is the number of observations.

        2. π is the probability of a success.

    B. The four conditions for a binomial distribution are:

        1. There are only two possible outcomes.

        2. π remains the same from trial to trial.

        3. The trials are independent.

        4. The distribution results from a count of the number of successes in a fixed number of trials.

    C. The mean and the variance of a binomial distribution are computed as follows:

$$\mu = n\pi$$

$$\sigma^2 = n\pi(1 - \pi)$$

    D. The continuity correction factor of .5 is used to extend the continuous value of X one-half unit in either direction. This correction compensates for estimating a discrete distribution by a continuous distribution.

❙ Chapter Exercises

21. Ball-Bearings, Inc. produces ball bearings automatically on a Kronar BBX machine. For one of the ball bearings, the arithmetic mean diameter is set at 20.00 mm (millimeters). The standard deviation of the production over a long period of time was computed to be 0.150 mm.

  a. What percent of the ball bearings will have diameters between 20.00 mm and 20.27 mm?
  b. What percent of the ball bearings will have diameters of 20.27 mm or more?
  c. What percent of the ball bearings will have diameters between 19.85 mm and 20.30 mm?
  d. What percent of the ball bearings will have diameters of 19.91 mm or less?

22. The accounting department at Weston, a national manufacturer of unattached garages, reports that it takes two construction workers a mean of 32 hours and a standard deviation of 2 hours to erect the Red Barn model.
  a. What percent of the garages take between 32 hours and 34 hours to erect?
  b. What percent of the garages take 28.7 hours or less to erect?
  c. What percent of the garages take between 29 hours and 34 hours to erect?
  d. Of the garages, 5 percent take how many hours or more to erect?

23. The net sales and the number of employees for aluminum fabricators with similar characteristics were organized into frequency distributions. Both were normally distributed. For the net sales, μ = $180 million and σ = $25 million. For the number of employees, μ = 1,500 and σ = 120. Clarion Fabricators had sales of $170 million and 1,850 employees.
  a. Convert Clarion's sales and number of employees to z values.
  b. Locate the two z values on a standard normal distribution.
  c. Compare Clarion's sales and number of employees with those of the other fabricators. What percent of the fabricators have more sales than Clarion? More employees?

24. A mechanical aptitude test designed for entering college students has a mean of 1,000 and a standard deviation of 150. An IQ test designed for college students has a mean of 110 and a standard deviation of 10. Shawn Bucci scored 1,310 on the mechanical aptitude test and 122 on the IQ test. Evaluate his test scores relative to those of others who took the tests.

25. A study of Furniture Wholesales, Inc. regarding the payment of invoices revealed that, on the average, an invoice was paid 20 days after it was received. The standard deviation equaled 5 days.
  a. What percent of the invoices are paid within 15 days of receipt?
  b. What is the probability of selecting any invoice and finding it was paid between 18 and 26 days after it was received?
  c. The management of Furniture Wholesales wants to encourage their customers to pay their monthly invoices as soon as possible. Therefore, it was announced that a 2 percent reduction in price would be in effect for customers who pay within 7 working days of the receipt of the invoice. Assuming the payments are normally distributed, out of 200 customers during July, how many would normally be eligible for the reduction?

26. The annual commissions per salesperson employed by Machine Products, which is a manufacturer of light machinery, averaged $40,000, with a standard deviation of $5,000. What percent of the salespersons earn between $32,000 and $42,000?

27. The weights of cans of Monarch pears are normally distributed with a mean of 1,000 grams and a standard deviation of 50 grams. Calculate the percentage of the cans that weigh:
  a. 860 grams or less.
  b. Between 1,055 and 1,100 grams.

28. Past experience with respect to the number of passengers on the *Queen Elizabeth II,* offering one-week cruises to the Caribbean, revealed that the mean number of passengers is 1,820 and the standard deviation of the normal distribution of the number of passengers is 120.
  a. What percent of the cruises will have between 1,820 and 1,970 passengers?
  b. What percent of the cruises will have 1,970 passengers or more?
  c. What percent of the Caribbean cruises will have 1,600 or fewer passengers?

29. Management at Gordon Electronics is considering adopting a bonus system to increase production. One suggestion is to pay a bonus on the highest 5 percent of production based on past experience. Past records indicate that, on the average, 4,000 units of a small assembly are produced during a week. The distribution of the weekly production is approximately normal with a standard deviation of 60 units. If the bonus is paid on the upper 5 percent of production, the bonus will be paid on how many units or more?

30. Fast Service Truck Lines uses the Ford Super 1310 exclusively. Management made a study of the maintenance costs using a sample. It revealed that the arithmetic mean number of kilometers traveled per truck during the year was 60,000. The distances traveled during the year were normally distributed. The standard deviation of the normally distributed distances in the sample of Ford 1310s was 2,000 kilometers.
    a. What percent of the Ford Super 1310s logged 65,200 kilometers or more?
    b. The truck line owns 3,500 Ford Super 1310s. Based on the sample findings, how many of them traveled 55,000 kilometers or less?
    c. How many of the Fords traveled 62,000 kilometers or less during the year?
31. The annual incomes of a large group of supervisors at Belco are normally distributed with a mean of $28,000 and a standard deviation of $1,200. The length of service of the same supervisors is also normally distributed with a mean of 20 years and a standard deviation of 5 years. John McMaster earns $30,400 annually and has 10 years of service.
    a. Compare his income with those of the other supervisors.
    b. Compare his length of service with those of the other supervisors.
32. An executive at Westinghouse drives from his home in the suburbs near Pittsburgh to his office in the center of the city. The driving times are normally distributed with a mean of 35 minutes and a standard deviation of 8 minutes.

    a. In what percent of the days will it take him 30 minutes or less to drive to work?
    b. In what percent of the days will it take 40 minutes or more to drive to work?
    c. Explain to the executive why the probability is nearly 0 that it will take him exactly 40 minutes to get to work.
    d. Since the executive didn't understand your answer to part c, how would you estimate the percent of days in which it takes 40 minutes to drive to work? (Hint: Within what range of values would the times be rounded to 40?)
    e. Some days there will be accidents or other delays, so the trip will take longer than usual. How long will the longest 10 percent of the trips take?
33. A large retailer offers a "no hassle" returns policy. The mean number of customers returning items is 10.3 per day with a standard deviation of 2.25 customers per day.
    a. In what percent of the days are there 8 or fewer customers returning items?
    b. In what percent of the days are there between 12 and 14 customers returning items?
    c. Is there any chance of a day with no returns?
34. A recent study showed that 20 percent of all employees steal from their company each year. If a company employs 50 people, what is the probability that:
    a. Fewer than 5 employees steal?
    b. More than 5 employees steal?
    c. Exactly 5 employees steal?
    d. More than 5 but fewer than 15 employees steal?
35. A recent study showed that 64 percent of American men over the age of 18 consider nutrition a top priority in their lives. A sample of 60 men is selected. What is the likelihood that:
    a. 32 or more consider diet important?
    b. 44 or more consider diet important?
    c. More than 32 but fewer than 43 consider diet important?
    d. Exactly 44 consider diet important?
36. Two-liter plastic bottles used for bottling cola are shipped in lots of 100. Suppose the lots are 5 percent defective. Some bottles leak, some are too small, and so forth.
    a. What is the probability that a shipment of plastic bottles contains 8 or more defectives?
    b. What is the probability that between 8 and 10 bottles are defective?
    c. What is the probability that there are exactly 8 defectives?
    d. What is the probability of no defectives?
37. At Casper State College 20 percent of the students drop basic statistics the first time they enroll. There are 50 students enrolled in Dr. Corbell's statistics class this semester. Compute the following probabilities.
    a. What is the probability that at least 8 drop?

    b. What is the probability that exactly 8 drop?

    c. What is the probability that 8 or fewer drop?

38. Assume that 10 percent of those taking the statistics part of the examination to qualify as a certified public accountant fail. Sixty students are taking the exam this Saturday.

    a. What is the probability that exactly two students will fail?

    b. What is the probability at least two students will fail?

39. The Tri-State county traffic division reported that 40 percent of the high-speed chases involving automobiles result in a minor or major accident. During a month in which 50 high-speed chases occur, what is the probability that 25 or more will result in a minor or major accident?

40. Cruise ships of the Royal Viking line report that 80 percent of their rooms are occupied during September. For a cruise ship having 800 rooms, what is the probability that 665 or more are occupied in September?

41. The goal at U.S. airports handling international flights is to clear these flights within 45 minutes. Let's interpret this to mean that 95 percent of the flights are cleared in 45 minutes, so 5 percent of the flights take longer to clear. Let's also assume that the distribution of times is normal.

    a. If the standard deviation of the time to clear an international flight is 5 minutes, what is the mean time to clear a flight?

    b. Suppose the standard deviation is 10 minutes, not the 5 minutes suggested in part a. What is the new mean?

    c. If an executive has 30 minutes from the time her flight landed to catch her limousine, assuming the information in part b, what is the likelihood that she will be cleared in time?

42. An Air Force study indicated that the probability of a disaster such as the January 28, 1986, explosion of the space shuttle *Challenger* was 1 in 35. Use the normal approximation to the binomial to compute the probability of at least one disaster in 25 missions.

43. The registrar at Elmwood University studied the grade point averages (GPAs) of students over many years. He has discovered that the distribution is approximately normal with a mean of 2.80 and a standard deviation of 0.40.

    a. What is the probability that a randomly selected student has a GPA of from 2.00 up to 3.00?

    b. What percent of the students are on probation, that is, have a GPA less than 2.00?

    c. The student population at EU is 10,000. How many students are on the dean's list, that is, have GPAs of 3.70 or higher?

    d. To qualify for a Bell scholarship, a student must be in the top 10 percent of the student body. What GPA must a student have to qualify for a Bell scholarship?

44. Mr. Jon Molnar will graduate from Eastwood High School this year. He took the American College Test (ACT) for college admission and received a score of 30. The high school principal informed him that only 2 percent of the students taking the exam receive a higher score. The mean score for all students taking the exam is 18.3. Jon's friends Karrie and George also took the test but were not given any information by the principal other than their scores. Karrie scored 25 and George 18. Based on this information, what were Karrie's and George's percentile ranks? What assumption is necessary?

45. Canned hams processed at the Henline Ham Company are normally distributed with a mean of 9.20 pounds and a standard deviation of 0.25 pound. The label weight is given as 9.00 pounds.

    a. What proportion of the hams actually weigh less than the amount claimed on the label?

    b. The owner, Glen Henline, is considering two proposals to reduce the proportion of hams below label weight. He can increase the mean weight to 9.25 and leave the standard deviation the same, or he can leave the mean weight at 9.20 and reduce the standard deviation from 0.25 pound to 0.15. Which change would you recommend?

46. A newspaper article reported that the mean number of hours worked per week by those employed full-time is 43.9. The article further indicated that about one third of those employed full-time work less than 40 hours per week. Given this information and assuming that number of hours worked is normally distributed, what is the standard deviation of

the number of hours worked? The article also indicated that 20 percent of those working full-time work more than 49 hours. Determine the standard deviation with this information. Are the two estimates of the standard deviation similar? What would you conclude if they are not?

47. Most four-year automobile leases allow up to 60,000 miles. If the lessee goes beyond this amount, a penalty of 10 cents per mile is added to the lease cost. Suppose the distribution of miles driven on four-year leases is normal with a mean of 52,000 miles and a standard deviation of 5,000 miles.
    a. What percent of the leases will yield a penalty because of excess mileage?
    b. If the lessor wanted to change the terms so that 25 percent of the leases went over the limit, where should the new upper limit be set?
    c. One definition of a low-mileage car is one that is four years old and has been driven less than 45,000 miles. What percent of the cars returned are considered low-mileage?

48. The price of Blair Corporation stock is normally distributed throughout the year with a mean of $42.00 per share and a standard deviation of $2.25 per share.
    a. What percent of the days is the price over $45.00? If stock is traded 240 days out of the year, how many days is the price over $45.00?
    b. What percent of the days is the price between $38.00 and $40.00?
    c. What is the stock's value on the highest 15 days of the year? (Again assume that there are 240 trading days in a year.)

49. The annual sales of romance novels are normally distributed with an unknown mean and an unknown standard deviation. Forty percent of the time sales are more than 470,000, and 10 percent of the time sales are more than 500,000. What are the mean and the standard deviation?

50. In establishing warranties on TV sets the manufacturer wants to set the limits so that few will need repair at manufacturer expense. On the other hand, the warranty period must be long enough to make the purchase attractive to the buyer. For a new TV the mean number of months until repairs are needed is 36.84 with a standard deviation of 3.34 months. Where should the warranty limits be set so that only 10 percent of the TVs need repairs at the manufacturer's expense?

51. DeKorte Marketing, a telephone sales firm, is considering purchasing a machine that randomly selects and automatically dials telephone numbers. DeKorte Marketing makes most of its calls during the evening, so calls to business phones are wasted. The manufacturer of the machine claims that its programming reduces the business phone calling rate to 15 percent of the calls. As a test, a sample of 150 numbers selected by the machine is checked. If the manufacturer's claim is true, what is the likelihood that more than 30 of the phone numbers selected will be for businesses?

▎ Computer Data Exercises

52. Refer to Data Set 1, which reports information on homes sold in the Venice, Florida, area during the last year.
    a. The mean selling price (in $thousands) of the homes was computed earlier to be $221.10, with a standard deviation of $47.11. Use the normal distribution to estimate the percent of homes selling for more than $280. Compare this to the actual results. Does the normal distribution yield a good approximation of the actual results?
    b. The mean distance from the center of the city is 14.629 miles with a standard deviation of 4.874 miles. Use the normal distribution to estimate the number of homes more than 18 miles but less than 22 miles from the center of the city. Compare this to the actual results. Does the normal distribution yield a good approximation of the actual results?

53. Refer to Data Set 2, which reports information on the 28 Major League Baseball teams for the 1997 season.
    a. The mean attendance per team for the season was 2.257 (in millions) with a standard deviation of .792. Use the normal distribution to estimate the number of teams with

attendance of more than 3.5. Compare that estimate with the actual number. Comment on the accuracy of your estimate.

b. The mean team salary was $38.58 million with a standard deviation of $13.74 million. Use the normal distribution to estimate the number of teams with a team salary of more than $50.0 million. Compare that estimate with the actual number. Comment on the accuracy of your estimate.

54. Refer to Data Set 3, which reports information on the circulation of 48 magazines.

a. The mean circulation of the 48 magazines is 3,048 (in thousands) with a standard deviation of 3,756. Use the normal distribution to estimate the number of magazines with a circulation of more than 5,000. Compare that with the actual percent. Comment on the accuracy of the estimate.

b. The mean percent of the 48 magazines whose readers have a college education is 42.75 percent with a standard deviation of 13.74 percent. Use the normal distribution to estimate the number of magazines where more than 75 percent of readership has a college education. Compare that with the actual percent. Comment on the accuracy of the estimate.

55. Refer to Data Set 4, which reports information on the 94 school districts in Northwest Ohio.

a. The mean amount spent on instruction is $2,725 with a standard deviation of $1,095. Use the normal distribution to estimate the percentage of school districts that spend more than $3,000 on instruction. Compare this estimate with the actual proportion. Does the normal distribution appear accurate in this case? Explain.

b. The mean number of students per school district is 2,134 with a standard deviation of 3,895. Use the normal distribution to estimate the percentage of school districts with more than 2,000 students enrolled. Compare this estimate with the actual proportion. Does the normal district appear accurate in this case? Explain.

CHAPTER 7   *Answers to Self-Review*

7–1   (a) 2.25, found by:

$$z = \frac{\$1,225 - \$1,000}{\$100} = \frac{\$225}{\$100} = 2.25$$

(b) −2.25, found by:

$$z = \frac{\$775 - \$1,000}{\$100} = \frac{-\$225}{\$100} = -2.25$$

7–2   (a) $36,400 and $38,000, found by $37,200 ± 1($800).
(b) $35,600 and $38,800, found by $37,200 ± 2($800).
(c) $34,800 and $39,600, found by $37,200 ± 3($800).
(d) $37,200. Mean, median, and mode are equal for a normal distribution.
(e) Yes, a normal distribution is symmetrical.

7–3   (a) Computing z:

$$z = \frac{482 - 400}{50} = +1.64$$

Referring to Appendix D, the area is .4495.
(b) .0505, found by .5000 − .4495.
(c)

7–4   (a) 98.16%, found by 0.4938 + 0.4878.

(b) 14.65%, found by 0.4878 − 0.3413.

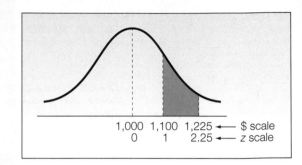

7–5   85.24 (instructor would no doubt make it 85). The closest area to .4000 is .3997; z is 1.28. Then:

$$1.28 = \frac{X - 75}{8}$$

$$10.24 = X - 75$$

$$X = 85.24$$

7–6   (a) $z = 0.60$ for PE ratio, found by:

$$z = \frac{11.2 - 10.0}{2.0} = 0.60$$

$z = 2.50$ for percent change, found by:

$$z = \frac{75 - 50}{10} = 2.50$$

(b)

(c) Compared with the other selected stocks, Radnor's PE ratio is slightly above average; the percent increase is well above average.

7–7 (a) .0465, found by $\mu = n\pi = 200(.80) = 160$, and $\sigma^2 = n\pi(1 - \pi) = 200(.80)(1 - .80) = 32$. Then,

$$\sigma = \sqrt{32} = 5.66$$

$$z = \frac{169.5 - 160}{5.66} = 1.68$$

Area from Appendix D is .4535. Subtracting from .5000 gives .0465.

(b) .9686, found by .4686 + .5000. First calculate z:

$$z = \frac{149.5 - 160}{5.66} = -1.86$$

Area from Appendix D is .4686.

This section is a review of the major concepts, terms, symbols, and equations introduced in Chapters 5, 6, and 7. These three chapters are concerned with methods of dealing with uncertainty. As an example of the uncertainty in business, consider the role of the quality assurance department in most mass-production firms. Usually, the department has neither the personnel nor the time to check, say, all 200 plug-in modules produced during a two-hour period. Standard procedure may call for selecting a sample of 5 modules and shipping all 200 modules if the 5 operate correctly. However, if 1 or more in the sample are defective, all 200 are checked. Assuming that all 5 function correctly, quality assurance personnel cannot be absolutely certain that their action (allowing shipment of the modules) will prove to be correct. It could be that the 5 selected at random are the only ones out of the 200 that function properly! Probability theory lets us measure the uncertainty involved, in this case, of shipping out defective modules. Also, probability as a measurement of uncertainty comes into play when Gallup, Harris, and other pollsters predict that Jim Barstow will win the vacant senatorial seat in Georgia.

Chapter 5 noted that a *probability* is a value between 0 and 1, inclusive, that expresses one's belief that a particular event will occur. A weather forecaster might state that the probability of rain tomorrow is .20. The project director of a firm bidding on a subway station in Bangkok might assess the firm's chance of being awarded the contract at .50. We looked at the ways probabilities can be combined using rules of addition and multiplication, some principles of counting, and the importance of Bayes' theorem.

Chapter 6 presented *discrete* probability distributions — the *binomial distribution,* the *hypergeometric distribution,* and the *Poisson distribution.* Other probability distributions will be discussed in forthcoming chapters (*t* distribution, chi-square distribution, etc.). Probability distributions are listings of all the possible outcomes of an experiment and the probability associated with each outcome. A probability distribution allows us to evaluate sample results.

As an example, suppose a consumer research firm, such as National Family Opinion (NFO), conducted a survey to find whether grocery shoppers can identify the brand name of a product if the name does not appear on the can, box, or package. For question 1, NFO deleted the name of a soup and gave the shopper five choices: (1) Campbell's, (2) Knorr, (3) Progresso, (4) Chalet Suzanne, and (5) Heinz.

There were six similar questions, and 1,000 shoppers participated in the experiment. There is a possibility that shoppers unfamiliar with various labels and brand names would select a name at random —that is, guess the brand name. So a binomial probability distribution is generated to see what a random distribution of choices would look like. These probabilities are in column 2 of the following table; the numbers expected are in column 3. Note that we expect only 2 of the 1,000 shoppers to *guess* five of the six questions correctly. We expect practically no shoppers to guess six out of six. The actual distribution of responses is in column 4. A comparison of columns 3 and 4 indicates that a large percentage of the shoppers can identify the brand name of the product by looking at the label. NFO would conclude that it is highly unlikely for such a large number of shoppers to select so many correct brand names by chance.

1 Number of Correct Identifications	2 Probability*	3 Expected Number by Chance	4 Actual Number in Survey
0	.262	262	5
1	.393	393	16
2	.246	246	10
3	.082	82	27
4	.015	15	81
5	.002	2	346
6	.000	0	515
	1.000	1,000	1,000

*Probabilities from Appendix A.

In Chapter 7 we described the *normal probability distribution,* which is a continuous distribution. Some phenomena, such as the tensile strength of wires and the weights of the contents of cans and bottles, approximate a normal, bell-shaped distribution. Actually, there is a family of normal distributions —each with its own mean and standard deviation. There is a normal distribution, for example, for a mean of $100 and a standard deviation of $5, another for a mean of $149 and a standard deviation of $5.26, and so on. It was noted that a normal probability distribution is bell-shaped and symmetrical about its mean and that the tails of the normal curve extend in either direction infinitely. Since there are an unlimited number of normal distributions, it is difficult to compare two or more distributions directly. Instead, the distributions of interest are *standardized.* The distribution of these standardized values is called the *standard normal distribution.* The standard normal distribution has a mean of 0 and a standard deviation of 1. It is very useful, for example, for comparing distributions in different units. The distribution of the incomes of middle managers and the distribution of their efficiency ratings is an example of distributions in different units. It is also used to compute the probability that various events will happen.

▌ Glossary

Chapter 5

Bayes' theorem   Developed by Reverend Bayes in the 1700s, it is designed to find the probability of one event, *A,* occurring, given that another event, *B,* has already occurred.

Classical probability   Probability based on the assumption that each of the outcomes is equally likely. Using this concept of probability, if there are *n* possible outcomes, the probability of a particular outcome is $1/n$. Thus, on the toss of a coin, the probability of a head is $1/n = \frac{1}{2}$.

Combination formula   A formula to count the number of possible outcomes. If the order *a, b, c* is considered the same as *b, a, c,* or *c, b, a,* and so on, the number of arrangements is found by:

$$_nC_x = \frac{n!}{x!(n-x)!}$$

Conditional probability   The likelihood that an event will occur given that another event has already occurred.

Event   A collection of one or more outcomes of an experiment. For example, an event may be three defective valves in an incoming shipment of valves for a 351 cu. in. Ford V8 engine.

Experiment   An activity that is either observed or measured. An experiment may be counting the number of correct responses to a question, for example.

Empirical probability   A concept of probability based on past experience. For example, the Metropolitan Life Insurance Company reported that during the year, 100.2 of every 100,000 persons in Wyoming died of accidental death (motor vehicle accidents, falls, drowning, firearms, etc.). Based on this experience, Metropolitan can estimate the probability of accidental death for a particular person in Wyoming: $100.2/100,000 = .001002$.

General rule of addition   Used to find the probabilities of complex events made up of *A* or *B.*

$$P(A \text{ or } B) = P(A) + P(B) - P(A \text{ and } B)$$

General rule of multiplication   Used to find the probabilities of complex events made up of *A* or *B.* Example: It is known that there are 3 defective radios in a box containing 10 radios. What is the probability of selecting 2 defective radios on the first two selections from the box?

$$P(A \text{ and } B) = P(A)P(B \mid A) = \frac{3}{10} \times \frac{2}{9} = \frac{6}{90} = .067$$

where $P(B \mid A)$ means "the probability of *B* occurring given that *A* has already occurred."

Independent   The occurrence of one event has no effect on the probability of the occurrence of another event.

Multiplication formula   One of the formulas used to count the number of possible outcomes of an experiment. It states that if there are *m* ways of doing one thing and *n* ways of doing another, there are $m \times n$ ways of doing both. Example: A sports shop offers two sport coats and three contrasting pants for $400. How many different outfits can there be? Answer: $m \times n = 2 \times 3 = 6$.

Outcome   A particular result of an experiment.

Permutation formula   A formula to count the number of possible outcomes. If *a, b, c* is one arrangement, *b, a, c* another, *c, a, b* another, and so on, the total number of arrangements is determined by

$$_nP_r = \frac{n!}{(n-r)!}$$

Probability   A value between 0 and 1, inclusive, that reports the likelihood that a specific event will occur.

Special rule of addition   For this rule to apply, the events must be mutually exclusive. For two events, the probability of *A* or *B* occurring is found by:

$$P(A \text{ or } B) = P(A) + P(B)$$

Example: The probability of a one-spot or a two-spot occurring on the toss of one die is

$$P(A \text{ or } B) = \frac{1}{6} + \frac{1}{6} = \frac{2}{6} = \frac{1}{3}$$

Special rule of multiplication   If two events are not related—that is, they are independent—this rule can be applied to determine the probability of their joint occurrence.

$$P(A \text{ and } B) = P(A)P(B)$$

Example: The probability of two heads on two tosses of a coin is:

$$P(A \text{ and } B) = P(A)P(B) = \frac{1}{2} \times \frac{1}{2} = \frac{1}{4}$$

Subjective probability   The chance of an event happening based on whatever information is available—hunches, personal opinion, opinions of others, rumors, and so on.

Chapter 6

Binomial probability distribution   A discrete random variable with the following characteristics:

1.   Each outcome can be classified into one of two mutually exclusive categories.
     Example: The answer to a multiple-choice question is either correct or wrong.
2.   The distribution is the result of counting the number of successes. The counts may be, for example, the number of correct answers to a 10-question multiple-choice test. The counts listed would be 0, 1, 2, . . . 10.
3.   Each trial is independent, meaning that the answer to trial 1 (correct or wrong) in no way affects the answer to trial 2, for example.
4.   The probability of a success stays the same from trial to trial. Example: For a multiple-choice quiz having four choices per question, the probability of guessing the answer to question 1 is .25, that of guessing the answer to question 2 is also .25, and so on.

Continuous random variable   A random variable that may assume an infinite number of values within a given range. Example: The height of the power forward on Indiana's basketball team may be 78.0 inches, 78.01 inches, 78.014 inches, and so on, depending on the accuracy of the measuring device being used.
Discrete random variable   A random variable that can assume only certain separate values. Example: A family can consists of 1, 2, 3, . . . persons, not −14 or 2¼ persons.

Hypergeometric probability distribution   A probability distribution based on a discrete random variable. Its major characteristics are:

1.   There is a fixed number of trials.
2.   The probability of success is not the same from trial to trial.

Poisson distribution   A distribution often used to approximate binomial probabilities when n is large and π is small. What is considered "large" or "small" is not precisely defined, but a general rule is that n should be equal to or greater than 20 and π equal to or less than .05.
Probability distribution   A listing of the possible outcomes of an experiment and the probability associated with each outcome.
Random variable   A quantity obtained from an experiment that may, by chance, result in different values. For example, a count of the number of accidents (the experiment) on I-75 during a week might be 10, or 11, or 12, or some other number.

Chapter 7

Continuity correction factor   Used to improve the accuracy of the approximation of a discrete distribution (binomial) by a continuous distribution (normal).
Normal probability distribution   A continuous distribution that is bell-shaped, with the mean dividing the distribution into two equal parts. Further, the normal curve extends infinitely in either direction; that is, it never touches the X-axis. By converting a normal distribution to a *standard normal distribution,* we can, for example, compare two or more distributions having significantly different means or that are in different units (such as incomes and years of service).
z value   The distance between a selected value and the population mean measured in units of the standard deviation.

▮ Exercises

Part I — Fill in the Blanks

1.   Based on your assessment of the stock market, you state that chances are 50–50 that stock prices will start to go down within two months. This concept of probability based on your belief is called _____.
2.   A study of absenteeism from the classroom is being conducted. In our study of probability, this particular activity is called _____.
3.   Refer to Exercise 2. It was found that 126 students were absent from Monday morning classes. This number (126) is called _____.
4.   To apply this rule of addition:

$$P(A \text{ or } B \text{ or } C) = P(A) + P(B) + P(C)$$

     the events must be _____.
5.   Management claims that the probability of a defective relay is only .001. The name of the rule

used for finding the probability of the relay *not* being defective is _____. The formula for that rule is _____. The probability of a particular relay not being defective is _____.

6. For a probability distribution, the sum of the probabilities of all possible outcomes must equal _____.

7. Is the binomial distribution a discrete or continuous probability distribution? _____.

8. The characteristics of a binomial probability distribution are: _____, _____, _____, _____.

9. The Poisson probability distribution is (discrete or continuous)? _____.

10. To construct a Poisson distribution, you need _____.

11. The characteristics of a normal probability distribution and its accompanying normal curve are: _____, _____, _____.

12. If we convert values of a normal distribution to a distribution that has a mean of 0 and a standard deviation of 1, this probability distribution is called the _____.

Part II — Problems

13. A self-study course on management principles was offered to all employees of TMC Electronics. At the end of the time period, the employees were tested, with the following results:

Course Grade	Number of Employees
A	20
B	35
C	90
D	40
F	10
Withdrew	5

What is the probability that an employee selected at random:
    a. Earned an A?
    b. Earned a C or better?
    c. Did not fail or withdraw?

14. It is claimed that Aldradine, a new medicine for acne, is 80 percent effective — that is, of every 100 persons who apply it, 80 show significant improvement. It is applied to the affected area of a group of 15 people. What is the probability that:
    a. All 15 will show significant improvement?
    b. Fewer than 9 of 15 will show significant improvement?
    c. That 12 or more people will show significant improvement?

15. First National Bank thoroughly investigates its applicants for small home-improvement loans. Their default record is very impressive: the probability that a homeowner will default is only .005. The bank has approved 400 small home-improvement loans. Assuming the Poisson probability distribution applies to this problem:
    a. What is the probability that no homeowners out of the 400 will default?
    b. How many of the 400 are expected not to default?
    c. What is the probability that 3 or more homeowners will default on their small home-improvement loans?

16. A study of the attendance at The University of Toledo's basketball games revealed that the distribution of attendance is normally distributed with a mean of 10,000 and a standard deviation of 2,000.
    a. What is the probability a particular game has an attendance of 13,500 or more?
    b. What percent of the games have an attendance between 8,000 and 11,500?
    c. Ten percent of the games have an attendance of how many or less?

17. The following table shows a breakdown of the U.S. Congress by party affiliation and branch prior to the Clinton administration.

	Party	
	Democrats	Republicans
House	258	177
Senate	54	46

a. A member of Congress is selected at random. What is the probability of selecting a Republican member of Congress?
b. Given that the person selected is a member of the House of Representatives, what is the probability he or she is a Republican?
c. What is the probability of selecting a member of the House of Representatives or a Democrat?

18. The Internal Revenue Service has set aside 200 tax returns where the amount of charitable contributions seemed excessive. A sample of six returns is selected from the group. If two or more of this sampled group have "excessive" amounts deducted for charitable contributions, the entire group will be audited. What is the probability that the entire group will be audited, if the true proportion of "excessive" deductions is 20 percent? What if the true proportion is 30 percent?

19. The Daniel-James Insurance Company will insure an offshore Mobil Oil production platform against weather losses for one year. The president of Daniel-James estimates the following losses for that platform (in millions of dollars) with the accompanying probabilities:

Amount of Loss ($ millions)	Probability of Loss
0	.98
40	.016
300	.004

a. What is the expected amount Daniel-James will have to pay to Mobil in claims?
b. What is the likelihood that Daniel-James will actually lose less than the expected amount?
c. Given that Daniel-James suffers a loss, what is the likelihood that it is for $300 million?
d. Daniel-James has set the annual premium at $2.0 million. Does that seem like a fair premium? Will it cover their risk?

20. The distribution of the number of school-age children per family in the Whitehall Estates area of Boise, Idaho, is:

Number of children	0	1	2	3	4
Percent of families	40	30	15	10	5

a. Determine the mean and standard deviation of the number of school-age children per family in Whitehall Estates.
b. A new school is planned in Whitehall Estates. An estimate of the number of school-age children is needed. There are 500 family units. How many children would you estimate?
c. Some additional information is needed about only the families having children. Convert the preceding distribution to one for families with children. What is the mean number of children among families that have children?

▌ Cases

A. Century National Bank

Refer to the Century National Bank data. Is it reasonable that the distribution of checking account balances approximates a normal distribution? Determine the mean and the standard deviation for the sample of 60 customers. Compare the actual distribution with the theoretical distribution. Cite some specific examples and comment on your findings.

Divide the account balances into three groups, of about 20 each, with the smallest third of the balances in the first group, the middle third in the second group, and those with the largest balances in the third group. Next, develop a table that shows the number in each of the categories of the account balances by branch. Does it appear that account balances are related to the branch? Cite some examples and comment on your findings.

Avondale	Midway	Kingston
9	19	38
14	22	39
11	23	41
8	14	39
14	22	41
6	17	39
10	15	39
13	20	
8	18	
8		
9		
12		
7		
13		

B. Elections Auditor

An item such as an increase in taxes, recall of elected officials, or an expansion of public services can be placed on the ballot if a required number of valid signatures are collected on the petition. Unfortunately, many people will sign the petition even though they are not registered to vote in that particular district, or they will sign the petition more than once.

Sara Ferguson, the elections auditor in Venango County, must certify the validity of these signatures after the petition is officially presented. Not surprisingly, her staff is overloaded, so she is considering using statistical methods to validate the pages of 200 signatures, instead of validating each individual signature. At a recent professional meeting, she found that in some communities in the state, election officials were checking only five signatures on each page and rejecting the entire page if two or more signatures were invalid. Some people are concerned that five may not be enough to make a good decision. They suggest that you should check 10 signatures and reject the page if three or more are invalid.

In order to investigate these methods, Sara asks her staff to pull the results from the last election and sample 30 pages. It happens that the staff selected 14 pages from the Avondale district, 9 pages from the Midway district, and 7 pages from the Kingston district. Each page had 200 signatures, and the data below show the number of invalid signatures on each.

Use the data to evaluate Sara's two proposals. Calculate the probability of rejecting a page under each of the approaches. Would you get about the same results by examining every single signature? Offer a plan of your own, and discuss how it might be better or worse than the two plans proposed by Sara.

C. Geoff "Applies" His Education

Geoff Brown is the manager for a small telemarketing firm and is evaluating the sales rate of experienced workers in order to set minimum standards for new hires. During the past few weeks, he has recorded the number of successful calls per hour for the staff. These data appear below along with some summary statistics he worked out with a statistical software package. Geoff has been a student at the local community college and has heard of what seem like many different kinds of probability distributions (binomial, normal, hypergeometric, Poisson, etc.). Could you give Geoff some advice on which distribution to use to fit these data as well as possible and how to decide when a probationary employee should be accepted as having reached full production status. This is important because it means a pay raise for the employee, and there have been some probationary employees in the past who have quit because of discouragement that they would never meet the standard.

Successful sales calls per hour during the week of August 14:

4 2 3 1 4 5 5 2 3 2 2 4 5 2 5 3 3 0 1 3 2 8 4 5 2 2 4 1 5 5 4 5 1 2 4

Descriptive statistics:

N	MEAN	MEDIAN	TRMEAN	STDEV	SEMEAN
35	3.229	3.000	3.194	1.682	0.284
MIN	MAX	Q1	Q3		
0.0	8.000	2.000	5.000		

Which distribution do you think Geoff should use for his analysis?

D. CNP Bank Card

Before banks issue a credit card, they usually rate or score the customer in terms of his or her projected probability of being a profitable customer. A typical scoring table appears below.

Age	Under 25 (12 pts.)	25–29 (5 pts.)	30–34 (0 pts.)	35+ (18 pts.)
Time at same address	< 1 yr. (9 pts.)	1–2 yrs. (0 pts.)	3–4 yrs. (13 pts.)	5+ yrs. (20 pts.)
Auto age	None (18 pts.	0–1 yr. (12 pts.)	2–4 yrs. (13 pts.)	5+ yrs. (3 pts.)
Monthly car payment	None (15 pts.)	$1–$99 (6 pts.)	$100–$299 (4 pts.)	$300+ (0 pts.)
Housing cost	$1–$199 (0 pts.)	$200–399 (10 pts.)	Owns (12 pts.)	Lives with relatives (24 pts.)
Checking/ savings accounts	Both (15 pts.)	Checking only (3 pts.)	Savings only (2 pts.)	Neither (0 pts.)

The score is the sum of the points on the six items. For example, Sushi Brown is under 25 years old (12 pts.), has lived at the same address for 2 years (0 pts.), owns a 4-year-old car (13 pts.), with car payments of $75 (6 pts.), housing cost of $200 (10 pts.), and a checking account (3 pts.). She would score 44.

A second chart is then used to convert scores into the probability of being a profitable customer. A sample chart of this type appears below.

Score	30	40	50	60	70	80	90
Probability	.70	.78	.85	.90	.94	.95	.96

Sushi's score of 44 would translate into a probability of being profitable of approximately .81. In other words 81 percent of customers like Sushi will make money for the bank card operations.

Here are the interview results for three potential customers.

Name	David Born	Edward Brendan	Ann McLaughlin
Age	42	23	33
Time at same address	9	2	5
Auto age	2	3	7
Monthly car payment	$140	$99	$175
Housing cost	$300	$200	Owns clear
Checking/savings accounts	Both	Checking only	Neither

a. Score each of these customers and estimate their probability of being profitable.
b. What is the probability that all three are profitable?
c. What is the probability that none of them are profitable?
d. Find the entire probability distribution for the number of profitable customers among this group of three.

Chapter Eight

Sampling Methods and Sampling Distributions

GOALS

When you have completed this chapter, you will be able to:

ONE
Explain why a sample is the only feasible way to learn about a population.

TWO
Explain methods for selecting a sample.

THREE
Define and construct a sampling distribution of the sample means.

FOUR
Explain the central limit theorem.

FIVE
Calculate confidence intervals for means and proportions.

SIX
Determine the sample size for attribute and variable sampling.

In a poll to estimate presidential popularity, each person in a random sample of 1,000 was asked to agree with one of three statements: The president is doing a good job, poor job, or no opinion. Five hundred and sixty people selected the first statement. How would you construct a confidence interval for the proportion of respondents who feel the president is doing a good job? (See Goal 5 and Exercise 61.)

▮ Introduction

Chapters 1 through 4 emphasized techniques to describe data. To illustrate these techniques, we organized the prices for the 80 vehicles sold last month at Whitner Pontiac into a frequency distribution and computed various measures of location and measures of dispersion. Such measures as the mean and the standard deviation described the typical selling price and the spread in the selling prices. In these chapters the emphasis was on describing the condition of the data. That is, we described something that had already happened.

In Chapter 5 we started to lay the foundation for statistical inference with the study of probability. Recall that in statistical inference our goal is to determine something about a *population* based on the *sample.* The population is the entire group of individuals or objects under consideration and the sample is a part or subset of that population. In Chapter 6 we extended the probability concepts by describing three discrete probability distributions: the binomial, the hypergeometric, and the Poisson. In Chapter 7 we described the normal probability distribution, which is a widely applicable continuous probability distribution. Probability distributions encompass all possible outcomes of an experiment and the probability associated with each outcome. We use probability distributions to evaluate something that might occur in the future.

In this chapter we begin our study of sampling. A sample is a tool to infer something about a population by selecting a sample from that population. We begin by discussing methods of selecting a sample from a population. Next, we construct a distribution of the sample means to understand how the sample means tend to cluster around the population mean and that the shape of this distribution tends to follow the normal distribution. We will construct confidence intervals, which define a range of values within which the population value will likely occur. Finally, we define formulas that determine the number of observations required for various sampling situations.

▮ Sampling the Population

In many cases sampling is the only way to determine something about the population. Some of the major reasons why sampling is necessary are:

1. **The destructive nature of certain tests.** If the wine tasters at the Sutter Home Winery in California drank all the wine to evaluate the vintage, they would consume the entire crop, and none would be available for sale. In the area of industrial production, steel plates, wires, and similar products must often have a certain minimum tensile strength. To ensure that the product meets the minimum standard, a small sample is selected. Each piece is stretched until it breaks, and the breaking point (usually measured in pounds per square inch) recorded. Obviously, if all the wire or all the plates were tested for tensile strength, none would be available for sale or use. For the same reason, only a sample of photographic film is selected by Kodak to determine the quality of all the film produced, and only a few seeds are tested for germination by Burpee prior to the planting season.
2. **The physical impossibility of checking all items in the population.** The populations of fish, birds, snakes, mosquitoes, and the like are large and are constantly moving, being born, and dying. Instead of even attempting to count all the ducks in Canada or all the fish in Lake Erie, we make estimates using various techniques—such as counting all the ducks on a pond picked at random, making creel checks, or setting nets at predetermined places in the lake.
3. **The cost of studying all the items in a population is often prohibitive.** Public opinion polls and consumer testing organizations, such as Gallup Polls and Marketing Facts, usually contact fewer than 2,000 families of approximately 50 million families in the United States. One consumer panel-type organization charges about

$40,000 to mail samples and tabulate responses in order to test a product (such as breakfast cereal, cat food, or perfume). The same product test using all 50 million families would cost about $1 billion.

4. **The adequacy of sample results.** Even if funds were available, it is doubtful the additional accuracy of a 100 percent sample—that is, studying the entire population — is essential in most problems. For example, the federal government uses a sample of grocery stores scattered throughout the United States to determine the monthly index of food prices. The prices of bread, beans, milk, and other major food items are included in the index. It is unlikely that the inclusion of all grocery stores in the United States would significantly affect the index, since the prices of milk, bread, and other major foods usually do not vary by more than a few cents from one chain store to another.

5. **To contact the whole population would often be time consuming.** A candidate for a national office may wish to determine her chances for election. A sample poll using the regular staff and field interviews of a professional polling firm would take only one or two days. By using the same staff and interviewers and working seven days a week, it would take nearly 200 years to contact all the voting population!

Even if a large staff of interviewers could be assembled, the cost of contacting all of the voters would probably not be worth the expense. If the candidate were extremely popular, the sample poll might indicate that she would most certainly receive between 79 percent and 81 percent of the popular vote. The additional expense and time needed to find she might receive exactly 80 percent of the popular vote does not seem justified.

▌ Probability Sampling Methods

In general, there are two types of samples: a *probability sample* and a *nonprobability sample.* What is a probability sample?

> **Probability sample**   A sample selected in such a way that each item or person in the population has a known (nonzero) likelihood of being included in the sample.

The results from nonprobability sampling may be biased.

If probability sampling is done, each item in the population has a chance of being chosen. If **nonprobability methods** are used, not all items or people have a chance of being included in the sample. In such instances the results may be **biased,** meaning that the sample results may not be representative of the population. Panel sampling and convenience sampling are two nonprobability methods. For example, a panel may consist of 2,000 cat owners or mothers of new babies. The panel is formed to solicit opinions on a newly developed cat food or a disposable baby diaper. Selection of panel members is based on the judgment of the person conducting the research, and the sample results may therefore not be representative of the entire population of cat owners or new mothers (since not all cat owners or new mothers have a chance of being chosen). The statistical procedures used in this text are based on probability sampling. Therefore, only the methods of probability sampling will be discussed in the following section.

There is no one "best" method of selecting a probability sample from a population of interest. A method used to select a sample of invoices in a file drawer might not be the most appropriate method for choosing a national sample of voters. However, all probability sampling methods have a similar goal, namely, *to allow chance to determine the items or persons to be included in the sample.*

Simple Random Sampling

The most widely used type of sampling is a **simple random sample.**

> **Simple random sample**   A sample selected so that each item or person in the population has the same chance of being included.

To illustrate simple random sampling and selection, suppose a population consists of 845 employees of Nitra Industries. A sample of 52 employees is to be selected from that population. One way of ensuring that every employee in the population has a chance of being chosen is to first write the name of each one on a small slip of paper and deposit all of the slips in a box. After they have been thoroughly mixed, the first selection is made by drawing a slip out of the box without looking at it. This process is repeated until the sample of size 52 is chosen.

A table of random numbers is an efficient way to select members of the sample.

A more convenient method of selecting a random sample is to use the identification number of each employee and a **table of random numbers** such as the one in Appendix E. As the name implies, these numbers have been generated by a random process (in this case, by a computer). For each digit of a number, the probability of 0, 1, 2, . . . ,9 is the same. Thus, the probability that employee number 011 will be selected is the same as for employee 722 or employee 382. Bias is eliminated from the selection process.

A portion of a table of random numbers is shown in the following illustration. To use this table to select a sample of employees, you must first choose a starting point in the table. Any starting point will do. Suppose the time is 3:04. You might look at the third column and then move down to the fourth set of numbers. The number is 03759. Since there are only 845 employees, we will use the first three digits of a five-digit random number. Thus, 037 is the number of the first employee to be a member of the sample. To continue selecting employees, you could move in any direction. Suppose you move right. The first three digits of the number to the right of 03759 are 447 — the number of the employee selected to be the second member of the sample. The next three-digit number to the right is 961. You skip 961 because there are only 845 employees. You continue to the right and select employee 784, then 189, and so on. Another way of selecting the starting point is to close your eyes and point at a number in the table.

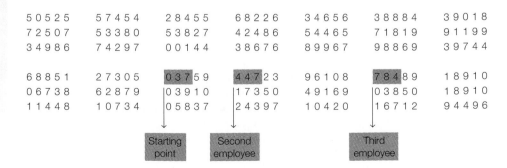

A study conducted by Marion Bryson and Robert Mason further illustrates the use of a table of random numbers and simple random sampling.

Located in 18 warehouses on a U.S. Army depot were 186,810 different military supply items such as tires, nuts, bolts, tank treads, and tire irons. In each warehouse there were bays, and in each bay there were bins. For example, in warehouse 17, motor vehicle parts were stored. Bay 260, bin 2, contained Jeep cranks. Bay 260, bin 3, had Jeep radiator caps.

The problem involved selecting a bin at random from a warehouse and counting the items found in the bin. This physical count was compared with the count that computer inventory records indicated should be on hand. Thus, the problem was essentially a physical inventory problem involving sampling methods. The objective of the research project was to determine how accurate the computer records were.

To ensure that each bin had an equal chance of being selected, a table of random numbers was used to choose the warehouse, bay, and bin.

If warehouse 5, bay 455, and bin 6 were selected, a checker went to that location and counted the number of items in that bin.

Using a table of random numbers to prevent bias

Why was such a time-consuming method used to select the bins to sample? The alternative would have been to allow the checkers to count the items in any bins they wished. No doubt the checkers would have avoided counting the items in bins containing heavy or greasy parts. And they probably would have shunned the top bins, 20 feet from the floor of the warehouse. The omission of the items in these bins from this physical inventory research project might have biased the results — that is, their omission might have given a false picture of the accuracy of the computer records.

SELF-REVIEW 8–1

The class roster, found at the top of page 262, lists the students enrolled in an introductory course in business statistics. Three students are to be randomly selected and asked various questions regarding course content and method of instruction.

(a) The numbers 00 through 45 are handwritten on slips of paper and placed in a bowl. The three numbers selected are 31, 7, and 25. Which students would be included in the sample?

(b) Now use the table of random digits, Appendix E, to select your own sample.

(c) What would you do if you encountered the number 59 in the table of random digits?

Systematic Random Sampling

The simple random sampling procedure may be awkward in certain research situations. For example, suppose the population of interest consists of 2,000 invoices located in file drawers. Drawing a simple random sample would first require numbering the invoices from 0000 to 1999. Using a table of random numbers, a sample of, say, 100 numbers would then have to be selected. An invoice to match each of these 100 numbers would have to be located in the file drawers. This would be a very time-consuming task. Instead, a **systematic random sample** could be selected by simply going through the file drawers and selecting every 20th invoice for study. The first invoice should be chosen using a random process — a table of random numbers, for example. If the 10th invoice were chosen as the starting point the sample would consist of the 10th, 30th, 50th, 70th, . . . invoices. Since the first item is chosen at random, all items have the same likelihood of being selected for the sample. Thus, it is a probability sample.

In a systematic sample the first item is chosen at random.

> **Systematic random sample** The items or individuals of the population are arranged in some way — alphabetically, in a file drawer by date received, or by some other method. A random starting point is selected, and then every *k*th member of the population is selected for the sample.

```
                    CSPM 264 01 BUSINESS & ECONOMIC STAT

                 8:00 AM  9:40 AM MW    ST 118   LIND D

RANDOM                                RANDOM
NUMBER  NAME                CLASS RANK NUMBER  NAME                CLASS RANK
 00     ANDERSON, RAYMOND       SO      23     MEDLEY, CHERYL ANN      SO
 01     ANGER, CHERYL RENEE     SO      24     MITCHELL, GREG R        FR
 02     BALL, CLAIRE JEANETTE   FR      25     MOLTER, KRISTI MARIE    SO
 03     BERRY, CHRISTOPHER G    FR      26     MULCAHY, STEPHEN ROBERT SO
 04     BOBAK, JAMES PATRICK    SO      27     NICHOLAS, ROBERT CHARLES JR
 05     BRIGHT, M. STARR        JR      28     NICKENS, VIRGINIA       SO
 06     CHONTOS, PAUL JOSEPH    SO      29     PENNYWITT, SEAN PATRICK SO
 07     DETLEV, BRIAN HANS      JR      30     POTEAU, KRIS E          JR
 08     DUDAS, VIOLA            SO      31     PRICE, MARY LYNETTE     SO
 09     DULBS, RICHARD ZALFA    JR      32     RISTAS, JAMES           SR
 10     EDINGER, SUSAN KEE      SR      33     SAGER, ANNE MARIE       SO
 11     FINK, FRANK JAMES       SR      34     SMILLIE, HEATHER MICHELLE SO
 12     FRANCIS, JAMES P        JR      35     SNYDER, LEISHA KAY      SR
 13     GAGHEN, PAMELA LYNN     JR      36     STAHL, MARIA TASHERY    SO
 14     GOULD, ROBYN KAY        SO      37     ST. JOHN, AMY J         SO
 15     GROSENBACHER, SCOTT ALAN SO     38     STURDEVANT, RICHARD R   SO
 16     HEETFIELD, DIANE MARIE  SO      39     SWETYE, LYNN MICHELE    SO
 17     KABAT, JAMES DAVID      JR      40     WALASINSKI, MICHAEL     SO
 18     KEMP, LISA ADRIANE      FR      41     WALKER, DIANE ELAINE    SO
 19     KILLION, MICHELLE A     SO      42     WARNOCK, JENNIFER MARY  SO
 20     KOPERSKI, MARY ELLEN    SO      43     WILLIAMS, WENDY A       SO
 21     KOPP, BRIDGETTE ANN     SO      44     YAP, HOCK BAN           SO
 22     LEHMANN, KRISTINA MARIE JR      45     YODER, ARLAN JAY        JR
```

A systematic sample should not be used, however, if there is a pattern to the population. For example, in the physical inventory study mentioned previously, some of the warehouses in the depot have bays six bins high. In the bottom row of bins are fast-moving items, such as grease, touch-up spray paint, and hardware. These items are stored on the floor-level bins to speed the work of the pickers who must fill the requisitions. In the top row of bins are slow-moving items, such as tire rims, half-track treads, and firing pins. The middle four rows are stocked with moderately fast-moving items, such as tires, headlights, and cotter pins. If a systematic sample is used to check the inventory, then it is quite possible that a biased sample will be selected. Suppose the sampling procedure called for a selection of every third bin, and bin 1 is selected first. Then bins 1, 4, 7, 10, 13, 16, 19 and 22 would be selected systematically.

The systematic procedure automatically selected 4 bins filled with moderately fast-moving items and a total of 4 bins filled with either fast-moving or slow-moving items. This 50-50 division of the sample does not coincide with the actual population characteristics. The population consists of 16 bins of moderately fast-moving items, 4 bins of fast-moving items, and 4 bins of slow-moving items. The sample results would undoubtedly be biased toward the slow- and fast-moving items.

Stratified Random Sampling

Another type of probability sampling is referred to as **stratified random sampling.**

> **Stratified random sample** A population is divided into subgroups, called strata, and a sample is selected from each stratum.

After the population has been divided into strata, either a *proportional* or a *nonproportional* sample can be selected. As the name implies, a proportional sampling procedure requires that the number of items in each stratum be in the same proportion as in the population. For instance, the problem might be to study the advertising expenditures of the 352 largest companies in the United States. Suppose the objective of the study is to determine whether firms with high returns on equity (a measure of profitability) spent more of each sales dollar on advertising than firms with a low return or a deficit. Assume that the 352 firms were divided into five strata. (See Table 8–1.) If, say, 50 firms are to be selected for intensive study, then 1 firm with a level of profitability of 30 percent or more would be included, 5 firms in the 20–30 percent stratum would be selected at random, and so on.

Table 8–1   Number Selected for a Proportional Stratified Random Sample

Stratum	Profitability (return on equity)	Number of Firms	Percent of Total	Number Sampled
1	30 percent and over	8	2	1*
2	20 up to 30 percent	35	10	5*
3	10 up to 20 percent	189	54	27
4	0 up to 10 percent	115	33	16
5	Deficit	5	1	1
	Total	352	100	50

*2 percent of 50 = 1; 10 percent of 50 = 5; etc.

In a *nonproportional* stratified sample, the number of items chosen in each stratum is disproportionate to the respective numbers in the population. We then weight the sample results according to the stratum's proportion of the total population. For example, if nonproportional sampling were used in the preceding case, we would weight the results of stratum 1 by 2/100, stratum 2 by 10/100, stratum 3 by 54/100, and so on. Regardless of whether a proportional or a nonproportional sampling procedure is used, every item or person in the population has a chance of being selected for the sample.

Stratified sampling has the advantage, in some cases, of more accurately reflecting the characteristics of the population than does simple random or systematic random sampling. Note in Table 8–1 that 2 percent of the firms have a return on equity of 30 percent or more (stratum 1), and 1 percent have a deficit (stratum 5). If a simple random sample of 50 were taken, we might not *by chance* select any firms in stratum 1 or 5. A stratified random sample, however, would ensure that at least one firm in stratum 1 and one firm in stratum 5 are represented in the sample.

Cluster Sampling

Cluster sampling reduces sampling cost.

Another common type of sampling is **cluster sampling.** It is often employed to reduce the cost of sampling a population scattered over a large geographic area. Suppose you want to determine the views of industrialists in a state about state and federal environmental protection policies. Selecting a random sample of industrialists in the state and personally contacting each one would be time consuming and very expensive. Instead, you could employ cluster sampling by subdividing the state into small units — either counties or regions. These are often called *primary units.* Suppose you divided the state into 12 primary units, then selected at random four regions — 2, 7, 4, and 12 — and concentrated your efforts in these primary units. You could take a random sample of the industrialists in each of these regions and interview them. (Note that this is a combination of cluster sampling and simple random sampling.)

Many other sampling methods

The discussion of sampling methods in the preceding sections did not include all the sampling methods available to a researcher. Should you become involved in a major research project in marketing, finance, accounting, or other areas, you would need to consult books devoted solely to sample theory and sample design.

SELF-REVIEW 8-2

Refer to Self-Review 8–1 and the class roster on page 262. Suppose a sample is to consist of every ninth student enrolled in the class. Initially, the fourth student on the list was selected at random. That student is numbered 03. Remembering that the random numbers start with 00, which students will be chosen to be members of the sample?

▌ Exercises

1. The following is a list of Marco's Pizza stores in Lucas County. Also noted is whether the store is corporate-owned (C) or manager-owned (M). A sample of four locations is to be selected and inspected for customer convenience, safety, cleanliness, and other features.

ID No.	Address	Type	ID No.	Address	Type
00	2607 Starr Av	C	12	2040 Ottawa River Rd	C
01	309 W Alexis Rd	C	13	2116 N Reynolds Rd	C
02	2652 W Central Av	C	14	3678 Rugby Dr	C
03	630 Dixie Hwy	M	15	1419 South Av	C
04	3510 Dorr St	C	16	1234 W Sylvania Av	C
05	5055 Glendale Av	C	17	4624 Woodville Rd	M
06	3382 Lagrange St	M	18	5155 S Main	M
07	2525 W Laskey Rd	C	19	106 E Airport Hwy	C
08	303 Louisiana Av	C	20	6725 W Central	M
09	149 Main St	C	21	4252 Monroe	C
10	835 S McCord Rd	M	22	2036 Woodville Rd	C
11	3501 Monroe St	M	23	1316 Michigan Av	M

a. The random numbers selected are 08, 18, 11, 54, 02, 41, and 54. Which stores are selected?

b. Use the table of random numbers to select your own sample of locations.

c. A sample is to consist of every seventh location. The number 03 is the starting point. Which locations will be included in the sample?

d. Suppose a sample is to consist of three locations, of which two are corporate-owned and one is manager-owned. Select a sample accordingly.

2. The following is a list of hospitals in the Cincinnati (Ohio) and Northern Kentucky Region. Also included is whether the hospital is a general medical/surgical hospital (M/S) or a specialty hospital (S).

ID Number	Name	Address	Type	ID Number	Name	Address	Type
00	Bethesda North	10500 Montgomery Cincinnati, Ohio 45242	M/S	15	Providence Hospital	2446 Kipling Avenue Cincinnati, Ohio 45239	M/S
01	Ft. Hamilton–Hughes	630 Eaton Avenue Hamilton, Ohio 45013	M/S	16	St. Francis–St. George Hospital	3131 Queen City Avenue Cincinnati, Ohio 54238	M/S
02	Jewish Hospital–Kenwood	4777 East Galbraith Rd. Cincinnati, Ohio 45236	M/S	17	St. Elizabeth Medical Center, North Unit	401 E. 20th Street Covington, Kentucky 41014	M/S
03	Mercy Hospital–Fairfied	3000 Mack Road Fairfield, Ohio 45014	M/S	18	St. Elizabeth Medical Center, South Unit	One Medical Village Edgewood, Kentucky 41017	M/S
04	Mercy Hospital–Hamilton	100 Riverfront Plaza Hamilton, Ohio 45011	M/S	19	St. Luke's Hospital West	7380 Turfway Dr. Florence, Kentucky 41075	M/S
05	Middletown Regional	105 McKnight Drive Middletown, Ohio 45044	M/S	20	St. Luke's Hospital East	85 North Grand Avenue Ft. Thomas, Kentucky 41042	M/S
06	Clermont Mercy Hospital	3000 Hospital Dr. Batavia, Ohio 45103	M/S	21	Care Unit Hospital Cinti.	3156 Glenmore Avenue Cincinnati, Ohio 45211	S
07	Mercy Hospital–Anderson	7500 State Road Cincinnati, Ohio 45255	M/S	22	Emerson Behavioral Service	2446 Kipling Avenue Cincinnati, Ohio 45239	S
08	Bethesda Oak Hospital	619 Oak Street Cincinnati, Ohio 45206	M/S	23	Pauline Warfield Lewis Center for Psychiatric Treat.	1101 Summit Rd. Cincinnati, Ohio 45237	S
09	Children's Hospital Medical Center	3333 Burnet Avenue Cincinnati, Ohio 45229	M/S	24	Children's Psychiatric No. Kentucky	502 Farrell Drive Covington, Kentucky 41011	S
10	Christ Hospital	2139 Auburn Avenue Cincinnati, Ohio 45219	M/S	25	Drake Center Rehab—Long Term	151 W. Galbraith Road Cincinnati, Ohio 45216	S
11	Deaconess Hospital	311 Straight Street Cincinnati, Ohio 45219	M/S	26	No. Kentucky Rehab Hospital—Short Term	201 Medical Village Edgewood, Kentucky	S
12	Good Samaritan Hospital	375 Dixmyth Avenue Cincinnati, Ohio 45220	M/S	27	Shriners Burns Institute	3229 Burnet Avenue Cincinnati, Ohio 45229	S
13	Jewish Hospital	3200 Burnet Avenue Cincinnati, Ohio 45229	M/S	28	VA Medical Center	3200 Vine Cincinnati, Ohio 45220	S
14	University Hospital	234 Goodman Street Cincinnati, Ohio 45267	M/S				

a. A sample of five hospitals is to be randomly selected. The random numbers are: 09, 16, 00, 49, 54, 12, and 04. Which hospitals are included in the sample?

b. Use a table of random numbers to develop your own sample of five hospitals.

c. A sample is to consist of every fifth location. We select 02 as the starting point. Which hospitals will be included in the sample?

d. A sample is to consist of four medical and surgical hospitals and one specialty hospital. Select an appropriate sample.

3. Listed below are the 35 members of the Metro Toledo Automobile Dealers Association.

ID Number	Dealer	ID Number	Dealer	ID Number	Dealer
00	Dave White Acura	12	Spurgeon Chevrolet Motor Sales, Inc.	24	Lexus of Toledo
01	Autofair Nissan	13	Dunn Chevrolet-Olds	25	Mathews Ford Oregon, Inc.
02	Autofair Toyota-Suzuki	14	Don Scott Chevrolet-Pontiac-Geo, Inc.	26	Northtowne Chevrolet-GEO
03	George Ballis Buick GMC Truck	15	Dave White Chevrolet Co.	27	Quality Ford Sales, Inc.
04	Yark Automotive Group	16	Dick Wilson Pontiac	28	Rouen Chrysler Plymouth Jeep Eagle
05	Bob Schmidt Chevrolet	17	Doyle Pontiac Buick	29	Saturn of Toledo
06	Bowling Green Lincoln Mercury Jeep Eagle	18	Franklin Park Lincoln Mercury	30	Ed Schmidt Pontiac Jeep Eagle
07	Brondes Ford	19	Genoa Motors	31	Southside Lincoln Mercury
08	Brown Honda	20	Great Lakes Ford Nissan	32	Valiton Chrysler Plymouth
09	Brown Mazda	21	Grogan Towne Chrysler	33	Vin Divers
10	Charlie's Dodge	22	Hatfield Olds-Honda	34	Whitman Ford
11	Thayer Chevrolet Geo Toyota	23	Kistler Ford, Inc.		

a. We want to select a random sample of five dealers. The random numbers are: 05, 20, 59, 21, 31, 28, 49, 38, 66, 08, 29, and 02. Which dealers would be included in the sample?

b. Use the table of random numbers to select your own sample of five dealers.

c. A sample is to consist of every 7th dealer. The number 04 is selected as the starting point. Which dealers are included in the sample?

4. Listed below are the 27 Nationwide Insurance agents in the Toledo, Ohio, metropolitan area.

ID Number	Agent	ID Number	Agent	ID Number	Agent
00	**Bly Scott** 3332 W Laskey Rd	09	**Harris Ev** 2026 Albon Rd	18	**Priest Harvey** 5113 N Summit St
01	**Coyle Mike** 5432 W Central Av	10	**Heini Bernie** 7110 W Central	19	**Riker Craig** 2621 N Reynolds Rd
02	**Denker Brett** 7445 Airport Hwy	11	**Hinckley Dave** 14 N Holland Sylvania Rd	20	**Schwab Dave** 572 W Dussel Dr
03	**Denker Rollie** 7445 Airport Hwy	12	**Joehlin Bob** 3358 Navarre Av	21	**Seibert John H** 201 S Main
04	**Farley Ron** 1837 W Alexis Rd	13	**Keisser David** 3030 W Sylvania Av	22	**Smithers Bob** 229 Superior St
05	**George Mark** 7247 W. Central Av	14	**Keisser Keith** 5901 Sylvania Av	23	**Smithers Jerry** 229 Superior St
06	**Gibellato Carlo** 6616 Monroe St 3521 Navarre Av	15	**Lawrence Grant** 342 W Dussel Dr	24	**Wright Steve** 105 S Third St
07	**Glemser Cathy** 5602 Woodville Rd	16	**Miller Ken** 2427 Woodville Rd	25	**Wood Tom** 112 Louisiana Av
08	**Green Mike** 4149 Holland Sylvania Rd	17	**O'Donnell Jim** 7247 W Central Av	26	**Yoder Scott** 6 Willoughby Av

a. We want to select a random sample of four agents. The random numbers are: 02, 59, 51, 25, 14, 29, 77, 69, and 18. Which dealers would be included in the sample?

b. Use the table of random numbers to select your own sample of four agents.

c. A sample is to consist of every 5th dealer. The number 02 is selected as the starting point. Which agents will be included in the sample?

▮ Sampling "Error"

The previous discussion stressed the importance of selecting a sample so that every item or individual in the population has a known chance of being selected. To accomplish this, we could choose a simple random sample, a systematic sample, a stratified sample, a cluster sample, or a combination of these methods. However, it is unlikely that the mean of a sample would be *identical* to the population mean. Likewise, the sample standard deviation or other measure computed from a sample would probably not be *exactly* equal to the corresponding population value. We can therefore expect some difference between a *sample statistic,* such as the sample mean or sample standard deviation, and the corresponding *population parameter.* The difference between a sample statistic and a population parameter is called **sampling error.**

> **Sampling error**   The difference between a sample statistic and its corresponding population parameter.

Suppose a population of five production employees had efficiency ratings of 97, 103, 96, 99, and 105. Further suppose that a sample of two ratings—97 and 105—is selected to estimate the population mean rating. The mean of that sample would be 101, found by $(97 + 105)/2$. Another sample of two is selected: 103 and 96, with a sample mean of 99.5. The mean of all the ratings (the population mean) is 100, found by: $(97 + 103 + 96 + 99 + 105)/5 = 500/5 = 100$. The sampling error for the first sample is 1.0, determined by $\bar{X} - \mu = 101 - 100$. The second sample has a sampling error of -0.5. Each of these differences, 1.0 and -0.5, is the error made in estimating the population mean based on a sample mean, and these sampling errors are due to chance. The amount of these errors will vary from one sample to the next.

Now that we have discovered the possibility of a sampling error when sample results are used to estimate a population parameter, how can we make an accurate prediction about the possible success of a newly developed toothpaste or other product, based only on sample results? How can the quality-assurance department in a mass-production firm release a shipment of microchips based only on a sample of 10 chips? How can Gallup or Harris polls make an accurate prediction about a presidential race based on a sample of 2,000 registered voters out of a voting population of nearly 90 million? To answer these questions, we first develop a *sampling distribution of the sample means.*

▮ Sampling Distribution of the Sample Means

Sample means vary from sample to sample.

The efficiency rating example showed the means for samples of a specified size vary from sample to sample. The mean efficiency rating of the first sample of two employees was 101, and the second sample mean was 99.5. A third sample would probably result in a different mean. The population mean was 100. If we organized the means of all possible samples of 2 ratings into a probability distribution, we would obtain the **sampling distribution of the sample means.**

> **Sampling distribution of the sample means**   A probability distribution of all possible sample means of a given sample size and the probability of occurrence for each sample mean.

The following example illustrates the construction of a sampling distribution of sample means.

Example

Tartus Industries has seven production employees (considered the population). The hourly earnings of each employee are given in Table 8–2.

Table 8–2   **Hourly Earnings of the Production Employees of Tartus Industries**

Employee	Hourly Earnings
Joe	$7
Sam	7
Sue	8
Bob	8
Jan	7
Art	8
Ted	9

1. What is the population mean?
2. What is the sampling distribution of the sample means for samples of size 2?
3. What is the mean of the sampling distribution?
4. What observations can be made about the population and the sampling distribution?

Solution

1. The population mean is $7.71, found by:

$$\mu = \frac{\$7 + \$7 + \$8 + \$8 + \$7 + \$8 + \$9}{7}$$

2. To arrive at the sampling distribution of the sample means, all possible samples of 2 were selected without replacement from the population, and their means were computed. There are 21 possible samples, found by using formula (5–10) on page 171.

$$_NC_n = \frac{N!}{n!(N-n)!} = \frac{7!}{2!(7-2)!} = 21$$

where $N = 7$ is the number of items in the population and $n = 2$ is the number of items in the sample.

The 21 distinct sample means from all possible samples of 2 that can be drawn from the population are shown in Table 8–3. This probability distribution is the sampling distribution of the sample means and is summarized in Table 8–4.

Table 8–3   **Sample Means for All Possible Samples of 2 Employees**

Sample	Employees	Hourly Earnings	Sum	Mean	Sample	Employees	Hourly Earnings	Sum	Mean
1	Joe, Sam	$7, $7	$14	$7.00	12	Sue, Bob	$8, $8	$16	$8.00
2	Joe, Sue	7, 8	15	7.50	13	Sue, Jan	8, 7	15	7.50
3	Joe, Bob	7, 8	15	7.50	14	Sue, Art	8, 8	16	8.00
4	Joe, Jan	7, 7	14	7.00	15	Sue, Ted	8, 9	17	8.50
5	Joe, Art	7, 8	15	7.50	16	Bob, Jan	8, 7	15	7.50
6	Joe, Ted	7, 9	16	8.00	17	Bob, Art	8, 8	16	8.00
7	Sam, Sue	7, 8	15	7.50	18	Bob, Ted	8, 9	17	8.50
8	Sam, Bob	7, 8	15	7.50	19	Jan, Art	7, 8	15	7.50
9	Sam, Jan	7, 7	14	7.00	20	Jan, Ted	7, 9	16	8.00
10	Sam, Art	7, 8	15	7.50	21	Art, Ted	8, 9	17	8.50
11	Sam, Ted	7, 9	16	8.00					

Table 8–4   Sampling Distribution of the Sample Mean for $n = 2$

	Number of	
Sample Mean	Means	Probability
$7.00	3	.1429
7.50	9	.4285
8.00	6	.2857
8.50	3	.1429
	21	1.0000

3. The mean of the sampling distribution of the sample mean is obtained by summing the various sample means and dividing the sum by the number of samples. The mean of all the sample means is usually written $\mu_{\bar{X}}$. The μ reminds us that it is a population value because we have considered all possible samples. The subscript $\bar{X}$ indicates that it is the sampling distribution of mean.

$$\mu_{\bar{X}} = \frac{\text{Sum of all sample means}}{\text{Total number of samples}} = \frac{\$7.00 + \$7.50 + \cdots + \$8.50}{21}$$

$$= \frac{\$162}{21} = \$7.71$$

Refer to Chart 8–1.

Population mean is equal to the mean of the sample means

Sample means approximate a normal distribution

Chart 8–1   Distributions of Population Values and Sample Means

4. These observations can be made:
   a. The mean of the sample means ($7.71) is equal to the mean of the population: $\mu = \mu_{\bar{X}}$.
   b. The spread in the distribution of the sample means is less than the spread in the population values. The sample means range from $7.00 to $8.50, while the population values vary from $7.00 up to $9.00. In fact, the standard deviation of the distribution of the sample means is equal to the population standard deviation divided by the square root of the sample size. So the formula for the standard deviation of the distribution of sample means is $\sigma/\sqrt{n}$. Notice, as we increase the size of the sample, the spread of the distribution of the sample means becomes smaller.
   c. The shape of the sampling distribution of the sample means and the shape of the frequency distribution of the population values are different. The distribution of sample means tends to be more bell-shaped and to approximate the normal probability distribution.

In summary, we took all possible random samples from a population and for each sample calculated a sample statistic (the mean amount earned). Because each possible sample has a chance of being selected, the probability that the mean amount earned will be values such as $7.27, $8.50, $6.50, and so on can be determined. The distribution of the mean amounts earned is called the sampling distribution of the sample means.

Even though in practice we see only one particular random sample, in theory any of the samples could arise. Consequently, we view the sampling process as repeated sampling of the statistic from its sampling distribution. This sampling distribution is then used to measure how likely a particular outcome might be.

SELF-REVIEW 8–3

The lengths of service of all the executives employed by Standard Chemicals are:

Name	Years
Mr. Snow	20
Ms. Tolson	22
Mr. Kraft	26
Ms. Irwin	24
Mr. Jones	28

(a) Using the combination formula, how many samples of size 2 are possible?
(b) List all possible samples of 2 executives from the population and compute their means.
(c) Organize the means into a sampling distribution.
(d) Compare the population mean and the mean of the sample means.
(e) Compare the dispersion in the population with that in the distribution of sample means.
(f) A chart portraying the population values follows. Is the distribution of population values normally distributed (bell-shaped)?

(g) Is the distribution of sample means computed in part (c) starting to show some tendency toward being bell-shaped?

▌ Exercises

5. A population consists of the following four values: 12, 12, 14, and 16.
   a. List all samples of size 2, and compute the mean of each sample.

   b. Compute the mean of the distribution of sample means and the population mean. Compare the two values.

   c. Compare the dispersion in the population with that of the sample means.

6. A population consists of the following five values: 2, 2, 4, 4, and 8.

   a. List all samples of size 2, and compute the mean of each sample.

   b. Compute the mean of the distribution of sample means and the population mean. Compare the two values.

   c. Compare the dispersion in the population with that of the sample means.

7. A population consists of the following five values: 12, 12, 14, 15, and 20.

   a. List all samples of size 3, and compute the mean of each sample.

   b. Compute the mean of the distribution of sample means and the population mean. Compare the two values.

   c. Compare the dispersion in the population with that of the sample means.

8. A population consists of the following five values: 0, 0, 1, 3, 6.

   a. List all samples of size 3, and compute the mean of each sample.

   b. Compute the mean of the distribution of sample means and the population mean. Compare the two values.

   c. Compare the dispersion in the population with that of the sample means.

9. In the law firm Tybo and Associates, there are six partners. Listed below is the number of cases each associate actually tried in court last month.

Associate	Number of Cases
Ruud	3
Austin	6
Sass	3
Palmer	3
Wilhelms	0
Schueller	1

   a. How many different samples of 3 are possible?

   b. List all possible samples of size 3, and compute the mean number of cases in each sample.

   c. Compare the mean of the distribution of sample means to the population mean.

   d. On a chart similar to Chart 8–1, compare the dispersion in the population with that of the sample means.

10. There are five sales representatives at Mid-Motors Ford. The five representatives and the number of cars they sold last week are:

Sales Representative	Cars Sold
Pete Hankish	8
Connie Stallter	6
Ron Eaton	4
Ted Barnes	10
Peggy Harmon	6

   a. How many different samples of size 2 are possible?

   b. List all possible samples of size 2, and compute the mean of each sample.

   c. Compare the mean of the sampling distribution of the sample means with that of the population.

   d. On a chart similar to Chart 8–1, compare the dispersion in the sample means with that in the population.

▮ The Central Limit Theorem

In this section, we examine the **central limit theorem.** Its application to the sampling distribution of the sample means, introduced in the previous section, allows us to use the normal probability distribution to create confidence intervals for the population mean. The central limit theorem states that, for large random samples, the shape of the sampling distribution of the sample means is close to a normal probability distribution. The approximation is more accurate for large samples than for small samples. This is one of the most useful conclusions in statistics. We can reason about the distribution of the sample means with absolutely no information about the shape of the original distribution from which the sample is taken. In other words, the central limit theorem is true for all distributions.

A formal statement of the central limit theorem follows.

> **Central Limit Theorem**   If all samples of a particular size are selected from any population, the sampling distribution of the sample means is approximately a normal distribution. This approximation improves with larger samples.

If the population is a normal probability distribution, then for any sample size the sampling distribution of the mean will also be normally distributed. If the population distribution is symmetrical (but not normal), you will see the normal shape of the central limit theorem emerge with samples as small as 10. On the other hand, if you start with a distribution that is skewed or has thick tails, it may require samples of at least 30 to observe the normality feature. Most statisticians consider a sample of 30 or more large enough for the central limit theorem to be employed.

The idea that the distribution of sample means from a population that is not normal will converge to normality is illustrated in Charts 8–2, 8–3, and 8–4. We will discuss this example in more detail shortly, but Chart 8–2 is a graph of a discrete probability distribution that is positively skewed. There are many possible samples of 5 that might be selected from this population. Suppose we randomly select 10 samples of 5 each and compute the mean of each sample. These results are shown in Chart 8–3. Notice that the shape of the distribution of the sample means has changed from the original population even though we only selected 10 of the many possible samples. To put it another way, we selected 10 random samples of 5 each from a population that is positively skewed and found the distribution of the sample means has changed from the shape of the population. As we take more samples, we will find the distribution of sample means will approach the normal distribution. Chart 8–4 is a histogram that shows the results of 30 random samples of 5 observations from the same population. Observe the clear trend toward the normal distribution. This is the point of the central limit theorem. The following example will underscore this condition.

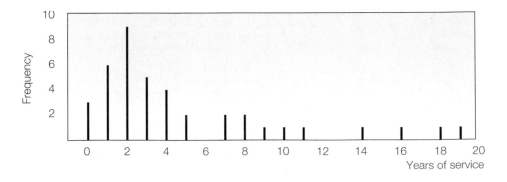

Chart 8–2   Length of Service of Spence Sprockets, Inc. Employees

Chart 8–3 Mean Length of Service of 10 Samples of Five Spence Sprockets, Inc. Employees

Example

Ed Spence began his sprocket business 20 years ago. The business has grown over the years and now employs 40 people. Spence Sprockets, Inc. faces some major decisions regarding health care for these employees. Before making a final decision on what health care plan to purchase, Ed decides to form a committee of five representative employees. The committee will be asked to study the health care issue carefully and make a recommendation as to what plan best fits the employee's needs. Ed feels the views of younger employees toward health care may differ from those of older employees. If Ed randomly selects this committee, what can he expect in terms of the mean years with Spence Sprockets for those on the committee? How does the shape of the distribution of years of experience of all employees compare with the shape of the sampling distribution of the means? The lengths of service (rounded to the nearest year) of the 40 employees currently on the Spence Sprockets, Inc. payroll are as follows.

11	4	18	2	1	2	0	2	2	4
3	4	1	2	2	3	3	19	8	3
7	1	0	2	7	0	4	5	1	14
16	8	9	1	1	2	5	10	2	3

Solution

Chart 8–2 shows the distribution of the years of experience for the 40 current employees. Observe that the distribution of lengths of service is positively skewed. There are a few employees who have worked at Spence Sprockets for some time. Specifically, six employees have been with the company 10 years or more. However, because the business has grown, the number of employees has increased in the last few years. Of the 40 employees, 18 have been with the company two years or less.

Let's consider the first of Ed Spence's problems. He would like to form a committee of five employees to look into the health care question and suggest what type of insurance would be most appropriate for the majority of workers. How should he select the committee? If he selects the committee randomly, what might he expect in terms of mean length of service for those on the committee?

To begin, Ed writes the length of service for each of the 40 employees on a piece of paper and puts them into an old baseball hat. Next, he shuffles the pieces of paper around and randomly selects 5 slips of paper. The lengths of service for these five employees are: 4, 1, 0, 14, and 9 years. So the mean length of service for these five employees is 5.60 years. How does that compare with the population mean? At

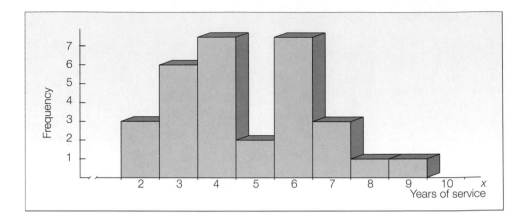

Chart 8–4   Histogram of Mean Length of Service for 30 Samples of Employees at
Spence Sprockets, Inc.

this point Ed does not know the population mean, but the number of employees in the population is only 40, so he decides to calculate the mean length of service for all his employees. It is 4.80 years, found by adding the lengths of service for all the employees and dividing the total by 40. That is $\mu = (11 + 4 + 18 + \cdots + 2 + 3)/40 = 192/40 = 4.80$. The difference between the sample mean, $\overline{X}$, and the population mean, μ, is called **sampling error.** In other words, the difference of 0.80 years between the population mean of 4.80 and the sample mean of 5.60 is the sampling error. It is due to chance. Thus, if Ed selected these five employees to constitute the committee, their mean length of service would be somewhat more than the population mean.

What would happen if Ed put the five pieces of paper back into the baseball hat and selected another sample? Would you expect the mean of this second sample to be exactly the same as the previous one? Suppose he selects another sample of five employees and finds the lengths of service in this sample to be 8, 3, 1, 1, and 14. This sample mean is 5.40 years. The result of selecting 10 samples of 5 employees each is shown in Chart 8–3. Notice the difference in the shape of the population and the distribution of these sample means. The population of the lengths of service for employees (Chart 8–2) is positively skewed, but the distribution of these 10 sample means does not reflect the same positive skew. In fact, it is negatively skewed.

Table 8–5 shows the result of selecting 30 more samples of 5 employees each and computing their sample means. These sample means are then organized into a histogram (Chart 8–4). Compare the shape of this frequency polygon to that of the population of employees in Chart 8–2. You should observe two important features:

1. The shape of the distribution of the 30 sample means is different from that of the population. In Chart 8–2 the distribution of all employees is positively skewed. However, the sampling distribution of the sample means, Chart 8–4, is more nearly a normal distribution. This illustrates the central limit theorem.
2. There is less dispersion in the sampling distribution of sample means than in the population distribution. In the population, the lengths of service ranged from 0 to 19 years. In the sampling distribution of sample means, the sample means ranged from 2.2 years to 9.2 years.

Table 8–5 Random Samples and Sample Means of 30 Samples of
Five Spence Sprockets, Inc. Employees

Sample Number	Sample Data (length of service)					Sample Mean $\bar{X}$	Sample Number	Sample Data (length of service)					Sample Mean $\bar{X}$
1	4	1	0	14	9	5.6	16	2	2	10	11	0	5.0
2	8	3	1	1	14	5.4	17	4	2	3	8	1	3.6
3	2	4	2	4	2	2.8	18	0	0	4	3	5	2.4
4	11	1	5	2	3	4.4	19	1	4	2	3	1	2.2
5	2	1	7	3	3	3.2	20	2	7	0	2	3	2.8
6	11	2	10	1	4	5.6	21	5	16	2	4	11	7.6
7	4	3	11	2	9	5.8	22	9	3	0	2	8	4.4
8	8	3	14	2	2	5.8	23	5	1	2	10	0	3.6
9	1	7	8	2	2	4.0	24	2	1	2	0	8	2.6
10	14	1	2	10	2	5.8	25	19	4	3	3	1	6.0
11	8	2	18	5	0	6.6	26	0	4	9	11	8	6.4
12	3	1	4	2	7	3.4	27	4	9	4	3	2	4.4
13	0	4	3	3	1	2.2	28	2	5	2	7	2	3.6
14	11	4	9	2	8	6.8	29	18	8	1	11	8	9.2
15	7	1	2	5	1	3.2	30	14	16	0	2	3	7.0

We can also compare the mean of the sample means to the population mean. The mean of the 30 samples reported in Table 8–5 is 4.7133 years, found by $\mu_{\bar{X}} = (5.6 + 5.4 + \cdots + 9.2 + 7.0)/30$. We use the symbol $\mu_{\bar{X}}$ to represent the mean of the sample means. The subscript reminds us that the distribution is of sample means. It is read "mu sub X bar." We observe that the mean of the sample means, 4.7133 years, is very close to the population mean of 4.80 years.

What can we conclude from this example? The central limit theorem indicates that, regardless of the shape of the population, the sampling distribution of the sample means will approximate the normal distribution. The larger these samples, the stronger the convergence. Spence Sprockets, Inc. is empirical evidence of how the central limit theorem works. We began this illustration with a positively skewed population (Chart 8–2). Next, we selected a small number of samples and looked at that distribution of sample means. We could observe a *change* in the shape of the population to the distribution of sample means (compare Charts 8–3 and 8–4). When we increase the number of samples from 10 to 30, we begin to see the normality feature. The shape of the distribution of the 30 sample means reported in Chart 8–4 is clearly moving toward a normal distribution as we increase the sample size.

The central limit theorem (reread the definition on page 272) does not say anything about the dispersion of the distribution of sample means or about a comparison of the mean of the sample means to the mean of the population. However, in our Example/Solution, we did observe there was less dispersion in the distribution of sample means than in the population by comparing the range of the population and the range of the sample means. We also observed that the mean of all the sample means was close to the population mean. It can be shown that if the dispersion in the population is σ, the dispersion in the sample means is $\sigma/\sqrt{n}$, where n is the size of the sample. From this relationship, you can see that, as the sample size increases, the dispersion of the sample means decreases. It can also be proven that the mean of the population is exactly equal to the mean of all the sample means. To put it another way, the mean of all the sample means is equal to the population mean.

▮ The Central Limit Theorem — A Second Example

The example just completed gives you some idea of the importance of the central limit theorem. It is worthwhile, however, to consider another example. In this second example we see the central limit theorem in a classical setting.

Example

Suppose we have a fair die, roll it twice, and look at the sum of the number of spots. Thus, if the first roll comes up a 3 and the second a 4, we are interested in the total, i.e., 7. What is the shape of the population of the number of spots? What are the possible outcomes to the experiment? What is the shape of the distribution of the sum of the number of spots when a single die is rolled twice?

Solution

This is actually a sampling situation. The population is a uniform distribution, with each of the whole numbers from 1 through 6 having an equal likelihood of occurrence. The following table and graph show the various outcomes in the population and their corresponding probabilities.

Possible Outcomes	Probability
1	1/6 = .1667
2	1/6 = .1667
3	1/6 = .1667
4	1/6 = .1667
5	1/6 = .1667
6	1/6 = .1667

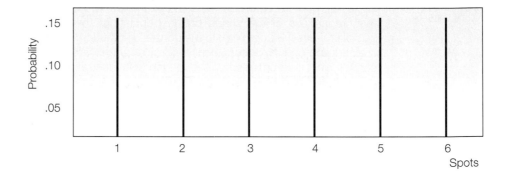

Now, if we roll the die twice, the total number of spots appearing can be summarized as follows.

Total number of spots

First roll						
6	7	8	9	10	11	12
5	6	7	8	9	10	11
4	5	6	7	8	9	10
3	4	5	6	7	8	9
2	3	4	5	6	7	8
1	2	3	4	5	6	7
	1	2	3	4	5	6

Second roll

For example, if the first roll of the die is a 4 and the second roll a 6, the total is 10. Next, we wish a distribution for the total number of spots appearing. From the table, there are 36 possible outcomes. On one occasion the total number of spots appearing is 2, and on one occasion the total is 12. There are 3 occasions when the total is 4, 6 occasions when the total is 7, and so on. By now you have probably noticed that we can find the number of outcomes by looking at the diagonals from upper left to lower right. The total number of spots and the probability of each are summarized in the following table and chart.

Possible Outcomes	Number of Times Appearing	Probability
2	1	1/36 = .0278
3	2	2/36 = .0556
4	3	3/36 = .0833
5	4	4/36 = .1111
6	5	5/36 = .1389
7	6	6/36 = .1667
8	5	5/36 = .1389
9	4	4/36 = .1111
10	3	3/36 = .0833
11	2	2/36 = .0556
12	1	1/36 = .0278

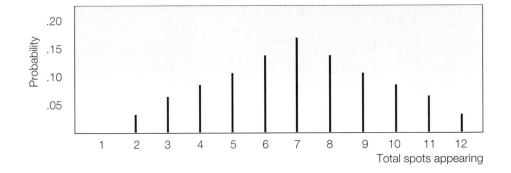

Notice the change in the shape of the distribution of the sums from that of the population. We began with a population that was uniform for the discrete whole numbers 1 through 6. When we rolled the die twice and looked at the total number of spots, the distribution changed to a triangular-shaped distribution. Incidentally, we could have used the average number of spots on the two rolls and obtained the same shape of the distribution.

Without reporting the details, suppose we roll the same die three times and report the distribution of the sum of the number of spots. First, we know that the smallest possible sum is 3 and the largest possible sum 18. The sums of 10 and 11 will each have a probability of occurrence of .1250, which is the highest probability. Chart 8–5 depicts the probability distribution for the sum of three rolls as well as for both one and two. Again, observe the clear effects of the central limit theorem. When we move from one to two and then to three rolls of a die, the shape of the distribution changes and moves toward the bell-shaped, normal probability distribution — an interesting result that intrigued the mathematicians of the 17th century and results in many modern applications.

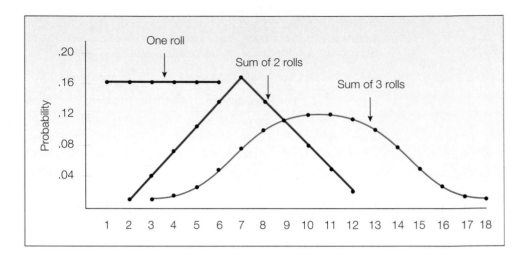

Chart 8–5   Sum of Spots Appearing in One, Two, and Three Rolls of a Fair Die

---

SELF-REVIEW 8–4

Refer to the Spence Sprockets, Inc. data on page 273. Select 10 random samples of 5 employees each. Use the methods described earlier in this chapter and the Table of Random Numbers (Appendix E) to find the employees to include in the samples. Compute the mean of each sample and plot the sample means on a chart similar to Chart 8–3.

▌ Exercises

11. Appendix E is a table of random numbers. Hence, each integer from 0 to 9 has the same likelihood of occurrence.
    a. Draw a graph showing the population distribution. What is the population mean?
    b. Below are the first 10 rows of five digits from Appendix E. Assume that these are 10 random samples of five values each. Determine the mean of each sample and plot the means on a chart similar to Chart 8–3. Compare the mean of the sampling distribution of the sample means with the population mean.

0	2	7	1	1
9	4	8	7	3
5	4	9	2	1
7	7	6	4	0
6	1	5	4	5
1	7	1	4	7
1	3	7	4	8
8	7	4	5	5
0	8	9	9	9
7	8	8	0	4

12. The Scrapper Elevator Company has 20 sales representatives who sell their product throughout the United States and Canada. The number of units sold last month by each representative is listed below. Assume these sales figures to be population values.

    2   3   2   3   3   4   2   4   3   2   2   7   3   4   5   3   3   3   3   5

    a. Draw a graph of the population.
    b. Compute the mean of the population.
    c. Select five random samples of 5 each and compute the mean of each sample. Use the methods described earlier in the chapter and Appendix E to determine the items in each sample.
    d. Compare the mean of the sampling distribution of the sample means to the population mean. Would you expect them to be exactly equal?
    e. Draw a histogram of the sample means. Do you notice a difference in the shape of the sample means compared to the population?

▌ Point Estimates and Confidence Intervals

The data on the length of service of Spence Sprockets employees, presented in the Example on page 273, are a population because we report the length of service for all 40 of the company employees. In this case we can easily compute the population mean. We have all the data and the population is not too large. However, in most cases we need to estimate the population mean. This population parameter is usually unknown. A single number used to estimate a population parameter is called a **point estimate.**

▌**Point Estimate**   The value, computed from sample information, that is used to estimate the population parameter.

The sample mean, $\bar{X}$, is a point estimate of the population mean, μ; p is a point estimate of π; and s is a point estimate of σ. Suppose Best Buy, Inc. wants to estimate the mean age of buyers of stereo equipment. They select a random sample of 50 recent purchasers, determine the age of each purchaser, and compute the mean age of the buyers in the sample. The mean of this sample is a point estimate of the mean of the population.

A point estimate, however, tells only part of the story. While we expect the point estimate to be close to the population parameter, we would like to measure how close it is. A confidence interval serves this purpose.

▌**Confidence Interval**   A range of values constructed from sample data so the parameter occurs within that range at a specified probability. The specified probability is called the *level of confidence.*

For example, we estimate the mean yearly income for construction workers in the New York–New Jersey area is $65,000. The range of this estimate might be from $61,000 to $69,000. We can describe how confident we are that the population parameter is in the interval by making a probability statement. We might say, for instance, that we are 90 percent sure that the mean yearly income of construction workers in the New York–New Jersey area is between $61,000 and $69,000.

The information developed about the shape of a sampling distribution of the sample means, that is the sampling distribution of $\bar{X}$, allows us to locate an interval that has a specified probability of containing the population mean μ. For reasonably large samples, we can use the central limit theorem and state the following:

1. Ninety-five percent of the sample means selected from a population will be within 1.96 standard deviations of the population mean μ.
2. Ninety-nine percent of the sample means will lie within 2.58 standard deviations of the population mean.

The standard deviation discussed here is the standard deviation of the sampling distribution of the sample mean. Intervals computed in this fashion are called the **95 percent confidence interval** and the **99 percent confidence interval.** How are the values of 1.96 and 2.58 obtained? The *95 percent* and *99 percent* refer to the percent of the time that similarly constructed intervals would include the parameter being estimated. The *95 percent,* for example, refers to the middle 95 percent of the observations. Therefore, the remaining 5 percent are equally divided between the two tails. See the following diagram.

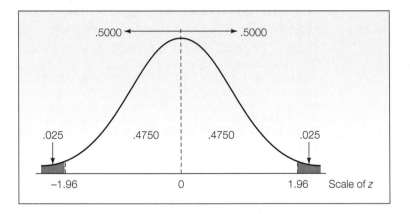

The central limit theorem states that the sampling distribution of the sample mean is approximately normal. Therefore, we can use Appendix D to find the appropriate *z* values. Locate .4750 in the body of the table, then read the corresponding row and column values. It is 1.96. So the probability of finding a *z* value between 0 and 1.96 is .4750. Likewise, the probability of being in the interval between −1.96 and 0 is also .4750. When we combine these two, the probability of being in the interval −1.96 to 1.96 is .9500. The *z* value corresponding to .99 is determined in a similar way.

How do you compute the 95 percent confidence interval? To illustrate, assume your research involves the annual starting salary of business school graduates. You have computed the sample mean to be $27,000 and the standard deviation of the sample means to be $200. The 95 percent confidence interval is between $26,608 and $27,392, found by $27,000 \pm 1.96(\$200)$. If 100 samples of the same size were selected from the population of interest and the corresponding 100 confidence intervals determined, we could expect to find the population mean in 95 of the 100 confidence intervals.

The Standard Error of the Sample Mean

In the previous section, the standard deviation of the sampling distribution of the sample means was given as $200. It is called the **standard error of the sample mean** and denoted by the symbol $\sigma_{\bar{X}}$, read "sigma sub X bar." It is often shortened to the **standard error.**

Standard Error of the Sample Mean   The standard deviation of the sampling distribution of sample mean.

The standard error is a measure of the variability of the sampling distribution of the sample mean. It is computed by

STANDARD ERROR OF THE MEAN, POPULATION STANDARD DEVIATION KNOWN	$\sigma_{\overline{X}} = \dfrac{\sigma}{\sqrt{n}}$	**[8–1]**

where:

$\sigma_{\overline{X}}$ is the standard error of the mean also called the standard deviation of the sampling distribution of the mean.

σ is the population standard deviation.

n is the sample size.

In most situations, the population standard deviation is not known. So we replace it with the sample standard deviation — that is, we replace σ with s. We then write formula (8–1) as follows:

STANDARD ERROR OF THE MEAN BASED ON THE SAMPLE STANDARD DEVIATION	$s_{\overline{X}} = \dfrac{s}{\sqrt{n}}$	**[8–2]**

The size of the standard error is affected by two values. The first is the standard deviation. If the standard deviation is large, then the standard error will also be large. However, the standard error is also affected by the sample size. As the sample size is increased, the standard error decreases, indicating that there is less variability in the distribution of sample means. This conclusion is logical, because an estimate made with a large sample should be more precise than one made from a small sample.

When the sample size, n, is at least 30, it is generally accepted that the central limit theorem will ensure a normal distribution of the sample means. This is an important consideration. If the sample means are normally distributed, we can use the standard normal distribution, that is, z, in our calculations.

The 95 percent and 99 percent confidence intervals are computed as follows, when $n \geq 30$.

95 PERCENT CONFIDENCE INTERVAL FOR A MEAN	$\overline{X} \pm 1.96 \dfrac{s}{\sqrt{n}}$	**[8–3]**

99 PERCENT CONFIDENCE INTERVAL FOR THE MEAN	$\overline{X} \pm 2.58 \dfrac{s}{\sqrt{n}}$	**[8–4]**

As discussed earlier, the values 1.96 and 2.58 are the z values corresponding to the middle 95 percent and 99 percent of the observations, respectively.

We can use other levels of confidence. For those cases the value of z changes accordingly. In general, a confidence interval for the mean is computed by:

CONFIDENCE INTERVAL FOR A MEAN	$\overline{X} \pm z \dfrac{s}{\sqrt{n}}$	**[8–5]**

where z is the level of confidence. So for a 92 percent confidence interval, the formula becomes:

$$\bar{X} \pm 1.75 \frac{s}{\sqrt{n}}$$

The value of 1.75 is from Appendix D. The table is based on half the normal distribution, so .9200/2 = .4600. The closest value in the body of the table is .4599, and the corresponding z value is 1.75.

Frequently we also use the 90 percent level of confidence. In this case, we want the area between 0 and z to be .4500, found by 90/2. To find the z value for this level of confidence, move down the left column of Appendix D to 1.6 and then over to the columns headed 0.04 and 0.05. The area corresponding to a z value of 1.64 is .4495, and for 1.65 it is .4505. To be conservative we use 1.65. Try looking up the following z values, check your answers against those on the right.

Confidence Interval	Closest Number	z Value
80 percent	.3997	1.28
94 percent	.4699	1.88
96 percent	.4798	2.05

Example

An experiment involves selecting a random sample of 256 middle managers. One item of interest is annual income. The sample mean is $45,420, and the sample standard deviation is $2,050.

1. What is the estimated mean income of all middle managers (the population)? That is, what is the point estimate?
2. What is the 95 percent confidence interval for the population mean (rounded to the nearest $10)?
3. What are the 95 percent confidence limits for the population mean?
4. What degree of confidence is being used?
5. Interpret the findings.

Solution

1. The point estimate of the population mean is $45,420.
2. The confidence interval is between $45,170 and $45,670, found by:

$$\bar{X} \pm 1.96 \frac{s}{\sqrt{n}} = \$45,420 \pm 1.96 \frac{\$2,050}{\sqrt{256}}$$

$$= \$45,420 \pm 251.125$$

$$= \$45,168.875 \text{ and } \$45,671.125$$

These endpoints are frequently rounded and, in this case, would be recorded as $45,170 and $45,670.

3. The endpoints of the confidence interval are called the *confidence limits*. In this example, $45,170 and $45,670 are the confidence limits.
4. The measure of confidence a person has is referred to as the *degree of confidence* or the *level of confidence*. In this case it is .95.
5. Interpretation: If we had time to select many samples of size 256 from the population of middle managers and compute the sample means and confidence

intervals, the population mean annual income would be in about 95 of the 100 confidence intervals. Either an interval contains the population mean or not. About 5 of 100 confidence intervals would *not* contain the population mean annual income, μ. This is shown in the following diagram. Note that the fifth confidence interval does not include the population mean.

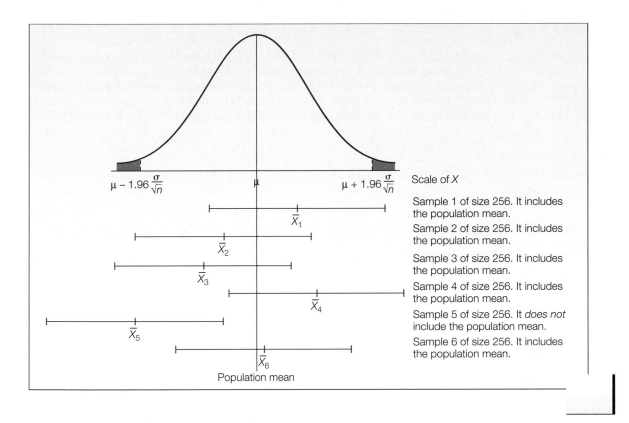

A Computer Simulation

With the aid of a computer, we can randomly select samples from a population, quickly compute the confidence interval, and show how confidence intervals usually, but not always, include the population parameter. The following example will help to explain.

Example

From many years in the automobile leasing business, Town Bank knows that the mean distance driven on a four-year lease is 50,000 miles and the standard deviation is 5,000. Suppose, using the MINITAB statistical software system, we want to find what proportion of the 95 percent confidence intervals will include the population mean of 50. We select 60 random samples of size 30, from a population with a mean of 50 and a standard deviation of 5. (To make the calculations easier to understand, we'll conduct the study in thousands of miles, instead of miles.)

Solution

The results of 60 random samples of 30 are in the table below. Of 60 confidence intervals with a 95 percent confidence level produced, 4 or 6.67 percent, did not include the population mean of 50. The intervals that do not include the population mean are highlighted. Another set of 60 confidence intervals would have a different result. The 6.67 percent is close to the estimate that 5 percent of the intervals will not include the population mean and the 56 of 60, or 93.33 percent is close to 95 percent.

To explain the calculation in more detail: MINITAB began by selecting a random sample of 30 observations from a population with a mean of 50 and a standard deviation of 5. These values were stored in the column c1. The mean of these 30 observations was 48.653. Hence, the sampling error was 1.347, found by 50 − 48.653. The interval 46.863 to 50.442 is determined by using formula (8–3) but using σ instead of s. There is a slight discrepancy, due to rounding, between the calculated interval below and that reported by MINITAB.

$$\bar{X} \pm 1.96 \frac{\sigma}{\sqrt{n}} = 48.653 \pm 1.96 \frac{5}{\sqrt{30}}$$

$$= 48.653 \pm 1.789 = 46.864 \text{ up to } 50.442$$

This process is repeated 59 more times.

STATISTICS IN ACTION

Many survey results reported in newspapers, in news magazines, and on TV use confidence intervals. For example, a recent survey of 800 viewers reported that for a large city 44 percent of the viewers watched the late local news on the CBS affiliate. The article went on to say the "margin of error was 3.4 percent." The margin of error is actually the amount that is added and subtracted from the point estimate to find the end points of the confidence interval. See formula (8–8).

$$z \sqrt{\frac{p(1 - p)}{n}} =$$

$$1.96 \sqrt{\frac{.44(1 - .44)}{800}} =$$

0.034

Thus, we conclude that the level of confidence is 95 percent.

```
Confidence Intervals

The assumed sigma = 5.00
Variable      N       Mean     StDev    SE Mean        95.0 % CI
C1           30     48.653     4.770     0.913    ( 46.863,  50.442)
C2           30     51.507     4.308     0.913    ( 49.717,  53.296)
C3           30     50.021     5.240     0.913    ( 48.232,  51.811)
C4           30     50.046     5.004     0.913    ( 48.257,  51.836)
C5           30     51.029     4.102     0.913    ( 49.240,  52.818)
C6           30     49.772     4.596     0.913    ( 47.983,  51.562)
C7           30     50.824     4.487     0.913    ( 49.034,  52.613)
C8           30     49.030     4.629     0.913    ( 47.240,  50.819)
C9           30     49.147     4.862     0.913    ( 47.357,  50.936)
C10          30     50.517     4.888     0.913    ( 48.727,  52.306)
C11          30     48.294     5.079     0.913    ( 46.504,  50.083)
C12          30     47.609     4.045     0.913    ( 45.819,  49.398)*
C13          30     50.136     4.579     0.913    ( 48.347,  51.926)
C14          30     50.054     5.443     0.913    ( 48.265,  51.844)
C15          30     49.353     5.191     0.913    ( 47.563,  51.142)
C16          30     49.711     4.586     0.913    ( 47.922,  51.501)
C17          30     49.794     4.848     0.913    ( 48.005,  51.584)
C18          30     50.190     5.834     0.913    ( 48.401,  51.980)
C19          30     49.569     4.333     0.913    ( 47.780,  51.359)
C20          30     49.670     4.392     0.913    ( 47.881,  51.460)
C21          30     49.862     5.448     0.913    ( 48.072,  51.651)
C22          30     51.285     4.991     0.913    ( 49.496,  53.075)
C23          30     50.566     5.315     0.913    ( 48.776,  52.355)
C24          30     49.848     4.788     0.913    ( 48.059,  51.638)
C25          30     49.964     4.913     0.913    ( 48.175,  51.754)
C26          30     49.587     5.931     0.913    ( 47.797,  51.376)
C27          30     52.375     4.703     0.913    ( 50.586,  54.165)*
C28          30     49.480     5.752     0.913    ( 47.690,  51.269)
C29          30     49.417     3.932     0.913    ( 47.627,  51.206)
C30          30     51.621     4.318     0.913    ( 49.832,  53.411)
```

```
Variable      N      Mean     StDev   SE Mean      95.0 % CI
C31          30    49.227    4.277    0.913    ( 47.437, 51.016)
C32          30    47.967    5.193    0.913    ( 46.178, 49.756)*
C33          30    49.627    5.038    0.913    ( 47.837, 51.416)
C34          30    51.333    4.645    0.913    ( 49.544, 53.122)
C35          30    50.808    4.959    0.913    ( 49.018, 52.597)
C36          30    50.775    5.442    0.913    ( 48.986, 52.564)
C37          30    50.853    4.855    0.913    ( 49.063, 52.642)
C38          30    50.539    5.142    0.913    ( 48.749, 52.328)
C39          30    50.776    5.440    0.913    ( 48.987, 52.566)
C40          30    50.629    3.608    0.913    ( 48.839, 52.418)
C41          30    51.424    4.902    0.913    ( 49.634, 53.213)
C42          30    48.798    5.310    0.913    ( 47.008, 50.587)
C43          30    50.166    5.003    0.913    ( 48.377, 51.955)
C44          30    49.332    4.364    0.913    ( 47.543, 51.122)
C45          30    50.013    5.047    0.913    ( 48.224, 51.802)
C46          30    50.299    4.280    0.913    ( 48.509, 52.088)
C47          30    50.436    5.002    0.913    ( 48.646, 52.225)
C48          30    50.177    6.091    0.913    ( 48.388, 51.966)
C49          30    50.957    4.936    0.913    ( 49.168, 52.746)
C50          30    50.457    5.328    0.913    ( 48.668, 52.246)
C51          30    48.919    4.414    0.913    ( 47.130, 50.708)
C52          30    48.929    4.143    0.913    ( 47.139, 50.718)
C53          30    50.572    5.284    0.913    ( 48.782, 52.361)
C54          30    50.871    5.468    0.913    ( 49.082, 52.661)
C55          30    50.719    5.680    0.913    ( 48.929, 52.508)
C56          30    49.611    5.437    0.913    ( 47.822, 51.401)
C57          30    48.004    5.206    0.913    ( 46.215, 49.794)*
C58          30    50.662    4.113    0.913    ( 48.872, 52.451)
C59          30    49.667    4.498    0.913    ( 47.878, 51.457)
C60          30    50.133    5.468    0.913    ( 48.344, 51.923)

*Does not include the population mean.
```

SELF-REVIEW 8–5

The wildlife department is feeding a special food to rainbow trout fingerlings in a pond. A sample of the weights of 40 trout revealed that the sample mean is 402.7 grams and the sample standard deviation 8.8 grams.

(a) What is the estimated mean weight of the population? What is that estimate called?
(b) What is the 99 percent confidence interval?
(c) What are the 99 percent confidence limits?
(d) What degree of confidence is being used?
(e) Interpret your findings.

▌ Exercises

13. A sample of 49 observations is taken from a normal population. The sample mean is 55, and the sample standard deviation is 10. Determine the 99 percent confidence interval for the population mean.
14. A sample of 81 observations is taken from a normal population. The sample mean is 40, and the sample standard deviation is 5. Determine the 95 percent confidence interval for the population mean.
15. A sample of 10 observations is selected from a normal population for which the population standard deviation is known to be 5. The sample mean is 20.

    a.   Determine the standard error of the mean.

    b.   Explain why we can use formula (8–3) to determine the 95 percent confidence interval even though the sample is less than 30.

    c.   Determine the 95 percent confidence interval for the population mean.

16. Suppose you wanted to use a 90 percent confidence level instead of the 95 percent and 99 percent intervals used in formulas (8–3) and (8–4). What value would you use to multiply the standard error of the mean?

17. A research firm conducted a survey to determine the mean amount steady smokers spend on cigarettes during a week. A sample of 49 steady smokers revealed that $\bar{X} = \$20$ and $s = \$5$.

    a.   What is the point estimate? Explain what it indicates.

    b.   Using the 95 percent level of confidence, determine the confidence interval for μ. Explain what it indicates.

18. Refer to the previous exercise. Suppose that 64 smokers (instead of 49) had been surveyed, and the sample mean and the sample standard deviation remained the same ($20 and $5, respectively).

    a.   What is the 95 percent confidence interval estimate of μ?

    b.   Explain why this confidence interval is narrower than the one determined in the previous exercise.

19. Al Fishhaber is the owner of Al's Marathon gas station. Al would like to estimate the mean number of gallons of gasoline sold to his customers. From his records he selects a sample of 60 sales and finds that the mean number of gallons sold is 8.60 and the standard deviation is 2.30 gallons.

    a.   What is the estimate of the population mean?

    b.   Develop a 99 percent confidence interval for the population mean.

    c.   Interpret the meaning of part b.

20. An English professor counted the number of misspelled words on an essay he recently assigned. For his class of 40 students, the mean number of misspelled words was 6.05 and the standard deviation 2.44. Construct a 95 percent confidence interval for the mean number of misspelled words in the population of students.

▎ Confidence Interval for a Population Proportion

The theory for determining a point estimator and an interval estimator for a *population proportion* are quite similar to those described in the previous section. A point estimate for the population proportion is found by dividing the number of successes in the sample by the total number sampled. Suppose 100 of 400 sampled said they liked a new cola better than their regular cola. The best estimate of the population proportion favoring the new cola is .25, or 25 percent, found by 100/400. Recall that a proportion is based on a *count* of the number of successes relative to the total number sampled.

How is the **confidence interval for a population proportion** estimated?

CONFIDENCE INTERVAL USING A POPULATION PROPORTION	$p \pm z\sigma_{\bar{p}}$	**[8–6]**

where $\sigma_{\bar{p}}$ is the standard error of the proportion:

STANDARD ERROR OF THE SAMPLE PROPORTION	$\sigma_{\bar{p}} = \sqrt{\dfrac{p(1 - p)}{n}}$	**[8–7]**

Therefore, the confidence interval is constructed by:

CONFIDENCE INTERVAL FOR A SAMPLE PROPORTION $\qquad p \pm z \sqrt{\dfrac{p(1-p)}{n}}$ **[8–8]**

---

where:

    p is the sample proportion.

    z is the z value for the degree of confidence selected.

    n is the sample size.

Example

Suppose 1,600 of 2,000 union members sampled said they plan to vote for the proposal to merge with the UMA. Using the .95 level of confidence, what is the interval estimate for the population proportion? Based on the confidence interval, what conclusion can be drawn?

Solution

Using formula (8–8), the interval is computed as follows.

$$p \pm z \sqrt{\frac{p(1-p)}{n}} = .80 \pm 1.96 \sqrt{\frac{.80(1-.80)}{2,000}}$$

$$= .80 \pm 1.96 \sqrt{.00008}$$

$$= .782 \text{ and } .818.$$

Confidence limits: 78.2 and 81.8 percent

Assume that at least 75 percent of the union members must approve of the merger. Based on the sample results, when all union members vote, the proposal will probably pass because .75 lies below the interval .782 and .818.

SELF-REVIEW 8–6

A market survey was conducted to estimate the proportion of homemakers who could recognize the brand name of a cleanser based on the shape and color of the container. Of the 1,400 homemakers, 420 were able to identify the brand name.

(a) Using the .99 degree of confidence, the population proportion lies within what interval?
(b) What are the confidence limits?
(c) Interpret your findings.

▌ Exercises

21. In Exercise 19, the owner of Al's Marathon determined the mean number of gallons of gasoline purchased by his customers. He is also interested in the proportion of women who pump their own gasoline. He surveyed 100 women and found that 80 indicated they pump their own gasoline.
    a. What is the estimated proportion of women in the population who pump their own gasoline?
    b. Develop a 95 percent confidence interval for the proportion of women who pump their own gasoline. Interpret.
22. Ms. Maria Wilson is considering running for mayor of the town of Bear Gulch, Montana. Before completing the petitions, she decides to conduct a survey of voters in Bear Gulch. A sample of 400 voters revealed that 300 would support her in the November election.

a.   What proportion of the population of voters in Bear Gulch do you estimate would support Ms. Wilson?

b.   Develop a 99 percent confidence interval for the proportion of voters in the population who would support Ms. Wilson.

c.   In part (b) note that both of the endpoints of the confidence interval are greater than .50. What importance would she attach to this?

23.   Suppose the Fox TV network is considering replacing one of its prime-time shows with a new family-oriented comedy. Before a final decision is made, a random sample of 400 prime-time viewers is conducted. After seeing a preview of the comedy, 250 indicated that they would watch it.

a.   What is your estimate of the proportion of viewers in the population who will watch the new show?

b.   Develop a 95 percent confidence interval for the proportion of viewers who will watch the new show.

24.   A silkscreen printer purchases plastic cups on which to print logos for sporting events and other special occasions. The printer received a large shipment this morning and would like to estimate the percent defective. A sample of 200 revealed 30 of the cups to be defective.

a.   What proportion of the shipment is estimated to be defective?

b.   Develop a 95 percent confidence interval for defective cups.

▌ Finite-Population Correction Factor

Infinite population

The populations we have sampled so far have been very large or assumed to be *infinite*. What if the sampled population is not infinite, or not even very large? In such instances we need to make some adjustments in the way we compute the standard error of the sample means and the standard error of the sample proportions.

Finite population

A population that has a fixed upper bound is said to be **finite.** For example, there are 21,376 students enrolled at Eastern Illinois University, and the Chrysler-Jeep Corp. manufactured 917 units at the Arkansas plant last year. A finite population can be rather small; it could be all the students registered for this class. It can also be very large, such as all senior citizens living in Florida.

For a finite population, where the total number of objects is N and the size of the sample is $n,$ the following adjustment is made to the standard errors of the sample means and the proportion:

STANDARD ERROR OF THE SAMPLE MEANS, USING A CORRECTION FACTOR	$\sigma_{\overline{X}} = \dfrac{\sigma}{\sqrt{n}} \sqrt{\dfrac{N-n}{N-1}}$	**[8–9]**

STANDARD ERROR OF THE SAMPLE PROPORTIONS, USING A CORRECTION FACTOR	$\sigma_p = \sqrt{\dfrac{p(1-p)}{n}} \sqrt{\dfrac{N-n}{N-1}}$	**[8–10]**

Finite-population correction factor

This adjustment is called the **finite-population correction factor.** Why is it necessary to apply a factor, and what is its effect? Logically, if the sample is a substantial percentage of the population, then estimates are more precise than those for a smaller sample. Note the effect of the term $(N - n)/(N - 1)$. Suppose the population is 1,000 and the sample is 100. Then this ratio is $(1,000 - 100)/(1,000 - 1)$, or 900/999. Taking the square root gives the correction factor, .9492. Multiplying by the standard error reduces the error by about 5 percent $(1 - .9492 \cong .05)$. This reduction in the size of the standard error yields a smaller range of values in estimating the population mean. If the sample is 200, the correction factor is .8949, meaning that the standard error has been reduced by more than 10 percent. Table 8–5 shows the effects of various sizes of samples on the correction factor. Note that when the sample is less than about 5 percent of the population, the impact of the correction factor is quite small. The usual rule is that if the ratio n/N is less than .05, the finite-population correction factor is ignored.

Table 8–5 Computation of the Finite-Population Correction Factor for Selected Sample Sizes When the Population Is 1,000

Sample Size	Fraction of Population	Correction Factor
10	.010	.9955
25	.025	.9879
50	.050	.9752
100	.100	.9492
200	.200	.8949
500	.500	.7075

Example

There are 250 families in the small town of Scandia. A poll of 40 families revealed the mean annual church contribution is $450 with a standard deviation of $75. Construct a 95 percent confidence interval for the mean annual contribution.

Solution

First note the population is finite. That is, there is a limit to the number of people in Scandia. Second, note that the sample constitutes more than 5 percent of the population; that is, $n/N = 40/250 = .16$. Hence, the finite-population correction factor is used. The 95 percent confidence interval is constructed as follows, using formulas (8–3) and (8–9).

$$\bar{X} \pm z \frac{s}{\sqrt{n}} \left(\sqrt{\frac{N - n}{N - 1}} \right) = \$450 \pm 1.96 \frac{\$75}{\sqrt{40}} \left(\sqrt{\frac{250 - 40}{250 - 1}} \right)$$

$$= \$450 \pm \$23.243(\sqrt{.8434})$$

$$= \$450 \pm \$21.35$$

$$= [\$428.65, \$471.35]$$

SELF-REVIEW 8–7

The same study of church contributions in Scandia revealed that 15 of the 40 families sampled attend church regularly. Construct the 95 percent confidence interval for the proportion of families attending church regularly. Should the finite-population correction factor be applied? Why or why not?

▌ Exercises

25. A population consists of 300 items. A sample of size 36 is selected. The mean is 35 and the standard deviation 5. Develop a 95 percent confidence interval for the population mean.
26. A population consists of 500 items. A sample of size 49 is selected. The mean is 40 and the standard deviation 9. Develop a 99 percent confidence interval for the population mean.
27. The attendance at the Durham Bulls minor league baseball game last night was 400. A random sample of 50 of those in attendance revealed that the mean number of soft drinks consumed was 1.86 with a standard deviation of 0.50. Develop a 99 percent confidence interval for the mean number of soft drinks consumed.
28. There are 300 welders employed at the Maine Shipyards Corporation. A sample of 30 welders revealed that 18 graduated from a registered welding course. Construct the 95 percent confidence interval for the proportion of all welders who graduated from a registered welding course.

▌ Choosing an Appropriate Sample Size

A concern that usually arises when designing a statistical study is "How many items should be in the sample?" If a sample is too large, money is wasted collecting the data. Similarly, if the sample is too small, the resulting conclusions will be uncertain. The correct sample size depends on three factors:

1. The level of confidence desired.
2. The margin of error the researcher will tolerate.
3. The variability in the population being studied.

You, the researcher, select the level of confidence. As noted in the previous section, confidence levels of 95 percent and 99 percent are most often selected. A 95 percent level of confidence corresponds to a z value of ± 1.96, and a 99 percent level of confidence corresponds to a z value of ± 2.58. The higher the level of confidence, the larger the size of the sample.

The maximum allowable error, designated as E, is the amount that is added and subtracted from the sample mean to determine the end points of the confidence interval. It is the amount of error the researcher is willing to tolerate. It is also one-half the width of the corresponding confidence interval. A small allowable error will require a large sample, and a large allowable error will permit a smaller sample.

The third factor in determining the size of a sample is the population standard deviation. If the population is widely dispersed, a large sample is required. On the other hand, if the population is concentrated (homogeneous), the required sample size will be smaller. However, finding an estimate for the population standard deviation may be necessary. Here are three suggestions.

Use the *comparable study* approach when there is an estimate of the dispersion available from another study. Suppose we want to estimate the number of hours worked per week by refuse workers. Perhaps information from certain state or federal agencies who regularly sample the workforce might be useful to provide an estimate of the standard deviation. If a standard deviation observed in a previous study is thought to be reliable, it can be used in the current study to help provide an approximate sample size.

If no value from previous experience is available, a *range-based approximation* might be appropriate. To use this approach we need to know or have an estimate of the largest and smallest values in the population. Recall from Chapter 4, where we described the Empirical Rule, that virtually all the observations could be expected to be within ± 3 standard deviations of the mean, assuming that the distribution was approximately bell-shaped, i.e., normal. So the distance between the largest and the smallest values is 6σ. We could estimate the standard deviation as one-sixth of the range. For example, suppose the director of operations of a bank wants an estimate of the number of checks written per month by college students. She believes that the distribution is approximately normal, the minimum number of checks written is 2 per month, and the most is 50. The range of the number of checks written per month is 48, found by 50 − 2. The estimate of the standard deviation then would be 8 checks per month, 48/6.

The third approach to estimating the standard deviation is to conduct a *pilot study.* This is the most common method. Suppose we want an estimate of the number of hours per week worked by students enrolled in the College of Business at The University of Texas. To test the validity of our questionnaire, we use it on a small sample of students. From this small sample we compute the standard deviation of the number of hours worked and use this value to determine the appropriate sample size.

We can express the interaction among these three factors and the sample size in the following formula.

$$E = z \frac{s}{\sqrt{n}}$$

Solving this equation for *n,* we obtain the required sample size.

SAMPLE SIZE FOR ESTIMATING A MEAN	$n = \left(\dfrac{z \cdot s}{E}\right)^2$	**[8–11]**

where:
  n   is the size of the sample.
  z   is the standard normal value corresponding to the desired level of confidence.
  s   is an estimate of the population standard deviation.
  E   is the maximum allowable error.

The result of this calculation is not always a whole number. When the outcome is not a whole number the usual practice is to round up any fractional result. For example, 201.22 would be rounded up to 202.

Example

A student in public administration wants to determine the mean amount members of city councils earn. The error in estimating the mean is to be less than $100 with a 95 percent level of confidence. The student found a report by the Department of Labor that estimated the standard deviation to be $1,000. What is the required sample size?

Solution

The maximum allowable error, *E,* is $100. The value of *z* for a 95 percent level of confidence is 1.96, and the estimate of the standard deviation is $1,000. Substituting these values into formula (8–11), the required sample size is:

$$n = \left(\frac{(1.96)(\$1,000)}{\$100}\right)^2 = (19.6)^2 = 384.16$$

The computed value of 384.16 is rounded up to 385. A sample of 385 is required to meet the specifications. If a higher level of confidence is desired, say 99 percent, then a larger sample is also required.

$$n = \left(\frac{(2.58)(\$1,000)}{\$100}\right)^2 = (25.8)^2 = 665.64$$

We recommend a sample of 666. Observe how much the change in the level of confidence increased the sample size. An increase from the 95 percent to the 99 percent level of confidence resulted in an increase of 281 observations. This could greatly increase the cost of the study, both in terms of time and money. Hence, the level of confidence should be carefully considered.

The procedure just described can be adapted to determine the sample size for a proportion. Again, three items need to be specified:

1. The desired level of confidence, usually 95 percent or 99 percent.
2. The margin of error in the population proportion that is required.
3. An estimate of the population proportion.

The formula to determine the sample size of a proportion is:

SAMPLE SIZE FOR A PROPORTION	$n = p(1 - p)\left(\dfrac{z}{E}\right)^2$	**[8–12]**

If such an estimate of π is available from a pilot study or some other source, it can be used. Otherwise, .50 is used because the term $p(1 - p)$ can never be larger than when $p = .50$. For example, if $p = .30$, then $p(1 - p) = .30(1 - .30) = .21$, but when $p = .50$, $p(1 - p) = .50(1 - .50) = .25$.

Example

The study in the previous example also estimates the proportion of cities that have private refuse collectors. The student wants the estimate to be within .10 of the population proportion, the desired level of confidence is 90 percent, and no estimate is available for the population proportion. What is the required sample size?

Solution

The estimate of the population proportion is to be within .10, so $E = .10$. The desired level of confidence is .90, which corresponds to a z value of 1.65. Because no estimate of the population proportion is available .50 will be used. The required sample size is

$$n = (.50)(.50)\left(\frac{1.65}{.10}\right)^2 = 68.0625$$

The student needs a random sample of 69 cities.

SELF-REVIEW 8–8

Will you assist the college registrar in determining how many transcripts to study? The registrar wants to estimate the arithmetic mean grade point average of all graduating seniors during the past 10 years. GPAs range between 2.0 and 4.0. The mean grade point average is to be estimated within plus and minus 0.05 of the population mean.

The .99 degree of confidence is to be used. Thus, the registrar wants to report something like this (hypothetical): "With a probability of .99, the mean grade point average of graduating seniors is in the interval between 2.45 and 2.55." The standard deviation of a small pilot survey is 0.279. How many transcripts should be sampled?

▌ Exercises

29. A population is estimated to have a standard deviation of 10. We want to estimate the population mean within 2, with a 95 percent level of confidence. How large a sample is required?

30. We want to estimate the population mean within 5, with a 99 percent level of confidence. The population standard deviation is estimated to be 15. How large a sample is required?

31. The estimate of the population proportion is to be within ± .05, with a 95 percent level of confidence. The best estimate of the population proportion is .15. How large a sample is required?

32. The estimate of the population proportion is to be within ± .10, with a 99 percent level of confidence. The best estimate of the population proportion is .45. How large a sample is required?

33. A survey is being planned to determine the mean amount of time corporation executives watch television. A pilot survey indicated that the mean time per week is 12 hours, with a standard deviation of 3 hours. It is desired to estimate the mean viewing time within one-quarter hour. The .95 degree of confidence is to be used. How many executives should be surveyed?

34. A processor of carrots cuts the green top off each carrot, washes the carrots, and inserts six to a package. Twenty packages are inserted in a box for shipment. To test the weight of the boxes, a few were checked. The mean weight was 20.4 pounds, the standard deviation 0.5 pounds. How many boxes must the processor sample to be 95 percent confident that the sample mean does not differ from the population mean by more than 0.2 pounds?

35. Suppose the President wants an estimate of the proportion of the population who support his current policy toward Haiti. The President wants the estimate to be within .04 of the true proportion. Assume a 95 percent level of confidence. The Secretary of State estimated the proportion supporting current policy to be .60.
    a. How large a sample is required?
    b. How large would the sample have to be if the estimate by the Secretary of State were not available?

36. Past surveys revealed that 30 percent of tourists going to Las Vegas to gamble during a weekend spent more than $1,000. Management wants to update that percentage.
    a. Using the .90 degree of confidence, management wants to estimate the percentage of tourists spending more than $1,000 within 1 percent. What sample size should be employed?
    b. Management said that the sample size suggested in part (a) is much too large. Suggest something that could be done to reduce the sample size. Based on your suggestion, recalculate the sample size.

▌ Chapter Outline

I. There are many reasons for sampling a population.
   A. Often testing destroys the sampled item and it cannot be returned to the population.
   B. It may be impossible to check or locate all the members of the population.
   C. The cost of studying all the items in the population may be prohibitive.
   D. The results of a sample may adequately estimate the population parameter, thus saving time and money.
   E. It may be too time consuming to contact all the members of the population.

II. There are two types of samples: probability and nonprobability.
   A. In a probability sample all members of the population have a chance of being selected for the sample. There are several probability sampling methods.
      1. In a simple random sample all members of the population have the same chance of being selected for the sample.

2. In a systematic sample a random starting point is selected, and then every kth item is selected for the sample.
3. In a stratified sample the population is divided into several groups, or strata, and then a sample is selected from each stratum.
4. In cluster sampling the population is divided into primary units, and then samples are drawn from the primary units.
   B. In nonprobability sampling, inclusion in the sample is based on the judgment of the person conducting the sample. Nonprobability samples may lead to biased results.
III. The difference between the population parameter and the sample statistic is called the sampling error.
IV. The sampling distribution of the sample means is a probability distribution showing all possible sample means and their probabilities of occurrence.
   A. For a given sample size, the mean of all possible means selected from the population is exactly equal to the population mean.
   B. There is less variation in the distribution of the sample means than in the population.
      1. The standard deviation of the distribution of sample means is called the standard error of the mean.
      2. It is computed by the following formula.

$$\sigma_{\bar{X}} = \frac{\sigma}{\sqrt{n}} \qquad \text{[8-1]}$$

   C. The central limit theorem states that if all samples of a reasonably large ($n \geq 30$) size are selected from any population, the distribution of the sample means is approximately normal.
      1. The approximation improves with larger samples.
      2. Sampling from a normal population leads directly to a normal distribution of the sample means.
V. A point estimate is a single value (statistic) used to estimate a population value (parameter).
VI. A confidence interval estimate is a range of values within which the population parameter is expected to occur.
   A. The factors that determine a confidence interval for a mean are:
      1. The number of observations in the sample, n.
      2. The variability in the population, usually estimated by the sample standard deviation, s.
      3. The level of confidence. It is represented by the z value.
   B. A confidence interval for the mean is

$$\bar{X} \pm z \frac{s}{\sqrt{n}} \qquad \text{[8-5]}$$

   C. The factors that determine a confidence interval for a proportion are:
      1. The number of observations in the sample.
      2. The value of p is computed by dividing the number of successes in the sample, X, by the number of observations in the sample, n.
      3. The level of confidence. It is represented by the z value.
   D. A confidence interval for a proportion is

$$p \pm z \sqrt{\frac{p(1-p)}{n}} \qquad \text{[8-8]}$$

VII. The required size of a sample can be determined for both means and proportions.
   A. The factors that determine the size of the sample for a mean are:
      1. The desired level of confidence, z.
      2. The maximum allowable error, E.
      3. The variation in the population (usually estimated by s).

B. The formula for sample size for a mean is:

$$n = \left(\frac{z \cdot s}{E}\right)^2 \qquad \text{[8–11]}$$

C. The factors that determine the size of the sample for a proportion are:
1. The desired level of confidence, z.
2. The maximum allowable error, E.
3. An estimate of the population proportion. If no estimate is available, then .50 is used.

D. The formula for sample size for a proportion is:

$$n = p(1 - p)\left(\frac{z}{E}\right)^2 \qquad \text{[8–12]}$$

E. The finite-population correction factor is applied if n/N is more than .05. The correction factor is

$$\sqrt{\frac{N - n}{N - 1}}$$

▌ Pronunciation Key

SYMBOL	MEANING	PRONUNCIATION
$\mu_{\bar{X}}$	Mean of the distribution of sample means	*mu sub X bar*
$\sigma_{\bar{X}}$	Population standard error of the sample means	*sigma sub X bar*
$s_{\bar{X}}$	The sample standard error of the sample means	*s sub X bar*
σ_p	Standard error of the sample proportion	*sigma sub p*

▌ Chapter Exercises

37. The retail stores located in the North Towne Square Mall are:

Number	Store	Number	Store	Number	Store
00	Elder-Beerman	09	Lion Store	17	Dollar Tree
01	Montgomery Ward	10	Bootleggers	18	County Seat
02	Deb Shop	11	Formal Man	19	Kid Mart
03	Frederick's of Hollywood	12	Leather Ltd.	20	Lerner
04	Petries	13	B Dalton Bookseller	21	Coach House Gifts
05	Easy Dreams	14	Pat's Hallmark	22	Spence Gifts
06	Summit Stationers	15	Things Remembered	23	CPI Photo Finish
07	E B Brown Opticians	16	Pearle Vision Express	24	Regis Hairstylists
08	Kay-Bee Toy & Hobby				

a. If the following random numbers are selected, which retail stores should be contacted for a survey? 11 65 86 62 06 10 12 77 04
b. Select a random sample of four retail stores. Use Appendix E.
c. A systematic sampling procedure is to be used. The first store is to be contacted and then every 3rd store. Which stores will be contacted?

38. The following is a list of family-practice physicians. Three physicians are to be randomly selected and contacted regarding their charge for a routine office visit. The 39 physicians have been coded from 00 to 38. Also noted is whether they are in practice by themselves (S), have a partner (P), or are in a group practice (G).

Number	Physician	Type of Practice	Number	Physician	Type of Practice
00	R. E. Scherbarth, M.D.	S	20	Gregory Yost, M.D.	P
01	Crystal R. Goveia, M.D.	P	21	J. Christian Zona, M.D.	P
02	Mark D. Hillard, M.D.	P	22	Larry Johnson, M.D.	P
03	Jeanine S. Huttner, M.D.	P	23	Sanford Kimmel, M.D.	P
04	Francis Aona, M.D.	P	24	Harry Mayhew, M.D.	S
05	Janet Arrowsmith, M.D.	P	25	Leroy Rodgers, M.D.	S
06	David DeFrance, M.D.	S	26	Thomas Tafelski, M.D.	S
07	Judith Furlong, M.D.	S	27	Mark Zilkoski, M.D.	G
08	Leslie Jackson, M.D.	G	28	Ken Bertka, M.D.	G
09	Paul Langenkamp, M.D.	S	29	Mark DeMichiei, M.D.	G
10	Philip Lepkowski, M.D.	S	30	John Eggert, M.D.	P
11	Wendy Martin, M.D.	S	31	Jeanne Fiorito, M.D.	P
12	Denny Mauricio, M.D.	P	32	Michael Fitzpatrick, M.D.	P
13	Hasmukh Parmar, M.D.	P	33	Charles Holt, D.O.	P
14	Ricardo Pena, M.D.	P	34	Richard Koby, M.D.	P
15	David Reames, M.D.	P	35	John Meier, M.D.	P
16	Ronald Reynolds, M.D.	G	36	Douglas Smucker, M.D.	S
17	Mark Steinmetz, M.D.	G	37	David Weldy, M.D.	P
18	Geza Torok, M.D.	S	38	Cheryl Zaborowski, M.D.	P
19	Mark Young, M.D.	P			

a. If the random numbers 31, 94, 43, 36, 03, 24, 17, and 09 are obtained from Appendix E, which physicians should be contacted?

b. Select a random sample of four physicians using the random numbers of Appendix E.

c. A sample is to consist of every fifth physician. The number 04 is selected as the starting point. Which physicians will be contacted?

d. A sample is to consist of two physicians in solo practice (S), two in partnership (P), and one in group practice. Select a sample accordingly. Explain your procedure.

39. What is sampling error? Could the value of the sampling error be zero? If it were zero, what would this mean?

40. List the reasons for sampling. Give an example of each reason for sampling.

41. The commercial banks in Region III are to be surveyed. Some of them are very large, with assets of more than $500 million; others are medium-size, with assets between $100 million and $500 million; and the remaining banks have assets of less than $100 million. Explain how you would select a sample of these banks.

42. Plastic Products is concerned about the inside diameter of the plastic PVC pipe it produces. A machine extrudes the pipe, which is then cut into 10-foot lengths. About 720 pipes are produced per machine during a two-hour period. How would you go about taking a sample from the two-hour production period?

43. A study of motel facilities in a metropolitan area showed there were 25 facilities. The city's convention and visitors bureau is studying the number of rooms at each location. The results

are as follows: 90, 72, 75, 60, 75, 72, 84, 72, 88, 74, 105, 115, 68, 74, 80, 64, 104, 82, 48, 58, 60, 80, 48, 58, and 108.

- a. Using a table of random numbers (Appendix E), select a random sample of size 5 from this population.
- b. Obtain a systematic sample by selecting a random starting point among the first five motels, and then select every fifth motel.
- c. Suppose the last five motels listed are "cut-rate" motels. Describe how you would select a random sample of three regular motels and two cut-rate motels.

44. Ten passengers are to be selected at random from the New York–Los Angeles Delta flight and interviewed in depth regarding airport facilities, service, food, and so on. Each passenger boarding the aircraft was given a number. The numbers started with 001 and ended with 250.
- a. Select 10 useable numbers at random using the table of random numbers in Appendix E.
- b. The sample of 10 could have been chosen using a systematic sample. Choose the first number using Appendix E, and then list the numbers to be interviewed.
- c. Evaluate the two methods by giving the advantages and possible disadvantages.
- d. In what other way could a random sample be selected from the 250 passengers?

45. Suppose your statistics instructor gave six examinations during the semester. You received the following grades (percent correct): 79 64 84 82 92 77. Instead of averaging the six scores, the instructor indicated he would randomly select two grades and report that grade to the student records office.
- a. How many different samples of 2 test grades are possible?
- b. List all possible samples of size 2 and compute the mean of each.
- c. Compute the mean of the sample means and compare it with the population mean.
- d. If you were a student, would you like this arrangement? Would the result be different from dropping the lowest score? Write a brief report.

46. At the downtown office of First National Bank there are five tellers. Last week the tellers made the following number of errors each: 2 3 5 3 5.
- a. How many different samples of 2 tellers are possible?
- b. List all possible samples of size 2 and compute the mean of each.
- c. Compute the mean of the sample means and compare it with the population mean.

47. Dr. Lamberg has five students doing special independent study this semester. To evaluate their reading progress, Dr. Lamberg gave the students a five-question true/false test. The number of correct answers for each student is given below.

Student	Number Correct
Taylor	4
Hurley	3
Fowler	5
Rousche	3
Telatko	2

- a. How many samples of 2 students are possible from this population?
- b. List all possible samples of size 2, and compute the sample means.
- c. Organize the sample means into a sampling distribution.
- d. Compute the mean of the sample means, and compare it with the population mean.
- e. Compare the shape of the population and the shape of the sampling distribution of the sample means.

48. The ages of the six executives of the Ace Manufacturing Company (considered the population) are:

Name	Age
Mr. Jones	54
Ms. Smith	50
Mr. Kirk	52
Ms. Small	48
Mr. Hugh	50
Mr. Sioto	52

    a. How many samples of size 2 are possible?

    b. Select all possible samples of size 2 from the population of executives, and compute the means.

    c. Organize the means into a sampling distribution.

    d. What is the mean of the population? Of the sample means?

    e. What is the shape of the population?

    f. What is the shape of the sampling distribution?

49. A random sample of 85 group leaders, supervisors, and similar personnel at Amana revealed that, on the average, a person spent 6.5 years on the job before being promoted. The standard deviation of the sample was 1.7 years. Construct a 95 percent confidence interval.

50. The Iowa state meat inspector has been given the assignment of estimating the mean net weight of packages of ground chuck labeled "3 pounds." Of course, he realizes that the weights cannot be precisely 3 pounds. A sample of 36 packages revealed the mean weight to be 3.01 pounds, with a standard deviation of 0.03 pounds.

    a. What is the estimated population mean?

    b. Using the .95 degree of confidence, what are the confidence limits for the population mean?

51. A recent study of 50 self-service gasoline stations in the Cincinnati, Ohio, area revealed that the mean price of unleaded gas was $1.179 per gallon, and the standard deviation was $0.03 per gallon. Determine a 99 percent confidence interval for the population mean price per gallon of unleaded gasoline.

52. A recent survey of 50 unemployed male executives showed that it took a mean of 26 weeks to find another position. The standard deviation was 6.2 weeks. Find the 95 percent confidence interval for the mean time it will take executives to find another job.

53. The Badik Construction Company limits its business to repairing driveways, installing patios, and building decks. The mean time for each of these three jobs is 12 hours, but the standard deviation is 3 hours for repairing a driveway, 6 hours for a patio, and 8 hours for a deck. This information is based on samples of 40 of each type of job.

    a. Before you do any calculation, which of the three types of jobs will have the smallest range of values for a 99 percent confidence interval for mean construction time?

    b. Compute a confidence interval for the mean construction time for each type of job.

54. The American Restaurant Association collected information on the number of meals eaten outside the home per week by young married couples. A survey of 60 couples showed the sample mean number of meals eaten outside the home was 2.76 per week, with a standard deviation of 0.75 meals. Construct a 97 percent confidence interval for the population mean.

55. Suppose the National Collegiate Athletic Association (NCAA) reported that the mean number of hours spent per week on coaching and recruiting by college football assistant coaches during the season is 70. A random sample of 50 assistant coaches showed the sample mean to be 68.6 hours, with a standard deviation of 8.2 hours.

    a. Using the sample data, construct a 99 percent confidence interval for the population mean.

    b. Does the 99 percent confidence interval include the value suggested by the NCAA? Does this cast doubt or reinforce the statement by the NCAA?

    c. Without doing any calculation, would changing the level of confidence from 99 percent to 95 percent increase or decrease the width of the confidence interval? What value would change in the calculation?

56. The Human Relations Department of Electronics, Inc. would like to include a dental plan as part of the benefits package. The question is: How much does a typical employee and their family spend per year on dental expenses? A sample of 45 employees showed the mean amount spent last year was $1,820, with a standard deviation of $660.
   a. Construct a 95 percent confidence interval for the population mean.
   b. The information from part (a) was given to the president of Electronics, Inc. He indicated he could afford $1,700 of employee dental expenses per year. Is it possible that the population mean could be $1,700? Justify your answer.

57. Of 900 consumers surveyed, 414 said they were very enthusiastic about a new home decor scheme. Construct the 99 percent confidence interval for the population proportion.

58. There are 20,000 eligible voters in the fifth precinct. A sample of 500 voters is selected. Of the 500 surveyed, 350 said they are going to vote for the Democratic incumbent. Using the .99 degree of confidence, set the confidence limits for the proportion who plan to vote for the Democratic incumbent.

59. In a survey of 1,200 voters in Oklahoma, 792 were able to name their two U.S. Senators. Develop a 95 percent confidence interval for the proportion of all voters in Oklahoma who can identify their senators.

60. Dr. Fowler, a professor of management, is studying the relationship between work schedules and family life. In a sample of 120 people who worked the night shift only, she found the following:
   a. The mean weekly amount of time (in hours) they spent caring for their children was 27.2 hours, with a standard deviation of 10.3 hours. Determine a 95 percent confidence interval for the mean number of hours spent caring for their children.
   b. A total of 18 indicated that their parents had also worked the night shift. Determine the 90 percent confidence interval for the proportion of workers whose parents also worked nights.

61. In a poll to estimate presidential popularity, each person in a random sample of 1,000 was asked to agree with one of the following statements:
   1. The President is doing a good job.
   2. The President is doing a poor job.
   3. I have no opinion.
   A total of 560 respondents selected the first statement, indicating they thought the President was doing a good job.
   a. Construct a 95 percent confidence interval for the proportion of respondents who feel the President is doing a good job.
   b. Based on your interval in part (a), is it reasonable to conclude that a majority (more than half) of the population believe the president is doing a good job?

62. Police Chief Kress of River City reports that 500 traffic citations were issued last month. A sample of 35 of these citations showed the mean amount of the fine to be $54, with a standard deviation of $4.50. Construct a 95 percent confidence interval for the mean amount of a citation in River City.

63. The First National Bank of Wilson has 650 checking account customers. A recent sample of 50 of these customers showed 26 to have a Visa card with the bank. Construct the 99 percent confidence interval for the proportion of checking account customers who have a Visa card with the bank.

64. It is estimated that 60 percent of U.S. households now can get cable TV. You would like to verify this statement for your class in mass communications. If you want your estimate to be within ± 5 percentage points, with a 95 percent level of confidence, how large a sample is required?

65. The mean number of travel days per year for outside salespeople is to be estimated. The .90 degree of confidence is to be used. The mean of a small pilot study was 150 days, with a standard deviation of 14 days. If the population mean is to be estimated within 2 days, how many outside salespeople should be sampled?

66. A sample survey is to be conducted to determine the mean family income in an area. The question is, how many families should be sampled? In order to get more information about

the area, a small pilot survey was conducted, and the standard deviation of the sample was computed to be $500. The sponsor of the survey wants you to use the .95 degree of confidence. The estimate is to be within $100. How many families should be interviewed?

67. You plan to conduct a survey to find what proportion of the workforce has two or more jobs. You decide on the .95 degree of confidence and state that the estimated proportion must be within 2 percent of the population proportion. A pilot survey reveals that 5 of the 50 sampled hold two or more jobs. How many in the workforce should be interviewed to meet your requirements?

68. The proportion of public accountants who had changed companies within three years is to be estimated within 3 percent. The .95 degree of confidence is to be used. A study conducted several years ago revealed that the percent of public accountants changing companies within three years was 21.
   a. To update this study, the files of how many public accountants should be studied?
   b. How many public accountants would be contacted if no previous estimates were available?

69. The Hunington National Bank, like most other large banks, found that using automatic teller machines (ATMs) reduces the cost of routine bank transactions. Hunington installed an ATM in the corporate offices of the Fun Toy Company. The ATM is for the exclusive use of Fun's 605 employees. After several months of operation, a sample of 100 employees revealed the following use of the ATM machine by Fun employees in a month.

Number of Times ATM Used	Frequency
0	25
1	30
2	20
3	10
4	10
5	5
Total	100

   a. What is the estimate of the proportion of employees who do not use the ATM in a month?
   b. Develop a 95 percent confidence interval for this estimate. Can Hunington be sure that at least 40 percent of the employees of Fun Toy Company will use the ATM?
   c. How many transactions does the average Fun employee make per month?
   d. Develop a 95 percent confidence interval for the mean number of transactions per month.
   e. Is it possible that the population mean is 0? Explain.

www.**Exercises**.com

70. Go to a Web site, such as *www.dbc.com/cgi-bin/htx.exe/dbcfiles/dowt.html?SOURCE=/blq/usawww,* which lists the 30 stocks that comprise the Dow. Compute the mean price of the 30 stocks. Use the Table of Random Numbers, Appendix E, to select five random samples of five stocks. Compute the mean of these samples. Compare them to the population mean. What did you find?

I Computer Data Exercises

71. Refer to Data Set 1, which reports information on the homes sold in the Venice, Florida, area last year.

a. Develop a 95 percent confidence interval for the mean selling price of the homes.
b. Develop a 95 percent confidence interval for the mean distance the home is from the center of the city.
c. Develop a 95 percent confidence interval for the proportion of homes with an attached garage.

72. Refer to Data Set 2, which reports information on the 28 Major League Baseball teams for the 1997 season. Suppose you were asked to determine the 95 percent confidence interval for the mean number of stolen bases by each team.
    a. Could you provide this estimate? What would be the difficulty in providing this estimate?
    b. In spite of the difficulty suggested in part (a), develop a 90 percent confidence interval for the mean number of stolen bases per team.

73. Refer to Data Set 3, which reports information on the circulation of magazines.
    a. Determine the 95 percent confidence interval for the mean number of other magazines read by women. To explain, if your were a reader of *Time* and read three other magazines, you would receive a 3 for this variable.
    b. Determine the 95 percent confidence interval for the mean cost of black-and-white advertising.
    c. Determine the 95 percent confidence interval for the mean percent of subscribers who attended college.

74. Refer to Data Set 4, which refers to the 94 school districts in Northwest Ohio. Assume that these data are a sample. Select the variable referring to percent of students who are on welfare. Compute the mean and the standard deviation for this variable, *but do not include Lima, Sandusky, Toledo, and Fostoria* in the calculation. Develop a 99 percent confidence interval for the mean percent on welfare, based on this information. Is the percent of students on welfare in the excluded school districts in this interval? Does it appear that the percent on welfare in the omitted school districts is different from the others? Why or why not?

❚ Computer Commands

1. The MINITAB commands to generate the 60 columns of 30 random numbers on page 284.
    a. Select **Calc, Random Data,** and then click on **Normal.**
    b. From the dialog box **Generate** *30* rows of data, **Store** the data in columns C1–C60, the **Mean** is *50,* and the **Standard Deviation** is *5.0,* then click **OK.**

Normal Distribution	
C1	**Generate** 30 rows of data
C2	
C3	**Store in column(s):**
C4	c1–c60
C5	
C6	
C7	
C8	
C9	
C10	
C11	
C12	
C13	
C14	
C15	**Mean:** 50.0
C16	**Standard deviation:** 5.0
C17	

Select

Help **OK** **Cancel**

2. The MINITAB commands to create the 60 confidence intervals on page 284.
   a. Select **Stat, Basic Statistics,** and then click on **1-Sample z.**
   b. From the dialog box select **Variables**C1–C60, set the **Level for the Confidence Interval** at 95.0, let **Sigma** be 5.0, and then click **OK.**

1-Sample z		
C1 C2 C3 C4 C5 C6 C7 C8 C9 C10 C11 C12 C13 C14 C15 C16 C17	**Variables:** C1–C60	
	⦿ **Confidence interval** **Level:** 95.0	
	○ **Test mean:** 0.0 Alternative: not equal	
Select	**Sigma:** 5	Graphs...
Help		OK Cancel

CHAPTER 8 *Answers to Self-Review*

8–1 (a) Students selected are Price, Detlev, and Molter.
(b) Answers will vary.
(c) Skip it and move to the next random number.

8–2 The students selected are: Berry, Francis, Kopp, Poteau, and Swetye.

8–3 (a) 10, found by:

$$\frac{5!}{2!(5-2)!}$$

(b)

	Service	Sample Mean
Snow, Tolson	20, 22	21
Snow, Kraft	20, 26	23
Snow, Irwin	20, 24	22
Snow, Jones	20, 28	24
Tolson, Kraft	22, 26	24
Tolson, Irwin	22, 24	23
Tolson, Jones	22, 28	25
Kraft, Irwin	26, 24	25
Kraft, Jones	26, 28	27
Irwin, Jones	24, 28	26

(c)

Mean	Number	Probability
21	1	.10
22	1	.10
23	2	.20
24	2	.20
25	2	.20
26	1	.10
27	1	.10
	10	1.00

(d) Identical: population mean, μ, is 24, and mean of sample means is also 24.
(e) Sample means range from 21 to 27. Population values go from 20 to 28.
(f) Nonnormal.
(g) Yes.

8–4 The answers will vary. Here is one solution.

	Sample Number									
	1	2	3	4	5	6	7	8	9	10
	8	2	2	19	3	4	0	4	1	2
	19	1	14	9	2	5	8	2	14	4
	8	3	4	2	2	4	1	14	4	1
	0	3	2	3	1	2	16	1	2	3
	2	1	7	2	19	18	18	16	3	7
Total	37	10	29	35	29	33	43	37	24	17
$\overline{X}$	7.4	2	5.8	7.0	5.8	6.6	8.6	7.4	4.8	3.4

8–5 (a) 402.7 grams. The point estimate.
(b) The interval is between 399.11 and 406.29 grams, found by:

$$\overline{X} \pm 2.58 \frac{s}{\sqrt{n}} = 402.7 \pm 2.58 \frac{8.8}{\sqrt{40}}$$

(c) 399.11 and 406.29 grams.
(d) .99.
(e) If we were to construct 100 similar intervals, about 99 should include the population mean.

8–6 (a) Between .268 and .332, found by:

$$.30 \pm 2.58 \sqrt{\frac{.30(1-.30)}{1,400}} = .30 \pm 2.58(.01225)$$

(b) .268 and .332.
(c) If we were to construct 100 similar intervals, about 99 should include the population proportion.

8–7 About 23.7 and 51.3 percent, found by:

$$.375 \pm 1.96 \sqrt{\frac{.375(.625)}{40}} \sqrt{\frac{250-40}{250-1}}$$

$$= .375 \pm 1.96(.0765)(.9184)$$

$$= .375 \pm .138 = [.237, .513]$$

The correction factor was applied because 40/250 > .05.

8–8 208, found by:

$$n = \left[\frac{(2.58)(0.279)}{0.05}\right]^2$$

$$= 207.26, \text{ which is rounded up to 208.}$$

Chapter Nine

Tests of Hypothesis

Large Samples

GOALS

When you have completed this chapter, you will be able to:

ONE

Define a hypothesis and hypothesis testing.

TWO

Describe the five-step hypothesis testing procedure.

THREE

Distinguish between a one-tailed and a two-tailed test of hypothesis.

FOUR

Conduct a test of hypothesis about a population mean and a population proportion.

FIVE

Conduct a test of hypothesis about the difference between two population means and two population proportions.

SIX

Define Type I and Type II errors.

SEVEN

Compute the probability of a Type II error.

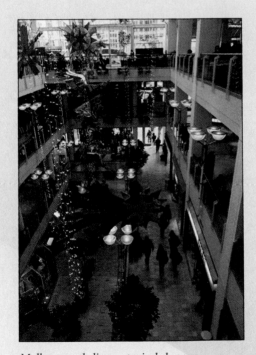

Mall owners believe a typical shopper spends 0.75 hours with a standard deviation of 0.10 hours at the mall. Specialty restaurants were introduced to keep shoppers longer. A sample of 45 shoppers revealed the mean time increased to 0.80 hours. Develop a hypothesis test to determine if the mean time spent is more than 0.75 hours. (See Goal 4 and Exercise 55.)

▌ Introduction

In Chapter 8 we began our study of statistical inference. We described how we could select a random sample and from this sample estimate the value of a population parameter. For example, we selected a sample of five employees at Spence Sprocket, found the number of years of company service of each sampled employee, computed the mean years of service of those in the sample, and used the sample mean to estimate the mean of all employees. In other words, we estimated a population parameter from a sample statistic. In addition, we developed a range of values, called a confidence interval, within which we expected the population value to be located.

In this chapter we continue our study of statistical inference. However, instead of developing a range of values within which we expect the population parameter to occur, we will conduct a test of hypothesis regarding a statement about a population parameter. Some examples of statements that we might illustrate using the methods of hypothesis testing are:

1. The mean number of miles driven on a Goodyear steel belted radial tire is more than 60,000 miles.
2. The typical American family lives in a home more than 11.8 years.
3. The mean starting salary for graduates with a four-year baccalaureate business degree is $26,000 per year.
4. Advil will relieve the symptoms of a headache in less than 20 minutes.

This chapter and several of the following chapters are concerned with hypothesis testing. We will first examine what is meant by a hypothesis and hypothesis testing. Next, we will outline the steps to test a hypothesis. Then we will conduct a test of hypothesis (1) comparing a sample mean to a hypothesized value and (2) comparing two sample means to determine whether they are equal. Finally, we explore statistical errors in testing a hypothesis.

▌ What Is a Hypothesis?

A hypothesis is a statement about a population parameter.

A hypothesis is a statement about a population. Data are then used to check the reasonableness of the statement. To begin we need to define the word *hypothesis.* In the United States legal system, a person is innocent until proven guilty. A jury hypothesizes that a person charged with a crime is innocent and subjects this hypothesis to verification by reviewing the evidence and hearing testimony before reaching a verdict. In a similar sense, a patient goes to his or her physician and reports various symptoms. Based on the symptoms, the physician will order certain diagnostic tests, then based on the symptoms and the test results, determine the treatment to be followed.

In statistical analysis we make a claim, that is, state a hypothesis, then follow up with tests to verify the assertion or to determine that it is untrue. We define a statistical hypothesis as follows.

▌ **Hypothesis**   A statement about a population developed for the purpose of testing. ▌

In most cases the population is so large that it is not feasible to study all the items, objects, or persons in the population. For example, it would not be possible to contact every systems analyst in the United States to find his or her monthly income. Likewise, the quality assurance department cannot check the breaking strength of each ampul produced to determine whether it is between 5 and 20 psi.

As noted in Chapter 8, an alternative to measuring or interviewing the entire population is to take a sample from the population. We can, therefore, test a statement to determine whether the empirical evidence from the sample does or does not support the statement concerning the population.

What Is Hypothesis Testing?

The terms *hypothesis testing* and *testing a hypothesis* are used interchangeably. Hypothesis testing starts with a statement, or assumption, about a population parameter — such as the population mean. As noted, this statement is referred to as a *hypothesis.* A hypothesis might be that the mean monthly commission of salespeople in retail computer stores, such as Computerland, is $2,000. We cannot contact all these salespeople to ascertain that the mean is in fact $2,000. The cost of locating and interviewing every computer salesperson in the United States would be exorbitant. To test the validity of the assumption (μ = $2,000), we must select a sample from the population of all computer salespeople, calculate sample statistics, and based on certain decision rules accept or reject the hypothesis. A sample mean of $1,000 for the computer salespeople would certainly cause rejection of the hypothesis. However, suppose the sample mean is $1,995. Is that close enough to $2,000 for us to accept the assumption that the population mean is $2,000? Can we attribute the difference of $5 between the two means to sampling error, or is that difference statistically significant?

> **Hypothesis Testing** A procedure based on sample evidence and probability theory to determine whether the hypothesis is a reasonable statement.

Five-Step Procedure for Testing a Hypothesis

A systematic procedure

There is a five-step procedure that systematizes hypothesis testing; when we get to step 5, we are ready to reject or not reject the hypothesis. However, hypothesis testing as used by statisticians does not provide proof that something is true, in the manner in which a mathematician "proves" a statement. It does provide a kind of "proof beyond a reasonable doubt," in the manner of the court system. Hence, there are specific rules of evidence, or procedures, that are followed. The steps are shown in the following diagram. We will discuss in detail each of the steps.

Step 1: State the Null Hypothesis (H_0) and the Alternate Hypothesis (H_1)

The first step is to state the hypothesis being tested. It is called the **null hypothesis,** designated H_0, and read "H sub-zero." The capital letter H stands for hypothesis, and the subscript zero implies "no difference." There is usually a "not" or a "no" term in the null hypothesis, meaning that there is "no change." In the first example in the introduction to this chapter, the null hypothesis is that the mean number of miles driven on the steel belted tire is not different from 60,000. The null hypothesis would be written H_0: μ = 60,000. Generally speaking, the null hypothesis is developed for the purpose of testing. We either reject or fail to reject the null hypothesis. The null hypothesis is a statement that is not rejected if our sample data fail to provide convincing evidence that it is false.

We should emphasize that if the null hypothesis is not rejected, based on the sample data, we cannot say that the null hypothesis is true. To put it another way, failing to reject the null hypothesis does not prove that H_0 is true, it means we have *failed to disprove H_0*. To prove without any doubt the null hypothesis is true, the population parameter would have to be known. To actually determine it, we would have to test, survey, or count every item in the population. This is usually not feasible. The alternative is to take a sample from the population.

It should also be noted that we often begin the null hypothesis by stating, "There is no *significant* difference between . . . ," or "The mean impact strength of the glass is not *significantly* different from. . . ." When we select a sample from a population, the sample statistic is usually numerically different from the hypothesized population parameter. As an illustration, suppose the hypothesized impact strength of a glass plate is 70 psi, and the mean impact strength of a sample of 12 glass plates is 69.5 psi. We must make a judgment about the difference of 0.5 psi. Is it a true difference, that is, a significant difference, or is the difference between the sample statistic (69.5) and the hypothesized population parameter (70.0) due to chance (sampling)? As noted, to answer this question we conduct a test of significance, commonly referred to as a test of hypothesis. To define what is meant by a null hypothesis:

| **Null Hypothesis**   A statement about the value of a population parameter. |

The **alternate hypothesis** describes what you will conclude if you reject the null hypothesis. It is written H_1 and is read "H sub-one." It is also referred to as the research hypothesis. The alternate hypothesis is accepted if the sample data provide us with enough statistical evidence that the null hypothesis is false.

| **Alternate hypothesis**   A statement that is accepted if the sample data provide enough evidence that the null hypothesis is false. |

The following example will help clarify what is meant by the null hypothesis and the alternate hypothesis. A recent article indicated the mean age of U.S. commercial aircraft is 15 years. To conduct a statistical test regarding this statement, the first step is to determine the null and the alternate hypotheses. The null hypothesis represents the current or reported condition. It is written H_0: $\mu = 15$. The alternate hypothesis is that the statement is not true, that is, H_1: $\mu \neq 15$. It is important to remember that no matter how the problem is stated, *the null hypothesis will always contain the equal sign*. The equality sign (=) will never appear in the alternate hypothesis. Why? Because the null hypothesis is the statement being tested. We turn to the alternate hypothesis only if we prove the null hypothesis to be untrue.

Step 2: Select the Level of Significance

Select a level of significance or risk

After setting up the null hypothesis and alternate hypothesis, the next step is to state the level of significance.

| **Level of Significance**   The probability of rejecting the null hypothesis when it is true. |

The level of significance is designated α, the Greek letter alpha. It is also sometimes called the level of risk. This may be a more appropriate term because it is the risk you take of rejecting the null hypothesis when it is really true.

There is no one level of significance that is applied to all tests. A decision is made to use the .05 level (often stated as the 5 percent level), the .01 level, the .10 level, or any other level between 0 and 1. Traditionally, the .05 level is selected for consumer research projects, .01 for quality assurance, and .10 for political polling. You, the researcher, must decide on the level of significance *before* formulating a decision rule and collecting sample data.

To illustrate how it is possible to reject a true hypothesis, suppose a firm manufacturing home computers uses a large number of printed circuit boards. Suppliers bid on the boards, and the one with the lowest bid is awarded a sizable contract. Suppose the contract specifies that the computer manufacturer's quality-assurance department will sample all incoming shipments of circuit boards. If more than 6 percent of the boards sampled are substandard, the shipment will be rejected. The null hypothesis is that the incoming shipment of boards contains 6 percent or less substandard boards. The alternate hypothesis is that more than 6 percent of the boards are defective.

A sample of 50 circuit boards received July 21 from Allied Electronics revealed that 4 boards, or 8 percent, were substandard. The shipment was rejected because it exceeded the maximum of 6 percent substandard printed circuit boards. If the shipment was actually substandard, then the decision to return the boards to the supplier was correct. However, suppose the 4 substandard printed circuit boards selected in the sample of 50 were the only substandard boards in the shipment of 4,000 boards. Then only $1/10$ of 1 percent were defective (4/4,000 = .001). In that case, less than 6 percent of the entire shipment was substandard and rejecting the shipment was an error. In terms of hypothesis testing, we rejected the null hypothesis that the shipment was not substandard when we should have accepted the null hypothesis. By rejecting a true hypothesis, we committed a Type I error. The probability of committing a Type I error is α.

▌ **Type I Error**   Rejecting the null hypothesis, H_0, when it is true.   ▌

The probability of committing another type of error, called a Type II error, is designated by the Greek letter beta (β).

▌ **Type II Error**   Accepting the null hypothesis when it is false.   ▌

The firm manufacturing home computers would commit a Type II error if, unknown to the manufacturer, an incoming shipment of printed circuit boards from Allied Electronics contained 15 percent substandard boards, yet the shipment was accepted. How could this happen? Suppose 2 of the 50 boards in the sample (4 percent) tested were substandard, and 48 of the 50 were good boards. According to the stated procedure, because the sample contained less than 6 percent substandard boards, the shipment was accepted. It could be that *by chance* the 48 good boards selected in the sample were the only acceptable ones in the entire shipment consisting of thousands of boards!

In retrospect, the researcher cannot study every item or individual in the population. Thus, there is a possibility of two types of error—a Type I error, wherein the null hypothesis is rejected when it should have been accepted, and a Type II error, wherein the null hypothesis is accepted when it should have been rejected.

We often refer to the probability of these two possible errors as *alpha,* α, and *beta,* β. Alpha (α) is the probability of making a Type I error, and beta (β) is the probability of making a Type II error.

The following table summarizes the decisions the researcher could make and the possible consequences.

Null Hypothesis	Researcher	
	Accepts H_0	*Rejects* H_0
H_0 is true	Correct decision	Type I error
H_0 is false	Type II error	Correct decision

Step 3: Compute the Test Statistic

There are many test statistics. In this chapter we use z as the test statistic. In other chapters we will use such test statistics as t, F, and χ^2, called chi-square.

| **Test Statistic** A value, determined from sample information, used to determine whether to reject the null hypothesis. |

In hypothesis testing for the mean (μ), the test statistic z is computed by:

| z DISTRIBUTION AS A TEST STATISTIC | $$z = \frac{\bar{X} - \mu}{\sigma/\sqrt{n}}$$ | **[9–1]** |

The z value is based on the sampling distribution of $\bar{X}$, which is normally distributed when the sample is reasonably large with a mean ($\mu_{\bar{x}}$) equal to μ, and a standard deviation $\sigma_{\bar{x}}$, which is equal to $\sigma/\sqrt{n}$. We can thus determine whether the difference between $\bar{X}$ and μ is statistically significant by finding the number of standard deviations $\bar{X}$ is from μ using formula (9–1).

Step 4: Formulate the Decision Rule

The decision rule states the conditions when H_0 is rejected. A decision rule is a statement of the conditions under which the null hypothesis is rejected and the conditions under which it is not rejected. The region or area of rejection defines the location of all those values that are so large or so small that the probability of their occurrence under a true null hypothesis is rather remote.

Chart 9–1 portrays the rejection region for a test of significance that will be conducted later in the chapter.

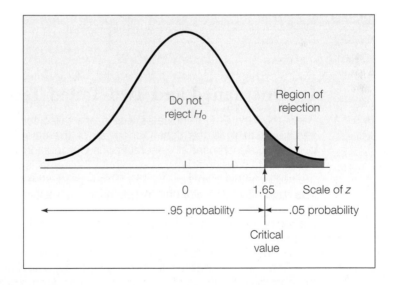

Chart 9–1 Sampling Distribution for the Statistic z, a Right-Tailed Test, .05 Level of Significance

Note in the chart that:

1. The area where the null hypothesis is not rejected is to the left of 1.65. We will explain how to get the 1.65 value shortly.
2. The area of rejection is to the right of 1.65.
3. A one-tailed test is being applied. (This will also be explained later.)
4. The .05 level of significance was chosen.

5. The sampling distribution of the statistic z is normally distributed.
6. The value 1.65 separates the regions where the null hypothesis is rejected and where it is not rejected.
7. The value 1.65 is called the **critical value.**

| **Critical value**   The dividing point between the region where the null hypothesis is rejected and the region where it is not rejected. |

Step 5: Make a Decision

The fifth and final step in hypothesis testing is making a decision to reject or not to reject the null hypothesis. Referring to Chart 9–1, if, based on sample information, z is computed to be 2.34, the null hypothesis is rejected at the .05 level of significance. The decision to reject H_0 was made because 2.34 lies in the region of rejection, that is, beyond 1.65. We would reject the null hypothesis, reasoning that it is highly improbable that a computed z value this large is due to sampling variation (chance).

Had the computed value been 1.65 or less, say 0.71, the null hypothesis would not be rejected. It would be reasoned that such a small computed value could be attributed to chance, that is, sampling variation.

As noted, only one of two decisions is possible in hypothesis testing—either accept or reject the null hypothesis. Instead of "accepting" the null hypothesis, H_0, some researchers prefer to phrase the decision as: "Do not reject H_0," "We fail to reject H_0," or "The sample results do not allow us to reject H_0."

It should be reemphasized that there is always a possibility that the null hypothesis is rejected when it should not be rejected (a Type I error). Also, there is a definable chance that the null hypothesis is accepted when it should be rejected (a Type II error).

Before actually conducting a test of hypothesis, we will differentiate between a one-tailed test of significance and a two-tailed test.

One-Tailed and Two-Tailed Tests of Significance

Refer to Chart 9–1. It indicates that a one-tailed test is being applied. The region of rejection is only in the right (upper) tail of the curve. To illustrate, suppose that the packaging department at General Foods Corporation is concerned that some boxes of Grape Nuts are significantly overweight. The cereal is packaged in 453-gram boxes, so the null hypothesis is H_0: $\mu \leq 453$. This is read, "the population mean (μ) is equal to or less than 453." The alternate hypothesis is, therefore, H_1: $\mu > 453$. This is read, "μ is greater than 453." Note that the inequality sign in the alternate hypothesis $>$ points to the region of rejection in the upper tail. (See Chart 9–1.) Also note that the null hypothesis includes the equal sign. That is, H_0: $\mu \leq 453$. This will always be the case. The equality condition always appears in H_0, never in H_1.

Chart 9–2 portrays a situation where the rejection region is in the left (lower) tail of the normal distribution. As an illustration, consider the problem of automobile manufacturers, large automobile leasing companies, and other organizations that purchase large quantities of tires. They want the tires to average, say, 40,000 miles of wear under normal usage. They will, therefore, reject a shipment of tires if accelerated-life tests reveal that the life of the tires is significantly below 40,000 miles on the average. They gladly accept a shipment if the mean life is greater than 40,000 miles! They are not concerned with this possibility, however. They are concerned only if they have sample evidence to conclude that the tires will average less than 40,000 miles of useful life. Thus, the test is set up to satisfy the concern of the automobile manufacturers and others that *the mean life of the tires is less than 40,000 miles.* The null and alternate hypotheses are written H_0: $\mu \geq 40,000$ and H_1: $\mu < 40,000$.

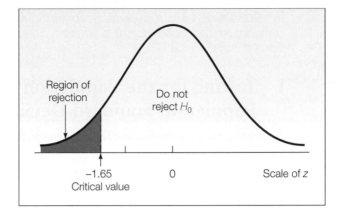

Chart 9–2 Sampling Distribution for the Statistic *z*, Left-Tailed Test,
.05 Level of Significance

Test is one-tailed if
H₁ states μ > or μ <

If H₁ states a direction,
test is one-tailed

One way to determine the location of the rejection region is to look at the direction in which the inequality sign in the alternate hypothesis is pointing (either < or >). In this problem it is pointing to the left, and the rejection region is therefore in the left tail.

In summary, a test is one-tailed when the alternate hypothesis, H_1, states a direction, such as:

H_0: The mean income of women is less than or equal to the mean income of men.

H_1: The mean income of men is *greater than* the mean income of women.

If no direction is specified in the alternate hypothesis, a *two-tailed test* is applied. Changing the previous alternate hypothesis to illustrate:

H_0: There is *no difference* between the mean income of males and the mean income of females.

Test is two-tailed if
H₁ does not state
a direction

H_1: There *is a difference* between the mean income of males and the mean income of females.

If the null hypothesis is rejected and H_1 accepted in this two-tailed case, the mean income of males could be greater than that of females or vice versa. To accommodate these two possibilities, the 5 percent area of rejection is divided equally into the two tails of the sampling distribution (2.5 percent each). Chart 9–3 shows the two areas and the critical values. Note that the total area in the normal distribution is 1.000, found by .95 + .025 + .025.

Chart 9–3 Regions of Nonrejection and Rejection for a Two-Tailed Test,
.05 Level of Significance

We will now test a hypothesis about the mean of a population by taking a large sample from that population. It is generally agreed that a sample of 30 or more is considered large.

▌ Testing for the Population Mean: Large Sample, Population Standard Deviation Known

Answering these questions involves a population mean:

- Is the mean income of top executives in manufacturing $325,000?
- Is the mean length of the slugs being sheared 2.0000 inches?
- Is the mean age of the inmates of federal prisons less than 40 years?
- Is the mean amount owed by credit card holders greater than $1,000?
- Is the mean weekly production of Model A325 desks at Jamestown Steel Company 200?

We use the five-step hypothesis-testing procedure to test the last question. The phrasing of the question requires a two-tailed test.

A Two-Tailed Test

The following example illustrates how to set the null hypothesis and the alternate hypothesis and how to use the statistical hypothesis testing procedure.

Example

The Jamestown Steel Company manufactures and assembles desks and other office equipment at several plants in the western New York State area. The weekly production of the Model A325 desk at the Fredonia Plant is normally distributed, with a mean of 200 and a standard deviation of 16. Recently, due to market expansion, new production methods have been introduced and new employees hired. The vice president of manufacturing would like to investigate whether there has been an overall change in the weekly production of the Model A325 desk. To put it another way, is the mean number of desks produced at the Fredonia Plant different from 200? Use the .01 significance level.

Solution

We use the statistical hypothesis testing procedure to investigate whether the production rate has changed from 200 per month.

Step 1. The null hypothesis is "The population mean is 200." The alternate hypothesis is "The mean is different from 200" or "The mean is not 200." These two hypotheses are written:

$H_0: \mu = 200$

$H_1: \mu \neq 200$

This is a *two-tailed test* because the alternate hypothesis does not state a direction. In other words, it does not state whether the mean production is greater than 200 or less than 200. The vice president only wants to find out whether the production rate is different from 200.

Step 2. As noted, the .01 level of significance is used. This is α, the probability of committing a Type I error. That is, it is the probability of rejecting a true hypothesis.

Step 3. The test statistic for this type of problem is z. It was discussed at length in Chapter 7. Transforming the production data to standard units (z values) permits their use not only in this problem but also in other hypothesis-testing problems. Formula (9–1) for *z* is repeated below with the various letters identified.

Formula for the test statistic

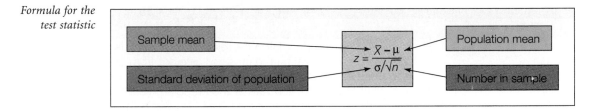

$$z = \frac{\bar{X} - \mu}{\sigma / \sqrt{n}}$$

Sample mean · Population mean · Standard deviation of population · Number in sample

Step 4. The decision rule is formulated by finding the critical value of *z* from Appendix D. Since this is a two-tailed test, half of .01, or .005, is in each tail. The area where H_0 is not rejected, located between the two tails, is therefore .99. Appendix D is based on just half of the area under the curve, or .5000. Then, .5000 − .005 is .4950, so .4950 is the area between 0 and the critical value. Locate .4950 in the body of the table. The value nearest to .4950 is .4951. Then read the critical value in the row and column corresponding to .4951. It is 2.58. For your convenience Appendix D, Areas under the Normal Curve, is repeated in the inside back cover.

All the facets of this problem are shown in the form of a diagram in Chart 9–4.

Chart 9–4 Decision Rule for the .01 Significance Level

The decision rule is, therefore: Reject the null hypothesis and accept the alternate hypothesis (which states that the population mean is not 200) if the computed value of *z* does not fall in the region between −2.58 and +2.58. Do not reject the null hypothesis if *z* falls between −2.58 and +2.58.

Step 5. Take a sample from the population (weekly production), compute *z*, and, based on the decision rule, arrive at a decision to reject H_0 or not to reject H_0. The mean number of desks produced over the last year (50 weeks, because the plant was shut down 2 weeks for vacation) is 203.5. The standard deviation of the population is 16 desks per month. Computing the z value from formula (9–1):

$$z = \frac{\overline{X} - \mu}{\sigma/\sqrt{n}} = \frac{203.5 - 200}{16/\sqrt{50}} = 1.55$$

Because 1.55 does not fall in the rejection region, H_0 is not rejected. We conclude that the population mean is *not* different from 200. So we would report to the vice president of manufacturing that the sample evidence does not show that the production rate at the Fredonia Plant has changed from 200 per week. The difference of 3.5 units between the historical weekly production rate and that last year can reasonably be attributed to chance. This information is summarized in the following chart.

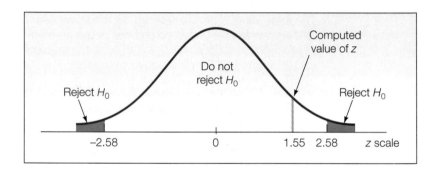

Did we prove that the assembly rate is still 200 per week? Not really. What we did, technically, was *fail to disprove the null hypothesis.* Failing to disprove the hypothesis that the population mean is 200 is not the same thing as proving it to be true. As we suggested in the chapter introduction, the conclusion is analogous to the American judicial system. To explain, suppose a person is accused of a crime but is acquitted by a jury. If a person is acquitted of a crime, the conclusion is that there was not enough evidence to prove the person guilty. The trial did not prove that the individual was innocent, only that there was not enough evidence to prove the defendant guilty. That is what we do in statistical hypothesis testing when we do not reject the null hypothesis. The correct interpretation is that we have failed to disprove the null hypothesis.

We selected the significance level, .01 in this case, before setting up the decision rule and sampling the population. This is the appropriate strategy. The significance level should be set by the investigator, but it should be determined *before* gathering the sample evidence and not changed based on the sample evidence.

How does the hypothesis testing procedure just described compare with that of confidence intervals discussed in the previous chapter? When we conducted the test of hypothesis regarding the production of desks we changed the units from desks per month to a z value. Then we compared the computed value of the test statistic (1.55) to that of the critical values (−2.58 and 2.58). Because the computed value was in the region where the null hypothesis was not rejected, we concluded that the population mean could be 200. To use the confidence interval approach, on the other hand, we would develop a confidence interval, based on formula (8–5). The interval would be from 197.66 to 209.34, found by $203.5 \pm 2.58(16/\sqrt{50})$. Note that the proposed population value, 200, is within this interval. Hence, we would conclude that the population mean could reasonably be 200.

In general, H_0 is rejected if the confidence interval does not include the hypothesized value. If the confidence interval includes the hypothesized value, then H_0 is not rejected. So the "do not reject region" for a test of hypothesis is equivalent to the confidence interval. The primary difference lies in whether the interval is centered around the sample statistic, such as $\overline{X}$ or around 0, as in the test of hypothesis.

SELF-REVIEW 9–1

The mean annual turnover rate of the 200-count bottle of Bayer Aspirin was reported to be 6.0. (This indicates that the stock of Bayer turns over on the pharmacy shelves an average of 6 times per year.) The standard deviation is 0.50. It is suspected that the mean turnover has changed and is not 6.0. The .05 significance level is to be used to test this hypothesis.

a. State the null hypothesis and the alternate hypothesis.
b. What is the probability of a Type I error?
c. Give the formula for the test statistic.
d. State the decision rule.
e. A random sample of 64 bottles of the 200-count size Bayer Aspirin showed a mean of 5.84. Shall we reject the hypothesis that the population mean is 6.0?
   Interpret the result.

A One-Tailed Test

In the previous Example, we emphasized that we were only concerned with reporting to the vice president whether there had been a change in the mean number of desks assembled at the Fredonia Plant. We were not concerned with whether the change was an increase or a decrease in the production.

To illustrate a one-tailed test, let's change the problem. Suppose the vice president wants to know whether there has been an *increase* in the number of units assembled. To put it another way, can we conclude, because of the improved production methods, that the mean number of desks assembled in the last 50 weeks was more than 200? Look at the difference in the way the problem is formulated. In the first case we wanted to know whether there was a *difference* in the mean number assembled, but now we want to know whether there has been an *increase*. Because we are investigating different questions, we need to set our hypotheses differently. The biggest difference occurs in the alternate hypothesis. Before, we stated the alternate hypothesis as "different from" now we want to state it as "greater than." In symbols:

A two-tailed test	A one-tailed test
H_0: $\mu = 200$	H_0: $\mu \leq 200$
H_1: $\mu \neq 200$	H_1: $\mu > 200$

The critical values for a one-tailed test are different from those of a two-tailed test at the same significance level. In the previous Example, we split the significance level in half and put half in the lower tail and half in the upper tail. In a one-tailed test we put all the rejection region in one tail. See the following diagram.

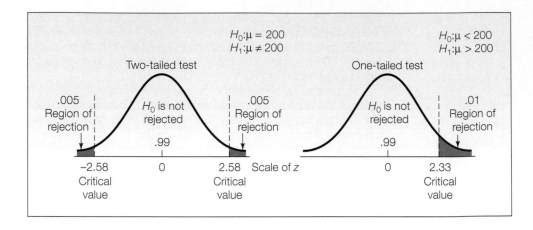

Chart 9–5   Rejection Regions for Two-Tailed and One-Tailed Tests, α = .01

For the one-tailed test, the critical value is 2.33, found by: (1) subtracting .01 from .5000 and (2) finding the z value corresponding to .4900.

▌ *p*-Value in Hypothesis Testing

In testing a hypothesis, we compared the test statistic to a critical value. A decision is made to either reject the null hypothesis or not to reject it. So, for example, if the critical value is 1.96 and the computed value of the test statistic is 2.19, the decision is to reject the null hypothesis.

In recent years, spurred by the availability of computer software, additional information is often reported on the strength of the rejection. That is, how confident were we in rejecting the null hypothesis? This approach reports the probability (assuming that the null hypothesis is true) of getting a value of the test statistic at least as extreme as the value actually obtained. This process compares the probability, called the **p-value,** with the significance level. If the *p*-value is smaller than the significance level, H_0 is rejected. If it is larger than the significance level, H_0 is not rejected.

▌ **p-value**   The probability of observing a sample value as extreme as, or more extreme than, the value observed, given that the null hypothesis is true.   ▌

Determining the *p*-value not only results in a decision regarding H_0, but it gives us additional insight into the strength of the decision. A very small *p*-value, such as .0001, indicates that there is little likelihood the H_0 is true. On the other hand, a *p*-value of .2033 means that H_0 is not rejected, and there is little likelihood that it is false.

How do we compute the *p*-value? To illustrate we will use the example in which we tested the null hypothesis that the mean number of desks produced per week at Fredonia was 200. We did not reject the null hypothesis, because the value of *z* of 1.55 fell in the region between −2.58 and 2.58. We agreed not to reject the null hypothesis if the computed value of *z* fell in this region. The probability of finding a *z* value of 1.55 or more is .0606, found by .5000 − .4394. That is, the probability of obtaining an $\overline{X}$ greater than 203.5 if μ = 200 is .0606. To compute the *p*-value, we need to be concerned with the region less than −1.55 as well as the values greater than 1.55 (because the rejection region is in both tails). The *p*-value is .1212, found by 2(.0606). The *p*-value of .1212 is greater than the significance level of .01 decided upon initially, so H_0 is not rejected. The details are shown in the following graph.

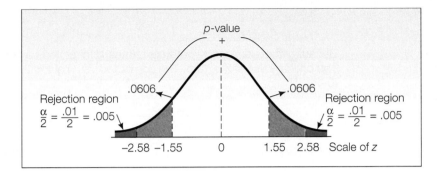

A *p*-value is a way to express the likelihood that H_0 is not true. But how do we interpret a *p*-value? We have already said that if the *p*-value is less than the significance level, then we reject H_0; if it is greater than the significance level, then we do not reject H_0. Also, if the *p*-value is very large then it is likely that H_0 is true. If the *p*-value is small, then it is likely that H_0 is not true. The following box will help to interpret *p*-values.

INTERPRETING THE WEIGHT OF EVIDENCE AGAINST H_0	If the *p*-value is less than (a) .10, we have *some* evidence that H_0 is not true. (b) .05, we have *strong* evidence that H_0 is not true. (c) .01, we have *very strong* evidence that H_0 is not true. (d) .001, we have *extremely strong evidence* that H_0 is not true.

Testing for the Population Mean: Large Sample, Population Standard Deviation Unknown

In the preceding problems, we knew σ, the population standard deviation. In most cases, however, it is unlikely that the population standard deviation would be known. Thus, σ must be based on prior studies or estimated by the sample standard deviation, *s*. The population standard deviation in the following example is not known, so the sample standard deviation is used to estimate σ. As long as the sample size, *n*, is greater than 30, *s* can be substituted for σ, as illustrated in the following formula:

z STATISTIC, σ UNKNOWN	$$z = \frac{\bar{X} - \mu}{s/\sqrt{n}}$$	**[9–2]**

Example

The Thompson's Discount Store chain issues its own credit card. The credit manager wants to find whether the mean monthly unpaid balance is more than $400. The level of significance is set at .05. A random check of 172 unpaid balances revealed the sample mean is $407 and the standard deviation of the sample is $38. Should the credit manager conclude the population mean is greater than $400, or is it reasonable that the difference of $7 ($407 − $400 = $7) is due to chance?

Solution   The null and alternate hypotheses are:

H_0: $\mu \le \$400$

H_1: $\mu > \$400$

Because the alternate hypothesis states a direction, a one-tailed test is applied. The critical value of z is 1.65. The computed value of z is 2.42, found by using formula (9–2):

$$z = \frac{\bar{X} - \mu}{s/\sqrt{n}} = \frac{\$407 - \$400}{\$38/\sqrt{172}} = \frac{\$7}{\$2.8975} = 2.42$$

The decision rule is portrayed graphically in the following chart.

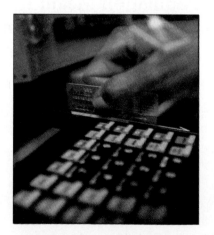

Because the computed value of the test statistic (2.42) is larger than the critical value (1.65), the null hypothesis is rejected. The credit manager can conclude the mean unpaid balance is greater than $400.

The *p*-value provides additional insight into the decision. Recall the *p*-value is the probability of finding a test statistic as large or larger than that obtained, when the null hypothesis is true. So we find the probability of a *z* value greater than 2.42. From Appendix D the probability of a *z* value between 0 and 2.42 is .4922. We want to determine the likelihood of a value *greater than* 2.42, so .5000 − .4922 = .0078. We conclude that the likelihood of finding a *z* value of 2.42 or larger when the null hypothesis is true is 0.78 percent. It is unlikely, therefore, that the null hypothesis is true.

SELF-REVIEW 9–2

Refer to Self-Review 9–1.

(a) Suppose the hypothesis-testing problem was changed to a one-tailed test. How would the null hypothesis be written symbolically if it read, "The population mean is equal to or greater than 6.0"?

(b) How would the alternate hypothesis be written symbolically if it read, "The population mean is less than 6.0"?

(c) Show the decision rule graphically. Show the rejection region and indicate the critical value.

▌ Exercises

For Exercises 1–4 answer the following questions: a. Is this a one- or two-tailed test? b. What is the decision rule? c. What is the value of the test statistic? d. What is your decision regarding H_0? e. What is the *p*-value? Interpret it.

1. The following information is available.

   $H_0: \mu = 50$

   $H_1: \mu \neq 50$

   The sample mean is 49, and the sample size is 36. The population standard deviation is 5. Use the .05 significance level.

2. The following information is available.

   $H_0: \mu \leq 10$

   $H_1: \mu > 10$

   The sample mean is 12 for a sample of 36. The population standard deviation is 3. Use the .02 significance level.

3. A sample of 36 observations is selected from a normal population. The sample mean is 21, and the sample standard deviation is 5. Conduct the following test of hypothesis using the .05 significance level.

   $H_0: \mu \leq 20$

   $H_1: \mu > 20$

4. A sample of 64 observations is selected from a normal population. The sample mean is 215, and the sample standard deviation is 15. Conduct the following test of hypothesis using the .03 significance level.

   $H_0: \mu \geq 220$

   $H_0: \mu < 220$

For Exercises 5–8 answer the following: a. State the null hypothesis and the alternate hypothesis. b. State the decision rule. c. Compute the value of the test statistic. d. What is your decision regarding H_0? e. What is the *p*-value? Interpret it.

5. The manufacturer of the X-15 steel-belted radial truck tire claims that the mean mileage the tire can be driven before the tread wears out is 60,000 miles. The standard deviation of the mileage is 5,000 miles. The Crosset Truck Company bought 48 tires and found that the mean mileage for their trucks is 59,500 miles. Is Crosset's experience different from that claimed by the manufacturer at the .05 significance level?

6. The MacBurger restaurant chain claims that the mean waiting time of customers for service is normally distributed, with a mean of 3 minutes and a standard deviation of 1 minute. The quality-assurance department found in a sample of 50 customers at the Warren Road MacBurger that the mean waiting time was 2.75 minutes. At the .05 significance level, can we conclude that the mean waiting time is less than 3 minutes?

7. A recent national survey found that high school students watched an average (mean) of 6.8 videos per month. A random sample of 36 college students revealed that the mean number of videos watched last month was 6.2, with a standard deviation of 0.5. At the .05 significance level, can we conclude that college students watch fewer videos a month than high school students?

8. At the time she was hired as a server at the Grumney Family Restaurant, Beth Brigden was told, "You can average more than $20 a day in tips." Over the first 35 days she was employed at the restaurant, the mean daily amount of her tips was $24.85, with a standard deviation of $3.24. At the .01 significance level, can Ms. Brigden conclude that she is earning more than $20 in tips?

❚ Hypothesis Testing: Two Population Means

The following illustration, involving a test comparing two population means, typifies a practical industrial problem.

Concrete blocks are used in the foundations of several buildings. The specifications state that the minimum mean compressive strength of the blocks must be 1,000 pounds per square inch (psi). If two companies submit samples of blocks that have mean compressive strengths over the minimum (1,000 psi), then the specifications state that one of two actions will be taken: (1) If a statistical test applied to the sampling results indicates that both samples could have come from the same, or identical, populations, the contract for the blocks will be divided equally. (2) If the sample statistics indicate that the means are not equal, the company submitting the blocks having the higher compressive strength will be awarded the contract.

A large construction project requires a large number of concrete blocks. The Stanblock Corporation and the Hicompressive Company have supplied blocks to the builder in the past, and both are interested in providing blocks for the new construction project. Before the blocks are tested for compressive strength, null and alternate hypotheses will be stated, a level of significance selected, an appropriate statistical test decided upon, and a decision rule formulated.

Follow the usual five-step testing procedure

Step 1: State the Null Hypothesis and the Alternate Hypothesis   The null hypothesis is that there is *no* difference between the mean compressive strength of the concrete blocks manufactured by the Stanblock Company and the mean compressive strength of the concrete blocks manufactured by the Hicompressive Company. The alternate hypothesis, H_1, is that there *is* a significant difference between the two mean compressive strengths. Symbolically:

$H_0: \mu_1 = \mu_2$

$H_1: \mu_1 \neq \mu_2$

Since the alternate hypothesis does not specify a direction (such as that the mean compressive strength of the blocks from Stanblock is greater than the mean of the Hicompressive blocks), a two-tailed test is used.

Step 2: Select the Level of Significance   The .01 level of significance has been chosen. This is the same as saying that the probability of committing a Type I error is .01.

Step 3: Compute the Statistical Test   At least 30 blocks (n_1) will be selected at random from the Stanblock Company, and at least 30 will be selected from Hicompressive (n_2). As noted previously, when n_1 and n_2 are 30 or more, the samples are considered large and the sampling distributions of $\bar{X}_1$ and $\bar{X}_2$ as well as their differences will be normal. Thus, the sample standard deviations, s_1 and s_2, can be substituted for σ_1 and σ_2, and z used as the test statistic. The selection process also meets one other assumption underlying the z test, namely, independence. This means that the two populations are not related. The z test assumes that the data are at least interval-scaled. Of course, either of the two populations could be called number 1. However, once you have labeled a particular population number 1, you must continue to call it that.

The idea underlying the sampling distribution of z (the critical value) will be examined briefly. It states in part:

> If a large number of independent random samples are selected from the two populations, the distribution of the differences between the two sample means divided by the standard error of the difference between the two means will approximate the standard normal distribution.

The corresponding formula for z is:

THE DIFFERENCE BETWEEN TWO MEANS	$z = \dfrac{\bar{X}_1 - \bar{X}_2}{\sqrt{\dfrac{s_1^2}{n_1} + \dfrac{s_2^2}{n_2}}}$	**[9–3]**

The numerator of formula (9–3) is the difference in the sample means. The denominator is the standard deviation of the distribution of these differences. It is called the **standard error of the differences in sample means.** For large samples this test statistic follows the z distribution.

To illustrate this theory, assume that many samples of size 100 were taken from the Stanblock Company, and many samples of 100 blocks were taken from the Hicompressive Company. For the sake of simplicity, assume that the standard deviation for each sample was computed to be 20 psi. (The sample means are hypothetical and are included merely to show the computation of z.) Then compute the z values:

Sample	$\bar{X}_1$	$\bar{X}_2$	$\bar{X}_1 - \bar{X}_2$	$\dfrac{\bar{X}_1 - \bar{X}_2}{\sqrt{\dfrac{s_1^2}{n_1} + \dfrac{s_2^2}{n_2}}}$	z
1	1,020	1,020	0	$\dfrac{0}{2.8} =$	0
2	1,022	1,020	+2	$\dfrac{+2}{2.8} =$	+0.71
3	1,030	1,021	+9	$\dfrac{+9}{2.8} =$	+3.21
4	1,018	1,021	−3	$\dfrac{-3}{2.8} =$	−1.07

Thus, in theory, if the two population means are equal and if the z values of 0, +0.71, +3.21, −1.07, and so on were plotted, the distribution of these z values would approximate a normal distribution.

Reference to the normal curve (Appendix D) reveals that 68 percent of the z values would fall within 0 ± 1.0; 95 percent would fall within 0 ± 1.96; and 99 percent would fall within 0 ± 2.58. (See Chart 9–6.)

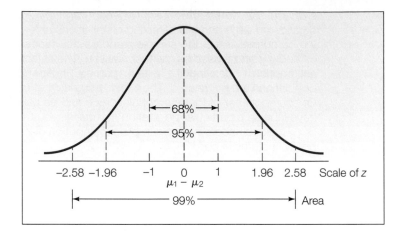

Chart 9–6   Distribution of z When $\mu_1 - \mu_2 = 0$

Step 4: Formulate the Decision Rule   Recall we selected the .01 level of significance. A two-tailed test is used (because the alternate hypothesis, H_1, does not state that the mean compressive strength of the blocks of one company is greater than the mean compressive strength of the other firm's blocks). It was noted in step 3 that 99 percent of the computed z values will be between -2.58 and $+2.58$ under the assumption that there is no difference between the means of the two populations. So if the computed z value does fall within the region between plus and minus 2.58, the null hypothesis is not rejected. Thus, it would be concluded that the difference between the two sample means is due to chance.

On the other hand, if the computed z value is greater than 2.58, the null hypothesis is *rejected.* The null hypothesis would be rejected on the basis that it is highly unlikely that a computed z value could be 2.58 or greater *by chance.* Of course, H_0 is also rejected if the computed z is to the left of -2.58. This decision rule is portrayed in Chart 9–7. (Note that we have inserted the *p*-value in the two tails. Computation for the *p*-value is shown on the next page.)

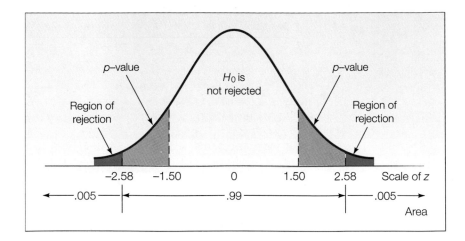

Chart 9–7   Two-Tailed Test, Areas of Nonrejection and Rejection, with a .01 Significance Level

Select samples from the
two populations

Step 5: Compute the Sample Results and Make the Decision A total of 81 blocks were selected at random from the Stanblock Company production, and the compressive strength of each was determined. The standard deviation of the sample and the mean compressive strength were computed. Sixty-four blocks from the Hicompressive Company were selected, and the same procedure was followed. The sample statistics are:

Stanblock Company	Hicompressive Company
$\bar{X}_1 = 1,070$ psi	$\bar{X}_2 = 1,055$ psi
$n_1 = 81$	$n_2 = 64$
$s_1 = 63$ psi	$s_2 = 57$ psi

Using formula (9–3), the test statistic (z) is 1.50. The calculations are:

$$z = \frac{\bar{X} - \bar{X}_2}{\sqrt{\dfrac{s_1^2}{n_1} + \dfrac{s_2^2}{n_2}}}$$

$$= \frac{1,070 - 1,055}{\sqrt{\dfrac{(63)^2}{81} + \dfrac{(57)^2}{64}}} = \frac{15}{9.99} = 1.50$$

The computed z value of 1.50 is in the area where the null hypothesis is not rejected. So we cannot reject the null hypothesis that the mean compressive strength of blocks from the two companies is the same. The difference of 15 psi, found by $1,070 - 1,055$, is attributed to chance. We have not shown that there is a difference in the two population means. Hence, the final decision is to split the contract between the two suppliers.

What is the p-value for the problem? Recall that we had a two-tailed test, so we need to find the area to the left of -1.50 and the area to the right of 1.50. Referring to Appendix D, the area between z values of 0 and 1.50 is .4332. So the area to the right of 1.50 is .0668, found by $.5000 - .4332$. The area to the left of -1.50 is also .0668, so the p-value is $.0668 + .0668 = .1336$. As expected, the p-value is larger than the significance level (.01) when the null hypothesis is not rejected. The p-value is shown in orange in Chart 9–7.

SELF-REVIEW 9–3

Corngrow is a chemical specifically designed to add weight to corn during the growing season. Alternate acres were treated with Corngrow during the growing season. In order to determine whether or not Corngrow was effective, 400 ears of corn receiving the Corngrow treatment were selected at random. Each was weighed, and the mean weight was computed to be 16 ounces, with a standard deviation of 1 ounce. Likewise, 100 ears of untreated corn were weighed. The mean was 15.7 ounces, and the standard deviation was 1.2 ounces.

(a) Using a one-tailed test and the .05 level, can we say that Corngrow was effective in adding weight to the corn?
(b) Show the decision rule graphically.
(c) Compute the p-value. Interpret it.

▌ Exercises

9. A sample of 40 observations is selected from one population. The sample mean is 102, and the sample standard deviation is 5. A sample of 50 observations is selected from a second population. The sample mean is 99, and the sample standard deviation is 6. Conduct the following test of hypothesis using the .04 significance level.

$H_0: \mu_1 = \mu_2$

$H_1: \mu_1 \neq \mu_2$

a. Is this a one-tailed or a two-tailed test?
b. State the decision rule.
c. Compute the value of the test statistic.
d. What is your decision regarding H_0?
e. What is the p-value?

10. A sample of 65 observations is selected from one population. The sample mean is 2.67, and the sample standard deviation is 0.75. A sample of 50 observations is selected from a second population. The sample mean is 2.59, and the sample standard deviation is 0.66. Conduct the following test of hypothesis using the .08 significance level.

$H_0: \mu_1 \leq \mu_2$

$H_1: \mu_1 > \mu_2$

a. Is this a one-tailed or a two-tailed test?
b. State the decision rule.
c. Compute the value of the test statistic.
d. What is your decision regarding H_0?
e. What is the p-value?

11. The Metro Real Estate Association is preparing a pamphlet that they feel might be of interest to prospective home buyers in the Rossford and Northwood areas of the city. One item of interest is the length of time the seller occupied the home. A sample of 40 homes sold recently in Rossford revealed that the mean length of ownership was 7.6 years, with a standard deviation of 2.3 years. A sample of 55 homes in Northwood revealed that the mean length of ownership was 8.1 years, with a standard deviation of 2.9 years. At the .05 significance level, can we conclude that the Rossford residents owned their homes for a shorter period of time? Use the five-step hypothesis-testing procedure. Compute the p-value and interpret it.

12. A study is made comparing the cost to rent a one-bedroom apartment in Cincinnati with the corresponding cost of similar apartments in Pittsburgh. A sample of 35 apartments in Cincinnati showed the mean rental rate to be $370, with a standard deviation of $30. A sample of 40 apartments in Pittsburgh showed the mean rate to be $380, with a standard deviation of $26. At the .05 significance level, is there a difference in the mean rental rate between Cincinnati and Pittsburgh? Use the five-step hypothesis-testing procedure.

13. A financial analyst is interested in comparing the turnover rates, in percent, for shares of oil-related stocks versus other stocks, such as GE and IBM. She selected 32 oil-related stocks and 49 other stocks. The mean turnover rate of oil-related stocks is 31.4 percent and the standard deviation 5.1 percent. For the other stocks, the mean rate was computed to be 34.9 percent and the standard deviation 6.7 percent. Is there a significant difference in the turnover rates of the two types of stock? The null and alternate hypotheses are:

$H_0: \mu_1 = \mu_2$

$H_1: \mu_1 \neq \mu_2$

a. Is this a one-tailed or a two-tailed test? What is your reasoning?
b. Using the .01 level of significance, what is the decision rule?

c. Determine the value of the test statistic, and arrive at a decision regarding H_0. Explain the meaning of your decision.

▌ Tests Concerning Proportions

The material presented so far in this chapter has used the interval or the ratio scale of measurement. That is, we used variables such as weights, incomes, distances, and ages. We now want to consider situations such as the following:

- The career services director at Southern Technical College reports that 80 percent of its graduates enter the job market in a position directly related to their field of study.
- A company representative claims that more than 45 percent of Burger King sales are made at the drive-through window.
- A large company wants to know whether there is a difference in the proportions of male and female executives willing to move to a different city to gain a promotion.

These problems are illustrations of the nominal scale of measurement. Recall that for the nominal scale of measurement the observation is recorded in one of two or more categories. For example, a person is classified as being male or female, or a potential voter is classified as Republican, Democrat, independent, or other.

| **Proportion** A fraction, ratio, or percentage that indicates the part of the population or sample having a particular trait of interest. |

As an example of a proportion, suppose 92 of 100 surveyed favor daylight savings time during the summer. The sample proportion is 92/100, or .92, or 92 percent. If we let p stand for the sample proportion, then:

SAMPLE PROPORTION	$$p = \frac{\text{Number of successes in the sample}}{\text{Number sampled}}$$	**[9–4]**

Some assumptions must be made and conditions met before testing a population proportion. To test a hypothesis about a population proportion, a random sample is chosen from the population. This is called the experiment. It is assumed that the binomial assumptions discussed in Chapter 6 are met: (1) the sample data collected are the result of counts; (2) an outcome of an experiment is classified into one of two mutually exclusive categories — a "success" or a "failure"; (3) the probability of a success is the same for each trial; and (4) the trials are independent, meaning the outcome of one trial does not affect the outcome of any other trial.

$n\pi$ and $n(1 - \pi)$ must be at least 5   The test we will conduct shortly is appropriate when both $n\pi$ and $n(1 - \pi)$ are at least 5. n is the sample size, and π is the population proportion. This test is introduced here because it is a special extension of the test presented earlier in this chapter and also is widely used. The test is a good example of the case where the normal probability distribution is applied to approximate a binomial probability distribution with a great deal of accuracy.

Example

Suppose prior elections in a state indicated it is necessary for a candidate for governor to receive at least 80 percent of the vote in the northern section of the state to be elected. The incumbent governor is interested in assessing his chances of returning to office and plans to conduct a survey of 2,000 registered voters in the northern section of the state.

Using the hypothesis-testing procedure, assess the governor's chances of reelection.

Solution   The following test of hypothesis can be conducted because both $n\pi$ and $n(1 - \pi)$ exceed 5. In this problem, $n = 2,000$ and $\pi = .80$ (π is the proportion of the vote in the northern part of the state, or 80 percent, needed to be elected). Thus, $n\pi = 2,000(.80) = 1,600$ and $n(1 - \pi) = 2,000 (1 - .80) = 400$. Both 1,600 and 400 are greater than 5.

Step 1   The null hypothesis, H_0, is that the population proportion π is .80. The alternate hypothesis, H_1, is that the proportion is less than .80. From a practical standpoint, the incumbent governor is concerned only when the sample proportion is less than .80. If it is equal to or greater than .80, he will have no problem; that is, the sample data would indicate he will probably be reelected. These hypotheses are written symbolically as:

$H_0: \pi \geq .80$

$H_1: \pi < .80$

H_1 states a direction. Thus, as noted previously, the test is one-tailed with the inequality sign pointing to the tail of the distribution containing the region of rejection.

Step 2   The level of significance is .05. This is the likelihood that a true hypothesis will be rejected.

Step 3 z is the appropriate statistic, found by:

| TEST OF HYPOTHESIS, ONE PROPORTION | $z = \dfrac{p - \pi}{\sigma_p}$ | **[9–5]** |

where:

    π is the population proportion.

    p is the sample proportion.

    n is the sample size.

    σ_π is the standard error of the population proportion. It is computed by $\sqrt{\pi(1 - \pi)/n}$, so the formula for z becomes:

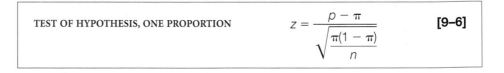

| TEST OF HYPOTHESIS, ONE PROPORTION | $z = \dfrac{p - \pi}{\sqrt{\dfrac{\pi(1 - \pi)}{n}}}$ | **[9–6]** |

Finding the critical value   **Step 4**   The critical value or values of z form the dividing point or points between the regions where H_0 is rejected and where it is not rejected. Since the alternate hypothesis states a direction, this is a one-tailed test. The sign of the inequality points to the left, so only the left half of the curve is used. (See Chart 9–8.) Alpha was given as .05 in step 2. This probability is in the left tail and determines the region of rejection. The area between zero and the critical value is .4500, found by .5000 − .0500. Referring to Appendix D and searching for .4500, we find the critical value of z is 1.65. The decision rule is, therefore: Reject the null hypothesis and accept the alternate hypothesis if the computed value of z falls to the left of −1.65; otherwise do not reject H_0.

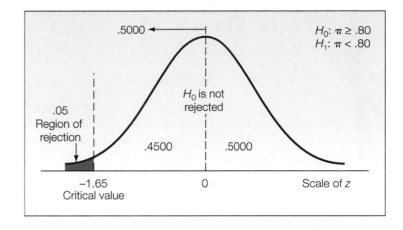

Chart 9–8 Rejection and Nonrejection Regions for the .05 Level of Significance, One-Tailed Test

Select a sample and make a decision regarding H_0

Step 5 Select a sample and make a decision about H_0. A sample survey of 2,000 potential voters in the northern part of the state revealed that 1,550 planned to vote for the incumbent governor. Is the proportion of .775 (found by 1,550/2,000) close enough to .80 to conclude that the difference is due to chance? In this problem:

- p is .775, the proportion in the sample who plan to vote for the governor.
- n is 2,000, the number of voters surveyed.
- π is .80, the hypothesized population proportion.
- z is a normally distributed test statistic when the hypothesis is true and the other assumptions are true.

Using formula (9–6) and computing z:

$$z = \frac{p - \pi}{\sqrt{\dfrac{\pi(1 - \pi)}{n}}} = \frac{\dfrac{1{,}550}{2{,}000} - .80}{\sqrt{\dfrac{.80(1 - .80)}{2{,}000}}} = \frac{.775 - .80}{\sqrt{.00008}} = \frac{-.025}{.0089443} = -2.80$$

The computed value of z (-2.80) is in the rejection region, so the null hypothesis is rejected at the .05 level. The difference of 2.5 percentage points between the sample percent (77.5 percent) and the hypothesized population percent in the northern part of the state necessary to carry the state (80 percent) is statistically significant. It is probably not due to sampling variation. To put it another way, the evidence at this point does not support the claim that the incumbent governor will return to the governor's mansion for another four years.

The p-value is the probability of finding a z value less than -2.80. From Appendix D, the probability of a z value between 0 and -2.80 is .4974. So the p-value is .0026, found by .5000 − .4974. The governor cannot be confident of reelection!

SELF-REVIEW 9-4

This claim is to be investigated at the .01 level: "Forty percent or more of those persons who retired from an industrial job before the age of 60 would return to work if a suitable job were available." Seventy-four persons out of the 200 sampled said they would return to work.

(a) Can z be used as the test statistic? Why or why not?

(b) State the null and alternate hypotheses.

(c) Show the decision rule graphically.

(d) Compute z and arrive at a decision.

(e) Compute the p-value. Interpret it.

▌ Exercises

14. The following hypotheses are given.

$H_0: \pi \le .70$

$H_1: \pi > .70$

A sample of 100 observations revealed that $p = .75$. At the .05 significance level, can the null hypothesis be rejected?

a. State the decision rule.
b. Compute the value of the test statistic.
c. What is your decision regarding the null hypothesis?

15. The following hypotheses are given.

$H_0: \pi = .40$

$H_1: \pi \ne .40$

A sample of 120 observations revealed that $p = .30$. At the .05 significance level, can the null hypothesis be rejected?

a. State the decision rule.
b. Compute the value of the test statistic.
c. What is your decision regarding the null hypothesis?

Note: It is recommended that the five-step hypothesis-testing procedure be used in solving the following problems.

16. The National Safety Council reported that 52 percent of American turnpike drivers are men. A sample of 300 cars traveling eastbound on the Ohio Turnpike yesterday revealed that 170 were driven by men. At the .01 significance level, can we conclude that a larger proportion of men were driving on the Ohio Turnpike than the national statistics indicate?

17. A recent article in *USA Today* reported that a job awaits only one in three new college graduates. The major reasons given were an overabundance of college graduates and a weak economy. A survey of 200 recent graduates from your school revealed that 80 students had jobs. At the .02 significance level, can we conclude that a larger proportion of students at your school have jobs?

18. Chicken Delight claims that 90 percent of its orders are delivered within 10 minutes of the time the order is placed. A sample of 100 orders revealed that 82 were delivered within the promised time. At the .10 significance level, can we conclude that less than 90 percent of the orders are delivered in less than 10 minutes?

19. Research at the University of Toledo indicates that 50 percent of the students change their major area of study after their first year in a program. A random sample of 100 students in

the College of Business revealed that 48 had changed their major area of study after their first year of the program. Has there been a significant decrease in the proportion of students who change their major after the first year in this program? Test at the .05 level of significance.

A Test Involving the Difference between Two Population Proportions

Several typical cases involving population proportions follow.

- A mock model of a proposed new automobile was shown to two groups of 150 persons each. One group consisted of a random sample of persons between 18 and 25 years of age, and the other group consisted of a random sample of persons more than 50 years old. Eighty percent of the younger group rated the styling satisfactory, but only 50 percent of the older group gave it a similar rating. In evaluating the market potential of this proposed automobile, is it reasonable to expect that it would appeal primarily to younger persons? Or is it possible that this difference of 30 percentage points could be due to sampling; that is, might not the two age groups in the population like the proposed automobile equally well?

- Manelli has developed a new perfume named Heavenly. A number of comparison tests indicate that the perfume has good market potential. The marketing and adver-

tising departments, however, want to plan their strategy so as to reach and impress the largest possible segment of the buying public. One of the questions is whether the perfume is preferred by a larger proportion of younger women or a larger proportion of older women. There are two populations, therefore — a population consisting of young women and one consisting of older women. A standard scent test is used. Women selected at random are asked to sniff several perfumes in succession, including the one they most frequently use and, of course, Heavenly. The names of the perfumes are known only to the person administering the test. Each woman selects the perfume she likes best.

- Two new high-speed machines designed by different companies are being considered for purchase. One factor in the final choice is the percent defective that each machine produces. A sample of the output of one of the machines revealed that 6 percent were defective. A sample of the output of the other machine indicated that 10 percent of the total were defective. Is the machine with the 6 percent scrap significantly better than the one with the 10 percent scrap? Or is there a chance that the two machines are producing an equal percent defective?

The procedures followed in making a statistical decision involving the difference between two proportions will now be examined. The perfume problem has been selected.

The usual five steps **Step 1: State H_0 and H_1** In this problem the null hypothesis is "There is no difference between the proportion of young women who prefer Heavenly and the proportion of older women who prefer it." If the proportion of young women in the population is designated as π_1 and the proportion of older women is π_2, then the null hypothesis is $\pi_1 = \pi_2$. The alternate hypothesis is that the two proportions are not equal, or $\pi_1 \neq \pi_2$. (Note again the Greek letter π represents the population proportions.)

Step 2: Select the Level of Significance   It was decided to use the .05 level.

Step 3: Compute the Statistical Test   When the samples are reasonably large, the *z* distribution is the appropriate test statistic. It approximates the standard normal distribution and is computed by:

TEST OF HYPOTHESIS, TWO PROPORTIONS $$z = \frac{p_1 - p_2}{\sqrt{\dfrac{p_c(1 - p_c)}{n_1} + \dfrac{p_c(1 - p_c)}{n_2}}}$$ **[9–7]**

---

where:

    n_1 is the number of young women selected in the sample.

    n_2 is the number of older women selected in the sample.

    X_1 is the number of young women (sample 1) who prefer Heavenly.

    X_2 is the number of older women (sample 2) who prefer Heavenly.

    p_c is the *weighted* mean of the two sample proportions, computed by:

POOLED PROPORTION $$p_c = \frac{\text{Total number of successes}}{\text{Total number in samples}} = \frac{X_1 + X_2}{n_1 + n_2}$$ **[9–8]**

---

p_c = combined (pooled) estimate

    p_c is generally referred to as the *pooled estimate of the population proportion*. This is the best estimate of the proportion of women in the population who prefer Heavenly, and it does not consider whether they are old or young. Hence, it is a "pooled," or "combined," estimate.

Step 4: Formulate the Decision Rule   Recall that the null hypothesis, H_0, states that $\pi_1 = \pi_2$ and the alternate hypothesis, H_1, is $\pi_1 \neq \pi_2$. Since H_1 does not state any direction (such as $\pi_1 < \pi_2$), the test is *two-tailed*. Thus, the critical values for the .05 level are -1.96 and $+1.96$. As before, if the computed *z* value falls in the region between $+1.96$ and -1.96, the null hypothesis is not rejected. If that does occur, it is assumed that any difference between the two sample proportions is due to chance variation (see Chart 9–9).

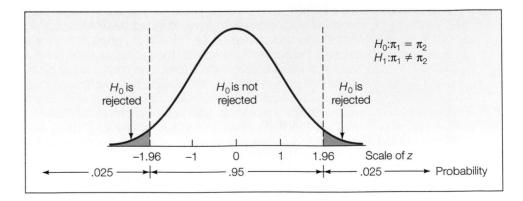

Chart 9–9   Two-Tailed Test, Areas of Rejection and Nonrejection, .05 Level of Significance

Step 5: Make a Decision A total of 100 young women were selected at random, and each was given the standard scent test. Twenty of the 100 young women chose Heavenly as the perfume they liked best.

X_1 is the number preferring Heavenly = 20.

n_1 is the number in the sample = 100.

$$p_1 = \frac{X_1}{n_1} = \frac{20}{100} = .20$$

Two hundred older women were selected at random, and each was given the same standard scent test. Of the 200 older women, 100 preferred Heavenly.

X_2 is the number preferring Heavenly = 100.

n_2 is the number in the sample = 200.

$$p_2 = \frac{X_2}{n_2} = \frac{100}{200} = .50$$

The pooled or weighted proportion, p_c, is computed using formula (9–8).

$$p_c = \frac{X_1 + X_2}{n_1 + n_2} = \frac{20 + 100}{100 + 200} = \frac{120}{300} = .40$$

Note that the weighted proportion of .40 is closer to .50 than to .20. This is because more older women than younger women were sampled.

Computing z using formula (9–7):

$$z = \frac{p_1 - p_2}{\sqrt{\dfrac{p_c(1 - p_c)}{n_1} + \dfrac{p_c(1 - p_c)}{n_2}}}$$

$$= \frac{.20 - .50}{\sqrt{\dfrac{.40(1 - .40)}{100} + \dfrac{.40(1 - .40)}{200}}}$$

$$= \frac{-.30}{.06} = -5.00$$

Reject H_0; it is unlikely that difference between .20 and .50 is due to sampling error

The computed z of −5.00 is in the area of rejection, that is, to the left of −1.96. Therefore, the null hypothesis is rejected at the .05 level of significance. To put it another way, the hypothesis that the proportion of young women in the population who prefer Heavenly is equal to the proportion of older women in the population who prefer Heavenly is rejected at the .05 level. It is highly unlikely that such a large difference between the two sample proportions (.30) could be due to chance (sampling).

The probability of committing a Type I error is .05, which is the same as the level of significance selected before the project started. This indicates there is a 5 percent risk of rejecting the true hypothesis that $\pi_1 = \pi_2$. The p-value is 0, because the probability of finding a z less than −5.00 or greater than 5.00 is virtually 0. There is very little likelihood that the null hypothesis is true.

SELF-REVIEW 9–5

Of 150 adults who tried a new peach-flavored peppermint patty, 87 rated it excellent. Of 200 children sampled, 123 rated it excellent. Using the .10 level of significance, can we conclude that there is a significant difference in the proportion of adults versus children who rate the new flavor as excellent?

(a) What is the null hypothesis? What is the alternate hypothesis?

(b) What is the probability of a Type I error?

(c) Is this a one-tailed test or a two-tailed test? Why?

(d) What is the critical value?

(e) Should the null hypothesis be rejected or not rejected?

(f) What is the *p*-value? Explain its meaning.

▌ Exercises

20. The stated hypotheses are:

    $H_0: \pi_1 \leq \pi_2$
    $H_1: \pi_1 > \pi_2$

    A sample of 100 observations from the first population indicated that X_1 is 70. A sample of 150 observations from the second population revealed X_2 to be 90. Use the .05 significance level to test the hypothesis.
    a. State the decision rule.
    b. Compute the pooled proportion.
    c. Compute the value of the test statistic.
    d. What is your decision regarding the null hypothesis?

21. The hypotheses H_0 and H_1 are:

    $H_0: \pi_1 = \pi_2$

    $H_1: \pi_1 \neq \pi_2$

    A sample of 200 observations from the first population revealed X_1 to be 170. A sample of 150 observations from the second population resulted in an X_2 of 110. Use the .05 significance level.
    a. State the decision rule.
    b. Compute the pooled proportion.
    c. Compute the value of the test statistic.
    d. What is your decision regarding the null hypothesis?

Note: It is recommended that the five-step hypothesis-testing procedure be used in solving the following problems.

22. The Damon family owns a large grape vineyard in western New York. The grapevines must be sprayed at the beginning of the growing season to protect against various insects and diseases. Two new insecticides have just been marketed: Pernod 5 and Action. To test their effectiveness, three long rows were selected and sprayed with Pernod 5, and three others were sprayed with Action. When the grapes ripened, 400 of the vines treated with Pernod 5 were checked for infestation. Likewise, a sample of 400 vines sprayed with Action were checked. The results are:

Insecticide	Number of Vines Checked (sample size)	Number of Infested Vines
Pernod 5	400	24
Action	400	40

At the .05 significance level, can we conclude that there is a difference in the proportion of vines infested using Pernod 5 as opposed to Action?

23. The Roper Organization conducted identical surveys in 1977 and 1997. One question asked women was "Are most men basically kind, gentle, and thoughtful?" The 1977 survey revealed that, of the 3,000 women surveyed, 2,010 said that they were. In 1997 1,530 of the 3,000 women surveyed thought that men were kind, gentle, and thoughtful. At the .05 level, can we conclude that women think men are less kind, gentle, and thoughtful in 1997 compared with 1977?

24. A nationwide sample of influential Republicans and Democrats were asked as a part of a comprehensive survey whether they favored lowering environmental standards so that high-sulfur coal could be burned in coal-fired power plants. The results were:

	Republicans	Democrats
Number sampled	1,000	800
Number in favor	200	168

At the .02 level of significance, can we conclude that there is a larger proportion of Democrats in favor of lowering the standards?

25. The research department at the home office of New Hampshire Insurance conducts ongoing research on the causes of automobile accidents, the characteristics of the drivers, and so on. A random sample of 400 policies written on single persons was selected. It was discovered that in the previous three-year period, 120 of them had at least one accident. Similarly, a sample of 600 policies written on married persons revealed that 150 had been in at least one accident. At the .05 level, is there a significant difference in the proportions of single and married persons having an accident during a three-year period?

▌ Type II Error

Recall that the level of significance, identified by the symbol α, is the probability that the null hypothesis is rejected when it is true. This is called a Type I error. The most common levels of significance are .05, and .01.

In a hypothesis-testing situation there is also the possibility that a null hypothesis is not rejected when it is actually false. That is, we accept a false null hypothesis. This is called a Type II error. The probability of a Type II error is identified by the Greek letter beta (β).

To illustrate the computation of beta, suppose a manufacturer purchases steel bars to make cotter pins. Past experience indicates that the mean tensile strength of all incoming shipments is 10,000 psi and that the standard deviation, σ, is 400 psi.

In order to make a decision about incoming shipments of steel bars, the manufacturer set up this rule for the quality-control inspector to follow: "Take a sample of 100 steel bars. If the sample mean ($\overline{X}$) strength falls between 9,922 psi and 10,078 psi, accept the lot. Otherwise the lot is to be rejected." Refer to Chart 9–10 and the region labeled *A*. It shows the region where each lot is rejected and where it is not rejected. The mean of this distribution is designated μ_0. The tails of the curve represent the probability of making a Type I error, that is, rejecting the incoming lot of steel bars when in fact it is a good lot, with a mean of 10,000 psi.

How is the probability of a Type II error computed? (Recall that it is the probability of accepting an incoming lot as a "good lot" when in fact the mean is not 10,000 psi.)

Example

Suppose the unknown population mean of an incoming lot, designated μ_1, is really 9,900 psi. What is the probability that the quality-control inspector will fail to reject the shipment (a Type II error)?

Solution

Computations for β
(Type II error)

The probability of committing a Type II error, as represented by the green area in Chart 9–10, region *B,* can be computed by determining the area under the normal curve that lies above 9,922 pounds. The calculation of the areas under the normal curve was discussed in Chapter 7. Reviewing briefly, it is necessary first to determine the probability of the sample mean falling between 9,900 and 9,922. Then this probability is subtracted from .5000 (which represents all the area beyond the mean of 9,900) to arrive at the probability of making a Type II error in this case.

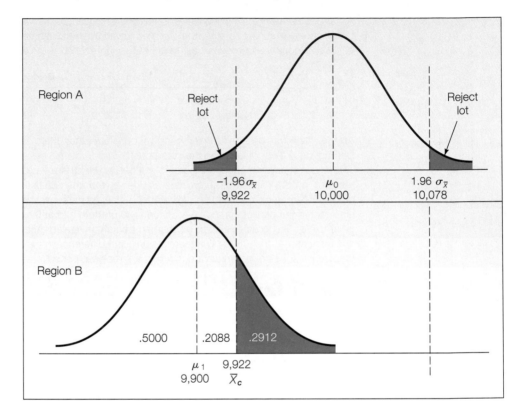

Chart 9–10   Charts Showing Type I and Type II Errors

The number of standard units (*z* value) between the mean of the incoming lot (9,900), designated μ_1, and $\overline{X}_c$, representing the critical value for 9,922, is computed by:

TYPE II ERROR	$z = \dfrac{\overline{X}_c - \mu_1}{\sigma/\sqrt{n}}$	**[9–9]**

With $n = 100$ and $\sigma = 400$, the value of *z* is 0.55:

$$z = \frac{\overline{X}_c - \mu_1}{\sigma/\sqrt{n}}$$

$$= \frac{9,922 - 9,900}{400/\sqrt{100}} = \frac{22}{40} = 0.55$$

The area under the curve between 9,900 and 9,922 (a z value of 0.55) is .2088 (from Appendix D).

The area under the curve beyond 9,922 pounds is $.5000 - .2088$, or .2912; this is the probability of making a Type II error—that is, accepting an incoming lot of steel bars when the population mean is 9,900 psi.

Another illustration in Chart 9–11, region C, depicts the probability of accepting a lot when the population mean is 10,120. To find the probability:

$$z = \frac{\overline{X}_c - \mu_1}{\sigma/\sqrt{n}} = \frac{10,078 - 10,120}{400/\sqrt{100}} = -1.05$$

The probability that z is less than -1.05 is .1469, found by $.5000 - .3531$.

Using the methods illustrated by Charts 9–10B and 9–11C, the probability of accepting a hypothesis as true when it is actually false can be determined for any value of μ_1.

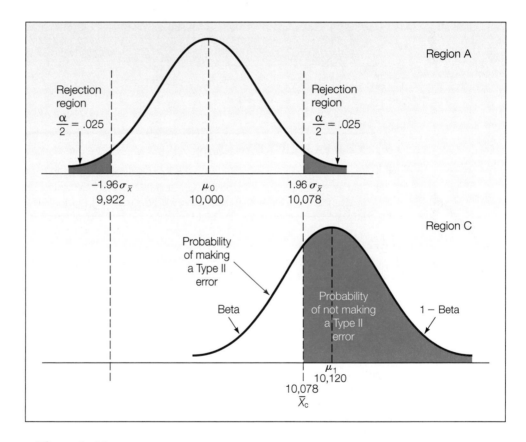

Chart 9–11 Type I and Type II Errors (Another Example)

Type II error probabilities are shown in the center column of Table 9–1 for selected values of μ, given in the left column. The right column gives the probability of not making a Type II error.

Table 9–1 Probabilities of a Type II Error for $\mu_0 = 10,000$ Pounds and Selected Alternative Means, .05 Level of Significance

Selected Alternative Mean (pounds)	Probability of Type II Error (β)	Probability of Not Making a Type II Error ($1 - \beta$)
9,820	.0054	.9946
9.880	.1469	.8531
9,900	.2912	.7088
9,940	.6736	.3264
9,980	.9194	.0806
10,000	—*	—
10,020	.9194	.0806
10,060	.6736	.3264
10,100	.2912	.7088
10,120	.1469	.8531
10,180	.0054	.9946

*It is not possible to make a Type II error when $\mu = \mu_0$.

SELF-REVIEW 9–6

Suppose the true mean of an incoming lot of steel bars is 10,180 psi. What is the probability that the quality control inspector will accept the bars as having a mean of 10,000 psi? (It sounds implausible that steel bars will be rejected if the tensile strength is higher than specified. However, it may be that the cotter pin has a dual function in an outboard motor. It may be designed not to shear off if the motor hits a small object, but to shear off it hits a rock. Therefore, the steel should not be *too* strong.)

The light area in Chart 9–11C represents the probability of falsely accepting the hypothesis that the mean tensile strength of the incoming lot of steel is 10,000 psi. What is the probability of committing a Type II error?

Exercises

26. Refer to Table 9–1 and the example just completed. With $n = 100$, $\sigma = 400$, $\bar{X}_c = 9,922$, and $\mu_1 = 9,880$, verify that the probability of a Type II error is .1469.
27. Refer to Table 9–1 and the example just completed. With $n = 100$, $\sigma = 400$, $\bar{X}_c = 9,922$, and $\mu_1 = 9,940$, verify that the probability of a Type II error is .6736.

Chapter Outline

I. The objective of hypothesis testing is to check the validity of statements about a population parameter.
II. The steps in hypothesis testing are:
    A. State the null hypothesis (H_0) and the alternate hypothesis (H_1).
    B. Select the level of significance.
        1. The level of significance is the probability of rejecting a true null hypothesis.

2. The most frequently used significance levels are .01, .05, and .10, but any value between 0 and 1.00 is possible.
C. Select the test statistic.
1. The test statistic is a value determined from sample information that is used to determine whether to reject the null hypothesis.
2. The standard normal distribution, z, is used as the test statistic for large samples.
D. State the decision rule.
1. The decision rule indicates the condition or conditions when the null hypothesis is rejected.
2. In a two-tailed test the rejection region is evenly split between the upper and the lower tail.
3. In a one-tailed test all the rejection region is in either the upper or the lower tail.
E. Select a sample, compute the value of the test statistic, make a decision on the null hypothesis, and interpret the result.
III. A *p*-value is the probability that the value of the test statistic is as large or larger than that obtained, when the null hypothesis is true.
IV. Testing a hypothesis about the population mean.
A. If the population standard deviation, σ, is known, the test statistic approximates the standard normal distribution, z, and is determined from:

$$z = \frac{\bar{X} - \mu}{\sigma/\sqrt{n}}$$ **[9–1]**

B. If σ is not known, the sample standard deviation, s, is substituted, provided n is greater than 30.

$$z = \frac{\bar{X} - \mu}{s/\sqrt{n}}$$ **[9–2]**

V. Testing a hypothesis about two population means.
A. The objective is to determine whether there is a difference between two sample means.
B. Both samples need to be at least 30.
C. The test statistic is:

$$z = \frac{\bar{X}_1 - \bar{X}_2}{\sqrt{\dfrac{s_1^2}{n_1} + \dfrac{s_2^2}{n_2}}}$$ **[9–3]**

VI. Testing a hypothesis about a proportion.
A. Both $n\pi$ and $n(1 - \pi)$ must be at least 5.
B. The test statistic is

$$z = \frac{p - \pi}{\sqrt{\dfrac{\pi(1 - \pi)}{n}}}$$ **[9–6]**

VII. Testing a hypothesis about two proportions.
A. The two samples are pooled by the following formula:

$$p_c = \frac{X_1 - X_2}{n_1 + n_2}$$ **[9–8]**

B. The test statistic is

$$z = \frac{p_1 - p_2}{\sqrt{\dfrac{p_c(1 - p_c)}{n_1} + \dfrac{p_c(1 - p_c)}{n_2}}}$$ **[9–7]**

VIII. Type I and Type II errors.
   A. A Type I error occurs when a true null hypothesis is rejected.
      1. It is equal to the level of significance.
      2. It is designated by the letter α.
   B. A Type II error occurs when a false null hypothesis is not rejected.
      1. It is designated as β.
      2. The likelihood of a Type II error is found from

$$z = \frac{\bar{X}_c - \mu_1}{\sigma/\sqrt{n}}$$ [9–9]

Pronunciation Key

SYMBOL	MEANING	PRONUNCIATION
H_0	Null hypothesis	*H sub zero*
H_1	Alternate hypothesis	*H sub one*
$\alpha/2$	Two-tailed significance level	*Alpha over 2*
p_c	Pooled proportion	*p sub c*
$\bar{X}_c$	Limit of the sample mean	*X bar sub c*
μ_0	Assumed population mean	*mu naught*

Chapter Exercises

Note: It is suggested that the five-step hypothesis testing procedure be followed for these exercises.

28. A new weight-watching company, Weight Reducers International, advertises that those who join will lose, on the average, 10 pounds the first two weeks. A random sample of 50 people who joined the new weight reduction program revealed the mean loss to be 9 pounds. The standard deviation of the sample was computed to be 2.8 pounds. At the .05 level of significance, can we conclude that those joining Weight Reducers on average will lose less than 10 pounds? Determine the *p*-value.

29. Dole Pineapple, Inc. is concerned that the 16-ounce can of sliced pineapple is being overfilled. The quality-control department took a random sample of 50 cans and found that the arithmetic mean weight was 16.05 ounces, with a sample standard deviation of 0.03 ounces. At the 5 percent level of significance, can we conclude that the mean weight is greater than 16 ounces? Determine the *p*-value.

30. The Peoria Board of Education wants to consider a new academic program funded by the U.S. Department of Education. In order to be eligible for the federal grant, the arithmetic mean income per household must not be more than $15,000. The board hired a research firm to gather the required data. In its report the firm indicated that the arithmetic mean income in the district is $17,000. They further reported that 75 households were surveyed and that the standard deviation of the sample was $3,000. Can the board argue that the difference between the mean income resulting from the sample survey and the mean specified by the Department of Education is due to chance (sampling)? Use the .05 level.

31. A statewide real estate sales agency, Farm Associates, specializes in selling farm property in the state of Nebraska. Their records indicate that the mean selling time of farm property is 90 days. Because of recent drought conditions, they believe that the mean selling time is now greater than 90 days. A statewide survey study of 100 farms sold recently revealed that the mean selling time was 94 days, with a standard deviation of 22 days. At the .10 significance level, can we conclude that the selling time has increased?

32. According to the local union president, the mean gross income of plumbers in the Salt Lake City area is normally distributed, with a mean of $30,000 and a standard deviation of $3,000. A recent investigative reporter for a TV station found, for a sample of 120 plumbers, the mean gross income was $30,500. At the .10 significance level can we conclude that the mean income is not equal to $30,000? Determine the *p*-value.

33. A recent article in *Vitality* magazine reported that the mean amount of leisure time per week for American men is 40.0 hours. You believe this figure is too large and decide to conduct your own test. In a random sample of 60 men, you find that the mean is 37.8 hours of leisure per week and that the standard deviation of the sample is 12.2 hours. Can you conclude that the information in the article is untrue? Use the .05 significance level. Determine the *p*-value and explain its meaning.

34. NBC TV news, in a segment on the price of gasoline, reported last evening that the mean price nationwide is $1.25 per gallon for self-serve regular unleaded. A random sample of 35 stations in the Salt Lake City area revealed that the mean price was $1.27 per gallon and that the standard deviation was $0.05 per gallon. At the .05 significance level, can we conclude that the price of gasoline is higher in the Salt Lake City area? Determine the *p*-value.

35. The Rutter Nursery Company packages their pine bark mulch in 50-pound bags. From a long history, the packaging department reports that the distribution is normal and the standard deviation of this process is 3 pounds per bag. At the end of each day Jeff Rutter, the production manager, weighs 10 bags and computes the mean weight of the sample. Below are the weights of 10 bags from today's production.

45.6	47.7	47.6	46.3	46.2
47.4	49.2	55.8	47.5	48.5

   a. Can Mr. Rutter conclude that the mean weight of the bags is less than 50 pounds? Use the .01 significance level.
   b. In a brief report, tell why Mr. Rutter can use the *z* distribution as the test statistic.
   c. Compute the *p*-value.

36. In a recent national survey the mean weekly allowance for a nine-year-old child from his or her parents was reported to be $3.65. A random sample of 45 nine-year-olds in the Tampa, Florida, area revealed the mean allowance to be $3.69 with a standard deviation of $0.24. At the .05 significance level, is there a difference in the mean allowance nationally and the mean allowance in the Tampa area for nine-year-olds?

37. The Air Force trains enlisted computer personnel at two bases — Cass AFB and Kingston AFB. A common final examination is administered. As part of an ongoing study of the training program, a comparison of the final test scores is to be made. Is there any significant difference in the final results of the two educational programs? Use the .04 significance level. Determine the *p*-value. Explain your decision to the committee studying the program.

	Cass AFB	Kingston AFB
Number sampled	40	50
Mean score	114.6	117.9
Sample standard deviation	9.1	10.4

38. Corrigan Industries has been awarded a large contract to supply pipeline parts to Angus Oil, a company drilling in the Scotland-Ireland area. In the past, two subcontractors specializing in steel products have provided Corrigan Industries with high-quality supplies such as nuts, bolts, steel bars, and casing. One of the concerns of Corrigan is the delivery time of the two subcontractors, Jackson Steel and Alabama Distributors. The question to be explored is whether there is a difference in the delivery times of the two subcontractors.

Random samples from the files of Corrigan Industries revealed these statistics about delivery times:

	Jackson Steel	Alabama Distributors
Number in sample	45	50
Mean delivery time (days)	20	21
Sample standard deviation (days)	4	3

At the .05 significance level, is there a difference in the delivery times? Determine the p-value.

39. An official of the Iowa Department of Highways wants to compare the useful life, in months, of two brands of paint used for striping roads. The mean number of months Cooper Paint lasted was 36.2, with a standard deviation of 1.14 months. The official reviewed 35 road stripes. For King Paint, the mean number of months was 37.0, with a standard deviation of 1.3 months. The official reviewed 40 road stripes. At the .01 significance level, is there a difference in the useful life of the two paints? Compute the p-value.

40. Clark Heter is an industrial engineer at Lyons Products. He would like to determine whether there are more units produced on the afternoon shift than on the day shift. A sample of 54 day-shift workers showed that the mean number of units produced was 345, with a standard deviation of 21. A sample of 60 afternoon-shift workers showed that the mean number of units produced was 351, with a standard deviation of 28 units. At the .05 significance level, is the number of units produced on the afternoon shift larger?

41. Fry Brothers Heating and Air Conditioning, Inc. employs Larry Clark and George Murnen to make service calls to repair furnaces and air conditioning units in homes. Tom Fry, the owner, would like to know whether there is a difference in the mean number of service calls they make per day. A random sample of 40 days last year showed that Larry Clark made an average of 4.77 calls per day, with a standard deviation of 1.05 calls per day. For a sample of 50 days George Murnen made an average of 5.02 calls per day, with a standard deviation of 1.23 calls per day. At the .05 significance level, is there a difference in the mean number of calls per day between the two employees? What is the p-value?

42. A coffee manufacturer is interested in finding out whether the mean daily consumption of regular-coffee drinkers is less than that of decaffeinated-coffee drinkers. A random sample of 50 regular-coffee drinkers showed a mean of 4.35 cups per day, with a standard deviation of 1.20 cups per day. A sample of 40 decaffeinated-coffee drinkers showed a mean of 5.84 cups per day, with a standard deviation of 1.36 cups per day. Use the .01 significance level. Compute the p-value.

43. The board of directors at the Anchor Pointe Marina is studying the usage of boats among its members. A sample of 30 members who have boats 10 to 20 feet in length showed that they used their boats an average of 11 days last July. The standard deviation of the sample was 3.88 days. For a sample of 40 members with boats 21 to 40 feet in length, the average number of days they used their boats in July was 7.67, with a standard deviation of 4.42 days. At the .02 significance level, can the board of directors conclude that those with the smaller boats used their crafts more frequently?

44. The *fog index* is used to measure the reading difficulty of written text. Calculating the index involves the following steps: (1) Find the mean number of words per sentence. (2) Find the percent of words with three or more syllables. (3) The fog index is 40 percent of the sum of 1 and 2.

The fog index for a sample of 36 articles from a scientific journal showed a sample mean of 11.0 and a standard deviation of 2.65. A sample of 40 articles from trade publications showed a mean of 8.9 and a standard deviation of 1.64. At the .01 significance level, is the fog index in the scientific journal significantly higher?

45. Tina Dennis is the chief accountant for Meek Industries. She believes that the current cash-flow problems of MI are due to the slow collection of accounts receivable. She believes that more than 60 percent of the accounts are in arrears more than three months. A sample of

200 accounts showed that 140 were more than three months old. At the .01 significance level, can we conclude that more than 60 percent of the accounts are in arrears for more than three months?

46. The policy of the Suburban Transit Authority is to add a bus route if more than 55 percent of the potential commuters indicate they would use the particular route. A sample of 70 commuters revealed that 42 would use a proposed route from Bowman Park to the downtown area. Does the Bowman-to-downtown route meet the STA criteria? Use the .05 significance level.

47. Past experience at the Crowder Travel Agency indicated that 44 percent of those persons who wanted the agency to plan a vacation for them wanted to go to Europe. During the most recent busy season, a sampling of 1,000 plans was selected at random from the files. It was found that 480 persons wanted to go to Europe on vacation. Has there been a significant shift upward in the percentage of persons who want to go to Europe? Test at the .05 level.

48. From past experience a television manufacturer found that 10 percent or less of its sets needed any type of repair in the first two years of operation. In a sample of 50 sets manufactured two years ago, 9 need repair. At the .05 significance level, has the percent of sets needing repair increased? Determine the p-value.

49. An urban planner claims that, nationally, 20 percent of all families renting condominiums move during a given year. A random sample of 200 families renting condominiums in Dallas revealed that 56 had moved during the past year. At the .01 significance level, does this evidence suggest that a larger proportion of condominium owners moved in the Dallas area? Determine the p-value.

50. Suppose the manufacturer of Advil developed a new formulation of the drug that is claimed to be more effective in relieving a headache than the one currently sold. To evaluate the new drug a sample of 200 current users is asked to try it. After a one-month trial, 180 indicated the new drug was more effective in relieving a headache. At the same time a sample of 300 current Advil users is given the current drug but told it is the new formulation. From this group, 261 said it was an improvement. At the .05 significance level can we conclude that the new drug is more effective?

51. Suppose a random sample of 1,000 American-born citizens revealed that 198 favored resumption of full diplomatic relations with Cuba. Similarly, 117 of a sample of 500 foreign-born citizens favored it. At the .05 significance level, is there a difference in the proportion of American-born versus foreign-born citizens who favor restoring diplomatic relations with Cuba?

52. Is there a difference in the proportion of college men versus college women who smoke at least a pack of cigarettes a day at Northern State University? A sample of 400 women revealed 72 smoked at least one pack per day. A sample of 500 men revealed that 70 smoked at least a pack of cigarettes a day. At the .05 significance level, is there a difference between the proportion of men and the proportion of women who smoke at least a pack of cigarettes a day, or can the difference in the proportions be attributed to sampling error?

53. One of the major U.S. automakers is studying its two-year/24,000-mile warranty policy. The warranty covers the engine, transmission, and drive train of all new cars for up to two years or 24,000 miles, whichever comes first. The manufacturer's quality-assurance department believes that the mean number of miles driven by owners is more than 24,000. A sample of 35 cars revealed that the mean number of miles was 24,421 with a standard deviation of 1,944 miles.

    a. At the .05 significance level, conduct the following hypothesis test.

$$H_0: \mu \le 24{,}000$$

$$H_1: \mu > 24{,}000$$

    b. Using the .05 significance level, what is the largest sample mean for which H_0 is not rejected?

    c. The population mean shifts to 25,000 miles. What is the probability that this change will not be detected?

54. A cola-dispensing machine is set to dispense 9.00 ounces of cola per cup, with a standard deviation of 1.00 ounces. The manufacturer of the machine would like to set the control limit in such a way that for samples of 36, 5 percent of the sample means will be greater than the upper control limit, and 5 percent of the sample means will be less than the lower control limit.
    a. At what value should the control limit be set?
    b. What is the probability that if the population mean shifts to 8.9, this change will not be detected?
    c. What is the probability that if the population mean shifts to 9.3, this change will not be detected?

55. The owners of the Franklin Park Mall are studying the shopping habits of their customers. From earlier studies the owners are under the impression that a typical shopper spends 0.75 hours at the mall, with a standard deviation of 0.10 hours. Recently the mall owners have added some specialty restaurants designed to keep shoppers in the mall longer. A consulting firm, Brunner and Swanson Marketing Enterprises, has been hired to evaluate the effects of the restaurants. A sample of 45 shoppers by Brunner and Swanson revealed that the mean time spent in the mall had increased to 0.80 hours.
    a. Develop a test of hypothesis to determine if the mean time spent in the mall is more than 0.75 hours. Use the .05 significance level.
    b. Suppose the mean shopping time actually increased from 0.75 hours to 0.77 hours. What is the probability this increase would not be detected?
    c. When Brunner and Swanson reported the information in part (b) to the mall owners, they were upset with the statement that a survey could not detect a change from 0.75 to 0.77 hours of shopping time. How could this probability be reduced?

56. The following null and alternate hypotheses are given.

    H_0: $\mu \leq 50$

    H_1: $\mu > 50$

    Suppose the population standard deviation is 10. The probability of a Type I error is set at .01 and the probability of a Type II error at .30. Assume the population mean shifts from 50 to 55. How large a sample is necessary to meet these requirements?

www.Exercises.com

57. The following Web site presents information on licensed nursing facilities in New Mexico: *http://lib.stat.cmu.edu/DASL/Datafiles/nursinghomedat.html*. Remember, this address is sensitive to capital letters, so enter as shown.
    a. Would it be reasonable for the New Mexico Director of Public Health to conclude that the mean number of beds per facility is less than 100? Set up and conduct an appropriate test of hypothesis. Use the .05 significance level in your test of hypothesis. Write a brief interpretation of the results.
    b. Would it be reasonable to conclude that the mean number of in-patient days (reported in hundreds) is more than 150 per facility? Conduct an appropriate test of hypothesis. Would it make any difference in your conclusion if you selected the .05 or the .01 significance level? Write a brief interpretation of the results.

58. The *USA Today (http://USAtoday.com/sports/mlb.htm)* and major league baseball's *(http://www.majorleaguebaseball.com)* regularly report information on individual player salaries. Go to one of these sites and find individual salaries for your favorite team. Compute the mean and the standard deviation. Is it reasonable to conclude that the mean salary per player on your favorite (or local team) is more than $1,500,000?

▌ Computer Data Exercises

59. Refer to Data Set 1, which reports information on the homes sold in the Venice, Florida, area last year.
    a. A recent article in the *Tampa Times* indicated that the mean selling price of homes on the west coast of Florida is more than $220,000. Can we conclude that the mean selling price in the Venice area is more than $220,000? Use the .01 significance level. What is the *p*-value?
    b. The same article reported that the mean size of the homes was more than 2,100 square feet. Can we conclude that the mean size of the homes sold in the Venice area is more than 2,100 square feet? Use the .01 significance level. What is the *p*-value?
    c. Determine the proportion of homes that have an attached garage. At the .05 significance level, can we conclude that more than 60 percent of the homes have an attached garage? What is the *p*-value?
    d. Determine the proportion of homes that have a pool. At the .05 significance level, can we conclude that more than 60 percent of the homes have a pool? What is the *p*-value?
60. Refer to Data Set 2, which reports information on the 28 Major League Baseball teams for the 1997 season. Suppose you want to determine whether the mean salary of the 28 teams is more than $40.0 million. Write a brief report indicating why, given the restrictions in this chapter this is not possible.
61. Refer to Data Set 3, which reports information on the circulation of magazines.
    a. At the .05 significance level, can we conclude that the mean number of magazines read by men is more than 2.5?
    b. At the .05 significance level can we conclude that the mean age of all magazine readers is less than 40 years?
62. Refer to Data Set 4, which includes information on the 94 school districts in northwest Ohio. Use the .01 significance level.
    a. If we assume that the 94 school districts are a sample, can we conclude that the mean salary in the region is less than $35,000?
    b. If we assume that the 94 school districts are a sample, can we conclude that the typical district has less than 10 percent of their population on welfare?
    c. If we assume that the 94 school districts are a sample, can we conclude that the typical school district has more than 60 percent of the students passing the proficiency exam?
    d. Divide the school districts into two groups, those with less than 2,000 students and those with 2,000 or more students. Is there a difference in the proportion of students passing the proficiency exam in the two groups?

CHAPTER 9   *Answers to Self-Review*

9–1 (a) H_0: $\mu = 6.0$; H_1: $\mu \neq 6.0$.
   (b) .05.
   (c) $z = \dfrac{\overline{X} - \mu}{\sigma/\sqrt{n}}$
   (d) Do not reject the null hypothesis if the computed z value falls between -1.96 and $+1.96$.
   (e) Yes. Computed $z = -2.56$, found by:

$$\frac{5.84 - 6.0}{0.5/\sqrt{64}} = \frac{-0.16}{.0625} = -2.56$$

   Reject H_0 at the .05 level. Accept H_1. The mean turnover rate is not equal to 6.0.

9–2 (a) H_0: $\mu \geq 6.0$
   (b) H_1: $\mu < 6.0$.
   (c) Note that the inequality sign ($<$) in the alternate hypothesis points in the direction of the region of rejection. To determine the critical value: $.5000 - .05 = .4500$. z from Appendix D is about -1.65.

9–3 (a) H_0: $\mu_1 \leq \mu_2$; H_1: $\mu_1 > \mu_2$, where population 1 is Corngrow. H_0 is rejected if computed z is > 1.65.

$$z = \frac{16.0 - 15.7}{\sqrt{\dfrac{(1)^2}{400} + \dfrac{(1.2)^2}{100}}}$$

$$= \frac{0.3}{0.13} = 2.31$$

   Since $2.31 > 1.65$ (critical value), the null hypothesis of $\mu_1 \leq \mu_2$ is rejected; the alternate, $\mu_1 > \mu_2$, is accepted. Corngrow is effective.

(b)

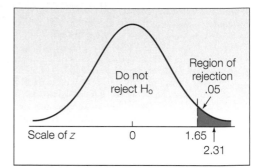

   (c) The p-value is .0104, found by $.5000 - .4896$. There is strong evidence that Corngrow is effective in adding weight to the corn.

9–4 (a) Yes, because both $n\pi$ and $n(1 - \pi)$ exceed 5: $n\pi = 200(.40) = 80$, and $n(1 - \pi) = 200(.60) = 120$.
   (b) H_0: $\pi \geq .40$
      H_1: $\pi < .40$
   (c)

   (d) $z = -0.87$, found by:

$$z = \frac{.37 - .40}{\sqrt{\dfrac{.40(1 - .40)}{200}}} = \frac{-.03}{\sqrt{.0012}} = -0.87$$

   Do not reject H_0.
   (e) The p-value is .1922, found by $.5000 - .3078$.

9–5 (a) H_0: $\pi_1 = \pi_2$; H_1: $\pi_1 \neq \pi_2$
   (b) .10.
   (c) Two-tailed because we are not concerned about the direction.

(d) −1.65 and +1.65.

(e) Not rejected. Computed $z = -0.66$.

$$p_c = \frac{87 + 123}{150 + 200} = \frac{210}{350} = .60$$

Then:

$$z = \frac{.58 - .615}{\sqrt{\dfrac{.60(.40)}{150} + \dfrac{.60(.40)}{200}}}$$

$$= \frac{-.035}{\sqrt{.0028}} = -0.66$$

H_0 is not rejected.

(f) The *p*-value is .5092. First find the area between 0 and .66; it is .2454. Then $2(.5000 - .2454) = .5092$. The probability of obtaining a difference at least this great when there actually is no difference is .5092.

9–6 .0054, found by determining the area under the curve between 10,078 and 10,180 (Chart 9–11B).

$$z = \frac{\overline{X}_c - \mu_1}{\sigma/\sqrt{n}}$$

$$= \frac{10,078 - 10,180}{400/\sqrt{100}} = -2.55$$

The area under the curve for a z of −2.55 is .4946 (Appendix D), and $.5000 - .4946 = .0054$.

SECTION 3
A REVIEW OF CHAPTERS 8 AND 9

Why sampling is often imperative

This section is a review of the major concepts and terms introduced in Chapters 8 and 9. Chapter 8 explored why it is almost impossible to study every item, or individual, in some populations. It would be too expensive and time consuming, for example, to contact and record the annual incomes of all U.S. bank officers. To estimate a population parameter, therefore, we sample the population. A sample is just part of the population. Care must be taken to ensure that every member of our population has a chance of being selected; otherwise the conclusions might be biased. A number of probability-type sampling methods can be used, including *simple random, systematic, stratified,* and *cluster sampling.*

Sampling methods

Sampling error

Regardless of the sampling method selected, it is unlikely that a sample mean will be exactly the same as the population mean. The difference between this sample statistic and the population parameter is the *sampling error.* If the means of all possible samples of a specified size selected from a population are organized in a distribution, called the *sampling distribution of the sample means,* the mean of the sampling distribution will be equal to the population mean. If the sample size is large enough, the distribution of sample means is approximately normally distributed.

These concepts are the essence of the *central limit theorem,* which is the theoretical foundation of *statistical inference.* Briefly, statistical inference is concerned with inferring something about a population parameter based on a sample statistic. Chapter 8 discussed one facet of statistical inference: *estimation.* Chapter 9 concentrated on the other facet of statistical inference: *hypothesis testing.*

Point estimate

Interval estimate
Confidence limits

We may want to estimate a particular population parameter. For example, if, based on a sample, we estimate that the mean annual income of all professional house painters (the population) is $35,300, that estimate is called a *point estimate.* If we state that the population mean is probably in the interval between $35,200 and $35,400, that estimate is called an *interval estimate.* The two endpoints ($35,200 and $35,400) are called the *confidence limits* for the population mean.

Hypothesis testing: A systematic procedure followed to arrive at a decision

A *hypothesis* is a statement about a population parameter or parameters. One such statement is "The mean net weight of Campbell's canned green pea soup is 319 grams." Using a systematic procedure called *hypothesis testing,* we decide whether to reject this hypothesis. The procedure calls for stating the null hypothesis and the alternate hypothesis, selecting a level of significance and the appropriate test statistic, formulating a decision rule, taking a sample, and (based on the sample results) deciding whether to reject the null hypothesis. Chapter 9 presented tests of hypotheses about one population mean, two population means, one population proportion, and two population proportions.

❙ Glossary

Chapter 8

Bias A possible consequence if certain members of the population are denied the chance to be selected for the sample. As a result, the sample may not be representative of the population.

Central limit theorem If the size of the sample is sufficiently large, the sampling distribution of the sample means will approach a normal distribution regardless of the shape of the population.

Cluster sampling A method often used to lower the cost of sampling if the population is dispersed over a wide geographic area. The area is divided into smaller units (counties, precincts, blocks, etc.) called primary units. Then a few primary units are chosen, and a random sample is selected from each unit.

Interval estimate The interval within which a population parameter probably lies, based on sample information. Example: Based on sample data, the population mean is in the interval between 1.9 and 2.0 pounds.

Point estimate A single value computed from a sample and used to estimate a population parameter. Example: If the sample mean is 1,020 psi, it is the best estimate of the mean tensile strength of the population.

Probability sample A sample of items or individuals chosen so that each member of the population has a chance of being included in the sample.

Sampling distribution of the sample means A probability distribution consisting of all possible means of samples of a given size selected from the population and their corresponding probabilities of occurrence.

Sampling error The difference between a sample statistic and the corresponding population parameter. Example: The sample mean income is $22,100; the population mean is $22,000. The sampling error is $22,100 − $22,000 = $100. This error can be attributed to sampling, that is, chance.

Simple random sampling A sampling scheme in which every member of the population has the same chance of being selected.

Stratified random sampling A population is first divided into subgroups called strata. A sample is then chosen from each stratum. If, for example, the population of interest consisted of all undergraduate students, the sample design might call for sampling 62 freshmen, 51 sophomores, 40 juniors, and 39 seniors.

Systematic random sampling Assuming the population is arranged in some way, such as alphabetically, by height, or in a file drawer, a random starting point is selected. Then every kth member becomes a member of the sample. If a sample design called for interviewing every ninth household on Main Street starting with 932 Main, the sample would consist of households at 932 Main, 941 Main, 950 Main, etc.

Chapter 9

Critical value A value that is the dividing point between the region where the null hypothesis is not rejected and the region where it is rejected. For a one-tailed test, there is only one critical value, such as 1.65. For a two-tailed test, there are two critical values — one in each tail — such as −1.96 and +1.96.

Hypothesis A statement about the value of a population parameter. Examples: 40.7 percent of all persons 65 years old and older live alone. The mean number of persons per family is 3.33.

Hypothesis testing A statistical procedure, based on sample evidence and probability theory, used to determine whether the statement about the population parameter is a reasonable statement.

One-tailed test Used when the alternate hypothesis states a direction, such as H_1: $\mu > 40$. Here the rejection region is only in one tail (the right tail).

Proportion A fraction or percentage of a sample or a population having a particular trait. If 5 out of 50 in a sample liked a new cereal, the proportion is 5/50, or .10.

***p*-value** The probability of getting a value of the test statistic at least as extreme as the one found in the sample data when the null hypothesis is true.

Two-tailed test Used when the alternate hypothesis does not state a direction, such as H_1: $\mu \neq \$75$, read "the population mean is not equal to $75." There is a region of rejection in each tail.

Type I error Occurs when a true H_0 is rejected.

Type II error Occurs when a false H_0 is accepted.

▌ Exercises

Part I — Multiple Choice

1. Each new employee is given an identification number. The personnel files are arranged sequentially starting with employee number 0001. To sample the employees, the number 0153 was first selected. Then numbers 0253, 0353, 0453, and so on became members of the sample. This type of sampling is called:
   a. Simple random sampling.
   b. Systematic sampling.
   c. Stratified random sampling.
   d. Cluster sampling.
   e. None of these is correct.

2. You divide a precinct into blocks. Then you select 12 blocks at random and concentrate your sampling efforts in those 12 blocks. This type of sampling is called:
   a. Simple random sampling.
   b. Systematic sampling.
   c. Stratified random sampling.
   d. Cluster sampling.
   e. Nonprobability sampling.

3. "Sampling error" as used in statistical inference:
   a. Indicates that a Type I error has been made.
   b. Indicates that a Type II error has been made.
   c. Is the difference between a sample statistic and its corresponding population parameter.
   d. Indicates that the z test must be used.
   e. None of these is correct.

4. Of 180 calculators sampled, 5 were defective. The proportion of defects is found by:
   a. $\dfrac{\text{Number of defects in sample}}{\text{Number sampled}}$
   b. $n = \left(\dfrac{z \cdot s}{E}\right)^2$
   c. $s/\sqrt{n}$
   d. $\dfrac{X_1 + X_2}{n_1 + n_2}$
   e. None of these is correct.

5. The endpoints of a confidence interval are called:
   a. Confidence levels.
   b. The test statistics.
   c. The degrees of confidence.
   d. The confidence limits.
   e. None of these is correct.

6. If a one-tailed test is used, and the level of significance is .01, the critical value is either:
   a. -1.96 or $+1.96$.
   b. -1.65 or $+1.65$.
   c. -2.58 or $+2.58$.
   d. 0 or 1.
   e. None of these is correct.

7. A Type II error is committed if we:
   a. Reject a true null hypothesis.
   b. Accept a true alternate hypothesis.
   c. Reject a true alternate hypothesis.
   d. Accept both the null and alternate hypotheses at the same time.
   e. None of these is correct.

8. The hypotheses are H_0: $\mu = 240$ pounds of pressure; H_1: $\mu \neq 240$ pounds of pressure.
   a. A one-tailed test is being applied.
   b. A two-tailed test is being applied.
   c. A three-tailed test is being applied.
   d. The wrong test is being applied.
   e. None of these is correct.

9. The .01 significance level is used in an experiment, and a one-tailed test with the rejection region in the lower tail is applied. Computed z is -1.8. This indicates:
   a. H_0 should not be rejected.
   b. We should reject H_0 and accept H_1.
   c. We should take a larger sample.
   d. We should have used the .05 level of significance.
   e. None of these is correct.

10. To test a hypothesis involving proportions, both $n\pi$ and $n(1 - \pi)$ should:
    a. Be at least 30.
    b. Be at least 5.
    c. Lie in the range from 0 to 1.
    d. Be at least -2.58.
    e. None of these is correct.

Part II — Problems

11. A machine is programmed to produce tennis balls so that the mean bounce is 36 inches when the ball is dropped from a platform. The supervisor suspects that the mean bounce has changed and is less than 36 inches. An experiment is conducted using 42 tennis balls. The 5 percent significance level is to be used to test the hypothesis. The sample mean was computed to be 35.5 inches and the standard deviation of the sample 0.9 inches. Is the supervisor correct?

12. Research by the Illinois Banking Corp. home office revealed that only 8 percent of the corporation's customers wait more than five minutes to do their banking during rush hours. They consider this a reasonable percent and will add no new part-time tellers unless the proportion becomes significantly greater than 8 percent. One branch manager believes that more than 8 percent of customers wait more than five minutes, and she requested additional help during rush hours. The home office decided to test the hypothesis at the 1 percent level. A random sample of 100 incoming customers were timed, and it was found that 10 waited more than five minutes.
    a. State the null and alternate hypotheses.
    b. State the level of significance.
    c. Give the formula for the test statistic.
    d. State the decision rule.
    e. Do the necessary calculations and arrive at a decision about the null hypothesis.
    f. Explain the difference between the sample proportion and the hypothesized population proportion.

13. You are updating a study of the errors in the company's invoices. The study made several years ago revealed that 5 percent of the invoices contained at least one error. You decide to use the .05 level, and the error in your prediction is not to exceed plus or minus 2 percent of the population proportion.
    a. How many invoices should be examined?
    b. Suppose the sample size you computed in part (a) would be too time-consuming. What could you do to reduce the sample size?

14. You want to determine the mean amount sports fans spend on snacks and drinks at a professional football game. You decide to use the .01 level and estimate the mean within plus or minus 20 cents. How many fans should be sampled if the standard deviation of a pilot survey was 50 cents?

15. A firm with plants in two metropolitan areas adjusts the hourly wages paid their employees in one area if there is a significant difference between the two population mean hourly wages. Based on the following sample data, is there a difference between the two mean wages? To solve, answer these questions:
    a. What are the null and alternate hypotheses?
    b. Is this a one-tailed or a two-tailed test? Why?
    c. What is the test statistic?
    d. Using the .05 level, what is the critical value or values?
    e. What is your decision regarding the null hypothesis?

Metropolitan Area	Sample Mean Hourly Wage	Sample Standard Deviation	Number in Sample
Bradenton	$10.92	$0.78	180
Venice	$11.05	$0.39	200

16. A wholesale automobile parts distributor has warehouses in Chicago and Dallas. Although perpetual inventories are taken, the number of items on the shelves and the number stored in the computer records are sometimes off by a few items. For example, if computer records indicate there are 122 boxes of GE #5 headlight bulbs on the shelf, but a count revealed 124, the computer record for that item is in error. An experiment is to be conducted to find whether there is a difference between the proportion of items in error in Chicago and the proportion of items in error in the Dallas warehouse.
   a. State the null and alternate hypotheses.
   b. Is this a one-tailed or a two-tailed test? Why?
   c. Give the formula for the test statistic.
   d. Using the .05 level, state the decision rule.
   e. A sample of 200 automotive items in the Chicago warehouse revealed that the computer records and the count did not differ for 180 of the 200 items. A random sample of 100 items in the Dallas warehouse revealed that the computer records and the shelf count did not differ for 87 of the 100 items. What decision should be made regarding the null hypothesis? Explain.

▌ Cases

A.   Century National Bank

Refer to the description of the Century National Bank at the end of the Review of Chapters 1–4 on page 139. When Mr. Selig took over as president of Century several years ago, the use of debit cards was just beginning. He would like an update on the use of these cards. Develop a 95 percent confidence interval for the proportion of customers using these cards. On the basis of the confidence interval, is it reasonable to conclude that more than half of the customers use a debit card? Interpret the results.

With many other options available, customers no longer let their money sit in a checking account. For many years the mean checking balance has been $1,600. Does the sample data indicate that the mean account balance has declined from this value?

Recent years have also seen an increase in the use of ATM machines. When Mr. Selig took over the bank, the mean number of transactions per month per customer was 8; now he believes it has increased to more than 10. In fact, the advertising agency that prepares TV commercials for Century would like to use this on the new commercial being designed. Is there sufficient evidence to conclude that the mean number of transactions per customer is more than 10 per month? What is the *p*-value? Could the advertising agency say the mean is more than 9 per month?

B.   Klein's Marking Research

Marsh and Kazmaier's are old and bitter rivals for the grocery business in the Los Angeles area. Each sponsors many commercials on radio and TV claiming the lowest prices. Recently they have become involved in a lawsuit over the right to claim the "lowest prices in town." As part of the trial, Klein's Marketing Research, Inc. is hired to make an impartial study. To begin, the research firm, using a one-week shopping plan (grocery list), makes identical purchases at a sample of stores. The total costs of the shopping plan are shown below. What can you conclude? Write a report summarizing the results.

Marsh

$127.23	$125.63	$132.39	$128.43	$133.83	$131.28	$138.58
129.16	129.99	140.09	132.48	123.35	121.63	130.71
129.38	136.56	127.39	137.74	129.18	132.75	131.51
129.68	126.08	135.94	123.77	120.79	128.67	137.28
134.82	133.34	136.91	129.12	136.16	135.64	133.33

Kazmaier's

$132.53	$133.19	$145.15	$138.22	$137.61	$129.36	$125.79
126.25	140.97	135.23	128.22	126.48	133.62	141.07
132.15	135.11	131.97	127.37	133.08	134.04	127.98
134.41	130.61	140.77	124.42	131.95	132.36	133.69
136.86	128.50	129.72	130.55	125.10	132.49	129.44
134.47	129.94	141.42				

C.   Levenson Brothers Department Store

Banks, financial institutions, department stores, and financial planners, as well as psychologists are concerned with the amount of debt in the United States. In 1996 the amount of credit offered by banks and other financial institutions totaled more than $1.02 trillion. The average credit card holder carries a balance of $3,900 on each credit card and only about one third of the customers pay their balances at the end of the month. Levenson Brothers, Inc., located at the corner of Liberty Street and Second Avenue in downtown Warren, is a full-line department store. They sell such items as stereo equipment, perfume, men's shirts, ladies' dresses, watches, children's apparel, and so forth. They also offer their own credit card. The conditions on the credit card are 18 percent interest on the unpaid balance and no interest if the account is paid at the end of the month. Bill Levenson, Vice-President of Finance at Levenson

Brothers, would like to know how customers at Levenson Brothers compare to the national statistics. Do Levenson Brothers' customers have lower balances? Do more customers pay off their balances at the end of the month? A random sample of 50 card holders at Levenson Brothers revealed the following balances at the end of last month. Also included is information on whether the customer paid the entire balance the previous month (1 = yes, 0 = no). Write a brief report summarizing the Levenson Brothers experience.

Customer	Balance	Paid	Customer	Balance	Paid
1	$2,354.01	0	13	534.29	0
2	2,844.38	0	14	421.74	0
3	845.17	0	15	815.26	0
4	147.70	1	16	2,014.56	0
5	3,041.68	1	17	420.92	1
6	200.92	0	18	240.66	0
7	32.65	1	19	1,152.86	1
8	3,554.87	0	20	188.96	0
9	534.03	0	21	55.28	0
10	1,615.75	0	22	287.51	1
11	17.64	0	23	71.94	0
12	387.75	1	24	1,011.26	1

Customer	Balance	Paid	Customer	Balance	Paid
25	24.52	0	38	1,641.63	1
26	$2,425.20	0	39	1,088.54	0
27	1,369.85	0	40	74.33	1
28	3,393.34	0	41	156.38	1
29	105.12	1	42	1,703.64	0
30	1,557.37	0	43	2,436.08	0
31	298.07	0	44	1,726.08	1
32	1,061.88	1	45	2,140.75	1
33	2,202.18	0	46	903.75	0
34	1,078.99	0	47	697.12	0
35	85.25	1	48	522.20	0
36	538.45	0	49	1,663.70	1
37	546.23	0	50	1,469.91	1

Chapter Ten

Tests of Hypothesis

Small Samples

GOALS

When you have completed this chapter, you will be able to

ONE
Describe the characteristics of Student's *t* distribution.

TWO
Understand the difference between dependent and independent samples.

THREE
Understand the assumptions necessary to conduct a test of hypothesis regarding a population mean when the number of observations is small.

FOUR
Conduct a test of hypothesis about a population mean.

FIVE
Conduct a test of hypothesis about the difference in the means of two independent samples.

SIX
Conduct a test of hypothesis regarding the mean difference between paired observations.

Two chemical solutions designed to increase the life of CDs were developed. Sample disks were treated, with results in hours given for both. At the .10 significance level, can we conclude that there is a difference in the length of time the two types of treatment lasted? (See Goal 5 and Exercise 40.)

❚ Introduction

Chapter 9 began our study of hypothesis testing. In that chapter we introduced statistical hypothesis testing. In that chapter the standard normal distribution, that is the *z* distribution, was used as the test statistic. To employ the *z* distribution, we need either to know the population standard deviation (σ) or to have a large sample (at least 30 observations). In many situations, however, σ is unknown and the number of observations in the sample is less than 30. We can use the sample standard deviation *s* as an estimate of σ, but we cannot use the *z* distribution as the test statistic. The appropriate test statistic is **Student's *t*,** or just the ***t* distribution,** as it is usually called. When we use Student's *t* distribution, we assume that the population is normally distributed.

To begin this chapter we will describe the characteristics of the *t* distribution. Then we will discuss three hypothesis testing situations where it is appropriate as the test statistic.

❚ Characteristics of Student's *t* Distribution

Student's *t* distribution was developed by William S. Gossett. He was a brewmaster for the Guinness Brewery in Ireland and published it in 1908 using the pen name "Student." Gossett was concerned with the exact behavior of

$$\frac{\overline{X} - \mu}{s/\sqrt{n}}$$

when *s* had to be used as an estimator of σ. He was especially worried about the discrepancy between *s* and σ when *s* was calculated from a very small sample. The *t* distribution and the standard normal distribution are shown graphically in Chart 10–1. Note particularly that the *t* distribution is flatter, more spread out, than the normal *z* distribution.

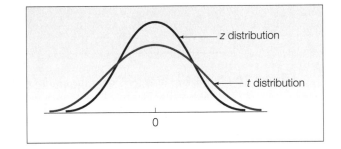

Chart 10–1   The Standard Normal Distribution and Student's *t* Distribution

The following characteristics of the *t* distribution are based on the assumption that the population of interest is normal, or nearly normal.

Characteristics of the t *distribution*

1. It is, like the *z* distribution, a continuous distribution.
2. It is, like the *z* distribution, bell-shaped and symmetrical.
3. There is not one *t* distribution, but rather a "family" of *t* distributions. All have the same mean of zero, but their standard deviations differ according to the sample size *n*. There is a *t* distribution for a sample size of 20, another for a sample size of 22, and so on.
4. The *t* distribution is more spread out and flatter at the center than is the standard normal distribution (see Chart 10–1). As the sample size increases, however, the *t* distribution approaches the standard normal distribution.

As noted, Student's *t* distribution has a greater spread than the *z* distribution. As a result, the critical values of *t* for a given level of significance are larger in magnitude than the corresponding *z* critical values. Chart 10–2 shows the rejection region for a one-tailed test using the .05 level of significance. The critical value for the *z* test is 1.65, but for *t* it is 2.132. (Determining the critical *t* value of 2.132 will be discussed shortly.)

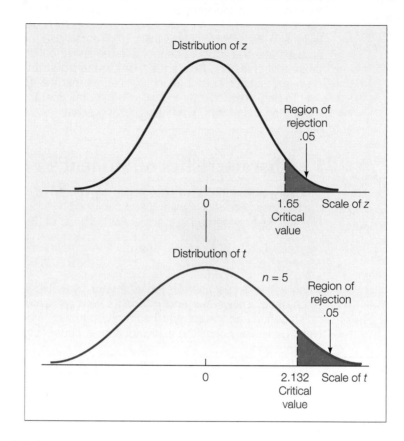

Chart 10–2   Regions of Rejection for the *z* and *t* Distributions, .05 Level of Significance, One-Tailed Test

Of what importance is the fact that the critical value for a given level of significance is greater for small samples than for large samples? The following statements hold true for small samples (which employ the *t* distribution): (1) The confidence interval will be wider than for large samples using the *z* distribution. (2) The region where H_0 is not rejected is wider than for large samples using the *z* distribution. (3) A larger computed *t* value will be needed to reject the null hypothesis than for large samples using *z*. In other words, because there is more variability in sample means computed from smaller samples, we have less confidence in the resulting estimates and are less apt to reject the null hypothesis.

▌ A Test for the Population Mean

Suppose we want to compare a sample mean with a hypothesized population mean, and the number of observations in the sample is less than 30. We can assume that the population is approximately normal, but the population standard deviation, σ, is not known. We can substitute *s,* the sample standard deviation, for the population standard deviation, but we will need to use the *t* distribution as the test statistic. The following example will show the details of the test.

| **Example** | The claims department at McFarland Insurance Company reports that the mean cost to process a claim, handle all the paperwork, pay the investigator, and so on is $60. An industry comparison showed this amount was larger than most other insurance companies, so they instituted cost-cutting measures. To evaluate the effect of the cost-cutting measures, MacFarland selected a random sample of 26 claims and found the mean of this sample was $57 and the standard deviation $10. At the |

.01 significance level should they conclude the cost-cutting measures actually reduced the cost? Or, should they conclude that the difference of $3 between the sample mean ($57) and the population mean ($60) is due to chance?

Solution

The usual five-step hypothesis-testing procedure is used.

Step 1: State the Null and the Alternate Hypothesis   The null hypothesis H_0, is that the population mean is at least $60. The alternate hypothesis, H_1, is that the population mean is less than $60. This is written:

H_0: $\mu \geq$ $60

H_1: $\mu <$ $60

The test is *one-tailed* because we want to determine whether there has been a *reduction* in cost. The inequality in the alternate hypothesis points to the region of rejection in the left tail of the distribution.

Step 2: Select the Level of Significance   The .01 level is to be used.

Step 3: Give the Test Statistic   The test statistic is Student's *t* distribution because (1) the population standard deviation is unknown, and (2) the sample size is small (under 30). The formula for *t* is:

ONE SAMPLE TEST OF MEAN	$t = \dfrac{\bar{X} - \mu}{s/\sqrt{n}}$	**[10–1]**

Step 4: Formulate the Decision Rule   The critical values of *t* are given in Appendix F, and a portion of that appendix is shown in Table 10–1. (Appendix F is also repeated on the back inside cover of the text.) The far left column of the table is labeled "Degrees of Freedom, *df.*" The number of degrees of freedom is the total number of observations in the sample minus the number of samples, written $n - 1$. In this case the number of observations in the sample is 26, so there are $26 - 1 =$

25 degrees of freedom.[1] To find the critical value, first locate the row with the appropriate degrees of freedom. This row is shaded in Table 10–1. Next, determine whether the test is one-tailed or two-tailed. In this case, we have a one-tailed test. So find the portion of the table that is labeled "one-tailed." Locate the column with the selected significance level. In this example the significance level is .01. Move down the column labeled ".01" until it intersects the row with 25 degrees of freedom. The value is 2.485. Because this is a one-tailed test and the rejection region is in the left tail, the critical value is negative. The decision rule is to reject H_0 if the value of t is less than -2.485. This is shown schematically in Chart 10–3.

Table 10–1 A Portion of the t Distribution Table

			Critical Values of t			
		Level of Significance for One-Tailed Test				
Degrees of Freedom,	.10	.05	.025	.01	.005	.0005
		Level of Significance for Two-Tailed Test				
df	.620	.10	.05	.02	.01	.001
21	1.323	1.721	2.080	2.518	2.831	3.819
22	1.321	1.717	2.074	2.508	2.819	3.792
23	1.319	1.714	2.069	2.500	2.807	3.767
24	1.318	1.711	2.064	2.492	2.797	3.745
25	1.316	1.708	2.060	2.485	2.787	3.725
26	1.315	1.706	2.056	2.479	2.779	3.707
27	1.314	1.703	2.052	2.473	2.771	3.690
28	1.313	1.701	2.048	2.467	2.763	3.674

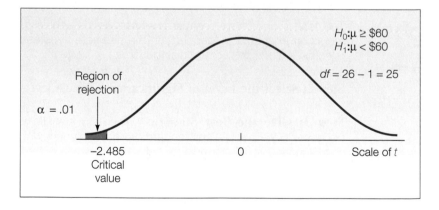

Chart 10–3 Rejection Region, t Distribution, .01 Significance Level

---

[1]In brief summary, because sample statistics are being used, it is necessary to determine the number of variables that are *free to vary*. To illustrate: Assume that the mean of four numbers is known to be 5. The four numbers are 7, 4, 1, and 8. The deviations of these numbers from the mean must total 0. The deviations of $+2$, -1, -4, and $+3$ do total 0. If the deviations of $+2$, -1, and -4 are known, then the value of $+3$ is fixed (restricted) in order to satisfy the condition that the sum of the deviations must equal 0. Thus, 1 degree of freedom is lost in a sampling problem involving the standard deviation of the sample because one number (the arithmetic mean) is known.

Step 5: Compute *t* and Arrive at a Decision   Recall that *t* is computed by formula (10–1):

$$t = \frac{\overline{X} - \mu}{s/\sqrt{n}}$$

with $n - 1$ degrees of freedom, where:

$\overline{X}$ is the mean of the sample.
μ is the hypothesized population mean.
s is the standard deviation of the sample.
n is the sample size.

In this problem:

$\overline{X} = \$57$, the sample mean.
$\mu = \$60$, the hypothesized population mean.
$s = \$10$, the sample standard deviation.
$n = 26$, the number of items in the sample.

The value of *t* is -1.530, found by:

$$t = \frac{\overline{X} - \mu}{s/\sqrt{n}} = \frac{\$57 - \$60}{\$10/\sqrt{26}} = -1.530$$

Because -1.530 lies in the region to the right of the critical value of -2.485, the null hypothesis is not rejected at the .01 significance level. There is not a statistically significant difference between $\overline{X}$ and μ. This indicates that the cost-cutting measures have not reduced the mean cost per claim to less than $60 based on the sample results. The difference of $3 between the sample mean and the population mean is due to chance.

SELF-REVIEW 10–1

From past records it is known that the mean life of a battery used in a digital clock is 305 days. The lives of the batteries are normally distributed. The battery was recently modified to last longer. A sample of 20 modified batteries were tested. It was discovered that the mean life was 311 days, and the sample standard deviation was 12 days. At the .05 level of significance, did the modification increase the mean life of the battery?

(a) State the null and alternate hypotheses.
(b) Show the decision rule graphically.
(c) Compute *t* and reach a decision. Briefly summarize your findings.

Exercises

1. The following hypotheses are given:

   $H_0: \mu \leq 10$

   $H_1: \mu > 10$

   For a random sample of 10 observations the sample mean was 12 and the sample standard deviation 3. Using the .05 significance level:
   a. State the decision rule.
   b. Compute the value of the test statistic.
   c. What is your decision regarding the null hypothesis?

2. You are given the following hypotheses:

H_0: $\mu = 400$

H_1: $\mu \neq 400$

For a random sample of 12 observations, the sample mean was 407 and the sample standard deviation 6. Using the .01 significance level:
a. State the decision rule.
b. Compute the value of the test statistic.
c. What is your decision regarding the null hypothesis?

3. The Rocky Mountain district sales manager of John C. Rath, Inc., a college book publishing company, claims that each of his sales representatives makes 40 calls on professors per week. Several reps said that this estimate is too low. To investigate, a random sample of 28 sales representatives revealed that the mean number of calls made last week was 42. The standard deviation of the sample was 2.1 calls. At the .05 level of significance, can we conclude that the mean number of calls per salesperson per week is more than 40?

4. The management of White Industries is considering a new method of assembling its three-wheel golf cart. The present method requires 42.3 minutes, on the average, to assemble a cart. The new method was introduced, and a time and motion study was conducted on a random sample of 24 carts. The mean assembly time was computed to be 40.6 minutes. The standard deviation of the sample was 2.7 minutes. Using the .10 level of significance, can it be said that the assembly time under the new method is significantly less than before?

5. The records of Yellowstone Trucks revealed that the mean life of a set of spark plugs is 22,100 miles. The distribution of the life of the plugs is approximately normal. A spark plug manufacturer claimed that its plugs have a mean life in excess of 22,100 miles. The fleet owner purchased a large number of sets. A sample of 18 sets revealed that the sample mean life was 23,400 miles and the sample standard deviation was 1,500 miles. Is there enough evidence to substantiate the manufacturer's claim at the .05 level?

6. Fast Service, a chain of automotive tune-up shops, advertises that its personnel can change the oil, replace the oil filter, and lubricate any standard automobile in 15 minutes, on the average. The National Business Bureau received complaints from customers that service takes considerably longer. To check the Fast Service claim, the bureau had service done on 21 unmarked cars. The mean service time was 18 minutes, and the standard deviation of the sample was 1 minute. Use the .05 level to check the reasonableness of the Fast Service claim.

In the previous examples, the mean and standard deviation of the sample were given in the problem. The following example requires that they be computed from the sample observations.

Example

The mean length of a small counterbalance bar is 43 millimeters. There is concern that the adjustments of the machine producing the bars have changed. The null hypothesis is that there has been no change in the mean length ($\mu = 43$). The alternate hypothesis is that there has been a change ($\mu \neq 43$). Test at the .02 level.

Twelve bars were randomly selected from production. Their lengths, in millimeters, were:

| 42 | 39 | 42 | 45 | 43 | 40 | 39 | 41 | 40 | 42 | 43 | 42 |

Solution

We begin by stating the null hypothesis and the alternate hypothesis.

$$H_0: \mu = 43$$
$$H_1: \mu \neq 43$$

The alternate hypothesis does not state a direction, so the test is two-tailed. There are 11 degrees of freedom, found by $n - 1 = 12 - 1 = 11$. Then — referring to Appendix F for a two-tailed test at the .02 level with 11 degrees of freedom — the critical value is 2.718. The critical values for the .02 level are shown in Chart 10–4. The decision rule is therefore to reject the null hypothesis if the computed t is to the left of -2.718 or to the right of 2.718.

STATISTICS IN ACTION

There is a difference between *statistically significant* and *practically significant*. To explain, suppose we develop a new diet pill and test it on 100,000 people. We conclude that the typical person taking the pill for two years lost one pound. Do you think many people would be interested in taking the pill to lose one pound? The results of using the new pill were statistically significant but not practically significant.

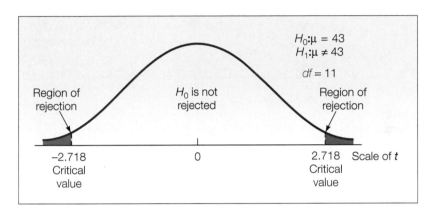

$$H_0: \mu = 43$$
$$H_1: \mu \neq 43$$

$df = 11$

Region of rejection — H_0 is not rejected — Region of rejection

-2.718 0   2.718   Scale of t
Critical value   Critical value

Chart 10–4   Regions of Rejection, Two-Tailed Test, Student's t Distribution, $\alpha = .02$

The standard deviation of the sample can be determined either by squaring the deviations from the mean or by an equivalent formula using the squares of the actual values. The two formulas from Chapter 4, (4–5) and (4–7), are:

Using squared deviations from mean:

$$s = \sqrt{\frac{\Sigma(X - \bar{X})^2}{n - 1}}$$

Using squares of raw data:

$$s = \sqrt{\frac{\Sigma X^2 - \dfrac{(\Sigma X)^2}{n}}{n - 1}}$$

The necessary calculations for these two methods are shown in Table 10–2 on the next page. The mean, $\bar{X}$, is 41.5 millimeters, and the standard deviation, s, is 1.78 millimeters.

Now we are ready to compute t, using formula (10–1).

$$t = \frac{\bar{X} - \mu}{s/\sqrt{n}} = \frac{41.5 - 43.0}{1.78/\sqrt{12}} = -2.92$$

The null hypothesis that the population mean is 43 millimeters is rejected at the .02 level because the computed t of -2.92 lies in the area of the tail beyond the critical value of -2.718. The alternate hypothesis that the mean is not 43 millimeters is accepted. Based on the sample results, we conclude the machine is out of adjustment.

Sample standard deviation computed using two methods

Table 10–2   Calculations of the Sample Standard Deviation

X (mm)	$X - \bar{X}$	$(X - \bar{X})^2$	X^2
42	0.5	0.25	1,764
39	-2.5	6.25	1,521
42	0.5	0.25	1,764
45	3.5	12.25	2,025
43	1.5	2.25	1,849
40	-1.5	2.25	1,600
39	-2.5	6.25	1,521
41	-0.5	0.25	1,681
40	-1.5	2.25	1,600
42	0.5	0.25	1,764
43	1.5	2.25	1,849
42	0.5	0.25	1,764
498	0	35.00	20,702

$$\bar{X} = \frac{498}{12} = 41.5 \text{ mm}$$

Squared deviation method:

$$s = \sqrt{\frac{\Sigma(X - \bar{X})^2}{n - 1}} = \sqrt{\frac{35}{12 - 1}} = 1.78$$

Squaring raw data:

$$s = \sqrt{\frac{\Sigma X^2 - \frac{(\Sigma X)^2}{n}}{n - 1}} = \sqrt{\frac{20,702 - \frac{(498)^2}{12}}{12 - 1}}$$

$$= 1.78$$

A Computer Solution

The MINITAB statistical software system, used in earlier chapters, provides an efficient way of conducting a one-sample test of hypothesis for a population mean. The steps to generate the following output are shown in the Computer Commands section at the end of the chapter. Note that the computed value of t (-2.91) is approximately the same as the value found using formula (10–1) (-2.92). The slight difference is due to rounding.

```
T Test of the Mean
Test of mu = 43.000 vs mu not = 43.000

Variable      N      Mean      StDev     SE Mean        T           P
Length       12     41.500     1.784      0.515      -2.91      0.014
```

An additional feature of MINITAB, and most other statistical software packages, is to output the p-value, which gives additional information on the null hypothesis. The p-value is the probability of a t value as large or larger than that computed, given that the null hypothesis is true. In this case, the p-value of .014 is the likelihood of a t value of -2.91 or less plus the likelihood of a t value of 2.91 or larger, given a population mean of 43. Thus, comparing the p-value to the significance level tells us whether the null hypothesis was close to being rejected, barely rejected, and so on.

To explain further, refer to the diagram at the top of the next page, in which the p-value of .014 is shown in green and the significance level is the orange area plus the green area. Because the p-value of .014 is less than the significance level of .02, the null hypothesis is rejected. Had the p-value been larger than the significance level—say, .06, .19, or .57 — the null hypothesis would not be rejected. If the significance level had initially been selected as .01, the null hypothesis would not be rejected.

In the preceding example the alternate hypothesis was two-tailed, so there were rejection areas in both the upper and the lower tails. To determine the p-value, it was necessary to determine the area to the left of -2.91 for a t distribution with 11 degrees of freedom and add to it the value to the right of 2.91, also with 11 degrees of freedom.

What if we were conducting a one-tailed test, so that the entire rejection region would be in either the upper or the lower tail? In that case, we would report the area from only the one tail. In the counterbalance example, if H_1 were stated as $\mu < 43$, the inequality would point to the left. Thus, we would have reported the p-value as the area to the left of -2.91. This value is .007, found by .014/2. Thus, the p-value for a one-tailed test would be .007.

A software package such as MINITAB has extensive tables to accurately estimate p-values. How can we estimate a p-value without a computer? To illustrate, recall that, in the example regarding the length of a counterbalance, we rejected the null hypothesis that $\mu = 43$ and accepted the alternate hypothesis that $\mu \neq 43$. The significance level was .02, so logically the p-value is less than .02. To estimate the p-value more accurately, go to Appendix F and find the row with 11 degrees of freedom. The computed t value of 2.91 is between 2.718 and 3.106. (A portion of Appendix F is reproduced as Table 10–3.) The two-tailed significance level corresponding to 2.718 is .02 and for 3.106 it is .01. Therefore, the p-value is between .01 and .02. The usual practice is to report that the p-value is *less* than the larger of the two significance levels. So we would report that "the p-value is less than .02." MINITAB reports the exact p-value as .014.

Table 10–3 A Portion of Student's *t* Distribution

	Level of Significance for One-Tailed Test					
	0.100	0.050	0.025	0.010	0.005	0.0005
	Level of Significance for Two-Tailed Test					
df	0.20	0.10	0.05	0.02	0.01	0.001
⋮	⋮	⋮	⋮	⋮	⋮	⋮
6	1.440	1.943	2.447	3.143	3.707	5.959
7	1.415	1.895	2.365	2.998	3.499	5.408
8	1.397	1.860	2.306	2.896	3.355	5.041
9	1.383	1.833	2.262	2.821	3.250	4.781
10	1.372	1.812	2.228	2.764	3.169	4.587
11	1.363	1.796	2.201	2.718	3.106	4.437
12	1.356	1.782	2.179	2.681	3.055	4.318
13	1.350	1.771	2.160	2.650	3.012	4.221
14	1.345	1.761	2.145	2.624	2.977	4.410
15	1.341	1.753	2.131	2.602	2.947	4.073
⋮	⋮	⋮	⋮	⋮	⋮	⋮

SELF-REVIEW 10–2

A machine is set to fill a small bottle with 9.0 grams of medicine. It is claimed that the mean weight is less than 9.0 grams. The hypothesis is to be tested at the .01 level. A sample revealed these weights (in grams): 9.2, 8.7, 8.9, 8.6, 8.8, 8.5, 8.7, and 9.0.

(a) State the null and alternate hypotheses.

(b) How many degrees of freedom are there?

(c) Give the decision rule.

(d) Compute t and arrive at a decision.

(e) Estimate the p-value.

▌ Exercises

7. The following null and alternate hypotheses are being considered:

H_0: $\mu \geq 20$

H_1: $\mu < 20$

A random sample of five observations was: 18, 15, 12, 19, and 21. At the .01 significance level, can we conclude that the population mean is less than 20?
a. State the decision rule.
b. Compute the value of the test statistic.
c. What is your decision about the null hypothesis?
d. Estimate the p-value.

8. The following null and alternate hypotheses are to be considered:

H_0: $\mu = 100$

H_1: $\mu \neq 100$

The following random sample of six observations was selected: 118, 105, 112, 119, 105, and 111. At the .05 significance level, can we conclude that the population mean is different from 100?
a. State the decision rule.
b. Compute the value of the test statistic.
c. What is your decision about the null hypothesis?
d. Estimate the p-value.

9. Experience raising New Jersey Red chickens revealed the average weight of the chickens at age five months to be 4.35 pounds. The weights are normally distributed. In an effort to increase their weight, a special additive was mixed with the chicken feed. The subsequent weights of a sample of five-month-old chickens were (in pounds): 4.41, 4.37, 4.33,

4.35, 4.30, 4.39, 4.36, 4.38, 4.40, and 4.39. At the .01 level, has the special additive increased the weight of the chickens? Estimate the *p*-value.

10. The liquid chlorine added to swimming pools to combat algae has a relatively short shelf life before it loses its effectiveness. Records indicate that the mean shelf life of a 5-gallon jug of chlorine is 2,160 hours (90 days). As an experiment, Holdlonger was added to the chlorine to find whether it would increase the shelf life. A sample of nine jugs of chlorine had these shelf lives (in hours): 2,159, 2,170, 2,180, 2,179, 2,160, 2,167, 2,171, 2,181, and 2,185. At the .025 level, has Holdlonger increased the shelf life of the chlorine? Estimate the *p*-value.

11. Wyoming fisheries contend that the mean number of cutthroat trout caught during a full day of fly-fishing on the Snake, Buffalo, and other rivers and streams in the Jackson Hole area is 4.0. To make their yearly update, the fishery personnel asked a sample of fly-fishermen to keep a count of the number caught during the day. The numbers were: 4, 4, 3, 2, 6, 8, 7, 1, 9, 3, 1, and 6. At the .05 level, is there convincing evidence that the number of trout caught daily has increased? Estimate the *p*-value.

12. Hugger Polls contends that an agent conducts a mean of 53 in-depth home surveys every week. A streamlined survey form has been introduced, and Hugger wants to evaluate its effectiveness. The number of in-depth surveys conducted during a week by a random sample of agents are: 53, 57, 50, 55, 58, 54, 60, 52, 59, 62, 60, 60, 51, 59, and 56. At the .05 level of significance, can we conclude that the mean number of interviews conducted by the agents is more than 53 per week? Estimate the *p*-value.

▌ Comparing Two Independent Population Means

In the previous section we selected a single random sample and compared the mean of that sample to a hypothesized value of the population mean. That is, we asked the question: Is it likely that a sample with a given mean could have come from a population with the proposed mean? In this section we extend that idea to two samples. The question we investigate is whether the means of the two samples are equal. Or, to put it another way, could the two sample means come from identical populations? To conduct this test, three assumptions are required:

1. The sampled populations are normally or approximately normally distributed.
2. The two populations are independent.
3. The standard deviations of the two populations are equal.

The *t* statistic for the two-sample case is similar to that employed in Chapter 9, formula (9–3), for the *z* statistic, except we require an additional calculation. The two sample variances must be pooled to form a single estimate of the unknown population variance. In essence, we compute a weighted mean of the two sample standard deviations and use this weighted estimate of the population standard deviation. Why do we need to pool the standard deviations? In most cases when the samples each have fewer than 30 observations, the population standard deviations are not known. So we calculate *s*, the sample standard deviation, and substitute it for σ, the population standard deviation. Because we assume that the two populations have equal standard deviations, the best estimate we can make of that value is to combine or pool all the information we have about the value of the population standard deviation.

The following formula is used to pool the sample variances. Notice that two factors are involved: the number of observations in each sample and the sample standard deviations themselves.

POOLED VARIANCE	$$s_p^2 = \frac{(n_1 - 1)(s_1^2) + (n_2 - 1)(s_2^2)}{n_1 + n_2 - 2}$$	**[10–2]**

where:

s_1^2 is the first sample variance.

s_2^2 is the second sample variance.

The value of t is:

TWO-SAMPLE TEST OF MEANS

$$t = \frac{\bar{X}_1 - \bar{X}_2}{\sqrt{s_p^2 \left(\dfrac{1}{n_1} + \dfrac{1}{n_2} \right)}}$$

[10–3]

---

where:

$\bar{X}_1$ is the mean of the first sample.

$\bar{X}_2$ is the mean of the second sample.

n_1 is the number in the first sample.

n_2 is the number in the second sample.

s_p^2 is the pooled estimate of the population variance.

The number of degrees of freedom in the test is equal to the total number of items sampled minus the number of samples. Because there are two samples, there are $n_1 + n_2 - 2$ degrees of freedom.

Example

Owens Lawn Care, Inc. manufactures and assembles lawnmowers, which are shipped to dealers throughout the United States and Canada. Two different procedures have been proposed for mounting the engine on the frame of the lawnmower. The question is: Is there a difference in the mean time to mount the engines on the frames of the lawnmowers? The first procedure was developed by Welles (designated as procedure 1), and the other procedure was developed by Atkins (designated as procedure 2). To evaluate the two methods, it was decided to conduct a time and motion study. A sample of five employees was timed using procedure 1, and six were timed using procedure 2. The results, in minutes, are shown below. Is there a difference in the mean mounting times? Use the .10 significance level.

Procedure 1 (minutes)	Procedure 2 (minutes)
2	3
4	7
9	5
3	8
2	4
	3

Solution

The null hypothesis states there is no difference in mean mounting time between the Welles procedure and the Atkins procedure. The alternate indicates that there is a difference.

H_0: $\mu_1 = \mu_2$

H_1: $\mu_1 \neq \mu_2$

The required assumptions are: (1) The observations in the Welles sample are *independent* of the observations in the Atkins sample, and of each other. (2) The two populations are approximately normal. (3) The two populations have equal standard deviations.

Is there a difference between the mean assembly times using the Welles and the Atkins methods? The degrees of freedom are equal to the total number of items sampled minus the number of samples. In this case that is $n_1 + n_2 - 2$. Five assemblers used the Welles method and six the Atkins method. Thus, there are 9 degrees of freedom, found by $5 + 6 - 2$. The critical values of t, from Appendix F for $df = 9$, a two-tailed test, and the .10 level of significance, are $+1.833$ and -1.833. The decision rule is portrayed graphically in Chart 10–5. We do not reject the null hypothesis if the computed t value falls between -1.833 and $+1.833$. Otherwise, H_0 is rejected.

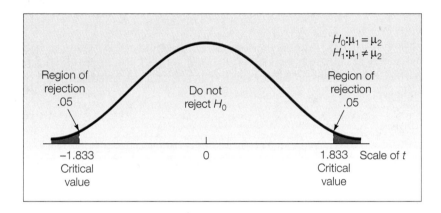

Chart 10–5 Regions of Rejection, Two-Tailed Test (9 degrees of freedom, $\alpha = .10$)

Determining Student's t is accomplished in three steps.

Step 1: Calculate the Sample Standard Deviations.

Procedure 1		Procedure 2	
X_1	X_1^2	X_2	X_2^2
2	4	3	9
4	16	7	49
9	81	5	25
3	9	8	64
2	4	4	16
20	114	3	9
		30	172

$$s_1 = \sqrt{\frac{\Sigma X_1^2 - \frac{(\Sigma X_1)^2}{n_1}}{n_1 - 1}} \qquad s_2 = \sqrt{\frac{\Sigma X_2^2 - \frac{(\Sigma X_2)^2}{n_2}}{n_2 - 1}}$$

$$= \sqrt{\frac{114 - \frac{(20)^2}{5}}{5 - 1}} \qquad = \sqrt{\frac{172 - \frac{(30)^2}{6}}{6 - 1}}$$

$$= 2.9155 \qquad = 2.0976$$

Step 2: Pool the Sample Variances. Applying formula (10–2),

$$s_p^2 = \frac{(n_1 - 1)s_1^2 + (n_2 - 1)s_2^2}{n_1 + n_2 - 2}$$

$$= \frac{(5 - 1)(2.9155)^2 + (6 - 1)(2.0976)^2}{5 + 6 - 2} = 6.2222$$

Step 3: Determine *t*. Using formula (10–3) with $\bar{X}_1 = 20/5 = 4$ and $\bar{X}_2 = 30/6 = 5$.

$$t = \frac{\bar{X}_1 - \bar{X}_2}{\sqrt{s_p^2\left(\frac{1}{n_1} + \frac{1}{n_2}\right)}} = \frac{4 - 5}{\sqrt{6.2222\left(\frac{1}{5} + \frac{1}{6}\right)}} = -0.662$$

The decision is not to reject the null hypothesis, because -0.662 falls in the region between -1.833 and $+1.833$. We conclude that there is no difference in the mean time to mount the engine on the frame between the two methods.

We can also estimate the *p*-value using Appendix F. Locate the row with 9 degrees of freedom and use the significance level for two-tailed tests. Find the *t* value, disregarding the sign, that is closest to our computed value of -0.66. It is 1.383, corresponding to a significance level of .20. So even had we used the 20 percent significance level we would not have rejected the null hypothesis of equal means. We would report that the *p*-value is greater than .20.

Software Example Using Excel

Excel has a procedure called "t-Test: Two-Sample Assuming Equal Variances" that will perform the calculations of formulas (10–2) and (10–3). The data are input in the first two columns of an Excel spreadsheet, labeled "One" and "Two." The output is as follows. The value of *t*, called the "t Stat," is -0.66205, and the actual two-tailed *p*-value is .524526. As we would expect, the *p*-value is larger than the significance level of .10 when the null hypothesis is not rejected.

One	Two			
2	3	t-Test: Two-Sample Assuming Equal Variances		
4	7			
9	5		One	Two
3	8	Mean	4	5
2	4	Variance	8.5	4.4
	3	Observations	5	6
		Pooled Variance	6.22222	
		Hypothesized Mean Difference	0	
		df	9	
		t Stat	-0.66205	
		P(T<=t) one-tail	0.26226	
		t Critical one-tail	1.38303	
		P(T<=t) two-tail	0.52453	
		t Critical two-tail	1.83311	

SELF-REVIEW 10–3

The production supervisor at Corry Steel Company, a manufacturer of steel desks, wants to compare the number of defective desks produced on the day shift with the number produced on the afternoon shift. A sample of the production from 6 day shifts and 8 afternoon shifts revealed the following information.

Day	5	8	7	6	9	7		
Afternoon	8	10	7	11	9	12	14	9

At the .05 significance level, is there a difference in the mean number of defects per shift? Estimate the *p*-value.

▌ Exercises

For Exercises 13 and 14: (a) state the decision rule, (b) compute the pooled estimate of the population variance, (c) compute the test statistic, (d) state your decision about the null hypothesis, (e) estimate the *p*-value.

13. The null hypothesis and the alternate hypothesis are:

    $H_0: \mu_1 = \mu_2$

    $H_1: \mu_1 \neq \mu_2$

    A random sample of 10 observations from one population revealed a sample mean of 23 and a sample deviation of 4. A random sample of 8 observations from another population revealed a sample mean of 26 and a sample standard deviation of 5. At the .05 significance level, is there a difference in the population means?

14. The null hypothesis and the alternate hypothesis are:

    $H_0: \mu_1 = \mu_2$

    $H_1: \mu_1 \neq \mu_2$

    A random sample of 15 observations from the first population revealed a sample mean of 350 and a sample standard deviation of 12. A random sample of 17 observations from the second population revealed a sample mean of 342 and a sample standard deviation of 15. At the .10 significance level, is there a difference in the population means?

15. A sample of scores on an examination given in Statistics 201 are:

Males	72	69	98	66	85	76	79	80	77
Females	81	67	90	78	81	80	76		

    At the .01 significance level, is the mean grade of the women higher than that of the men?

16. A recent study compared the time spent together by single- and dual-earner couples. According to the records kept by the wives during the study, the mean amount of time spent together watching television among the single-earner couples was 61 minutes per day, with a standard deviation of 15.5 minutes. For the dual-earner couples the mean number of minutes spent watching television was 48.4 minutes, with a standard deviation of 18.1 minutes. At the .01 significance level, can we conclude that the single-earner couples on average spend more time watching television together? Fifteen single-earner and 12 dual-earner couples were studied.

17. Ms. Lisa Monnin is the budget director for the New Process Company. She would like to compare the daily travel expenses for the sales staff and the audit staff. She collected the following sample information.

Sales ($)	131	135	146	165	136	142	
Audit ($)	130	102	129	143	149	120	139

At the .10 significance level, can she conclude that the mean daily expenses are greater for the sales staff. What is the *p*-value?

18. The Tampa Bay (Florida) Area Chamber of Commerce wanted to know whether the mean weekly salary of nurses was larger than that of grade school teachers. To investigate, they collected the following sample information. Is it reasonable to conclude that the mean weekly salary of nurses is higher? Use the .01 significance level. What is the *p*-value?

Grade school teachers ($)	545	526	527	575	484	509	502	520	529	530	542	532
Nurses ($)	541	590	521	471	550	559	525	529				

▮ Hypothesis Testing with Dependent Samples

In the previous section, we tested the difference between the means from two independent samples. The difference in the mean time required to mount an engine using the Welles method was compared to the time to mount the engine using the Atkins method. The samples were *independent,* meaning that the sample of assembly times using the Welles method was in no way related to the sample of assembly times using the Atkins method.

There are situations, however, in which the samples are not independent. To put it another way, the samples are **dependent** or related. As an example, Nickel Savings and Loan employs two firms, Schadek Appraisals and Bowyer Real Estate, to appraise the value of the real estate properties on which they make loans. It is important that these two firms are similar in their appraisal values. To review the consistency of the two appraisal firms, Nickel Savings randomly selects ten homes and has both Schadek Appraisals and Bowyer Real Estate appraise the value of the selected homes. For each home, there will be a pair of appraisal values. That is, for the first home there will be an appraised value from Schadek Appraisals and from Bowyer Real Estate. The appraised values depend on, or are related to, the home selected. This is also referred to as a **paired sample.**

For the purpose of hypothesis testing, we are interested in the distribution of the *differences* in the appraised value. Hence, there is only one sample. To put it more formally, we are interested in investigating whether the mean of the distribution of differences in the appraised values is 0. The sample is made up of the *differences* between the appraised values determined by Schadek Appraisals and the values from Bowyer Real Estate. If the two appraisal firms are actually reporting similar estimates, then sometimes Schadek Appraisals will be the higher value and sometimes Bowyer Real Estate will have the higher value. However, the mean of the distribution of differences will be about 0. On the other hand, if one of the firms consistently reports the larger appraisal values, then the mean of the distribution of the differences will not be 0.

We will use the symbol μ_d to indicate the mean of the population of the distribution of differences. The test statistic follows Student's *t* distribution. We calculate the test statistic from the following formula:

PAIRED *t* TEST	$$t = \frac{\bar{d}}{s_d/\sqrt{n}}$$	**[10–4]**

There are $n - 1$ degrees of freedom and

$\bar{d}$ is the mean of the difference between paired or related observations.

s_d is the standard deviation of the distribution of the differences between the paired or related observations.

n is the number of paired observations.

The standard deviation of the differences, s_d, is computed using formula (4–9) except that d is substituted for X. The formula is

$$s_d = \sqrt{\frac{\Sigma d^2 - \frac{(\Sigma d)^2}{n}}{n - 1}}$$

As with the two earlier tests, we assume that the distribution of the population of differences is normal. The following example involving Nickel Savings and Loan and their problem with consistent real estate appraisals will illustrate the details.

Example

Recall that Nickel Savings and Loan wants to compare the two companies they use to appraise the value of residential homes. Nickel Savings selected a sample of ten residential properties and scheduled both firms for an appraisal. The results, reported in $000, are:

Appraised Value ($ thousands)		
Home	Schadek	Bowyer
1	135	128
2	110	105
3	131	119
4	142	140
5	105	98
6	130	123
7	131	127
8	110	115
9	125	122
10	149	145

At the .05 significance level, can we conclude that there is a difference in the mean appraised values of the homes?

Solution

The first step is to state the null and the alternate hypotheses. In this case a two-tailed alternative is appropriate because we are interested in determining whether there is a *difference* in the appraised values. We are not interested in showing whether one particular firm appraises property at a higher value than the other. The question is whether the sample differences in the appraised values could have come from a population with a mean of 0. If the population mean of the differences is 0, then we conclude that there is no mean difference in the appraised values. The null and alternate hypotheses are:

$H_0: \mu_d = 0$

$H_1: \mu_d \neq 0$

There are 10 homes that were appraised by both firms, $n = 10$, and $df = n - 1 = 10 - 1 = 9$. We have a two-tailed test and the significance level is .05. To determine the critical value, go to Appendix F, move across the row with 9 degrees of freedom to the column for a two-tailed test and the .05 significance level. The value at the intersection is 2.262. The decision rule is to reject the null hypothesis if the computed value of t is less than -2.262 or greater than 2.262.

Home	Appraised Value ($ thousands) Schadek	Bowyer	Difference, d	Difference Squared, d^2
1	135	128	7	49
2	110	105	5	25
3	131	119	12	144
4	142	140	2	4
5	105	98	7	49
6	130	123	7	49
7	131	127	4	16
8	110	115	-5	25
9	125	122	3	9
10	149	145	4	16
			46	386

$$\bar{d} = \frac{\Sigma d}{n} = \frac{46}{10} = 4.60$$

$$s_d = \sqrt{\frac{\Sigma d^2 - \frac{(\Sigma d)^2}{n}}{n - 1}} = \sqrt{\frac{386 - \frac{(46)^2}{10}}{10 - 1}} = 4.402$$

Using formula (10–4), the value of t is 3.305, found by:

$$t = \frac{\bar{d}}{s_d/\sqrt{n}} = \frac{4.6}{4.402/\sqrt{10}} = \frac{4.6}{1.3920} = 3.305$$

Because the computed value of t falls in the rejection region beyond the critical value, the null hypothesis is rejected. The population distribution of differences does not have a mean of 0. We conclude that there is a difference in the appraised values of the homes. There is a difference in the appraisors' values. The largest difference of $12,000 is in Home 3. Perhaps that would be an appropriate place to begin the review.

To find the p-value we use Appendix F and the section for a two-tailed test. Move along the row with 9 degrees of freedom and find the values of t that bracket our calculated value. For a .01 significance level, the value of t is 3.250, and for a .001 significance level, the value of t is 4.781. Our computed value of 3.305 falls between these two values. Hence, we report that the p-value is less than .01 and greater than .001. This information is summarized in Table 10–4.

Table 10–4 A Portion of the Student's *t* Distribution

df	\multicolumn{6}{c}{Level of Significance for One-Tailed Test}
	.10	.05	.025	.01	.005	.0005
	\multicolumn{6}{c}{Level of Significance for Two-Tailed Test}
	.20	.10	.05	.02	.01	.001
1	3.078	6.314	12.706	31.821	63.657	636.619
2	1.886	2.920	4.303	6.965	9.925	31.599
3	1.638	2.353	3.182	4.541	5.841	12.924
4	1.533	2.132	2.776	3.747	4.604	8.610
5	1.476	2.015	2.571	3.365	4.032	6.869
6	1.440	1.943	2.447	3.143	3.707	5.959
7	1.415	1.895	2.365	2.998	3.499	5.408
8	1.397	1.860	2.306	2.896	3.355	5.041
9	1.383	1.833	2.262	2.821	3.250	4.781
10	1.372	1.812	2.228	2.764	3.169	4.587
11	1.363	1.796	2.201	2.718	3.106	4.437
12	1.356	1.782	2.179	2.681	3.055	4.318
13	1.350	1.771	2.160	2.650	3.012	4.221
14	1.345	1.761	2.145	2.624	2.977	4.140
15	1.341	1.753	2.131	2.602	2.947	4.073

Comparing Dependent and Independent Samples

Beginning students are often confused by the difference between tests for independent samples (formula [10–3]) and tests for dependent samples (formula [10–4]). How do we tell the difference between dependent and independent samples? There are two types of dependent samples: (1) those characterized by a measurement, an intervention of some type, and then another measurement; and (2) a matching or pairing of the observations. To explain further:

1. The first type of dependent sample is characterized by a measurement followed by an intervention of some kind and then another measurement. Two examples will help to clarify. Suppose we want to show that, by placing speakers in the production area and playing soothing music, we were able to increase production. We begin by selecting a sample of workers and measuring their output under the current conditions. The speakers are then installed in the production area, and then we measure the output of the same workers again. There are two measurements, before placing the speakers in the production area and after. The intervention is placing speakers in the production area. A second example involves an educational firm that offers courses designed to increase test scores and reading ability. Suppose the firm wants to offer a course that will help high school juniors increase their SAT scores. To begin, each student takes the SAT in the junior year in high school. During the summer between the junior and senior year, they participate in the course that gives them tips on taking tests. Finally, during the fall of their senior year in high school, they retake the SAT. Again the procedure is characterized by a measurement (taking the SAT as a junior), an intervention (the summer workshops), and another measurement (taking the SAT during their senior year).

2. The second type of dependent sample is characterized by matching or pairing observations. Nickel Savings in the previous Example is a dependent sample of this type. They selected a property for appraisal and then had two appraisals on the same property. As a second example, suppose an industrial psychologist is studying the intellectual similarities of newly married couples. To begin, she selects a sample of newlyweds. Next, she administers a standard intelligence test to both the man and woman to determine the difference in the scores. Notice the matching that occurred—comparing the scores of the man and the woman.

Why do we prefer dependent samples over independent samples? The answer is that, by using dependent samples, we are able to reduce the variation in the sampling distribution. To illustrate we will use the Nickel Saving and Loan Example just completed. Suppose we assume that we have two independent samples of real estate property for appraisal and conduct the following test of hypothesis, using formula (10–3). The null and alternate hypotheses are:

$$H_0: \mu_1 = \mu_2$$
$$H_1: \mu_1 \neq \mu_2$$

There are two samples of 10 each, so the total number of degrees of freedom is $10 + 10 - 2 = 18$. From Appendix D, using the .05 significance level, H_0 is rejected if t is less than -2.101 or greater than 2.101.

The mean of the appraised value of the 10 properties by Schadek is $126,800, and the standard deviation is $14,500. For Bowyer Real Estate the mean appraised value is $122,200, and the standard deviation is $14,300. To make the calculations easier we use $000 instead of $. The value of the pooled estimate of the variance from formula (10–2) is

$$s_p^2 = \frac{(n_1 - 1)s_1^2 + (n_2 - 1)s_2^2}{n_1 + n_2} = \frac{(10 - 1)14.5^2 + (10 - 1)14.3^2}{10 - 10 - 2} = 207.37$$

Using formula (10–3), t is 0.714.

$$t = \frac{\bar{X}_1 - \bar{X}_2}{\sqrt{s_p^2\left(\frac{1}{n_1} + \frac{1}{n_2}\right)}} = \frac{126.8 - 122.2}{\sqrt{207.37\left(\frac{1}{10} + \frac{1}{10}\right)}} = \frac{4.60}{6.4403} = 0.714$$

The computed value of t (0.714) is less than 2.101, so the null hypothesis is not rejected. We have failed to show that there is a difference in the mean appraisal value. That is not the same conclusion that we got before! Why does this happen? The numerator is the same in the paired observations test (4.6). However, the denominator is smaller. In the paired test the denominator is 1.3920 (see the calculations on page 370). In the case of the independent samples the denominator is 6.4403. This accounts for the difference in the t values and the difference in the statistical decisions. The denominator measures the standard error of the statistic. When the samples are not paired, two kinds of variation are present: differences between the two appraisal firms and the difference in the value of the real estate. Properties numbered 4 and 10 have relatively high values, whereas number 5 is relatively low. These data show how different the values of the property are, but we are really interested in the difference between the two appraisal firms.

The trick is to pair the values to reduce the variation among the properties. The paired test uses only the difference between the two appraisal firms for the same property. Thus, the paired or dependent statistic focuses on the variation between Schadek Appraisals and Bowyer Real Estate. Thus, its standard error is always smaller. That, in turn, leads to a larger test statistic and a greater chance of rejecting the null hypothesis. So whenever possible you should pair the data.

There is a bit of bad news here. In the paired observations test, the degrees of freedom are half of what they are if the samples are not paired. For the real estate example the degrees of freedom drop from 18 to 9 when the observations are paired. However, in most cases, this is a small price to pay for a better test.

SELF-REVIEW 10–4

Advertisements by Sylph Physical Fitness Center claim that completing their course will result in losing weight. A random sample of 8 recent students showed the following body weights before entering the course and after completing the course. At the .01 significance level, can we conclude that the students lost weight?

Name	Before	After
Hunter	155	154
Cashman	228	207
Mervine	141	147
Massa	162	157
Creola	211	196
Peterson	164	150
Redding	164	150
Poust	172	165

(a) State the null hypothesis and the alternate hypothesis.
(b) What is the critical value of t?
(c) What is the computed value of t?
(d) Interpret the result. What is the p-value?

▌ Exercises

For Exercises 19 and 20, (a) state the decision rule, (b) compute the standard deviation of the differences in the paired values, (c) compute the test statistic, (d) state your decision about the null hypothesis, and (e) estimate the p-value.

19. The null and the alternate hypothesis are:

$H_0: \mu_d \leq 0$

$H_1: \mu_d > 0$

The following sample information represents the number of defective units produced on the day shift and the afternoon shift for a sample of four days.

		Day		
	1	2	3	4
Day	10	12	15	19
Afternoon	8	9	12	15

At the .05 significance level, can we conclude that there are more defects on average produced on the day shift?

20. The null and alternate hypothesis are:

    H_0: $\mu_d = 0$

    H_1: $\mu_d \neq 0$

    The following paired sample observations show the number of citations given for speeding by Officer Dhondt and Officer Meredith of the Ohio Highway Patrol for the last five months.

Officer Dhondt	30	22	25	19	26
Officer Meredith	26	19	20	15	19

    At the .05 significance level, is there a difference in the mean number of citations given by the two officers?

21. A survey is conducted at North Central University to measure the effect of the change in environment on international students. One of the facets of the study is a comparison of student weights upon arrival on campus with weights one year later. It is suspected that the richer American food will cause an increase in weights. The .01 level is used. A random sample of 11 international students is chosen for the study. What is your conclusion?

Name	Weight on Arrival	Weight One Year Later	Name	Weight on Arrival	Weight One Year Later
Nassar	124	142	Farouk	149	150
O'Toole	157	157	Thatcher	176	184
Obie	98	96	Sambul	200	209
Silverman	190	212	Onassis	180	180
Kim	103	116	Pierre	256	269
Gross	135	134			

22. The management of Discount Furniture, a chain of discount furniture stores in the Northeast, designed an incentive plan for salespeople. To evaluate this innovative plan, 12 salespeople were selected at random, and their weekly incomes before and after the plan were recorded.

Salesperson	Weekly Income Before	Weekly Income After	Salesperson	Weekly Income Before	Weekly Income After
Sid Mahone	$320	$340	Peg Mancuso	$625	$631
Carol Quick	290	285	Anita Loma	560	560
Tom Jackson	421	475	John Cuso	360	365
Andy Jones	510	510	Carl Utz	431	431
Jean Sloan	210	210	A. S. Kushner	506	525
Jack Walker	402	500	Fern Lawton	505	619

    Was there a significant increase in the average salesperson's weekly income due to the innovative incentive plan? Use the .05 significance level. Estimate the p-value, and interpret it.

23. Calorie Watchers, a national chain of exercise and diet centers, has a new weight-reduction program designed to produce dramatic results within three weeks. As a result of their advertisements, over 1,000 persons signed up. Each was weighed before and after the initial three-week period. The results of a sample of 10 enrollees are:

Name	Weight Before	Weight After		Name	Weight Before	Weight After
Evie Gorky	190	196		Pat O'Leary	126	129
Bob Mack	250	240		Kim Dennis	186	189
Lou Brandon	345	345		Connie Kaye	116	115
Karl Unger	210	212		Tom Dama	196	194
Sue Koontz	114	113		Maxine Sims	125	124

At the .01 level of significance, can we say that the new weight-reduction program is a success?

24. A study of high-crime locations in Miami, Florida, was conducted. The number of crimes in each of the eight sample areas during a one-year period was recorded. Then a neighborhood watch program was inaugurated. The number of crimes before and after the watch are indicated in the table that follows. Has there been a decrease in the number of crimes since the program was inaugurated?

	A	B	C	D	E	F	G	H
				Number of Crimes by Area				
Before watch	14	7	4	5	17	12	8	9
After watch	2	7	3	6	8	13	3	5

Use the .01 significance level. Estimate the *p*-value.

▌ Chapter Outline

I. The *t* distribution is used as the test statistic when:
   A. The sampled population approximates the normal distribution.
   B. The population standard deviation is not known.
   C. The sample contains less than 30 observations.
II. The characteristics of the *t* distribution are:
   A. It is a continuous distribution.
   B. It is mound-shaped and symmetrical.
   C. It is flatter, or more spread out, than the standard normal distribution.
   D. There is a family of *t* distributions, depending on the number of degrees of freedom.
III. In a one-sample test, a single sample mean is compared to a population mean.
   A. The formula for the test statistic *t* is:

$$t = \frac{\bar{X} - \mu}{s/\sqrt{n}}$$ [10–1]

   where $\bar{X}$ is the sample mean, μ the population mean, s the sample standard deviation, and n the number of observations in the sample.
   B. The degrees of freedom is $n - 1$.
IV. In a two-sample test, the two sample means are compared to determine whether the sample came from populations with equal means.
   A. The required assumptions are:
      1. Both populations are normally distributed.
      2. The populations are independent.
      3. The standard deviations are the same in both populations.

  B. Because we assume that the populations have equal standard deviations, the sample standard deviations are pooled.

    1. The formula for the pooled variance (the standard deviation squared) is

$$s_p^2 = \frac{(n_1 - 1)s_1^2 + (n_2 - 1)s_2^2}{n_1 + n_2 - 2} \qquad \textbf{[10–2]}$$

      where n_1 and n_2 refer to the sample sizes and s_1 and s_2 to the two sample standard deviations.

    2. The value of the test statistic is computed from

$$t = \frac{\bar{X}_1 - \bar{X}_2}{\sqrt{s_p^2\left(\dfrac{1}{n_1} + \dfrac{1}{n_2}\right)}} \qquad \textbf{[10–3]}$$

      where $\bar{X}_1$ and $\bar{X}_2$ refer to the two independent sample means, s_p^2 to the pooled sample variance, and n_1 and n_2, the two sample sizes.

 V. If the samples are paired or dependent, the value of t, the test statistic, is computed by

$$t = \frac{\bar{d}}{s_d/\sqrt{n}} \qquad \textbf{[10–4]}$$

where $\bar{d}$ is the mean of the differences, s_d is the standard deviation of the sample differences, and n is the sample size.

▎ Pronunciation Key

SYMBOL	MEANING	PRONUNCIATION
s_p^2	Pooled sample variance	*s sub p squared*
$\bar{X}_1$	Mean of first sample	*X bar sub 1*
$\bar{X}_2$	Mean of second sample	*X bar sub 2*
n_1	Number of observations in the first sample	*n sub 1*
n_2	Number of observations in the second sample	*n sub 2*
$\bar{d}$	Mean of the difference between dependent observations	*d bar*
s_d	Standard deviation of the difference between dependent observations	*s sub d*

▎ Chapter Exercises

25. The manufacturer of the Ososki motorcycle advertises that the cycle will average 87 miles per gallon on long trips. The mileages on eight long trips were 88, 82, 81, 87, 80, 78, 79, and 89. At the .05 level, is the mean mileage less than the advertised 87 miles per gallon?

26. The Myers Summer Casual Furniture Store tells customers that a special order will take six weeks (42 days). During recent months the owner has received several complaints that the special orders are taking longer than 42 days. A sample of 12 special orders delivered in the last month showed that the mean waiting time was 51 days with a standard deviation of 8 days. At the .05 significance level, are customers waiting an average of more than 42 days? Estimate the *p*-value.

27. A recent article in *The Wall Street Journal* reported that the prime rate for large banks now exceeds 9 percent. A sample of eight small banks in the Midwest revealed the following

prime rates: 10.1, 9.3, 9.2, 10.2, 9.3, 9.6, 9.4, and 8.8. At the .01 significance level, can we conclude that the prime rate for small banks also exceeds 9 percent? Estimate the p-value.

28. A typical college student drinks an average of 27 gallons of coffee each year, or 2.25 gallons per month. A sample of 12 students at Northwestern State University revealed the following amounts of coffee consumed last month.

1.75	1.96	1.57	1.82	1.85	1.82	2.43	2.65	2.60	2.24	1.69	2.66

At the .05 significance level, is there a significant difference between the average amount consumed at Northwestern and the national average?

29. The postanesthesia care area (recovery room) at St. Luke's Hospital in Maumee, Ohio, was recently enlarged. The hope was that with the enlargement the mean number of patients per day would be more than 25. A random sample of 15 days revealed the following numbers of patients. At the .01 significance level, can we conclude that the mean number of patients per day is more than 25? Estimate the p-value and interpret it.

25	27	25	26	25	28	28	27	24	26	25	29	25	27	24

30. A recent survey found that the typical grandparents live a 6½-hour drive from their grand-children. A sample of 12 Ohio grandparents revealed the following driving times, in hours. At the .01 significance level, can we conclude that Ohio grandparents live closer to their grandchildren?

0	4	3	4	9	4	5	9	1	6	7	10

31. During recent seasons, Major League Baseball has been criticized for the length of the games. A report indicated that the average game lasts 3 hours and 30 minutes. A sample of 17 games revealed the following times to completion. (Note that the minutes have been changed to fractions of hours, so that a game that lasted 2 hours and 24 minutes is reported at 2.40 hours.)

2.98	2.40	2.70	2.25	3.23	3.17	2.93	3.18	2.80
2.38	3.75	3.20	3.27	2.52	2.58	4.45	2.45	

Can we conclude that the mean time for a game is less than 3.50 hours? Use the .05 significance level.

32. The Watch Corporation of Switzerland claims that their watches on average will neither gain or lose time during a week. A sample of 18 watches provided the following gains (+) or losses (−) in seconds per week. Is it reasonable to conclude that the mean gain or loss in time for the watches is 0? Use the .05 significance level. Estimate the p-value.

−0.38	−0.20	−0.38	−0.32	+0.32	−0.23	+0.30	+0.25	−0.10
−0.37	−0.61	−0.48	−0.47	−0.64	−0.04	−0.20	−0.68	+0.05

33. Listed below is the rate of return for one year (reported in percent) for a sample of 12 mutual funds that are classified as taxable money market funds. Using the .05 significance level is it reasonable to conclude that the rate of return is more than 4.50 percent?

4.63	4.15	4.76	4.70	4.65	4.52
4.70	5.06	4.42	4.51	4.24	4.52

34. A study of the health benefits packages for employees of large and small firms was recently completed by Pohlman Associates, a management consulting firm. Among the 15 large firms studied, the benefits package costs an average of 17.6 percent of salary, with a standard deviation of 2.6 percent. Among the 12 small firms studied, the benefits package averaged 16.2 percent of salary, with a standard deviation of 3.3 percent. Is there a significant difference between the mean percent of the employees' salaries spent by large firms and by small firms on health benefits? Use the .05 level of significance.

35. The manager of a package courier service believes that packages shipped at the end of the month are heavier than those shipped early in the month. As an experiment, he weighed a random sample of 20 packages at the beginning of the month. He found that the mean weight was 20.25 pounds and that the standard deviation was 5.84 pounds. Ten packages randomly selected at the end of the month had a mean weight of 24.80 pounds and a standard deviation of 5.67 pounds. At the .05 significance level, can we conclude that the packages shipped at the end of the month weigh more?

36. Hamburger sales per day at two locations of the Bun 'N' Run were compared. The mean number sold for 10 randomly selected days at the Northside site was 83.55, and the standard deviation was 10.50. For a random sample of 12 days at the Southside location, the mean number sold was 78.80 and the standard deviation was 14.25. At the .05 significance level, is there a difference in the mean number of hamburgers sold at the two locations?

37. The Commercial Bank and Trust Company is studying the use of its automatic teller machines (ATMs). Of particular interest is whether young adults (under 25 years) use the machines more than senior citizens. To investigate further, samples of customers under 25 years of age and customers over 60 years of age were selected. The number of ATM transactions last month was determined for each selected individual, and the results are shown below. At the .01 significance level, can bank management conclude that younger customers use the ATMs more?

Age	Number of Transactions										
Under 25	10	10	11	15	7	11	10	9			
Over 60	4	8	7	7	4	5	1	7	4	10	5

38. Two boats, the *Sea Hawk* and the *Sea Queen,* are competing for a spot in the upcoming *America's Cup* race. To decide which will represent the United States, they race over a part of the course several times. Below are the sample times in minutes. At the .05 significance level, can we conclude that there is a difference in their mean times?

Boat	Time (minutes)										
Sea Hawk	12.9	12.5	11.0	13.3	11.2	11.4	11.6	12.3	14.2	11.3	
Sea Queen	14.1	14.1	14.2	17.4	15.8	16.7	16.1	13.3	13.4	13.6	10.8	19.0

39. The manufacturer of a compact disc player wanted to know whether a 10 percent reduction in price is enough to increase the sales of their product. To investigate, the owner randomly selected eight outlets and sold the disc player at the reduced price. At seven randomly selected outlets, the regular price was charged. Reported below is the number of units sold last month at the selected outlets. At the .01 significance level, can the manufacturer conclude that the price reduction resulted in an increase in sales?

Regular price	138	121	88	115	141	125	96	
Reduced price	128	134	152	135	114	106	112	120

40. The Engineering Department at Sims Software, Inc. has developed two chemical solutions designed to increase the usable life of computer disks. A sample of disks treated with the first solution lasted 86, 78, 66, 83, 84, 81, 84, 109, 65, and 102 hours. Those treated with the second solution lasted 91, 71, 75, 76, 87, 79, 73, 76, 79, 78, 87, 90, 76, and 72 hours. At the .10 significance level, can we conclude that there is a difference in the length of time the two types of treatment lasted?

41. The Willow Run Outlet Mall has two Haggar Outlet Stores, one located on Peach Street and the other on Plum Street. The two stores are laid out differently, but both store managers claim their layout maximizes the amounts customers will purchase on impulse. A sample of 10 customers at the Peach Street store revealed they spent the following amounts more than planned: $17.58, $19.73, $12.61, $17.79, $16.22, $15.82, $15.40, $15.86, $11.82, $15.85. A sample of 14 customers at the Plum Street store revealed they spent the following amounts more than they planned: $18.19, $20.22, $17.38, $17.96, $23.92, $15.87, $16.47, $15.96, $16.79, $16.74, $21.40, $20.57, $19.79, $14.83. At the .01 significance level, is there a difference in the mean amounts purchased on an impulse at the two stores?

42. A number of minor automobile accidents occur at various high-risk intersections in Teton County despite traffic lights. The traffic department claims that a modification in the type of light will reduce these accidents. The county commissioners have agreed to a proposed experiment. Eight intersections were chosen at random, and the lights at those intersections were modified. Use the .01 significance level. The numbers of minor accidents during a six-month period before and after the modifications were:

	Number of Accidents, by Intersection							
	A	B	C	D	E	F	G	H
Before modification	5	7	6	4	8	9	8	10
After modification	3	7	7	0	4	6	8	2

43. Reginald "Bud" Owens is vice president for human resources for a large manufacturing company. In recent years he has noticed an increase in absenteeism that he thinks is related to the general health of the employees. Four years ago, in an attempt to improve the situation, he began a fitness program in which employees exercise during their lunch hour. To evaluate the program, he selected a random sample of eight participants and found the number of days each was absent in the six months before the exercise program began and in the last six months. Below are the results. At the .05 significance level, can he conclude that the number of absences has declined? Estimate the p-value.

Employee	Before Program	After Program	Employee	Before Program	After Program
1	6	5	5	4	3
2	6	2	6	3	6
3	7	1	7	5	3
4	7	3	8	6	7

44. Scott Seggity, owner of Seggity Software, Inc., recently purchased a special math co-processor chip advertised to "drastically reduce processing time." To test the chip, he selected a sample of 12 programs. The selected programs were run on two identical computers, one with the chip and the other without it. The processing times are reported below, in seconds. At the .05 significance level, can Mr. Seggity conclude that the new coprocessor will reduce the processing time? Estimate the p-value.

Program	Without Chip	With Chip		Program	Without Chip	With Chip
1	1.23	0.60		7	1.30	0.60
2	0.69	0.93		8	1.37	1.35
3	1.28	0.95		9	1.29	0.67
4	1.19	1.37		10	1.17	0.89
5	0.78	0.62		11	1.14	1.29
6	1.02	0.99		12	1.09	1.00

45. Dr. Thomas Sharkey, Dean of the College of Business at Genoa University, wants to study the effect on student grade point averages (GPAs) of moving from the quarter system to the semester system. (Under the quarter system the academic year is divided into three ten-week sessions, whereas under the semester system there are two fifteen-week sessions.) Genoa U. recently switched from the quarter to the semester system. To investigate, Dean Sharkey selected a sample of 10 students enrolled in the fall quarter last year and the fall semester this year. Listed below are the grades. At the .05 significance level, is there evidence that the student grades declined after the conversion?

Student	Last Fall	This Fall		Student	Last Fall	This Fall
Asad, Shelley	2.98	3.17		Volmer, Mary Jo	2.09	2.08
Becka, Joseph	2.34	2.04		Anderson, Robin	2.45	2.88
Bowerman, Jon	3.68	3.62		Bolger, T. J.	2.96	3.15
Sweede, Ronald	3.13	3.19		Palmer, Robert	2.80	2.49
Davis, Carolyn	3.34	2.90		Weis, Fran	4.00	3.98

46. The president of the American Insurance Institute wants to compare the yearly cost of auto insurance offered by two leading companies. He selects a sample of 15 families, some with only a single insured driver, others with several teenagers, and pays these families a stipend to contact the two companies and ask for a price quote. To make the data comparable, certain features, such as the amount deductible, are standardized. The sample information is reported below. At the .10 significance level, can we conclude that there is a difference in the amounts quoted?

Family	American Car Insurance	St. Paul Mutual Insurance		Family	American Car Insurance	St. Paul Mutual Insurance
Becker	$2,090	$1,610		King	$1,018	1,956
Berry	1,683	1,247		Kucic	1,881	1,772
Cobb	1,402	2,327		Meridieth	1,571	1,375
Debuck	1,830	1,367		Obeid	854	1,527
Dibucci	930	1,461		Price	1,579	1,767
Eckroate	697	1,789		Phillips	1,577	1,636
German	1,741	1,621		Tresize	860	1,188
Glasson	1,129	1,914				

www.Exercises.com

47. Listed below are 11 prominent companies and their stock prices in early 1998. Go to the Web and look up the price as of today's date. There are many sources to find stock prices. One is *Yahoo*. The address is *http://quote.yahoo.com*. Enter the symbol identification, and the current price will be reported. At the .01 significance level, can we conclude that the prices have increased?

Company	Symbol	Stock Price*	Company	Symbol	Stock Price*
Coca-Cola	KO	$67.938	IBM	IBM	$103.000
Walt Disney	DIS	95.750	McDonald's	MCD	46.250
Eastman Kodak	EK	58.125	McGraw-Hill Publishing	MHP	70.688
Ford Motor Company	F	2.375	Oracle	ORCL	21.813
General Motors	GM	59.750	Monsanto	MTC	40.375
Goodyear Tire	GT	62.188			

*The stock prices are reported as decimals rather than as fractions.

48. Listed below are nine companies in the auto industry and their stock prices in early 1998. Go to the Web and find the current price. At the .05 significance level, can we conclude that the price has increased since early 1998? Hint: You can locate the stock prices at *http://quote.yahoo.com* by entering the company's symbol identification.

Company	Symbol	Stock Price*	Company	Symbol	Stock Price*
General Motors	GM	$59.688	Honda	HMC	$ 72.813
Ford	FORD	2.375	Volkswagen	VLKAY	109.750
Chrysler	C	34.500	Mitsubishi	MSBHY	14.750
Nissan	NSANY	7.875	Volvo	VOLVY	27.000
Toyota	TOYOY	57.250			

*The stock prices are reported as decimals rather than as fractions.

▌ Computer Data Exercises

49. Refer to Data Set 1, which reports information on homes sold in Venice, Florida, during last year.
   a. At the .05 significance level, can we conclude that the mean selling price of a home with a pool is different from the mean selling price of a home without a pool?
   b. At the .05 significance level, can we conclude that the mean selling price of a home with a garage is different from the mean selling price of a home without a garage?
   c. At the .05 significance level, can we conclude that the mean selling price of a home in Township 1 is different from the mean selling price of a home in Township 2?
50. Refer to Data Set 2, which reports information on the 28 Major League Baseball teams for the 1997 season.
   a. At the .05 significance level, can we conclude that there is a difference in the mean number of stolen bases by National League teams and American League teams?
   b. At the .05 significance level, can we conclude that there is a difference in the mean team batting average for National League teams and American League teams?
   c. At the .05 significance level, can we conclude that there is a difference in the mean attendance for National League teams and American League teams?
   d. At the .05 significance level, is there a difference in the mean number of stolen bases by teams that have turf playing surfaces in their stadiums versus those that have natural grass?
51. Refer to Data Set 3, which reports information on the circulation of 48 popular magazines.
   a. Create a new variable that divides the male readership into two groups. The first group includes those magazines whose readership is less than 50 percent men. The second group includes magazines for which 50 percent or more of the readership is men. Conduct a test of hypothesis to determine whether the mean cost of color advertising is different for these two groups. Use the .01 significance level.
   b. Using the same variable created in part (a) above, is there a difference in the mean circulation between the two groups? Use the .01 significance level.

    c.   Using the same variable created in part (a) above, is there a difference in the mean age of the subscribers? Use the .01 significance level.

52.   Refer to Data Set 4, which reports information on the 94 school districts in northwest Ohio.
    a.   Sample every fifth school district in the data set, beginning with number 2. At the .05 significance level, can we conclude that the mean amount spent on instruction per pupil is different from $3,000?
    b.   Is there a difference in the mean teacher salary for the "large" districts (3,000 or more students) and the small districts (less than 1,000 students)?
    c.   Is there a difference in the mean amount spent on instruction per pupil for the large and the small districts? Use the .05 significance level and the same definition of large and small developed in part (b) above.
    d.   Is there a difference in the mean daily attendance for the large and the small districts? Use the .05 significance level.

▌ Computer Commands

1.   The MINITAB commands for the *t* test on page 360 are:
    a.   Enter the data by typing **Set C1** and hitting the return key.
    b.   Enter each observation, separated by a space. When all the observations have been entered, hit **Enter** and then type the word **End.**
    c.   Enter the command **Name C1 'Length.'**

```
MTB > Set c1
DATA> 42 39 42 45 43 40 39 41 40 42 43 42
DATA> end
MTB > name c1 'Length'
```

    d.   From the menu bar select **Stat, Basic Statistics, 1-Sample *t*,** then hit **Enter.** The following dialog box will appear.

    e.   Select the variable **Length,** select **Test mean,** insert **43,** and click **OK.**

2. The Excel commands for the two-sample *t*-test on page 366 are:
   a. Enter the data into columns A and B (or any other columns) in the spreadsheet, with the variables named in the first row.
   b. From the menu bar select **Tools** and **Data Analysis.** Select **t-Test: Two-Sample Assuming Equal Variances,** then click **OK.**
   c. In the dialog box indicate that the range of **Variable 1** is from A1 to A6 and **Variable 2** is from B1 to B7, the **Hypothesized Mean Difference** is 0, the **Labels** are in the first row, **Alpha** is .10, and the **Output Range** is D2. Click **OK.**

t-Test: Two-Sample Assuming Equal Variances	? ✕

Input

Variable 1 Range:	$A$1:$A$6		OK
Variable 2 Range:	$B$1:$B$7		Cancel
Hypothesized Mean Difference:	0		Help

☑ Labels

Alpha: 0.1

Output options

◉ Output Range: $D$2

○ New Worksheet Ply:

○ New Workbook

CHAPTER 10　*Answers to Self-Review*

10–1　(a) H_0: $\mu \le 305$, H_1: $\mu > 305$.
　　　(b) $df = 19$

(c) $t = \dfrac{\overline{X} - \mu}{s/\sqrt{n}} = \dfrac{311 - 305}{12/\sqrt{20}} = 2.236$

Reject H_0 because $2.236 > 1.729$. The modification increased the mean battery life to more than 305 days.

10–2　(a) H_0: $\mu \ge 9.0$, H_1: $\mu < 9.0$.
　　　(b) 7, found by $n - 1 = 8 - 1 = 7$.
　　　(c) Reject H_0 if $t < -2.998$.

(d) $t = -2.494$, found by:

$$s = \sqrt{\dfrac{619.88 - \dfrac{(70.4)^2}{8}}{8 - 1}} = 0.2268$$

$$\overline{X} = \dfrac{70.4}{8} = 8.8$$

Then

$$t = \dfrac{8.8 - 9.0}{0.2268/\sqrt{8}} = -2.494$$

Since -2.494 lies to the right of -2.998, H_0 is not rejected. We have not shown that the mean is less than 9.0

(e) The *p*-value is between .025 and .010.

10–3　H_0: $\mu_1 = \mu_2$, H_1: $\mu_1 \ne \mu_2$. H_0 is rejected if $t > 2.179$ or $t < -2.179$. There are 12 degrees of freedom.

	Day	Afternoon
Mean	7.00	10.00
Standard deviation	1.4142	2.2678
n	6	8

$$s_p^2 = \dfrac{(6 - 1)(1.4142)^2 + (8 - 1)(2.2678)^2}{6 + 8 - 2} = 3.8334$$

$$t = \dfrac{7.00 - 10.00}{\sqrt{3.8334\left(\dfrac{1}{6} + \dfrac{1}{8}\right)}} = \dfrac{-3.00}{1.0574} = -2.837$$

H_0 is rejected. the mean number of units produced is not the same on the two shifts. The *p*-value is less than 0.02.

10–4　(a) H_0: $\mu_d \le 0$, H_1: $\mu_d > 0$.
　　　(b) Reject H_0 if $t > 2.998$

(c) Name	Before	After	d	d^2
Hunter	155	154	1	1
Cashman	228	207	21	441
Mervine	141	147	-6	36
Massa	162	157	5	25
Creola	211	196	15	225
Peterson	164	150	14	196
Redding	184	170	14	196
Poust	172	165	7	49
			71	1,169

$$\overline{d} = \dfrac{71}{8} = 8.875$$

$$s_d = \sqrt{\dfrac{1169 - \dfrac{(71)^2}{8}}{8 - 1}} = 8.774$$

$$t = \dfrac{8.875}{8.774/\sqrt{8}} = 2.861.$$

(d) Do not reject H_0. We cannot conclude that the students lost weight. The *p*-value is less than .025.

Chapter Eleven

Analysis of Variance

GOALS

When you have completed this chapter, you will be able to:

ONE
Discuss the general idea of analysis of variance.

TWO
List the characteristics of the *F* distribution.

THREE
Conduct a test of hypothesis to determine whether two sample variances came from equal populations.

FOUR
Organize data into a one-way and a two-way ANOVA table.

FIVE
Define the terms *treatments* and *blocks*.

SIX
Conduct a test of hypothesis among three or more treatment means.

SEVEN
Develop confidence intervals for the difference between treatment means.

EIGHT
Conduct a test of hypothesis to determine whether there is a difference among block means.

The mean rate of return on 10 oil stocks was 12.6 percent with a standard deviation of 3.9 percent. The mean rate of return of 8 utility stocks was 10.9 percent with a standard deviation of 3.5 percent. At the .05 significance level, can we conclude there is more variation in oil stocks? (See Goal 3 and Exercise 6.)

▮ Introduction

In this chapter we continue our discussion of hypothesis testing. Recall that in Chapter 9 we examined the general theory of hypothesis testing. We described the case where a large sample was selected from the population. We used the z distribution (the standard normal distribution) to determine whether it was reasonable to conclude that the mean calculated from a particular sample came from the hypothesized population. Also, we tested whether two sample means came from equal populations. We also conducted both one- and two-sample tests for proportions, again using the standard normal distribution as the test statistic. In Chapter 10 we described methods for conducting tests of means where the populations were assumed normal but the samples were small (contained less than 30 observations). In the last case the t distribution was used as the test statistic. In this chapter we expand further our idea of hypothesis tests. We describe a test for variances and then a test that simultaneously compares several means to determine if they came from equal populations.

▮ The *F* Distribution

The probability distribution used in this chapter is the F distribution. It was named to honor Sir Ronald Fisher, one of the founders of modern-day statistics. This probability distribution is used as the test statistic for several situations. It is used to test whether two samples are from populations having equal variances, and it is also applied when we want to compare several population means simultaneously. The simultaneous comparison of several population means is called **analysis of variance (ANOVA).** In both of these situations, the populations must be normal, and the data must be at least interval-scale.

Characteristics of the F distribution

What are the characteristics of the F distribution?

1. There is a "family" of F distributions. A particular member of the family is determined by two parameters: the degrees of freedom in the numerator and the degrees of freedom in the denominator. The shape of the distribution is illustrated by the following graph. There is one F distribution for the combination of 29 degrees of freedom in the numerator and 28 degrees of freedom in the denominator. There is another F distribution for 19 degrees in the numerator and 6 degrees of freedom in the denominator. Note that the shape of the curves changes as the degrees of freedom change.

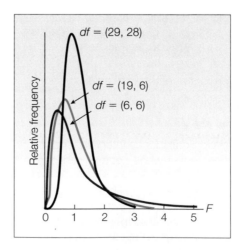

2. F cannot be negative, and it is a continuous distribution.
3. The F distribution is positively skewed.
4. Its values range from 0 to ∞. As the values increase, the curve approaches the X-axis but never touches it.

▍ Comparing Two Population Variances

The F distribution is used in this section to test the hypothesis that the variance of one normal population equals the variance of another normal population. Thus, this test is useful for determining whether one normal population has more variation than another. The following examples show the use of this test:

- Two Barth shearing machines are set to produce steel bars of the same length. The bars, therefore, should have the same mean length. We want to ensure that in addition to having the same mean length, they have similar variation.

- The mean rate of return on investment of two types of stock may be the same, but there may be more variation in the return of one than the other. A sample of 10 aerospace stocks and 10 utility stocks might show the same mean rate of return, but it is likely there is more variation in the rate of return of aerospace stocks.

Similarly, the F distribution is used to validate assumptions for certain statistical tests. As an example, recall that the t test described in Chapter 10 is used to determine whether the means of two independent populations differ. To employ that test, it is necessary to assume that the two population variances are the same. See this list of assumptions on page 363.

Regardless of whether we want to determine if one population has more variation than another population or validate an assumption for a statistical test, we first state the null hypothesis. The null hypothesis is that the variance of one normal population, σ_1^2, equals the variance of the other normal population, σ_2^2. The alternate hypothesis could be that the variances differ. This test of hypothesis is written:

$$H_0: \sigma_1^2 = \sigma_2^2$$
$$H_1: \sigma_1^2 \neq \sigma_2^2$$

To conduct the test, a random sample of n_1 observations is obtained from one population, and a sample of n_2 observations is obtained from the second population. The test statistic is s_1^2/s_2^2, where s_1^2 and s_2^2 are the respective sample variances. If the null hypothesis is true ($H_0: \sigma_1^2 = \sigma_2^2$), the test statistic follows the F distribution with $n_1 - 1$ and $n_2 - 1$ degrees of freedom. In order to reduce the size of the table of critical values, the *larger* sample variance is placed in the numerator; hence, the F ratio is always larger than 1.00. Thus, the upper-tail critical value is the only one required. The critical value of F is found by dividing the significance level in half ($\alpha/2$) and then referring to the appropriate numbers of degrees of freedom in Appendix G. An example will illustrate.

Example

Lammers Limos offers limousine service from the city hall in Toledo, Ohio, to Metro Airport in Detroit. Sean Lammers, president of the company, is considering two routes. One is via U.S. 25 and the other via I-75. He wants to study both routes and then compare the results. He collected the following sample data. Using the .10 significance level, is there a difference in the variation in the two routes?

Route	Mean Time (minutes)	Standard Deviation (minutes)	Sample Size
U.S. 25	56	12	7
I-75	58	5	8

Solution

Lammers noted that the mean times seem very similar, but there is more variation, as measured by the standard deviation, in the U.S. 25 route than in the I-75 route. This is somewhat consistent with his knowledge of the two routes; the U.S. 25 route contains more stoplights, whereas I-75 is a limited-access interstate highway. However, the I-75 route is several miles longer. It is important that the service offered be both timely and consistent, so he decides to conduct a statistical test to determine whether there really is a difference in the variation of the two routes.

The usual five-step hypothesis-testing procedure will be employed.

Step 1. The null hypothesis and the alternate hypothesis are stated. The test is two-tailed because we are looking for a difference in the variation of the two routes. We are not trying to show that one particular or specific route has more variation than the other.

$H_0: \sigma_1^2 = \sigma_2^2$

$H_1: \sigma_1^2 \neq \sigma_2^2$

Step 2: The .10 significance level is selected.

Step 3: The appropriate test statistic is s_1^2/s_2^2, which follows the F distribution when H_0 is true.

Step 4: The critical value is obtained from Appendix G, a portion of which is reproduced as Table 11–1. Because we are using a two tailed test, the significance level is .05, found by $\alpha/2 = .10/2 = .05$. There are $n_1 - 1 = 7 - 1 = 6$ degrees of freedom in the numerator, and $n_2 - 1 = 8 - 1 = 7$ degrees of freedom in the denominator. To find the critical value, move horizontally across the top portion of the F table (Table 11–1 or Appendix G) for the .05 significance level to 6 degrees of freedom in the numerator. Then move down that column to the critical value opposite 7 degrees of freedom in the denominator. The critical value is 3.87. Thus, the decision rule is: If the ratio of the sample variances, s_1^2/s_2^2, exceeds 3.87, the null hypothesis is rejected.

Table 11–1   Critical Values of the F Distribution, $\alpha = .05$

Degrees of Freedom for Denominator	Degrees of Freedom for Numerator			
	5	6	7	8
1	230	234	237	239
2	19.3	19.3	19.4	19.4
3	9.01	8.94	8.89	8.85
4	6.26	6.16	6.09	6.04
5	5.05	4.95	4.88	4.82
6	4.39	4.28	4.21	4.15
7	3.97	3.87	3.79	3.73
8	3.69	3.58	3.50	3.44
9	3.48	3.37	3.29	3.23
10	3.33	3.22	3.14	3.07

Step 5: Determine the value of the test statistic by taking the ratio of the two sample variances, as shown in formula (11–1).

TEST FOR EQUAL VARIANCES	$F = \dfrac{s_1^2}{s_2^2}$	**[11–1]**

The computed value of the F statistic is 5.76, found by

$$F = \frac{s_1^2}{s_2^2} = \frac{12^2}{5^2} = 5.76$$

The null hypothesis is rejected and the alternate accepted. We conclude that there is a difference in the variation in the travel time along the two routes.

As noted, the usual practice is to determine the F ratio by putting the larger of the two variances in the numerator. This will force the F ratio to be larger than 1.00. This allows us to always use the upper, or right-hand, tail of the F statistic, thus avoiding the need for more extensive F tables.

A logical question arises regarding one-tailed tests. For example, suppose in the previous problem we suspected that the variance of the times using the U.S. 25 route is *larger* than the variance of the times along the I-75 route. We would state the null and the alternate hypothesis as

H_0: $\sigma_1^2 \le \sigma_2^2$

H_0: $\sigma_1^2 > \sigma_2^2$

The test statistic is computed as s_1^2/s_2^2. The F ratio will be larger than 1.00, so we can use the upper tail of the F distribution. Under these conditions, it is not necessary to divide the significance level in half. Because Appendix G gives us only the .05 and .01 significance levels, we are restricted to these levels for one-tailed tests and .10 and .02 for two-tailed tests unless you consult a more complete table.

SELF-REVIEW 11–1

The Treece Company assembles electrical components. For the last 10 days Mark Treece has averaged 9 rejects with a standard deviation of 2 rejects. Debbie Thorton averaged 8.5 rejects with a standard deviation of 1.5 rejects over the same period. At the .05 significance level, can we conclude that there is more variation in the number of rejects per day attributed to Mark?

▌ Exercises

1. Using a two-tailed test and the .10 significance level, what is the critical F value for a sample of six observations in the numerator and four in the denominator?
2. Using a one-tailed test and the .01 significance level, what is the critical F value for a sample of four observations in the numerator and seven in the denominator?
3. The following hypotheses are given.

H_0: $\sigma_1^2 = \sigma_2^2$

H_1: $\sigma_1^2 \ne \sigma_2^2$

A random sample of eight observations from the first sample resulted in a standard deviation of 10. A random sample of six observations from the second sample gave a standard deviation of 7. At the .02 significance level, is there a difference in the variation of the two populations?

4. The following hypotheses are given.

$$H_0: \sigma_1^2 \le \sigma_2^2$$

$$H_1: \sigma_1^2 > \sigma_2^2$$

A random sample of five observations from the first sample resulted in a standard deviation of 12. A random sample of seven observations from the second sample showed a standard deviation of 7. At the .01 significance level, is there more variation in the first population?

5. Stargell Research Associates conducted a study of the radio listening habits of men and women. One facet of the study involved the mean listening time. It was discovered that the mean listening time for men is 35 minutes per day. The standard deviation of the sample of the 10 men studied was 10 minutes per day. The mean listening time for the 12 women studied was also 35 minutes, but the standard deviation of the sample was 12 minutes. At the .10 significance level, can we conclude that there is a difference in the variation in the number of minutes men and women listen to the radio?

6. A stockbroker at Critical Securities reported that the mean rate of return on a sample of 10 oil stocks was 12.6 percent with a standard deviation of 3.9 percent. The mean rate of return on a sample of 8 utility stocks was 10.9 percent with a standard deviation of 3.5 percent. At the .05 significance level, can we conclude that there is more variation in the oil stocks?

❙ ANOVA Assumptions

Another use of the *F* distribution is the analysis of variance (ANOVA) technique where we compare three or more sample means to determine whether they came from equal populations. To use ANOVA, we assume the following:

1. The populations are normally distributed.
2. The populations have equal standard deviations (σ).
3. The samples are selected independently.

When these conditions are met, *F* is used as the test statistic. ANOVA had its beginning in agriculture and many of the terms related to that context remain. In particular the term *treatment* is used to identify the populations being examined.

❙ **Treatment**   A specific source of variation in a set of data.   ❙

The following illustration will clarify the term *treatment* and demonstrate an application of ANOVA.

Bruce Kuhlman, the owner of Kuhlman Farms, wants to use the brand of fertilizer that will produce the maximum yield per acre of wheat. Mr. Kuhlman can select from three different commercial brands: Wolfe, White, and Korosa. To begin, Mr. Kuhlman divides his field into 12 plots of equal size. The wheat is then planted at the same time in the same manner. The only difference in the plots is that he randomly assigns the Wolfe brand of fertilizer to four plots, the White brand to four plots, and the Korosa brand to four plots. At the end of the growing season, the number of bushels of wheat produced on each plot is recorded. In this illustration there are three treatments. That is, the three different brands of fertilizer are the three different treatments. The results, in bushels at the end of the growing season are:

Wolfe	White	Korosa
55	66	47
54	76	51
59	67	46
56	71	48

Is there a difference in the mean number of bushels of wheat produced? Chart 11–1 illustrates how the populations would appear if there was a difference in the treatment means. Note that the populations are approximately normal and the variation in each population is the same, but the fertilizer (treatment) means are *not* the same.

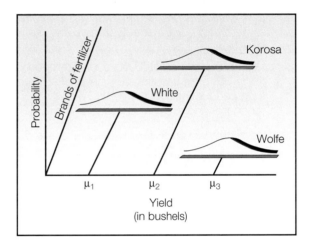

Chart 11–1   Case Where Treatment Means Are Different

Suppose the populations are the same. That is, there is no difference in the fertilizer (treatment) means. This is shown in Chart 11–2. This would indicate that the population means are the same. Note again that the populations are approximately normal and the variation in each of the populations is the same.

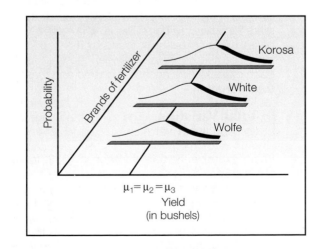

Chart 11–2   Case Where Treatment Means Are the Same

Why do we need to study ANOVA? Why can't we just use the *t* distribution, discussed in Chapter 10, to compare the treatment means two at a time? The major reason is the unsatisfactory buildup of Type I error. To explain further, suppose we have four different methods (A, B, C, and D) of training new recruits to be firefighters. We randomly assign each of the 40 recruits in this year's class to one of the four methods. At the end of the training program, a common test to measure understanding of firefighting techniques is given to the four groups. The question to be explored is: Is there a difference in the mean test scores among the four groups? An answer to this question will allow us to compare the four training methods.

Using the *t* distribution to compare the four sample means, we would have to run six different *t* tests. That is, we would need to compare the mean scores for the four methods as follows: A versus B, A versus C, A versus D, B versus C, B versus D, and C versus D. If we set α at .05, the probability of a correct statistical decision is .95, found by $1 - .05$. The probability that we do *not* make an incorrect decision due to sampling in any of the six independent tests is $(.95)^6 = .735$. Thus, the probability of at least one incorrect decision due to sampling is $1 - .735 = .265$. So if we conduct six independent tests using the *t* distribution, the likelihood of at least one sampling error is increased from .05 to an unsatisfactory level of .265. It is obvious that we need a better method than conducting six *t* tests. ANOVA will allow us to compare the treatment means simultaneously and avoid the buildup of the Type I error.

▌ The ANOVA Test

How does the ANOVA test work? Recall that we want to determine whether the various sample means came from a single population or populations with different means. We actually compare these sample means through their variances. To explain, recall on page 390, we listed the assumptions required for ANOVA. One of those assumptions was that the standard deviations of the various populations had to be the same. We take advantage of this requirement in the ANOVA test. The underlying strategy is to estimate the population variance (standard deviation squared) two ways and then find the ratio of these two estimates. If this ratio is about 1, then logically the two estimates are the same, and we conclude that the sample means are the same. If the ratio is quite different from 1, then we conclude that the sample means are not the same. The *F* distribution tells us when the ratio is too much larger than 1 to have occurred by chance.

Refer to the Kuhlman Farms example in the previous section. The owner of the farm wants to determine whether there is a difference in the mean yields of wheat for the various fertilizers. He has 12 plots of land and randomly assigned four plots to each of three fertilizers. To begin, find the overall mean wheat yield, in bushels, of the 12 plots of land. It is 58 bushels, found by $(55 + 54 + \cdots + 48)/12$. Next, for each of the 12 plots find the difference between the yield for the particular plot and the overall mean. Each of these differences is squared and these squares summed. This term is called the **total variation.**

▌ **Total Variation**   The sum of the squared differences between each observation and the overall mean. ▌

In our example the total variation is 1082, found by $(55 - 58)^2 + (54 - 58)^2 + \cdots + (48 - 58)^2$.

Next, break this total variation into two components: that which is due to the **treatments,** and that which is **random.** To find these two components, determine the mean of each of the treatments. In our Kuhlman Farms example, we calculate the mean wheat yield of the four plots that were fertilized with the Wolfe brand, the mean yield of the four plots using the White brand, and the mean yield of the four plots using the Korosa brand. The first source of variation is due to the treatments.

| **Treatment Variation** The sum of the squared differences between each treatment mean and the overall mean.

In the fertilizer example the variation due to the treatments is the sum of the squared differences between the mean of each fertilizer and the overall mean. This term is 992. To calculate it we first find the mean yield of each of the four treatments. The mean yield for Wolfe is 56 bushels, found by $(55 + 54 + 59 + 56)/4$. The other means are 70 bushels and 48 bushels, respectively. The sum of the squares due to the treatments is $(56 - 58)^2 + (56 - 58)^2 + \cdots + (48 - 58)^2 = 4(56 - 58)^2 + 4(70 - 58)^2 + 4(48 - 58)^2 = 992$. If there is considerable variation between the treatments, it is logical that this term will be a large value. If the treatment means are similar, this term will be a small value. The smallest value possible is zero. This would occur when all the treatment means were the same.

The other source of variation is referred to as the random component, or the error component.

| **Random Variation** The sum of the squared differences between each observation and its treatment mean.

In the fertilizer example this term is the sum of the squared differences between the wheat yield for each plot and the mean yield for the particular treatment. The error variation is 90, found by $(55 - 56)^2 + (54 - 56)^2 + \cdots + (48 - 48)^2$.

We determine the F statistic, which is the ratio of the two estimates of the population variance from the following equation.

$$F = \frac{\text{Estimate of the population variance based on the differences among the sample means}}{\text{Estimate of the population variance based on the variation within samples}}$$

Our first estimate of the population variance is based on the treatments, that is the difference *between* the means. It is 992/2. Why did we divide by 2? Recall in Chapter 4 that, to find a sample variance (formula [4–6]), we divide by the number of observations minus one. In this case there are three treatments, so we divide by 2. Our first estimate of the population variance is 992/2.

The variance estimate *within* the treatments is the random variation divided by the total number of observations less the number of treatments. That is 90/(12 − 3). Hence, our second estimate of the population variance is 90/9. The last step is to take the ratio of these two estimates.

$$F = \frac{992/2}{90/9} = 49.6$$

Because this ratio is quite different from 1, we can conclude that the treatment means are not the same. There is a difference in the mean yield of the three fertilizers.

The above conceptual view of ANOVA is fairly difficult to carry out. That is, the calculations can be quite tedious, particularly when the overall mean and the treatment means are not whole numbers. There are two alternatives to avoid the extensive calculations. In the following Example we provide an efficient method for solving the ANOVA problem where the calculations are minimized. We could also use a spreadsheet or statistical software package. Later in the chapter we will provide such an example.

Here's another example, which shows some shortcut computational formulas and also deals with samples of different sizes.

Example

A professor had students in a large marketing class rate his performance as excellent, good, fair, or poor. A graduate student collected the ratings and assured the students that the professor would not receive them until after course grades had been sent to the records office. The rating (i.e., the treatment) a student gave the professor was matched with his or her course grade, which could range from 0 to 100. The sample information is reported below. Is there a difference in the mean score of the students in each of the four rating categories? Use the .01 significance level.

	Course Grades		
Excellent	Good	Fair	Poor
94	75	70	68
90	68	73	70
85	77	76	72
80	83	78	65
	88	80	74
		68	65
		65	

Solution

We will follow the usual five-step hypothesis-testing procedure.

Step 1: State the null hypothesis and the alternate hypothesis. The null hypothesis is that the mean scores are the same for the four ratings.

$$H_0: \mu_1 = \mu_2 = \mu_3 = \mu_4$$

The alternate hypothesis is that the mean scores are not all the same for the four ratings.

H_1: The mean scores are not all equal.

If the null hypothesis is not rejected, we conclude that there is no difference in the mean course grades based on the instructor ratings. If H_0 is rejected, we conclude that there is a difference in at least one pair of mean ratings, but at this point we do not know which pair or how many pairs differ.

Step 2: Select the level of significance. We selected the .01 significance level.

Step 3: Determine the test statistic. The test statistic is the F distribution.

Step 4: Determine the decision rule. To determine the decision rule, we need the critical value. The critical value for the F statistic is found in Appendix G. The critical values for the .05 significance level are found on the first page and the .01 significance level on the second page. To use this table we need to know the degrees of freedom in the numerator and the denominator. The degrees of freedom in the numerator equals the number of treatments, designated as k, minus 1. The degrees of freedom in the denominator is the total number of observations, n, minus the number of treatments. For this problem there are four treatments and a total of 22 observations.

Degrees of freedom in the numerator = $k - 1 = 4 - 1 = 3$
Degrees of freedom in the denominator = $n - k = 22 - 4 = 18$

Refer to Appendix G and the .01 significance level. Move horizontally across the top of the page to 3 degrees of freedom in the numerator. Then move down that column to the row with 18 degrees of freedom. The value at this intersection is 5.09. So the decision rule is to reject H_0 if the computed value of F exceeds 5.09.

Step 5: Select the sample, perform the calculations, and make a decision. It is convenient to summarize the calculations of the F statistic in an **ANOVA table**. The format for an ANOVA table is as follows.

ANOVA Table

Source of Variation	Sum of Squares	Degrees of Freedom	Mean Square	F
Treatments	SST	$k - 1$	$SST/(k - 1) = MST$	MST/MSE
Error	SSE	$n - k$	$SSE/(n - k) = MSE$	
Total	SS total	$n - 1$		

There are three values, called the **sum of squares,** that are required to compute F. We can determine these values by finding SS total and SST, then finding SSE by subtraction. The SS total term is the total variation, SST is the variation due to the treatments, and SSE is the variation among the treatments.

To find the value of F, we actually work our way across the table. The degrees of freedom for the numerator and the denominator are the same as those for finding the critical values of F. The term **mean square** is another expression for an estimate of the variance. The mean square for the treatment is SST divided by its degrees of freedom. The result is called the **mean square for treatments** and is written MST. We compute the **mean square error** (MSE) similarly. We divide the SSE term by its degrees of freedom. To complete the process and find F, we divide MST by MSE.

We usually start the process by finding SS total. This is the sum of the squared differences between each observation and the overall mean. The formula for finding SS total is

SUM OF SQUARES TOTAL	$$\text{SS total} = \Sigma X^2 - \frac{(\Sigma X)^2}{n}$$	**[11–2]**

where:

ΣX^2 is the X values squared and then summed.

$(\Sigma X)^2$ is the X values summed and then squared.

n is the total number of observations.

Next we determine SST, called the sum of squares due to the treatments. The formula for finding SST is

SUM OF SQUARES TREATMENT	$$\text{SST} = \Sigma\left(\frac{T_c^2}{n_c}\right) - \frac{(\Sigma X)^2}{n}$$	**[11–3]**

where:

T_c is the column total for each treatment.

n_c is the number of observations (sample size) for each treatment.

Finally we determine SSE, the sum of squares error, by subtraction. The formula for finding SSE is

SUM OF SQUARES ERROR	$$\text{SSE} = \text{SS total} - \text{SST}$$	**[11–4]**

The detailed calculations for this example are shown in Table 11–2.

Table 11–2 Calculations Necessary for Computing the Value of F

	Excellent		Good		Fair		Poor		Total
	X	X²	X	X²	X	X²	X	X²	
	94	8,836	75	5,625	70	4,900	68	4,624	
	90	8,100	68	4,624	73	5,329	70	4,900	
	85	7,225	77	5,929	76	5,776	72	5,184	
	80	6,400	83	6,889	78	6,084	65	4,225	
			88	7,744	80	6,400	74	5,476	
					68	4,624	65	4,225	
					65	4,225			
T_c	349		391		510		414		1664
n_c	4		5		7		6		22
X^2		30,561		30,811		37,338		28,634	127,344

The entries for the ANOVA table are computed as follows. First, using formula (11–2), we compute the total variation:

$$\text{SS total} = \Sigma X^2 - \frac{(\Sigma X)^2}{n} = 127,344 - \frac{1,664^2}{22} = 1,485.09$$

Next, using formula (11–3), we compute the treatment variation.

$$\text{SST} = \Sigma\left(\frac{T_c^2}{n_c}\right) - \frac{(\Sigma X)^2}{n} = \frac{349^2}{4} + \frac{391^2}{5} + \frac{510^2}{7} + \frac{414^2}{6} - \frac{1,664^2}{22} = 890.68$$

Finally, by subtraction, we determine the error variation.

$$\text{SSE} = \text{SS total} - \text{SST} = 1,485.09 - 890.68 = 594.41$$

Inserting these values into an ANOVA table and computing the value of F:

Source of Variation	Sum of Squares	Degrees of Freedom	Mean Square	F
Treatments	890.68	3	296.89	8.99
Error	594.41	18	33.02	
Total	1,485.09	23		

The computed value of F is 8.99, which is greater than the critical value of 5.09, so the null hypothesis is rejected. We conclude the population means are not all equal. The mean scores are not the same in each of the four ratings groups. It is likely that the grades students earned in the course are related to the opinion they have of the overall competency and classroom performance of the instructor. At this point we can only conclude there is a difference in the treatment means. We cannot determine which treatment groups differ or how many treatment groups differ.

As you noted from the previous example, the calculations become very tedious if the number of observations in each treatment is large. Below is the MINITAB output to the student ratings example. The output is in the form of an ANOVA table.

```
One-Way Analysis of Variance

Analysis of Variance
Source       DF      SS      MS          F         P
Factor        3    890.7   296.9        8.99     0.001
Error        18    594.4    33.0
Total        21   1485.1
                                 Individual 95% CIs For Mean
                                 Based on Pooled StDev
Level        N     Mean    StDev   ----------+---------+---------+------
Excellent     4   87.250   6.076                          (------*------)
Good          5   78.200   7.662                 (------*-- ----)
Fair          7   72.857   5.490           (----- *-----)
Poor          6   69.000   3.688   (-----*---- -)
                                 ----------+---------+---------+------
Pooled StDev =     5.747           72.0      80.0      88.0
```

The MINITAB system uses the term *factor* instead of *treatment,* with the same intended meaning. The *p*-value is .001 and is located under the heading "P." How do we interpret this value? It is the probability of finding an F value to the right of 8.99 with 3 degrees of freedom in the numerator and 18 in the denominator, given that H_0 is true. So the likelihood of committing a Type I error by rejecting a true H_0 is 0.1 percent — a very small likelihood indeed!

SELF-REVIEW 11–2

Clean All is a new all-purpose cleaner being test marketed by placing sales displays in three different locations within various supermarkets. The number of 12-ounce bottles sold from each location within each of the supermarkets is reported below.

Location	Sales			
Near the bread	20	15	24	18
Near the beer	12	18	10	15
With other cleaners	25	28	30	32

At the .05 significance level, is there a difference in the mean number of bottles sold at the three locations?

(a) State the null hypothesis and the alternate hypothesis.
(b) What is the decision rule?
(c) Compute the values of SS total, SST, and SSE.
(d) Develop an ANOVA table.
(e) What is your decision regarding the null hypothesis?
(f) Interpret the result.

I Exercises

7. The following is sample information. Test the hypothesis that the treatment means are equal. Use the .05 significance level.

Treatment 1	Treatment 2	Treatment 3
8	3	3
6	2	4
10	4	5
9	3	4

a. State the null hypothesis and the alternate hypothesis.
b. What is the decision rule?
c. Compute SST, SSE, and SS total.
d. Complete an ANOVA table.
e. State your decision regarding the null hypothesis.

8. The following is sample information. Test the hypothesis that the treatment means are equal. Use the .05 significance level.

Treatment 1	Treatment 2	Treatment 3
9	13	10
7	20	9
11	14	15
9	13	14
12		15
10		

a. State the null hypothesis and the alternate hypothesis.
b. What is the decision rule?
c. Compute SST, SSE, and SS total.
d. Complete an ANOVA table.
e. State your decision regarding the null hypothesis.

9. A real estate developer is considering investing in a shopping mall on the outskirts of Atlanta, Georgia. Three parcels of land are being evaluated. Of particular importance is the income in the area surrounding the proposed mall. A random sample of four families is selected near each proposed mall. Following are the sample results. At the .05 significance level, can the developer conclude there is a difference in the mean income? Use the usual five step hypothesis-testing procedure. (Of course, in actual practice more than four families would be selected.)

Southwyck Area ($ thousands)	Franklin Park ($ thousands)	Old Orchard ($ thousands)
34	44	45
38	41	50
40	39	46
30	40	48

10. The manager of a computer software company is studying the number of hours top executives spend at their computer terminals by type of industry. A sample of five executives from each of three industries is obtained. At the .05 significance level, can the manager conclude there is a difference in the mean number of hours spent at a terminal per week by industry?

Banking	Retail	Insurance
12	8	10
10	8	8
10	6	6
12	8	8
10	10	10

▌ Inferences about Treatment Means

Suppose in carrying out the ANOVA procedure, we make the decision to reject the null hypothesis. This allows us to conclude that all the treatment means are not the same. Sometimes we may be satisfied with this conclusion, but in other instances we may want to know which treatment means differ. This section provides the details for such a test.

Recall in the example regarding student opinions and grades there was a difference in the treatment means. That is, the null hypothesis was rejected and the alternate hypothesis accepted. If the student opinions do differ, the question is: Between which groups do the treatment means differ?

Several procedures are available to answer this question. Perhaps the simplest is through the use of confidence intervals. From the computer output of the previous example (see page 397), note that the mean score for those students rating the instruction excellent is 87.250, and for those rating the instruction poor it is 69.000. Thus, those students who rated the instruction excellent seemingly earned higher grades than those who rated the instruction poor. Is there enough difference to justify the conclusion that there is a difference in the mean scores of the two groups?

The t distribution, described in Chapter 10, is used as the basis for this test. Recall that one of the basic assumptions of ANOVA is that the population variances are the same for all treatments. This common population value is called the **mean square error,** or MSE, and is determined by $SSE/(n - k)$. A confidence interval for the difference between two population means is found by:

$$\text{COMPARISON OF TREATMENT MEANS} \qquad (\bar{X}_1 - \bar{X}_2) \pm t \sqrt{\text{MSE}\left(\frac{1}{n_1} + \frac{1}{n_2}\right)} \qquad \textbf{[11–5]}$$

where:

$\bar{X}_1$ is the mean of the first treatment.

$\bar{X}_2$ is the mean of the second treatment.

t is obtained from Appendix F. The number of degrees of freedom is equal to $n - k$.

MSE is the mean square error obtained from the ANOVA table [$SSE/(n - k)$].

n_1 is the number of observations in the first treatment.

n_2 is the number of observations in the second treatment.

How do we decide whether there is a difference in the treatment means? If the confidence interval includes zero, there is *not* a difference between the treatment means. For example, if the lower endpoint of the confidence interval has a negative sign and the upper endpoint has a positive sign, the two means do not differ. So if we developed a confidence interval from formula (11–5) and found that the difference in the treatment means was 5.00, that is $\bar{X}_1 - \bar{X}_2 = 5$, and that $t \sqrt{\text{MSE}(1/n_1 + 1/n_2)} = 12$, the confidence interval would range from -7.00 up to 17.00. To put it another way:

$$(\bar{X}_1 - \bar{X}_2) \pm t \sqrt{\text{MSE}\left(\frac{1}{n_1} + \frac{1}{n_2}\right)} = 5 \pm 12$$

$$= -7.00 \text{ up to } 17.00$$

Note that zero is included in this interval. Therefore, we would conclude that there is no significant difference in the selected treatment means.

On the other hand, if the endpoints of the confidence interval have the *same* sign, this demonstrates that the treatment means differ. For example, if $\bar{X}_1 - \bar{X}_2 = -0.35$ and

$t\sqrt{MSE(1/n_1 + 1/n_2)} = 0.25$, the confidence interval would range from -0.60 to -0.10. Because -0.60 and -0.10 have the same sign (both negative), we conclude that these two means differ.

Using the previous student opinion example and the .95 level of confidence, the endpoints of the confidence interval are 10.46 and 26.04, found by:

$$(\bar{X}_1 - \bar{X}_2) \pm t\sqrt{MSE\left(\frac{1}{n_1} + \frac{1}{n_2}\right)} = (87.25 - 69.00) \pm 2.101 \sqrt{33.0\left(\frac{1}{4} + \frac{1}{6}\right)}$$

$$= 18.25 \pm 7.79 = 10.46 \text{ up to } 26.04$$

where:

$\bar{X}_1 = 87.25$

$\bar{X}_2 = 69.00$

$t = 2.101$ from Appendix F ($N - k = 22 - 4 = 18$ degrees of freedom)

$MSE = 33.0$, from the ANOVA table

$n_1 = 4$

$n_2 = 6$

The 95 percent confidence interval ranges from 10.46 up to 26.04. Both endpoints are positive; hence, we can conclude these treatment means differ significantly. That is, students who rated the instructor excellent have significantly higher grades than those who rated the instructor as poor.

Likewise, approximate results can be obtained from the MINITAB output on page 397. On the bottom of the MINITAB output a confidence interval for each mean is provided. The endpoints of the dotted line indicate the endpoints of a confidence interval for each treatment mean. These endpoints are identified by the symbols "(" and ")". In those instances where the intervals overlap (that is, contain a common area) the treatment means do not differ. In this example, the students who rated the instructor excellent had a significantly different mean grade from that of those who rated him fair.

SELF-REVIEW 11–3

The following data represent the tuition charges (in thousands of dollars) for a sample of private colleges in various regions of the United States. At the .05 significance level, can we conclude there is a difference in the mean tuition charge?

Northeast ($ thousands)	Southeast ($ thousands)	West ($ thousands)
10	8	7
11	9	8
12	10	6
10	8	7
12		6

(a) State the null and alternate hypotheses.
(b) What is the decision rule?
(c) What is the computed value of the test statistic?
(d) What is your decision regarding the null hypothesis?
(e) Could there be a significant difference between the mean tuition in the Northeast and that in the West? If so, develop a 95 percent confidence interval for that difference.

Also, the mean grade of those who rated the instruction excellent differed from the mean of those rating it poor.

Caution: The investigation of differences in treatment means is a step-by-step process. The initial step is to conduct the ANOVA test. Only if the null hypothesis that the treatment means are equal is rejected should any analysis of the individual treatment means be attempted.

▮ Exercises

11. The following sample information is given. Test the hypothesis that the treatment means are equal at the .05 significance level.

Treatment 1	Treatment 2	Treatment 3
8	3	3
11	2	4
10	1	5
	3	4
	2	

a. State the null hypothesis and the alternate hypothesis.
b. What is the decision rule?
c. Compute SST, SSE, and SS total.
d. Complete an ANOVA table.
e. State your decision regarding the null hypothesis.
f. If H_0 is rejected, can we conclude that treatment 1 and treatment 2 differ? Use the 95 percent level of confidence.

12. The following is sample information. Test the hypothesis that the treatment means are equal at the .05 significance level.

Treatment 1	Treatment 2	Treatment 3
3	9	6
2	6	3
5	5	5
1	6	5
3	8	5
1	5	4
	4	1
	7	5
	6	
	4	

a. State the null hypothesis and the alternate hypothesis.
b. What is the decision rule?
c. Compute SST, SSE, and SS total.
d. Complete an ANOVA table.
e. State your decision regarding the null hypothesis.
f. If H_0 is rejected, can we conclude that treatment 2 and treatment 3 differ? Use the 95 percent level of confidence.

13. A senior accounting major at Midsouth State University has job offers from four CPA firms. To explore the offers further, she asked a sample of recent trainees how many months each worked for the firm before receiving a raise in salary. The sample information is

Number of Months before First Raise in Salary			
CPA, Inc.	AB Intl.	Acct Ltd.	Pfisters
12	14	18	12
10	12	12	14
14	10	16	16
12	10		

At the .05 level of significance, is there a difference in the mean number of months before a raise was granted among the four CPA firms?

14. A stock analyst wants to determine whether there is a difference in the mean rate of return for three types of stock: utility, retail, and banking stocks. The following sample information is collected.

Rates of Return		
Utility	Retail	Banking
14.3	11.5	15.5
18.1	12.0	12.7
17.8	11.1	18.2
17.3	11.9	14.7
19.5	11.6	18.1
		13.2

a. Using the .05 level of significance, is there a difference in the mean rate of return among the three types of stock?

b. Suppose the null hypothesis is rejected. Can the analyst conclude there is a difference between the mean rates of return for the utility and the retail stocks? Explain.

▌ Two-Way Analysis of Variance

In the student ratings example, we divided the total variation into two categories: the variation between the treatments and the variation within the treatments. We also called the variation within the treatments the error or the random variation. To put it another way, we considered only two sources of variation, those due to the treatments and the random. In the student ratings example there may be other causes of variation in the student grades beside the instructor rating. These factors might include the number of hours per week the student studied, the mathematics ability of the student, or the gender of the student.

The benefit of considering other factors is that we can reduce the error variance. That is, if we can reduce the denominator of the F statistic (reducing the error variance or more directly the SSE term) the value of F will be larger, causing us to reject the hypothesis of equal treatment means. An example will clarify the reduction in the error variance. In other words, if we can explain more of the variation, then there is less "error."

Example

WARTA, the Warren Area Regional Transit Authority, is expanding bus service from the suburb of Starbrick into the central business district of Warren. There are four routes being considered from Starbrick to downtown Warren: (1) via U.S. 6, (2) via the west end, (3) via the Hickory Street bridge, and (4) via Rte. 59. WARTA conducted test runs to determine whether there was a difference in the travel times along the four routes. Because there will be many different drivers the test was set up so each driver drove along each of the four routes. The travel times, in minutes, for each of the driver–route combinations is shown below.

Travel Time from Starbrick to Warren (minutes)

Driver	U.S. 6	West End	Hickory St.	Rte. 59
Deans	18	20	20	22
Snaverly	21	22	24	24
Ormson	20	23	25	23
Zollaco	25	21	28	25
Filbeck	26	24	28	25

At the .05 significance level is there a difference in the mean travel time along the four routes? If we remove the effect of the drivers, is there a difference in the mean travel time?

Solution

To begin, we conduct a test of hypothesis using a one-way ANOVA. That is, we consider only the four routes. Under this condition the variation is either due to the treatments or it is random. The null hypothesis and the alternate hypothesis for comparing the mean travel time along the four routes are

$H_0: \mu_1 = \mu_2 = \mu_3 = \mu_4$

H_1: At least one is different

There are four routes, so the numerator the degrees of freedom is $k - 1 = 4 - 1 = 3$. There are 20 observations, so the degrees of freedom in the denominator is $n - k = 20 - 4 = 16$. From Appendix G, with the .05 significance level the critical value of F is 3.24. The decision rule is to reject the null hypothesis if the computed value of F is greater than 3.24. The details of the treatment totals and squares are reported in Table 11–3.

Table 11–3 Calculations Needed for a One-Way and a Two-Way ANOVA

Driver	Travel Time from Starbrick to Warren (minutes)				
	U.S. 6	West End	Hickory St.	Rte. 59	Row Sum, B_r
Deans	18	20	20	22	80
Snaverly	21	22	24	24	91
Ormson	20	23	25	23	91
Zollaco	25	21	28	25	99
Filbeck	26	24	28	25	103
Column total, T_c	110	110	125	119	464
Sum of squares	2,466	2,430	3,169	2,839	10,904

The entries for the ANOVA table are computed as follows. First, using formula (11–2), we determine the total variation:

$$\text{SS total} = \Sigma X^2 - \frac{(\Sigma X)^2}{n} = 10{,}904 - \frac{464^2}{20} = 139.2$$

Next, using formula (11–3), we compute the treatment variation:

$$\text{SST} = \Sigma\left(\frac{T_c^2}{n_c}\right) - \frac{(\Sigma X)^2}{n} = \frac{110^2}{5} + \frac{110^2}{5} + \frac{125^2}{5} + \frac{119^2}{5} - \frac{464^2}{20} = 32.4$$

Finally, by subtraction, we determine the error variation.

$$\text{SSE} = \text{SS total} - \text{SST} = 139.2 - 32.4 = 106.8$$

Inserting these values into an ANOVA table and computing the value of F:

Source of Variation	Sum of Squares	Degrees of Freedom	Mean Square	F
Treatments	32.4	3	10.8	1.618
Error	106.8	16	6.675	
Total	139.2	19		

Because the computed F value of 1.618 is less than the critical value of 3.24 we do not reject the null hypothesis. WARTA can conclude that there is no difference in the mean travel time along the four routes. There is no reason to select one of the routes as faster than the others.

In the above Example we considered the variation due to the treatments (routes) and took all the remaining variation to be random. However, we did set up the trials so that each of the five drivers drove along each of the four routes. If we could consider the effect of the several drivers, this would allow us to reduce the SSE term, which would lead to a larger value of F. The second treatment variable, the drivers in this case, is referred to as a **blocking variable.**

Blocking Variable   A second treatment variable that when included in the ANOVA analysis will have the effect of reducing the SSE term.

In this case we let the drivers be the blocking variable, and removing the effect of the drivers from the SSE term will change the F ratio for the treatment variable. First, we need to determine the sum of squares due to the blocks. The equation for determining the sum of squares blocks is quite similar to the equation for the sum of squares for treatments.

SUM OF SQUARES BLOCKS	$\text{SSB} = \Sigma\left(\dfrac{B_r^2}{k}\right) - \dfrac{(\Sigma X)^2}{n}$	**[11–6]**

where B_r refers to the block total, that is the total for the row, and k is the number of items in each block.

The same format is used in the two-way ANOVA table as in the one-way case, except there is an additional row for the blocking variable. SS total and SST are calculated as before, and SSB is found from formula (11–6). The SSE term is found by subtraction.

SUM OF SQUARES ERROR, TWO-WAY	SSE = SS total − SST − SSB	**[11–7]**

The values for the various components of the ANOVA table are computed as follows.

Source of Variation	Sum of Squares	Degrees of Freedom	Mean Square	F
Treatments	SST	$k - 1$	$SST/(k - 1) = MST$	MST/MSE
Blocks	SSB	$b - 1$	$SSB/(b - 1) = MSB$	MSB/MSE
Error	SSE	$(k - 1)(b - 1)$	$SSE/(k - 1)(b - 1) = MSE$	
Total	SS total	$n - 1$		

SSB is found by formula (11–6).

$$SSB = \Sigma\left(\frac{B_r^2}{k}\right) - \frac{(\Sigma X)^2}{n} = \left(\frac{80^2}{4} + \frac{91^2}{4} + \frac{91^2}{4} + \frac{99^2}{4} + \frac{103^2}{4}\right) - \frac{464^2}{20} = 78.2$$

SSE is found by formula (11–7).

$$SSE = SS\ total - SST - SSB = 139.2 - 32.4 - 78.2 = 28.6$$

Source of Variation	(1) Sum of Squares	(2) Degrees of Freedom	(3) Mean Square (1)/(2)
Treatments	32.4	3	10.80
Blocks	78.2	4	19.550
Error	28.6	12	2.383
Total	139.2		

There is disagreement at this point. If the purpose of the blocking variable (the drivers in this example) was only to reduce the error variation, we should not conduct a test of hypothesis for the difference in block means. That is, if our goal was to reduce the MSE term, then we should not test a hypothesis regarding the blocking variable. On the other hand, we may wish to give the blocks the same status as the treatments and conduct a test of hypothesis. In the latter case, when the blocks are important enough to be considered as a second factor, we refer to this as a **two-factor experiment.** In many cases the decision is not clear. In our example we are concerned about the differences in the travel time for the different drivers, so we will conduct the test of hypothesis. The two sets of hypotheses are:

1. H_0: The treatment means are the same ($\mu_1 = \mu_2 = \mu_3 = \mu_4$).
   H_1: The treatment means are not the same.
2. H_0: The block means are the same ($\mu_1 = \mu_2 = \mu_3 = \mu_4 = \mu_5$).
   H_1: The block means are not the same.

First we will test the hypothesis concerning the treatment means. There are $k - 1 = 4 - 1 = 3$ degrees of freedom in the numerator and $(b - 1)(k - 1) = (5 - 1)(4 - 1) = 12$ degrees of freedom in the denominator. Using the .05 significance level, the critical value of F is 3.49. The null hypothesis that the mean times for the four routes are the same is rejected if the F ratio exceeds 3.49.

$$F = \frac{MST}{MSE} = \frac{10.80}{2.383} = 4.53$$

The null hypothesis is rejected and the alternate accepted. It is concluded that the mean travel time is not the same for all routes. WARTA will want to conduct some tests to determine which treatment means differ.

Next, we test to find out whether the travel time is the same for the various drivers. The degrees of freedom in the numerator for blocks is $b - 1 = 5 - 1 = 4$. The degrees of freedom for the denominator is the same as before: $(b - 1)(k - 1) = (5 - 1)(4 - 1) = 12$. The null hypothesis that the block means are the same is rejected if the F ratio exceeds 3.26.

$$F = \frac{MSB}{MSE} = \frac{19.550}{2.383} = 8.20$$

The null hypothesis is rejected, and the alternate is accepted. The mean time is not the same for the various drivers. Thus, WARTA management can conclude, based on the sample results, that there is a difference in the routes and in the drivers.

The Excel Spreadsheet has a two-factor ANOVA procedure. The output for the WARTA example just completed is repeated below. The results are the same as reported earlier. In addition the Excel output reports the p-values. The p-value for the null hypothesis regarding the drivers is .002 and .024 for the routes. These p-values confirm the hypothesis that the null hypotheses for treatments and blocks should both be rejected at the .05 significance level.

Anova: Two-Factor Without Replication

SUMMARY	Count	Sum	Average	Variance
Deans	4	80	20	2.666667
Snaverly	4	91	22.75	2.25
Ormson	4	91	22.75	4.25
Zollaco	4	99	24.75	8.25
Filbeck	4	103	25.75	2.916667
U.S. 6	5	110	22	11.5
West end	5	110	22	2.5
Hickory St.	5	125	25	11
Rte. 59	5	119	23.8	1.7

ANOVA						
Source of Variation	SS	df	MS	F	P-value	F crit
Rows	78.2	4	19.55	8.202797	0.001989	3.25916
Columns	32.4	3	10.8	4.531469	0.024065	3.4903
Error	28.6	12	2.383333			

SELF-REVIEW 11-4

Rudduck Shampoo sells three shampoos — for dry, normal, and oily hair. Sales, in millions of dollars, for the past five months are given in the following table.

Month	Sales ($ million)		
	Dry	Normal	Oily
June	7	9	12
July	11	12	14
August	13	11	8
September	8	9	7
October	9	10	13

Using the .05 level, apply the ANOVA procedure to test whether:

(a) The mean sales for dry, normal, and oily hair are the same.
(b) The mean sales are the same for each of the five months.

▌ Exercises

For exercises 15 and 16, conduct a test of hypothesis to determine whether the block and the treatment means differ. Use the .05 significance level and: (a) State the null and alternate hypotheses for treatments; (b) State the decision rule for treatments; (c) State the null and alternate hypotheses for blocks. Also, state the decision rule for blocks; (d) Compute SST, SSB, SS total, and SSE; (e) Complete an ANOVA table; (f) What is your decision regarding the two sets of hypotheses?

15. The following data are given for a two-factor ANOVA.

	Treatment	
Block	1	2
A	46	31
B	37	26
C	44	35

16. The following data are given for a two-factor ANOVA.

	Treatment		
Block	1	2	3
A	12	14	8
B	9	11	9
C	7	8	8

17. The Brunner Manufacturing Company operates 24 hours a day, five days a week. The workers rotate shifts each week. Management is interested in whether there is a difference in the number of units produced when the employees work on various shifts. A sample of five workers is selected and their output recorded on each shift. At the .05 significance level,

can we conclude there is a difference in the mean production by shift and in the mean production by employee?

| | Units Produced | | |
Employee	Day	Afternoon	Night
Skaff	31	25	35
Lum	33	26	33
Clark	28	24	30
Treece	30	29	28
Morgan	28	26	27

18. There are three hospitals in the Tulsa area. The following data show the number of outpatient surgeries performed at each hospital last week. At the .05 significance level, can we conclude that there is a difference in the mean number of surgeries performed among the three hospitals and in the mean number of surgeries by day of the week?

| | Number of Surgeries Performed | | |
Day	St. Luke's	St. Vincent	Mercy
Monday	14	18	24
Tuesday	20	24	14
Wednesday	16	22	14
Thursday	18	20	22
Friday	20	28	24

❚ Chapter Outline

I. The characteristics of the F distribution are:
   A. It is continuous.
   B. Its values cannot be negative.
   C. It is positively skewed.
   D. There is a family of F distributions. Each time the degrees of freedom in either the numerator or the denominator changes, a new distribution is created.

II. The F distribution is used to test whether two sample variances come from equal populations.
   A. The sampled populations must be normal.
   B. The ratio of the two sample variances is computed and the result compared to the critical value of F.
   C. The larger of the two sample variances is placed in the numerator, forcing the ratio to be greater than 1.00.
   D. The value of F is computed using the following equation:

$$F = \frac{s_1^2}{s_2^2}$$ [11–1]

III. A one-way ANOVA is used to compare several treatment means to see whether they came from the same or equal populations.
   A. A treatment is a source of variation.
   B. The assumptions underlying ANOVA are:
      1. The samples are from normally distributed populations.
      2. The populations have equal standard deviations.
      3. The populations are independent.
   C. The information for finding the value of F is summarized in an ANOVA table.
      1. The formula for SS total, the sum of squares total is:

$$\text{SS total} = \Sigma X^2 - \frac{(\Sigma X)^2}{n}$$ [11–2]

2. The formula for the SST, the sum of squares treatment is:

$$SST = \Sigma\left(\frac{T_c^2}{n_c}\right) - \frac{(\Sigma X)^2}{n}$$ **[11–3]**

3. The SSE, the sum of squares error, is found by subtraction.

$$SSE = SS\ total - SST$$ **[11–4]**

4. This information is summarized in the following table and the value of *F* determined.

Source of Variation	Sum of Squares	Degrees of Freedom	Mean Square	*F*
Treatments	SST	$k - 1$	$SST/(k - 1) = MST$	MST/MSE
Error	SSE	$n - k$	$SSE/(n - k) = MSE$	
Total	SS total	$n - 1$		

IV. If a null hypothesis of equal treatment means is rejected, we can identify the pairs that differ from the following confidence interval.

$$(\bar{X}_1 - \bar{X}_2) \pm t\ \sqrt{MSE\left(\frac{1}{n_1} + \frac{1}{n_2}\right)}$$ **[11–5]**

V. In a two-way ANOVA we consider a second treatment variable.
   A. The second treatment variable is called the blocking variable.
   B. It is determined using the following equation

$$SSB = \Sigma\left(\frac{B_r^2}{k}\right) - \frac{(\Sigma X)^2}{n}$$ **[11–6]**

   C. The SSE term, or sum of squares error is found from the following equation.

$$SSE = SS\ total - SST - SSB$$ **[11–7]**

   D. The *F* statistics for the treatment variable and the blocking variable are determined in the following table.

Source of Variation	Sum of Squares	Degrees of Freedom	Mean Square	*F*
Treatments	SST	$k - 1$	$SST/(k - 1) = MST$	MST/MSE
Blocks	SSB	$b - 1$	$SSB/(b - 1) = MSB$	MSB/MSE
Error	SSE	$(k - 1)(b - 1)$	$SSE/(k - 1)(b - 1) = MSE$	
Total	SS total	$n - 1$		

▌ Pronunciation Key

SYMBOL	MEANING	PRONUNCIATION
SS total	Sum of squares total	S S total
SST	Sum of squares treatment	S S T
SSE	Sum of squares error	S S E
T_c^2	Column totals squared	T sub c squared
n_c	Number of observations in each treatment	n sub c
MSE	Mean square error	M S E
SSB	Block sum of squares	S S B

▌ Chapter Exercises

19. A real estate agent in the coastal area of the Carolinas wants to compare the variation in the selling price of homes on the ocean front with those between one and three blocks from the ocean. A sample of 21 ocean-front homes sold within the last year revealed that the standard deviation of the selling prices was $45,600. A sample of 18 homes, also sold within the last year, that were one to three blocks from the ocean revealed that the standard deviation was $21,330. At the .01 significance level, can we conclude that there is more variation in the selling prices of the ocean-front homes?

20. A computer manufacturer is about to unveil a new, faster personal computer. The new machine clearly is faster, but initial tests indicate there is more variation in the processing time. The processing time depends on the particular program being run, the amount of input data, and the amount of output. A sample of 16 computer runs, covering a range of production jobs, showed that the standard deviation of the processing time was 22 (hundredths of a second) for the new machine and 12 (hundredths of a second) for the current machine. At the .05 significance level can we conclude that there is more variation in the processing time of the new machine?

21. There are two Chevrolet dealers in Jamestown, New York. The mean weekly sales at Sharkey Chevy and Dave White Chevrolet are about the same. However, Tom Sharkey, the owner of Sharkey Chevy, believes his sales are more consistent. Below is the number of new cars sold at Sharkey in the last seven months and for the last eight months at Dave White. Do you agree with Mr. Sharkey? Use the .01 significance level.

Sharkey	98	78	54	57	68	64	70	
Dave White	75	81	81	30	82	46	58	101

22. Random samples of five were selected from each of three populations. The sum of squares total was 100. The sum of squares due to treatment was 40.
    a. Set up the null hypothesis and the alternate hypothesis.
    b. What is the decision rule? Use the .05 significance level.
    c. Complete an ANOVA table. What is the value of F?
    d. What is your decision regarding the null hypothesis?

23. In an ANOVA table MSE was equal to 10. Random samples of six were selected from four populations, where the SS total was 250.
    a. Set up the null hypothesis and the alternate hypothesis.
    b. What is the decision rule?
    c. Complete an ANOVA table. What is the value of F?
    d. What is your decision regarding the null hypothesis?

24. Following is a partial ANOVA table.

Source	Sum of Squares	df	Mean Square	F
Treatment		2		
Error			20	
Total	500	11		

Complete the table, and answer the following questions. Use the .05 significance level.
    a. How many treatments are there?
    b. What was the total sample size?
    c. What is the critical value of F?
    d. Write out the null and alternate hypotheses.
    e. What is your conclusion regarding the null hypothesis?

25. A consumer organization wants to know whether there is a difference in the price of a particular toy at three different types of stores. The price of the toy was checked in a sample

of five discount toy stores, five variety stores, and five department stores. The results are shown below.

Discount Toy	Variety	Department
$12	$15	$19
13	17	17
14	14	16
12	18	20
15	17	19

Use the .05 significance level to conduct the test.

26. A physician who specializes in weight control has three different diets she recommends. As an experiment, she randomly selected 15 patients and then assigned 5 to each diet. After three weeks the following weight losses, in pounds, were noted. At the .05 significance level, can she conclude that there is a difference in the mean amount of weight loss among the three diets?

Plan A	Plan B	Plan C
5	6	7
7	7	8
4	7	9
5	5	8
4	6	9

27. The City of Maumee comprises four districts. Chief of Police Andy North wants to determine whether there is a difference in the mean number of crimes committed among the four districts. He recorded the number of crimes reported in each district for a sample of six days. At the .05 significance level, can the chief of police conclude there is a difference in the mean number of crimes?

Number of Crimes			
Rec Center	Key Street	Monclova	Whitehouse
13	21	12	16
15	13	14	17
14	18	15	18
15	19	13	15
14	18	12	20
15	19	15	18

28. The personnel director of Cander Machine Products is investigating "perfectionism" on the job. A test designed to measure perfectionism was administered to a random sample of 18 employees. The scores ranged from 20 to about 40. One of the facets of the study involved the early background of each employee. Did the employee come from a rural background, a small city, or a large city? The scores are:

Rural Area	Small Urban Area	Large Urban Area
35	28	24
30	24	28
36	25	26
38	30	30
29	32	34
34	28	
31		

a. At the .05 level, can it be concluded that there is a difference in the three mean scores?
b. If the null hypothesis is rejected, can you state that the mean score of those with a rural background is different from the score of those with a large-city background?

29. It can be shown that when only two treatments are involved, ANOVA and the Student t test (Chapter 10) result in the same conclusions. Also, $t^2 = F$. As an example, suppose that 14 randomly selected students were divided into two groups, one consisting of 6 students and the other of 8. One group was taught using a combination of lecture and programmed instruction, the other using a combination of lecture and television. At the end of the course, each group was given a 50-item test. The following is a list of the number correct for each of the two groups.

Lecture and Programmed Instruction	Lecture and Television
19	32
17	28
23	31
22	26
17	23
16	24
	27
	25

a. Using analysis of variance techniques, test H_0 that the two mean test scores are equal; $\alpha = .05$.
b. Using the t test from Chapter 10, compute t.
c. Interpret the results.

30. One reads that a business school graduate with an undergraduate degree earns more than a high school graduate with no additional education, and a person with a master's degree or a doctorate earns even more. To test this, a random sample of 25 executives from companies with assets over $1 million was selected. Their incomes, classified by highest level of education, follow.

Income ($ thousands)		
High School or Less	Undergraduate Degree	Master's Degree or More
45	49	51
47	57	73
53	85	82
62	73	59
39	81	94
43	84	89
54	89	89
	92	95
	62	73

Test at the .05 level of significance that there is no difference in the arithmetic mean salaries of the three groups. If the null hypothesis is rejected, conduct further tests to determine which groups differ.

31. Shank's, Inc., a nationwide advertising firm, wants to know whether the size of an advertisement and the color of the advertisement make a difference in the response of magazine readers. A random sample of readers is shown ads of four different colors and three different

sizes. Each reader is asked to give the particular combination of size and color a rating between 1 and 10. Assume that the ratings are approximately normally distributed. The rating for each combination is shown in the following table (for example, the rating for a small red ad is 2).

| | Color of Ad | | | |
Size of Ad	Red	Blue	Orange	Green
Small	2	3	3	8
Medium	3	5	6	7
Large	6	7	8	8

Is there a difference in the effectiveness of an advertisement by color and by size? Use the .05 level of significance.

32. There are four McBurger restaurants in the Columbus, Georgia, area. The numbers of burgers sold at the respective restaurants for each of the last six weeks are shown below. At the .05 significance level, is there a difference in the mean number sold among the four restaurants, when the factor of week is considered?

| | Restaurant | | | |
Week	Metro	Interstate	University	River
1	124	160	320	190
2	234	220	340	230
3	430	290	290	240
4	105	245	310	170
5	240	205	280	180
6	310	260	270	205

a. Is there a difference in the treatment means?
b. Is there a difference in the block means?

33. The city of Tucson, Arizona, employs people to assess the value of homes for the purpose of establishing real estate tax. The city manager routinely sends each assessor to five homes and then compares the results. The information is given below, in thousands of dollars. Can we conclude that there is a difference in the assessors, at $\alpha = .05$?

| | Assessor | | | |
Home	Zawodny	Norman	Cingle	Holiday
A	$53.0	$55.0	$49.0	$45.0
B	50.0	51.0	52.0	53.0
C	48.0	52.0	47.0	53.0
D	70.0	68.0	65.0	64.0
E	84.0	89.0	92.0	86.0

a. Is there a difference in the treatment means?
b. Is there a difference in the block means?

34. Martin Motors has in stock three cars of the same make and model. The president would like to compare the gas consumption of the three cars (labeled car A, car B, and car C) using four different types of gasoline. For each trial, a gallon of gasoline was added to an empty tank, and the car was driven until it ran out of gas. The following table shows the number of miles driven in each trial.

Types of Gasoline	Distance (miles)		
	Car A	Car B	Car C
Regular	22.4	20.8	21.5
Super regular	17.0	19.4	20.7
Unleaded	19.2	20.2	21.2
Premium unleaded	20.3	18.6	20.4

Using the .05 level of significance:
a. Is there a difference among types of gasoline?
b. Is there a difference in the cars?

35. A research firm wants to compare the miles per gallon of unleaded regular, mid-grade, and super premium gasolines. Because of differences in the performance of different automobiles, seven different automobiles were selected and treated as blocks. Therefore, each brand of gasoline was tested with each type of automobile. The results of the trials, in miles per gallon, are shown in the following table. At the .05 significance level, is there a difference in the gasolines and automobiles?

Automobile	Regular	Mid-grade	Super Premium
1	21	23	26
2	23	22	25
3	24	25	27
4	24	24	26
5	26	26	30
6	26	24	27
7	28	27	32

36. Three supermarket chains in the Denver area each claim to have the lowest overall prices. As part of an investigative study on supermarket advertising, the *Denver Daily News* conducted a study. First, a random sample of nine grocery items was selected. Next, the price of each selected item was checked at each of the three chains on the same day. At the .05 significance level, is there a difference in the mean prices at the supermarkets and for the items?

Item	Super$	Ralph's	Lowblaws
1	$1.12	$1.02	$1.07
2	1.14	1.10	1.21
3	1.72	1.97	2.08
4	2.22	2.09	2.32
5	2.40	2.10	2.30
6	4.04	4.32	4.15
7	5.05	4.95	5.05
8	4.68	4.13	4.67
9	5.52	5.46	5.86

37. Listed below are the weights (in grams) of a sample of M&M's Plain candies, classified according to color. Use a statistical software system to determine whether there is a difference in the mean weights of candies of different colors. Use the .05 significance level.

Red	Orange	Yellow	Brown	Tan	Green
0.946	0.902	0.929	0.896	0.845	0.935
1.107	0.943	0.960	0.888	0.909	0.903
0.913	0.916	0.938	0.906	0.873	0.865
0.904	0.910	0.933	0.941	0.902	0.822
0.926	0.903	0.932	0.838	0.956	0.871
0.926	0.901	0.899	0.892	0.959	0.905
1.006	0.919	0.907	0.905	0.916	0.905
0.914	0.901	0.906	0.824	0.822	0.852
0.922	0.930	0.930	0.908		0.965
1.052	0.883	0.952	0.833		0.898
0.903		0.939			
0.895		0.940			
		0.882			
		0.906			

38. There are four radio stations in Midland. The stations have different formats (hard rock, classical, country/western, and easy listening), but each is concerned with the number of minutes of music played per hour. From a sample of 10 hours from each station, the following sample means were offered.

$$\bar{X}_1 = 51.43 \qquad \bar{X}_2 = 44.64 \qquad \bar{X}_3 = 47.2 \qquad \bar{X}_4 = 50.85$$
$$\text{SS total} = 650.75$$

   a. Determine SST.
   b. Determine SSE.
   c. Complete an ANOVA table.
   d. At the .05 significance level, is there a difference in the treatment means?
   e. Is there a difference in the mean amount of music time between station 1 and station 4? Use the .05 significance level.

www.**Exercises**.com

39. The following Web site presents information on the number of calories and the amount of sodium in hot dogs. The hot dogs are classified by three types: beef, poultry, and meat (mostly pork and beef, but up to 15 percent poultry meat). At the .05 significance level, is there a difference in the mean number of calories and the mean amount of sodium by type of hot dog? The Web site is: *http://lib.stat.cmu.edu/DASL/Datafiles/Hotdogs.html.* (Remember that the site requires the capital letters as shown.)

40. Many real estate companies and rental agencies now publish their listings on the Web. One example is the Dunes Realty Company, located in Garden City and Surfside Beaches in South Carolina. Go to the Web site *http:www.dunes.com,* select **Cottage Search,** then indicate 5 bedroom, accommodations for 14 people, second row (this means it is across the street from the beach), no pool or floating dock, select a period in July and August, indicate that you are willing to spend $5,000 per week, and then click on **Search the Cottages.** The output should include details on the cottages that met your criteria. At the .05 significance level is there a difference in the mean rental prices for the different number of bedrooms? (You may want to combine some of the larger homes, such as 8 or more bedrooms.) Which pairs of means differ?

▌ Computer Data Exercises

41. Refer to Data Set 1, which reports information on the homes sold in the Venice, Florida, area last year.
    a. At the .02 significance level, is there a difference in the variability of the selling prices of the homes that have a pool versus those that do not have a pool?
    b. At the .02 significance level, is there a difference in the variability of the selling prices of the homes with an attached garage versus those that do not have an attached garage?
    c. At the .05 significance level, is there a difference in the mean selling price of the homes among the five townships?

42. Refer to Data Set 2, which reports information on the 28 Major League Baseball teams for the 1997 season.
    a. At the .10 significance level, is there a difference in the variation of the number of stolen bases among the teams that play their home games on natural grass versus on artificial grass?
    b. Create a variable that classifies a team's total attendance into three groups: less than 2.0 (million), 2.0 up to 3.0, and 3.0 or more. At the .05 significance level, is there a difference in the mean number of games won among the three groups?
    c. Using the same attendance variable developed in part (b), is there a difference in the mean number of stolen bases?
    d. Using the same attendance variable developed in part (b), is there a difference in the mean salary of the three groups?

43. Refer to Data Set 3, which reports information on the circulation of magazines. Create a variable that divides the percent of male readership into three groups: less than 33 percent male, 33 percent up to 67 percent male, and 67 percent or more.
    a. Is there a difference in the mean circulation for the three groups? Use the .05 significance level. If the null hypothesis is rejected, determine which pair or pairs of means differ.
    b. Is there a difference in the mean color advertising cost for the three groups? Use the .05 significance level. If the null hypothesis is rejected, determine which pair or pairs of means differ.
    c. Compare the variation of the median income of readers of magazines with less than 33 percent male readership with the variation in the median income of readers of magazines with 67 percent or more male readership. Use the .02 significance level.

44. Refer to Data Set 4, which reports information on 94 school districts in northwest Ohio.
    a. Create a variable related to the size of the school district. The three groups are: (1) small (less than 1000 students), (2) medium (1000 up to 3000 students), and (3) large (more than 3000 students). Is there a difference in the mean amount spent on instruction for these three groups? If the null hypothesis is rejected, determine which pair or pairs of means differ.
    b. Using the size variable created in part (a), is there a difference in the means of the salaries of the three groups? Use the .05 significance level. If the null hypothesis is rejected, determine which pair or pairs of means differ.

▌ Computer Commands

1. The MINITAB commands for the one-way ANOVA on page 397 are:
    a. Input the data, using the **Set** command, into four columns.
    b. Use the **Name** command to identify the columns as Excellent, Good, Fair, and Poor.
    c. Use the mouse to select **Stat, Anova,** and **Oneway (Unstacked).**
    d. Select all four variables and then click **OK.**

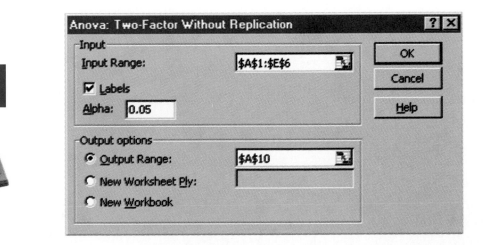

2. The Excel commands for the two-way ANOVA on page 406 are:
   a. In the first row of the first column write the word **Drivers,** then list the five drivers in the first column. In the first row of the next four columns, input the route names. Enter the data under the various routes as on page 403.
   b. Select **Tools, Data Analysis,** and **ANOVA: Two-Factor Without Replication** and then click **OK.**
   c. In the dialog box the **Input Range** is A1:E6. Select **Labels,** select *A10* for the **Output Range,** and then click **OK.**

CHAPTER 11   *Answers to Self-Review*

11-1 Let Mark's assemblies be population 1. then H_0: $\sigma_1^2 \leq \sigma_2^2$; H_1: $\sigma_1^2 > \sigma_2^2$; $df_1 = 10 - 1 = 9$; and df_2 also equals 9. H_0 is rejected if $F > 3.18$.

$$F = \frac{(2.0)^2}{(1.5)^2} = 1.78$$

H_0 is not rejected. The variation is the same for both employees.

11-2 (a) H_0: $\mu_1 = \mu_2 = \mu_3$
     H_1: At least one treatment mean is different.
(b) Reject H_0 if $F > 4.26$
(c) SS total $= 5651 - \dfrac{(247)^2}{12} = 566.92$

$$SST = \frac{(77)^2}{4} + \frac{(55)^2}{4} + \frac{(115)^2}{4} - \frac{(247)^2}{12}$$

$$= 460.67$$

$$SSE = 566.92 - 460.67 = 106.25$$

(d)

Source	Sum of Squares	Degrees of Freedom	Mean Square	F
Treatment	460.67	2	230.335	19.510
Error	106.25	9	11.806	

(e) H_0 is rejected.
(f) There is a difference in the mean number of bottles sold at the various locations.

11-3 (a) H_0: $\mu_1 = \mu_2 = \mu_3$
     H_1: Not all means are equal.
(b) H_0 is rejected if $F > 3.98$.
(c) SS total $= 1{,}152 - \dfrac{(124)^2}{14} = 53.71$

$$SST = \frac{(55)^2}{5} + \frac{(35)^2}{4} + \frac{(34)^2}{5}$$

$$- \frac{(124)^2}{14} = 44.16$$

$$SSE = 53.71 - 44.16 = 9.55$$

Source	Sum of Squares	df	Mean Square	F
Treatment	44.16	2	22.08	25.43
Error	9.55	11	0.8682	
Total	53.71	13		

(d) H_0 is rejected. The treatment means differ.
(e) $(11.0 - 6.8) \pm 2.201 \sqrt{0.8682(\frac{1}{5} + \frac{1}{5})}$
     $= 4.2 \pm 1.30 = 2.90$ and 5.50.
These treatment means differ because both endpoints of the confidence interval are of the same sign — positive in this problem.

11-4 For types:

H_0: $\mu_1 = \mu_2 = \mu_3$
H_1: The treatment means are not equal.

Reject H_0 if $F > 4.46$.
For months:

H_0: $\mu_1 = \mu_2 = \mu_3 = \mu_4 = \mu_5$
H_1: The block means are not equal.

Reject H_0 if $F > 3.84$.
     The analysis of variance table is as follows:

Source	df	SS	MS	F
Types	2	3.60	1.80	0.39
Months	4	31.73	7.93	1.71
Error	8	37.07	4.63	
Total	14	72.40		

The null hypotheses cannot be rejected for either types or months. There is no difference in the mean sales among types or months.

This section is a review of the major concepts and terms introduced in Chapters 10 and 11. Chapter 10 continued the subject of hypothesis testing started in Chapter 9. Chapter 9 dealt with large samples (30 and more).

Less than 30 is a small sample

Chapter 10 was concerned with small samples (less than 30). In the small-sample case, it is assumed that the standard deviation of the population is unknown. The major difference between the testing procedures for large samples (Chapter 9) and small samples (Chapter 10) is the test statistic used. For large samples it is *z*, and for small samples it is the *Student t*.

Paired difference test used for dependent samples

Testing for the reasonableness of a mean involving a small sample, or the difference between two means, also requires that the samples be *independent*. For *dependent* samples, we applied the *paired difference test,* which also uses *t* as the test statistic. One typical paired sample problem calls for recording an individual's blood pressure before administering antihypertensive medication and then again afterward in order to evaluate the effectiveness of the medication. Another typical problem using the paired difference test involves recording the production of an individual using method A and then using method B. The purpose of the experiment is to find out whether the difference in production between method A and method B is statistically significant.

The ANOVA procedure

Chapter 10 dealt with either one mean or the difference between two means. Chapter 11 presented a procedure called the *analysis of variance,* or *ANOVA,* used to simultaneously determine whether several populations have identical means. This is accomplished by comparing the variances of the random samples selected from these populations. The usual five-step hypothesis-testing procedure is applied, but we use a probability distribution called the *F* distribution as the test statistic. Before beginning the calculations for *F,* we set up an ANOVA table to organize the calculations into a convenient form.

As an example of the analysis of variance, a test could be conducted to find whether there is any difference in effectiveness among five fertilizers on the weight of popcorn ears. This type of analysis is referred to as *one-factor ANOVA* because we are able to draw conclusions about only one factor, called a *treatment.* If we want to draw conclusions about the simultaneous effects of more than one factor or variable, the *two-factor ANOVA* technique is applied. Both the one-factor and two-factor tests use the *F distribution* as the test statistic. The *F* distribution is also the test statistic used to find whether one normal population has more variation than another. In addition, it is applied when we want to test the assumption that the variances of two populations are equal.

Glossary

Chapter 10

Degrees of freedom   The number of items in a sample that are free to vary. Suppose there are two items in a sample, and we know the mean. We are free to specify only one of the two values because the other value is automatically determined (since the two values total twice the mean). Example: If the mean is $6, we are free to choose only one value. Choosing $4 makes the other value $8 because $4 + $8 = 2($6). So there is 1 degree of freedom in this illustration. It could have been determined by $n - 1 = 2 - 1 = 1$ degree of freedom. If n is 4, then there are 3 degrees of freedom, found by $n - 1 = 4 - 1 = 3$.

Dependent samples   Samples chosen from several populations in such a way that they are dependent of each other. Paired samples are dependent because the same individual or item is a member of both samples. Example: If the test scores of 10 individuals were recorded before a new teaching method was introduced, and then their test scores after using the new method were recorded, the two paired samples would be considered dependent.

Independent samples   The samples chosen at random are in no way related to each other. A sample of the ages of 28 inmates in the Auburn maximum security prison and a sample of the ages of 19 students at Mid-South University are examples of two independent samples.

Paired difference test   A test of hypothesis conducted using paired samples. It is especially useful for "before and after" problems and to test whether method A and method B are equally effective.

***t* distribution**   Investigated and reported by William S. Gossett in 1908 and published under the pseudonym *Student,* it is similar to the normal distribution presented in Chapter 7. The major characteristics of *t* are:

1. It is a continuous distribution.
2. It can assume values between $-\infty$ and ∞
3. It is symmetrical about its mean of zero. However, it is more spread out and flatter at the apex than the normal distribution.
4. It approaches the standard normal distribution as n gets larger.

5. There is a "family" of t distributions. One t distribution exists for a sample of 15, another for a sample of 16, and so on.

Chapter 11

Analysis of variance (ANOVA)   A technique used to test simultaneously whether the means of several populations are equal. It uses the F distribution as the test statistic.
Block   A second source of variation, in addition to treatments.
F distribution   Used as the test statistic for ANOVA problems, it has the following characteristics:

1. The value of F is never negative.
2. The F distribution is a continuous distribution approaching the X-axis but never touching it.
3. It is positively skewed.
4. Like the t distribution, there is a "family" of F distributions. There is one distribution for 17 degrees of freedom in the numerator and 9 degrees of freedom in the denominator, there is another F distribution for 7 degrees of freedom in the numerator and 12 degrees of freedom in the denominator, and so on.

Treatment   A cause or specific source of variation in the data.

▌ Exercises

Part I — Multiple Choice

For Exercises 1 through 12, give the letter representing the correct answer.

1. The test statistic for testing a hypothesis for small sample means when the population standard deviation is not known is:
   a. z.
   b. t.
   c. F.
   d. $A > B$.
   e. None of these is correct.
2. We want to test a hypothesis for the difference between two population means. The null and alternate hypotheses are stated as H_0: $\mu_1 - \mu_2$ and H_1: $\mu_1 \neq \mu_2$.
   a. A left-tailed test should be applied.
   b. A two-tailed test should be applied.
   c. A right-tailed test should be applied.
   d. We cannot determine whether a left-, right-, or two-tailed test should be applied based on the information given.
   e. None of these is correct.
3. The F distribution:
   a. Cannot be negative.
   b. Cannot be positive.
   c. Is the same as the t distribution.
   d. Is the same as the z distribution.
   e. None of these is correct.
4. As the sample size increases, the t distribution approaches:
   a. ANOVA.
   b. The standard normal or z distribution.
   c. The Poisson distribution.
   d. Zero.
   e. None of these is correct.
5. To conduct a paired difference test, the samples must be:
   a. Infinitely large.
   b. Equal to ANOVA.
   c. Independent.

   d.   Dependent.
   e.   None of these is correct.
6.   An ANOVA test was conducted with respect to the population means. The null hypothesis was rejected. This indicates that:
   a.   There were too many degrees of freedom.
   b.   There is no difference between the population means.
   c.   There is a difference between at least two population means.
   d.   A larger sample should be selected.
   e.   None of these is correct.

Use the following information for Exercises 7, 8, and 9. The Rochester Builders Association stated that the mean cost of erecting a multistory apartment building in the area is no more than $80 per square foot. A building contractor claims that the mean cost per square foot is more than $80. A sample of 21 apartment buildings resulted in the sample mean of $81.

7.   The alternate hypothesis is:
   a. H_1: $\mu <$ $80.
   b. H_1: $\mu \neq$ $80.
   c. H_1: $\mu \geq$ $80.
   d. H_1: $\mu >$ $80.
   e.   None of these is correct.
8.   The number of degrees of freedom for this problem is:
   a.   80.
   b.   0
   c.   21.
   d.   20.
   e.   None of these is correct.
9. t was computed to be 1.90. At the .05 level, the null hypothesis is:
   a.   Not rejected.
   b.   Rejected.
   c.   Both accepted and rejected.
   d.   None of these is correct.

Exercises 10, 11, and 12 are based on the following. A preliminary study of the hourly wages paid unskilled employees in three metropolitan areas was conducted. Seven employees were included from area A, 9 from area B, and 12 from area C. The objective of the study is to find whether there is a significant difference in the mean hourly wage in the three areas. The .01 level of significance is to be applied. The test statistic was computed to be 4.91.

10.   For this type of problem we would use as the test statistic the:
   a. z distribution.
   b. t distribution.
   c. χ^2 distribution.
   d. F distribution.
   e.   None of these is correct.
11.   At the .01 level, the critical value is:
   a.   1.96.
   b.   −1.96.
   c.   5,000.
   d.   5.00.
   e.   None of these is correct.
12.   We would conclude that:
   a.   The mean hourly wages of unskilled employees in the three areas are equal.
   b.   The mean hourly wages in at least two metropolitan areas are different.
   c.   More degrees of freedom are needed.
   d.   None of these is correct.

Part II — Problems

13. It was hypothesized that university clerical employees did not engage in productive work 20 minutes on the average out of every hour. Some claimed the time lost was greater than 20 minutes. An actual study was conducted at a midwestern university using a stopwatch and other ways of checking the work habits of the clerical employees. A random check of the employees revealed the following unproductive times, in minutes, during a one-hour period (exclusive of regularly scheduled breaks): 10, 25, 17, 20, 28, 30, 18, 23, and 18. Test at the .05 level that the mean unproductive time is 20 minutes, against the alternate hypothesis that it is greater than 20 minutes.

14. A test is to be conducted involving the mean holding power of two glues designed for plastic. First, a small plastic hook was coated at one end with Epox glue and fastened to a sheet of plastic. After it dried, weight was added to the hook until it separated from the sheet of plastic. The weight was then recorded. This was repeated until 12 hooks were tested. The same procedure was followed for Holdtite glue, but only 10 hooks were used. The sample results, in pounds, were:

	Epox	Holdtite
Sample mean	250	252
Sample standard deviation	5	8
Number in sample	12	10

At the .01 level, is there a difference between the mean holding power of Epox and that of Holdtite?

15. An additive formulated to add to the life of paints used in the South is to be tested. The top half of a piece of wood was painted using the regular paint. The bottom half was painted with the paint including the additive. The same procedure was followed for a total of 10 pieces. Then each piece was subjected to high-pressure water and brilliant light. The data, number of hours each piece lasted before it faded beyond a certain point, follow:

	Number of Hours by Sample									
	A	B	C	D	E	F	G	H	I	J
Without additive	325	313	320	340	318	312	319	330	333	319
With additive	323	313	326	343	310	320	313	340	330	315

Using the .05 level, determine whether the additive is effective in prolonging the life of the paint.

16. The Buffalo, N.Y., cola distributor is featuring a super-special sale on 12-packs. She wonders where to place the cola for maximum attention. Should it be near the front door of the grocery stores, in the cola section, at the checkout registers, or near the milk and other dairy products? Four stores with similar total sales cooperated in an experiment. In one store the 12-packs were stacked near the front door, in another they were placed near the checkout registers. and so on. Sales were checked at specified times in each store for exactly four minutes. The results were:

Cola at Door	Cola in Cola Section	Cola Near Registers	Cola Near Dairy Products
$6	$ 5	$ 7	10
8	10	10	9
3	12	9	6
7	4	4	11
	9	5	
		7	

The Buffalo distributor wants to find out whether there is a difference in the mean sales for cola stacked at the four locations in the store. Use the .05 significance level.

17. An agriculture economist wants to determine whether soil condition and type of fertilizer have an effect on the yield of blueberries. The following results were obtained, in boxes per acre, from a study of 15 combinations of soil conditions and fertilizer types. Use the .05 significance level.

Soil Conditions	Yield (boxes) by Fertilizer Type				
	A	B	C	D	E
Dry	15	13	7	16	9
Moderate	10	11	8	15	10
Moist	18	14	6	19	12

18. A recent study by the dean of students at Napa Valley College showed that the mean number of hours attempted by a sample of 28 engineering majors was 12.2, and the standard deviation was 2.85 hours. A study of 23 nursing art majors at Napa Valley showed the mean number of hours attempted was nearly the same — 12.8 — but the standard deviation was much larger — 3.9 hours. The dean speculated that this was because many nursing students were able to find part-time work nights and weekends at a local hospital and elected to take fewer hours. Also, some of the nursing students apparently were anxious to complete their program because jobs were plentiful in the field and took an excessive number of hours. At the .05 significance level, can the dean conclude that there is more variation in the number of hours attempted by nursing majors compared with engineering majors?

▌ Cases

A. Century National Bank

Refer to the description of Century National Bank at the end of the Review of Chapters 1–4 on page 139. The bank has branch offices in four different cities: Cincinnati, Ohio; Atlanta, Georgia; Louisville, Kentucky; and Erie, Pennsylvania. Mr. Selig would like to know whether there is a difference in the mean checking account balance among the four branches. If there are differences, between which branches do these differences occur?

Mr. Selig is also interested in the ATMs. Is there a difference in the ATM use among the branches? Also, do customers who have debit cards tend to use the ATMs differently from those who do not have debit cards? Is there a difference in ATM use by those with checking accounts that pay interest versus those that do not?

B. Bell Grove Medical Center

Ms. Jean Dempsey manages the emergency care center at Bell Grove Medical Center. One of her responsibilities is to staff enough nurses so that incoming patients needing service can be handled promptly. It is stressful for patients to wait a long time for emergency care even when their care needs are not life threatening. Ms. Dempsey gathered the following information regarding the number of patients over the last several weeks. The center is not open on weekends. Does it appear that there are any differences in the number of patients served by the day of the week? If there are differences, which days seem to be the busiest?

Date	Day	Patients	Date	Day	Patients
9-29-97	Monday	38	10-13-97	Monday	37
9-30-97	Tuesday	28	10-14-97	Tuesday	29
10-1-97	Wednesday	28	10-15-97	Wednesday	27
10-2-97	Thursday	30	10-16-97	Thursday	28
10-3-97	Friday	35	10-17-97	Friday	35
10-6-97	Monday	35	10-20-97	Monday	37
10-7-97	Tuesday	25	10-21-97	Tuesday	26
10-8-97	Wednesday	22	10-22-97	Wednesday	28
10-9-97	Thursday	21	10-23-97	Thursday	23
10-10-97	Friday	32	10-24-97	Friday	33

Chapter Twelve

Linear Regression and Correlation

GOALS

When you have completed this chapter, you will be able to:

ONE

Draw a scatter diagram.

TWO

Understand and interpret the terms *dependent* and *independent variable*.

THREE

Calculate and interpret the coefficient of correlation, the coefficient of determination, and the standard error of estimate.

FOUR

Conduct a test of hypothesis to determine whether the population coefficient of correlation is different from zero.

FIVE

Calculate the least squares regression line.

SIX

Construct and interpret confidence intervals and prediction intervals for the dependent variable.

SEVEN

Set up and interpret an ANOVA table.

A study of twenty worldwide financial institutions showed the correlation between their assets and pretax profit to be .86. At the .05 significance level, can we conclude there is a positive correlation? (See Goal 4 and Exercise 10).

▌ Introduction

Chapters 2 through 4 dealt with *descriptive statistics.* We organized raw data into a frequency distribution, and computed several measures of central tendency and measures of dispersion to describe the major characteristics of the data. Chapter 5 started the study of *statistical inference.* The main emphasis was on inferring something about a population parameter, such as the population mean, based on a sample. We tested for the reasonableness of a population mean or a population proportion, the difference between two population means, or whether several population means were equal. All of these tests involved just *one* interval- or ratio-level variable, such as the weight of a plastic soft drink bottle, the income of bank presidents, or the number of patients admitted to a particular hospital.

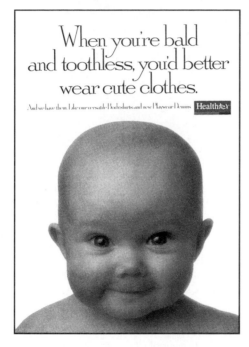

We shift our emphasis in this chapter. Here we study the *relationship between two or more variables and develop an equation that allows us to estimate one variable based on another.* Is there a relationship between the amount Heathtex spends on advertising and its sales? Can we estimate the cost to heat a home in January in the upper Midwest based on the number of square feet in the home? Is there a relationship between the number of years a production worker has been on the job and the number of units produced? Note in each of these instances there are two variables — for example, the number of years on the job and the number of units produced.

We begin this chapter by examining the meaning and purpose of **correlation analysis.** Then we look at a chart designed to portray the relationship between two variables: a **scatter diagram.** We continue our study by developing a mathematical equation that will allow us to estimate the value of one variable based on the value of another. This is called **regression analysis.** We will (1) determine the equation of the straight line that best fits the data, (2) estimate the value of one variable based on another, (3) measure the error in our estimate, and (4) establish confidence and prediction intervals for our estimate.

▌ What is Correlation Analysis?

An example will illustrate correlation analysis. Suppose the sales manager of Copier Sales of America, which has a large sales force throughout the United States and Canada, wants to determine whether there is a relationship between the number of sales calls made in a month and the number of copiers sold that month. The manager selects a random sample of 10 representatives and determines the number of sales calls each representative made last month and the number of copiers sold. The sample information is shown in Table 12–1.

Table 12–1   Sales Calls and Copiers Sold for Ten Salespeople

Sales Representative	Number of Sales Calls	Number of Copiers Sold
Tom Keller	20	30
Jeff Hall	40	60
Brian Virost	20	40
Greg Fish	30	60
Susan Welch	10	30
Carlos Ramirez	10	40
Rich Niles	20	40
Mike Kiel	20	50
Mark Reynolds	20	30
Soni Jones	30	70

There does seem to be some relationship between the number of sales calls and the number of units sold. That is, the salespeople who made the most sales calls sold the most units. The relationship is not "perfect" or exact, however. For example, Soni Jones made fewer sales calls than Jeff Hall, but she sold more units.

Instead of talking in generalities, as we have been doing up to this point, we will develop some statistical measures to portray more precisely the relationship between the two variables, sales calls and copiers sold. This group of statistical techniques is called **correlation analysis.**

| **Correlation Analysis**   A group of techniques to measure the strength of the association between two variables. |

The basic idea of correlation analysis is to report the strength of the association between two variables. The usual first step is to plot the data in a scatter diagram.

| **Scatter Diagram**   A chart that portrays the relationship between two variables. |

An example will show how a scatter diagram is used.

Example

Copier Sales of America, Inc., sells copiers to businesses of all sizes throughout the United States and Canada. Ms. Marcy Bancer was recently promoted to the position of national sales manager. At the upcoming sales meeting, the sales representatives from all over the country will be in attendance. She would like to impress upon them the importance of making that extra sales call each day. She decides to gather some information on the relationship between the number of sales calls and the number of copiers sold. She selected a random sample of 10 sales representatives and determined the number of sales calls they made last month and the number of copiers they sold. The sample information is reported in Table 12–1. Portray this information in a scatter diagram. What observations can you make about the relationship between the number of sales calls and the number of copiers sold?

Solution

Based on the information in Table 12–1, Ms. Bancer suspects there is a relationship between the number of sales calls made in a month and the number of copiers sold. Soni Jones sold the most copiers last month, and she was one of three representatives making 30 or more sales calls. On the other hand, Susan Welch and Carlos Ramirez made only 10 sales calls last month. Ms. Welch had the lowest number of copiers sold among the sampled representatives.

The implication is that the number of copiers sold is related to the number of sales calls made. As the number of sales calls increases, the number of copiers sold also increases. We refer to number of sales calls as the *independent variable* and number of copiers sold as the *dependent variable.*

| **Dependent Variable**   The variable that is being predicted or estimated.   **|**

| **Independent Variable**   A variable that provides the basis for estimation. It is the predictor variable.   **|**

It is common practice to scale the dependent variable (copiers sold) on the vertical or Y-axis and the independent variable (number of sales calls) on the horizontal or X-axis. To develop the scatter diagram of the Copier Sales of America sales information, we begin with the first sales representative, Tom Keller. Tom made 20 sales calls last month and sold 30 copiers, so $X = 20$ and $Y = 30$. To plot this point, move along the horizontal axis to $X = 20$, then go vertically to $Y = 30$ and place a dot at the intersection. This process is continued until all the paired data are plotted, as shown in Chart 12–1.

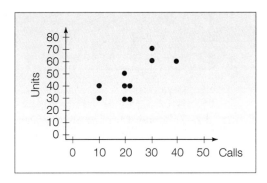

Chart 12–1   Scatter Diagram Showing Sales Calls and Copiers Sold

The scatter diagram shows that the sales representatives who make more calls tend to sell more copiers. It is reasonable for Ms. Bancer, the national sales manager at Copier Sales of America, to tell her salespeople that the more sales calls they make the more copiers they can expect to sell. Note that while there appears to be a positive relationship between the two variables, all the points do not fall on a straight line. In the following section you will measure the strength and direction of this relationship between two variables by determining the coefficient of correlation.

| The Coefficient of Correlation

Interval- or ratio-level data is required.

Originated by Karl Pearson about 1900, the **coefficient of correlation** describes the strength of the relationship between two sets of interval-scaled or ratio-scaled variables. Designated *r,* it is often referred to as *Pearson's r* and as the *Pearson product-moment correlation coefficient.* It can assume any value from −1.00 to +1.00 inclusive. A correlation coefficient of −1.00 or +1.00 indicates *perfect correlation.* For example, a correlation coefficient for the preceding example computed to be +1.00 would indicate that the number of sales calls was a perfect predictor of the number of copiers sold. That is, the number of sales calls and the number of copiers sold are perfectly related in a positive linear sense. A computed value of −1.00 reveals that the independent variable *X* and the dependent variable *Y* are perfectly related in a negative linear way. How the

Characteristics of r

scatter diagram would appear if the relationship between the two sets of data were linear and perfect is shown in Chart 12–2.

If there is absolutely no relationship between the two sets of variables, Pearson's r will be zero. A coefficient of correlation r close to 0 (say, .08) shows that the relationship is quite weak. The same conclusion is drawn if $r = -.08$. Coefficients of $-.91$ and $+.91$ have equal strength; both indicate very strong correlation between the two sets of variables. Thus, *the strength of the correlation does not depend on the direction (either $-$ or $+$).*

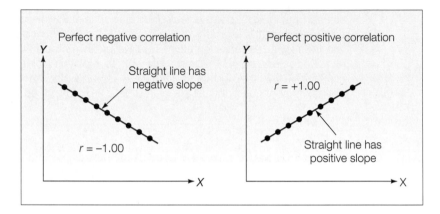

Chart 12–2   Scatter Diagrams Showing Perfect Negative Correlation and Perfect Positive Correlation

Scatter diagrams for $r = 0$, a weak r (say, $-.23$), and a strong r (say, $+.87$) are shown in Chart 12–3. Note that if the correlation is weak, there is considerable scatter about a straight line drawn through the center of the data. For the scatter diagram representing a strong relationship, there is very little scatter about the straight line. This indicates, in the example shown on the chart, that high school GPA is a good predictor of performance in college.

Examples of degrees of correlation

Chart 12–3   Scatter Diagrams Depicting Zero, Weak, and Strong Correlation

The following drawing summarizes the strength and direction of the coefficient of correlation.

Coefficient of Correlation　A measure of the strength of the linear relationship between two variables.

To determine the numerical value of the coefficient of correlation, we use the following formula. The formula for r is:

$$\text{CORRELATION COEFFICIENT} \qquad r = \frac{n(\Sigma XY) - (\Sigma X)(\Sigma Y)}{\sqrt{[n(\Sigma X^2) - (\Sigma X)^2][n(\Sigma Y^2) - (\Sigma Y)^2]}} \qquad \text{[12–1]}$$

where:

n　is the number of paired observations.

ΣX　is the X variable summed.

ΣY　is the Y variable summed.

(ΣX^2)　is the X variable squared and the squares summed.

$(\Sigma X)^2$　is the X variable summed and the sum squared.

(ΣY^2)　is the Y variable squared and the squares summed.

$(\Sigma Y)^2$　is the Y variable summed and the sum squared.

ΣXY　is the sum of the products of X and Y.

Example

Refer to the previous Example, where we developed a scatter diagram depicting the relationship between the number of sales calls and the number of copiers sold. Determine the coefficient of correlation and interpret its value.

Solution

Table 12–2 repeats the information on the number of sales calls and the number of copiers sold. Also included are additional totals necessary to determine the coefficient of correlation.

Table 12–2 Sales Calls and Copiers Sold for 10 Salespeople

Sales Representative	Sales Calls (X)	Copiers Sold (Y)	X^2	Y^2	XY
Tom Keller	20	30	400	900	600
Jeff Hall	40	60	1,600	3,600	2,400
Brian Virost	20	40	400	1,600	800
Greg Fish	30	60	900	3,600	1,800
Susan Welch	10	30	100	900	300
Carlos Ramirez	10	40	100	1,600	400
Rich Niles	20	40	400	1,600	800
Mike Kiel	20	50	400	2,500	1,000
Mark Reynolds	20	30	400	900	600
Soni Jones	30	70	900	4,900	2,100
Total	220	450	5,600	22,100	10,800

The coefficient of correlation is 0.759, found by using formula (12–1).

$$r = \frac{n\Sigma XY - \Sigma X \Sigma Y}{\sqrt{[n(\Sigma X^2) - (\Sigma X)^2][n(\Sigma Y^2) - (\Sigma Y)^2]}}$$

$$= \frac{10(10,800) - (220)(450)}{\sqrt{[10(5,600) - (220)^2][10(22,100) - (450)^2]}}$$

$$= 0.759$$

How do we interpret a correlation of 0.759? First, it is positive, so we see there is a direct relationship between the number of sales calls and the number of copiers sold. This confirms our reasoning based on the scatter diagram, Chart 12–1. The value of 0.759 is fairly close to 1.00, so we conclude that the association is strong. To put it another way, a 25 percent increase in calls will likely lead to 25 percent more sales.

The Coefficient of Determination

In the previous Example regarding the relationship between the number of sales calls 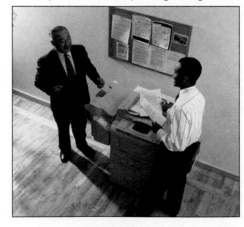 and the units sold, the coefficient of correlation, 0.759, was interpreted as being "strong." Terms such as *weak, moderate,* and *strong,* however, do not have precise meaning. A measure that has a more easily interpreted meaning is the **coefficient of determination.** It is computed by squaring the coefficient of correlation. In the example, the coefficient of determination, r^2, is 0.576, found by $(0.759)^2$. This is a proportion or a percent; we can say that 57.6 percent of the variation in the number of copiers sold is explained, or accounted for, by the variation in the number of sales calls.

> **Coefficient of Determination** The proportion of the total variation in the dependent variable *Y* that is explained, or accounted for, by the variation in the independent variable *X*.

Further discussion of the coefficient of determination is found later in the chapter.

A Word of Caution

If there is a strong relationship (say, .91) between two variables, we are tempted to assume that an increase or decrease in one variable *causes* a change in the other variable. For example, it can be shown that the consumption of Georgia peanuts and the consumption of aspirin have a large correlation. However, this does not indicate that an increase in the consumption of peanuts *caused* the consumption of aspirin to increase. Likewise, the incomes of professors and the number of inmates in mental institutions have increased proportionately. Further, as the population of donkeys has decreased, there has been an increase in the number of doctoral degrees granted. Relationships such as these are called **spurious correlations.** What we can conclude when we find two variables with a strong correlation is that there is a relationship between the two variables, not that a change in one causes a change in the other. So, Ms. Bancer, the sales manager of Copier Sales of America, can conclude that there is a positive relationship between sales calls and copiers sold. She cannot conclude that more sales calls cause more copiers to be sold.

SELF-REVIEW 12–1

Reliable Furniture is a family business that has been selling to retail customers in the Chicago area for many years. They advertise extensively on radio and TV, emphasizing their low prices and easy credit terms. The owner would like to review the relationship between sales and the amount spent on advertising. Below is information on sales and advertising expense for the last four months.

Month	Advertising Expense ($ million)	Sales Revenue ($ million)
July	2	7
August	1	3
September	3	8
October	4	10

(a) The owner wants to forecast sales based on advertising expense. Which variable is the dependent variable? Which variable is the independent variable?
(b) Draw a scatter diagram.
(c) Determine the coefficient of correlation.
(d) Interpret the strength of the correlation coefficient.
(e) Determine the coefficient of determination. Interpret.

▮ Exercises

1. The following sample observations were randomly selected.

X:	4	5	3	6	10
Y:	4	6	5	7	7

Determine the coefficient of correlation and the coefficient of determination. Interpret.

2. The following sample observations were randomly selected.

X:	5	3	6	3	4	4	6	8
Y:	13	15	7	12	13	11	9	5

Determine the coefficient of correlation and the coefficient of determination. Interpret.

3. Bi-lo Appliance Stores has outlets in several large metropolitan areas. The general sales manager plans to air a camcorder television commercial on selected local stations at least twice prior to a gigantic sale starting on Saturday and ending Sunday. She plans to get the figures for Saturday–Sunday camcorder sales at the various outlets and pair them with the number of times the advertisement was shown on the local TV stations. The basic purpose of the research is to find whether there is any relationship between the number of times the advertisement was aired and camcorder sales. The pairings are:

Location of TV Station	Number of Airings	Saturday-Sunday Sales ($ thousands)
Buffalo	4	15
Albany	2	8
Erie	5	21
Syracuse	6	24
Rochester	3	17

a. What is the dependent variable?
b. Draw a scatter diagram.
c. Determine the coefficient of correlation.
d. Determine the coefficient of determination.
e. Interpret these statistical measures.

4. The production department of NDB Electronics wants to explore the relationship between the number of employees who assemble a subassembly and the number produced. As an experiment, two employees were assigned to assemble the subassemblies. They produced 15 during a one-hour period. Then four employees assembled them. They produced 25 during a one-hour period. The complete set of paired observations follows.

Number of Assemblers	One-Hour Production (units)
2	15
4	25
1	10
5	40
3	30

The dependent variable is production; that is, it is assumed that the level of production depends upon the number of employees.

a. Draw a scatter diagram.
b. Based on the scatter diagram, does there appear to be any relationship between the number of assemblers and production? Explain.
c. Compute the coefficient of correlation.
d. Evaluate the strength of the relationship by computing the coefficient of determination.

5. The city council of Pine Bluffs is considering increasing the number of police in an effort to reduce crime. Before making a final decision, the council asks the Chief of Police to survey other cities of similar size to determine the relationship between the number of police and the number of crimes reported. The Chief gathered the following information.

City	Police	Number of Crimes	City	Police	Number of Crimes
Oxford	15	17	Holgate	17	7
Starksville	17	13	Carey	12	21
Danville	25	5	Whistler	11	19
Athens	27	7	Woodville	22	6

   a. If we want to estimate crimes based on the number of police, which variable is the dependent variable and which is the independent variable?
   b. Draw a scatter diagram.
   c. Determine the coefficient of correlation.
   d. Determine the coefficient of determination.
   e. Interpret these statistical measures. Does it surprise you that the relationship is inverse?

6. The owner of Maumee Motors wants to study the relationship between the age of a car and its selling price. Listed below is a random sample of 12 used cars sold at Maumee Motors during the last year.

Car	Age (years)	Selling Price ($000)	Car	Age (years)	Selling Price ($000)
1	9	8.1	7	8	7.6
2	7	6.0	8	11	8.0
3	11	3.6	9	10	8.0
4	12	4.0	10	12	6.0
5	8	5.0	11	6	8.6
6	7	10.0	12	6	8.0

   a. If we want to estimate selling price based on the age of the car, which variable is the dependent variable and which is the independent variable?
   b. Draw a scatter diagram.
   c. Determine the coefficient of correlation.
   d. Determine the coefficient of determination.
   e. Interpret these statistical measures. Does it surprise you that the relationship is inverse?

Testing the Significance of the Correlation Coefficient

Recall the sales manager of Copier Sales of America found the correlation between the number of sales calls and the number of copiers sold was 0.759. This indicated a strong association between the two variables. However, only 10 salespeople were sampled. Could it be that the correlation in the population is actually 0? This would mean the correlation of 0.759 was due to chance. The population in this example is all the salespeople employed by the firm.

Could the correlation in the population be zero?

Resolving this dilemma requires a test to answer the obvious question: Could there be zero correlation in the population from which the sample was selected? To put it another way, did the computed *r* come from a population of paired observations with zero correlation? To continue our convention of allowing Greek letters to represent a population value, we will let ρ represent the correlation in the population. It is pronounced "rho."

We will continue with the illustration involving sales calls and copiers sold. The null hypothesis and the alternate hypothesis are:

H_0: ρ = 0 (The correlation in the population is zero.)

H_1: ρ ≠ 0 (The correlation in the population is different from zero.)

From the way H_1 is stated, we know that the test is two-tailed.

The formula for *t* is:

t TEST FOR THE COEFFICIENT OF CORRELATION	$t = \dfrac{r\sqrt{n-2}}{\sqrt{1-r^2}}$ with $n-2$ degrees of freedom	**[12–2]**

Using the .05 level of significance, the decision rule states that if the computed *t* falls in the area between plus 2.306 and minus 2.306, the null hypothesis is not rejected. To locate the critical value of 2.306, refer to Appendix F for $df = n - 2 = 10 - 2 = 8$. See Chart 12–4.

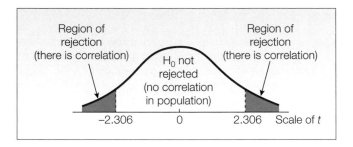

Chart 12–4 Decision Rule for Test of Hypothesis at .05 Significance Level and 8 *df*

Applying formula (12–2) to the problem of sales calls and units sold:

$$t = \frac{r\sqrt{n-2}}{\sqrt{1-r^2}} = \frac{.759\sqrt{10-2}}{\sqrt{1-(.759)^2}} = 3.297$$

The computed *t* falls in the rejection region. Thus, H_0 is rejected at the .05 significance level. This means that the correlation in the population is not zero. From a practical standpoint, it indicates to the sales manager that there definitely is correlation in the population of salespeople with respect to the number of sales calls made and the number of copiers sold.

We can also interpret the test of hypothesis in terms of *p*-values. Recall, we discussed *p*-values in Chapters 9 and 10. To review, it is the likelihood of finding a value of the test statistic this large or larger, when H_0 is true. To determine the *p*-value, go to the *t* distribution in Appendix F and find the row for 8 degrees of freedom. The value of the test statistic is 3.297, so in the row for 8 degrees of freedom and a two-tailed test, find the value closest to 3.297.

For a two-tailed test at the .02 significance level, the critical value is 2.896, and the critical value at the .01 significance level is 3.355. We conclude that the *p*-value is less than .02.

SELF-REVIEW 12–2

A sample of 25 mayoral campaigns in cities with populations larger than 50,000 showed that the correlation between the percent of the vote received and the amount spent on the campaign by the candidate was .43. At the .05 significance level, is there a positive association between the variables?

Exercises

7. The following hypotheses are given.

   $H_0: \rho \leq 0$

   $H_1: \rho > 0$

   A random sample of 12 paired observations indicated a correlation of .32. Can we conclude that the correlation in the population is greater than zero? Use the .05 significance level.

8. The following hypotheses are given.

   $H_0: \rho \geq 0$

   $H_1: \rho < 0$

   A random sample of 15 paired observations have a correlation of $-.46$. Can we conclude that the correlation in the population is less than zero? Use the .05 significance level.

9. The Pennsylvania Refining Company is studying the relationship between the pump price of gasoline and the number of gallons sold at a particular gasoline station. For a sample of 20 stations last Tuesday, the correlation was .78. At the .01 significance level, is the correlation in the population greater than zero?

10. A study of 20 worldwide financial institutions showed the correlation between their assets and pretax profit to be .86. At the .05 significance level, can we conclude that there is positive correlation in the population?

Regression Analysis

We are going to develop next an equation to express the relationship between two variables and estimate the value of the dependent variable Y based on a selected value of the independent variable X. The technique used to develop the equation for the straight line and make these predictions is called **regression analysis.**

In Table 12–1 we reported the number of sales calls and the number of units sold for a sample of 10 sales representatives employed by Copier Sales of America. Chart 12–1 portrayed this information in a scatter diagram. Now we want to develop an equation that expresses the relationship between the number of sales calls and the number of units sold. The equation for the line used to estimate Y based on X is referred to as the **regression equation.**

| **Regression Equation** An equation that defines the relationship between two variables. |

Straight line drawn by hand to fit scatter plots

The scatter diagram in Chart 12–1 is reproduced in Chart 12–5, with a line drawn with a ruler through the dots to illustrate that a straight line would probably fit the data. However, the line drawn using a straight edge has one disadvantage: Its position is based in part on the judgment of the person drawing the line. The hand-drawn lines in Chart 12–6 represent the judgments of four people. All the lines except line A seem to be reasonable. Each would, however, give a different estimate of units sold.

Chart 12–5 Sales Calls and Copiers Sold for 10 Sales Representatives

Chart 12–6 Four Lines Superimposed on the Scatter Diagram

Least Squares Principle

Least squares line gives "best" fit; subjective method is unreliable

Judgment is eliminated by determining the regression line using a mathematical method called the **least squares principle.** This method gives what is commonly referred to as the "best-fitting" straight line.

> **Least Squares Principle** Determining a regression equation by minimizing the sum of the squares of the vertical distances between the actual Y values and the predicted values of Y.

To illustrate this concept, the same data are plotted in the three charts that follow. The regression line in Chart 12–7 was determined using the least squares method. It is the best-fitting line because the sum of the squares of the vertical deviations about it is at a minimum. The first plot ($X = 3$, $Y = 8$) deviates by 2 from the line, found by $10 - 8$. The deviation squared is 4. The squared deviation for the plot $X = 4$, $Y = 18$ is 16. The squared deviation for the plot $X = 5$, $Y = 16$ is 4. The sum of the squared deviations is 24, found by $4 + 16 + 4$.

Chart 12–7 The Least Squares Line

Chart 12–8 Line Drawn Using a Straight Edge

Chart 12–9 Line Drawn Using a Straight Edge

Assume that the straight lines in Charts 12–8 and 12–9 were drawn using a straight edge. The sum of the squared vertical deviations in Chart 12–8 is 44. For Chart 12–9 it is 132. Both sums are greater than the sum for the line in Chart 12–7, found using the least squares method.

The general form of the regression equation is:

GENERAL FORM OF LINEAR REGRESSION EQUATION	$Y' = a + bX$	[12–3]

where:

Y' read Y prime, is the predicted value of the Y variable for a selected X value.

a is the Y-intercept. It is the estimated value of Y when $X = 0$. Another way to put it is: a is the estimated value of Y where the regression line crosses the Y-axis when X is zero.

b is the slope of the line, or the average change in Y' for each change of one unit (either increase or decrease) in the independent variable X.

X is any value of the independent variable that is selected.

It should be noted that the linear regression equation for the sample of salespeople is just an estimate of the relationship between the two variables in the population. Thus, the values of a and b in the regression equation are usually referred to as the **estimated regression coefficients,** or the just the **regression coefficients.**

The formulas for b and a are:

SLOPE OF THE REGRESSION LINE	$b = \dfrac{n(\Sigma XY) - (\Sigma X)(\Sigma Y)}{n(\Sigma X^2) - (\Sigma X)^2}$	[12–4]

Y-AXIS INTERCEPT	$a = \dfrac{\Sigma Y}{n} - b\dfrac{\Sigma X}{n}$	[12–5]

where:

X is a value of the independent variable.

Y is a value of the dependent variable.

n is the number of items in the sample.

Example

Recall the problem involving Copier Sales of America. The sales manager gathered information on the number of sales calls made and the number of copiers sold for a random sample of 10 sales representatives. As a part of her presentation at the upcoming sales meeting, Ms. Bancer, the sales manager, would like to offer specific information about the relationship between the number of sales calls and the number of copiers sold. Use the least squares method to determine a linear equation to express the relationship between the two variables. What is the expected number of copiers sold by a representative who makes 20 calls?

Solution

Table 12–3 repeats the sample information from Table 12–2. It also includes the sums needed in formulas (12–4) and (12–5) to calculate the regression equation. The calculations necessary to determine the regression equation are as follows:

$$b = \frac{n(\Sigma XY) - \Sigma X \Sigma Y}{n\Sigma X^2 - (\Sigma X)^2} = \frac{10(10,800) - (220)(450)}{10(5,600) - (220)^2} = 1.1842$$

$$a = \frac{\Sigma Y}{n} - b\frac{\Sigma X}{n} = \frac{450}{10} - (1.1842)\frac{220}{10} = 18.9476$$

Table 12–3   Calculations Needed for Determining the Least Squares Regression Equation

Sales Representative	Sales Calls (X)	Copiers Sold (Y)	X^2	Y^2	XY
Tom Keller	20	30	400	900	600
Jeff Hall	40	60	1,600	3,600	2,400
Brian Virost	20	40	400	1,600	800
Greg Fish	30	60	900	3,600	1,800
Susan Welch	10	30	100	900	300
Carlos Ramirez	10	40	100	1,600	400
Rich Niles	20	40	400	1,600	800
Mike Kiel	20	50	400	2,500	1,000
Mark Reynolds	20	30	400	900	600
Soni Jones	30	70	900	4,900	2,100
Total	220	450	5,600	22,100	10,800

Thus, the regression equation is $Y' = 18.9476 + 1.1842X$. So if a salesperson makes 20 calls, they can expect to sell 42.6316 copiers, found by $Y' = 18.9476 + 1.1842X = 18.9476 + 1.1842(20)$. The b value of 1.1842 means that for each additional sales call made the sales representative can expect to increase the number of copiers sold by about 1.2. To put it another way five additional sales calls in a month will result in about six more copiers being sold [$1.1842(5) = 5.921$].

The a value of 18.9476 is the point where the equation crosses the Y-axis. A literal translation is that if no sales calls are made, that is, $X = 0$, 18.9476 copiers will be sold. Note that $X = 0$ is outside the range of values included in the sample and, therefore, should not be used to estimate the number of copiers sold. The sales calls ranged from 10 to 40, so estimates should be made within that range.

Drawing the Line of Regression

The least squares equation, $Y' = 18.9476 + 1.1842X$, can be drawn on the scatter diagram. The first sales representative in the sample is Tom Keller. He made 20 calls. His estimated number of copiers sold is $Y' = 18.9476 + 1.1842(20) = 42.6316$. The plot $X = 20$ and $Y = 42.6316$ is located by moving to 20 on the X-axis and then going vertically to 42.6316. The other points on the regression equation can be determined by substituting the particular value of X into the regression equation.

Sales Representative	Sales Calls (X)	Estimated Sales (Y')	Sales Representative	Sales Calls (X)	Estimated Sales (Y')
Tom Keller	20	42.6316	Carlos Ramirez	10	30.7896
Jeff Hall	40	66.3156	Rich Niles	20	42.6316
Brian Virost	20	42.6316	Mike Kiel	20	42.6316
Greg Fish	30	54.4736	Mark Reynolds	20	42.6316
Susan Welch	10	30.7896	Soni Jones	30	54.4736

All the other points are connected to give the straight line. See Chart 12–10.

Chart 12–10   The Line of Regression Drawn on the Scatter Diagram

This line has some interesting features. As we have discussed, there is no other line through the data for which the sum of the squared deviations is less. In addition, this line will pass through the points represented by the mean of the X values and the mean of the Y values, that is, $\bar{X}$ and $\bar{Y}$. In this example $\bar{X} = 22.0$ and $\bar{Y} = 45.0$.

SELF-REVIEW 12–3

Refer to Self-Review 12–1, where the owner of the Reliable Furniture Company was studying the relationship between sales and the amount spent on advertising. The sales information for the last four months is repeated below.

Month	Advertising Expense ($ million)	Sales Revenue ($ million)
July	2	7
August	1	3
September	3	8
October	4	10

(a) Determine the regression equation.
(b) Interpret the values of *a* and *b*.
(c) Estimate sales when 3 million dollars is spent on advertising.

▌ Exercises

Note: It is suggested that you save your values for ΣX, ΣX^2, ΣXY, ΣY, and ΣY^2, as these problems will be referred to later in the chapter.

11.   The following sample observations were randomly selected.

X:	4	5	3	6	10
Y:	4	6	5	7	7

    a.   Determine the regression equation.

    b.   Determine the value of Y' when X is 7.

12.   The following sample observations were randomly selected.

X:	5	3	6	3	4	4	6	8
Y:	13	15	7	12	13	11	9	5

    a.   Determine the regression equation.

    b.   Determine the value of Y' when X is 7.

13.   The Bradford Electric Illuminating Company is studying the relationship between kilowatt-hours (thousands) and the number of rooms in a private single-family residence. A random sample of 10 homes yielded the following.

Number of Rooms	Kilowatt-Hours (thousands)	Number of Rooms	Kilowatt-Hours (thousands)
12	9	8	6
9	7	10	8
14	10	10	10
6	5	5	4
10	8	7	7

    a.   Determine the regression equation.

    b.   Determine the number of kilowatt-hours, in thousands, for a six-room house.

14.   Mr. James McWhinney, president of Daniel-James Financial Services, believes there is a relationship between the number of client contacts and the dollar amount of sales. To document this assertion, Mr. McWhinney gathered the following sample information. The X column indicates the number of client contacts last month, and the Y column shows the value of sales ($ thousands) last month for each client sampled.

Number of Contacts, X	Sales ($ thousands), Y	Number of Contacts, X	Sales ($ thousands), Y
14	24	23	30
12	14	48	90
20	28	50	85
16	30	55	120
46	80	50	110

    a.   Determine the regression equation.

    b.   Determine the estimated sales if 40 contacts are made.

15.   A recent article in *Business Week* listed the "Best Small Companies." We are interested in the current results of the companies' sales and earnings. A random sample of 12 companies was selected and the sales and earnings, in millions of dollars are reported below.

Company	Sales ($ millions)	Earnings ($ millions)	Company	Sales ($ millions)	Earnings ($ millions)
Papa John's International	$89.2	$4.9	Checkmate Electronics	$17.5	$ 2.6
Applied Innovation	18.6	4.4	Royal Grip	11.9	1.7
Integracare	18.2	1.3	M-Wave	19.6	3.5
Wall Data	71.7	8.0	Serving-N-Slide	51.2	8.2
Davidson Associates	58.6	6.6	Daig	28.6	6.0
Chico's Fas	46.8	4.1	Cobra Golf	69.2	12.8

Let sales be the independent variable and earnings be the dependent variable.
a. Draw a scatter diagram.
b. Compute the coefficient of correlation.
c. Compute the coefficient of determination.
d. Interpret your findings in parts b. and c.
e. Determine the regression equation.
f. For a small company with $50.0 million in sales, estimate the earnings.

16. We are studying mutual bond funds for the purpose of investing in several funds. For this particular study, we want to focus on the assets of a fund and its five-year performance. The question is: Can the five-year rate of return be estimated based on the assets of the fund? Nine mutual funds were selected at random, and their assets and rates of return are shown below.

Fund	Assets ($ millions)	Return (%)	Fund	Assets ($ millions)	Return (%)
AARP High Quality Bond	$622.2	10.8	MFS Bond A	$494.5	11.6
Babson Bond L	160.4	11.3	Nichols Income	158.3	9.5
Compass Capital Fixed Income	275.7	11.4	T. Raive Price Short-term	681.0	8.2
Galaxy Bond Retail	433.2	9.1	Thompson Income B	241.3	6.8
Keystone Custodian B-1	437.9	9.2			

a. Draw a scatter diagram.
b. Compute the coefficient of correlation.
c. Compute the coefficient of determination.
d. Write a brief report of your findings for parts b. and c.
e. Determine the regression equation. Use assets as the independent variable.
f. For a fund with $400.0 million in sales, determine the five-year rate of return (in percent).

17. Refer to Exercise 5.
a. Determine the regression equation.
b. Estimate the number of crimes for a city with 20 police.
c. Interpret the regression equation.

18. Refer to Exercise 6.
a. Determine the regression equation.
b. Estimate the selling price of a 10-year-old car.
c. Interpret the regression equation.

❙ The Standard Error of Estimate

Note in the preceding scatter diagram (Chart 12–10) all of the points do not lie exactly on the regression line. If they all were on the line, and if the number of observations were sufficiently large, there would be no error in estimating the number of units sold. To put it another way, if all the points were on the regression line, units sold could be predicted with 100 percent accuracy. Thus, there would be no error in predicting the Y variable based on an X variable. This is true in the following hypothetical case (see Chart 12–11). Theoretically, if $X = 6$, then an exact Y of 200 could be predicted with 100 percent confidence. Or if $X = 10$, then $Y = 800$. Because there is no difference between the observed values and the predicted values, there is no error in this estimate.

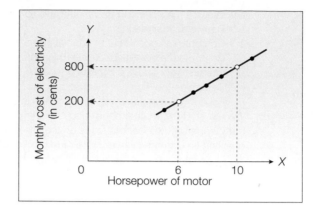

Chart 12–11   Example of Perfect Prediction: Horsepower of Motor and Cost of Electricity

Perfect prediction unrealistic in business   Perfect prediction in economics and business is practically impossible. For example, the revenue for the year from gasoline sales (Y) based on the number of automobile registrations (X) as of a certain date could no doubt be approximated fairly closely, but the prediction would not be exact to the nearest dollar, or probably even to the nearest thousand dollars. Even predictions of tensile strength of steel wires based on the outside diameters of the wires are not always exact due to slight differences in the composition of the steel.

What is needed, then, is a measure that indicates how precise the prediction of Y is based on X or, conversely, how inaccurate the estimate might be. This measure is called the **standard error of estimate.** The standard error of estimate, symbolized by $s_{y \cdot x}$, is the same concept as the standard deviation discussed in Chapter 4. The standard deviation measures the dispersion around the mean. The standard error of estimate measures the dispersion about the regression line.

| **Standard Error of Estimate**   A measure of the scatter, or dispersion, of the observed values around the line of regression. |

The standard error of estimate is found by the following equation. Note that the equation is quite similar to the one for the standard deviation of a sample.

| **STANDARD ERROR OF ESTIMATE** | $s_{y \cdot x} = \sqrt{\dfrac{\Sigma(Y - Y')^2}{n - 2}}$ | **[12–6]** |

Example   Recall the example involving Copier Sales of America. The sales manager determined the least squares regression equation to be $Y' = 18.9476 + 1.1842X$, where Y refers to the number of copiers sold and X the number of sales calls made. Determine the standard error of estimate as a measure of how well the values fit the regression line.

Solution   The standard deviation is based on squared deviations from the mean, whereas the standard error of estimate is based on squared deviations from the regression line. If the squared deviations result in a small total, this means that the regression line is representative of the data. If the squared deviations are a large value, then the regression line may not be representative of the data.

To find the standard error, we begin by finding the difference between the value, Y, and the value estimated from the regression equation, Y'. Next we square this difference, that is, $(Y - Y')^2$. We do this for each of the n observations and sum the results. That is, we compute $\Sigma(Y - Y')^2$, which is the numerator of formula (12–6). Finally, we divide by the number of observations minus 2. Why minus 2? We lose a degree of freedom each for estimating the intercept value, *a*, and the slope value, *b*. The details of the calculations are summarized in Table 12–4.

Table 12–4 Computations Needed for the Standard Error of Estimate

Sales Representative	Actual Sales (Y)	Estimated Sales (Y')	Deviation (Y − Y')	Deviation Squared (Y − Y')²
Tom Keller	30	42.6316	−12.6316	159.557
Jeff Hall	60	66.3156	−6.3156	39.887
Brian Virost	40	42.6316	−2.6316	6.925
Greg Fish	60	54.4736	5.5264	30.541
Susan Welch	30	30.7896	−0.7896	0.623
Carlos Ramirez	40	30.7896	9.2104	84.831
Rich Niles	40	42.6316	−2.6316	6.925
Mike Kiel	50	42.6316	7.3684	54.293
Mark Reynolds	30	42.6316	−12.6316	159.557
Soni Jones	70	54.4736	15.5264	241.069
			0.000	784.208

The standard error of estimate is 9.901, found by using formula (12–6).

$$s_{y \cdot x} = \sqrt{\frac{\Sigma(Y - Y')^2}{n - 2}} = \sqrt{\frac{784.208}{10 - 2}} = 9.901$$

The deviations $(Y - Y')$ are the vertical deviations from the regression line. To illustrate, the 10 deviations from Table 12–4 are shown in Chart 12–12. Note in Table 12–4 that the sum of the signed deviations is zero. This indicates that the positive deviations (above the regression line) are offset by the negative deviations (below the regression line).

Formula (12–6) for the standard error of estimate was applied to show the similarity in concept and computation between the standard deviation and the standard error of estimate. Suppose a large number of observations are being studied, and the numbers are large. Computing each Y' point on the regression line and then squaring the differences — that is, $(Y - Y')^2$ — would be rather tedious. The following formula is algebraically equivalent to formula (12–6) but is much easier to use.

COMPUTATION FORMULA FOR THE STANDARD ERROR OF ESTIMATE	$s_{y \cdot x} = \sqrt{\dfrac{\Sigma Y^2 - a(\Sigma Y) - b(\Sigma XY)}{n - 2}}$	**[12–7]**

The squares, sums, and other numbers for the Copier Sales of America Example were calculated in Table 12–3. Inserting these values into the formula:

$$s_{x \cdot y} = \sqrt{\frac{22{,}100 - 18.9476(450) - 1.1842(10{,}800)}{10 - 2}}$$

$$= 9.901$$

This is the same standard error of estimate as computed previously.

Chart 12–12   Sales Calls and Copiers Sold for 10 Salespeople

▌ Assumptions Underlying Linear Regression

For a better understanding of the application of the standard error of estimate of 9.901 in regression analysis, the underlying assumptions about linear regression and correlation should be stated.

Assumptions required to apply linear regression analysis

1. For each value of *X,* there is a group of *Y* values, and these *Y* values are *normally distributed.*
2. The *means* of these normal distributions of *Y* values all lie on the straight line of regression.
3. The *standard deviations* of these normal distributions are *equal.*
4. The *Y* values are statistically *independent.* This means that in the selection of a sample, the *Y* values chosen for a particular *X* value do not depend on the *Y* values for any other *X* value.

Chart 12–13 illustrates these assumptions. Note that these statements are true for each of the three *X* values: (1) The *Y* values are normally distributed. (2) The means are all on the line of regression. (3) The standard deviations, as represented by the standard error of estimates, $s_{y \cdot x}$, are equal.

Visual presentation of the assumptions

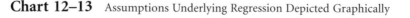

Chart 12–13   Assumptions Underlying Regression Depicted Graphically

Recall from Chapter 7 that if the values are normally distributed:

$\bar{X} \pm 1s$ encompasses approximately the middle 68 percent of the values.

$\bar{X} \pm 2s$ encompasses approximately the middle 95.5 percent of the values.

$\bar{X} \pm 3s$ encompasses virtually all of the values.

The same relationships exist between the average predicted value, Y', and the standard error of estimate, $s_{y \cdot x}$. Again, if the scatter about the regression line is somewhat normally distributed and the sample is large, then:

$Y' \pm 1s_{y \cdot x}$ encompasses the middle 68 percent of the observed values.

$Y' \pm 2s_{y \cdot x}$ encompasses the middle 95.5 percent of the observed values.

$Y' \pm 3s_{y \cdot x}$ encompasses virtually all of the observed values.

We can now relate these assumptions to Copier Sales of America where we were studying the relationship between the number of sales calls and the number of copiers sold. Assume that we took a much larger sample than $n = 10$, but that the standard error of estimate was still 9.901. If we drew a parallel line 9.901 units above the regression line and another 9.901 units below the regression line, about 68 percent of the points would fall between the two lines. Similarly, a line 19.802 [$2s_{y \cdot x} = 2(9.901)$] units above the regression line and another 19.802 units below the regression line should include about 95 percent of the data values. As a rough check refer to the second column from the right in Table 12–4 on page 443, i.e., the column headed "Deviation." Three of the 10 deviations exceed one standard error of estimate. That is, the deviation of -12.6316 for Tom Keller, -12.6316 for Mark Reynolds, and $+15.5264$ for Soni Jones all exceed the value of 9.901, which is one standard error from the regression line. So, to put it another way, seven of the ten deviations in the sample are within one standard error of the regression line—a good result for a relatively small sample.

SELF-REVIEW 12–4

Refer to Self-Reviews 12–1 and 12–3, where the owner of Reliable Furniture was studying the relationship between sales and the amount spent on advertising. Determine the standard error of estimate.

▌ Exercises

19. Refer to Exercise 11.
    a. Determine the standard error of estimate.
    b. Suppose a large sample is selected (instead of just five). About 68 percent of the predictions would be between what two values?

20. Refer to Exercise 12.
    a. Determine the standard error of estimate.
    b. Suppose a large sample is selected (instead of just eight). About 95 percent of the predictions would be between what two values?

21. Refer to Exercise 13.
    a. Determine the standard error of estimate.
    b. Suppose a large sample is selected (instead of just 10). About 95 percent of the predictions regarding kilowatt-hours would occur between what two values?

22. Refer to Exercise 14.
    a. Determine the standard error of estimate.
    b. Suppose a large sample is selected (instead of just 10). About 95 percent of the predictions regarding sales would occur between what two values?

23. Refer to Exercise 5. Determine the standard error of estimate.

24. Refer to Exercise 6. Determine the standard error of estimate.

▌ Confidence Intervals and Prediction Intervals

The standard error of estimate is also used to establish confidence intervals when the sample size is large and the scatter around the regression line approximates the normal distribution. In our example involving the number of sales calls and the number of copiers sold, the sample size is small; hence, we need a correction factor to account for the size of the sample. In addition, when we move away from the mean of the independent variable, our estimates are subject to more variation, and we also need to correct for this.

We are interested in providing interval estimates of two types. The first, which is called a **confidence interval,** reports the *mean* value of Y for a given X. The second type of estimate is called a **prediction interval,** and it reports the range of values of Y for a *particular* value of X. To explain further, suppose we estimate the salary of executives in the retail industry based on their years of experience. If we want an interval estimate of the salary of *all* retail executives with 20 years of experience, we calculate a confidence interval. If we want an estimate of the salary of Curtis Bender, a particular retail executive with 20 years of experience, we calculate a prediction interval.

To determine the confidence interval for the mean value of Y for a given X, the formula is:

| A CONFIDENCE INTERVAL FOR THE MEAN OF Y, GIVEN X. | $Y' \pm t(s_{y \cdot x}) \sqrt{\dfrac{1}{n} + \dfrac{(X - \bar{X})^2}{\Sigma X^2 - \dfrac{(\Sigma X)^2}{n}}}$ | **[12–8]** |

where:

Y' is the predicted value for any selected X value.

X is any selected value of X.

$\bar{X}$ is the mean of the Xs, found by $\Sigma X/n$.

n is the number of observations.

$s_{y \cdot x}$ is the standard error of estimate.

t is the value of t from Appendix F with $n - 2$ degrees of freedom.

It is sufficient to again note that the concept of t was developed by William Gossett in the early 1900s. He noticed that $\bar{X} \pm z(s)$ was not precisely correct for small samples. He observed, for example, for samples of size 120, that 95 percent of the items fell within $\bar{X} \pm 1.98s$ instead of $\bar{X} \pm 1.96s$. This is not too critical, but note what happens as the sample size becomes smaller:

df	t
120	1.980
60	2.000
21	2.080
10	2.228
3	3.182

This is logical. The smaller the sample, the larger the possible error. The increase in the t value compensates for this possibility.

Example

We return to the Copier Sales of America illustration. Determine a 95 percent confidence interval for all sales representatives who make 25 calls and for Sheila Baker, a West Coast sales representative who made 25 calls.

Solution

We use formula (12–8) to determine a confidence interval. Table 12–5 includes the necessary totals and a repeat of the information of Table 12–2 on page 430.

Table 12–5 Calculations Needed for Determining the Confidence Interval and Prediction Interval

Sales Representative	Sales Calls (X)	Copiers Sold (Y)	X^2	Y^2	XY
Tom Keller	20	30	400	900	600
Jeff Hall	40	60	1,600	3,600	2,400
Brian Virost	20	40	400	1,600	800
Greg Fish	30	60	900	3,600	1,800
Susan Welch	10	30	100	900	300
Carlos Ramirez	10	40	100	1,600	400
Rich Niles	20	40	400	1,600	800
Mike Kiel	20	50	400	2,500	1,000
Mark Reynolds	20	30	400	900	600
Soni Jones	30	70	900	4,900	2,100
Total	220	450	5,600	22,100	10,800

The first step is to determine the number of copiers we expect a sales representative to sell if he or she makes 25 calls. It is 48.5526, found by $Y' = 18.9476 + 1.1842X = 18.9476 + 1.1842(25)$.

To find the *t* value, we need to first know the number of degrees of freedom. In this case the degrees of freedom is $n - 2 = 10 - 2 = 8$. We set the confidence level at 95 percent. Appendix F reports the significance level, which is found by one minus the level of confidence. We use the two-tailed category. To find the value of *t*, move down the left-hand column to 8 degrees of freedom, then move across to the column with the two-tailed significance level of .05. The value of *t* is 2.306.

In the previous section we calculated the standard error of estimate to be 9.901, $X = 25$, and from Table 12–5 $\Sigma X = 220$ and $\Sigma X^2 = 5,600$. In addition $\overline{X} = \Sigma X/n = 220/10 = 22$. Inserting these values in formula (12–8), we can determine the confidence interval.

$$\text{Confidence interval} = Y' \pm t s_{y \cdot x} \sqrt{\frac{1}{n} + \frac{(X - \overline{X})^2}{\Sigma X^2 - \frac{(\Sigma X)^2}{n}}}$$

$$= 48.5526 \pm 2.306(9.901) \sqrt{\frac{1}{10} + \frac{(25 - 22)^2}{5,600 - \frac{(220)^2}{10}}}$$

$$= 48.5526 \pm 7.6356$$

Thus, the 95 percent confidence interval for all sales representatives who make 25 calls is from 40.9170 up to 56.1882. To interpret, let's round the values. If a sales representative makes 25 calls, he or she can expect to sell 48.6 copiers. It is likely his sales will range from 40.9 to 56.2 copiers.

To determine the prediction interval for a particular value of Y for a given X, formula (12–8) is modified slightly: A "1" is added under the radical. The formula becomes:

PREDICTION INTERVAL FOR Y, GIVEN X	$Y' \pm t s_{y \cdot x} \sqrt{1 + \dfrac{1}{n} + \dfrac{(X - \bar{X})^2}{\sum X^2 - \dfrac{(\sum X)^2}{n}}}$	**[12–9]**

Suppose we want to estimate the number of copiers sold by Sheila Baker, who made 25 sales calls. The 95 percent prediction interval is determined as follows:

$$\text{Prediction interval} = Y' \pm t s_{y \cdot x} \sqrt{1 + \frac{1}{n} + \frac{(X - \bar{X})^2}{\sum X^2 - \dfrac{(\sum X)^2}{n}}}$$

$$= 48.5526 \pm 2.306(9.901) \sqrt{1 + \frac{1}{10} + \frac{(25 - 22)^2}{5{,}600 - \dfrac{(220)^2}{10}}}$$

$$= 48.5526 \pm 24.0746$$

Thus, the interval is from 24.478 up to 72.627 copiers. We conclude that the number of copiers sold will be between about 24 and 73 for a particular sales representative. This interval is quite large. It is much larger than the interval for all sales representatives who made 25 calls. It is logical, however, that there should be more variation in the sales estimate for an individual than for a group.

Again, there is an important distinction between a confidence interval and a prediction interval. A confidence interval refers to all cases with a given value of X and is computed using formula (12–8). A prediction interval refers to a particular case for a given value of X and is computed using formula (12–9). The prediction interval will have a wider range, as a result of the extra "1" under the radical.

SELF-REVIEW 12-5

Refer to the sample data in Self-Reviews 12–1, 12–3, and 12–4, where the owner of Reliable Furniture was studying the relationship between sales and the amount spent on advertising. The sales information for the last four months is repeated below.

Month	Advertising Expense ($ millions)	Sales Revenue ($ millions)
July	2	7
August	1	3
September	3	8
October	4	10

The regression equation was computed to be $Y' = 1.5 + 2.2X$, and the standard error is 0.9487. Both variables are reported in millions of dollars. Determine the 90 percent confidence interval for the typical month in which $3 million was spent on advertising.

Exercises

25. Refer to Exercise 11.
    a. Determine the .95 confidence interval for the mean predicted when $X = 7$.
    b. Determine the .95 prediction interval for an individual predicted when $X = 7$.
26. Refer to Exercise 12.
    a. Determine the .95 confidence interval for the mean predicted when $X = 7$.
    b. Determine the .95 prediction interval for an individual predicted when $X = 7$.
27. Refer to Exercise 13.
    a. Determine the .95 confidence interval, in thousands of kilowatt-hours, for the mean of all six-room homes.
    b. Determine the .95 prediction interval, in thousands of kilowatt-hours, for a particular six-room home.
28. Refer to Exercise 14.
    a. Determine the .95 confidence interval, in thousands of dollars, for the mean of all sales personnel who make 40 contacts.
    b. Determine the .95 prediction interval, in thousands of dollars, for a particular salesperson who makes 40 contacts.

More on the Coefficient of Determination

Formula (12–1) is a convenient computational formula to determine the coefficient of correlation, r. The coefficient of determination is found by squaring the coefficient of correlation.

To further examine the basic concept of the coefficient of determination, suppose there is interest in the relationship between years on job, X, and weekly production, Y. Sample data revealed:

Employee	Years on Job, X	Weekly Production, Y
Gordon	14	6
James	7	5
Ford	3	3
Salter	15	9
Artes	11	7

The sample data were plotted in a scatter diagram. Since the relationship between X and Y appears to be linear, a straight line was drawn through the plots (see Chart 12–14). The equation is $Y' = a + bX$ or $2 + 0.4X$.

Note in Chart 12–14 that if we were to use that straight line to predict weekly production for an employee, in no case would our prediction be exact. That is, there would be some error in each of our predictions. As an example, for Gordon, who has been with the company 14 years, we would predict weekly production to be 7.6 units; however, he produces only 6 units.

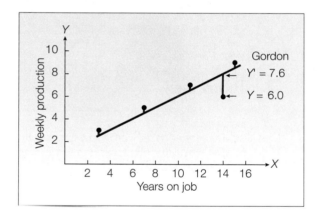

Chart 12–14   Observed Data and the Least Squares Line

To measure the overall error in our prediction, every deviation from the straight line is squared and the squares summed. The predicted point on the straight line is designated Y', read Y prime, and the observed point is designated Y. For Gordon, $(Y - Y')^2 = (6 - 7.6)^2 = (-1.6)^2 = 2.56$. Logically, this variation cannot be explained by the independent variable, so it is referred to as the *unexplained variation*. Specifically, we cannot explain why Gordon's production of 6 units is 1.6 units below his predicted production of 7.6 units, based on the number of years he has been on the job.

Unexplained variation

The sum of the squared deviations, $\Sigma(Y - Y')^2$, is 4.00. (See Table 12–6.) The term $\Sigma(Y - Y')^2 = 4.00$ is the variation in Y (production) that cannot be predicted from X. It is the "unexplained" variation in Y.

Table 12–6 Computations Needed for the Unexplained Variation

	X	Y	Y'	Y − Y'	(Y − Y')²
Gordon	14	6	7.6	−1.6	2.56
James	7	5	4.8	0.2	0.04
Ford	3	3	3.2	−0.2	0.04
Salter	15	9	8.0	1.0	1.00
Artes	11	7	6.4	0.6	0.36
Total	50	30		0.0*	4.00

*Must be 0.

Now suppose *only* the Y values (weekly production, in this problem) are known and we want to predict production for every employee. The actual production figures for the employees are 6, 5, 3, 9, and 7 (from Table 12–6). To make these predictions, we could assign the mean weekly production (6 units, found by $\Sigma Y/n = 30/5 = 6$) to each employee. This would keep the sum of the squared prediction errors at a minimum. (Recall from Chapter 3 that the sum of the squared deviations from the arithmetic mean for a set of numbers is smaller than the sum of the squared deviations from any other value, such as the median.) Table 12–7 shows the necessary calculations. The sum of the squared deviations is 20, as shown in Table 12–7. The value 20 is referred to as the

Total variation in Y   *total variation in Y.*

Table 12–7 Calculations Needed for the Total Variation in Y

Name	Weekly Production, Y	Mean Weekly Production, $\bar{Y}$	Y − $\bar{Y}$	(Y − $\bar{Y}$)²
Gordon	6	6	0	0
James	5	6	−1	1
Ford	3	6	−3	9
Salter	9	6	3	9
Artes	7	6	1	1
Total			0*	20

*Must be 0.

What we did to arrive at the total variation in Y is shown diagrammatically in Chart 12–15.

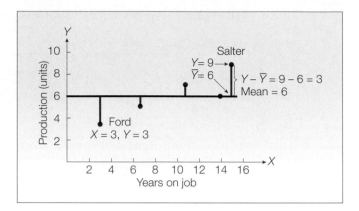

Chart 12–15   Plots Showing Deviations from the Mean of Y

Logically, the total variation in Y can be subdivided into unexplained variation and explained variation. To arrive at the explained variation, since we know the total variation and unexplained variation, we simply subtract: Explained variation = Total variation − Unexplained variation. Dividing the explained variation by the total variation gives the coefficient of determination, r^2, which is a proportion. In terms of a formula:

COEFFICIENT OF DETERMINATION

$$r^2 = \frac{\text{Total variation} - \text{Unexplained variation}}{\text{Total variation}}$$

$$= \frac{\Sigma(Y - \bar{Y})^2 - \Sigma(Y - Y')^2}{\Sigma(Y - \bar{Y})^2}$$

[12–10]

In this problem:

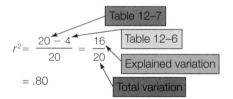

As mentioned, .80 is a proportion. We say that 80 percent of the variation in weekly production, Y, is determined, or accounted for, by its linear relationship with X (years on the job).

As a check, the computational formula (12–1) for the coefficient of correlation could be used. Squaring r gives the coefficient of determination. Exercise 29 offers a check on the preceding problem.

▌ Exercises

29.   Using the preceding problem, involving years on the job and weekly production, verify that the coefficient of determination is in fact .80.

30.   The number of shares of Icom, Inc., turned over during a month, and the price at the end of the month, are listed in the following table. Also, the Y′ plots on the straight line going through observed data are given.

Turnover (thousands of shares), X	Actual Price, Y	Estimated Price, Y'
4	$2	$2.7
1	1	0.6
5	4	3.4
3	2	2.0
2	1	1.3

a. Draw a scatter diagram. Plot a straight line through the dots.
b. Compute the coefficient of determination using formula (12–10).
c. As a check, use the computational formula (12–1) for *r*.
d. Interpret the coefficient of determination.

▌ The Relationships among the Coefficient of Correlation, the Coefficient of Determination, and the Standard Error of Estimate

In an earlier section, we discussed the standard error of estimate, which measures how close the actual values are to the regression line. When the standard error is small, it indicates that the two variables are closely related. In the calculation of the standard error, the key term is $\Sigma(Y - Y')^2$. If the value of this term is small, then the standard error will also be small.

The correlation coefficient measures the strength of the association between two variables. When the points on the scatter diagram appear close to the straight line, we note that the correlation coefficient tends to be large. Thus, the standard error of estimate and the coefficient of correlation relate the same information but use a different scale to report the strength of the association. However, both measures involve the term $\Sigma(Y - Y')^2$.

We also noted that the square of the correlation coefficient is the coefficient of determination. The coefficient of determination measures the percent of the variation in Y that is explained by the variation in X.

A convenient vehicle for showing the relationship among these three measures is an ANOVA table. This table is similar to the analysis of variance table developed in Chapter 11. In that chapter, the variation was divided into two components: that due to the *treatments* and that due to *random error*. The concept is similar in regression analysis. The total variation, $\Sigma(Y - Y')^2$, is divided into two components: (1) that explained by the *regression* (explained by the independent variable) and (2) the *error*, or unexplained variation. These two categories are identified in the first column of the ANOVA table that follows. The column headed "DF" refers to the degrees of freedom associated with each category. The total number of degrees of freedom is $n - 1$. The number of degrees of freedom in the regression is 1, since there is only one independent variable. The number of degrees of freedom associated with the error term is $n - 2$. The term "SS" located in the middle of the ANOVA table refers to the sum of squares—the variation. The terms are computed as follows:

$$\text{Regression} = \quad \text{SSR} = \Sigma(Y' - \bar{Y})^2$$

$$\text{Error variation} = \quad \text{SSE} = \Sigma(Y - Y')^2$$

$$\text{Total variation} = \text{SS total} = \Sigma(Y - \bar{Y})^2$$

The format for the ANOVA table is:

Source	DF	SS	MS
Regression	1	SSR	SSR/1
Error	$n - 2$	SSE	SSE/$(n - 2)$
Total	$n - 1$	SS total*	

*SS total = SSR + SSE.

The coefficient of determination, r^2, can be obtained directly from the ANOVA table by:

COEFFICIENT OF DETERMINATION	$r^2 = \dfrac{\text{SSR}}{\text{SS total}} = 1 - \dfrac{\text{SSE}}{\text{SS total}}$	**[12–11]**

The term "SSR/SS total" is the proportion of the variation in Y *explained* by the independent variable, X. Note the effect of the SSE term on r^2. As SSE decreases, r^2 will increase. Conversely, as the standard error decreases, the r^2 term increases.

The standard error of estimate can also be obtained from the ANOVA table using the following equation:

STANDARD ERROR OF ESTIMATE	$s_{y \cdot x} = \sqrt{\dfrac{\text{SSE}}{n - 2}}$	**[12–12]**

The Copier Sales of America Example is used to illustrate the computations of the coefficient of determination and the standard error of estimate from an ANOVA table.

Example

In the Copier Sales of America Example we studied the relationship between the number of sales calls made and the number of copiers sold. Use a computer software package to determine the least squares regression equation and the ANOVA table. Identify the regression equation, the standard error of estimate, and the coefficient of determination on the computer output. From the ANOVA table on the computer output, determine the coefficient of determination and the standard error of estimate using formulas (12–11) and (12–12).

Solution

Following is the output from the MINITAB system.

```
Regression Analysis
                                    Regression equation

The regression equation is
Units = 18.9 + 1.18 Calls


Predictor          Coef          StDev          T          P
Constant         18.947          8.499       2.23      0.056
Calls            1.1842          0.3591      3.30      0.011

                                                           Coefficient of
    S = 9.901          R-Sq = 57.6%    R-Sq(adj) = 52.3%   determination

Analysis of Variance

SOURCE            DF             SS            MS          F          P
Regression         1         1065.8        1065.8      10.87      0.011
Error              8          784.2          98.0
Total:             9         1850.0        1850.0
```
Standard error of estimate

Using formula (12–11), the coefficient of determination is .576, found by

$$r^2 = \frac{\text{SSR}}{\text{SS total}} = \frac{1065.8}{1850.0} = .576$$

This is the same value we computed earlier in the chapter, when we found the coefficient of determination by squaring the coefficient of correlation. Again, the interpretation is that the independent variable, *Calls,* explains 57.6 percent of the variation in the number of copiers sold. If we needed the coefficient of correlation, we could find it by taking the square root of the coefficient of determination:

$$r = \sqrt{r^2} = \sqrt{.576} = .759$$

A problem does remain, and that involves the sign for the coefficient of correlation. Recall that the square root of a value could have either a positive or a negative sign. The sign of the coefficient of correlation will always be the same as that of the slope. That is, b and r will always have the same sign. In this case the sign is positive, so the coefficient of determination is .759.

To find the standard error of estimate, we use formula (12–12).

$$s_{y \cdot x} = \sqrt{\frac{\text{SSE}}{n - 2}} = \sqrt{\frac{784.2}{10 - 2}} = 9.901$$

Again, this is the same value calculated earlier in the chapter. These values are identified on the MINITAB computer output.

Exercises

31. Given the following ANOVA table:

SOURCE	DF	SS	MS	F
Regression	1	1000.0	1000.00	26.00
Error	13	500.0	38.46	
Total	14	1500.0		

   a.　Determine the coefficient of determination.
   b.　Assuming a direct relationship between the variables, what is the coefficient of correlation?
   c.　Determine the standard error of estimate.

32. On the first statistics exam the coefficient of determination between the hours studied and the grade earned was 80 percent. The standard error of estimate was 10. There were 20 students in the class. Develop an ANOVA table.

Chapter Outline

  I.　A scatter diagram is a graphic tool used to portray the relationship between two variables.
    A.　The dependent variable is scaled on the *Y*-axis and is the variable being estimated.
    B.　The independent variable is scaled on the *X*-axis and is the variable used as the estimator.
  II.　The coefficient of correlation measures the strength of the association between two variables.
    A.　Both variables must be at least the interval scale of measurement.
    B.　The coefficient of correlation can range from -1.00 up to 1.00.
    C.　If the correlation between two variables is 0, there is no association between them.
    D.　A value of 1.00 indicates perfect positive correlation, and -1.00 perfect negative correlation.
    E.　A positive sign means there is a direct relationship between the variables, and a negative sign means there is an inverse relationship.
    F.　It is designated by the letter *r* and found by the following equation:

$$r = \frac{n\Sigma XY - \Sigma X \Sigma Y}{\sqrt{[n\Sigma X^2 - (\Sigma X)^2][n\Sigma Y^2 - (\Sigma Y)^2]}}$$　　**[12–1]**

    G.　The following test statistic is used to determine whether the correlation in the population is different from 0.

$$t = \frac{r\sqrt{n-2}}{\sqrt{1-r^2}}$$　　**[12–2]**

  III.　The coefficient of determination is the fraction of the variation in one variable that is explained by the other variable.
    A.　It ranges from 0 to 1.0.
    B.　It is the square of the coefficient of correlation.
  IV.　In regression analysis we estimate one variable based on another variable.
    A.　The variable being estimated is the dependent variable.
    B.　The variable used to make the estimate is the independent variable.
      1.　The relationship between the variables must be linear.
      2.　Both the independent and the dependent variable must be interval or ratio scale.
      3.　The least squares criterion is used to determine the regression equation.

V. The least squares regression line is of the form $Y' = a + bX$.
   A. Y' is the estimated value of Y for a selected value of X.
   B. a is the constant or intercept.
      1. It is the value of Y' when $X = 0$.
      2. a is computed using the following equation.

$$a = \frac{\Sigma Y}{n} - b\frac{\Sigma X}{n}$$ **[12–4]**

   C. b is the slope of the line.
      1. It shows the amount of change in Y' for a change of 1 in X.
      2. A positive value for b indicates a direct relationship between the two variables, and a negative value an inverse relationship.
      3. The sign of b and the sign of r, the coefficient of correlation, are always the same.
      4. b is computed using the following equation.

$$b = \frac{n(\Sigma XY) - (\Sigma X)(\Sigma Y)}{n(\Sigma X^2) - (\Sigma X)^2}$$ **[12–4]**

   D. X is the value of the independent variable.
VI. The standard error of estimate measures the variation around the regression line.
   A. It is in the same units as the dependent variable.
   B. It is based on squared deviations from the regression line.
   C. Small values indicate that the points cluster closely about the regression line.
   D. It is computed using the following formula.

$$s_{y \cdot x} = \sqrt{\frac{\Sigma Y^2 - a(\Sigma Y) - b(\Sigma XY)}{n - 2}}$$ **[12–7]**

VII. Inference about linear regression is based on the following assumptions.
   A. For a given value of X, the values of Y are normally distributed about the line of regression.
   B. The standard deviation of each of the normal distributions is the same for all values of X and is estimated by the standard error of estimate.
   C. The deviations from the regression line are independent, with no pattern to the size or direction.
VIII. There are two types of interval estimates.
   A. In a confidence interval the mean value of Y is estimated for a given value of X.
      1. It is computed from the following formula.

$$Y' \pm ts_{y \cdot x} \sqrt{\frac{1}{n} + \frac{(X - \bar{X})^2}{\Sigma X^2 - \frac{(\Sigma X)^2}{n}}}$$ **[12–8]**

      2. The width of the interval is affected by the level of confidence, the size of the standard error of estimate, and the size of the sample, as well as the value of the independent variable.
   B. In a prediction interval the individual value of Y is estimated for a given value of X.
      1. It is computed from the following formula.

$$Y' \pm ts_{y \cdot x} \sqrt{1 + \frac{1}{n} + \frac{(X - \bar{X})^2}{\Sigma X^2 - \frac{(\Sigma X)^2}{n}}}$$ **[12–9]**

      2. The difference between formulas (12–8) and (12–9) is the 1 under the radical.
         a. The prediction interval will be wider than the confidence interval.
         b. The prediction interval is also based on the level of confidence, the size of the standard error of estimate, the size of the sample, and the value of the independent variable.

Pronunciation Key

SYMBOL	MEANING	PRONUNCIATION
ΣXY	Sum of the products of X and Y	*Sum X Y*
ρ	Coefficient of correlation in the population	*Rho*
Y'	Estimated value of Y	*Y prime*
$s_{y \cdot x}$	Standard error of estimate	*s y dot x*
r^2	Coefficient of determination	*r square*

Chapter Exercises

33. A major airline selected a random sample of 25 flights and found that the correlation between the number of passengers and the total weight, in pounds, of luggage stored in the luggage compartment is 0.94. Using the .05 significance level, can we conclude that there is a positive association between the two variables?

34. A sociologist claims that the success of students in college (measured by their GPA) is related to their family's income. For a sample of 20 students, the coefficient of correlation is 0.40. Using the 0.01 significance level, can we conclude that there is a positive correlation between the variables?

35. An Environmental Protection Agency study of 12 automobiles revealed a correlation of 0.47 between the engine size and performance. At the .01 significance level, can we conclude that there is a positive association between these variables? What is the *p*-value? Interpret.

36. A study of college soccer games revealed the correlation between the number of shots attempted and the number of goals scored to be 0.21 for a sample of 20 games. Is it reasonable to conclude that there is a positive correlation between the two variables? Use the .05 significance level. Determine the *p*-value.

37. A sample of 30 used cars sold by Northcut Motors in 1998 revealed that the correlation between the selling price and the number of miles driven was −.45. At the .05 significance level, can we conclude that there is a negative association in the population between the two variables?

38. For a sample of 32 large U.S. cities, the correlation between the mean number of square feet per office worker and the mean monthly rental rate in the central business district is −.363. At the .05 significance level, can we conclude that there is a negative association in the population between the two variables?

39. What is the relationship between the amount spent per week on food and the size of the family? Do larger families spend more on food? A sample of 10 families in the Chicago area revealed the following figures for family size and the amount spent on food per week.

Family Size	Amount Spent on Food	Family Size	Amount Spent on Food
3	$ 99	3	$111
6	104	4	74
5	151	4	91
6	129	5	119
6	142	3	91

a. Compute the coefficient of correlation.
b. Determine the coefficient of determination.
c. Can we conclude that there is a positive association between the amount spent on food and the family size? Use the .05 significance level.

40. A sample of 12 homes sold last week in St. Paul, Minnesota, is selected. Can we conclude that as the size of the home (reported below in thousands of square feet) increases, the selling price (reported in $ thousands) also increases?

Home Size (thousands of square feet)	Selling Price ($ thousands)	Home Size (thousands of square feet)	Selling Price ($ thousands)
1.4	100	1.3	110
1.3	110	0.8	85
1.2	105	1.2	105
1.1	120	0.9	75
1.4	80	1.1	70
1.0	105	1.1	95

   a. Compute the coefficient of correlation.
   b. Determine the coefficient of determination.
   c. Can we conclude that there is a positive association between the size of the home and the selling price? Use the .05 significance level.

41. The manufacturer of Cardio Glide exercise equipment wants to study the relationship between the number of months since the glide was purchased and the length of time the equipment was used last week.

Person	Months Owned	Hours Exercised	Person	Months Owned	Hours Exercised
Rupple	12	4	Massa	2	8
Hall	2	10	Sass	8	3
Bennett	6	8	Karl	4	8
Longnecker	9	5	Malrooney	10	2
Phillips	7	5	Veights	5	5

   a. Plot the information on a scatter diagram. Let hours of exercise be the dependent variable. Comment on the graph.
   b. Determine the coefficient of correlation. Interpret.
   c. At the .01 significance level, can we conclude that there is a negative association between the variables?

42. The following regression equation was computed from a sample of 20 observations:

$$Y' = 15 - 5X$$

   SSE was found to be 100 and SS total 400.
   a. Determine the standard error of estimate.
   b. Determine the coefficient of determination.
   c. Determine the coefficient of correlation. (Caution: Watch the sign!)

43. An ANOVA table is:

SOURCE	DF	SS	MS	F
Regression	1	50		
Error				
Total	24	500		

   a. Complete the ANOVA table.
   b. How large was the sample?
   c. Determine the standard error of estimate.
   d. Determine the coefficient of determination.

44. Following is a regression equation.

$$Y' = 17.08 + 0.16X$$

This information is also available: $s_{y \cdot x} = 4.05$, $\Sigma X = 210$, $\Sigma X^2 = 9,850$, and $n = 5$.
   a. Estimate the value of Y' when $X = 50$.
   b. Develop a 95 percent prediction interval for an individual value of Y for $X = 50$.

45. The National Highway Association is studying the relationship between the number of bidders on a highway project and the winning (lowest) bid for the project. Of particular interest is whether the number of bidders increases or decreases the amount of the winning bid.

Project	Number of Bidders, X	Winning Bid ($ millions), Y	Project	Number of Bidders, X	Winning Bid ($ millions), Y
1	9	5.1	9	6	10.3
2	9	8.0	10	6	8.0
3	3	9.7	11	4	8.8
4	10	7.8	12	7	9.4
5	5	7.7	13	7	8.6
6	10	5.5	14	7	8.1
7	7	8.3	15	6	7.8
8	11	5.5			

   a. Determine the regression equation. Interpret the equation. Do more bidders tend to increase or decrease the amount of the winning bid?
   b. Estimate the amount of the winning bid if there were seven bidders.
   c. A new turnpike entrance is to be constructed on the Ohio Turnpike. There are seven bidders on the project. Develop a 95 percent prediction interval for the winning bid.
   d. Determine the coefficient of determination. Interpret its value.

46. Mr. William Profit is studying companies going public for the first time. He is particularly interested in the relationship between the size of the offering and the price per share. A sample of 15 companies that recently went public revealed the following information.

Company	Size ($ millions), X	Price per Share, Y	Company	Size ($ millions), X	Price per Share, Y
1	9.0	10.8	9	160.7	11.3
2	94.4	11.3	10	96.5	10.6
3	27.3	11.2	11	83.0	10.5
4	179.2	11.1	12	23.5	10.3
5	71.9	11.1	13	58.7	10.7
6	97.9	11.2	14	93.8	11.0
7	93.5	11.0	15	34.4	10.8
8	70.0	10.7			

   a. Determine the regression equation.
   b. Determine the coefficient of determination. Do you think Mr. Profit should be satisfied with using the size of the offering as the independent variable?

47. The Bardi Trucking Co., located in Cleveland, Ohio, makes deliveries in the Great Lakes region, the Southeast, and the Northeast. Jim Bardi, the president, is studying the relationship between the distance a shipment must travel and the length of time, in days, it takes the shipment to arrive at its destination. To investigate, Mr. Bardi selected a random sample of 20 shipments made last month. Shipping distance is the independent variable, and shipping time is the dependent variable. The results are as follows:

Shipment	Distance (miles)	Shipping Time (days)	Shipment	Distance (miles)	Shipping Time (days)
1	656	5	11	862	7
2	853	14	12	679	5
3	646	6	13	835	13
4	783	11	14	607	3
5	610	8	15	665	8
6	841	10	16	647	7
7	785	9	17	685	10
8	639	9	18	720	8
9	762	10	19	652	6
10	762	9	20	828	10

a. Draw a scatter diagram. Based on these data, does it appear that there is a relationship between how many miles a shipment has to go and how long it takes to arrive at its destination?

b. Determine the coefficient of correlation. Can we conclude that there is a positive correlation between distance and time?

c. Determine and interpret the coefficient of determination.

d. Determine the standard error of estimate.

48. Following is a summary of the total assets, in millions of dollars, for the 26 credit unions located in Toledo, Ohio. Also reported are the capital ratio, a financial measure showing the ratio of total equity to total liabilities, and the profit for each credit union for the year 1997 in thousands of dollars.

Credit Union	Assets ($ millions)	Capital Ratio	1997 Profit ($ thousands)
Toledo Area Catholic	74.139	8.759	1,147
Sun Federal	69.624	7.505	589
Glass City Federal	58.033	8.185	789
OC Federal	49.235	9.207	449
Toledo Telephone Employees	37.639	12.572	414
Erie Shores Federal	30.650	13.537	191
Champion	27.070	13.631	259
Mutual Federal	22.008	8.451	105
UT-MCO Federal	21.288	8.441	232
AP Federal (AP Parts)	21.092	12.635	218
Great Lakes Federal	20.153	7.711	181
Toledo Fire Fighters	19.923	9.075	180
Sohio Toledo Refinery	19.153	10.808	283
Toledo Metro Federal	13.788	10.110	98
Toledo Hospital Employees	11.990	9.116	199
Conrail Toledo	11.887	14.705	206
General Mills Toledo	11.695	9.987	139
Jeep Federal	11.234	11.786	353
Toledo Police Federal	10.734	11.608	189
Toledo St. Vincent Federal	9.631	9.179	109
United Services Federal	8.724	8.517	22
Blade Federal	8.584	10.916	85
North West Federal	8.342	11.496	76
Co-Op Toledo	8.422	10.057	81
Sylvania Education and Municipal Employees	7.291	8.874	130
Local 50 Plumbers and Steamfitters	5.812	8.448	44

   a. Determine the correlation between the total assets of the credit unions and their 1997 profits. Can we conclude that there is a significant positive correlation between these two variables? Plot the variabies in the form of a scatter diagram. Do you see any problems? Use the .05 significance level.

   b. Determine the correlation between capital ratio and 1997 profits. Can we conclude that there is a significant negative correlation between the two variables? Use the .05 significance level.

49. A recent report by the *Business Journal* of Santa Clara County, California, reported the number of local employees and the number of square feet cleaned per night (reported in millions) for 21 janitorial firms in the county. The information is reported below.

Company	Employees	Square Feet Cleaned
Commercial Building Maintenance	800	15.00
Acme Building Maintenance	665	22.00
Pacific Maintenance	500	8.30
American Building Maintenance	380	10.40
Jani-King of California	300	6.00
Service Performance Co.	206	5.00
Centennial Contract Services	196	6.70
United Maintenance Co.	160	5.50
Continental Building Maintenance	160	4.80
Regional Building Maintenance	125	4.50
Tiger Maintenance Co.	92	2.00
California Janitorial Service	81	1.10
Cave Imaging Systems	80	2.80
Polaris Building Maintenance	71	1.60
Pro Clean Enterprises	65	3.00
California Building Maintenance	63	0.83
Environmental Control Building Maintenance	48	1.00
Valley Building Maintenance Co.	47	1.70
Univorsal Maintenance	45	1.20
Associated Building Maintenance	45	1.30
Salinas Valley Corp.	42	1.50

   a. Determine the regression equation. Let the number of square feet cleaned be the dependent variable. How much additional area does each additional employee clean?

   b. Determine the coefficients of determination and correlation. Can you conclude that the correlation between the area cleaned and the number of employees is greater than 0? Use the .05 significance level.

www.Exercises.com

50. Small companies are defined as those with annual sales greater than $5 million and less than $350 million. The 60 top companies were ranked according to their 5-year return on investment. Reported at the Web location *http://lib.stat.cmu.edu/DASL/Datafiles/ceodat.html* is information on the age of the chief executive officer of these 60 companies and their salaries, including bonuses. The total salary is reported in thousands of dollars. Determine the correlation between these two variables. At the .05 significance level, can you conclude that it is greater than zero?

51. Many real estate companies and rental agencies now publish their listings on the Web. One example is the Dunes Realty Company, located in Garden City and Surfside Beaches in South Carolina. Go to the Web site *http://www.dunes.com* and select **Cottage Search.** Then

indicate 5 bedroom, accommodations for 14 people, second row (this means it is across the street from the beach), and no pool or floating dock; select a period in July or August; indicate that you are willing to spend $5,000 per week; and then click on **Search the Cottages.** The output should include details on the cottages that met your criteria.

a. Determine the correlation between the number of baths in each cottage and the weekly rental price. Can you conclude that the correlation is greater than zero at the .05 significance level? Determine the coefficient of determination.

b. Determine the regression equation using the number of bathrooms as the independent variable and the price per week as the dependent variable. Interpret the regression equation.

c. Calculate the correlation between the number of people the cottage will accommodate and the weekly rental price. At the .05 significance level can you conclude that it is different from zero?

▌ Computer Data Exercises

52. Refer to Data Set 1, which reports information on homes sold in Venice, Florida last year.
    a. Let selling price be the dependent variable and size of the home the independent variable. Determine the regression equation. Estimate the selling price for a home with an area of 2,200 square feet. Determine the 95 percent confidence interval and the 95 percent prediction interval for the selling price of a home with 2,200 square feet.
    b. Let selling price be the dependent variable and distance from the center of the city the independent variable. Determine the regression equation. Estimate the selling price of a home 20 miles from the center of the city. Determine the 95 percent confidence interval and the 95 percent prediction interval for homes 20 miles from the center of the city.
    c. Can you conclude that the independent variables "distance from the center of the city" and "selling price" are negatively correlated and that the area of the home and the selling price are positively correlated? Use the .05 significance level. Report the p-value of the test.

53. Refer to Data Set 2, which reports information on the 1997 Major League Baseball season.
    a. Let number of games won be the dependent variable and total team salary, in millions of dollars, be the independent variable. Can you conclude that there is a positive association between the variables? Determine the regression equation. About how many additional wins will an additional $5 million in salary bring?
    b. Determine the correlation between games won and ERA and games won and team batting average. Which has the stronger correlation? Can we conclude that there is a positive correlation between wins and team batting and a negative correlation between wins and ERA? Use the .05 significance level.
    c. Let number of games won be the dependent variable and attendance the independent variable. Can we conclude that the correlation between these two variables is greater than 0? Use the .05 significance level. What is the p-value?

54. Refer to Data Set 3, which refers to information on the circulation of magazines.
    a. Determine the correlations between the magazine circulation and the cost of (1) the color and (2) the black-and-white advertisements. Can you conclude that both of the correlations are significant? Use the .05 significance level.
    b. Determine the correlation between the magazine circulation and the median income of subscribers. Can you show that there is a significant negative association? Use the .05 significance level. What is the p-value?

55. Refer to Data Set 4, which includes information on the 94 school districts in northwestern Ohio.
    a. Let the independent variable be the percent of families on welfare in the school district and the number of students in the district be the dependent variable.
        1. Determine the regression equation. Comment on the values you found for the slope and the intercept. Are they reasonable?

2. Estimate the number of students in the school district in which 10 percent of the families are on welfare.
3. Develop a 95 percent confidence interval and a 95 percent prediction interval for all schools that have 10 percent of families on welfare.

b. Let the independent variable be the attendance rate and the dependent variable be the percent passing the proficiency examination.
1. Determine the regression equation. Comment on the values you found for *a* and *b*. Are they reasonable?
2. Estimate the percent of students passing the proficiency examination if the attendance rate is 90 percent.
3. Develop a 95 percent confidence interval and a 95 percent prediction interval for the percentage passing the proficiency examination, if the attendance rate is 90 percent.

c. At the .01 significance level can we conclude that there is a positive association between the variables "attendance rate" and "percent passing the proficiency examination"?

▌ Computer Commands

1. The MINITAB commands for the regression output on page 455:
    a. Use the **Set** command to enter the data in columns C1 and C2.
    b. Use the **Name** command to identify the first column as "Calls" and the second column as "Units."
    c. Select "Units" as the **Response** variable and "Calls" as the **Predictor** variable and then click **OK.**

CHAPTER 12   *Answers to Self-Review*

12–1 (a) Advertising expense is the independent variable and sales revenue is the dependent variable.

(b)

(c)

X	Y	XY	X²	Y²
2	7	14	4	49
1	3	3	1	9
3	8	24	9	64
4	10	40	16	100
10	28	81	30	222

$r = .96$, found by

$$r = \frac{4(81) - (10)(28)}{\sqrt{[4(30) - (10)^2][4(222) - (28)^2]}}$$

$$= \frac{44}{\sqrt{2{,}080}} = \frac{44}{45.607017} = .9648$$

(d) There is a strong correlation between the advertising expense and sales.

(e) $r^2 = .93$, 93% of the variation in sales is "explained" by variation in advertising.

12-2 $H_0: \rho \le 0$, $H_1: \rho > 0$. H_0 is rejected if $t > 1.714$.

$$t = \frac{.43\sqrt{25 - 2}}{\sqrt{1 - (.43)^2}} = 2.284$$

H_0 is rejected. There is a positive correlation between the percent of the vote received and the amount spent on the campaign.

12-3 (a) See the calculations in Self-Review 12–1, part (c).

$$b = \frac{4(81) - (10)(28)}{4(30) - (10)^2} \qquad a = \frac{28}{4} - 2.2\left(\frac{10}{4}\right)$$

$$= \frac{324 - 280}{120 - 100} = 2.2 \qquad = 7 - 5.5 = 1.5$$

(b) The slope is 2.2. This indicates that an increase of $1 million in advertising will result in an increase of $2.2 million in sales. The intercept is 1.5. If there was no expenditure for advertising, sales would be $1.5 million.

(c) $Y' = 1.5 + 2.2(3) = 8.1$

12-4 0.9487, found by:

$$s_{y \cdot x} = \sqrt{\frac{\Sigma Y^2 - a(\Sigma Y) - b(\Sigma XY)}{n - 2}}$$

$$= \sqrt{\frac{222 - 1.5(28) - 2.2(81)}{4 - 2}}$$

$$= \sqrt{\frac{1.8}{2}} = 0.9487$$

12-5 1. 6.58 and 9.52, since Y' for an X of 3 is 8.1, found by $Y' = 1.5 + 2.2(3) = 8.1$, then $\overline{X} = 2.5$. and $\Sigma X^2 = 30$ and $\Sigma X = 10$.

t from Appendix F for $4 - 2 = 2$ degrees of freedom at the .10 level is 2.920.

$$Y' \pm t(s_{y \cdot x})\sqrt{\frac{1}{n} + \frac{(X - \overline{X})^2}{\Sigma X^2 - \frac{(\Sigma X)^2}{n}}}$$

$$= 8.1 \pm 2.920(0.9487)\sqrt{\frac{1}{4} + \frac{(3 - 2.5)^2}{30 - \frac{(10)^2}{4}}}$$

$$= 8.1 \pm 2.920(0.9487)(0.5477)$$

$$= 6.58 \text{ and } 9.62 \text{ (in \$ millions)}$$

Chapter Thirteen

Multiple Regression and Correlation Analysis

GOALS

When you have completed this chapter, you will be able to:

ONE

Describe the relationship between several independent variables and a dependent variable using a multiple regression equation.

TWO

Compute and interpret the multiple standard error of estimate and the coefficient of determination.

THREE

Interpret a correlation matrix.

FOUR

Set up and interpret an ANOVA table.

FIVE

Conduct a test of hypothesis to determine whether regression coefficients differ from zero.

SIX

Conduct a test of hypothesis on each of the regression coefficients.

In working with those who work on sophisticated machinery, the production department needed to know if age, length of service, mechanical aptitude, or prior on the job rating as a machine operator are important to determine performance on the machines. How many dependent and independent variables are there? (See Goal 1 and Exercise 2.)

Introduction

In the previous chapter we described the relationship between two sets of interval- or ratio-scaled measurements. One was designated the independent variable and the other the dependent variable. We noted that if the relationship between the two variables is linear, the regression equation $Y' = a + bX$ can predict the dependent variable, Y, based on the independent variable, X. Further, the coefficient of correlation is one measure we examined that reveals whether the relationship is strong, moderate, or weak. A coefficient near plus or minus 1.00 indicates a very strong linear relationship between X and Y. A coefficient near 0 (say, $-.12$ or $+.12$) means that the relationship is quite weak.

Use of only one independent variable to predict the dependent variable ignores the relationship of other variables to the dependent variable. This chapter expands our study of correlation and regression by examining the influence of *two or more* independent variables on the dependent variable. This approach is referred to as **multiple regression and correlation analysis.** We present multiple regression analysis first by developing and explaining the use of the multiple regression equation and the multiple standard error of estimate. Then we measure the strength of the relationship between the independent variables and the dependent variable using the multiple coefficient of determination. Finally, we present and analyze several computer applications using MINITAB and Excel.

Multiple Regression Analysis

Recall from Chapter 12 the linear regression equation using one independent variable has the form $Y' = a + bX$. The multiple regression case extends the equation to include additional independent variables. For two independent variables, the general form of the **multiple regression equation** is:

MULTIPLE REGRESSION EQUATION WITH TWO INDEPENDENT VARIABLES	$Y' = a + b_1X_1 + b_2X_2$	**[13–1]**

where:

X_1, X_2 are the two independent variables.

a is the Y-intercept, the point of intercept with the Y-axis.

b_1 is the net change in Y for each unit change in X_1, holding X_2 *constant* (unchanged). It is called a **partial regression coefficient,** a **net regression coefficient,** or just a **regession coefficient.**

b_2 is the net change in Y for each unit change in X_2, *holding X_1 constant* (unchanged). It is also referred to as a partial regression coefficient, or just a regression coefficient.

b *is called a regression coefficient*

To illustrate the interpretation of a and the two regression coefficients, suppose a vehicle's mileage per gallon of gasoline is directly related to the octane rating of the gasoline being used (X_1) and inversely related to the weight of the automobile (X_2). Assume the multiple regression equation is $Y' = 6.3 + 0.2X_1 + (-0.001)X_2$. The a value of 6.3 indicates that the regression plane intercepts the Y-axis at 6.3 when both X_1 and X_2 are zero. Of course, it does

Negative b indicates inverse relationship

not make any physical sense to own an automobile that has no (zero) weight and to use gasoline with no octane. It is important to keep in mind that a regression equation is not generally used outside the range of the sample values.

The b_1 of 0.2 indicates that for each increase of 1 in the octane rating of the gasoline, the automobile would travel 2/10 of a mile more per gallon, *regardless of the weight of the vehicle.* That is, the vehicle's weight is held constant. The b_2 value of -0.001 reveals that for each increase of one pound in the vehicle's weight, the number of miles traveled per gallon decreases by .0001, *regardless of the octane of the gasoline being used.*

As an example, an automobile with 92-octane gasoline in the tank and weighing 2,000 pounds would travel an average 22.7 miles per gallon, found by:

$$Y' = a + b_1X_1 + b_2X_2$$

$$= 6.3 + 0.2(92) + (-0.001)2,000$$

$$= 22.7 \text{ miles per gallon}$$

We can expand the number of independent variables. For three independent variables designated X_1, X_2, and X_3, the general multiple regression equation is:

MULTIPLE REGRESSION EQUATION WITH THREE INDEPENDENT VARIABLES	$Y' = a + b_1X_1 + b_2X_2 + b_3X_3$	[13–2]

This can be extended for any number of independent variables (k), with the general multiple regression equation being:

MULTIPLE REGRESSION EQUATION WITH k INDEPENDENT VARIABLES	$Y' = a + b_1X_1 + b_2X_2 + b_3X_3 + \cdots + b_kX_k$	[13–3]

As in Chapter 12, the least squares method of estimating a, b_1, b_2, and so forth minimizes the sum of the squares of the vertical deviations about the straight line. The same applies to multiple regression. To arrive at a, b_1 and b_2 in the multiple regression equation, however, the many calculations are very tedious — even using a hand calculator. As an example, for two independent variables, three equations must be solved simultaneously, namely:

$$\Sigma Y = na + b_1\Sigma X_1 + b_2\Sigma X_2$$

$$\Sigma X_1Y = a\Sigma X_1 + b_1\Sigma X_1^2 + b_2\Sigma X_1X_2$$

$$\Sigma X_2Y = a\Sigma X_2 + b_1\Sigma X_1X_2 + b_2\Sigma X_2^2$$

There are many computer software packages available to perform the calculations and output the results. MINITAB, SAS, and SPSS are three of the most widely used packages. The format of the output is fairly standard. We begin the discussion of multiple regression by describing a situation involving three independent variables.

Example

Salsberry Realty sells homes along the east coast of the United States. One of the questions most frequently asked by prospective buyers is: If we purchase this home, how much can we expect to pay to heat it during the winter? The research department at Salsberry has been asked to develop some guidelines regarding heating costs for single family homes. Three variables are thought to relate to the heating costs: (1) the mean daily outside temperature, (2) the number of inches of insulation in the attic, and (3) the age of the furnace. To investigate, Salsberry's research department selected a random sample of 20 recently sold homes. They determined the cost to heat the home last January, as well as the January outside temperature in the region, the number of inches of insulation in the attic, and the age of the furnace. The sample information is reported in Table 13–1.

Table 13–1 Factors in January Heating Cost for a Sample of 20 Homes

Home	Heating Cost ($)	Mean Outside Temperature (°F)	Attic Insulation (inches)	Age of Furnace (years)
1	$250	35	3	6
2	360	29	4	10
3	165	36	7	3
4	43	60	6	9
5	92	65	5	6
6	200	30	5	5
7	355	10	6	7
8	290	7	10	10
9	230	21	9	11
10	120	55	2	5
11	73	54	12	4
12	205	48	5	1
13	400	20	5	15
14	320	39	4	7
15	72	60	8	6
16	272	20	5	8
17	94	58	7	3
18	190	40	8	11
19	235	27	9	8
20	139	30	7	5

Determine the multiple regression equation. Which variable or variables are the independent variable? Which variable or variables are the dependent variable? Discuss the regression coefficients. What does it indicate that some are positive and some are negative? What is the intercept value? What is the estimated heating cost for a home where the mean outside temperature is 30 degrees, there are 5 inches of insulation in the attic, and the furnace is 10 years old?

Solution

The MINITAB statistical software system generates the output on page 470. The dependent variable is the January heating cost. There are three independent variables. They are the mean outside temperature, the number of inches of insulation in the attic, and the age of the furnace.

The general form of a multiple regression equation with three independent variables is $Y' = a + b_1X_1 + b_2X_2 + b_3X_3$. In this case the multiple regression equation is $Y' = 427 - 4.58X_1 - 14.80X_2 + 6.10X_3$. The intercept value is 427. This is the place that the regression equation crosses the Y-axis. The regression coefficients for the mean outside temperature and the amount of attic insulation are both negative.

This is not surprising. As the outside temperature increases, the cost to heat the home will go down. Hence, we would expect an inverse relationship. For each degree the mean temperature increases, we expect the heating cost to decrease $4.58 per month. So if the mean temperature in Boston is 25 degrees and it is 35 degrees in Philadelphia, all other things being the same, we expect the cost would be $45.80 *less* in Philadelphia.

```
Regression Analysis

The regression equation is
Cost = 427 − 4.58 Temp − 14.8 Insul + 6.10 Age

Predictor            Coef          StDev             T             P
Constant           427.19          59.60          7.17         0.000
Temp               −4.5827         0.7723         −5.93         0.000
Insulation         −14.831         4.754          −3.12         0.007
Age                  6.101         4.012           1.52         0.148


S = 51.05           R-Sq = 80.4%           R-Sq(adj) = 76.7%


Analysis of Variance

Source         DF           SS            MS            F             P
Regression      3       171220         57073         21.90         0.000
Error          16        41695          2606
Total          19       212916
```

The variable "attic insulation" also shows an inverse relationship. The more insulation we put in the attic, the less the cost to heat the home. So the negative sign for this coefficient is logical. For each additional inch of insulation, we expect the cost of heating the home to decline $14.80 per month, regardless of the outside temperature or the age of the furnace.

The furnace variable shows a direct relationship. As the age of the furnace increases, so does the heating cost. For each additional year old the furnace is, we expect the cost to increase $6.10 per month.

We can estimate the home heating cost if the mean outside temperature for the month is 30 degrees, there are 5 inches of insulation in the attic, and the furnace is 10 years old. We substitute these values in the regression equation, and our estimated cost is $Y' = 427 − 4.58X_1 − 14.8X_2 + 6.10X_3 = 427 − 4.58(30) − 14.8(5) + 6.10(10) = 276.60$. We conclude that the estimated heating cost is $276.60 for the month.

SELF-REVIEW 13–1

The quality control engineer at Bethel Steel is interested in estimating the tensile strength of steel wire based on its outside diameter and the amount of molybdenum in the steel. As an experiment, she selected twenty-five pieces of wire, measured the outside diameters, and determined the molybdenum content. Then she measured the tensile strength of each piece. The results of the first four were:

Piece	Tensile Strength (psi), Y	Outside Diameter (mm), X_1	Amount of Molybdenum (units), X_2
A	11	.3	6
B	9	.2	5
C	16	.4	8
D	12	.3	7

Suppose the multiple regression equation is $Y' = -0.5 + 20X_1 + 1X_2$.

(a) Based on the equation, what is the predicted tensile strength of a steel wire having an outside diameter of .35 mm and 6.4 units of molybdenum?

(b) Interpret the value of b_1 in the equation.

STATISTICS IN ACTION

Exercises

1. The director of marketing at Reeves Wholesale Products is studying the monthly sales of his company's six regions. Three independent variables were selected as predictors of sales: regional population, per-capita income, and regional unemployment rate. The regression equation was computed to be (in dollars):

$$Y' = 64,100 + 0.394X_1 + 9.6X_1 - 11,600X_3$$

   a. What is the full name of the equation?
   b. Interpret the number 64,100.
   c. What are the estimated monthly sales for region IV? The region has a population of 796,000, per-capita income of $6,940, and an unemployment rate of 6.0 percent.

2. Thompson Machine Works purchased several new, highly sophisticated machines. The production department needed some guidance with respect to qualifications needed by an operator. Is age a factor? Is the length of service as a machine operator important? In order to explore further the factors needed to estimate performance on the new machines, four variables were listed:

   X_1 = Length of time employee was a machinist. X_3 = Prior on-the-job rating.
   X_2 = Mechanical aptitude test score. X_4 = Age.

   Performance on the new machine is designated Y.

   Thirty machinists were selected at random. Data were collected for each, and their performances on the new machines were recorded. A few results are:

Name	Performance on New Machine, Y	Length of Time as a Machinist, X_1	Mechanical Aptitude Score, X_2	Prior On-the-Job Performance, X_3	Age, X_4
Andy Kosin	112	12	312	121	52
Sue Annis	113	2	380	123	27

Suppose the equation is:

$$Y' = 11.6 + 0.4X_1 + 0.286X_2 + 0.112X_3 + 0.002X_4$$

a. What is the full designation of the equation?
b. How many dependent variables are there? Independent variables?
c. What is the number 0.286 called?
d. As age increases by one year, how much does estimated performance on the new machine increase?
e. Carl Knox applied for a job on a new machine. He has been a machinist for six years, and he scored 280 on the mechanical aptitude test. Carl's prior on-the-job performance rating is 97, and he is 35 years old. Estimate Carl's performance on the new machine.

3. A sample of widowed senior citizens was studied to determine their degree of satisfaction with their present life. A special index, called the index of satisfaction, was used to measure satisfaction. Six factors were studied, namely, age at the time of first marriage (X_1), annual income (X_2), number of children living (X_3), value of all assets (X_4), status of health in the form of an index (X_5), and the average number of social activities per week — such as bowling and dancing (X_6). Suppose the multiple regression equation is:

$$Y' = 16.24 + 0.017X_1 + 0.0028X_2 + 42X_3 + 0.0012X_4 + 0.19X_5 + 26.8X_6$$

a. What is the estimated index of satisfaction for a person who first married at 18, has an annual income of $26,500, has three children living, has assets of $156,000, has an index of health status of 141, and has 2.5 social activities a week on the average?
b. Which would add more to satisfaction, an additional income of $10,000 a year or two more social activities a week?

4. Cellulon, a manufacturer of a new type of home insulation, wants to develop guidelines for builders and consumers regarding the effects on natural gas consumption (1) of the thickness of the insulation in the attic of a home and (2) of the outdoor temperature. In the laboratory they varied the insulation thickness and temperature. A few of the findings are:

Monthly Natural Gas Consumption (cubic feet), Y	Thickness of Insulation (inches), X_1	Outdoor Temperature (°F), X_2
30.3	6	40
26.9	12	40
22.1	8	49

Based on the sample results, the regression equation is:

$$Y' = 62.65 - 1.86X_1 - 0.52X_2$$

a. How much natural gas can homeowners expect to use per month if they install 6 inches of insulation and the outdoor temperature is 40 degrees F?

b. What effect would installing 7 inches of insulation instead of 6 have on the monthly natural gas consumption (assuming the outdoor temperature remains at 40 degrees F)?

c. Why are the regression coefficients b_1 and b_2 negative? Is this logical?

▌ Multiple Standard Error of Estimate

Returning to the Salsberry Realty example, we found the estimated cost to heat a home during the month of January where the mean outside temperature was 30 degrees, that had 5 inches of attic insulation, and a 10-year-old furnace was $276.60. We would expect to find some random error in this estimate. Sometimes a home with these statistics would cost more than $276.60 to heat and other times less. The error in this estimate is measured by the **multiple standard error of estimate.** The standard error, as it is usually called, is denoted $s_{y \cdot 123}$. The subscripts indicate that three independent variables are being used to estimate the value of Y.

Recall from Chapter 12 that the standard error of estimate described the variation around the regression line. A small standard error indicated that the points were close to the regression line, whereas a large value indicated the points were scattered about the regression line. The same concept is true in multiple regression. If we have two independent variables, then we can think of the variation around a regression plane. If there are more than two independent variables, we do not have a geometric interpretation of the equation, but the standard error is still a measure of the "error" or variability in the prediction.

The formula to compute the standard error is similar to that used in the previous chapter. See formula (12–6) on page 442. The numerator is the sum of the squared differences between the estimated and the actual values of the dependent variable. In the denominator, we adjust for the fact that we are considering several, that is, k, independent variables.

MULTIPLE STANDARD ERROR OF ESTIMATE	$s_{y \cdot 12 \cdots k} = \sqrt{\dfrac{\Sigma(Y - Y')^2}{n - (k + 1)}}$	**[13–4]**

where:

Y is the observation

Y' is the value estimated from the regression equation.

n is the number of observations in the sample.

k is the number of independent variables.

In the Salsberry Realty example, $k = 3$.

Again, we use the Salsberry Realty problem to illustrate. The first home had a mean outside temperature of 35 degrees, 3 inches of attic insulation, and a 6-year-old furnace. Substituting these values into the regression equation, the estimated heating cost is $258.90, determined by $427 - 4.58(35) - 14.80(3) + 6.10(6)$. The Y' values for the other homes are found similarly and are reported in Table 13–2.

The actual heating cost for the first home is $250, in contrast to the estimated cost of $258.90. That is, the error in the prediction is −$8.90, found by ($250 − $258.90). This difference between the actual heating cost and the estimated heating cost is called the **residual.** To find the multiple standard error of estimate, we determine the residual for each of the sampled homes, square the residual, and then total the squared residuals. The total is reported in the lower right corner of Table 13–2.

Table 13–2 Calculations Needed for the Multiple Standard Error of Estimate

Home	Temperature (°F)	Insulation (inches)	Age (years)	Cost, Y	Y'	(Y − Y')	(Y − Y')²
1	35	3	6	$250	258.90	−8.90	79.21
2	29	4	10	360	295.98	64.02	4,098.56
3	36	7	3	165	176.82	−11.82	139.71
4	60	6	9	43	118.30	−75.30	5,670.09
5	65	5	6	92	91.90	0.10	0.01
6	30	5	5	200	246.10	−46.10	2,125.21
7	10	6	7	355	335.10	19.90	396.01
8	7	10	10	290	307.94	−17.94	321.84
9	21	9	11	230	264.72	−34.72	1,205.48
10	55	2	5	120	176.00	−56.00	3,136.00
11	54	12	4	73	26.48	46.52	2,164.11
12	48	5	1	205	139.26	65.74	4,321.75
13	20	5	15	400	352.90	47.10	2,218.41
14	39	4	7	320	231.88	88.12	7,765.13
15	60	8	6	72	70.40	1.60	2.56
16	20	5	8	272	310.20	−38.20	1,459.24
17	58	7	3	94	76.06	17.94	321.84
18	40	8	11	190	192.50	−2.50	6.25
19	27	9	8	235	218.94	16.06	257.92
20	30	7	5	139	216.50	−77.50	6,006.25
Total							41,695.58

In this problem $n = 20$ and $k = 3$ (three independent variables), so the multiple standard error of estimate is:

$$s_{y \cdot 123} = \sqrt{\frac{\Sigma(Y - Y')^2}{n - (k + 1)}} = \sqrt{\frac{41,695.58}{20 - (3 + 1)}} = 51.05$$

How do we interpret the 51.05? It is the typical "error" we make when we use this equation to predict the cost. First, the units are the same as the dependent variable, so the standard error is in dollars. Second, if the errors are normally distributed, about 68 percent of the residuals should be less than ±51.05 and about 95 percent should be less than ±2(51.05) or ±102.10. Refer to the second column from the right in Table 13–2, the column headed $(Y - Y')$. Of the 20 residuals reported in this column, 14 are less than ±51.05 and all are less than ±102.10, which is quite close to the guidelines of 68 percent and 95 percent.

In Chapter 12 we used the standard error of estimate to construct confidence intervals and predictions intervals. We will not detail these procedures for multiple regression, but they are available on statistical software systems, such as MINITAB.

▌ Assumptions about Multiple Regression and Correlation

Before continuing our discussion of multiple correlation, we list the assumptions underlying both multiple regression and multiple correlation. As noted in several previous chapters, we identify the assumptions because if they are not fully met, the results might be biased. For instance, in selecting a sample, we assume that all the items in the population have a chance of being selected. If our research involves surveying all those who ski, but we ignore those over 40 because we believe they are "too old," we would be biasing the responses toward the younger skiers. It should be mentioned, however, that in practice strict adherence to the following assumptions is not always possible in multiple regression and correlation problems involving the ever-changing business climate. But the statistical techniques discussed in this chapter appear to work well even when one or more of the assumptions are violated. Even if the values in the multiple regression equation are "off" slightly, our estimates based on the equation will be closer than any that could otherwise be made.

Each of the following assumptions will be discussed in more detail as we progress through the chapter.

1. The independent variables and the dependent variables have a linear relationship.
2. The dependent variable is continuous and at least interval scale.
3. The variation in the difference between the actual and the predicted values is the same for all fitted values of Y. That is, $(Y - Y')$ must be approximately the same for all values of Y'. When this is the case, differences exhibit **homoscedasticity.**

Homoscedasticity

4. The residuals, computed by $Y - Y'$, are normally distributed with a mean of 0.
5. Successive observations of the dependent variable are uncorrelated. Violation of this assumption is called **autocorrelation.** Autocorrelation often happens when data are collected successively over periods of time.

Autocorrelation

Statistical tests are available to detect homoscedasticity and autocorrelation. For those interested, these tests are covered in more advanced textbooks such as *Applied Linear Regression Models* by Neter, Kutner, Nachtscheim, and Wasserman (4th ed., 1996, published by Richard D. Irwin, Inc.).

▌ The ANOVA Table

As mentioned previously, the multiple regression calculations are lengthy. Fortunately, many computer software systems are available to perform the calculations. Most of the systems output the results in a fairly standard format. The following output from the MINITAB system, reported earlier, is typical. It includes the regression equation, the standard error of estimate, the coefficient of determination, as well as an analysis of variance table. We have already described the meaning of the regression coefficients in the equation $Y' = 427 - 4.58X_1 - 14.8X_2 + 6.10X_3$. We will discuss the "Coef," "StDev," and "T" (i.e., t ratio) columns later in the chapter. At this point we concentrate on the analysis of variance table.

```
Regression Analysis

The regression equation is
Cost = 427 - 4.58 Temp - 14.8 Insul + 6.10 Age

Predictor            Coef          StDev              T           P
Constant           427.19          59.60           7.17       0.000
Temp               -4.5827         0.7723          -5.93       0.000
Insulation        -14.831          4.754           -3.12       0.007
Age                  6.101         4.012            1.52       0.148

S = 51.05              R-Sq = 80.4%           R-Sq(adj) = 76.7%

Analysis of Variance

SOURCE            DF          SS            MS            F           P
Regression         3      171220         57073        21.90       0.000
Error             16       41695          2606
Total             19      212916
```

First, let's focus on the analysis of variance table. It is similar to the ANOVA table described in Chapter 10. In that chapter the variation was divided in two components: that due to the *treatments* and that due to random *error.* Here the total is also divided into two components: that explained by the **regression,** that is, the independent variables, and the **error,** or unexplained variation. These two categories are identified in the "SOURCE" column of the analysis of variance table. In the example there are 20 observations, so $n = 20$. The *total* number of degrees of freedom is $n - 1$, or $20 - 1 = 19$. The number of degrees of freedom in the "Regression" row is the number of independent variables. We let k represent the number of independent variables, so $k = 3$. The number of degrees of freedom in the "Error" row is $n - (k + 1) = 20 - (3 + 1) = 16$ degrees of freedom.

The heading "SS" in the middle of the ANOVA table refers to the sum of squares, or the variation.

Total variation = SS total = $\Sigma(Y - \overline{Y})^2 = 212,916$
Error variation = SSE = $\Sigma(Y - Y')^2 = 41,695$
Regression variation = SSR = SS total − SSE = $212,916 - 41,695 = 171,220$

The column headed "MS" (mean square) is determined by dividing the SS term by the *df* term. Thus, MSR, the mean square regression, is equal to SSR/k, and MSE equals SSE/$[n - (k + 1)]$. The general format of the ANOVA table is:

Source	df	SS	MS	F
Regression	k	SSR	MSR = SSR/k	MSR/MSE
Error	$n - (k + 1)$	SSE	MSE = SSE/$[n - (k + 1)]$	
Total	$n - 1$	SS total		

The **coefficient of multiple determination,** written as R^2, is the percent of the variation explained by the regression. It is the sum of squares due to the regression divided by the sum of squares total.

$$R^2 = \frac{\text{SSR}}{\text{SS total}} = \frac{171{,}220}{212{,}916} = .804$$

The multiple standard error of estimate may also be found directly from the ANOVA table.

$$s_{y \cdot 123} = \sqrt{\frac{\text{SSE}}{n - (k + 1)}} = \sqrt{\frac{41{,}695}{[(20 - (3 + 1)]}} = 51.05$$

These values, $R^2 = .804$ and $s_{y \cdot 123} = 51.05$, are included in the MINITAB output.

SELF-REVIEW 13-2

Refer to the following ANOVA table.

SOURCE	DF	SS	MS	F
Regression	4	10	2.50	10.0
Error	20	5	0.25	
Total	24	15		

(a) How large was the sample?
(b) How many independent variables are there?
(c) Compute the coefficient of multiple determination.
(d) Compute the multiple standard error of estimate.

Exercises

5. Refer to the following ANOVA table.

SOURCE	DF	SS	MS	F
Regression	3	21	7.0	2.33
Error	15	45	3.0	
Total	18	66		

a. How large was the sample?
b. How many independent variables are there?
c. Compute the coefficient of multiple determination.
d. Compute the multiple standard error of estimate.
6. Refer to the following ANOVA table.

SOURCE	DF	SS	MS	F
Regression	5	60	12	1.714
Error	20	140	7	
Total	25	200		

a. How large was the sample?
b. How many independent variables are there?
c. Compute the coefficient of multiple determination.
d. Compute the multiple standard error of estimate.

▌ Evaluating the Regression Equation

Earlier in the chapter we described a problem in which Salsberry Realty developed, using multiple regression techniques, an equation to express the cost to heat a home during the month of January based on the mean temperature, the number of inches of attic insulation, and the age of the furnace. The equation seemed reasonable, but we wish to verify that the multiple coefficient of determination is significantly larger than zero, evaluate the regression coefficients to see which are not equal to zero, and verify that the regression assumptions are met.

Using a Scatter Diagram

There are three independent variables, designated X_1, X_2, and X_3. The dependent variable, the heating cost, is designated Y. In order to visualize the relationships between the dependent variable and each of the independent variables, we drew the following scatter diagrams.

Of the three independent variables, the strongest association is between heating cost and the mean outside temperature. The relationships between cost and temperature and cost and insulation both are inverse. That is, as the independent variable increases, the dependent variable decreases. The relationship between the heating cost and the age of the furnace is direct. As the furnace gets older, it costs more to heat the home.

Correlation Matrix

A correlation matrix is useful in analyzing the factors involved in the cost to heat a home.

▌ **Correlation Matrix**   A matrix showing the coefficients of correlation between all pairs of variables.

The correlation matrix for the Salsberry Realty problem follows. The matrix was developed using the Excel system.

	Cost	Temperature	Insulation	Age
Cost	1			
Temperature	−0.811509	1		
Insulation	−0.257101	−0.10301613	1	
Age	0.5367276	−0.4859877	0.063617	1

Cost is the dependent variable, *Y.* We are particularly interested in independent variables that have a strong correlation with the dependent variable. We may wish to develop a simpler multiple regression equation using fewer independent variables and the correlation matrix helps us identify which may be relatively more important. As indicated in the output, temperature has the strongest correlation with cost, $-.811509$. The negative sign indicates the inverse relationship we were expecting. Age has a stronger correlation with cost than insulation and, again as we expected, the correlation between cost and the age of the furnace is direct. It is 0.5367276.

A second use of the correlation matrix is to check for **multicollinearity.**

| **Multicollinearity**   Correlation among the independent variables. |

Multicollinearity can distort the standard error of estimate and may, therefore, lead to incorrect conclusions as to which independent variables are statistically significant. In this case, the correlation between the age of the furnace and the temperature is the strongest, but it is not large enough to cause a problem. A common rule of thumb is that correlations among the independent variables between $-.70$ and .70 do not cause difficulties. The usual remedy for multicollinearity is to drop one of the independent variables that are strongly correlated and recompute the regression equation.

Global Test: Testing Whether the Multiple Regression Model Is Valid

The ability of the independent variables $X_1, X_2, \ldots, X_k$ to explain the behavior of the dependent variable Y can be tested. To put this in question form: Can the dependent variable be estimated without relying on the independent variables? The test used is referred to as the **global test.** Basically, it investigates whether it is possible all the independent variables have zero net regression coefficients. To put it another way, could the amount of explained variation, R^2, occur by chance?

To relate this question to the heating cost problem, we will test whether the independent variables (amount of insulation in the attic, mean daily outside temperature, and age of furnace) are capable of effectively estimating home heating costs.

Recall that in testing a hypothesis, we first state the null hypothesis and the alternate hypothesis. In the heating cost problem, there are three independent variables. Recall that b_1, b_2, and b_3 are sample net regression coefficients. The corresponding coefficients in the population are given the symbols β_1, β_2, and β_3. We now test whether the net regression coefficients in the population are zero. The null hypothesis is:

$$H_0\colon \beta_1 = \beta_2 = \beta_3 = 0$$

The alternate hypothesis is:

$$H_1\colon \text{Not all the } \beta \text{s are 0.}$$

If the null hypothesis is true, it implies the regression coefficients are all zero and, logically, are of no use in estimating the dependent variable (heating cost). Should that be the case, we would have to search for some other independent variables — or take a different approach — to predict home heating costs.

To test the null hypothesis that the multiple regression coefficients are all zero, we employ the F distribution introduced in Chapter 11. We will use the .05 level of significance. Recall these characteristics of the F distribution:

Characteristics of the F distribution
1. It is positively skewed, with the critical value for the .05 level located in the right tail. The critical value is the point that separates the region where H_0 is not rejected from the region of rejection.
2. It is constructed by knowing the number of degrees of freedom in the numerator and the number of degrees of freedom in the denominator.

The degrees of freedom for the numerator and the denominator may be found in the computer summary in the analysis of variance table. That portion of the table is included below. The top number in the column marked "DF" is 3, indicating that there are 3 degrees of freedom in the numerator. The middle number in the "DF" column (16) indicates that there are 16 degrees of freedom in the denominator. The number 16 is found by $n - (k + 1) = 20 - (3 + 1) = 16$. The number 3 corresponds to the number of independent variables.

```
Analysis of Variance

SOURCE          DF          SS          MS          F          P
Regression       3      171220       57073      21.90      0.000
Error           16       41695        2606
Total           19      212916
```

The value of F is computed by dividing the MSR term by MSE.

$$F = \frac{SSR/k}{SSE/[n - (k + 1)]} = \frac{171{,}220/3}{41{,}695/[20 - (3 + 1)]} = 21.90$$

The critical value of F is found in Appendix G. Using the table for the .05 level, move horizontally to 3 degrees of freedom in the numerator, then down to 16 degrees of freedom in the denominator, and read the critical value. It is 3.24. The region where H_0 is not rejected and the region where H_0 is rejected are shown in the following diagram.

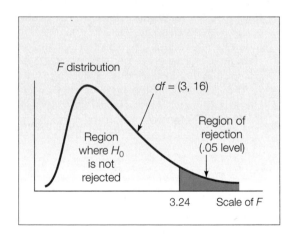

Continuing with the global test, the decision rule is: Do not reject the null hypothesis that all the regression coefficients are 0 if the computed value of F is less than or equal to 3.24. If the computed F is greater than 3.24, reject H_0 and accept the alternate hypothesis, H_1.

The computed value of F is 21.90, which is in the rejection region. The null hypothesis that all the multiple regression coefficients are zero is therefore rejected. The p-value is 0.000 from the above analysis of variance table, so it is quite unlikely that H_0 is true. The alternate hypothesis is accepted, indicating that not all the regression coefficients are zero. From a practical standpoint, this means that the independent variables (amount of insulation, etc.) do have the ability to explain the variation in the dependent variable (heating cost). We expected this decision. Logically, the outside temperature, the amount of insulation, and age of the furnace have a great bearing on heating costs. The global test assures us that they do.

Evaluating Individual Regression Coefficients

So far we have shown that some, but not necessarily all, of the regression coefficients are not equal to zero and thus useful for predictions. The next step is to test the variables *individually* to determine which regression coefficients may be 0 and which are not.

Why is it important to find whether it is possible that any of the βs equal 0? If a β could equal 0, it implies that this particular independent variable is of no value in explaining any variation in the dependent value. If there are coefficients for which H_0 cannot be rejected, we may want to eliminate them from the regression equation.

We will now conduct three separate tests of hypothesis — for temperature, for insulation, and for the age of the furnace.

For temperature:	For insulation:	For furnace age:
H_0: $\beta_1 = 0$	H_0: $\beta_2 = 0$	H_0: $\beta_3 = 0$
H_1: $\beta_1 \neq 0$	H_1: $\beta_2 \neq 0$	H_1: $\beta_3 \neq 0$

We will test the hypotheses at the .05 level. The way the alternate hypothesis is stated indicates that the test is two-tailed.

The test statistic is the Student t distribution with $n - (k + 1)$ degrees of freedom. The number of sample observations is n. There are 20 homes in the study, so $n = 20$. The number of independent variables is k, which is 3. Thus, there are $n - (k + 1) = 20 - (3 + 1) = 16$ degrees of freedom.

The critical value for t is in Appendix F. For a two-tailed test with 16 degrees of freedom using the .05 significant level, H_0 is rejected if t is less than -2.120 or greater than 2.120. The MINITAB system produced the following output.

Predictor	Coef	StDev	T	P
Constant	427.19	59.60	7.17	0.000
Temp	−4.5827	0.7723	−5.93	0.000
Insulation	−14.831	4.754	−3.12	0.007
Age	6.101	4.012	1.52	0.148

The column headed "Coef" gives the multiple regression equation:

$$Y' = 427.19 - 4.5827X_1 - 14.831X_2 + 6.101X_3$$

Interpreting the term $-4.5827X_1$ in the equation: For each degree the temperature increases, it is expected that the heating cost will decrease about $4.58, holding the two other variables constant.

The column on the MINITAB output labeled "StDev" indicates the standard deviation of the sample regression coefficient. Recall that Salsberry Realty selected a sample of 20 homes along the east coast of the United States. If they were to select a second sample at random and compute the regression coefficients of that sample, the values would not be exactly the same. If they repeated the sampling process many times, however, we could design a sampling distribution of the regression coefficients. The column labeled "StDev" estimates the variability of these regression coefficients. The sampling distribution of Coef/StDev follows the t distribution with $n - (k + 1)$ degrees of freedom. Hence, we are able to test the independent variables individually to determine whether the net regression coefficients differ from zero. The computed t ratio is -5.93 for temperature and -3.12 for insulation. Both of these t values are in the rejection region to the left of -2.120. Thus, we conclude that the regression coefficients for the temperature and insulation variables are *not* zero. The computed t for age of the furnace is 1.52, so we conclude that β_3 could equal 0. The independent variable "age of the furnace" is not a significant predictor of heating cost. It can be dropped from the analysis.

In Self-Review 13–3, we run the multiple regression problem again using MINITAB, but only two variables—"temperature" and "insulation"—are included. These two variables explained 77.6 percent of the variation in heating cost. Using all three variables—temperature, insulation, and furnace age—a total of 80.4 percent of the variation is explained. The additional variable increased R^2 by only 2.8 percent—a rather small increase for the addition of an independent variable.

At this point we should also develop a strategy for deleting independent variables. In the Salsberry Realty case there were three independent variables and one (age) had a regression coefficient that did not differ from 0. It is clear that we should drop that variable. So we delete that variable and rerun the regression equation. However, in some instances it may not be as clear-cut which variable to delete.

To explain, suppose we developed a multiple regression equation based on five independent variables. We conducted the global test and found that some of the regression coefficients were different from zero. Next, we tested the regression coefficients individually and found that three were significant and two were not. The preferred procedure is to drop the single independent variable with the *smallest absolute t* value or largest *p*-value and rerun the regression equation with the four remaining variables. Then, on the new regression equation with four independent variables, conduct the global test and the individual tests. If there are still regression coefficients that are not significant, again drop the variable with the smallest absolute *t* value. To describe the process in another way, we should delete only one variable at a time. Each time we delete a variable, we need to rerun the regression equation and check the remaining variables.

SELF-REVIEW 13–3

The multiple regression and correlation data for the preceding heating cost problem were rerun using only the first two significant independent variables—temperature and insulation. (See the following MINITAB output.)

(a) What is the new multiple regression equation? (Temperature is X_1 and insulation X_2.)
(b) What is the coefficient of multiple determination? Interpret.
(c) How can you tell that these two independent variables are of value in predicting heating costs?
(d) What is the *p*-value of insulation? Interpret.

```
The regression equation is
Cost = 490 − 5.15 Temp − 14.7 Insul
Predictor          Coef          StDev               T               P
Constant          490.29         44.41           11.04           0.000
Temp             −5.1499        0.7019           −7.34           0.000
Insul            −14.718         4.934           −2.98           0.008


S = 52.98          R-Sq = 77.6%               R-Sq(adj) = 74.9%


Analysis of Variance
SOURCE          DF          SS          MS          F          p-value
Regression       2        165195       82597      29.42        0.000
Error           17         47721        2807
Total           19        212916
```

Qualitative Independent Variables

The three variables used in the Salsberry Realty problem were all quantitative; that is, numerical in nature. Frequently we wish to use nominal-scale variables — such as gender, whether the home has a swimming pool, or whether the sports team was the home or the visiting team — in our analysis. These are called *qualitative variables* because they describe a particular quality, such as male or female. To use a qualitative variable in regression analysis, we use a scheme of **dummy variables** in which one of the two possible conditions is coded 0 and the other 1.

Dummy Variable   A variable in which there are only two possible outcomes. For analysis, one of the outcomes is coded a 1 and the other a 0.

For example, we might be interested in estimating an executive's salary based on years of job experience and whether he or she graduated from college. "Graduation from college" can take on only one of two conditions: yes or no. Thus, it is considered a qualitative variable.

Is it possible to use a qualitative variable with more than two possible outcomes? Yes, but the coding scheme becomes more complex and will require a series of dummy variables. To explain, suppose a company is studying its sales as they relate to adver-tising expense by quarter for the last five years. Let sales be the dependent variable and advertising expense be the first independent variable, X_1. To include the qualitative infor-mation regarding the quarter, we will need three additional independent variables. For the variable X_2, the five observations referring to the first quarter of each of the five years are coded 1 and the other quarters 0. Similarly, for X_3 the five observations referring to the second quarter are coded 1 and the other quarters 0. For X_4 the five observations referring to the third quarter are coded 1 and the other quarters 0. An observation that does not refer to any of the first three quarters must refer to the fourth quarter, so a distinct independent variable referring to this quarter is not necessary.

Suppose in the Salsberry Realty example that the independent variable "garage" is added. For those homes without an attached garage, 0 is used; for homes with an attached garage, a 1 is used. We will refer to the "garage" variable as X_4. The data from Table 13–3 are entered into the MINITAB system.

Table 13–3   Home Heating Costs, Temperature, Insulation, and Presence of a Garage for a Sample of 20 Homes

Cost, Y	Temperature, X_1	Insulation, X_2	Garage, X_4
$250	35	3	0
360	29	4	1
165	36	7	0
43	60	6	0
92	65	5	0
200	30	5	0
355	10	6	1
290	7	10	1
230	21	9	0
120	55	2	0
73	54	12	0
205	48	5	1
400	20	5	1
320	39	4	1
72	60	8	0
272	20	5	1
94	58	7	0
190	40	8	1
235	27	9	0
139	30	7	0

The output from MINITAB is:

```
Regression Analysis

The regression equation is
Cost = 394 − 3.96 Temp − 11.3 Insul + 77.4 Garage

Predictor            Coef          StDev              T            P
Constant           393.67          45.00           8.75        0.000
Temp              −3.9628         0.6527          −6.07        0.000
Insul             −11.334          4.002          −2.83        0.012
Garage             77.43          22.78           3.40        0.004

S = 41.62           R-Sq = 87.0%            R-Sq(adj) = 84.5%

Analysis of Variance

SOURCE          DF          SS            MS           F            P
Regression       3       185202         61734       35.64       0.000
Error           16        27713          1732
Total           19       212916
```

What is the effect of the variable "garage"? Should it be included in the analysis? To show the effect of the variable, suppose we have two houses exactly alike next to each other in Buffalo, New York; one has an attached garage, and the other does not. Both homes have 3 inches of insulation, and the mean January temperature in Buffalo is 20 degrees. For the house without an attached garage, a 0 is substituted for X_4 in the regression equation. The estimated heating cost is $280.90, found by:

$$Y' = 394 − 3.96X_1 − 11.3X_2 + 77.4X_4$$

$$= 394 − 3.96(20) − 11.3(3) + 77.4(0) = 280.90$$

For the house with an attached garage, a 1 is substituted for X_4 in the regression equation. The estimated heating cost is $385.30, found by:

$$Y' = 394 − 3.96X_1 − 11.3X_2 + 77.4X_4$$

$$= 394 − 3.96(20) − 11.3(3) + 77.4(1) = 358.30$$

The difference between the estimated heating costs is $77.40 ($358.30 − $280.90). Hence, we can expect the cost to heat a house with an attached garage to be $77.40 more than the cost for an equivalent house without a garage.

We have shown the difference between the two types of homes to be $77.40, but is the difference significant? We conduct the following test of hypothesis.

H_0 $\beta_4 = 0$

H_1 $\beta_4 \neq 0$

The information necessary to answer this question can be found in the MINITAB output above. The computed t ratio is 3.40. There are three independent variables in the analysis, so there are $n − (k + 1) = 20 − (3 + 1) = 16$ degrees of freedom. The critical value from Appendix F is 2.120. The decision rule, using a two-tailed test and the .05 significance level, is to reject H_0 if the computed t is to the left of −2.120 or to the right of 2.120. Since the computed value of 3.40 is to the right of 2.120, the null hypothesis is rejected. It is concluded that the regression coefficient is not zero. The independent variable "garage" should be included in the analysis.

▌ Exercises

7. Refer to the following information:

Predictor	Coef	StDev
Constant	20.00	10.00
X_1	−1.00	0.25
X_2	12.00	8.00
X_3	−15.00	5.00

SOURCE	DF	SS	MS	F
Regression	3	7,500.00		
Error	18			
Total	21	10,000.0		

    a. Complete the ANOVA table.
    b. Conduct a global test of hypothesis, using the .05 significance level. Can you conclude that any of the net regression coefficients are different from zero?
    c. Conduct a test of hypothesis on each of the regression coefficients. Could you delete any of the variables?
8. Refer to the following information:

Predictor	Coef	StDev
Constant	−150	90
X_1	2000	500
X_2	−25	30
X_3	5	5
X_4	−300	100
X_5	0.60	0.15

SOURCE	DF	SS	MS	F
Regression	5	1,500.0		
Error	15			
Total	20	2,000.0		

    a. Complete the ANOVA table.
    b. Conduct a global test of hypothesis, using the .05 significance level. Can you conclude that any of the net regression coefficients are different from zero?
    c. Conduct a test of hypothesis on each of the regression coefficients. Could you delete any of the variables?

▌ Analysis of Residuals

In an earlier section we described the assumptions required for regression and correlation analysis. These assumptions are:

1. There is a linear relationship between the dependent variable and the independent variables.

2. The dependent variable is of interval- or ratio-scale.
3. Successive observations of the dependent variable are not correlated.
4. The differences between the actual values and estimated values, that is, the residuals, are normally distributed.
5. The variation in the residuals is the same for all fitted values of Y'. That is, the distribution of $(Y - Y')$ is the same for all values of Y'.

The last two assumptions can be verified by plotting the residuals. That is, we want to confirm that the residuals follow a normal distribution and that residuals have the same variation whether the Y' value is large or small. We present the necessary data in Table 13–4. The column headed "Actual Cost" is the original heating cost, first presented in Table 13–1. The next column, labeled "Estimated Cost," is the cost to heat the home as estimated from the regression equation. This is also referred to as the fitted value and is Y'. The value for the first home is found by substituting the actual values of the three variables into the regression equation. For example, from Table 13–3, for the first home the mean outside temperature was 35 degrees, it had 3 inches of attic insulation, and did not have an attached garage. The actual heating cost was $250, and the estimated heating cost is $221.08, found by

$$Y' = 393.67 - 3.96(35) - 11.33(3) + 77.43(0) = 221.08$$

The residual is in the last column. It is 28.92, found by $250 - 221.08$. The residuals for the 19 other values are computed similarly.

Table 13–4   Summary of Actual Costs, Estimated Costs, and Residuals for Salsberry Realty Problem

Home	Actual Cost, Y	Estimated Cost, Y'	Residual, $Y - Y'$
1	250	221.08	28.92
2	360	310.94	49.06
3	165	171.80	−6.80
4	43	88.09	−45.09
5	92	79.62	12.38
6	200	218.22	−18.22
7	355	363.52	−8.52
8	290	330.08	−40.08
9	230	208.54	21.46
10	120	153.21	−33.21
11	73	43.87	29.13
12	205	224.37	−19.37
13	400	335.25	64.75
14	320	271.34	48.66
15	72	65.43	6.57
16	272	335.25	−63.25
17	94	84.68	9.32
18	190	222.06	−32.06
19	235	184.78	50.22
20	139	195.56	−56.56

We can use the last column, the residuals, to verify the normality assumption. Chart 13–1 is a stem-and-leaf display and Chart 13–2 is a histogram of the residuals. Both charts indicate that the distribution of the residuals is somewhat normal, as required in the assumptions. To interpret the histogram in Chart 13–2, note that it is constructed so that the residuals are tallied into classes: -70 up to -50, with a midpoint of -60; -50 up to -30 with a midpoint of -40; and so on. The details of the first three classes are:

Class	Midpoint	Residuals	Count
-70 up to -50	-60	$-63.25, -56.56$	2
-50 up to -30	-40	$-45.09, -40.08, -33.21, -32.06$	4
-30 up to -10	-20	$-19.37, -18.22$	2

```
Stem-and-leaf of Residuals   N = 20
Leaf Unit = 10


         1    -0  6
         4    -0  544
         6    -0  33
        10    -0  1100
        10     0  001
         7     0  222
         4     0  445
         1     0  6
```

Chart 13–1   Stem-and-Leaf Display of the Residuals

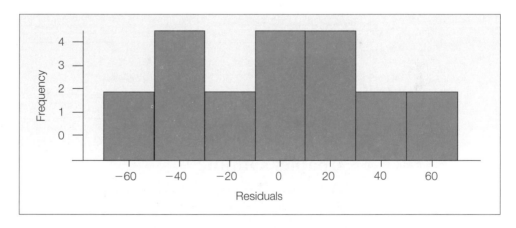

Chart 13–2   Histogram of Residuals

Homoscedasticity   The assumptions for regression analysis also require that the residuals remain constant for all values of Y'. Recall that this condition is called **homoscedasticity.** To check for homoscedasticity, the residuals are plotted against the fitted values of Y (see Chart 13–3). Because there is no more variation around large values of Y' than around small values of Y', we can conclude that this assumption is met.

Following are two examples where the homoscedasticity requirement is not met. Note that in the first example, the plot of residuals is funnel-shaped. That is, as the fitted Y values increase, so does the variation in the residuals. In the second example, there is a pattern to the residuals. The residuals seem to take the shape of a polynomial, or second-degree equation.

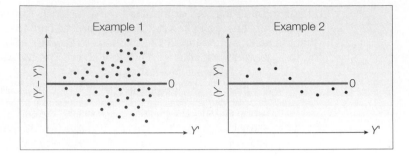

What problems are caused by residuals that fail to show homoscedasticity? The standard deviations of the regression coefficients will be understated (too small), causing potential independent variables to appear to be significant when they may not be. The remedy for this condition is to select other independent variables or to transform some of the variables. For a more detailed discussion of residual analysis, refer to an advanced text, such as *Applied Linear Regression Models* by Neter, Kutner, Nachtsheim, and Wasserman (Richard D. Irwin, 1996).

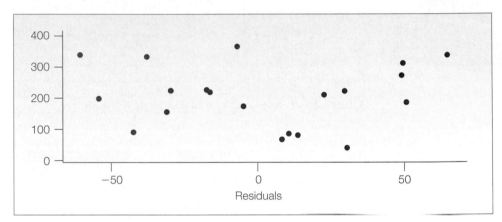

Chart 13–3   Fitted Values of Y' and Residuals

I Chapter Outline

I. Multiple regression and correlation analysis is based on these assumptions.
  A. There is a linear relationship between the independent variables and the dependent variable.
  B. The dependent variable is continuous and of interval scale.
  C. The residual variation is the same for all fitted values of Y.
  D. The residuals are normally distributed.
  E. Successive observations of the dependent variable are uncorrelated.

II. The general form of the multiple regression equation is:

$$Y' = a + b_1X_1 + b_2X_2 + \cdots + b_kX_k \qquad \textbf{[13–3]}$$

where Y' is the estimated value, a is the Y-intercept, the bs are the sample regression coefficients, and the Xs represent the values of the various independent variables.
  A. There can be any number of independent variables.
  B. The least squares criterion is used to develop the equation.
  C. A computer is needed to determine a and the various b values.

III. There are two measures of the effectiveness of the regression equation.

    A. The multiple standard error of estimate is similar to the standard deviation.
      1. It is measured in the same units as the dependent variable.
      2. It is difficult to determine what is a large value and what is a small value of the standard error.
    B. The coefficient of determination may range from 0 to 1.
      1. It shows the fraction of the variation in Y that is explained by the set of independent variables.
      2. It does not reveal the direction of the relationship.
IV. The ANOVA table gives the variation in the dependent variable explained by the regression equation.
V. A correlation matrix shows all possible simple correlation coefficients between pairs of variables.
VI. A global test is used to investigate whether any of the independent variables have significant regression coefficients.
    A. The null hypothesis is: All the regression coefficients are zero.
    B. The alternate hypothesis is: At least one regression coefficient is not zero.
    C. The test statistic is the F distribution with k (the number of independent variables) and $n - (k + 1)$ degrees of freedom, where n is the sample size.
VII. The test for individual variables determines which independent variables have nonzero regression coefficients.
    A. The variables that have zero regression coefficients are usually dropped from the analysis.
    B. The test statistic is the t distribution with $n - (k + 1)$ degrees of freedom.
VIII. Dummy variables are used to represent qualitative variables and can assume only one of two possible conditions.
IX. A residual is the difference between the actual value of Y and the predicted value of Y'.
    A. Residuals should be approximately normally distributed. Histograms and stem-and-leaf charts are useful in checking this requirement.
    B. A plot of the residuals and their corresponding Y' values is useful for showing that there are no trends or patterns in the residuals.

▌ Pronunciation Key

SYMBOL	MEANING	PRONUNCIATION
b_1	Regression coefficient for the first independent variable	b sub 1
b_k	Regression coefficient for any independent variable	b sub k
$s_{y \cdot 12 \cdots k}$	Multiple standard error of estimate	s sub y dot 1, 2 . . .

▌ Chapter Exercises

9. A multiple regression equation yields the following partial results.

Source	Sum of Squares	df
Regression	750	4
Error	500	35

    a. What is the total sample size?
    b. How many independent variables are being considered?
    c. Compute the coefficient of determination.
    d. Compute the standard error of estimate.
    e. Test the hypothesis that none of the regression coefficients is equal to zero. Let $\alpha = .05$.

10. In a multiple regression equation two independent variables are considered, and the sample size is 25. The regression coefficients and the standard errors are as follows.

$$b_1 = 2.676 \qquad s_{b_1} = 0.56$$

$$b_2 = -0.880 \qquad s_{b_2} = 0.71$$

Conduct a test of hypothesis to determine whether either independent variable has a coefficient equal to zero. Would you consider deleting either variable from the regression equation? Use the .05 significance level.

11. The following output was obtained.

```
Analysis of variance

SOURCE            DF         SS         MS
Regression         5        100         20
Error             20         40          2
Total             25        140


Predictor       Coef     StDev     t-ratio
Constant        3.00      1.50        2.00
  X₁            4.00      3.00        1.33
  X₂            3.00      0.20       15.00
  X₃            0.20      0.05        4.00
  X₄           -2.50      1.00       -2.50
  X₅            3.00      4.00        0.75
```

a. What is the sample size?
b. Compute the value of R^2.
c. Compute the multiple standard error of estimate.
d. Conduct a global test of hypothesis to determine whether any of the regression coefficients are significant. Use the .05 significance level.
e. Test the regression coefficients individually. Would you consider omitting any variable(s)? If so, which one(s)? Use the .05 significance level.

12. In a multiple regression equation $k = 5$ and $n = 20$, the MSE value is 5.10, and SS total is 519.68. At the .05 significance level, can we conclude that any of the regression coefficients are not equal to 0?

13. The district manager of Jasons, a large discount retail chain, is investigating why certain stores in her region are performing better than others. She believes that three factors are related to total sales: the number of competitors in the region, the population in the surrounding area, and the amount spent on advertising. From her district, consisting of several hundred stores, she selects a random sample of 30 stores. For each store she gathered the following information.

Y = total sales last year (in $ thousands).

X_1 = number of competitors in the region.

X_2 = population of the region (in millions).

X_3 = advertising expense (in $ thousands).

The sample data were run on the MINITAB software package, with the following results.

```
Analysis of variance

SOURCE             DF          SS          MS
Regression          3     3050.00      762.50
Error              26     2200.00       84.62
Total              29     5250.00


Predictor        Coef       StDev      t-ratio
Constant        14.00        7.00         2.00
    X₁          -1.00        0.70        -1.43
    X₂          30.00        5.20         5.77
    X₃           0.20        0.08         2.50
```

a. What are the estimated sales for the Bryne Store, which has four competitors, a regional population of 0.4 (400,000), and advertising expense of 30 ($30,000)?
b. Compute the R^2 value.
c. Compute the multiple standard error of estimate.
d. Conduct a global test of hypothesis to determine whether any of the regression coefficients are not equal to zero. Use the .05 level of significance.
e. Conduct tests of hypotheses to determine which of the independent variables have significant regression coefficients. Which variables would you consider eliminating? Use the .05 significance level.

14. Suppose that the sales manager of a large automotive parts distributor wants to estimate as early as April the total annual sales of a region. Based on regional sales, the total sales for the company can also be estimated. If, based on past experience, it is found that the April estimates of annual sales are reasonably accurate, then in future years the April forecast could be used to revise production schedules and maintain the correct inventory at the retail outlets.

   Several factors appear to be related to sales, including the number of retail outlets in the region stocking the company's parts, the number of automobiles in the region registered as of April 1, and the total personal income for the first quarter of the year. Five independent variables were finally selected as being the most important (according to the sales manager). Then the data were gathered for a recent year. The total annual sales for that year for each region were also recorded. Note in the following table that for region 1 there were 1,739 retail outlets stocking the company's automotive parts, there were 9,270,000 registered automobiles in the region as of April 1, and sales for that year were $37,702,000.

Annual Sales ($ millions), Y	Number of Retail Outlets, X_1	Number of Automobiles Registered (millions), X_2	Personal Income ($ billions), X_3	Average Age of Automobiles (years), X_4	Number of Supervisors, X_5
37.702	1,739	9.27	85.4	3.5	9.0
24.196	1,221	5.86	60.7	5.0	5.0
32.055	1,846	8.81	68.1	4.4	7.0
3.611	120	3.81	20.2	4.0	5.0
17.625	1,096	10.31	33.8	3.5	7.0
45.919	2,290	11.62	95.1	4.1	13.0
29.600	1,687	8.96	69.3	4.1	15.0
8.114	241	6.28	16.3	5.9	11.0
20.116	649	7.77	34.9	5.5	16.0
12.994	1,427	10.92	15.1	4.1	10.0

The MINITAB software system was used to generate the following output.

a. Consider the following correlation matrix. Which single variable has the strongest corre-
    lation with the dependent variable? The correlations between the independent variables
    "outlets" and "income" and between "cars" and "outlets" are fairly strong. Could this be
    a problem? What is this condition called?

	sales	outlets	cars	income	age
outlets	0.899				
cars	0.605	0.775			
income	0.964	0.825	0.409		
age	−0.323	−0.489	−0.447	−0.349	
bosses	0.286	0.183	0.395	0.155	0.291

b. The following regression equation was obtained using the five independent variables.
    What percent of the variation is explained by the regression equation?

```
The regression equation is
sales = −19.7 − 0.00063 outlets + 1.74 cars + 0.410 income
        + 2.04 age − 0.034 bosses

        Predictor          Coef          StDev        t-ratio
        Constant         −19.672         5.422         −3.63
        outlets       −0.000629         0.002638       −0.24
        cars             1.7399         0.5530          3.15
        income          0.40994         0.04385         9.35
        age              2.0357         0.8779          2.32
        bosses          −0.0344         0.1880         −0.18

Analysis of Variance
        SOURCE          DF          SS            MS
        Regression       5       1593.81        318.76
        Error            4          9.08          2.27
        Total            9       1602.89
```

c. Conduct a global test of hypothesis to determine whether any of the regression coeffi-
    cients are not zero. Use the .05 significance level.
d. Conduct a test of hypothesis on each of the independent variables. Would you consider
    eliminating "outlets" and "bosses"? Use the .05 significance level.
e. The regression has been rerun below with "outlets" and "bosses" eliminated. Compute
    the coefficient of determination. How much has R^2 changed from the previous analysis?

```
The regression equation is
        sales = -18.9 + 1.61 cars + 0.400 income + 1.96 age

            Predictor              Coef            StDev          t-ratio
            Constant            -18.924            3.636            -5.20
            Cars                 1.6129           0.1979             8.15
            Income              0.40031          0.01569            25.52
            Age                  1.9637           0.5846             3.36

Analysis of Variance

            SOURCE            DF             SS               MS
            Regression         3        1593.66           531.22
            Error              6           9.23             1.54
            Total              9        1602.89
```

f. Following is a histogram and a stem-and-leaf chart of the residuals. Does the normality assumption appear reasonable?

```
Histogram of residual N = 10      Stem-and-leaf of residual N = 10
                                  Leaf Unit = 0.10


Midpoint  Count
   -1.5      1   *                1   -1   7
   -1.0      1   *                2   -1   2
   -0.5      2   **               2   -0
   -0.0      2   **               5   -0   440
    0.5      2   **               5    0   24
    1.0      1   *                3    0   68
    1.5      1   *                1    1
                                  1    1   7
```

g. Following is a plot of the fitted values of Y (i.e., Y') and the residuals. Do you see any violations of the assumptions?

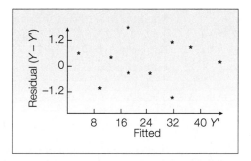

15. The administrator of a new paralegal program at Seagate Technical College wants to estimate the grade point average in the new program. He thought that high school GPA, the verbal score on the Scholastic Aptitude Test (SAT), and the mathematics score on the SAT would be good predictors of paralegal GPA. The data on nine students are:

Student	High School GPA	SAT Verbal	SAT Math	Paralegal GPA
1	3.25	480	410	3.21
2	1.80	290	270	1.68
3	2.89	420	410	3.58
4	3.81	500	600	3.92
5	3.13	500	490	3.00
6	2.81	430	460	2.82
7	2.20	320	490	1.65
8	2.14	530	480	2.30
9	2.63	469	440	2.33

The MINITAB software system was used to generate the following output.

a. The following correlation matrix was obtained. Which variable has the strongest correlation with the dependent variable? Some of the correlations among the independent variables are strong. Does this appear to be a problem?

```
           legal       gpa      verbal
gpa        0.911
verbal     0.616     0.609
math       0.487     0.636     0.599
```

b. Consider the following output. Compute the coefficient of multiple determination.

```
The regression equation is
legal = -0.411 + 1.20 gpa + 0.00163 verbal - 0.00194 math

Predictor              Coef            StDev        t-ratio
Constant            -0.4111           0.7823          -0.53
gpa                  1.2014           0.2955           4.07
verbal               0.001629         0.002147         0.76
math                -0.001939         0.002074        -0.94

Analysis of Variance

SOURCE        DF        SS          MS
Regression     3     4.3595      1.4532
Error          5     0.7036      0.1407
Total          8     5.0631
```

c. Conduct a global test of hypothesis from the preceding output. Does it appear that any of the regression coefficients are not equal to zero?
d. Conduct a test of hypothesis on each independent variable. Would you consider eliminating the variables "verbal" and "math"? Let $\alpha = .05$.
e. The analysis has been rerun without "verbal" and "math." See the following output. Compute the coefficient of determination. How much has R^2 changed from the previous analysis?

```
The regression equation is
legal = -0.454 + 1.16 gpa

   Predictor         Coef        StDev      t-ratio
   Constant       -0.4542       0.5542        -0.82
   gpa             1.1589       0.1977         5.86


Analysis of Variance

SOURCE            DF           SS           MS
Regression         1       4.2061       4.2061
Error              7       0.8570       0.1224
Total              8       5.0631
```

f. Following are a histogram and a stem-and-leaf diagram of the residuals. Does the normality assumption for the residuals seem reasonable?

```
Histogram of residual N = 9

Midpoint         Count
    -0.4           1 *
    -0.2           3 ***
     0.0           3 ***
     0.2           1 *
     0.4           0
     0.6           1 *


Stem-and-leaf of residual N = 9
Leaf unit = 0.10

   1      -0 4
   2      -0 2
  (3)     -0 110
   4       0 00
   2       0
   1       0
   1       0 6
```

g. Following is a plot of the residuals and the Y' values. Do you see any violation of the assumptions?

The following problems require a software package.

16. Mr. Mike Wilde is president of the teachers' union for Otsego School District. In preparing for upcoming negotiations, he would like to investigate the salary structure of classroom teachers in the district. He believes there are three factors that affect a teacher's salary: years of experience, a rating of teaching effectiveness given by the principal, and whether the teacher has a master's degree. A random sample of 20 teachers resulted in the following data.

Salary ($ thousands), Y	Years of Experience, X_1	Principal's Rating, X_2	Master's Degree,* Y_3
21.1	8	35	0
23.6	5	43	0
19.3	2	51	1
33.0	15	60	1
28.6	11	73	0
35.0	14	80	1
32.0	9	76	0
26.8	7	54	1
38.6	22	55	1
21.7	3	90	1
15.7	1	30	0
20.6	5	44	0
41.8	23	84	1
36.7	17	76	0
28.4	12	68	1
23.6	14	25	0
31.8	8	90	1
20.7	4	62	0
22.8	2	80	1
32.8	8	72	0

*1 = yes, 0 = no.

a. Develop a correlation matrix. Which independent variable has the strongest correlation with the dependent variable? Does it appear there will be any problems with multicollinearity?

b. Determine the regression equation. What salary would you estimate for a teacher with five years' experience, a rating by the principal of 60, and no master's degree?

c. Conduct a global test of hypothesis to determine whether any of the net regression coefficients differ from zero. Use the .05 significance level.

d. Conduct a test of hypothesis for the individual regression coefficients. Would you consider deleting any of the independent variables? Use the .05 significance level.

e. If your conclusion in part (d) was to delete one or more independent variables, run the analysis again without those variables.

f. Determine the residuals for the equation of part (e). Use a stem-and-leaf chart or a histogram to verify that the distribution of the residuals is approximately normal.

g. Plot the residuals computed in part (f) in a scatter diagram with the residuals on the Y-axis and the Y' values on the X-axis. Does the plot reveal any violations of the assumptions of regression?

17. The district sales manager for a major automobile manufacturer is studying car sales. Specifically, he would like to determine what factors affect the number of cars sold at a dealership. To investigate, he randomly selects 12 dealers. From these dealers he obtains the number of cars sold last month, the minutes of radio advertising purchased last month, the number of full-time salespeople employed in the dealership, and whether the dealer is located in the city. The information is as follows:

Cars Sold Last Month, Y	Advertising, X_1	Sales Force, X_2	City, X_3	Cars Sold Last Month, Y	Advertising, X_1	Sales Force, X_2	City, X_3
127	18	10	Yes	161	25	14	Yes
138	15	15	No	180	26	17	Yes
159	22	14	Yes	102	15	7	No
144	23	12	Yes	163	24	16	Yes
139	17	12	No	106	18	10	No
128	16	12	Yes	149	25	11	Yes

a. Develop a correlation matrix. Which independent variable has the strongest correlation with the dependent variable? Does it appear there will be any problems with multicollinearity?

b. Determine the regression equation. How many cars would you expect to be sold by a dealership employing 20 salespeople, purchasing 15 minutes of advertising, and located in a city?

c. Conduct a global test of hypothesis to determine whether any of the net regression coefficients differ from zero. Let $\alpha = .05$.

d. Conduct a test of hypothesis for the individual regression coefficients. Would you consider deleting any of the independent variables? Let $\alpha = .05$.

e. If your conclusion in part (d) was to delete one or more independent variables, run the analysis again without those variables.

f. Determine the residuals for the equation of part (e). Use a stem-and-leaf chart or a histogram to verify that the distribution of the residuals is approximately normal.

g. Plot the residuals computed in part (f) in a scatter diagram with the residuals on the Y-axis and the Y' values on the X-axis. Does the plot reveal any violations of the assumptions of regression?

18. Fran's Convenience Marts are located throughout metropolitan Erie, Pennsylvania. Fran, the owner, would like to expand into other communities in northwestern Pennsylvania and southwestern New York, such as Jamestown, Corry, Meadville, and Warren. As part of her presentation to the local bank, she would like to better understand the factors that make a particular outlet profitable. She must do all the work herself, so she will not be able to study all her outlets. She selects a random sample of 15 marts and records the average daily sales (Y), the floor space (area), the number of parking spaces, and the median income of families in that ZIP code region for each. The sample information is reported below.

Sampled Mart	Daily Sales	Store Area	Parking Spaces	Income ($ thousands)
1	$1,840	532	6	44
2	1,746	478	4	51
3	1,812	530	7	45
4	1,806	508	7	46
5	1,792	514	5	44
6	1,825	556	6	46
7	1,811	541	4	49
8	1,803	513	6	52
9	1,830	532	5	46
10	1,827	537	5	46
11	1,764	499	3	48
12	1,825	510	8	47
13	1,763	490	4	48
14	1,846	516	8	45
15	1,815	482	7	43

a. Determine the regression equation.
b. What is the value of R^2? Comment on the value.
c. Conduct a global hypothesis test to determine if any of the independent variables are different from zero.
d. Conduct individual hypothesis tests to determine if any of the independent variables can be dropped.
e. If variables are dropped, recompute the regression equation and R^2.

19. Mr. Steve Douglas has been hired as a management trainee by a large brokerage firm. As his first project, he is asked to study the gross profit of firms in the chemical industry. What factors affect profitability in that industry? Steve selects a random sample of 16 firms and obtains data on the number of employees, number of consecutive common stock dividends paid, the total value of inventory at the start of the current year, and the gross profit for each firm. His findings are:

Company	Gross Profit ($ thousands), Y	Number of Employees, X_1	Consecutive Dividends, X_2	Beginning Inventory ($ thousands), X_3
1	2,800	140	12	1,800
2	1,300	65	21	320
3	1,230	130	42	820
4	1,600	115	80	76
5	4,500	390	120	3,600
6	5,700	670	64	8,400
7	3,150	205	43	508
8	640	40	14	870
9	3,400	480	88	5,500
10	6,700	810	98	9,875
11	3,700	120	44	6,500
12	6,440	590	110	9,130
13	1,280	440	38	1,200
14	4,160	280	24	890
15	3,870	650	60	1,200
16	980	150	24	1,300

a. Determine the regression equation. The Master Chemical Company employs 220 people, has paid 64 consecutive common stock dividends, and has an inventory valued at $1,500,000 at the start of the year. What is the estimate of the gross profit?
b. Conduct a global test of hypothesis to determine whether any of the net regression coefficients differ from zero.
c. Conduct a test of hypothesis for the individual regression coefficients. Would you consider deleting any of the independent variables?
d. If your conclusion in part (c) was to delete one or more independent variables, run the analysis again, deleting those variables.
e. Determine the residuals for the equation of part (d). Use a stem-and-leaf chart or a histogram to verify that the distribution of the residuals is approximately normal.
f. Plot the residuals computed in part (e) in a scatter diagram with the residuals on the Y-axis and the Y' values on the X-axis. Does the plot reveal any violations of the assumptions of regression?

20. The *Times-Observer* is a daily newspaper in Metro City. Like many city newspapers, the *Times-Observer* is suffering through difficult financial times. The circulation manager is studying other papers in similar cities in the United States and Canada. She is particularly interested in what variables relate to the number of subscriptions to the paper. She is able to obtain the following sample information on 25 newspapers in similar cities. The following notation is used:

Sub = Number of subscriptions (in thousands).

Popul = The metropolitan population (in thousands).

Adv = The advertising budget of the paper (in $ hundreds).

Income = The median family income in the metropolitan area (in $ thousands).

Paper	Sub	Popul	Adv	Income	Paper	Sub	Popul	Adv	Income
1	37.95	588.9	13.2	35.1	14	38.39	586.5	15.4	35.5
2	37.66	585.3	13.2	34.7	15	37.29	544.0	11.0	34.9
3	37.55	566.3	19.8	34.8	16	39.15	611.1	24.2	35.0
4	38.78	642.9	17.6	35.1	17	38.29	643.3	17.6	35.3
5	37.67	624.2	17.6	34.6	18	38.09	635.6	19.8	34.8
6	38.23	603.9	15.4	34.8	19	37.83	598.9	15.4	35.1
7	36.90	571.9	11.0	34.7	20	39.37	657.0	22.0	35.3
8	38.28	584.3	28.6	35.3	21	37.81	595.2	15.4	35.1
9	38.95	605.0	28.6	35.1	22	37.42	520.0	19.8	35.1
10	39.27	676.3	17.6	35.6	23	38.83	629.6	22.0	35.3
11	38.30	587.4	17.6	34.9	24	38.33	680.0	24.2	34.7
12	38.84	576.4	22.0	35.4	25	40.24	651.2	33.0	35.8
13	38.14	570.8	17.6	35.0					

a. Determine the regression equation.

b. Conduct a global test of hypothesis to determine whether any of the net regression coefficients are not equal to zero.

c. Conduct a test for the individual coefficients. Would you consider deleting any coefficients?

d. Determine the residuals and plot them against the fitted values. Do you see any problems?

e. Develop a histogram of the residuals. Do you see any problems with the normality assumption?

21. The *Toledo* (Ohio) *Blade* recently ran an advertisement indicating that they had openings for carriers. "Wake up to opportunities," the advertisement said. "With a *Blade* route, you'll work about an hour a day—in the morning, when you can afford the time." The announcement went on to list the following available carrier routes. Let the average weekly profit be the dependent variable and the number of daily customers and the number of Sunday customers the independent variables.

Route	Average Weekly Profit	Number of Daily Customers	Number of Sunday Customers
Greenwood	$47.00	66	78
Oswald	70.00	98	117
Neveda	24.00	32	45
Forsythe	30.00	42	51
Idaho	25.00	34	44
Valleywood	44.00	60	76
Oak Hill	26.00	40	40
Burbank	19.50	30	30
Burke Glen	33.20	46	57
Penelope	35.00	48	61

a. Develop a correlation matrix. Do you see any problems with multicollinearity?

b. Determine the regression equation. How much profit would you estimate for a route that had 50 daily customers and 100 Sunday customers?

c. Can we conclude that the two variables account for all of the variation in weekly profit?

d. How much does an additional Sunday customer add to the profit per week? How much does each daily customer add to weekly profit?

e. The R^2 value is very large. Does this surprise you? Would you consider adding any other independent variables?

22. A mortgage department of a large bank is studying its recent loans. Of particular interest is how such factors as the value of the home (in thousands of dollars), education level of the head of the household, age of the head of the household, current monthly mortgage payment (in dollars), and sex of the head of the household (male = 1, female = 0) relate to the family income. Are these variables effective predictors of the income of the household? A random sample of 25 recent loans is obtained.

Income ($ thousands)	Value ($ thousands)	Years of Education	Age	Mortgage Payment	Sex
$40.3	$190	14	53	$230	1
39.6	121	15	49	370	1
40.8	161	14	44	397	1
40.3	161	14	39	181	1
40.0	179	14	53	378	0
38.1	99	14	46	304	0
40.4	114	15	42	285	1
40.7	202	14	49	551	0
40.8	184	13	37	370	0
37.1	90	14	43	135	0
39.9	181	14	48	332	1
40.4	143	15	54	217	1
38.0	132	14	44	490	0
39.0	127	14	37	220	0
39.5	153	14	50	270	1
40.6	145	14	50	279	1
40.3	174	15	52	329	1
40.1	177	16	47	274	0
41.7	188	15	49	433	1
40.1	153	15	53	333	1
40.6	150	16	58	148	0
40.4	173	13	42	390	1
40.9	163	14	46	142	1
40.1	150	15	50	343	0
38.5	139	14	45	373	0

a. Determine the regression equation.

b. What is the value of R^2? Comment on the value.

c. Conduct a global hypothesis test to determine whether any of the independent variables are different from zero.

d. Conduct individual hypothesis tests to determine whether any of the independent variables can be dropped.

e. If variables are dropped, recompute the regression equation and R^2.

23. Mr. Fred G. Hire is the manager of human resources at St. Luke's Medical Center. As part of his yearly report to the president of the medical center, he is required to present an analysis of the salaried employees. Because there are over 1,000 employees, he does not have the staff to gather information on each salaried employee, so he selects a random sample of 30. For each employee, he records monthly salary; service at St. Luke's, in months; sex (1 = male, 0 = female); and whether the employee has a technical or clerical job. Those working technical jobs are coded 1, and those who are clerical 0.

Sampled Employee	Monthly Salary	Length of Service	Age	Sex	Job
1	$1,769	93	42	1	0
2	1,740	104	33	1	0
3	1,941	104	42	1	1
4	2,367	126	57	1	1
5	2,467	98	30	1	1
6	1,640	99	49	1	1
7	1,756	94	35	1	0
8	1,706	96	46	0	1
9	1,767	124	56	0	0
10	1,200	73	23	0	1
11	1,706	110	67	0	1
12	1,985	90	36	0	1
13	1,555	104	53	0	0
14	1,749	81	29	0	0
15	2,056	106	45	1	0
16	1,729	113	55	0	1
17	2,186	129	46	1	1
18	1,858	97	39	0	1
19	1,819	101	43	1	1
20	1,350	91	35	1	1
21	2,030	100	40	1	0
22	2,550	123	59	1	0
23	1,544	88	30	0	0
24	1,766	117	60	1	1
25	1,937	107	45	1	1
26	1,691	105	32	0	1
27	1,623	86	33	0	0
28	1,791	131	56	0	1
29	2,001	95	30	1	1
30	1,874	98	47	1	0

a. Determine the regression equation, using salary as the dependent variable and the other four variables as independent variables.

b. What is the value of R^2? Comment on this value.

c. Conduct a global test of hypothesis to determine whether any of the independent variables are different from 0.

d. Conduct an individual test to determine whether any of the independent variables can be dropped.

e. Rerun the regression equation, using only the independent variables that are significant. How much more does a man earn per month than a woman? Does it make a difference whether the employee has a technical or a clerical job?

www.Exercises.com

24. As cheese ages, various chemical reactions take place to determine the final flavor of the cheese. Go to the following Web site to locate information on the taste of cheese and three variables thought to be related to the flavor of cheese: *http://lib.stat.cmu.edu/DSAL/ Data files/Cheese.html.* (Remember that the Web address is sensitive to capitalization.) Determine the multiple linear regression equation, using taste as the dependent variable and the other three variables as independent variables. Conduct both the global and the individual tests, using the .05 significance level. Would you consider deleting any of the independent variables?

25. As described in the examples in Chapters 11 and 12, many real estate companies and rental agencies now publish their listings on the Web. One example is the Dunes Realty Company, located in Garden City and Surfside Beaches in South Carolina. Go to the Web site *http://www.dunes.com,* select **Cottage Search,** then indicate 5 bedroom, accommodations for 14 people, oceanfront, and no pool or floating dock, select a period in July and August, indicate that you are willing to spend $5,000 per week, and then click on **Search the Cottages.** The output should include details on the cottages that met your criteria. Develop a multiple linear regression equation using the rental price per week as the dependent variable and number of bedrooms, number of bathrooms, and how many people the cottage will accommodate as independent variables. Analyze the regression equations. Would you consider deleting any independent variables? What is the coefficient of determination? If you delete any of the variables, rerun the regression equation and discuss the new equation.

▌ Computer Data Exercises

26. Refer to Data Set 1, which reports information on homes sold in the Venice, Florida, area during the last year. Use the selling price of the home as the dependent variable and determine the regression equation with number of bedrooms, size of the house, whether there is a pool, whether there is an attached garage, distance from the center of the city, and number of bathrooms as independent variables.
  a. Write out the regression equation. Discuss each of the variables. For example, are you surprised that the regression coefficient for distance from the center of the city is negative? How much does a garage or a swimming pool add to the selling price of a home.
  b. Determine the value of R^2. Interpret.
  c. Develop a correlation matrix. Which independent variables have strong or weak correlations with the dependent variable? Do you see any problems with multicollinearity?
  d. Conduct the global test on the set of independent variables. Interpret.
  e. Conduct a test of hypothesis on each of the independent variables. Would you consider deleting any of the variables? If so, which ones?
  f. Rerun the analysis until only significant net regression coefficients remain in the analysis. Identify these variables.
  g. Develop a histogram or a stem-and-leaf display of the residuals from the final regression equation developed in part (f). Is it reasonable to conclude that the normality assumption has been met?
  h. Plot the residuals against the fitted values from the final regression equation developed in part (f) against the fitted values of Y'. Plot the residuals on the vertical axis and the fitted values on the horizontal axis.

27. Refer to Data Set 2, which reports information on the 28 Major League Baseball teams for the 1997 season. Let the number of games won be the dependent variable and the following variables be independent variables: team batting average, number of stolen bases, number of errors committed, team ERA, and whether the team's home field is natural grass or artificial turf.
  a. Write out the regression equation. Discuss each of the variables. For example, are you surprised that the regression coefficient for ERA is negative? How many wins does playing on natural grass for a home field add to or subtract from the total wins for the season?
  b. Determine the value of R^2. Interpret.
  c. Develop a correlation matrix. Which independent variables have strong or weak correlations with the dependent variable? Do you see any problems with multicollinearity?
  d. Conduct a global test on the set of independent variables. Interpret.
  e. Conduct a test of hypothesis on each of the independent variables. Would you consider deleting any of the variables? If so, which ones?

    f.   Rerun the analysis until only significant net regression coefficients remain in the analysis. Identify these variables.

    g.   Develop a histogram or a stem-and-leaf display of the residuals from the final regression equation developed in part (f). Is it reasonable to conclude that the normality assumption has been met?

    h.   Plot the residuals against the fitted values from the final regression equation developed in part (f) against the fitted values of Y'. Plot the residuals on the vertical axis and the fitted values on the horizontal axis.

28.   Refer to Data Set 3, which reports information on the circulation of 48 popular magazines. Let circulation be the dependent variable and percent of male readers, median age, percent of readers who attended college, the cost of color advertising, and the cost of black and white advertising be the independent variables.

    a.   Write out the regression equation. Discuss each of the variables.

    b.   Determine the value of R^2. Interpret.

    c.   Develop a correlation matrix. Which independent variables have strong or weak correlations with the dependent variable? Do you see any problems with multicollinearity?

    d.   Conduct a global test on the independent variables. Interpret.

    e.   Conduct a test of hypothesis on each of the independent variables. Would you consider deleting any of the variables? If so, which ones?

    f.   Rerun the analysis until only significant net regression coefficients remain in the analysis. Identify these variables.

    g.   Develop a histogram or a stem-and-leaf display of the residuals from the final regression equation developed in part (f). Is it reasonable to conclude that the normality assumption has been met?

    h.   Plot the residuals against the fitted values from the final regression equation developed in part (f) against the fitted values of Y'. Plot the residuals on the vertical axis and the fitted values on the horizontal axis.

29.   Refer to Data Set 4, which reports information on the 94 school districts in northwest Ohio. Let the dependent variable be the percent passing the state proficiency test. The independent variables are the average teacher's salary, the percent on welfare in the district, the instructional cost per student in the district, and the percent attendance in the district.

    a.   Write out the regression equation. Discuss each of the variables.

    b.   Determine the value of R^2. Interpret.

    c.   Develop a correlation matrix. Which independent variables have strong or weak correlations with the dependent variable? Do you see any problems with multicollinearity?

    d.   Conduct a global test on the set of independent variables. Interpret.

    e.   Conduct a test of hypothesis on each of the independent variables. Would you consider deleting any of the variables? If so, which ones?

    f.   Rerun the analysis until only significant net regression coefficients remain in the analysis. Identify these variables.

    g.   Develop a histogram or a stem-and-leaf display of the residuals from the final regression equation developed in part (f). Is it reasonable to conclude that the normality assumption has been met?

    h.   Plot the residuals against the fitted values from the final regression equation developed in part (f) against the fitted values of Y'. Plot the residuals on the vertical axis and the fitted values on the horizontal axis.

▌ Computer Commands

1.   MINITAB commands for the multiple regression output on page 476.

    a.   Import the data from the data disk. The file name is **Tbl13-1.**

    b.   Select **Stat, Regression,** and then click on **Regression.**

c. Select **Cost** as the **Response** variable and **Temp, Insul,** and **Age** as the **Predictor** variables. Then click **OK.**

Regression

C1	Cost	**Response:**	Cost
C2	Temp	**Predictors:**	Temp-Age
C3	Insul		
C4	Age		
C5	Garage		
C10	Y prime		
C11			
C12			
C15	Fitted		
C16	Residuals		

Select   Graphs...   Options...

Help   OK   Storage...   Cancel

2. Excel commands to develop the correlation matrix on page 478.
    a. Import the data from the data disk. The file name is **Tbl13-1.**
    b. Select **Tools, Data Analysis** and then hit **Enter.** Select **Correlation** and then hit **OK.**
    c. The **Input range** is a1:d21, grouped by **Columns,** check the **Labels** box, select the **Output Range** as b25.

Correlation

Input

Input Range: $A$1:$D$21

Grouped By: ● Columns   ○ Rows

☑ Labels in First Row

Output options

● Output Range: b25

○ New Worksheet Ply:

○ New Workbook

OK   Cancel   Help

3. MINITAB commands for the multiple regression output on page 484.
    a. Import the data from the data disk. The file name is **Tbl13-1.**
    b. Select **Stat, Regression,** and then click on **Regression.**

c. Select **Cost** as the **Response** variable and **Temp, Insul,** and **Garage** as the **Predictor** variables. Then click **OK.**

Regression

C1	Cost
C2	Temp
C3	Insul
C4	Age
C5	Garage
C10	Y prime
C11	
C12	
C15	Fitted
C16	Residuals

Response: Cost

Predictors: Temp Insul Garage

Options...

Select

Graphs... Storage...

Help OK Cancel

CHAPTER 13   *Answers to Self-Review*

13–1 (a) 12.9 psi, found by $Y' = -0.5 + 20(.35) + 1(6.4)$.

(b) The b_1 of 20 indicates that the tensile strength of the wire will increase 20 psi for each increase of 1 mm in outside diameter, with the amount of molybdenum held constant. That is, tensile strength will increase 20 psi regardless of the amount of molybdenum in the wire.

13–2 (a) $n = 25$

(b) 4

(c) $R^2 = \dfrac{10}{15} = 0.667$

(d) $s_{y \cdot 1234} = \sqrt{\dfrac{5}{20}} = 0.50$

13–3 (a) $Y' = 490 - 5.15X_1 - 14.7X_2$

(b) .776. A total of 77.6% of the variation in heating cost is explained by temperature and insulation.

(c) The results of the global test indicate that at least one of the regression coefficients is not zero. To arrive at that conclusion, we first stated the null hypothesis as $H_0: \beta_1 = \beta_2 = 0$. The critical value of F is 3.59, and the computed value 29.4, found by 82,597/2,807. Since 29.4 lies in the region of rejection beyond 3.59, we reject H_0.

(d) The p-value is .008. The probability of a t-value less than -2.98 or greater than 2.98, with 17 degrees of freedom, is .008.

SECTION 5
A REVIEW OF CHAPTERS 12 AND 13

Simple regression and correlation examines the relationship between two variables.

This section is a review of the major concepts and terms introduced in Chapters 12 and 13. Chapter 12 noted that the strength of the relationship between the independent variable and the dependent variable can be measured by the *coefficient of correlation.* Developed by Karl Pearson, Pearson's *r* can assume any value between -1.00 and $+1.00$ inclusive. Coefficients of -1.00 and $+1.00$ indicate perfect relationship, and 0 indicates no relationship. A value near 0, such as $-.14$ or $.14$, indicates a weak relationship. A value near -1 or $+1$, such as $-.90$ or $+.90$, indicates a strong relationship. Squaring *r* gives the *coefficient of determination,* also called r^2. It indicates the proportion of the total variation in the dependent variable explained by the independent variable.

Multiple regression and correlation is concerned with relationship between two or more independent variables and the dependent variable.

Likewise, the strength of the relationship between several independent variables and a dependent variable is measured by the *coefficient of multiple determination, R^2.* It measures the proportion of the variation in *Y* explained by two or more independent variables.

The linear relationship in the simple case involving one independent variable and one dependent variable is described by the equation $Y' = a + bX$. For three independent variables, X_1, X_2, and X_3, the sample multiple regression equation is

$$Y' = a + b_1X_1 + b_2X_2 + b_3X_3$$

Computer invaluable in multiple regression and correlation

Solving for b_1, b_2, b_3, . . . ,b_k would involve tedious calculations. Fortunately, this type of problem can be quickly solved using one of the many statistical packages and spreadsheet packages available for the computer. The independent variable most highly correlated with the dependent variable is brought in first, and only independent variables with nonzero net regression coefficients are used in the analysis. Various measures, such as the coefficient of determination, the multiple standard error of estimate, the results of the global test, and the test of the individual variable are reported in the output of most computer software programs.

Glossary

Chapter 12

Coefficient of correlation   A measure of the strength of association between two variables. It is computed by:

$$r = \frac{n(\Sigma XY) - (\Sigma X)(\Sigma Y)}{\sqrt{[n(\Sigma X^2) - (\Sigma X)^2][n(\Sigma Y^2) - (\Sigma Y)^2]}}$$ [12–1]

Coefficient of determination   The proportion of the total variation in the dependent variable that is explained by the independent variable. It can assume any value between 0 and $+1.00$ inclusive. A coefficient of .82 indicates that 82 percent of the variation in *Y* is accounted for by *X*. This coefficient is computed by squaring the coefficient of correlation, *r*.

Correlation analysis   A group of statistical techniques used to measure the strength of the relationship between two variables.

Least squares method   A technique used to arrive at the regression equation by minimizing the sum of the squares of the vertical distances between the actual *Y* values and the predicted *Y* values.

Linear regression equation   A mathematical equation that defines the relationship between two variables. It has the form $Y' = a + bX$. It is used to predict *Y* based on a selected *X* value. *Y* is the dependent variable and *X* the independent variable.

Scatter diagram   A chart that visually depicts the relationship between two variables.

Standard error of estimate   Measures the dispersion of the actual *Y* values about the regression line. It is reported in the same units as the dependent variable.

Test of significance of *r*   A formula to answer the question: Is the correlation in the population from which the sample was selected zero? The test statistic is *t,* and the number of degrees of freedom is $n - 2$.

$$t = \frac{r\sqrt{n-2}}{\sqrt{1-r^2}}$$ [12–2]

Chapter 13

Autocorrelation   Correlation of successive residuals. This condition frequently occurs when time is involved in the analysis.

Correlation matrix   A listing of all possible simple coefficients of correlation. A correlation matrix includes the correlations between each of the independent variables and the dependent variable, as well as those among all the independent variables.

Homoscedasticity   The standard error of estimate is the same for all fitted values of the dependent variable.

Multicollinearity   A condition that occurs in multiple regression analysis if the independent variables are themselves correlated.

Multiple regression equation The relationship in the form of a mathematical equation between several independent variables and a dependent variable. The general form is $Y' = a + b_1X_1 + b_2X_2 + b_3X_3 + \cdots + b_kX_k$. It is used to estimate Y given selected X values and k independent variables.

Qualitative variables A nominal-scale variable that can assume only one of two possible outcomes. For example, a person is considered either employed or unemployed.

Residual The difference between the actual value of the dependent variable and the estimated value of the dependent variable, that is $Y - Y'$.

▌ Exercises

Part I — Fill in the Blanks and Discussion

1. The strength of the relationship between a set of independent variables X and a dependent variable Y is measured by the _____.
2. A coefficient of correlation was computed to be $-.90$. Comment.
3. Pearson's r for a problem involving 60 pairs of data was computed to be .40. Comment. Is the correlation in the population zero? Give evidence.
4. The coefficient of determination was computed to be .38 in a problem involving one independent and one dependent variable. What does this mean?
5. What is the relationship between the coefficient of correlation and the coefficient of determination?

Exercises 6 through 10 are based on the following table. The accounting division for a large chain of department stores is trying to predict the net profit for each of the chain's many stores based on the number of employees in the store, overhead cost, and so on. A few statistics from some of the stores are:

Store	Net Profit ($ thousands)	Number of Employees	Overhead Cost ($ thousands)	Average Markup (percent)	Theft Loss ($ thousands)
1	$846	143	$79	69	$52
2	513	110	64	50	45

6. The dependent variable is _____.
7. The general equation for this problem is _____.
8. The multiple regression equation was computed to be $Y' = 67 + 8X_1 - 10X_2 + 0.004X_3 - 3X_4$. What is predicted sales for a store with 112 employees, an overhead cost of $65,000, a markup rate of 50 percent, and a loss from theft of $50,000?
9. Suppose R^2 was computed to be .86. Explain.
10. Suppose that the multiple standard error of estimate was 3 (in $ thousands). Explain what this means in this problem.

Part II — Problems

11. Quick-print firms in a large downtown business area spend most of their advertising dollars on advertisements on bus benches. A research project involves predicting monthly sales based on the annual amount spent on placing ads on bus benches. A sample of quick-print firms revealed these advertising expenses and sales:

Firm	Annual Bus Bench Advertising ($ thousands)	Monthly Sales ($ thousands)
A	2	10
B	4	40
C	5	30
D	7	50
E	3	20

    a. Draw a scatter diagram.
    b. Determine the coefficient of correlation.
    c. What is the coefficient of determination?
    d. Compute the regression equation.
    e. Estimate the monthly sales of a quick-print firm that spends $4,500 on bus bench advertisements.
    f. Summarize your findings.
  12. The following ANOVA output is given.

SOURCE	Sum of Squares	DF	MS
Regression	1050.8	4	262.70
Error	83.8	20	4.19
Total	1134.6	24	

Predictor	Coef	St.Dev.	t-ratio
Constant	70.06	2.13	32.89
X_1	0.42	0.17	2.47
X_2	0.27	0.21	1.29
X_3	0.75	0.30	2.50
X_4	0.42	0.07	6.00

    a. Compute the coefficient of determination.
    b. Compute the multiple standard error of estimate.
    c. Conduct a test of hypothesis to determine whether any of the net regression coefficients are different from zero.
    d. Conduct a test of hypothesis on the individual regression coefficients. Can any of the variables be detected?

▌ Cases

A. The Century National Bank

Refer to the Century National Bank data. Using checking account balance as the dependent variable and using the number of ATM transactions, the number of other services used, whether the individual has a debit card, and whether interest is paid on the particular account as independent variables, write a report indicating which of the variables seem related to the account balance and how well they explain the variation in account balances. Should all of the independent variables proposed be used in the analysis or can some be dropped?

B. Terry and Associates: The Time to Deliver Medical Kits

Terry and Associates is a specialized medical testing center in Denver, Colorado. One of their major sources of revenue is a kit used to test for elevated amounts of lead in the blood. Workers in auto body shops, those in the lawn care industry, and commercial house painters are exposed to large amounts of lead and thus must be randomly tested. It is expensive to conduct the test, so the kits are delivered on demand to a variety of locations throughout the Denver area.

Kathleen Terry, the owner, is concerned about appropriate costing of each delivery. To investigate, Ms. Terry gathered information on a random sample of 50 recent deliveries. Factors thought to be related to the cost of delivering a kit are:

Prep The time between when the customized order is phoned into the company and when it is ready for delivery.

Delivery The actual travel time from Terry's plant to the customer.

Mileage The distance in miles from Terry's plant to the customer.

Sample Number	Cost	Prep	Delivery	Mileage
1	$32.60	10	51	20
2	23.37	11	33	12
3	31.49	6	47	19
4	19.31	9	18	8
5	28.35	8	88	17
6	22.63	9	20	11
7	22.63	9	39	11
8	21.53	10	23	10
9	21.16	13	20	8
10	21.53	10	32	10
11	28.17	5	35	16
12	20.42	7	23	9
13	21.53	9	21	10
14	27.55	7	37	16
15	23.37	9	25	12
16	17.10	15	15	6
17	27.06	13	34	15
18	15.99	8	13	4
19	17.96	12	12	4
20	25.22	6	41	14
21	24.29	3	28	13
22	22.76	4	26	10
23	28.17	9	54	16
24	19.68	7	18	8
25	25.15	6	50	13
26	20.36	9	19	7

Sample Number	Cost	Prep	Delivery	Mileage
27	21.16	3	19	8
28	25.95	10	45	14
29	18.76	12	12	5
30	18.76	8	16	5
31	24.29	7	35	13
32	19.56	2	12	6
33	22.63	8	30	11
34	21.16	5	13	8
35	21.16	11	20	8
36	19.68	5	19	8
37	18.76	5	14	7
38	17.96	5	11	4
39	23.37	10	25	12
40	25.22	6	32	14
41	27.06	8	44	16
42	21.96	9	28	9
43	22.63	8	31	11
44	19.68	7	19	8
45	22.76	8	28	10
46	21.96	13	18	9
47	25.95	10	32	14
48	26.14	8	44	15
49	24.29	8	34	13
50	24.35	3	33	12

a. Develop a multiple linear regression equation that describes the relationship between the cost of delivery and the other variables. Do these three variables explain a reasonable amount of the variation in the dependent variable? Estimate the delivery cost for a kit that takes 10 minutes for preparation, takes 30 minutes to deliver, and must cover a distance of 14 miles.

b. Test to determine that some of the set of net regression coefficients differ from zero. Also test to see whether any of the variables can be dropped from the analysis. If some of the variables can be dropped, rerun the regression equation until only significant variables are included. Write a brief report interpreting the final regression equation.

Chapter Fourteen

Nonparametric Methods

Chi-Square Applications

Five percent of credit card holders have had some high school, 15 percent have completed high school, 25 percent have had some college, and 55 percent have completed college. Of 500 card holders who failed to pay their charges, 50 had some high school, 100 had completed high school, 190 had some college, and 160 had completed college. Can we conclude that the distribution of nonpaying card holders is different from the rest? (See Goal 2 and Exercise 11.)

▌ Introduction

Chapters 8 through 11 dealt with data that were at least interval scale, such as weights, incomes, and ages. We conducted a number of tests of hypotheses about a population mean and two or more population means. For these tests it was assumed that the population was normal. Can tests of hypotheses be made if the data are not interval scale, but are nominal or ordinal scale, and if no assumptions are made about the shape of the parent population?

To answer this question, there are tests for nominal and ordinal levels of measurement, and no assumptions need be made about the shape of the population. Recall from Chapter 1 that *nominal*-level data are the "lowest" type of data. This type of data can only be classified into categories, such as Republican, Democrat, and "all others," or male and female. The *ordinal* level of measurement assumes that one category is ranked higher than the next one. As an example, a sample of joggers are asked by Marketing Research Associates to rate a newly developed shoe as either outstanding, good, fair, or unsatisfactory. It is implied that a ranking of outstanding is higher than good, good is higher than fair, and so on.

Tests of hypotheses concerned with nominal or ordinal levels of measurement are called **nonparametric tests** or **distribution-free tests.** The latter name implies that these tests are free of assumptions regarding the distribution of the parent population. These distribution-free tests are relatively easy to apply, and the computations are generally easy to perform.

▌ Goodness-of-Fit Test: Equal Expected Frequencies

The **goodness-of-fit test** is one of the most commonly used nonparametric tests. Developed by Karl Pearson in the early 1900s, it can be used for any level of data. The first test of significance involves *equal expected frequencies.*

As the full name implies, the purpose of the goodness-of-fit test is to determine how well an *observed* set of data fits an *expected* set of data. An illustration can describe the hypothesis-testing situation.

Example

Ms. Jan Kilpatrick is the marketing manager for a manufacturer of sports cards. She plans to begin a series of cards with pictures and playing statistics of former major league baseball players. One problem is the selection of the former players. At the baseball card show at the Southwyck Mall last weekend, she set up a booth and offered cards of the following six Hall of Fame baseball players: Dizzy Dean, Bob Feller, Phil Rizzuto, Warren Spahn, Mickey Mantle, and Willie Mays. At the end of the first day she sold a total of 120 cards. The number of cards sold for each old-time player is shown in Table 14–1. Can she conclude that the sales of cards are the same for the six players, or should she conclude that the sales are not the same?

Table 14–1 Number of Cards Sold for Each Player

Player	Cards Sold
Dizzy Dean	13
Bob Feller	33
Phil Rizzuto	14
Warren Spahn	7
Mickey Mantle	36
Willie Mays	17
Total	120

If there is no significant difference between the observed frequencies and the expected frequencies, we would expect that the observed frequencies (f_0) would be equal — or nearly equal. That is, we would expect to sell as many cards for Phil Rizzuto as for Dizzy Dean. Thus, any discrepancy in the set of observed and expected frequencies could be attributed to sampling (chance).

Because there are 120 cards in the sample, we expect that 20 cards will fall in each of the six categories. These categories are called **cells.** An examination of the set of observed frequencies in Table 14–2 indicates that the card for Warren Spahn is sold rather infrequently, whereas the cards for Mickey Mantle and Bob Feller are sold more often. Is the difference in sales due to chance, or can we conclude that there is a preference for the cards of certain players?

Table 14–2 Observed and Expected Frequencies for the 120 Cards Sold

Player	Cards Sold, f_0	Expected Number Sold, f_e
Dizzy Dean	13	20
Bob Feller	33	20
Phil Rizzuto	14	20
Warren Spahn	7	20
Mickey Mantle	36	20
Willie Mays	17	20
Total	120	120

Solution   The same systematic five-step hypothesis-testing procedure followed in Chapters 9 through 11 will be used.

Step 1: State the Null Hypothesis and the Alternate Hypothesis.   The null hypothesis, H_0, is that there is no difference between the set of observed frequencies and the set of expected frequencies; that is, any differences between the two sets of frequencies can be attributed to sampling (chance). The alternate hypothesis, H_1, is that there is a difference between the observed and expected sets of frequencies. If

H_0 is rejected and H_1 is accepted, it means that sales are not equally distributed among the six categories (cells).

Step 2: Select the Level of Significance.   We selected the .05 level, which is the same as the Type I error probability. Thus, the probability is .05 that a true null hypothesis will be rejected.

Step 3: Select the Test Statistic.   It is the chi-square distribution, designated as χ^2:

CHI-SQUARE TEST STATISTIC	$\chi^2 = \sum \left[\dfrac{(f_0 - f_e)^2}{f_e} \right]$	**[14–1]**

with $k - 1$ degrees of freedom, where:

   k is the number of categories, and
   f_0 is an observed frequency in a particular category.
   f_e is an expected frequency in a particular category.

We will examine the characteristics of the chi-square distribution in more detail shortly.

Step 4: Formulate the Decision Rule.   Recall the decision rule in hypothesis testing requires finding a number that separates the region where we do not reject H_0 from the region of rejection. This number is called the *critical value.* As we will soon see, the chi-square distribution is really a family of distributions. Each distribution has a different shape, depending on the number of degrees of freedom. The number in this type of problem is found by $k - 1$, where k stands for the number of categories. In this particular problem there are six. Since there are six categories, there are $k - 1 = 6 - 1 = 5$ degrees of freedom. As noted, a category is called a *cell,* so there are six cells. The critical value for 5 degrees of freedom and the .05 level of significance is found in Appendix I. A portion of that table is shown in Table 14–3. The critical value is 11.070, found by locating 5 degrees of freedom in the left margin and then moving horizontally (to the right) and reading the critical value in the .05 column.

Table 14–3   **A Portion of the Chi-Square Table**

Degrees of Freedom, df	Right-Tail Area			
	.10	.05	.02	.01
1	2.706	3.841	5.412	6.635
2	4.605	5.991	7.824	9.210
3	6.251	7.815	9.837	11.345
4	7.779	9.488	11.668	13.277
5	9.236	11.070	13.388	15.086

The decision rule, therefore, is: Do not reject the null hypothesis if the computed value of chi-square is equal to or less than 11.070. If it is greater than 11.070, reject H_0 and accept the alternate hypothesis, H_1. Chart 14–1 shows the two regions.

Chart 14–1 Chi-Square Probability Distribution for 5 Degrees of Freedom, Showing the Region of Rejection, .05 Level of Significance

In essence, the decision rule indicates that if there are large differences between the observed and expected frequencies, resulting in a computed χ^2 of more than 11.070, the null hypothesis should be rejected. However, if the differences between f_0 and f_e are small, the computed χ^2 value will be 11.070 or less, and the null hypothesis should not be rejected. The reasoning is that such small differences between the observed and expected frequencies are probably due to chance.

Step 5: Select a Sample, Compute the Value of Chi-Square, and Make a Decision to Reject or Not Reject the Null Hypothesis.   Of the 120 cards sold in the sample, we counted the number of times Bob Feller, Willie Mays, and each of the others were sold. The counts were reported in Table 14–1. The calculations for chi-square follow. (Note again that the expected frequencies are the same for each cell.)

Column 1:   Determine the differences between f_0 and f_e. The sum of these differences is zero.

Column 2:   Square the difference between each observed and expected frequency. That is $(f_0 - f_e)^2$.

Column 3:   Divide the results of column 2 by the expected frequency, and sum these values. The sum, 34.40 in this case, is the value of chi-square.

Baseball Player	f_0	f_e	(1) $f_0 - f_e$	(2) $(f_0 - f_e)^2$	(3) $\dfrac{(f_0 - f_e)^2}{f_e}$
Dizzy Dean	13	20	−7	49	49/20 = 2.45
Bob Feller	33	20	13	169	169/20 = 8.45
Phil Rizzuto	14	20	−6	36	36/20 = 1.80
Warren Spahn	7	20	−13	169	169/20 = 8.45
Mickey Mantle	36	20	16	256	256/20 = 12.80
Willie Mays	17	20	−3	9	9/20 = 0.45
			0		34.40

Must be

χ^2

The computed χ^2 of 34.40 is in the rejection region beyond the critical value of 11.070. The decision, therefore, is to reject H_0 at the .05 level and to accept H_1. The difference between the observed and the expected frequencies is not due to chance. Rather, the differences between f_0 and f_e are large enough to be considered significant. The chance of these differences being due to sampling is very small. So we conclude that it is unlikely that card sales are the same among the six players.

Both the example solution and self-review involved *equal* expected frequencies. Before considering problems with *unequal* expected frequencies, we will look briefly at the characteristics of the chi-square distribution.

The chi-square distribution, which is used as the test statistic in this chapter, has the following characteristics.

1. Chi-square is never negative, because the difference between f_0 and f_e is squared, that is, $(f_0 - f_e)^2$.
2. There is a family of chi-square distributions. There is a chi-square distribution for 1 degree of freedom, another for 2 degrees of freedom, another for 3 degrees of freedom, and so on. In this type of problem the number of degrees of freedom is determined by $k - 1$, where k is the number of categories. Therefore, the shape of the chi-square distribution does *not* depend on the size of the sample. For example, if 200 employees of an airline were classified into one of three categories — flight personnel, ground support, and administrative personnel—there would be $k - 1 = 3 - 1 = 2$ degrees of freedom.
3. The chi-square distribution is *positively skewed*. However, as the number of degrees of freedom increases, the distribution begins to approximate the normal distribution. Chart 14–2 shows the distributions for selected degrees of freedom. Notice that for 10 degrees of freedom the curve is approaching a normal distribution.

Shape of χ^2 distribution approaches normal distribution as df becomes larger

Chart 14–2   Chi-Square Distributions for Selected Degrees of Freedom

SELF-REVIEW 14-1

The personnel manager is concerned about absenteeism. She decides to sample the records to determine whether absenteeism is distributed evenly throughout the six-day workweek. The null hypothesis to be tested is: Absenteeism is distributed evenly throughout the week. The .01 level is to be used. The sample results are:

	Number Absent			Number Absent
Monday	12		Thursday	10
Tuesday	9		Friday	9
Wednesday	11		Saturday	9

(a) What are the numbers 12, 9, 11, 10, 9, and 9 called?
(b) How many categories (cells) are there?
(c) What is the *expected* frequency for each day?
(d) How many degrees of freedom are there?
(e) What is the chi-square critical value at the 1 percent level?
(f) Compute the χ^2 test statistic.
(g) Is the null hypothesis rejected?
(h) Specifically, what does this indicate to the personnel manager?

▌ Exercises

1. In a particular chi-square goodness-of-fit test there are four categories and 200 observations. Use the .05 significance level.
   a. How many degrees of freedom are there?
   b. What is the critical value of chi-square?
2. In a particular chi-square goodness-of-fit test there are six categories and 500 observations. Use the .01 significance level.
   a. How many degrees of freedom are there?
   b. What is the critical value of chi-square?
3. The null hypothesis and the alternate are:

   H_0: The cell categories are equal.

   H_1: The cell categories are not equal.

Category	f_0
A	10
B	20
C	30

   a. State the decision rule, using the .05 significance level.
   b. Compute the value of chi-square.
   c. What is your decision regarding H_0?
4. The null hypothesis and the alternate are:

   H_0: The cell categories are equal.

   H_1: The cell categories are not equal.

Category	f_0
A	10
B	20
C	30
D	20

a. State the decision rule, using the .05 significance level.
b. Compute the value of chi-square.
c. What is your decision regarding H_0?

5. A six-sided die is rolled 30 times and the numbers 1 through 6 appear as shown in the following frequency distribution. At the .10 significance level, can we conclude that the die is fair?

Outcome	Frequency	Outcome	Frequency
1	3	4	3
2	6	5	9
3	2	6	7

6. The director of human resources collected the following data on absenteeism by day of the week. At the .05 significance level, can she conclude that there is a difference in the absence rate by day of the week?

Day	Frequency
Monday	124
Tuesday	74
Wednesday	104
Thursday	98
Friday	120

7. A group of department store buyers viewed a new line of dresses and gave their opinions of them. The results were:

Opinion	Number of Buyers	Opinion	Number of Buyers
Outstanding	47	Good	39
Excellent	45	Fair	35
Very good	40	Undesirable	34

Because the largest number (47) indicated the new line is outstanding, the head designer thinks that this is a mandate to go into mass production of the dresses. The head sweeper (who somehow became involved in this) believes that there is not a clear mandate and claims that the opinions are evenly distributed among the six categories. He further states that the slight differences among the various counts are probably due to chance. Test the null hypothesis that there is no significant difference among the opinions of the buyers. Test at the .01 level of risk. Follow a formal approach; that is, state the null hypothesis, the alternate hypothesis, and so on.

8. The safety director of Honda USA took samples at random from the file of minor accidents and classified them according to the time the accident took place.

Time	Number of Accidents		Time	Number of Accidents
8 up to 9 A.M.	6		1 up to 2 P.M.	7
9 up to 10 A.M.	6		2 up to 3 P.M.	8
10 up to 11 A.M.	20		3 up to 4 P.M.	19
11 up to 12 P.M.	8		4 up to 5 P.M.	6

Using the goodness-of-fit test and the .01 level of significance, determine whether the accidents are evenly distributed throughout the day. Write a brief explanation of your conclusion.

▌ Goodness-of-Fit Test: Unequal Expected Frequencies

The expected frequencies (f_e) in the previous problem involving baseball cards were all equal (20). Theoretically, it was expected that a picture of Dizzy Dean would appear 20 times at random, the picture of Willie Mays would appear 20 times out of 120 trials, and so on. The chi-square test can also be used if the expected frequencies are not equal.

Expected frequencies not equal in this problem

The following example illustrates the case of unequal frequencies and also gives a practical use of chi-square—namely, to find out whether a local experience differs from the national experience.

Example

A national study of hospital admissions during a two-year period revealed these statistics concerning senior citizens who resided in care centers and who were hospitalized anytime during the period: Forty percent were admitted only once in the two-year period. Twenty percent were admitted twice. Fourteen percent were admitted three times, and so on. The complete percentage distribution is given in Table 14–4.

Table 14–4　National Study: Admissions of Senior Citizens to Hospitals in a Two-Year Period

Number of Times Admitted	Percent of Total
1	40
2	20
3	14
4	10
5	8
6	6
7	2
	100

Table 14–5　Local Study: Admissions to the Bartow County Hospital during a Two-Year Period

Number of Times Admitted	Number of Senior Citizens, f_0
1	165
2	79
3	50
4	44
5	32
6	20
7	10
	400

The administrator of the local hospital is anxious to compare her Bartow County Hospital experience with the national pattern or distribution. She selected 400 senior citizens in local care centers who needed hospitalization and determined the number of times during a two-year period each was admitted to her hospital. The observed frequencies are listed in Table 14–5.

The chi-square statistic is used to compare this local experience with the national experience. The question is: How can the locally observed frequencies in Table 14–5 be compared with the national percentages in Table 14–4? We will use the .05 level of significance.

Solution

Determining expected frequencies

Obviously, the *number* of observed frequencies resulting from the study of local senior citizens cannot be compared directly with the *percentages* given for the nation's hospitals. However, the percentages for the nation in Table 14–4 can be converted to expected frequencies, f_e. Table 14–4 shows that 40 percent of the senior citizens who required hospitalization went only once in a two-year period. Thus, if there is *no* difference between the experience at Bartow County Hospital and the national experience, then 40 percent of the 400 sampled by the hospital administrator (160 senior citizens) would have been admitted just once in the period. Further, 20 percent of the 400 sampled (80 people) would have been admitted twice, and so on. The observed local frequencies and the expected local frequencies based on the percents in the national study are given in Table 14–6.

Table 14–6 Observed and Expected Frequencies for Bartow County Hospital

Number of Times Admitted	Observed Number of Admissions, f_0	Expected Number of Admissions, f_e
1	165	160 ⟵ 40% × 400
2	79	80 ⟵ 20% × 400
3	50	56 ⟵ 14% × 400
4	44	40 ⟵ 10% × 400
5	32	32 ⟵ 8% × 400
6	20	24 ⟵ 6% × 400
7	10	8 ⟵ 2% × 400
	400	400

Must be equal

The null and alternate hypotheses are:

H_0: There is no difference between the local experience and the national experience.

H_1: There is a difference between the local experience and the national experience.

To find the decision rule we use Appendix I. There are seven admitting categories, so the degree of freedom is $df = k - 1 = 7 - 1 = 6$. The critical value is 12.592.

Therefore, the decision rule is to reject H_0 if $\chi^2 > 12.592$. The decision rule is portrayed graphically in Chart 14–3.

Chart 14–3   Decision Criteria for the Bartow County Hospital Research Study

Now to compute the chi-square test statistic:

Number of Times Admitted	f_0	f_e	$f_0 - f_e$	$(f_0 - f_e)^2$	$\dfrac{(f_0 - f_e)^2}{f_e}$
1	165	160	+5	25	0.156
2	79	80	−1	1	0.013
3	50	56	−6	36	0.643
4	44	40	+4	16	0.400
5	32	32	0	0	0.000
6	20	24	−4	16	0.667
7	10	8	+2	4	0.500
			0		$\chi^2 = 2.379$

The computed value of chi-square (2.379) lies to the left of 12.592 and is, therefore, in the region where we cannot reject H_0. The null hypothesis, that there is no difference between the local experience at Bartow County Hospital and the national experience, is therefore not rejected. The hospital administrator would conclude that the local situation with respect to the hospitalization of senior citizens in care centers is like that in other parts of the country.

▮ Limitations of Chi-Square

Be careful in applying χ^2 to some problems.

If there is an unusually small expected frequency in a cell, chi-square (if applied) might result in an erroneous conclusion. This can happen because f_e appears in the denominator, and dividing by a very small number makes the quotient quite large! Two generally accepted rules regarding small cell frequencies are:

1. If there are only two cells, the *expected* frequency in each cell should be 5 or more. The computation of chi-square would be permissible in the following problem, involving a minimum f_e of 6.

Individual	f_0	f_e
Literate	643	642
Illiterate	7	6

2. For more than two cells, χ^2 should not be applied if more than 20 percent of the f_e cells have expected frequencies less than 5. According to this rule, it would be permissible to compute χ^2 for the management data in the left-hand table below. Only one out of six cells, or 17 percent, contains a frequency less than 5.

Level of Management	Number f_0	f_e
Foreman	18	16
Supervisor	39	37
Manager	8	13
Middle management	6	4
Assistant vice president	82	78
Vice president	10	15
	163	163

Level of Management	Number f_0	f_e
Foreman	30	32
Supervisor	110	113
Manager	86	87
Middle management	23	24
Assistant vice president	5	2
Vice president	5	4
Senior vice president	4	1

Chi-square should not be used for the management data in the right-hand table because three of the seven expected frequencies, or 43 percent, are less than 5.

Using this example to develop the reasoning behind the rule, note that most of the paired observed and expected frequencies in the right-hand table are almost equal. The largest difference is just 3. One might conclude, therefore, that there is no significant difference between the observed set and the expected set of frequencies. However, actually computing chi-square and evaluating it against the appropriate critical value will refute that conclusion. Instead, it would be concluded that there is a difference between the frequencies observed in the sample and the expected frequencies. This conclusion, however, does not seem logical.

The dilemma can be resolved if the data are such that some of the categories can be combined. This seems to be the case in the management problem above. The three vice-presidential levels were combined into one category in order to satisfy the 20 percent rule.

Level of Management	Number in Sample, f_0	Expected Number, f_e
Foreman	30	32
Supervisor	110	113
Manager	86	87
Middle management	23	24
Vice president	14	7

The computed value of chi-square for the revised set of frequencies is 7.26. This is less than the critical value of 9.488 for the .05 level. The null hypothesis is, therefore, not rejected at the .05 level of significance. This indicates that there is no difference between the observed sample results and the expected results. The small differences between the observed and expected observations can be attributed to sampling. This is, of course, a more logical conclusion.

SELF-REVIEW 14-2

The American Accounting Association classifies accounts receivable as "current," "late," and "not collectible." Industry figures show that 60 percent of accounts receivable are current, 30 percent are late, and 10 percent are not collectible. Massa and Barr, attorneys in Greenville, Ohio, has 500 accounts receivable: 320 are current, 120 are late, and 60 are not collectible. Are these numbers in agreement with the industry distribution? Use the .05 significance level.

▌ Exercises

9. The following hypotheses are given:

   H_0: Forty percent of the observations are in category A, 40 percent are in B, and 20 percent are in C.

   H_1: The observations are not as described in H_0.

   We took a sample of 60, with the following results.

Category	f_0
A	30
B	20
C	10

   a. State the decision rule using the .01 significance level.
   b. Compute the value of chi-square.
   c. What is your decision regarding H_0?

10. The chief of security of a large shopping mall was directed to study the problem of missing goods. He selected a sample of 100 boxes that had been tampered with and ascertained that for 60 of the boxes, the missing pants, shoes, and so on were attributed to shoplifting. For 30 other boxes employees had stolen the goods, and for the remaining 10 boxes he blamed poor inventory control.

    In his report to the mall management, can he say that shoplifting is *twice* as likely to be the cause of the loss as compared with employee theft or poor inventory control? Use the .02 level.

11. The bank credit card department of Carolina Bank knows from long experience that 5 percent of the card holders have had some high school, 15 percent have completed high school, 25 percent have had some college, and 55 percent have completed college. Of the 500 card holders whose cards have been called in for failure to pay their charges this month, 50 had some high school, 100 had completed high school, 190 had some college, and 160 had completed college. Can we conclude that the distribution of card holders who do not pay their charges is different from all others? Use the .01 significance level.

12. For many years TV executives used the guideline that 30 percent of the audience were watching each of the prime-time networks and 10 percent cable stations on a weekday night. A random sample of 500 viewers in the Tampa-St. Petersburg, Florida, area last Monday night showed that 165 homes were tuned in to the ABC affiliate, 140 to the CBS affiliate, 125 to the NBC affiliate, and the remainder were viewing a cable station. At the .05 significance level, can we conclude that the guideline is still reasonable?

▌ Using the Goodness-of-Fit Test to Test for Normality

We can also use the goodness-of-fit test to determine whether a set of observed frequencies matches a set of expected frequencies that conforms to a normal distribution. To put it another way, do the observed values in a frequency distribution coincide with the expected values based on a normal distribution? Recall in earlier chapters we often assumed that the sampled populations were normally distributed. This test offers a way to check that assumption.

Example

Dr. Beth McPherson, president of Duval University, collected data on the annual salaries of full professors at 160 colleges. Using a statistical software package, she determined that the mean salary was $54.03 (in thousands) and that the standard deviation was $13.76 (in thousands). The frequency distribution for these annual salaries is shown in Table 14–7.

Table 14–7   Average Annual Salaries of Professors at 160 Colleges

Salary ($ thousands)	Number of Colleges
20 up to 30	4
30 up to 40	20
40 up to 50	41
50 up to 60	44
60 up to 70	29
70 up to 80	16
80 up to 90	2
90 up to 100	4
Total	160

Do the observed frequencies coincide with the expected frequencies based on the normal probability distribution?

Solution

The mean and standard deviation are inserted into formula (7–1) (the formula for finding z). X in the formula is the lower or the upper class limit. To illustrate the computation of the z values, we selected the "70 up to 80" class.

$$z = \frac{X - \mu}{\sigma}$$

where X is the particular salary class limit, such as $70 (thousand), μ is the mean (54.03), and σ is the standard deviation (13.76).

The z value for 70, the lower limit of the "70 up to 80" class, is 1.16, found by

$$z = \frac{X - \mu}{\sigma} = \frac{70 - 54.03}{13.76} = 1.16$$

This indicates that 70 is 1.16 standard deviations above the mean of 54.03.

For the upper limit of the "70 up to 80" class, $z = 1.89$, found by

$$z = \frac{X - \mu}{\sigma} = \frac{80 - 54.03}{13.76} = 1.89$$

Thus, 80 is 1.89 standard deviations above the mean of 54.03.

To determine the area in the standard normal distribution from 0 to 1.16, refer to Appendix D or the standard normal distribution on the back inside cover of this book. Go down the left margin to 1.1, then horizontally to 0.06, and read the area. It is .3770. This is also the area under the curve between the mean of 54.03 and 70.00.

Next, the area between 54.03 (the mean) and 80 is .4706. To find the area under the curve between 1.16 and 1.89, we subtract $.4706 - .3770 = .0936$. Thus we expect .0936 or 9.36 percent of the salaries to be between 1.16 and 1.89 standard deviations from the mean. Thus, the expected number of salaries between $70 and $80 (thousand) is 14.976, found by 160(.0936). This information is summarized in the following drawing. The expected frequencies for all the other categories are listed in Table 14–8.

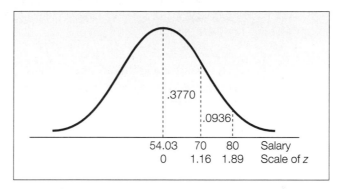

Before continuing, we should emphasize one of the limitations of tests using chi-square as the test statistic. The second limitation on page 522 indicates that if more than 20 percent of the cells have *expected frequencies* of less than 5, some of the categories should be combined. In Table 14–7 there are three cases where the *observed frequencies* are less than 5. To avoid the possibility that there will be too many cells with expected frequencies less than 5, the two largest salary categories are combined in Table 14–8. So the groups "80 up to 90" and "90 up to 100" are combined into a single group of "80 or more." The details for determining the expected frequency (f_e) for each of the categories are shown in Table 14–8.

Table 14–8 Salaries, z Values, Normal Areas, and f_e

Salary ($ thousands)	z Value	Area	Expected Frequency, f_e
Under 30	Under −1.75	.0401	6.416 ← .0401 × 160
30 to 40	−1.75 to −1.02	.1138	18.208 ← .1138 × 160
40 to 50	−1.02 to −0.29	.2320	37.120 ← .2320 × 160
50 to 60	−0.29 to 0.43	.2805	44.880 ← .2805 × 160
60 to 70	0.43 to 1.16	.2106	33.696 ← .2106 × 160
70 to 80	1.16 to 1.89	.0936	14.976 ← .0936 × 160
80 or more	Over 1.89	.0294	4.704 ← .0294 × 160
		1.0000	160.000

Now to compute the value of chi-square: (See Table 14–9.) Column 2 shows the observed frequency and column 3 the expected frequency for each of the salary categories. Columns 4, 5, and 6 show the computations for the chi-square value. Computed chi-square is 2.590.

Table 14–9   Calculations for Chi-Square

(1) Salary ($ thousands)	(2) f_0	(3) f_e	(4) $f_0 - f_e$	(5) $(f_0 - f_e)^2$	(6) $\dfrac{(f_0 - f_e)^2}{f_e}$
Under 30	4	6.416	−2.416	5.837	0.910
30 to 40	20	18.208	1.792	3.211	0.176
40 to 50	41	37.120	3.880	15.054	0.406
50 to 60	44	44.880	−0.880	0.774	0.017
60 to 70	29	33.696	−4.696	22.052	0.654
70 to 80	16	14.976	1.024	1.049	0.070
80 and over	6	4.704	1.296	1.680	0.357
	160	160			2.590

Must be equal

χ^2

As usual, the null and the alternate hypotheses are stated:

H_0:   The population is normally distributed.

H_1:   The population is not normally distributed.

To find the critical value of chi-square, we need to know the degrees of freedom. In this case there are 7 categories (see Table 14–9), so the degrees of freedom is $7 - 1 = 6$. In addition, the values $54.03, the mean salary, and $13.76, the standard deviation of the salaries of full professors, were computed from this sample all the professors. When we estimate population parameters from sample data, we lose a degree of freedom for each estimate. So we lose two more degrees of freedom for estimating the population mean and the population standard deviation. Thus, the number of degrees of freedom in this problem is 4, found by $k - 2 - 1 = 7 - 2 - 1 = 4$.

From Appendix I, using the .05 significance level, the critical value of χ^2 is 9.488. H_0 is rejected if the computed value of chi-square is greater than 9.488. In this case we computed χ^2 to be 2.590, so the null hypothesis is not rejected. We conclude that the distribution of full professors' salaries follows the normal distribution.

To expand on the calculation of the number of degrees of freedom, suppose we knew the mean and standard deviation of a population but wished to find whether some sample information conformed to the normal distribution. In this case the degrees of freedom is k, the number of categories minus 1. On the other hand, suppose we have sample data grouped into a frequency distribution, but we do not know the population mean or the population standard deviation. We wish to test whether the sample data are normally distributed. Because we are estimating the population mean and the population standard deviation from the sample data, the number of degrees of freedom is $k - 2 - 1$. In general, when we use sample statistics to estimate population parameters, the number of degrees of freedom is found by $k - p - 1$, where p represents the number of population parameters being estimated from the sample data.

SELF-REVIEW 14–3

Refer to the problem of salaries of full professors. Verify the expected number of salaries between $60 and $70 (thousand).

▌ Exercises

13. The manufacturer of a computer terminal reports in its advertising that the mean life of the terminal, under normal use, is 6 years, with a standard deviation of 1.4 years. A sample of 90 units sold 10 years ago revealed the following distribution of the lengths of life. At the .05 significance level, can the manufacturer conclude that the terminal lives are normally distributed?

Length of Life (years)	Frequency
Up to 4	7
4 up to 5	14
5 up to 6	25
6 up to 7	22
7 up to 8	16
8 or more	6

14. The commissions for sales of new cars are reported to average $1,500 per month with a standard deviation of $300. A sample of 500 sales representatives in the Northwest revealed the following distribution of commissions. At the .01 significance level, can we conclude that the population is normally distributed, with a mean of $1,500 and a standard deviation of $300?

Commission ($)	Frequency
Less than 900	9
900 up to 1,200	63
1,200 up to 1,500	165
1,500 up to 1,800	180
1,800 up to 2,100	71
2,100 or more	12
Total	500

▌ Contingency Table Analysis

The goodness-of-fit tests applied in the previous sections were concerned with only a single variable and a single trait. The chi-square test can also be used for a research project involving *two* traits. As examples:

- Is there any relationship between the grade point average students earn in college and their income 10 years after graduation? The two traits measured for each individual are grade point average and income.

- Does a male released from federal prison make a better adjustment to civilian life if he returns to his hometown or if he goes elsewhere to live? The two traits are adjustment to civilian life and place of residence. Note that both traits are measured on the nominal scale.

Example

Suppose the Federal Correction Agency wants to investigate the first question cited above: Does a male released from federal prison make better adjustment to civilian life if he returns to his hometown or if he goes elsewhere to live? To put it another way, is there a relationship between adjustment to civilian life and place of residence after release from prison?

Solution

As before, the first step in hypothesis testing is to state the null and alternate hypotheses.

H_0:   There is no relationship between adjustment to civilian life and where the individual lives after being released from prison.

H_1:   There is a relationship between adjustment to civilian life and where the individual lives after being released from prison.

The .01 level of significance will be used to test the hypothesis. Recall that this is the probability of a Type I error (i.e., the probability is .01 that a true null hypothesis is rejected).

The agency's psychologists interviewed 200 randomly selected former prisoners. Using a series of questions, the psychologists classified the adjustment of each individual to civilian life as outstanding, good, fair, or unsatisfactory. The classifications for the 200 former prisoners were tallied as follows. Joseph Camden, for example, returned to his hometown and has shown outstanding adjustment to civilian life. His case is one of the 27 tallies in the upper left box.

Residence after Release from Prison	Adjustment to Civilian Life			
	Outstanding	Good	Fair	Unsatisfactory
Hometown	⊬⊬ ⊬⊬ ⊬⊬ ⊬⊬ ⊬⊬ //	⊬⊬ ⊬⊬ ⊬⊬ ⊬⊬ ⊬⊬ ⊬⊬ ⊬⊬	⊬⊬ ⊬⊬ ⊬⊬ ⊬⊬ ⊬⊬ ⊬⊬ ///	⊬⊬ ⊬⊬ ⊬⊬ ⊬⊬ ⊬⊬
Not hometown	⊬⊬ ⊬⊬ ///	⊬⊬ ⊬⊬ ⊬⊬	⊬⊬ ⊬⊬ ⊬⊬ ⊬⊬ ⊬⊬ //	⊬⊬ ⊬⊬ ⊬⊬ ⊬⊬ ⊬⊬

Contingency table consists of count data

The tallies in each box, or *cell*, were counted. The counts are given in the following **contingency table.** (See Table 14–10.) In this case, the Federal Correction Agency wondered whether adjustment to civilian life is *contingent on* where the prisoner goes after release from prison.

Table 14–10   Adjustment to Civilian Life and Place of Residence

Residence after Release from Prison	Adjustment to Civilian Life				Total
	Outstanding	Good	Fair	Unsatisfactory	
Hometown	27	35	33	25	120
Not hometown	13	15	27	25	80
Total	40	50	60	50	200

Once we know how many rows (2) and how many columns (4) there are in the contingency table, the critical value and the decision rule can be determined. For a chi-square test of significance where two traits are classified in a contingency table, the degrees of freedom are found by:

$$df = (\text{number of rows} - 1)(\text{number of columns} - 1) = (r - 1)(c - 1)$$

In this problem:

$$df = (r - 1)(c - 1) = (2 - 1)(4 - 1) = 3$$

To find the critical value for 3 degrees of freedom and the .01 level (selected earlier), refer to Appendix I. It is 11.345. The decision rule is, therefore: Do not reject the null hypothesis if the computed value of χ^2 is equal to or less than 11.345; reject H_0 and accept H_1 if it is greater than 11.345. The decision rule is portrayed graphically in Chart 14–4.

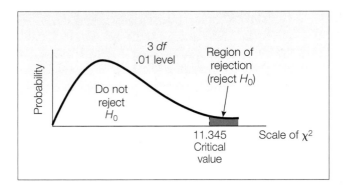

Chart 14–4   Chi-Square Distribution for 3 Degrees of Freedom

Now to find the computed value of χ^2: The observed frequencies, f_0, are shown in Table 14–10. How are the corresponding expected frequencies, f_e, determined? Note in the "Total" column of Table 14–10 that 120 of the 200 former prisoners (60 percent) returned to their hometowns. *If there were no relationship whatsoever* between adjustment and residency after release from prison, we would expect 60 percent of the 40 ex-prisoners who made outstanding adjustment to civilian life to reside in their hometowns. Thus, the expected frequency f_e for the upper left cell is .60 × 40 = 24. Likewise, if there were no relationship between adjustment and present residence, we would expect 60 percent of the 50 ex-prisoners (30) who had "good" adjustment to civilian life to reside in their hometowns.

Further, notice that 80 of the 200 ex-prisoners studied (40 percent) did not return to their hometowns to live. Thus, of the 60 considered by the psychologists to have made "fair" adjustment to civilian life, .40 × 60, or 24, would be expected not to return to their hometowns.

The expected frequency for any cell can be determined by

EXPECTED FREQUENCY	Expected frequency for a cell $= \dfrac{(\text{Row total})(\text{Column total})}{\text{Grand total}}$	**[14–2]**

Using this formula, the expected frequency for the upper left cell in Table 14–10 is:

$$\text{Expected frequency} = \frac{(\text{Row total})(\text{Column total})}{\text{Grand total}} = \frac{(120)(40)}{200} = 24$$

The observed frequencies, f_0, and the expected frequencies, f_e, for all of the cells in the contingency table are listed in Table 14–11.

Table 14–11 Observed and Expected Frequencies

Residence after Release from Prison	Adjustment to Civilian Life									
	Out-standing		Good		Fair		Unsatis-factory		Total	
	f_0	f_e	f_0	f_e	f_0	f_e	f_0	f_e	f_0	f_e
Hometown	27	24	35	30	33	36	25	30	120	120
Not hometown	13	16	15	20	27	24	25	20	80	80
Total	40	40	50	50	60	60	50	50	200	200

Must be equal

$\dfrac{(80)(50)}{200}$

Must be equal

Recall the computed value of chi-square using formula (14–1) is found by:

$$\chi^2 = \Sigma \left[\frac{(f_0 - f_e)^2}{f_e} \right]$$

Starting with the upper left cell:

$$\chi^2 = \frac{(27 - 24)^2}{24} + \frac{(35 - 30)^2}{30} + \frac{(33 - 36)^2}{36} + \frac{(25 - 30)^2}{30}$$

$$+ \frac{(13 - 16)^2}{16} + \frac{(15 - 20)^2}{20} + \frac{(27 - 24)^2}{24} + \frac{(25 - 20)^2}{20}$$

$$= 0.375 + 0.833 + 0.250 + 0.833 + 0.563 + 1.250 + 0.375 + 1.250$$

$$= 5.729$$

Because the computed value of chi-square (5.729) lies in the region to the left of 11.345, the null hypothesis is not rejected at the .01 level. We conclude there is no relationship between adjustment to civilian life and where the prisoner resides after being released from prison. For the Federal Correction Agency's advisement program, adjustment to civilian life is not related to where the ex-prisoner lives.

The following output is from the MINITAB system.

```
Chi-Square Test

Expected counts are printed below observed counts

                 C1       C2       C3       C4    Total
       1         27       35       33       25      120
               24.00    30.00    36.00    30.00

       2         13       15       27       25       80
               16.00    20.00    24.00    20.00

    Total        40       50       60       50      200


Chi-Sq =   0.375 + 0.833 + 0.250 + 0.833 +
           0.562 + 1.250 + 0.375 + 1.250 = 5.729
  DF = 3,  P-Value = 0.126
```

Observe the value of chi-square is the same as that computed earlier. In addition, the *p*-value is reported, .126. So, the probability of finding a value of the test statistic this large or larger is .126, when H_0 is true.

SELF-REVIEW 14–4

A sociologist was researching this question: Is there any relationship between the level of education and social activities of an individual? She decided on three levels of education: attended or completed college, attended or completed high school, and attended or completed grade school or less. Each individual kept a record of his or her social activities, such as bowling with a group, dancing, and church functions. The sociologist divided them into above-average frequency, average frequency, and below-average frequency.

	Social Activity		
Education	Above Average	Average	Below Average
College	18	12	10
High school	17	15	13
Grade school	9	9	22

(a) What is the table called?
(b) State the null hypothesis.
(c) Should the null hypothesis be rejected at the .05 significance level? Cite figures to substantiate your decision.
(d) What specifically does this indicate in this problem?

❚ Exercises

15. The marketing director for a metropolitan daily newspaper is studying the relationship between the type of community the reader lives in and the portion of the paper he or she reads first. For a sample of readers the following information was collected.

	National News	Sports	Comics
Urban	170	124	90
Rural	120	112	100
Farm	130	90	88

At the .05 significance level, can we conclude there is a relationship between the type of community where the person resides and the portion of the paper read first?

16. Four brands of light bulbs are being considered for use in a large manufacturing plant. The director of purchasing asked for samples of 100 from each manufacturer. The numbers of acceptable and unacceptable bulbs from each manufacturer are shown below. At the .05 significance level, is there a difference in the quality of the bulbs?

	Manufacturer			
	A	B	C	D
Acceptable	12	8	5	11
Unacceptable	88	92	95	89
Total	100	100	100	100

17. The Quality Control Department at Food Town, Inc., a grocery chain in upstate New York, conducts a monthly check on the comparison of scanned prices to posted prices. The chart below summarizes the results of a sample of 500 items last month. Company management would like to know whether there is any relationship between error rates on regular priced items and specially priced items. Use the .01 significance level.

	Regular Price	Advertised Special Price
Undercharge	20	10
Overcharge	15	30
Correct price	200	225

18. The use of cellular phones in automobiles has increased dramatically in the last few years. Of concern to traffic experts, as well as manufacturers of cellular phones, is the effect on accident rates. Is someone who is using a cellular phone more likely to be involved in a traffic accident? What is your conclusion from the following sample information? Use the .05 significance level.

	Had Accident in the Last Year	Did Not Have an Accident in the Last Year
Cellular phone in use	25	300
Cellular phone not in use	50	400

▌ Chapter Outline

I. The characteristics of the chi-square distribution are:
   A. The value of chi-square is never negative.
   B. The chi-square distribution is positively skewed.
   C. There is a family of chi-square distributions.
      1. Each time the degrees of freedom change, a new distribution is formed.
      2. As the degrees of freedom increase, the distribution approaches the normal distribution.

II.   A goodness-of-fit test will show whether an observed set of frequencies could have come from a hypothesized discrete distribution.
  A.   The degrees of freedom are $k - 1$, where k is the number of categories.
  B.   The formula for computing the value of chi-square is

$$\chi^2 = \Sigma \frac{(f_0 - f_e)^2}{f_e}$$ **[14–1]**

III. A goodness-of-fit test can also be used to determine whether the sample observations came from a continuous distribution such as the normal distribution.
  A.   To conduct the test for a normal distribution, find the mean and standard deviation of the distribution.
  B.   Group the data into a frequency distribution.
  C.   Convert the class limits to z values.
  D.   Multiply the probability for finding a value in each class by the total number of observations to find the expected frequency.
  E.   Use formula (14–1) to determine the value of chi-square.
  F.   The degrees of freedom is equal to $k - 3$ if the mean and the standard deviation are estimated from the data..

IV.   A contingency table is used to test whether two traits or characteristics are related.
  A.   Each observation is classified according to two traits.
  B.   The expected frequency is determined as follows:

$$f_e = \frac{(\text{Row total})(\text{Column total})}{(\text{Grand total})}$$ **[14–2]**

  C.   The degrees of freedom are found by:

$$df = (\text{Rows} - 1)(\text{Columns} - 1)$$

  D.   The usual hypothesis testing procedure is used.

▌ Pronunciation Key

SYMBOL	MEANING	PRONUNCIATION
χ^2	Probability distribution	*chi square*
f_0	Observed frequency	*f sub zero*
f_e	Expected frequency	*f sub e*

▌ Chapter Exercises

19.   Vehicles heading west on Front Street may turn right, left, or go straight ahead at Elm Street. The city traffic engineer believes that half of the vehicles will continue straight through the intersection. Of the remaining half, equal proportions will turn right and left. Two hundred vehicles were observed, with the following results. Use the .10 significance level. Can we conclude that the traffic engineer is correct?

	Straight	Right Turn	Left Turn
Frequency	112	48	40

20.   The publisher of a sports magazine plans to offer new subscribers one of three gifts: a sweatshirt with the logo of their favorite team, a coffee cup with the logo of their favorite team, or a pair of earrings also with the logo of their favorite team. In a sample of 500 new subscribers,

the number selecting each gift is reported below. At the .05 significance level, is there a preference for the gifts or should we conclude that the gifts are equally well liked?

Gift	Frequency
Sweatshirt	183
Coffee cup	175
Earrings	142

21. In a particular television market there are three commercial television stations, each with its own evening news program from 6:00 to 6:30 P.M. According to a report in this morning's local newspaper, a random sample of 150 viewers last night revealed 53 watched the news on WNAE (channel 5), 64 watched on WRRN (channel 11), and 33 on WSPD (channel 13). At the .05 significance level, is there a difference in the proportion of viewers watching the three channels?

22. There are four entrances to the Government Center Building in downtown Philadelphia. The building maintenance supervisor would like to know if the entrances are equally utilized. To investigate, 400 people were observed entering the building. The number using each entrance is reported below. At the .01 significance level, is there a difference in the use of the four entrances?

Entrance	Frequency
Main Street	140
Broad Street	120
Cherry Street	90
Walnut Street	50
Total	400

23. The owner of a mail-order catalog would like to compare her sales with the geographic distribution of the population. According to the United States Bureau of the Census, 21 percent of the population lives in the Northeast, 24 percent in the Midwest, 35 percent in the South, and 20 percent in the West. Listed below is a breakdown of a sample of 400 orders randomly selected from those shipped last month.

Region	Frequency
Northeast	68
Midwest	104
South	155
West	73
Total	400

At the .01 significance level, does the distribution of the orders reflect the population?

24. Southern Medical Services performed 3,459 abortions last year. The number of previous abortions reported by the same patients were:

Abortions	Patients
0	2,441
1	784
2	184
3	50

Are these data consistent with the national figures, which indicate that 67 percent of the patients never had an abortion before, 27 percent had one previous abortion, 5 percent had two previous abortions, and 1 percent had 3 or more previous abortions? Use the .05 significance level.

25. Did you ever purchase a bag of M&M's peanut candies and wonder about the distribution of the colors? The manufacturer reports that 30 percent are brown, 30 percent yellow, and 10 percent each are blue, orange, red, and green. A 6.0 ounce bag of M&M's peanut candies purchased at the BP Station at the Junction of I-75 and U.S. 20 in Perrysburg, Ohio, had 17 brown, 20 yellow, 13 blue, 9 orange, 6 green, and 7 red, for a total of 72 candies. At the .05 significance level, can we conclude the actual breakdown by color of the candies agrees with the expected distribution?

26. The American Association of Television Broadcasters recently reported the mean number of television sets per household in the United States is 2.30 sets and that the standard deviation is 1.474 sets. A sample of 100 homes In Boise, Idaho, revealed the following number of sets per household:

Number of Television Sets	Number of Households	Number of Television Sets	Number of Households
0	7	3	18
1	27	4	10
2	28	5 or more	10

At the .05 significance level, is it reasonable to conclude that the number of television sets per household follows the normal distribution. (*Hint:* Use limits such as 0.50, 1.5, etc.)

27. The Eckel Manufacturing believes that their hourly wages follow a normal probability distribution. To confirm this, 300 workers were sampled and the results organized into the following frequency distribution. Find the mean and the standard deviation of these data grouped into a frequency distribution. At the .10 significance level, is it reasonable to conclude that the distribution of hourly wages approximates the normal distribution?

Hourly Wage ($)	Frequency
5.50 up to 6.50	20
6.50 up to 7.50	54
7.50 up to 8.50	130
8.50 up to 9.50	68
9.50 up to 10.50	28
Total	300

28. A recent study by a large retailer designed to determine whether there was a relationship between the importance a store manager placed on advertising and the size of the store revealed the following sample information:

	Important	Not Important
Small	40	52
Medium	106	47
Large	67	32

What is your conclusion? Use the .05 significance level.

29. Two hundred men selected at random from various levels of management were interviewed regarding their concern about environmental issues. The response of each person was tallied into one of three categories: no concern, some concern, and great concern. The results were:

Level of Management	No Concern	Some Concern	Great Concern
Top management	15	13	12
Middle management	20	19	21
Supervisor	7	7	6
Group leader	28	21	31

Use the .01 significance level to determine whether there is a relationship between management level and environmental concern.

30. A study regarding the relationship between age and the amount of pressure sales personnel feel in relation to their jobs revealed the following sample information. At the .01 significance level, is there a relationship between job pressure and age?

| Age (years) | Degree of Job Pressure | | |
	Low	Medium	High
Less than 25	20	18	22
25 up to 40	50	46	44
40 up to 60	58	63	59
60 and older	34	43	43

31. The claims department at the Wise Insurance Company believes that younger drivers have more accidents and, therefore, should be charged higher insurance rates. Investigating a sample of 1,200 Wise policyholders revealed the following breakdown on whether a claim had been filed in the last three years and the age of the policyholder. Is it reasonable to conclude that there is a relationship between the age of the policyholder and whether or not the person filed a claim? Use the .05 significance level.

Age Group	No Claim	Claim
16 up to 25	170	74
25 up to 40	240	58
40 up to 55	400	44
55 or older	190	24
Total	1,000	200

32. A sample of employees at a large chemical plant was asked to indicate a preference for one of three pension plans. The results are given in the following table. Does it seem that there is a relationship between the pension plan selected and the job classification of the employees? Use the .01 significance level.

| Job Class | Pension Plan | | |
	Plan A	Plan B	Plan C
Supervisor	10	13	29
Clerical	19	80	19
Labor	81	57	22

www.Exercises.com

33. A sample of Montana residents was asked whether their personal financial status was worse, the same, or better than a year ago, and whether they thought the state economic outlook was better for the next year. This information can be accessed at the following Web site: *http://lib.stat.cmu.edu/DASL/Datafiles/montanadat.html.* (Remember this address is sensitive to capitalization.) At the .05 significance level, is there a relationship between the personal financial condition and the sampled resident's view of economic conditions?

34. As described in earlier chapters, many real estate companies and rental agencies now publish their listings on the Web. One example is the Dunes Realty Company, located in Garden City and Surfside Beaches in South Carolina. Go to the Web site *http://www.dunes. com,* select **Cottage Search,** then indicate 5 bedroom, accommodations for 14 people, oceanfront, and no pool or floating dock; select a period in July and August; indicate that you are willing to spend $5,000 per week; and then click on **Search the Cottages**. The output should include details on the cottages that met your criteria. Organize the selling prices into a frequency distribution. Is it reasonable to conclude that the distribution is normal with a population mean of $3,000 and standard deviation of $900?

▌ Computer Data Exercises

35. Refer to Data Set 1, which reports information on homes sold in the Venice, Florida, area last year.
   a. Develop a contingency table that shows whether a home has a pool and the township in which the house is located. Is there an association between the variables "pool" and "township"? Use the .05 significance level.
   b. Develop a contingency table that shows whether a home has an attached garage and the township in which the home is located. Is there an association between the variables "attached garage" and "township"? Use the .05 significance level.

36. Refer to Data Set 2, which reports information on the 28 Major League Baseball teams for the 1997 season. Set up a variable that divides the teams into two groups, those that had a winning season and those that did not. There are 162 games in the season, so define a winning season as having won more than 81 games. Next, divide the teams into two groups according to team salary. That is let the 14 teams with the largest team salaries be in one group and the 14 with the lowest salaries be in the second group. At the .05 significance level, is there a relationship between salaries and winning?

37. Refer to Data Set 4, which has information on 94 school districts in northwest Ohio.
   a. Group the districts based on the percent of students on welfare: "low" (less than 5 percent), "moderate" (5 up to 10 percent), and "high" (10 percent or more). Conduct a test of hypothesis to determine whether the three categories are equally represented in the sample. Use the .05 significance level.
   b. Identify each district as "small" (less than 1,000 students), "medium" (1,000 up to 3,000), or "large" (more than 3,000 students). Create a table that shows the districts cross-classified by both percent of students on welfare and the size of the district. At the .05 significance level, can we conclude that the two characteristics are related?

█ Computer Commands

1. The MINITAB commands for the chi-square analysis on page 531 are:
    a. Enter the data into the MINITAB spreadsheet by entering the values 27, 35, 33, and 25 in row 1 of columns c1 through c4. Enter the values 13, 15, 27, and 25 in row 2 of the same columns.
    b. Select **Stat** and **Table**, and then click on **Chisquare Test.**
    c. Select columns c1, c2, c3, and c4 and then click **OK.**

CHAPTER 14 *Answers to Self-Review*

14–1 (a) Observed frequencies.
(b) Six (six days of the week).
(c) 10. Total observed frequencies $\div$ 6 = 60/6 = 10.
(d) 5; $k - 1 = 6 - 1 = 5$.
(e) 15.086 (from the chi-square table in Appendix I).
(f)

$$\chi^2 = \Sigma \left[\frac{(f_0 - f_e)^2}{f_e} \right] = \frac{(12 - 10)^2}{10} + \cdots + \frac{(9 - 10)^2}{10} = 0.8$$

(g) No. We do not reject H_0.
(h) Absenteeism is distributed evenly throughout the week. The observed differences are due to sampling variation.

14–2 H_0: $P_C = .60$, $P_L = .30$, and $P_U = .10$.

H_1: Distribution is not as above.

Reject H_0 if $\chi^2 > 5.991$.

Category	f_0	f_e	$\frac{(f_0 - f_e)^2}{f_e}$
Current	320	300	1.33
Late	120	150	6.00
Uncollectible	60	50	2.00
	500	500	9.33

Reject H_0. The accounts receivable data does not reflect the national average.

14–3 33.696, found by $z = (60 - 54.03)/13.76 = 0.43$ and $z = (70 - 54.03)/13.76 = 1.16$. Then $.3770 - .1664 = .2106$ and $.2106 \times 160 = 33.696$.

14–4 (a) Contingency table
(b) There is no relationship between the level of education and the frequency of social activity.
(c) The value of chi-square is completed from the following table:

Education	Social Activity						Total
	Above Average		Average		Below Average		
	f_0	f_e	f_0	f_e	f_0	f_e	
College	18	14.08	12	11.52	10	14.40	40
High school	17	15.84	15	12.96	13	16.20	45
Grade school	9	14.08	9	11.52	22	14.40	40
	44	44.00	36	36.00	45	45.00	125

$$\chi^2 = \frac{(18 - 14.08)^2}{14.08} + \frac{(12 - 11.52)^2}{11.52} + \cdots + \frac{(22 - 14.40)^2}{14.40}$$

$$= 9.889$$

The critical value of chi-square is 9.448, so H_0 is rejected.
(d) There is a relationship between the level of education and the frequency of social activity.

Chapter Fifteen

Nonparametric Methods:

Analysis of Ranked Data

GOALS

When you have completed this chapter, you will be able to:

ONE

Conduct the sign test for dependent samples using the binomial and normal distributions as the test statistics.

TWO

Conduct a test of hypothesis for dependent samples using the Wilcoxon signed-rank test.

THREE

Conduct the Wilcoxon rank-sum test for independent samples.

FOUR

Conduct the Kruskal-Wallis test for several independent samples.

FIVE

Compute and interpret Spearman's coefficient of rank correlation.

SIX

Conduct a test of hypothesis to determine whether the correlation among the ranks in the population is different from zero.

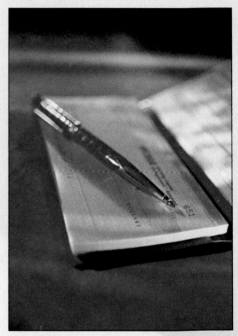

Given the turnover rates of samples selected from four branches of a bank, determine if there is a difference in the turnover rates of the personal checking accounts among the four branches. (See Goal 4 and Self Review 15–6).

▌ Introduction

Chapter 14 introduced nonparametric, or distribution-free, tests of hypotheses. We stressed that the goodness-of-fit test is especially useful for *nominal* level of measurement. (Recall from Chapter 1 that nominal level of measurement implies that the data can only be classified into categories, and there is no particular order to the categories.) The purpose of these tests is to determine whether an observed set of frequencies, f_0, is significantly different from a corresponding set of expected frequencies, f_e. Likewise, if you are interested in the relationship between two characteristics — such as the age of an individual and his or her music preference — you would tally the data into a contingency table and use the chi-square distribution as the test statistic. For both these types of problems, no assumptions need to be made about the shape of the population. We do not have to assume, for example, that the population of interest is normally distributed, as was done with tests of hypotheses in Chapters 9 through 11.

This chapter is a continuation of tests of hypotheses designed especially for nonparametric data. However, instead of being applicable to nominal-level data, these tests require that the responses be at least *ordinal level.* That is, the responses can be ranked from low to high. An example of ranking is the executive title. Executives are ranked assistant vice president, vice president, senior vice president, and president. A vice president is ranked higher than an assistant vice president, a senior vice president is ranked higher than a vice president, and so on.

Five distribution-free tests will be considered in this chapter: the sign test, the median test, the Wilcoxon signed-rank test, the Wilcoxon rank-sum test, the Kruskal-Wallis analysis of variance by ranks, and the Spearman coefficient of rank correlation.

▌ The Sign Test

The **sign test** is based on the sign of a difference between two related observations. We usually designate a plus sign for a positive difference and a minus sign for a negative difference. If, for example, sales increased from $34,698 in October to $51,276 in November, we record the $16,578 difference as a plus sign. If production dropped from 98,000 computers in the first quarter to 51,000 in the second quarter, a minus sign is recorded. For a sign test, we are not concerned with the magnitude of the difference, only the direction of the difference.

The sign test has many applications. One is for "before/after" experiments. To illustrate, suppose an evaluation is to be made on a new tune-up program for automobiles. The number of miles traveled per gallon of gasoline is recorded before the tune-up and again after the tune-up. If the tune-up is not effective, that is, had no effect on performance, then about half of the automobiles tested would show an increase in miles per gallon and the other half a decrease. A "+" sign is assigned to an increase, a "−" sign to a decrease.

A product-preference experiment illustrates another use of the sign test. Taster's Choice markets two kinds of coffee in a 4-ounce jar: decaffeinated and regular. Their market research department wants to determine whether coffee drinkers prefer decaffeinated or regular coffee. Coffee drinkers are given two small, unmarked cups of coffee, and each is asked his or her preference. Preference for decaffeinated could be coded "+" and preference for regular "−." In a sense the data are ordinal level because the coffee drinkers give their preferred coffee the higher rank; they rank the other kind below it. Here again, if the population of consumers do not have a preference, we would expect half of the sample of coffee drinkers to prefer decaffeinated and the other half regular coffee.

We can best show the application of the sign test by an example. We will use a "before/after" experiment.

Example

Top management at Samuelson Chemicals recommended that an in-plant computer training program be instituted for managers, with the objective of improving their knowledge of computer usage in accounting, procurement, production, and so on. Some managers thought it would be a worthwhile program; others resisted it, saying it would be of no value. Despite these objections, it was announced that the computer sessions would commence the first of the month.

A sample of 15 managers was selected at random. The general level of competence of each manager with respect to the computer was determined by a panel of experts before the program started. Their competence and understanding were rated as being either outstanding, excellent, good, fair, or poor. (See Table 15–1.) After the three-month training program, the same panel of computer experts rated each manager again. The two ratings (before and after) are shown along with the sign of the difference. A "+" sign indicates improvement, and a "−" sign indicates that the manager's competence on the computer had declined after the training program.

Table 15–1   Competence before and after the Computer Training Program

Name	Before	After	Sign of Difference
T. J. Bowers	Good	Outstanding	+
Sue Jenkins	Fair	Excellent	+
James Brown	Excellent	Good	−
Tad Jackson	Poor	Good	+
Andy Love	Excellent	Excellent	0
Sarah Truett	Good	Outstanding	+
John Sinshi	Poor	Fair	+
Jean Unger	Excellent	Outstanding	+
Coy Farmer	Good	Poor	−
Troy Archer	Poor	Good	+
V. A. Jones	Good	Outstanding	+
Coley Casper	Fair	Excellent	+
Candy Fry	Good	Fair	−
Arthur Seiple	Good	Outstanding	+
Sandy Gumpp	Poor	Good	+

(Dropped from analysis: Andy Love)

We are interested in whether the in-plant computer training program was effective in increasing the competence of the managers on the computer. That is, are the managers more competent after the training program than before?

Solution

We will use the five-step hypotheses testing procedure.

Step 1:   State the Null Hypothesis and the Alternate Hypothesis.

Hypothesis	Meaning
H_0: $\pi \le .50$	There is no increase in competence as a result of the in-plant computer training program.
H_1: $\pi > .50$	The computer competence of the managers has increased.

If we *do not reject* the null hypothesis, it will indicate the training program has produced no change in the level of computer competence, or competence actually decreased. If we *reject* the null hypothesis, it will indicate that the computer competence of the managers has increased as a result of the training program.

The binomial distribution discussed in Chapter 6 is used as the test statistic. It is appropriate because the sign test meets all the binomial assumptions, namely:

1. There are only two outcomes: a "success" and a "failure." A manager either increased in computer competence (a success) or did not.
2. For each trial the probability of success is assumed to be .50. Thus, the probability of a success is the same for all trials (managers in this case).
3. The total number of trials is fixed (15 in this experiment).
4. Each trial is independent. This means, for example, that Arthur Seiple's performance in the three-month course is unrelated to Sandy Gumpp's performance.

Step 2: Select a Level of Significance.   We chose the .10 level.

Step 3: Decide on the Test Statistic.   It is *the number of plus signs* resulting from the experiment (11 in this case).

Step 4: Formulate a Decision Rule.   Fifteen managers were enrolled in the computer course, but Andy Love showed no increase or decrease in competence. (See Table 15–1.) He was, therefore, eliminated from the study, so $n = 14$. From the binomial probability distribution table in Appendix A, for an n of 14 and a probability of .50, we copied the binomial probability distribution in Table 15–2. The number of successes is in column 1, the probability of success in column 2, and the cumulative probabilities in column 3. To arrive at the cumulative probabilities, we *add up* the probabilities of success in column 2 from the bottom. For illustration, to get the cumulative probability of 11 or more successes, we add .000 + .001 + .006 + .022 = .029.

This is a one-tailed test because the alternate hypothesis gives a direction. The inequality (>) points to the right. Thus, the region of rejection is in the upper tail. If the inequality sign pointed toward the left tail (<), the region of rejection would be in the lower tail. If that were the case, we would add the probabilities in column 2 *down* to get the cumulative probabilities in column 3.

Recall that we selected the .10 level of significance. To arrive at the decision rule for this problem, we go to the cumulative probabilities in Table 15–2, column 3. We read up from the bottom until we come to the *cumulative probability nearest to but not exceeding the level of significance (.10).* That cumulative probability is .090. The number of successes (plus signs) corresponding to .090 in column 1 is 10. Therefore, the decision rule is: If the number of pluses in the sample is 10 or more, the null hypothesis is rejected and the alternate hypothesis accepted.

Table 15–2   Binomial Probability Distribution for $n = 14$, $\pi = .50$

(1) Number of Successes	(2) Probability of Success	(3) Cumulative Probability	
0	.000	1.000	
1	.001	.999	
2	.006	.998	
3	.022	.992	
4	.061	.970	
5	.122	.909	
6	.183	.787	
7	.209	.604	
8	.183	.395	
9	.122	.212	
10	.061	.090	
11	.022	.029	← .000 + .001 +
12	.006	.007	.006 + .022
13	.001	.001	
14	000	.000	

To repeat: We add the probabilities up from the bottom because the direction of the inequality ($>$) is toward the right, indicating that the region of rejection is in the upper tail. If the number of plus signs in the sample is 10 or more, we reject the null hypothesis; otherwise, we do not reject H_0. The region of rejection is portrayed in Chart 15–1.

Chart 15–1   Region of Rejection, $n = 14$, $\pi = .50$

What procedure is followed for a two-tailed test? We combine (add) the probabilities of success in the two tails until we come as close to α as possible without exceeding it. In this example α is .10. The probability of 3 or fewer successes is .029, found by .000 + .001 + .006 + .022. The probability of 11 or more successes is also .029. Adding the two probabilities gives .058. This is the closest we can come to .10 without exceeding it. (Had we included the probabilities of 4 and 10 successes, the total would be .180, which exceeds .10.) Hence, the decision rule for a two-tailed test would be to reject the null hypothesis if there are 3 or fewer plus signs, or 11 or more plus signs.

Step 5: Make a Decision Regarding the Null Hypothesis.   Eleven out of the 14 managers in the computer course increased their computer competency. The number 11 is in the rejection region, which starts at 10, so H_0 is rejected. The three-month computer course was effective. It increased the computer competency of the managers.

It should be noted again that if the alternate hypothesis does not give a direction — for example, H_0: $\pi = .50$ and H_1: $\pi \neq .50$ — the test of hypothesis is *two-tailed*. In such cases there will be two rejection regions — one in the lower tail and one in the upper tail. If $\alpha = .10$ and the test is two-tailed, the area in each tail is .05 ($\alpha/2 = .10/2 = .05$). Self-Review 15–1 illustrates this.

SELF-REVIEW 15–1

Recall the Taster's Choice example described on page 541, involving a consumer test to determine the preference for decaffeinated versus regular coffee. The null and alternate hypotheses are:

H_0: π = .50 n = 12

H_1: π ≠ .50 α = .10

(a) Is this a one-tailed or a two-tailed test of hypothesis?
(b) Show the decision rule in a chart.
(c) Letting consumer preference for decaffeinated coffee be a "+" and preference for regular coffee a "−," it was found that two customers preferred decaffeinated. What is your decision? Explain.

▌ Exercises

1. The following hypothesis-testing situation is given: H_0: π ≤ .50 and H_1: π > .50. The significance level is .10, and the sample size is 12.
   a. What is the decision rule?
   b. There were nine successes. What is your decision regarding the null hypothesis? Explain.
2. The following hypothesis-testing situation is given: H_0: π = .50 and H_1: π ≠ .50. The significance level is .05, and the sample size is 9.
   a. What is the decision rule?
   b. There were five successes. What is your decision regarding the null hypothesis?
3. Calorie Watchers has low-calorie breakfasts, lunches, and dinners. If you join the club, you receive two packaged meals a day. CW claims that you can eat anything you want for the third meal and still lose at least five pounds the first month. Members of the club are weighed before commencing the program and again at the end of the first month. The experiences of a random sample of 11 enrollees are:

Name	Weight Change	Name	Weight Change
Foster	Lost	Hercher	Lost
Taoka	Lost	Camder	Lost
Lange	Gained	Hinckle	Lost
Rousos	Lost	Hinkley	Lost
Stephens	No change	Justin	Lost
Cantrell	Lost		

We are interested in whether there has been a weight loss as a result of the Calorie Watchers program.
   a. State H_0 and H_1.
   b. Using the .05 level of significance, what is the decision rule?
   c. What is your conclusion about the Calorie Watchers program?
4. Many new stockbrokers resist giving presentations to bankers and certain other groups. Sensing this lack of self-confidence, management arranged to have a confidence-building seminar for a sample of new stockbrokers and enlisted Career Boosters for a three-week course. Before the first session, Career Boosters measured the level of confidence of each participant. It was measured again after the three-week seminar. The before and after levels of self-confidence for the 14 in the course are shown below. Self-confidence was classified as being either negative, low, high, or very high.

Stockbroker	Before Seminar	After Seminar	Stockbroker	Before Seminar	After Seminar
J. M. Martin	Negative	Low	F. M. Orphey	Low	Very high
T. D. Jagger	Negative	Negative	C. C. Ford	Low	High
A. D. Hammer	Low	High	A. R. Utz	Negative	Low
T. A. Jones, Jr.	Very high	Low	M. R. Murphy	Low	High
J. J. Cornwall	Low	High	P. A. Arms	Negative	Low
D. A. Skeen	Low	High	B. K. Pierre	Low	High
C. B. Simmer	Negative	High	N. S. Walker	Low	Very high

The purpose of this study is to find whether Career Boosters was effective in raising the self-confidence of the new stockbrokers. That is, was the level of self-confidence higher after the seminar than before it? Use the .05 significance level.

a. State the null and alternate hypotheses.
b. Using the .05 level of significance, state the decision rule — either in words or in chart form.
c. Draw conclusions about the seminar offered by Career Boosters.

Using the Normal Approximation to the Binomial

If the number of observations in the sample is larger than 10, the normal distribution can be used to approximate the binomial. Recall in Chapter 6, we computed the mean of the binomial distribution from $\mu = \pi n$ and the standard deviation from $\sigma = \sqrt{n\pi(1 - \pi)}$. In this case $\pi = .50$, so the equations reduce to $\mu = .50n$ and $\sigma = .5\sqrt{n}$, respectively.

The test statistic z is

SIGN TEST, LARGE SAMPLE	$z = \dfrac{(X \pm .50) - \mu}{\sigma}$	**[15–1]**

If the number of pluses or minuses *is more than* $n/2$, we use the following form as the test statistic:

SIGN TEST, LARGE SAMPLE, + SIGNS MORE THAN $n/2$	$z = \dfrac{(X - .50) - \mu}{\sigma} = \dfrac{(X - .50) - .50n}{.50\sqrt{n}}$	**[15–2]**

If the number of pluses or minuses is *less than* $n/2$, the test statistic z is

SIGN TEST, LARGE SAMPLE, + SIGNS LESS THAN $n/2$	$z = \dfrac{(X + .50) - \mu}{\sigma} = \dfrac{(X + .50) - .50n}{.50\sqrt{n}}$	**[15–3]**

In the preceding formulas, X is the number of plus (or minus) signs. The value $+.50$ or $-.50$ is the *continuity correction factor,* discussed in Chapter 7. Briefly, it is applied when a continuous distribution such as the normal distribution (which we are using) is used to approximate a discrete distribution (the binomial).

Example

The market research department of Cola, Inc. has been given the assignment of testing a new soft drink. Two versions of the drink are considered — a rather sweet drink and a somewhat bitter one. A preference test is to be conducted consisting of a sample of 64 consumers. Each will taste both the sweet cola (labeled A) and the bitter one (labeled B) and indicate a preference. How will the test of hypothesis be conducted, and what cola, if any, should be marketed?

Solution

Step 1: State the Null and Alternate Hypotheses.

H_0: $\pi = .50$ There is no preference.

H_1: $\pi \neq .50$ There is a preference.

Step 2: Select a Level of Significance.   It is the .05 level.

Step 3: The Test Statistic is Selected.   It is z, given in formula (15–1).

$$z = \frac{(X \pm .50) - \mu}{\sigma}$$

where $\mu = .50n$ and $\sigma = .50\sqrt{n}$.

Step 4: Formulate the Decision Rule.   Referring to Appendix D, Areas under the Normal Curve, for a two-tailed test (because H_1, states that $\pi \neq .50$) and the .05 significance level, the critical values are $+1.96$ and -1.96. Recall from Chapter 9 that for a two-tailed test we split the rejection region in half and place one half in each tail. That is, $\alpha/2 = .05/2 = .025$. Continuing, $.5000 - .4750$. Searching for .4750 in the body of the table and reading the z value in the left margin gives 1.96, the critical value. Therefore, do not reject H_0 if the computed z value is between $+1.96$ and -1.96. Otherwise, reject H_0 and accept H_1.

Step 5: Compute z, Compare the Computed Value with the Critical Value, and Make a Decision Regarding H_0.   Preference for cola A was given a "+" sign and preference for B a "−" sign. Out of the 64 in the sample, 42 preferred the sweet cola, A. Therefore, there are 42 pluses. Since 42 is *more than* $n/2 = 64/2 = 32$, we use formula (15–2) for z:

$$z = \frac{(X - .50) - .50n}{.50\sqrt{n}} = \frac{(42 - .50) - .50(64)}{.50\sqrt{64}} = 2.38$$

The computed z of 2.38 is beyond the critical value of 1.96. Therefore, the null hypothesis of no difference is rejected at the .05 significance level. We conclude there is a difference in consumer preference. That is, we conclude consumers prefer one cola over another.

The p-value is the probability of finding a z value larger than 2.38 or smaller than -2.38. From Appendix D, the probability of finding a z value greater than 2.38 is $.5000 - .4913 = .0087$. Thus, the two-tailed p-value is .0174. So the probability that the null hypothesis is true is less than 2 percent.

SELF-REVIEW 15–2

The Human Resources Department in a large automobile assembly plant began blood pressure screening and education for the 100 employees in the Paint Department the first of the year. As a follow-up, in July the same 100 employees were again screened for blood pressure and 80 showed a reduction. Can we conclude the screening was effective in reducing blood pressure readings?

(a)   State the null hypothesis and the alternate hypothesis.
(b)   What is the decision rule for a significance level of .05?
(c)   Compute the value of the test statistic.
(d)   What is your decision regarding the null hypothesis?
(e)   Interpret your decision.

▌ Exercises

5. A sample of 45 overweight men participated in an exercise program. A total of 32 had lost weight at the end of the program. At the .05 significance level, can we conclude the program is effective?
    a. State the null hypothesis and the alternate hypothesis.
    b. State the decision rule.
    c. Compute the value of the test statistic.
    d. What is your decision regarding the null hypothesis?

6. A sample of 60 college students was given a special training program designed to improve their study and time management skills. One month after completing the course the students were contacted and asked whether the skills learned in the program were effective. A total of 42 responded yes. At the .05 significance level, can we conclude the program is effective?
    a. State the null hypothesis and the alternate hypothesis.
    b. State the decision rule.
    c. Compute the value of the test statistic.
    d. What is your decision regarding the null hypothesis?

7. Pierre's Restaurant announced that on Thursday night the menu would consist of unusual gourmet items, such as squid, rabbit, snails from Scotland, and dandelion greens. As part of a larger survey, a sample of 81 regular customers was asked whether they preferred the regular menu or the gourmet menu. Forty-three preferred the gourmet menu. Using the sign test and the .02 level, test whether the customers liked the gourmet menu better than the regular menu. Justify your conclusion.

8. Assembly workers at Computer Associates assemble just one or two subassemblies and insert them in a frame. The executives at CA think that the employees would have more pride in their work if they assembled all of the subassemblies and tested the complete computer. A sample of 25 employees was selected to experiment with the idea. The null hypothesis is that the employees have no preference. After a training program, each was asked his or her preference. Twenty liked assembling the entire unit and testing it. At the .05 level, use the sign test to arrive at a decision regarding employee preference. Explain the steps you used to arrive at your decision.

Testing a Hypothesis about a Median

Most of the tests of hypothesis we have conducted so far involved the population mean or a proportion. The sign test is one of the few tests that can be used to test the value of a median. Recall from Chapter 3 that the median is the value above which half of the observations lie and below which the other half lie. For hourly wages of $7, $9, $11, and $18, the median is $10. Half of the wages are above $10 an hour and the other half below $10.

To conduct a test of hypothesis, a value above the median is assigned a plus sign, and a value below the median is assigned a minus sign. If a value is the same as the median, it is dropped from further analysis. The procedure is identical to that followed in the small-sample and large-sample cases just discussed.

Example

The district manager of Superior Grocers hypothesized that the median weekly grocery bill of the customers in his region is $123. He wants to investigate his hypothesis. The null hypothesis to be tested is H_0: Median = $123. If the population median weekly grocery bill is $123, half of the bills will be less than $123 and the other half will be more than $123. Suppose, however, that the manager randomly selected 102 grocery bills and found that 50 were over the median and 52 were under the median of $123. Is that sufficient evidence to reject the null hypothesis that the median is $123, or could this slight imbalance be due to sampling error? What if the sample survey revealed that 55 grocery bills were greater than the median and 47 were less than the median? Should we reject H_0?

When the district manager did randomly select 102 grocery bills, he found that 60 of them were above his hypothesized median of $123, 40 were below $123, and 2 were exactly $123. Based on these sample results, should we conclude that the median weekly grocery bill is not $123? That is, is this imbalance (60 above, 40 below the median) so great that we need to reject H_0 and accept H_1, which states that the median is not equal to $123? We will use the .10 significance level.

Solution The null and alternate hypotheses are:

H_0: Median = $123.

H_1: Median ≠ $123.

This is a two-tailed test because the alternate hypothesis does not state a direction (either less than or more than $123.00).

The critical values are ±1.65, found by $\alpha/2 = .10/2 = .05$. Then $.5000 - .05 = .4500$. Find .4500 in Appendix D and read the critical value of z. It is 1.65.

As noted previously, the district manager selected 102 grocery bills. Because 2 were exactly $123 (the hypothesized median), they are omitted. Thus, $102 - 2 = 100$, which is n. Substituting 100 for n and solving for the mean, μ, and the standard deviation, σ:

$$\mu = .50n = .50(100) = 50$$
$$\sigma = .50\sqrt{n} = .50\sqrt{100} = 5$$

We use formula (15–2) for z because 60 is greater than $n/2$ (100/2 = 50).

$$z = \frac{(X - .50) - .50n}{.50\sqrt{n}} = \frac{(60 - .50) - .50(100)}{.50\sqrt{100}} = 1.90$$

Because 1.90 is in the area beyond 1.65, the null hypothesis is rejected at the .10 significance level. The median grocery weekly bill is not $123.

SELF-REVIEW 15–3

The owner of the local Churchill's Super Markets wants to compare the results of the district manager's study to the local experience. A sample of 64 local Churchill's customers showed that 42 spent more than $123 on groceries. At the .05 significance level, can the owner of the local Churchill's conclude that the median amount spent per week is more than $123?

(a) State the null hypothesis and the alternate hypothesis.
(b) What is the decision rule?
(c) Compute the value of the test statistic.
(d) What is your decision regarding the null hypothesis?
(e) Interpret your decision.

▌ Exercises

9. It is claimed that the median annual income of computer programmers with at least five years of experience is $40,000. The claim is being challenged by the programmers, who say the median annual income is greater than $40,000. To resolve the controversy, a random sample

of 205 programmers was selected. It was found that 170 had incomes above $40,000, 5 earned exactly $40,000, and the remaining number had incomes under $40,000.
   a.   State the null and alternate hypotheses.
   b.   Using the .05 level, state the decision rule in words.
   c.   Do the necessary computations, and write out your conclusions.
10.   Central Airlines claims that the median price of a round-trip ticket to Jackson Hole, Wyoming, is $503. This claim is being challenged by the Association of Travel Agents, who believe the median price is less than $503. To resolve the issue, a random sample of 400 round-trip tickets was selected. Of these, 160 tickets were below $503. None of the tickets were exactly $503. Let $\alpha = .05$.
   a.   State the null and alternate hypotheses.
   b.   Reach a decision regarding the controversy.

▌ Wilcoxon Signed-Rank Test

The paired *t* test, described in Chapter 10, had two requirements. First, the samples must be dependent. Recall that dependent samples are characterized by a measurement, some type of intervention, and then another measurement. For example, a large company began a "wellness" program at the start of the year. Suppose 20 workers enrolled in the weight reduction portion of the program. To begin, all participants were weighed. Next they dieted, did the exercise, and so forth in an attempt to lose weight. At the end of the program, which lasted 6 months, all participants were weighed again. The difference in their weight between the start and the end of the program is the variable of interest. Note that there is a measurement, an intervention, and then another measurement.

The second requirement for the paired *t* test is that the distribution of the differences follow a normal distribution. In the company wellness example in the previous paragraph, this would require that the differences in the weights of the 20 participants follow the normal distribution. In that case this assumption is reasonable. However, there are instances where we want to study the differences between dependent observations where we cannot assume that the distribution of the differences approximates a normal distribution. Frequently we encounter a problem with the normality assumption when the level of measurement in the samples is ordinal, rather than interval or ratio. For example, suppose there are 10 surgical patients on 3 East today. The nursing supervisor asks Nurse Benner and Nurse Jurris to rate each of the 10 patients on a scale of 1 to 10, based on the difficulty of patient care. The distribution of the differences probably would not approximate the normal distribution, and, therefore, the paired *t* test would not be appropriate.

In 1945, Frank Wilcoxon developed a nonparametric test, based on the differences in dependent samples, where the normality assumption is not required. This test is called the **Wilcoxon signed-rank test.** The following example details its application.

Example   Fricker's is a family restaurant located primarily in the southeastern part of the United States. They offer a full dinner menu, but their specialty is chicken. Recently, Bernie Frick, the owner and founder, developed a new spicy flavor for the batter in which the chicken is cooked. Before replacing the current flavor, he wants to conduct some tests to be sure that patrons will like the spicy flavor better.

To begin, Bernie selects a random sample of 15 people. He is careful that this sample is representative of his customers. Each member of the sample is given a small sample of the current chicken and asked to rate its overall taste on a scale of 1 to 20. A value near 20 indicates the participant liked the flavor, whereas a score near 0 indicates they did not like the flavor. Next, the same 15 participants are given a sample of the new chicken with the spicier flavor and again asked to rate its taste on a scale of 1 to 20. The results are reported below. Is it reasonable to conclude that the spicy flavor is preferred? Use the .05 significance level.

Participant	Spicy Flavor Score	Current Flavor Score	Participant	Spicy Flavor Score	Current Flavor Score
Arquette	14	12	Garcia	19	10
Jones	8	16	Sundar	18	10
Fish	6	2	Miller	16	13
Wagner	18	4	Peterson	18	2
Badenhop	20	12	Boggart	4	13
Hall	16	16	Hein	7	14
Fowler	14	5	Whitten	16	4
Virost	6	16			

Solution

The samples are dependent or related. That is, the participants are asked to rate both flavors of chicken. Thus, if we compute the difference between the rating for the spicy flavor and the current flavor, the resulting value shows the amount the participants favor one flavor over the other. If we choose to subtract the current flavor score from the spicy flavor score, a positive result is the "amount" the participant favors the spicy flavor. Negative difference scores indicate the participant favored the current flavor. Because of the somewhat subjective nature of the scores, we are not sure the distribution of the differences follows the normal distribution. We decide to use the nonparametric Wilcoxon signed-rank test.

As usual, we will use the five-step hypothesis-testing procedure. The null hypothesis is that there is no difference in the rating of the chicken flavors by the participants. That is, as many participants in the study rated the spicy flavor higher as rated the regular flavor higher. The alternate hypothesis is that the ratings are higher for the spicy flavor. More formally:

H_0: There is no difference in the ratings of the two flavors.

H_1: The spicy ratings are higher.

This is a one-tailed test. Why? Because Bernie Frick, the owner of Fricker's, will want to change his chicken flavor only if the sample participants show that the population of customers like the new flavor better. The significance level is .05, as stated in the problem above.

The steps to conduct the Wilcoxon signed-rank test are as follows.

1. Compute the difference between the spicy flavor score and the current flavor score for each participant. These differences are shown in column 4 of Table 15–3.
2. Only the positive and negative differences are considered further. That is, if the difference in flavor scores is 0, that participant is dropped from the analysis and the number in the sample reduced. From Table 15–3, Hall, the sixth participant, scored both the spicy and the current flavor a 16. Hence, Hall is dropped from the study and the sample size reduced from 15 to 14.
3. Determine the absolute differences for the values computed in column 4. Recall that in an absolute difference we ignore the sign of the difference. The absolute differences are shown in column 5.
4. Next, rank the absolute differences from smallest to largest. Arquette, the first participant scored the spicy chicken a 14 and the current a 12. The difference

Table 15–3   Flavor Rating for Current and Spicy Flavors

(1) Participant	(2) Spicy Score	(3) Current Score	(4) Difference in Score	(5) Absolute Difference	(6) Rank	(7) Signed Rank R^+	R^-
Arquette	14	12	2	2	1	1	
Jones	8	16	−8	8	6		6
Fish	6	2	4	4	3	3	
Wagner	18	4	14	14	13	13	
Badenhop	20	12	8	8	6	6	
Hall	16	16	*	*	*	*	
Fowler	14	5	9	9	9	9	
Virost	6	16	−10	10	11		11
Garcia	19	10	9	9	9	9	
Sundar	18	10	8	8	6	6	
Miller	16	13	3	3	2	2	
Peterson	18	2	16	16	14	14	
Boggart	4	13	−9	9	9		9
Hein	7	14	−7	7	4		4
Whitten	16	4	12	12	12	12	
Total						75	30

of 2 in the two scores is the smallest absolute difference, so it is given a ranking of 1. The next largest difference is 3, given by Miller, so it is given a rank of 2. The other differences are ranked in a similar manner. There are three participants who rated the difference in the flavor as 8. That is, Jones, Badenhop, and Sundar each had a difference of 8 between their rating of the spicy flavor and the current flavor. To resolve this problem, we average the ranks involved and report the average rank for each. This situation involves the ranks 5, 6, and 7, so all three participants are assigned the rank of 6. The same situation occurs for those participants with a difference of 9. The ranks involved are 8, 9, and 10, so three participants are assigned a rank of 9.

5.   Each assigned rank in column 6 is then given the same sign as the original difference, and the results are reported in column 7. For example, the second participant has a difference score of −8 and a rank of 6. This value is located in the R^- section of column 7.

6.   The R^+ and the R^- columns are totaled. The sum of the positive ranks is 75 and the sum of the negative ranks is 30. The smaller of the two rank sums is used as the test statistic and referred to as T.

The critical values for the Wilcoxon signed-rank test are located in Appendix H. A portion of that table is repeated at the top of the following page. The α row is used for one-tailed tests and the 2α row for two-tailed tests. In this case we want to show that customers like the spicy taste better, which is a one-tailed test, so we select the α row. We chose the .05 significance level, so move to the right to the column headed .05. Go down that column to the row where n is 14. (Recall that one person in the study rated the chicken flavors the same and was dropped from the study, making the sample size 14.) The value at the intersection is 25, so the critical value is 25. The decision rule is to reject the null hypothesis if the *smaller* of the rank sums is 25 or less. The value obtained from Appendix H is the *largest value in the rejection region*. In this case the smaller rank sum is 30, so the decision is not to reject the null hypothesis. We cannot conclude there is a difference in the flavor ratings between the current and the spicy. Mr. Frick has not shown that customers prefer the new flavor.

n	2 α .15 / α .075	.10 / .050	.05 / .025	.04 / .020	.03 / .015	.02 / .010	.01 / .005
4	0						
5	1	0					
6	2	2	0	0			
7	4	3	2	1	0	0	
8	7	5	3	3	2	1	0
9	9	8	5	5	4	3	1
10	12	10	8	7	6	5	3
11	16	13	10	9	8	7	5
12	19	17	13	12	11	9	7
13	24	21	17	16	14	12	9
14	28	25	21	19	18	15	12
15	33	30	25	23	21	19	15
16	39	35	29	28	26	23	19
17	45	41	34	33	30	27	23

SELF-REVIEW 15–4

A record of the production for each machine operator was kept over a period of time. Certain changes in the production procedure were suggested, and 11 operators were picked as an experimental test group to determine whether the new procedures were worthwhile. Their production rates before and after the new procedures were established are as follows:

Operator	Production Before	Production After	Operator	Production Before	Production After
S. M.	17	18	U. Z.	10	22
D. J.	21	23	Y. U.	20	19
M. D.	25	22	U. T.	17	20
B. B.	15	25	Y. H.	24	30
M. F.	10	28	Y. Y.	23	26
A. A.	16	16			

(a) How many usable pairs are there? That is, what is n?
(b) Using the Wilcoxon signed-rank test, determine whether the new procedures actually increased production. Use the .05 level and a one-tailed test.

❙ Exercises

11. A random sample of seven young urban professional couples (yuppies) who own their homes is selected. The size of their home (square feet) is compared with that of their parents. At the .05 significance level, can we conclude that the yuppies live in larger homes?

Couple Name	Professional	Parent	Couple Name	Professional	Parent
Gordon	1,725	1,175	Kuhlman	1,290	1,360
Sharkey	1,310	1,120	Welch	1,880	1,750
Uselding	1,670	1,420	Anderson	1,530	1,440
Bell	1,520	1,640			

12. One of the major car manufacturers is studying the effect of regular versus high-octane gasoline in its economy cars. Ten executives are selected and asked to maintain records on the number of miles traveled per gallon of gas. The results are:

	Miles per Gallon				Miles per Gallon	
Executive	Regular	High-Octane			Regular	High-Octane
Bowers	25	28		Rau	38	40
Demars	33	31		Greolke	29	29
Grasser	31	35		Burns	42	37
DeToto	45	44		Snow	41	44
Kleg	42	47		Lawless	30	44

At the .05 significance level, is there a difference in the number of miles traveled per gallon between regular and high-octane gasoline?

13. A new assembly-line procedure has been suggested by Mr. Mump. To test whether the new procedure is superior to the old procedure, a sample group of 15 men was selected at random. First their production under the old system was determined. Then the new Mump procedure was introduced. After an appropriate break-in period, their production was measured again. The results were:

	Production				Production	
Employee	Old System	Mump Method		Employee	Old System	Mump Method
A	60	64		I	87	84
B	40	52		J	80	80
C	59	58		K	56	57
D	30	37		L	21	21
E	70	71		M	99	108
F	78	83		N	50	56
G	43	46		O	56	62
H	40	52				

At the .05 significance level can we conclude the production is greater using the Mump method?
   a. State the null and alternate hypotheses.
   b. State the decision rule.
   c. Arrive at a decision regarding the null hypothesis.

14. It has been suggested that daily production of a subassembly would be increased if better portable lighting were installed and background music and free coffee and doughnuts were provided during the day. Management agreed to try the scheme for a limited time. The numbers of subassemblies produced per week by a small test group of employees are as follows.

Employee	Past Production Record	Production after Installing Lighting, Music, etc.		Employee	Past Production Record	Production after Installing Lighting, Music, etc.
JD	23	33		WWJ	21	25
SB	26	26		OP	25	22
MD	24	30		CD	21	23
RCF	17	25		PA	16	17
MF	20	19		RRT	20	15
UHH	24	22		AT	17	9
IB	30	29		QQ	23	30

Using the Wilcoxon signed-rank test, determine whether the suggested changes are worthwhile.

a. State the null hypothesis.
b. You decide on the alternate hypothesis.
c. You decide on the level of significance.
d. State the decision rule.
e. Compute T and arrive at a decision.

▌ Wilcoxon Rank-Sum Test

One test specifically designed to determine whether two independent samples came from equal populations is the **Wilcoxon rank-sum test.** This test is an alternative to the two-sample t test described in Chapter 10. Recall the t test requires the two populations be normally distributed and have equal population variances. These conditions are not required for the Wilcoxon rank-sum test.

Test using independent samples   The Wilcoxon rank-sum test is based on the average of ranks. The data are ranked as if the observations were part of a single sample. If the null hypothesis is true, then the ranks will be about evenly distributed between the two samples, and the average of the ranks for the two samples will be about the same. That is, the low, medium, and high ranks should be about equally divided between the two samples. If the alternate hypothesis is true, one of the samples will have more of the lower ranks and, thus, a smaller rank total. The other sample will have more of the higher ranks and, therefore, a larger total. If each of the samples contains *at least eight observations,* the standard normal distribution is used as the test statistic. The formula is:

WILCOXON RANK-SUM TEST	$$z = \dfrac{W - \dfrac{n_1(n_1 + n_2 + 1)}{2}}{\sqrt{\dfrac{n_1 n_2(n_1 + n_2 + 1)}{12}}}$$	**[15–4]**

where:

n_1 is the number of observations from the first population.
n_2 is the number of observations from the second population.
W is the sum of the ranks from the first population.

Example

Mr. Dan Thompson, the president of CEO Airlines, recently noted an increase in the number of no-shows for flights out of Atlanta. He is particularly interested in determining whether there are more no-shows for flights that originate from Atlanta compared with flights leaving Chicago. A sample of nine flights from Atlanta and eight from Chicago are reported in Table 15–4. At the .05 significance level, can we conclude that there are more no-shows for the flights originating in Atlanta?

Table 15–4 Number of No-Shows for Scheduled Flights

Atlanta	Chicago	Atlanta	Chicago
11	13	20	9
15	14	24	17
10	10	22	21
18	8	25	
11	16		

Solution   If we were to assume the populations of no-shows were normally distributed and had equal variances, the two-sample *t* test, discussed in Chapter 10, would be appropriate. In this case Mr. Thompson believes these two conditions cannot be met. Therefore, a nonparametric test, the Wilcoxon rank-sum test, is appropriate.

If the number of no-shows is the same for Atlanta and Chicago, then we expect the means of the two ranks to be about the same. If the number of no-shows is not the same, we expect the two sums of ranks to be quite different.

Mr. Thompson believes there are more no-shows for Atlanta flights. Thus, a one-tailed test is appropriate, with the rejection region located in the upper tail. The null and alternate hypotheses are:

H_0: The distribution of no-shows is the same for Atlanta and Chicago.

H_1: The distribution of no-shows is larger for Atlanta than for Chicago.

The test statistic follows the standard normal distribution. At the .05 significance level, we find from Appendix D the critical value of *z* is 1.65. The null hypothesis is rejected if the computed value of *z* is greater than 1.65.

The alternate hypothesis is that there are more no-shows in Atlanta, which means that distribution is larger and is located to the right of the Chicago distribution. The value of *W* is calculated for the Atlanta group and is found to be 96.5, which is the sum of the ranks for the no-shows for the Atlanta flights. (See Table 15–5.) The details of rank assignment are shown in Table 15–5. We rank the observations from *both* samples as if they were a single group. The Chicago flight with only 8 no-shows had the fewest, so it is assigned a rank of 1. The Chicago flight with 9 no-shows is ranked 2, and so on. The Atlanta flight with 25 no-shows is the highest, so it is assigned the largest rank, 17. There are also two instances of tied ranks. There are an Atlanta and a Chicago flight that each had 10 no-shows and two Atlanta flights with 11 no-shows. How do we handle these ties? The solution is to average the ranks involved and assign the average rank to both flights. In the case involving 10 no-shows the ranks involved are 3 and 4. The mean of these ranks is 3.5, so a rank of 3.5 is assigned to both the Atlanta and the Chicago flights with 10 no-shows.

Table 15–5   Ranked Number of No-Shows for Scheduled Flights

Atlanta		Chicago	
No-Shows	Rank	No-Shows	Rank
11	5.5	13	7
15	9	14	8
10	3.5	10	3.5
18	12	8	1
11	5.5	16	10
20	13	9	2
24	16	17	11
22	15	21	14
25	17		
	96.5		56.5

Note from Table 15–5 there are nine flights originating in Atlanta and eight in Chicago, so $n_1 = 9$ and $n_2 = 8$. Computing *z* from formula (15–4) gives:

$$z = \frac{W - \dfrac{n_1(n_1 + n_2 + 1)}{2}}{\sqrt{\dfrac{n_1 n_2(n_1 + n_2 + 1)}{12}}} = \frac{96.5 - \dfrac{9(9 + 8 + 1)}{2}}{\sqrt{\dfrac{9(8)(9 + 8 + 1)}{12}}} = 1.49$$

Because the computed z value (1.49) is less than 1.65, the null hypothesis is not rejected. The evidence does not show a difference in the typical number of no-shows. That is, it appears that the number of no-shows is the same in Atlanta as in Chicago. The p-value is .0681, found by determining the area to the right of 1.49 $(.5000 - .4319)$.

In using the Wilcoxon rank-sum test, you may number the two populations in either order. However, once you have made a choice, W must be the sum of the ranks identified as population 1. If, in the no-show example, the population of Chicago was identified as number 1, the direction of the alternate hypothesis would be changed, but the *absolute value of z* remains the same.

H_0: The distribution of no-shows is the same for Chicago and Atlanta.

H_1: The distribution of no-shows is smaller for Chicago than for Atlanta.

The computed value of z is -1.49, found by:

$$z = \frac{W - \dfrac{n_1(n_1 + n_2 + 1)}{2}}{\sqrt{\dfrac{n_1 n_2(n_1 + n_2 + 1)}{12}}} = \frac{56.5 - \dfrac{8(8 + 9 + 1)}{2}}{\sqrt{\dfrac{8(9)(8 + 9 + 1)}{12}}} = -1.49$$

SELF-REVIEW 15–5

The research director for a golf ball manufacturer wants to know whether there is a difference in the distribution of the distances traveled by two of the company's golf balls. Eight of their Dino brand and eight of their Maxi brand balls were hit by an automatic driver. The distances (in yards) were as follows:

Dino: 252, 263, 279, 273, 271, 265, 257, 280

Maxi: 262, 242, 256, 260, 258, 243, 239, 265

Assume the distributions are not normally distributed. At the .05 significance level, is there a difference between the two distributions?

▌ Exercises

15. The following observations were selected from populations that were not necessarily normally distributed. Use the .05 significance level, a two-tailed test, and the Wilcoxon rank-sum test to determine whether there is a difference between the two populations.

    Population A: 38, 45, 56, 57, 61, 69, 70, 79

    Population B: 26, 31, 35, 42, 51, 52, 57, 62

16. The following observations were selected from populations that are not necessarily normally distributed. Use the .05 significance level, a two-tailed test, and the Wilcoxon rank-sum test to determine whether there is a difference between the two populations.

    Population A: 12, 14, 15, 19, 23, 29, 33, 40, 51

    Population B: 13, 16, 19, 21, 22, 33, 35, 43

17. Two groups of professional musicians—rock and country-western—are being studied. One facet of the study involves the age of those in the two groups. Assume the populations of

ages are not normally distributed. A sample of 10 rock and 12 country-western musicians revealed the following ages, in years.

Rock: 28, 16, 42, 29, 31, 22, 50, 42, 23, 25

Country-western: 26, 42, 65, 38, 29, 32, 59, 42, 27, 41, 46, 18

At the .05 significance level, can we conclude the country-western singers are older?

18. One group was taught an assembly procedure using a standard sequence of steps and another group was taught a new experimental technique. The time to complete the assembly, in seconds, for a sample of workers is shown below.

Current method: 41, 36, 42, 39, 36, 48, 49, 38

Experimental: 21, 27, 36, 20, 19, 21, 39, 24, 22

At the .05 significance level, can we conclude the experimental method is faster? Assume that the distribution of assembly lines is not normal.

▌ Kruskal-Wallis Test: Analysis of Variance by Ranks

Kruskal-Wallis test less restrictive than ANOVA

The analysis of variance (ANOVA) procedure discussed in Chapter 11 was concerned with whether several population means are equal. The data were interval or ratio level, and it was assumed the populations were normally distributed and the standard deviations of those populations were equal. What if the data are ordinal scale and/or the populations are not normal? W. H. Kruskal and W. A. Wallis reported a nonparametric test in 1952 requiring only ordinal-level (ranked) data. No assumptions about the shape of the populations are required by that test. The test is referred to as the **Kruskal-Wallis one-way analysis of variance by ranks.**

For the Kruskal-Wallis test to be applied, the samples selected from the populations must be *independent.* For example, if samples from three groups — executives, staff, and supervisors — are to be selected and interviewed, the responses of one group (say, the executives) must in no way influence the responses of the others.

To compute the Kruskal-Wallis test statistic, (1) all the samples are combined, (2) the combined values are ordered from low to high, and (3) the ordered values are *replaced by ranks, starting with 1 for the smallest value.* An example will clarify the procedure.

Example

A management seminar consisting of a large number of executives from manufacturing, finance, and trade is to be conducted. Before scheduling the seminar sessions, the seminar leader is interested in whether the three groups are equally knowledgeable about management principles. Plans are to take samples of the executives in manufacturing, in finance, and in trade and to administer a test to each executive. If there is no difference in the scores for the three distributions, the seminar leader will conduct just one session. However, if there is a difference in the scores, separate sessions will be given.

We will use the Kruskal-Wallis test instead of ANOVA because the seminar leader is unwilling to assume that (1) the populations of management scores are normally distributed or (2) the population variances are the same.

Solution

The usual first step in hypothesis testing is to state the null and the alternate hypotheses.

H_0: The distributions of the management scores for the populations of executives in manufacturing, finance, and trade are equal.

H_1: The distributions are not all equal.

The seminar leader selected the .05 level of risk.

The test statistic used for the Kruskal-Wallis test is designated H. Its formula is:

$$
\begin{array}{l}
\text{KRUSKAL-} \\
\text{WALLIS} \\
\text{TEST}
\end{array}
\quad
H = \frac{12}{n(n+1)} \left[\frac{(\Sigma R_1)^2}{n_1} + \frac{(\Sigma R_2)^2}{n_2} + \cdots + \frac{(\Sigma R_k)^2}{n_k} \right] - 3(n+1)
\quad \textbf{[15–5]}
$$

with $k - 1$ degrees of freedom (k is the number of populations), where:

$\Sigma R_1, \Sigma R_2, \ldots, \Sigma R_k$ are the sums of the ranks of samples 1, 2, . . . , k, respectively.

$n_1, n_2, \ldots, n_k$ are the sizes of samples 1, 2, . . . , k, respectively.

n is the combined number of observations for all samples.

Chi-square used if every sample is at least 5

The distribution of the sample H statistic is very close to the chi-square distribution with $k - 1$ degrees of freedom *if every sample size is at least 5*. Therefore, we will use chi-square in formulating the decision rule. In this problem there are three populations—a population of executives in manufacturing, another for executives in finance, and a third population of trade executives. Thus, there are $k - 1$, or $3 - 1 = 2$ degrees of freedom. Refer to the chi-square table of critical values in Appendix I. The critical value for 2 degrees of freedom and the .05 level of risk is 5.991. Do not reject H_0 if the computed value of the test statistic H is less than or equal to 5.991. Reject H_0 if the computed value of H is greater than 5.991, and accept H_1.

The next step is to select samples from the three populations. A sample of seven manufacturing, eight finance, and six trade executives was selected. Their scores on the test are recorded in Table 15–6.

Table 15–6   Management Test Scores for Manufacturing, Finance, and Trade Executives

Manufacturing Executives	Finance Executives	Trade Executives
56	103	42
39	87	38 ← tie for next lowest
48	51	89
38 ← tie for next lowest	95	75
73	68	35 ← lowest
50	42	61
62	107 ← highest score	
	89	

Considering the scores as a single population, the trade executive with a score of 35 is the lowest, so it is ranked 1. There are two scores of 38. To resolve this tie, each score is given a rank of 2.5, found by $(2 + 3)/2$. This process is continued for all scores. The highest score is 107, and that finance executive is given a rank of 21. The scores, the ranks, and the sum of the ranks for each of the three samples are given in Table 15–7.

Table 15–7   Scores, Ranks, and Sums of Ranks for Management Test Scores

Manufacturing Executives		Finance Executives		Trade Executives	
Scores	Ranks (R_1)	Scores	Ranks (R_2)	Scores	Ranks (R_3)
56	10.0	103	20.0	42	5.5
39	4.0	87	16.0	38	2.5
48	7.0	51	9.0	89	17.5
38	2.5	95	19.0	75	15.0
73	14.0	68	13.0	35	1.0
50	8.0	42	5.5	61	11.0
62	12.0	107	21.0		
		89	17.5		
	$\Sigma R_1 = 57.5$		$\Sigma R_2 = 121.0$		$\Sigma R_3 = 52.5$

Solving for H:

$$H = \frac{12}{n(n+1)}\left[\frac{(\Sigma R_1)^2}{n_1} + \frac{(\Sigma R_2)^2}{n_2} + \frac{(\Sigma R_3)^2}{n_3}\right] - 3(n+1)$$

$$= \frac{12}{21(21+1)}\left[\frac{57.5^2}{7} + \frac{121^2}{8} + \frac{52.5^2}{6}\right] - 3(21+1) = 5.736$$

Because the computed value of H (5.736) is not beyond 5.991, the null hypothesis is not rejected. There is no difference among the executives from manufacturing, finance, and trade with respect to their typical knowledge of management principles. From a practical standpoint, the seminar leader should consider offering only one session including executives from all areas.

The Kruskal-Wallis procedure is available on the MINITAB system. Output for the previous Example regarding the knowledge of management principles of executives from several industries follows. The computed value of H is 5.74 and the p-value reported on the output is .057. This agrees with our earlier calculations.

```
Kruskal-Wallis Test on Scores

Groups      N       Median      Ave Rank            Z
1           7       50.00            8.2        -1.45
2           8       88.00           15.1         2.39
3           6       51.50            8.7        -1.05
Overall    21                       11.0


H = 5.74    DF = 2     P = 0.057
H = 5.75    DF = 2     P = 0.057 (adjusted for ties)
```

Recall from Chapter 11 that for the analysis of variance technique to apply, we assume that: (1) the populations are normally distributed, (2) these populations have equal standard deviations, and (3) the samples are selected independently. If these assumptions are met, we use the F distribution as the test statistic. If these assumptions cannot be met, we apply the distribution-free test by Kruskal-Wallis. To highlight the similarities between the two approaches, we will solve the Example regarding executive knowledge of management principles using the ANOVA technique.

To begin, we state the null and the alternate hypotheses for the three groups.

H_0: $\mu_1 = \mu_2 = \mu_3$

H_1: The treatment means are not all the same.

Using the .05 significance level, with $k - 1 = 3 - 1 = 2$ degrees of freedom in the numerator and $n - k = 21 - 3 = 18$ degrees of freedom in the denominator, the critical value of F is 3.16. The decision rule is to reject the null hypothesis if the computed value of F is greater than 3.16. The output from the Excel system follows.

SUMMARY					
Groups	Count	Sum	Average	Variance	
Manufacturing	7	366	52.28571	156.9048	
Finance	8	642	80.25	577.3571	
Trade	6	340	56.66667	486.6667	
ANOVA					
Source of Variation	SS	df	MS	F	P-value
Between Groups	3394.976	2	1697.488	4.119971	0.033635
Within Groups	7416.262	18	412.0146		
Total	10811.24	20			

From the above output, the computed value of F is 4.12 (rounded) and the p-value is .034 (also rounded). Our decision is to reject the null hypothesis and accept the alternate hypothesis. Using this test we conclude that the treatment means are not the same. That is, the knowledge of management principles is different among the three executive groups.

We have contradictory conclusions on the same data. How can this happen? If we compare the results using p-values, the answers are similar. For the Kruskal-Wallis test the p-value was .057, which is only slightly more than the significance level of .05, but our decision was not to reject H_0. The p-value using ANOVA is .034, which is not far beyond the critical value into the rejection region. So to summarize, we just missed rejecting H_0 with the Kruskal-Wallis test, and we were just in the rejection region using ANOVA. The difference in the p-values is .023. Thus, the results are actually quite close in terms of the p-values.

SELF-REVIEW 15–6

The regional bank manager of Statewide Financial is interested in the turnover rate of personal checking accounts in four of the large branch banks. (Turnover rate is the speed at which the money in an account is deposited and withdrawn. An extremely active account may have a rate of 300; if only one or two checks were written, the rate could be about 30.) The turnover rates of the samples selected from the four branch banks are shown. Using the .01 level and the Kruskal-Wallis test, determine whether there is a difference in the turnover rates of the personal checking accounts among the four branches.

Englewood Branch	West Side Branch	Great Northern Branch	Sylvania Branch
208	91	302	99
307	62	103	116
199	86	319	189
142	91	340	103
91	80	180	100
296			131

▮ Exercises

19. Under what conditions should the Kruskal-Wallis test be used instead of analysis of variance?
20. Under what conditions should the Kruskal-Wallis test be used instead of the Wilcoxon rank-sum test?
21. The following sample data were obtained from three populations that were not necessarily normal.

Sample 1	Sample 2	Sample 3
50	48	39
54	49	41
59	49	44
59	52	47
65	56	51
	57	

    a. State the null hypothesis.
    b. Using the .05 level of risk, state the decision rule.
    c. Compute the value of the test statistic.
    d. What is your decision on the null hypothesis?
22. The following sample data were obtained from three populations where the variances were not equal, and you wish to compare the populations.

Sample 1	Sample 2	Sample 3
21	15	38
29	17	40
35	22	44
45	27	51
56	31	53
71		

a. State the null hypothesis.
b. Using the .01 level of risk, state the decision rule.
c. Compute the value of the test statistic.
d. What is your decision on the null hypothesis?

23. An outboard motor manufacturer has developed an epoxy painting process for corrosion protection on exhaust components. The engineers want to determine whether the distributions of the length of life for the paint are equal for three different conditions: salt water, fresh water without weeds, and fresh water with a heavy concentration of weeds. Accelerated-life tests were conducted in the laboratory, and the number of hours the paint lasted before peeling was recorded.

Salt Water	Fresh Water	Fresh Water with Weeds
167.3	160.6	182.7
189.6	177.6	165.4
177.2	185.3	172.9
169.4	168.6	169.2
180.3	176.6	174.7

Use the Kruskal-Wallis test and the .01 level to determine whether the lasting quality of the paint is the same for the three water conditions.

24. The National Turkey Association wants to experiment with three different food mixtures for very young turkeys. Since no experience exists regarding the three food mixtures, no assumptions can be made about the shape of the distribution of weights. The Kruskal-Wallis test must be used to test whether the turkeys are equal in weight after eating the food for a specified length of time. Five young turkeys were given food A, six were given food B, and five were given food C. Test at the .05 level whether the mean weights of the turkeys who ate food A, food B, and food C are equal.

Weight (in pounds)		
Food Mixture A	Food Mixture B	Food Mixture C
11.2	12.6	11.3
12.1	10.8	11.9
10.9	11.3	12.4
11.3	11.0	10.6
12.0	12.0	12.0
	10.7	

Rank-Order Correlation

In Chapter 12 we discussed r, the coefficient of correlation, which measures the association between two interval- or ratio-scaled variables. For example, the coefficient of correlation reports the association between the salary of executives and their years of experience, or the association between the number of miles a shipment had to travel and the number of days it took to arrive at its destination.

Charles Spearman, a British statistician, introduced a measure of correlation for ordinal-level data. This measure allows us to study the relationship between sets of ranked data. For example, two staff members in the Office of Research at the University of the Valley are asked to rank 10 faculty research proposals. We want to study the association between the ratings of the two staff members. That is, do the two staff members rate the same proposals as the most worthy and the least worthy of funding? Spearman's coefficient of rank correlation, denoted r_s, provides a measure of the association.

The coefficient of rank correlation is computed using the following formula.

SPEARMAN'S COEFFICIENT OF RANK CORRELATION	$r_s = 1 - \dfrac{6\Sigma d^2}{n(n^2 - 1)}$	[15–6]

where:

d is the difference between the ranks for each pair.

n is the number of paired observations.

Like the coefficient of correlation, the coefficient of rank correlation can assume any value from -1.00 up to 1.00. A value of -1.00 indicates perfect negative correlation and a value of 1.00 perfect positive correlation among the ranks. A rank correlation of 0 indicates that there is no strong association among the ranks. Rank correlations of $-.84$ and $.84$ indicate a strong association, but the former indicates an inverse relationship between the ranks and the latter a direct relationship.

Example

A composite rating is given by executives to each college graduate joining a plastics manufacturing firm. The executive rating is an expression of the future potential of the college graduate. The ratings represent, of course, the ordinal level of measurement. The recent college graduate then enters an in-plant training program and is given another composite rating based on tests, opinions of group leaders, training officers, and so on. The executive ratings and the in-plant training ratings are given in Table 15–8.

Table 15–8 Executive Ratings and In-Plant Training Ratings for a Selected Group of College Graduates

Graduate	Executive Rating, X	Training Rating, Y	Graduate	Executive Rating, X	Training Rating, Y
A	8	4	G	11	9
B	10	4	H	7	6
C	9	4	I	8	6
D	4	3	J	13	9
E	12	6	K	10	5
F	11	9	L	12	9

Determine the relationship between the ratings college graduates received from the executives before they entered the in-plant training program (X) and the ratings they received in the training program (Y). That is, what is the coefficient of rank correlation?

Solution

It was decided to rank the variables from low to high. The lowest rating given by the executives was a 4 to graduate D, so it was ranked 1. The next lowest was a 7 to graduate H, so it was ranked 2. There were two graduates rated 8. The tie is resolved by giving each a rank of 3.5, which is the average of ranks 3 and 4. The same procedure is followed when there are more than two ratings tied. For example, note that the lowest training rating is 3, and it is given a rank of 1. Then there are three ratings of 4. The average of the three tied ranks is 3, found by $(2 + 3 + 4)/3$. This is illustrated along with the necessary calculations for r_s in Table 15–9.

Table 15–9 Calculations Needed for r_s

Graduate	Executive Rating, X	Training Rating, Y	Rank Executive	Rank Training	Difference between Ranks, d	Difference Squared, d^2
A	8	4	3.5	3.0	0.5	0.25
B	10	4	6.5	3.0	3.5	12.25
C	9	4	5.0	3.0	2.0	4.00
D	4	3	1.0	1.0	0	0
E	12	6	10.5	7.0	3.5	12.25
F	11	9	8.5	10.5	−2.0	4.00
G	11	9	8.5	10.5	−2.0	4.00
H	7	6	2.0	7.0	−5.0	25.00
I	8	6	3.5	7.0	−3.5	12.25
J	13	9	12.0	10.5	1.5	2.25
K	10	5	6.5	5.0	1.5	2.25
L	12	9	10.5	10.5	0	0
					0.0	78.50

r_s is computed to be .726, found by:

$$r_s = 1 - \frac{6\Sigma d^2}{n(n^2 - 1)} = 1 - \frac{6(78.50)}{12(143)} = .726$$

The value of .726 indicates a strong positive association between the ratings of the executives and the ratings of the training staff. The graduate that received high ratings from the executives also received high ratings from the training staff.

Testing the Significance of r_s

Testing whether correlation in the population is zero In an earlier chapter we tested the significance of Pearson's r. For ranked data the question also arises whether the correlation in the population is actually zero. For instance, there were only 12 graduates sampled in the preceding example. In the solution to the example, the rank correlation coefficient of .726 indicates a rather strong relationship between the two sets of ranks. Is it possible that the correlation of .726 is due to chance and that the correlation in the population is really 0? We will now conduct a test of significance to answer that question.

"Large" samples— 10 or more For a sample of 10 or more, the significance of r_s is determined by computing t using the following formula. The sampling distribution of r_s follows the t distribution with $n - 2$ degrees of freedom.

HYPOTHESES TEST, RANK CORRELATION	$t = r_s \sqrt{\dfrac{n - 2}{1 - r_s^2}}$	**[15–7]**

The null and the alternate hypotheses are:

H_0: The rank correlation in the population is zero.

H_1: The rank correlation in the population is greater than zero.

The decision rule is to reject H_0 if the computed value of t is greater than 1.812 (from Appendix F, .05 significance level, one-tailed test, and 10 degrees of freedom, found by $n - 2 = 12 - 2 = 10$.

The computed value of t is 3.338:

$$t = r_s \sqrt{\frac{n-2}{1-r_s^2}} = .726 \sqrt{\frac{12-2}{1-(.726)^2}} = 3.338$$

H_0 is rejected because the computed t of 3.338 is greater than 1.812. H_1 is accepted. There is positive correlation between the ranks given by the executives and the ranks assigned during training.

SELF-REVIEW 15–7

A small sample of individuals revealed the following scores on an eye perception test (X) and a mechanical aptitude test (Y):

Subject	Eye Perception	Mechanical Aptitude	Subject	Eye Perception	Mechanical Aptitude
001	805	23	006	810	28
002	777	62	007	805	30
003	820	60	008	840	42
004	682	40	009	777	55
005	777	70	010	820	51

(a) Compute the coefficient of rank correlation.
(b) At the .05 significance level, can we conclude that the correlation in the population is different from 0?

Exercises

25. The ABC network television research staff wants to pretest a questionnaire to be mailed to several thousand viewers. One question involves the ranking of male and female senior citizens with respect to the popularity of certain prime-time programs. The composite rankings of a small group of senior citizens are:

Program	Ranking by Males	Ranking by Females
"Monday Night Football"	1	5
"Robin Crest"	4	1
"Simon and Sandor"	3	2
Evening News	2	4
"Our Hero"	5	3

a. Draw a scatter diagram. Let the rankings by males be X.
b. Compute Spearman's rank-order correlation coefficient. Interpret.

26. Far West University offers both day and evening classes in business administration. An extensive survey is to be conducted. One question involves sophomore students and how they perceive the prestige associated with certain careers. Each student was asked to rank the careers from 1 to 8, with 1 having the most prestige and 8 the least prestige. The composite results were:

Career	Ranking by Day Students	Ranking by Evening Students	Career	Ranking by Day Students	Ranking by Evening Students
Accountant	6	3	Statistician	1	7
Computer programmer	7	2	Marketing researcher	4	8
Branch bank manager	2	6	Stock analyst	3	5
Hospital administrator	5	4	Production manager	8	1

Find the coefficient correlation.

27. New representatives for the John Ford Metal and Wheel Company attend a brief training program before being assigned to a regional office. At the end of such a program, each representative was ranked with respect to future sales potential. At the end of the first sales year, their rankings were paired with their annual sales:

Representative	Annual Sales ($ thousands)	Ranking in Training Program	Representative	Annual Sales ($ thousands)	Ranking in Training Program
Kitchen	319	3	Arden	300	10
Bond	150	9	Crane	280	5
Gross	175	6	Arthur	200	2
Arbuckle	460	1	Keene	190	7
Greene	348	4	Knopf	300	8

a. Compute and interpret Spearman's rank correlation coefficient.
b. At the .05 significance level, can we conclude that there is a positive association among the ranks?

28. The University of Winston has five scholarships available for the women's basketball team. The coach provided two scouts with the names of 10 high school players with potential. Each scout attended at least three games and then ranked the players with respect to potential.

Player	Rank, by Scout Jean Cann	Rank, by Scout John Cannelli	Player	Rank, by Scout Jean Cann	Rank, by Scout John Cannelli
Cora Jean Seiple	7	5	Candy Jenkins	3	1
Bette Jones	2	4	Rita Rosinski	5	7
Jeannie Black	10	10	Anita Lockes	4	2
Norma Tidwell	1	3	Brenda Towne	8	9
Kathy Marchal	6	6	Denise Ober	9	8

a. Determine Spearman's rank correlation coefficient.
b. At the .05 significance level, can we conclude there is a positive association between the ranks?

▌ Chapter Outline

I. The sign test.
   A. No assumptions need be made about the shape of the two populations.
   B. It is based on paired or dependent samples.
   C. For small samples find the number of + or − signs and refer to the binomial distribution for the critical value.

D. For large samples (more than 10) use the standard normal distribution and the following formula.

$$z = \frac{(X \pm .50) - .50n}{.50\sqrt{n}}$$ **[15–2] [15–3]**

II. The median test is used to test a hypothesis about a population median.
   A. The normal approximation to the binomial distribution is used.
   B. The z distribution is used as the test statistic.
   C. The value of z is computed from the following formula, where X is the number of observations above or below the median.

$$z = \frac{(X \pm .50) - \mu}{\sigma}$$ **[15–1]**

III. The Wilcoxon signed-rank test.
   A. Data must be at least ordinal scale, and the samples must be dependent.
   B. The steps to conduct the test are:
      1. Rank absolute differences between the related observations.
      2. Recognize ties, and give ranks appropriate signs.
      3. Sum negative ranks and positive ranks.
      4. The smaller of the two sums is the computed T value.
      5. Refer to Appendix J for the critical value, and make a decision regarding H_0.

IV. The Wilcoxon rank-sum test is used to test whether two independent samples came from equal populations.
   A. No assumption about the shape of the population is required.
   B. To apply the test, the data must be at least ordinal scale.
   C. Each sample must contain at least eight observations.
   D. To determine the value of the test statistic W, all data values are ranked from low to high as if they were from a single population.
   E. The sum of ranks for each of the two samples is determined.
   F. W is used to compute z, where W is the sum of the ranks for population 1, from

$$z = \frac{W - \dfrac{n_1(n_1 + n_2 + 1)}{2}}{\sqrt{\dfrac{n_1 n_2 (n_1 + n_2 + 1)}{12}}}$$ **[15–4]**

   G. The z distribution is used as the test statistic.

V. The Kruskal-Wallis one-way ANOVA by ranks.
   A. No assumptions regarding the shape of the population are required.
   B. The samples must be independent and at least ordinal scale.
   C. It is used to test whether several populations are the same.
   D. The sample observations are ranked from smallest to largest as though they were a single group.
   E. The chi-square distribution can be used as the test statistic, provided there are at least 5 observations in each sample.
   G. The value of the test statistic is computed from the following:

$$H = \frac{12}{n(n + 1)}\left[\frac{(\Sigma R_1)^2}{n_1} + \frac{(\Sigma R_2)^2}{n_2} + \cdots + \frac{(\Sigma R_k)^2}{n_k}\right] - 3(n + 1)$$ **[15–5]**

VI. Spearman's coefficient of rank correlation is a measure of the association between two ordinal-scale variables.
   A. It can range from -1 up to 1.
      1. A value of 0 indicates there is no association between the variables.
      2. A value of -1 indicates perfect negative correlation, and 1 is perfect positive correlation.

B. The value of r_s is computed from the following formula.

$$r_s = 1 - \frac{6\Sigma d^2}{n(n^2 - 1)}$$ **[15–6]**

C. Provided the sample size is at least 10, we can conduct a test of hypothesis using the following formula:

$$t = r_s \sqrt{\frac{n - 2}{1 - r_s^2}}$$ **[15–7]**

1. The test statistic is the t distribution.
2. There are $n - 2$ degrees of freedom.

▌ Pronunciation Key

SYMBOL	MEANING	PRONUNCIATION
$(\Sigma R_1)^2$	Square of the total of the first column ranks	*Sigma R sub 1 squared*
r_s	Coefficient of rank correlation	*r sub s*

▌ Chapter Exercises

29. The program director at NBC is finalizing the prime-time schedule for next fall. She has decided to include a Western but is unsure which of two possibilities to select. She has a pilot called "The Loner" and another called "Cattleman." To help her make a final decision, a sample of 20 viewers from throughout the United States is asked to watch the two pilots and indicate which show they prefer. The results were that 12 liked "The Loner," 7 liked "Cattleman," and one had no preference. Is there a preference for one of the two shows? Use the .10 significance level.

30. Suppose Merrill Lynch wants to award a substantial contract for fine-line pens to be used nationally in their offices. Two suppliers, Bic and Pilot, have submitted the lowest bids. To determine the preference of office employees, brokers, and others, a personal preference test is to be conducted using a randomly selected sample of 20 employees. The .05 level of significance is to be used.
     a. If the alternate hypothesis states that Bic is preferred over Pilot, is the sign test to be conducted as a one-tailed or a two-tailed test? Explain.
     b. As each of the sample members told the researchers his or her preference, a "+" was recorded if it was Bic and a "−" if it was the Pilot fine-line pen. A count of the pluses revealed that 12 employees preferred Bic, 5 preferred Pilot, and 3 were undecided. What is n?
     c. What is the decision rule in words.
     d. What conclusion did you reach regarding pen preference? Explain.

31. Cornwall and Hudson, a large department store chain, wants to handle just one brand of high-quality compact disc player. The list has been narrowed to two brands: Sony and Pioneer. To help make a decision, a panel of 16 audio experts met. A passage using Sony components (labeled A) was played. Then the same passage was played using Pioneer components (labeled B). A "+" in the following table indicates an individual's preference for the Sony components, a "−" indicates preference for Pioneer, and a 0 signifies no preference.

							Expert								
1	2	3	4	5	6	7	8	9	10	11	12	13	14	15	16
+	−	+	−	+	+	−	0	−	+	−	+	+	−	+	−

Conduct a test of hypothesis at the .10 significance level to determine whether there is a difference in preference between the two brands.

32. The South Carolina Real Estate Association claims that the median rental for three-bedroom condominiums in the metropolitan area is more than $1,200 a month. To check this, a random sample of 149 units was selected. Of the 149, 5 rented for exactly $1,200 a month, and 75 rented for more than $1,200. At the .05 level, test the statement that the median rental is $1,200.
   a. State H_0 and H_1.
   b. Give the decision rule.
   c. Do the necessary calculations, and arrive at a decision.

33. The Citrus Council wants to find whether consumers prefer plain orange juice or juice with some orange pulp in it. A random sample of 212 consumers was selected. Each member of the sample tasted a small, unlabeled cup of one kind and then tasted the other kind. Twelve consumers said they had no preference, 40 preferred plain juice, and the remainder liked the juice with pulp better. Test at the .05 level that the preferences for plain juice and for orange juice with pulp are equal.

34. A research project involving community responsibility is to be conducted. The objective is to find whether women are more community conscious before marriage or after five years of marriage. A test to measure community consciousness was administered to a sample of women before marriage, and the same test was given to them five years after marriage. The test scores are:

Name	Before Marriage	After Marriage		Name	Before Marriage	After Marriage
Beth	110	114		Carol	186	196
Jean	157	159		Lisa	116	116
Sue	121	120		Sandy	100	140
Cathy	96	103		Petra	149	142
Mary	130	139				

Test at the .05 level. H_0 is: There is no difference in community consciousness before and after marriage. H_1 is: There is a difference.

35. Is there a difference in the annual divorce rates in predominantly rural counties among three geographic regions, namely, the Southwest, the Southeast, and the Northwest? Test at the .05 level. Annual divorce rates per 1,000 population for randomly selected counties are:

   Southwest: 5.9, 6.2, 7.9, 8.6, 4.6

   Southeast: 5.0, 6.4, 7.3, 6.2, 8.1, 5.1

   Northwest: 6.7, 6.2, 4.9, 8.0, 5.5

36. The idle times during the eight-hour day shift and the night shift are to be compared. A time study revealed the following numbers of minutes of idle time for eight-hour periods.

   Day shift: 92, 103, 116, 81, 89

   Night shift: 96, 114, 80, 82, 88, 91

   Is there a difference in the idle time between the two shifts? Test at the .05 level.

37. The mobility of executives in stock exchanges, in service, in heavy construction, and in air transportation is to be researched. Samples from each of these industries were selected, and

the number of times an executive moved during a 10-year period was converted to an index. An index of 0 would indicate no movement, whereas 100 would indicate almost constant movement from one location to another or one firm to another. The indexes for the four groups are:

Stock Exchange	Service	Heavy Construction	Air Transportation
4	3	62	30
17	12	40	38
8	40	81	46
20	17	96	40
16	31	76	21
	19		

We cannot assume that the indexes are normally distributed. Thus, we must use a nonparametric test. Using the .05 level, determine whether the four populations of mobility indexes are identical.

38. A series of questions on sports and world events was asked of a randomly selected group of male senior citizens. The results were translated into a "knowledge" score. The scores were:

Citizen	Sports	World Events	Citizen	Sports	World Events
J. C. McCarthy	47	49	L. M. Zaugg	87	75
A. N. Baker	12	10	J. B. Simon	59	86
B. B. Beebe	62	76	J. Goulden	40	61
L. D. Gaucet	81	92	A. A. Davis	87	18
C. A. Jones	90	86	A. M. Carbo	16	75
J. N. Narko	35	42	A. O. Smithy	50	51
A. F. Nissen	61	61	J. J. Pascal	60	61

a. Determine the degree of association between how the senior citizens ranked with respect to knowledge of sports and how they ranked on world events.
b. At the .05 significance level, is the rank correlation in the population greater than zero?

39. Early in the basketball season, 12 teams appeared to be outstanding. A panel of sportswriters and a panel of college basketball coaches were asked to rank the 12 teams. Their composite rankings were as follows.

Team	Coaches	Sportswriters	Team	Coaches	Sportswriters
Duke	1	1	Syracuse	7	10
UNLV	2	5	Georgetown	8	11
Indiana	3	4	Villanova	9	7
North Carolina	4	6	LSU	10	12
Louisville	5	3	St. Johns	11	8
Ohio State	6	2	Michigan	12	9

Determine the correlation between the rankings of the coaches and the sportswriters. At the .05 significance level, can we conclude it is different from zero?

40. Professor Bert Forman believes the students who complete his examinations in the shortest time receive the highest grades and those who take the longest to complete them receive the lowest grades. To verify his suspicion, he assigns a rank to the order of finish and then grades the examinations. The results are shown below:

Student	Order of Completion	Score (50 possible)	Student	Order of Completion	Score (50 possible)
Gromney	1	48	Smythe	7	39
Bates	2	48	Arquette	8	30
MacDonald	3	43	Govito	9	37
White	4	49	Gankowski	10	35
Harris	5	50	Bonfigilo	11	36
Cribb	6	47	Hineman	12	33

Convert the test scores to a rank and find the coefficient of rank correlation. At the .05 significance level, can Professor Forman conclude there is a positive association between the order of finish and the test scores?

www.Exercises.com

41. Is there a correlation between the starting position in an auto race and the order of finish? To investigate, use the results of the most recent Indianapolis 500 race. To obtain the result go to *http://www.indy 500.com/,* go to the section called Record book, select race results and box scores, then select the latest race. For example, select "1997—Luyendyk."
    a. Compute the coefficient of rank correlation between starting position and rank at the end of the race.
    b. Conduct a test of hypothesis to determine whether the rank correlation is greater than zero.
    c. Write a brief report summarizing the results.
42. A public policy group is studying the per pupil spending by the 50 states and the District of Columbia. Information on this variable can be found at the Web site: *http://lib.stat.cmu.edu/ DASL/Datafiles/teacherpaydat.html.* Assume the distribution of per pupil spending is not normally distributed. The states are grouped by regions. Conduct a test of hypothesis to determine whether there is a difference in the per pupil spending by region.

▌ Computer Data Exercises

43. Refer to Data Set 1, which reports information on homes sold in the Venice, Florida, area during the last year.
    a. Use an appropriate nonparametric test to determine whether there is a difference in the typical selling price of the homes in the several townships. Assume the selling prices are not normally distributed. Use the .05 significance level.
    b. Combine the homes with 6 or more bedrooms into one group and determine whether there is a difference in the typical selling prices of the homes. Use the .05 significance level and assume the distribution of selling prices is not normally distributed.
    c. Assume that the distribution of the distance from the center of the city is positively skewed. That is, the normality assumption is not reasonable. Compare the distribution of the homes that have a pool with those that do not have a pool. Can we conclude that there is a difference in the distributions? Use the .05 significance level.
44. Refer to Data Set 2, which reports information on the 1997 Major League Baseball season.
    a. Rank the teams by the number of wins and their total team salary. Compute the coefficient of rank correlation between the two variables. At the .01 significance level, can you conclude that it is greater than zero?
    b. Assume that the distributions of team salaries for the American League and the National League do not approximate the normal distribution. Conduct a test of hypothesis to see whether there is a difference in the two distributions.
45. Refer to Data Set 3, which reports information on the circulation of 48 popular magazines.
    a. Rank the 48 magazines in terms of circulation and the cost of color advertising. Compute the coefficient of rank correlation between the two variables. At the .05 significance level, can you conclude that it is not equal to zero?

   b. In Exercise 51 in Chapter 10 you created a variable that divided the male readership into two groups. The first group included those magazines whose readership was less than 50 percent men. The second group includes magazines for which 50 percent or more of the readership was men. Conduct a test of hypothesis to determine whether there is a difference in the magazine circulation of these two groups. Assume that the distribution of the circulation does not follow the normal distribution. Use the .05 significance level.

46. Refer to Data Set 4, which reports information on 94 school districts in northwest Ohio.
   a. Group the data by size of the school district: "large" is 3,000 or more students, "medium" is 1,000 up to 3,000 students, and "small" is less than 1,000 students. Now compare the distributions of amount spent on instruction for the three groups. At the .05 significance level, is there a difference? Assume that the distributions of amount spent on instruction do not follow the normal distribution.
   b. Use the same grouping regarding size and compare the distributions of salary. Use the .05 significance level.
   c. Compute the coefficient of rank correlation between the number of students in the district and mean salary of the teachers in the district. Can you conclude there is a significant positive association? Use the .01 significance level.

▮ Computer Commands

1. The MINITAB commands for the Kruskal-Wallis test on page 560 are:
   a. Enter all the scores in column 1 and the number corresponding to their group in column 2.
   b. Enter the command **Name c5 'Scores' and c6 'Groups'** and hit **Enter.**
   c. From the menu bar select **Stat,** then **Nonparametric,** then **Kruskal-Wallis,** and then hit **Enter.** The following dialog box will appear.
   d. Select the variable **Scores** as the response variable and **Groups** as the Factor variable and then click **OK.**

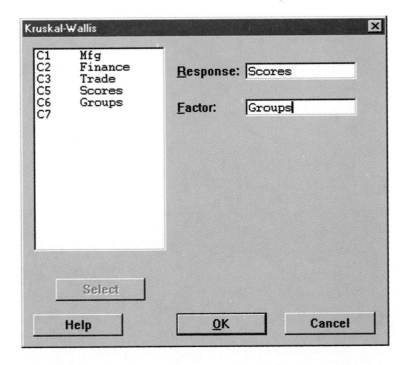

2. The Excel commands for the one-way ANOVA on page 561 are:
    a. In the first row, columns A, B, and C, enter the names of the variables: *Manufacturing, Finance,* and *Trade.* Enter the data in the respective columns.
    b. Select **Tools, Data Analysis,** and **ANOVA: Single Factor** and then click **OK.**
    c. In the dialog box the **Input Range** is a1:c9, select **Labels in First Row,** and enter **B12** as the **Output Range,** then click **OK.**

Anova: Single Factor   ? ✕

Input

Input Range: $A$1:$C$9

Grouped By: ⦿ Columns
                    ◯ Rows

☑ Labels in First Row

Alpha: 0.05

Output options

⦿ Output Range: b12
◯ New Worksheet Ply:
◯ New Workbook

OK
Cancel
Help

CHAPTER 15 *Answers to Self-Review*

15–1 (a) Two-tailed because H_1 does not state a direction.

(b)

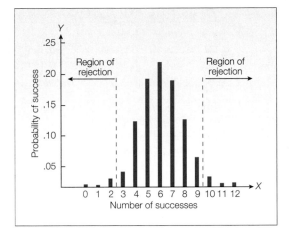

Adding down, $.000 + .003 + .016 = .019$. This is the largest cumulative probability up to but not exceeding .050, which is half the level of significance.

(c) Reject H_0; accept H_1. There is a preference.

15–2 (a) $H_0: \pi \leq 0.50$, $H_1: \pi > 0.50$.

(b) Reject H_0 if $z > 1.65$.

(c) Since 80 is more than $n/2 = 100/2 = 50$, we use:

$$z = \frac{(80 - .50) - .50(100)}{.50\sqrt{100}} = \frac{29.5}{5} = 5.9$$

(d) H_0 is rejected.

(e) The screening was effective.

15–3 (a) H_0: The median $= \$123$, H_1: The median is more than $123.

(b) Reject H_0 if $z > 1.65$.

(c) $z = \dfrac{(42 - .50) - 32}{.50\sqrt{64}} = \dfrac{9.5}{4} = 2.38$

(d) Reject H_0.

(e) The median bill is more than $123.

15–4 (a) $n = 10$ (because there was no change for A.A.)

(b)

Before	After	Difference	Absolute Difference	Rank of Absolute Difference	Negative Ranks	Positive Ranks
17	18	−1	1	1.5	1.5	
21	23	−2	2	3.0	3.0	
25	22	3	3	5.0		5.0
15	25	−10	10	8.0	8.0	

Before	After	Difference	Absolute Difference	Rank of Absolute Difference	Negative Ranks	Positive Ranks
10	28	−18	18	10.0	10.0	
16	16	—	—	—	—	—
10	22	−12	12	9.0	9.0	
20	19	1	1	1.5		1.5
17	20	−3	3	5.0	5.0	
24	30	−6	6	7.0	7.0	
23	26	−3	3	5.0	5.0	
					48.5	6.5

H_0: Production is the same.
H_1: Production has increased.
The sum of the positive signed ranks is 6.5; the negative sum is 48.5. From Appendix J, one-tailed test, $n = 10$, the critical value is 10. Since 6.5 is less than 10, reject the null hypothesis and accept the alternate. New procedures did increase production.

15–5 H_0: There is no difference in the distances traveled by Dino and by Maxi.

H_1: There is a difference in the distances traveled by Dino and by Maxi.

Do not reject H_0 if the computed z is between 1.96 and −1.96 (from Appendix D); otherwise, reject H_0 and accept H_1. $n_1 = 8$, the number of observations in the first sample.

Dino		Maxi	
Distance	Rank	Distance	Rank
252	4	262	9
263	10	242	2
279	15	256	5
273	14	260	8
271	13	258	7
265	11.5	243	3
257	6	239	1
280	16	265	11.5
Total	89.5		46.5

$W = 89.5$

$$z = \cfrac{89.5 - \cfrac{8(8 + 8 + 1)}{2}}{\sqrt{\cfrac{(8)(8)(8 + 8 + 1)}{12}}}$$

$$= \frac{21.5}{9.52} = 2.26$$

Reject H_0; accept H_1. There is a difference in the distances traveled by the two golf balls.

15–6

		Great	
Ranks			
Englewood	**West Side**	**Northern**	**Sylvania**
17	5	19	7
20	1	9.5	11
16	3	21	15
13	5	22	9.5
5	2	14	8
18			12

$$\Sigma R_1 = 89 \quad \Sigma R_2 = 16 \quad \Sigma R_3 = 85.5 \quad \Sigma R_4 = 62.5$$

$$n_1 = 6 \quad n_2 = 5 \quad n_3 = 5 \quad n_4 = 6$$

H_0: The distributions are the same.

H_1: The distributions are not the same.

$$H = \frac{12}{22(22 + 1)} \left[\frac{(89)^2}{6} + \frac{(16)^2}{5} + \frac{(85.5)^2}{5} + \frac{(62.5)^2}{6} \right]$$

$$- 3(22 + 1)$$

$$= 13.635$$

The critical value of chi-square for $k - 1 = 4 - 1 = 3$ degrees of freedom is 11.345. Since the computed value of 13.635 is greater than 11.345, the null hypothesis is rejected. We conclude that the distributions are not the same.

15–7 (a)

		Rank			
X	**Y**	**X**	**Y**	**d**	**d²**
805	23	5.5	1	4.5	20.25
777	62	3.0	9	-6.0	36.00
820	60	8.5	8	0.5	0.25
682	40	1.0	4	-3.0	9.00
777	70	3.0	10	-7.0	49.00
810	28	7.0	2	5.0	25.00
805	30	5.5	3	2.5	6.25
840	42	10.0	5	5.0	25.00
777	55	3.0	7	-4.0	16.00
820	51	8.5	6	2.5	6.25
				0	193.00

$$r_s = 1 - \frac{6(193)}{10(99)} = -.170$$

(b) H_0: $\rho = 0$; H_1: $\rho \neq 0$. Reject H_0 if $t < -2.306$ or $t > 2.306$.

$$t = -0.170 \sqrt{\frac{10 - 2}{1 - (-0.170)^2}} = -0.488$$

H_0 is not rejected. We have not shown a relationship between the two tests.

A REVIEW OF CHAPTERS 14 AND 15

Goodness-of-fit test and contingency table analysis applicable to nominal-level data

This section is a review of the major concepts and terms introduced in Chapters 14 and 15. Chapter 14 began the study of *nonparametric,* or *distribution-free,* tests by discussing the *chi-square goodness-of-fit test* This test is applied to a set of observed frequencies, f_0, and a corresponding set of frequencies, f_e, to test how well the sets fit. This test involves only one characteristic possessed by an individual, such as education. If we are interested in two characteristics, such as a relationship between education level and income, the data are cross-classified into a contingency table, and the chi-square test for independence is applied. For these two lists, no assumption about the shape of the population is needed; they require only that the data be nominal level. The chi-square goodness-of-fit test is also used to determine whether a set of observed frequencies is normally distributed.

Five tests for ordinal-level data

Chapter 15 presented five nonparametric tests of hypothesis and the coefficient of rank correlation, all of which require the ordinal level of measurement. That is, the data must be ranked from low to high. The tests discussed were the *sign test,* the *median test,* the *Wilcoxon rank-sum test,* the *Kruskal-Wallis analysis of variance test,* and the *Wilcoxon signed-rank test.*

▌ Glossary

Chapter 14

Chi-square distribution A distribution with these characteristics: (1) Its value can only be positive. (2) There is a family of chi-square distributions, a different one for each different degree of freedom. (3) The distributions are positively skewed, but as the number of degrees of freedom increases, the distribution approaches the normal distribution.

Chi-square goodness-of-fit test A test with the objective of determining how well an observed set of frequencies fits an expected set of frequencies. It is concerned with one nominal-scale variable, such as the color of a car.

Contingency table If two characteristics, such as education and income, are cross-classified into a table, the result is called a contingency table. The chi-square test statistic is used to investigate whether the two characteristics are related.

Nominal level of measurement The "lowest" level of measurement. Such data can only be classified into categories, and there is no particular order for the categories. For example, it makes no difference whether the categories "male" and "female" are listed in that order, or female first and male second. The categories are mutually exclusive—meaning, in this illustration, that a person cannot be a male and a female at the same time.

Nonparametric or distribution-free tests Hypothesis tests involving nominal- and ordinal-level data. No assumptions need be made about the shape of the population; that is, we do not assume the population is normally distributed.

Chapter 15

Kruskal-Wallis one-way analysis of variance by ranks A test used when the assumptions for the parametric analysis of variance (ANOVA) cannot be met. Its purpose is to test whether several populations are equal. Again, the data must be at least ordinal scale.

Sign test A test used for dependent samples. The sign test is used to find whether there is a brand preference for two products or to determine whether performance after an experiment is greater than before the experiment. Also, the sign test is used to test a hypothesis about the median.

Spearman's coefficient of rank correlation A measure of the association between the ranks of two variables. It can range from −1.00 to 1.00. A value of −1.00 indicates a perfect negative association among the ranks and a value of 1.00 a perfect positive association among the ranks. A value of 0 indicates no association among the ranks.

Wilcoxon matched-pair signed-rank test A nonparametric test requiring at least ordinal-level data. Its purpose is to find whether there is any difference between two sets of paired (related) observations. It is used if the assumptions required for the paired t test cannot be met.

Wilcoxon rank-sum test A nonparametric test requiring independent samples. The data must be at least ordinal level. That is, the data must be capable of being ranked. The test is used when the assumptions for the parametric Student t test cannot be met. The objective of the test is to find whether two independent samples can be considered as coming from the same population.

▎ Exercises

1. For a chi-square test, what do f_0 and f_e stand for?
2. The following is an example of what?

Political Affiliation	Amount Contributed to Campaign		
	$1–$99	$100–$999	$1,000 and More
Republican	42	87	342
Democrat	596	302	116
Socialist	42	49	36
All others	19	17	11

3. Refer to Exercise 2. What test statistic would be used to find whether there is any relationship between political affiliation and the amount contributed?
4. Refer to Exercise 2. How many degrees of freedom are there?
5. Refer to Exercise 2. Suppose the computed value of χ^2 is 11.248, and the .05 level is being used. Should the null hypothesis be rejected?
6. For a goodness-of-fit test, the computed value of chi-square is 8.403, and the critical value is 5.991. The .05 level is being used. Is the null hypothesis rejected?
7. Refer to Exercise 6. What is the null hypothesis?
8. What level of measurement is required for the parametric tests of hypotheses discussed in Chapters 10 and 11?
9. What level of measurement is required for the goodness-of-fit test?
10. What level of measurement is required for the Wilcoxon rank-sum test?
11. What is the purpose of the Wilcoxon rank-sum test?
12. What assumptions are made about the shape of the populations in using the Kruskal-Wallis test?
13. What is the objective of the Kruskal-Wallis test?
14. What is the objective of the Wilcoxon signed-rank test?
15. Of the following nonparametric tests (sign test, Wilcoxon rank-sum, Kruskal-Wallis, and Wilcoxon signed-rank), which one deals with three or more samples?
16. Refer to Exercise 15. Which test deals with paired data?
17. Refer to Exercise 15. Can these tests be applied to interval- and ratio-level data?
18. For a Wilcoxon rank-sum test, the alternate hypothesis is: The women have better eye perception than the men. Would a one-tailed or a two-tailed test be applied?
19. The chi-square distribution for 5 degrees of freedom is approximately normally distributed. Is that statement true?
20. How are the degrees of freedom for a goodness-of-fit test determined?
21. Describe the steps followed, using a simple example, to test a hypothesis involving the median.

▎ Cases

A. Century National Bank

Is there a relationship between the location of the branch bank and whether the customer has a debit card? Based on the information available, develop a table that shows the relationship between these two variables. At the .05 significance level, can we conclude there is a relationship be-

tween the branch location and whether the customer uses a debit card?

B. Thomas Testing Labs

John Thomas, the owner of Thomas Testing, has for some time done contract work for insurance companies regarding drunk driving. To improve his research capabilities, he recently purchased the Rupple Driving Simulator. This device will allow a subject to take a "road test" and provide a score, indicating the number of driving errors committed during the test drive. Higher scores indicate more driving errors. Driving errors would include: not coming to a complete stop at a stop sign, not using turning signals, not exercising caution on wet or snowy pavement, and so on. During the road test, problems appear at random and not all problems appear in each road test. These are major advantages to the Rupple Driving Simulator because subjects do not gain any advantage by taking the test several times.

With the new driving simulator, Mr. Thomas would like to study in detail the problem of drunk driving. He begins by selecting a random sample of 25 drivers. He asks each of the selected individuals to take the test drive on the Rupple Driving Simulator. The number of errors for each driver is recorded below. Next, he has each of the individuals in the group drink 3 16-ounce cans of beer in a 60-minute period and return to the Rupple Driving Simulator for another test drive. The number of driving errors after drinking the beer is also shown below. The research question is: Does alcohol impair the driver's ability and, therefore, increase the number of driving errors?

Mr. Thomas believes the distribution of scores on the test drive does not follow a normal distribution and, there-fore, a nonparametric test should be used. Because the observations are paired, he decides to use both the sign test and the Wilcoxon signed-rank test. Compare the results using these two procedures. Which statistical test would you suggest? What conclusion would you make regarding the effects of drunk driving? Write a brief report summarizing your findings.

| | Driving Errors | | | Driving Errors | |
| | Without | With | | Without | With |
Subject	Alcohol	Alcohol	Subject	Alcohol	Alcohol
1	75	89	14	72	106
2	78	83	15	83	89
3	89	80	16	99	89
4	100	90	17	75	77
5	85	84	18	58	78
6	70	68	19	93	108
7	64	84	20	69	69
8	79	104	21	86	84
9	83	81	22	97	86
10	82	88	23	65	92
11	83	93	24	96	97
12	84	92	25	85	94
13	80	103			

Chapter Sixteen

Statistical Quality Control

GOALS

When you have completed this chapter, you will be able to:

ONE
Discuss the role of quality control in production and service operations.

TWO
Define and understand the terms chance causes, assignable causes, in control and out of control, attribute, and variable.

THREE
Construct and interpret a Pareto chart.

FOUR
Construct and interpret a fishbone diagram.

FIVE
Construct and interpret a mean chart and a range chart.

SIX
Construct and interpret a percent defective chart and a *c*-bar chart.

SEVEN
Discuss acceptance sampling.

EIGHT
Construct an operating characteristic curve for various sampling plans.

Every hour the quality control inspector measures the outside diameter of four parts. Given results of the measurements, how would you determine whether the measurements are within control limits? (See Goal 5 and Self Review 16–2)

▌ Introduction

Throughout this text we have presented many applications of hypothesis testing. In Chapter 9 we described methods for testing a hypothesis about a population mean when the sample was large. In Chapter 10 we discussed testing a hypothesis about a population mean when the sample was small. In Chapter 12 we described tests of hypothesis regarding the coefficient of correlation. In this chapter we present another, somewhat different application of hypothesis testing, called **statistical process control** or **SPC.**

Statistical process control is a collection of strategies, techniques, and actions taken by an organization to ensure they are producing a quality product or providing a quality service. It begins at the product planning stage, when we specify the attributes of the product or service. It continues through the production stage. Each attribute throughout the process contributes to the overall quality of the product. To effectively use quality control, measurable attributes and specifications must be developed against which the actual attributes of the product or service can be compared.

▌ A Brief History of Quality Control

Prior to the 1900s U.S. industry was largely characterized by small shops making relatively simple products, such as candles or furniture. In these small shops the individual worker was generally a craftsman who was completely responsible for the quality of the work. The worker could ensure the quality through the personal selection of the materials, skillful manufacturing, and selective fitting and adjustment.

In the early 1900s factories sprang up, where people with limited training were formed into large assembly lines. Products became much more complex. The individual worker no longer had complete control over the quality of the product. A semi-professional staff, usually called the Inspection Department, became responsible for the quality of the product. The quality responsibility was usually fulfilled by a 100 percent inspection of all the important characteristics. If there were any discrepancies noted, these problems were handled by the manufacturing department supervisor. In essence, quality was attained by "inspecting the quality into the product."

During the 1920s Dr. Walter A. Shewhart, of the Bell Telephone Laboratories, developed the concepts of statistical quality control. He introduced the concept of "controlling" the quality of a product as it was being manufactured, rather than inspecting the quality into the product after it was manufactured. For the purpose of controlling quality, Shewhart developed charting techniques for controlling in-process manufacturing operations. In addition, he introduced the concept of statistical sample inspection to estimate the quality of a product as it was being manufactured. This replaced the old method of inspecting each part after it was completed in the production operation.

Statistical quality control really came into its own during World War II. The need for mass-produced war related items, such as bomb sights, accurate radar, and other electronic equipment, at the lowest possible cost hastened the use of statistical sampling and quality control charts. Since World War II these statistical techniques have been refined and sharpened. The use of computers in the last decade has also widened the use of these techniques.

World War II virtually destroyed the Japanese production capability. Rather than retool their old production methods, the Japanese enlisted the aid of the late Dr. W. Edwards Deming, of the United States Department of Agriculture, to help them develop an overall plan. In a series of seminars with Japanese planners he stressed a philosophy that is known today as Deming's 14 points. These 14 points are listed below. He emphasized that quality originates from improving the process, not from inspection. Also, that quality is determined by the customers. The manufacturer must be able, via market research, to anticipate the needs of customers. Upper management has the responsibility for long-term improvement. Another of his points, and one that the Japanese strongly endorsed, is that every member of the company must contribute to the long-term improvement. To achieve this improvement, ongoing education and training are necessary.

Deming had some ideas that did not mesh with contemporary management philosophies in the United States. Two areas where Deming's ideas differed from U.S. management philosophy were with production quotas and merit ratings. He claimed these two practices, which are both common in the United States, are not productive and should be eliminated. He also pointed out that U.S. managers are mostly interested in good news. Good news, however, does not provide an opportunity for improvement. On the other hand, bad news opens the door for new products and allows for company improvement.

Listed below, in a condensed form, are Dr. Deming's 14 points. He was adamant that the 14 points needed to be adopted as a package in order to be successful. The underlying theme is cooperation, teamwork, and the belief that workers want to do their jobs in a quality fashion.

1. Create constancy of purpose for the continual improvement of products and service to society.
2. Adopt a philosophy that we can no longer live with commonly accepted levels of delays, mistakes, defective materials, and defective workmanship.
3. Eliminate the need for mass inspection as the way to achieve quality. Instead achieve quality by building the product correctly in the first place.
4. End the practice of awarding business solely on the basis of price. Instead, require meaningful measures of quality along with the price.
5. Improve constantly and forever every process for planning, production, and service.
6. Institute modern methods of training on the job for all employees, including managers. This will lead to better utilization of each employee.
7. Adopt and institute leadership aimed at helping people do a better job.
8. Encourage effective two-way communication and other means to drive out fear throughout the organization so that everyone may work more effectively and more productively for the company.
9. Break down barriers between departments and staff areas.
10. Eliminate the use of slogans, posters, and exhortations demanding Zero Defects and new levels of productivity without providing methods.
11. Eliminate work standards that prescribe quotas for the workforce and numerical goals for people in management. Substitute aids and helpful leadership in order to achieve continual improvement in quality and productivity.
12. Remove the barriers that rob hourly workers and the people in management of their right to pride of workmanship.
13. Institute a vigorous program of education and encourage self-improvement for everyone. What an organization needs is good people and people who are improving with education. Advancement to a competitive position will have its roots in knowledge.
14. Define clearly management's permanent commitment to ever-improving quality and productivity to implement all of these principles.

Deming's 14 points did not ignore statistical quality control, which is often abbreviated as SQC, TQC, or just QC. The objective of statistical quality control is to monitor production through many stages of manufacturing. We use the tools of statistical quality control, such as X-bar and R charts, to monitor the quality of many processes and services. Control charts allow us to identify when a process or service is "out of control," that is, when the point is reached where an excessive number of defective units are being produced.

Interest in quality has accelerated dramatically in the United States since the late 1980s. Turn on the television and watch the commercials sponsored by GM, Ford, and

Chrysler to verify the emphasis on quality control on the assembly line. It is now one of the "in" topics in all facets of business. V. Daniel Hunt, president of Technology Research Corporation, wrote in his book *Quality in America* that in the United States, 20 to 25 percent of the costs of production is currently spent finding and correcting mistakes. And, he added, the additional cost incurred in repairing or replacing faulty products in the field drives the total cost of poor quality to nearly 30 percent. In Japan, he indicates, this cost is about 3 percent!

In recent years companies have been motivated to improve quality by the challenge of being recognized for their quality achievements. The Malcolm Baldrige National Quality Award, established in 1988, is awarded annually to U.S. companies that demonstrate excellence in quality achievement and management. The award categories include manufacturing, service, and small business. Past winners include Motorola, Xerox, IBM, Federal Express, and Cadillac. But the award is not limited to large companies. One of the most recent winners is a small firm in Minneapolis, Minnesota, that employs only 100 workers.

What is quality? There is no commonly agreed upon definition of quality. To cite a few diverse definitions: From Westinghouse, "Total quality is performance leadership in meeting the customer requirements by doing the right things right the first time." From AT&T, "Quality is meeting customer expectations." Historian Barbara W. Tuchman says, "Quality is achieving or reaching the highest standard as against being satisfied with the sloppy or fraudulent."

▌ Causes of Variation

No two parts are *exactly* the same. There is some variation. The weight of each McDonald's Quarter Pounder is not exactly 0.25 pounds. Some will weigh more than 0.25 pounds, others less. The standard time for the TARTA (Toledo Area Regional Transit Authority) bus run from downtown Toledo, Ohio, to Perrysburg is 25 minutes. However, each run does not take *exactly* 25 minutes. Some runs take longer. Other times the TARTA driver must wait in Perrysburg before returning to Toledo. In some cases there is a reason for the bus being late, an accident on the expressway or a snowstorm, for example. In other cases the driver may not "hit" the green lights or the traffic is unusually heavy and slow for no apparent reason. There are two general causes of variation in a process—chance and assignable.

▌ **Chance Variation**   Variation that is random in nature. This type of variation cannot be completely eliminated unless there is a major change in the equipment or material used in the process. ▌

Internal machine friction, slight variations in material or process conditions (such as the temperature of the mold being used to make glass bottles), atmospheric conditions (such as temperature, humidity, and the dust content of the air), and vibrations transmitted to a machine from a passing forklift are a few examples of sources of chance variation.

If the hole drilled in a piece of steel is too large due to a dull drill, the drill may be sharpened or a new drill inserted. An operator who continually sets up the machine incorrectly can be replaced or retrained. If the roll of steel to be used in the process does not have the correct tensile strength, it can be rejected. These are examples of assignable variation.

| **Assignable Variation**   Variation that is not random. It can be eliminated or reduced by investigating the problem and finding the cause. |

There are several reasons we should be concerned with variation.

1. It will change the shape, dispersion, and central tendency of the distribution of the product characteristic being measured.
2. Assignable variation is usually correctable, whereas chance variation usually cannot be corrected or stabilized economically.

▌ Diagnostic Charts

There are a variety of diagnostic techniques available to investigate quality problems. Two of the more prominent of these techniques are *Pareto charts* and *fishbone diagrams.*

Pareto Charts

Pareto analysis is a technique for tallying the number and type of defects that happen within a product or service. The chart is named after a 19th-century Italian scientist, Vilfredo Pareto. He noted that most of the "activity" in a process is caused by relatively few of the "factors." His concept, often called the 80–20 rule, is that 80 percent of the activity is caused by 20 percent of the factors. By concentrating on 20 percent of the factors, managers can attack 80 percent of the problem. For example, Emily's Family Restaurant, located at the junction of Interstates 75 and 70, is investigating "customer complaints." The five complaints heard most frequently are: discourteous service, cold food, long wait for seating, few menu choices, and unruly young children. Suppose discourteous service was mentioned most frequently and cold food second. These two factors total more than 85 percent of the complaints and hence are the two that should be addressed first because this will yield the largest reduction in complaints.

To develop a Pareto chart, we begin by tallying the type of defects. Next, we rank the defects in terms of frequency of occurrence from largest to smallest. Finally, we produce a vertical bar chart, with the height of the bars corresponding to the frequency of each defect. The following example illustrates these ideas.

| **Example** | The city manager of Grove City, Utah, is concerned with water usage, particularly in single family homes. She would like to develop a plan to reduce the water usage in Grove City. To investigate, she selects a sample of 100 homes and determines the typical daily water usage for various purposes. These sample results are as follows. |

Reasons for Water Usage	Gallons per Day	Reasons for Water Usage	Gallons per Day
Laundering	24.9	Swimming pool	28.3
Watering lawn	143.7	Dishwashing	12.3
Personal bathing	106.7	Car washing	10.4
Cooking	5.1	Drinking	7.9

What is the area of greatest usage? Where should she concentrate her efforts to reduce the water usage?

Solution   A Pareto chart is useful for identifying the major areas of water usage and focusing on those areas where the greatest reduction can be achieved. The first step is to convert each of the activities to a percent and then to order them from largest to smallest. The total water usage per day is 339.3 gallons, found by totaling the gallons used in the eight activities. The activity with the largest use is watering lawns. It accounts for 143.7 gallons of water per day, or 42.4 percent of the amount of water used. The next largest category is personal bathing, which accounts for 31.4 percent of the water used. These two activities account for 73.8 percent of the water usage.

Reasons for Water Usage	Gallons per Day	Percent
Laundering	24.9	7.3
Watering lawn	143.7	42.4
Personal bathing	106.7	31.4
Cooking	5.1	1.5
Swimming pool usage	28.3	8.3
Dishwashing	12.3	3.6
Car washing	10.4	3.1
Drinking	7.9	2.3
Total	339.3	100.0

To draw the Pareto chart, we begin by scaling the number of gallons used on the left vertical axis and the corresponding percent on the right vertical axis. Next we draw a vertical bar with the height of the bar corresponding to the activity with the largest number of occurrences. In the Grove City example, we draw a vertical bar for the activity watering lawns to a height of 143.7 gallons. (We call this the count.) We continue this procedure for the other activities, as shown in Chart 16–1.

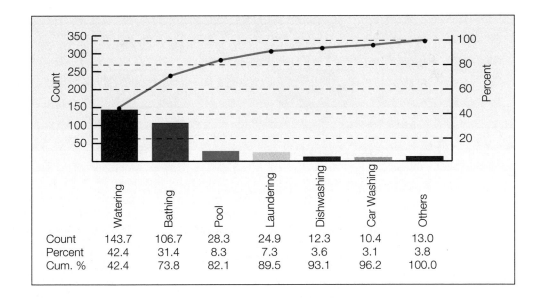

	Watering	Bathing	Pool	Laundering	Dishwashing	Car Washing	Others
Count	143.7	106.7	28.3	24.9	12.3	10.4	13.0
Percent	42.4	31.4	8.3	7.3	3.6	3.1	3.8
Cum. %	42.4	73.8	82.1	89.5	93.1	96.2	100.0

Chart 16–1   Pareto Chart for Water Usage, Grove City, Utah

Below the chart we list the activities, their frequency of occurrence, and the percent of the time each activity occurs. In the last row we list the cumulative percentage. This cumulative row will allow us to quickly determine which set of activities account for most of the activity. These cumulative percents are plotted above the vertical bars. In the Grove City example, the activities of watering lawn, personal bathing, and pools account for 82.1 percent of the water usage. The city manager can attain the greatest gain by looking to reduce the water usage in these three areas.

Fishbone Diagram

Another diagnostic chart is a **cause-and-effect diagram** or a **fishbone diagram.** It is called a cause-and-effect diagram to emphasize the relationship between an effect and a set of possible causes that produce the particular effect. This diagram is useful to help organize ideas and to identify relationships. It is a tool that encourages open "brainstorming" for ideas. By identifying these relationships we can determine factors that are the cause of variability in our process. The name *fishbone* comes from the manner in which the various causes and effects are organized on the diagram. The effect is usually a particular problem, or perhaps a goal, and it is shown on the right-hand side of the diagram. The major causes are listed on the left-hand side of the diagram.

The usual approach to a fishbone diagram is to consider four problem areas, namely, methods, materials, equipment, and personnel. The problem, or the effect, is the head of the fish. See Chart 16–2.

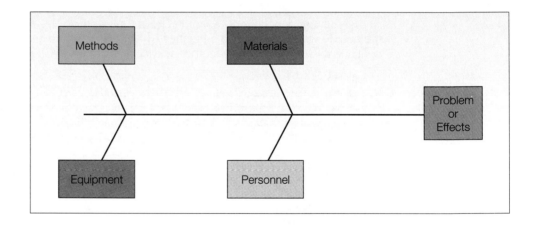

Chart 16–2   Fishbone Diagram

Under each of the possible causes are subcauses that are identified and investigated. The subcauses are factors that may be producing the particular effect. Information is gathered about the problem and used to fill in the fishbone diagram. Each of the subcauses is investigated and those that are not important eliminated, until the real cause of the problem is identified.

Chart 16–3 illustrates the details of a fishbone diagram. Suppose a family restaurant, such as those found along an interstate highway, has recently been experiencing complaints from customers that the food being served is cold. Notice each of the subcauses are listed as assumptions. Each of these subcauses must be investigated to find the real problem regarding the cold food. In a fishbone diagram there is no weighting of the subcauses.

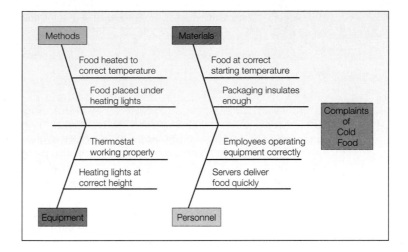

Chart 16–3   Fishbone Diagram for a Restaurant Investigation of Cold Food Complaints

SOURCE: Adapted from M. A. Vonderembse and G. P. White, *Operations Management,* 3rd Ed. (South Western College Publishing, 1996), p. 489.

SELF-REVIEW 16–1

Patients at the Rouse Home have been complaining recently about the conditions at the home. The administrator would like to use a Pareto chart to investigate. When a patient or patient's relative has a complaint, they are asked to complete a complaint form. Listed below is a summary of the complaint forms received during the last 12 months.

Complaint	Number	Complaint	Number
Nothing to do	45	Dirty conditions	63
Poor care by staff	71	Poor quality food	84
Medication error	2	Lack of respect by staff	35

Develop a Pareto chart. What complaints would you suggest the administrator work on to achieve the most significant improvement?

▍ Exercises

1. Tom Sharkey is the owner of Sharkey Chevy. At the start of the year Tom instituted a customer opinion program to find ways to improve service. One week after the service is performed, Tom's administrative assistant calls the customer to find out whether the service was performed satisfactorily and how the service might be improved. Listed below is a summary of the complaints for the first six months. Develop a Pareto chart. What complaints would you suggest that Tom work on to improve the quality of service?

Complaint	Frequency		Complaint	Frequency
Problem not corrected	38		Price too high	23
Error on invoice	8		Wait too long for service	10
Unfriendly atmosphere	12			

2. Out of 110 diesel engines tested, the manufacturer found 9 had leaky radiators, 15 had faulty cylinders, 4 had ignition problems, 52 had oil leaks, and 30 had cracked blocks. Draw a Pareto chart to identify the key problem is the production process.

▌ Purpose and Types of Quality Control Charts

Control charts identify when assignable causes of variation or changes have entered the process. For example, the Wheeling Company makes vinyl-coated aluminum replacement windows for older homes. The vinyl coating must have a thickness between certain limits. If the coating becomes too thick, it will cause the windows to jam. On the other hand, if the coating becomes too thin, the window will not seal properly. The mechanism that determines how much coating is put on each window becomes worn and begins making the coating too thick. Thus, a change has occurred in the process. Control charts are useful for detecting the change in process conditions. It is important to know when changes have entered the process, so that the cause may be identified and corrected before a large number of unacceptable items are produced.

Control charts may be compared to the scoreboard in a baseball game. By looking at the scoreboard, the fans, coaches, and players can tell which team is winning the game. However, the scoreboard can do nothing to win or lose the game. Control charts provide a similar function. These charts indicate to the workers, group leaders, quality control engineers, production supervisor, and management whether the production of the part or service is "in control" or "out of control." If the production is "out of control," the control chart will not fix the situation; it is just a piece of paper with figures and dots on it. Instead, the person responsible will adjust the machine manufacturing the part or do what is necessary to return production to "in control."

There are two types of control charts. A **variable control chart** portrays measurements, such as the amount of cola in a two liter bottle or the time it takes a nurse at Mt. Carmel Hospital to respond to a patient's call. A variable control chart requires the interval or the ratio scale of measurement. An **attribute control chart** classifies a product or service as either acceptable or unacceptable. It is based on the nominal scale of measurement. Patients in a hospital are asked to rate the meals served as acceptable or unacceptable, bank loans are either repaid or they are defaulted.

Control Charts for Variables

To develop control charts for variables, we rely on the sampling theory discussed in connection with the Central Limit Theorem in Chapter 8. Suppose a sample of five pieces is selected each hour from the production process and the mean of each sample computed. The sample means are $\bar{X}_1$, $\bar{X}_2$, $\bar{X}_3$, and so on. The mean of these sample means is denoted as $\bar{\bar{X}}$. We use k to indicate the number of sample means. The overall or grand mean is found by:

$$\textbf{GRAND MEAN} \qquad \bar{\bar{X}} = \frac{\Sigma \text{ of the means of the subgroups}}{\text{Number of sample means}} = \frac{\Sigma \bar{X}}{k} \qquad \textbf{[16–1]}$$

The standard error of the distribution of the sample means is designated by $s_{\bar{x}}$. It is found by:

STANDARD ERROR OF THE MEAN	$s_{\bar{x}} = \dfrac{s}{\sqrt{n}}$	**[16–2]**

These relationships allow limits to be set up around the sample means to show how much variation can be expected for a given sample size. These expected limits are called the **upper control limit** (*UCL*) and the **lower control limit** (*LCL*). An example will illustrate the use of control limits and how the limits are determined.

Example

Statistical Software, Inc., offers a toll-free number where customers can call with problems involving the use of their products from 7 A.M. until 11 P.M. daily. It is impossible to have every call answered immediately by a technical representative, but it is important customers do not wait too long for a person to come on the line. Customers become upset when they hear the message "Your call is important to us. The next available representative will be with you shortly" too many times. To understand their process, Statistical Software decides to develop a control chart describing the total time from when a call is received until the representative answers the caller's question. Yesterday, for the 16 hours of operation, five calls were sampled each hour. This information is reported below, in minutes until a call was answered.

Time	Sample Number				
	1	2	3	4	5
A.M. 7	8	9	15	4	11
8	7	10	7	6	8
9	11	12	10	9	10
10	12	8	6	9	12
11	11	10	6	14	11
P.M. 12	7	7	10	4	11
1	10	7	4	10	10
2	8	11	11	7	7
3	8	11	8	14	12
4	12	9	12	17	11
5	7	7	9	17	13
6	9	9	4	4	11
7	10	12	12	12	12
8	8	11	9	6	8
9	10	13	9	4	9
10	9	11	8	5	11

Based on this information, develop a control chart for the mean duration of the call. Does there appear to be a trend in the calling times? Is there any period in which it appears that customers wait longer than others?

Solution

A mean chart has two limits, an upper control limit (*UCL*) and a lower control limit (*LCL*). These upper and lower control limits are computed by:

CONTROL LIMITS FOR THE MEAN	$UCL = \overline{\overline{X}} + 3\dfrac{s}{\sqrt{n}}$ and $LCL = \overline{\overline{X}} - 3\dfrac{s}{\sqrt{n}}$	**[16–3]**

where s is an estimate of the standard deviation of the population, σ. Notice that in the calculation of the upper and lower control limits the number 3 appears. It represents the 99.74 percent confidence limits. The limits are often called the 3-sigma limits. However, other levels of confidence (such as 90 or 95 percent) can be used. Rather than calculate the standard deviation from each sample as a measure of variation, it is easier to use the range. For fixed sized samples there is a constant relationship between the range and the standard deviation, so we can use the following formulas to determine the 99.74 percent control limits for the mean. It can be demonstrated that the term $3\dfrac{s}{\sqrt{n}}$ from formula 16–3 is equivalent to $A_2\overline{R}$ in the following formula.

CONTROL LIMITS FOR THE MEAN	$UCL = \overline{\overline{X}} + A_2\overline{R}$ $LCL = \overline{\overline{X}} - A_2\overline{R}$	**[16–4]**

where:

A_2 is a constant used in computing the upper and the lower control limits. It is based on the average range, $\overline{R}$. The factors for various sample sizes can be found in Appendix B. (Note: n in this table refers to the number in the sample.) A portion of Appendix B is shown below. To locate the A_2 factor for this problem, find the sample size for n in the left margin. It is 5. Then move horizontally to the A_2 column, and read the factor. It is 0.577.

n	A_2	d_2	D_3	D_4
2	1.880	1.128	0	3.267
3	1.023	1.693	0	2.575
4	0.729	2.059	0	2.282
5	0.577	2.326	0	2.115
6	0.483	2.534	0	2.004

$\overline{\overline{X}}$ is the mean of the sample means, computed by $\Sigma\overline{X}/k$, where k is the number of samples selected. In this problem a sample of 5 observations is taken each hour for 16 hours, so $k = 16$.

$\overline{R}$ is the mean of the ranges of the sample. It is $\Sigma R/k$. Remember the range is the difference between the largest and the smallest value in each sample. It describes the variability occurring in that particular sample.

Table 16–1 Duration of 16 Samples of Five Help Sessions

Time	1	2	3	4	5	Mean	Range
A.M. 7	8	9	15	4	11	9.4	11
8	7	10	7	6	8	7.6	4
9	11	12	10	9	10	10.4	3
10	12	8	6	9	12	9.4	6
11	11	10	6	14	11	10.4	8
P.M. 12	7	7	10	4	11	7.8	7
1	10	7	4	10	10	8.2	6
2	8	11	11	7	7	8.8	4
3	8	11	8	14	12	10.6	6
4	12	9	12	17	11	12.2	8
5	7	7	9	17	13	10.6	10
6	9	9	4	4	11	7.4	7
7	10	12	12	12	12	11.6	2
8	8	11	9	6	8	8.4	5
9	10	13	9	4	9	9.0	9
10	9	11	8	5	11	8.8	6
Total						150.60	102

The centerline for the chart is $\overline{\overline{X}}$. It is 9.4125 minutes, found by 150.60/16. The mean of the ranges ($\overline{R}$) is 6.375 minutes, found by 102/16. Thus, the upper control limit of the *X* bar chart is:

$$UCL = \overline{\overline{X}} + A_2\overline{R} = 9.4125 + 0.577(6.375) = 13.0909$$

The lower control limit of the *X* bar chart is:

$$LCL = \overline{\overline{X}} - A_2\overline{R} = 9.4125 - 0.577(6.375) = 5.7341$$

$\overline{\overline{X}}$, *UCL,* and *LCL,* and the sample means are portrayed in Chart 16–4. The mean, $\overline{\overline{X}}$, is 9.4125 minutes, the upper control limit is located at 13.0909 minutes, and the lower control limit is located at 5.7341. There is some variation in the duration of the calls, but all sample means are within the control limits. Thus, based on 16 samples of five calls, we conclude that 99.74 percent of the time the mean length of a sample of 5 calls will be between 5.7341 minutes and 13.0909 minutes.

Chart 16–4   Control Chart for Mean Length of Customer Calls to Statistical Software, Inc.

Because the statistical theory is based on the normality of large samples, control charts should be based on a stable process, that is, a fairly large sample, taken over a long period of time. One rule of thumb is to design the chart after at least 25 samples have been selected.

In addition to the central tendency in a sample, we must also monitor the amount of variation from sample to sample.

Range Chart

A **range chart** shows the variation in the sample ranges. If the points representing the ranges fall between the upper and the lower limits, it is concluded that the operation is in control. According to chance, about 997 times out of 1,000 the range of the samples will fall within the limits. If the range should fall above the limits, we conclude that an assignable cause affected the operation and an adjustment to the process is needed. Why are we not as concerned about the lower limit of the range? For small samples the lower limit is often zero. Actually, for any sample of six or less, the lower control limit is 0. If the range is zero, then logically all the parts are the same and there is not a problem with the variability of the operation.

The upper and lower limits of the range chart are determined from the following equations.

CONTROL CHART FOR RANGES	$UCL = D_4\bar{R} \qquad LCL = D_3\bar{R}$	**[16–5]**

The values for D_3 and D_4 are found in Appendix B or in the table on page 590.

Example

The length of time customers of Statistical Software, Inc. waited from the time their call was answered until a technical representative answered their question or solved their problem is recorded in Table 16–1. Develop a control chart for the range. Does it appear that there is any time when there is too much variation in the operation?

Solution

The first step is to find the mean of the sample ranges. The range for the five calls sampled in the 7 A.M. hour is 11 minutes. The longest call selected from that hour was 15 minutes and the shortest 4 minutes; the difference in the lengths is 11 minutes. In the 8 A.M. hour the range is 4 minutes. The total of the 16 ranges is 102 minutes, so the average range is 6.375 minutes, found by $\bar{R} = 102/16$. Referring to Appendix B or the partial table on page 590, D_3 and D_4 are 0 and 2.115, respectively. The lower and upper control limits are 0 and 13.4831.

$$UCL = D_4\bar{R} = 2.115(6.375) = 13.4831$$
$$LCL = D_3\bar{R} = 0(6.375) = 0$$

The range chart with the 16 sample ranges plotted is shown in Chart 16–5. This chart shows all the ranges are well within the control limits. Hence, we conclude the variation in the time to service the customer's calls is within normal limits, that is "in control." Of course, we should be determining the control limits based on one set of data and then applying them to evaluate future data, not the data we already know.

Chart 16–5   Control Chart for Ranges of Length of Customer Calls to
Statistical Software, Inc.

▌ Some In-Control and Out-of-Control Situations

Following are three illustrations of in-control and out-of-control processes.

Everything OK   1.   The mean chart and the range chart together indicate that the process is in control.
Note the sample means and sample ranges are clustered close to the centerlines.
Some are above and some below the centerlines, indicating the process is quite
stable. That is, there is no visible tendency for the means and ranges to move
toward the "out of control" areas.

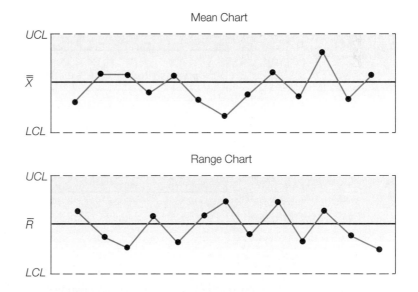

Considerable   2.   The sample means are in control, but the ranges of the last two samples are out of
variation in ranges   control. This indicates there is considerable variation from piece to piece. Some
pieces are large; others are small. An adjustment in the process is probably
necessary.

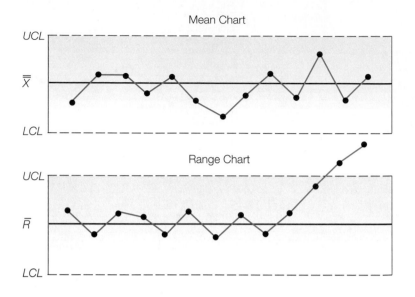

3. The mean weight was in control for the first samples, but there is an upward trend toward *UCL*. The mean weights of the last two were out of control. An adjustment in the process is indicated.

Mean out of control

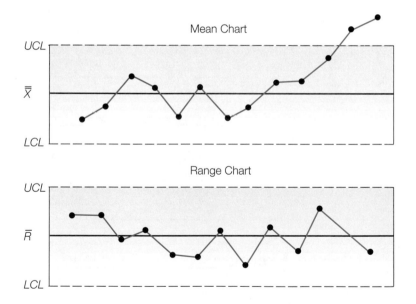

   The above chart for the mean is an example in which the control chart offers some additional information. Note the direction of the last five observations of the mean. They are all above $\overline{X}$ and increasing, and, in fact, the last two observations are out of control. The fact that the sample means were increasing for seven consecutive observations is an indication that the process is out of control.

   MINITAB will draw a control chart for the mean and the range. Below is the output for the Statistical Software example. There are some minor differences in the limits, which are due to rounding.

Mean and Range Charts for Call Times at Statistical Software

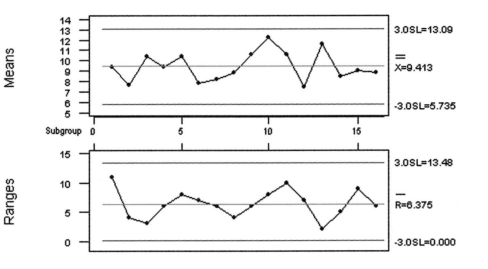

SELF-REVIEW 16–2

Every hour a quality control inspector measures the outside diameter of four parts. The results of the measurements are shown below.

		Sample Piece		
Time	1	2	3	4
9 A.M.	1	4	5	2
10 A.M.	2	3	2	1
11 A.M.	1	7	3	5

(a) Compute the mean outside diameter, the mean range, and determine the control limits for the mean and the range.
(b) Are the measurements within the control limits? Interpret the chart.

▌ Exercises

3. Describe the difference between assignable variation and chance variation.
4. Describe the difference between an attribute control chart and a variable control chart.
5. Samples of size $n = 4$ are selected from a production line.
   a. What is the value of the A_2 factor used to determine the upper and lower control limits or the mean?
   b. What are the values of the D_3 and D_4 factors used to determine the upper and lower control limits for the range?
6. Samples of size 5 are selected from a manufacturing process. The mean of the sample ranges is .50. What is the estimate of the standard deviation of the population?
7. A new industrial oven has just been installed at the Piatt Bakery. To develop experience regarding the oven temperature, an inspector reads the temperature at four different places

inside the oven each half hour. The first reading, taken at 8:00 A.M., was 340 degrees Fahrenheit. (Only the last two digits are given in the following table to make the computations easier.)

	Reading			
Time	1	2	3	4
8:00 A.M.	40	50	55	39
8:30 A.M.	44	42	38	38
9:00 A.M.	41	45	47	43
9:30 A.M.	39	39	41	41
10:00 A.M.	37	42	46	41
10:30 A.M.	39	40	39	40

    a. Based on this initial experience, determine the control limits for the mean temperature. Determine the grand mean. Plot the experience on a chart.

    b. Interpret the chart. Does there seem to be a time when the temperature is out of control?

8. Refer to exercise 7.

    a. Based on this initial experience, determine the control limits for the range. Plot the experience on a chart.

    b. Does there seem to be a time when there is too much variation in the temperature?

❙ Attribute Control Charts

Often the data we collect are the result of counting, rather than measuring. That is, we observe the presence or absence of some attribute. For example, the screw top on a bottle of shampoo either fits onto the bottle and does not leak (an "acceptable" condition) or does not seal and a leak results (an "unacceptable" condition), or a bank makes a loan to a customer and the loan is either repaid or it is not repaid. In other cases we are interested in the number of defects in a sample. British Airways might count the number of its flights arriving late per day at Gatwick Airport in London. In this section we discuss two types of attribute charts: the p (percent defective) and the c (number of defectives).

Percent Defective Chart

If the item recorded is the fraction of unacceptable parts made in a batch of larger parts, the appropriate control chart is the percent defective chart. This chart is based on the binomial distribution, discussed in Chapter 6, and proportions, discussed in Chapter 10. The centerline is at $\bar{p}$, the mean proportion defective. The $\bar{p}$ replaces the $\bar{X}$ of the variable control chart. The mean proportion defective is found by:

$$\textbf{MEAN PROPORTION DEFECTIVE} \qquad \bar{p} = \frac{\text{Total number defective}}{\text{Total number of items sampled}} \qquad \textbf{[16--6]}$$

The variation in the sample proportion is described by the standard error of a proportion. It is found by:

$$\textbf{STANDARD ERROR OF THE PROPORTION} \qquad s_p = \sqrt{\frac{\bar{p}(1 - \bar{p})}{n}} \qquad \textbf{[16--7]}$$

Hence, the upper control limit (*UCL*) and the lower control limit (*LCL*) are computed as the mean percent defective plus or minus three times the standard error of the percents (proportions). The formula for the control limits is:

CONTROL LIMITS FOR PROPORTIONS	$LCL, UCL = \bar{p} \pm 3 \sqrt{\dfrac{\bar{p}(1 - \bar{p})}{n}}$	[16–8]

An example will show the details of the calculations and the conclusions.

Example

The Credit Department at Global National Bank is responsible for entering each transaction charged to the customer's monthly statement. Of course, accuracy is critical and errors will make the customer very unhappy! To guard against errors, each data entry clerk rekeys a sample of 1,500 of their batch of work a second time and a computer program checks that the numbers match. The program also prints a report of the number and size of any discrepancy. Seven people were working last hour and here are their results:

Inspector	Number Inspected	Number Mismatched
Mullins	1,500	4
Rider	1,500	6
Gankowski	1,500	6
Smith	1,500	2
Reed	1,500	15
White	1,500	4
Reading	1,500	4

Construct the percent defective chart for this process. What are the upper and the lower control limits? Interpret the results. Does it appear any of the data entry clerks are "out of control?"

Solution

The first step is to determine the mean proportion defective $\bar{p}$, using formula (16–6). It is .0039, found by 41/10,500.

Inspector	Number Inspected	Number Mismatched	Proportion Defective
Mullins	1,500	4	.00267
Rider	1,500	6	.00400
Gankowski	1,500	6	.00400
Smith	1,500	2	.00133
Reed	1,500	15	.01000
White	1,500	4	.00267
Reading	1,500	4	.00267
Total	10,500	41	

The upper and lower control limits are computed using formula (16–8).

$$LCL, UCL = \bar{p} \pm 3 \sqrt{\frac{\bar{p}(1 - \bar{p})}{n}}$$

$$= \frac{41}{10,500} \pm 3 \sqrt{\frac{.0039(1 - .0039)}{1,500}} = .0039 \pm .0048$$

From the above calculations, the upper control limit is .0087, found by .0039 + .0048. The lower control limit is 0. Why? The lower limit by formula is determined by

.0039 − .0048, which is equal to −0.0009. A negative proportion defective is not possible, so the smallest value is 0. We set the control limit at 0. Thus any data entry clerk, whose proportion defective is between 0 and .0087 is "in control." Clerk number 5, whose name is Reed, is out of control. Her proportion defective is .01, or 1.0 percent, which is outside the upper control limit. Perhaps she should receive additional training or be transferred to another position. This information is summarized in Chart 16–6.

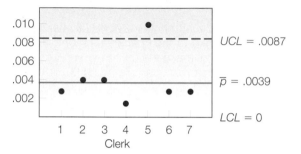

Chart 16–6   Control Chart for Proportion of Entries Defective among Data Entry Clerks, Global National Bank

c-Bar Chart

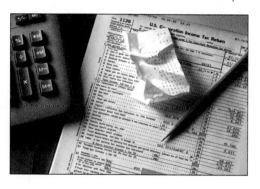

The *c*-bar chart plots the number of defects or failures per unit. It is based on the Poisson distribution discussed in Chapter 6. The number of bags mishandled on a flight by Southwest Airlines might be monitored by a *c*-bar chart. The "unit" under consideration is the flight. On most flights there are not any bags mishandled. On others there may be only one, on others two, and so on. The Internal Revenue Service might count and develop a control chart for the number of errors in arithmetic per tax return. Most returns will not have any errors, some returns will have a single error, others will have two, and so on. We let $\bar{c}$ be the mean number of defects per unit. Thus, $\bar{c}$ is the mean number of bags mishandled by Southwest Airlines per flight or the mean number of arithmetic errors per tax return. Recall from Chapter 6 that the standard deviation of a Poisson distribution is the square root of the mean. Thus, we can determine the 3 sigma, or 99.74 percent limits on a *c*-bar chart by:

CONTROL LIMITS FOR THE NUMBER OF DEFECTS PER UNIT	$LCL, UCL = \bar{c} \pm 3\sqrt{\bar{c}}$	**[16–9]**

Example

The publisher of the *Oak Harbor Daily Telegraph* is concerned about the number of misspelled words in the daily newspaper. They do not print a paper on Saturday or Sunday. In an effort to control the problem and promote the need for correct spelling, a control chart is to be instituted. The number of misspelled words found in the final edition of the paper for the last 10 days is: 5, 6, 3, 0, 4, 5, 1, 2, 7, and 4. Determine the appropriate control limits and interpret the chart. Were there any days during the period that the number of misspelled words was out of control?

Solution   The sum of the number of misspelled words over the 10-day period is 37. So the mean number of defects, $\bar{c}$, is 3.7. The square root of this number is 1.924. So the upper control limit is:

$$UCL = \bar{c} + 3\sqrt{\bar{c}} = 3.7 + 3\sqrt{3.7} = 3.7 + 5.77 = 9.47$$

The computed lower control limit would be $3.7 - 3(1.924) = -2.07$. However, the number of misspelled words cannot be less than 0, so we use 0 as the lower limit. The lower control limit is 0 and the upper limit is 9.47. When we compare each of the data points to the value of 9.47, we see they are all less than the upper control limit; the number of misspelled words is "in control." Of course, newspapers are going to strive to eliminate all misspelled words, but control charting techniques offer a means of tracking daily results and determining whether there has been a change. For example, if a new proofreader was hired, her work could be compared with others. These results are summarized in Chart 16–7.

Chart 16–7   *c*-Bar Chart for Number of Misspelled Words per Edition of the *Oak Harbor Daily Telegraph*

SELF-REVIEW   16–3

The Auto-Lite Company manufactures car batteries. At the end of each shift the Quality Assurance Department selects a sample of batteries and tests them. The number of defective batteries found over the last 12 shifts is 2, 1, 0, 2, 1, 1, 7, 1, 1, 2, 6, and 1. Construct a control chart for the process and comment on whether the process is in control.

| Exercises

9. A bicycle manufacturer randomly selects 10 frames each day and tests for defects. The number of defective frames found over the last 14 days are 3, 2, 1, 3, 2, 2, 8, 2, 0, 3, 5, 2, 0, 4. Construct a control chart for this process and comment on whether the process is "in control."

10. Scott Paper tests its toilet paper by subjecting 15 rolls to a wet stress test to see whether and how often the paper tears during the test. Following are the number of defectives found over the last 15 days: 2, 3, 1, 2, 2, 1, 3, 2, 2, 1, 2, 2, 1, 0, and 0. Construct a control chart for the process and comment on whether the process is "in control."

11. Sam's Supermarkets tests its checkout clerks by randomly examining the printout receipts for scanning errors. The following numbers are the number of errors on each receipt for October 27: 0, 1, 1, 0, 0, 1, 1, 1, 0, 1, 1, 0. Construct a control chart for this process and comment on whether the process is "in control."

12. Dave Christi runs a car wash chain scattered throughout Chicago. He is concerned that some local managers are giving away free washes to their friends. He decides to collect data on the number of "voided" sales receipts. Of course, some of them are legitimate voids. Would the following data indicate a reasonable number of "voids" at his facilities: 3, 8, 3, 4, 6, 5, 0, 1, 2, 4? Construct a control chart for this process and comment on whether the process is "in control."

▌ Acceptance Sampling

STATISTICS
IN ACTION

It was reported during the late 1980s that a Canadian firm ordered some parts from a Japanese company with instructions that there should be "no more than three defective parts per one thousand." When the parts arrived, there was a note attached that said, "Your three defective parts are wrapped separately in the upper left compartment of the shipment." This is a far cry from the days when "Made in Japan" meant cheap.

The previous section was concerned with maintaining the *quality of the product as it is being produced.* In many business situations we are also concerned with the *quality of the incoming finished product.* What do the following cases have in common?

*   Sims Software, Inc., purchased diskettes from Diskettes International. The normal purchase order is for 100,000 diskettes, packaged in lots of 1,000. Todd Sims, president, does not expect each diskette to be perfect. In fact, he has agreed to accept lots of 1,000 with up to 10 percent defective. He would like to develop a plan to inspect incoming lots, to ensure that the quality standard is met. The purpose of the inspection procedure is to separate the acceptable from the unacceptable lots.
*   Zenith Electric purchases magnetron tubes from Bono Electronics for use in their new microwave oven. The tubes are shipped to Zenith in lots of 10,000. Zenith allows the incoming lots to contain up to 5 percent defective tubes. They would like to develop a sampling plan to determine which lots meet the criterion and which do not.
*   General Motors purchases windshields from many suppliers. GM insists that the windshields be in lots of 1,000. They are willing to accept 50 or fewer defects in each lot, that is, 5 percent defective. They would like to develop a sampling procedure to verify that incoming shipments meet the criterion.

The common thread in these cases is a need to verify that an incoming product meets the stipulated requirements. The situation can be likened to a screen door, which allows the warm summer air to enter the room while keeping the bugs out. Acceptance sampling lets the lots of acceptable quality into the manufacturing area and screens out lots that are not acceptable.

Of course, the situation in modern business is more complex. The buyer wants protection against accepting lots that are below the quality standard. The best protection against inferior quality is 100 percent inspection. Unfortunately, the cost of 100 percent inspection is often prohibitive. Another problem with checking each item is that the test may be destructive. If all light bulbs were tested until burning out before they were shipped, there would be none left to sell. Also, 100 percent inspection may not lead to the identification of all defects, because boredom might cause a loss of perception on the part of the inspectors. Thus, complete inspection is rarely employed in practical situations.

Acceptance sampling

Acceptance number

The usual procedure is to screen the quality of incoming parts by using a statistical sampling plan. According to this plan, a sample of n units is randomly selected from the lots of N units (the population). This is called **acceptance sampling.** The inspection will determine the number of defects in the sample. This number is compared with a predetermined number called the **critical number** or the **acceptance number.** The acceptance number is usually designated c. If the number of defects in the sample of size n is less than or equal to c, the lot is accepted. If the number of defects exceeds c, the lot is rejected and returned to the supplier, or perhaps submitted to 100 percent inspection.

Acceptance sampling is a decision-making process. There are two possible decisions: accept or reject the lot. In addition, there are two situations under which the decision is made: the lot is good or the lot is bad. These are the states of nature. If the lot is good and the sample inspection reveals the lot to be good, or if the lot is bad and the sample inspection indicates it is bad, then a correct decision is made. However, there are two other possibilities. The lot may actually contain more defects than it should, but it is accepted. This is called **consumer's risk.** Similarly, the lot may be within the agreed-upon limits, but it is rejected during the sample inspection. This is called the **producer's risk.** The following summary table for acceptance decisions shows these possibilities.

Consumer's risk

Producer's risk

	States of Nature	
Decision	Good Lot	Bad Lot
Accept lot	Correct	Consumer's risk
Reject lot	Producer's risk	Correct

OC curve

To evaluate a sampling plan and determine that it is fair to both the producer and the consumer, the usual procedure is to develop an **operating characteristic curve,** or an **OC curve** as it is usually called. An OC curve reports the percent defective along the horizontal axis and the probability of accepting that percent defective along the vertical axis. A smooth curve is usually drawn connecting all the possible levels of quality. The binomial distribution is used to develop the probabilities for an OC curve.

Example

Sims Software, as mentioned earlier, purchases diskettes from Diskettes International. The diskettes are packaged in lots of 1,000 each. Todd Sims, president of Sims Software, has agreed to accept lots with 10 percent or fewer defective diskettes. Todd has directed his inspection department to select a random sample of 20 diskettes and examine them carefully. He will accept the lot if it has two or fewer defects in the sample. Develop an OC curve for this inspection plan. What is the probability of accepting a lot that is 10 percent defective?

Solution

This type of sampling is called **attribute sampling** because the sampled item, a diskette in this case, is classified as acceptable or unacceptable. No "reading" or "measurement" is obtained on the diskette. Let's structure the problem in terms of the states of nature. Let π represent the actual proportion defective in the population.

Attribute sampling

The lot is good if $\pi \leq .10$.

The lot is bad if $\pi > .10$.

Decision rule

Let X be the number of defects in the sample. The decision rule is:

Reject the lot if $X \geq 3$.

Accept the lot if $X \leq 2$.

Here the acceptable lot is one with 10 percent or fewer defective diskettes. If the lot is acceptable when it has exactly 10 percent defectives, it would be even more acceptable if it contained fewer than 10 percent defectives. Hence, it is the usual practice to work with the upper limit of the percent of defectives.

The binomial distribution is used to compute the various values on the OC curve. Recall that for us to use the binomial there are four requirements:

1. There are only two possible outcomes. Here the diskette is either acceptable or unacceptable.
2. There is a fixed number of trials. In this instance the number of trials is the sample size of 20.
3. There is a constant probability of success. A success is the probability of finding a defective part. It is assumed to be .10.
4. The trials are independent. The probability of obtaining a defective diskette on the third one selected is not related to the likelihood of finding a defect on the fourth diskette selected.

Appendix A gives the various binomial probabilities. We need to convert the acceptance sampling vocabulary to that used in Chapter 6 for discrete probability distributions. Let $\pi = .10$, the probability of a success, and $n = 20$, the number of trials. c is the number of defects allowed — two in this case. We will now determine the probability of accepting an incoming lot that is 10 percent defective using a sample size of 20 and allowing zero, one, or two defects. First, locate within Appendix A the case where $n = 20$ and $\pi = .10$. Find the row where X, the number of defects, is 0. The probability is .122. Next find the probability of one defect, that is, where $X = 1$. It is .270. Similarly, the probability of $X = 2$ is .285. To find the probability of two or fewer defects, we need to add these three probabilities. The total is .677. Hence, the probability of accepting a lot that is 10 percent defective is .677. The probability of rejecting this lot is .323, found by $1 - .677$. This result is usually written in shorthand notation as follows (the bar, |, means "given that"):

$$P(X \le 2 \mid \pi = .10 \text{ and } n = 20) = .677$$

The OC curve in Chart 16–8 shows various values of π and the corresponding probabilities of accepting a lot of that quality. Management of Sims Software will be able to quickly evaluate the probabilities of various quality levels.

Chart 16–8   OC Curve for Sampling Plan ($n = 20$, $c = 2$)

SELF-REVIEW   16–4

Compute the probability of accepting a lot of diskettes that is actually 30 percent defective, using the sampling plan for Sims Software.

▌ Exercises

13. Determine the probability of accepting lots that are 10 percent, 20 percent, 30 percent, and 40 percent defective using a sample of size 12 and an acceptance number of 2.
14. Determine the probability of accepting lots that are 10 percent, 20 percent, 30 percent, and 40 percent defective using a sample of size 14 and an acceptance number of 3.
15. Warren Electric manufactures fuses for many customers. To ensure the quality of the outgoing product, they test 10 fuses each hour. If no more than one fuse is defective, they package the fuses and prepare them for shipment. Develop an OC curve for this sampling plan. Compute the probabilities of accepting lots that are 10 percent, 20 percent, 30 percent, and 40 percent defective. Draw the OC curve for this sampling plan using the four quality levels.
16. Grills Radio Products purchases transistors from Mira Electronics. According to his sampling plan, Art Grills, owner of Grills Radio, will accept a shipment of transistors if three or fewer are defective in a sample of 25. Develop an OC curve for these percents defective: 10 percent, 20 percent, 30 percent, and 40 percent.

▌ Chapter Outline

I. The objective of statistical quality control is to control the quality of the product or service as it is being developed.
II. A Pareto chart is a technique for tallying the number and type of defects that happen within a product or service.
 A. This chart was named after an Italian scientist, Vilfredo Pareto.
 B. The concept of the chart is that 80 percent of the activity is caused by 20 percent of the factors.
III. A fishbone diagram emphasizes the relationship between a possible problem cause that will produce the particular effect.
 A. It is also called a cause-and-effect diagram.
 B. The usual approach is to consider four problem areas: methods, materials, equipment, and personnel.
IV. The purpose of a control chart is to portray graphically the quality of a product or service.
 A. There are two types of control charts.
  1. A variable control chart is the result of a measurement.
  2. An attribute chart shows whether the product or service is acceptable or not acceptable.
 B. There are two sources of variation in the quality of a product or service.
  1. Chance variation is random in nature and cannot be controlled or eliminated.
  2. Assignable variation is not due to random causes and can be eliminated.
 C. Four control charts were considered in this chapter.
  1. A mean chart shows the mean of a variable, and a range chart shows the range of the variable.
   a. The upper and lower control limits are set at plus or minus 3 standard errors from the mean.
   b. The formulas for the upper and lower control limits for the mean are:

$$UCL = \bar{\bar{X}} + A_2\bar{R} \qquad LCL = \bar{\bar{X}} - A_2\bar{R} \qquad \textbf{[16–4]}$$

   c. The formulas for the upper and lower control limits for the range are:

$$UCL = D_4\bar{R} \qquad LCL = D_3\bar{R} \qquad \textbf{[16–5]}$$

2. A percent defective chart is an attribute chart that shows the proportion of the product or service that does not conform to the standard.
   a. The mean percent defective is found by

   $$\bar{p} = \frac{\text{Total number defective}}{\text{Total number of items sampled}}$$ **[16–6]**

   b. The control limits for the proportion defective are determined from the equation

   $$LCL, UCL = \bar{p} \pm 3 \sqrt{\frac{\bar{p}(1 - \bar{p})}{n}}$$ **[16–8]**

3. A *c*-bar chart refers to the number of defects per unit.
   a. It is based on the Poisson distribution.
   b. The mean number of defects per unit is $\bar{c}$.
   c. The control limits are determined from the following equation.

   $$LCL, UCL = \bar{c} \pm 3 \sqrt{\bar{c}}$$ **[16–9]**

V. Acceptance sampling is a method to determine whether an incoming lot of a product meets specified standards.
   A. It is based on random sampling techniques.
   B. A random sample of *n* units is selected from a population of *N* units.
   C. *c* is the maximum number of defective units that may be found in the sample of *n* and the lot still considered acceptable.
   D. An OC (operating characteristic) curve is developed using the binomial probability distribution in order to determine the probability of accepting lots of various quality levels.

▌ Pronunciation Key

SYMBOL	MEANING	PRONUNCIATION
$\bar{\bar{X}}$	Mean of the sample means	*X double bar*
$s_{\bar{X}}$	Standard error of the mean	*s sub X bar*
A_2	Constant used to determine the upper and lower control limit for the mean	*A sub 2*
$\bar{R}$	Mean of the sample ranges	*R bar*
D_4	Constant used to determine the upper control limit for the range	*D sub 4*
$\bar{p}$	Mean of the sample proportions	*p bar*
$\bar{c}$	Mean number of defects per unit	*c bar*

▌ Chapter Exercises

17. The production supervisor at Westburg Electric, Inc., noted an increase in the number of electric motors rejected at the time of final inspection. Of the last 200 motors rejected, 80 of the defects were due to poor wiring, 60 contained a short in the coil, 50 involved a defective plug, and 10 involved other defects. Develop a Pareto chart to show the major problem areas.

18. The manufacturer of athletic shoes conducted a study on their newly developed jogging shoe. Listed below are the type and frequency of the nonconformities and failures found. Develop a Pareto chart to show the major problem areas.

Type of Nonconformity	Frequency	Type of Nonconformity	Frequency
Sole separation	34	Lace breakage	14
Heel separation	98	Eyelet failure	10
Sole penetration	62	Other	16

19. Wendy's fills their soft drinks with an automatic machine that operates based on the weight of the soft drink. When the process is in control, the machine fills each cup so that the grand mean is 10.0 ounces and the mean range is 0.25 for samples of 5.
    a. Determine the upper and lower control limits for the process for both the mean and the range.
    b. The manager of the I-280 store tested five soft drinks served last hour and found that the mean was 10.16 ounces and the range was 0.35 ounces. Is the process in control? Should other action be taken?

20. A new machine has just been installed to cut and rough-shape large slugs. The slugs are then transferred to a precision grinder. One of the critical measurements is the outside diameter. The quality control inspector randomly selected five slugs each hour, measured the outside diameter, and recorded the results. The measurements (in millimeters) for the period 8:00 A.M. to 10:30 A.M. follow.

Time	Outside Diameter (millimeters)				
	1	2	3	4	5
8:00	87.1	87.3	87.9	87.0	87.0
8:30	86.9	88.5	87.6	87.5	87.4
9:00	87.5	88.4	86.9	87.6	88.2
9:30	86.0	88.0	87.2	87.6	87.1
10:00	87.1	87.1	87.1	87.1	87.1
10:30	88.0	86.2	87.4	87.3	87.8

    a. Determine the control limits for the mean and the range.
    b. Plot the control limits for the mean outside diameter and the range.
    c. Are there any points on the mean or the range chart that are out of control? Comment on the chart.

21. The Long Last Tire Company, as part of its inspection process, tests its tires for tread wear under simulated road conditions. Twenty samples of three tires each were selected from different shifts over the last month of operation. The tread wear is reported below in hundredths of an inch.

Sample	Tread Wear			Sample	Tread Wear		
1	44	41	19	11	11	33	34
2	39	31	21	12	51	34	39
3	38	16	25	13	30	16	30
4	20	33	26	14	22	21	35
5	34	33	36	15	11	28	38
6	28	23	39	16	49	25	36
7	40	15	34	17	20	31	33
8	36	36	34	18	26	18	36
9	32	29	30	19	26	47	26
10	29	38	34	20	34	29	32

a. Determine the control limits for the mean and the range.
b. Plot the control limits for the mean outside diameter and the range.
c. Are there any points on the mean or the range chart that are out of control? Comment on the chart.

22. The Charter National Bank has a staff of loan officers located in its branch offices throughout the Southwest. The vice president in charge of the loan officers would like some information on the typical amount of loans and the range in the amount of the loans. A staff analyst of the vice president selected a sample of 10 loan officers and from each officer selected a sample of five loans he or she made last month. The data are reported below. Develop a control chart for the mean and the range of each loan officer. Do any of the officers appear to be "out of control?" Comment on your findings.

Officer	Loan Amount ($000)					Officer	Loan Amount ($000)				
	1	2	3	4	5		1	2	3	4	5
Weinraub	59	74	53	48	65	Bowyer	66	80	54	68	52
Visser	42	51	70	47	67	Kuhlman	74	43	45	65	49
Moore	52	42	53	87	85	Ludwig	75	53	68	50	31
Brunner	36	70	62	44	79	Longnecker	42	65	70	41	52
Wolf	34	59	39	78	61	Simonetti	43	38	10	19	47

23. The producer of a candy bar, called the Mickey Mantle Bar, reports on the package that the calorie content is 420 per 2-ounce bar. A sample of 5 bars from each of the last 10 days is sent for a chemical analysis of the calorie content. The results are shown below. Does it appear that there are any days where the calorie count is out of control? Develop an appropriate control chart and analyze your findings.

Sample	Calorie Count					Sample	Calorie Count				
	1	2	3	4	5		1	2	3	4	5
1	426	406	418	431	432	6	427	417	408	418	422
2	421	422	415	412	411	7	422	417	426	435	426
3	425	420	406	409	414	8	419	417	412	415	417
4	424	419	402	400	417	9	417	432	417	416	422
5	421	408	423	410	421	10	420	422	421	415	422

24. The Early Morning Delivery Service guarantees delivery of small packages by 10:30 A.M. Of course, some of the packages are not delivered by 10:30 A.M. For a sample of 200 packages delivered each of the last 15 working days, the following number of packages were delivered after the deadline: 9, 14, 2, 13, 9, 5, 9, 3, 4, 3, 4, 3, 3, 8, and 4.
a. Determine the mean proportion of packages delivered after 10:30 A.M.
b. Determine the control limits for the proportion of packages delivered after 10:30 A.M. Were any of the sampled days out of control?
c. If 10 packages out of 200 in the sample were delivered after 10:30 A.M. today, is this sample within the control limits?

25. An automatic machine produces 5.0 millimeter bolts at a high rate of speed. A quality control program has been started to control the number of defectives. The quality control inspector selects 50 bolts at random and determines how many are defective. The number of defective in the first 10 samples are 3, 5, 0, 4, 1, 2, 6, 5, 7, and 7.
a. Design a percent defective chart. Insert the mean percent defective, *UCL,* and *LCL.*
b. Plot the percent defective for the first 10 samples on the chart.
c. Interpret the chart.

26. The Inter State Moving and Storage Company is setting up a control chart to monitor the proportion of residential moves that result in written complaints due to late delivery, lost items, or damaged items. A sample of 50 moves is selected for each of the last 12 months. The number of written complaints in each sample is 8, 7, 4, 8, 2, 7, 11, 6, 7, 6, 8, and 12.
    a. Design a percent defective chart. Insert the mean percent defective, *UCL,* and *LCL.*
    b. Plot the proportion of written complaints in the last 12 months.
    c. Interpret the chart. Does it appear that the number of complaints is out of control for any of the months?

27. Eric's Cookie House sells chocolate chip cookies in shopping malls. Of concern is the number of chocolate chips in each cookie. Eric, the owner and president, would like to establish a control chart for the number of chocolate chips per cookie. He selects a sample of 15 cookies from today's production and counts the number of chocolate chips in each. The results are as follows: 6, 8, 20, 12, 20, 19, 11, 23, 12, 14, 15, 16, 12, 13, and 12.
    a. Determine the centerline and the control limits.
    b. Develop a control chart and plot the number of chocolate chips per cookie.
    c. Interpret the chart. Does it appear that the number of chocolate chips is out of control in any of the cookies sampled?

28. The number of "near misses" recorded for the last 20 months at the Lima International Airport are 3, 2, 3, 2, 2, 3, 5, 1, 2, 2, 4, 4, 2, 6, 3, 5, 2, 5, 1, and 3. Develop an appropriate control chart. Determine the mean number of misses per month and the limits on the number of misses per month. Are there any months where the number of near misses is out of control?

29. The following number of robberies were reported during the last 10 days to the Robbery Division of the Metro City Police: 10, 8, 8, 7, 8, 5, 8, 5, 4, and 7. Develop an appropriate control chart. Determine the mean number of robberies reported per day and determine the control limits. Are there any days when the number of robberies reported is out of control?

30. Seiko purchases watch stems for their watches in lots of 10,000. Seiko's sampling plan calls for checking 20 stems, and if 3 or fewer stems are defective, the lot is accepted.
    a. Based on their sampling plan, what is the probability that a lot of 40 percent defective will be accepted?
    b. Design an OC curve for incoming lots that have zero, 10 percent, 20 percent, 30 percent, and 40 percent defective stems.

31. Automatic Screen Door Manufacturing Company purchases door latches from a number of vendors. The purchasing department is responsible for inspecting the incoming latches. Automatic purchases 10,000 door latches per month and inspects 20 latches selected at random. Develop an OC curve for the sampling plan if three latches can be defective and the incoming lot is still accepted.

32. At the beginning of each football season Team Sports, the local sporting goods store, purchases 5,000 footballs. A sample of 25 balls is selected, and they are inflated, tested, and then deflated. If more than two balls are found defective, the lot of 5,000 is returned to the manufacturer. Develop an OC curve for this sampling plan.
    a. What are the probabilities of accepting lots that are 10 percent, 20 percent, and 30 percent defective?
    b. Estimate the probability of accepting a lot that is 15 percent defective.
    c. John Brennen, owner of Team Sports, would like the probability of accepting a lot that is 5 percent defective to be more than 90 percent. Does this appear to be the case with this sampling plan?

▌ Computer Commands

1. The MINITAB commands for the *X*-bar and *R* charts on page 595 are:
    a. Use the set command to enter the data in a single column. Label this column *Minutes.*
    b. Select **Stat, Control Charts,** and **Xbar-R** and then hit **Enter.**

c. Select the **single column** format and indicate that the subgroup size is 5.
d. Click on **Options** and write the title for the chart in the space provided, then click **OK.**
e. Click **OK** in the dialog box.

Xbar/R Chart

| C1   Minutes | **Data are arranged as** | **Tests...** |

⊙ **Single column:**   Minutes   **Tests...**

Subgroup size: 5   **Estimate...**

[use a constant or an ID column]   **Stamp...**

○ **Subgroups across rows of:**   **Options...**

Historical mean: [   ] (optional)

Historical sigma: [   ] (optional)

Select

Help   **OK**

Cancel

CHAPTER 16 *Answers to Self-Review*

16–1

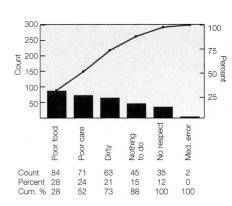

	Poor food	Poor care	Dirty	Nothing to do	No respect	Med. error
Count	84	71	63	45	35	2
Percent	28	24	21	15	12	0
Cum. %	28	52	73	88	100	100

Seventy-two percent of the complaints involve poor food, poor care, or dirty conditions. These are the factors the administrator should address.

16–2 (a)

Sample Piece

	1	2	3	4	Total	Average	Range
1	4	5	2		12	3	4
2	3	2	1		8	2	2
1	7	3	5		16	4	6
						9	12

$$\overline{\overline{X}} = \frac{9}{3} = 3 \qquad \overline{R} = \frac{12}{3} = 4$$

$$UCL \text{ and } LCL = \overline{\overline{X}} \pm A_2\overline{R}$$

$$= 3 \pm 0.729(4)$$

$$UCL = 5.916 \qquad LCL = 0.084$$

$$LCL = D_3\overline{R} = 0(4) = 0$$

$$UCL = D_4\overline{R} = 2.282(4) = 9.128$$

(b) Yes. Both the mean chart and the range chart indicate that the process is in control.

16–3 $\bar{c} = \frac{25}{12} = 2.083$

$$UCL = 2.083 + 3\sqrt{2.083} = 6.413$$

$$LCL = 2.083 - 3\sqrt{2.083} = 0$$

The shift with 7 defects is out of control.

16–4 $P(X \le 2/\pi = .30 \text{ and } n = 20) = .036$

Chapter Seventeen

Index Numbers

An index of clothing and shoe prices for 1998 needs to be prepared. Given the prices and quantities consumed in 1995, what is the aggregate price index for the two years? (See Goal 2 and Self Review 17–2.)

▌ Introduction

In this chapter we will examine a useful descriptive tool called an **index.** No doubt you are familiar with indexes such as the **Consumer Price Index,** which is released monthly. There are many other indexes, such as the **Dow Jones Industrial Average** and **Standard & Poor's 500 Stock Average.** Indexes are published on a regular basis by the federal government and by business publications such as *Business Week* and *Forbes.*

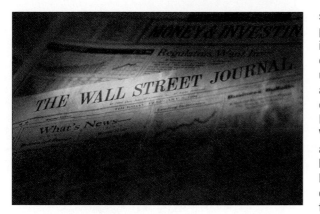

Of what importance is an index? Why is the Consumer Price Index so important and so widely reported? As the name implies, it measures the change in the price of a large group of items consumers purchase. The Federal Reserve Board, consumer groups, unions, management, senior citizens organizations, and others in business and economics are very concerned about changes in prices. The Consumer Price Index and the **Producer Price Index** (formerly the **Wholesale Price Index**), which measures price fluctuations at all stages of production, are closely watched by these groups. To combat sharp price increases, the Federal Reserve often raises the interest rate to "cool down" the economy. Likewise, the Dow Jones Industrial Average, which is published daily, describes the overall change in common stock prices of 30 large companies during the day.

A few stock market indexes appear daily in the financial section of most newspapers. They are updated at least every 15 minutes on many web sites such as the business section of *USA Today* (*http://www.usatoday.com/money/mfront.htm*). Shown are the Dow Jones Industrial Average, Nasdaq, and S&P 500.

▌ Simple Index Numbers

What is an index number?

▌ **Index Number** A number that expresses the relative change in price, quantity, or value from one period to another.

If the index number is used to measure the relative change in just one variable—such as hourly wages in manufacturing—we refer to this as a **simple index.** It is the ratio of two variables and that ratio converted to a percentage. The following four examples will serve to illustrate the use of index numbers.

Example

As noted in the definition, the main use of an index number in business is to show the percent change in one or more items from one time period to another. According to the Bureau of Labor Statistics, in January 1987 the average hourly earnings of production workers was $8.90. In September 1997 it was $12.39. What is the index of hourly earnings of production workers for September 1997 based on January 1987?

Solution

It is 139.2, found by:

$$P = \frac{\text{Average hourly earnings of production workers in September 1997}}{\text{Average hourly earnings of production workers in January 1987}} \times 100$$

$$= \frac{\$12.39}{\$8.90}(100) = 139.2$$

Thus, hourly earnings of production workers in September 1997 compared to January 1987 were 139.2 percent. This means there was a 39.2 percent increase in hourly earnings during the period, found by $139.2 - 100 = 39.2$.

Example

The Bureau of the Census reported the farm population dropped from 30,529,000 in 1930 to an estimated 4,900,000 in 1997. What is the index of farm population for 1997 based on 1930?

Solution

The index is 16.1, found by

$$\frac{1997 \text{ population}}{1930 \text{ population}} \times 100 = \frac{4,900,000}{30,529,000} \times 100 = 16.1$$

This indicates the farm population in 1997 compared with 1930 was 16.1 percent, or it decreased 83.9 percent during the period, found by $100.0 - 16.1$.

Example

An index can also be used to compare one thing with another: The population of the Canadian province of British Columbia is estimated to be 3,668,000; for Ontario, 10,928,000. What is the population of British Columbia compared with that of Ontario?

Solution

The index of population for British Columbia is 33.6, found by:

$$\frac{\text{Population of British Columbia}}{\text{Population of Ontario}} \times 100 = \frac{3,668,000}{10,928,000} \times 100 = 33.6$$

This indicates the population of British Columbia is 33.6 percent (about one third) of the population of Ontario, or the population of British Columbia is 66.4 percent less than the population of Ontario ($100.0 - 33.6 = 66.4$).

Example

The number of passengers arriving and departing at Chicago's O'Hare International Airport, the busiest in the United States, is 65,091,168 a year; for the eighth busiest, JFK in New York, the number is 26,796,036. What is the arrival and departure rate for O'Hare compared with that of JFK, expressed as an index?

Solution

The index for O'Hare is 242.9, found by:

$$\frac{\text{Arrive/depart O'Hare}}{\text{Arrive/depart JFK}} \times 100 = \frac{65,091,168}{26,796,036} \times 100 = 242.9$$

This indicates the number of arrivals and departures from Chicago's O'Hare is 242.9 percent of that of New York's JFK; that is, O'Hare's arrival and departure rate is 142.9 percent greater than that for JFK.

Note from the previous discussion that:

1. The index of average hourly earnings of production workers (139.2) and the index of farm population (16.1) are actually percentages. However, the percent sign is usually omitted.
2. Each index has a **base period.** In the example regarding the average hourly earnings of production workers, we used January 1987 as the base period. Until recently the base period for the Consumer Price Index was the period 1982–84. In January 1999 it was revised to 1993–95. The parity ratio, which is the ratio of prices received by farmers to the prices paid by farmers, still has 1910–14 as the base period.
3. Most business and economic indexes are computed to either the nearest whole number, such as 214 or 96, or to the nearest tenth of a percent, such as 97.5 or 178.6.

Why Convert Data to Indexes?

Indexes allow us to express a change in price, quantity, or value as a percent

Compiling index numbers is not a recent innovation. An Italian, G. R. Carli, is credited with originating the first index numbers in 1764. They were incorporated in a report he made regarding price fluctuations in Europe from 1500 to 1750. No systematic approach to collecting and reporting data in index form was evident in the United States until about 1900. The cost-of-living index (now called the Consumer Price Index) was introduced in 1913, and a long list of indexes have been compiled since then.

Why convert data to indexes? An index is a convenient way to express a change in a heterogenous group of items. The Consumer Price Index (CPI), for example, encompasses about 400 items — including golf balls, lawn mowers, hamburgers, funeral services, and dentists' fees. Prices are expressed in dollars per pound, box, yard, and many other different units. Only by converting the prices of these many diverse goods and services to one index number every month can the federal government and others concerned with inflation keep informed of the overall movement of consumer prices.

Converting data to indexes also makes it easier to assess the trend in a series composed of exceptionally large numbers. For example, suppose retail sales for the first six months of 1997 were $185,679,432,621.87 and 1992 six-month sales were $185,500,000,000.00. The increase of $179,432,621.87 appears significant. Yet if the 1997 sales total were expressed as an index based on 1992 sales, the increase would be less than one tenth of 1 percent!

$$\frac{\text{Retail sales in 1997}}{\text{Retail sales in 1992}} = \frac{\$185,679,432,621.87}{\$185,500,000,000.00} \times 100 = 100.09$$

SELF-REVIEW 17-1

1. The annual sales for a few selected industrial corporations are:

Company	Sales ($ million)	Company	Sales ($ million)
GM	101,781.9	IBM	54,217.0
Exxon	76,416.0	Daimler–Chrysler	26,257.7
Ford	71,643.4		

(a) Express the annual sales of GM as an index, using the sales of IBM as the base (denominator). Interpret.
(b) Express the annual sales of Daimler-Chrysler as an index, using the sales of IBM as the base. Interpret.

2. The average hourly earnings in the retail trade for selected periods are:

Year	Average Hourly Earnings	Year	Average Hourly Earnings
1988	$5.16	1990	5.44
1989	5.30	1998 (April)	9.45

(a) Using 1988 as the base period, determine the index number for April 1998 that might aptly be called the index of average hourly earnings in retail trade. Interpret this index.
(b) Using the average of 1988 and 1989 (that is, 1988–89 = 100), determine the index for April 1998.
(c) What is the index for April 1998, using 1990 = 100? Interpret.

❙ Exercises

1. In 1990 the sales of Johnson and Johnson Co., in millions, were $1,461; in 1995 sales increased to $2,403; and by 1996 sales were $2,887. Using 1990 as the base, develop a simple index for the change in sales at Johnson and Johnson for the years 1995 and 1996, based on 1990 sales.
2. In 1992 the net sales, in millions, at Pepsico were $21,885; in 1995 net sales increased to $30,225; and by 1996 they had increased to $31,645. Use 1995 as the base year. Compute an index for each year. What percent less were 1992 sales than 1995 sales? What percent more were 1996 sales than 1995 sales?
3. Listed below is information on gross profit, in millions, at IBM for the years 1994 through 1996.

Year	1996	1995	1994
Gross profit	$30,539	$30,367	$25,284

Use a 1994–95 average as the base and determine a simple index for 1996.
4. In January 1994 the price for fresh whole chicken was $0.899 per pound. This was the U.S. average. In September 1997 the price for the same chicken was $0.992. Use the January 1994 price as the base period. Develop a simple index. By what percent had the cost of chicken increased?

Construction of Index Numbers

We already discussed the construction of a simple price index. The price in a selected year (such as 1998) is divided by the price in the base year.

The base-period price is designated as p_0, and a price other than the base period is often referred to as the *given period* or *selected period* and designated p_t. To calculate the simple price index P for any given period:

SIMPLE INDEX	$P = \dfrac{p_t}{p_0} \times 100$	**[17–1]**

Suppose that the price of a standard lot at the Shady Rest Cemetery in 1990 was $450. The price rose to $795 in 1998. What is the price index for 1998 using 1990 as the base period? It is 176.7, found by:

$$P = \frac{p_t}{p_0}(100) = \frac{\$795}{\$450}(100) = 176.7$$

Interpreting this result, the price of a cemetery lot increased 76.7 percent from 1990 to 1998.

The base period need not be a single year. Note in Table 17–1 that if we use 1980–81 = 100, the base price for the stapler would be $21 [found by determining the mean price of 1980 and 1981, ($20 + $22)/2 = $21]. The prices $20, $22, and $23 would be averaged if 1980–82 had been selected as the base. The mean price would be $21.67. The indexes constructed using the three different base periods are presented in Table 17–1. (Note that when 1980–82 = 100, the index numbers for 1980, 1981, and 1982 average 100.0, as we would expect.) Logically, the index numbers for 1998 using the three different bases are not the same.

Table 17–1 Prices of a Benson Automatic Stapler, Model 3, Converted to Indexes Using Three Different Base Periods

Year	Price of Stapler	Price Index (1980 = 100)	Price index (1980–81 = 100)	Price index (1980–82 = 100)
1975	$18	90.0	$\dfrac{18}{21} \times 100 = 85.7$	$\dfrac{18}{21.67} \times 100 = 83.1$
1980	20	100.0	$\dfrac{20}{21} \times 100 = 95.2$	$\dfrac{20}{21.67} \times 100 = 92.3$
1981	22	110.0	$\dfrac{22}{21} \times 100 = 104.8$	$\dfrac{22}{21.67} \times 100 = 101.5$
1982	23	115.0	$\dfrac{23}{21} \times 100 = 109.5$	$\dfrac{23}{21.67} \times 100 = 106.1$
1998	38	190.0	$\dfrac{38}{21} \times 100 = 181.0$	$\dfrac{38}{21.67} \times 100 = 175.4$

Unweighted Indexes

In many situations we wish to combine several items and develop an index to compare the cost of a group of items in two different time periods. For example, we might be interested in an index for items that relate to the expense of running and maintaining an automobile. The items in the index might include tires, oil changes, and gasoline prices. Or we might be interested in a college student index. This index might include the cost of books, tuition, housing, meals, and entertainment. There are several ways we can combine the items to determine the index.

Simple Average of the Price Relatives

Table 17–2 reports the prices for several food items for the years 1995 and 1998. We would like to develop an index for this group of food items for 1998, using 1995 as the base. This is written 1995 = 100.

Table 17–2   Computation of Index for Food Price 1998, 1995 = 100

Item	1995 Price	1998 Price	Simple Index
Bread, white, cost per pound	$0.77	$0.89	115.6
Eggs, dozen	1.85	1.84	99.5
Milk, gallon, white	.88	1.01	114.8
Apples, Red Delicious, 1 pound	1.46	1.56	106.8
Orange Juice, 12 oz concentrate	1.58	1.70	107.6
Coffee, 100% ground roast, 1 pound	4.40	4.62	105.0
Total	$10.94	$11.62	

We could begin by computing a **simple average of the price relatives** for each item, using 1995 as the base year and 1998 as the given year. The simple index for bread is 115.6, found by using formula (17–1).

$$P = \frac{p_t}{p_0}(100) = \frac{\$0.89}{\$0.77}(100) = 115.6$$

We compute the simple index for the other items in Table 17–2 similarly. The largest price increase was for bread, 15.6 percent, and milk was a close second with 14.8 percent. The price of eggs dropped by a half a percent in the three-year period, found by 100.0 − 99.5 = 0.5. Then it would be natural to average the simple indexes. The formula is:

SIMPLE AVERAGE OF THE PRICE RELATIVES	$P = \dfrac{\Sigma P_i}{n}$	**[17–2]**

where P_i refers to the index for each of the items and n the number of items. In our example the index is 108.2, found by:

$$P = \frac{\Sigma P_i}{n} = \frac{115.6 + \cdots + 105.0}{6} = \frac{649.3}{6} = 108.2$$

This indicates that the mean of the group of indexes increased 8.2 percent from 1995 to 1998.

A positive feature of the simple average of price relatives is we would obtain the same value for the index regardless of the units of measure. In the above index, if apples were priced in tons, instead of pounds, the impact of apples on the average would not change. That is, the commodity "apples" represents one of six items in the index, so the impact of the item is not related to the units. A negative feature of this index is that it fails to consider the relative importance of the items included in the index. For example, milk and eggs receive the same weight, even though a typical family might spend far more over the year on milk than on eggs.

Simple Aggregate Index

A second possibility is to sum the prices for the two periods (rather than the indexes) and then determine the index based on the totals. The formula is

SIMPLE AGGREGATE INDEX	$P = \dfrac{\Sigma p_t}{\Sigma p_0} \times 100$	[17–3]

This is called a **simple aggregate index.** The index for the above food items is found by summing the prices in 1995 and 1998. The sum of the prices for the base period is $10.94 and for the given period it is $11.62. The simple aggregate index is 106.2. This means that the aggregate group of prices had increased 6.2 percent in the three-year period.

$$P = \frac{\Sigma p_t}{\Sigma p_0}(100) = \frac{\$11.62}{\$10.94}(100) = 106.2$$

Because the value of a simple aggregate index can be influenced by the units of measurement, it is not used frequently. In our example the value of the index would differ significantly if we were to report the price of apples in tons rather than pounds. Also, note the effect of coffee on the total index. For both the current year and the base year, the value of coffee is about 40 percent of the total index, so a change in the price of coffee will drive the index much more than any other item. So we need a way to appropriately "weight" the items according to their relative importance.

▌ Weighted Indexes

Two methods of computing a **weighted price index** are the **Laspeyres** method and the **Paasche** method. They differ only with respect to the period used for weighting. The Laspeyres method uses *base-period weights*; that is, the original prices and quantities of the items bought are used to find the percent change over a period of time in either price or quantity consumed, depending on the problem. The Paasche method uses *current-year weights* for the denominator of the weighted index.

Laspeyres' Price Index

Etienne Laspeyres developed a method in the latter part of the 18th century to determine a weighted index using base-period weights. Applying his method, a weighted price index is computed by:

LASPEYRES' PRICE INDEX	$P = \dfrac{\Sigma p_t q_0}{\Sigma p_0 q_0} \times 100$	[17–4]

where:

P is the price index.
p_t is the current price.
p_0 is the price in the base period.
q_0 is the quantity consumed in the base period.

Example

The prices for the six food items from Table 17–2 are repeated below in Table 17.3. Also included is the number of units of each consumed by a typical family in 1995 and 1998.

Table 17–3   Computation of Laspeyres and Paasche Indexes of Food Price, 1995 = 100

Item	1995 Price	1995 Quantity	1998 Price	1998 Quantity
Bread, white, cost per pound	$0.77	50	$0.89	55
Eggs, dozen	1.85	26	1.84	20
Milk, gallon, white	.88	102	1.01	130
Apples, Red Delicious, 1 pound	1.46	30	1.56	40
Orange Juice, 12 oz concentrate	1.58	40	1.70	41
Coffee, 100% ground roast, 1 pound	4.40	12	4.62	12

Determine a weighted price index using the Laspeyres method. Interpret the result.

Solution

First we determine the total amount spent for the six items in the base period, 1995. To find this value we multiply the base period price for bread ($0.77) by the base period quantity of 50. The result is $38.50. This indicates that a total of $38.50 was spent in the base period on bread. We continue that for all items and total the results. The base period total is $336.16. The current period total is computed in a similar fashion. For the first item, bread, we multiply the quantity in 1995 by the price of bread in 1998, that is $0.89(50). The result is $44.50. We make the same calculation for each item and total the result. The total is $365.60. Because of the repetitive nature of these calculations a spreadsheet is effective for carrying out the calculations. Below is a copy of the Excel output.

```
                              Laspeyres' Index

Item          Price-95 Quantity-95 Price-Qty-95 Price-98 Quantity-98 Pr-98*Qty-95

Bread           0.77       50          38.5       0.89        55         44.5

Eggs            1.85       26          48.1       1.84        20         47.84

Milk            0.88      102          89.76      1.01       130        103.02

Apples          1.46       30          43.8       1.56        40         46.8

Orange Juice    1.58       40          63.2       1.7         41         68

Coffee          4.4        12          52.8       4.62        12         55.44

                                      336.16                            365.6
```

The weighted price index for 1998 is 108.8, found by

$$P = \frac{\Sigma p_t q_0}{\Sigma p_0 q_0}(100) = \frac{\$365.60}{\$336.16}(100) = 108.8$$

Based on this analysis we conclude that the price of this group of items has increased 8.8 percent in the three year period. The advantage of this method over the simple aggregate index is that the weight of each of the items is considered. In the simple aggregate index coffee had about 40 percent of the weight in determining the index. In the Laypeyres index the item with the most weight is milk, because the product of the price and the units sold is the largest.

The major disadvantage of the Laypeyres index is it assumes that the base-period quantities are still realistic in the given period. That is, the quantities used for the six items are about the same in 1995 as 1998. In this case notice that the quantity of eggs purchased declined by 23 percent, the quantity of milk increased by nearly 28 percent, and the number of apples increased by 33 percent.

Paasche's Price Index

The Paasche index is an alternative. The procedure is similar, but instead of using base period weights, we use current period weights. We use the sum of the products of the 1995 prices and the 1998 quantities. This has the advantage of using the more recent quantities. If there has been a change in the quantities consumed since the base period, such a change is reflected in the Paasche index.

PAASCHE'S PRICE INDEX	$P = \dfrac{\Sigma p_t q_t}{\Sigma p_0 q_t} \times 100$	**[17–5]**

Example

Use the information from Table 17–3 to determine the Paasche Index. Discuss which of the indexes should be used.

Solution

Again, because of the repetitive nature of the calculations, Excel is used to perform the calculations. The results are shown in the following output.

	Paasche's Index					
Item	Price-95	Quanty-95	Price95*Qty98	Price-98	Quantity-98	Price98*Qty98
Bread	0.77	50	42.35	0.89	55	48.95
Eggs	1.85	26	37	1.84	20	36.8
Milk	0.88	102	114.4	1.01	130	131.3
Apples	1.46	30	58.4	1.56	40	62.4
Orange Juice	1.58	40	64.78	1.7	41	69.7
Coffee	4.4	12	52.8	4.62	12	55.44
			369.73			404.59

The Paasche index is 109.4, found by

$$P = \frac{\Sigma p_t q_t}{\Sigma p_0 q_t}(100) = \frac{\$404.59}{\$369.73}(100) = 109.4$$

This result indicates that there has been an increase of 9.4 percent in the price of this market basket of goods between 1995 and 1998. That is, it costs 9.4 percent more to purchase these items in 1998 than it did in 1995. All things considered, because of the change in the quantities purchased between 1995 and 1998, the Paasche index is more reflective of the current situation. It should be noted that the Laspeyres index is more widely used. The Consumer Price Index, the most widely reported index, is an example of a Laspeyres' index.

How do we decide which index to use? When is Laspeyres' most appropriate and when is Paasche's the better choice?

Laspeyres'

Advantages   Requires quantity data from only the base period. This allows a more meaningful comparison over time. The changes in the index can be attributed to changes in the price.

Disadvantages	Does not reflect changes in buying patterns over time. Also, it may overweight goods whose prices increase.

Paasche's

Advantages	Because it uses quantities from the current period, it reflects current buying habits.
Disadvantages	It requires quantity data for each year, which may be difficult to obtain. Because different quantities are used each year, it is impossible to attribute changes in the index to changes in price alone. It tends to overweight the goods whose prices have declined. It requires the prices to be recomputed each year.

Fisher's Ideal Index

As noted above, Laspeyres' index tends to overweight goods whose prices have increased. Paasche's index, on the other hand, tends to overweight goods whose prices have gone down. In an attempt to offset these shortcomings, Irving Fisher, in his book *The Making of Index Numbers,* published in 1922, proposed an index called **Fisher's Ideal Index.** It is the geometric mean of the Laspeyres and Paasche indexes. We described the geometric mean in Chapter 3. It is determined by taking the *k*th root of the product of *k* positive numbers.

$$\text{Fisher's ideal index} = \sqrt{(\text{Laspeyres' index})(\text{Paasche's index})} \qquad \textbf{[17–6]}$$

Fisher's index seems to be theoretically ideal because it combines the best features of both Laspeyres' and Paasche. That is, it balances the effects of the two indexes. However, it is rarely used in practice because it has the same basic set of problems as the Paasche index. It requires that a new set of quantities be determined for each year.

Example / *Solution*

Determine Fisher's ideal index for the data in Table 17–3.

Fisher's ideal index is 102.3.

$$\text{Fisher's ideal index} = \sqrt{(\text{Laspeyres' index})(\text{Paasche's index})}$$

$$= \sqrt{(108.8)(109.4)} = 109.1$$

SELF-REVIEW 17–2

An index of clothing prices for 1998 based on 1995 is to be constructed. The clothing items considered are shoes and dresses. The information for prices and quantities for both years is given below. Use 1995 as the base period.

	1995		1998	
Item	Price	Quantity	Price	Quantity
Dress (each)	$75	500	$85	520
Shoes (pair)	40	1,200	45	1,300

(a) Determine the simple average of the price relatives.
(b) Determine the aggregate price indexes for the two years.
(c) Determine Laspeyres' price index.
(d) Determine the Paasche price index.
(e) Determine Fisher's ideal index.

▌ Exercises

For exercises 5–8:

a. Determine the simple price relatives.

b. Determine the simple aggregate price indexes for the two years.

c. Determine Laspeyres' price index.

d. Determine the Paasche price index.

e. Determine Fisher's ideal index.

5. Below are the prices of toothpaste (9 oz), shampoo (7 oz), cough tablets (package of 100), and antiperspirant (2 oz) for August 1996 and August 1999. Also included are the quantity purchased. Use August 1996 as the base.

Item	August 1996 Price	August 1996 Quantity	August 1999 Price	August 1999 Quantity
Toothpaste	$2.49	6	$2.69	6
Shampoo	3.29	4	3.59	5
Cough tablets	1.59	2	1.79	3
Antiperspirant	1.79	3	2.29	4

6. Fruit prices and the amounts consumed for 1990 and 1998 are below. Use 1990 as the base.

Fruit	1990 Price	1990 Quantity	1998 Price	1998 Quantity
Bananas (pound)	$0.23	100	$0.35	120
Grapefruit (each)	0.29	50	0.27	55
Apples (pound)	0.35	85	0.35	85
Strawberries (basket)	1.02	8	1.40	10
Oranges (bag)	0.89	6	0.99	8

7. The prices and the numbers of various items produced by a small machine and stamping plant are reported below. Use 1992 as the base.

Item	1992 Price	1992 Quantity	1999 Price	1999 Quantity
Washer	$0.07	17,000	$0.10	20,000
Cotter pin	0.04	125,000	0.03	130,000
Stove bolt	0.15	40,000	0.15	42,000
Hex nut	0.08	62,000	0.10	65,000

8. Following are the quantities and prices for the years 1995 and 1999 for Kinzua Valley Geriatrics. Use 1995 as the base period.

Item	1995 Price	1995 Quantity	1999 Price	1999 Quantity
Syringes (dozen)	$6.10	1,500	$6.50	2,000
Thermometers	8.10	10	8.90	12
Advil (bottle)	4.00	250	4.40	250
Patient record forms (box)	6.00	1,000	6.50	900
Computer paper (box)	12.00	30	13.00	40

▮ Value Index

Value index measures percent change in value

A **value index** measures changes in both the price and quantities involved. A value index, such as the index of department store sales, needs the original base-year prices, the original base-year quantities, the present-year prices, and the present-year quantities for its construction. Its formula is:

VALUE INDEX	$$V = \frac{\sum p_t q_t}{\sum p_0 q_0} \times 100$$	**[17–7]**

Example

The prices and quantities sold at the Waleska Department Store for various items of apparel for May 1992 and May 1998 are:

Item	1992 Price, p_0	1992 Quantity Sold (thousands), q_0	1998 Price, p_t	1998 Quantity Sold (thousands), q_t
Ties (each)	$ 1	1,000	$ 2	900
Suits (each)	30	100	40	120
Shoes (pair)	10	500	8	500

What is the index of value for May 1998 using May 1992 as the base period?

Solution

Total sales in May 1998 were $10,600,000, and the comparable figure for 1992 is $9,000,000. (See Table 17–4.) Thus, the index of value for May 1998 using 1992 = 100 is 117.8. The value of apparel sales in 1998 was 117.8 percent of the 1992 sales. To put it another way, the value of apparel sales increased 17.8 percent from May 1992 to May 1998.

$$V = \frac{\sum p_t q_t}{\sum p_0 q_0}(100) = \frac{\$10,600,000}{\$9,000,000}(100) = 117.8$$

Table 17–4   **Construction of a Value Index for 1998 (1992 = 100)**

Item	1992 Price, p_0	1992 Quantity Sold (thousands), q_0	$p_0 q_0$ ($ thousands)	1998 Price, p_t	1998 Quantity Sold (thousands), q_t	$p_t q_t$ ($ thousands)
Ties (each)	$ 1	1,000	$1,000	$ 2	900	$ 1,800
Suits (each)	30	100	3,000	40	120	4,800
Shoes (pair)	10	500	5,000	8	500	4,000
			$9,000			$10,600

SELF-REVIEW 17-3

The number of items produced by Houghton Products for 1996 and 1999 and the whole-sale prices for the two periods are:

	Price		Number Produced	
Item Produced	1996	1999	1996	1999
Shear pins (box)	$ 3	$4	10,000	9,000
Cutting compound (pound)	1	5	600	200
Tie rods (each)	10	8	3,000	5,000

(a) Find the index of the value of production for 1999 using 1996 as the base period.
(b) Interpret the index.

▌ Exercises

9. The prices and production of grains for August 1995 and August 1999 are:

Grain	1995 Price	1995 Quantity Produced (millions of bushels)	1999 Price	1999 Quantity Produced (millions of bushels)
Oats	$1.52	200	$1.87	214
Wheat	2.10	565	2.05	489
Corn	1.48	291	1.48	203
Barley	3.05	87	3.29	106

Using 1995 as the base period, find the value index of grains produced for August 1999.

10. The Johnson Wholesale Company manufactures a variety of products. The prices and quantities produced for April 1994 and April 1998 are:

Product	1994 Price	1998 Price	1994 Quantity Produced	1998 Quantity Produced
Small motor (each)	$23.60	$28.80	1,760	4,259
Scrubbing compound (gallon)	2.96	3.08	86,450	62,949
Nails (pound)	0.40	0.48	9,460	22,370

Using April 1994 as the base period, find the index of the value of goods produced for April 1998.

▌ Special Purpose Indexes

Many important indexes are prepared and published by private organizations. J. D. Power & Associates surveys automobile purchasers to determine how satisfied customers are with their vehicle after one year of ownership. This special index is called the *Consumer Satisfaction Index*. Financial institutions, utility companies, and university bureaus of research often prepare indexes on employment, factory hours and wages, and retail sales for the regions they serve. Many trade associations prepare indexes of price and quantity that are vital to their particular area of interest. How are these special indexes prepared? An example, simplified of course, will help to explain some of the details.

Example

The Seattle Chamber of Commerce wants to develop a measure of general business activity for the northwest portion of the United States. The Director of Economic Development has been assigned to develop the index. It will be called the *General Business Activity Index of the Northwest.*

Solution

After considerable thought and research, the director has concluded that four factors should be considered: the regional department store sales (which are reported in $ millions), the regional employment index (which has a 1990 base and is reported by the Commonwealth of Washington), the freight car loadings (reported in millions), and exports for the Seattle Harbor (reported in thousands of tons). Recent information on these variables is reported in Table 17–5.

Table 17–5   Data for the Computation of the General Business Activity Index of the Northwest

Year	Department Store Sales	Index of Employment	Freight Car Loadings	Exports
1990	20	100	50	500
1995	41	110	30	900
1998	44	125	18	700

After review and consultation the director assigned weights of 40 percent to department store sales, 30 percent to employment, 10 percent to freight car loadings, and 20 percent to exports.

To develop the General Business Activity Index of the Northwest for 1998 using 1990 = 100, each 1998 value is expressed as a percentage, with the base-period value as the denominator. For illustration, department store sales for 1998 are converted to a percentage by ($44/$20)(100) = 220. This means that department store sales have increased 120 percent in the eight-year period. This percentage is then adjusted by the appropriate weight. For the department store sales this is (220)(.40) = 88.0. The details of the calculations for the years 1995 and 1998 are shown below.

	1995		1998	
Department store sales	($41/$20)(100)(.40) =	82.0	($44/$20)(100)(.40) =	88.0
Employment	(110/100)(100)(.30) =	33.0	(125/100)(100)(.30) =	37.5
Freight car loadings	(30/50)(100)(.10) =	6.0	(18/50)(100)(.10) =	3.6
Exports	(900/500)(100)(.20) =	36.0	(700/500)(100)(.20) =	28.0
Total		157.0		157.1

The General Business Activity Index of the Northwest for 1995 is 157.0 and for 1998 it is 157.1. Interpreting, business activity has increased 57.0 percent from 1990 to 1995 and 57.1 percent from the base period of 1990 to 1998.

As we stated at the start of the section, there are many special-purpose indexes. Here are a few examples.

Consumer Price Index	This index is reported monthly by the U.S. Bureau of Labor Statistics. It describes the changes in prices from one period to another for a "market basket" of goods and services. We discuss its history and detail and present some applications in the next section.
Producer Price Index	Formerly called the Wholesale Price Index, it dates back to 1890 and is also published by the U.S. Bureau of Labor Statistics. It reflects the prices of over 3,400 commodities. Price data are collected from the seller of the commodities, and it usually refers to the first large-volume transaction for each commodity. It is a Laspeyres type index.
Dow Jones Industrial Average	This is an index of stock prices, but perhaps it would be better to say it is an "indicator" than an index. It is supposed to be the mean price of 30 specific industrial stocks. However, today its value cannot be calculated by summing the 30 stocks and dividing by 30. This is because of stock splits, mergers, and stocks being added or dropped. When changes occur, adjustments are made in the denominator used with the average. Today the DJIA is more of a psychological indicator than a representation of the general price movement on the New York Stock Exchange. The lack of representativeness of the stocks on the DJIA is one of the reasons for the development of the **New York Stock Exchange Index.** This index was developed as an average price of *all* stocks on the New York Stock Exchange.
S & P 500 Index	The full name of this index is the Standard and Poor's Composite Index of Stock Prices. It reports the composite price of 500 common stocks. It, too, is probably a better reflection of the market than is the DJIA.

SELF-REVIEW 17–4

As an intern in the Fulton County Economic Development Office, you have been asked to develop a special-purpose index for your county. Three economic series seem to hold promise as the basis of an index. These data are the price of cotton (per pound), the number of new automobiles sold in the county, and the rate of money turnover (published by the local bank). After discussing the project with your supervisor and the director, you decide that money turnover should have a weight of .60, the number of new automobiles sold a weight of .30, and the cotton price .10. The base period is 1992.

Year	Cotton Price	Automobiles Sold	Money Turnover
1992	$0.20	1,000	80
1996	0.25	1,200	90
1998	0.50	900	75

(a) Construct the index for 1996 and 1998.
(b) Interpret the index for 1996 and 1998.

❙ Exercises

11. The index of leading economic indicators, compiled and published by the U.S. National Bureau of Economic Research, is composed of 12 time series, such as the average work

hours of production in manufacturing, manufacturers' new orders, and money supply. This index and similar indexes are designed to move up or down before the economy begins to move the same way. Thus, an economist has statistical evidence to forecast future trends.

You want to construct a leading indicator for Erie County in upstate New York. The index is to be based on 1989 data. Because of the time and work involved, you decide to use only four time series. As an experiment, you select these four series: unemployment in the county, a composite index of county stock prices, county price index, and retail sales. Here are the figures for 1989 and 1999.

	1989	1999
Unemployment rate (percent)	5.3	6.8
Composite county stocks	265.88	362.26
County Price Index (1982 = 100)	109.6	125.0
Retail sales ($ millions)	529,917.0	622,864.0

The weights you assigned are: unemployment rate 20 percent, stock prices 40 percent, County Price Index 25 percent, and retail sales 15 percent.
a.   Using 1989 as the base period, construct a leading economic indicator for 1999.
b.   Interpret your leading index.

12.   You are employed by the state bureau of economic development. There is a demand for a leading economic index to review past economic activity and to forecast future economic trends in the state. You decide that several key factors should be included in the index: number of new businesses started during the year, number of business failures, state income tax receipts, college enrollment, and the state sales tax receipts. The data for 1997 and the present year are:

	1997	Present Year
New businesses	1,088	1,162
Business failures	627	520
State income tax receipts ($ millions)	191.7	162.6
College student enrollment	242,119	290,841
State sales tax ($ millions)	41.6	39.9

a.   Decide on the weights to be applied to each item in the leading index.
b.   Compute the leading economic indicator for the present year.
c.   Interpret the indexes for 1997 and the present year.

▌ Consumer Price Index

There are two consumer price indexes.

Frequent mention has been made of the Consumer Price Index (CPI) in the preceding pages. It measures the change in price of a fixed market basket of goods and services from one period to another. In January 1978 the Bureau of Labor Statistics began publishing CPIs for two groups of the population. One index, called the Consumer Price Index—All Urban Consumers for all urban consumers, covers about 80 percent of the total population. The other index is for urban wage earners and clerical workers and covers about 32 percent of the population.

In brief, the CPI serves several major functions. It allows consumers to determine the degree to which their purchasing power is being eroded by price increases. In that respect, it is a yardstick for revising wages, pensions, and other income payments to keep pace with changes in price. Equally important, it is an economic indicator of the rate of inflation in the United States.

The index includes about 400 items, and about 250 part-time and full-time agents collect price data monthly. Prices are collected from more than 21,000 retail establishments and 60,000 housing units in 91 urban areas across the country. The prices of baby cribs, bread, beer, cigars, gasoline, haircuts, mortgage interest rates, physicians' fees, taxes, and operating-room charges are just a few of the items included in what is often termed a typical "market basket" of goods and services that you purchase.

The CPI originated in 1913 and has been published regularly since 1921. The standard reference period (the base period) has been updated periodically. Beginning with the release of the CPI for January 1999, the base period was changed to 1993–95 = 100. The earlier base periods were: 1982–84, 1967, 1957–59, 1947–49, 1935–39, and 1925–29. Why is it necessary to change the base? Our expenditure patterns change dramatically, and these changes must be reflected in the index. The most recent revision includes consumer items, such as VCRs, home computers, and cell phones. Earlier versions of the CPI did not include these items. By changing the base, the CPI captures the most recent expenditure patterns.

The CPI is actually not just one index. There are Consumer Price Indexes for New York, Chicago, Seattle, and Atlanta, as well as a number of other large cities. There are also price indexes for food, apparel, medical care, and other items. A few of them are shown below, 1982–84 = 100, for April 1998.

Item	CPI-U
All items	162.5
Food and beverage	160.2
Apparel and upkeep	135.8
Transportation	141.5
Medical care	240.7
Housing	159.5

A perusal of this listing shows that a weighted average of all items has increased 62.5 percent since 1982–84; medical care has increased the most, 140.7 percent; and apparel and upkeep went up the least, 35.8 percent. You can find the latest information on the CPI by going the U.S. Bureau of Labor Statistics Web site at: *http://stats.bls.gov/cpihome.htm.*

Special Uses of the Consumer Price Index

In addition to measuring changes in the prices of goods and services, both consumer price indexes have a number of other applications. The CPI is used to determine real disposable personal income, to deflate sales or other series, to find the purchasing power of the dollar, and to establish cost-of-living increases. We first discuss the use of the CPI in determining **real income.**

Real income

Real Income   As an example of the meaning and computation of *real income,* assume for the sake of simplicity that the Consumer Price Index is presently 200 with 1982–84 = 100. Also, assume that Ms. Watts earned $20,000 in the base period of 1982, 1983, and 1984. She has a current income of $40,000. Note that although her

Money income

money income has doubled since the base period of 1982–84, the prices she paid for food, gasoline, clothing, and other items have also doubled. Thus, Ms. Watts' standard of living has remained the same from the base period to the present time. Price increases have exactly offset an increase in income, so her present buying power (real income) is still $20,000. (See Table 17–6 for computations.)

In general:

REAL INCOME	$\text{Real income} = \dfrac{\text{Money income}}{\text{CPI}} \times 100$	**[17–8]**

Table 17–6 Computation of Real Income for 1982–84 and Present Year

Year	Money Income	Consumer Price Index (1982–84 = 100)	Real Income	Computation of Real Income
1982–84	$20,000	100	$20,000	$\dfrac{\$20,000}{100}(100)$
Present year	40,000	200	20,000	$\dfrac{\$40,000}{200}(100)$

Deflated income and real income are the same   The concept of real income is sometimes called *deflated income,* and the CPI is called the *deflator.* Also, a popular term for deflated income is *income expressed in constant dollars.* Thus, in Table 17–6, to determine whether Ms. Watts' standard of living changed, her money income was converted to constant dollars. We found that her purchasing power, expressed in 1982–84 dollars (constant dollars), remained at $20,000.

SELF-REVIEW 17–5

The take-home pay of Jon Greene and the CPI for 1986 and 1998 are:

Year	Take-Home Pay	CPI (1982–84 = 100)
1986	$25,000	109.60
1998	41,200	160.00

(a)   What was Jon's real income in 1986?
(b)   What was his real income in 1998?
(c)   Interpret your findings.

Deflated sales important for showing the trend in "real" sales   **Deflating Sales**   A price index can also be used to "deflate" sales or similar money series. Deflated sales are determined by

USING AN INDEX AS A DEFLATOR	$\text{Deflated sales} = \dfrac{\text{Actual sales}}{\text{An appropriate index}} \times 100$	**[17–9]**

Example   The sales of Eugene Enterprises, a small manufacturer, increased from $1,482,000 in 1982 (the base period) to $1,502,000 in September 1997. Eugene Enterprises knows that the price of raw materials used in production has also risen since 1982, so Eugene Enterprises wants to deflate the September 1997 sales to account for the rise in raw material prices. What are the deflated sales for September 1997? That is, what are the September 1997 sales expressed in constant 1982 dollars?

Solution   The Producer Price Index (PPI) is an index released every month and published in the *Monthly Labor Review* and is also available at the Bureau of Labor Statistics Web site. The prices included in the PPI reflect the prices charged the manufacturer for the metals, rubber, and other items purchased. So the PPI seems an appropriate index to use to deflate the manufacturer's sales. The manufacturer's sales are listed in the second column of Table 17–7, and the PPI is in the third column. The next column shows sales divided by the Producer Price Index, and the deflated sales are in the extreme right column.

Table 17–7 Computations for Deflating Sales

Year	Sales	PPI* (1982 = 100)	Computation of Deflated Sales	Sales in Constant 1982 Dollars
1982	$1,482,000	100.0	$\frac{\$1,482,000}{100.0} \times 100 =$	$1,482,000
1990 (Jan.)	1,491,000	117.6	$\frac{\$1,491,000}{117.6} \times 100 =$	$1,267,857
1997 (Sept.)	1,502,000	131.8	$\frac{\$1,502,000}{131.8} \times 100 =$	$1,139,605

The conclusion is that although the actual dollar sales of Eugene Enterprises increased from 1982 to September 1997, sales deflated for the rise in prices the company paid for raw materials actually declined (from about $1,482,000 down to about $1,139,605). This is so because the prices Eugene paid for raw materials increased at a more rapid rate than did sales.

What has happened to the purchasing power of your dollar?

Purchasing Power of the Dollar The Consumer Price Index is also used to determine the *purchasing power of the dollar.*

USING AN INDEX TO FIND PURCHASING POWER	Purchasing power of dollar $= \dfrac{\$1}{\text{CPI}} \times 100$	**[17–10]**

Example

Suppose the Consumer Price Index this month is 200.0 (1982–84 = 100). What is the purchasing power of the dollar?

Solution

Using formula (17–10), it is 50 cents, found by:

$$\text{Purchasing power of dollar} = \frac{\$1}{200.0}(100) = \$0.50$$

The CPI of 200.0 indicates that prices have doubled from the years 1982–84 to this month. Thus, the purchasing power of a dollar has been cut in half. That is, a 1982–84 dollar is worth only 50 cents this month. To put it another way, if you lost $1,000 in the period 1982–84 and just found it, the $1,000 could only buy half of what it could have bought in the years 1982, 1983, and 1984.

CPI used to adjust wages, pensions, and so on

Cost-of-Living Adjustments The Consumer Price Index is also the basis for cost-of-living adjustments in many management-union contracts. The specific clause in the contract is often referred to as the "escalator clause." About 31 million Social Security beneficiaries, 2.5 million retired military and federal civil service employees and survivors, and 600,000 postal workers have their incomes or pensions pegged to the Consumer Price Index.

The CPI is also used to adjust alimony and child support payments; attorneys' fees; workers' compensation payments; rentals on apartments, homes, and office buildings; welfare payments; and so on. In brief, say a retiree receives a pension of $500 a month and the Consumer Price Index increases 5 points from 165 to 170. Suppose for each point (percent) that the CPI increases the pension benefits increase 1.0 percent, so the monthly increase in benefits will be $25, found by $500 (5 points)(.01). Now the retiree will receive $525 per month.

SELF-REVIEW   17–6

Suppose the Consumer Price Index for the latest month is 158.3 (1982–84 = 100). What is the purchasing power of the dollar? Interpret.

▌ Shifting the Base

If two or more time series have the same base period, they can be compared directly. As an example, suppose we are interested in the trend in the prices of food and beverages, housing, medical care, and so on since the base period, 1982–84. Note in Table 17–8 that all of the consumer price indexes use the same base. Thus, it can be said that the price of all consumer items combined increased 61.2 percent from the base period (1982–84) to September 1997. Likewise, housing prices increased 57.7 percent, medical care 135.4 percent, and so on.

Table 17–8   Trend in Consumer Prices to 1995 (1982–84 = 100)

Year	All Items	Food and Beverages	Housing	Apparel and Upkeep	Medical Care
1982–84	100.0	100.0	100.0	100.0	100.0
1986	109.6	109.1	110.9	105.9	122.0
1987	113.6	113.5	114.2	110.6	130.1
1994 (Nov.)	149.7	145.9	145.5	134.2	214.7
1997 (Sept.)	161.2	158.4	157.7	133.0	235.4

A problem arises, however, when two or more series being compared do not have the same base period.

Example

We want to compare the price changes on the New York Stock Exchange and the American Stock Exchange since 1985. The two price indexes are as follows.

	Year			
Index	1985	1987	1993	1997
New York Stock Exchange (Dec. 31, 1965 = 50)	108.09	161.70	244.72	478.29
American Stock Exchange (Aug. 31, 1973 = 50)	229.10	316.61	418.54	678.27

Solution

Price indexes on different base years cannot be compared directly.

Note again that the two price indexes have different base periods — the New York base period is 1965, and the American base is 1973. Thus, a direct comparison of 478.29 and 678.27 is not appropriate. We want to compare the movement of price since 1985, so the logical thing to do is to let the base period be 1985 for both series. For the New York price series 108.09 becomes the base, and for the American series the base is 229.10.

The calculations for the 1997 American Stock Exchange price index using 1985 = 100 are:

$$\frac{678.27}{229.10} \times 100 = 296.1$$

The complete set of indexes using 1985 = 100 is:

	Year			
Index	1985	1987	1993	1997
New York Stock Exchange	100.0	149.6	226.4	442.5
American Stock Exchange	100.0	138.2	182.7	296.1

We can now conclude that common stock prices on both the New York Stock Exchange and the American Stock Exchange since 1985 have risen, with the rise on the New York Stock Exchange being significantly greater (342.5 percent compared with 196.1 percent on the American exchange).

SELF-REVIEW 17–7

1. In the preceding example, verify that the New York Stock Exchange price index for 1993, using 1985 as the base period, is 226.4.
2. The changes in industrial production and in the prices manufacturers have paid for raw materials since 1982 are to be compared. Unfortunately, the index of industrial production, which measures changes in production, and the Producer Price Index, which measures the change in the prices of raw materials, have different base periods. The production index has a 1977 base period, and the Producer Price Index uses 1982 as the base period. Shift the base and make the two series comparable. Interpret.

Year	Industrial Production Index (1977 = 100)	Producer Price Index (1982 = 100)
1982	115.3	100.0
1987	129.8	105.4
1994	142.8	119.2
1997	172.3	131.2

▌ Exercises

13. In August 1997 the mean salary for an experienced registered nurse with a bachelor's degree was $32,000. The Consumer Price Index for August 1997 was 158.3 (1982–84 = 100). The mean annual salary for a nurse in the base period of 1982–84 was $19,800. What was the real income of the nurse in 1997? How much had the mean salary increased?

14. The Trade Union Association of Orlando, Florida, maintains indexes on the hourly wages for a number of the trades. Unfortunately, the indexes do not all have the same base periods. Listed below is information on plumbers and electricians. Shift the base periods to 1995 and compare the hourly wage increases.

Year	Plumbers (1990 = 100)	Electricians (1992 = 100)
1995	133.8	126.0
1998	159.4	158.7

15. In 1990 the mean salary of classroom teachers in the Tinora School District was $23,650. By 1995 the mean salary increased to $28,972, and further increased in 1999 to $32,382. The American Federation of Classroom Teachers maintains information on the trends throughout the United States in classroom teacher salaries. Their index, which has a base of 1990, was 122.5 for 1995 and 136.9 for 1999. Compare the Tinora teachers to the national trends.

16. Sam Steward is a freelance computer programmer. Listed below are his yearly wages for the years 1995 through 1999. Also included is an industry index for computer programmers that reports the rate of wage inflation in the industry. This index has a base of 1990.

Year	Wage ($000)	Index (1990 = 100)
1995	125.0	148.3
1996	134.8	160.6
1997	145.2	173.6
1998	156.6	187.9
1999	168.8	203.3

Compute Sam's real income for the period. Did his wages keep up with inflation, or did he lose ground?

Chapter Outline

I. An index number measures the relative change from one period to another.
   A. The major characteristics of an index are:
      1. It is a percentage, but the percent sign is usually omitted.
      2. It has a base period.
      3. Most indexes are reported to the nearest tenth of a percent, such as 153.1.
      4. The base of most indexes is 100.
   B. The reasons for computing an index are:
      1. It facilitates the comparison of unlike series.
      2. If the numbers are very large, often it is easier to comprehend the change of the index than the actual numbers.
II. There are two types of price indexes, unweighted and weighted.
   A. In an unweighted index we do not consider the quantities.
      1. In a simple index we compare the base period to the given period.

$$P = \frac{p_t}{p_0} \times 100 \qquad \text{[17–1]}$$

where p_t refers to the price in the current period, and p_0 is the price in the base period.
      2. In the simple average of price relatives, we add the simple indexes for each item and divide by the number of items.

$$P = \frac{\sum P_i}{n} \qquad \text{[17–2]}$$

3. In a simple aggregate price index the price of the items in the group are totaled for both periods and compared.

$$P = \frac{\sum p_t}{\sum p_0} \times 100 \qquad \text{[17–3]}$$

B. In a weighted index the quantities are considered.
   1. In the Laspeyres method the base period quantities are used in both the base period and the given period.

$$P = \frac{\sum p_t q_0}{\sum p_0 q_0} \times 100 \qquad \text{[17–4]}$$

   2. In the Paasche method current period quantities are used.

$$P = \frac{\sum p_t q_t}{\sum p_0 q_t} \times 100 \qquad \text{[17–5]}$$

   3. Fisher's ideal index is the geometric mean of Laspeyres' index and Paasche's index.

$$\text{Fisher's ideal index} = \sqrt{(\text{Laspeyres' index})(\text{Paasche's index})} \qquad \text{[17–6]}$$

C. A value index uses both base period and current period quantities

$$V = \frac{\sum p_t q_t}{\sum p_0 q_0} \qquad \text{[17–7]}$$

III. The most widely reported index is the Consumer Price Index (CPI).
   A. It is often used to show the rate of inflation in the United States.
   B. It is reported monthly by the U.S. Bureau of Labor Statistics.
   C. Through 1998 the base period is 1982–84, but starting with the reports in 1999, the base will change to 1993–95.
   D. It is tied to the Social Security system, so when the CPI changes, retirement benefits also change.

▌ Chapter Exercises

The following information was taken from the 1993 and 1996 Johnson and Johnson annual reports. The principal office of Johnson and Johnson is in New Brunswick, New Jersey. Their common stock is listed on the New York Stock Exchange, using the symbol JNJ.

	Sales		
Year	Domestic ($ million)	International ($ million)	Employees (000)
1983	3,611	2,362	77.4
1984	3,736	2,389	74.2
1985	3,990	2,431	74.9
1986	3,972	3,031	77.1
1987	4,167	3,845	78.2
1988	4,576	4,424	81.3
1989	4,881	4,876	83.1
1990	5,427	5,805	82.2
1991	6,248	6,199	82.7
1992	6,903	6,850	84.9
1993	7,203	6,935	81.6
1994	7,812	7,922	81.5
1995	9,190	9,652	82.3
1996	10,899	10,721	89.3

17. Refer to the Johnson and Johnson data set on the previous page. Use 1983 as the base period and compute a simple index for domestic sales for each year from 1984 until 1996. Interpret the trend in domestic sales.
18. Refer to the Johnson and Johnson data set. Use the period 1983–85 as the base period and compute a simple index for domestic sales for each year from 1986 to 1996.
19. Refer to the Johnson and Johnson data set. Use 1983 as the base period and compute a simple index for international sales for each year from 1984 until 1996. Interpret the trend in international sales.
20. Refer to the Johnson and Johnson data set. Use the period 1983–85 as the base period and compute a simple index for international sales for each year from 1986 to 1996.
21. Refer to the Johnson and Johnson data set. Use 1983 as the base period and compute a simple index for the number of employees for each year from 1984 until 1996. Interpret the trend in the number of employees.
22. Refer to the Johnson and Johnson data set. Use the period 1983–85 as the base period and compute a simple index for the number of employees for each year from 1986 to 1996.

The following information is from the PNC Bank annual report for 1996. PNC Bank has corporate offices in Pittsburgh, Pennsylvania, and is traded on the New York Stock Exchange under the symbol PNC.

Year	Income ($ millions)	Earnings (per share)
1992	388	1.08
1993	899	1.175
1994	884	1.31
1995	408	1.40
1996	992	1.42

23. Compute a simple index for income of PNC Bank. Use 1992 as the base period. What can you conclude about the change in income over the period?
24. Compute a simple index for income of PNC Bank using the period 1992–93 as the base. What can you conclude about the change in income over the period?
25. Compute a simple index for earnings per share of PNC Bank. Use 1992 as the base period. What can you conclude about the change in earnings per share over the period?
26. Compute a simple index for earnings of PNC Bank using the period 1992–93 as the base. What can you conclude about the change in earnings per share over the period?

The U.S. Department of Labor reported the following information on food items for the years 1995 and 1999.

Item	1995		1999	
	Price	Quantity	Price	Quantity
Margarine (pound)	$0.81	18	$0.89	27
Shortening (pound)	.84	5	.94	9
Milk (½ gallon)	1.44	70	1.43	65
Potato chips	2.91	27	3.07	33

27. Compute a simple price index for each of the four items. Use 1995 as the base period.
28. Compute a simple aggregate price index. Use 1995 as the base period.
29. Compute Laspeyres' price index for 1999, using 1995 as the base period.
30. Compute Paasche's index for 1999, using 1995 as the base period.
31. Determine Fisher's ideal index, using the values for the Laspeyres and Paasche indexes computed in the two previous problems.
32. Determine a value index for 1999, using 1995 as the base period.

Betts Electronics purchases three replacement parts for robotic machines used in their manufacturing process. Information on the price of the replacement parts and the quantity purchased is given below.

	Price		Quantity	
Part	1995	1999	1995	1999
RC-33	$0.50	$0.60	320	340
SM-14	1.20	0.90	110	130
WC50	0.85	1.00	230	250

33. Compute a simple price index for each of the three items. Use 1995 as the base period.
34. Compute a simple aggregate price index for 1999. Use 1995 as the base period.
35. Compute Laspeyres' price index for 1999, using 1995 as the base period.
36. Compute Paasche's index for 1999, using 1995 as the base period.
37. Determine Fisher's ideal index, using the values for the Laspeyres and Paasche indexes computed in the two previous problems.
38. Determine a value index for 1999, using 1995 as the base period.

Prices for selected foods for 1995 and 1999 are given in the following table.

	Price		Quantity	
Item	1995	1999	1995	1999
Cabbage (pound)	$0.06	$0.05	2,000	1,500
Carrots (bunch)	0.10	0.12	200	200
Peas (quart)	0.20	0.18	400	500
Endive (bunch)	0.15	0.15	100	200

39. Compute a simple price index for each of the four items. Use 1995 as the base period.
40. Compute a simple aggregate price index. Use 1995 as the base period.
41. Compute Laspeyres' price index for 1999, using 1995 as the base period.
42. Compute Paasche's index for 1999, using 1995 as the base period.
43. Determine Fisher's ideal index, using the values for the Laspeyres and Paasche indexes computed in the two previous problems.
44. Determine a value index for 1999, using 1995 as the base period.

The prices of selected items for 1980 and 1999 follow. Production figures for those two periods are also given.

	Price		Quantity	
Item	1980	1999	1980	1999
Aluminum (cents per pound)	$0.287	$0.76	1,000	1,200
Natural gas (1,000 cu. ft.)	0.17	2.50	5,000	4,000
Petroleum (barrel)	3.18	26.00	60,000	60,000
Platinum (troy ounce)	133.00	490.00	500	600

45. Compute a simple price index for each of the four items. Use 1980 as the base period.
46. Compute a simple aggregate price index. Use 1980 as the base period.
47. Compute Laspeyres' price index for 1999, using 1980 as the base period.
48. Compute Paasche's index for 1999, using 1980 as the base period.
49. Determine Fisher's ideal index, using the values for the Laspeyres and Paasche indexes computed in the two previous problems.

50. Determine a value index for 1999, using 1980 as the base period.
51. A special-purpose index is to be designed to monitor the overall economy of the Southwest. Four key series were selected. After considerable deliberation it was decided to weight retail sales 20 percent, total bank deposits 10 percent, industrial production in the area 40 percent, and nonagricultural employment 30 percent. The data for 1990 and 1999 are:

Year	Retail Sales ($ millions)	Bank Deposits ($ billions)	Industrial Production (1977 = 100)	Employment
1990	1,159.0	87	110.6	1,214,000
1999	1,971.0	91	114.7	1,501,000

Construct a special-purpose index for 1999 using 1990 as the base period and interpret.
52. We are making a historical study of certain facets of the American economy from 1950 to 1980. Data on prices, the labor force, productivity, and the GNP were collected. Note in the following table that the CPI is on a 1967 base, employment is in millions of persons, and so on. A direct comparison, therefore, is not feasible.
   a. Make whatever calculations are necessary to compare the trend in the four series from 1950 to 1980.
   b. Interpret.

Year	Consumer Price Index (1967 = 100)	Total Labor Force (millions)	Index of Productivity in Manufacturing (1967 = 100)	Gross National Product ($ billions)
1950	72.1	64	64.9	286.2
1967	100.0	81	100.0	789.6
1971	121.3	87	110.3	1,063.4
1975	161.2	95	114.9	1,516.3
1980	246.8	107	146.6	2,626.0

53. The management of Ingalls Super Discount stores, with several stores in the Oklahoma City area, wants to construct an index of economic activity for the metropolitan area. Management contends that if the index reveals that the economy is slowing down, inventory should be kept at a low level.

   Three series seem to hold promise as predictors of economic activity—area retail sales, bank deposits, and employment. All of these data can be secured monthly from the U.S. government. Retail sales is to be weighted 40 percent, bank deposits 35 percent, and employment 25 percent. Seasonally adjusted data for the first three months of the year are:

Month	Retail Sales ($ millions)	Bank Deposits ($ billions)	Employment (thousands)
January	8.0	20	300
February	6.8	23	303
March	6.4	21	297

Construct an index of economic activity for each of the three months, using January as the base period.
54. The following table gives information on the Consumer Price Index and the monthly take-home pay of Bill Martin, an employee at the Jeep Corporation.

Year	Consumer Price Index (1982–84 = 100)	Mr. Martin's Monthly Take-Home Pay
1982–84	100.0	$ 600
1997 (Sept.)	131.8	2,000

    a.   What is the purchasing power of the dollar for September 1997 based on the period 1982–84?

    b.   Determine Mr. Martin's "real" monthly income for each of the time periods.

55.   Suppose that the Producer Price Index and the sales of Hoskin's Wholesale Distributors for 1983 and 1999 are:

Year	Producer Price Index	Sales
1983	120.0	$2,400,000
1999	320.6	3,500,000

What are Hoskin's real sales (also called deflated sales) for the two years?

www.Exercises.com

56.   Listed below are the monthly sales for the Master Chemical Company for 1996 and the first six months of 1997. Go to the U.S. Bureau of Labor statistics (*http://stats.bls.gov/ datahome.htm*), then select "Most Requested Series" and find the **Consumer Price Index — All Urban Consumers** (CPI-U) for the corresponding period. Select all items with the 1982–84 base and a period that includes 1996 and 1997. Adjust the CPI-U to a base of January 1996. Adjust the sales values to the same base. Write a brief report detailing the change in sales during the 18-month period in terms of constant dollars.

Month	Year	Sales ($ million)	Month	Year	Sales ($ million)	Month	Year	Sales ($ million)
Jan	1996	28.3	Jul	1996	44.0	Jan	1997	48.2
Feb	1996	38.1	Aug	1996	42.6	Feb	1997	53.5
Mar	1996	37.5	Sep	1996	48.3	Mar	1997	55.6
Apr	1996	39.0	Oct	1996	46.7	Apr	1997	54.7
May	1996	40.1	Nov	1996	51.3	May	1997	64.2
Jun	1996	41.9	Dec	1996	52.1	Jun	1997	58.3

▌ Computer Commands

1.   The Excel commands for the spreadsheet on page 618 are:

    a.   Enter the data for the price and quantities. We entered the label "Item" in cell A3, and the item names in cells A4 through A9. The label "Price-95" was entered in B3, and the price data for 1995 in cells B4 through B9. The label "Quantity-95" was entered in cell C3, with the 1995 quantities in cells C4 through C9. Cell D3 was labeled "Price*Qty-95".

    b.   To determine the product of the 1995 prices and quantities, highlight the cells from D4 to D9. With this group of cells still highlighted, type "=B4*C4" in cell D4 and hit **Enter.** The value "38.5" should appear. This is the product of the price of bread ($0.77) and the quantity of bread (50) sold in 1995.

    c.   With cells D4 through D9 still highlighted select **Edit,** then **Fill,** then **Down** and hit **Enter.** The remaining products should appear.

    d.   Move to cell D10, click on Σ on the toolbar, and hit **Enter.** The value 336.16 will appear. This is the denominator for the Laspeyres price index. The other products and column totals are determined in a similar manner.

Chapter 17 *Answers to Self-Review*

17–1 1. (a) 187.7, found by ($101,781.9/$54,217.0) × 100. Sales of GM are 87.7 percent greater than sales of IBM.
  (b) 48.4, found by ($26,257.7/$54,217.0)100. Sales of Chrysler are 51.6 percent below IBM sales.
2. (a) 183.1, found by ($9.45/$5.16)100. Earnings increased 83.1 percent.
  (b) The base is ($5.16 + $5.30)/2 = $5.23. The index is 180.7, found by ($9.45/$5.23)100.
  (c) 173.7, found by ($9.45/$5.44)(100). Earnings increased 73.7 percent.

17–2 (a) $P_1 = ($85/$75)(100) = 113.3$, $P_2 = ($45/$40)(100) = 112.5$, $P = (113.3 + 112.5)/2 = 112.9$
  (b) $P = ($130/$115)(100) = 113.0$
  (c) $P = \dfrac{$85(500) + $45(1,200)}{$75(500) + $40(1,200)}(100)$

  $= \dfrac{$96,500}{85,500}(100) = 112.9$

  (d) $P = \dfrac{$85(520) + $45(1,300)}{$75(520) + $40(1,300)}(100)$

  $= \dfrac{$102,700}{$91,000}(100) = 112.9$

  (e) $P = \sqrt{(112.9)(112.9)} = 112.9$

17–3 (a) $P = \dfrac{$4(9,000) + $5(200) + $8(5,000)}{$3(10,000) + $1(600) + $10(3,000)}(100)$

  $= \dfrac{$77,000}{60,600}(100) = 127.1$

  (b) The value of sales has gone up 27.1 percent from 1996 to 1999.

17–4 (a)

For 1998	
Item	**Weight**
Cotton	($0.50/$0.20)(100)(.10) = 25.00
Autos	(900/1,000)(100)(.30) = 27.00
Money turnover	(75/80)(100)(.60) = 56.25
	108.25

For 1996	
Item	**Weight**
Cotton	($0.25/$0.20)(100)(.10) = 12.5
Autos	(1,200/1,000)(100)(.30) = 36.0
Money turnover	(90/80)(100)(.60) = 67.5
	116.0

  (b) Business activity increased 16 percent from 1992 to 1996. It increased 8.25 percent from 1992 to 1998.

17–5 (a) $22,810, found by ($25,000/109.6)(100).
  (b) $25,750, found by ($41,200/160.0)(100).
  (c) In terms of the base period, Jon's salary was $22,810 in 1986 and $25,750 in 1998. This indicates that his take-home pay increased at a faster rate than the price he paid for food, transportation, etc.

17–6 $0.63, found by ($1/158.3)(100).

17–7 1. (244.72/108.09)100 = 226.4
2. (a) Using 1982 as the base period for both series:

	Industrial Production Index	Producer Price Index
1982	100.0	100.0
1987	112.6	105.4
1994	123.9	119.2
1997	149.4*	131.2

*$P = (172.3/115.3)(100) = 149.4$

  (b) From the base of 1982 to 1997, industrial production increased at a faster rate (49.4 percent) than prices (31.2 percent).

Chapter Eighteen

Time Series and Forecasting

GOALS

When you have completed this chapter, you will be able to:

ONE

Define the four components of a time series.

TWO

Determine a linear trend equation.

THREE

Compute a moving average.

FOUR

Compute the trend equation for a nonlinear trend.

FIVE

Use trend equations to forecast future time periods and to develop seasonally adjusted forecasts.

SIX

Determine and interpret a set of seasonal indexes.

SEVEN

Deseasonalize data using a seasonal index.

Given the sales of aluminum by quarter since 1991, determine the typical seasonal patterns for sales using the ratio-to-moving-average method. (See Goal 6 and Exercise 26.)

▎ Introduction

The emphasis in this chapter is on time series analysis and forecasting. A **time series** is a collection of data recorded over a period of time — weekly, monthly, quarterly, or yearly. Two examples of time series are (1) the sales by quarter of the Appliance Center since its opening in 1962 and (2) the annual production of sulfuric acid since 1970. The computer image in the photo shows the volume of data traveling into the National Science Foundation network in one month. The colors represent traffic

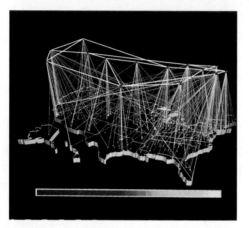

volume from zero bytes (purple) to 100 billion bytes (white).

An analysis of history — a time series — can be used by management to make current decisions and for long-term forecasting and planning. We usually assume past patterns will continue into the future. Long-term forecasts extend more than 1 year into the future; 5-, 10-, 15-, and 20-year projections are common. Long-range predictions are essential to allow sufficient time for the procurement, manufacturing, sales, finance, and other departments of a company to develop plans for possible new plants, financing, development of new products, and new methods of assembling.

Forecasting the level of sales, both short-term and long-term, is practically dictated by the very nature of business organizations in the United States. Competition for the consumer's dollar, stress on earning a profit for the stockholders, a desire to procure a larger share of the market, and the ambitions of executives are some of the prime motivating forces in business. Thus, a forecast (a statement of the goals of management) is necessary in order to have the raw materials, production facilities, and staff available to meet the projected demand.

This chapter deals with the use of data to forecast future events. First, we look at the components of a time series. Then, we examine some of the techniques used in analyzing data. Finally, we project future events.

▎ Components of a Time Series

There are four components to a time series: the trend, the cyclical variation, the seasonal variation, and the irregular variation.

Secular Trend

The long-term trends of sales, employment, stock prices, and other business and economic series follow various patterns. Some move steadily upward, others decline, and still others stay the same over time.

▎ **Secular Trend**   The smooth long-term direction of a time series.   ▎

The following are several examples of a secular trend.

- The chart on the next page shows the number of GTE cellular phone subscribers (in millions) in the United States from 1992 until 1996. The number increased from 1.09 million in 1992 to 3.75 million in 1996. This is an increase of 2.66 million subscribers, or 244 percent. The long-run direction of the time series is increasing.

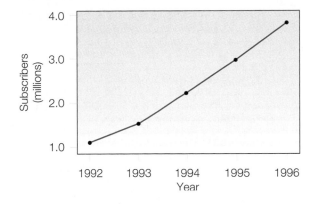

- The chart below shows the amount of the average tax refund for the years from 1990 to 1997. Again the long-run direction is increasing. The average refund in 1990 was $916. By 1997 the average refund was $1,375. This is an increase of $459, or 50 percent.

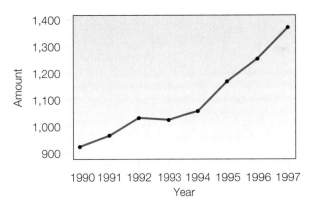

- This chart is an example of a declining long-run trend. In 1992 Gaughn's Drug Stores, a large retail chain in the Northwest, operated 245 stores. At the end of 1997 Gaughn's was operating 204 stores. This is a decline of 41 stores, or 16.7 percent.

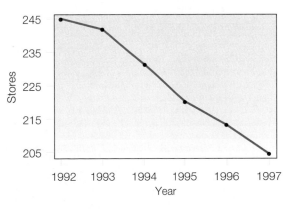

- The chart on the following page shows the total car production in both Japan and Western Europe for the five-year period from 1992 to 1996. The production in Western Europe increased about a million cars over the period, from 13.1 million in 1992 to 14.1 million in 1996. There was a decline in 1993 and 1994. In Japan there has been a steady decline in car production. In 1992, 9.4 million were produced. By 1996 this had declined to 7.9 million. This is a decline of 1.5 million or an average decline of 0.3 million per year.

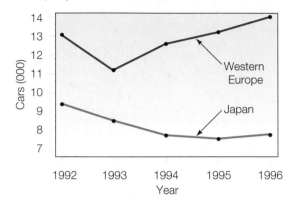

Cyclical Variation

The second component of a time series is cyclical variation. A typical business cycle consists of a period of prosperity followed by periods of recession, depression, and then recovery. There are sizable fluctuations unfolding over more than one year in time above and below the secular trend. In a recession, for example, employment, production, the Dow Jones Industrial Average, and many other business and economic series are below the long-term trend lines. Conversely, in periods of prosperity they are above their long-term trend lines.

> **Cyclical Variation** The rise and fall of a time series over periods longer than one year.

Chart 18–1 shows the number of batteries sold by National Battery Sales, Inc. from 1980 through 1997. The cyclical nature of business is highlighted. There are periods of recovery, followed by prosperity, then recession, and finally the cycle bottoms out with depression.

Seasonal Variation

The third component of a time series is the seasonal component. Many sales, production, and other series fluctuate with the seasons. The unit of time reported is either quarterly or monthly.

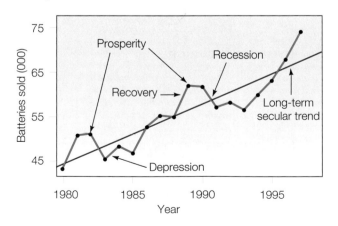

Chart 18–1 Battery Sales by National Battery Sales, Inc., 1980–1997

Seasonal Variation Patterns of change in a time series within a year. These patterns tend to repeat themselves each year.

Almost all businesses tend to have recurring seasonal patterns. Men's and boys' clothing, for example, have extremely high sales just prior to Christmas and relatively low sales just after Christmas and during the summer. Toy sales is another example with an extreme seasonal pattern. More than half of the business for the year is usually done in the months of November and December. The lawn care business is seasonal in the northeast and north-central states. Many businesses try to even out the seasonal effects by engaging in an offsetting seasonal business. In the Northeast you will see the operator of a lawn care business with a snowplow on the front of the truck in an effort to earn income in the off-season. In northern Michigan and other ski areas, you will often find golf courses nearby. The owners of the lodges try to rent to skiers in the winter and golfers in the summer. This is an effective method of spreading their fixed costs over the entire year rather than a few months.

Chart 18–2 shows the quarterly sales, in millions of dollars, of Hercher Sporting Goods, Inc. They are a Chicago area sporting goods company that specializes in selling baseball and softball equipment to high schools, colleges, and youth leagues. They also have several retail outlets in some of the larger shopping malls. There is a distinct seasonal pattern to their business. Most of their sales are in the first and second quarters of the year, when schools and organizations are purchasing equipment for the upcoming season. During the early summer, they keep busy by selling replacement equipment. They do some business during the holidays (fourth quarter). The late summer (third quarter) is their slow season.

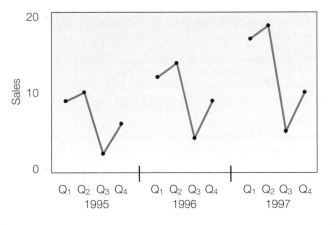

Chart 18–2 Sales of Baseball and Softball Equipment, Hercher Sporting Goods, 1995–97 by Quarter

Irregular Variation

Many analysts prefer to subdivide the **irregular variation** into *episodic* and *residual* variations. Episodic fluctuations are unpredictable, but they can be identified. The initial impact on the economy of a major strike or a war can be identified, but a strike or war cannot be predicted. After the episodic fluctuations have been removed, the remaining variation is called the residual variation. The residual fluctuations, often called chance fluctuations, are unpredictable, and they cannot be identified. Of course, neither episodic nor residual variation can be projected into the future.

▎ Linear Trend

The long-term trend of many business series, such as sales, exports, and production, often approximates a straight line. If so, the equation to describe this growth is:

LINEAR TREND EQUATION	$Y' = a + bt$	**[18–1]**

where:

Y' read Y prime, is the projected value of the Y variable for a selected value of t.

a is the Y-intercept. It is the estimated value of Y when $t = 0$. Another way to put it is: a is the estimated value of Y where the line crosses the Y-axis when t is zero.

Slope of trend line is b

b is the slope of the line, or the average change in Y' for each change of one unit (either increase or decrease) in t.

t is any value of time that is selected.

To illustrate the meaning of Y', a, b, and t in a time-series problem, a line has been drawn in Chart 18–3 to represent the typical trend of sales. Assume that this company started in business in 1990. This beginning year (1990) has been arbitrarily designated as year 1. Note that sales increased $2 million on the average every year; that is, based on the straight line drawn through the sales data, sales increased from $3 million in 1990 to $5 million in 1991, to $7 million in 1992, to $9 million in 1993, and so on. The slope, or b, is therefore 2. Note too that the line intercepts the Y-axis (when $t = 0$) at $1 million. This point (1) is a. Another way of determining b is to locate the starting place of the straight line in year (1). It is 3 for 1990 in this problem. Then locate the value on the straight line for the last year. It is 19 for 1998. Sales went up $19 million − $3 million, or $16 million, in eight years (1990 to 1998). Thus, 16 ÷ 8 = 2, which is the slope of the line, or b.

The equation for the line in Chart 18–3 is:

$$Y' = 1 + 2t \text{ (in millions)}$$

where:

Sales are in millions of dollars. The origin, or year 0, is 1989.

t increases by one unit for each year.

Chart 18–3   A Straight Line Fitted to Sales Data

In Chapter 12 we drew a line through points on a scatter diagram to approximate the regression line. We stressed, however, that this method for determining the regression equation has a serious drawback—namely, the position of the line depends on the judgment of the individual who drew the line. Three people would probably draw three different lines through the scatter plots. Likewise, the line we drew through the sales data in Chart 18–3 might not be the "best-fitting" line.

Because of the subjective judgment involved, this method should be used only when a quick approximation of the straight-line equation is needed, or to check the reasonableness of the least squares line, which is discussed next.

▌ Least Squares Method

The **least squares method** of computing the equation for a line through the data of interest gave the "best-fitting" line. Two equations may be solved simultaneously to arrive at the least squares trend equation. They are:

EQUATIONS FOR THE TREND LINE	$\sum Y = na + b\sum t$ $\sum tY = a\sum t + b\sum t^2$	**[18–2]**

You may recognize these as the normal equations discussed in Chapter 12, with t replacing X in the equations. As we described in Chapter 12, using the normal equations to determine a and b can be tedious. A better approach is to use the following computational equations.

THE SLOPE	$b = \dfrac{\sum tY - (\sum Y)(\sum t)/n}{\sum t^2 - (\sum t)^2/n}$	**[18–3]**

THE INTERCEPT	$a = \dfrac{\sum Y}{n} - b\left(\dfrac{\sum t}{n}\right)$	**[18–4]**

If the number of years is large—say, 15 or more—and the magnitude of the numbers is also large, a computer software package is recommended.

Example

The sales of Jensen Foods, a small grocery chain, since 1994 are:

Year	Sales ($ millions)
1994	7
1995	10
1996	9
1997	11
1998	13

Determine the least squares trend-line equation.

Solution

To simplify the calculations, the years are replaced by *coded* values. That is, we let 1994 be 1, 1995 be 2, and so forth. This reduces the size of the values of $\sum t$, $\sum t^2$, and $\sum tY$. (See Table 18–1.) This is often referred to as the **coded method.**
Determining a and b using formulas (18–3) and (18–4):

$$b = \frac{\sum tY - (\sum Y)(\sum t)/n}{\sum t^2 - (\sum t)^2/n} = \frac{163 - 50(15)/5}{55 - (15)^2/5} = 1.30$$

$$a = \frac{\sum Y}{n} - b\left(\frac{\sum t}{n}\right) = \frac{50}{5} - 1.30\left(\frac{15}{5}\right) = 6.1$$

Table 18–1   Computations Needed for Determining the Trend Equation

Year	Sales ($ millions), Y	t	tY	t^2
1994	7	1	7	1
1995	10	2	20	4
1996	9	3	27	9
1997	11	4	44	16
1998	13	5	65	25
	50	15	163	55

The trend equation is therefore $Y' = 6.1 + 1.30t$, where:

Sales are millions of dollars.

The origin, or year 0, is in the middle of 1993 (i.e., July 1, 1993), and *t* increases by one unit for each year.

How do we interpret the equation? The value of 1.30 indicates sales increased at a rate of $1.3 million per year. The value 6.1 is the estimated sales when $t = 0$. That is, the estimated sales amount for 1993 (the base year) is $6.1 million.

Plotting the Line

The least squares equation can be used to find points on the line going through the middle of the data. The sales data from Table 18–1 are repeated in Table 18–2 to show the procedure. The equation determined earlier is $Y' = 6.1 + 1.30t$. To get the coordinates of the point on the line for 1997, for example, insert the *t* value of 4 in the equation. Then $Y' = 6.10 + 1.30(4) = 11.3$.

Table 18–2   Calculations Needed for Determining the Points on the Straight Line Using the Coded Method

Year	Sales ($ millions), Y	t	Y'		Found by
1994	$ 7	1	7.4	←	6.10 + 1.30(1)
1995	10	2	8.7	←	6.10 + 1.30(2)
1996	9	3	10.0	←	6.10 + 1.30(3)
1997	11	4	11.3	←	6.10 + 1.30(4)
1998	13	5	12.6	←	6.10 + 1.30(5)

The actual sales and the trend in sales as represented by the line are shown in Chart 18–4. The first point on the line has the coordinates $t = 1$, $Y' = 7.4$. Another point is $t = 3$, $Y' = 10$.

Estimation

If the sales, production, or other data tend to approximate a linear trend, the equation developed by the least squares method can be used to estimate sales for some future period.

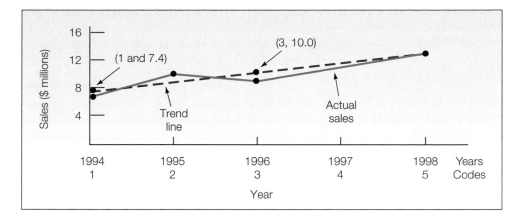

Chart 18–4 Actual Sales and Linear Trend

Example

Refer to the sales data in Table 18–1. The year 1994 is coded 1, and 1995 is coded 2. What is the sales forecast for 2001?

Solution

The year 1996 is coded 3, 1997 is logically coded 4, 1998 is coded 5, 1999 is coded 6, 2000 is coded 7, and 2001 is coded 8. Thus, in 2001 $t = 8$. Substituting the period 8 in the equation [formula (18–1)]:

$$Y' = a + bt = 6.1 + 1.30(8) = 16.5$$

Thus, based on past sales, the estimate for 2001 is $16.5 million.

In this time series problem, there were five years of sales data. Based on those five sales figures, we estimated sales for 2001. Many researchers suggest that we do not project sales, production, and other business and economic series more than $n/2$ time periods into the future. If, for example, there are 10 years of data, we would make estimates only up to 5 years into the future ($n/2 = 10/2 = 5$). Others suggest the forecast may be for no longer than 2 years, especially in rapidly changing economic times.

SELF-REVIEW 18–1

Annual production of king-size rockers by Wood Products, Inc. since 1991 follows.

Year	Production (thousands)	Year	Production (thousands)
1991	4	1995	11
1992	8	1996	9
1993	5	1997	11
1994	8	1998	14

(a) Plot the production data.
(b) Determine the least squares equation.
(c) Determine the points on the straight line for 1991 and 1997. Connect the two points to arrive at the line.
(d) Based on the equation for the line, what is the estimated production for 2001?

▌ Exercises

1. The numbers of bank failures for the years 1994 through 1998 are given below. Determine the least squares equation and estimate the number of failures in 2001.

Year	Code	Number of Failures
1994	1	79
1995	2	120
1996	3	138
1997	4	184
1998	5	200

2. The personal consumption expenditures for telephone and telegraph, in billions of dollars, in the United States for the years 1993 to 1998 are given below. Determine the least squares equation, and estimate the expenditure for 2001.

Year	Code	Expenditures ($ billions)
1993	1	37.9
1994	2	39.8
1995	3	40.4
1996	4	42.7
1997	5	44.1
1998	6	47.1

3. The following table gives the annual amount of scrap produced by Machine Products, Inc.

Year	Code	Scrap (tons)
1994	1	2.0
1995	2	4.0
1996	3	3.0
1997	4	5.0
1998	5	6.0

Determine the least squares trend equation. Estimate the amount of scrap for the year 2000.

4. The amounts spent in vending machines in the United States, in billions of dollars, for the years 1994 through 1998 are given below. Determine the least squares equation, and estimate vending sales for 2000.

Year	Code	Vending Machine Sales ($ billions)
1994	1	17.5
1995	2	19.0
1996	3	21.0
1997	4	22.7
1998	5	24.5

▌ The Moving-Average Method

Moving-average method smooths out fluctuations

The **moving-average method** is not only useful in smoothing out a time series; it is the basic method used in measuring the seasonal fluctuation, described later in the chapter. In contrast to the least squares method, which expresses the trend in terms of a mathematical equation ($Y' = a + bt$), the moving-average method merely smooths out the fluctuations in the data. This is accomplished by "moving" the arithmetic mean values through the time series.

To apply the moving-average method to a time series, the data should follow a fairly linear trend and have a definite rhythmic pattern of fluctuations (repeating, say, every three years). The data in the following example have three components — trend, cycle, and irregular, abbreviated *T, C,* and *I*. There is no seasonal variation, because the data are recorded annually. What the moving-average method does, in effect, is average out *C* and *I*. The residual is trend.

If the duration of the cycles is constant, and if the amplitudes of the cycles are equal, the cyclical and irregular fluctuations can be removed entirely using the moving-average method. The result is a line. For example, in the following time series the cycle repeats itself every seven years, and the amplitude of each cycle is 4; that is, there are exactly four units from the trough (lowest time period) to the peak. The seven-year moving average, therefore, averages out the cyclical and irregular fluctuations perfectly, and the residual is a linear trend.

Compute mean of first seven years

The first step in computing the seven-year moving average is to determine the seven-year moving totals. The total sales for the first seven years (1973–79 inclusive) are $22 million, found by 1 + 2 + 3 + 4 + 5 + 4 + 3. (See Table 18–3.) The total of $22 million is divided by 7 to determine the arithmetic mean sales per year. The seven-year total (22) and the seven-year mean (3.143) are positioned opposite the middle year for that group of seven, namely, 1976, as shown in Table 18–3. Then the total sales for the next seven years (1974–80 inclusive) are determined. [A convenient way of doing this is to subtract the sales for 1973 ($1 million) from the first seven-year total ($22 million) and add the sales for 1980 ($2 million), to give the new total of $23 million.] The mean of this total, $3.286 million, is positioned opposite the middle year, 1977.

Table 18–3   The Computations for the Seven-Year Moving Average

Year	Sales ($ millions)	Seven-Year Moving Total	Seven-Year Moving Average
1973	$1		
1974	2		
1975	3		
1976	4	22	3.143
1977	5	23	3.286
1978	4	24	3.429
1979	3	25	3.571
1980	2	26	3.714
1981	3	27	3.857
1982	4	28	4.000
1983	5	29	4.143
1984	6	30	4.286
1985	5	31	4.429
1986	4	32	4.571
1987	3	33	4.714
1988	4	34	4.857
1989	5	35	5.000
1990	6	36	5.143
1991	7	37	5.286
1992	6	38	5.429
1993	5	39	5.571
1994	4	40	5.714
1995	5	41	5.857
1996	6		
1997	7		
1998	8		

This procedure is repeated until all possible seven-year totals and their means are found. (Note that there are no totals for the first three years and the last three years.) See Table 18–3 and Chart 18–5.

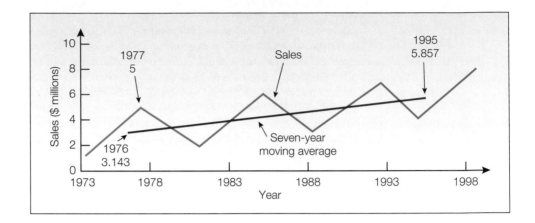

Chart 18–5   Sales and Seven-Year Moving Average

A three-year and a five-year moving average are shown in Table 18–4 and depicted in Chart 18–6.

Table 18–4   A Three-Year Moving Average and a Five-Year Moving Average

Year	Production, Y	Three-Year Moving Total	Three-Year Moving Average	Five-Year Moving Total	Five-Year Moving Average
1980	5				
1981	6	19	6.3		
1982	8	24	8.0	34	6.8
1983	10	23	7.7	32	6.4
1984	5	18	6.0	33	6.6
1985	3	15	5.0	35	7.0
1986	7	20	6.7	37	7.4
1987	10	29	9.7	43	8.6
1988	12	33	11.0	49	9.8
1989	11	32	10.7	55	11.0
1990	9	33	11.0	60	12.0
1991	13	37	12.3	66	13.2
1992	15	46	15.3	70	14.0
1993	18	48	16.0	72	14.4
1994	15	44	14.7	73	14.6
1995	11	40	13.3	75	15.0
1996	14	42	14.0	79	15.8
1997	17	53	17.7		
1998	22				

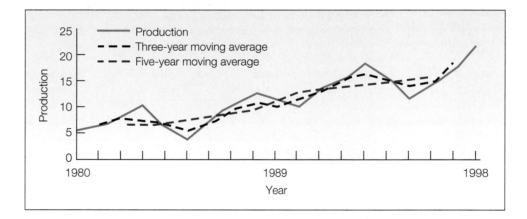

Chart 18–6 A Three-Year Moving Average and a Five-Year Moving Average

SELF-REVIEW 18–2

Compute a three-year moving average for the following production series. Plot both the original data and the moving average.

Year	Number Produced (thousands)	Year	Number Produced (thousands)
1993	2	1996	5
1994	6	1997	3
1995	4	1998	10

Sales, production, and other economic and business series usually do not have (1) periods of oscillation that are of equal length or (2) oscillations that have identical amplitudes. Thus, in actual practice, the application of the moving-average method to data does not result precisely in a line. For example, the production series in Table 18–4 repeats about every five years, but the amplitude of the data varies from one oscillation to another. The trend appears to be upward and somewhat linear. Both moving averages—the three-year and the five-year—seem to adequately describe the trend in production since 1980.

Determining a moving average for an even-numbered period, such as four years

Four-year, six-year, and other even-numbered-year moving averages present one minor problem regarding the centering of the moving totals and moving averages. Note in Table 18–5 that there is no center time period, so the moving totals are positioned *between* two time periods. The total for the first four years ($42) is positioned between 1988 and 1989. The total for the next four years is $43. The averages of the first four years and the second four years ($10.50 and $10.75, respectively) are averaged, and the resulting figure is centered on 1989. This procedure is repeated until all possible four-year averages are computed.

Table 18–5   A Four-Year Moving Average

Year	Sales, Y	Four-Year Moving Total	Four-Year Moving Average	Centered Four-Year Moving Average
1987	$ 8			
1988	11			
		$42 (8 + 11 + 9 + 14)	$10.50 ($42 ÷ 4)	
1989	9			10.625
		43 (11 + 9 + 14 + 9)	10.75 ($43 ÷ 4)	
1990	14			10.625
		42	10.50	
1991	9			10.625
		43	10.75	
1992	10			10.000
		37	9.25	
1993	10			9.625
		40	10.00	
1994	8			
1995	12			

To summarize the technique of using moving averages, its purpose is to help identify the long-term trend in a time series (because it smooths out short-term fluctuations). It is used to reveal any cyclical and seasonal fluctuations.

Nonlinear Trends

The emphasis in the previous discussion was on a time series whose growth or decline approximated a line. A linear trend equation is used to represent the time series when it is believed that the data are increasing (or decreasing) by *equal amounts,* on the average, from one period to another.

Data that increase (or decrease) by *increasing amounts* over a period of time appear *curvilinear* when plotted on paper having an arithmetic scale. To put it another way, data that increase (or decrease) by *equal percents or proportions* over a period of time appear curvilinear on arithmetic paper. (See Chart 18–7.)

The trend equation for a time series that does approximate a curvilinear trend, such as the one portrayed in Chart 18–7, can be computed by using the logarithms of the data and the least squares method.

The general equation for the logarithmic trend equation is:

LOG TREND EQUATION	$\log Y' = \log a + \log b(t)$	**[18–5]**

The logarithmic equation can be determined for the import data in Chart 18–7 using MINITAB. The first step is to enter the data, then find the log base 10 of each year's imports. Finally, use the regression procedure to find the least squares equation. To put it another way, we take the log of each year's data then use the logs as the dependent variable and the coded year as the independent variable.

Year	Imports	Year	Imports
1986	3.0	1993	31.0
1987	4.2	1994	44.6
1988	5.7	1995	60.1
1989	8.3	1996	84.3
1990	11.5	1997	118.6
1991	16.0	1998	163.9
1992	22.4		

Chart 18–7 Imports from 1986 to 1998 on an Arithmetic Scale

Row	Year	Code	Imports	Log-Imports
1	1986	1	3.0	0.47712
2	1987	2	4.2	0.62325
3	1988	3	5.7	0.75587
4	1989	4	8.3	0.91908
5	1990	5	11.5	1.06070
6	1991	6	16.0	1.20412
7	1992	7	22.4	1.35025
8	1993	8	31.0	1.49136
9	1994	9	44.6	1.64933
10	1995	10	60.1	1.77887
11	1996	11	84.3	1.92583
12	1997	12	118.6	2.07408
13	1998	13	163.9	2.21458

```
The regression equation is
Log-Imports = 0.333 + 0.145 Code

Predictor             Coef              StDev              T              P
Constant          0.332549          0.003381          98.36          0.000
Code              0.145069          0.000426         340.56          0.000


S = 0.005747      R-Sq = 100.0%      R-Sq(adj) = 100.0%
Analysis of Variance

SOURCE           DF           SS           MS              F              P
Regression        1       3.8302       3.8302      115980.20          0.000
Error            11       0.0004       0.0000
Total            12       3.8306
```

The regression equation is $Y' = 0.332549 + 0.145069X$, which is the log form. We now have a trend equation in terms of percent change. That is, the value 0.145069 is the percent change in Y' for each unit change in t. This value is similar to the geometric mean described in Chapter 3.

The log of b is 0.145069 and its antilog or inverse is 1.3966. If we subtract 1 from this value, as we did in Chapter 3, the value .3966 indicates the geometric mean rate of increase from 1986 to 1998. We conclude that imports increased at a rate of 39.66 percent annually during the period.

We can also use the logarithmic equation to make estimates of future values. Suppose we want to estimate the imports in the year 2003. The first step is to determine the code for the year 2003, which is 18. How did we get 18? The year 1998 has a code of 13 and the year 2003 is five years later, so $13 + 5 = 18$. The log of imports for the year 2003 is

$$Y' = .332549 + .145069(t) = .332549 + .145069(18) = 2.943791$$

To find the estimated imports for the year 2003, we need the antilog of 2.943791. It is 878.6. This is our estimate of the number of imports for 2003. Recall the data was in thousands of dollars, so the estimate is $878,600.

SELF-REVIEW 18–3

Sales at Tomlin Manufacturing since 1994 are:

Year	Sales ($ millions)
1994	2.13
1995	18.10
1996	39.80
1997	81.40
1998	112.00

(a) Determine the logarithmic equation for the sales data.
(b) Sales increased by what percent annually?
(c) What is the projected sales amount for 1999?

▌ Exercises

5. Sally's Software, Inc. is a rapidly growing supplier of computer software to the Sarasota area. Sales for the last five years are given below.

Year	Sales ($ millions)
1993	1.1
1994	1.5
1995	2.0
1996	2.4
1997	3.1

    a. Determine the logarithmic equation.
    b. By what percent did sales increase, on the average, during the period?
    c. Estimates sales for the year 2000.

6. It appears that the imports of carbon black have been increasing by about 10 percent annually.

Year	Imports of Carbon Black (thousands of tons)	Year	Imports of Carbon Black (thousands of tons)
1987	92.0	1991	135.0
1988	101.0	1992	149.0
1989	112.0	1993	163.0
1990	124.0	1994	180.0

    a. Determine the logarithmic equation.
    b. By what percent did imports increase, on the average, during the period?
    c. Estimate imports for the year 1997.

▌ Seasonal Variation

We mentioned that *seasonal variation* is another of the components of a time series. Business series, such as automobile sales, shipments of soft-drink bottles, and residential construction, have periods of above-average and below-average activity each year.

In the area of production, one of the reasons for analyzing seasonal fluctuations is to have a sufficient supply of raw materials on hand to meet the varying seasonal demand. The glass container division of a large glass company, for example, manufactures nonreturnable beer bottles, iodine bottles, aspirin bottles, bottles for rubber cement, and so on. The production scheduling department must know how many bottles to produce and when to produce each kind. A run of too many bottles of one kind may cause a serious storage problem. Production cannot be based entirely on orders on hand, because many orders are telephoned in for immediate shipment. Since the demand for many of the bottles varies according to the season, a forecast a year or two in advance, by month, is essential to good scheduling.

An analysis of seasonal fluctuations over a period of years can also help in evaluating current sales. The typical sales of department stores in the United States, excluding mail-order sales, are expressed as indexes in Table 18–6. Each index represents the average sales for a period of several years. The actual sales for some months were above average (which is represented by an index over 100.0), and the sales for other months were below average. The index of 126.8 for December indicates that, typically, sales for December are 26.8 percent above an average month; the index of 86.0 for July indicates that department store sales for July are typically 14 percent below an average month.

Table 18–6 Typical Seasonal Indexes for U.S. Department Store Sales, Excluding Mail-Order Sales

January	87.0	July	86.0
February	83.2	August	99.7
March	100.5	September	101.4
April	106.5	October	105.8
May	101.6	November	111.9
June	89.6	December	126.8

Suppose an enterprising store manager, in an effort to stimulate sales during December, introduced a number of unique promotions, including bands of carolers strolling through the store singing holiday songs, large mechanical exhibits, and clerks dressed in Santa Claus costumes. When the index of sales was computed for that December, it was 150.0. Compared with the typical sales of 126.8, it was concluded that the promotional program was a huge success.

Determining a Seasonal Index

Objective: To determine a set of "typical" seasonal indexes

A typical set of monthly indexes consists of 12 indexes that are representative of the data for a 12-month period. Logically, there are four typical seasonal indexes for data reported quarterly. Each index is a percent, with the average for the year equal to 100.0; that is, each monthly index indicates the level of sales, production, or another variable in relation to the annual average of 100.0. A typical index of 96.0 for January indicates that sales (or whatever the variable is) are usually 4 percent below the average for the year. An index of 107.2 for October means that the variable is typically 7.2 percent above the annual average.

Several methods have been developed to measure the typical seasonal fluctuation in a time series. The method most commonly used to compute the typical seasonal pattern is called the **ratio-to-moving-average method.** It eliminates the trend, cyclical, and irregular components from the original data (Y). In the following discussion, T refers to trend, C to cyclical, S to seasonal, and I to irregular variation. The numbers that result are called the *typical seasonal index.*

We will discuss in detail the steps followed in arriving at typical seasonal indexes using the ratio-to-moving-average method. As before, simple figures are used to illustrate.

The data of interest might be monthly or quarterly. To illustrate, we have chosen the quarterly sales of Toys International. First, we will show the steps needed to arrive at a set of typical quarterly indexes. Then we will apply a procedure by Hall from *Computerized Business Statistics,* a statistical software package published by Irwin/McGraw-Hill.

Example

Table 18–7 shows the quarterly sales for Toys International for the years 1993 through 1998. The sales are reported in millions of dollars. Determine a quarterly seasonal index using the ratio-to-moving-average method.

Table 18–7   Quarterly Sales of Toys International ($ millions)

Year	Winter	Spring	Summer	Fall
1993	6.7	4.6	10.0	12.7
1994	6.5	4.6	9.8	13.6
1995	6.9	5.0	10.4	14.1
1996	7.0	5.5	10.8	15.0
1997	7.1	5.7	11.1	14.5
1998	8.0	6.2	11.4	14.9

Solution   Chart 18–8 depicts the quarterly sales for Toys International over the six-year period. Notice the seasonal nature of the sales. For each year the fourth-quarter sales are the largest and the second-quarter sales are the smallest. Also, there is a moderate increase in the sales from one year to the next. To observe this feature, look only at the six fourth-quarter sales values. Over the six-year period the sales in the fourth quarter increased. If you connect these points in your mind as we did in Chart 18–8, you can visualize fourth-quarter sales increasing for 1999.

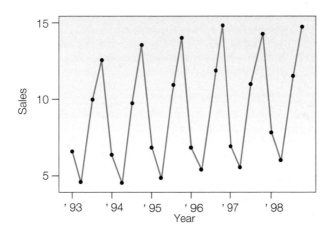

Chart 18–8   Quarterly Sales ($ millions) of Toys International

There are six steps to determine the quarterly seasonal indexes.

Step 1   For the following discussion, refer to Table 18–8. The first step is to determine the four-quarter moving total for 1993. Starting with the winter quarter of 1993, we add $6.7, $4.6, $10.0, and $12.7. The total is $34.0 (million). The four-quarter total is "moved along" by adding the spring, summer, and fall sales of 1993 to the winter sales of 1994. The total is $33.8 (million), found by 4.6 + 10.0 + 12.7 + 6.5. This procedure is continued for the quarterly sales for each of the six years. Column 2 of Table 18–8 shows all of the moving totals. Note that the moving total 34.0 is positioned between the spring and summer sales of 1993. The next moving total, 33.8, is positioned between sales for summer and fall of 1993, and so on. Check the totals frequently to avoid arithmetic errors.

Table 18–8   Computations Needed for the Specific Seasonal Indexes

		(1) Sales ($ millions)	(2) Four-Quarter Moving Total	(3) Four-Quarter Moving Average	(4) Centered Moving Average	(5) Specific Seasonal
Year	Quarter					
1993	Winter	6.7				
	Spring	4.6				
			34.0	8.500		
	Summer	10.0			8.4750	1.1799
			33.8	8.450		
	Fall	12.7			8.4500	1.5030
			33.8	8.450		
1994	Winter	6.5			8.4250	0.7715
			33.6	8.400		
	Spring	4.6			8.5125	0.5404
			34.5	8.625		
	Summer	9.8			8.6750	1.1297
			34.9	8.725		
	Fall	13.6			8.7750	1.5499
			35.3	8.825		
1995	Winter	6.9			8.9000	0.7753
			35.9	8.975		
	Spring	5.0			9.0375	0.5533
			36.4	9.100		
	Summer	10.4			9.1125	1.1413
			36.5	9.125		
	Fall	14.1			9.1875	1.5347
			37.0	9.250		
1996	Winter	7.0			9.3000	0.7527
			37.4	9.350		
	Spring	5.5			9.4625	0.5812
			38.3	9.575		
	Summer	10.8			9.5875	1.1265
			38.4	9.600		
	Fall	15.0			9.6250	1.5584
			38.6	9.650		
1997	Winter	7.1			9.6875	0.7329
			38.9	9.725		
	Spring	5.7			9.6625	0.5899
			38.4	9.600		
	Summer	11.1			9.7125	1.1429
			39.3	9.825		
	Fall	14.5			9.8875	1.4665
			39.8	9.950		
1998	Winter	8.0			9.8875	0.8010
			40.1	10.025		
	Spring	6.2			10.0750	0.6154
			40.5	10.125		
	Summer	11.4				
	Fall	14.9				

Step 2   Each quarterly moving total in column 2 is divided by 4 to give the four-quarter moving average. (See column 3.) All the moving averages are still positioned between the quarters. For example, the first moving average (8.500) is positioned between spring and summer of 1993.

Step 3   The moving averages are then centered. The first centered moving average is found by (8.500 + 8.450)/2 = 8.4750 and centered opposite Summer 1993. The second moving average is found by (8.450 + 8.450)/2 = 8.450. The others are found similarly. Note in column 4 that a centered moving average is positioned on a particular quarter.

Step 4   The **specific seasonal** for each quarter is then computed by dividing the sales in column 1 by the centered moving average in column 4. The specific seasonal reports the ratio of the original time series value to the moving average. To explain further, if the time series is represented by *TSCI* and the moving average by *TCI*, then, algebraically, if we compute *TSCI/TCI*, the result is the seasonal component. The specific seasonal for the summer quarter of 1993 is 1.1799, found by 10.0/8.4750.

Step 5   The specific seasonals are organized in a table. (See Table 18–9.) This table will help us locate the specific seasonals for the corresponding quarters. The values 1.1799, 1.1297, 1.1413, 1.1265, and 1.1429 all represent estimates of the typical seasonal index for the summer quarter. A reasonable method to find a typical seasonal index is to average these values. So we find the typical index for the summer quarter by (1.1799 + 1.1297 + 1.1413 + 1.1265 + 1.1429)/5 = 1.1441. We used the arithmetic mean, but the median or a modified mean can also be used.

Table 18–9   Calculations Needed for the Typical Quarterly Indexes

Year	Winter	Spring	Summer	Fall	
1993			1.1799	1.5030	
1994	0.7715	0.5404	1.1297	1.5499	
1995	0.7753	0.5533	1.1413	1.5347	
1996	0.7527	0.5812	1.1265	1.5584	
1997	0.7329	0.5899	1.1429	1.4665	
1998	0.8010	0.6154			
Total	3.8334	2.8802	5.7203	7.6125	
Mean	0.7667	0.5760	1.1441	1.5225	4.0093
Typical index	76.49	57.47	114.14	151.90	4.0000

Step 6   The four quarterly means (0.7667, 0.5760, 1.1441, and 1.5225) should theoretically total 4.00 because the average is set at 1.0. The total of the four quarterly means may not exactly equal 4.00 due to rounding. In this problem the total of the means is 4.0093. A *correction factor* is therefore applied to each of the four means to force them to total 4.00.

CORRECTION FACTOR FOR ADJUSTING QUARTERLY MEANS	Correction factor $= \dfrac{4.00}{\text{Total of four means}}$	**[18–6]**

In this problem,

$$\text{Correction factor} = \frac{4.00}{4.0093} = 0.99768$$

The adjusted winter quarterly index is, therefore, $(0.7667)(0.99768) = 0.7649$. Each of the means is adjusted downward so that the total of the four quarterly means is 4.00. Usually indexes are reported as percentages, so each value in the last row of Table 18–9 has been multiplied by 100. So the index for the winter quarter is 76.49 and for the fall it is 151.90. How are these values interpreted? Sales for the fall quarter are 51.90 percent above the typical quarter, and for winter they are 23.51 below the typical quarter $(100.0 - 76.49)$. These findings should not surprise you. The period prior to Christmas (the fall quarter) is when toy sales are brisk. After Christmas (the winter quarter) sales of the toys decline drastically.

Now to briefly summarize the reasoning underlying the preceding calculations. The original data in column 1 of Table 18–8 contain trend (T), cycle (C), seasonal (S), and irregular (I) components. The ultimate objective is to remove seasonal (S) from the original sales valuation.

Columns 2 and 3 in Table 18–8 were concerned with deriving the centered moving average given in column 4. Basically, we "averaged out" the seasonal and irregular fluctuations from the original data in column 1. Thus, in column 4 we have only trend and cycle (TC).

Next, we divided the sales data in column 1 ($TCSI$) by the centered fourth-quarter moving average in column 4 (TC) to arrive at the specific seasonals in column 5 (SI). In terms of letters, $TCSI/TC = SI$. We multiplied SI by 100.0 in order to express the typical seasonal in index form.

Finally, we took the mean of all the winter typical indexes, all the spring indexes, and so on. This averaging eliminates most of the irregular fluctuations from the seasonals, and the resulting four indexes indicate the typical seasonal sales pattern.

SELF-REVIEW   18 – 4

Teton Village, Wyoming, near Grand Teton Park and Yellowstone Park, contains shops, restaurants, and motels. They have two peak seasons — winter, for skiing on the 10,000-foot slopes, and summer, for tourists visiting the parks. The specific seasonals with respect to the total sales volume for recent years are:

Year	Winter	Spring	Summer	Fall
1994	117.0	80.7	129.6	76.1
1995	118.6	82.5	121.4	77.0
1996	114.0	84.3	119.9	75.0
1997	120.7	79.6	130.7	69.6
1998	125.2	80.2	127.6	72.0

(a) Develop the typical seasonal pattern for Teton Village using the ratio-to-moving-average method.
(b) Explain the typical index for the winter season.

▌ Exercises

7. Victor Anderson, the owner of Anderson Belts, Inc., is studying absenteeism among his employees. His workforce is small, consisting of only five employees. For the last three years he recorded the following number of employee absences, in days, for each quarter.

	Quarter			
Year	I	II	III	IV
1996	4	10	7	3
1997	5	12	9	4
1998	6	16	12	4

Determine a typical seasonal index for each of the four quarters.

8. The Appliance Center sells a variety of electronic equipment and home appliances. For the last four years the following quarterly sales (in $ millions) were reported.

	Quarter			
Year	I	II	III	IV
1995	5.3	4.1	6.8	6.7
1996	4.8	3.8	5.6	6.8
1997	4.3	3.8	5.7	6.0
1998	5.6	4.6	6.4	5.9

Determine a typical seasonal index for each of the four quarters.

A Computer Solution As noted previously, a statistical software package called *Computerized Business Statistics,* developed by Hall, has a routine for computing seasonal indexes. The following is the output obtained for the previous Example. Much of the same information on the trend and seasonal-irregular components is shown. The final answers differ slightly, due to rounding, from those in Table 18–9. Use of a software package such as Hall's will greatly reduce computational time and the possibility of an error in arithmetic. The seasonal values obtained from the Hall software package will be used in the analyses later in the chapter.

```
CBSW                        Time Series                        6/2/98

                             Results

        Seasonal Indices                     Periods = 24

    Period        Quarter          Value         Trend          S-I
      1              1              6.7            -              -
                     2              4.6            -              -
                     3              10           8.4750        1.1799
                     4              12.7         8.4500        1.5030
      2              1              6.5          8.4250        0.7715
                     2              4.6          8.5125        0.5404
                     3              9.8          8.6750        1.1297
                     4              13.6         8.7750        1.5499
      3              1              6.9          8.900         0.7753
                     2              5            9.0375        0.5533
                     3              10.4         9.1125        1.1413
                     4              14.1         9.1875        1.5347
      4              1              7            9.3000        0.7527
                     2              5.5          9.4625        0.5812
                     3              10.8         9.5875        1.1265
                     4              15           9.6250        1.5584
      5              1              7.1          9.6875        0.7329
                     2              5.7          9.6625        0.5899
                     3              11.1         9.7125        1.1429
                     4              14.5         9.8775        1.4665
      6              1              8            9.9875        0.8010
                     2              6.2          10.0750       0.6154
                     3              11.4           -              -
                     4              14.9           -              -
```

| | Seasonal Index | | |
Quarter	Average S-I	Seasonal Factor	Seasonal Index
1	0.7667	0.7667	76.67
2	0.5760	0.5760	57.60
3	1.1440	1.1440	114.40
4	1.5225	1.5225	152.25

Deseasonalizing Data

A set of typical indexes is very useful in adjusting a sales series, for example, for seasonal fluctuations. The resulting sales series is called **deseasonalized sales** or **seasonally adjusted sales.** The reason for deseasonalizing the sales series is to remove the seasonal fluctuations so that the trend and cycle can be studied. To illustrate the procedure, the quarterly sales totals of Toys International from Table 18–7 are repeated in column 1 of Table 18–10.

Table 18–10 Actual and Deseasonalized Sales for Toys International

Year	Quarter	(1) Sales	(2) Seasonal Index	(3) Deseasonalized Sales
1993	Winter	6.7	0.7667	8.7387
	Spring	4.6	0.5760	7.9861
	Summer	10.0	1.1440	8.7413
	Fall	12.7	1.5225	8.3415
1994	Winter	6.5	0.7667	8.4779
	Spring	4.6	0.5760	7.9861
	Summer	9.8	1.1440	8.5664
	Fall	13.6	1.5225	8.9327
1995	Winter	6.9	0.7667	8.9996
	Spring	5.0	0.5760	7.6806
	Summer	10.4	1.1440	9.0909
	Fall	14.1	1.5225	9.2611
1996	Winter	7.0	0.7667	9.1300
	Spring	5.5	0.5760	9.5486
	Summer	10.8	1.1440	9.4406
	Fall	15.0	1.5225	9.8522
1997	Winter	7.1	0.7667	9.2605
	Spring	5.7	0.5760	9.8958
	Summer	11.1	1.1440	9.7028
	Fall	14.5	1.5225	9.5238
1998	Winter	8.0	0.7667	10.4343
	Spring	6.2	0.5760	10.7639
	Summer	11.4	1.1440	9.9650
	Fall	14.9	1.5225	9.7865

To remove the effect of seasonal variation, the sales amount for each quarter (which contains trend, cyclical, irregular, and seasonal effects) is divided by the seasonal index for that quarter, that is, *TSCI/S*. For example, the actual sales for the first quarter of 1993 were $6.7 million. The seasonal index for the winter quarter is 76.67, using the Hall results on page 662. The index of 76.67 indicates that sales for the first quarter are typically 23.33 percent below the average for a typical quarter. By dividing the actual sales of $6.7 million by 76.67 and multiplying the result by 100, we find the *deseasonalized sales* value for the first quarter of 1993. It is $8,738,750, found by ($6,700,000/76.67)100. We continue this process for the other quarters in column 3 of Table 18–10, with the results reported in millions of dollars. Because the seasonal component has been removed (divided out) from the quarterly sales, the deseasonalized sales figure contains only the trend (*T*), cyclical (*C*), and irregular (*I*) components. Scanning the deseasonalized sales in column 3 of Table 18–10, we see that the sales of toys showed a moderate increase over the six-year period. Chart 18–9 shows both the actual sales and the deseasonalized sales. It is clear that removing the seasonal factor allows us to focus on the overall long-term trend of sales. We will also be able to determine the regression equation of the trend data and use it to forecast future sales.

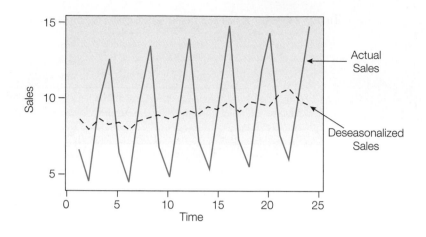

Chart 18–9 Actual Sales and Deseasonalized Sales for Toys International, 1993 to 1998

Using Deseasonalized Data to Forecast The procedure for identifying trend and the seasonal adjustments can be combined to yield seasonally adjusted forecasts. To identify the trend, we determine the least squares trend equation on the deseasonalized historical data. Then we project this trend into future periods, and finally we adjust these trend values to account for the seasonal factors. The following example will help to clarify.

Example	Toys International would like to forecast their sales for each quarter of 1999. Use the information in Table 18–10 to determine the forecast.
Solution	The first step is to use the deseasonalized data in column 3 of Table 18–10 to determine the least squares trend equation. The deseasonalized trend equation is:

$$Y' = a + bt$$

where:

    Y' is the estimated trend for Toys International sales for period t.

    a is the intercept of the trend line at time 0.

    b is the slope of the trend line.

The winter quarter of 1993 is the period $t = 1$, and $t = 24$ corresponds to the fall quarter of 1998. (See column 1 in Table 18–11.) The sums needed to compute a and b are also shown in Table 18–11.

$$b = \frac{\Sigma tY - (\Sigma Y)(\Sigma t)/n}{\Sigma t^2 - (\Sigma t)^2/n} = \frac{2{,}866.9626 - (221.1069)(300)/24}{4{,}900 - (300)^2/24} = 0.0897$$

$$a = \frac{\Sigma Y}{n} \quad b\left(\frac{\Sigma t}{n}\right) = \frac{221.1069}{24} - 0.0897\left(\frac{300}{24}\right) = 8.0915$$

Table 18–11 Deseasonalized Sales for Toys International: Data Needed for Determining Trend Line

Year	Quarter	(1) t	(2) Y	(3) tY	(4) t^2
1993	Winter	1	8.7387	8.7387	1
	Spring	2	7.9861	15.9722	4
	Summer	3	8.7413	26.2239	9
	Fall	4	8.3415	33.3660	16
1994	Winter	5	8.4779	42.3895	25
	Spring	6	7.9861	47.9166	36
	Summer	7	8.5664	59.9648	49
	Fall	8	8.9327	71.4616	64
1995	Winter	9	8.9996	80.9964	81
	Spring	10	8.6806	86.8060	100
	Summer	11	9.0909	99.9999	121
	Fall	12	9.2611	111.1332	144
1996	Winter	13	9.1300	118.6900	169
	Spring	14	9.5486	133.6804	196
	Summer	15	9.4406	141.6090	225
	Fall	16	9.8522	157.6352	256
1997	Winter	17	9.2605	157.4285	289
	Spring	18	9.8958	178.1244	324
	Summer	19	9.7028	184.3532	361
	Fall	20	9.5238	190.4760	400
1998	Winter	21	10.4343	219.1203	441
	Spring	22	10.7639	236.8058	484
	Summer	23	9.9650	229.1950	529
	Fall	24	9.7865	234.8760	576
Total		300	221.1069	2,866.9626	4,900

The trend equation is:

$$Y' = 8.0915 + 0.0897t$$

The slope of the trend line is 0.0897. This shows that over the 24 quarters the deseasonalized sales increased at a rate of 0.0897 ($ millions) per quarter, or $89,700 per quarter. The value of 8.0915 is the intercept of the trend line on the Y-axis (i.e., for $t = 0$).

Of course, we can use a statistical software package to determine the regression equation. The following output is from the Excel system. Using a software package will reduce the possibility of an error in arithmetic. In addition, we can use the value of R^2 to give an indication of the fit of the data. Because this is *not* sample information, technically, we should not use R^2 for judging a regression equation. It will serve, however, to quickly evaluate the fit of the deseasonalized data. In this instance the R^2 value is 78.5 percent, which indicates that time does a good job of explaining the variation in the deseasonalized data.

```
                        SUMMARY OUTPUT

                     Regression Statistics

         Multiple R              0.88614511
         R Square                0.78525315
         Adjusted R Square       0.77549193
         Standard Error          0.33905327
         Observations                    24
```

ANOVA

	df	SS	MS	F	Significance F
Regression	1	9.247864404	9.247864	80.44621	8.40734E-09
Residual	22	2.529046642	0.114957		
Total	23	11.77692105			

	Coefficients	Standard Error	t Stat	P-value
Intercept	8.09184891	0.14286026	56.64171	2.47E-25
Time	0.08967509	0.009998135	8.969181	8.41E-09

If we assume that the past 24 periods are a good indicator of future sales, we can use the trend equation to estimate future sales. For example, for the winter quarter of 1999, the value of t is 25. The estimated sales total for that period is $10,334,000, found by

$$Y' = 8.0915 + 0.0897(25) = 10.334$$

Using the trend equation, we can forecast sales at Toys International for the four quarters of 1999. These estimates are shown in Table 18–12.

Table 18–12 Quarterly Forecast for Toys International for 1999

Quarter	t	Estimated Sales	Seasonal Index	Quarterly Forecast
Winter	25	10.3340	0.7667	7.923
Spring	26	10.4237	0.5760	6.004
Summer	27	10.5134	1.1440	12.027
Fall	28	10.6031	1.5225	16.143

Now that we have the forecasts for the four quarters of 1999, we can seasonally adjust them. The index for the winter quarter is 0.7667 (see the Hall computer solution earlier in the chapter), so we can estimate the sales in this quarter by 10.3340(0.7667) = 7.923. The estimates for the four quarters of 1999 are shown in the last column of Table 18–12. Notice how the seasonal adjustments drastically increase the sales estimates for the last two quarters of the year.

SELF-REVIEW 18–5

The Westberg Electric Company sells electric motors to customers in the Jamestown, New York, area. The monthly trend equation, based on five years of monthly data, is

$$Y' = 4.40 + 0.50t$$

The seasonal factor for the month of January is 120, and it is 95 for February. Determine the seasonally adjusted forecast for January and February of the sixth year.

Exercises

9. The planning department of Padget and Kure Shoes, the manufacturer of an exclusive brand of women's shoes, developed the following trend equation, in millions of pairs, based on five years of quarterly data.

$$Y' = 3.30 + 1.75t$$

The following table gives the seasonal factors for each quarter.

	\multicolumn{4}{c}{Quarter}			
	I	II	III	IV
Index	110.0	120.0	80.0	90.0

Determine the seasonally adjusted forecast for each of the four quarters of the sixth year.
10. Team Sports, Inc. sells sporting goods to high schools and colleges via a nationally distributed catalog. Management at Team Sports estimates they will sell 2,000 Wilson Model A2000 catcher's mitts next year. The deseasonalized sales are projected to be the same for each of the four quarters next year. The seasonal factor for the second quarter is 145. Determine the seasonally adjusted sales for the second quarter of next year.
11. Refer to Exercise 7, regarding the absences at Anderson Belts, Inc. Use the seasonal indexes you computed to determine the deseasonalized absences. Determine the trend equation based on the quarterly data for the three years. Forecast the seasonally adjusted absences for 1999.
12. Refer to Exercise 8, regarding sales at the Appliance Center. Use the seasonal indexes you computed to determine the deseasonalized sales. Determine the trend equation based on the quarterly data for the four years. Forecast the seasonally adjusted sales for 1999.

Chapter Outline

I. A time series is a collection of data over a period of time.
   A. The trend is the long-run direction of the time series.
   B. The cyclical component is the fluctuation above and below the long-term trend line.
   C. The seasonal variation is the pattern in a time series within a year. These patterns tend to repeat themselves from year to year for most businesses.
   D. The irregular variation is divided into two components.
      1. The episodic variations are unpredictable, but they can usually be identified. A flood is an example.
      2. The residual variations are random in nature.
II. The linear trend equation is $Y' = a + bt$, where a is the Y-intercept, b is the slope of the line, and t is the time.

A. The trend equation is determined using the least squares principle.

B. If the trend is not linear, but rather the increases tend to be a constant percent, the *Y* values are converted to logarithms, and a least squares equation is determined using the logs.

III. A moving average is used to smooth the trend in a time series.

IV. A seasonal factor can be estimated using the ratio-to-moving-average method.

A. The six-step procedure yields a seasonal index for each period.

1. Seasonal factors are usually computed on a monthly or a quarterly basis.

2. The seasonal factor is used to adjust forecasts, taking into account the effects of the season.

❚ Chapter Exercises

13. Refer to the following diagram.

a. Estimate the linear equation for the following production series by drawing a straight line through the data.

b. What is the average annual decrease in production?

c. Based on the trend equation, what is the forecast for the year 2000?

14. a. Estimate the trend equation for the following personal income series.

b. What is the average annual increase in personal income?

15. The asset turnovers, excluding cash and short-term investments, for the RNC Company from 1987 to 1997 are:

1987	1988	1989	1990	1991	1992	1993	1994	1995	1996	1997
1.11	1.28	1.17	1.10	1.06	1.14	1.24	1.33	1.38	1.50	1.65

a. Plot the data.
b. Determine the least squares trend equation.
c. Calculate the points on the trend line for 1990 and 1995, and plot the line on the graph.

d. Estimate the asset turnover for 2002.
e. How much did the asset turnover increase per year, on the average, from 1987 to 1997?

16. The sales, in billions of dollars, of Keller Overhead Door, Inc. for 1992 to 1997 are:

Year	Sales	Year	Sales
1992	7.45	1995	7.94
1993	7.83	1996	7.76
1994	8.07	1997	7.90

a. Plot the data.
b. Determine the least squares trend equation.
c. Use the trend equation to calculate the points for 1994 and 1996. Plot them on the graph and draw the regression line.

d. Estimate the net sales for 2000.
e. By how much have sales increased (or decreased) per year on the average during the period?

17. The number of employees, in thousands, of Keller Overhead Door, Inc. for the years 1992 to 1997 are:

Year	Employees	Year	Employees
1992	45.6	1995	39.3
1993	42.2	1996	34.0
1994	41.1	1997	30.0

a. Plot the data.
b. Determine the least squares trend equation.
c. Use the trend equation to calculate the points for 1994 and 1996. Plot them on the graph and draw the regression line.

d. Estimate the number of employees in 2000.
e. By how much has the number of employees increased (or decreased) per year on the average during the period?

18. Since 1988 the annual value of merchandise trade from Canada to the United States, in billions of Canadian dollars, is:

Year	Merchandise Value	Year	Merchandise Value
1988	121.9	1993	168.2
1989	123.8	1994	183.3
1990	129.6	1995	194.3
1991	127.6	1996	201.1
1992	142.2		

a. Plot the data.
b. Determine the least squares trend equation.
c. Calculate the points for the years 1990 and 1992 based on the trend equation. Plot them on the graph and draw the regression line.

d. Estimate the trade in 2000.
e. By how much has the trade increased (or decreased) per year on the average during the period?

19. If plotted on arithmetic paper, the following sales series would appear curvilinear. This indicates that sales are increasing at a somewhat constant annual rate (percent). To fit the sales, therefore, a logarithmic straight-line equation should be used.

Year	Sales ($ millions)	Year	Sales ($ millions)
1988	8.0	1994	39.4
1989	10.4	1995	50.5
1990	13.5	1996	65.0
1991	17.6	1997	84.1
1992	22.8	1998	109.0
1993	29.3		

a. Determine the logarithmic equation.
b. Determine the coordinates of the points on the logarithmic straight line for 1991 and 1996.
c. By what percent did sales increase per year, on the average, during the period from 1988 to 1998?
d. Based on the equation, what are the estimated sales for 1999?

20. Reported below are the amounts spent on advertising ($ billions) from 1987 to 1997.

Year	Amount	Year	Amount
1987	88.1	1993	132.6
1988	94.7	1994	141.9
1989	102.1	1995	150.9
1990	109.8	1996	157.9
1991	118.1	1997	162.6
1992	125.6		

a. Determine the logarithmic trend equation.
b. Estimate the advertising expenses for 2000.
c. By what percent per year did advertising expense increase during the period?

21. The numbers of households (in millions) in the United States with videocassette recorders (VCRs) for each year from 1980 to 1996 are shown below.

Year	Number	Year	Number
1980	0.8	1989	58.4
1981	1.4	1990	63.2
1982	3.0	1991	67.1
1983	4.6	1992	72.3
1984	8.9	1993	75.9
1985	17.6	1994	79.7
1986	30.9	1995	86.1
1987	42.6	1996	91.3
1988	51.4		

a. Determine the logarithmic trend equation.
b. Estimate the number of households with VCRs in 2000.
c. By what percent per year did the number of households with VCRs increase during the period?

22. The production of the Reliable Manufacturing Company for 1994 and part of 1995 follows.

Month	1994 Production (thousands)	1995 Production (thousands)	Month	1994 Production (thousands)	1995 Production (thousands)
January	6	7	July	3	4
February	7	9	August	5	
March	12	14	September	14	
April	8	9	October	6	
May	4	5	November	7	
June	3	4	December	6	

a. Using the ratio-to-moving-average method, determine the specific seasonals for July, August, and September 1994.

b. Assume that the specific seasonal indexes in the following table are correct. Insert in the table the specific seasonals you computed in part (a) for July, August, and September 1994, and determine the 12 typical seasonal indexes.

Year	Jan.	Feb.	Mar.	Apr.	May	June	July	Aug.	Sept.	Oct.	Nov.	Dec.
1994							?	?	?	92.1	106.5	92.9
1995	88.9	102.9	178.9	118.2	60.1	43.1	44.0	74.0	200.9	90.0	101.9	90.9
1996	87.6	103.7	170.2	125.9	59.4	48.6	44.2	77.2	196.5	89.6	113.2	80.6
1997	79.8	105.6	165.8	124.7	62.1	41.7	48.2	72.1	203.6	80.2	103.0	94.2
1998	89.0	112.1	182.9	115.1	57.6	56.9						

c. Interpret the typical seasonal index.

23. The Sales of Andre's Boutique for 1993 and part of 1994 are:

Month	1993 Sales (thousands)	1994 Sales (thousands)	Month	1993 Sales (thousands)	1994 Sales (thousands)
January	78	65	July	81	65
February	72	60	August	85	61
March	80	72	September	90	75
April	110	97	October	98	
May	92	86	November	115	
June	86	72	December	130	

a. Using the ratio-to-moving-average method, determine the specific seasonals for July, August, September, and October 1993.

b. Assume that the specific seasonals in the following table are correct. Insert in the table the specific seasonals you computed in part (a) for July, August, September, and October 1993, and determine the 12 typical seasonal indexes.

Year	Jan.	Feb.	Mar.	Apr.	May	June	July	Aug.	Sept.	Oct.	Nov.	Dec.
1993							?	?	?	?	123.6	150.9
1994	83.9	77.6	86.1	118.7	99.7	92.0	87.0	91.4	97.3	105.4	124.9	140.1
1995	86.7	72.9	86.2	121.3	96.6	92.0	85.5	93.6	98.2	103.2	126.1	141.7
1996	85.6	65.8	89.2	125.6	99.6	94.4	88.9	90.2	100.2	102.7	121.6	139.6
1997	77.3	81.2	85.8	115.7	100.3	89.7						

c. Interpret the typical seasonal index.

24. The quarterly production of pine lumber, in millions of board feet, by Northwest Lumber since 1993 is:

	Quarter			
Year	Winter	Spring	Summer	Fall
1993	7.8	10.2	14.7	9.3
1994	6.9	11.6	17.5	9.3
1995	8.9	9.7	15.3	10.1
1996	10.7	12.4	16.8	10.7
1997	9.2	13.6	17.1	10.3

a. Determine the typical seasonal pattern for the production data using the ratio-to-moving-average method.
b. Interpret the pattern.
c. Deseasonalize the data and determine the linear trend equation.
d. Project the seasonally adjusted production for the four quarters of 1998.

25. Work Gloves Corp. is reviewing its quarterly sales of Toughie, the most durable glove they produce. The numbers of pairs produced (in thousands) by quarter are:

	Quarter			
	I	II	III	IV
Year	Jan.–Mar.	Apr.–June	July–Sept.	Oct.–Dec.
1992	142	312	488	208
1993	146	318	512	212
1994	160	330	602	187
1995	158	338	572	176
1996	162	380	563	200
1997	162	362	587	205

a. Using the ratio-to-moving-average method, determine the four typical quarterly indexes.
b. Interpret the typical seasonal pattern.

26. Sales of aluminum, by quarter, since 1991 are shown below (in $ millions).

	Quarter			
Year	I	II	III	IV
1991	210	180	60	246
1992	214	216	82	230
1993	246	228	91	280
1994	258	250	113	298
1995	279	267	116	304
1996	302	290	114	310
1997	321	291	120	320

a. Determine the typical seasonal patterns for sales using the ratio-to-moving-average method.
b. Deseasonalize the data and determine the trend equation.
c. Project the sales for 1998, and then seasonally adjust each quarter.

27. The inventory turnover rates for Bassett Wholesale Enterprises, by quarter, are:

Year	Quarter I	II	III	IV
1993	4.4	6.1	11.7	7.2
1994	4.1	6.6	11.1	8.6
1995	3.9	6.8	12.0	9.7
1996	5.0	7.1	12.7	9.0
1997	4.3	5.2	10.8	7.6

   a. Arrive at the four typical quarterly turnover rates for the Bassett Company using the ratio-to-moving-average method.
   b. Deseasonalize the data and determine the trend equation.
   c. Project the turnover rates for 1998, and seasonally adjust each quarter of 1998.
28. The following is the enrollment at the University of Toledo from 1967 through 1997. Develop both a linear and a logarithmetic trend equation. Estimate the enrollment for 1998 using both equations. Which trend equation would you recommend? Why? Plot the data and comment on your forecast.

Year	Enrollment	Year	Enrollment
1967	12,755	1983	21,589
1968	13,501	1984	21,039
1969	14,489	1985	21,238
1970	15,158	1986	21,176
1971	14,903	1987	21,740
1972	14,669	1988	22,806
1973	14,343	1989	23,928
1974	15,730	1990	24,781
1975	17,109	1991	24,969
1976	17,204	1992	24,541
1977	17,498	1993	24,188
1978	17,257	1994	23,107
1979	18,246	1995	21,991
1980	20,270	1996	21,343
1981	21,117	1997	20,040
1982	21,386		

29. Ray Anderson, owner of the Anderson Ski Lodge in upstate New York, is interested in forecasting the number of visitors for the upcoming year. The following data are available, by quarter since 1991. Develop a seasonal index for each quarter. How many visitors would you expect for each quarter of 1998, if Ray projects that there will be a 10 percent increase from the total number of visitors in 1997? Determine the trend equation, project the number of visitors for 1998, and seasonally adjust the forecast. Which forecast would you choose?

Year	Quarter	Visitors	Year	Quarter	Visitors
1991	I	86	1995	I	188
	II	62		II	172
	III	28		III	128
	IV	94		IV	198
1992	I	106	1996	I	208
	II	82		II	202
	III	48		III	154
	IV	114		IV	220
1993	I	140	1997	I	246
	II	120		II	240
	III	82		III	190
	IV	154		IV	252
1994	I	162			
	II	140			
	III	100			
	IV	174			

30. The enrollment in the College of Business at Midwestern University by quarter since 1993 is:

Year	Quarter			
	Winter	Spring	Summer	Fall
1993	2,033	1,871	714	2,318
1994	2,174	2,069	840	2,413
1995	2,370	2,254	927	2,704
1996	2,625	2,478	1,136	3,001
1997	2,803	2,668	—	—

Using the ratio-to-moving-average method:
a. Determine the four quarterly indexes.
b. Interpret the quarterly pattern of enrollment. Does the seasonal variation surprise you?
c. Compute the trend equation, and forecast the 1998 enrollment by quarter.

31. The Jamie Farr Kroger Classic is an LPGA (Women's Professional Golf) tournament played in Toledo, Ohio, each year. Listed below are the total purse and the prize for winner for the 11 years from 1987 through 1997. Develop a trend equation for both variables. Which variable is increasing at a faster rate? Project both the amount of the purse and the prize for the winner in 2000. Find the ratio of the winner's prize to the total purse. What do you find? Which variable can we estimate more accurately, the size of the purse or the winner's prize?

Year	Purse	Prize	Year	Purse	Prize
1987	$225,000	$33,750	1993	$450,000	$ 67,500
1988	275,000	41,250	1994	500,000	75,000
1989	275,000	41,250	1995	500,000	75,000
1990	325,000	48,750	1996	575,000	86,250
1991	350,000	52,500	1997	700,000	105,000
1992	400,000	60,000			

www.**Exercises**.com

32. The following Web site presents information on annual world crude oil production from 1880 to 1973: *http://lib.stat.cmu.edu/DASL/Stories/Oilproduction.html.* Download these data and plot them. Note that the relationship does not appear to be linear. Develop a regression equation where the independent variable is the log of annual world crude oil production. Discuss the regression equation and develop a forecast for the next several periods.

33. Listed below are the total number of units (this means cars and trucks) sold in North America by Ford Motor Company between 1986 and 1996. The data are reported in thousands of units. You should be able to update the sales by accessing Ford's Web site at: *http://www.ford.com/finaninvest/stockholder/stock96/contents.htm.* Select financial results and click on the selection that includes the "Vehicle Sales Summary." Determine the trend equation. What is the yearly rate of increase? Plot the data. Does it appear that we can effectively forecast the total number of units sold with this equation?

Year	1986	1987	1988	1989	1990	1991	1992	1993	1994	1995	1996
Units sold	3,876	4,040	4,313	4,131	3,632	3,212	3,693	4.131	4,591	4,279	4,222

▌ Computer Commands

1. The MINITAB commands to determine the logs of the number of imports and determine the regression equation on page 653 are:
   a. Use the **Set** command to enter the years:
      Set Cl
      1986:1998
   b. Use the **Set** command to enter the import data:
      Set C2
      3.0 4.2 5.7 . . . 163.9
   c. Find the logarithm of each import value in column C2 and put it in C3.
      Logten C2 C3
   d. Select **Stat,** then **Regression,** and then hit **Enter.** You will get the following dialog box.

Regression		✕
C1 Year	**R̲esponse:**	'Log-Imports'
C2 Code	**Predj̲ctors:**	Code
C3 Imports		
C4 Log-Imports		
		Options...
Select	Graphs...	S̲torage...
Help	O̲K	Cancel

e. Select 'Log-Imports' as the **Response** variable, 'Code' as the **Predictor** and then click **OK.**

2. The Excel commands to determine the regression equation on page 666 are:
   a. Enter the variable names **Year, Quarters, Times,** and **Sales** in row 1 of columns A, B, C, and D.
   b. In cell A2 type the year, which is 1993, in A6 type 1994, in A10 type 1995, in A14 type 1996, in A18 type 1997, and in A22 type 1998.
   c. In column B type the quarter the data represents. For example, the data in cell B13 is the fourth quarter of 1995 so it is coded as a 4.
   d. In cells C2 through C25 record the digits 1 through 24. These values represent the consecutive time periods.
   e. In cells D2 through D25 record the sales data.
   f. Click on **Tools,** then **Data Analysis,** then select **Regression** and click **OK.**
   g. In the dialog box, the **Input Y Range** is D1:D25, while the **Input X Range** is C1:C25. Check **Labels.** The **Output Range** is C30. Then click **OK.**
   h. The dialog box appears as follows.

Regression		? X
Input		**OK**
Input Y Range:	d1:d25	**Cancel**
Input X Range:	c1:c25	**Help**
☑ Labels ☐ Constant is Zero		
☐ Confidence Level 95 %		
Output options		
⦿ Output Range:	c30	
○ New Worksheet Ply:		
○ New Workbook		
Residuals		
☐ Residuals ☐ Residual Plots		
☐ Standardized Residuals ☐ Line Fit Plots		
Normal Probability		
☐ Normal Probability Plots		

   i. The **Input** ranges are d1 to d25 and c1 to c25, check **Labels,** c30 as the **Output,** and then click **OK.**

CHAPTER 18 *Answers to Self-Review*

18–1 (a)

(b) $Y' = a + bt = 3.3928 + 1.905t$ (in thousands)

$$b = \frac{365 - 36(70)/8}{204 - (36)^2/8} = \frac{50}{42} = 1.1905$$

$$a = \frac{70}{8} - 1.1905\left(\frac{36}{8}\right) = 3.3928$$

(c) For 1991:

$$Y' = 3.3928 + 1.1905(1) = 4.5833$$

for 1997:

$$Y' = 3.3928 + 1.1905(7) = 11.7263$$

(d) For 2001, $t = 11$, so

$$Y' = 3.3928 + 1.1905(11) = 16.4883$$

or 16,488 king-size rockers.

18–2

Year	Production (thousands)	Three-Year Moving Total	Three-Year Moving Average
1993	2	—	—
1994	6	12	4
1995	4	15	5
1996	5	12	4
1997	3	18	6
1998	10	—	—

18–3 (a)

Year	Y	log Y	t	t log Y	t^2
1994	2.13	0.3284	1	0.3284	1
1995	18.10	1.2577	2	2.5154	4
1996	39.80	1.5999	3	4.7997	9
1997	81.40	1.9106	4	7.6424	16
1998	112.00	2.0492	5	10.2460	25
		7.1458	15	25.5319	55

$$b = \frac{25.5319 + (7.1458)(15)/5}{55 - (15)^2/5} = \frac{4.0945}{10} = 0.40945$$

$$a = \frac{7.1458}{5} - 0.40945\left(\frac{15}{5}\right) = 0.20081$$

(b) About 156.7 percent. The antilog of 0.40945 is 2.567. Subtracting 1 yields 1.567.

(c) About 454.5, found by $Y' = 0.20081 + .40945(6) = 2.65751$. The antilog of 2.64751 is 454.5.

18–4 (a) The following values are from the Hall software package. Due to rounding, your figures might be slightly different.

	Winter	Spring	Summer	Fall
Mean	119.35	81.66	125.31	74.24
Typical seasonal	119.35	81.66	125.31	74.24

No correction is needed.

(b) Total sales at Teton Village for the winter season are typically 19.35 percent above the annual average.

18–5 The forecast value for January of the sixth year is 34.9, found by

$$Y' = 4.40 + 0.5(61) = 34.9$$

Seasonally adjusting the forecast, $34.9(120)/100 = 41.88$. For February, $Y' = 4.40 + 0.50(62) = 35.4$. Then $(35.4)95/100 = 33.63$.

An Introduction to Decision Making

GOALS

When you have completed this chapter, you will be able to:

ONE

Define the terms *state of nature, event, act,* and *payoff.*

TWO

Organize information into a payoff table or a decision tree.

THREE

Determine the expected payoff of an act.

FOUR

Compute opportunity loss and expected opportunity loss.

FIVE

Assess the value of information.

Given the expected payoffs for three stocks (chemicals, construction, and electronics) how would you verify that the expected payoff for the Rim Homes stock is $1,760? (See Goal 3 and Self-Review 19–1.)

▌ Introduction

A branch of statistics called **statistical decision theory** has developed rapidly since the early 1950s. The term **Bayesian statistics** is also used to indicate this branch of statistics. As the name implies, the focus is on the process of making decisions and explicitly includes the payoffs that may result. In contrast, classical statistics focuses on estimating a parameter, such as the population mean, constructing a confidence interval, or conducting a hypothesis test. Classical statistics does not address the financial consequences.

Statistical decision theory is concerned with determining which decision, from a set of possible alternatives, is optimal for a particular set of conditions. Consider the following examples of decision-theory problems.

- Ford Motor Company must decide whether to purchase assembled door locks for the new model Ford Escort or to manufacture and assemble the parts at their Sandusky, Ohio, plant. If sales of the Escort continue to increase, it will be more profitable to manufacture and assemble the parts. If sales level off or decline, it will be more profitable to purchase the door locks assembled. Which decision should be made?
- Haggar slacks developed a new line of wool slacks that are very popular in the cold-weather regions of the country. Haggar would like to purchase commercial television time during the upcoming Super Bowl. If both teams that play in the Super Bowl are from warm parts of the country, Haggar estimates that only a small proportion of the viewers will be interested in the wool slacks. However, a match-up between two teams who come from cold climates would reach a large proportion of viewers who wear wool slacks. What decision should Haggar make?
- General Electric is considering three options regarding the prices of refrigerators for next year. GE could (1) raise the prices 5 percent, (2) raise the prices 2.5 percent, or (3) leave the prices as they are. The final decision will be based on sales estimates and on GE's knowledge of what other refrigerator manufacturers might do.

In each of these cases the decision is characterized by several alternative courses of action and several factors not under the control of the decision maker. For example, Haggar has no control over which teams reach the Super Bowl. These cases characterize the nature of decision making. Possible decision alternatives can be listed, possible future events determined, and even probabilities established, but *the decisions are made in the face of uncertainty.*

▌ Elements of a Decision

There are three components to any decision-making situation: (1) the choices available, or alternatives; (2) the states of nature, which are not under the control of the decision maker; and (3) the payoffs. These concepts will be explained in the following paragraphs.

The **alternatives,** or **acts,** are the choices available to the decision maker. Ford can decide to manufacture and assemble the door locks in Sandusky, or they can decide to purchase them. To simplify our presentation, we are going to assume that the decision maker can select from a rather small number of outcomes. With the help of computers, however, the decision alternatives can be expanded to a large number of possibilities.

The **states of nature** are the uncontrollable future events. The state of nature that actually happens is outside the control of the decision maker. Ford does not know whether demand will remain high for the Escort. Haggar cannot determine whether warm-weather or cold-weather teams will play in the Super Bowl.

A **payoff** is needed for each combination of decision alternative and state of nature. Ford may estimate that if they assemble door locks at their Sandusky Plant and the demand for Escorts is low, the payoff will be $40,000. Conversely, if they purchase the door locks assembled and the demand is high, the payoff is estimated to be $22,000.

The main elements of the decision problem under conditions of uncertainty are identified schematically:

	Explanatory Statements
Event	{ Uncertainty regarding future demand. State of nature (future demand) unknown. Decision maker has no control over state of nature.
Act	{ Two or more courses of action open to decision maker. Decision maker must evaluate alternatives. Decision maker selects a course of action based on certain criteria. Depending on the set of circumstances, these criteria may be quantitative, psychological, sociological, and so on.
Outcome Payoff Consequence	{ Profit. Breakeven. Loss.

In many cases we can make better decisions if we establish probabilities for the various states of nature. These probabilities may be based on historical data or subjective estimates. Ford may estimate the probability of continued high demand as .70. GE may estimate the probability to be .25 that Sears and other manufacturers will raise the prices of their refrigerators.

▌ A Case Involving Decision Making under Conditions of Uncertainty

At the outset it should be emphasized that this case description includes only the fundamental concepts found in a decision-making problem. The purpose of examining the case is to explain the logical procedure that might be followed. In many problems there are other variables to consider.

The first step is to set up a payoff table.

Payoff Table

Bob Hill, a small investor, has $1,100 to invest. He has studied several common stocks and narrowed his choices to three, namely, Kayser Chemicals, Rim Homes, and Texas Electronics. He estimated that if his $1,100 were invested in Kayser Chemicals and a strong bull market developed by the end of the year (that is, stock prices increased drastically), the value of his Kayser stock would more than double, to $2,400. However, if there were a bear market (i.e., stock prices declined), the value of his Kayser stock could conceivably drop to $1,000 by the end of the year. His predictions regarding the value of his $1,100 investment for the three stocks for a bull market and for a bear market are shown in Table 19–1. This table is a **payoff table.**

Table 19–1 Payoff Table for Three Common Stocks under Two Market Conditions

Purchase	Bull Market, S_1	Bear Market, S_2
Kayser Chemicals (A_1)	$2,400	$1,000
Rim Homes (A_2)	2,200	1,100
Texas Electronics (A_3)	1,900	1,150

The various choices are called the **decision alternatives** or the **acts.** There are three in this problem. Let A_1 be the purchase of Kayser Chemicals, A_2 the purchase of Rim Homes, and A_3 the purchase of Texas Electronics. Whether the market turns out to be bear or bull is not under the control of Bob Hill. These uncontrolled future events are the states of nature. Let the bull market be represented by S_1 and the bear market by S_2.

Expected Payoff

If the payoff table were the only information available, the investor might take a conservative action and buy Texas Electronics in order to be assured of at least $1,150 at the end of the year (a slight profit). A speculative venture, however, might be to buy Kayser Chemicals, with the possibility of more than doubling the $1,100 investment.

Any decision regarding the purchase of one of the three common stocks made solely on the information in the payoff table would ignore the valuable historical records kept by Moody's, Value Line, and other investment services relative to stock price movements over a long period. A study of these records, for example, revealed that during the past 10 years stock market prices increased six times and declined only four times. Thus, it can be said that the probability of a market rise is .60 and the probability of a market decline is .40.

Assuming these historical frequencies are somewhat typical, we see that the payoff table and the probability estimates (.60 and .40) can be combined to arrive at the **expected payoff** of buying each of the three stocks. Expected payoff is also called **expected monetary value,** shortened to EMV. It can also be described as the **mean payoff.** The calculations needed to arrive at the expected payoff for the act of purchasing Kayser Chemicals are shown in Table 19–2.

Table 19–2 Expected Payoff for the Act of Buying Kayser Chemicals, EMV (A_1)

State of Nature	Payoff	Probability of State of Nature	Expected Value
Market rise, S_1	$2,400	.60	$1,440
Market decline, S_2	1,000	.40	400
			$1,840

To explain one expected monetary value calculation, note that if the investor had purchased Kayser Chemicals and the market prices declined, the value of the stock would be only $1,000 at the end of the year (from Table 19–1). Past experience, however, revealed that this event (a market decline) occurred only 40 percent of the time. In the long run, therefore, a market decline would contribute $400 to the total expected payoff from the stock, found by $1,000 × .40. Adding the $400 to the $1,440 expected under rising market conditions gives $1,840, the total payoff in the long run.

These calculations are summarized as follows.

EXPECTED MONETARY VALUE	$EMV(A_i) = \Sigma[P(S_j) \times V(A_i, S_j)]$	[19–1]

where:

$EMV(A_i)$ refers to the expected monetary value of the various decision alternatives. There may be many decisions possible. We will let 1 stand for the first decision, 2 for the second, and so on. The lower-case letter i represents the entire set of decisions.

$P(S_j)$ refers to the probability of the various states of nature. There can be an unlimited number, so we will let j represent the various possible outcomes.

$V(A_i, S_j)$ refers to the value of the various payoffs. Note that each payoff is the result of a combination of a decision alternative and a state of nature.

$EMV(A_1)$, the expected monetary value for the decision alternative of purchasing Kayser Chemicals stock, is computed by:

$$EMV(A_1) = P(S_1) \times V(A_1, S_1) + P(S_2) \times V(A_1, S_2)$$
$$= .60(\$2,400) + .40(\$1,000) = \$1,840$$

Purchasing Kayser Chemicals stock is only one possible choice. The expected payoffs for the acts of buying Kayser Chemicals, Rim Homes, and Texas Electronics are given in Table 19–3.

Table 19–3   Expected Payoffs for Three Stocks

Purchase	Expected Payoff
Kayser Chemicals	$1,840
Rim Homes	1,760
Texas Electronics	1,600

An analysis of the expected payoffs in Table 19–3 indicates that purchasing Kayser Chemicals would yield the greatest expected profit. This outcome is based upon (1) the investor's estimated future value of the stocks and (2) historical experience with respect to the rise and decline of stock prices. It should be emphasized that although purchasing Kayser stock represents the best action under the expected-value criterion, the investor still might decide to buy Texas Electronics stock in order to minimize the risk of losing some of the $1,100 investment.

SELF-REVIEW 19–1

Verify the conclusion, shown in Table 19–3, that the expected payoff for the act of purchasing Rim Homes stock is $1,760.

▌ Exercises

1. The following payoff table was developed. Let $P(S_1) = .30$, $P(S_2) = .50$, and $P(S_3) = .20$. Compute the expected monetary value for each of the alternatives. What decision would you recommend?

| | State of Nature | | |
Alternative	S_1	S_2	S_3
A_1	$50	$70	$100
A_2	90	40	80
A_3	70	60	90

2. The Wilhelms Cola Company plans to market a new pineapple-flavored cola this summer. The decision is whether to package the cola in returnable or in no-return bottles. Currently, the state legislature is considering eliminating no-return bottles. Tybo Wilhelms, president of Wilhelms Cola Company, has discussed the problem with his state representative and established the probability to be .70 that no-return bottles will be eliminated. The following table shows the estimated monthly profits (in thousands of dollars) if the pineapple cola is bottled in returnable versus no-return bottles. Of course, if the law is passed and the decision is to bottle the cola in no-return bottles, all profits would be from out-of-state sales. Compute the expected profit for both bottling decisions. Which decision do you recommend?

Alternative	Law Is Passed ($000) ($S_1$)	Law Is Not Passed ($000) ($S_2$)
Returnable bottle	80	40
No-return bottle	25	60

Opportunity Loss

Another way of arriving at a decision regarding which common stock to purchase is to determine the profit that might be lost because the exact state of nature (the market behavior) was not known at the time the investor bought the stock. This potential loss is called **opportunity loss** or **regret.** To illustrate, suppose the investor had purchased the common stock of Rim Homes, and a bull market developed. Further, suppose the value of his Rim Homes stock increased from $1,100 to $2,200, as anticipated. But had the investor bought Kayser Chemicals stock and market values increased, the value of his Kayser stock would be $2,400 (from Table 19–1). Thus, the investor missed making an extra profit of $200 by buying Rim Homes instead of Kayser Chemicals. To put it another way, the $200 represents the opportunity loss for not knowing the correct state of nature. If market prices did increase, the investor would have *regretted* buying Rim Homes. However, had the investor bought Kayser Chemicals and market prices increased, he would have had no regret, that is, no opportunity loss.

The opportunity losses corresponding to this example are given in Table 19–4. Each amount is the outcome (opportunity loss) of a particular combination of acts and a state of nature, that is, stock purchase and market reaction.

It is apparent that the stock of Kayser Chemicals would be a good investment choice in a rising (bull) market, Texas Electronics would be the best buy in a declining (bear) market, and Rim Homes is somewhat of a compromise.

Table 19–4   Opportunity Losses for Various Combinations of Stock Purchase and Market Movement

| | Opportunity Loss | |
Purchase	Market Rise	Market Decline
Kayser Chemicals	$ 0	$150
Rim Homes	200	50
Texas Electronics	500	0

SELF-REVIEW 19–2

Refer to Table 19–4. Verify that:
(a)   The opportunity loss for Rim Homes given a market decline is $50.
(b)   The opportunity loss for Texas Electronics given a market rise is $500.

▌ Exercises

3.   Refer to Exercise 1. Develop an opportunity loss table. Determine the opportunity loss for each decision.
4.   Refer to Exercise 2, involving the Wilhelms Cola Company. Develop an opportunity loss table, and determine the opportunity loss for each decision.

Expected Opportunity Loss

The opportunity losses in Table 19–4 again ignore the historical experience of market movements. Recall the probability of a market rise is .60 and that of a market decline .40. These probabilities and the opportunity losses are combined to determine the **expected opportunity loss.** These calculations are shown in Table 19–5 for the decision to purchase Rim Homes. The expected opportunity loss is $140.

Interpreting, the expected opportunity loss of $140 means that, in the long run, the investor would lose the opportunity to make an additional profit of $140 if he decided to buy Rim Homes stock. This expected loss would be incurred because the investor was unable to accurately predict the trend of the stock market. In a bull market, he could earn an additional $200 by purchasing the common stock of Kayser Chemicals, but in a bear market an investor could earn an additional $50 by buying Texas Electronics stock. When weighted by the probability of the event, the expected opportunity loss is $140.

Table 19–5   Expected Opportunity Loss for the Act of Buying Rim Homes Stock

State of Nature	Opportunity Loss	Probability of State of Nature	Expected Opportunity Loss
Market rise, S_1	$200	.60	$120
Market decline, S_2	50	.40	20
			$140

These calculations are summarized as follows:

EXPECTED OPPORTUNITY LOSS	$EOL(A_i) = \sum[P(S_j) \times R(A_i, S_j)]$	**[19–2]**

where:

$EOL(A_i)$ refers to the expected opportunity loss for a particular decision alternative.

$P(S_j)$ refers to the probability associated with the various states of nature.

$R(A_i, S_j)$ refers to the regret or loss for a particular combination of a state of nature and a decision alternative.

$EOL(A_2)$, the regret, or expected opportunity loss, for selecting Rim Homes, is computed as follows:

$$EOL(A_2) = P(S_1) \times R(A_2, S_1) + P(S_2) \times R(A_2, S_2)$$

$$= .60(\$200) + .40(\$50) = \$140$$

The expected opportunity losses for the three decision alternatives are given in Table 19–6. The lowest expected opportunity loss is $60, meaning that the investor would experience the least regret on average if he purchased Kayser Chemicals.

Table 19–6   Expected Opportunity Losses for the Three Stocks

Purchase	Expected Opportunity Loss
Kayser Chemicals	$ 60
Rim Homes	140
Texas Electronics	300

Incidentally, note that the decision to purchase Kayser Chemicals stock because it offers the lowest expected opportunity loss reinforces the decision made previously, that Kayser stock would ultimately result in the highest expected payoff ($1,840). These two approaches (lowest expected opportunity loss and highest expected payoff) will always lead to the same decision concerning which course of action to follow.

SELF-REVIEW 19–3

Referring to Table 19–6, verify that the expected opportunity loss for the act of purchasing Texas Electronics is $300.

I Exercises

5. Refer to Exercises 1 and 3. Compute the expected opportunity losses.
6. Refer to Exercises 2 and 4. Compute the expected opportunity losses.

Maximin, Maximax, and Minimax Regret Strategies

Maximin strategy

Several financial advisors consider the purchase of Kayser Chemicals stock too risky. They note that the payoff might not be $1,840, but only $1,000 (from Table 19–1). Arguing that the stock market is too unpredictable, they urge the investor to take a more conservative position and buy Texas Electronics. This is called a **maximin strategy:** it maximizes the minimum gain. Based on the payoff table (Table 19–1), they reason that the investor would be assured of at least a $1,150 return, that is, a small profit. Those who subscribe to this somewhat pessimistic strategy are sometimes called **maximiners.**

Maximax strategy

At the other extreme are the optimistic *maximaxers,* who would select the stock that maximizes the maximum gain. If their **maximax strategy** were followed, the investor would purchase Kayser Chemicals stock. These optimists stress that there is a possibility of selling the stock in the future for $2,400 instead of only $1,150, as advocated by the maximiners.

Minimax strategy

Another possible strategy is the **minimax regret strategy.** Financial advisors advocating this approach would scan the opportunity losses in Table 19–4 and select the stock that minimizes the maximum regret. In this example it would be Kayser Chemicals stock, with a maximum opportunity loss of $150. Recall that you wish to *avoid* opportunity losses! The maximum regrets were $200 for Rim Homes and $500 for Texas Electronics.

Value of Perfect Information

How much is "perfect" information worth?

Before deciding on a stock and purchasing it, the investor might want to consider ways of predicting the movement of the stock market. If he knew precisely what the market would do, he could maximize profit by always purchasing the correct stock. The question is: What is this advance information worth? The dollar value of this information is called the **expected value of perfect information,** written EVPI. In this problem, it would mean that Bob Hill knew beforehand whether the stock market would rise or decline in the near future.

An acquaintance who is an analyst with a large brokerage firm said that he would be willing to supply Bob with information that he might find quite valuable in predicting market rises and declines. Of course, there would be a fee, as yet undetermined, for this information, regardless of whether the investor used it. What is the maximum amount that Bob should pay for this special service? $10? $100? $500?

The value of the information from the analyst is, in essence, the expected value of perfect information, because the investor would then be assured of buying the most profitable stock. The value of perfect information is defined as the *difference between the maximum payoff under conditions of certainty and the maximum payoff under uncertainty.* In this problem it is the difference between the maximum value of the stock at the end of the year under conditions of certainty and the value associated with the optimum decision using the expected-value criterion.

From a practical standpoint, the maximum expected value under conditions of certainty means that the investor would buy Kayser Chemicals if a market rise were predicted and Texas Electronics if a market decline were imminent. The expected payoff under conditions of certainty is $1,900. (See Table 19–7.)

Table 19–7   Calculations for the Expected Payoff under Conditions of Certainty

State of Nature	Payoff	Probability of State of Nature	Expected Payoff
Market rise, S_1	$2,400	.60	$1,440
Market decline, S_2	1,150	.40	460
			$1,900

Recall that if the actual behavior of the stock market were unknown (conditions of uncertainty), the stock to buy would be Kayser Chemicals; its expected value at the end of the period was computed to be $1,840 (from Table 19–3). The value of perfect information is, therefore, $60, found by:

$1,900   Expected value of stock purchased under conditions of certainty
$\underline{-1,840}$ Expected value of purchase (Kayser) under conditions of uncertainty
$ 60   Expected value of perfect information

In general, the expected value of perfect information is computed as follows:

EXPECTED VALUE OF PERFECT INFORMATION	EVPI = Expected value under conditions of certainty − Optimal decision under conditions of uncertainty	**[19–3]**

It would be worth up to $60 for the information the stock analyst might supply. In essence, the analyst would be "guaranteeing" a selling price on average of $1,900, and if the analyst asked $40 for the information, the investor would be assured of a $1,860 payoff, found by $1,900 − $40. Thus, it would be worthwhile for the investor to agree to this fee ($40) because the expected outcome ($1,860) would be greater than the expected value under conditions of uncertainty ($1,840). However, if his acquaintance wanted a fee of $100 for the service, the investor would realize only $1,800 on average, found by $1,900 − $100. Logically, the service would not be worth $100, because the investor could expect $1,840 on average without agreeing to this financial arrangement.

It should be noted that the expected value of perfect information ($60) is the same as the minimum of the expected regrets (Table 19–6). That is not an accident.

The calculations in the preceding investment problem were mainly kept at a minimum to emphasize the new terms and the decision-making procedures. When the number of decision alternatives and the number of states of nature become large, a computer package is recommended. The output for the investment problem using *Computerized Business Statistics,* developed by Hall and described in the previous chapter, is used as an example. The required inputs are: the decision alternatives, the states of nature and the corresponding probabilities, and the payoffs.

```
CBSW                      Decision Analysis              05-04-98

                  Decision Making      Under Risk     Maximization

No. Alternatives              3
No. States                    2

State Probabilities
S1 = 0.6
S2 = 0.4

Payoff Table

                      Kayser            Rim             Texas
S1                    2400             2200            1900
S2                    1000             1100            1150

                                    Results
Criteria              Kayser            Rim             Texas
EMV                   1840             1760            1600
EOL                     60              140             300
EPPI                  1900             1900            1900

              Optimal Decision     Kayser (#1)
```

Note that the results for EMV are the same as in Table 19–3, the EOL figures are the same as in Table 19–6, and EPPI (EVPI) is the same as in Table 19–7.

Sensitivity Analysis

Expected payoffs are not highly sensitive.

In the foregoing stock selection problem, the set of probabilities applied to the payoff values was derived from historical experience with similar market conditions. Objections may be voiced, however, that future market behavior may be different from past experiences. Despite these differences, *the expected payoffs are not highly sensitive to any changes within a plausible range.* As an example, suppose the investor's brother believes that instead of a 60 percent chance of a market rise and a 40 percent chance of a decline, the reverse is true—that is, there is a .40 probability that the stock market will rise and a .60 probability of a decline. Further, the investor's cousin thinks the probability of a market rise is .50 and that of a decline is .50. A comparison of the original expected payoffs (left column), the expected payoffs for the set of probabilities suggested by the investor's brother (center column), and those cited by the cousin (right column) is shown in Table 19–8. The decision is the same in all three cases—purchase Kayser Chemicals.

Table 19–8 Expected Payoffs for Three Sets of Probabilities

	Expected Payoffs		
Purchase	Historical Experience (probability of .60 rise, .40 decline)	Brother's Estimate (probability of .40 rise, .60 decline)	Cousin's Estimate (probability of .50 rise, .50 decline)
Kayser Chemicals	$1,840	$1,560	$1,700
Rim Homes	1,760	1,540	1,650
Texas Electronics	1,600	1,450	1,525

SELF-REVIEW 19–4

Referring to Table 19–8, verify that:
(a) The expected payoff for Texas Electronics for the brother's set of probabilities is $1,450.
(b) The expected payoff for Kayser Chemicals for the cousin's set of probabilities is $1,700.

A comparison of the three sets of expected payoffs in Table 19–8 reveals the best alternative would still be to purchase Kayser Chemicals. As might be expected, there are some differences in the expected future values for each of the three stocks.

If there are drastic changes in the assigned probabilities, the expected values and the optimal decision may change. As an example, suppose the prognostication for a market rise was .20 and for a market decline .80. The expected payoffs would be as shown in Table 19–9. In the long run, the best alternative would be to buy Rim Homes stock. Thus, sensitivity analysis lets you see how accurate the probability estimates need to be in order to feel comfortable with your choice.

Table 19–9 Expected Values for Purchasing the Three Stocks

Purchase	Expected Payoff
Kayser Chemicals	$1,280
Rim Homes	1,320
Texas Electronics	1,300

SELF-REVIEW 19–5

Is there any choice of probabilities for which the best alternative would be to purchase Texas Electronics stock? (*Hint:* This can be arrived at algebraically or using a trial-and-error method. Try a somewhat extreme probability for a market rise.)

Exercises

7. Refer to Exercises 1, 3, and 5. Compute the expected value of perfect information.
8. Refer to Exercises 2, 4, and 6. Compute the expected value of perfect information.
9. Refer to Exercise 1. Revise the probabilities as follows: $P(S_1) = .50$, $P(S_2) = .20$, and $P(S_3) = .30$. Does this change the decision?

10.   Refer to Exercise 2. Reverse the probabilities; that is, let $P(S_1) = .30$ and $P(S_2) = .70$. Does this alter your decision?

▌ Decision Trees

Decision tree: A picture of all possible outcomes

An analytic tool introduced in Chapter 5 that is very useful for studying a decision situation is a *decision tree.* Basically, it is a picture of all the possible courses of action and the consequent possible outcomes. A box is used to indicate the point at which a decision must be made, and the branches going out from the box indicate the alternatives under consideration. Referring to Chart 19–1, on the left is the box with three branches radiating from it, representing the acts of purchasing Kayser Chemicals, Rim Homes, or Texas Electronics.

Decision tree shows Kayser Chemicals best buy

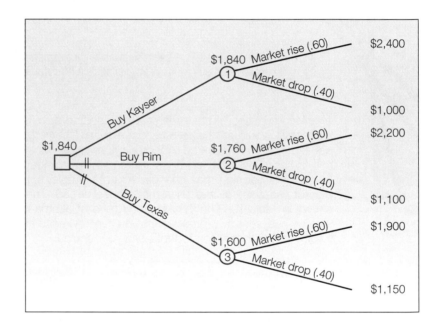

Chart 19–1   Decision Tree for the Investor's Decision

The three nodes, or circles, numbered 1, 2, and 3, represent the expected payoff of each of the three stocks. The branches going out to the right of the nodes show the chance events (market rise or decline) and their corresponding probabilities in parentheses. The numbers at the extreme ends of the branches are the estimated future values of stopping the decision process at those points. This is sometimes called the *conditional payoff* to denote that the payoff depends on a particular choice of action and a particular chance outcome. Thus, if the investor purchased Rim Homes stock and the market rose, the estimated value of the stock would be $2,200.

After the decision tree has been constructed, the optimal decision strategy can be found by what is termed *backward induction.* For example, suppose the investor is considering the act of purchasing Texas Electronics. Starting at the lower right in Chart 19–1 with the anticipated payoff given a market rise ($1,900) versus a market decline ($1,150) and going backward (moving left), the appropriate probabilities are applied to give the expected payoff of $1,600 [found by .60($1,900) + .40($1,150)]. The investor would mark the expected value of $1,600 above circled node 3 as shown in Chart 19–1. Similarly, the investor would determine the expected values for Rim Homes and Kayser Chemicals.

Assuming the investor wants to maximize the expected future value of his stock purchase, $1,840 would be preferred over $1,760 or $1,600. Continuing to the left toward the box, the investor would draw a double bar across branches representing the two alternatives he rejected (numbers 2 and 3, representing Rim Homes and Texas Electronics). The unmarked branch that leads to the box is clearly the best action to follow, namely, buy Kayser Chemicals stock.

The expected value under *conditions of certainty* can also be portrayed via a decision tree analysis (see Chart 19–2). Recall that under conditions of certainty the investor would know *before the stock is purchased* whether the stock market will rise or decline. Hence, he would purchase Kayser Chemicals in a rising market and Texas Electronics in a falling market, and the expected payoff would be $1,900. Again, backward induction would be used to arrive at the expected payoff of $1,900.

If perfect information is available: Buy Kayser in rising market; buy Texas in declining market.

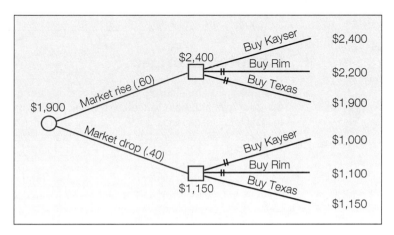

Chart 19–2 Decision Tree Given Perfect Information

The monetary difference based on perfect information in Chart 19–2 and the decision based on imperfect information in Chart 19–1 is $60, found by $1,900 − $1,840. Recall that the $60 is the value of perfect information.

Decision tree analysis provides an alternative way to perform the calculations presented earlier in the chapter. Some managers find these graphic sketches help them in following the decision path.

▌ Chapter Outline

I. Statistical decision theory is concerned with making decisions from a set of possible alternatives.
  A. The various courses of action are called the acts or alternatives.
  B. The uncontrollable future events are called the states of nature. Probabilities are usually assigned to the various states of nature.
  C. The combination of a particular decision alternative and state of nature is called the payoff.
  D. All possible combinations of decision alternatives and states of nature result in a payoff table.
II. There are several criteria for selecting the optimal decision.
  A. In the expected monetary value (EMV) criterion, the expected value for each decision alternative is computed, and the optimal (largest if profits, smallest if cost) is selected.
  B. An opportunity loss table can be developed.
    1. An opportunity loss table is constructed by taking the difference between the optimal decision for each state of nature and the other decision alternatives.

2. The difference between the optimal decision and any other decision is the opportunity loss or regret due to making a decision other than the optimum.
3. The expected opportunity loss (EOL) is similar to the expected monetary value. The opportunity loss is combined with the probabilities of the various states of nature for each decision alternative to determine the expected opportunity loss.

C. The strategy of maximizing the minimum gain is referred to as maximin.
D. The strategy of maximizing the maximum gain is called maximax.
E. The strategy that minimizes the maximum regret is designated minimax regret.

III. The expected value of perfect information (EVPI) is the difference between the expected payoff if the state of nature is known and the optimal decision under conditions of uncertainty.

IV. Sensitivity analysis examines the effects of various probabilities for the states of nature on the expected values.

V. Decision trees are useful for structuring the various alternatives. They present a picture of the various courses of action and the possible states of nature.

▍ Chapter Exercises

11. The Twenge Manufacturing Company is considering introducing two new products. The company can add both to the current line, neither, or just one of the two. The success of these products depends on the general economy and on consumers' reactions to the products. These reactions can be summarized as "good," $P(S_1) = .30$; "fair," $P(S_2) = .50$; or "poor," $P(S_3) = .20$. The company's revenues, in thousands of dollars, are estimated in the following payoff table.

	State of Nature		
Decision	S_1	S_2	S_3
Neither	0	0	0
Product 1 only	125	65	30
Product 2 only	105	60	30
Both	220	110	40

a. Compute the expected monetary value for each decision.
b. What decision would you recommend?
c. Develop an opportunity loss table.
d. Compute the expected opportunity loss for each decision.
e. Compute the expected value of perfect information.

12. A financial executive lives in Boston but frequently must travel to New York. She can go to New York by car, train, or plane. The cost for a plane ticket from Boston to New York is $100, and it is estimated that the trip takes 30 minutes in good weather and 45 minutes in bad weather. The cost for a train ticket is $50, and the trip takes an hour in good weather and two hours in bad weather. The cost to drive her own car from Boston to New York is $20, and this trip takes three hours in good weather and four in bad weather. The executive places a cost of $30 per hour on her time. The weather forecast is for a 60 percent chance of bad weather tomorrow.

What decision would you recommend? (*Hint:* Set up a payoff table, and remember that you want to minimize costs.) What is the expected value of perfect information?

13. The Thomas Manufacturing Company has $100,000 available to invest. Doctor Thomas, the president and CEO of the company, would like to either expand his production, invest the money in stocks, or purchase a certificate of deposit from the bank. Of course, the unknown is whether the economy will continue at a high level or there will be a recession. He estimates the likelihood of a recession at .20. Whether there is a recession or not, the certificate of deposit will result in a gain of 6 percent. If there is a recession, he predicts 10 percent loss if he expands his production and a 5 percent loss if he invests in stocks. If there is not a

recession, an expansion of production will result in a 15 percent gain, and stock investment will produce a 12 percent gain.

    a.   What decision should he make if he uses the maximin strategy?

    b.   What decision should Doctor Thomas make if the maximax strategy is used?

    c.   What decision would be made if he uses the expected-monetary-value criterion?

    d.   What is the expected value of perfect information?

14.   The quality-assurance department at Malcomb Products must either inspect each part in a lot or not inspect any of the parts. That is, there are two decision alternatives: inspect all the parts or inspect none of the parts. The proportion of parts defective in the lot, S_j, is known from historical data to assume the following probability distribution.

State of Nature, S_j	Probability, $P(S_j)$
.02	.70
.04	.20
.06	.10

For the decision not to inspect any parts, the cost of quality is $C = NS_jK$. For inspecting all the items in the lot, it is $C = Nk$,

where

$$N = 20 \text{ (lot size)}$$

$$K = \$18.00 \text{ (the cost of finding a defect)}$$

$$k = \$0.50 \text{ (the cost of sampling one item)}$$

    a.   Develop a payoff table.

    b.   What decision should be made if the expected-value criterion is used?

    c.   What is the expected value of perfect information?

15.   Dude Ranches Incorporated was founded on the idea that many families in the eastern and southern areas of the United States do not have a sufficient amount of vacation time to drive to the dude ranches in the Southwest and Rocky Mountain areas for their vacations. Various surveys indicated, however, that there was a considerable interest in this type of family vacation, which includes horseback riding, cattle drives, swimming, fishing, and the like. Dude Ranches Incorporated bought a large farm near several eastern cities and constructed a lake, a swimming pool, and other facilities. However, to build a number of family cottages on the ranch would have required a considerable investment. Further, they reasoned that most of this investment would be lost should the ranch-farm complex be a financial failure. Instead, they decided to enter into an agreement with the Mobile Homes Manufacturing Company to supply a very attractive authentic ranch-type mobile home. Mobile Homes agreed to deliver a mobile home on Saturday for $300 a week. Mobile Homes must know early Saturday morning how many mobile homes Dude Ranches Incorporated wants for the forthcoming week. They have other customers to supply and can only deliver the homes on Saturday. This presents a problem. Dude Ranches will have some reservations by Saturday, but indications are that many families do not make them. Instead, they prefer to examine the facilities before making a decision. An analysis of the various costs involved indicated that $350 a week should be charged for a ranch home, including all privileges. The basic problem is how many mobile ranch homes to order from Mobile Homes each week. Should Dude Ranches Incorporated order 10 (considered the minimum), 11, 12, 13, or 14 (considered the maximum)?

    Any decision made solely on the information in the payoff table would ignore, however, the valuable experience that Dude Ranches Incorporated has acquired in the past four years (about 200 weeks) actually operating a dude ranch in the Southwest. Their records showed that they always had nine advance reservations. Also, they never had a demand for 15 or more cottages. The occupancy of 10, 11, 12, 13, or 14 ranch cottages, in part, represented families who drove in and inspected the facilities before renting. A frequency distribution showing the number of weeks in which 10, 11, . . . , 14 ranch cottages were rented during the 200-week period is found in the following table.

Number of Cottages Rented	Number of Weeks
10	26
11	50
12	60
13	44
14	20
	200

    a. Construct a payoff table.
    b. Determine the expected payoffs, and arrive at a decision.
    c. Set up an opportunity loss table.
    d. Compute the expected opportunity losses, and arrive at a decision.
    e. Determine the value of perfect information.

16. The proprietor of the newly built Ski and Swim Lodge has been considering purchasing or leasing several snowmobiles for the use of guests. The owner found that other financial obligations made it impossible to purchase the machines. Snowmobiles Incorporated (SI) will lease a machine for $20 a week, including any needed maintenance. According to SI, the usual rental charge to the guests of the lodge is $25 a week. Gasoline and oil are extra. Snowmobiles Incorporated only leases a machine for the full season. The proprietor of Ski and Swim, knowing that leasing an excessive number of snowmobiles might cause a net loss for the lodge, investigated the records of other resort owners. The combined experience at several other lodges was found to be:

Number of Snowmobiles Demanded by Guests	Number of Weeks
7	10
8	25
9	45
10	20

    a. Design a payoff table.
    b. Compute the expected profits for leasing 7, 8, 9, and 10 snowmobiles based on the cost of leasing of $20, the rental charge of $25, and the experience of other lodges.
    c. Which alternative is the most profitable?
    d. Design an opportunity loss table.
    e. Find the expected opportunity losses for leasing 7, 8, 9, and 10 snowmobiles.
    f. Which act would give the least expected opportunity loss?
    g. Determine the value of perfect information.
    h. Suggest a course of action to the proprietor of the Ski and Swim Lodge. Include in your explanation the various figures, such as expected profit.

17. A furniture store has had numerous inquiries regarding the availability of furniture and equipment that could be rented for large outdoor summer parties. This includes such items as folding chairs and tables, a deluxe grill, propane gas, and lights. No rental equipment of this

nature is available locally, and the management of the furniture store is considering forming a subsidiary to handle rentals.

An investigation revealed that most people interested in renting wanted a complete group of party essentials (about 12 chairs, four tables, a deluxe grill, a bottle of propane gas, tongs, etc.). Management decided not to buy a large number of complete sets because of the financial risk involved. That is, if the demand for the rental groups was not as large as anticipated, a large financial loss might be incurred. Further, outright purchase would mean that the equipment would have to be stored during the off-season.

It was then discovered that a firm in Boston leased a complete party set for $560 for the summer season. This amounts to about $5 a day. In the promotional literature from the Boston firm, a rental fee of $15 was suggested. For each set rented, a profit of $10 would thus be earned. It was then decided to lease from the Boston firm, at least for the first season.

The Boston firm suggested that, based on the combined experience of similar rental firms in other cities, either 41, 42, 43, 44, 45, or 46 complete sets be leased for the season. Based on this suggestion, management must now decide on the most profitable number of complete sets to lease for the season.

The leasing firm in Boston also made available some additional information gathered from several rental firms similar to the newly formed subsidiary. Note in the following table (which is based on the experience of the other rental firms) that for 360 days of the total of 6,000 days' experience — or about 6 percent of the days — these rental firms rented out 41 complete party sets. On 10 percent of the days during a typical summer, they rented 42 complete sets, and so on.

Number of Sets Rented	Number of Days	Number of Sets Rented	Number of Days
40	0	44	2,400
41	360	45	1,500
42	600	46	300
43	840	47	0

a. Construct a payoff table. (As a check figure, for the act of having 41 complete sets available and the event of renting 41, the payoff is $410.)

b. The expected daily profit for leasing 43 complete sets from the Boston firm is $426.70; for 45 sets, $431.70; and for 46 sets, $427.45. Organize these expected daily profits into a table, and complete the table by finding the expected daily profit for leasing 41, 42, and 44 sets from the Boston firm.

c. Based on the expected daily profit, what is the most profitable action to take?

d. The expected opportunity loss for leasing 43 party sets from the Boston firm is $11.60; for 45 sets, $6.60; for 46 sets, $10.85. Organize these into an expected opportunity loss table, and complete the table by computing the expected opportunity loss for 41, 42, and 44.

e. Based on the expected opportunity loss table, what is the most profitable course of action to take? Does this agree with your decision for part (c)?

f. Determine the value of perfect information. Explain what it indicates in this problem.

18. Tim Waltzer owns and operates Waltzer's Wrecks, a discount car rental agency near the Cleveland Hopkins International Airport. He rents a wreck for $20 a day. He has an arrangement with Landrum Leasing to purchase used cars at $6,000 each. His cars receive only needed maintenance and, as a result, are worth only $2,000 at the end of the year of operation. Tim has decided to sell all his wrecks every year and purchase a complete set of used cars from Landrum Leasing.

His clerk-accountant provided him with a probability distribution with respect to the number of cars rented per day.

	Numbers of Cars Rented per Day			
	20	21	22	23
Probability	.10	.20	.50	.20

Tim is an avid golfer and tennis player. He is either on the golf course on weekends or playing tennis indoors. Thus, his car rental agency is only open weekdays. Also, he closes for two weeks during the summer and goes on a golfing tour.

The clerk-accountant estimated that it cost $1.50 per car rental for minimal maintenance and cleaning.

a. How many cars should he purchase to maximize profit?

b. What is the expected value of perfect information?

CHAPTER 19   *Answers to Self-Review*

19–1

Event	Payoff	Probability of Event	Expected Value
Market rise	$2,200	.60	$1,320
Market decline	1,100	.40	440
			$1,760

19–2 (a) Suppose the investor purchased Rim Homes stock, and the value of the stock in a bear market dropped to $1,100 as anticipated (Table 19–1). Instead, had the investor purchased Texas Electronics and the market declined, the value of the Texas Electronics stock would be $1,150. The difference of $50, found by $1,150 − $1,100, represents the investor's regret for buying Rim Homes stock.

(b) Suppose the investor purchased Texas Electronics stock, and then a bull market developed. The stock rose to $1,900, as anticipated (Table 19–1). However, had the investor bought Kayser Chemicals stock and the market value increased to $2,400 as anticipated, the difference of $500 represents the extra profit the investor could have made by purchasing Kayser Chemicals stock.

19–3

Event	Payoff	Probability of Event	Expected Opportunity Loss
Market rise	$500	.60	$300
Market decline	0	.40	0
			$300

19–4 (a)

Event	Payoff	Probability of Event	Expected Value
Market rise	$1,900	.40	$ 760
Market decline	1,150	.60	690
			$1,450

(b)

Event	Payoff	Probability of Event	Expected Value
Market rise	$2,400	.50	$1,200
Market decline	1,000	.50	500
			$1,700

19–5 For probabilities of a market rise (or decline) down to .333, Kayser Chemicals stock would provide the largest expected profit. For probabilities .333 to .143, Rim Homes would be the best buy. For .143 and below, Texas Electronics would give the largest expected profit. Algebraic solutions:

Kayser: $2,400p + (1 − p)1,000$
Rim: $2,200p + (1 − p)1,100$

$1,400p + 1,000 = 1,100p + 1,100$
$p = .333$

Rim: $2,200p + (1 − p)1,100$
Texas: $1,900p + (1 − p)1,150$

$1,100p + 1,100 = 750p + 1,150$
$p = .143$

Appendixes

APPENDIX A

Binomial Probability Distribution

n = 1
Probability

x	0.05	0.10	0.20	0.30	0.40	0.50	0.60	0.70	0.80	0.90	0.95
0	0.950	0.900	0.800	0.700	0.600	0.500	0.400	0.300	0.200	0.100	0.050
1	0.050	0.100	0.200	0.300	0.400	0.500	0.600	0.700	0.800	0.900	0.950

n = 2
Probability

x	0.05	0.10	0.20	0.30	0.40	0.50	0.60	0.70	0.80	0.90	0.95
0	0.903	0.810	0.640	0.490	0.360	0.250	0.160	0.090	0.040	0.010	0.003
1	0.095	0.180	0.320	0.420	0.480	0.500	0.480	0.420	0.320	0.180	0.095
2	0.003	0.010	0.040	0.090	0.160	0.250	0.360	0.490	0.640	0.810	0.903

n = 3
Probability

x	0.05	0.10	0.20	0.30	0.40	0.50	0.60	0.70	0.80	0.90	0.95
0	0.857	0.729	0.512	0.343	0.216	0.125	0.064	0.027	0.008	0.001	0.000
1	0.135	0.243	0.384	0.441	0.432	0.375	0.288	0.189	0.096	0.027	0.007
2	0.007	0.027	0.096	0.189	0.288	0.375	0.432	0.441	0.384	0.243	0.135
3	0.000	0.001	0.008	0.027	0.064	0.125	0.216	0.343	0.512	0.729	0.857

n = 4
Probability

x	0.05	0.10	0.20	0.30	0.40	0.50	0.60	0.70	0.80	0.90	0.95
0	0.815	0.656	0.410	0.240	0.130	0.063	0.026	0.008	0.002	0.000	0.000
1	0.171	0.292	0.410	0.412	0.346	0.250	0.154	0.076	0.026	0.004	0.000
2	0.014	0.049	0.154	0.265	0.346	0.375	0.346	0.265	0.154	0.049	0.014
3	0.000	0.004	0.026	0.076	0.154	0.250	0.346	0.412	0.410	0.292	0.171
4	0.000	0.000	0.002	0.008	0.026	0.063	0.130	0.240	0.410	0.656	0.815

n = 5
Probability

x	0.05	0.10	0.20	0.30	0.40	0.50	0.60	0.70	0.80	0.90	0.95
0	0.774	0.590	0.328	0.168	0.078	0.031	0.010	0.002	0.000	0.000	0.000
1	0.204	0.328	0.410	0.360	0.259	0.156	0.077	0.028	0.006	0.000	0.000
2	0.021	0.073	0.205	0.309	0.346	0.313	0.230	0.132	0.051	0.008	0.001
3	0.001	0.008	0.051	0.132	0.230	0.313	0.346	0.309	0.205	0.073	0.021
4	0.000	0.000	0.006	0.028	0.077	0.156	0.259	0.360	0.410	0.328	0.204
5	0.000	0.000	0.000	0.002	0.010	0.031	0.078	0.168	0.328	0.590	0.774

APPENDIX A

Binomial Probability Distribution (continued)

n = 6

Probability

x	0.05	0.10	0.20	0.30	0.40	0.50	0.60	0.70	0.80	0.90	0.95
0	0.735	0.531	0.262	0.118	0.047	0.016	0.004	0.001	0.000	0.000	0.000
1	0.232	0.354	0.393	0.303	0.187	0.094	0.037	0.010	0.002	0.000	0.000
2	0.031	0.098	0.246	0.324	0.311	0.234	0.138	0.060	0.015	0.001	0.000
3	0.002	0.015	0.082	0.185	0.276	0.313	0.276	0.185	0.082	0.015	0.002
4	0.000	0.001	0.015	0.060	0.138	0.234	0.311	0.324	0.246	0.098	0.031
5	0.000	0.000	0.002	0.010	0.037	0.094	0.187	0.303	0.393	0.354	0.232
6	0.000	0.000	0.000	0.001	0.004	0.016	0.047	0.118	0.262	0.531	0.735

n = 7

Probability

x	0.05	0.10	0.20	0.30	0.40	0.50	0.60	0.70	0.80	0.90	0.95
0	0.698	0.478	0.210	0.082	0.028	0.008	0.002	0.000	0.000	0.000	0.000
1	0.257	0.372	0.367	0.247	0.131	0.055	0.017	0.004	0.000	0.000	0.000
2	0.041	0.124	0.275	0.318	0.261	0.164	0.077	0.025	0.004	0.000	0.000
3	0.004	0.023	0.115	0.227	0.290	0.273	0.194	0.097	0.029	0.003	0.000
4	0.000	0.003	0.029	0.097	0.194	0.273	0.290	0.227	0.115	0.023	0.004
5	0.000	0.000	0.004	0.025	0.077	0.164	0.261	0.318	0.275	0.124	0.041
6	0.000	0.000	0.000	0.004	0.017	0.055	0.131	0.247	0.367	0.372	0.257
7	0.000	0.000	0.000	0.000	0.002	0.008	0.028	0.082	0.210	0.478	0.698

n = 8

Probability

x	0.05	0.10	0.20	0.30	0.40	0.50	0.60	0.70	0.80	0.90	0.95
0	0.663	0.430	0.168	0.058	0.017	0.004	0.001	0.000	0.000	0.000	0.000
1	0.279	0.383	0.336	0.198	0.090	0.031	0.008	0.001	0.000	0.000	0.000
2	0.051	0.149	0.294	0.296	0.209	0.109	0.041	0.010	0.001	0.000	0.000
3	0.005	0.033	0.147	0.254	0.279	0.219	0.124	0.047	0.009	0.000	0.000
4	0.000	0.005	0.046	0.136	0.232	0.273	0.232	0.136	0.046	0.005	0.000
5	0.000	0.000	0.009	0.047	0.124	0.219	0.279	0.254	0.147	0.033	0.005
6	0.000	0.000	0.001	0.010	0.041	0.109	0.209	0.296	0.294	0.149	0.051
7	0.000	0.000	0.000	0.001	0.008	0.031	0.090	0.198	0.336	0.383	0.279
8	0.000	0.000	0.000	0.000	0.001	0.004	0.017	0.058	0.168	0.430	0.663

APPENDIX A

Binomial Probability Distribution (continued)

$n = 9$
Probability

x	0.05	0.10	0.20	0.30	0.40	0.50	0.60	0.70	0.80	0.90	0.95
0	0.630	0.387	0.134	0.040	0.010	0.002	0.000	0.000	0.000	0.000	0.000
1	0.299	0.387	0.302	0.156	0.060	0.018	0.004	0.000	0.000	0.000	0.000
2	0.063	0.172	0.302	0.267	0.161	0.070	0.021	0.004	0.000	0.000	0.000
3	0.008	0.045	0.176	0.267	0.251	0.164	0.074	0.021	0.003	0.000	0.000
4	0.001	0.007	0.066	0.172	0.251	0.246	0.167	0.074	0.017	0.001	0.000
5	0.000	0.001	0.017	0.074	0.167	0.246	0.251	0.172	0.066	0.007	0.001
6	0.000	0.000	0.003	0.021	0.074	0.164	0.251	0.267	0.176	0.045	0.008
7	0.000	0.000	0.000	0.004	0.021	0.070	0.161	0.267	0.302	0.172	0.063
8	0.000	0.000	0.000	0.000	0.004	0.018	0.060	0.156	0.302	0.387	0.299
9	0.000	0.000	0.000	0.000	0.000	0.002	0.010	0.040	0.134	0.387	0.630

$n = 10$
Probability

x	0.05	0.10	0.20	0.30	0.40	0.50	0.60	0.70	0.80	0.90	0.95
0	0.599	0.349	0.107	0.028	0.006	0.001	0.000	0.000	0.000	0.000	0.000
1	0.315	0.387	0.268	0.121	0.040	0.010	0.002	0.000	0.000	0.000	0.000
2	0.075	0.194	0.302	0.233	0.121	0.044	0.011	0.001	0.000	0.000	0.000
3	0.010	0.057	0.201	0.267	0.215	0.117	0.042	0.009	0.001	0.000	0.000
4	0.001	0.011	0.088	0.200	0.251	0.205	0.111	0.037	0.006	0.000	0.000
5	0.000	0.001	0.026	0.103	0.201	0.246	0.201	0.103	0.026	0.001	0.000
6	0.000	0.000	0.006	0.037	0.111	0.205	0.251	0.200	0.088	0.011	0.001
7	0.000	0.000	0.001	0.009	0.042	0.117	0.215	0.267	0.201	0.057	0.010
8	0.000	0.000	0.000	0.001	0.011	0.044	0.121	0.233	0.302	0.194	0.075
9	0.000	0.000	0.000	0.000	0.002	0.010	0.040	0.121	0.268	0.387	0.315
10	0.000	0.000	0.000	0.000	0.000	0.001	0.006	0.028	0.107	0.349	0.599

APPENDIX A

Binomial Probability Distribution (continued)

$n = 11$
Probability

x	0.05	0.10	0.20	0.30	0.40	0.50	0.60	0.70	0.80	0.90	0.95
0	0.569	0.314	0.086	0.020	0.004	0.000	0.000	0.000	0.000	0.000	0.000
1	0.329	0.384	0.236	0.093	0.027	0.005	0.001	0.000	0.000	0.000	0.000
2	0.087	0.213	0.295	0.200	0.089	0.027	0.005	0.001	0.000	0.000	0.000
3	0.014	0.071	0.221	0.257	0.177	0.081	0.023	0.004	0.000	0.000	0.000
4	0.001	0.016	0.111	0.220	0.236	0.161	0.070	0.017	0.002	0.000	0.000
5	0.000	0.002	0.039	0.132	0.221	0.226	0.147	0.057	0.010	0.000	0.000
6	0.000	0.000	0.010	0.057	0.147	0.226	0.221	0.132	0.039	0.002	0.000
7	0.000	0.000	0.002	0.017	0.070	0.161	0.236	0.220	0.111	0.016	0.001
8	0.000	0.000	0.000	0.004	0.023	0.081	0.177	0.257	0.221	0.071	0.014
9	0.000	0.000	0.000	0.001	0.005	0.027	0.089	0.200	0.295	0.213	0.087
10	0.000	0.000	0.000	0.000	0.001	0.005	0.027	0.093	0.236	0.384	0.329
11	0.000	0.000	0.000	0.000	0.000	0.000	0.004	0.020	0.086	0.314	0.569

$n = 12$
Probability

x	0.05	0.10	0.20	0.30	0.40	0.50	0.60	0.70	0.80	0.90	0.95
0	0.540	0.282	0.069	0.014	0.002	0.000	0.000	0.000	0.000	0.000	0.000
1	0.341	0.377	0.206	0.071	0.017	0.003	0.000	0.000	0.000	0.000	0.000
2	0.099	0.230	0.283	0.168	0.064	0.016	0.002	0.000	0.000	0.000	0.000
3	0.017	0.085	0.236	0.240	0.142	0.054	0.012	0.001	0.000	0.000	0.000
4	0.002	0.021	0.133	0.231	0.213	0.121	0.042	0.008	0.001	0.000	0.000
5	0.000	0.004	0.053	0.158	0.227	0.193	0.101	0.029	0.003	0.000	0.000
6	0.000	0.000	0.016	0.079	0.177	0.226	0.177	0.079	0.016	0.000	0.000
7	0.000	0.000	0.003	0.029	0.101	0.193	0.227	0.158	0.053	0.004	0.000
8	0.000	0.000	0.001	0.008	0.042	0.121	0.213	0.231	0.133	0.021	0.002
9	0.000	0.000	0.000	0.001	0.012	0.054	0.142	0.240	0.236	0.085	0.017
10	0.000	0.000	0.000	0.000	0.002	0.016	0.064	0.168	0.283	0.230	0.099
11	0.000	0.000	0.000	0.000	0.000	0.003	0.017	0.071	0.206	0.377	0.341
12	0.000	0.000	0.000	0.000	0.000	0.000	0.002	0.014	0.069	0.282	0.540

APPENDIX A

Binomial Probability Distribution (continued)

$n = 13$
Probability

x	0.05	0.10	0.20	0.30	0.40	0.50	0.60	0.70	0.80	0.90	0.95
0	0.513	0.254	0.055	0.010	0.001	0.000	0.000	0.000	0.000	0.000	0.000
1	0.351	0.367	0.179	0.054	0.011	0.002	0.000	0.000	0.000	0.000	0.000
2	0.111	0.245	0.268	0.139	0.045	0.010	0.001	0.000	0.000	0.000	0.000
3	0.021	0.100	0.246	0.218	0.111	0.035	0.006	0.001	0.000	0.000	0.000
4	0.003	0.028	0.154	0.234	0.184	0.087	0.024	0.003	0.000	0.000	0.000
5	0.000	0.006	0.069	0.180	0.221	0.157	0.066	0.014	0.001	0.000	0.000
6	0.000	0.001	0.023	0.103	0.197	0.209	0.131	0.044	0.006	0.000	0.000
7	0.000	0.000	0.006	0.044	0.131	0.209	0.197	0.103	0.023	0.001	0.000
8	0.000	0.000	0.001	0.014	0.066	0.157	0.221	0.180	0.069	0.006	0.000
9	0.000	0.000	0.000	0.003	0.024	0.087	0.184	0.234	0.154	0.028	0.003
10	0.000	0.000	0.000	0.001	0.006	0.035	0.111	0.218	0.246	0.100	0.021
11	0.000	0.000	0.000	0.000	0.001	0.010	0.045	0.139	0.268	0.245	0.111
12	0.000	0.000	0.000	0.000	0.000	0.002	0.011	0.054	0.179	0.367	0.351
13	0.000	0.000	0.000	0.000	0.000	0.000	0.001	0.010	0.055	0.254	0.513

$n = 14$
Probability

x	0.05	0.10	0.20	0.30	0.40	0.50	0.60	0.70	0.80	0.90	0.95
0	0.488	0.229	0.044	0.007	0.001	0.000	0.000	0.000	0.000	0.000	0.000
1	0 359	0.356	0.154	0.041	0.007	0.001	0.000	0.000	0.000	0.000	0.000
2	0.123	0.257	0.250	0.113	0.032	0.006	0.001	0.000	0.000	0.000	0.000
3	0.026	0.114	0.250	0.194	0.085	0.022	0.003	0.000	0.000	0.000	0.000
4	0.004	0.035	0.172	0.229	0.155	0.061	0.014	0.001	0.000	0.000	0.000
5	0.000	0.008	0.086	0.196	0.207	0.122	0.041	0.007	0.000	0.000	0.000
6	0.000	0.001	0.032	0.126	0.207	0.183	0.092	0.023	0.002	0.000	0.000
7	0.000	0.000	0.009	0.062	0.157	0.209	0.157	0.062	0.009	0.000	0.000
8	0.000	0.000	0.002	0.023	0.092	0.183	0.207	0.126	0.032	0.001	0.000
9	0.000	0.000	0.000	0.007	0.041	0.122	0.207	0.196	0.086	0.008	0.000
10	0.000	0.000	0.000	0.001	0.014	0.061	0.155	0.229	0.172	0.035	0.004
11	0.000	0.000	0.000	0.000	0.003	0.022	0.085	0.194	0.250	0.114	0.026
12	0.000	0.000	0.000	0.000	0.001	0.006	0.032	0.113	0.250	0.257	0.123
13	0.000	0.000	0.000	0.000	0.000	0.001	0.007	0.041	0.154	0.356	0.359
14	0.000	0.000	0.000	0.000	0.000	0.000	0.001	0.007	0.044	0.229	0.488

APPENDIX A

Binomial Probability Distribution (continued)

$n = 15$
Probability

x	0.05	0.10	0.20	0.30	0.40	0.50	0.60	0.70	0.80	0.90	0.95
0	0.463	0.206	0.035	0.005	0.000	0.000	0.000	0.000	0.000	0.000	0.000
1	0.366	0.343	0.132	0.031	0.005	0.000	0.000	0.000	0.000	0.000	0.000
2	0.135	0.267	0.231	0.092	0.022	0.003	0.000	0.000	0.000	0.000	0.000
3	0.031	0.129	0.250	0.170	0.063	0.014	0.002	0.000	0.000	0.000	0.000
4	0.005	0.043	0.188	0.219	0.127	0.042	0.007	0.001	0.000	0.000	0.000
5	0.001	0.010	0.103	0.206	0.186	0.092	0.024	0.003	0.000	0.000	0.000
6	0.000	0.002	0.043	0.147	0.207	0.153	0.061	0.012	0.001	0.000	0.000
7	0.000	0.000	0.014	0.081	0.177	0.196	0.118	0.035	0.003	0.000	0.000
8	0.000	0.000	0.003	0.035	0.118	0.196	0.177	0.081	0.014	0.000	0.000
9	0.000	0.000	0.001	0.012	0.061	0.153	0.207	0.147	0.043	0.002	0.000
10	0.000	0.000	0.000	0.003	0.024	0.092	0.186	0.206	0.103	0.010	0.001
11	0.000	0.000	0.000	0.001	0.007	0.042	0.127	0.219	0.188	0.043	0.005
12	0.000	0.000	0.000	0.000	0.002	0.014	0.063	0.170	0.250	0.129	0.031
13	0.000	0.000	0.000	0.000	0.000	0.003	0.022	0.092	0.231	0.267	0.135
14	0.000	0.000	0.000	0.000	0.000	0.000	0.005	0.031	0.132	0.343	0.366
15	0.000	0.000	0.000	0.000	0.000	0.000	0.000	0.005	0.035	0.206	0.463

$n = 16$
Probability

x	0.05	0.10	0.20	0.30	0.40	0.50	0.60	0.70	0.80	0.90	0.95
0	0.440	0.185	0.028	0.003	0.000	0.000	0.000	0.000	0.000	0.000	0.000
1	0.371	0.329	0.113	0.023	0.003	0.000	0.000	0.000	0.000	0.000	0.000
2	0.146	0.275	0.211	0.073	0.015	0.002	0.000	0.000	0.000	0.000	0.000
3	0.036	0.142	0.246	0.146	0.047	0.009	0.001	0.000	0.000	0.000	0.000
4	0.006	0.051	0.200	0.204	0.101	0.028	0.004	0.000	0.000	0.000	0.000
5	0.001	0.014	0.120	0.210	0.162	0.067	0.014	0.001	0.000	0.000	0.000
6	0.000	0.003	0.055	0.165	0.198	0.122	0.039	0.006	0.000	0.000	0.000
7	0.000	0.000	0.020	0.101	0.189	0.175	0.084	0.019	0.001	0.000	0.000
8	0.000	0.000	0.006	0.049	0.142	0.196	0.142	0.049	0.006	0.000	0.000
9	0.000	0.000	0.001	0.019	0.084	0.175	0.189	0.101	0.020	0.000	0.000
10	0.000	0.000	0.000	0.006	0.039	0.122	0.198	0.165	0.055	0.003	0.000
11	0.000	0.000	0.000	0.001	0.014	0.067	0.162	0.210	0.120	0.014	0.001
12	0.000	0.000	0.000	0.000	0.004	0.028	0.101	0.204	0.200	0.051	0.006
13	0.000	0.000	0.000	0.000	0.001	0.009	0.047	0.146	0.246	0.142	0.036
14	0.000	0.000	0.000	0.000	0.000	0.002	0.015	0.073	0.211	0.275	0.146
15	0.000	0.000	0.000	0.000	0.000	0.000	0.003	0.023	0.113	0.329	0.371
16	0.000	0.000	0.000	0.000	0.000	0.000	0.000	0.003	0.028	0.185	0.440

APPENDIX A

Binomial Probability Distribution (continued)

$n = 17$
Probability

x	0.05	0.10	0.20	0.30	0.40	0.50	0.60	0.70	0.80	0.90	0.95
0	0.418	0.167	0.023	0.002	0.000	0.000	0.000	0.000	0.000	0.000	0.000
1	0.374	0.315	0.096	0.017	0.002	0.000	0.000	0.000	0.000	0.000	0.000
2	0.158	0.280	0.191	0.058	0.010	0.001	0.000	0.000	0.000	0.000	0.000
3	0.041	0.156	0.239	0.125	0.034	0.005	0.000	0.000	0.000	0.000	0.000
4	0.008	0.060	0.209	0.187	0.080	0.018	0.002	0.000	0.000	0.000	0.000
5	0.001	0.017	0.136	0.208	0.138	0.047	0.008	0.001	0.000	0.000	0.000
6	0.000	0.004	0.068	0.178	0.184	0.094	0.024	0.003	0.000	0.000	0.000
7	0.000	0.001	0.027	0.120	0.193	0.148	0.057	0.009	0.000	0.000	0.000
8	0.000	0.000	0.008	0.064	0.161	0.185	0.107	0.028	0.002	0.000	0.000
9	0.000	0.000	0.002	0.028	0.107	0.185	0.161	0.064	0.008	0.000	0.000
10	0.000	0.000	0.000	0.009	0.057	0.148	0.193	0.120	0.027	0.001	0.000
11	0.000	0.000	0.000	0.003	0.024	0.094	0.184	0.178	0.068	0.004	0.000
12	0.000	0.000	0.000	0.001	0.008	0.047	0.138	0.208	0.136	0.017	0.001
13	0.000	0.000	0.000	0.000	0.002	0.018	0.080	0.187	0.209	0.060	0.008
14	0.000	0.000	0.000	0.000	0.000	0.005	0.034	0.125	0.239	0.156	0.041
15	0.000	0.000	0.000	0.000	0.000	0.001	0.010	0.058	0.191	0.280	0.158
16	0.000	0.000	0.000	0.000	0.000	0.000	0.002	0.017	0.096	0.315	0.374
17	0.000	0.000	0.000	0.000	0.000	0.000	0.000	0.002	0.023	0.167	0.418

$n = 18$
Probability

x	0.05	0.10	0.20	0.30	0.40	0.50	0.60	0.70	0.80	0.90	0.95
0	0.397	0.150	0.018	0.002	0.000	0.000	0.000	0.000	0.000	0.000	0.000
1	0.376	0.300	0.081	0.013	0.001	0.000	0.000	0.000	0.000	0.000	0.000
2	0.168	0.284	0.172	0.046	0.007	0.001	0.000	0.000	0.000	0.000	0.000
3	0.047	0.168	0.230	0.105	0.025	0.003	0.000	0.000	0.000	0.000	0.000
4	0.009	0.070	0.215	0.168	0.061	0.012	0.001	0.000	0.000	0.000	0.000
5	0.001	0.022	0.151	0.202	0.115	0.033	0.004	0.000	0.000	0.000	0.000
6	0.000	0.005	0.082	0.187	0.166	0.071	0.015	0.001	0.000	0.000	0.000
7	0.000	0.001	0.035	0.138	0.189	0.121	0.037	0.005	0.000	0.000	0.000
8	0.000	0.000	0.012	0.081	0.173	0.167	0.077	0.015	0.001	0.000	0.000
9	0.000	0.000	0.003	0.039	0.128	0.185	0.128	0.039	0.003	0.000	0.000
10	0.000	0.000	0.001	0.015	0.077	0.167	0.173	0.081	0.012	0.000	0.000
11	0.000	0.000	0.000	0.005	0.037	0.121	0.189	0.138	0.035	0.001	0.000
12	0.000	0.000	0.000	0.001	0.015	0.071	0.166	0.187	0.082	0.005	0.000
13	0.000	0.000	0.000	0.000	0.004	0.033	0.115	0.202	0.151	0.022	0.001
14	0.000	0.000	0.000	0.000	0.001	0.012	0.061	0.168	0.215	0.070	0.009
15	0.000	0.000	0.000	0.000	0.000	0.003	0.025	0.105	0.230	0.168	0.047
16	0.000	0.000	0.000	0.000	0.000	0.001	0.007	0.046	0.172	0.284	0.168
17	0.000	0.000	0.000	0.000	0.000	0.000	0.001	0.013	0.081	0.300	0.376
18	0.000	0.000	0.000	0.000	0.000	0.000	0.000	0.002	0.018	0.150	0.397

APPENDIX A

Binomial Probability Distribution (continued)

$n = 19$

						Probability					
x	0.05	0.10	0.20	0.30	0.40	0.50	0.60	0.70	0.80	0.90	0.95
0	0.377	0.135	0.014	0.001	0.000	0.000	0.000	0.000	0.000	0.000	0.000
1	0.377	0.285	0.068	0.009	0.001	0.000	0.000	0.000	0.000	0.000	0.000
2	0.179	0.285	0.154	0.036	0.005	0.000	0.000	0.000	0.000	0.000	0.000
3	0.053	0.180	0.218	0.087	0.017	0.002	0.000	0.000	0.000	0.000	0.000
4	0.011	0.080	0.218	0.149	0.047	0.007	0.001	0.000	0.000	0.000	0.000
5	0.002	0.027	0.164	0.192	0.093	0.022	0.002	0.000	0.000	0.000	0.000
6	0.000	0.007	0.095	0.192	0.145	0.052	0.008	0.001	0.000	0.000	0.000
7	0.000	0.001	0.044	0.153	0.180	0.096	0.024	0.002	0.000	0.000	0.000
8	0.000	0.000	0.017	0.098	0.180	0.144	0.053	0.008	0.000	0.000	0.000
9	0.000	0.000	0.005	0.051	0.146	0.176	0.098	0.022	0.001	0.000	0.000
10	0.000	0.000	0.001	0.022	0.098	0.176	0.146	0.051	0.005	0.000	0.000
11	0.000	0.000	0.000	0.008	0.053	0.144	0.180	0.098	0.017	0.000	0.000
12	0.000	0.000	0.000	0.002	0.024	0.096	0.180	0.153	0.044	0.001	0.000
13	0.000	0.000	0.000	0.001	0.008	0.052	0.145	0.192	0.095	0.007	0.000
14	0.000	0.000	0.000	0.000	0.002	0.022	0.093	0.192	0.164	0.027	0.002
15	0.000	0.000	0.000	0.000	0.001	0.007	0.047	0.149	0.218	0.080	0.011
16	0.000	0.000	0.000	0.000	0.000	0.002	0.017	0.087	0.218	0.180	0.053
17	0.000	0.000	0.000	0.000	0.000	0.000	0.005	0.036	0.154	0.285	0.179
18	0.000	0.000	0.000	0.000	0.000	0.000	0.001	0.009	0.068	0.285	0.377
19	0.000	0.000	0.000	0.000	0.000	0.000	0.000	0.001	0.014	0.135	0.377

APPENDIX A

Binomial Probability Distribution (continued)

$n = 20$

					Probability						
x	0.05	0.10	0.20	0.30	0.40	0.50	0.60	0.70	0.80	0.90	0.95
0	0.358	0.122	0.012	0.001	0.000	0.000	0.000	0.000	0.000	0.000	0.000
1	0.377	0.270	0.058	0.007	0.000	0.000	0.000	0.000	0.000	0.000	0.000
2	0.189	0.285	0.137	0.028	0.003	0.000	0.000	0.000	0.000	0.000	0.000
3	0.060	0.190	0.205	0.072	0.012	0.001	0.000	0.000	0.000	0.000	0.000
4	0.013	0.090	0.218	0.130	0.035	0.005	0.000	0.000	0.000	0.000	0.000
5	0.002	0.032	0.175	0.179	0.075	0.015	0.001	0.000	0.000	0.000	0.000
6	0.000	0.009	0.109	0.192	0.124	0.037	0.005	0.000	0.000	0.000	0.000
7	0.000	0.002	0.055	0.164	0.166	0.074	0.015	0.001	0.000	0.000	0.000
8	0.000	0.000	0.022	0.114	0.180	0.120	0.035	0.004	0.000	0.000	0.000
9	0.000	0.000	0.007	0.065	0.160	0.160	0.071	0.012	0.000	0.000	0.000
10	0.000	0.000	0.002	0.031	0.117	0.176	0.117	0.031	0.002	0.000	0.000
11	0.000	0.000	0.000	0.012	0.071	0.160	0.160	0.065	0.007	0.000	0.000
12	0.000	0.000	0.000	0.004	0.035	0.120	0.180	0.114	0.022	0.000	0.000
13	0.000	0.000	0.000	0.001	0.015	0.074	0.166	0.164	0.055	0.002	0.000
14	0.000	0.000	0.000	0.000	0.005	0.037	0.124	0.192	0.109	0.009	0.000
15	0.000	0.000	0.000	0.000	0.001	0.015	0.075	0.179	0.175	0.032	0.002
16	0.000	0.000	0.000	0.000	0.000	0.005	0.035	0.130	0.218	0.090	0.013
17	0.000	0.000	0.000	0.000	0.000	0.001	0.012	0.072	0.205	0.190	0.060
18	0.000	0.000	0.000	0.000	0.000	0.000	0.003	0.028	0.137	0.285	0.189
19	0.000	0.000	0.000	0.000	0.000	0.000	0.000	0.007	0.058	0.270	0.377
20	0.000	0.000	0.000	0.000	0.000	0.000	0.000	0.001	0.012	0.122	0.358

APPENDIX A

Binomial Probability Distribution (concluded)

$n = 25$
Probability

x	0.05	0.10	0.20	0.30	0.40	0.50	0.60	0.70	0.80	0.90	0.95
0	0.277	0.072	0.004	0.000	0.000	0.000	0.000	0.000	0.000	0.000	0.000
1	0.365	0.199	0.024	0.001	0.000	0.000	0.000	0.000	0.000	0.000	0.000
2	0.231	0.266	0.071	0.007	0.000	0.000	0.000	0.000	0.000	0.000	0.000
3	0.093	0.226	0.136	0.024	0.002	0.000	0.000	0.000	0.000	0.000	0.000
4	0.027	0.138	0.187	0.057	0.007	0.000	0.000	0.000	0.000	0.000	0.000
5	0.006	0.065	0.196	0.103	0.020	0.002	0.000	0.000	0.000	0.000	0.000
6	0.001	0.024	0.163	0.147	0.044	0.005	0.000	0.000	0.000	0.000	0.000
7	0.000	0.007	0.111	0.171	0.080	0.014	0.001	0.000	0.000	0.000	0.000
8	0.000	0.002	0.062	0.165	0.120	0.032	0.003	0.000	0.000	0.000	0.000
9	0.000	0.000	0.029	0.134	0.151	0.061	0.009	0.000	0.000	0.000	0.000
10	0.000	0.000	0.012	0.092	0.161	0.097	0.021	0.001	0.000	0.000	0.000
11	0.000	0.000	0.004	0.054	0.147	0.133	0.043	0.004	0.000	0.000	0.000
12	0.000	0.000	0.001	0.027	0.114	0.155	0.076	0.011	0.000	0.000	0.000
13	0.000	0.000	0.000	0.011	0.076	0.155	0.114	0.027	0.001	0.000	0.000
14	0.000	0.000	0.000	0.004	0.043	0.133	0.147	0.054	0.004	0.000	0.000
15	0.000	0.000	0.000	0.001	0.021	0.097	0.161	0.092	0.012	0.000	0.000
16	0.000	0.000	0.000	0.000	0.009	0.061	0.151	0.134	0.029	0.000	0.000
17	0.000	0.000	0.000	0.000	0.003	0.032	0.120	0.165	0.062	0.002	0.000
18	0.000	0.000	0.000	0.000	0.001	0.014	0.080	0.171	0.111	0.007	0.000
19	0.000	0.000	0.000	0.000	0.000	0.005	0.044	0.147	0.163	0.024	0.001
20	0.000	0.000	0.000	0.000	0.000	0.002	0.020	0.103	0.196	0.065	0.006
21	0.000	0.000	0.000	0.000	0.000	0.000	0.007	0.057	0.187	0.138	0.027
22	0.000	0.000	0.000	0.000	0.000	0.000	0.002	0.024	0.136	0.226	0.093
23	0.000	0.000	0.000	0.000	0.000	0.000	0.000	0.007	0.071	0.266	0.231
24	0.000	0.000	0.000	0.000	0.000	0.000	0.000	0.001	0.024	0.199	0.365
25	0.000	0.000	0.000	0.000	0.000	0.000	0.000	0.000	0.004	0.072	0.277

APPENDIX B

Factors for Control Charts

| Number of Items in Sample, n | Chart for Averages | Chart for Ranges | | |
| | Factors for Control Limits | Factors for Central Line | Factors for Control Limits | |
	A_2	d_2	D_3	D_4
2	1.880	1.128	0	3.267
3	1.023	1.693	0	2.575
4	.729	2.059	0	2.282
5	.577	2.326	0	2.115
6	.483	2.534	0	2.004
7	.419	2.704	.076	1.924
8	.373	2.847	.136	1.864
9	.337	2.970	.184	1.816
10	.308	3.078	.223	1.777
11	.285	3.173	.256	1.744
12	.266	3.258	.284	1.716
13	.249	3.336	.308	1.692
14	.235	3.407	.329	1.671
15	.223	3.472	.348	1.652

SOURCE: Adapted from American Society for Testing and Materials, *Manual on Quality Control of Materials*, 1951, Table B2, p. 115. For a more detailed table and explanation, see Acheson J. Duncan, *Quality Control and Industrial Statistics*, 3d ed. (Homewood, Ill.: Richard D. Irwin, 1974), Table M, p. 927.

APPENDIX C

Poisson Distribution

					μ				
x	0.1	0.2	0.3	0.4	0.5	0.6	0.7	0.8	0.9
0	0.9048	0.8187	0.7408	0.6703	0.6065	0.5488	0.4966	0.4493	0.4066
1	0.0905	0.1637	0.2222	0.2681	0.3033	0.3293	0.3476	0.3595	0.3659
2	0.0045	0.0164	0.0333	0.0536	0.0758	0.0988	0.1217	0.1438	0.1647
3	0.0002	0.0011	0.0033	0.0072	0.0126	0.0198	0.0284	0.0383	0.0494
4	0.0000	0.0001	0.0003	0.0007	0.0016	0.0030	0.0050	0.0077	0.0111
5	0.0000	0.0000	0.0000	0.0001	0.0002	0.0004	0.0007	0.0012	0.0020
6	0.0000	0.0000	0.0000	0.0000	0.0000	0.0000	0.0001	0.0002	0.0003
7	0.0000	0.0000	0.0000	0.0000	0.0000	0.0000	0.0000	0.0000	0.0000

					μ				
x	1.0	2.0	3.0	4.0	5.0	6.0	7.0	8.0	9.0
0	0.3679	0.1353	0.0498	0.0183	0.0067	0.0025	0.0009	0.0003	0.0001
1	0.3679	0.2707	0.1494	0.0733	0.0337	0.0149	0.0064	0.0027	0.0011
2	0.1839	0.2707	0.2240	0.1465	0.0842	0.0446	0.0223	0.0107	0.0050
3	0.0613	0.1804	0.2240	0.1954	0.1404	0.0892	0.0521	0.0286	0.0150
4	0.0153	0.0902	0.1680	0.1954	0.1755	0.1339	0.0912	0.0573	0.0337
5	0.0031	0.0361	0.1008	0.1563	0.1755	0.1606	0.1277	0.0916	0.0607
6	0.0005	0.0120	0.0504	0.1042	0.1462	0.1606	0.1490	0.1221	0.0911
7	0.0001	0.0034	0.0216	0.0595	0.1044	0.1377	0.1490	0.1396	0.1171
8	0.0000	0.0009	0.0081	0.0298	0.0653	0.1033	0.1304	0.1396	0.1318
9	0.0000	0.0002	0.0027	0.0132	0.0363	0.0688	0.1014	0.1241	0.1318
10	0.0000	0.0000	0.0008	0.0053	0.0181	0.0413	0.0710	0.0993	0.1186
11	0.0000	0.0000	0.0002	0.0019	0.0082	0.0225	0.0452	0.0722	0.0970
12	0.0000	0.0000	0.0001	0.0006	0.0034	0.0113	0.0263	0.0481	0.0728
13	0.0000	0.0000	0.0000	0.0002	0.0013	0.0052	0.0142	0.0296	0.0504
14	0.0000	0.0000	0.0000	0.0001	0.0005	0.0022	0.0071	0.0169	0.0324
15	0.0000	0.0000	0.0000	0.0000	0.0002	0.0009	0.0033	0.0090	0.0194
16	0.0000	0.0000	0.0000	0.0000	0.0000	0.0003	0.0014	0.0045	0.0109
17	0.0000	0.0000	0.0000	0.0000	0.0000	0.0001	0.0006	0.0021	0.0058
18	0.0000	0.0000	0.0000	0.0000	0.0000	0.0000	0.0002	0.0009	0.0029
19	0.0000	0.0000	0.0000	0.0000	0.0000	0.0000	0.0001	0.0004	0.0014
20	0.0000	0.0000	0.0000	0.0000	0.0000	0.0000	0.0000	0.0002	0.0006
21	0.0000	0.0000	0.0000	0.0000	0.0000	0.0000	0.0000	0.0001	0.0003
22	0.0000	0.0000	0.0000	0.0000	0.0000	0.0000	0.0000	0.0000	0.0001

APPENDIX D

Areas under the Normal Curve

Example:
If $z = 1.96$, then
$P(0$ to $z) = 0.4750$

0.4750

$z \longrightarrow$ 0   1.96

z	0.00	0.01	0.02	0.03	0.04	0.05	0.06	0.07	0.08	0.09
0.0	0.0000	0.0040	0.0080	0.0120	0.0160	0.0199	0.0239	0.0279	0.0319	0.0359
0.1	0.0398	0.0438	0.0478	0.0517	0.0557	0.0596	0.0636	0.0675	0.0714	0.0753
0.2	0.0793	0.0832	0.0871	0.0910	0.0948	0.0987	0.1026	0.1064	0.1103	0.1141
0.3	0.1179	0.1217	0.1255	0.1293	0.1331	0.1368	0.1406	0.1443	0.1480	0.1517
0.4	0.1554	0.1591	0.1628	0.1664	0.1700	0.1736	0.1772	0.1808	0.1844	0.1879
0.5	0.1915	0.1950	0.1985	0.2019	0.2054	0.2088	0.2123	0.2157	0.2190	0.2224
0.6	0.2257	0.2291	0.2324	0.2357	0.2389	0.2422	0.2454	0.2486	0.2517	0.2549
0.7	0.2580	0.2611	0.2642	0.2673	0.2704	0.2734	0.2764	0.2794	0.2823	0.2852
0.8	0.2881	0.2910	0.2939	0.2967	0.2995	0.3023	0.3051	0.3078	0.3106	0.3133
0.9	0.3159	0.3186	0.3212	0.3238	0.3264	0.3289	0.3315	0.3340	0.3365	0.3389
1.0	0.3413	0.3438	0.3461	0.3485	0.3508	0.3531	0.3554	0.3577	0.3599	0.3621
1.1	0.3643	0.3665	0.3686	0.3708	0.3729	0.3749	0.3770	0.3790	0.3810	0.3830
1.2	0.3849	0.3869	0.3888	0.3907	0.3925	0.3944	0.3962	0.3980	0.3997	0.4015
1.3	0.4032	0.4049	0.4066	0.4082	0.4099	0.4115	0.4131	0.4147	0.4162	0.4177
1.4	0.4192	0.4207	0.4222	0.4236	0.4251	0.4265	0.4279	0.4292	0.4306	0.4319
1.5	0.4332	0.4345	0.4357	0.4370	0.4382	0.4394	0.4406	0.4418	0.4429	0.4441
1.6	0.4452	0.4463	0.4474	0.4484	0.4495	0.4505	0.4515	0.4525	0.4535	0.4545
1.7	0.4554	0.4564	0.4573	0.4582	0.4591	0.4599	0.4608	0.4616	0.4625	0.4633
1.8	0.4641	0.4649	0.4656	0.4664	0.4671	0.4678	0.4686	0.4693	0.4699	0.4706
1.9	0.4713	0.4719	0.4726	0.4732	0.4738	0.4744	0.4750	0.4756	0.4761	0.4767
2.0	0.4772	0.4778	0.4783	0.4788	0.4793	0.4798	0.4803	0.4808	0.4812	0.4817
2.1	0.4821	0.4826	0.4830	0.4834	0.4838	0.4842	0.4846	0.4850	0.4854	0.4857
2.2	0.4861	0.4864	0.4868	0.4871	0.4875	0.4878	0.4881	0.4884	0.4887	0.4890
2.3	0.4893	0.4896	0.4898	0.4901	0.4904	0.4906	0.4909	0.4911	0.4913	0.4916
2.4	0.4918	0.4920	0.4922	0.4925	0.4927	0.4929	0.4931	0.4932	0.4934	0.4936
2.5	0.4938	0.4940	0.4941	0.4943	0.4945	0.4946	0.4948	0.4949	0.4951	0.4952
2.6	0.4953	0.4955	0.4956	0.4957	0.4959	0.4960	0.4961	0.4962	0.4963	0.4964
2.7	0.4965	0.4966	0.4967	0.4968	0.4969	0.4970	0.4971	0.4972	0.4973	0.4974
2.8	0.4974	0.4975	0.4976	0.4977	0.4977	0.4978	0.4979	0.4979	0.4980	0.4981
2.9	0.4981	0.4982	0.4982	0.4983	0.4984	0.4984	0.4985	0.4985	0.4986	0.4986
3.0	0.4987	0.4987	0.4987	0.4988	0.4988	0.4989	0.4989	0.4989	0.4990	0.4990

APPENDIX E

Table of Random Numbers

02711	08182	75997	79866	58095	83319	80295	79741	74599	84379
94873	90935	31684	63952	09865	14491	99518	93394	34691	14985
54921	78680	06635	98689	17306	25170	65928	87709	30533	89736
77640	97636	37397	93379	56454	59818	45827	74164	71666	46977
61545	00835	93251	87203	36759	49197	85967	01704	19634	21898
17147	19519	22497	16857	42426	84822	92598	49186	88247	39967
13748	04742	92460	85801	53444	65626	58710	55406	17173	69776
87455	14813	50373	28037	91182	32786	65261	11173	34376	36408
08999	57409	91185	10200	61411	23392	47797	56377	71635	08601
78804	81333	53809	32471	46034	36306	22498	19239	85428	55721
82173	26921	28472	98958	07960	66124	89731	95069	18625	92405
97594	25168	89178	68190	05043	17407	48201	83917	11413	72920
73881	67176	93504	42636	38233	16154	96451	57925	29667	30859
46071	22912	90326	42453	88108	72064	58601	32357	90610	32921
44492	19686	12495	93135	95185	77799	52441	88272	22024	80631
31864	72170	37722	55794	14636	05148	54505	50113	21119	25228
51574	90692	43339	65689	76539	27909	05467	21727	51141	72949
35350	76132	92925	92124	92634	35681	43690	89136	35599	84138
46943	36502	01172	46045	46991	33804	80006	35542	61056	75666
22665	87226	33304	57975	03985	21566	65796	72915	81466	89205
39437	97957	11838	10433	21564	51570	73558	27495	34533	57808
77082	47784	40098	97962	89845	28392	78187	06112	08169	11261
24544	25649	43370	28007	06779	72402	62632	53956	24709	06978
27503	15558	37738	24849	70722	71859	83736	06016	94397	12529
24590	24545	06435	52758	45685	90151	46516	49644	92686	84870
48155	86226	40359	28723	15364	69125	12609	57171	86857	31702
20226	53752	90648	24362	83314	00014	19207	69413	97016	86290
70178	73444	38790	53626	93780	18629	68766	24371	74639	30782
10169	41465	51935	05711	09799	79077	88159	33437	68519	03040
81084	03701	28598	70013	63794	53169	97054	60303	23259	96196
69202	20777	21727	81511	51887	16175	53746	46516	70339	62727
80561	95787	89426	93325	86412	57479	54194	52153	19197	81877
08199	26703	95128	48599	09333	12584	24374	31232	61782	44032
98883	28220	39358	53720	80161	83371	15181	11131	12219	55920
84568	69286	76054	21615	80883	36797	82845	39139	90900	18172
04269	35173	95745	53893	86022	77722	52498	84193	22448	22571
10538	13124	36099	13140	37706	44562	57179	44693	67877	01549
77843	24955	25900	63843	95029	93859	93634	20205	66294	41218
12034	94636	49455	76362	83532	31062	69903	91186	65768	55949
10524	72829	47641	93315	80875	28090	97728	52560	34937	79548
68935	76632	46984	61772	92786	22651	07086	89754	44143	97607
89450	65665	29190	43709	11172	34481	95977	47535	25658	73898
90696	20451	24211	97310	60446	73530	62865	96574	13829	72226
49006	32047	93086	00112	20470	17136	28255	86328	07293	38809
74591	87025	52368	59416	34417	70557	86746	55809	53628	12000
06315	17012	77103	00968	07235	10728	42189	33292	51487	64443
62386	09184	62092	46617	99419	64230	95034	85481	07857	42510
86848	82122	04028	36959	87827	12813	08627	80699	13345	51695
65643	69480	46598	04501	40403	91408	32343	48130	49303	90689
11084	46534	78957	77353	39578	77868	22970	84349	09184	70603

APPENDIX F

Student's t *Distribution*

df	Level of Significance for One-Tailed Test					
	0.100	0.050	0.025	0.010	0.005	0.0005
	Level of Significance for Two-Tailed Test					
	0.20	0.10	0.05	0.02	0.01	0.001
1	3.078	6.314	12.706	31.821	63.657	636.619
2	1.886	2.920	4.303	6.965	9.925	31.599
3	1.638	2.353	3.182	4.541	5.841	12.924
4	1.533	2.132	2.776	3.747	4.604	8.610
5	1.476	2.015	2.571	3.365	4.032	6.869
6	1.440	1.943	2.447	3.143	3.707	5.959
7	1.415	1.895	2.365	2.998	3.499	5.408
8	1.397	1.860	2.306	2.896	3.355	5.041
9	1.383	1.833	2.262	2.821	3.250	4.781
10	1.372	1.812	2.228	2.764	3.169	4.587
11	1.363	1.796	2.201	2.718	3.106	4.437
12	1.356	1.782	2.179	2.681	3.055	4.318
13	1.350	1.771	2.160	2.650	3.012	4.221
14	1.345	1.761	2.145	2.624	2.977	4.140
15	1.341	1.753	2.131	2.602	2.947	4.073
16	1.337	1.746	2.120	2.583	2.921	4.015
17	1.333	1.740	2.110	2.567	2.898	3.965
18	1.330	1.734	2.101	2.552	2.878	3.922
19	1.328	1.729	2.093	2.539	2.861	3.883
20	1.325	1.725	2.086	2.528	2.845	3.850
21	1.323	1.721	2.080	2.518	2.831	3.819
22	1.321	1.717	2.074	2.508	2.819	3.792
23	1.319	1.714	2.069	2.500	2.807	3.768
24	1.318	1.711	2.064	2.492	2.797	3.745
25	1.316	1.708	2.060	2.485	2.787	3.725
26	1.315	1.706	2.056	2.479	2.779	3.707
27	1.314	1.703	2.052	2.473	2.771	3.690
28	1.313	1.701	2.048	2.467	2.763	3.674
29	1.311	1.699	2.045	2.462	2.756	3.659
30	1.310	1.697	2.042	2.457	2.750	3.646
40	1.303	1.684	2.021	2.423	2.704	3.551
60	1.296	1.671	2.000	2.390	2.660	3.460
120	1.289	1.658	1.980	2.358	2.617	3.373
∞	1.282	1.645	1.960	2.326	2.576	3.291

APPENDIX G

Critical Values of the F Distribution at a 5 Percent Level of Significance

Degrees of Freedom for the Numerator

	1	2	3	4	5	6	7	8	9	10	12	15	20	24	30	40
1	161	200	216	225	230	234	237	239	241	242	244	246	248	249	250	251
2	18.5	19.0	19.2	19.2	19.3	19.3	19.4	19.4	19.4	19.4	19.4	19.4	19.4	19.5	19.5	19.5
3	10.1	9.55	9.28	9.12	9.01	8.94	8.89	8.85	8.81	8.79	8.74	8.70	8.66	8.64	8.62	8.59
4	7.71	6.94	6.59	6.39	6.26	6.16	6.09	6.04	6.00	5.96	5.91	5.86	5.80	5.77	5.75	5.72
5	6.61	5.79	5.41	5.19	5.05	4.95	4.88	4.82	4.77	4.74	4.68	4.62	4.56	4.53	4.50	4.46
6	5.99	5.14	4.76	4.53	4.39	4.28	4.21	4.15	4.10	4.06	4.00	3.94	3.87	3.84	3.81	3.77
7	5.59	4.74	4.35	4.12	3.97	3.87	3.79	3.73	3.68	3.64	3.57	3.51	3.44	3.41	3.38	3.34
8	5.32	4.46	4.07	3.84	3.69	3.58	3.50	3.44	3.39	3.35	3.28	3.22	3.15	3.12	3.08	3.04
9	5.12	4.26	3.86	3.63	3.48	3.37	3.29	3.23	3.18	3.14	3.07	3.01	2.94	2.90	2.86	2.83
10	4.96	4.10	3.71	3.48	3.33	3.22	3.14	3.07	3.02	2.98	2.91	2.85	2.77	2.74	2.70	2.66
11	4.84	3.98	3.59	3.36	3.20	3.09	3.01	2.95	2.90	2.85	2.79	2.72	2.65	2.61	2.57	2.53
12	4.75	3.89	3.49	3.26	3.11	3.00	2.91	2.85	2.80	2.75	2.69	2.62	2.54	2.51	2.47	2.43
13	4.67	3.81	3.41	3.18	3.03	2.92	2.83	2.77	2.71	2.67	2.60	2.53	2.46	2.42	2.38	2.34
14	4.60	3.74	3.34	3.11	2.96	2.85	2.76	2.70	2.65	2.60	2.53	2.46	2.39	2.35	2.31	2.27
15	4.54	3.68	3.29	3.06	2.90	2.79	2.71	2.64	2.59	2.54	2.48	2.40	2.33	2.29	2.25	2.20
16	4.49	3.63	3.24	3.01	2.85	2.74	2.66	2.59	2.54	2.49	2.42	2.35	2.28	2.24	2.19	2.15
17	4.45	3.59	3.20	2.96	2.81	2.70	2.61	2.55	2.49	2.45	2.38	2.31	2.23	2.19	2.15	2.10
18	4.41	3.55	3.16	2.93	2.77	2.66	2.58	2.51	2.46	2.41	2.34	2.27	2.19	2.15	2.11	2.06
19	4.38	3.52	3.13	2.90	2.74	2.63	2.54	2.48	2.42	2.38	2.31	2.23	2.16	2.11	2.07	2.03
20	4.35	3.49	3.10	2.87	2.71	2.60	2.51	2.45	2.39	2.35	2.28	2.20	2.12	2.08	2.04	1.99
21	4.32	3.47	3.07	2.84	2.68	2.57	2.49	2.42	2.37	2.32	2.25	2.18	2.10	2.05	2.01	1.96
22	4.30	3.44	3.05	2.82	2.66	2.55	2.46	2.40	2.34	2.30	2.23	2.15	2.07	2.03	1.98	1.94
23	4.28	3.42	3.03	2.80	2.64	2.53	2.44	2.37	2.32	2.27	2.20	2.13	2.05	2.01	1.96	1.91
24	4.26	3.40	3.01	2.78	2.62	2.51	2.42	2.36	2.30	2.25	2.18	2.11	2.03	1.98	1.94	1.89
25	4.24	3.39	2.99	2.76	2.60	2.49	2.40	2.34	2.28	2.24	2.16	2.09	2.01	1.96	1.92	1.87
30	4.17	3.32	2.92	2.69	2.53	2.42	2.33	2.27	2.21	2.16	2.09	2.01	1.93	1.89	1.84	1.79
40	4.08	3.23	2.84	2.61	2.45	2.34	2.25	2.18	2.12	2.08	2.00	1.92	1.84	1.79	1.74	1.69
60	4.00	3.15	2.76	2.53	2.37	2.25	2.17	2.10	2.04	1.99	1.92	1.84	1.75	1.70	1.65	1.59
120	3.92	3.07	2.68	2.45	2.29	2.18	2.09	2.02	1.96	1.91	1.83	1.75	1.66	1.61	1.55	1.50
∞	3.84	3.00	2.60	2.37	2.21	2.10	2.01	1.94	1.88	1.83	1.75	1.67	1.57	1.52	1.46	1.39

Degrees of Freedom for the Denominator

APPENDIX G

Critical Values of the F Distribution at a 1 Percent Level of Significance

Degrees of Freedom for the Numerator

	1	2	3	4	5	6	7	8	9	10	12	15	20	24	30	40
1	4052	5000	5403	5625	5764	5859	5928	5981	6022	6056	6106	6157	6209	6235	6261	6287
2	98.5	99.0	99.2	99.2	99.3	99.3	99.4	99.4	99.4	99.4	99.4	99.4	99.4	99.5	99.5	99.5
3	34.1	30.8	29.5	28.7	28.2	27.9	27.7	27.5	27.3	27.2	27.1	26.9	26.7	26.6	26.5	26.4
4	21.2	18.0	16.7	16.0	15.5	15.2	15.0	14.8	14.7	14.5	14.4	14.2	14.0	13.9	13.8	13.7
5	16.3	13.3	12.1	11.4	11.0	10.7	10.5	10.3	10.2	10.1	9.89	9.72	9.55	9.47	9.38	9.29
6	13.7	10.9	9.78	9.15	8.75	8.47	8.26	8.10	7.98	7.87	7.72	7.56	7.40	7.31	7.23	7.14
7	12.2	9.55	8.45	7.85	7.46	7.19	6.99	6.84	6.72	6.62	6.47	6.31	6.16	6.07	5.99	5.91
8	11.3	8.65	7.59	7.01	6.63	6.37	6.18	6.03	5.91	5.81	5.67	5.52	5.36	5.28	5.20	5.12
9	10.6	8.02	6.99	6.42	6.06	5.80	5.61	5.47	5.35	5.26	5.11	4.96	4.81	4.73	4.65	4.57
10	10.0	7.56	6.55	5.99	5.64	5.39	5.20	5.06	4.94	4.85	4.71	4.56	4.41	4.33	4.25	4.17
11	9.65	7.21	6.22	5.67	5.32	5.07	4.89	4.74	4.63	4.54	4.40	4.25	4.10	4.02	3.94	3.86
12	9.33	6.93	5.95	5.41	5.06	4.82	4.64	4.50	4.39	4.30	4.16	4.01	3.86	3.78	3.70	3.62
13	9.07	6.70	5.74	5.21	4.86	4.62	4.44	4.30	4.19	4.10	3.96	3.82	3.66	3.59	3.51	3.43
14	8.86	6.51	5.56	5.04	4.69	4.46	4.28	4.14	4.03	3.94	3.80	3.66	3.51	3.43	3.35	3.27
15	8.68	6.36	5.42	4.89	4.56	4.32	4.14	4.00	3.89	3.80	3.67	3.52	3.37	3.29	3.21	3.13
16	8.53	6.23	5.29	4.77	4.44	4.20	4.03	3.89	3.78	3.69	3.55	3.41	3.26	3.18	3.10	3.02
17	8.40	6.11	5.18	4.67	4.34	4.10	3.93	3.79	3.68	3.59	3.46	3.31	3.16	3.08	3.00	2.92
18	8.29	6.01	5.09	4.58	4.25	4.01	3.84	3.71	3.60	3.51	3.37	3.23	3.08	3.00	2.92	2.84
19	8.18	5.93	5.01	4.50	4.17	3.94	3.77	3.63	3.52	3.43	3.30	3.15	3.00	2.92	2.84	2.76
20	8.10	5.85	4.94	4.43	4.10	3.87	3.70	3.56	3.46	3.37	3.23	3.09	2.94	2.86	2.78	2.69
21	8.02	5.78	4.87	4.37	4.04	3.81	3.64	3.51	3.40	3.31	3.17	3.03	2.88	2.80	2.72	2.64
22	7.95	5.72	4.82	4.31	3.99	3.76	3.59	3.45	3.35	3.26	3.12	2.98	2.83	2.75	2.67	2.58
23	7.88	5.66	4.76	4.26	3.94	3.71	3.54	3.41	3.30	3.21	3.07	2.93	2.78	2.70	2.62	2.54
24	7.82	5.61	4.72	4.22	3.90	3.67	3.50	3.36	3.26	3.17	3.03	2.89	2.74	2.66	2.58	2.49
25	7.77	5.57	4.68	4.18	3.85	3.63	3.46	3.32	3.22	3.13	2.99	2.85	2.70	2.62	2.54	2.45
30	7.56	5.39	4.51	4.02	3.70	3.47	3.30	3.17	3.07	2.98	2.84	2.70	2.55	2.47	2.39	2.30
40	7.31	5.18	4.31	3.83	3.51	3.29	3.12	2.99	2.89	2.80	2.66	2.52	2.37	2.29	2.20	2.11
60	7.08	4.98	4.13	3.65	3.34	3.12	2.95	2.82	2.72	2.63	2.50	2.35	2.20	2.12	2.03	1.94
120	6.85	4.79	3.95	3.48	3.17	2.96	2.79	2.66	2.56	2.47	2.34	2.19	2.03	1.95	1.86	1.76
∞	6.63	4.61	3.78	3.32	3.02	2.80	2.64	2.51	2.41	2.32	2.18	2.04	1.88	1.79	1.70	1.59

Degrees of Freedom for the Denominator

APPENDIX H

Wilcoxon T *Values*

n	2α .15 α .075	.10 .050	.05 .025	.04 .020	.03 .015	.02 .010	.01 .005
4	0						
5	1	0					
6	2	2	0	0			
7	4	3	2	1	0	0	
8	7	5	3	3	2	1	0
9	9	8	5	5	4	3	1
10	12	10	8	7	6	5	3
11	16	13	10	9	8	7	5
12	19	17	13	12	11	9	7
13	24	21	17	16	14	12	9
14	28	25	21	19	18	15	12
15	33	30	25	23	21	19	15
16	39	35	29	28	26	23	19
17	45	41	34	33	30	27	23
18	51	47	40	38	35	32	27
19	58	53	46	43	41	37	32
20	65	60	52	50	47	43	37
21	73	67	58	56	53	49	42
22	81	75	65	63	59	55	48
23	89	83	73	70	66	62	54
24	98	91	81	78	74	69	61
25	108	100	89	86	82	76	68
26	118	110	98	94	90	84	75
27	128	119	107	103	99	92	83
28	138	130	116	112	108	101	91
29	150	140	126	122	117	110	100
30	161	151	137	132	127	120	109
31	173	163	147	143	137	130	118
32	186	175	159	154	148	140	128
33	199	187	170	165	159	151	138
34	212	200	182	177	171	162	148
35	226	213	195	189	182	173	159
40	302	286	264	257	249	238	220
50	487	466	434	425	413	397	373
60	718	690	648	636	620	600	567
70	995	960	907	891	872	846	805
80	1,318	1,276	1,211	1,192	1,168	1,136	1,086
90	1,688	1,638	1,560	1,537	1,509	1,471	1,410
100	2,105	2,045	1,955	1,928	1,894	1,850	1,779

SOURCE: Abridged from Robert L. McCormack, "Extended Tables of the Wilcoxon Matched-Pair Signed Rank Statistic," *Journal of the American Statistical Association*, September 1965, pp. 866–67.

APPENDIX I

Critical Values of Chi-Square

This table contains the values of χ^2 that correspond to a specific right-tail area and specific number of degrees of freedom.

χ^2
Possible values of χ^2

Degrees of Freedom, df	Right-Tail Area			
	0.10	0.05	0.02	0.01
1	2.706	3.841	5.412	6.635
2	4.605	5.991	7.824	9.210
3	6.251	7.815	9.837	11.345
4	7.779	9.488	11.668	13.277
5	9.236	11.070	13.388	15.086
6	10.645	12.592	15.033	16.812
7	12.017	14.067	16.622	18.475
8	13.362	15.507	18.168	20.090
9	14.684	16.919	19.679	21.666
10	15.987	18.307	21.161	23.209
11	17.275	19.675	22.618	24.725
12	18.549	21.026	24.054	26.217
13	19.812	22.362	25.472	27.688
14	21.064	23.685	26.873	29.141
15	22.307	24.996	28.259	30.578
16	23.542	26.296	29.633	32.000
17	24.769	27.587	30.995	33.409
18	25.989	28.869	32.346	34.805
19	27.204	30.144	33.687	36.191
20	28.412	31.410	35.020	37.566
21	29.615	32.671	36.343	38.932
22	30.813	33.924	37.659	40.289
23	32.007	35.172	38.968	41.638
24	33.196	36.415	40.270	42.980
25	34.382	37.652	41.566	44.314
26	35.563	38.885	42.856	45.642
27	36.741	40.113	44.140	46.963
28	37.916	41.337	45.419	48.278
29	39.087	42.557	46.693	49.588
30	40.256	43.773	47.962	50.892

APPENDIX J

Data Set 1 — Real Estate

x_1 = Selling price in $000

x_2 = Number of bedrooms

x_3 = Size of the home in square feet

x_4 = Pool (1 = yes, 0 = no)

x_5 = Distance from the center of the city

x_6 = Township

x_7 = Garage attached (1 = yes, 0 = no)

x_8 = Number of bathrooms

x_1	x_2	x_3	x_4	x_5	x_6	x_7	x_8
263.115	4	2,349	0	17	5	1	2
182.385	4	2,102	1	19	4	0	2
242.055	3	2,271	1	12	3	0	2
213.57	2	2,188	1	16	2	0	2.5
139.86	2	2,148	1	28	1	0	1.5
245.43	2	2,117	0	12	1	1	2
327.24	6	2,484	1	15	3	1	2
271.755	2	2,130	1	9	2	1	2.5
221.13	3	2,254	0	18	1	0	1.5
266.625	4	2,385	1	13	4	1	2
292.41	4	2,108	1	14	3	1	2
208.98	2	1,715	1	8	4	1	1.5
270.81	6	2,495	1	7	4	1	2
246.105	4	2,073	1	18	3	1	2
194.4	2	2,283	1	11	3	0	2
281.34	3	2,119	1	16	2	1	2
172.665	4	2,189	0	16	3	0	2
207.495	5	2,316	0	21	4	0	2.5
198.855	3	2,220	0	10	4	1	2
209.25	6	1,901	0	15	4	1	2
252.315	4	2,624	1	8	4	1	2
192.915	4	1,938	0	14	2	1	2.5
209.25	5	2,101	1	20	5	0	1.5
345.33	8	2,644	1	9	4	1	2
326.295	6	2,141	1	11	5	1	3
173.07	2	2,198	0	21	5	1	1.5
186.975	2	1,912	1	26	4	0	2
257.175	2	2,117	1	9	4	1	2
233.01	3	2,162	1	14	3	1	1.5
180.36	2	2,041	1	11	5	0	2
233.955	2	1,712	1	19	3	1	2
207.09	2	1,974	1	11	5	1	2
247.725	5	2,438	1	16	2	1	2
166.185	3	2,019	0	16	2	1	2
177.12	2	1,919	1	10	5	1	2

x_1	x_2	x_3	x_4	x_5	x_6	x_7	x_8
182.655	4	2,023	0	14	4	0	2.5
216	4	2,310	1	19	2	0	2
312.12	6	2,639	1	7	5	1	2.5
199.8	3	2,069	1	19	3	1	2
273.24	5	2,182	1	16	2	1	3
206.01	3	2,090	0	9	3	0	1.5
232.2	3	1,928	0	16	1	1	1.5
198.315	4	2,056	0	19	1	1	1.5
205.065	3	2,012	0	20	4	0	2
175.635	4	2,262	0	24	4	1	2
307.8	3	2,431	0	21	2	1	3
269.19	5	2,217	1	8	5	1	3
224.775	3	2,157	1	17	1	1	2.5
171.585	3	2,014	0	16	4	0	2
216.81	3	2,221	1	15	1	1	2
192.645	6	2,236	0	14	1	0	2
236.385	5	2,189	1	20	3	1	2
172.395	3	2,218	1	23	3	0	2
251.37	3	1,937	1	12	2	1	2
245.97	6	2,296	1	7	3	1	3
147.42	6	1,749	0	12	1	0	2
176.04	4	2,230	1	15	1	1	2
228.42	3	2,263	1	17	5	1	1.5
166.455	3	1,593	0	19	3	0	2.5
189.405	4	2,221	1	24	1	1	2
312.12	7	2,403	1	13	3	1	3
289.845	6	2,036	1	21	3	1	3
269.865	5	2,170	0	11	4	1	2.5
154.305	2	2,007	1	13	2	0	2
222.075	2	2,054	1	9	5	1	2
209.655	5	2,247	0	13	2	1	2
190.89	3	2,190	0	18	3	1	2
254.34	4	2,495	0	15	3	1	2
207.495	3	2,080	0	10	2	0	2
209.655	4	2,210	0	19	2	1	2
294.03	2	2,133	1	13	2	1	2.5
176.31	2	2,037	0	17	3	0	2
294.3	7	2,448	1	8	4	1	2
223.965	3	1,900	0	6	1	1	2
125.01	2	1,871	1	18	4	0	1.5
236.8035	4	2,583.9	0	17	5	1	2
164.1465	4	2,312.2	1	19	4	0	2
217.8495	3	2,498.1	1	12	3	0	2
192.213	2	2,406.8	1	16	2	0	2.5
125.874	2	2,362.8	1	28	1	0	1.5
220.887	2	2,328.7	0	12	1	1	2

APPENDIX J

Data Set 1 — Real Estate (concluded)

x_1	x_2	x_3	x_4	x_5	x_6	x_7	x_8	x_1	x_2	x_3	x_4	x_5	x_6	x_7	x_8
294.516	6	2,732.4	1	15	3	1	2	178.9695	3	2,442	0	10	4	1	2
244.5795	2	2,343	1	9	2	1	2.5	188.325	6	2,091.1	0	15	4	1	2
199.017	3	2,479.4	0	18	1	0	1.5	227.0835	4	2,886.4	1	8	4	1	2
239.9625	4	2,623.5	1	13	4	1	2	173.6235	4	2,131.8	0	14	2	1	2.5
263.169	4	2,318.8	1	14	3	1	2	188.325	5	2,311.1	1	20	5	0	1.5
188.082	2	1,886.5	1	8	4	1	1.5	310.797	8	2,908.4	1	9	4	1	2
243.729	6	2,744.5	1	7	4	1	2	293.6655	6	2,355.1	1	11	5	1	3
221.4945	4	2,280.3	1	18	3	1	2	178.9695	3	2,442	1	8	4	1	2
174.96	2	2,511.3	1	11	3	0	2	188.325	6	2,091.1	0	14	2	1	2.5
253.206	3	2,330.9	1	16	2	1	2	227.0835	4	2,886.4	1	20	5	0	1.5
155.3985	4	2,407.9	0	16	3	0	2	173.6235	4	2,131.8	1	9	4	1	2
186.7455	5	2,547.6	0	21	4	0	2.5	188.325	5	2,311.1	1	11	5	1	3

APPENDIX K

Data Set 2 — 1997 Major League Baseball

x_1 = Team
x_2 = Team batting average
x_3 = Team earned run average
x_4 = Number of stolen bases
x_5 = Errors committed
x_6 = Number of wins for the season
x_7 = Team salary ($)
x_8 = Team salary in $ millions
x_9 = Team attendance in millions
x_{10} = Playing surface (1 = artificial, 0 = grass)
x_{11} = League (1 = American, 0 = National)
x_{12} = Year
x_{13} = Average player salary ($)

x_1	x_2	x_3	x_4	x_5	x_6	x_7	x_8	x_9	x_{10}	x_{11}		x_{12}	x_{13}
Colorado	0.288	5.25	137	111	83	41,567,334	41.56733	3.888453	0	0		1989	512,804
San Diego	0.271	4.98	140	132	76	31,713,672	31.71367	2.089336	0	0		1990	578,930
Atlanta	0.27	3.18	108	114	101	52,171,000	52.171	3.463988	0	0		1991	891,188
Los Angeles	0.268	3.62	131	116	88	48,385,304	48.3853	3.318886	0	0		1992	1,084,408
Chicago Cubs	0.263	4.44	116	112	68	30,816,000	30.816	2.190308	0	0		1993	1,120,254
New York Mets	0.262	3.95	97	120	88	39,209,500	39.2095	1.766174	0	0		1994	1,188,679
Pittsburgh	0.262	4.28	160	131	79	12,174,166	12.17417	1.657022	1	0		1995	1,071,029
Houston	0.259	3.66	171	131	84	34,182,500	34.1825	2.046811	1	0		1996	1,176,967
Florida	0.259	3.83	115	116	92	53,490,000	53.49	2.364387	0	0		1997	1,383,578
San Francisco	0.258	4.39	121	125	90	44,121,713	44.12171	1.690831	0	0			
Montreal	0.258	4.14	75	132	78	18,460,500	18.4605	1.497609	1	0			
Philadelphia	0.255	4.85	92	108	68	30,681,500	30.6815	1.490638	1	0			
St. Louis	0.255	3.88	164	123	73	48,274,167	48.27417	2.658357	0	0			
Cincinnati	0.253	4.41	190	106	76	31,713,672	31.71367	1.785788	1	0			
Boston	0.291	4.85	68	135	78	40,011,351	40.01135	2.226136	0	1			
New York Yankees	0.287	3.84	99	104	96	64,989,577	64.98958	2.580445	0	1			
Cleveland	0.286	4.73	118	106	86	58,465,056	58.46506	3.40475	0	1			
Seattle	0.28	4.78	89	126	90	45,574,660	45.57466	3.198995	1	1			
Texas	0.274	4.69	72	121	77	42,913,425	42.91343	2.945228	0	1			
Chicago White Sox	0.273	4.73	106	127	80	41,899,500	41.8995	1.865222	0	1			
Anaheim	0.272	4.52	126	123	84	39,234,000	39.234	1.767324	0	1			
Minnesota	0.27	5.01	151	101	68	31,797,500	31.7975	1.411064	1	1			
Baltimore	0.268	3.91	63	97	98	62,961,399	62.9614	3.711132	0	1			
Kansas City	0.264	4.7	130	91	67	35,205,000	35.205	1.517638	0	1			
Milwaukee	0.26	4.22	103	121	78	26,688,736	26.68874	1.444027	0	1			
Oakland	0.26	4.58	71	122	65	13,594,000	13.594	1.261219	0	1			
Detroit	0.258	4.56	161	92	79	16,185,500	16.1855	1.365157	0	1			
Toronto	0.244	3.93	134	94	76	43,814,833	43.81483	2.589297	1	1			

APPENDIX L

Data Set 3 — Magazine Circulation

$x_1 =$ Name of magazine

$x_2 =$ Circulation (000)

$x_3 =$ Percent male readership

$x_4 =$ Percent female readership

$x_5 =$ Number of other magazines read by men

$x_6 =$ Number of other magazines read by women

$x_7 =$ Percent in-home readers

$x_8 =$ Median age of subscribers

$x_9 =$ Median income of subscribers ($)

$x_{10} =$ Percent of subscribers who are college graduates

$x_{11} =$ Black and white advertising cost per page ($)

$x_{12} =$ Color advertising cost per page ($)

x_1	x_2	x_3	x_4	x_5	x_6	x_7	x_8	x_9	x_{10}	x_{11}	x_{12}
Better Homes and Gardens	8,000	22	78	1.21	3.23	62	41	23,241	36	61,030	73,820
Business Week	845	72	28	4.85	2.1	37	39	30,884	68	23,120	35,140
Car and Driver	725	88	12	4.84	0.53	41	31	25,982	45	15,450	23,795
Cosmopolitan	2,250	17	83	1.19	4.26	56	28	22,785	46	21,535	28,980
Ebony	1,250	42	58	2.6	3.48	62	33	16,505	29	16,200	21,886
Family Circle	7,450	13	87	0.75	3.51	72	42	21,785	34	53,780	62,750
Field and Stream	2,000	79	21	5.38	1.79	49	34	24,337	29	22,240	33,760
Forbes	700	74	26	2.53	1.29	40	42	36,783	74	16,520	25,090
Fortune	670	71	29	4.01	1.96	29	40	35,204	72	10,760	30,040
Glamour	1,800	6	94	0.49	4.52	49	27	21,828	44	17,250	24,340
Golf Digest	1,025	82	18	2.47	0.99	59	43	32,949	54	17,750	26,625
Good Housekeeping	5,000	13	87	1.25	4.89	62	39	21,980	35	46,235	58,020
Harper's Bazaar	650	8	92	1.71	2.57	36	35	25,358	55	11,200	16,200
Hot Rod	850	78	22	6.12	1.33	49	27	23,056	24	12,750	20,400
House & Garden	1,000	19	81	2.78	7.72	47	41	23,726	39	17,290	25,430
House Beautiful	800	16	84	1.94	8.44	45	40	24,198	42	13,525	19,775
Ladies Home Journal	5,000	12	88	0.62	3.55	62	39	21,583	36	39,000	48,000
Mademoiselle	1,000	9	91	0.53	4.04	48	29	23,660	50	11,130	16,280
McCalls	6,200	12	88	0.55	3.19	62	40	20,690	32	48,670	59,830
Mechanix Illustrated	1,600	81	19	3.84	0.89	51	38	22,568	38	17,500	24,815
Money	1,000	58	42	4.01	2.45	46	37	31,587	58	16,450	25,740
Motor Trend	750	84	16	5.18	0.83	42	33	23,878	40	13,690	21,905
Ms.	450	16	84	0.65	4.26	51	30	24,107	56	6,500	7,845
National Enquirer	4,637	40	60	1.57	2.9	68	36	19,969	24	21,000	26,500
National Geographic	8,400	55	45	1.86	1.65	64	42	26,294	51	73,520	95,575
National Lampoon	580	72	27	6.78	1.47	39	25	22,888	49	6,700	9,900
Newsweek	2,950	62	38	4.12	3.17	45	36	26,719	53	40,930	63,850
Outdoor Life	1,500	82	18	4.17	1.4	51	35	23,596	29	16,520	28,475
Parents Magazine	1,650	22	78	1.08	4.13	43	29	20,779	37	22,240	36,960
People	2,350	40	60	4.19	6.5	48	32	23,971	40	43,775	56,425

APPENDIX L

Data Set 3 — Magazine Circulation (concluded)

x_1	x_2	x_3	x_4	x_5	x_6	x_7	x_8	x_9	x_{10}	x_{11}	x_{12}
Playboy	5,000	78	22	3.25	0.97	59	31	24,051	43	39,780	55,710
Playgirl	650	36	64	2.13	4.26	53	30	19,329	36	5,415	7,220
Popular Mechanics	1,600	81	19	5.81	1.65	50	38	25,474	36	18,966	26,932
Popular Science	1,800	80	20	3.97	1.15	49	37	26,542	44	18,910	26,820
Reader's Digest	17,900	44	56	1.38	1.75	75	46	21,802	34	81,399	97,700
Redbook	3,800	11	89	0.66	3.26	61	35	22,794	35	32,270	42,675
Road & Track	630	89	11	6.06	0.65	61	30	28,093	35	11,945	18,775
Rolling Stone	700	66	34	4.65	2.61	48	25	24,074	47	11,915	17,770
Scientific American	720	68	32	4.01	1.91	40	35	29,531	78	16,000	24,000
Seventeen	1,500	9	91	0.84	3.98	51	29	21,251	33	13,325	19,250
Sports Illustrated	2,250	80	20	5.25	1.66	53	32	26,275	46	34,720	54,165
The Star	3,400	35	65	1.02	1.99	72	35	19,156	20	17,400	21,350
Time	4,400	56	44	2.92	2.29	52	36	26,908	53	55,045	85,870
True Story	1,400	18	82	0.77	3.98	69	39	14,325	10	10,330	13,435
TV Guide	17,345	45	55	1.24	1.47	87	35	20,461	31	65,000	77,400
U.S. News and World Report	2,050	63	37	3.25	1.75	45	42	26,998	57	26,935	42,510
Vogue	950	11	89	0.88	5.75	40	31	23,452	48	12,500	18,000
Woman's Day	7,125	8	92	0.66	5.29	46	39	21,910	47	51,740	60,435

APPENDIX M

Data Set 4 — Northwest Ohio School Districts

x_1 = Name of district

x_2 = Number of students

x_3 = Mean family income in the district ($)

x_4 = Mean property value in the district ($)

x_5 = Percent of families receiving welfare

x_6 = Mean salary of classroom teachers ($)

x_7 = Amount spent per pupil ($)

x_8 = Mean daily attendance

x_9 = Percent passing 12th grade proficiency exam

x_1	x_2	x_3	x_4	x_5	x_6	x_7	x_8	x_9
Bluffton	1,132	24,487	62,678	1.8	31,221	2,130	95.7	85
Shawnee	2,472	29,777	130,910	2.6	34,860	2,570	94.7	73
Spencerville	1,026	23,161	51,645	5.4	30,155	2,262	95.5	68
Delphos	1,104	21,792	88,453	6.2	32,273	2,506	96.5	65
Elida	3,204	24,446	65,550	8.9	32,876	2,250	94.1	62
Lima	5,963	18,394	44,138	33.8	33,142	2,657	92.3	40
Northeastern	1,194	26,428	88,789	1.7	30,919	2,431	96.1	72
Ayersville	921	28,228	82,707	3.9	32,850	2,693	95.6	68
Defiance	3,046	23,812	56,333	11.2	34,750	2,438	94.2	63
Hicksville	990	22,448	56,411	7	34,224	2,351	95.7	59
Central	1,216	24,189	53,923	4.6	34,430	2,496	94.8	56
Berlin-Milan	1,593	25,223	76,878	4	32,166	2,564	96.1	77
Perkins	2,038	25,586	117,545	3.3	39,352	2,861	95.8	74
Huron	1,494	27,135	105,588	4.6	33,433	2,968	95.4	74
Margaretta	1,560	23,849	74,601	2.8	37,084	2,464	95.5	66
Sandusky	4,426	19,529	72,425	25.2	36,042	2,766	93	37
Kelleys Island	20	19,854	802,081	11.4	27,144	11,226	95	100
Pettisville	503	25,079	53,948	3.9	31,159	2,834	96.1	78
Wauseon	1,864	23,408	60,896	4.9	32,499	2,252	95.3	75
Evergreen	1,238	23,826	69,432	5.2	32,353	2,250	95	72
Archbold-Area	1,401	26,706	107,547	4.1	35,982	2,837	96.2	69
Pike-Delta-York	1,559	23,396	48,638	6.1	31,310	2,309	94.8	66
Gorham-Fayette	487	22,405	57,221	6.9	33,166	2,492	94.6	51
Swanton	1,725	24,596	69,320	6.3	33,690	2,615	94.9	50
Arlington	685	26,175	55,478	2.7	31,821	2,205	96.5	84
Vanlue	346	24,709	49,606	4.1	28,411	2,420	96.2	83
Liberty-Benton	954	28,718	77,503	1.5	30,330	2,063	96.7	78
Van Buren	840	28,964	151,992	1.8	33,447	2,584	96.4	75
Cory-Rawson	794	23,904	69,242	2.4	31,241	2,416	96.4	73
Arcadia	597	24,305	78,102	2.5	30,738	2,752	95.9	64
McComb	805	23,754	69,347	5.7	28,986	2,321	95.9	61
Findlay	5,758	24,269	92,648	7.6	35,879	2,860	94.9	60
Ada	855	23,029	52,655	5.3	28,479	2,380	95.9	69
Kenton	2,228	20,418	61,155	13.8	30,907	2,512	93.7	54

APPENDIX M

Data Set 4— Northwest Ohio School Districts (continued)

x_1	x_2	x_3	x_4	x_5	x_6	x_7	x_8	x_9
Liberty Center	1,009	24,723	57,685	4.1	30,904	2,431	95.8	82
Patrick Henry	1,176	23,061	63,134	5.2	31,895	2,552	95.9	75
Napoleon Area	2,331	25,304	84,245	6.6	32,773	2,422	94.6	73
Holgate	605	23,962	49,709	6	31,324	2,454	94.9	71
Monroeville	686	22,942	63,103	4.3	30,838	2,474	95.8	64
Bellevue	2,276	24,025	66,912	6.9	32,164	2,374	95.1	55
Willard	2,300	23,304	58,832	14.3	35,042	2,347	94.6	53
Norwalk	2,650	21,551	72,266	12.2	37,145	2,384	94	50
Ottawa Hills	933	45,723	122,356	0.2	43,256	4,150	95.7	95
Anthony Wayne	3,178	29,215	88,004	3.1	35,617	2,844	95.3	75
Sylvania	7,822	32,114	101,503	3.8	39,684	2,943	95.5	72
Maumee	3,009	27,604	117,921	3.9	41,634	3,933	95	69
Oregon	3,594	24,525	123,599	8.7	35,848	2,941	94.7	52
Washington	7,154	23,507	102,485	11.8	39,155	2,997	93.7	51
Springfield	3,575	26,048	98,346	12.2	34,437	2,774	93.8	49
Toledo	36,790	21,079	62,668	42.8	36,190	2,611	90.7	28
Benton Carroll Salem	2,063	23,899	237,206	4.7	42,734	3,444	95.6	81
Danbury	635	21,325	182,360	3.2	34,971	3,158	95.3	65
Genoa	1,584	25,321	53,120	4.8	34,661	2,845	95.9	65
Port Clinton	2,238	20,941	129,961	10.5	39,542	2,926	94.5	50
Put-in-Bay	70	19,266	426,419	1.4	30,242	7,824	94.5	33
Paulding	1,993	22,677	46,163	8.6	32,928	2,560	94.5	59
Ottoville	610	24,128	46,582	0.2	26,125	2,588	99.8	86
Columbus Grove	866	23,562	55,568	8.4	30,476	2,174	96.2	84
Kalida	775	24,456	44,267	0.7	28,962	2,274	96.8	81
Continental	792	23,625	37,277	10	28,945	2,225	95.5	79
Ottawa-Glandorf	1,749	25,363	64,288	6.5	31,185	2,154	96.5	77
Pandora-Gilboa	632	23,806	55,446	1.2	27,693	2,078	96.5	67
Leipsic	748	20,941	62,648	16.1	30,282	2,811	93.9	47
Gibsonburg	983	23,312	46,098	17.8	31,244	2,242	94.4	71
Lakota	1,332	22,678	55,933	10.5	30,765	2,306	95.2	66
Fremont	5,156	22,327	74,874	16.2	37,759	2,616	94.7	57
Woodmore	1,141	26,460	90,484	10.9	32,296	2,227	96.5	56
Clyde-Green Springs	2,368	23,854	55,724	7	33,998	2,383	94.6	47
Bettsville	347	22,103	37,269	6.1	27,466	2,394	95.8	83
Seneca East	1,183	22,656	50,895	4.8	29,940	2,435	95.9	80
Old Fort	540	23,208	50,712	19.3	28,195	2,743	96	78
Hopewell-Loudon	870	22,103	72,201	4.7	30,644	2,564	94.6	74
New Riegel	459	23,314	41,376	2.7	29,099	2,501	97	73
Tiffin	3,632	21,246	65,291	9	35,513	2,506	94.7	67
Fostoria	2,742	20,809	62,268	20.4	34,241	2,455	92.7	34
Van Wert	2,504	22,728	67,932	7.1	33,885	2,511	95.3	61
Edon-Northwest	744	23,035	38,462	2.7	30,833	1,916	95.1	73
Milcreek-West Unity	788	21,302	40,239	3.2	31,582	2,382	95.9	71
Bryan	2,266	22,607	81,152	4.2	32,643	2,706	95.2	69
North Central	757	21,871	59,396	2.9	31,978	2,349	95.6	68

APPENDIX M

Data Set 4 — Northwest Ohio School Districts (concluded)

x_1	x_2	x_3	x_4	x_5	x_6	x_7	x_8	x_9
Montpelier	1,172	20,787	44,383	8.2	33,243	2,654	94.8	67
Edgerton	767	22,429	54,040	4.1	28,975	2,470	95.9	61
Stryker	579	24,084	65,532	3.4	33,855	2,617	95.7	47
Perrysburg	3,839	32,773	97,888	2.6	40,320	3,011	96.1	98
Elmwood	1,237	22,179	47,644	7.5	30,434	2,643	95.2	68
Bowling Green	3,534	21,307	84,682	7.5	37,983	2,849	94.7	68
Otsego	1,643	24,614	57,601	5	36,065	2,539	95.4	64
Northwood	1,091	25,905	77,077	7.9	35,536	2,979	94.9	61
Eastwood	1,739	25,043	67,929	4.7	35,742	2,499	95.9	60
Lake	1,665	23,559	95,859	6.2	38,046	2,820	95.2	55
Rossford	2,087	25,360	123,725	7.2	39,476	3,258	94.9	54
North Baltimore	839	22,075	58,383	10.6	29,579	2,331	94.5	50
Upper Sandusky	1,801	21,063	68,348	3.9	32,778	2,267	95.6	62
Carey	915	21,658	51,497	6	30,968	2,513	95.5	59

APPENDIX N

Banking Data Set—Case

x_1 = Account balance in $

x_2 = Number of ATM transactions in the month

x_3 = Number of other bank services used

x_4 = Has a debit card (1 = yes, 0 = no)

x_5 = Receives interest on the account

x_6 = City where banking is done*

	x_1	x_2	x_3	x_4	x_5	x_6		x_1	x_2	x_3	x_4	x_5	x_6
1	1,756	13	4	0	1	2	31	1,958	6	2	1	0	2
2	748	9	2	1	0	1	32	634	2	7	1	0	4
3	1,501	10	1	0	0	1	33	580	4	1	0	0	1
4	1,831	10	4	0	1	3	34	1,320	4	5	1	0	1
5	1,622	14	6	0	1	4	35	1,675	6	7	1	0	2
6	1,886	17	3	0	1	1	36	789	8	4	0	0	4
7	740	6	3	0	0	3	37	1,735	12	7	0	1	3
8	1,593	10	8	1	0	1	38	1,784	11	5	0	0	1
9	1,169	6	4	0	0	4	39	1,326	16	8	0	0	3
10	2,125	18	6	0	0	2	40	2,051	14	4	1	0	4
11	1,554	12	6	1	0	3	41	1,044	7	5	1	0	1
12	1,474	12	7	1	0	1	42	1,885	10	6	1	1	2
13	1,913	6	5	0	0	1	43	1,790	11	4	0	1	3
14	1,218	10	3	1	0	1	44	765	4	3	0	0	4
15	1,006	12	4	0	0	1	45	1,645	6	9	0	1	4
16	2,215	20	3	1	0	4	46	32	2	0	0	0	3
17	137	7	2	0	0	3	47	1,266	11	7	0	0	4
18	167	5	4	0	0	4	48	890	7	1	0	1	1
19	343	7	2	0	0	1	49	2,204	14	5	0	0	2
20	2,557	20	7	1	0	4	50	2,409	16	8	0	0	2
21	2,276	15	4	1	0	3	51	1,338	14	4	1	0	2
22	1,494	11	2	0	1	1	52	2,076	12	5	1	0	2
23	2,144	17	3	0	0	3	53	1,708	13	3	1	0	1
24	1,995	10	7	0	0	2	54	2,138	18	5	0	1	4
25	1,053	8	4	1	0	3	55	2,375	12	4	0	0	2
26	1,526	8	4	0	1	2	56	1,455	9	5	1	1	3
27	1,120	8	6	1	0	3	57	1,487	8	4	1	0	4
28	1,838	7	5	1	1	3	58	1,125	6	4	1	0	2
29	1,746	11	2	0	0	2	59	1,989	12	3	0	1	2
30	1,616	10	4	1	1	2	60	2,156	14	5	1	0	2

*Cincinnati = 1.

Atlanta = 2.

Louisville = 3.

Erie, Pennsylvania = 4.

ANSWERS

to Odd-Numbered Chapter Exercises

CHAPTER 1

1. **a.** Interval
    b. Ratio
    c. Interval
    d. Nominal
    e. Ordinal
    f. Ratio
3. Answers will vary.
5. Qualitative data is not numerical, whereas quantitative data is numerical. Examples will vary by student.
7. Nominal, ordinal, interval, and ratio. Examples will vary.
9. A categorization is exhaustive if every object appears in some category.
11. Based on these sample findings, we can infer that 270/300, or 90 percent, of the executives would move.
13. Discrete variables can assume only certain values, but continuous variables can assume any values within some range. Examples will vary.
15. **a.** Township is a qualitative variable, the others are quantitative.
    b. Township is a nominal level variable, the others are ratio level variables.
17. **a.** The name of the magazine is a qualitative variable, the others are quantitative.
    b. The name of the magazine is a nominal level variable, the others are ratio level variables.

CHAPTER 2

1. $2^5 = 32, 2^6 = 64$
    $\therefore$ 6 classes
3. $\dfrac{\$567 - \$235}{1 + 3.322(\log 230)} = \dfrac{\$332}{8.846} = \$37.53$
    Suggest an interval of $40.
5. **a.** Using the formula $2^k \geq n$, we suggest 4 classes (although a minimum of 5 classes is usually preferred).
    b. Using formula (2-1), the suggested class interval would be 1.5, found by $(31 - 25)/4$. For ease of computations, 2.0 would be better.
    c. 24
    d.

	f	Relative Frequency
24 up to 26	2	.125
26 up to 28	8	.500
28 up to 30	4	.250
30 up to 32	2	.125
Total	16	1.000

e. The largest concentration of scores is in the 26 up to 28 class (8).

7. **a.**

Number of Shoppers	f
0 up to 3	9
3 up to 6	21
6 up to 9	13
9 up to 12	4
12 up to 15	3
15 up to 18	1
Total	51

b. The largest group of shoppers (21) shop at Food Queen 3, 4 or 5 times during a two-week period. Some customers visit the store only 1 time during the two weeks, but others shop as many as 15 times.

c.

Number of Shoppers	Percent of Total
0 up to 3	17.65
3 up to 6	41.18
6 up to 9	25.49
9 up to 12	7.84
12 up to 15	5.88
15 up to 18	1.96
Total	100.00

9. **a.** 620 to 629
    b. 5
    c. 621, 623, 623, 627, 629
11. **a.** 25
    b. one
    c. 38, 106
    d. 60, 61, 63, 63, 65, 65, 69
    e. No values
    f. 9
    g. 9
    h. 76
    i. 16
13.

Stem	Leaves
0	5
1	28
2	
3	0024789
4	12366
5	2

There were a total of 16 calls studied. The number of calls ranged from 5 to 52 received. Seven of the 16 subscribers received between 30 and 39 calls.

15. **a.** Histogram
 b. 100
 c. 5
 d. 28
 e. 0.28
 f. 12.5
 g. 13

17. **a.** 50
 b. 1.5 days
 c. Using lower limits on the *X*-axis:

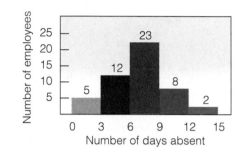

 d. *X* = 1.5, *Y* = 5
 e.

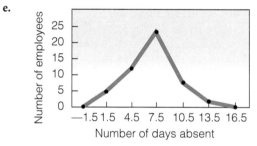

 f. For the 50 employees about half were absent between 6 up to 9 days. Five employees were absent less than 3 days, and two were absent 12 or more days.

19. **a.** 40
 b. 5
 c. 11 or 12
 d. about $18/hr
 e. about $9/hr
 f. about 75%

21. **a.** 5, 17
 b.

Days Absent	f	CF
0 up to 3	5	5
3 up to 6	12	17
6 up to 9	23	40
9 up to 12	8	48
12 up to 15	2	50

c.

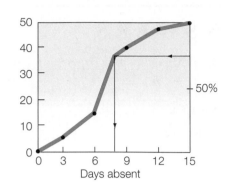

 d. about 8.7 days

23.
Corporation Performance

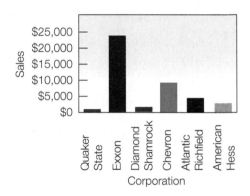

Exxon far exceeds the other corporations in sales. Quaker State and Diamond Shamrock are the two corporations with the least amount of 4th quarter sales.

25.
Homicides in Toledo, Ohio

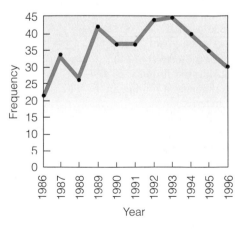

Homicides reached the highest number in 1993. They decreased from 1993 to 1996.

27.
Population Growth in the United States

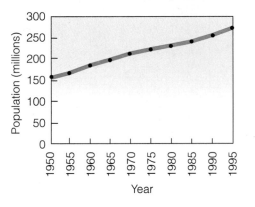

Population in the United States has increased steadily since 1950.

29. $2^6 = 64$ and $2^7 = 128$ Suggest 7 classes.

31. **a.** 5, because $2^4 = 16 < 25$ and $2^5 = 32 > 25$.

   b. 6, found by $\dfrac{(48-16)}{(48-16)/5}$ or 7, found by $\dfrac{(48-16)}{[1 + 3.322\log(25)]}$

   c. 15

   d.

Class		Frequency
15 up to 22	III	3
22 up to 29	⊬⊬ III	8
29 up to 36	⊬⊬ II	7
36 up to 43	⊬⊬	5
43 up to 50	II	2
		25

   e. It is fairly symmetrical, with most of the values between 22 and 36.

33. **a.** 70
   b. one
   c. 0, 145
   d. 30, 30, 32, 39
   e. 24
   f. 21
   g. 77
   h. 25

35. **a.** 56
   b. 10 (found by $60 - 50$)
   c. 55
   d. 17

37. **a.** \$36.60, found by $(\$265 - \$82)/5$.
   b. \$40.
   c.

\$ 80 up to \$120	8
120 up to 160	19
160 up to 200	10

\$200 up to 240	6
240 up to 280	1
Total	44

   d. The purchases ranged from a low of about \$80 to a high of about \$280. The concentration is in the \$120 up to \$160 class.

39.

Note: You could also use a bar chart. Repair represents the largest expense, and insurance and repairs represent over half the expenses.

41. unit = 0.10

3	76	149
3	77	
4	78	1
(2)	79	77
6	80	14
4	81	04
2	82	77

The lowest percent of on time is 76.1%, the largest is 82.7%. The typical airline is on time 79.7% of the time.

43.
Enrollment University at Toledo, 1979–1997

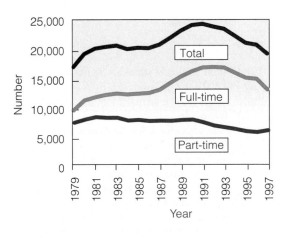

Enrollment increased up to 1992. From 1995 to 1997 enrollment decreased mostly because full-time students decreased.

45.

All others:
License 2.9%
Death/Gift 0.6
Property 0.4

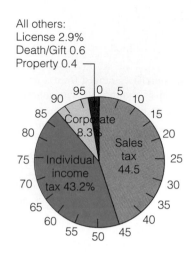

Sales tax and income tax dominate the total revenues for the state of Georgia.

47. There are 50 observations, so the recommended number of classes is 6. However, there are several states that have many more farms than the others, so it may be useful to have an open-ended class. One possible frequency distribution is:

Farms in USA

(000)	Frequency
0 up to 20	16
20 up to 40	13
40 up to 60	8
60 up to 80	6
80 up to 100	4
100 or more	3
Total	50

Twenty-nine of the 50 states, or 58 percent, have fewer than 40,000 farms. There are three states that have more than 100,000 farms. Most states have around 40,000 farms.

49. In 1990 the prices for a Toyota Camry and a Ford Taurus were about the same, a little more than $11,000 each. Since that time, the prices of both cars have increased, but the rate of increase of the Camry has been larger than the Taurus. The difference in the selling price between the two cars was the largest in 1996, about $6500. From 1996 to 1997 the selling price of a Camry decreased about $500, the only price decrease for either car during the 9-year period.

51.

```
Stem-and-leaf of Run-up   N = 95
Leaf Unit = 1.0

    1    −1  1
    3    −0  96
   14    −0  33332211000
   45     0  000111112222233333333333444444
  (26)    0  55555666667777788888899999
   24     1  0000011122334
   11     1  5666799
    4     2  24
    2     2
    2     3
    2     3
    2     4  2
    1     4
    1     5
    1     5
    1     6
    1     6
    1     7  0
```

The percentage of waste, or run-up, ranged from −11.0 percent to 70.0 percent. The middle value is 0.5 percent. Fifty-seven of the 95 observations are between 0 and 9 percent.

53. **a.** $2^5 = 32$

$$i = \frac{64.9896 - 12.1742}{1 + 3.322 \log(28)} = \frac{52.8154}{5.8075} = 9.09$$

Use an interval of 10.0.

Team Salary

($ million)	*f*	*CF*
10.0 up to 20.0	4	4
20.0 up to 30.0	1	5
30.0 up to 40.0	9	14
40.0 up to 50.0	9	23
50.0 up to 60.0	3	26
60.0 up to 70.0	2	28
	28	

1. The salaries ranged from about $10,000,000 per team to nearly $70,000,000 per team. Nine of the 28 teams or 36% had team salaries between $40,000,000 and $50,000,000.

2. There is a very large difference in the salaries, $60,000,000, but no team seems really out of line to all others.

b.

1. Forty percent of the teams have total salaries less than about $38,000,000.
2. 23 of the teams have total salaries of less than $50,000,000.
3. The five lowest teams pay less than $30,000,000.

55. a. The salaries are in $000.

```
1    26 1
4    27 146
11   28 1449999
14   29 059
29   30 122344677889999
40   31 11222335889
(12) 32 112234677889
42   33 112446889
33   34 22446789
25   35 05567889
17   36 001
14   37 0179
10   38 0
9    39 13456
4    40 3
3    41 6
2    42 7
1    43 2
```

1. The lowest salary ($000) is $26.1 and the largest is $43.2.
2. A typical salary is about $32.6.
3. Fourteen districts have salaries of less than $30, so 80 have salaries of 30.0 or more.
4. The teacher salaries in ($000) ranged from a low of $26.1 to a high of $43.2. The typical salary is about $32,000. There were 14 districts where the average salary was less than $30,000 and 4 where the salary was more than $40,000.

CHAPTER 3

1. $\mu = 5.4$, found by 27/5.
3. **a.** Mean = 7.0, found by 28/4.
   b. $(5 - 7) + (9 - 7) + (4 - 7) + (10 - 7) = 0$
5. 14.58, found by 43.74/3.
7. **a.** 15.4, found by 154/10.
   b. Population parameter, since it includes all the salespersons at Midtown Ford.
9. **a.** $54.55, found by $1,091/20.
   b. A sample statistic—assuming that the power company serves more than 20 customers.
11. $0.775, found by ($10 + $37.50 + $30)/100.
13. $11.50, found by ($400 + $500 + $1,400)/200 = $2,300/200.
15. **a.** No mode
    b. The given value would be the mode.
    c. 3 and 4 bimodal.
17. Median = 5, Mode = 5
19. **a.** Median = 2.9
    b. 2.9
21. 11.18, found by $\sqrt[5]{8(12)(14)(26)(5)} = 11.18$
23. .0284, or 2.84%, found by $\sqrt[46]{\dfrac{185}{51}} - 1$
25. $GM = \sqrt[12]{\dfrac{14.0}{3.9}} - 1$

    $1.112 - 1 = .112$ or 11.2%
27. Because the exact values in a frequency distribution are not known, the computed mean is an estimate.

29.

Class	f	X	fX
20 up to 30	7	25	175
30 up to 40	12	35	420
40 up to 50	21	45	945
50 up to 60	18	55	990
60 up to 70	12	65	780
	70		3310

$$\overline{X} = \frac{3310}{70} = 47.2857$$

31.

Class	f	X	fX
20 up to 30	1	25	25
30 up to 40	15	35	525
40 up to 50	22	45	990
50 up to 60	8	55	440
60 up to 70	4	65	260
	50		2240

$$\overline{X} = \frac{2240}{50} = 44.8$$

33.

Class	f	CF
0 up to 5	2	2
5 up to 10	7	9
10 up to 15	12	21
15 up to 20	6	27
20 up to 25	3	30
	30	

$$\text{Median} = 10 + \frac{\frac{30}{2} - 9}{12}(5) = 12.5$$

$$\text{Mode} = 12.5$$

35.

Amount	f	CF
$ 0 up to $ 2,000	4	4
$ 2,000 up to $ 4,000	15	19
$ 4,000 up to $ 6,000	18	37
$ 6,000 up to $ 8,000	10	47
$ 8,000 up to $10,000	4	51
$ 10,000 up to $12,000	3	54

a. $\text{Median} = \$4,000 + \dfrac{\frac{54}{2} - 19}{18}(\$2,000)$

$= \$4,889$

b. Mode = $5,000.00

37. a. Mean = 5, found by $(6 + 4 + 3 + 7 + 5)/5$.
Median is 5, found by rearranging the values and selecting the middle value.
b. Population, because all partners were included.
c. $\Sigma(X - \mu) = (6 - 5) + (4 - 5) + (3 - 5) + (7 - 5) + (5 - 5) = 0$.

39. $\bar{X} = \dfrac{545}{16} = 34.06$
Median = 37.50

41. 370.08, found by 18,504/50.

43. $\bar{X}_w = \dfrac{\$5(270) + \$6.50(300) + \$8.00(100)}{270 + 300 + 100} = \$6.12$

45. $\bar{X}_w = \dfrac{[15,300(4.5) + 10,400(3.0) + 150,600(10.2)]}{176,300}$

$= 9.28$

47. 3.38% found by $(3.25 + 3.51)/2$

49. Earthquake mean size = 7.0, found by 168.2/24.
Median size = 7.05.
Earthquake deaths: mean = 5,607.79; median = 1,100.
Mean for the size and the median for deaths because of all the extreme values listed.

51. 61.68 percent

53. 83.215

55.

Weights	f	X	fX	CF
130 up to 140	2	135	270	2
140 up to 150	8	145	1,160	10
150 up to 160	20	155	3,100	30
160 up to 170	15	165	2,475	45
170 up to 180	9	175	1,575	54
180 up to 190	7	185	1,295	61
190 up to 200	3	195	585	64
200 up to 210	2	205	410	66
	66		10,870	

a. $\bar{X} = \dfrac{10,870}{66} = 164.697$

b. $\text{Median} = 160 + \dfrac{33 - 30}{15}(10) = 162.0$

57.

Income	Alaska Percent	CF
Less than $20,000	18.3	18.3
$20,000 up to $30,000	21.2	39.5
30,000 up to 40,000	18.4	57.9
40,000 up to 50,000	15.1	73.0
50,000 up to 60,000	11.3	84.3
60,000 or greater	15.7	100.0

$$\text{Median} = \$30,000 + \dfrac{50.0 - 39.5}{18.4}(\$10,000) = \$35,706.52$$

The mode is $25,000.

59.

Monthly Mortgage	f	X	fX	CF
$ 100 up to $ 500	1	300	300	1
500 up to 900	9	700	6,300	10
900 up to 1,300	11	1,100	12,100	21
1,300 up to 1,700	23	1,500	34,500	44
1,700 up to 2,100	11	1,900	20,900	55
2,100 up to 2,500	4	2,300	9,200	59
2,500 up to 2,900	1	2,700	2,700	60
	60		86,000	

a. $\bar{X} = \dfrac{\$86,000}{60} = \$1,433$

b. $\text{Median} = \$1,300 + \dfrac{30 - 21}{23}(\$400) = \$1,456.52$

61. Answers will vary. The paragraphs should discuss issues such as: The average is higher for part-time nurses compared to full-time nurses. This may be because there are not as many part-time nurses. Therefore, when you calculate the mean, it will be higher. Also, as the number of beds increases, the average hourly wage increases. Again, this could be because there are not many hospitals with 500 or more beds. On the other hand, the lowest average is the hospital located in the rural setting. The type of hospital dictates the average, too. The private, nonprofit hospital has a greater hourly wage compared to the public hospital.

63. Johnson & Johnson:

$$\overline{X}_w = \frac{1(6) + 2(10) + 3(7)}{23} = \frac{47}{23} = 2.04$$

Pepsico:

$$\overline{X}_w = \frac{1(10) + 2(7) + 3(6)}{23} = \frac{42}{23} = 1.83$$

The Pepsico stock has the better rating.

65. **a.** $\overline{X} = \$221.1$ and the median is $\$213.57$ (answers in 000). Either measure is acceptable.
  b. $\overline{X} = 3.8$, median $= 4$.
  c. $\overline{X} = 2.08$, median $= 2$.
  d. $\overline{X} = 14.6$ miles, and the median is 15.0 miles.
67. **a.** $\overline{X} = 3{,}048{,}000$, and the median is 1,600,000. The median is more representative. The two large values distort the mean.
  b. $\overline{X} = \$26{,}622{,}000$, and the median is $\$17{,}625{,}000$. Again the median is the more representative.
  c. $\overline{X} = 36{,}629{,}000$, and the median is 26,722,000. The median is more representative.

CHAPTER 4

1. **a.** 7, found by $10 - 3$.
  b. 6, found by 30/5.
  c. 2.4, found by 12/5.
  d. The difference between the highest number sold (10) and the smallest number sold (3) is 7. On the average the number of service reps on duty deviates by 2.4 from the mean of 6.
3. **a.** 30, found by $54 - 24$.
  b. 38, found by 380/10.
  c. 7.2 found by 72/10.
  d. The difference of 54 and 24 is 30. On the average the number of minutes required to install a door deviates 7.2 minutes from the mean of 38 minutes.
5. **a.** 15, found by $41 - 26$.
  b. 33.9, found by 339/10.
  c. 4.12, found by 41.2/10.
  d. The ratings deviates 4.12 from the mean of 33.9 on the average.
7. **a.** 5
  b. 4.4, found by

$$\frac{(8 - 5)^2 + (3 - 5)^2 + (7 - 5)^2 + (3 - 5)^2 + (4 - 5)^2}{5}$$

9. **a.** $2.77
  b. 1.26, found by

$$\frac{\begin{array}{c}(2.68 - 2.77)^2 + (1.03 - 2.77)^2 + (2.26 - 2.77)^2 \\ + (4.30 - 2.77)^2 + (3.58 - 2.77)^2\end{array}}{5}$$

11. **a.** Range: 7.3, found by $11.6 - 4.3$. Arithmetic mean: 6.94, found by 34.7/5. Variance: 6.5944, found by 32.972/5. Standard deviation: 2.568, found by $\sqrt{6.5944}$.
  b. Dennis has a higher mean return ($11.76 > 6.94$). However, Dennis has greater spread in their returns on equity ($16.89 > 6.59$).
13. **a.** $\overline{X} = 4$

$$s^2 = \frac{(7 - 4)^2 + \cdots + (3 - 4)^2}{5 - 1} = 5.5$$

  b. $s^2 = \dfrac{102 - \dfrac{(20)^2}{5}}{5 - 1} = 5.50$

  c. $s = 2.3452$
15. **a.** $\overline{X} = 38$

$$s^2 = \frac{(28 - 38)^2 + \cdots + (42 - 38)^2}{10 - 1} = 82.6667$$

  b. $s^2 = \dfrac{15{,}184 - \dfrac{(380)^2}{10}}{10 - 1} = 82.6667$

  c. $s = 9.0921$
17. **a.** $\overline{X} = 124$

$$s^2 = \frac{(124 - 124)^2 + \cdots + (121 - 124)^2}{10 - 1} = 4.6667$$

  b. $s^2 = \dfrac{153{,}802 - \dfrac{(1240)^2}{10}}{10 - 1} = 4.6667$

  c. $s = \sqrt{4.6667} = 2.1602$
19. **a.** 25, found by $25 - 0$.
  b. 5.331, found by

$$\sqrt{\frac{5{,}637.50 - \dfrac{(380)^2}{30}}{30 - 1}}$$

  c. 28.42, found by 5.331^2
21. **a.** 12 minutes, found by $14 - 2$.
  b. 2.5959 minutes, found by:

$$\sqrt{\frac{2{,}594 - \dfrac{(312)^2}{42}}{42 - 1}}$$

  c. 6.7387, found by $(2.5959)^2$.
23. About 69%, found by $1 - 1/(1.8)^2$.
25. **a.** About 95%.
  b. 47.5%, 2.5%.
27. 8.06%, found by $(.25/3.10)(100)$.
29. **a.** Because the two series are in different units of measurement.
  b. P.E. ratio 16.51%.
    ROI 20.8% Less spread in the P.E. ratios.
31. Symmetrical, because mean, median, and mode are equal. The coefficient of skewness is zero.

33. **a.** Positively skewed.
   b. 2.949. A large positive skewness.
35. Median = 53, found by $(11 + 1)(\frac{1}{2})$ ∴ 6 value in from lowest.
   $Q_1 = 49$, found by $(11 + 1)(\frac{1}{4})$ ∴ 3 value in from lowest.
   $Q_3 = 55$, found by $(11 + 1)(\frac{3}{4})$ ∴ 9 value in from lowest.
37. **a.** $Q_1 = 33.25$, $Q_3 = 50.25$
   b. $D_2 = 27.8$, $D_8 = 52.6$
   c. $P_{67} = 47$
39. **a.** 350
   b. $Q_1 = 175$, $Q_3 = 930$
   c. $930 - 175 = 755$
   d. Less than 0, or more than about 2060.
   e. There are no outliers.
   f. The distribution is positively skewed.
41.

```
        +--------------------------+
        |                          |
--------|    |          |         |---------------
        |                          |
-----+--------+---------+---------+---------+---------+---
   14.0     21.0     28.0      35.0      42.0      49.0
```

   The distribution is somewhat positively skewed. Note that dashed line above 35 is longer than below 18.
43. Line 2
45. 239.2 and 240.8
47. 239.9, 240.1
49. 1.6, found by $\dfrac{3.9}{242.9}(100)$.
51. 9, found by 3^2.
53. Negatively skewed. The mean is smaller than the median. The longer tail is to the left.
55. **a.** 55, found by $72 - 17$.
   b. 14.4, found by 144/10, where $\overline{X} = 43.2$.
   c. 17.6245.
57. **a.** Population.
   b. 183.47.
   c. 94.92%.
59. Range is $25 - 0 = 25$.
   $$s = \sqrt{\dfrac{13,637.50 - \dfrac{(910)^2}{70}}{69}} = 5.118$$
61. $Q_1 = 44.25$, $Q_3 = 68.5$, and the median is 55.50. The distribution is approximately symmetric. The box plot is as follows.

```
-------------------|       +       |----------------
---+---------+---------+---------+---------+---------+-----
   24        36        48        60        72        84 miles
```

   The above results are found using MINITAB.
63. The distribution is positively skewed. The first quartile is approx. $20 and the third quartile is approx. $90. There is one outlier located at $255. The median is about $50.

65. **a.** -18.6434, 78.76104, found by $30.05882 \pm 2(24.35111)$.
   b. 81%, found by $\dfrac{24.35111}{30.05882}(100)$.
   The standard deviation is 81% of the mean.
   c. Positive skewness because the mean is greater than the median.
67. **a.** $\overline{X} = \dfrac{857.90}{50} = 17.158$, median = 16.35
   b. $s = \sqrt{\dfrac{20,206.73 - \dfrac{(857.90)^2}{50}}{50 - 1}} = 10.58$
   c. $17.158 \pm (1.5)(10.58) = 1.288$ up to 33.028
   d. $17.158 \pm (2)(10.58) = 17.158 \pm 21.16 = -4.002$, 38.318
   e. $CV = \dfrac{10.58}{17.158}(100) = 61.66$
   f. $sk = \dfrac{3(17.158 - 16.35)}{10.58} = 0.23$
   g. $L_P = (50 + 1)\dfrac{25}{100} = 12.75$ $Q_1 = 7.825$
   $L_P = (50 + 1)\dfrac{75}{100} = 38.25$ $Q_3 = 27.400$

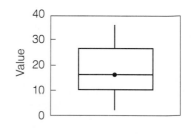

   h. The distribution is nearly symmetrical. The mean is 17.158, the median is 16.35 and the standard deviation is 10.58. About 75 percent of the companies have a value less than 27.4, and 25 percent have a value less than 7.825.
69. **a.** $\overline{X} = \$67.26$, median = $63.62
   $s = \$21.46$, $Q_1 = \$49.72$, and $Q_3 = \$78.28$
   $sk = \dfrac{3(67.26 - 63.62)}{21.46} = 0.51$
   There is some positive skewness and one outlier. This is the stock price of JP Morgan.

b. The standard deviation is $21.46. The coefficient of variation is 31%.

c. Answers will vary.

71. **a. 1.** $\overline{X} = 38.58$ ($ million), median = 39.62 ($ million), $s = 13.74$

   2. $sk = \dfrac{3(38.58 - 39.62)}{13.74} = -0.23$

   3. Minimum team salary is 12.17 and the maximum is 64.99. $Q_1 = 31.04$ and $Q_3 = 47.60$

```
Character Boxplot
   12.17              31.    39.6  47.60              65
     ↓                 ↓      ↓     ↓                  ↓
                    -------------------
     -----------------I    +     I-----------------
                    -------------------
     +---------+---------+---------+---------+---------+------Sal-Mil
    10        20        30        40        50        60
```

   4. A typical team salary is about 40 million dollars. The distribution is symmetrical and the team salaries range from 12.17 million dollars to 64.99 million dollars.

   b. 1. $\overline{X} = 2.26$ million, median = 2.07 million, $s = 0.79$ million

   2. $sk = \dfrac{3(2.26 - 2.07)}{0.79} = -0.72$

   The distribution is negatively skewed.

   3. The largest attendance is 3.89 million and the smallest is 1.26 million. $Q_1 = 1.55$ and $Q_3 = 2.87$.

```
Character Boxplot
  1.26   1.55        2.1   2.87             3.89
    ↓      ↓          ↓     ↓                ↓
         --------------------
  -------I     +     I--------------------
         --------------------
  --------+---------+---------+---------+-------Attendance
        1.50      2.00      2.50      3.00      3.50
```

   4. The typical attendance was a little more than 2.0 million. The attendance ranged from 1.26 million up to almost 6.5 million spectators. The standard deviation was 0.79 million.

73. **a. 1.** $\overline{X} = \$33,181$, median = 32,708, and $s = 3,549$

   2. $sk = \dfrac{3(33,181 - 32,708)}{3,549} = 0.40$

   3. The largest salary is $43,256 and the smallest is $26,125. $Q_1 = 30,816$ and $Q_3 = 35,519$. There are two outliers, in the positive direction.

```
Character Boxplot
        26,125     30,816    35,519              43,256
          ↓          ↓         ↓                   ↓
                  ---------------
        -------------I    +     I----------------- * *
                  ---------------
   +--------+---------+---------+---------+---------+------Salary
 24500    28000     31500     35000     38500     42000
```

4. The typical teacher salary is about $33,000. The salaries range from $26,125 up to $43,256. There are two outliers on the positive side.

b. 1. $\overline{X} = 2134$, median = 1227, and $s = 3895$

   2. $sk = \dfrac{3(2134 - 1227)}{3895} = 0.70$

   3. The range of students is quite large. The smallest number of students in a district is 20 and the largest is 36,790. The box plot shows several outliers and extreme outliers. $Q_1 = 794$ and $Q_3 = 2282$.

```
Character Boxplot
  794 2282                                        36,790
   ↓ ↓                        Approximate            ↓
   ---
  -I+I---***OO                                       O
   ---
  +---------+---------+---------+---------+---------+------Students
  0        7000     14000     21000     28000     35000
```

4. There is a wide range in the data. The number of students in the Toledo system is much larger than the others. This increases the standard deviation.

CHAPTER 5

1.

	Person	
Outcome	1	2
1	A	A
2	A	F
3	F	A
4	F	F

3. **a.** 176, found by $\dfrac{6}{34}$

   b. Empirical.

5. **a.** The experiment is asking the 500 citizens whether they favor or oppose widening Indiana Avenue to three lanes.

   b. Possible outcomes include 321 favor the widening, 387 favor the widening, 444 favor the widening, and so on.

   c. Answers will vary, but two possibilities are: a majority favor the widening, which would be 251 or more, and more than 300 favor the widening.

7. **a.** Empirical.

   b. Classical.

   c. Classical.

   d. Subjective, because this is someone's opinion.

9. **a.** $13/52 = .25$.

   b. $1/52 = .019$.

   c. Classical.

11. **a.** The survey of 40 people about abortion.

   b. 26 or more respond yes, for example.

c. $10/40 = .25.$

d. Empirical.

e. The events are not equally likely, but they are mutually exclusive.

13. a. Answers will vary. Here are some possibilities: 123, 124, 125, 999.

b. $\left(\dfrac{1}{10}\right)^3$

c. Classical.

15. $P(A \text{ or } B) = P(A) + P(B)$
$$= .30 + .20$$
$$= .50$$
$P(\text{neither}) = 1 - .50 = .50.$

17. a. $102/200 = .51$

b. $.49$, found by $61/200 + 37/200 = .305 + .185.$ Special rule of addition.

19. a. 80%, found by 50% + 30%.

b. 80%, found by 100% − 20%.

21. Events A and C; B and C are mutually exclusive. Events B and C are complements.

23. $P(A \text{ or } B) = P(A) + P(B) - P(A \text{ and } B)$
$$= .20 + .30 - .15$$
$$= .35$$

25. When two events are mutually exclusive, it means that if one occurs the other event cannot occur. Therefore, the probability of their joint occurrence is zero.

27. a. $.65$ found by $.35 + .40 - .10.$

b. A joint probability.

c. No, an executive might read more than one magazine.

29. $P(A \text{ and } B) = P(A) \times P(B|A)$
$$= .40 \times .30$$
$$= .12$$

31. $.90$, found by $(.80 + .60) - .5.$
$.10$, found by $(1 - .90).$

33. a. $P(A_1) = 3/10 = .30$

b. $P(B_1|A_2) = 1/3 = .33$

c. $P(B_2 \text{ and } A_3) = 1/10 = .10$

35. a. A contingency table.

b. $.27$, found by $300/500 \times 135/300.$

c. The tree diagram would appear as:

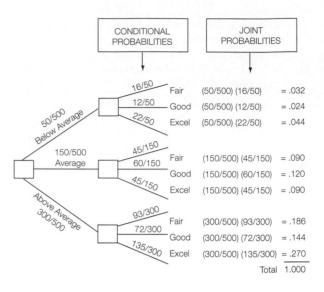

37. Probability the first presentation wins $= 3/5 = .60.$
Probability the second presentation wins $= 2/5 (3/4) = .30.$
Probability the third presentation wins $= (2/5)(1/4)(3/3) = .10.$

39. $.4286$, found by:
$$P(A_1|B_1) = \frac{P(A_1) \times P(B_1|A_1)}{P(A_1) \times P(B_1|A_1) + P(A_2) \times P(B_1|A_2)}$$
$$= \frac{.60 \times .05}{(.60 \times .05) + (.40 \times .10)}$$

41. $.5645$, found by:
$$P(\text{night}|\text{win}) = \frac{P(\text{night})P(\text{win}|\text{night})}{P(\text{night})P(\text{win}|\text{night}) + P(\text{day})P(\text{win}|\text{day})}$$
$$= \frac{(.70)(.50)}{[(.70)(.50)] + [(.30)(.90)]}$$

43. $.1053$, found by:
$$P(\text{cash})|> \$50) = \frac{P(\text{cash}) \, P(> \$50|\text{cash})}{\begin{array}{l} P(\text{cash}) \, P(> \$50|\text{cash}) \\ + P(\text{check}) \, P(> \$50|\text{check}) \\ + P(\text{charge}) \, P(> \$50|\text{charge}) \end{array}}$$
$$= \frac{(.30)(.20)}{[(.30)(.20)] + [(.30)(.90)] + [(.40)(.60)]}$$

45. a. 78,960,960

b. 840, found by $(7)(6)(5)(4)$. That is $7!/3!$.

c. 10, found by $5!/3!2!$.

47. 210, found by $(10)(9)(8)(7)/(4)(3)(2).$

49. 120, found by $5!$.

51. 10,897,286,400, found by $_{15}P_{10} = (15)(14)(13)(12)(11)(10)(9)(8)(7)(6).$

53. a. Asking teenagers their reactions to a newly developed soft drink.
  b. Answers will vary. One possibility is more than half of the respondents like it.
55. Subjective.
57. 3/6 or 1/2, found by 1/6 + 1/6 + 1/6. Classical.
59. a. The likelihood an event will occur, assuming that another event has already occurred.
  b. The collection of one or more outcomes of an experiment.
  c. A measure of the likelihood that two or more events will happen concurrently.
61. a. .8145, found by $(.95)^4$.
  b. Special rule of multiplication.
  c. P(A and B and C and D) = P(A) $\times$ P(B) $\times$ P(C) $\times$ P(D).
63. a. .08, found by .80 $\times$ .10.
  b.

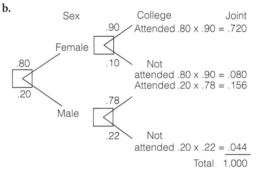

  c. Yes, because all the possible outcomes are shown on the tree diagram.
65. .99, found by 57/100 + 40/100 + 2/100.
67. All hit = .4096, found by $(.80)^4$. None hit = .0016, found by $(.20)^4$.
69. a. .3818, found by (9/12)(8/11)(7/10).
  b. .6182, found by 1 − .3818.
71. a. .5467, found by 82/150.
  b. .76, found by (39/150) + (75/150).
  c. .6267, found by 82/150 + 39/150 − 27/150. General rule of addition.
  d. .3293, found by 27/82.
  e. .2972, found by (82/150)(81/149).
73. $P(\text{poor}|\text{profit}) = \dfrac{(.10)(.20)}{[(.10)(.20)] + [(.60)(.80)] + [(.30)(.60)]}$

  $= .0294$
75. a. P(pizza or soft drink)

  = P(pizza) P(no drink) + P(no pizza) P(drink)

  $= \left(\dfrac{1}{50}\right)\left(\dfrac{9}{10}\right) + \left(\dfrac{49}{50}\right)\left(\dfrac{1}{10}\right) = .116$

  b. $P(\text{no prize}) = \left(\dfrac{9}{10}\right)\left(\dfrac{49}{50}\right) = .882$

  c. P(no prize on 3 visits) = $(.882)^3$ = .686
  d. P(at least one prize) = 1 − P(no prize) = 1 − .686 = .314
77. 24, found by 4!.
79. .4545, found by:

  $$\dfrac{(.50)(.625)}{(.50)(.625) + (.50)(.75)} = \dfrac{.3125}{.6875}$$

81. Yes. 256 is found by 2^8.
83. 2,520, found by:

  $$_7P_5 = \dfrac{7!}{(7-5)!}$$

85. .9744, found by 1 − $(.40)^4$.
87. a. .185, found by (.15)(.95) + (.05)(.85).
  b. .0075, found by (.15)(.05).
89. a. P(F and >60) = .25, found by solving with the general rule of multiplication:
  P(F) · P(>60|F) = (.5)(.5)
  b. 0
  c. .3333, found by 1/3.
91. a. .3034, found by 18.9/62.3.
  b. .7047, found by 5.8/62.3 + 43.4/62.3 − 5.3/62.3.
  c. .3346, found by $\dfrac{4.3 + 2.6 + 1.7}{12.5 + 8.0 + 5.2}$.
  d. $P(F) = \dfrac{8.2 + 5.4 + 3.5}{43.4} = .3940$

  $P(R) = \dfrac{4.3 + 2.6 + 1.7}{18.9} = .4550$

  Therefore, this is a repeat offender.
  e. .4853, found by $\left(\dfrac{43,400}{62,300}\right)\left(\dfrac{43,399}{62,299}\right)$.
93. For the system to operate, both components in the series must work. The probability they both work is 0.81, found by P(A) $\times$ P(B) = (.90)(.90).
95. 1/3,628,800
97. See diagram below.
  a. P(Buys) = P(S)P(Buy|S) + P(NS)P(Buy|NS)

  = (.05)(.01) + (.95)(.005) = .00525

  b. $P(S|\text{Buy}) = \dfrac{(.05)(.01)}{(.05)(.01) + (.95)(.005)} = .0952$

  c. $P(S|\text{Not buy}) = \dfrac{(.05)(.99)}{(.05)(.99) + (.95)(.995)} = .0498$

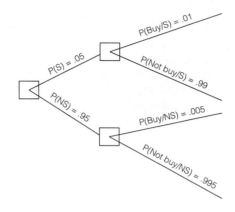

$P(Buy/S) = .01$

$P(S) = .05$

$P(Not\ buy/S) = .99$

$P(NS) = .95$

$P(Buy/NS) = .005$

$P(Not\ buy/NS) = .995$

99. a. P(male) = 140/182 = .7692

b. P(35 and 54) = 112/182 = .6154

c. P(male and 35 and 54) = $\frac{87}{182}$ = .4780

d. P(female and over 54) = $\frac{3}{182}$ = .0165

e. P(male or 35 and 54) = $\frac{140}{182} + \frac{112}{182} - \frac{87}{182}$

= .9066

f. P(female or over 54) = $\frac{42}{182} + \frac{29}{182} - \frac{3}{182}$

= .3736

g. P(male | under 35) = $\frac{27}{41}$ = .6585

h. P(male | over 54) = $\frac{26}{29}$ = .8966

i. P(over 54 | male) = $\frac{26}{140}$ = .1857

j. P(over 54 | female) = $\frac{3}{42}$ = .0714

k. P(M) = $\frac{140}{182}$ = .769   P(M | 35 to 54) = $\frac{87}{112}$ = .777

Probabilities are very close, they could be independent.

l. P(F) = $\frac{42}{182}$ P(F | over 54) = $\frac{3}{29}$ = .103

The events are not independent.

m. No, there are some members that are both male and over 54.

n. Yes. You must either be male or female.

101. a.

	Attendance			
	< 1.5 million	1.5 up to 2.5	2.5 or More	Total
Losing	6	7	3	16
Winning	0	5	7	12
	6	12	10	28

1. P(win) = $\frac{12}{28}$ = .4286

2. P(win or 2.5 or more) = $\frac{12}{28} + \frac{10}{28} - \frac{7}{28}$ = $\frac{15}{28}$ = .5357

3. P(win | 2.5 or more) = 0.70

4. P(losing and <1.5) = $\frac{6}{28}$ = .2143

b.

	Grass	Artificial Turf	Total
Losing	10	6	16
Winning	10	2	12
	20	8	28

1. P(Turf) = $\frac{8}{28}$ = .2857

2. P(W | Grass) = $\frac{10}{20}$ = .50

P(W | Turf) = $\frac{2}{8}$ = .25

3. P(Win or Turf) = $\frac{12}{28} + \frac{8}{28} - \frac{2}{28} = \frac{18}{28}$

= .6429

103. a. The first step is to group the 94 school districts by the percent of students on welfare.

Welfare Group	Frequency	Mean Percent Passing
Low	43	72.0
Moderate	32	64.0
High	19	54.0
Total	94	66.0

To explain these values, there were 19 districts in which the percent on welfare was more than 10 percent. The mean passing rate in these 19 schools was 54.0.

1. From the above chart, among the 94 districts the mean percent passing is 66.0. So we estimate the probability that a randomly selected student passes the exam is 0.66.

2. From the above chart, among the Low group, 72 percent passed the test. So we estimate the probability of passing the exam as 0.72.

3. The probability a student from a high welfare district passes is 0.54

4. First, to find the probability that a student is from a moderate district and failed the exam, we multiply the likelihood of being from the moderate group and failed. That is 32/94 = 0.34 times the probability a student in the moderate group fails (1 − probability he or she passes = 1 − 0.66 = 0.34). The result is 0.34 × 0.34 = 0.12. To find the probability a student failed or is from the moderate group: P(Moderate or Fail) = P(Moderate) + P(Fail) − P(Moderate and Fail) = 0.34 + .034 − 0.12 = 0.56.

b. First, we create the following table, which shows the districts by welfare and size.

Welfare	Size of District			Total
	Small	Medium	Large	
Low	22	17	4	43
Moderate	9	18	5	32
High	5	7	7	19
Total	36	42	16	94

1. $P(\text{Small}) = \dfrac{36}{94}(100) = 38\%$

2. $P(\text{Low/Small}) = \dfrac{22}{36}(100) = 61\%$

3. $P(\text{Small and Low}) = \dfrac{22}{94}(100) = 23\%$

4. $P(\text{Small or Low}) = \dfrac{36}{94} + \dfrac{43}{94} - \dfrac{22}{94} = \dfrac{57}{94}$

$= 0.61$

5. $P(\text{3 Medium}) = \left(\dfrac{42}{94}\right)\left(\dfrac{41}{93}\right)\left(\dfrac{40}{92}\right) = 0.0856$

CHAPTER 6

1. Mean = 1.3, variance = .81, found by:

$\mu = \Sigma XP(X) = 0(.20) + 1(.40) + 2(.30) + 3(.10)$

$= 1.3$

$\sigma^2 = \Sigma(X - \mu)^2 P(X)$

$= (0 - 1.3)^2(.2) + (1 - 1.3)^2(.4)$

$+ (2 - 1.3)^2(.3) + (3 - 1.3)^2(.1)$

$= .81$

3. a. The second, or middle, one.
b. .2, .4, .9
c. $\mu = 14.5$, variance = 27.25, found by:

$\mu = 5(.1) + 10(.3) + 15(.2) + 20(.4) = 14.5$

$\sigma^2 = (5 - 14.5)^2(.1) + (10 - 14.5)^2(.3)$

$+ (15 - 14.5)^2(.2) + (20 - 14.5)^2(.4)$

$= 27.25$

$\sigma = 5.22$, found by $\sqrt{27.25}$

5. $\mu = 0(.3) + 1(.4) + 2(.2) + 3(.1)$

$= 1.1$

$\sigma^2 = (0 - 1.1)^2(.3) + (1 - 1.1)^2(.4)$

$+ (2 - 1.1)^2(.2) + (3 - 1.1)^2(.1)$

$= 0.89$

$\sigma = .943$.

7. a. .20
b. .55
c. .95
d. $\mu = 48$, found by:
0(.45) + 10(.30) + 100(.20) + 500(.05)
$\sigma^2 = 12{,}226$, found by:

$(0 - 48)^2(.45) + (10 - 48)^2(.3)$

$+ (100 - 48)^2(.2) + (500 - 48)^2(.05)$

$\sigma = 110.57$, found by $\sqrt{12{,}226}$

9. a. 0, 1, 2, 3
b.

Number of Minority	Probability
0	.1667
1	.5000
2	.3000
3	.0333

c. .5, .8333, .3333
d. $\mu = 0(.1667) + 1(.5) + 2(.30) + 3(.0333)$

$= 1.1999$

$\sigma^2 = (0 - 1.1999)^2(.1667) + (1 - 1.1999)^2(.5)$

$+ (2 - 1.1999)^2(.3) + (3 - 1.1999)^2(.0333)$

$= 0.5599$

$\sigma = 0.7483$

11. a. $P(2) = \dfrac{4!}{2!(4 - 2)!}(.25)^2(.75)^{4-2} = .2109$

b. $P(3) = \dfrac{4!}{3!(4 - 3)!}(.25)^3(.75)^{4-3} = .0469$

13. a.

X	P(X)
0	.064
1	.288
2	.432
3	.216

b. $\mu = 1.8$

$\sigma^2 = 0.72$

$\sigma = \sqrt{0.72} = .8485$

15. a. .2668, found by $P(2) = \dfrac{9!}{(9 - 2)!2!}(.3)^2(.7)^7$

b. .1715, found by $P(4) = \dfrac{9!}{(9-4)!4!}(.3)^4(.7)^5$

c. .0404, found by $P(0) = \dfrac{9!}{(9-0)!0!}(.3)^0(.7)^9$

17. a. .2824, found by $P(0) = \dfrac{12!}{(12-0)!0!}(.10)^0(.9)^{12}$

b. .3766, found by $P(1) = \dfrac{12!}{(12-1)!1!}(.10)^1(.9)^{11}$

c. .2301, found by $P(2) = \dfrac{12!}{(12-2)!2!}(.10)^2(.9)^{10}$

d. $\mu = 1.2$, found by $12(.10)$
$\sigma = 1.0392$, found by $\sqrt{1.08}$

19. a. Number of production employees absent.
b. Discrete, because the number absent can only assume certain values, such as 1, 2, 3, and so on. There cannot be a fractional number of employees absent on a particular day.
c. .349, found by referring to Appendix A, an n of 10, an X of 0, and a π of 0.10.
d.

X	P(X)
0	.349
1	.387
2	.194
3	.057
4	.011
5	.001

e. $\mu = 1.00$, found by $n\pi = (10)(.10)$
$\sigma^2 = .90$, found by $n\pi(1-\pi) = (10)(.10)(.90)$
$\sigma = .949$, found by $\sqrt{.90}$

21. a. .296, found by using Appendix A with n of 8, π of .30, and X of 2.
b. $P(X \le 2) = .058 + .198 + .296$

$$= .552$$

c. .448, found by $P(X \ge 3) = 1 - P(X \le 2) = 1 - .552$.

23. a. .387, found from Appendix A with n of 9, π of .90, and an X of 9.
b. $P(X < 5) = .001$
c. .992, found by $1 - .008$
d. .947, found by $1 - .053$

25. $P(2) = \dfrac{[_6C_2][_4C_1]}{_{10}C_3} = \dfrac{15(4)}{120} = .50$

27. $P(0) = \dfrac{[_7C_2][_3C_0]}{[_{10}C_2]} = \dfrac{21(1)}{45} = .4667$

29. $P(2) = \dfrac{[_9C_3][_6C_2]}{[_{15}C_5]} = \dfrac{84(15)}{3003} = .4196$

31. a. .6703
b. .3297

33. a. .0613
b. .0803

35. $\mu = 6$, $P(X \ge 5) = .7149 = 1 - (.0025 + .0149 + .0446 + .0892 + .1339)$

37. a. $P(2) = \dfrac{[_8C_2][_4C_2]}{[_{12}C_4]} = \dfrac{28(6)}{495} = 0.3394$

b. $\dfrac{[_8C_0][_4C_4]}{[_{12}C_4]} = \dfrac{1}{495} = .0020$

c. $P(1) = \dfrac{[_8C_3][_4C_1]}{[_{12}C_4]} = \dfrac{(56)(4)}{495} = .4525$

$P(0) = \dfrac{[_8C_4][_4C_0]}{[_{12}C_4]} = \dfrac{(70)(1)}{495} = .1414$

$P(X \le 1) = P(0) + P(1) = .1414 + .4525 = .5939$

Using a binomial with $n = 12$, and $\pi = \dfrac{4}{12} = .3333$

a. $P(2) = [_4C_2](.3333)^2(.6667)^2 = .2963$
b. $P(4) = [_4C_4](.3333)^4(.6667)^0 = .0123$
c. $P(X \le 1) = [_4C_0](.3333)^0(.6667)^4$
$\qquad\qquad + [_4C_1](.3333)^1(.6667)^3$

$$= .1975 + .3951 = .5926$$

Binomial estimates are not very close.

39. When n is large and π is small, the Poisson and the binomial distribution will yield approximately the same results.

41. $\mu = 0(.1) + 1(.2) + 2(.3) + 3(.4) = 2$.

$\sigma^2 = (0-2)^2(.1) + \cdots + (3-2)^2(.4) = 1.0$

$\sigma = 1$

43. $\mu = 0(.4) + 1(.2) + 2(.2) + 3(.1) + 4(.1) = 1.3$

$\sigma^2 = (0-1.3)^2(.4) + \cdots + (4-1.3)^2(.1) = 1.81$

$\sigma = 1.3454$

45. a. .001
b. .001

47. $P(2) = \dfrac{[_6C_2][_4C_2]}{[_{10}C_4]} = \dfrac{(15)(6)}{210} = .4286$

49. a. $P(1) = \dfrac{[_7C_2][_3C_1]}{[_{10}C_3]} = \dfrac{(21)(3)}{120} = .5250$

b. $P(0) = \dfrac{[_7C_3][_3C_0]}{[_{10}C_3]} = \dfrac{(35)(1)}{120} = .2917$

$P(X \ge 1) = 1 - P(0) = 1 - .2917 = .7083$

51. $P(X = 0) = \dfrac{[_8C_4][_4C_0]}{[_{12}C_4]} = \dfrac{70}{495} = .141$

53. a. .0498
b. .7746, found by $(1 - .0498)^5$

55. $\mu = 4.0$ from Appendix C.
a. .0183
b. .1954

c. .6289
d. .5665

57. For NASA, $\mu = n\pi = 25(1/60,000) = .0004$

$$P(0) = \frac{.0004^0 e^{-.0004}}{0!} = .9996$$

$$P(X \geq 1) = 1 - .9996 = .0004$$

For Air Force, $\mu = 25\left(\frac{1}{35}\right) = .7143$

$$P(0) = \frac{.7143^0 e^{-.7143}}{0!} = .4895$$

$$P(X \geq 1) = 1 - .4895 = .5105$$

Summarizing, Air Force estimate is .5105, and NASA estimate is .0004.

59. Let $\mu = n\pi = 155\left(\frac{1}{3709}\right) = .042$

$$P(4) = \frac{.042^4 e^{-.042}}{4!} = .0080001$$

Very unlikely!

61. Eight of the 28 teams have artificial turf home fields.

$$P(2) = \frac{[_8C_2][_{20}C_3]}{[_{28}C_5]} = \frac{(28)(1,140)}{98,280} = 0.3248$$

CHAPTER 7

1. The actual shape of a normal distribution depends on its mean and standard deviation. Thus, there is a normal distribution, and an accompanying normal curve, for a mean of 7 and a standard deviation of 2. There is another normal curve for a mean of $25,000 and a standard deviation of $1,742, and so on.

3. a. 490 and 510, found by $500 \pm 1(10)$.
b. 480 and 520, found by $500 \pm 2(10)$.
c. 470 and 530, found by $500 \pm 3(10)$.

5. a. 1.25, found by:

$$z = \frac{25 - 20}{4.0} = 1.25$$

b. .3944, found in Appendix D.
c. .3085, found by:

$$z = \frac{18 - 20}{4.0} = -0.5$$

Find .1915 in Appendix D for $z = -0.5$, then $.5000 - .1915 = .3085$.

7. a. .3413, found by:

$$z = \frac{\$20 - \$16.50}{\$3.50} = 1.00$$

Then find .3413 in Appendix D for $z = 1$.
b. .1587, found by $.5000 - .3413 = .1587$.
c. .3336, found by:

$$z = \frac{\$15.00 - \$16.50}{\$3.50} = -0.43$$

Find .1664 in Appendix D for $z = -0.43$, then $.5000 - .1664 = .3336$.

9. a. .8276. First, find $z = -1.5$, found by $(44 - 50)/4$ and $z = 1.25 = (55 - 50)/4$. The area between -1.5 and 0 is .4332 and the area between 0 and 1.25 is .3944, both from Appendix D. Adding the two areas, we find that $.4332 + .3944 = .8276$.
b. .1056, found by $.5000 - .3944$, where $z = 1.25$.
c. .2029. Recall that the area for $z = 1.25$ is .3944. And the area for $z = .5$, found by $(52 - 50)/4$, is .1915. Then subtract $.3944 - .1915$ to get .2029.
d. $X = 56.60$, found by adding .5000 (the area left of the mean) and then finding a z value that forces 45% of the data to fall inside the curve. Solving for X: $1.65 = (X - 50)/4 = 56.60$

11. a. .1525, found by subtracting $.4938 - .3413$, which are the areas associated with z values of 2.5 and 1, respectively.
b. .0062, found by $.5000 - .4938$.
c. .9710, found by recalling that the area for the z value of 2.5 is .4938. Then find $z = -2.00$, found by $(6.8 - 7.0)/.1$. Then add the area for $z = 2.5$ and $z = -2$. Thus, $.4938 + .4772 = .9710$.
d. 7.233. Find a z value where .4900 of area is between 0 and z. That value is $z = 2.33$. Then solve for X: $2.33 = (X - 7)/.1$ so $X = 7.233$.

13. a. .0764, found by $z = (20 - 15)/3.5 = 1.43$. Then $.5000 - .4236 = .0764$.
b. .9236, found by $.5000 + .4236$, where $z = 1.43$.
c. .1185, found by $z = (12 - 15)/3.5 = -0.86$. The area under the curve is .3051. Then $z = (10 - 15)/3.5 = -1.43$. The area is .4236. Finally, $.4236 - .3051 = .1185$.
d. About 16.82 minutes, found by solving for X where $z = .52$. This point forces .20 of the area to fall under the curve between 0 and z. First multiplying $.52 \times 3.5$ and then adding 15, we find $X = 16.82$.

15. a. $\mu = n\pi = 50(.25) = 12.5$

$$\sigma^2 = n\pi(1 - \pi) = 12.5(1 - .25) = 9.375.$$

$$\sigma = \sqrt{9.375} = 3.0619.$$

b. .2578, found by $(14.5 - 12.5)/3.0619 = .65$. The area is .2422. Then $.5000 - .2422 = .2578$.
c. .2578, found by $(10.5 - 12.5)/3.0619 = -0.65$. The area is .2422. Then $.5000 - .2422 = .2578$.

17. a. .0655, found by $(9.5 - 6)/2.32 = 1.51$. The area is .4345. Then $.5000 - .4345 = .0655$.
b. .1401, found by $(8.5 - 6)/2.32 = 1.08$. The area is .3599. Then $.5000 - .3599 = .1401$.

c. .0746, found by .4345 − .3599 = .0746. This is the probability of getting exactly 9 errors.

19. a. Yes. (1) There are two mutually exclusive outcomes: overweight and not overweight. (2) It is the result of counting the number of successes (overweight members). (3) Each trial is independent. (4) The probability of .30 remains the same for each trial.

b. .0084, found by μ = 500(.30) = 150. σ^2 = 500(.30)(.70) = 105. Standard deviation = 10.24695, found by $\sqrt{105}$.

$$z = \frac{X - \mu}{\sigma} = \frac{174.5 - 150}{10.24695} = 2.39$$

Area under the curve for 2.39 is .4916. Then .5000 − .4916 = .0084.

c. .8461, found by:

$$z = \frac{139.5 - 150}{10.24695} = -1.02$$

The area between 139.5 and 150 is .3461. Adding, .3461 + .5000 = .8461.

21. a. 46.41%, found by (20.27 − 20.00)/.15 = 1.8
b. 3.59%, found by .5000 − .4641.
c. 81.85%, found by .3413 + .4772.
d. 27.43%, found by .5000 − .2257.

23. a. −0.4 for net sales, found by (170 − 180)/25. And 2.92 for employees, found by (1,850 − 1,500)/120.
b. Net sales are 0.4 standard deviations below the mean. Employees is 2.92 standard deviations above the mean.
c. 65.54% of the aluminum fabricators have greater net sales compared with Clarion, found by .1554 + .5000. Only 0.18% have more employees than Clarion, found by .5000 − .4982.

25. a. 15.87%, found by (15 − 20)/5 = −1.0. The area for −1.0 is .3413. Then .5000 − .3413 = .1587.
b. .5403. First, the area between 18 and 20 is .1554. The area between 20 and 26 is .3849. Adding, .1554 + .3849 = .5403.
c. About 1 person, found by z = (7 − 20)/5 = −2.6, for which the area is .4953. Then .5000 − .4953 = .0047. Finally, 200(.0047) = 0.94, which is about 1 person.

27. a. (860 − 1,000)/50 = −2.8. The area below 860 is .0026, found by .5000 − .4974, or .26 percent.
b. (1,055 − 1,000)/50 = 1.1. The area between 1000 and 1055 is .3643. The area between 1,000 and 1,100 is .4772. Subtracting: .4772 − .3643 gives .1129 or 11.29%.

29. About 4,099 units found by solving for X.
1.65 = (X − 4,000)/60

31. a. Only 2.28% earn more than John: ($30,400 − $28,000)/$1,200 = 2.00. Then .5000 − .4772 = .0228.
b. Of the other supervisors, 97.72% have more service. (10 − 20)/5 = −2.00. Then .4772 + .5000 = .9772.

33. a. 15.39%, found by (8 − 10.3)/2.25 = −1.02. Then .5000 − .3461 = .1539.
b. 17.31%, found by:

z = (12 − 10.3)/2.25 = 0.76. Area is .2764.
z = (14 − 10.3)/2.25 = 1.64. Area is .4495.
The area between 12 and 14 is .1731, found by .4495 − .2764.

c. Yes, but it is rather remote. Reasoning: On 99.73% of the days, returns are between 3.55 and 17.03, found by 10.3 ± 3(2.25). Thus, the chance of less than 3.55 returns is rather remote.

35. a. .9678, found by:

$$\mu = 60(.64) = 38.4$$
$$\sigma^2 = 60(.64)(.36) = 13.824$$
$$\sigma = \sqrt{13.824} = 3.72.$$

Then (31.5 − 38.4)/3.72 = −1.85, for which the area is .4678. Then .5000 + .4678 = .9678.
b. .0853, found by (43.5 − 38.4)/3.72 = 1.37, for which the area is .4147. Then .5000 − .4147 = .0853.
c. .8084, found by adding .4441 and .3643.
d. .0348 = .4495 − .4147.

37. a. .8106, where μ = 10, variance = 8, standard deviation = 2.8284. z − (7.5 − 10)/2.8284 = −.88. The area is = .3106. Then .5000 + .3106 = .8106.
b. .1087, found by: z = (8.5 − 10)/2.8284 = −.53. Then .3106 − .2019 = .1087.
c. .2981, found by .5000 − .2019.

39. .0968, found by:

$$\mu = 50(.40) = 20$$
$$\sigma^2 = 50(.40)(.60) = 12$$
$$\sigma = \sqrt{12} = 3.4641.$$
$$z = (24.5 - 20)/3.4641 = 1.30.$$

The area is .4032. Then for 25 or more, .5000 − .4032 = .0968.

41. a. 1.65 = (45 − μ)/5
μ = 36.75
b. 1.65 = (45 − μ)/10
μ = 28.5
c. z = (30 − 28.5)/10 = .15
Then .5000 + .0596 = .5596

43. a. .6687, found by: $z = (2.00 - 2.80)/.40 = -2.00$. And, $(3.00 - 2.80)/.40 = .50$. Then $.4772 + .1915 = .6687$.

b. .0228, found by: $(2.00 - 2.80)/.40 = -2.00$ The probability is $.5000 - .4772 = .0228$.

c. 122, found by: $z = (3.70 - 2.80)/.40 = 2.25$, so $.5000 - .4878 = .0122$. Then $10,000 \times .0122 = 122$.

d. 3.312, found by: $1.28 = (X - 2.8)/.40$.

45. a. 21.19 percent, found by: $z = (9.00 - 9.20)/.25 = -0.80$. Then $.5000 - .2881 = .2119$.

b. Increase the mean. $z = (9.00 - 9.25)/.25 = 1.00$; probability is $.5000 - .3413 = .1587$.
Reduce the standard deviation. $z = (9.00 - 9.20)/.15 = 1.33$; the probability is $.5000 - .4082 = .0918$.
Reducing the standard deviation is better because a smaller percent of the hams will be below the limit.

47. a. $z = (52 - 60)/5 = 1.60$. Then, $.5000 - .4452 = .0548$

b. Let $z = 0.67$, so $0.67 = (X - 52)/5$ and $X = 55.35$. Set mileage at 55,350.

c. $z = (45 - 52)/5 = -1.40$. Then $.5000 - .4192 = .0808$.

49.
$$\frac{470 - \mu}{\sigma} = 0.25$$

$$\frac{500 - \mu}{\sigma} = 1.28$$

$\sigma = 29.126$ and $\mu = 462.719$

51. $\mu = 150(.15) = 22.5$

$\sigma = \sqrt{150(.15)(.85)} = 4.3732$

$z = (30.5 - 22.5)/4.3732 = 1.83$

$P(z > 1.83) = .5000 - .4664 = .0336$

53. a. $z = (3.5 - 2.257)/0.792 = 1.57$
$P(z > 1.57) = .5000 - .4418 = .0582$
Two of the 28 teams, or 7 percent, had attendance of over 2.0 million. The approximation is quite accurate.

b. $z = (50.0 - 38.58)/13.74 = 0.83$
$P(z > 0.83) = .5000 - .2967 = .2033$
Five teams had salaries of over $50.0 million. The actual percent is 18 percent, versus an estimate of 20 percent.

55. a. $z = (3,000 - 2,725)/1,095 = 0.25$
$P(z > 0.25) = .5000 - .0987 = 0.4013$
Only eight schools, or 8.5 percent, spent more than $3,000 per student. Estimate is not very accurate.

b. $z = (2,000 - 2,134)/3,895 = -0.03$
$P(z > -.03) = .0120 + .5000 = .5120$
There are actually 30 school districts, or about 32 percent, so the estimate is not accurate.

CHAPTER 8

1. a. 303 Louisiana, 5155 S. Main, 3501 Monroe, 2652 W. Central

b. Answers will vary.

c. 630 Dixie Hwy, 835 S. McCord Rd, 4624 Woodville Rd

d. Answers will vary.

3. a. Bob Schmidt Chevrolet
Great Lakes Ford Nissan
Grogan Towne Chrysler
Southside Lincoln Mercury
Rouen Chrysler Plymouth Jeep Eagle

b. Answers will vary.

c. York Automotive
Thayer Chevrolet Geo Toyota
Franklin Park Lincoln Mercury
Mathews Ford Oregon Inc
Valiton Chrysler Plymouth

5. a.

Sample	Values	Sum	Mean
1	12, 12	24	12
2	12, 14	26	13
3	12, 16	28	14
4	12, 14	26	13
5	12, 16	28	14
6	14, 16	30	15

b. $\mu_{\bar{X}} = (12 + 13 + 14 + 13 + 14 + 15)/6 = 13.5$
$\mu = (12 + 12 + 14 + 16)/4 = 13.5$

c. More dispersion with population data compared to the sample means. The sample means vary from 12 to 15, whereas the population varies from 12 to 16.

7. a.

Sample	Values	Sum	Mean
1	12, 12, 14	38	12.66
2	12, 12, 15	39	13.0
3	12, 12, 20	44	14.66
4	14, 15, 20	49	16.33
5	12, 14, 15	41	13.66
6	12, 14, 15	41	13.66
7	12, 15, 20	47	15.66
8	12, 15, 20	47	15.66
9	12, 14, 20	46	15.33
10	12, 14, 20	46	15.33

b. $\mu_{\bar{X}} = \dfrac{(12.66 + \cdots + 15.33 + 15.33)}{10}$
$= 14.6$
$\mu = (12 + 12 + 14 + 15 + 20)/5 = 14.6$

c. The dispersion of the population is greater than that of the sample means. The sample means vary from 12.6 to 16.3, whereas the population varies from 12 to 20.

9. a. 20, found by $_6C_3$

b.

Sample	Cases	Sum	Mean
Ruud, Austin, Sass	3, 6, 3	12	4.0
Ruud, Sass, Palmer	3, 3, 3	9	3.0
⋮	⋮	⋮	⋮
Sass, Palmer, Schueller	3, 3, 1	7	2.33

c. $\mu_{\bar{x}} = 2.63$, found by $\dfrac{52.63}{20}$.

$\mu = 2.66$, found by $(3 + 6 + 3 + 3 + 1)/6$.

They are equal.

d.

Population

Distribution of Sample Means

Sample Mean	Number of Means	Probability
1.33	3	.1500
2.00	3	.1500
2.33	5	.2500
3.00	3	.1500
3.33	3	.1500
4.00	3	.1500
	20	1.0000

The population has more dispersion than the sample means. The sample means vary from 1.33 to 4.0. The population varies from 0 to 6.

11. a.

$$\mu = \frac{0 + 1 + \cdots + 9}{10} = 4.5$$

b.

Sample	Sum	$\bar{X}$
1	11	2.2
2	31	6.2
3	21	4.2
4	24	4.8
5	21	4.2
6	20	4.0
7	23	4.6
8	29	5.8
9	35	7.0
10	27	5.4

The mean of the 10 sample means is 4.84, which is close to the population mean of 4.5. The sample means range from 2.2 to 7.0, whereas the population values range from 0 to 9. From the above graph, the sample means tend to cluster between 4 and 5.

13. 51.314 and 58.686, found by $55 \pm 2.58(10/\sqrt{49})$.

15. a. 1.581, found by $\sigma_{\bar{x}} = 5/\sqrt{10}$

b. The population is normally distributed and the population variance is known.

c. 16.901 and 23.099, found by 20 ± 3.099.

17. a. $20. It is our best estimate of the population mean.

b. $18.60 and $21.40, found by $\$20 \pm 1.96(\$5/\sqrt{49})$. About 95 percent of the intervals similarly constructed will include the population mean.

19. **a.** 8.60 gallons.
   b. 7.83 and 9.37, found by $8.60 \pm 2.58(2.30/\sqrt{60})$.
   c. If 100 such intervals were determined, the population mean would be included in about 99 intervals.
21. **a.** .80, found by 80/100.
   b. .7216 and .8784, found by:
   $.80 \pm 1.96\sqrt{[(.80)(.20)/100]}$
23. **a.** .625, found by 250/400.
   b. .578 and .672, found by:
   $.625 \pm 1.96\sqrt{[(.625)(.375)/400]}$
25. 33.465 and 36.535, found by

$$35 \pm 1.96(5/\sqrt{36})\sqrt{\frac{300-36}{300-1}}$$

27. 1.689 up to 2.031, found by

$$1.86 \pm 2.58(.50/\sqrt{50})\sqrt{\frac{400-50}{400-1}}$$

29. 97, found by $n = [(1.96 \cdot 10)/2]^2 = 96.04$.
31. 196, found by:

$$n = .15(.85)(1.96/.05)^2 = 195.9216$$

33. 554, found by $n = [(1.96 \cdot 3)/.25]^2 = 553.19$.
35. **a.** 577, found by:
   $n = .60(.40)(1.96/.04)^2 = 576.24$
   b. 601, found by:
   $n = .50(.50)(1.96/.04)^2 = 600.25$
37. **a.** Formal Man, Summit Stationers, Bootleggers, Leather Ltd, Petries.
   b. Answers may vary.
   c. Elder-Beerman, Frederick's of Hollywood, Summit Stationers, Lion Store, Leather Ltd., Things Remembered, County Seat, Coach House Gifts, Regis Hairstylists
39. The difference between a sample statistic and the population parameter. Yes, the difference could be zero. The sample mean and the population parameter are equal.
41. Use of either a proportional or nonproportional stratified random sample would be appropriate. For example, suppose the number of banks in Region III were as follows:

Assets	Number	Percent of Total
$500 million and more	20	2.0
$100–$499 million	324	32.4
Less than $100 million	656	65.6
	1,000	100.0

For a proportional stratified sample, if the sample size is 100, then two banks with assets of $500 million would be selected, 32 medium-size banks, and 66 small banks. For a nonproportional sample, 10 or even all 20 large banks could be selected and fewer medium- and small-size banks and the sample results weighted by the appropriate percents of the total.

43. **a.** We selected 60, 104, 75, 72, and 48. Answers will vary.
   b. We selected the third observation. So the sample consists of 75, 72, 68, 82, 48. Answers will vary.
   c. Number the first 20 motels from 00 to 19. Randomly select three numbers. Then number the last five numbers 20 to 24. Randomly select two numbers from that group.
45. **a.** 15, found by $_6C_2$
   b.

Sample	Value	Sum	Mean
1	79, 64	143	71.5
2	79, 84	163	81.5
.	.	.	.
.	.	.	.
.	.	.	.
15	92, 77	169	84.5
			1,195

   c. $\mu_{\bar{X}} = 79.67$, found by 1,195/15.

   $\mu = 79.67$, found by 478/6.
   They are equal.
   d. No. The student is not graded on all available information. He/she is as likely to get a lower grade based on the sample as a higher grade.
47. **a.** 10, found by $_5C_2$.
   b.

Number Correct	Mean	Number Correct	Mean
4, 3	3.5	3, 3	3.0
4, 5	4.5	3, 2	2.5
4, 3	3.5	5, 3	4.0
4, 2	3.0	5, 2	3.5
3, 5	4.0	3, 2	2.5

   c.

Sample Mean	Frequency	Probability
2.5	2	.20
3.0	2	.20
3.5	3	.30
4.0	2	.20
4.5	1	.10
	10	1.00

   d. $\mu_{\bar{X}} = (3.5 + 4.5 + \cdots + 2.5)/10 = 3.4$
   $\mu = (4 + 3 + 5 + 3 + 2)/5 = 3.4$
   The two means are equal.
   e. The population values are relatively uniform in shape. The distribution of sample means tends toward normality.

49. 6.14 years to 6.86 years, found by $6.5 \pm 1.96(1.7/\sqrt{85})$.

51. \$1.168 and \$1.190, found by $1.179 \pm 2.58(.03/\sqrt{50})$.

53. **a.** The driveway, because it has the smallest standard deviation.

     b. Driveway: 10.776 and 13.224 $(12 \pm 2.58[3/\sqrt{40}])$

        Patio: 9.552 and 14.448 $(12 \pm 2.58[6/\sqrt{40}])$

        Deck: 8.737 and 15.263 $(12 \pm 2.58[8/\sqrt{40}])$

55. **a.** 65.61 up to 71.59 hours, found by

$$68.6 \pm (2.58)\frac{8.2}{\sqrt{50}}.$$

     b. The value suggested by the NCAA is included in the confidence interval. Therefore, it is reasonable.

     c. Changing the confidence interval to 95 would reduce the width of the interval. The value of 2.58 would change to 1.96.

57. .42 and .50, found by:

$$.46 \pm 2.58\sqrt{\frac{.46(1 - .46)}{900}}.$$

59. .633 and .687, found by

$$.66 \pm 1.96\sqrt{\frac{.66(.34)}{1200}}.$$

61. **a.** .53 up to .59, found by

$$.56 \pm (1.96)\sqrt{\frac{(.56)(.44)}{1000}}.$$

     b. The lower point of the interval is greater than .50, so we can conclude the majority feel the president is doing a good job.

63. .345 and .695, found by:

$$.52 \pm 2.58\sqrt{\frac{.52(.48)}{50}}\sqrt{\frac{(650 - 50)}{(650 - 1)}}.$$

65. 134, found by $[(1.65 \times 14)/2]^2 = 133.4$.

67. 865, found by $.10(.90)\left(\frac{1.96}{.02}\right)^2$.

69. **a.** 25%, found by 25/100.

     b. .172 to .328, found by

$$.25 \pm 1.96\left(\sqrt{\frac{(.25)(.75)}{100}}\right)\left(\sqrt{\frac{605 - 100}{604}}\right)$$

        No, .40 is not in the interval.

     c. 1.65, found by 165/100.

     d. 1.387 to 1.913, found by

$$1.65 \pm 1.96\frac{1.4659}{\sqrt{100}}\left(\sqrt{\frac{505}{604}}\right)$$

Note: $s = 1.4659$

     e. No, because 0 is not in the interval between 1.387 and 1.91.

71. **a.** For selling price:

$$221.1 \pm (1.96)\frac{47.11}{\sqrt{105}}$$

$$= 221.1 \pm 9.01$$

$$= 212.09 \text{ up to } 230.11$$

     b. For distance:

$$14.629 \pm (1.96)\frac{4.874}{\sqrt{105}}$$

$$= 14.629 \pm .932$$

$$= 13.697 \text{ up to } 15.561$$

     c. For garage:

$$.6762 \pm 1.96\sqrt{\frac{.6762(1 - .6762)}{105}}$$

$$= .6762 \pm .0895$$

$$= .5867 \text{ up to } .7657$$

73. **a.** $2.904 \pm (1.96)\frac{1.804}{\sqrt{48}} = 2.904 \pm .510$.

        The interval is from 2.394 up to 3.414.

     b. $\$26,622 \pm 1.96\frac{\$18,858}{\sqrt{48}} = \$26,622 \pm \$5335$.

        The interval is from \$21,287 up to \$31,957.

     c. $42.75 \pm 1.96\frac{13.74}{\sqrt{48}} = 42.75 \pm 3.89$.

        The interval is from 38.86 up to 46.64.

CHAPTER 9

1. **a.** Two-tailed.

     b. Reject H_0 and accept H_1 when z does not fall in the region from -1.96 and 1.96.

     c. -1.2, found by:

$$z = \frac{49 - 50}{(5/\sqrt{36})} = -1.2$$

     d. Fail to reject H_0.

     e. $p = .2302$, found by $2(.5000 - .3849)$. A 23.02 percent chance of finding a z value this large when H_0 is true.

3. **a.** One-tailed.

     b. Reject H_0 and accept H_1 where $z > 1.65$.

     c. 1.2, found by:

$$z = \frac{21 - 20}{(5/\sqrt{36})} = 1.2$$

d. Fail to reject H_0 at the .05 significance level.

e. p = .1151, found by .5000 − .3849. An 11.51 percent chance of finding a z-value this large or larger.

5. a. H_0: $\mu = 60{,}000$

H_1: $\mu \neq 60{,}000$

b. Reject H_0 if $z < -1.96$ or $z > 1.96$.

c. −0.69, found by:

$$z = \frac{59{,}500 - 60{,}000}{(5{,}000/\sqrt{48})} = -0.69$$

d. Do not reject H_0.

e. p = .4902, found by 2(.5000 − .2549). Crosset's experience is not different from that claimed by the manufacturer. If H_0 is true, the probability of finding a value more extreme than this is .4902.

7. a. H_0: $\mu \geq 6.8$, H_1: $\mu < 6.8$

b. Reject H_0 if $z < -1.65$

c. $z = \dfrac{6.2 - 6.8}{0.5/\sqrt{36}} = -7.2$

d. H_0 is rejected.

e. p = 0. The mean number of videos watched is less than 6.8 per month. If H_0 is true, there is virtually no chance of getting a statistic this small.

9. a. Two-tailed test.

b. Reject H_0 if $z < -2.05$ or $z > 2.05$

c. 2.59, found by:

$$z = \frac{102 - 99}{\sqrt{\dfrac{5^2}{40} + \dfrac{6^2}{50}}} = 2.59$$

d. Reject H_0 and accept H_1.

e. p = .0096, found by 2(.5000 − .4952).

11. Step 1 H_0: $\mu_1 \geq \mu_2$
H_1: $\mu_1 < \mu_2$

Step 2 The .05 significance level was chosen.

Step 3 Reject H_0 and accept H_1 if $z < -1.65$.

Step 4 −0.94, found by:

$$z = \frac{7.6 - 8.1}{\sqrt{\dfrac{(2.3)^2}{40} + \dfrac{(2.9)^2}{55}}} = -0.94$$

Step 5 Fail to reject H_0. No difference in lengths of time that owners occupied their homes. p = .1736, found by .5000 − .3264

13. a. Two-tailed test, because we are trying to show that a difference exists between the two means.

b. Reject H_0 if $z < -2.58$ or $z > 2.58$.

c. −2.66, found by:

$$z = \frac{31.4 - 34.9}{\sqrt{\dfrac{(5.1)^2}{32} + \dfrac{(6.7)^2}{49}}} = -2.66$$

Reject H_0 at the .01 level. There is a difference in the mean turnover rate.

15. a. H_0 is rejected if $z < -1.96$ or $z > 1.96$.

b. $z = \dfrac{.30 - .40}{\sqrt{\dfrac{.40(.60)}{120}}} = -2.24$

c. H_0 is rejected.

17. H_0: $\pi \leq .33$, H_1: $\pi > .33$
H_0 is rejected if $z > 2.05$.

$$z = \frac{.40 - .3333}{\sqrt{\dfrac{.3333(.6667)}{200}}} = 2.00$$

H_0 is not rejected. The proportion of students with jobs is not larger at your school.

19. H_0: $\pi \geq .50$, H_1: $\pi < .50$
H_0 is rejected if $z < -1.65$

$$z = \frac{.48 - .50}{\sqrt{\dfrac{.50(.50)}{100}}} = -0.40$$

H_0 is not rejected. The proportion of students changing their major has not changed.

21. a. H_0 is rejected if $z < -1.96$ or $z > 1.96$

b. $p_c = \dfrac{170 + 110}{200 + 150} = .80$

c. $z = \dfrac{.85 - .7333}{\sqrt{\dfrac{.80(.20)}{200} + \dfrac{.80(.20)}{150}}} = 2.70$

d. H_0 is rejected.

23. a. H_0: $\pi_1 \geq \pi_2$ H_1: $\pi_1 < \pi_2$

b. H_0 is rejected if $z < -1.65$

$$p_c = \frac{1530 + 2010}{3000 + 3000} = .59$$

c. $z = \dfrac{.51 - .67}{\sqrt{\dfrac{.59(.41)}{3000} + \dfrac{.59(.41)}{3000}}} = -12.60$

d. H_0 is rejected. The proportion of women who think men are thoughtful has declined.

25. H_0: $\pi_s = \pi_m$ H_1: $\pi_s \neq \pi_m$
H_0 is rejected if $z < -1.96$ or $z > 1.96$.

$$\bar{p}_c = \frac{120 + 150}{400 + 600} = .27$$

$$z = \frac{.30 - .25}{\sqrt{\dfrac{.27(.73)}{400} + \dfrac{.27(.73)}{600}}} = 1.74$$

H_0 is not rejected. There is no difference in the proportion of married and single drivers who have accidents.

27. $z = (9{,}922 - 9{,}940)/(400/\sqrt{100}) = -0.45$. Then the area of $.1736 + .5000 = .6736$, which is the probability of a Type II error.

29. H_0: $\mu \le 16$
H_1: $\mu > 16$
Reject H_0 if $z > 1.65$
Computed $z = 11.79$, found by:

$$z = \frac{16.05 - 16.0}{(0.03/\sqrt{50})} = 11.79$$

Reject H_0. The cans are being overfilled. p-value is very close to 0.

31. H_0: $\mu \le 90$
H_1: $\mu > 90$
Reject H_0 if $z > 1.28$

$$z = \frac{94 - 90}{(22/\sqrt{100})} = 1.82$$

Reject H_0. At the .10 level we can conclude that the farm selling time has increased.

33. H_0: $\mu \ge 40$, H_1: $\mu < 40$. Reject H_0 if $z < -1.65$.

$$z = \frac{37.8 - 40.0}{(12.2/\sqrt{60})} = -1.40$$

H_0 is not rejected. The p-value $= .5000 - .4192 = .0808$. We cannot conclude that the mean leisure time is less than 40 hours per week.

35. **a.** H_0: $\mu \ge 50$, H_1: $\mu < 50$ Reject H_0 if $z < -2.33$.
$\overline{X} = 48.18$

$$z = \frac{48.18 - 50.00}{(3.00/\sqrt{10})} = -1.92$$

H_0 is not rejected. The mean weight is not less than 50 pounds.
b. Mr. Rutter can use the z distribution as the test statistic because the population standard deviation ($\sigma = 3$) is known and the population is normal.
c. p-value $= .5000 - .4726 = 0.0274$

37. H_0: $\mu_1 = \mu_2$
H_1: $\mu_1 \ne \mu_2$
Reject H_0 if $z < -2.05$ or $z > 2.05$.

$$z = \frac{114.6 - 117.9}{\sqrt{\dfrac{(9.1)^2}{40} + \dfrac{(10.4)^2}{50}}} = -1.60$$

Fail to reject H_0. There is no difference in the test scores. The p-value is .1096, found by $2(.5000 - .4452)$

39. H_0: $\mu_1 = \mu_2$, H_1: $\mu_1 \ne \mu_2$. Reject H_0 if $z < -2.58$ or $z > 2.58$.

$$z = \frac{36.2 - 37.0}{\sqrt{\dfrac{(1.14)^2}{35} + \dfrac{(1.30)^2}{40}}} = -2.84$$

Reject H_0. There is a difference in the useful life of the two brands of paint. p-value $= 2(.5000 - .4977) = .0046$.

41. H_0: $\mu_1 = \mu_2$, H_1: $\mu_1 \ne \mu_2$. Reject H_0 if $z < -1.96$ or $z > 1.96$.

$$z = \frac{4.77 - 5.02}{\sqrt{\dfrac{(1.05)^2}{40} + \dfrac{(1.23)^2}{50}}} = -1.04$$

H_0 is not rejected. There is no difference in the mean number of calls. p-value $= 2(.5000 - .3508) = .2984$.

43. H_0: $\mu_1 \le \mu_2$, H_1: $\mu_1 > \mu_2$. Reject H_0 if $z > 2.05$.

$$z = \frac{11.00 - 7.67}{\sqrt{\dfrac{(3.88)^2}{30} + \dfrac{(4.42)^2}{40}}} = 3.35$$

H_0 is rejected. Those with smaller boats use their boats more often. The p-value is less than .0001.

45. H_0: $\pi \le .60$ H_1: $\pi > .60$
H_0 is rejected if $z > 2.33$.

$$z = \frac{.70 - .60}{\sqrt{\dfrac{.60(.40)}{200}}} = 2.89$$

H_0 is rejected. Ms. Dennis is correct. More than 60% of the accounts are more than 3 months old.

47. H_0: $\pi \le .44$ H_1: $\pi > .44$
H_0 is rejected if $z > 1.65$.

$$z = \frac{.48 - .44}{\sqrt{\dfrac{.44(.56)}{1000}}} = 2.55$$

H_0 is rejected. We conclude that there has been an increase in the proportion of people wanting to go to Europe.

49. H_0: $\pi \le .20$, H_1: $\pi > .20$. Reject H_0 if $z > 2.33$.

$$z = \frac{\dfrac{56}{200} - .20}{\sqrt{\dfrac{.20(.80)}{200}}} = 2.83.$$

H_0 is rejected. More than 20 percent of the owners move during a particular year. p-value $= .5000 - .4977 = .0023$.

51. $H_0: \pi_a = \pi_f$ $H_1: \pi_a \neq \pi_f$
H_0 is rejected if $z < -1.96$ or $z > 1.96$.

$$p_c = \frac{198 + 117}{1000 + 500} = .21$$

$$z = \frac{.198 - .234}{\sqrt{\dfrac{.21(.79)}{1000} + \dfrac{.21(.79)}{500}}} = -1.61$$

H_0 is not rejected. There is no difference in the proportion of American-born citizens and foreign-born citizens who favor resumption of diplomatic relations with Cuba.

53. a. Reject H_0 where $z > 1.65$

$$z = \frac{24,421 - 24,000}{(1,944/\sqrt{35})} = 1.28$$

Fail to reject H_0.

b. 24,542, found by:

$$1.65 = \frac{\overline{X}_c - 24,000}{(1,944/\sqrt{35})}$$

$$\overline{X}_c = 24,542$$

c. $z = (24,542 - 25,000)/(1,944/\sqrt{35}) = -1.39$
$.5000 - .4177 = .0823$

55. a. $H_0: \mu \leq 0.75$, $H_1: \mu > 0.75$. Reject H_0 if $z > 1.65$.

$$z = \frac{.80 - .75}{.1/\sqrt{45}} = 3.35$$

Reject H_0. The shoppers are on average spending more than .75 hours in the mall.

b. $1.65 = (\overline{X}_c - 0.75)/(.1/\sqrt{45})$

$$\overline{X}_c = .0246 + 0.75 = .7746$$

then

$$z = (.7746 - .77)/(.1/\sqrt{45}) = 0.31$$

$$P(z < 0.31) = .1217 + .5000 = .6217$$

c. Increase the significance level to .10.

57. a. $H_0: \mu \geq 100$, $H_1: \mu < 100$. Reject H_0 if $z < -1.65$. From the MINITAB system, $\overline{X} = 93.27$ and $s = 40.85$.

$$z = \frac{93.27 - 100}{40.85/\sqrt{52}} = -1.19$$

H_0 is not rejected. We cannot conclude that the mean number of bids per facility is less than 100. The p-value is .1170, found by $.5000 - .3830$.

b. $H_0: \mu \leq 150$, $\mu > 150$, Reject H_0 if $z > 1.65$. From the MINITAB system, $\overline{X} = 183.9$ and $s = 87.0$

$$z = \frac{183.9 - 150.0}{87.0/\sqrt{52}} = 2.81$$

Reject H_0. The mean number of annual medical in-patient days is more than 150 (hundreds) per facility. The p-value is .0025, found by $.5000 - .4975$. H_0 is rejected at either significance level.

59. a. $H_0: \mu \leq 220.0$, $H_1: \mu > 220.0$, Reject H_0 if $z > 2.33$

$$z = \frac{221.00 - 220.0}{47.11/\sqrt{105}} = 0.24$$

Do not reject H_0. We cannot conclude that the mean selling price is more than \$220,000. The p-value is .4052, found by $.5000 - .0948$.

b. $H_0: \mu \leq 2100$, $H_1: \mu > 2100$. Reject H_0 if $z > 2.33$.

$$z = \frac{2231.4 - 2100}{249.3/\sqrt{105}} = 5.40$$

Reject H_0. The mean size of the home is greater than 2,100 square feet. The p-value is 0.

c. $H_0: \pi \leq 0.60$, $H_1: \pi > 0.60$, Reject H_0 if $z > 1.65$. Seventy-one homes have an attached garage, so $p = 71/105 = 0.6762$.

$$z = \frac{0.6762 - .60}{\sqrt{\dfrac{60(.40)}{105}}} = 1.59.$$

Do not reject H_0. We cannot conclude that more than 60 percent of the homes have an attached garage. The p-value is .0559, found by $.5000 - .4441$.

d. $H_0: \pi \leq 0.60$, $H_1: \pi > 0.60$. Reject H_0 if $z > 1.65$. $p = 67/105 = .6381$.

$$z = \frac{.6381 - .6000}{\sqrt{\dfrac{.60(.40)}{105}}} = 0.80$$

Do not reject H_0. We cannot conclude that more than 60 percent of the homes have a pool. The p-value is .2119, found by $.5000 - .2881$.

61. a. $H_0: \mu \leq 2.5$, $H_1: \mu > 2.5$. Reject H_0 if $z > 1.65$.

$$z = \frac{2.75 - 2.50}{(1.859/\sqrt{48})} = 0.93$$

H_0 is not rejected. The mean number of magazines read is not greater than 2.5 for men.

b. $H_0: \mu \geq 40$, $H_1: \mu < 40$. Reject H_0 if $z < -1.65$.

$$z = \frac{35.167 - 40.00}{(5.200/\sqrt{48})} = -6.44$$

H_0 is rejected. The mean age of readers is less than 40 years.

CHAPTER 10

1. **a.** Reject H_0 where $t > 1.833$

   b. $t = \dfrac{12 - 10}{(3/\sqrt{10})} = 2.108$

   c. Reject H_0. The mean is greater than 10.

3. $H_0: \mu \le 40$
   $H_1: \mu > 40$
   Reject H_0 if $t > 1.703$.

   $$t = \frac{42 - 40}{(2.1/\sqrt{28})} = 5.040$$

   Reject H_0 and conclude that the mean number of calls is greater than 40 per week.

5. $H_0: \mu \le 22{,}100$
   $H_1: \mu > 22{,}100$
   Reject H_0 if $t > 1.740$.

   $$t = \frac{23{,}400 - 22{,}100}{(1{,}500/\sqrt{18})} = 3.680$$

   Reject H_0. The mean life of the spark plugs is greater than 22,100 miles.

7. **a.** Reject H_0 if $t < -3.747$.

   b. $\overline{X} = 17$ and $s = \sqrt{(1495 - (85)^2/5)/(5 - 1)} = 3.536$

   $$t = \frac{17 - 20}{(3.536/\sqrt{5})} = -1.90$$

   c. Do not reject H_0. We cannot conclude the population mean is less than 20.

   d. Between .05 and .10, about .065

9. $H_0: \mu \le 4.35$
   $H_1: \mu > 4.35$
   Reject H_0 if $t > 2.821$.

   $$t = \frac{4.368 - 4.35}{(0.0339/\sqrt{10})} = 1.68$$

   Do not reject H_0. The additive did not increase the mean weight of the chickens. The p-value is between .10 and .05.

11. **a.** $H_0: \mu \le 4.0$
    $H_1: \mu > 4.0$
    Reject H_0 if $t > 1.796$.

    $$t = \frac{4.50 - 4.0}{(2.68/\sqrt{12})} = 0.65$$

    Do not reject H_0. Mean number of fish caught has not been shown to be greater than 4.0. The p-value is greater than .10.

13. **a.** Reject H_0 if $t > 2.120$ or $t < -2.120$

    $$df = 10 + 8 - 2 = 16$$

    b. $s_p^2 = \dfrac{(10 - 1)(4)^2 + (8 - 1)(5)^2}{10 + 8 - 2} = 19.9375$

    c. $t = \dfrac{23 - 26}{\sqrt{19.9375\left(\dfrac{1}{10} + \dfrac{1}{8}\right)}} = -1.416$

    d. Do not reject H_0.

    e. p-value is $> .10$ and $< .20$

15. $H_0: \mu_f \le \mu_m$, $H_1: \mu_f > \mu_m$. Reject H_0 if $t > 2.624$.
    $df = 9 + 7 - 2 = 14$.

    $$s_p^2 = \frac{(7 - 1)(6.88)^2 + (9 - 1)(9.49)^2}{7 + 9 - 2} = 71.749$$

    $$t = \frac{79 - 78}{\sqrt{71.749\left(\dfrac{1}{7} + \dfrac{1}{9}\right)}} = 0.234$$

    Do not reject H_0. There is no difference in the mean grades.

17. $H_0: \mu_s \le \mu_a$, $H_1: \mu_s > \mu_a$. Reject H_0 if $t > 1.363$.
    $df = 6 + 7 - 2 = 11$.

    $$s_p = \frac{(6 - 1)(12.2)^2 + (7 - 1)(15.8)^2}{6 + 7 - 2} = 203.82$$

    $$t = \frac{142.5 - 130.3}{\sqrt{203.82\left(\dfrac{1}{6} + \dfrac{1}{7}\right)}} = 1.536$$

    Reject H_0. The mean daily expenses are greater for the sales staff. The p-value is between .05 and .10.

19. **a.** Reject H_0 if $t > 2.353$. $df = 4 - 1 = 3$.

    b. $\overline{d} = \dfrac{12}{4} = 3.00$

    $$s_d = \sqrt{\frac{38 - \dfrac{(12)^2}{4}}{3}} = .816$$

    c. $t = \dfrac{3.00}{.816/\sqrt{4}} = 7.35$

    d. Reject H_0. There are more defective parts produced on the day shift.

    e. p-value is $< .005$, but $> .0005$.

21. $H_0: \mu_d \le 0$
    $H_1: \mu_d > 0$
    Reject H_0 if $t > 2.764$.
    $\overline{d} = 7.3636$, $s_d = 8.3699$.

    $$t = \frac{7.3636}{(8.3699/\sqrt{11})} = 2.92$$

    Reject H_0. The weights have increased.

23. $H_0: \mu_d \leq 0$
$H_1: \mu_d > 0$
Reject H_0 if $t > 2.821$.
$\bar{d} = 0.1$, $s_d = 4.28$.

$$t = \frac{0.10}{4.28/\sqrt{10}} = 0.07$$

Fail to reject H_0. There has been no reduction.

25. $H_0: \mu \geq 87$; $H_1: \mu < 87$.
Reject H_0 if $t < -1.895$.

$$\bar{X} = \frac{664}{8} = 83.0$$

$$s = \sqrt{\frac{55{,}244 - (664)^2/8}{8 - 1}} = 4.3425$$

$$t = \frac{83 - 87}{4.3425/\sqrt{8}} = -2.61$$

Reject H_0. The mileage is less than advertised.

27. $H_0: \mu \leq 9$; $H_1: \mu > 9$.
Reject H_0 if $t > 2.998$.
$\bar{X} = 9.488$, $s = .467$.

$$t = \frac{9.488 - 9.00}{.467/\sqrt{8}} = 2.95$$

Do not reject H_0. The mean prime rate for small banks is 9.0 percent. The p-value is less than .025.

29. $H_0: \mu \leq 25$; $H_1: \mu > 25$. Reject H_0 if $t > 2.624$.
$\bar{X} = 26.07$; $s = 1.5337$.

$$t = \frac{26.07 - 25.00}{1.5337/\sqrt{15}} = 2.702$$

Reject H_0. The mean number of patients per day is more than 25. The p-value is less than .01.

31. $H_0: \mu \geq 3.5$; $H_1: \mu < 3.5$. Reject H_0 if $t < -1.746$.

$$t = \frac{2.9553 - 3.5}{0.5596/\sqrt{17}} = -4.013$$

Reject H_0. The mean time to complete a game is less than 3.5 hours.

33. $H_0: \mu \leq 4.5\%$; $H_1: \mu > 4.5\%$.
Reject H_0 if $t > 1.796$
$\bar{X} = 4.5717$ and $s = 0.2405$

$$t = \frac{4.5717 - 4.50}{0.2405/\sqrt{12}} = 1.033$$

Do not reject H_0. The mean rate of return is not more than 4.5 percent.

35. $H_0: \mu_E \leq \mu_b$; $H_1: \mu_E > \mu_b$. Reject H_0 if $t > 1.701$.

$$s_p^2 = \frac{(20 - 1)(5.84)^2 + (10 - 1)(5.67)^2}{20 + 10 - 2} = 33.4767$$

$$t = \frac{24.80 - 20.25}{\sqrt{33.4767\left(\dfrac{1}{10} + \dfrac{1}{20}\right)}} = 2.031$$

H_0 is rejected. The packages shipped at the end of the month weigh more on average.

37. $H_0: \mu_1 \leq \mu_2$; $H_1: \mu_1 > \mu_2$. Reject H_0 if $t > 2.567$.

$$s_p^2 = \frac{(8 - 1)(2.2638)^2 + (11 - 1)(2.4606)^2}{8 + 11 - 2} = 5.672$$

$$t = \frac{10.375 - 5.636}{\sqrt{5.672(1/8 + 1/11)}} = 4.28$$

Reject H_0. The mean number of transactions by the young adults is more than for the senior citizens.

39. $H_0: \mu_1 \leq \mu_2$; $H_1: \mu_1 > \mu_2$. Reject H_0 if $t > 2.650$.
$\bar{X}_1 = 125.125$, $s_1 = 15.094$, $\bar{X}_2 = 117.714$, $s_2 = 19.914$.

$$s_p^2 = \frac{(8 - 1)(15.094)^2 + (7 - 1)(19.914)^2}{8 + 7 - 2} = 305.708$$

$$t = \frac{125.125 - 117.714}{\sqrt{305.708\left(\dfrac{1}{8} + \dfrac{1}{7}\right)}} = 0.819$$

H_0 is not rejected. There is no difference in the mean number sold at the regular price and the mean number sold at the reduced price.

41. $H_0: \mu_1 = \mu_2$; $H_1: \mu_1 \neq \mu_2$. Reject H_0 if $t > 2.819$ or $t < -2.819$.

$$s_p^2 = \frac{(10 - 1)(2.33)^2 + (14 - 1)(2.55)^2}{10 + 14 - 2} = 6.06$$

$$t = \frac{15.87 - 18.29}{\sqrt{6.06\left(\dfrac{1}{10} + \dfrac{1}{14}\right)}} = 2.374$$

Do not reject H_0. There is no difference in mean amount purchased.

43. $H_0: \mu_d \leq 0$; $H_1: \mu_d > 0$. Reject H_0 if $t > 1.895$.
$\bar{d} = 1.75$; $s_d = 2.9155$.

$$t = \frac{1.75}{2.9155/\sqrt{8}} = 1.698$$

H_0 is not rejected. There is no difference in the mean number of absences. The p-value is greater than .05.

45. $H_0: \mu_d \leq 0$; $H_1: \mu_d > 0$. Reject H_0 if $t > 1.833$.
$\bar{d} = 0.027$; $s_d = 0.2661$.

$$t = \frac{.027}{.2661/\sqrt{10}} = 0.321$$

Do not reject H_0. We have not shown a decline in grades.

47. Answers will vary. Developed 2/10/98
$H_0: \mu_d \leq 0$; $H_1: \mu_d > 0$. Reject H_0 if $t > 2.764$.
$\bar{d} = 4.02$; $s_d = 6.41$.

$$t = \frac{4.02}{6.41/\sqrt{11}} = 2.080$$

Cannot reject H_0. Stock prices have not significantly increased.

49. a. $\mu_1 =$ without pool; $\mu_2 =$ with pool.
$H_0: \mu_1 = \mu_2$; $H_1: \mu_1 \neq \mu_2$. Reject H_0 if $t > 2.000$ or $t < -2.000$.

$$\bar{X}_1 = 202.79 \qquad s_1 = 33.71 \qquad n = 38$$
$$\bar{X}_2 = 231.48 \qquad s_2 = 50.48 \qquad n = 67$$

$$s_p^2 = \frac{(38-1)(33.71)^2 + (67-1)(50.48)^2}{38 + 67 - 2} = 2041.05$$

$$t = \frac{202.79 - 231.48}{\sqrt{2041.05\left(\dfrac{1}{38} + \dfrac{1}{67}\right)}} = -3.12$$

Reject H_0. There is a difference in mean selling price for homes with and without a pool.

b. $\mu_1 =$ without garage; $\mu_2 =$ with garage.
$H_0: \mu_1 = \mu_2$; $H_1: \mu_1 \neq \mu_2$. Reject H_0 if $t > 2.00$ or $t < -2.00$.

$$\bar{X}_1 = 185.44 \qquad s_1 = 28.01$$
$$\bar{X}_2 = 238.18 \qquad s_2 = 44.88$$

$$s_p^2 = \frac{(34-1)(28.01)^2 + (71-1)(44.88)^2}{103} = 1620.25$$

$$t = \frac{185.44 - 238.18}{\sqrt{1620.25\left(\dfrac{1}{34} + \dfrac{1}{71}\right)}} = -6.28$$

Reject H_0. There is a difference in the mean selling price of homes with and without a garage.

c. $H_0: \mu_1 = \mu_2$; $H_1: \mu_1 \neq \mu_2$. Reject H_0 if $t < -2.036$ or $t > 2.036$.

$$\bar{X}_1 = 196.92 \qquad s_1 = 35.79 \qquad n = 15$$
$$\bar{X}_2 = 227.45 \qquad s_2 = 44.2 \qquad n = 20$$

$$s_p^2 = \frac{(15-1)(35.79)^2 + (20-1)(44.2)^2}{15 + 20 - 2} = 1668.24$$

$$t = \frac{196.92 - 227.45}{\sqrt{1668.24\left(\dfrac{1}{15} + \dfrac{1}{20}\right)}} = -2.188$$

Reject H_0. There is a difference in the mean selling price of homes in Township 1 and Township 2.

51. a. Let population 1 refer to $< 50\%$, $H_0: \mu_1 = \mu_2$; $H_1: \mu_1 \neq \mu_2$. Reject H_0 if $t < -2.021$ or $t > 2.021$. Note: Answer in \$000.

Less than 50% male: $\bar{X}_1 = 37.620$, $s = 24.527$, $n = 25$
50% or more: $\bar{X}_2 = 35.551$, $s = 21.653$, $n = 23$

$$s_p^2 = \frac{(25-1)(24.527)^2 + (23-1)(21.653)^2}{25 + 23 - 2} = 538.098$$

$$t = \frac{37.620 - 35.551}{\sqrt{538.098\left(\dfrac{1}{25} + \dfrac{1}{23}\right)}} = 0.309$$

Do not reject H_0. There is no difference in the mean cost of the two groups.

b. $H_0: \mu_1 = \mu_2$; $H_1: \mu_1 \neq \mu_2$. Reject H_0 if $t < -2.021$ or $t > 2.021$.

Less than 50: $\bar{X}_1 = 4{,}142$, $s_1 = 4679$, $n = 25$
50 or more: $\bar{X}_2 = 1{,}858$, $s_2 = 1850$, $n = 23$

$$s_p^2 = \frac{(25-1)(4679)^2 + (23-1)(1850)^2}{25 + 23 - 2} = 13{,}059{,}304$$

$$t = \frac{4{,}142 - 1{,}858}{\sqrt{13{,}059{,}304\left(\dfrac{1}{25} + \dfrac{1}{23}\right)}} = 2.188$$

Reject H_0. The mean circulation is not the same for the two groups of magazines.

c. $H_0: \mu_1 = \mu_2$; $H_1: \mu_1 \neq \mu_2$. Reject H_0 if $t < -2.021$ or $t > 2.021$.

Less than 50: $\bar{X}_1 = 35.20$, $s_1 = 5.23$, $n = 25$
50 or more: $\bar{X}_2 = 35.13$, $s_2 = 5.29$, $n = 23$

$$s_p^2 = \frac{(25-1)(5.23)^2 + (23-1)(5.29)^2}{25 + 23 - 2} = 27.6548$$

$$t = \frac{35.20 - 35.13}{\sqrt{27.6548\left(\dfrac{1}{25} + \dfrac{1}{23}\right)}} = 0.046$$

Do not reject H_0. There is no difference in the mean age of the two groups.

CHAPTER 11

1. 9.01, from Appendix G.

3. Reject H_0 if $F > 10.5$, where degrees of freedom in numerator are 7 and 5 in the denominator. Computed $F = 2.04$, found by:

$$F = \frac{s_1^2}{s_2^2} = \frac{(10)^2}{(7)^2} = 2.04$$

Do not reject H_0. There is no difference in the variations of the two populations.

5. $H_0: \sigma_1^2 = \sigma_2^2; H_1: \sigma_1^2 \neq \sigma_2^2$.
   Reject H_0 where $F > 3.10$. (3.10 is about halfway between 3.14 and 3.07.) Computed $F = 1.44$, found by:

$$F = \frac{(12)^2}{(10)^2} = 1.44$$

Do not reject H_0. There is no difference in the variations of the two populations.

7. **a.** $H_0: \mu_1 = \mu_2 = \mu_3; H_1$: Treatment means are not all the same.
   b. Reject H_0 if $F > 4.26$.
   c. & d.

Source	SS	df	MS	F
Treatment	62.17	2	31.08	21.94
Error	12.75	9	1.42	
Total	74.92	11		

   e. Reject H_0. The treatment means are not all the same.

9. $H_0: \mu_1 = \mu_2 = \mu_3; H_1$: Treatment means are not all the same. Reject H_0 if $F > 4.26$.

Source	SS	df	MS	F
Treatment	276.50	2	138.25	14.18
Error	87.75	9	9.75	

   Reject H_0. The treatment means are not all the same.

11. **a.** $H_0: \mu_1 = \mu_2 = \mu_3; H_1$: Not all means are the same.
    b. Reject H_0 if $F > 4.26$.
    c. SST $= 107.20$, SSE $= 9.47$, SS total $= 116.67$.
    d.

Source	SS	df	MS	F
Treatment	107.20	2	53.600	50.96
Error	9.47	9	1.052	
Total	116.67	11		

    e. Since $50.96 > 4.26$, H_0 is rejected. At least one of the means differs.
    f. $(\overline{X}_1 - \overline{X}_2) \pm t \sqrt{\text{MSE}(1/n_1 + 1/n_2)} = (9.667 - 2.20) \pm 2.262 \sqrt{1.052(1/3 + 1/5)} = 7.467 \pm 1.69 = [5.777, 9.157]$

    Yes, we can conclude that treatments 1 and 2 have different means.

13. $H_0: \mu_1 = \mu_2 = \mu_3 = \mu_4; H_1$: Not all means are equal. H_0 is rejected if $F > 3.71$.

Source	SS	df	MS	F
Treatment	32.33	3	10.77	2.36
Error	45.67	10	4.567	
Total	78.00	13		

Because 2.36 is less than 3.71, H_0 is not rejected. There is no difference in the mean number of weeks.

15. **a.** $H_0: \mu_1 = \mu_2; H_1$: Not all treatment means are equal.
    b. Reject H_0 if $F > 18.5$
    c. $H_0: \mu_1 = \mu_2 = \mu_3; H_1$: Not all block means are equal.
    H_0 is rejected if $F > 19.0$.
    d. $\text{SST} = \frac{(127)^2}{3} + \frac{(92)^2}{3} - \frac{(219)^2}{6} = 204.167$

    $\text{SSB} = \frac{(77)^2}{2} + \frac{(63)^2}{2} + \frac{(79)^2}{2} - \frac{(219)^2}{6} = 76$

    SS total $= 8{,}283 - (219)^2/6 = 289.5$
    SSE $= 289.5 - 204.167 - 76 = 9.333$
    e.

Source	SS	df	MS	F
Treatment	204.167	1	204.167	43.75
Blocks	76.000	2	38.000	8.14
Error	9.333	2	4.667	
Total	289.5000	5		

    f. $43.75 > 18.5$, so reject H_0. There is a difference in the treatments. $8.14 < 19.0$, so fail to reject H_0 for blocks. There is no difference among blocks.

17. For treatment   For blocks

$H_0: \mu_1 = \mu_2 = \mu_3$ $H_0: \mu_1 = \mu_2 = \mu_3 = \mu_4 = \mu_5$
H_1: Not all means equal H_1: Not all means equal
Reject if $F > 4.46$ Reject if $F > 3.84$

Source	SS	df	MS	F
Treatment	62.53	2	31.265	5.75
Blocks	33.73	4	8.4325	1.55
Error	43.47	8	5.4338	
Total	139.73			

There is a difference in shifts, but not by employee.

19. $H_0: \sigma_1^2 \leq \sigma_2^2; H_1: \sigma_1^2 > \sigma_2^2$. $df_1 = 21 - 1 = 20$; $df_2 = 18 - 1 = 17$. H_0 is rejected if $F > 3.16$.

$$F = \frac{(45{,}600)^2}{(21{,}330)^2} = 4.57$$

Reject H_0. There is more variation in selling price of oceanfront homes.

21. Sharkey: $n = 7$ $s_d = 14.79$
White: $n = 8$ $s_d = 22.95$

$H_0: \sigma_w^2 \le \sigma_s^2$; $H_1: \sigma_w^2 > \sigma_s^2$. $df_s = 7 - 1 = 6$; $df_w = 8 - 1 = 7$. Reject H_0 if $F > 8.26$.

$$F = \frac{(22.95)^2}{(14.79)^2} = 2.41$$

Cannot reject H_0. There is no difference in the variation of the weekly sales.

23. a. $H_0: \mu_1 = \mu_2 = \mu_3 = \mu_4$
  H_1: Treatment means are not all equal.
b. $\alpha = .05$ Reject H_0 if $F > 3.10$.
c.

Source	SS	df	MS	F
Treatment	50	$4 - 1 = 3$	50/3	$\frac{50/3}{10} = 1.67$
Error	200	$24 - 4 = 20$	10	
Total	250	$24 - 1 = 23$		

d. Do not reject H_0.

25. $H_0: \mu_1 = \mu_2 = \mu_3$; H_1: Not all treatment means are equal. H_0 is rejected if $F > 3.89$.

Source	df	SS	MS	F
Treatment	2	63.33	31.667	13.38
Error	12	28.40	2.367	
Total	14	91.73		

H_0 is rejected. There is a difference in the treatment means.

27. $H_0: \mu_1 = \mu_2 = \mu_3 = \mu_4$; H_1: Not all means are equal. H_0 is rejected if $F > 3.10$

Source	df	SS	MS	F
Factor	3	87.79	29.26	9.12
Error	20	64.17	3.21	
Total	23	151.96		

Because computed F of $9.12 > 3.10$, the null hypothesis of no difference is rejected at the .05 level.

29. a. $H_0: \mu_1 = \mu_2$; $H_1: \mu_1 \neq \mu_2$. Critical value of $F = 4.75$.

Source	SS	df	MS	F
Treatment	219.43	1	219.43	23.10
Error	114.00	12	9.5	
Total	333.43	13		

b. $t = \dfrac{19 - 27}{\sqrt{9.5\left(\dfrac{1}{6} + \dfrac{1}{8}\right)}} = -4.81$

Then $t^2 = F$. That is $(-4.81)^2 \simeq 23.10$ (actually 23.14. Difference due to rounding)
c. H_0 is rejected. There is a difference in the mean scores.

31. For color the critical value of F is 4.76, for size it is 5.14

Source	SS	df	MS	F
Treatment	25.0	3	8.3333	5.88
Blocks	21.5	2	10.75	7.59
Error	8.5	6	1.4167	
Total	55.0	11		

H_0 for both treatment and blocks (color and size) is rejected. At least one mean differs for color and at least one mean differs for size.

33. a. Critical value of F is 3.49. Computed F is .668. Do not reject H_0.
b. Critical value of F is 3.26. Computed F value is 100.204. Reject H_0 for block means.

35. For gasoline:
$H_0: \mu_1 = \mu_2 = \mu_3$; H_1: Mean mileage is not the same. Reject H_0 if $F > 3.89$.
For automobile:
$H_0: \mu_1 = \mu_2 = \cdots = \mu_7$; H_1: Mean mileage is not the same. Reject H_0 if $F > 3.00$.

ANOVA Table

Source	df	SS	MS	F
Gasoline	2	44.095	22.048	26.71
Autos	6	77.238	12.873	15.60
Error	12	9.905	0.825	
Total	20			

There is a difference in both autos and gasoline.

37. a. $H_0: \mu_1 = \mu_2 = \mu_3 = \mu_4 = \mu_5 = \mu_6$; H_1: The treatment means are not equal. Reject H_0 if $F > 2.37$.

Source	df	SS	MS	F
Treatment	5	0.03478	0.00696	3.86
Error	58	0.10439	0.0018	
Total	63	0.13917		

H_0 is rejected. There is a difference in the mean weight of the colors.

39. For calories: H_0: $\mu_B = \mu_M = \mu_P$; H_1: Not all means are the same. Reject H_0 if $F > 3.18$.

Source	SS	df	MS	F
Type	17,692	2	8846	16.07
Error	28,067	51	550	
Total	45,759	53		

Reject H_0. There is a difference in the mean number of calories. Poultry differs from both beef and meat.

For sodium: H_0: $\mu_B = \mu_M = \mu_P$; H_1: Not all means are the same. Reject H_0 if $F > 3.18$.

Source	SS	df	MS	F
Treatment	31,739	2	15,869	1.78
Error	455,249	51	8,926	

Do not reject H_0. Failed to show a difference in sodium for the three types.

41. a. H_0: $\sigma_P^2 = \sigma_{NP}^2$; H_1: $\sigma_P^2 \neq \sigma_{NP}^2$. Reject H_0 if $F > 2.21$. $df_1 = 67 - 1 = 66$; $df_2 = 38 - 1 = 37$.

$$F = \frac{(50.58)^2}{(33.71)^2} = 2.25$$

Reject H_0. There is a difference in the variance of the two selling prices.

b. H_0: $\sigma_g^2 = \sigma_{ng}^2$; H_1: $\sigma_g^2 \neq \sigma_{ng}^2$. Reject H_0 if $F > 2.21$.

$$F = \frac{(44.88)^2}{(28.01)^2} = 2.57$$

Reject H_0. There is a difference in the variance of the two selling prices.

c. H_0: $\mu_1 = \mu_2 = \mu_3 = \mu_4 = \mu_5$; H_1: Not all treatment means are equal. Reject H_0 if $F > 2.50$.

Source	SS	df	MS	F
Township	13,258	4	3314	1.52
Error	217,555	100	2176	
Total	230,812	104		

Do not reject H_0. There is no difference in the mean selling prices in the five townships.

43. a. H_0: $\mu_1 = \mu_2 = \mu_3$; H_1: Not all treatment means are the same. Reject H_0 if $F > 3.23$.

Source	DF	SS	MS	F
Treatment	2	105877149	52938574	4.27
Error	45	557332745	12385172	
Total	47	663209894		

Reject H_0. There is a difference in the treatment means. There is a difference between the 33 up to 67 percent male and the more than 67 percent male groups.

b. H_0: $\mu_1 = \mu_2 = \mu_3$; H_1: Not all treatment means are the same. Reject H_0 if $F > 3.23$.

Analysis of Variance				
Source	DF	SS	MS	F
Factor	2	3.194E+09	1.597E+09	3.33
Error	45	2.161E+10	480212090	
Total	47	2.480E+10		

Reject H_0. There is a difference in the 33 up to 67 percent male group and the more than 67 percent group.

c. H_0: $\sigma_1^2 = \sigma_2^2$; H_1: $\sigma_1^2 \neq \sigma_2^2$. Population 1 is the more than 67 percent group. Reject H_0 if $F > 3.31$.

$$F = \frac{(4429)^2}{(2345)^2} = 3.57$$

H_0 is rejected. The variation is not the same in the two groups.

CHAPTER 12

1. $\sum X = 28$, $\sum Y = 29$, $\sum X^2 = 186$, $\sum XY = 173$, $\sum Y^2 = 175$

$$r = \frac{5(173) - (28)(29)}{\sqrt{[5(186) - (28)^2][5(175) - (29)^2]}} = 0.75$$

The 0.75 coefficient indicates a rather strong positive correlation between X and Y. The coefficient of determination is 0.5625, found by $(0.75)^2$. More than 56 percent of the variation in Y is accounted for by X.

3. a. Sales.

b.

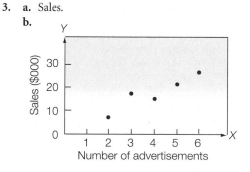

c. $n = 5$, $\sum X = 20$, $\sum X^2 = 90$, $\sum Y = 85$, $\sum Y^2 = 1595$, and $\sum XY = 376$, so:

$$r = \frac{5(376) - (20)(85)}{\sqrt{[5(90) - (20)^2][5(1595) - (85)^2]}} = 0.93$$

d. The coefficient of determination is 0.8649, found by $(0.93)^2$.

e. There is a strong positive association between the variables. About 86 percent of the variation in sales is explained by the number of airings.

5. a. Police is the independent variable and crime is the dependent variable.

b.

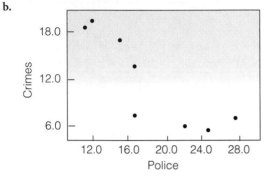

c. $n = 8$, $\sum X = 146$, $\sum X^2 = 2906$, $\sum Y = 95$, $\sum Y^2 = 1419$, and $\sum XY = 1502$

$$r = \frac{8(1502) - 146(95)}{\sqrt{[8(2906) - (146)^2][8(1419) - (95)^2]}}$$
$$= -.874$$

d. 0.76, found by $(-.874)^2$

e. Strong inverse relationship. As the number of police increases, the crime decreases.

7. Reject H_0 if $t > 1.812$.

$$t = \frac{.32\sqrt{12 - 2}}{\sqrt{1 - (.32)^2}} = 1.07$$

Do not reject H_0.

9. H_0: $\rho \leq 0$; H_1: $\rho > 0$. Reject H_0 if $t > 2.552$. $df = 18$.

$$t = \frac{.78\sqrt{20 - 2}}{\sqrt{1 - (.78)^2}} = 5.288$$

Reject H_0. There is a positive correlation between gallons sold and the pump price.

11. a. $Y' = 3.7671 + .3630X$

$$b = \frac{5(173) - (28)(29)}{5(186) - (28)^2} = 0.3630$$

$$a = \frac{29}{5} - (0.363)\frac{28}{5} = 3.7671$$

b. 6.3081, found by $Y' = 3.7671 + 0.3630(7)$

13. a. $b = \frac{10(718) - (91)(74)}{10(895) - (91)^2} = 0.667$

$$a = \frac{74}{10} - .667\left(\frac{91}{10}\right) = 1.333$$

b. $Y' = 1.333 + .667(6) = 5.333$

15. a.

b. $r = \dfrac{12(3306.35) - (501.10)(64.1)}{\sqrt{[12(28,459) - (501.10)^2][12(458.41) - (64.1)^2]}}$

$= 0.673$

c. $r^2 = (0.673)^2 = 0.4529$

d. A strong positive association between the variables. About 45 percent of the variation in earnings is accounted for by sales.

e. $b = \dfrac{12(3306.35) - (501.1)(64.1)}{5(28,459) - (501.1)^2} = 0.0836$

$$a = \frac{64.1}{12} - 0.0836\left(\frac{501.10}{12}\right) = 1.8507$$

f. $Y' = 1.8507 + 0.0836(50.0) = 6.0307$ ($ millions)

17. a. $b = \dfrac{8(1502) - (146)(95)}{8(2906) - (146)^2} = -0.9596$

$$a = \frac{95}{8} - (-0.9596)\left(\frac{146}{8}\right) = 29.3877$$

b. 10.1957, found by $29.3877 - 0.9596(20)$

c. For each policeman added, crime goes down by almost one.

19. a. $\sqrt{\dfrac{175 - 3.767(29) - 0.363(173)}{5 - 2}} = .993$

b. $Y' \pm .993$

21. a. $\sqrt{\dfrac{584 - 1.333(74) - 0.667(718)}{10 - 2}} = .898$

b. $Y' \pm 1.796$

23. $\sqrt{\dfrac{1419 - 29.3977(95) - (-.9596)(1502)}{8 - 2}} = 3.355$

25. a. $6.308 \pm (3.182)(.993)\sqrt{.2 + \dfrac{(7 - 5.6)^2}{186 - (784/5)}}$

$= 6.308 \pm 1.633$

$= [4.675, 7.941]$

b. $6.308 \pm (3.182)(.993)\sqrt{1 + 1/5 + .0671} = [2.751, 9.865]$

27. **a.** [4.2939, 6.3721]
   b. [2.9854, 7.6806]
29. Coefficient of correlation $r = .8944$, found by:

$$\frac{(5)(340) - (50)(30)}{\sqrt{[(5)(600) - (50)^2][(5)(200) - (30)^2]}}$$

Then, $(.8944)^2 = .80$, the coefficient of determination.

31. **a.** $r^2 = 1000/1500 = .667$
   b. .82, found by $\sqrt{.667}$

   c. 6.20, found by $s_{Y \cdot X} = \sqrt{\dfrac{500}{15 - 2}}$

33. H_0: $\rho \le 0$; H_1: $\rho > 0$. Reject H_0 if $t > 1.714$.

$$t = \frac{.94\sqrt{25 - 2}}{\sqrt{1 - (.94)^2}} = 13.213$$

Reject H_0. There is a positive correlation between passengers and weight of luggage.

35. H_0: $\rho \le 0$; H_1: $\rho > 0$. Reject H_0 if $t > 2.764$.

$$t = \frac{.47\sqrt{12 - 2}}{\sqrt{1 - (.47)^2}} = 1.684$$

Do not reject H_0. There is not a positive correlation between engine size and performance. p-value is greater than .05, but less than .10.

37. H_0: $\rho \ge 0$; H_1: $\rho < 0$. Reject H_0 if $t < -1.701$, $df = 28$.

$$t = \frac{-.45\sqrt{30 - 2}}{\sqrt{1 - .2025}} = -2.67$$

Reject H_0. There is a negative correlation between the selling price and the number of miles driven.

39. **a.** $r = 0.589$
   b. $r^2 = (0.589)^2 = 0.3469$
   c. H_0: $\rho \le 0$; H_1: $\rho > 0$. Reject H_0 if $t > 1.860$.

$$t = \frac{0.589\sqrt{10 - 2}}{\sqrt{1 - (.589)^2}} = 2.062$$

H_0 is rejected. There is a positive association between family size and the amount spent on food.

41. **a.**

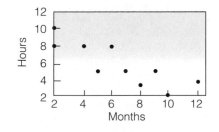

There is an inverse relationship between the variables. As the months owned increase, the number of hours exercised decreases.

b. $r = \dfrac{10(313) - (65)(58)}{\sqrt{[10(523) - (65)^2][10(396) - (58)^2]}}$

   $= -0.827$

c. H_0: $\rho \ge 0$; H_1: $\rho < 0$. Reject H_0 if $t < -2.896$.

$$t = \frac{-0.827\sqrt{10 - 2}}{\sqrt{1 - (-0.827)^2}} = -4.16$$

Reject H_0. There is a negative association between months owned and hours exercised.

43. **a.**

Source	SS	df	MS	F
Regression	50	1	50	2.5556
Error	450	23	19.5652	
Total	500	24		

b. $n = 25$
c. $s_{y \cdot x} = \sqrt{19.5652} = 4.4233$
d. $r^2 = \dfrac{50}{500} = 0.10$

45. **a.** $n = 15$, $\sum X = 107$, $\sum X^2 = 837$, $\sum Y = 118.6$, $\sum Y^2 = 969.92$, $\sum XY = 811.60$, $s_{y \cdot x} = 1.114$

$$b = \frac{15(811.60) - (107)(118.6)}{15(837.0) - (107)^2} = -0.4667$$

$$a = \frac{118.6}{15} - (-0.4667)\left(\frac{107}{15}\right) = 11.2358$$

b. $Y' = 11.2358 - 0.4667(7.0) = 7.9689$

c. $7.9689 \pm (2.160)(1.114)\sqrt{1 + \dfrac{1}{15} + \dfrac{(7 - 7.1333)^2}{837 - \dfrac{(107)^2}{15}}}$

   $= 7.9689 \pm 2.4854$
   $= [5.4835, 10.4543]$

d. $r^2 = 0.499$. Nearly 50 percent of the variation in the amount of the bid is explained by the number of bidders.

47. **a.**

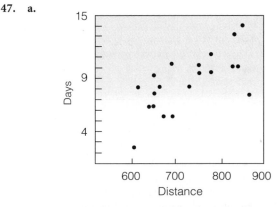

There appears to be a relationship between the two variables. As the distance increases, so does the shipping time.

b. $r = 0.692$

$H_0: \rho \leq 0$; $H_1: \rho > 0$. Reject H_0 if $t > 1.734$.

$$t = \frac{0.692\sqrt{20 - 2}}{\sqrt{1 - (0.692)^2}} = 4.067$$

H_0 is rejected. There is a positive association between shipping distance and shipping time.

c. $r^2 = 0.479$. Nearly half of the variation in shipping time is explained by shipping distance.

d. $s_{y \cdot x} = \sqrt{\dfrac{1550 - (-7.126)(168) - .0214(125,051)}{20 - 2}}$

$= 1.987$

49. a. $Y' = 0.546 + .0227X$. Each additional employee cleans .0227 square feet. This is in millions of square feet, so it is actually 22,700 square feet.

b. The correlation is 0.924.

$H_0: \rho \leq 0$; $H_1: \rho > 0$. Reject H_0 if $t > 1.729$.

$$t = \frac{.924\sqrt{21 - 2}}{\sqrt{1 - (.924)^2}} = 10.532$$

H_0 is rejected. There is a positive correlation between the number of employees and the area cleaned.

51. a. Answers will vary. At the time of publication there were 14 cottages, and $r = 0.668$. Reject H_0 if $t > 1.782$.

$$t = \frac{.668\sqrt{14 - 2}}{\sqrt{1 - (.668)^2}} = 3.11$$

Reject H_0. There is a positive correlation between price and baths.

b. $Y' = 758 + 347x$

c. $H_0: \rho \leq 0$; $H_1: \rho > 0$. Reject H_0 if $t > 1.782$.

$$t = \frac{.085\sqrt{14 - 2}}{\sqrt{1 - (0.085)^2}} = 0.269.$$

Do not reject H_0.

53. a. The correlation between wins and salary is 0.673, and $n = 28$. $H_0: \rho \leq 0$; $H_1: \rho > 0$. Reject H_0 if $t > 1.706$.

$$t = \frac{.673\sqrt{28 - 2}}{\sqrt{1 - (.673)^2}} = 4.640$$

Reject H_0. There is a positive association between wins and salary.

The regression equation is $Y' = 62.766 + .471X$. An additional \$5,000,000 would increase the number of wins by 2.355, found by .471(5.0).

b. The correlation between wins and team batting average is 0.325 and the correlation between wins

and ERA is -0.546. We conclude that the correlation is stronger between wins and ERA.

For batting average: $H_0: \rho \leq 0$; $H_1: \rho > 0$. Reject H_0 if $t > 1.706$.

$$t = \frac{.325\sqrt{28 - 2}}{\sqrt{1 - (.325)^2}} = 1.752$$

H_0 is rejected. We conclude the two variables are positively correlated. The p-value is between .025 and .05.

For ERA: $H_0: \rho \geq 0$; $H_1: \rho < 0$. Reject H_0 if $t < -1.706$.

$$t = \frac{-.546\sqrt{28 - 2}}{\sqrt{1 - (-.546)^2}} = -3.323$$

Reject H_0. There is a negative correlation between the variables. The p-value is less than .0005.

c. The correlation between wins and attendance is .590. $H_0: \rho \leq 0$; $H_1: \rho > 0$. Reject H_0 if $t > 1.706$.

$$t = \frac{.590\sqrt{28 - 2}}{\sqrt{1 - (.590)^2}} = 3.726$$

Reject H_0. There is a positive correlation between wins and attendance. The p-value is less than .0005.

55. a. $Y' = -699.2 + 391.71X$, $r^2 = .43$, 95 percent confidence interval is 2559 up to 3876. 95 percent prediction interval is -2691 to 9127.

b. $r^2 = .446$, $Y' = -718.7 + 8.235X$. Expected rate is 22.45. Bounds for a confidence interval are 12.22 and 32.68. Bounds for a prediction interval are -0.22 and 45.12.

c. $H_0: \rho \leq 0$; $H_1: \rho > 0$. Reject H_0 if $t > 2.326$.

$$t = \frac{-0.668\sqrt{94 - 2}}{\sqrt{1 - (-0.668)^2}} = -8.61$$

Reject H_0. There is a significant negative correlation between attendance and passing.

CHAPTER 13

1. a. Multiple regression equation.

b. The Y-intercept.

c. $Y' = 64,100 + 0.394(796,000) + 9.6(6,940) - 11,600(6.0) = \$374,748$

3. a. 497.736, found by

$Y' = 16.24 + 0.017(18)$
$+ 0.0028(26,500) + 42(3)$
$+ 0.0012(156,000)$
$+ 0.19(141) + 26.8(2.5)$

b. Two more social activities. Income added only 28 to the index; social activities added 53.6.

5. a. 19

b. 3

c. .318, found by 21/66

d. 1.732, found by $\sqrt{\dfrac{45}{[19 - (3 + 1)]}}$

7. a.

Source	SS	df	MS	F
Regression	7,500.0	3	2500	18
Error	2,500.0	18	138.89	
Total	10,000.0	21		

b. $H_0: \beta_1 = \beta_2 = \beta_3 = 0$; H_1: Not all βs are 0. Reject H_0 if $F > 3.16$.

Reject H_0. Not all net regression coefficients equal zero.

c.

For X_1:

$H_0: \beta_1 = 0$
$H_1: \beta_1 \neq 0$
$t = -4.00$

For X_2:

$H_0: \beta_2 = 0$
$H_1: \beta_2 \neq 0$
$t = 1.50$

For X_3:

$H_0: \beta_3 = 0$
$H_1: \beta_3 \neq 0$
$t = -3.00$

Reject H_0 if $t > 2.101$ or $t < -2.101$.
Delete variable 2, keep 1 and 3.

9. a. $n = 40$

b. 4

c. $R^2 = \dfrac{750}{1250} = .60$

d. $s_{y \cdot 1234} = \sqrt{500/35} = 3.7796$

e. $H_0: \beta_1 = \beta_2 = \beta_3 = \beta_4 = 0$
H_1: Not all the βs equal zero.
H_0 is rejected if $F > 2.65$.

$$F = \dfrac{750/4}{500/35} = 13.125$$

H_0 is rejected. At least one β_i does not equal zero.

11. a. $n = 26$.

b. $R^2 = 100/140 = .7143$

c. 1.4142, found by $\sqrt{2}$

d. $H_0: \beta_1 = \beta_2 = \beta_3 = \beta_4 = \beta_5 = 0$
H_1: Not all the βs are 0.
H_0 is rejected if $F > 2.71$.
Computed $F = 10.0$. Reject H_0. At least one regression coefficient is not zero.

e. H_0 is rejected in each case if $t < -2.086$ or $t > 2.086$. X_1 and X_5 should be dropped.

13. a. $28,000

b. $R^2 = \dfrac{SSR}{SStotal} = \dfrac{3,050}{5,250} = .5809$

c. 9.199, found by $\sqrt{84.62}$.

d. H_0 is rejected if $F > 2.97$ (approximately).

$$\text{Computed } F = \dfrac{762.50}{84.62} = 9.01$$

H_0 is rejected. At least one regression coefficient is not zero.

e. If computed t is to the left of -2.056 or to the right of 2.056, the null hypothesis in each of these cases is rejected. Computed t for X_2 and X_3 exceed the critical value. Thus, "population" and "advertising expenses" should be retained and "number of competitors," X_1, dropped.

15. a. The strongest correlation is between GPA and legal. No problem with multicollinearity.

b. $R^2 = \dfrac{4.3595}{5.0631} = .8610$

c. H_0 is rejected if $F > 5.41$.

$$F = \dfrac{1.4532}{0.1407} = 10.328.$$

At least one coefficient is not zero.

d. Any H_0 is rejected if $t < -2.571$ or $t > 2.571$. It appears that only GPA is significant. Verbal and math could be eliminated.

e. $R^2 = \dfrac{4.2061}{5.0631} = .8307.$

R^2 has only been reduced .0303.

f. The residuals appear slightly skewed (positive), but acceptable.

g. There does not seem to be a problem with the plot.

17. a. The correlation matrix is:

	cars	adv	sales
adv	0.808		
sales	0.872	0.537	
city	0.639	0.713	0.389

Size of sales force (0.872) has strongest correlation with cars sold. Fairly strong relationship between location of dealership and advertising (0.713). Could be a problem.

b. The regression equation is:
$Y' = 31.1328 + 2.1516adv + 5.0140sales + 5.6651city$
$Y' = 31.1328 + 2.1516(15) + 5.0140(20) + 5.6651(1) = 169.352$.

c. $H_0: \beta_1 = \beta_2 = \beta_3 = 0$; H_1: Not all βs are 0. Reject H_0 if computed $F > 4.07$.

Analysis of Variance

Source	SS	df	MS
Regression	5504.4	3	1834.8
Error	420.2	8	52.5
Total	5924.7	11	

$F = 1,834.8/52.5 = 34.95$.

Reject H_0. At least one regression coefficient is not 0.

d. H_0 is rejected in all cases if $t < -2.306$ or if $t > 2.306$. Advertising and sales force should be retained, city dropped. (Note that dropping city removes the problem with multicollinearity.)

Predictor	Coef	Stdev	t-ratio	P
Constant	31.13	13.40	2.32	0.049
adv	2.1516	0.8049	2.67	0.028
sales	5.0140	0.9105	5.51	0.000
city	5.665	6.332	0.89	0.397

e. The new output is

$$Y' = 25.2952 + 2.6187adv + 5.0233sales$$

Predictor	Coef	Stdev	t-ratio
Constant	25.30	11.57	2.19
adv	2.6187	0.6057	4.32
sales	5.0233	0.9003	5.58

Analysis of Variance

Source	SS	df	MS
Regression	5462.4	2	2731.2
Error	462.3	9	51.4
Total	5924.7	11	

f. Stem-and-leaf
Leaf unit = 1.0

1	−1	6
1	−1	
2	−0	5
5	−0	110
(5)	0	01224
2	0	58

The normality assumption is reasonable.

g.

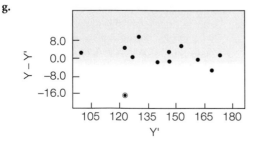

The circled value could be a problem. However, with a small sample the residual plot is acceptable.

19. a. The regression equation is
$$Y' = 965.3 + 2.865X_1 + 6.75X_2 + 0.2873X_3$$
$2,458,780

b.

Analysis of Variance

Source	SS	df	MS
Regression	45510096	3	15170032
Error	12215892	12	1017991
Total	57725984	15	

$$F = \frac{15170032}{1017991} = 14.902$$

H_0 is rejected because computed F of 14.9 is greater than the critical value of 3.49. At least one of the regression coefficients is not zero.

c. $H_0: \beta_1 = 0$ $H_0: \beta_2 = 0$ $H_0: \beta_3 = 0$
$H_1: \beta_1 \neq 0$ $H_1: \beta_2 \neq 0$ $H_1: \beta_3 \neq 0$
The H_0s are rejected if $t < -2.179$ or $t > 2.179$. Both workers and dividends are not significant variables. Inventory is significant. Delete dividends and rerun analysis.

d. The regression equation (if we used X_1 and X_3)

$$Y' = 1134.8 + 3.258X_1 + 0.3099X_3$$

Predictor	Coef	Stdev	t-ratio
Constant	1134.8	418.6	2.71
Workers	3.258	1.434	2.27
inv	0.3099	0.1033	3.00

Analysis of Variance

Source	SS	df	MS	F
Regression	45070624	2	22535312	23.15
Error	12655356	13	973489	
Total	57725968	15		

e.

```
Histogram of C12          N = 16
Midpoint                  Count
   −1500                    1   *
   −1000                    3   ***
    −500                    1   *
       0                    6   ******
     500                    2   **
    1000                    2   **
    1500                    0
    2000                    1   *
```

The normality assumption is reasonable.

f.

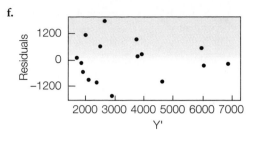

The plot of the residuals is acceptable.

21. a. The correlation matrix is:

	Profit	Daily
Daily	0.997	
Sunday	0.995	0.984

The two independent variables are highly correlated.

b. The regression equation is:
$Y' = -0.643 + 0.401X_1 + 0.269X_2$
$Y' = -0.643 + 0.401(50) + 0.269(100) = 46.307$
Or about $46.30 per week.

c. One hundred percent of the variation is accounted for by the two variables.

d. Each additional Sunday customer adds $0.269 profit per week, and a daily customer adds $0.401 per week.

e. The large R-square is expected. There really are not other variables to be added.

23. The computer output is:

Predictor	Coef	Stdev	t-ratio	p
Constant	651.9	345.3	1.89	0.071
Service	13.422	5.125	2.62	0.015
Age	−6.710	6.349	−1.06	0.301
Gender	205.65	90.27	2.28	0.032
Job	−33.45	89.55	−0.37	0.712

Analysis of Variance

SOURCE	DF	SS	MS	F	p
Regression	4	1066830	266708	4.77	0.005
Error	25	1398651	55946		
Total	29	2465481			

a. $Y' = 651.9 + 13.422X_1 - 6.710X_2 + 205.65X_3 - 33.45X_4$

b. $R^2 = .433$, which is somewhat low for this type of study.

c. $H_0: \beta_1 = \beta_2 = \beta_3 = \beta_4 = 0$; H_1: not all βs equal zero. Reject H_0 if $F > 2.76$.

$$F = \frac{1,066,830/4}{1,398,651/25} = 4.77$$

H_0 is rejected. Not all the β_is equal 0.

d. Using the .05 significance level, reject the hypothesis that the regression coefficient is 0 if $t < -2.060$ or $t > 2.060$. Service and gender should remain in the analyses, age and job should be dropped.

e. Following is the computer output using the independent variables service and gender.

Predictor	Coef	Stdev	t-ratio	p
Constant	784.2	316.8	2.48	0.020
Service	9.021	3.106	2.90	0.007
Gender	224.41	87.35	2.57	0.016

Analysis of Variance

SOURCE	DF	SS	MS	F	p
Regression	2	998779	499389	9.19	0.001
Error	27	1466703	54322		
Total	29	2465481			

A man earns $224 more per month than a woman. The difference between technical and clerical jobs is not significant.

25. The answers will vary. Here is one solution. The output is:

Predictor	Coef	StDev	T	P
Constant	1130.5	872.3	1.30	0.224
Bedrooms	138.5	126.8	1.09	0.300
Baths	295.1	104.3	2.83	0.018
People	−67.25	74.30	−0.91	0.387

$S = 306.4$ $R-S1 = 51.0\%$ $R-Sq(adj) = 36.3\%$

Analysis of Variance

Source	DF	SS	MS	F	P
Regression	3	977839	325946	3.47	0.059
Error	10	938804	93880		
Total	13	1916643			

To conduct the global test: $H_1: \beta_1 = \beta_2 = \beta_3 = 0$; H_1: some of the net regression coefficients do not equal 0. The null hypothesis is rejected if $F > 3.71$. The computed value of F is 3.47, so the null hypothesis cannot be rejected. We conclude that all the net regression coefficients could be equal to 0. The R-square value is .510.

If we look at the p-values associated with each of the net regression coefficients, it seems that the number of bathrooms may be a useful predictor of price. The following output uses only the independent variable *baths*.

```
Predictor        Coef      StDev         T        P
Constant        879.3      347.7      2.53    0.026
Baths          304.95      97.73      3.12    0.009


S = 296.9      R-Sq = 44.8%      R-Sq(adj) = 40.2%


Analysis of Variance


Source        DF        SS         MS        F        P
Regression     1     858548     858548     9.74    0.009
Error         12    1058095      88175
Total         13    1916643
```

The *p*-value is .009, so this variable is a useful estimator of the dependent variable *price*. The *R*-square value is .448.

27. The computer output is as follows:

```
Predictor        Coef      StDev         T        P
Constant        15.35      35.16      0.44    0.667
Average         505.0      134.2      3.76    0.001
ERA          -14.828      2.794     -5.31    0.000
Stolen      -0.00684    0.04100     -0.17    0.869
Errors      -0.0344      0.1007     -0.33    0.743
Turf          0.440       3.087      0.14    0.888


S = 6.593      R-Sq = 61.6%      R-Sq(adj) = 52.9%


Analysis of Variance


Source        DF        SS         MS        F        P
Regression     5    1535.44     307.09     7.06    0.000
Error         22     956.42      43.47
Total         27    2491.86
```

a. The regression equation is:

$$Y' = 15.4 + 505\ average - 14.8\ ERA$$
$$- 0.0068\ stolen - 0.033\ errors + 0.44\ turf.$$

For each additional point that the team batting average increases, the number of wins goes up by 5. The variable ERA is negatively related to wins. An increase in the number of stolen bases decreases the number of wins. An increase of 100 stolen bases would result in losing about 7 more games. Same with errors.

b. The coefficient of determination is .616. About 60 percent of the variation in the number of wins

is accounted for in the variation in the five independent variables.

c. The following is the correlation matrix.

```
             Wins    Average     ERA    Stolen   Errors
Average     0.325
ERA        -0.546     0.363
Stolen     -0.179    -0.334   -0.046
Errors      0.047     0.154    0.009   -0.172
Turf       -0.238    -0.365    0.037    0.279    0.026
```

The independent variable *ERA* has the strongest correlation with wins. The next strongest is between *average* and *wins*. There does not seem to be a problem with multicollinearity.

d. To conduct the global test: H_1: $\beta_1 = \beta_2 = \beta_3 = \beta_4 = \beta_5 = 0$; H_1: Some of the net regression coefficients do not equal 0. The null hypothesis is rejected if $F > 2.66$. The computed value of F is 7.06, so the null hypothesis is rejected. We conclude that not all the net regression coefficients are equal to 0.

e. In reviewing the individual net regression coefficients, the *p*-values for *ERA* and *average* are less than .05, but the *p*-values for *stolen bases, errors,* and *turf* are quite large. It seems reasonable that these three variables can be deleted from the analysis.

f. Below is the regression analysis with wins as the dependent variable and ERA and team batting average as the independent variables.

```
Predictor        Coef      StDev         T        P
Constant        12.25      27.43      0.45    0.659
Average         498.2      110.3      4.52    0.000
ERA          -14.742      2.569     -5.74    0.000


S = 6.204      R-Sq = 61.4%      R-Sq(adj) = 58.3%


Analysis of Variance


Source        DF        SS         MS        F        P
Regression     2    1529.73     764.86    19.87    0.000
Error         25     962.13      38.49
Total         27    2491.86
```

Both of the independent variables are significant (*p*-values less than .05), and there was little change in the *R*-square value. *R*-square decreased from .616 to .614.

g. The following is a histogram of the residuals for the regression equation in part (f). It is reasonable to conclude that it is normal.

```
Histogram of Residual for 28 observations

Midpoint  Count
    -10    3 ***
     -8    2 **
     -6    0
     -4    3 ***
     -2    4 ****
      0    3 ***
      2    6 ******
      4    2 **
      6    1 *
      8    2 **
     10    1 *
     12    0
     14    1 *
```

h. Below is a scatter diagram. The residuals are plotted on the vertical axis and the fitted values on the horizontal axis. There does not seem to be a pattern to the plotted data.

29. The computer output is as follows:

```
Predictor      Coef        StDev         T        P
Constant     -658.8        158.1     -4.17    0.000
Salary     0.0000571    0.0003227      0.18    0.860
Welfare      -0.2067       0.2545     -0.81    0.419
Instruct   0.0018732    0.0009636      1.94    0.055
Attend         7.548        1.593      4.74    0.000


S = 10.08      R-Sq = 47.5%      R-Sq(adj) = 45.2%


Analysis of Variance


Source        DF       SS        MS        F        P
Regression     4    8187.8    2047.0    20.16    0.000
Error         89    9037.4     101.5
Total         93   17225.2
```

a. The regression equation is:

$$Y' = -659 + 0.000057\ salary - 0.207\ welfare$$
$$+ 0.00187\ instruct + 7.55\ attend.$$

The percent of students passing in the district increases when the teacher salary is increased, when the instructional cost per student increases, and the percent attendance increases. The percent passing decreases when the percent on welfare in the district increases.

b. Less than half of the variation in percent passing is explained by the four independent variables. The *R*-square value is .475.

c. The following is the correlation matrix.

	Passing	Salary	Welfare	Instruct
Salary	−0.191			
Welfare	−0.560	0.091		
Instruct	0.093	0.033	0.006	
Attend	0.668	−0.329	−0.756	−0.095

There is a strong correlation between attendance and passing and between welfare and passing. There is also a strong correlation between these two independent variables. Salary and instructional cost do not show much correlation with the dependent variable.

d. The global test of hypothesis is: H_0: $\beta_1 = \beta_2 = \beta_3 = \beta_4 = 0$; H_1: Not all the net regression coefficients equal 0. The null hypothesis is rejected if the computed value of *F* is greater than 2.50. The computed value is 20.16, so the null hypothesis is rejected. We conclude that not all the net regression coefficients equal 0.

e. Comparing the *p*-values of the four independent variables, attendance is significant, salary and welfare are not significant, and instruction seems to be close (*p*-value is .055). Rerunning the regression equation with attendance and instruction as independent variables, the output is as follows. Both independent variables are significant at the .05 significance level.

```
Predictor      Coef        StDev         T        P
Constant     -741.57       90.31     -8.21    0.000
Instruct   0.0019553    0.0009521      2.05    0.043
Attend        8.4191       0.9449      8.91    0.000


S = 10.01      R-Sq = 47.1%      R-Sq(adj) = 45.9%


Analysis of Variance


Source        DF       SS        MS        F        P
Regression     2    8104.7    4052.4    40.43    0.000
Error         91    9120.5     100.2
Total         93   17225.2
```

f. The following is a histogram of the residuals. It seems reasonable to conclude that the distribution is normal.

```
Histogram of residual n = 94

Midpoint    Count
   -35        1  *
   -30        0
   -25        0
   -20        3  ***
   -15        2  **
   -10       16  ****************
    -5       15  ***************
     0       19  *******************
     5       17  *****************
    10       13  *************
    15        5  *****
    20        1  *
    25        2  **
```

g. The following is a plot showing the relationship between the fitted values of Y and the residuals. There do not seem to be any unusual patterns. We conclude that *instruction* and *attendance* are reasonable independent variables, but the value of R-square is less than we would have hoped.

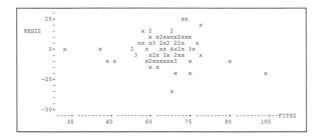

CHAPTER 14

1. a. 3
   b. 7.815
3. a. Reject H_0 if $\chi^2 > 5.991$.

   b. $\chi^2 = \dfrac{(10 - 20)^2}{20} + \dfrac{(20 - 20)^2}{20} + \dfrac{(30 - 20)^2}{20}$

   $= 10.0$

   c. Reject H_0. The proportions are not equal.
5. H_0: The outcomes are the same; H_1: The outcomes are not the same. Reject H_0 if $\chi^2 > 9.236$

$$\chi^2 = \frac{(3 - 5)^2}{5} + \cdots + \frac{(7 - 5)^2}{5} = 7.60$$

Do not reject H_0. Cannot reject H_0 that outcomes are the same.
7. H_0: There is no difference in the proportions; H_1: There is a difference in the proportions. Reject H_0 if $\chi^2 > 15.086$.

$$\chi^2 = \frac{(47 - 40)^2}{40} + \cdots + \frac{(34 - 40)^2}{40} = 3.400$$

Do not reject H_0. There is no difference in the proportions.
9. a. Reject H_0 if $\chi^2 > 9.210$.

   b. $\chi^2 = \dfrac{(30 - 24)^2}{24} + \dfrac{(20 - 24)^2}{24} + \dfrac{(10 - 12)^2}{12}$

   $= 2.50$

   c. Do not reject H_0.
11. H_0: Proportions are as stated; H_1: Proportions are not as stated. Reject H_0 if $\chi^2 > 11.345$.

$$\chi^2 = \frac{(50 - 25)^2}{25} + \frac{(100 - 75)^2}{75} + \frac{(190 - 125)^2}{125}$$

$$+ \frac{(160 - 275)^2}{275} = 115.22$$

Reject H_0. The proportions are not as stated.
13. H_0: Distribution is normally distributed. H_1: It is not normally distributed. Reject H_0 if $\chi^2 > 11.070$.

Time	z Areas	f_0	f_e	$\dfrac{(f_0 - f_e)^2}{f_e}$
Up to 4	.0764	7	6.9	.001
4 to 5	.1625	14	14.6	.025
5 to 6	.2611	25	23.5	.096
6 to 7	.2611	22	23.5	.096
7 to 8	.1625	16	14.6	.134
8 or more	.0764	6	6.9	.117
Total	1.000	90	90	.469

Computed $\chi^2 = .469$. Do not reject H_0 that the distribution is normal.
15. H_0: There is no relationship between size and section read. H_1: There is a relationship. Reject H_0 if $\chi^2 > 9.488$.

$$\chi^2 = \frac{(170 - 157.50)^2}{157.50} + \cdots + \frac{(88 - 83.62)^2}{83.62} = 7.340$$

Do not reject H_0. There is no relationship between size and section read.
17. H_0: No relationship between error rates and item type. H_1: There is a relationship between error rates and item type. Reject H_0 if $\chi^2 > 9.21$.

$$\chi^2 = \frac{(20 - 14.1)^2}{14.1} + \frac{(10 - 15.9)^2}{15.9} + \cdots + \frac{(200 - 199.75)^2}{199.75}$$

$$+ \frac{(225 - 225.25)^2}{225.25} = 8.033$$

Do not reject H_0. There is not a relationship between error rates and item type.

19. H_0: $\pi_s = 0.50$, $\pi_r = \pi_e = 0.25$
    H_a: Distribution is not as given above.
    $df = 2$. Reject H_0 if $\chi^2 > 4.605$.

Turn	f_o	f_e	$f_o - f_e$	$(f_o - f_e)^2/f_e$
Straight	112	100	12	1.44
Right	48	50	−2	0.08
Left	40	50	−10	2.00
Total	200	200		3.52

H_0 is not rejected. The proportions are as given in the null hypothesis.

21. H_0: There is no preference with respect to TV stations.
    H_1: There is a preference with respect to TV stations.
    $df = 3 - 1 = 2$. H_0 is rejected if $\chi^2 > 5.991$.

TV Station	f_o	f_e	$f_o - f_e$	$(f_o - f_e)^2$	$(f_o - f_e)^2/f_e$
WNAE	53	50	3	9	0.18
WRRN	64	50	14	196	3.92
WSPD	33	50	−17	289	5.78
	150	150	0		9.88

H_0 is rejected. There is a preference for TV stations.

23. H_0: $\pi_n = 0.21$, $\pi_m = 0.24$, $\pi_s = 0.35$, $\pi_w = 0.20$.
    H_1: The distribution is not as given.
    Reject H_0 if $\chi^2 > 11.345$.

Region	f_o	f_e	$f_o - f_e$	$(f_o - f_e)^2/f_e$
Northeast	68	84	−16	3.0476
Midwest	104	96	8	0.6667
South	155	140	15	1.6071
West	73	80	−7	0.6125
Total	400	400	0	5.9339

H_0 is not rejected. The distribution of order destinations reflects the population.

25. H_0: The proportion of colors is as reported; H_1: The proportions are not as reported. Reject H_0 if $\chi^2 > 11.070$.

$$\chi^2 = \frac{(17 - 21.6)^2}{21.6} + \frac{(20 - 21.6)^2}{21.6} + \cdots + \frac{(7 - 7.2)^2}{7.2}$$

$$= 6.426$$

Do not reject H_0. The actual breakdown of candies agrees with the expected distribution.

27. H_0: The distribution is normal; H_1: The distribution is not normal. Reject H_0 if $\chi^2 > 4.605$.

$$\bar{X} = \frac{2430}{300} = 8.10$$

$$s = \sqrt{\frac{19,994 - \frac{(2430)^2}{300}}{300 - 1}} = 1.02$$

Wage	f_o	Area	f_e	$\frac{(f_o - f_e)^2}{f_e}$
$5.50 up to $ 6.50	20	.0582	17.46	.370
6.50 up to 7.50	54	.2194	65.82	2.123
7.50 up to 8.50	130	.3741	112.23	2.814
8.50 up to 9.50	68	.2630	78.90	1.506
9.50 up to 10.50	28	.0853	25.59	0.227
	300			7.04

Reject H_0. We cannot conclude that the distribution is normal.

29. H_0: Levels of management and concern regarding the environment are not related. H_1: Levels of management and concern regarding the environment are related. Reject H_0 if $\chi^2 > 16.812$.

$$\chi^2 = \frac{(15 - 14)^2}{14} + \cdots + \frac{(31 - 28)^2}{28} = 1.550$$

Do not reject H_0. Levels of management and environmental concern are not related.

31. H_0: Whether a claim is filed and age are not related.
    H_1: Whether a claim is filed and age are related.
    Reject H_0 if $\chi^2 > 7.815$.

$$\chi^2 = \frac{(170 - 203.33)^2}{203.33} + \frac{(74 - 40.67)^2}{40.67} + \cdots + \frac{(24 - 35.67)^2}{35.67}$$

$$= 53.639$$

Reject H_0. Age is related to whether a claim is filed.

33. H_0: There is no relationship between financial condition and view of economic condition. H_1: There is a relationship between financial condition and view of economic condition. Reject H_0 if $\chi^2 > 5.991$.

Finance	Better	Not Better	Total
Worse	47	13	60
Same	41	21	62
Better	30	28	58
	118	62	180

$$\chi^2 = \frac{(47 - 39.33)^2}{39.33} + \cdots + \frac{(28 - 19.98)^2}{19.98} = 9.261$$

H_0 is rejected. There is a relationship between personal financial condition and view of the state economic condition.

35. **a.** H_0: There is no relationship between pool and township. H_1: There is a relationship between pool and township. Reject H_0 if $\chi^2 > 9.488$.

Pool	Township 1	2	3	4	5	Total
No	9	8	7	11	3	38
Yes	6	12	18	18	13	67
	15	20	25	29	16	105

$$\chi^2 = \frac{(9 - 5.43)^2}{5.43} + \cdots + \frac{(13 - 10.21)^2}{10.21} = 6.680$$

Do not reject H_0. There is no relationship between pool and township.

b. H_0: There is no relationship between attached garage and township. H_1: There is a relationship between attached garage and township. Reject H_0 if $\chi^2 > 9.488$.

Attached Garage	Township 1	2	3	4	5	Total
No	6	5	10	9	4	34
Yes	9	15	15	20	12	71
	15	20	25	29	16	105

$$\chi^2 = \frac{(6 - 4.86)^2}{4.86} + \cdots + \frac{(12 - 10.82)^2}{10.82} = 1.980$$

Do not reject H_0. There is no relationship between attached garage and township.

37. **a.** H_0: The proportions are the same. H_1: The proportions are not the same. Reject H_0 if $\chi^2 > 5.991$.

$$\chi^2 = \frac{(43 - 31.33)^2}{31.33} + \frac{(31 - 31.33)^2}{31.33} + \frac{(20 - 31.33)^2}{31.33}$$

$$= 8.448$$

Reject H_0. The proportions on welfare are not the same.

b. H_0: Welfare and size are not related. H_1: Welfare and size are related. Reject H_0 if $\chi^2 > 9.488$.

Welfare	Size Small	Medium	Large	Total
Low	22	17	4	43
Medium	8	18	5	31
High	6	7	7	20
	36	42	16	94

$$\chi^2 = \frac{(22 - 16.468)^2}{16.468} + \cdots + \frac{(7 - 3.404)^2}{3.404} = 10.716$$

Reject H_0. Conclude that welfare and size are related.

CHAPTER 15

1. **a.** If the number of pluses (successes) in the sample is 9 or more, reject H_0.
   b. Reject H_0 because the cumulative probability associated with nine or more successes (.073) does not exceed the significance level (.10).
3. **a.** H_0: $\pi \le .50$; H_1: $\pi > .50$; $n = 10$.
   b. H_0 is rejected if there are nine or more plus signs. A "+" represents a loss.
   c. Reject H_0. It is an effective program, because there were 9 people who lost weight.
5. **a.** H_0: $\pi \le .50$ (There is no change in weight.) H_1: $\pi > .50$ (There is a loss of weight.)
   b. Reject H_0 if $z > 1.65$.

   c. $z = \dfrac{(32 - .50) - .50(45)}{.50\sqrt{45}} = 2.68$

   d. Reject H_0. The weight loss program is effective.
7. **a.** H_0: $\pi \le .50$, H_1: $\pi > .50$. H_0 is rejected if $z > 2.05$.

   $$z = \frac{42.5 - 40.5}{4.5} = .44$$

   Because $.44 < 2.05$, do not reject H_0. No preference.
9. **a.** H_0: Median $\le$ \$40,000; H_1: Median $>$ \$40,000.
   b. H_0 is rejected if $z > 1.65$.

   c. $z = \dfrac{170 - .5 - 100}{7.07} = 9.83$

   H_0 is rejected. The median income is greater than \$40,000.

11.

Couple	Difference	Rank
1	550	7
2	190	5
3	250	6
4	−120	3
5	−70	1
6	130	4
7	90	2

Sums: -4, $+24$. So $T = 4$ (the smaller of the two sums). From Appendix J, .05 level, one-tailed test, $n = 7$, the critical value is 3. Since the T of $4 > 3$, do not reject H_0 (one-tailed test). There is no difference in square footage. Yuppies do not live in larger homes.

13. a. H_0: The production is the same for the two systems.

H_1: Production using the Mump method is greater.

b. H_0 is rejected if $T \le 21$, $n = 13$.

c. The calculations for the first three employees are:

Employee	Old	Mump	d	Rank	R^+	R^-
A	60	64	4	6	6	
B	40	52	12	12.5	12.5	
C	59	58	−1	2		2

The sum of the negative ranks is 6.5. Since 6.5 is less than 21, H_0 is rejected. Production using the Mump method is greater.

15. H_0: The distributions are the same. H_1: The distributions are not the same. Reject H_0 if $z < -1.96$ or $z > 1.96$.

A		B	
Score	Rank	Score	Rank
38	4	26	1
45	6	31	2
56	9	35	3
57	10.5	42	5
61	12	51	7
69	14	52	8
70	15	57	10.5
79	16	62	13
	86.5		49.5

$$z = \frac{86.5 - \dfrac{8(8 + 8 + 1)}{2}}{\sqrt{\dfrac{8(8)(8 + 8 + 1)}{12}}} = 1.943$$

H_0 is not rejected. There is no difference in the two populations.

17. H_0: The distributions are the same. H_1: The distribution of Country is to the right. Reject H_0 if $z > 1.65$.

Country		Rock	
Age	Rank	Age	Rank
26	6	28	8
42	16.5	16	1
65	22	42	16.5
38	13	29	9.5
29	9.5	31	11
32	12	22	3
59	21	50	20
42	16.5	42	16.5
27	7	23	4
41	14	25	5
46	19		94.5
18	2		
	158.5		

$$z = \frac{158.5 - \dfrac{12(12 + 10 + 1)}{2}}{\sqrt{\dfrac{12(10)(12 + 10 + 1)}{12}}} = 1.35$$

H_0 is not rejected. There is no difference in the distributions.

19. ANOVA requires that we have two or more populations, the data are interval or ratio-level, the populations are normally distributed, and the population standard deviations are equal. Kruskal-Wallis requires only ordinal-level data, and no assumptions are made regarding the shape of the populations.

21. a. H_0: The three population distributions are equal. H_1: Not all of the distributions are the same.

b. Reject H_0 if $H > 5.991$.

c.

Rank	Rank	Rank
8	5	1
11	6.5	2
14.5	6.5	3
14.5	10	4
16	12	9
64	13	19
	53	

$$H = \frac{12}{16(16 + 1)} \left[\frac{(64)^2}{5} + \frac{(53)^2}{6} + \frac{(19)^2}{5} \right] - 3(16 + 1)$$

$$= 59.98 - 51 = 8.98$$

d. Reject H_0 because $8.98 > 5.991$. The three distributions are not equal.

23. H_0: The distributions of the lengths of life are the same. H_1: The distributions of the lengths of life are not the same. H_0 is rejected if $H > 9.210$.

Salt		Fresh		Others	
Hours	Rank	Hours	Rank	Hours	Rank
167.3	3	160.6	1	182.7	13
189.6	15	177.6	11	165.4	2
177.2	10	185.3	14	172.9	7
169.4	6	168.6	4	169.2	5
180.3	12	176.6	9	174.7	8
	46		39		35

$$H = \frac{12}{15(16)} \left[\frac{(46)^2}{5} + \frac{(39)^2}{5} + \frac{(35)^2}{5} \right] - 3(16) = 0.62$$

H_0 is not rejected. There is no difference in the three distributions.

25. a.

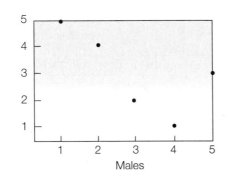

b.

Rank Males	Rank Females	d	d^2
1	5	−4	16
4	1	3	9
3	2	1	1
2	4	−2	4
5	3	2	4
			34

$$r_s = 1 - \frac{6(34)}{5(5^2 - 1)} = -0.7$$

Fairly strong negative correlation among the ranks.

27.

Representative	Sales	Rank	Training Rank	d	d^2
1	319	3	3	0	0
2	150	10	9	1	1
3	175	9	6	3	9
4	460	1	1	0	0
5	348	2	4	−2	4
6	300	4.5	10	−5.5	30.25
7	280	6	5	1	1
8	200	7	2	5	25
9	190	8	7	1	1
10	300	4.5	8	−3.5	12.25
					83.50

a. $r_s = 1 - \dfrac{6(83.5)}{10(10^2 - 1)} = 0.494$

A moderate positive correlation.

b. H_0: No correlation among the ranks. H_1: A positive correlation among the ranks. Reject H_0 if $t > 1.860$.

$$t = 0.494 \sqrt{\frac{10 - 2}{1 - (0.494)^2}} = 1.607$$

H_0 is not rejected. The correlation in population among the ranks could be 0.

29. H_0: $\pi = .50$; H_1: $\pi \neq .50$; $n = 19$. H_0 is rejected if there are either 5 or fewer "+" signs, or 14 or more. The total of 12 "+" signs falls in the acceptance region. H_0 is not rejected. There is no preference between the two shows.

31. H_0: $\pi = .50$
H_1: $\pi \neq .50$
H_0 is rejected if there are 12 or more or 3 or fewer plus signs. Because there are only 8 plus signs, H_0 is not rejected. There is no preference with respect to the two brands of components.

33. H_0: $\pi = .50$; H_1: $\pi \neq .50$. Reject H_0 if $z > 1.96$ or $z < -1.96$.

$$z = \frac{159.5 - 100}{7.071} = 8.415$$

Reject H_0. There is a difference in the preference for the two types of orange juice.

35. H_0: Rates are the same; H_1: The rates are not the same. H_0 is rejected if $H > 5.991$. $H = .082$. Do not reject H_0.

37. H_0: The populations are the same. H_1: The populations differ. Reject H_0 if $H > 7.815$. $H = 14.30$. Reject H_0, accept H_1.

39. $r_s = 1 - \dfrac{6(78)}{12(12^2 - 1)} = 0.727$

H_0: There is no correlation between the rankings of the coaches and of the sportswriters.
H_1: There is a positive correlation between the rankings of the coaches and of the sportswriters.
Reject H_0 if $t > 1.812$.

$$t = 0.727 \sqrt{\frac{12 - 2}{1 - (.727)^2}} = 3.348$$

H_0 is rejected. There is a positive correlation between the sportswriters and the coaches.

41. **a.** Answers will vary. For the 1997 race, $r_s = 0.355$.
  b. H_0: There is no correlation in the ranks; H_1: There is a positive correlation in the ranks. Reject H_0 if $t > 1.69$.

$$t = \frac{.355\sqrt{35-2}}{\sqrt{1-(.355)^2}} = 2.181$$

  c. There is a positive rank correlation between the starting position and the finishing position.

43. **a.** H_0: There is no difference in the distributions of the selling prices in the five townships. H_1: There is a difference in the distributions of the selling prices in the five townships. H_0 is rejected if H is greater than 9.448. The computed value of H is 4.70, so the null hypothesis is not rejected. The sample data does not suggest a difference in the distributions of selling prices.

  b. H_0: There is no difference in the distributions of the selling prices depending on the number of bedrooms. H_1: There is a difference in the distributions of the selling prices depending on the number of bedrooms. H_0 is rejected if H is greater than 9.448. The computed value of H is 16.34, so the null hypothesis is rejected. The sample data indicates there is a difference in the distributions of selling prices based on the number of bedrooms.

  c. H_0: There is no difference in the distributions of the distance from the center of the city depending on whether the home had a pool or not. H_1: There is a difference in the distributions of the distances from the center of the city depending on whether the home has a pool or not. H_0 is rejected if H is greater than 3.84. The computed value of H is 3.37, so the null hypothesis is not rejected. The sample data does not suggest a difference in the distributions of the distances.

45. **a.** The correlation between the ranks is 0.833.
  H_0: There is no correlation between circulation rank and color cost rank of magazines. H_1: There is a correlation between circulation rank and color cost rank of the magazines. Reject H_0 if $t > 2.021$ or $t < -2.021$.

$$t = .833 \sqrt{\frac{48-2}{1-(.833)^2}} = 10.211$$

Reject H_0. There is a correlation between circulation rank and rank of color advertising cost.

  b. H_0: The distributions are the same. H_1: The distributions are different. Reject H_0 if H > 3.841.
   The computed value of $H = 4.09$. Reject H_0. There is a difference in the magazine circulation between the 2 groups of male readers.

CHAPTER 16

1.

Count	38	23	12	10	8
Percent	42	25	13	11	9
Cum %	42	67	80	91	100

About 67% of the complaints concern the problem not being corrected and the price being too high.

3. Chance variation is random in nature; because the cause is a variety of factors, it cannot be entirely eliminated. Assignable variation is not random; it is usually due to a specific cause and can be eliminated.

5. **a.** The A_2 factor is 0.729.
  b. The value for D_3 is 0, and for D_4 it is 2.282.

7. **a.**

Time	$\bar{X}$, Arithmetic Means	R Range
8:00 A.M.	46	16
8:30 A.M.	40.5	6
9:00 A.M.	44	6
9:30 A.M.	40	2
10:00 A.M.	41.5	9
10:30 A.M.	39.5	1
	251.5	40

$$\bar{\bar{X}} = \frac{251.5}{6} = 41.92 \qquad \bar{R} = \frac{40}{6} = 6.67$$

UCL $= 41.92 + 0.729(6.67) = 46.78$
LCL $= 41.92 - 0.729(6.67) = 37.06$

b. Interpreting, the mean reading was 341.92 degrees Fahrenheit. If the oven continues operating as evidenced by the first six hourly readings, about 99.7 percent of the mean readings will lie between 337.06 degrees and 346.78 degrees.

9. $\bar{p} = \dfrac{37}{140} = .26$

$$.26 \pm 3\sqrt{\dfrac{.26(.74)}{10}} = .26 \pm .42$$

The control limits are from 0 to .68. The process is out of control on the seventh day.

11. $\bar{c} = \dfrac{6}{11} = 0.545$

$0.545 \pm 3\sqrt{0.545} = 0.545 \pm 2.215$

The control limits are from 0 to 2.760, so there are no receipts out of control.

13.

Percent Defective	Probability of Accepting Lot
10	.889
20	.558
30	.253
40	.083

15. $P(X \le 1 \mid n = 10, \pi = .10) = .736$
$P(X \le 1 \mid n = 10, \pi = .20) = .375$
$P(X \le 1 \mid n = 10, \pi = .30) = .149$
$P(X \le 1 \mid n = 10, \pi = .40) = .046$

17.

Count	80	60	50	10
Percent	40	30	25	5
Cum %	40	70	95	100

19. **a.** UCL $= 10.0 + 0.577(0.25) = 10.0 + 0.14425$

$= 10.14425$

LCL $= 10.0 - 0.577(0.25) = 10.0 - 0.14425$

$= 9.85575$

UCL $= 2.115(0.25) = 0.52875$

LCL $= 0(0.25) = 0$

b. The mean is 10.16, which is above the upper control limit and is out of control. There is too much cola in the soft drinks. The process is in control for variation; an adjustment is needed.

21. **a.** $\bar{\bar{X}} = \dfrac{611.23}{20} = 30.5665$

$\bar{R} = \dfrac{312}{20} = 15.6$

UCL $= 30.5665 + (1.023)(15.6) = 46.53$

LCL $= 30.5665 - (1.023)(15.6) = 14.61$

UCL $= 2.575(15.6) = 40.17$

b.

c. The points all seem to be within the control limits. No adjustments are necessary.

23. $\bar{\bar{X}} = \dfrac{4183}{10} = 418.3$

$\bar{R} = \dfrac{162}{10} = 16.2$

UCL = 418.3 + (0.577)(16.2) = 427.65

LCL = 418.3 − (0.577)(16.2) = 408.95

UCL = 2.115(16.2) = 34.26

All the points are in control for both the mean and the range.

25. a. $\bar{p} = \dfrac{40}{10(50)} = 0.08$

$3\sqrt{\dfrac{0.08(0.92)}{50}} = 0.115$

UCL = 0.08 + 0.115 = 0.195

LCL = 0.08 − 0.115 = 0

b.

c. There are no points that exceed the limits.

27. a. $\bar{c} = \dfrac{213}{15} = 14.2; 3\sqrt{14.2} = 11.30$

UCL = 14.2 + 11.3 = 25.5

LCL = 14.2 − 11.3 = 2.9

b.

c. All the points are in control.

29. $\bar{c} = \dfrac{70}{10} = 7.0$

UCL = $7.0 + 3\sqrt{7} = 14.9$

LCL = $7.0 - 3\sqrt{7} = 0$

31. $P(X \le 3 \mid n = 20, \pi = .10) = .867$
$P(X \le 3 \mid n = 20, \pi = .20) = .412$
$P(X \le 3 \mid n = 20, \pi = .30) = .108$

CHAPTER 17

1. 164.5, found by ($2,403/$1,461)(100)
197.6, found by ($2,887/$1,461)(100)

3. ($30,367 + $25,284)/2 = $27,825.50
$I = [($30,539)/27,825.50]100 = 109.75$

5. a. $P_t = \dfrac{2.69}{2.49}(100)$ $\qquad P_S = \dfrac{3.59}{3.29}(100)$

$= 108.03$ $\qquad\qquad = 109.12$

$P_C = \dfrac{1.79}{1.59}(100)$ $\qquad P_A = \dfrac{2.29}{1.79}(100)$

$= 112.58$ $\qquad\qquad = 127.93$

b. $P = \dfrac{10.36}{9.16}(100) = 113.1$

c. $P = \dfrac{\$2.69(6) + 3.59(4) + 1.79(2) + 2.29(3)}{\$2.49(6) + 3.29(4) + 1.59(2) + 1.79(3)} (100)$

$= 111.7$

d. $P = \dfrac{\$2.69(6) + 3.59(5) + 1.79(3) + 2.29(4)}{2.49(6) + 3.29(5) + 1.59(3) + 1.79(4)} (100)$

$= 112.2$

e. $I = \sqrt{112.2(111.7)} = 111.95$

7. a. $P_W = \dfrac{.10}{.07}(100)$ $P_C = \dfrac{.03}{.04}(100)$

$= 142.9$ $= 75.0$

$P_S = \dfrac{.15}{.15}(100)$ $P_H = \dfrac{.10}{.08}(100)$

$= 100$ $= 125.0$

b. $\dfrac{.38}{.34}(100) = 111.8$

c. $P = \dfrac{\begin{array}{l}.10(17,000) + .03(125,000) \\ + .15(40,000) + .10(62,000)\end{array}}{\begin{array}{l}.07(17,000) + .04(125,000) \\ + .15(40,000) + .08(62,000)\end{array}} (100) = 102.92$

d. $P = \dfrac{\begin{array}{l}.10(20,000) + .03(130,000) \\ + .15(42,000) + .10(65,000)\end{array}}{\begin{array}{l}.07(20,000) + .04(130,000) \\ + .15(42,000) + .08(65,000)\end{array}} (100) = 103.32$

e. $P = \sqrt{(102.92)(103.32)} = 103.12$

9. $V = \dfrac{\begin{array}{l}1.87(214) + 2.05(489) \\ + 1.48(203) + 3.29(106)\end{array}}{\begin{array}{l}\$1.52(200) + 2.10(565) \\ + 1.48(291) + 3.05(87)\end{array}} (100) = 93.8$

11. a. $I = \dfrac{6.8}{5.3}(.20) + \dfrac{362.26}{265.88}(.40)$

$+ \dfrac{125.0}{109.6}(.25) + \dfrac{622,864}{529,917}(.15)$

$= 1.263$

So index is 126.3.

b. Business activity increased 26.3 percent from 1989 to 1999.

13. $X = (\$32,000)/1.583 = \$20,214.78$
Salary increased $\$20,214.78 - \$19,800 = \$414.78$

15.

	Tinora		
Year	Salary	Index	National Index
1990	$23,650	100.0	100
1995	28,972	122.5	122.5
1999	32,382	136.9	136.9

The Tinora teachers received the same increase as the national average.

17. The index for selected years is:

Year	1983	1988	1993	1994	1995	1996
Index	100.00	126.72	199.47	216.34	254.50	301.83

Domestic sales increased by 201.83 percent from 1983 to 1996.

19. The index for selected years is:

Year	1983	1988	1993	1994	1995	1996
Index	100	187.30	293.61	335.39	408.64	453.90

International sales increased 353.90 percent from 1983 to 1996.

21. The index for selected years is:

Year	1983	1988	1993	1994	1995	1996
Index	100.00	105.04	105.43	105.30	106.33	115.37

The number of employees increased 15.37 percent during the period.

23. The index is as follows:

Year	1992	1993	1994	1995	1996
Index	100.00	231.70	227.84	105.15	255.67

Income increased 155.67 percent during the period.

25. The index is as follows:

Year	1992	1993	1994	1995	1996
Index	100.00	108.80	121.30	129.63	131.48

The earnings per share increased 31.48 percent during the period.

27. $P_{Ma} = \dfrac{\$0.89}{\$0.81}(100)$ $P_S = \dfrac{\$0.94}{\$0.84}(100)$

$= 109.88$ $= 111.90$

$P_{Mi} = \dfrac{1.43}{1.44}(100)$ $P_P = \dfrac{3.07}{2.91}(100)$

$= 99.31$ $= 105.50$

29. $P = \dfrac{.89(18) + .94(5) + 1.43(70) + (3.07)(27)}{.81(18) + .84(5) + 1.44(70) + (2.91)(27)} (100)$

$= 102.81$

31. $P = \sqrt{(102.81)(103.51)} = 103.16$

33. $P_r = \dfrac{.60}{.50}(100) = 120$ $\qquad$ $P_s = \dfrac{.90}{1.20}(100) = 75.0$

$P_w = \dfrac{1.00}{.85}(100) = 117.65$

35. $P = \dfrac{.60(320) + .90(110) + 1.00(230)}{.50(320) + 1.20(110) + .85(230)}(100) = 106.87$

37. $P = \sqrt{(106.87)(106.04)} = 106.45$

39. $P_{Cb} = \dfrac{.05}{.06}(100) = 83.33$ $\qquad$ $P_{Cr} = \dfrac{.12}{.10}(100) = 120$

$P_P = \dfrac{.18}{.20}(100) = 90.0$ $\qquad$ $P_E = \dfrac{.15}{.15}(100) = 100$

41. $P = \dfrac{.05(2000) + .12(200) + .18(400) + .15(100)}{.06(2000) + .10(200) + .20(400) + .15(100)}(100)$

$\quad = 89.79$

43. $P = \sqrt{(89.79)(91.25)} = 90.52$

45. $P_A = \dfrac{0.76}{0.287}(100) = 264.8$ $\qquad$ $P_N = \dfrac{2.50}{0.17}(100) = 1470.59$

$P_{Pe} = \dfrac{26.00}{3.18}(100) = 817.61$ $\qquad$ $P_{Pl} = \dfrac{490.00}{133.00}(100) = 368.42$

47. $P = \dfrac{\begin{array}{c}.76(1000) + 2.50(5000) \\ + \ 26(60{,}000) + 490(500)\end{array}}{\begin{array}{c}.287(1000) + .17(5000) \\ + \ 3.18(60{,}000) + 133(500)\end{array}}(100)$

$\quad = 703.56$

49. $P = \sqrt{(703.56)(686.58)} = 695.02$

51. $I = 100\left[\dfrac{1971.0}{1159.0}(.20) + \dfrac{91}{87}(.10) + \dfrac{114.7}{110.6}(.40) + \dfrac{1501}{1214}(.30)\right]$

$\quad = 123.05$

The economy is up 23.05 percent from 1990 to 1999.

53. February:

$I = 100\left[\dfrac{6.8}{8.0}(.40) + \dfrac{23.0}{20.0}(.35) + \dfrac{303}{300}(.25)\right] = 99.50$

March:

$I = 100\left[\dfrac{6.4}{8.0}(.40) + \dfrac{21.0}{20.0}(.35) + \dfrac{297}{300}(.25)\right] = 93.5$

55. For 1983: $2,000,000, found by $2,400,000/1.20
For 1999: $1,091,703, found by $3,500,000/3.206

CHAPTER 18

1. $b = \dfrac{2{,}469 - (721)(15)/5}{55 - (15)^2/5} = \dfrac{306}{10} = 30.6$

$a = \dfrac{721}{5} - 30.6\left(\dfrac{15}{5}\right) = 52.4$ $\qquad$ for 2001, $t = 8$

$Y' = 52.4 + 30.6t = 52.4 + 30.6(8) = 297.2$

3. $b = \dfrac{69 - (20)(15)/5}{55 - (15)^2/5} = \dfrac{9}{10} = 0.90$

$a = \dfrac{20}{5} - 0.90\left(\dfrac{15}{5}\right) = 1.30$

$Y' = 1.30 + 0.90t = 1.30 + 0.90(7) = 7.6(\text{tons})$

5. a. $b = \dfrac{5.274318 - (1.390087)(15)/5}{55 - (15)^2/5} = \dfrac{1.104057}{10}$

$\quad = 0.1104057$

$a = \dfrac{1.390087}{5} - 0.1104057\left(\dfrac{15}{5}\right) = -0.0531997$

b. 28.95%, found by $1.28945 - 1.0$
c. $Y' = -0.0531997 + 0.1104057t$
$Y' = -0.0531997 + 0.1104057(8)$
$\quad = 0.8300459$
Antilog of $0.8300459 = 6.76$

7. Using the CBS system, the final output is:

Quarter	Average SI Component	Seasonal Index
1	0.6859	0.6911
2	1.6557	1.6682
3	1.1616	1.1704
4	0.4732	0.4768

9.

t	Estimated Pairs (millions)	Seasonal Index	Quarterly Forecast (millions)
21	40.05	110.0	44.055
22	41.80	120.0	50.160
23	43.55	80.0	34.840
24	45.30	90.0	40.770

11. $Y' = 5.1658 + .37805t$. The following are the sales estimates.

Estimate	Index	Seasonally Adjusted
10.080	0.6911	6.966
10.458	1.6682	17.446
10.837	1.1704	12.684
11.215	0.4768	5.343

13. a. $Y' = 18,000 - 400t$, assuming the line starts at 18,000 in 1975 and goes down to 10,000 in 1995.
b. 400
c. 8,000, found by $18,000 - 400(25)$.

15. a.

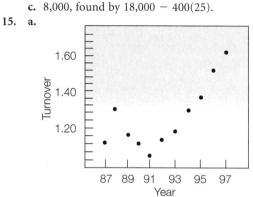

b. $Y' = 1.0045 + 0.04409t$, using $t = 1$ for 1987.
c. For 1990, $Y' = 1.18091$, and for 1995 $Y' = 1.40136$
d. For 2002, $Y' = 1.70999$
e. Each asset turned over .044 times.

17. a.

b. $Y' = 49.140 - 2.9829t$
c. For 1994, $Y' = 40.1913$, and for 1996 $Y' = 34.2255$
d. For 2000, $Y' = 22.2939$
e. The number of employees decreases at a rate of 2,983 per year.

19. a. $\text{Log } Y' = 0.790231 + 0.113669t$
b. $\text{Log } Y' = 1.244907$, antilog is 17.575
$\text{Log } Y' = 1.813252$, antilog is 65.05
c. 29.92, which is the antilog of .113669 minus 1.
d. $\text{Log } Y' = 2.154258$, antilog is 142.65

21. a. $\text{Log } Y' = 0.2639 + 0.12195t$
b. $\text{Log } Y' = 2.82485$, antilog is 668.1
c. 32.4 percent per year which is the antilog of 0.12195 minus 1.

23. a. July 87.5; August 92.9; September 99.3; October 109.1.
b.

Month	Total	Mean	Corrected
July	348.9	87.225	86.777
Aug.	368.1	92.025	91.552
Sept.	395.0	98.750	98.242
Oct.	420.4	105.100	104.560
Nov.	496.2	124.050	123.412
Dec.	572.3	143.075	142.340
Jan.	333.5	83.375	82.946
Feb.	297.5	74.375	73.993
March	347.3	86.825	86.379
April	481.3	120.325	119.707
May	396.2	99.050	98.541
June	368.1	92.025	91.552
		1,206.200	

Correction $= 1,200/1,206.2 = 0.99486$
c. April, November, and December are periods of high sales, while February's sales are lowest.

25. a.   **Seasonal Index by Quarter**

Quarter	Average SI Component	Seasonal Index
1	0.5014	0.5027
2	1.0909	1.0936
3	1.7709	1.7753
4	0.6354	0.6370

b. Production is the largest in the third quarter. It is 77.5 percent above the average quarter. The second quarter is also above average. The first and fourth quarters are well below average, with the first quarter at about 50 percent of a typical quarter.

27. a.   **Seasonal Index by Quarter**

Quarter	Average SI Component	Seasonal Index
1	0.5549	0.5577
2	0.8254	0.8296
3	1.5102	1.5178
4	1.0973	1.1029

b. $Y' = 7.667 + 0.0023t$
c.

Period	Production	Index	Forecast
21	7.7153	0.5577	4.3028
22	7.7176	0.8296	6.4025
23	7.7199	1.5178	11.7173
24	7.7222	1.1029	8.5168

29.

Seasonal Index by Quarter

Quarter	Average SI Component	Seasonal Index
1	1.1962	1.2053
2	1.0135	1.0212
3	0.6253	0.6301
4	1.1371	1.1457

The regression equation is: $Y' = 43.611 + 7.2153t$

Period	Visitors	Index	Forecast
29	252.86	1.2053	304.77
30	260.07	1.0212	265.58
31	267.29	0.6301	168.42
32	274.50	1.1457	314.50

In 1997 there were 928 visitors. A 10 percent increase in 1998 means there will be 1,021 visitors. The quarterly estimates are $1,021/4 = 255.25$ visitors per quarter.

Period	Visitors	Index	Forecast
Winter	255.25	1.2053	307.65
Spring	255.25	1.0212	260.66
Summer	255.25	0.6301	160.83
Fall	255.25	1.1457	292.44

The regression approach is probably superior because the trend is considered.

31. Log purse $= 2.32181 + .045529t$, $R^2 = .984$
Log prize $= 1.49790 + .045529t$, $R^2 = .984$
Purse in 2000 is \$910,366, prize is \$136,555.

33. $Y' = 3815.6 + 32.6t$, $R^2 = .079$, and units increase at a rate of 32.6 per year.

CHAPTER 19

1. $EMV(A_1) = .30(\$50) + .50(\$70) + .20(\$100) = \$70$

$EMV(A_2) = .30(\$90) + .50(\$40) + .20(\$80) = \$63$

$EMV(A_3) = .30(\$70) + .50(\$60) + .20(\$90) = \$69$

Decision: Choose alternative 1.

3.

Opportunity Loss

	S_1	S_2	S_3
A_1	\$40	\$ 0	\$ 0
A_2	0	30	20
A_3	20	10	10

5. (Answers in \$000)

$EOL(A_1) = .30(\$40) + 50(\$0) + .20(\$0) = \$12$

$EOL(A_2) = .30(\$0) + .50(\$30) + .20(\$20) = \$19$

$EOL(A_3) = .30(\$20) + .50(\$10) + .20(\$10) = \$13$

7. Expected value under conditions of certainty is \$82, found by $.30(\$90) + .50(\$70) + .20(\$100) = \$82$.

$$EVPI = \$82 - \$70 = \$12$$

9. Yes, it changes the decision. Choose alternative 2. (Answers in \$000).

$EMV(A_1) = .50(\$50) + .20(\$70) + .30(\$100) = \$69$

$EMV(A_2) = .50(\$90) + .20(\$40) + .30(\$80) = \$77$

$EMV(A_3) = .50(\$70) + .20(\$60) + .30(\$90) = \$74$

11. a. (Answers in \$000)

$EMV(\text{neither}) = .30(\$0) + .50(\$0) + .20(\$0) = \$0$

$EMV(1) = .30(\$125) + .50(\$65) + .20(\$30) = \$76.00$

$EMV(2) = .30(\$105) + .50(\$60) + .20(\$30) = \$67.50$

$EMV(\text{both}) = .30(\$220) + .50(\$110) + .20(\$40) = \$129.00$

b. Choose both.

c.

Opportunity Loss

	S_1	S_2	S_3
Neither	\$220	\$110	\$40
1	95	45	10
2	115	50	10
Both	0	0	0

d. $EOL(\text{neither}) = \$129.00$

$EOL(1) = \$53.00$

$EOL(2) = \$61.50$

$EOL(\text{both}) = \$0$

e. $EVPI = \$0$, found by $\$129 - \$129$.

Certainty $= .30(\$220) + .50(\$110) + .20(\$40)$

$= \$129$

13. The payoff table is as follows in \$000.

	Recession, S_1	No Recession, S_2
Production	\$-10.0	\$15.0
Stock	-5.0	12.0
CD	6.0	6.0

a. Purchase a CD
b. Increase production.
c. (Answers in $000)

$$EMV(Prod.) = .2(-10) + .8(15.0) = 10.0$$

$$EMV(Stock) = .2(-5) + .8(12.0) = 8.6$$

$$EMV(CD) = .2(6) + .8(6) = 6.0$$

Expand production.

d. $EVPI = [.2(6) + .8(15)] - [10.0] = 3.2$

15. a.

Act	Event 10	11	12	13	14
10	$500	$500	$500	$500	$500
11	200	550	550	550	550
12	−100	250	600	600	600
13	−400	−50	300	650	650
14	−700	−350	0	350	700

b.

Act	Expected Profit
10	$500.00
11	504.50
12	421.50
13	233.50
14	−31.50

Order 11 mobile homes because expected profit of $504.50 is the highest.

c.

Supply	Opportunity Loss 10	11	12	13	14
10	$ 0	$ 50	$100	$150	$200
11	300	0	50	100	150
12	600	300	0	50	100
13	900	600	300	0	50
14	1,200	900	600	300	0

d.

	Act 10	11	12	13	14
Expected opportunity loss	$95.50	$91	$174	$362	$627

Decision: Order 11 homes because the opportunity loss of $91 is the smallest.

e. $91, found by:

$595.50	profit under certainty
−504.50	profit under uncertainty
$ 91.00	value of perfect information

17. a.

Act	Event 41	42	43	44	45	46
41	$410	$410	$410	$410	$410	$410
42	405	420	420	420	420	420
43	400	415	430	430	430	430
44	395	410	425	440	440	440
45	390	405	420	435	450	450
46	385	400	415	430	445	460

b.

Act	Expected Profit
41	$410.00
42	419.10
43	426.70
44	432.20
45	431.70
46	427.45

c. Order 44 because $432.20 is the largest expected profit.

d. Expected opportunity loss:

41	42	43	44	45	46
$28.30	$19.20	$11.60	$6.10	$6.60	$10.85

e. Order 44 because the opportunity loss of $6.10 is the smallest. Yes, it agrees.

f. $6.10, found by:

$438.30	profit under certainty
−432.20	profit under uncertainty
$ 6.10	value of perfect information

The maximum we should pay for perfect information is $6.10.

ANSWERS

to Odd-Numbered Review Exercises

REVIEW OF CHAPTERS 1–4

1. a. Sample.
   b. Ratio.
   c. $11.60, found by $58/5.
   d. $11.70. Half of the employees earn below $11.70 an hour and the other half earn above $11.70 an hour.
   e. $s^2 = \dfrac{696.18 - \dfrac{(58)^2}{5}}{5 - 1} = 5.845$
   f. $sk = \dfrac{3(11.60 - 11.70)}{2.42} = -0.124$

3. a.

Rolls	Frequency
3 up to 6	2
6 up to 9	6
9 up to 12	8
12 up to 15	3
15 up to 18	1

   b.

   c. $\overline{X} = \dfrac{186}{20} = 9.3$
   d. median = 9
   e. 9 and 10, each occurs 4 times
   f. 14 using the frequency distribution, 13 using the actual data.
   g. $s^2 = \dfrac{1906 - \dfrac{(186)^2}{20}}{20 - 1} = 9.2736$
   h. $s = \sqrt{9.2736} = 3.045$
   i. $9.30 \pm 2(3.045)$. The limits are 3.21 up to 15.39.

5. a. 8.82%, found by 44.1/5.
   b. 7.479%.

   c. Geometric mean, because it is not highly influenced by the 19.5%.

7.

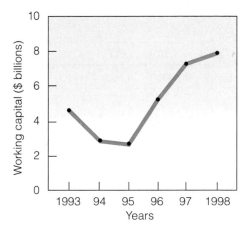

9. Ordinal.

11. Less-than-cumulative frequency polygon. About 45; about 35; 10; 35, found by 55 − 20.

13. 9.375%.

15. Coefficient of variation.

17. 92 and 108, found by $100 \pm 2(4)$.

19. a. The following histogram is from MINITAB.

```
Histogram of C1   N = 50
Midpoint      Count
       0         1 *
      40         7 *******
      80         3 ***
     120         8 ********
     160        15 ***************
     200        10 **********
     240         3 ***
     280         3 ***
```

   b. and c.

N	MEAN	MEDIAN	TRMEAN	STDEV	SEMEAN
50	147.90	148.50	146.11	69.24	9.79

MIN	MAX	Q1	Q3
14.00	299.00	106.00	186.25

The distribution is fairly symmetrical because the mean ($147.90) and the median ($148.50) are

777

quite close. The mean $\pm 2s$ indicates that the middle 95% of the deposits are between \$147.90 $\pm 2(\$69.24) = \$9.42$ and \$286.38. Range $= \$299.00 - \$14.00 = \$285.00$. There is a slight negative skewness (because the mean is less than the median).

21. a. From MINITAB:

	N	MEAN	MEDIAN	TRMEAN	STDEV	SEMEAN
C1	85	15.06	15.00	14.79	9.63	1.04

	MIN	MAX	Q1	Q3
C1	0.00	36.00	6.00	22.50

Typical length of service is about 15 years (mean or median).

   b. Range is 36 years, found by 36 (MAX) − 0 (MIN).
   c. Only slight positive skewness because the mean of 15.06 is slightly larger than the median (15.00).
   d.
```
Stem-and-leaf of C1      N = 85
Leaf Unit = 1.0
   12    0 011222333444
   30    0 555555566677788999
   42    1 000133334444
  (16)   1 5555566666788899
   27    2 00001233333
   16    2 6667889
    9    3 00123344
    1    3 6
```

23. The typical age is 55 years. The range is 27 years.

```
Variable    N   Mean Median Tr Mean StDev SE Mean
years      43 54.674 55.000  54.590 6.383   0.973


Variable    Min    Max    Q1     Q3
years    42.000 69.000 50.000 58.000


Stem-and-leaf of years    N = 43
Leaf Unit = 1.0

    2    4 23          18    5 6667777
    2    4             11    5 8
    6    4 6677        10    6 0111
    9    4 899          6    6 2
   15    5 001111       5    6 455
   17    5 22           2    6
   (8)   5 44445555     2    6 89
```

1. Subjective.
3. An outcome.
5. Complement rule. $1 - P(X) = .999$.
7. Discrete.
9. Discrete.
11. Bell-shaped, symmetrical, asymptotic.
13. a. .10, found by 20/200.
   b. .725, found by 145/200.
   c. .925, found by $1 - 15/200$.
15. a. .1353, found from Appendix C, where $\mu = 2.0$.
   b. 398, found by $400 - 2$.
   c. .3233, found by $1 - (.1353 + .2707 + .2707)$.
17. a. .417, found by 223/535.
   b. .407, found by 177/435.
   c. .914, found by 489/535.
19. a. \$1.84 million, found by $0 + .64 + 1.2$.
   b. .98.
   c. .20, found by .004/.02.
   d. Yes. The \$2 million premium is greater than the expected loss of \$1.84 million. Thus the expected profit is \$.16 million.

1. b
3. c
5. d
7. e
9. a
11. $H_0: \mu \geq 36$; $H_1: \mu < 36$. Reject H_0 if $z < -1.65$.

$$z = \frac{35.5 - 36.0}{.9/\sqrt{42}} = -3.60$$

Reject H_0. The mean height is less than 36 inches.

13. a. 457, found by $n = .05(1 - .05)\left(\dfrac{1.96}{.02}\right)^2$.
   b. Change the level of confidence to 90 percent, or raise the allowable error.
15. a. $H_0: \mu_b = \mu_v$; $H_1: \mu_b \neq \mu_v$
   b. Two-tailed. No direction given.
   c. $z = \dfrac{\overline{X}_b - \overline{X}_v}{\sqrt{\dfrac{s_b^2}{n_b} + \dfrac{s_v^2}{n_v}}}$
   d. $-1.96, +1.96$.
   e. $\dfrac{10.92 - 11.05}{\sqrt{\dfrac{(.78)^2}{180} + \dfrac{(.39)^2}{200}}} = -2.02$

Reject H_0 and accept H_1. The mean wages are not equal.

REVIEW OF CHAPTERS 10 AND 11

1. b   **7.** d

3. a   **9.** b

5. d   **11.** e

13. H_0: $\mu \le 20$; H_1: $\mu > 20$. Reject H_0 if $t > 1.860$.

$$\overline{X} = 21, s = 6.185$$

$$t = \frac{21 - 20}{6.185/\sqrt{9}} = 0.485$$

H_0 is not rejected. The mean amount of break time is not more than 20 minutes.

15. H_0: $\mu_d \le 0$; H_1: $\mu_d > 0$. Reject H_0 if $t > 1.833$.

$$\overline{d} = 0.4 \qquad s_d = 6.11 \qquad t = \frac{.4}{6.11/\sqrt{10}} = 0.21$$

H_0 is not rejected. There is no difference in the life of the paints.

17. H_0: $\mu_1 = \mu_1 = \mu_2 = \mu_3 = \mu_4 = \mu_5$
H_1: Means not equal. Reject if $F > 3.84$

H_0: $\mu_1 = \mu_2 = \mu_3$
H_1: Means not all equal. Reject if $F > 4.46$

Source	SS	df	MS	F
Treatments	165.73	4	41.43	11.098
Blocks	22.8	2	11.40	3.054
Error	29.87	8	3.73	
Total	218.40	14		

There is a difference in fertilizer types, but not soil conditions.

REVIEW OF CHAPTERS 12 AND 13

1. Coefficient of correlation or the coefficient of determination.

3. H_0: $\rho \le 0$; H_1: $\rho > 0$. Critical value of t is 1.671; computed $t = 3.324$. H_0 rejected. There is positive correlation.

5. The square of the coefficient of correlation is the coefficient of determination.

7. $Y' = a + b_1 X_1 + b_2 X_2 + b_3 X_3 + b_4 X_4$

9. About 86% of the variation in net profit is explained by the four variables.

11. a.

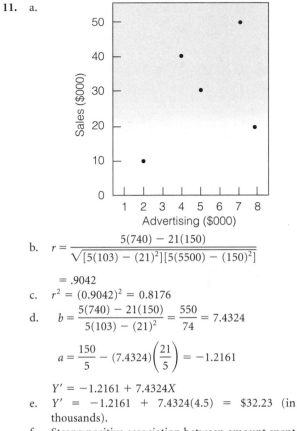

b. $r = \dfrac{5(740) - 21(150)}{\sqrt{[5(103) - (21)^2][5(5500) - (150)^2]}}$

= .9042

c. $r^2 = (0.9042)^2 = 0.8176$

d. $b = \dfrac{5(740) - 21(150)}{5(103) - (21)^2} = \dfrac{550}{74} = 7.4324$

$a = \dfrac{150}{5} - (7.4324)\left(\dfrac{21}{5}\right) = -1.2161$

$Y' = -1.2161 + 7.4324X$

e. $Y' = -1.2161 + 7.4324(4.5) = \$32.23$ (in thousands).

f. Strong positive association between amount spent on advertising and monthly sales. For each additional \$1,000 spent on advertising, sales increase \$7,432.40.

REVIEW OF CHAPTERS 14 AND 15

1. Frequency observed and frequency expected.

3. Chi-square distribution.

5. Not rejected, because 11.248 is less than 12.592.

7. There is no difference between the observed and the expected set of frequencies.

9. Nominal level.

11. To determine whether two independent populations are the same.

13. To determine whether three or more populations are the same.

15. Kruskal-Wallis

17. Yes.

19. No. It is positively skewed.

21. H_0: Median = \$27,000; H_1: Median ≠ \$27,000. Use .05 significance level and the sign test. The critical values are -1.96 and 1.96. Count the number of values above the median, compute z, assuming a large sample, and make a decision.

INDEX

PHOTO CREDITS

KEY FORMULAS Mason, Lind, and Marchal • Statistical Techniques in Business and Economics, 10th edition

CHAPTER 2

• Class interval

$$i = \frac{\text{Highest value} - \text{Lowest value}}{\text{Number of classes}}$$ [2–1]

• Class interval

$$i = \frac{\text{Highest value} - \text{Lowest value}}{1 + 3.322(\text{logarithm of total frequencies})}$$ [2–2]

CHAPTER 3

• Population mean, raw data

$$\mu = \frac{\Sigma X}{N}$$ [3–1]

• Sample mean, raw data

$$\bar{X} = \frac{\Sigma X}{n}$$ [3–2]

• Weighted mean

$$\bar{X}_w = \frac{w_1 X_1 + w_2 X_2 + \cdots + w_n X_n}{w_1 + w_2 + \cdots + w_n}$$ [3–4]

• Geometric mean

$$GM = \sqrt[n]{(X_1)(X_2)(X_3) \cdots (X_n)}$$ [3–5]

• Geometric mean rate of increase

$$GM = \sqrt[n]{\frac{\text{Value at end of period}}{\text{Value at start of period}}} - 1.0$$ [3–6]

• Sample mean grouped data

$$\bar{X} = \frac{\Sigma fX}{n}$$ [3–7]

• Median, grouped data

$$\text{Median} = L + \frac{\frac{n}{2} - CF}{f}(i)$$ [3–8]

CHAPTER 4

• Mean deviation

$$MD = \frac{\Sigma |X - \bar{X}|}{n}$$ [4–2]

• Population variance, raw data

$$\sigma^2 = \frac{\Sigma(X - \mu)^2}{N}$$ [4–3]

• Population standard deviation, raw data

$$\sigma = \sqrt{\frac{\Sigma(X - \mu)^2}{N}}$$ [4–4]

• Sample variance, raw data

$$s^2 = \frac{\Sigma(X - \bar{X})^2}{n - 1}$$ [4–5]

• Sample variance, raw data computational form

$$s^2 = \frac{\Sigma X^2 - \frac{(\Sigma X)^2}{n}}{n - 1}$$ [4–6]

• Sample standard deviation, raw data

$$s = \sqrt{\frac{\Sigma X^2 - \frac{(\Sigma X)^2}{n}}{n - 1}}$$ [4–7]

• Sample standard deviation, grouped data

$$s = \sqrt{\frac{\Sigma fX^2 - \frac{(\Sigma fX)^2}{n}}{n - 1}}$$ [4–8]

• Coefficient of variation

$$CV = \frac{s}{\bar{X}}(100)$$ [4–9]

• Coefficient of skewness

$$Sk = \frac{3(\bar{X} - \text{median})}{s}$$ [4–10]

• Location of percentile

$$L_p = (n + 1)\frac{P}{100}$$ [4–11]

CHAPTER 5

• Special rule of addition

$$P(A \text{ or } B) = P(A) + P(B)$$ [5–2]

• Complement rule

$$P(A) = 1 - P(\sim A)$$ [5–3]

• General rule of addition

$$P(A \text{ or } B) = P(A) + P(B) - P(A \text{ and } B)$$ [5–4]

• Special rule of multiplication

$$P(A \text{ and } B) = P(A)P(B)$$ [5–5]

• General rule of multiplication

$$P(A \text{ and } B) = P(A)P(B|A)$$ [5–6]

• Bayes' Theorem

$$P(A_1|B) = \frac{P(A_1) \cdot P(B|A_1)}{P(A_1) \cdot P(B|A_1) + P(A_2) \cdot P(B|A_2)}$$ [5–7]

• Number of permutations

$$_nP_r = \frac{n!}{(n - r)!}$$ [5–9]

- Number of combinations

$$_nC_r = \frac{n!}{r!(n-r)!}$$ **[5–10]**

- Sample size for proportion

$$n = p(1-p)\left(\frac{z}{E}\right)^2$$ **[8–12]**

CHAPTER 6

- Mean of a probability distribution

$$\mu = \Sigma[XP(X)]$$ **[6–1]**

- Variance of a probability distribution

$$\sigma^2 = \Sigma[(X-\mu)^2 P(X)]$$ **[6–2]**

- Binomial distribution

$$P(x) = \frac{n!}{x!(n-x)!}\,\pi^x(1-\pi)^{n-x}$$ **[6–3]**

- Mean of a binomial distribution

$$\mu = n\pi$$ **[6–4]**

- Variance of a binomial distribution

$$\sigma^2 = n\pi(1-\pi)$$ **[6–5]**

- Hypergeometric probability distribution

$$P(x) = \frac{(_SC_x)(_{N-S}C_{n-x})}{_NC_n}$$ **[6–6]**

- Poisson probability distribution

$$P(x) = \frac{\mu^x e^{-\mu}}{x!}$$ **[6–7]**

CHAPTER 7

- Standard normal value

$$z = \frac{X-\mu}{\sigma}$$ **[7–1]**

CHAPTER 8

- Standard error of the mean

$$s_{\bar{x}} = \frac{s}{\sqrt{n}}$$ **[8–2]**

- Confidence interval for mean

$$\bar{X} \pm z\frac{s}{\sqrt{n}}$$ **[8–5]**

- Confidence interval for proportion

$$p \pm z\sqrt{\frac{p(1-p)}{n}}$$ **[8–8]**

- Sample size for mean

$$n = \left(\frac{zs}{E}\right)^2$$ **[8–11]**

CHAPTER 9

- Single sample mean

$$z = \frac{\bar{X}-\mu}{s/\sqrt{n}}$$ **[9–2]**

- Two sample test of means

$$z = \frac{\bar{X}_1 - \bar{X}_2}{\sqrt{\dfrac{s_1^2}{n_1} + \dfrac{s_2^2}{n_2}}}$$ **[9–3]**

- Single sample, proportion

$$z = \frac{p-\pi}{\sqrt{\dfrac{\pi(1-\pi)}{n}}}$$ **[9–6]**

- Two sample test of proportions

$$z = \frac{p_1 - p_2}{\sqrt{\dfrac{p_c(1-p_c)}{n_1} + \dfrac{p_c(1-p_c)}{n_2}}}$$ **[9–7]**

- Pooled proportions

$$p_c = \frac{X_1 + X_2}{n_1 + n_2}$$ **[9–8]**

- Type II error

$$z = \frac{\bar{X}_c - \mu_1}{\sigma/\sqrt{n}}$$ **[9–9]**

CHAPTER 10

- One sample test of a mean

$$t = \frac{\bar{X}-\mu}{s/\sqrt{n}}$$ **[10–1]**

- Pooled variance

$$s_p^2 = \frac{(n_1-1)(s_1^2) + (n_2-1)(s_2^2)}{n_1 + n_2 - 2}$$ **[10–2]**

- Two sample test of means

$$t = \frac{\bar{X}_1 - \bar{X}_2}{\sqrt{s_p^2\left(\dfrac{1}{n_1} + \dfrac{1}{n_2}\right)}}$$ **[10–3]**

- Paired test

$$t = \frac{\bar{d}}{s_d/\sqrt{n}}$$ **[10–4]**

CHAPTER 11

- Test for equal variance

$$F = \frac{s_1^2}{s_2^2}$$ **[11–1]**

- Sum of squares, total

$$SS\ total = \sum X^2 - \frac{(\sum X)^2}{n}$$ **[11–2]**

- Sum of squares, treatments

$$SST = \sum \left[\frac{T_c^2}{n_c}\right] - \frac{(\sum X)^2}{n}$$ **[11–3]**

- Sum of squares, error

$$SSE = SS\ total - SST$$ **[11–4]**

- Confidence interval for means

$$(\bar{X}_1 - \bar{X}_2) \pm t\ \sqrt{MSE\left(\frac{1}{n_1} + \frac{1}{n_2}\right)}$$ **[11–5]**

- Sum of squares, blocks

$$SSB = \sum \left[\frac{B_r^2}{k}\right] - \frac{(\sum X)^2}{N}$$ **[11–6]**

- Sum of squares error, two way ANOVA

$$SSE = SS\ total - SST - SSB$$ **[11–7]**

CHAPTER 12

- Coefficient of correlation

$$r = \frac{n(\sum XY) - (\sum X)(\sum Y)}{\sqrt{[n(\sum X^2) - (\sum X)^2][n(\sum Y^2) - (\sum Y)^2]}}$$ **[12–1]**

- Correlation test of hypothesis

$$t = \frac{r\sqrt{n-2}}{\sqrt{1-r^2}}$$ **[12–2]**

- Linear regression equation

$$Y' = a + bX$$ **[12–3]**

- Slope of a regression line

$$b = \frac{n(\sum XY) - (\sum X)(\sum Y)}{n(\sum X^2) - (\sum X)^2}$$ **[12–4]**

- Intercept of a regression line

$$a = \frac{\sum Y}{n} - b\left(\frac{\sum X}{n}\right)$$ **[12–5]**

- Standard error of estimate

$$s_{y \cdot x} = \sqrt{\frac{\sum(Y - Y')^2}{n-2}},\ s_{y \cdot x} = \sqrt{\frac{SSE}{n-2}}$$ **[12–6], [12–12]**

or

$$s_{y \cdot x} = \sqrt{\frac{\sum Y^2 - a(\sum Y) - b(\sum XY)}{n-2}}$$ **[12–7]**

- Confidence interval

$$Y' \pm t(s_{y \cdot x})\ \sqrt{\frac{1}{n} + \frac{(X - \bar{X})^2}{\sum X^2 - \frac{(\sum X)^2}{n}}}$$ **[12–8]**

- Prediction interval

$$Y' \pm t(s_{y \cdot x})\ \sqrt{1 + \frac{1}{n} + \frac{(X - \bar{X})^2}{\sum X^2 - \frac{(\sum X)^2}{n}}}$$ **[12–9]**

- Coefficient of determination

$$r^2 = \frac{Total\ variation - Unexplained\ variation}{Total\ variation}$$ **[12–10]**

or

$$r^2 = \frac{SSR}{SS\ total} = 1 - \frac{SSE}{SS\ total}$$ **[12–11]**

CHAPTER 13

- Multiple regression equation

$$Y' = a + b_1 X_1 + b_2 X_2 + \cdots + b_k X_k$$ **[13–3]**

- Multiple standard error

$$s_{y \cdot 12 \cdots k} = \sqrt{\frac{\sum(Y - Y')^2}{n - (k+1)}}$$ **[13–4]**

- Coefficient of multiple determination

$$R^2 = \frac{SSR}{SS\ total}$$

- Global test of hypothesis

$$F = \frac{SSR/k}{SSE/(n - (k+1))}$$

- Testing for a particular regression coefficient

$$t = \frac{b_i}{s_{b_i}}$$

CHAPTER 14

- Chi-square test statistic

$$\chi^2 = \sum \left[\frac{(f_0 - f_e)^2}{f_e}\right]$$ **[14–1]**

- Expected frequency

$$f_e = \frac{(Row\ total)(Column\ total)}{Grand\ total}$$ **[14–2]**

CHAPTER 15

- Median test

$$z = \frac{(X \pm .50) - \mu}{\sigma}$$ **[15–1]**

- Wilcoxon rank-sum test

$$z = \frac{W - \dfrac{n_1(n_1 + n_2 + 1)}{2}}{\sqrt{\dfrac{n_1 n_2(n_1 + n_2 + 1)}{12}}}$$ **[15–4]**

- Kruskal-Wallis test

$$H = \frac{12}{n(n + 1)}\left[\frac{(\sum R_1)^2}{n_1} + \frac{(\sum R_2)^2}{n_2} + \cdots + \frac{(\sum R_k)^2}{n_k}\right] - 3(n + 1)$$ **[15–5]**

- Spearman rank correlation

$$r_s = 1 - \frac{6\sum d^2}{n(n^2 - 1)}$$ **[15–6]**

- Hypothesis test, rank correlation

$$t = r_s\sqrt{\frac{n - 2}{1 - r_s^2}}$$ **[15–7]**

CHAPTER 16

- Grand mean

$$\bar{\bar{X}} = \frac{\sum \bar{X}}{k}$$ **[16–1]**

- Control limits, mean

$$\text{UCL} = \bar{\bar{X}} + A_2\bar{R} \qquad \text{LCL} = \bar{\bar{X}} - A_2\bar{R}$$ **[16–4]**

- Control limits, range

$$\text{UCL} = D_4\bar{R} \qquad \text{LCL} = D_3\bar{R}$$ **[16–5]**

- Mean percent defective

$$\bar{p} = \frac{\text{Sum of the number defective}}{\text{Total number of items sampled}}$$ **[16–6]**

- Control limits, proportion

$$\text{UCL and LCL} = \bar{p} \pm 3\sqrt{\frac{\bar{p}(1 - \bar{p})}{n}}$$ **[16–8]**

- Control limits, c-bar chart

$$\text{UCL and LCL} = \bar{c} \pm 3\sqrt{\bar{c}}$$ **[16–9]**

CHAPTER 17

- Simple index

$$P = \frac{p_t}{p_0}(100)$$ **[17–1]**

- Simple average of price relatives

$$P = \frac{\sum P_i}{n}$$ **[17–2]**

- Simple aggregate index

$$p = \frac{\sum p_t}{\sum p_0}(100)$$ **[17–3]**

- Laspeyres price index

$$P = \frac{\sum p_t q_0}{\sum p_0 q_0}(100)$$ **[17–4]**

- Paasche price index

$$P = \frac{\sum p_t q_t}{\sum p_0 q_t}(100)$$ **[17–5]**

- Fisher's ideal index

$$\text{Fisher's ideal index} = \sqrt{(\text{Laspeyres price index})(\text{Paasche price index})}$$ **[17–6]**

- Value index

$$V = \frac{\sum p_t q_t}{\sum p_0 q_0}(100)$$ **[17–7]**

- Real income

$$\text{Real income} = \frac{\text{Money income}}{\text{CPI}}(100)$$ **[17–8]**

- Deflating sales

$$\text{Deflated sales} = \frac{\text{Actual sales}}{\text{An appropriate index}}(100)$$ **[17–9]**

- Purchasing power

$$\text{Purchasing power of dollar} = \frac{\$1}{\text{CPI}}(100)$$ **[17–10]**

CHAPTER 18

- Linear trend

$$Y' = a + bt$$ **[18–1]**

- Slope of a trend equation

$$b = \frac{\sum tY - (\sum Y)(\sum t)/n}{\sum t^2 - (\sum t)^2/n}$$ **[18–3]**

- Intercept of a trend equation

$$a = \frac{\sum Y}{n} - b\left(\frac{\sum t}{n}\right)$$ **[18–4]**

- Log trend equation

$$\log Y' = \log a + \log b(t)$$ **[18–5]**

CHAPTER 19

- Expected monetary value

$$\text{EMV}(A_i) = \sum[P(S_j) \cdot V(A_i, S_j)]$$ **[19–1]**

- Expected opportunity cost

$$\text{EOL}(A_i) = \sum(P(S_j) \cdot R(A_i, S_j))$$ **[19–2]**

- Expected value of perfect information

$$\text{EVPI} = \text{Expected value under conditions of certainty} - \text{Expected value of optimal decision under conditions of uncertainty}$$ **[19–3]**

AREAS UNDER THE NORMAL CURVE

Example:
If $z = 1.96$, then
$P(0$ to $z) = 0.4750$

z	0.00	0.01	0.02	0.03	0.04	0.05	0.06	0.07	0.08	0.09
0.0	0.0000	0.0040	0.0080	0.0120	0.0160	0.0199	0.0239	0.0279	0.0319	0.0359
0.1	0.0398	0.0438	0.0478	0.0517	0.0557	0.0596	0.0636	0.0675	0.0714	0.0753
0.2	0.0793	0.0832	0.0871	0.0910	0.0948	0.0987	0.1026	0.1064	0.1103	0.1141
0.3	0.1179	0.1217	0.1255	0.1293	0.1331	0.1368	0.1406	0.1443	0.1480	0.1517
0.4	0.1554	0.1591	0.1628	0.1664	0.1700	0.1736	0.1772	0.1808	0.1844	0.1879
0.5	0.1915	0.1950	0.1985	0.2019	0.2054	0.2088	0.2123	0.2157	0.2190	0.2224
0.6	0.2257	0.2291	0.2324	0.2357	0.2389	0.2422	0.2454	0.2486	0.2517	0.2549
0.7	0.2580	0.2611	0.2642	0.2673	0.2704	0.2734	0.2764	0.2794	0.2823	0.2852
0.8	0.2881	0.2910	0.2939	0.2967	0.2995	0.3023	0.3051	0.3078	0.3106	0.3133
0.9	0.3159	0.3186	0.3212	0.3238	0.3264	0.3289	0.3315	0.3340	0.3365	0.3389
1.0	0.3413	0.3438	0.3461	0.3485	0.3508	0.3531	0.3554	0.3577	0.3599	0.3621
1.1	0.3643	0.3665	0.3686	0.3708	0.3729	0.3749	0.3770	0.3790	0.3810	0.3830
1.2	0.3849	0.3869	0.3888	0.3907	0.3925	0.3944	0.3962	0.3980	0.3997	0.4015
1.3	0.4032	0.4049	0.4066	0.4082	0.4099	0.4115	0.4131	0.4147	0.4162	0.4177
1.4	0.4192	0.4207	0.4222	0.4236	0.4251	0.4265	0.4279	0.4292	0.4306	0.4319
1.5	0.4332	0.4345	0.4357	0.4370	0.4382	0.4394	0.4406	0.4418	0.4429	0.4441
1.6	0.4452	0.4463	0.4474	0.4484	0.4495	0.4505	0.4515	0.4525	0.4535	0.4545
1.7	0.4554	0.4564	0.4573	0.4582	0.4591	0.4599	0.4608	0.4616	0.4625	0.4633
1.8	0.4641	0.4649	0.4656	0.4664	0.4671	0.4678	0.4686	0.4693	0.4699	0.4706
1.9	0.4713	0.4719	0.4726	0.4732	0.4738	0.4744	0.4750	0.4756	0.4761	0.4767
2.0	0.4772	0.4778	0.4783	0.4788	0.4793	0.4798	0.4803	0.4808	0.4812	0.4817
2.1	0.4821	0.4826	0.4830	0.4834	0.4838	0.4842	0.4846	0.4850	0.4854	0.4857
2.2	0.4861	0.4864	0.4868	0.4871	0.4875	0.4878	0.4881	0.4884	0.4887	0.4890
2.3	0.4893	0.4896	0.4898	0.4901	0.4904	0.4906	0.4909	0.4911	0.4913	0.4916
2.4	0.4918	0.4920	0.4922	0.4925	0.4927	0.4929	0.4931	0.4932	0.4934	0.4936
2.5	0.4938	0.4940	0.4941	0.4943	0.4945	0.4946	0.4948	0.4949	0.4951	0.4952
2.6	0.4953	0.4955	0.4956	0.4957	0.4959	0.4960	0.4961	0.4962	0.4963	0.4964
2.7	0.4965	0.4966	0.4967	0.4968	0.4969	0.4970	0.4971	0.4972	0.4973	0.4974
2.8	0.4974	0.4975	0.4976	0.4977	0.4977	0.4978	0.4979	0.4979	0.4980	0.4981
2.9	0.4981	0.4982	0.4982	0.4983	0.4984	0.4984	0.4985	0.4985	0.4986	0.4986
3.0	0.4987	0.4987	0.4987	0.4988	0.4988	0.4989	0.4989	0.4989	0.4990	0.4990